West's Law School Advisory Board

WHITE COLLAR CRIME

CASES AND MATERIALS

Second Edition

By

Pamela H. Bucy
Bainbridge Professor of Law
University of Alabama, School of Law

AMERICAN CASEBOOK SERIES®

WEST
GROUP

ST. PAUL, MINN., 1998

American Casebook Series, and the West Group symbol are registered trademarks used herein under license.

 TEXT IS PRINTED ON 10% POST CONSUMER RECYCLED PAPER

1st Reprint — 2003

This book, and much more,
is dedicated to Pat, Julie, and Ben.

*

Preface

This book began eighteen years ago when I was sworn in as an Assistant United States Attorney for the Eastern District of Missouri. I spent most of my seven years as a federal prosecutor trying white collar criminal cases and I developed a fascination and love for the intrigue and subtley of this unique type of criminal case. I found that white collar criminal cases, unlike the narcotics and other "street crimes" I also prosecuted, bridged civil and criminal law and constantly forced me to analyze what could—and could not—be achieved by criminal prosecution. When I entered law teaching eleven years ago, I began using these materials, and have revised them every year since, incorporating my views and those of my students.

I have three goals for these materials. The first is to cover thoroughly the substantive law of white collar crime. Conspiracy and mail fraud, each with their own fascinating jurisprudence, are the foundation of almost every other white collar crime. One must develop an intuitive feel for these basic offenses so that, like Justice Stewart and pornography: one knows them when one sees them. Building from these offenses, one can master RICO, labor and benefit fund fraud, public corruption, money laundering, corporate crime, the False Claims Act, fraud upon financial institutions and tax fraud.

My second goal is to address the civil ramifications of white collar crime. These civil consequences are reflected in the few hybrid civil/criminal causes of action, and in the many civil and administrative consequences of any criminal action. RICO and the False Claims Act epitomize the hybrid causes of action: they both create a criminal cause of action to be pursued by the federal government and a civil cause of action to be pursued by federal or state governments or private citizens. Either way, the criminal and civil plaintiffs prove the same elements—simply with a different burden of proof and different remedies. Because of the substantial overlap of civil and criminal law, about 40% of the cases and materials in this book are concerned with collateral civil or administrative matters. Chapter 17, The Jurisprudence of White Collar Crime, is devoted entirely to the philosophical, policy and constitutional questions raised by the hybrid character of white collar crime.

My third goal is to convey some of the excitement of litigating the white collar case and some of the practical things I learned—sometimes the hard way—while in active practice. I have strived to select cases and commentary to demonstrate four points in particular: (1) Knowing the Paper. White collar criminal cases are document cases. An attorney handling these cases must know every minute piece of the "paper trail," and all possible tangents, backwards and forwards. (2) Developing a Theory of the Case. To avoid becoming engulfed by the minutia, it is essential to develop a "theory of the case" that focuses on the "big picture" and organizes everything—voir dire, opening statement, exhibits, objections, witnesses and closing argument—in a way that paints this "big picture." Regardless of how complex the case is, the plaintiff must convince the fact-finder that the defendant has lied, stolen, or cheated. The plaintiff's theory of the case should focus everything toward this clear, straightforward direction. If the plaintiff fails in achieving this, the defense wins. The defense theory of the case should target the weak points of the plaintiff's case and gear every aspect of its defense effort to attacking these points. (3) Avoiding Boredom and Confusion. This is not an easy matter in a case made up of documents—sone tedium for the fact-finder is usually inevitable. Too much boredom or confusion, however, is the way cases are lost. One cannot prevail if the fact-finder does not understand the strong points of a case or is inattentive during key portions of a case. Teaching the trial techniques of complex litigation is beyond the scope of this book, but I have made an effort throughout the notes following appropriate cases to focus on effective trial techniques for overcoming these inherent problems in the white collar criminal case. (4) Using—or Deflecting—Key Types of Evidence. This is directed primarily at those who anticipate defending the alleged white collar criminal. I found that defense attorneys who were outstanding litigators but unfamiliar with criminal trials were adept at virtually every aspect of the white collar case, which in many ways resembles the civil fraud trial, with two exceptions. These counsel were surprisingly unprepared for introduction of coconspirator's statements (Fed. R.Evid. 801(d)(2)(E)) and proof of similar "wrongs" (Fed.R.Evid. 404(b)). Lack of familiarity with these key types of evidence, which are often available and especially potent in the white collar criminal trial, can devastate the defense case. Thus, whenever possible, I have included notes and discussions covering the intricacies of coconspirator's statements and proof of similar "wrongs."

Many citations have been deleted without specific indication, but omission of anything more than a citation is indicated by brackets or ellipsis. Original footnote numbers have been retained in all quoted materials; my footnotes are lettered rather than numbered. Acknowledgements of permission to reprint excerpts from the literature appear at appropriate places in the text.

PAMELA H. BUCY

June, 1998

Acknowledgements

My thanks begin where I first learned about white collar crime—with the judges and my friends and colleagues at the federal courthouse in St. Louis, Missouri. As the years go by, I cherish all the more what they taught me about trying cases, and maintaining integrity and common sense. Tom Dittmeier, United States Attorney, gave support, guidance, and the chance to try cases I could learn from. Terry I. Adelman, First Assistant United States Attorney (now United States Magistrate), taught me how to be a good lawyer and a better person. Rick Buckles (now United States Magistrate), Kathianne Crane (now Judge, Missouri Court of appeals), Jim Crowe, Kevin O'Malley, Mike Reap, David Rosen, Jim Steitz, Mitch Stevens, and Tim Wilson (now Judge, St. Louis Circuit Court) all shared their experiences and unique perspectives. Many agents of the FBI, HHS, IRS and Postal Inspection Service, especially FBI Special Agents David F. Cunningham and Michael S. Clapp, taught me invaluable lessons about investigating fraud.

I cannot imagine a more supportive law school than the University of Alabama where I joined the faculty ten years ago. From the moment I began teaching, my colleagues and friends on the faculty, especially Dean Kenneth C. Randall, have been as excited about my professional interest in white collar crime as I am. Dean Randall and the Law School Foundation have graciously made available resources which have made both editions of this casebook possible.

A special acknowledgment is due to Melissa Harrison, Professor of Law, University of Montana School of Law. But for unforeseen circumstances, Melissa would have joined me as a co-author on the second edition of this casebook. Even so, Professor Harrison contributed substantially to Chapters 6 and 7 of this casebook and I am most grateful for her expertise, dedication, and friendship.

The joy of teaching for me is, and always will be, my students and I am indebted to the many students I've taught—for our terrific discussions and arguments, their helpful suggestions on these materials, and most recently, their encouragement as I have logged long hours. A special thanks goes to those students who in one way or another made special contributions to this book: Angela K. Aderholt, Karen F. Bean, Stacy S. Calvert, Sean P. Costello, David R. Hanbury, Stephanie M. Keller, Leslie Miller Klasing, Kimberly J. Johnson, Randal C. Johnson, Stephanie J. Larkins, Steven T. Marshal, Ellen M. Maus, Angela E. McFadden, Candance B. Stewart-Magee, Jill Ganus Teague, Robert C. Ward, J. Andrew Ware, and Nick C. Whitehead. Of all the students who have helped me with research, proofing, and more proofing, one stands out. I am most grateful to Melissa Kay (Misti) Atwood for her relentless help on copyright permissions and indefatigable good cheer.

Most especially, I thank Alesia Darling who labored many extra hours to help me meet deadlines. I cannot imagine how this edition would have happened without Alesia's professionalism, humor, and outstanding organizational, proofing and word processing skills. A special thank you is due to Alesia's family, her daughter, Rachel, and her husband, Bill, for sharing Alesia on the many nights and weekends she worked on this manuscript.

Lastly, I thank my family, my children, Julie and Ben, and my husband, Pat, for being supportive in more ways than words can express.

Summary of Contents

*

Table of Contents

Table of Cases

The principal cases are in bold type. Cases cited or discussed in the text are roman type. References are to pages. Cases cited in principal cases and within other quoted materials are not included.

*

WHITE COLLAR CRIME

CASES AND MATERIALS

Second Edition

*

Introduction

The term "white collar crime" was introduced by Edwin Sutherland in 1939.[a] Prior to the introduction of this concept, theories of criminal behavior focused on personal and social pathologies. As a result, criminal justice scholars emphasized "poverty [and] other social conditions and personal traits which are assumed to be associated with poverty" as the causes of crime.[b] Sutherland's definition of white collar crime also focused on the criminal actor. According to Sutherland, white collar crime was "committed by a person of respectability and high social status in the course of his occupation."[c] This definition has been criticized as overly restrictive because it fails to encompass all actors who commit white collar crimes and because it fails to focus on the conduct that constitutes white collar crime. Most other attempts to define white collar crime have focused on the conduct of the crime.[d] The following definition has been heralded as more inclusive and workable: "White collar violations * * * involve the use of a violator's position of significant power, influence or trust in the legitimate order * * * for the purpose of illegal gain, or to commit an illegal act for personal or organizational gain."[e]

"White collar crime is the fastest growing legal specialty in the United States."[f] Over the past twenty years, prosecutions of white collar crime have increased exponentially in volume and visibility. The front pages of newspaper Business sections are now filled with the charges, and intrigue, of insider trading and defense procurement scandals, fraud in the banking industry, public corruption, environmental and occupational crime. Prestigious law firms are building new litigation sections devoted to the civil prosecution or defense of white collar crimes. Increasingly, academic criminal law is tackling the jurisprudential question raised by white collar crime: What is the purpose of the criminal law and is prosecution of white collar crimes consistent with this purpose?[g]

a. *Geis & Goff, Introduction to E. Sutherland, White Collar Crime: The Unexpurgated Version* at IX (1983).

b. *E. Sutherland,* id. at 5.

c. Id.

d. *A. Reiss & A. Biderman, Data Sources on White Collar Law Breaking* 39–45 (1980); Edelhertz, *The Nature, Impact and Prosecution of White Collar Crime* in *Crime At The Top* 44–45 (1978).

e. *A. Reiss and A. Biderman, Data Sources on White Collar Law Breaking* at 4; cf. Edelhertz, *The Nature, Impact and Prosecution of White Collar Crime* in *Crime At The Top* at 44.

f. Paul R. Conolly, Chairman of the Section on Litigation of the American Bar Association (1977), *quoted in Malcolm Feeley, The Process is the Punishment* (New York: Russell Sage Foundation, 1979); cf. *Lateral Moves: Specialties Play an Increasing Role,* N.L.J. 38 (Oct. 22, 1990).

g. A comprehensive listing of academic literature tackling this issue is not possible here, but some of the more provocative recent works include *J. Braithwaite, Crime,*

In short, white collar crime is a growing field which is catapulting criminal law in new directions. This trend is not likely to change. Just as it is not possible to put the genie back in the bottle, it is highly unlikely that future prosecutors will turn their backs on acts which erode economic stability. You, as the new cadre of lawyers, will participate in this evolution of criminal law, whether by choice or not.

Those who choose to practice criminal law must be fluent in the nuances posed by white collar crime. The prosecution and defense of white collar crime is vastly different from the prosecution and defense of street crime. This is true for three major reasons. First, with street crime it is generally not difficult, once credible witnesses are located, to ascertain what conduct occurred (i.e., the suspect shot the victim, the suspect stole the car). With white collar crime, however, it is sometimes impossible to reconstruct what conduct occurred (i.e., was money funneled out of the country?, was a bribe offered?).

Second, with street crime, it is usually not difficult to determine whether the conduct is a crime (i.e., if the suspect hit someone, it is an assault; if the suspect killed someone, it is a homicide). With white collar crime, it can be difficult to determine whether the conduct, once identified, constitutes a crime at all. For example, in 1987 the Supreme Court overturned forty-year-old precedent of the courts of appeals when it held that conduct historically prosecuted as mail fraud was not an offense under the federal mail fraud statute. McNally v. United States, 483 U.S. 350 (1987). Likewise in Williams v. United States, 458 U.S. 279 (1982), the Supreme Court held that check kiting was not an offense under the statute charged although such conduct had been prosecuted as a violation of this statute for decades.

The third major difference between street crime and white collar crime is procedural. There is little or no grand jury investigation prior to filing of formal charges on the typical street crime, whereas most white collar crimes are preceded by months, if not years, of grand jury investigation. This may be the most crucial distinction yet because in this grand jury stage, both the prosecutor and defense counsel will confront legal issues and strategic considerations different from those dealt with by the lawyer specializing in traditional criminal law. Failure to appreciate these differences can prove disastrous for the attorney as well as the client.

It is not only the criminal law practitioner who should be familiar with the specialty of white collar crime, however. In fact, in some ways, it is the civil business lawyer who most needs to understand white collar crime. This lawyer will represent clients who, wittingly or unwittingly, cross the line between legitimate, aggressive business tactics, and criminal fraud. The good lawyer will be able to forewarn the client before this line is crossed, and will know how to defend this client if a grand jury

Shame and Reintegration (1989); *Corrigible Corporations and Unruly Law* (B. Fisse & P.A. French, eds. 1985); *White Collar Crime: An Agenda For Research* (H. Edelhertz & T.D. Overcast, eds. 1982).

begins to investigate possible criminal violations. In addition, this prepared civil lawyer will see when a client has suffered because of criminal fraud by others and will be able to help this client recover, perhaps even benefit, from such overreaching. Statutes such as RICO and the False Claims Act are prime examples of why the civil lawyer should be well versed in white collar crime. With awards of substantial damages, penalties and attorneys fees, these statutes encourage "private attorneys general" to discover and prove fraud. To use these statutes, however, the civil plaintiff must prove what is essentially criminal fraud.

It is important in studying white collar crime to recognize that it blurs the distinction between criminal and civil law. This is because the facts which give rise to the criminal action often also give rise to civil or administrative actions. For example, the criminal trial of a health care provider may involve the same acts for which patients of that provider have civil malpractice causes of action. This same provider may also be subject to substantial civil fines and administrative sanctions, in addition to criminal prosecution and private malpractice actions. Similarly, the criminal trial of a business-person may involve the same acts for which associates of that business-person have tort or breach of contract actions. Professionals such as lawyers, doctors, accountants, engineers, and architects who have been convicted of criminal fraud charges may lose their professional licenses because of—or instead of—criminal prosecution.

The fact that viable civil remedies exist for the victim of white collar crime or for governmental agencies which oversee a defendant's activity is significant. For example, defending oneself in civil litigation by testifying will waive the Fifth Amendment privilege in subsequent criminal proceedings. The criminal trial, on the other hand, presents a fruitful discovery opportunity for the civil plaintiff who is suing, or may sue, the criminal defendant. Navigating through the dangers and advantages of parallel proceedings requires knowledge of the law and an intuitive feel for how multiple legal systems work.

Because of the hybrid nature of white collar crimes, these materials focus on many issues of civil as well as criminal law, such as the False Claims Act and RICO, both of which encourage "private attorneys general"; the collateral estoppel and double jeopardy issues raised when one attempts to use—in the civil forum—a judgment obtained in the criminal forum; directors and officers liability issues; the civil and administrative collateral consequences of a conviction, such as professional licensure discipline, suspension or debarment from federal programs, and loss of indemnity insurance.

Seven years ago when I prepared the first edition of this casebook I became immersed in the field of white collar crime as I read hundreds of cases, law review articles, bar journals and CLE materials to choose topics and cases to include. It has been fascinating to undergo this same process seven years later. There have been some substantial and interesting changes. For example, although the money laundering and forfeitures statutes have covered white collar crime since 1970, there was little use of these statutes in the area of white collar crime even seven years ago. At that time the only significant reported cases were drug prosecutions. In preparing the second edition, however, I found a "wealth" of white collar money laundering prosecutions and forfeiture actions from which to choose cases for this book. Thus, not only are the money laundering and forfeiture chapters much improved but, because money laundering is included in most white collar prosecutions today, chapters throughout the book demonstrate money laundering's versatility as a prosecution tool.

Another change in the last seven years has been the explosion of "civil prosecution" of white collar crime by "private attorneys general," using statutes such as civil RICO and the *qui tam* provisions of the False Claims Act. The second edition of this casebook reflects this trend, with new materials on the use of civil RICO and increased and updated materials on the False Claims Act which strive to capture the dynamic nature of this boutique area of the law.

Sentencing issues now dominate the federal appellate caseload; this second edition reflects this fact with the inclusion of a new chapter on the legal and policy issues presented by the United States Sentencing Guidelines. One effect of the Sentencing Guidelines has been to encourage businesses of every size to implement corporate compliance plans and, when needed, to institute internal investigations for fraud. These plans and investigations have been described as "full employment acts for attorneys," and indeed a "cottage industry" has developed in the past few years from the need to service these plans and conduct these investigations. Both trends raise new questions about preserving the attorney-client privilege, avoiding conflicts of interest and fulfilling corporate directors duties. Chapters throughout this edition address these issues.

The last "sea change" I have observed is distressing. The hostility between prosecutors and the defense bar has increased decibels. Whereas seven years ago, one rarely saw claims of prosecutorial misconduct, at least in the reported court opinions, such claims are commonplace now. More alarming, however, are the plethora of prosecutions aimed at attorneys, so much so that this second edition includes a separate chapter on such prosecutions.

While these are the dramatic changes I noticed in making my recent review of white collar crime, the field has changed in more subtle ways that rendered the first edition amazingly out of date. Thus, while some of the topics remain the same, most of the cases in the second edition are new. One thing remains the same, however. It is imperative that the lawyers emerging from today's law schools be exposed to the nature, and peril, of white collar crime. As the cases that follow aptly demonstrate, the new lawyer is fortunate. While the philosophical and policy ramifications of vigorous pursuit of white collar crimes are hotly debated, all of those familiar with white collar crime agree on one point: white collar crime is fascinating.

Chapter 1

CONSPIRACY

Conspiracy is an agreement between two or more persons to commit an unlawful act. The essence of the offense is the agreement itself, not acts taken in furtherance of the agreement.[a]

Conspiracy may be a civil cause of action when the object of the conspiracy is a tort and the conspiracy causes proximate damage to the plaintiff. Conspiracy is also a criminal offense when the object of the conspiracy is the commission of a crime. Either way, the cause of action arises from certain planning activities that precede the tort or crime. Generally, there are three elements that must be proven to show that a conspiracy, civil or criminal, exists: (1) an agreement between two or more persons to commit a wrongful (civil) or illegal (criminal) act; (2) an intent to commit the wrongful or illegal act; (3) the commission of at least one overt act by one coconspirator which is in furtherance of the conspiracy. A typical criminal conspiracy statute reads as follows:

> "A person is guilty of criminal conspiracy if with the intent that conduct constituting an offense be performed, he agrees with one or more persons to engage in or cause the performance of such conduct, and any one or more of such persons does an overt act to effect an objective of the agreement."[b]

Some criminal conspiracy statutes are more limited. For example, the general conspiracy statute in the federal criminal code prohibits only conspiracies to commit an offense against the United States, 18 U.S.C. § 371. Another federal statute proscribes only conspiracies to commit a controlled substance offense, 21 U.S.C. § 846.[c]

---

a. For a discussion of the historical development of the conspiracy offense, see Francis B. Sayre, *Criminal Conspiracy*, 35 Harv. L. Rev. 393 (1921).

b. Ala.Code § 13A–4–3 1977.

c. The Supreme Court held that § 846, unlike most conspiracy statutes, does not contain an overt act requirement. United States v. Shabani, 513 U.S. 10 (1994). To reach its conclusion the Court looked to the statutory language, Congressional intent and the common law on conspiracy. It found that the terms of the statute did not require an overt act; and then focused on the "settled principle of statutory construction that, absent contrary indications, Congress intends to adopt the common law definition of statutory terms," and concluded by looking at history: "At common law it was neither necessary to aver nor prove an

The agreement to conspire need not be express or formal. It may be inferred from circumstances such as the relationship between the parties and the way the parties conduct themselves. While it is not necessary to establish that a conspirator had knowledge of the entire scope of the conspiracy or that a conspirator knew the identity or role of all of the coconspirators, it is necessary to prove that an actor had the requisite mens rea to commit the substantive offense which is the object of the conspiracy.

The overt act requirement usually is not difficult to prove once agreement and intent have been proven. An overt act need not itself be a criminal act; for example, it simply may be a telephone conversation or a meeting discussing the criminal conduct. The only function of the overt act requirement is to demonstrate that the conspiracy exists.

It is especially appropriate to begin a discussion of white collar crime with the conspiracy offense, not only because conspiracy is one of the most frequently charged crimes, but also because of the unique advantages this offense offers the prosecutor, and the distinct disadvantages it holds for the defendant. These advantages and disadvantages are amplified in complex cases such as white collar crimes.[d] The major advantage to the prosecutor of a conspiracy offense is that it permits the government to synthesize into one indictment many far-flung actors and types of conduct. This often allows the government to indict persons who could not otherwise be indicted and buttresses the government's case against all named defendants. Perhaps the most obvious manifestation of this advantage is an evidentiary one: once the existence of a conspiracy has been proven, it is possible to admit into evidence coconspirators' statements, which otherwise would be inadmissible hearsay.

Because conspiracy is charged so frequently by prosecutors, the question of whether coconspirators' statements should be admitted will arise often. Because of the subtlety of most white collar criminal cases, proof of criminal intent may be available only through the statements of the defendant and the defendant's colleagues. When a conspiracy is proven, the statements of these colleagues, which are in furtherance of a conspiracy, become admissible and supply important evidence of criminal intent.

A. PROVING A CONSPIRACY

Determining whether the government has proven a conspiracy is a highly fact-specific analysis and thus, difficult to demonstrate through a

overt act in furtherance of the conspiracy." *Id.* The Court also noted that other conspiracy offenses in the federal code contained explicit overt act requirements. *Id.* at 385.

d. For a general discussion of the use of the conspiracy offense in white collar criminal cases, see *White Collar Crime: Eighth Survey of Law,* 30 Am.L.Rev. 685–716

(1993); Sarah N. Welling, *Intracorporate Plurality in Criminal Conspiracy Law,* 33 Hastings L.Rev. 1155 (1982); G.E. Hale, *Joint Ventures: Collaborative Subsidiaries and the Antitrust Laws,* 42 Va.L.Rev. 927 (1956); Note, Conditional Objectives of Conspiracies, 94 Yale L.J. 895 (1985).

"typical" case. However, certain general principles are followed by the courts in assessing whether all elements of a conspiracy charge have been proven. The next case, United States v. Brown, 943 F.2d 1246 (10th Cir.1991), provides a helpful discussion of these principles. The United States Court of Appeals for the Tenth Circuit reversed Brown's conviction and ordered a new trial because of evidentiary errors made by the District Court. However, before reaching these issues, the court reviewed the evidence against the defendant and concluded that it was sufficient for the jury to convict on all charges, including conspiracy. As you read this opinion, determine at what point the defendant should have acted differently than he did, and what action he should have taken.

UNITED STATES v. BROWN

United States Court of Appeals, Tenth Circuit, 1991.
943 F.2d 1246.

SETH, CIRCUIT JUDGE.

This appeal involves various charges arising out of the representation of Gary and Marcee Levine by the law firm of Zimmerman & Schwartz. The grand jury returned a 50 count indictment charging the Levines, the law firm, certain members of the law firm, and other participants of conspiring to defraud the United States by concealing the financial transactions of the Levines. Appellant, who was an associate with the law firm, was named in 18 of the counts. In a joint trial with Steven Zimmerman, one of the senior partners of the law firm, appellant was convicted of four counts, conspiracy in violation of 18 U.S.C. § 371, two counts of bankruptcy fraud * * * and mail fraud * * *. On appeal, he challenges the sufficiency of the evidence as to each of those counts as well as various rulings by the trial court. * * *

STATEMENT OF FACTS

Due to the complex nature of the transactions, we limit our discussion of the facts to those relevant to this appellant * * *. Viewing the evidence in the light most favorable to the government, the following events occurred in relation to this appeal.

Gary and Marcee Levine operated a retail furniture store known as Levines Home Furnishings in Denver. The store's corporate name was Sofa Gallery, Inc. In 1985, they sought advice from David Schwartz, of Zimmerman & Schwartz, regarding payment of creditors and filing bankruptcy.

Based upon the advice of Schwartz, the Levines hired Sales Results and its principal, Stanley Lansing, to conduct a liquidation sale. Lansing and Sales Results were to receive 10% of the gross retail revenues and the net proceeds were to be paid to the Levines' creditors. Cherry Creek National Bank and Westinghouse Credit Corporation, two of Sofa Gallery's principal creditors, agreed to the sale. They released their secured interests in the unsold inventory and financed the acquisition of over two million dollars additional inventory for the sale.

During this time, the Levines and Lansing entered into an undisclosed kickback agreement whereby Lansing agreed to pay Marcee Levine one-third of his 10% commission. Upon the advice of Schwartz, Gary Levine received none of this money because of his impending bankruptcy.

The liquidation sale was conducted from July through December 1985. The sale resulted in a reported loss, with no proceeds paid to the creditors except for O. Wesley Box and the Rocky Mountain News. During the course of the sale, however, Marcee Levine received an undisclosed kickback of approximately $100,000 from Sales Results. This payment along with $150,000 from pre-liquidation sale accounts receivable was deposited in the law firm trust account for the Levines' personal use. No evidence was introduced that any of these financial transactions appeared in the law firm's ledger.

In 1985, Schwartz delegated two tasks relevant to the Levine transactions to appellant. Schwartz requested that appellant draft a quitclaim deed granting Gary Levine's interest in the house to Marcee Levine and draw up the Articles of Incorporation for a business known as Action Sales Group, Inc. for Stephen Forsey.

On February 19, 1986, Schwartz asked appellant to attend a meeting at the Marriott to take notes. During this meeting, Schwartz proposed that the Levines use money from the Sofa Gallery's employee pension plan to capitalize Action Sales Group, Inc. At trial, appellant testified that he stated at the meeting that this would be an improper use of pension funds and refused to draft the documents. Forsey, however, testified that appellant did not object to the use of the funds.

Thereafter, the Levines withdrew $425,000 from the pension plan and gave $300,000 to Forsey to fund Action Sales Group, Inc. The Levines put the other $125,000 in a secret trust account at the accounting firm of William C. Schlapman, P.C. This money was supplemented by corporate tax refunds and used for the Levines' personal use. In addition, the Levines and Schlapman entered into a plan to delay filing amended tax returns.

On April 17, 1986, Schwartz drafted a letter to the Levines stating that "Tom Brown [the defendant] has been fully briefed on all aspects of all of our transactions and is fully cognizant of all the problem areas in the event that there is any problem with either the new business or with the old negotiations."

On May 20, 1986, D. Bruce Coles, an attorney representing Colorado National Leasing, deposed Gary Levine. During his deposition, Gary Levine failed to disclose any of the trust accounts or interest in Action Sales Group, Inc. Although Schwartz attended the deposition with Gary Levine, the evidence showed that appellant met with Gary Levine prior to the deposition and met with Schwartz afterwards. Gary Levine subsequently filed for bankruptcy on September 26, 1986.

Schwartz continued his representation of the Levines until 1987 when he turned the Levine file over to appellant. On January 29, 1987, appellant met with Gary Levine to discuss his deposition concerning the bankruptcy proceedings. The following day, he attended the deposition with Gary Levine. Those present at the deposition were appellant, Gary Levine, Coles, and H. Christopher Clark, the bankruptcy trustee. They discussed the use of the employee pension plan funds to capitalize Action Sales Group, Inc.; however, Gary Levine denied any ownership or stock interest in Action Sales Group, Inc. He also failed to disclose either the law firm trust account or the Schlapman trust account.

After the liquidation sale, the Levines put their financial records in a storage locker. During the bankruptcy proceedings, they allowed numerous inspections of the records contained in the storage locker. In 1986, Cherry Creek National Bank reviewed, inspected and removed 20–25 boxes of documents. At his deposition in January 1987, Gary Levine agreed to turn over his storage locker key to the trustee. In March 1987, appellant wrote to the trustee and offered him the opportunity to inspect the records for the creditors.

On April 14, 1987, a creditors' meeting was held where Coles expressed his dissatisfaction with discovery. In an attempt to obtain more information about the Levines' assets, Coles made several discovery requests. On May 19, 1987, the bankruptcy court issued an order for Marcee Levine to appear at a deposition on June 9, 1987, and produce copies of all financial bookkeeping or accounting records and related documents.

During this time, Gary Levine told appellant that he did not want to pay rent on the storage locker and was going to destroy the remaining records. On May 23, 1987, appellant reviewed the records, determined that they were of no value to the bankruptcy proceedings and destroyed them at a landfill site.

On May 27, 1987, appellant wrote a letter to Coles advising him that he had filed a motion with the court to vacate the order authorizing the examination and that the court would not be able to act before the June 9 deposition date. Thereafter, Marcee Levine was served with two subpoenas dated June 2 and June 15, 1987.

Without the court ruling on appellant's motion, Marcee Levine was deposed on June 18, 1987. Marcee Levine, through appellant, did not produce all of the documents requested by Coles, asserting attorney-client privilege. Thereafter, appellant filed a motion for a protective order of the records until the court could make a determination of this issue. Coles did not oppose this motion because appellant subsequently agreed to supply Coles with the records he had requested.

During the course of the bankruptcy proceedings, the bankruptcy trustee requested information concerning the Levines' 1986 tax return. In response to these requests, appellant drafted a letter dated February 10, 1988 stating that:

"The reason for the delay has been that the accountant wants a wealth of information and documents which the Levines have not entirely been able to locate. Many of their financial records were in the storage locker and seem to have disappeared into the hands of the numerous attorneys and banks who were interested in those documents."

SUFFICIENCY OF THE EVIDENCE

Appellant challenges the sufficiency of the evidence to sustain his conviction on all four counts. We address each of these counts in turn. In reviewing a sufficiency of the evidence claim, we "view the proof presented in the light most favorable to the government to ascertain if there is sufficient substantial proof, direct and circumstantial, together with reasonable inferences to be drawn therefrom, from which a jury might find a defendant guilty beyond a reasonable doubt." United States v. Sullivan, 919 F.2d 1403, 1431 (10th Cir.1990).

Count 1

Count 1 charged appellant with conspiracy to defraud the United States under 18 U.S.C. § 371. Under this statute, the government was required to establish beyond a reasonable doubt that: (1) there was an agreement between two or more people, (2) to defraud the United States and (3) an overt act was committed by one of the conspirators in furtherance of that agreement. The defendant need not have knowledge of all the details or all the members of the conspiracy, United States v. Savaiano, 843 F.2d 1280, 1294 (10th Cir.1988), and the jury may presume that a defendant is a knowing participant in the conspiracy when he acts in furtherance of the objective of the conspiracy. "The connection of the defendant to the conspiracy need only be slight, if there is sufficient evidence to establish that connection beyond a reasonable doubt." However, "caution must be taken that the conviction not be obtained by piling inference upon inference." [internal quotation marks and citations omitted]

Appellant claims that the evidence was insufficient to support his conviction because he was not a knowing participant in the conspiracy. Specifically, he claims that the government's case was built on inferences involving his role as attorney for the Levines. He argues that any task performed by him in relation to the bankruptcy proceedings could not constitute an overt act in furtherance of the conspiracy to defraud the United States without his knowing participation.

We agree with appellant's argument that the government's case centers around his role as the Levines' attorney. While there is little direct evidence of appellant's involvement, we must conclude that there was sufficient circumstantial evidence for a jury to have found beyond a reasonable doubt that appellant knowingly and actively participated in the conspiracy to defraud the United States.

Viewing the evidence in the light most favorable to the government, a reasonable jury could infer that appellant was aware of the misuse of Sofa Gallery's employee pension plan funds, the Levines' interest in

Action Sales Group, Inc., the misuse of the law firm trust account to hide the proceeds from the liquidation sale and the Schlapman trust account from the following evidence presented at trial.

The evidence showed that appellant began working on the Levine bankruptcy case in 1985. His involvement in the Levine case gradually increased in 1986 when he attended a meeting at the Marriott with Schwartz, Forsey, and the Levines. During this meeting, it was suggested that Gary Levine use the Sofa Gallery's employee pension plan funds to capitalize Action Sales Group, Inc. Although appellant denies that he acquiesced to the use of those funds in that manner, Forsey testified that appellant did not object. Further, Forsey's testimony was corroborated by the letter dated April 17, 1986, which stated that appellant had been fully briefed on all aspects of the Levine transactions.

In addition to the letter drafted by Schwartz concerning appellant's knowledge of the Levine transactions, a reasonable jury could possibly infer that Schwartz "prepped" appellant on the Levine financial transactions when he turned the file over to him in 1987. Appellant's knowledge of Gary Levine's assets during the bankruptcy proceedings would be crucial to effective representation given the existing conspiracy to conceal a number of Gary Levine's assets.

Further, appellant met with Gary Levine to discuss his assets and go over "ground rules" for his deposition. Appellant also discussed Gary Levine's assets with Schlapman. A reasonable jury could infer that appellant was aware of Gary Levine's undisclosed assets from these discussions.

While we have previously held that knowledge or mere association is insufficient to convict on a charge of conspiracy, we believe that appellant's actions constitute more than mere knowledge given the following events and the inferences which may be derived therefrom.

During his first deposition, Gary Levine failed to disclose any information regarding his interest in Action Sales Group, Inc., the law firm trust account or the Schlapman trust account. While appellant did not attend this deposition, he did meet with Gary Levine prior to representing Gary Levine at his second deposition which took place on January 30, 1987. Again, Gary Levine failed to disclose any of the trust accounts. While they discussed the embezzlement scheme of the employee pension plan to fund Action Sales Group, Inc., Gary Levine denied any ownership or stock interest in the company. From this evidence, a reasonable jury could infer that appellant discussed Gary Levine's assets with him and how to conceal them during the deposition. They could further conclude that appellant was aware of the conspiracy to conceal Gary Levine's assets and actively participated in the conspiracy by failing to reveal the undisclosed assets to the bankruptcy trustee.

Lastly, the jury heard testimony concerning appellant's destruction of business records contained in the Levines' storage locker. A reasonable jury could conclude that appellant's destruction of records relating to the Levines' bankruptcy proceedings was probative of his involvement in the conspiracy and could infer from his actions that he actively participated in the conspiracy to defraud the United States.

Given the evidence presented and the reasonable inferences therefrom, a jury could have found beyond a reasonable doubt that appellant was aware of all of the Levines' financial transactions; that he agreed to defraud the United States by concealing their financial transactions; and that he aided the conspiracy in its objectives in violation of 18 U.S.C. § 371.

Notes

1.   At what point did Tommy Brown cease to be an unwitting associate acting at the orders of his boss, and become a coconspirator in mail fraud and bankruptcy fraud: When he destroyed records at the landfill (May 23, 1987)? When he failed to protest more vigorously about raiding the corporation's pension plan (February 19, 1986)? When he drafted the quitclaim deed granting Gary Levine's interest in a house to Marcee Levine and drew up the Articles of Incorporation for Action Sales Group (1985)?

2.   Exactly what should Tommy Brown have done? Talk to the partner, David Schwartz? Talk to other partners? Call his state bar's Ethic's Committee? Say nothing and move to another firm?

3.   In addition to criminal liability, Brown faces some probable ethical violations. Consider the following ABA Model Rules of Professional Conduct:

RULE 3.4 Fairness to Opposing Party and Counsel

A lawyer shall not:

* * * unlawfully obstruct another party's access to evidence or unlawfully alter, destroy or conceal a document or other material having potential evidentiary value. A lawyer shall not counsel or assist another person to do any such act.

RULE 5.2 Responsibilities of a Subordinate Lawyer

(a) A lawyer is bound by the rules of professional conduct notwithstanding that the lawyer acted at the direction of another person.

(b) A subordinate lawyer does not violate the rules of professional conduct if that lawyer acts in accordance with a supervisory lawyer's reasonable resolution of an arguable question of professional duty.

Do you believe Brown falls within Rule 5.2(b), i.e., was he acting "in accordance with [Schwartz's] reasonable resolution of an arguable question of professional duty"?

———

One of the more difficult aspects of pleading and proving conspiracy is determining the scope of the conspiracy. If the government charges the conspiracy too broadly, it will charge as defendants some who were not coconspirators, at least as to *that* conspiracy. If the government charges the conspiracy too narrowly, it will fail to charge all coconspirators. If the evidence at trial proves a conspiracy different in scope than the one charged, the variance may require reversal, depending on prejudice to defendants. The next case, United States v. Morrow, 39 F.3d 1228 (1st Cir.1994), discusses these "scope of the conspiracy" issues.

UNITED STATES v. MORROW

United States Court of Appeals, First Circuit, 1994.
39 F.3d 1228.

BOUDIN, CIRCUIT JUDGE.

* * *

This automobile fraud case poses a tricky issue in conspiracy law that may not have been clearly addressed in this circuit. We conclude that some evidence may have been admitted at trial against both appellants that was admissible only against one of the two, but we also find that the error was clearly harmless. Rejecting all other claims of error, we affirm.

I.

In March 1992, a federal grand jury indicted the two appellants— Charles Morrow and Jacob Nevcherlian—together with Rodney Andreoni, Vito DeLuca and Randal Lane for conspiracy to commit mail fraud. 18 U.S.C. § 371. Nevcherlian was also charged with two substantive violations of the mail fraud statute, 18 U.S.C. § 1341, and Morrow was similarly charged with one such violation.

DeLuca, Andreoni and Lane pled guilty. Morrow and Nevcherlian were tried together in January 1993. At trial, the government's chief witness was FBI agent Gary Brotan, who had pretended to participate in the scheme. His extensive testimony was supplemented by documents and by recordings of certain of the conversations among the indicted defendants. The government's evidence, if believed, tended to show the following.

In early 1991, the FBI began investigating a possible case of automobile insurance fraud. A confidential informant, Mark Vermilyea, introduced Brotan to Andreoni in March 1991. Andreoni was self-employed as an insurance adjustor. Brotan posed as Vermilyea's cousin from Boston and colleague in the subsequent activities. Andreoni described to Brotan how to conduct an insurance fraud scheme involving old but valuable "classic" cars.

Andreoni proposed that Brotan acquire from DeLuca a 1975 Corvette which had been used in prior frauds. It was suggested that Brotan or Vermilyea insure a less expensive car and then substitute the Corvette on the policy. The insured then would file a claim based on an alleged accident involving the Corvette, and shortly thereafter report the car stolen and collect again, presumably from a different insurer. The accident or loss had to be staged within three days of the purported acquisition of the car so that it would not be necessary to register the vehicle in Rhode Island or pay the state sales tax on the acquisition.

About ten days after the initial conversation, Andreoni introduced Brotan to DeLuca. Brotan made a $4,000 down payment to DeLuca to purchase a 1975 Corvette for $10,000. Although the car belonged to DeLuca, DeLuca had previously registered the car in Florida under Nevcherlian's name and with Nevcherlian's consent. DeLuca gave Brotan a receipt and a copy of the title purportedly signed by Nevcherlian. Several weeks later, in April 1991, Brotan paid the $6,000 balance to DeLuca and received from him a bill of sale, again purportedly signed by Nevcherlian, showing a spurious purchase price of $21,000.

In May 1991, Andreoni offered to stage an accident in which he backed his car into the 1975 Corvette in exchange for payment of $750. In June 1991, Andreoni notified his own insurer, Travelers Insurance Company, that such an accident had occurred on June 7. Shortly thereafter, Andreoni gave DeLuca a loss form sent to Andreoni by Travelers and Andreoni asked DeLuca to send it to Nevcherlian in case Nevcherlian, as the listed prior owner, was questioned by the insurance company.

On July 26, 1991, DeLuca, Andreoni, Nevcherlian, Brotan and Vermilyea met at DeLuca's home. Nevcherlian was not in the room at the outset of the discussion. Brotan asked that a new receipt for the down payment for the Corvette be prepared and redated June 3, 1991, to bring it close to the alleged June 7 accident. Brotan also asked that a new bill of sale be dated August 1, 1991, to cover a separate claim for the theft of the vehicle scheduled for August 2, 1991.

After this discussion, Nevcherlian joined the meeting and was introduced as the prior owner of the car. Thereafter, the question arose whether the Corvette's hard top should also be reported as stolen, Vermilyea saying that it would be strange to claim that the hard top was being used in August. Nevcherlian suggested that Vermilyea tell the insurance company that the car had air conditioning to explain the use of the hard top, and he further suggested that it could be falsely claimed that the car had a stereo system worth $1,000. Nevcherlian also suggested giving a false purchase price of $25,000 on the new bill of sale to be dated August 1, 1991.

On August 1, Travelers sent Vermilyea a check for just under $5,000 to cover the supposed June 7 accident and, on the same date, Vermilyea substituted the 1975 Corvette for another car on his own insurance policy. The following day he reported to the Narraganset police that the 1975 Corvette had been stolen. Shortly thereafter, Nevcherlian was contacted in Florida by telephone by a Narraganset police detective and he told the detective that he had sold the car a few years earlier but lacked details; in September 1991, Nevcherlian called the police department and told a sergeant that he had sold the 1975 Corvette to Vermilyea for $25,000. In response to a request for the paperwork, Nevcherlian then mailed a copy of the Florida title certificate to the Narraganset police.

In the meantime, a second fraudulent transaction was in preparation. On August 5, 1991, DeLuca introduced Brotan to Morrow, who was the owner of a car dealership in Rhode Island and apparently a business partner of DeLuca in other ventures. Morrow agreed to sell Brotan a 1958 Corvette for $15,000; Brotan explained how he intended to use it in an insurance fraud. Brotan then made a $10,000 down payment; Morrow said he could not release the car at once because he himself had a pending insurance claim relating to the car.

Later in August, Brotan took the 1958 Corvette to Lane's garage in New Hampshire; Lane agreed to strip the vehicle, have it found after Brotan reported it stolen, and then after insurance inspection replace the original parts, all in exchange for a fee of $2,500. In September 1991, after discussion of the planned fraud, Brotan gave Morrow $5,000—the balance of the $15,000 purchase price—and Morrow gave Brotan the title certificate and an undated bill of sale showing a fictitious purchase price of $28,500.

On October 4, 1991, Brotan reported to the Manchester, New Hampshire, police that the 1958 Corvette had been stolen and later that month received claim forms from Aetna Insurance Company for Brotan's claim for the alleged theft and stripping of the 1958 Corvette. DeLuca had earlier given Brotan a bill of sale for another car that Brotan did not own but proceeded to insure so that the 1958 Corvette could be substituted on the policy prior to filing the claim on the Corvette. Morrow subsequently advised an Aetna investigator that he had sold the 1958 Corvette to Brotan on October 3, 1991, for $28,500.

In his own defense, Nevcherlian denied complicity in any plot and testified that he had registered the 1975 Corvette in Florida as a favor to DeLuca. He admitted signing a bill of sale dated June 3, 1991, at the meeting at DeLuca's home on July 26, 1991, and admitted sending the title for the car to the Narraganset police in October 1991. Morrow also testified in his own defense and denied guilt. He acknowledged giving Brotan an undated bill of sale for the 1958 Corvette with a purported purchase price of $28,500 even though he had received only $15,000. Both Nevcherlian and Morrow admitted that they knew that insurance claims are routinely processed through the mail.

On January 21, 1993, the jury convicted Nevcherlian and Morrow on all of the counts charged against them. Thereafter, Morrow was sentenced to ten months' imprisonment and a fine of $2,000. Nevcherlian was sentenced to ten months' imprisonment, five of which were to be served in home confinement, and was fined $250. These appeals followed. Our discussion begins with the conspiracy count, then addresses the substantive counts and concludes with several miscellaneous claims of error.

II.

Count 1 of the indictment charged all of the defendants with being parties to a continuing conspiracy to commit mail fraud by inducing insurance companies to pay fraudulent claims of loss for purported automobile theft and damage. Both Nevcherlian and Morrow argue that the evidence was so weak as to require a directed judgment of acquittal. Morrow also argues, in the alternative, that a new trial should have been ordered. Both appellants also claim that the district court erred in refusing to grant a mistrial or give a limiting instruction because the evidence showed no single conspiracy that embraced both appellants.

In reviewing the sufficiency of the evidence, we resolve credibility issues and draw inferences in the government's favor, since the issue is whether a jury could reasonably have arrived at the verdict. Our analysis, for reasons that will become clear, starts not with appellants but with DeLuca and Andreoni. The evidence already summarized was ample to permit the jury to find that DeLuca and Andreoni were engaged in a conspiracy to defraud that contemplated the use of the mails in furtherance of the scheme.

Further, the jury could easily find that DeLuca and Andreoni were engaged in a single continuing conspiracy embracing both of the specific frauds attempted here. It is a commonplace that a single conspiracy may embrace multiple crimes. The similarity of the frauds, the core of common participants, the common location, and the overlap in timing all make it permissible to treat the conspiracy as an unbroken one under the criteria commonly used to distinguish between single and multiple conspiracies.

We now turn to consider the roles of Nevcherlian and Morrow. Although Nevcherlian argues that he was not guilty of any conspiracy, we think that the evidence permitted the jury to find that Nevcherlian did participate in a conspiracy to commit mail fraud with DeLuca and Andreoni. Nevcherlian was the prior title holder of the 1975 Corvette used in the first fraud, was familiar with the fraudulent plan as a result of the July 26 meeting, suggested three different ways in which the other participants could increase the fraudulent claim, and provided a false story of the sale to the police. By his own admission, the use of the mails to obtain insurance payments was reasonably foreseeable.

Morrow could also reasonably be found a party to a mail fraud conspiracy with DeLuca and Andreoni based on his role in the 1958 Corvette transaction. The evidence showed that he was familiar with the intended fraudulent use of the car, that he assisted in the fraudulent arrangements by providing phony bill of sale, and that he also knew that the mails were used to process and collect insurance payments. This is not by any means a case in which a defendant's involvement is based merely on the provision of some lawful object or commodity later used in a criminal manner.

While the evidence was thus adequate to show that each appellant participated in a mail fraud conspiracy with DeLuca and Andreoni, the hard question is whether a reasonable fact finder could conclude Nevcherlian and Morrow each participated in the same conspiracy. Put differently, each of the appellants has a colorable claim that, although guilty of conspiracy to commit mail fraud, neither participated in the overarching conspiracy charged in the indictment but rather each joined only in a smaller, separate conspiracy relating to a different car—Nevcherlian being associated with the 1975 Corvette and Morrow with the 1958 Corvette.

The law of conspiracy is fraught with difficulties but perhaps no aspect is more confusing than "the scope to be accorded to a combination, i.e., the singleness or multiplicities of the conspiratorial relationships. . . . " American Law Institute, Model Penal Code and Commentaries 423 (1985). One reason is that the "scope" issue is used to decide a variety of quite different issues, ranging from substantive responsibility for co-conspirator acts, overt act requirements, and double jeopardy, to admissibility of hearsay, venue, joinder and limitations issues. From a policy standpoint, not all should necessarily be treated in the same way.

Further, and perhaps more fundamental as a cause of confusion, is "the verbal ambiguity which leads courts [sometimes] to deal with the crime of conspiracy as though it were a group rather than an act [i.e., of agreement]." *Developments in the Law: Criminal Conspiracy*, 72 Harv. L.Rev. 920, 934 (1959). To emphasize "agreement," the core concept in conspiracy, implies that "scope" is to be resolved by asking what the defendant agreed to do, or at least knew to be likely. By contrast, if the "group" character of the crime is emphasized, "scope" may seem more to be a function of how the enterprise conducted itself rather than what any one individual had in mind.

In our view, the governing principle is this: at a minimum, a conspirator must have knowledge or foresight of the conspiracy's multiplicity of objectives before that defendant is convicted of a multiple-crime conspiracy. Conviction for such a multiple-crime conspiracy remains possible even if the conspiracy is open-ended (e.g., a conspiracy to rob banks) and the specifics of the future crimes (e.g., which banks) is undetermined or at least unknown to the defendant. But if a defendant agrees with others simply to commit a single crime (e.g., to rob one bank) and has no knowledge or foresight of the conspiracy's broader scope, that defendant is a member only of the narrower, one-crime conspiracy.

Our conclusion does not rest upon policy, for policies can be found on either side of the issue. Rather, our view derives in part from the core concept of agreement, for it seems to us hard for a conspirator to "agree" to multiple objectives if instead the conspirator believes that only one crime is intended. Our view is buttressed by precedents that hold or imply that knowledge is required, including language in our own prior cases. Whether anything more than knowledge may be required for agreement depends upon context and, in any event, is not at issue here. In this case the government has not attempted on appeal to point us to evidence to show that either Nevcherlian or Morrow was aware that the conspiracy embraced multiple frauds. No such evidence may exist as to Nevcherlian; Morrow is arguably a closer case but his broader knowledge is not unequivocally established. Nor is this the type of conspiracy, such as a drug ring, where knowledge that multiple crimes are intended may be rather easily inferred based on common practice. In sum, we think that we are not in a position to sustain the convictions here on the ground that Nevcherlian or Morrow engaged in a multiple-crime conspiracy.

This conclusion prolongs our discussion but does not alter the result. The indictment charged Nevcherlian and Morrow with conspiracy to commit mail fraud; and the jury, on ample evidence, convicted them of this very crime. Thus there was no constructive amendment of the indictment. Of course, the indictment charged each defendant with a single continuing multi-crime conspiracy, so as to Nevcherlian and Morrow there was a variance between the facts charged and the facts proved. But the indictment gave appellants ample notice of the events charged, and a variance warrants reversal only if shown to be prejudicial.

On appeal, the closest that either appellant comes to an assertion of prejudice relates to the admission of hearsay. In accordance with settled First Circuit practice, the district judge admitted provisionally a number of co-conspirator statements against both appellants—specifically, recordings or Brotan's testimony of what was said at various meetings. Ultimately, after all of the evidence was admitted, the district judge concluded (outside the presence of the jury) that a single conspiracy existed in which both appellants participated.

Such findings are normally reviewed only for clear error. But here the district court's explanation for its ruling suggests that the court believed it to be sufficient that an overarching conspiracy existed and that each appellant agreed to participate in a phase of its operation. Thus, our disagreement turns on an issue of law, namely our view that (in addition) knowledge of the multiple-crimes objective was requisite. In all events, the government has not pointed to evidence of such knowledge, so a contrary finding would be clearly erroneous.

It is therefore likely true that some of the hearsay relating to the first fraud and admitted against Morrow was not, as to him, covered by the co-conspirator exception to the hearsay rule; and, conversely, some of the hearsay on the second fraud was not admissible against Nevcherlian. Arguably, the co-conspirator hearsay exception is an historical anomaly, there being nothing especially reliable about such statements; but it is settled law, *see* Fed.R.Evid. 801(d)(2)(E), and the exception clearly requires that the defendant be (at some point) a member of the same conspiracy that generates the hearsay statement. *Id*. That condition has not been met here.

It remains to consider whether harm occurred. Normally, where evidence is wrongly admitted over objection, it is for the government to show that it was harmless. Here, however, we think that harmlessness is apparent from the distinctness of the two fraudulent schemes. The admissible evidence against each appellant amply proved his complicity in the narrow conspiracy relating to the car furnished by that appellant.

There is no indication that inadmissible evidence as to the first fraud came in against Nevcherlian or, as to the second, against Morrow.

It is true that in principle some of the evidence used to prove the second fraud was wrongly admitted against Nevcherlian; a limiting instruction excluding its use as to him would have been proper. But nothing tied Nevcherlian to that fraud, and it is a virtual certainty that the jury convicted him because of his involvement with the first fraud. The same is true, mutatis mutandis, of the case against Morrow. Nor is this an instance in which one of the frauds was doubtful and the proof of one depended upon proof of the other. If ever an error was harmless, this is it.

* * *

Notes

1. Do you agree with the First Circuit's method of determining whether there is more than one conspiracy? What evidence might show that Nevcherlian and Morrow participated in the same conspiracy? What evidence might dispute this?

2. The First Circuit found that Nevcherlian and Morrow were joined improperly to a conspiracy and that otherwise inadmissible hearsay (coconspirators' statements) was admitted against them because of the improper joinder. Yet, the court concluded there was no prejudice because of "the distinctness of the two fraudulent schemes." If the schemes are so distinct, why isn't joinder prejudicial enough to require reversal?

B. COCONSPIRATORS' STATEMENTS

In *Morrow*, the First Circuit spoke of the coconspirator hearsay exception as an "historical anomaly." Anomaly or not, use of this exception may be the greatest advantage a litigant (usually the government) obtains in proving the existence of a conspiracy. The next four cases discuss admission of coconspirators statements. Prior to reading these cases, it may be helpful to review, briefly, the evidentiary rules pertaining to hearsay.

"Hearsay is a statement, other than one made by the declarant while testifying at the trial or hearing, offered in evidence to prove the truth of the matter asserted." Fed.R.Evid. 801(c). Most often, the hearsay objection is made when one party attempts to solicit testimony of a statement made outside of the trial or hearing. Because such a statement is not under oath and is not subject to cross examination, it does not bear the indicia of reliability of sworn statements subject to cross examination, and generally is deemed to be inadmissible hearsay.

Federal Rule of Evidence 801, which defines hearsay, specifically provides that a party's own statement made outside of a trial or hearing (and thus not sworn or subject to cross-examination) and *offered against the party* is not hearsay, Fed.R.Evid. 801(d)(2). Rule 801 also provides that statements for which a party is properly deemed responsible are not hearsay. Such statements include those "in which the party has manifested an adoption or belief in its truth", Fed.R.Evid. 801(d)(2)(B) and, significant for our purposes, "a statement by a conspirator of a party [made] during the course and in furtherance of the conspiracy." Fed. R.Evid. 801(d)(2)(E).

An example may help demonstrate these definitional nuances. Assume that Andrew is indicted for delivering cocaine to Brian. Andrew admits he delivered a gym bag to Brian. Andrew claims, however, that he did not know that there was cocaine in the gym bag—he was merely returning Brian's bag which Brian left in Andrew's apartment the prior day.

Assume Chris, a neighbor of Andrew's, is called as a government witness. Chris testifies that she heard Andrew leaving his apartment (on the day in question) and muttering to himself, "I hope I got that hole in this gym bag fixed. I would hate to leave a trail of white powder." The evidentiary significance of this statement is obvious: it helps rebut Andrew's claim of ignorance regarding the contents of the gym bag.

Note that Andrew's overheard statement was not made at a trial or hearing, is not sworn, and is not subject to cross examination. As such it would appear to be inadmissible hearsay. Yet, it is not hearsay and therefore is admissible because, pursuant to Fed.R.Evid. 801(d)(2)(A), it is the statement of a party (Andrew) which is offered against Andrew.

Assume, now, that instead of overhearing Andrew's muttering, Chris overheard Debra, Andrew's close friend, speaking on the telephone. Chris hears Debra say, "Look, Brian, Andrew will be there in 30 minutes. He and I measured everything. There are 2 kilos of coke in the gym bag. You owe us $40,000. If you want more coke, tell Andrew and we will get it." At Andrew's trial, the government calls Chris as a witness, who testifies as to the statements she overheard Debra make in her telephone conversation. Debra's statements are not made at a trial or hearing, are not sworn, and are not subject to cross examination. Debra's statements may, at first glance, appear to be inadmissible hearsay. However, if Debra is a coconspirator with Andrew, and her statement was made during and in furtherance of the conspiracy, Debra's overheard statement is not hearsay and is admissible pursuant to Fed.R.Evid. 801(d)(2)(E).

Although the next case, United States v. Lindemann, 85 F.3d 1232 (7th Cir.1996), provides an excellent discussion of coconspirators' statements, note that the defendant, George Lindemann, was never charged with conspiracy. It is well settled that the government need not charge conspiracy to lay the necessary evidentiary foundation for admission of coconspirators' statements; it is only necessary that the government prove, by a *preponderance* of the evidence, that a conspiracy existed. Thus, when the government does not believe it can prove the existence of a conspiracy beyond a reasonable doubt and thus foregoes charging conspiracy in an indictment, all is not lost—from the government's perspective.

UNITED STATES v. LINDEMANN

United States Court of Appeals, Seventh Circuit, 1996.
85 F.3d 1232.

CUMMINGS, CIRCUIT JUDGE.

"Charisma," a show horse, died in its stall on the night of December 15, 1990. The insurance company that had issued a policy on Charisma's life concluded that the death was the result of natural causes and paid the $250,000 value of the policy. Subsequently, the Federal Bureau of Investigation uncovered an alleged conspiracy between Tommy Burns and Barney Ward to kill horses for pay, allowing the horses' owners to collect insurance proceeds. Burns gave the FBI information indicating that George Lindemann, Jr. ("Lindemann"), a partial owner of Charisma, had arranged the horse's death in order to gain the proceeds of its life insurance policy. Lindemann was tried and convicted of three counts of wire fraud in violation of 18 U.S.C. § 1343. He appeals that conviction and we affirm.

I.

The following is a synopsis of Burns' testimony at trial. Ward[1] had arranged for Burns to kill fourteen horses for pay prior to Charisma's death. On December 13, 1990, Ward called Burns in Chicago and told him that he could make a lot of money by coming to New York to kill a horse for a man Ward identified as "Lindemann." Burns then called Ward's travel agent in New York to book a flight from Chicago to White Plains, New York. Burns arrived in White Plains at 10:18 a.m. on December 15, 1990, and made his way by car to Ward's residence in Brewster, New York—"Castle Hill." The trip took him longer than expected because of icy road conditions. Upon his arrival, Ward told him to call "Cellular Farms," the horse farm of the Lindemann family, and to speak to Marion Hulick, Lindemann's horse trainer and a co-defendant in this action. Two sequential calls were then made by Burns to Hulick at Cellular Farms.

Hulick told Burns that "they had a horse which needed to be killed at their farm." One of Ward's employees drove Burns to Cellular Farms at around 4:00 p.m. where he was taken directly to Hulick's apartment. In the apartment, Burns met Gerald Shepard, an acquaintance who was inquiring about a position at Cellular Farms. Outside of Shepard's hearing, Hulick told Burns that the killing had to be completed that day because "George" wanted it done while he was in Asia and because Charisma was scheduled to travel to Florida the next day. Hulick told Burns that the amount of the insurance policy was $250,000 and Burns

---

1. Ward was a co-defendant in the original indictment, but his trial was severed from the trial of Lindemann and Hulick.

demanded ten percent of the proceeds in exchange for the killing. Hulick responded that "George" would pay whatever it took.

Burns, Hulick and Shepard then drove to a remote area of the farm so that Hulick could point out a back road by which Burns could enter the premises that night. The three then went to the stable area. To indicate which horse was to be killed, Hulick entered the stall of only one horse, whose name plate read "Charisma." Prior to Burns' departure, Hulick assured him that she would see to it that the staff was out that night and that she would lock up the dogs so that his presence would not be detected. Burns then checked into a nearby hotel and purchased electrical cords and other equipment. At about 10:00 p.m. that night, he entered Cellular Farms by way of the back road and electrocuted Charisma in its stall.

Burns' testimony was corroborated through the following testimony and evidence. A colleague of Burns, Harlow Arlie, testified that prior to December 15, 1990, Burns told him that he had arranged a profitable horse killing for "a man in New York who owned a phone corporation." Lindemann's father, George Lindemann, Sr., is a successful businessman in the cellular telephone industry, and Lindemann owns 20 percent of his father's corporation. Weather records confirmed that there were ice storms in the area around Cellular Farms on December 15, 1990. Phone records confirmed that two calls were made from Castle Hill to Cellular Farms at the time identified by Burns. Two of Lindemann's employees confirmed Burns' detailed description of the Cellular Farms premises, including the specifics of a statue in the courtyard and a description of the brass poles containing electrical outlets in each of the horses' stalls. Shepard testified that when Burns arrived at Cellular Farms, Burns and Hulick had a conversation out of his hearing. He also testified that Hulick then drove him and Burns to a remote area of the farm and told Burns, "This is a seldom used road. You can park here and come back." Shepard further confirmed that on the tour of the stables, Hulick entered the stall of only one horse—Charisma. Records confirmed that Lindemann was in Asia from November 23, 1990, to December 22, 1990, and that Charisma was scheduled to travel to Florida on December 16, 1990. Colleen Reed, an employee at Cellular Farms, testified that she was taken out to dinner by Hulick on the night of December 15, 1990. She testified that this was odd because it broke a strictly enforced Cellular Farms rule requiring someone to remain on the premises at all times. Reed testified that when she pointed out to Hulick that no one would be left to monitor the stables, Hulick brushed this fact aside. Reed then found Charisma dead in its stall the morning of December 16, 1990 and observed blood in its nostrils and manure. Finally, it was generally known at Cellular Farms that both Lyman Whitehead and Molly Ash had ridden Charisma in competitions. However, after Lindemann filed the insurance claim for Charisma's death, he specifically told Reed and another employee to lie to the insurance investigators by telling them that Lindemann and his sister were the only people who had ridden Charisma. Lindemann then told the investigators the same thing.

II.

* * *

The government's case against Lindemann was as follows: (1) Lindemann defrauded his insurance carrier by ordering Hulick to have Charisma killed; (2) Hulick carried out this order by bringing in Ward to aid in hiring a killer; (3) Ward brought in Burns; and (4) Burns admitted that he did the killing. Burns' testimony regarding his conversations with Ward, his meeting with Hulick at Cellular Farms, and his electrocution of Charisma was corroborated by other testimony and evidence. Furthermore, Lindemann stipulated to Burns' long relationship with Ward regarding the killing of numerous horses for pay. Thus the evidence strongly indicated that a conspiracy to kill Charisma existed, and that it contained the following members: (1) Burns, who did the killing; (2) Ward, who set up the contact between Cellular Farms and Burns; (3) Hulick, who pointed out to Burns the method of entrance to Cellular Farms and which of the horses was Charisma; and (4) some unknown conspiracy member, who ordered the killing and planned to pay Burns for doing it. Lindemann's contention is that the government presented insufficient evidence to prove that he was that unknown member.

Identification of the defendant as the person who committed the crime is certainly an essential element of any offense. However, in making a challenge to the sufficiency of the evidence, one bears a "heavy burden." United States v. James, 923 F.2d 1261, 1267 (7th Cir.1991). This Court will reverse a conviction for insufficient evidence only if, after reviewing the evidence in a light most favorable to the government, it is determined that no rational trier of fact could have found the defendant guilty beyond a reasonable doubt.

The evidence identifying Lindemann as the unknown member rested specifically on the following testimony of Burns: (1) Ward told Burns that he could make a lot of money coming to New York to kill a horse for a man named "Lindemann"; (2) Hulick told Burns that "George" wanted the killing done while he was in Asia; and (3) Hulick told Burns that "George" would pay whatever it took. Lindemann asserts that these statements were improperly admitted into evidence. If he is wrong, these statements clearly constitute sufficient evidence for the jury to conclude that it was indeed Lindemann who ordered the killing. Unfortunately for Lindemann, because he waived this issue by failing to object when the statements were admitted in the district court,[2] we must review the

---

2. Prior to the trial, the government filed a written proffer and motion in limine requesting that the statements be admitted pursuant to Fed.R.Evid. 801(d)(2)(E). The district court then held a hearing on the motion and specifically asked, "[I]s there anything that is in dispute or any question about the government's meeting its obligation to show the conspirators and the coconspirators as required by United States v. Santiago, [582 F.2d 1128 (7th Cir.

1978)]?" Counsel for Hulick answered in the negative and counsel for Lindemann remained silent. The court then granted the motion. Furthermore, neither Lindemann nor Hulick objected or requested a limiting instruction when the statements were elicited at trial.

Lindemann concedes that he did not object to the admission of the statements. He argues that he did not do so because "the

decision to admit the statements for plain error only. Under this standard, Lindemann must prove that there was an error, that it was plain, and that it affected his substantial rights and the fairness, integrity or public reputation of the judicial proceedings as a whole.

We pause initially to address Lindemann's contention that the statements were inadmissible because they did not satisfy the personal knowledge requirement of Fed.R.Evid. 602.[3] Lindemann contends that pursuant to Rule 602, the government was required to introduce evidence to prove that Ward and Hulick, as the declarants of the statements, had personal knowledge that it was Lindemann who ordered the killing. However, the Advisory Committee Notes to Rule 801(2)(d)(E) specifically refute this contention:

> "No *guarantee of trustworthiness is required in the case of an admission*. The freedom which admissions have enjoyed ... from the restrictive influence of the opinion rule *and the rule requiring firsthand knowledge*, when taken with the apparently prevalent satisfaction with the results, calls for generous treatment of this avenue to admissibility." (emphasis added).

Furthermore, every court that has addressed the issue has held that coconspirator statements are not subject to the requirements of Rule 602. Thus, Rule 602 did not require the government to present specific evidence of Ward's and Hulick's personal knowledge.

With that aside, we turn now to whether it was plain error to admit the statements pursuant to Fed.R.Evid. 801(d)(2)(E). The basis for excluding hearsay evidence is the notion that statements made while not under oath and while not subject to cross-examination are inherently unreliable. However, the Rules except admissions from the hearsay definition because it is disingenuous for a party to claim that a statement that he himself made is unreliable. This justification loses force in conspiracy situations, however, where the declarant is not the party against whom the statement is offered. But two concerns unrelated to reliability favor admission in conspiracy situations. First is the basic agency principle that acts by one conspirator are chargeable against all those who conspired. Pinkerton v. United States, 328 U.S. 640 (1946). Thus one conspirator's statements are admissible as evidence against the others. The second concern is necessity:

statements were admissible to show a conspiracy between certain alleged participants in the fraud scheme." However, he claims that his failure to object does not mean that he abandoned his claim that the statements were inadmissible to identify him as a participant in that scheme. Unfortunately, that is exactly what it means. Attempting to draw a distinction between admissibility regarding the conspiracy and admissibility regarding identification does not eliminate the most basic tenet of the law of waiver: If

one would like to preserve error regarding the admission of evidence, one must make a specific objection to that evidence at the time when it is offered. *See, e.g.*, United States v. Maholias, 985 F.2d 869, 877 (7th Cir.1993).

3. Rule 602 states that "[a] witness may not testify to a matter unless evidence is introduced sufficient to support a finding that the witness has personal knowledge of the matter." Fed.R.Evid. 602.

"Conspiracies are secretive; often their aim is to commit destructive crimes (drug dealing, kidnaping, extortion, murder); often they raise social costs and risks more than individual crimes; live testimony by active participants is hard to get. These reasons account for the crime of conspiracy, the leeway given to the government in prosecuting, and the [coconspirator] exception itself." Mueller and Kirkpatrick, Federal Evidence § 425 (2d ed.1994).

Because of these concerns, the Federal Rules of Evidence treat coconspirator statements as non-hearsay, despite the fact that the declarant is not the party against whom they are offered. Thus a court may admit such statements if it determines that the declarant and the defendant were involved in an existing conspiracy, and that the statement was made during and in furtherance of that conspiracy. Bourjaily v. United States, 483 U.S. 171, 175–176 (1987). The standard to be applied is a preponderance of the evidence. *Id.* Furthermore, in making its determination, the court may consider all non-privileged evidence, Fed.R.Evid. 104(a) ("[The court] is not bound by the rules of evidence except those with respect to privileges."), including the statements themselves. Id. at 181. However, to ensure an element of reliability in the statements, courts have required that some evidence, independent of the statements, exist to corroborate the conspiracy's existence.[4]

Given these principles, Judge Marovich's determination that the statements at issue were made in furtherance of a conspiracy between Lindemann, Hulick, Ward, and Burns, and thus admissible pursuant to Fed.R.Evid. 801(d)(2)(E), was not plain error. The evidence sufficiently demonstrated that Burns killed Charisma and was involved in a conspiracy with others in doing so: Burns admitted to being in the "horse killing business"; he admitted to killing Charisma for pay; Arlie testified that prior to leaving, Burns mentioned being paid to go kill a horse in New York; and Shepard testified that Burns was at Cellular Farms on December 15, 1990. Furthermore, there was sufficient evidence that the conspiracy involved both Hulick and Ward: Burns testified at length to the specific roles of both Hulick and Ward in the conspiracy; phone records confirm telephone calls from Ward's residence to Cellular Farms at the times indicated by Burns; Shepard corroborated that Hulick and Burns had a secretive conversation on December 15, 1990, and that Hulick pointed out to Burns a seldom used back road that he could use "to come back" that night; and Shepard further corroborated that while they were in the stables, Hulick entered Charisma's stall, and no other.

Finally, there is evidence that the conspiracy involved Lindemann. Most important, of course, are the statements themselves, which involved Ward and Hulick referring specifically to "George" and "Linde-

---

4. Although the Supreme Court expressly declined to decide whether a trial court could rely "solely upon [the declarant's] hearsay statements to determine that a conspiracy had been established by a preponderance of the evidence," *Bourjaily*, 483 U.S. at 181, nearly every Circuit Court of Appeals has answered the question in the negative and required some independent evidence to corroborate the conspiracy. [citations omitted]

mann" as the unknown conspiracy member. But the evidence does not end there. The government offered evidence corroborating many of the facts contained in the statements. One of Hulick's statements was that Burns had to kill Charisma on December 15, 1990, because "George want[ed] it done while he [wa]s in Asia," and because Charisma was scheduled to travel to Florida the next day. The government introduced independent evidence proving that Lindemann was in fact in Asia on December 15, 1990, and that he would return a few days later. It also introduced independent evidence that Charisma was scheduled to travel to Florida on December 16, 1990. Proving that particular elements of the statement did in fact occur satisfies the function of the independent evidence requirement: ensuring an element of reliability in the statement as a whole.

In addition, Arlie testified that prior to leaving for New York, Burns told him that he was going to New York to kill a horse for "a man who owned a phone company." The government offered proof that Lindemann owned 20 percent of his father's large cellular phone corporation. The government also introduced evidence that after Charisma's death, Lindemann intentionally lied, and ordered his employees to lie, to insurance investigators so that the insurance company would not be able to apply one of the policy's exceptions. While these actions did take place after Charisma's death, they aid in making it "more likely than not" that Lindemann was involved in the fraud.

Given the multiple statements referring to "George Lindemann," the evidence corroborating facts contained in the statements, and Burns' corroborated testimony regarding the rest of the conspiracy, Judge Marovich was entitled to conclude that, more likely than not, Ward and Hulick were involved in a conspiracy with Lindemann to kill Charisma. Judge Marovich was also entitled to conclude that the statements were made in furtherance of that conspiracy. Each statement was made to identify for Burns the party who would pay him for the killing. Such identifications facilitated Burns' decision to kill Charisma and were therefore in furtherance of the conspiracy. Thus Judge Marovich's determination that the statements were admissible pursuant to Fed.R.Evid. 801(d)(2)(E) was not plain error.

* * *

Notes

1. Proving the evidentiary foundation necessary to admit a coconspirator's statement may not be the only hurdle the government must overcome to obtain admission of such evidence. There also may be constitutional problems in admitting a coconspirator's statements. When a coconspirator's statement is admitted into evidence, the defendant has no opportunity to cross examine the declarant of the statement. This may violate the Sixth Amendment's guarantee that each defendant has the right "to be confronted with the witnesses against him."

The Ninth Circuit dealt with this constitutional hurdle in a securities fraud case, United States v. Weiner, 578 F.2d 757 (9th Cir.1978). Weiner and other accountants for Equity Funding Corporation (Equity Funding) were convicted for overstating the income and claiming non-existent assets so as to increase the market value of Equity Funding's stock. Statements highly incriminating to the defendants made outside of the trial by Stanley Goldblum, President of Equity Funding, were testified to by officers of Equity who appeared as witnesses for the government. The Ninth Circuit rejected the defendants' argument that admission of these statements violated their Sixth Amendment right of confrontation:

"Defendants * * * contend that the testimony of [Samuel] Lowell, [Michael] Sultan, John Templeton [the officers of Equity Funding who testified as government witnesses], and others concerning extrajudicial declarations by Goldblum violated their right of confrontation because the prosecution never called Goldblum as a witness.

"Goldblum was called by the defense but refused to testify after asserting his Fifth Amendment right against self-incrimination. Goldblum's extrajudicial statements were admissible * * * under the coconspirator exception.

"The admissibility of evidence under the coconspirator exception, however, does not automatically demonstrate compliance with the confrontation clause.

"In *Dutton v. Evans,* 400 U.S. 74 (1970), the Supreme Court dealt with a situation where a third party testified to a conversation with Evans' codefendant, Williams, who was tried separately. Williams did not testify at Evans' trial. The Court did not indicate whether Williams was available to testify, and did not address the issue. In dealing with the relationship between the coconspirator hearsay exception and the Sixth Amendment, the Court acknowledged that the confrontation clause does not bar the admission of all hearsay. Although the hearsay rule and the confrontation clause have a similar basis, the two do not precisely overlap. Under *Dutton* an analysis must be made to determine whether there are sufficient indicia of reliability to permit the introduction of the hearsay declarations in spite of the lack of opportunity for the defendant to cross-examine the declarant.

* * *

"Once Goldblum's refusal to testify and his resulting unavailability are established and cross-examination is thus precluded, the next question is whether there are sufficient indicia of reliability to permit introduction of his declarations without violating the Sixth Amendment.

' * * * The relevant factual inquiry is whether, under the circumstances, the unavailability of the declarant for cross-examination deprived the jury of a satisfactory basis for evaluating the truth of the extrajudicial declaration * * *.'

"Among the factors to be considered in determining the reliability of the hearsay declarations is whether the witness testifying would have had knowledge of the roles and identities of others within the conspiracy. Also significant is whether the witness's recollection of the declarant's statements is likely to be accurate and whether the declarant would have had any reason to have lied to the witness. The court must determine whether cross-examination of the declarant would be likely to show that the declarant's statements were unreliable. Another important determination is whether the evidence is 'crucial' or 'devastating' to the defense.

"Employing the *Dutton* approach, we hold that Goldblum's declarations contained sufficient indicia of reliability and were properly admitted. Each of the witnesses testifying about Goldblum's extrajudicial declarations was involved in the day-to-day running of the company. They were officers and employees of Equity Funding, and the conversations to which they testified were directed to the operation of the corporation and the maintenance of its financial records. The witnesses were talking from personal knowledge. Because of their position within the company and, in some cases, within the conspiracy, it is unlikely that Goldblum would have been lying to them. The testimony of Lowell, Evans, and others who were among the original persons charged also contained statements against their own penal interests, a further badge of reliability.

"Finally none of the declarations was 'crucial' or 'devastating.' There was abundant evidence regarding the manipulation of Equity Funding's financial recordkeeping, and the conversations with Goldblum were not a major component of proof against the defendants. In fact, so substantial was the other evidence that, even if error, the admission of Goldblum's declarations would have been error harmless beyond a reasonable doubt."

In 1990 the Supreme Court addressed the issue of whether admission of hearsay generally violates a defendant's rights under the Confrontation Clause of the Sixth Amendment. Idaho v. Wright, 497 U.S. 805, 808 (1990). The Court reaffirmed *Dutton*'s "indicia of reliability" test for determining whether admission of specific hearsay violates a defendant's rights:

"[Hearsay] is admissible only if it bears adequate 'indicia of reliability.' Reliability can be inferred * * * where the evidence falls within a firmly rooted hearsay exception. In other cases, the evidence must be excluded, at least absent a showing of particularized guarantees of trustworthiness." *Id.* at 815 *quoting* Ohio v. Roberts, 448 U.S. 56, 66 (1980).

2. Coconspirators' statements should be distinguished from *"Bruton"* statements. In 1968, the Supreme Court reversed the conviction of George William Bruton, holding that admission of a confession by Bruton's codefendant, Evans, which also implicated Bruton, violated Bruton's Sixth Amendment right of cross-examination. Evans did not testify at the joint trial in which Evans and Bruton were codefendants. Evan's confession, also implicating Bruton, was introduced into evidence, however. Because Evans invoked his Fifth Amendment privilege against self incrimination, Bruton was not able to call Evans to the stand and cross-examine him about the references to Bruton in Evans's confession.[5] It was this inability to cross

5. 391 U.S. 123, 126 (1968).

examine a key witness that led the Court to reverse Bruton's conviction as a violation of his Sixth Amendment right to counsel.

After this decision, if the government wishes to introduce confessions which implicate others besides the confessor, the government must *"Bruton-ize"* confessions by deleting all references to other criminal actors.

The key difference between proper admission of a coconspirator's statement pursuant to Federal Rule of Evidence 801(d)(2)(E) and improper admission of a codefendant's statement pursuant to *Bruton* is the circumstances under which the statement is made. If the statement is made during a conspiracy and in furtherance of it, it likely will qualify as a coconspirator's statement. If the statement is a confession, it is not made "in furtherance" of the conspiracy. Excerpts from the next case, United States v. Smith, 46 F.3d 1223 (1st Cir.1995), provide a helpful discussion of the *Bruton* issue:

"Between December 1985 and March 1991, James Smith, Richard Mangone, Robert Cohen, and Ambrose Devaney fraudulently obtained tens of millions of dollars in real estate loans from the Barnstable Community Federal Credit Union (BCCU) and the Digital Employees Federal Credit Union (Digital). Smith, a real estate developer, and Mangone, President of Digital, were co-founders of BCCU. Robert Cohen was general counsel to both credit unions. Smith and Mangone controlled much of BCCU's lending through Lynn Vasapolle, a coconspirator who was BCCU's manager. Devaney was a real estate developer, the only defendant who was an outsider to the credit unions.

"The loans were used in part to finance the purchase of commercial real estate on Cape Cod. To circumvent the credit unions' policies restricting 'insider' loans or limiting maximum borrowing by an individual, Smith, Mangone, and Devaney formed more than a dozen nominee trusts to create the impression that the loans were going to many different borrowers. Cohen, who served as closing attorney for the credit unions, prepared the trust instruments and closing binders. He also instructed Vasapolle what documents to include in her BCCU files.

"The conspirators concealed their interest in the trusts by representing the trustees as putative owners. At Mangone's direction, Vasapolle prepared false certificates of beneficial interest on a blank form that Cohen had provided. There was evidence that in some cases Cohen directly submitted false certificates to BCCU, while maintaining parallel sets of genuine and false certificates in his files. In one case where he served as trustee, Cohen signed a certificate misrepresenting himself and his wife as the beneficiaries of the trust.

"For their part, Smith and Vasapolle prepared false financial statements for BCCU showing that the trustees qualified for the loans. Smith altered the purchase and sale agreements, sometimes inflating the purchase price by millions of dollars, in order to obtain larger loans. The excess loan proceeds were usually deposited in Cohen's client account, transferred to one of Smith's accounts, and then distributed to Smith, Mangone, and Devaney.

"In the late 1980's, the real estate market on Cape Cod collapsed. Unable to sell the properties and faced with mounting debts, Smith,

Mangone, and Devaney resorted to a pyramid scheme. Cohen created new trusts that purported to buy subdivisions from the old trusts; the sham 'sales' were in turn financed by new loans from the credit unions. By March 1991, when BCCU was seized by regulators from the National Credit Union Administration (NCUA), the outstanding balance on the Smith–Mangone–Devaney loans had reached forty to sixty million dollars.

"On September 12, 1992, Smith, Mangone, Cohen, and Devaney were indicted for conspiracy (18 U.S.C. § 371) to commit bank fraud (18 U.S.C. § 1344); unlawful receipt of monies by a credit union officer (18 U.S.C. § 1006); and unlawful monetary transactions (money laundering) (18 U.S.C. § 1957). Each defendant was also charged with various offenses underlying the conspiracy. The case was tried on a redacted indictment that included a conspiracy count, seven bank fraud counts, seven parallel unlawful receipt counts (which concerned Mangone alone), and the money laundering charges. Vasapolle testified under a plea agreement and explained the workings of the conspiracy.

"Smith and Mangone were convicted on all counts. Cohen was convicted on all counts except for four money laundering counts. Devaney was convicted of conspiracy, three counts of bank fraud and one count of money laundering. Mangone fled before sentencing. Smith was sentenced to fifteen years imprisonment and three years supervised release, and ordered to pay up to twenty million dollars in restitution. Cohen was sentenced to ten years imprisonment. Devaney was sentenced to thirty-seven months imprisonment and three years supervised release, and was ordered to pay up to ten million dollars in restitution.

"We begin with Smith's claim of error under Bruton v. United States, 391 U.S. 123, (1968)—the heart of his argument for severance. *Bruton* held that, because of the substantial risk that a jury, despite contrary instructions, will look to a codefendant's incriminating extrajudicial statement in determining a defendant's guilt, admission of the codefendant's statement in a joint trial violates the defendant's right of cross-examination under the Confrontation Clause of the Sixth Amendment. As the Court emphasized in Richardson v. Marsh, 481 U.S. 200, 208, (1987), *Bruton* error occurs where the codefendant's statement 'expressly implicate[s]' the defendant, leaving no doubt that it would prove 'powerfully incriminating' (quoting *Bruton*, 391 U.S. at 124 n. 1, 135, 88 S.Ct. at 1622 n. 1, 1628). There is no *Bruton* error if the statement becomes incriminating 'only when linked with evidence introduced . . . at trial.' *Richardson*, 481 U.S. at 208.

"Against this backdrop, we turn to the claimed *Bruton* error. The trial began on May 17, 1993. During the government's case, Vasapolle testified that she, Cohen, Smith, and Mangone met twice after the BCCU takeover to discuss the possibility of removing or destroying loan documents from the BCCU's and Cohen's files. Cohen allegedly agreed to remove some of his documents, but advised his coconspirators that it would be impossible to purge all of the files. He also refused to destroy any documents because to do so would be an obstruction of justice.

"On June 28, 1993, the last day of testimony, Cohen called Professor Richard Huber, an authority on professional responsibility. Huber testified subject to a limiting instruction that his testimony 'has nothing to do with ... Mr. Smith [and] Mr. Devaney.' According to Huber, Cohen called him in late March of 1991 and 'indicated that he had a serious problem with professional responsibility that was facing him and he would like to have an opportunity to discuss it.' Cohen met with Huber on April 4, 1991. Huber testified:

'Mr. Cohen explained that he had been involved as a lawyer for a banking institution.... [O]n the 23rd of March [1991], a former officer of the bank, a former director of the bank, and a bank manager came in and spoke to him ... concerning activities that involved them and their work at the bank. * * * [E]ssentially it amounted to the issue that certain documents had been changed, the information had been changed, figures had been changed, data had been changed, that this had been done after preparation by Mr. Cohen and after they had been presumptively completed, as far as he was concerned, and were in file—in his files, the bank files. He indicated that it was a possibility, though he wasn't certain, as I can recall this, that there may have been also forgeries, in terms of signatures including possibly his own. But the main thrust ... was that documentation which he had prepared and which was complete and on file, had been changed by these three people in their indication to him when they met with him.'

"Cohen asked 'whether he could reveal any of this information, which had been received from these persons as clients.' Huber advised him that 'there was no way in which he could reveal confidences at that point in time,' but that he could do so 'if it was necessary to protect himself, that is, where he would be charged with crime or where he would be sued civilly.'

"After Huber testified, Cohen's codefendants moved for a mistrial, citing *Bruton*. The court deferred its ruling until Cohen's next witness had testified. Just before Cohen's closing argument, the court instructed counsel '[not to] argue what Cohen said to Huber,' because that evidence would be stricken. The court then stated, '[Y]ou may argue what Huber said to Cohen.' The next day, the court instructed the jury that Huber's testimony of what Cohen 'said to him about other persons [is] ... stricken entirely.' Left in evidence was 'the fact that Mr. Cohen went to Huber, the fact that he made disclosures to Mr. Huber about what he said to Mr. Cohen.... ' As it explained at sidebar, the court submitted the case to the jury because the *Bruton* error (if any) occurred during the last day of testimony in a lengthy trial, and might be mooted by an acquittal. In addition, the harmfulness of the error would be more apparent in light of the verdicts.

"All of the defendants were convicted, and Smith moved for a new trial. The district court opined that there had been an 'egregious error' under *Bruton*. In the court's view, however, the *Bruton* evidence was 'merely cumulative' of the government's case and therefore harmless beyond a reasonable doubt.

"In the classic *Bruton* scenario, Cohen would have made a detailed confession of bank fraud, naming Smith as an accomplice. The government could not introduce such an incriminating statement at a joint trial, even against Cohen alone. In fact, Cohen—not the government—offered his own statement that three unnamed clients came to him and essentially confessed to bank fraud. The government emphasizes the self-serving nature of this evidence, while Smith dwells on the power of a confession offered to one's own attorney at a time of presumed confidence. To us, these factors seem more or less a wash. We shall assume without deciding that the district court correctly found that *Bruton* error had occurred. Cohen's statement could be found to be 'powerfully incriminat[ing]' on its face, even without 'inferential incrimination' from other evidence in the case.

"We are nonetheless convinced that any error was harmless beyond a reasonable doubt. The jury convicted all the defendants on the conspiracy count, and Cohen on most of the substantive counts. Even if the jury threw the curative instructions to the wind and considered the stricken testimony as evidence against Smith, the scenario which implicates *Bruton*, it could not have believed Cohen's claim that the unnamed clients confessed to him at the close of the conspiracy. No one confesses to a partner in crime.

"Admittedly, Cohen's statement might tend to incriminate Smith and Devaney by showing that the coconspirators met to discuss damage control. In this sense, however, the statement falls far outside the pale of the 'powerfully incriminating' evidence detail to the coconspirators' meetings in the wake of the BCCU takeover. Thus, once Cohen's statement is considered as something other than an account of the codefendants' confessions, it becomes merely cumulative of the government's case and could not have produced *Bruton* error.

"The right of confrontation ensures that a criminal defendant can cross-examine his or her accusers. Had Cohen testified to the confession himself, Smith's cross-examination of Cohen would have sought to show that no confession ever occurred. The verdicts suggest that the jury, if it considered this evidence, found just that. The jury, even if it disregarded the limiting instructions, plainly did not believe Cohen's claim that his codefendants had confessed to him. It is clear, therefore, that any *Bruton* error was harmless beyond a reasonable doubt."

———

In *Lindemann, supra,* the Seventh Circuit referred to the Supreme Court's opinion in Bourjaily v. United States, 483 U.S. 171 (1987). As you read the Court's decision in *Bourjaily*, determine whether you agree with the majority or the dissent.

BOURJAILY v. UNITED STATES

United States Supreme Court, 1987.
483 U.S. 171.

REHNQUIST, CHIEF JUSTICE.

Federal Rule of Evidence 801(d)(2)(E) provides, "A statement is not hearsay if * * * [t]he statement is offered against a party and is * * * a statement by a coconspirator of a party during the course and in furtherance of the conspiracy." We granted certiorari to answer three questions regarding the admission of statements under Rule 801(d)(2)(E): * * * whether the court must determine by independent evidence that the conspiracy existed and that the defendant and the declarant were members of this conspiracy * * *.

In May 1984, Clarence Greathouse, an informant working for the Federal Bureau of Investigation, arranged to sell a kilogram of cocaine to Angelo Lonardo. Lonardo agreed that he would find individuals to distribute the drug. When the sale became imminent, Lonardo stated in a tape-recorded telephone conversation that he had a "gentleman friend" who had some questions to ask about the cocaine. In a subsequent telephone call, Greathouse spoke to the "friend" about the quality of the drug and the price. Greathouse then spoke again with Lonardo, and the two arranged the details of the purchase. They agreed that the sale would take place in a designated hotel parking lot, and Lonardo would transfer the drug from Greathouse's car to the "friend," who would be waiting in the parking lot in his own car. Greathouse proceeded with the transaction as planned, and FBI agents arrested Lonardo and petitioner immediately after Lonardo placed a kilogram of cocaine into petitioner's car in the hotel parking lot. In petitioner's car, the agents found over $20,000 in cash.

Petitioner was charged with conspiring to distribute cocaine, in violation of 21 U.S.C. § 846, and possession of cocaine with intent to distribute, a violation of 21 U.S.C. § 841(a)(1). The Government introduced, over petitioner's objection, Angelo Lonardo's telephone statements regarding the participation of the "friend" in the transaction. The District Court found that, considering the events in the parking lot and Lonardo's statements over the telephone, the Government had established by a preponderance of the evidence that a conspiracy involving Lonardo and petitioner existed, and that Lonardo's statements over the telephone had been made in the course of and in furtherance of the conspiracy. Accordingly, the trial court held that Lonardo's out-of-court statements satisfied Rule 801(d)(2)(E) and were not hearsay. Petitioner was convicted on both counts and sentenced to 15 years. The United States Court of Appeals for the Sixth Circuit affirmed. 781 F.2d 539 (1986). The Court of Appeals agreed with the District Court's analysis and conclusion that Lonardo's out-of-court statements were admissible under the Federal Rules of Evidence. The court also rejected petitioner's contention that because he could not cross-examine Lonardo, the admission of these statements violated his constitutional right to confront the witnesses against him. We affirm.

Before admitting a coconspirator's statement over an objection that it does not qualify under Rule 801(d)(2)(E), a court must be satisfied that the statement actually falls within the definition of the rule. There must be evidence that there was a conspiracy involving the declarant and the nonoffering party, and that the statement was made "during the course and in furtherance of the conspiracy." Federal Rule of Evidence 104(a) provides: "Preliminary questions concerning * * * the admissibility of evidence shall be determined by the court." Petitioner and respondent agree that the existence of a conspiracy and petitioner's involvement in it are preliminary questions of fact that, under Rule 104, must be resolved by the court. * * *

* * *

* * * [Petitioner] challenges the admission of Lonardo's statements. Petitioner argues that in determining whether a conspiracy exists and whether the defendant was a member of it, the court must look only to independent evidence—that is, evidence other than the statements sought to be admitted. Petitioner relies on Glasser v. United States, 315 U.S. 60 (1942), in which this Court first mentioned the so-called "bootstrapping rule." The relevant issue in *Glasser* was whether Glasser's counsel, who also represented another defendant, faced such a conflict of interest that Glasser received ineffective assistance. Glasser contended that conflicting loyalties led his lawyer not to object to statements made by one of Glasser's coconspirators. The Government argued that any objection would have been fruitless because the statements were admissible. The Court rejected this proposition:

> "[S]uch declarations are admissible over the objection of an alleged coconspirator, who was not present when they were made, only if there is proof aliunde that he is connected with the conspiracy * * *. Otherwise, hearsay would lift itself by its own bootstraps to the level of competent evidence." *Id.*

The Court revisited the bootstrapping rule in United States v. Nixon, 418 U.S. 683 (1974), where again, in passing, the Court stated: "Declarations by one defendant may also be admissible against other defendants upon a sufficient showing, *by independent evidence,* of a conspiracy among one or more other defendants and the declarant and if the declarations at issue were in furtherance of that conspiracy." *Id.* Read in the light most favorable to petitioner, *Glasser* could mean that a court should not consider hearsay statements at all in determining preliminary facts under Rule 801(d)(2)(E). Petitioner, of course, adopts this view of the bootstrapping rule. *Glasser,* however, could also mean that a court must have *some* proof aliunde, but may look at the hearsay statements themselves in light of this independent evidence to determine whether a conspiracy has been shown by a preponderance of the evidence. The Courts of Appeals have widely adopted the former view and held that in determining the preliminary facts relevant to coconspirators' out-of-court statements, a court may not look at the hearsay statements themselves for their evidentiary value.

Both *Glasser* and *Nixon,* however, were decided before Congress enacted the Federal Rules of Evidence in 1975. These Rules now govern the treatment of evidentiary questions in federal courts. Rule 104(a) provides: "Preliminary questions concerning * * * the admissibility of evidence shall be determined by the court * * *. In making its determination it is not bound by the rules of evidence except those with respect to privileges." Similarly, Rule 1101(d)(1) states that the Rules of Evidence (other than with respect to privileges) shall not apply to "[t]he determination of questions of fact preliminary to admissibility of evidence when the issue is to be determined by the court under rule 104." The question thus presented is whether any aspect of *Glasser*'s bootstrapping rule remains viable after the enactment of the Federal Rules of Evidence.

Petitioner concedes that Rule 104, on its face, appears to allow the court to make the preliminary factual determinations relevant to Rule 801(d)(2)(E) by considering any evidence it wishes, unhindered by considerations of admissibility. That would seem to many to be the end of the matter. Congress has decided that courts may consider hearsay in making these factual determinations. Out-of-court statements made by anyone, including putative coconspirators, are often hearsay. Even if they are, they may be considered, *Glasser* and the bootstrapping rule notwithstanding. But petitioner nevertheless argues that the bootstrapping rule, as most Courts of Appeals have construed it, survived this apparently unequivocal change in the law unscathed and that Rule 104, as applied to the admission of coconspirator's statements, does not mean what it says. We disagree.

Petitioner claims that Congress evidenced no intent to disturb the bootstrapping rule, which was embedded in the previous approach, and we should not find that Congress altered the rule without affirmative evidence so indicting. It would be extraordinary to require legislative history to *confirm* the plain meaning of Rule 104. The Rule on its face allows the trial judge to consider any evidence whatsoever, bound only by the rules of privilege. We think that the Rule is sufficiently clear that to the extent that it is inconsistent with petitioner's interpretation of *Glasser* and *Nixon*, the Rule prevails.

Nor do we agree with petitioner that this construction of Rule 104(a) will allow courts to admit hearsay statements without any credible proof of the conspiracy, thus fundamentally changing the nature of the coconspirator exception. Petitioner starts with the proposition that coconspirators' out-of-court statements are deemed unreliable and are inadmissible, at least until a conspiracy is shown. Since these statements are unreliable, petitioner contends that they should not form any part of the basis for establishing a conspiracy, the very antecedent that renders them admissible.

Petitioner's theory ignores two simple facts of evidentiary life. First, out-of-court statements are only *presumed* unreliable. The presumption may be rebutted by appropriate proof. See Fed.R.Evid. 803(24) (otherwise inadmissible hearsay may be admitted if circumstantial guarantees of trustworthiness demonstrated). Second, individual pieces of evidence, insufficient in themselves to prove a point, may in cumulation prove it. The sum of an evidentiary presentation may well be greater than its constituent parts. Taken together, these two propositions demonstrate that a piece of evidence, unreliable in isolation, may become quite probative when corroborated by other evidence. A per se rule barring consideration of these hearsay statements during preliminary fact-finding is not therefore required. Even if out-of-court declarations by coconspirators are presumptively unreliable, trial courts must be permitted to evaluate these statements for their evidentiary worth as revealed by the particular circumstances of the case. Courts often act as fact finders, and there is no reason to believe that courts are any less able to properly recognize the probative value of evidence in this particular area. The party opposing admission has an adequate incentive to point out the shortcomings in such evidence before the trial court finds the preliminary facts. If the opposing party is unsuccessful in keeping the evidence from the fact finder, he still has the opportunity to attack the probative value of the evidence as it relates to the substantive issue in the case. See, e.g., Fed.R.Evid. 806 (allowing attack on credibility of out-of-court declarant).

We think that there is little doubt that a coconspirator's statements could themselves be probative of the existence of a conspiracy and the participation of both the defendant and the declarant in the conspiracy. Petitioner's case presents a paradigm. The out-of-court statements of Lonardo indicated that Lonardo was involved in a conspiracy with a "friend." The statements indicated that the friend had agreed with Lonardo to buy a kilogram of cocaine and to distribute it. The statements also revealed that the friend would be at the hotel parking lot, in his car, and would accept the cocaine from Greathouse's car after Greathouse gave Lonardo the keys. Each one of Lonardo's statements may itself be unreliable, but taken as a whole, the entire conversation between Lonardo and Greathouse was corroborated by independent evidence. The friend, who turned out to be petitioner, showed up at the prearranged spot at the prearranged time. He picked up the cocaine, and a significant sum of money was found in his car. On these facts, the trial court concluded, in our view correctly, that the Government had established the existence of a conspiracy and petitioner's participation in it.

We need not decide in this case whether the courts below could have relied solely upon Lonardo's hearsay statements to determine that a conspiracy had been established by a preponderance of the evidence. To the extent that *Glasser* meant that courts could not look to the hearsay statements themselves for any purpose, it has clearly been superseded by Rule 104(a). It is sufficient for today to hold that a court, in making a preliminary factual determination under Rule 801(d)(2)(E), may examine the hearsay statements sought to be admitted. As we have held in other cases concerning admissibility determinations, "the judge should receive the evidence and give it such weight as his judgment and experience counsel." United States v. Matlock, 415 U.S. 164, 175 (1974). The courts below properly considered the statements of Lonardo and the subsequent events in finding that the Government had established by a preponderance of the evidence that Lonardo was involved in a conspiracy with petitioner. We have no reason to believe that the District Court's fact-finding of this point was clearly erroneous. We hold that Lonardo's out-of-court statements were properly admitted against petitioner.

* * *

The judgment of the Court of Appeals is affirmed.

JUSTICE BLACKMUN, with whom JUSTICE BRENNAN and JUSTICE MARSHALL join, dissenting.

I disagree with the Court * * *. I do not believe that the Federal Rules of Evidence changed the long- and well-settled law to the effect that the preliminary questions of fact, relating to admissibility of a nontestifying coconspirator's statement, must be established by evidence independent of that statement itself. * * * I disagree with the Court's conclusion that allowing the coconspirator's statement to be considered in the resolution of these factual questions will remedy problems of the statement's unreliability. In my view, the abandonment of the independent-evidence requirement will lead, instead, to the opposite result. This is because the abandonment will eliminate one of the few safeguards of reliability that this exemption from the hearsay definition possesses. * * *

* * *

* * * [W]hen Rule 801(d)(2)(E) and Rule 104(a) are considered together—an examination that the Court neglects to undertake—there appears to be a conflict between the fact that no change in the coconspirator hearsay exemption was intended by Rule 801(d)(2)(E) and the freedom that Rule 104(a) gives a trial court to rely on hearsay in resolving preliminary factual questions. Although one must be somewhat of an interpretative funambulist to walk between the conflicting demands of these Rules in order to arrive at a resolution that will satisfy their respective concerns, this effort is far to be preferred over accepting the easily available safety "net" of Rule 104(a)'s "plain meaning." The purposes of *both* Rules can be achieved by considering the relevant preliminary factual question for Rule 104(a) analysis to be the following: "whether a conspiracy that included the declarant and the defendant against whom a statement is offered has been demonstrated to exist on the basis of evidence *independent of the declarant's hearsay statements* "(emphasis added). S. Saltzburg & K. Redden, Federal Rules of Evidence Manual 735 (4th ed. 1986). This resolution sufficiently answers Rule 104(a)'s concern with allowing a trial court to consider hearsay in determining preliminary factual questions, because the only hearsay not available for its consideration is the statement at issue. The exclusion of the statement from the preliminary analysis maintains the common-law exemption unchanged.

* * *

* * * [One of] [t]he Court's * * * argument[s] in favor of abandonment of the independent-evidence rule might best be characterized as an attempt at pragmatic or "real world" analysis. The Court suggests that, while a coconspirator's statement might be presumed unreliable when considered in isolation, it loses this unreliability when examined together with other evidence of the conspiracy and the defendant's participation in it. In the Court's view, such a consideration of the statement will reveal its probative value, as the facts of this case demonstrate. Proceeding in this "real world" vein, the Court believes that the trial court is capable of detecting any remaining unreliability in the coconspirator's statement and that the defendant is afforded the opportunity to point out any shortcomings of the out-of-court statement.

I, too, prefer an approach that includes a realistic view of problems that come before the Court. I am inclined, however, to remain with the traditional exemption that has been shaped by years of "real world" experience with the use of coconspirator statements in trials and by a frank recognition to the possible unreliability of these statements.

As explained above, despite the recognized need by prosecutors for coconspirator statements, these statements often have been considered to be somewhat unreliable. It has long been understood that such statements in some cases may constitute, at best, nothing more than the "idle chatter" of a declarant or, at worst, malicious gossip. Moreover, when confronted with such a statement, an innocent defendant would have a difficult time defending himself against it, for, if he were not in the conspiracy, he would have no idea why the conspirator made the statement. Even an experienced trial judge might credit an incriminatory statement that a defendant could not explain, precisely because the defendant had no ready explanation for it. * * * The independent-evidence requirement was one * * * safeguard [against such unreliability.]

If this requirement is set aside, then one of the exemption's safeguards is lost. From a "real world" perspective, I do not believe that considering the statement together with the independent evidence will cure this loss. Contrary to the Court's suggestion, the situation in which a trial court now commonly will rely on the coconspirator's statement to establish the existence of a conspiracy in which the defendant participated will not be limited to instances in which the statement constitutes just another "piece of evidence," to be considered as no more important than the independent evidence. Rather, such a statement will serve the greatest purpose, and thus will be introduced most frequently, in situations where *all* the other evidence that the prosecution can muster to show the existence of a conspiracy will not be adequate. In this situation, despite the use of hearsay admissible under other exceptions and the defendant's and other conspirators' actions, the coconspirator's statement will be necessary to satisfy the trial court by a preponderance of the evidence that the defendant was a member of an existing conspiracy. Accordingly, the statement will likely *control* the interpretation of whatever other evidence exists and could well transform a series of innocuous actions by a defendant into evidence that he was participating in a criminal conspiracy. This is what "bootstrapping" is all about. Thus, the

Court removes one reliability safeguard from an exemption, even though the situation in which a coconspirator's statement will be used to resolve the preliminary factual questions is that in which the court will rely *most* on the statement.

It is at least heartening, however, to see that the Court reserves the question whether a coconspirator's statement alone, without *any* independent evidence, could establish the existence of a conspiracy and a defendant's participation in it. I have no doubt that, in this ultimate example of "bootstrapping," the statement could not pass the preliminary factual test for its own admissibility, even under the Court's reformulation. For the presumptively unreliable statement would have no corroborative independent evidence that would bring out its probative value. If the statement alone could establish its own foundation for admissibility, a defendant could be convicted of conspiracy on the basis of an unsupported remark by an alleged conspirator—a result that surely the Court could not countenance and that completely cuts the exception adrift from its agency mooring.

———

Notes

1. Can you identify the coconspirator's statements at issue? The coconspirator who made the statement? The witness who testified to the statements? The evidentiary significance of the statements?

2. Was Bourjaily's claim of error credible? Why or why not?

3. In his dissenting opinion, Justice Blackmun argues that Federal Rules of Evidence 104 and 801(d)(2)(e) should be read together. Presumably doing so would mean that the coconspirator's statement for which admission is being sought should not be used to show the foundation necessary to admit the statement (i.e., that a conspiracy exists and that the statement is in furtherance of the conspiracy), however, other hearsay would be admitted solely to establish this foundation. Perhaps the following example will help demonstrate this distinction.

Assume Evan and Frank are alleged to be coconspirators in an illegal drug business. Assume also that the government has located a witness, Gladys, who could testify about conversations she had with Frank wherein Frank implicated Evan in the drug business. To properly admit Gladys' testimony of conversations, the government must demonstrate that Frank and Evan were coconspirators and that Frank's statements to Gladys were made during and in furtherance of this conspiracy. Under Justice Blackmun's approach, Frank's statements to Gladys can not be used to establish this foundation.

However, assume also that Gladys overheard a mutual friend, Harry, say "Evan and Frank have a cocaine business." Harry is not available as a witness. His statement, made outside of a hearing or trial, is not sworn, or subject to cross examination, and is inadmissible hearsay (assuming none of the exceptions in Fed.R.Evid. 803 apply). Under Justice Blackmun's approach, Gladys' testimony as to what she heard Harry say is admissible, solely to show that a conspiracy existed between

Frank and Evan and that Frank's statement was made in furtherance of the conspiracy. Gladys' testimony as to Frank's statement, because it is the statement in issue, will not be eligible to show this foundation.

What do you think of Justice Blackmun's approach? Do you prefer it or the approach taken by the majority? Note that the question of whether the proper foundation has been laid for admission of a coconspirator's statement is an issue for the court. Thus, only the court, and not the jury, will hear the hearsay testimony that is admitted to establish this necessary foundation. In your mind, would this fact make the approach of the majority, or Justice Blackmun, preferable?

4. Also in his dissenting opinion, Justice Blackmun suggests that statements by coconspirators in furtherance of a conspiracy may not be reliable. Can you think of instances where this may be true? If true, is this reason to reject the majority's position?

5. As the Seventh Circuit indicated in *Lindemann*, *supra*, although the Supreme Court "expressly declined [in *Bourjaily*] to decide whether a trial court could rely 'solely upon [the declarant's] hearsay statements to determine that a conspiracy had been established by a preponderance of the evidence,' nearly every Circuit Court of Appeals has answered the question in the negative and required some independent evidence to corroborate the conspiracy." In this regard, the following discussion by the United States Court of Appeals for the Ninth Circuit is typical:

"This court has answered the question left open in *Bourjaily*. We have ruled that a coconspirator's out-of-court statement, standing alone, is insufficient to establish that the defendant had knowledge of and participated in a particular conspiracy. To abandon the requirement that *some* evidence aside from the proffered coconspirator's statements be presented to show that the defendant knowingly participated in the alleged conspiracy would be to render all such statements self-validating. Such a ruling would 'eliminate one of the few safeguards of reliability that this exemption from the hearsay definition possesses.' *Bourjaily*, 483 U.S. at 171. (Blackmun, J., joined by Brennan and Marshall, JJ., dissenting).

"Accordingly, in this circuit, when the proponent of the coconspirator's statement offers *no* additional proof of defendant's knowledge of and participation in the conspiracy, the statement must be excluded from evidence. Where, on the other hand, some additional proof is offered, the court must determine whether such proof, viewed in light of the coconspirator's statement itself, demonstrates by a preponderance of the evidence that defendant knew of and participated in the conspiracy."[e]

6. Do you think coconspirators' statements should be admitted against a defendant who is not a member of the conspiracy at the time the statements were made? A majority of federal courts of appeals hold that admission is permissible. The following discussion by the United States Court of Appeals for the Fifth Circuit is typical of the Courts' analysis of this question:

e. United States v. Silverman, 861 F.2d   571, 578 (9th Cir.1988).

"Holder [a defendant] also contends that, even if a conspiracy existed at the time of that telephone conversation, such conspiracy existed only between Chartrain and Cook [other defendants]. Holder's assertion that he was not a member of the conspiracy at the time of the telephone conversation does not help him. An otherwise admissible declaration of one coconspirator is admissible against members of the conspiracy who joined after the statement was made.[6]"

When one examines the requirements for admission of coconspirators' statements, this reasoning becomes clearer. Recall that the following must be shown for admission: (1) a conspiracy existed, (2) the coconspirator/declarant and the defendant were members of the conspiracy, and (3) the statement was made during the course and in furtherance of the conspiracy. Nowhere is it required that the defendant be a member of the conspiracy *at the time the statement was made*.

Do you agree with this reasoning and conclusion? Is there a legitimate distinction between disallowing admission of statements made by a coconspirator *after* the conspiracy has ended (*Krulewitch v. United States, infra*, disallows this) yet allowing admission of statements by one conspirator *before* the defendant joined the conspiracy? If so, what?

———

As the next case demonstrates, not every statement by coconspirators about their conspiracy will qualify for admission pursuant to Fed. R.Evid. 801(d)(2)(E).

KRULEWITCH v. UNITED STATES

United States Supreme Court, 1949.
336 U.S. 440.

MR. JUSTICE BLACK.

A federal district court indictment charged in three counts that petitioner and a woman defendant had (1) induced and persuaded another woman to go on October 20, 1941, from New York City to Miami, Florida, for the purpose of prostitution, in violation of 18 U.S.C. § 399;[f] (2) transported or caused her to be transported from New York to Miami for that purpose, in violation of 18 U.S.C. § 398;[g] and (3) conspired to commit those offenses in violation of 18 U.S.C. § 88.[h] Tried alone, the petitioner was convicted on all three counts of the indictment. The Court of Appeals affirmed. 167 F.2d 943. * * * We granted certiora-

---

6. United States v. Holder, 652 F.2d 449, 451 (5th Cir.1981). *See also* United States v. Murphy, 852 F.2d 1, 8–9 (1st Cir.1988); United States v. Badalamenti, 794 F.2d 821, 826–28 (2d Cir.1986); United States v. Osgood, 794 F.2d 1087, 1093 (5th Cir.1986); United States v. Balistrieri, 778 F.2d 1226, 1230–31 (7th Cir.1985); United States v. Jackson, 757 F.2d 1486, 1490 (4th Cir.1985); United States v. Leroux, 738 F.2d 943, 949–50 (8th Cir.1984); United States v. Jannotti, 729 F.2d 213, 221 (3d Cir.1984); United States v. Tombrello, 666 F.2d 485, 491 (11th Cir.1982); United States v. Anderson, 532 F.2d 1218, 1230 (9th Cir.1976).

f. Currently, 18 U.S.C. § 2422.

g. Currently, 18 U.S.C. § 2421.

h. Currently, 18 U.S.C. § 371.

ri limiting our review to consideration of alleged error in admission of certain hearsay testimony against petitioner over his timely and repeated objections.

The challenged testimony was elicited by the Government from its complaining witness, the person whom petitioner and the woman defendant allegedly induced to go from New York to Florida for the purpose of prostitution. The testimony narrated the following purported conversation between the complaining witness and petitioner's alleged coconspirator, the woman defendant.

"She asked me, she says, 'You didn't talk yet?' And I says, 'No.' And she says, 'Well, don't,' she says, 'until we get you a lawyer.' And then she says, 'Be very careful what you say.' And I can't put it in exact words. But she said, 'It would be better for us two girls to take the blame than Kay (the defendant) because he couldn't stand it, he couldn't stand to take it.' "

The time of the alleged conversation was more than a month and a half after October 20, 1941, the date the complaining witness had gone to Miami. Whatever original conspiracy may have existed between petitioner and his alleged coconspirator to cause the complaining witness to go to Florida in October, 1941, no longer existed when the reported conversation took place in December, 1941. For on this latter date the trip to Florida had not only been made—the complaining witness had left Florida, had returned to New York, and had resumed her residence there. Furthermore, at the time the conversation took place, the complaining witness, the alleged coconspirator, and the petitioner had been arrested. They apparently were charged in a United States District Court of Florida with the offense of which petitioner was here convicted.

It is beyond doubt that the central aim of the alleged conspiracy— transportation of the complaining witness to Florida for prostitution— had either never existed or had long since ended in success or failure when and if the alleged coconspirator made the statement attributed to her. The statement plainly implied that petitioner was guilty of the crime for which he was on trial. It was made in petitioner's absence and the Government made no effort whatever to show that it was made with his authority. The testimony thus stands as an unsworn, out-of-court declaration of petitioner's guilt. This hearsay declaration, attributed to a coconspirator, was not made pursuant to and in furtherance of objectives of the conspiracy charged in the indictment, because if made, it was after those objectives either had failed or had been achieved. Under these circumstances, the hearsay declaration attributed to the alleged coconspirator was not admissible on the theory that it was made in furtherance of the alleged criminal transportation undertaking.

Although the Government recognizes that the chief objective of the conspiracy—transportation for prostitution purposes—had ended in success or failure before the reported conversation took place, it nevertheless argues for admissibility of the hearsay declaration as one in furtherance of a continuing subsidiary objective of the conspiracy. Its argument runs this way. Conspirators about to commit crimes always expressly or implicitly agree to collaborate with each other to conceal facts in order to prevent detection, conviction and punishment. Thus the argument is that even after the central criminal objectives of a conspiracy have succeeded or failed, an implicit subsidiary phase of the conspiracy always survives, the phase which has concealment as its sole objective. The Court of Appeals adopted this view. It viewed the alleged hearsay declaration as one in furtherance of this continuing subsidiary phase of the conspiracy, as part of "the implied agreement to conceal." 167 F.2d 943, 948. It consequently held the declaration properly admitted.

We cannot accept the Government's contention. There are many logical and practical reasons that could be advanced against a special evidentiary rule that permits out-of-court statements of one conspirator to be used against another. But, however cogent these reasons, it is firmly established that where made in furtherance of the objectives of a going conspiracy, such statements are admissible as exceptions to the hearsay rule. This prerequisite to admissibility, that hearsay statements by some conspirators to be admissible against others must be made in furtherance of the conspiracy charged, has been scrupulously observed by federal courts. The Government now asks us to expand this narrow exception to the hearsay rule and hold admissible a declaration, not made in furtherance of the alleged criminal transportation conspiracy charged, but made in furtherance of an alleged implied but uncharged conspiracy aimed at preventing detection and punishment. No federal court case cited by the Government suggests so hospitable a reception to the use of hearsay evidence to convict in conspiracy cases. The Government contention does find support in some but not all of the state court opinions cited in the Government brief. But in none of them does there appear to be recognition of any such broad exception to the hearsay rule as that here urged. The rule contended for by the Government could have far-reaching results. For under this rule plausible arguments could generally be made in conspiracy cases that most out-of-court statements offered in evidence tended to shield coconspirators. We are not persuaded to adopt the Government's implicit conspiracy theory which in all criminal conspiracy cases would create automatically a further breach of the general rule against the admission of hearsay evidence.

It is contended that the statement attributed to the alleged coconspirator was merely cumulative evidence, that without the statement the case against petitioner was so strong that we should hold the error harmless under 28 U.S.C. § 391. In Kotteakos v. United States, 328 U.S. 750 (1946) we said that error should not be held harmless under the harmless error statute if upon consideration of the record the court is left in grave doubt as to whether the error had substantial influence in bringing about a verdict. We have such doubt here. The Florida District Court grand jury failed to indict. After indictment in New York petitioner was tried four times with the following results: mistrial; conviction; mistrial; conviction with recommendation for leniency. The revolting type of charges made against this petitioner by the complaining witness makes it difficult to believe that a jury convinced of a strong case against him would have recommended leniency. There was corroborative evidence of the complaining witness on certain phases of the case. But as to all vital phases, those involving the sordid criminal features, the jury was compelled to choose between believing the petitioner or the complaining witness. The record persuades us that the jury's task was difficult at best. We cannot say that the erroneous admission of the hearsay declaration may not have been the weight that tipped the scales against petitioner.

Reversed.

MR. JUSTICE JACKSON, concurring in the judgment and opinion of the Court.

This case illustrates a present drift in the federal law of conspiracy which warrants some further comment because it is characteristic of the long evolution of that elastic, sprawling and pervasive offense. Its history exemplifies the "tendency of a principle to expand itself to the limit of its logic." The unavailing protest of courts against the growing habit to indict for conspiracy in lieu of prosecuting for the substantive offense itself, or in addition thereto, suggests that loose practice as to this offense constitutes a serious threat to fairness in our administration of justice.

The modern crime of conspiracy is so vague that it almost defies definition.[3] Despite certain elementary and essential elements, it also, chameleon-like, takes on a special coloration from each of the many independent offenses on which it may be overlaid. It is always "predominantly mental in composition" because it consists primarily of a meeting of minds and an intent.

The crime comes down to us wrapped in vague but unpleasant connotations. It sounds historical undertones of treachery, secret plotting and violence on a scale that menaces social stability and the security of the state itself. "Privy conspiracy" ranks with sedition and rebellion in the Litany's prayer for deliverance. Conspiratorial movements do indeed lie back of the political assassination, the *coup d'état*, the *putsch*, the revolution, and seizures of power in modern times, as they have in all history.

But the conspiracy concept also is superimposed upon many concerted crimes having no political motivation. It is not intended to question that the basic conspiracy principle has some place in modern criminal law, because to unite, back of a criminal purpose, the strength, opportunities and resources of many is obviously more dangerous and more difficult to police than the efforts of a lone wrongdoer. It also may be

---

3. Albert J. Harno, *Intent in Criminal Conspiracy*, 89 U.Pa.L.Rev. 624 (1941): "In the long category of crimes there is none, not excepting criminal attempt, more difficult of confine within the boundaries of definitive statement than conspiracy." An English author—Wright, *Criminal Conspiracies* p. 11—gives up with the remark: "But no intelligible definition of 'conspiracy' has yet been established."

trivialized, as here, where the conspiracy consists of the concert of a loathsome panderer and a prostitute to go from New York to Florida to ply their trade and it would appear that a simple Mann Act prosecution would vindicate the majesty of federal law. However, even when appropriately invoked, the looseness and pliability of the doctrine present inherent dangers which should be in the background of judicial thought wherever it is sought to extend the doctrine to meet the exigencies of a particular case.

Conspiracy in federal law aggravates the degree of crime over that of unconcerted offending. The act of confederating to commit a misdemeanor, followed by even an innocent overt act in its execution, is a felony and is such even if the misdemeanor is never consummated. The more radical proposition also is well-established that at common law and under some statutes a combination may be a criminal conspiracy even if it contemplates only acts which are not crimes at all when perpetrated by an individual or by many acting severally.

Thus the conspiracy doctrine will incriminate persons on the fringe of offending who would not be guilty of aiding and abetting or of becoming an accessory, for those charges only lie when an act which is a crime has actually been committed.

Attribution of criminality to a confederation which contemplates no act that would be criminal if carried out by any one of the conspirators is a practice peculiar to Anglo–American law. "There can be little doubt that this wide definition of the crime of conspiracy originates in the criminal equity administered in the Star Chamber." [Citing 8 Holdsworth, History of English Law 382.] In fact, we are advised that "The modern crime of conspiracy is almost entirely the result of the manner in which conspiracy was treated by the Court of the Star Chamber." [*Id.* at 379.] The doctrine does not commend itself to jurists of civil-law countries, despite universal recognition that an organized society must have legal weapons for combating organized criminality. Most other countries have devised what they consider more discriminating principles upon which to prosecute criminal gangs, secret associations and subversive syndicates.

A recent tendency has appeared in this Court to expand this elastic offense and to facilitate its proof. In Pinkerton v. United States, 328 U.S. 640 (1946), it sustained a conviction of a substantive crime where there was no proof of participation in or knowledge of it, upon the novel and dubious theory that conspiracy is equivalent in law to aiding and abetting.

* * *

Of course, it is for prosecutors rather than courts to determine when to use a scatter gun to bring down the defendant, but there are procedural advantages from using it which add to the danger of unguarded extension of the concept.

An accused, under the Sixth Amendment, has the right to trial "by an impartial jury of the state and district wherein the crime shall have been committed." The leverage of a conspiracy charge lifts this limitation from the prosecution and reduces its protection to a phantom, for the crime is considered so vagrant as to have been committed in any district where any one of the conspirators did any one of the acts, however innocent, intended to accomplish its object. The Government may, and often does, compel one to defend at a great distance from any place he ever did any act because some accused confederate did some trivial and by itself innocent act in the chosen district. Circumstances may even enable the prosecution to fix the place of trial in Washington, D.C., where a defendant may lawfully be put to trial before a jury partly or even wholly made up of employees of the Government that accuses him.

When the trial starts, the accused feels the full impact of the conspiracy strategy. Strictly, the prosecution should first establish prima facie the conspiracy and identify the conspirators, after which evidence of acts and declarations of each in the course of its execution are admissible against all. But the order of proof of so sprawling a charge is difficult for a judge to control. As a practical matter, the accused often is confronted with a hodgepodge of acts and statements by others which he may never have authorized or intended or even known about, but which help to persuade the jury of existence of the conspiracy itself. In other words, a conspiracy often is proved by evidence that is admissible only upon assumption that conspiracy existed. The naive assumption that prejudicial effects can be overcome by instructions to the jury * * * all practicing lawyers know to be unmitigated fiction.

The trial of a conspiracy charge doubtless imposes a heavy burden on the prosecution, but it is an especially difficult situation for the defendant. The hazard from loose application of rules of evidence is aggravated where the Government institutes mass trials. Moreover, in federal practice there is no rule preventing conviction on uncorroborated testimony of accomplices, as there are in many jurisdictions, and the most comfort a defendant can expect is that the court can be induced to follow the "better practice" and caution the jury against "too much reliance upon the testimony of accomplices." Caminetti v. United States, 242 U.S. 470, 495 (1917).

A co-defendant in a conspiracy trial occupies an uneasy seat. There generally will be evidence of wrong-doing by somebody. It is difficult for the individual to make his own case stand on its own merits in the minds of jurors who are ready to believe that birds of a feather are flocked together. If he is silent, he is taken to admit it and if, as often happens, co-defendants can be prodded into accusing or contradicting each other, they convict each other. There are many practical difficulties in defending against a charge of conspiracy which I will not enumerate.

Against this inadequately sketched background, I think the decision of this case in the court below introduced an ominous expansion of the accepted law of conspiracy. The prosecution was allowed to incriminate the defendant by means of the prostitute's recital of a conversation with defendant's alleged coconspirator, who was not on trial. The conversation was said to have taken place after the substantive offense was accomplished, after the defendant, the coconspirator and the witness had all been arrested, and after the witness and the other two had a falling out. The Court of Appeals sustained its admission upon grounds stated as follows:

* * * We think that implicit in a conspiracy to violate the law is an agreement among the conspirators to conceal the violation after as well as before the illegal plan is consummated. Thus the conspiracy continues, at least for purposes of concealment, even after its primary aims have been accomplished. The statements of the coconspirator here were made in an effort to protect the appellant by concealing his role in the conspiracy. Consequently, they fell within the implied agreement to conceal and were admissible as evidence against the appellant. * * *

I suppose no person planning a crime would accept as a collaborator one on whom he thought he could not rely for help if he were caught, but I doubt that this fact warrants an inference of conspiracy for that purpose. Of course, if an understanding for continuous aid had been proven, it would be embraced in the conspiracy by evidence and there would be no need to imply such an agreement. Only where there is no convincing evidence of such an understanding is there need for one to be implied.

It is difficult to see any logical limit to the "implied conspiracy," either as to duration or means, nor does it appear that one could overcome the implication by express and credible evidence that no such understanding existed, nor any way in which an accused against whom the presumption is once raised can terminate the imputed agency of his associates to incriminate him. Conspirators, long after the contemplated offense is complete, after perhaps they have fallen out and become enemies, may still incriminate each other by deliberately harmful, but unsworn declarations, or unintentionally by casual conversations out of court. On the theory that the law will impute to the confederates a continuing conspiracy to defeat justice, one conceivably could be bound by another's unauthorized and unknown commission of perjury, bribery of a juror or witness, or even putting an incorrigible witness with damaging information out of the way.

Moreover, the assumption of an indefinitely continuing offense would result in an indeterminate extension of the statute of limitations. If the law implies an agreement to cooperate in defeating prosecution, it must imply that it continues as long as prosecution is a possibility, and prosecution is a possibility as long as the conspiracy to defeat it is implied to continue.

I do not see the slightest warrant for judicially introducing a doctrine of implied crimes or constructive conspiracies. It either adds a new crime or extends an old one. True, the modern law of conspiracy was largely evolved by the judges. But it is well and wisely settled that there can be no judge-made offenses against the United States and that every federal prosecution must be sustained by statutory authority. No statute authorizes federal judges to imply, presume or construct a conspiracy except as one may be found from evidence. To do so seems to approximate creation of a new offense and one that I would think of doubtful constitutionality even if it were created by Congress. And, at all events, it is one fundamentally and irreconcilably at war with our presumption of innocence.

There is, of course, strong temptation to relax rigid standards when it seems the only way to sustain convictions of evildoers. But statutes authorize prosecution for substantive crimes for most evil doing without the dangers to the liberty of the individual and the integrity of the judicial process that are inherent in conspiracy charges. We should disapprove the doctrine of implied or constructive crime in its entirety and in every manifestation. And I think there should be no straining to uphold any conspiracy conviction where prosecution for the substantive offense is adequate and the purpose served by adding the conspiracy charge seems chiefly to get procedural advantages to ease the way to conviction.

Although a reversal after four trials is, of course, regrettable, I cannot overlook the error as a harmless one. But I should concur in reversal even if less sure that prejudice resulted, for it is better that the crime go unwhipped of justice than that this theory of implied continuance of conspiracy find lodgment in our law, either by affirmance or by tolerance. Few instruments of injustice can equal that of implied or presumed or constructive crimes. The most odious of all oppression are those which mask as justice.

Notes

1. Can you identify the coconspirator's statement at issue? The coconspirator who made the statement? The witness who testified to the statement? The evidentiary significance of the statement?

2. What was the government's theory as to why the statement at issue was "in furtherance of the conspiracy?" Do you agree with the Supreme Court's rejection of this theory?

3. Consider the following case, United States v. Williams, 87 F.3d 249 (8th Cir.1996). Do you believe its facts are distinguishable from *Krulewitch*?

"Sometime during the late summer of 1993, Tommie Penson, a St. Louis resident, learned from a friend, Jobe Reid, that Joe Ellis had access to blank United States Treasury checks through his employment at the St. Louis post office. Penson told Reid he could cash the checks in Mexico. Reid promptly contacted Ellis, who then stole seven blank Treasury checks, beginning on October 1, 1993. Ellis understood from Reid that he would receive a portion of the proceeds raised by the checks.

"At some point, Penson discussed the Treasury checks with Williams, a longtime associate who lived in Texas. Penson and Williams had done business before, partly through an entity owned by Penson called the Royal Oaks Estates. After talking with Penson, Williams recruited a Mexican citizen, Genaro Alvarez, to cash one of the checks in exchange for part of the proceeds. Alvarez flew from Texas to Mexico City in October 1993, and met Maria Nelda San Martin, an associate of Penson and Williams. On October 29, Alvarez presented a Treasury check made payable to him in the amount of $1,165,000 at a money exchange house in Mexico City. He received a cashier's check for $50,000 in his name as an advance, and the check was later paid in full by the Federal Reserve Bank in Minneapolis, Minnesota. Williams spoke with Penson and told him to have the 'Treasuries' in place in Mexico. Williams then told his girlfriend, Elena Cantu, that he had to conclude a deal in Mexico, and he arrived on October 30 in Mexico City, where he met Penson and Nelda.

"During the first week of November 1993, Williams, Penson, and Nelda agreed on the disbursement of the $1,165,000 check. Penson channeled most of the funds into a Texas bank account maintained by Nelda's brother, Jose San Martin. From that account, Penson directed the disbursement of $400,000 to his St. Louis accounts and $95,000 to Nelda's account in Mexico City. On behalf of Williams, Penson made a series of wire transfers into bank accounts maintained by Williams, Elena Cantu, and Williams' ex-wife.

"On November 15, 1993, Penson flew back to St. Louis after arranging for Williams to become a signatory on his Royal Oaks Estates account at the Banco Mexicano in Mexico City. Penson then transferred $10,000 of the stolen money from his St. Louis account to the Royal Oaks account the following day. Penson and Williams communicated some twelve times by phone and fax during this period.

"Prior to Penson's departure from Mexico, he agreed with Williams and Nelda to obtain more stolen Treasury checks. Penson contacted Reid, who persuaded Ellis to steal approximately 60 blank checks on November 12, 1993. Nelda received the checks on November 14 and collaborated with Williams, Penson, and Alvarez to make six of the checks payable to Emilio Sanchez Martinez in amounts ranging from eight to eleven million dollars, the proceeds of which they agreed to share. On November 15, Alvarez unsuccessfully tried to pass two of these checks in Mexico.

"On November 17, 1993, the St. Louis postal center received a copy of one check for $10,000,000. Postal inspectors immediately began an investigation. They interviewed Alvarez on November 21, who told them about cashing the $1,165,000 check. Penson was arrested in St. Louis shortly thereafter on November 24. He told postal inspectors that he had no knowledge of the stolen Treasury checks, and he did not mention his association with Williams or Nelda.

"Following his arrest, Penson remained in contact with Williams through his friend, Eddie Walker. Williams, who was staying at Nelda's residence in Mexico City during November and December 1993, spoke to Penson and Walker some 90 times. Penson and Williams continued to disburse the funds from the $1,165,000 check and persuaded Jose San Martin to pay $12,000 of the stolen money to Penson's wife on December 1, 1993. They also attempted to cash another stolen check. Williams told Walker in December 1993 that Penson and Alvarez were his partners in an ongoing 'deal.' Around December 20, 1993, Penson had Walker contact Williams in New York about that deal. At that time, one of the stolen checks in the amount of $9,980,000 was being processed at the Banco Mexicano's New York office after having been presented at the bank in Mexico. Williams called the Banco Mexicano from New York several times, but the check did not clear.

"Williams was arrested over a year later, on January 9, 1995, as he attempted to enter the United States in San Diego. He was carrying a check written to his Mexico City landlord on the Royal Oaks Estates account, a hotel bill listing him as a representative of Royal Oaks, and other papers linking him to the conspirators in this case.

"At trial, Williams denied knowledge of, or participation in, any activity related to the stolen Treasury checks and their proceeds. He was found guilty on all counts (except one that had been dismissed). * * *

"Williams * * * contends that certain statements of Penson were improperly admitted as an exception to the hearsay rule and that this violated his Sixth Amendment right to confrontation. Following his arrest, Tommie Penson told investigators that he had funded wire transfers with money borrowed from an unidentified source, that he did not know about any stolen Treasury checks, and that he was not in Mexico when the $1,165,000 stolen check had been presented. Penson did not mention Williams or other conspirators. Although Penson did not testify at trial, his statements were admitted as those of a coconspirator under Fed.R.Evid. 801(d)(2)(E). Williams argues that Penson's statements were not made in furtherance of the conspiracy since he had already been arrested, and that he was therefore entitled to a cautionary instruction under the Sixth Amendment.

* * *

"The arrest of one coconspirator does not necessarily terminate the conspiracy. Rather, a conspiracy is presumed to exist until there has been an affirmative showing that it has been terminated so long as there is 'a continuity of purpose and a continued performance of acts.'

"Statements made during the concealment phase of the conspiracy may also be admissible under Rule 801(d)(2)(E). *Id.* In making this determination, courts must be careful to ensure that the statements occurred during an ongoing conspiracy and were made in furtherance of it. A conspiracy is ongoing where 'acts of concealment were undertaken to preserve the conspiracy and foil attempts at detection.' Such a case generally exists where the conspiracy is a continuing arrangement with a series of objectives, and concealment is essential to and in furtherance of the survival of its operation. Post-arrest confessions or statements incriminating others by one coconspirator are generally not made in furtherance of a conspiracy. [citations omitted].

"The purposes of the charged conspiracy in this case included the theft, receipt, forgery, and concealment of U.S. Treasury checks and the receipt and concealment of fraudulently obtained money. Williams was also charged with being a fugitive and communicating with other conspirators in an effort to conceal his involvement in the conspiracy and avoid detection by law enforcement authorities. Although Penson's statements to authorities were made after his arrest in November 1993, he did not confess to stealing the checks or to a conspiracy, nor did he incriminate any of his fellow conspirators. Rather, his denial of knowledge of the checks and his failure to mention Williams or other conspirators enabled the coconspirators to continue to pursue their common objectives. For example, on December 1, 1993, Penson and Williams persuaded Jose San Martin to pay $12,000 of the stolen funds to Penson's wife in an effort to conceal the money. Williams also attempted to cash a stolen Treasury check in New York in the amount of $9,980,-000 nearly three weeks after Penson's arrest, and Williams told one of Penson's associates that Penson and Alvarez were also involved in that deal.

"These actions demonstrate that the conspiracy was continuing to function actively at the time of Penson's statements, and that the statements were made in furtherance of the conspiracy's objectives to profit from the stolen checks and continue functioning without discovery."

Can you distinguish *Williams* from *Krulewitch*? How?

4. As *Krulewitch* holds, a statement made by one coconspirator to another *after* the conspiracy has ended is not properly admissible as a coconspirator's exception to the hearsay rule. As the next case demonstrates, neither is a statement from one coconspirator to another during the conspiracy which is not "in furtherance of the conspiracy" but is "mere conversation between conspirators." As you read the following excerpts from United States v. El—Zoubi, 993 F.2d 442 (5th Cir.1993), determine if you can tell whether the conversation at issue is "in furtherance of the conspiracy" or "mere conversation."

"Abdallah M. El–Zoubi (El–Zoubi) was charged in a superseding indictment with conspiracy, mail fraud, and arson, in violation of 18 U.S.C. §§ 371, 1341 [mail fraud], 844(I) [arson], and 2 [aiding and abetting], respectively. After a jury trial, he was convicted on all counts. On the arson count he received a sentence of 120 months of imprisonment, to be followed by five years of supervised release. His sentences on the conspiracy and mail fraud counts run concurrently with his arson sentence, and call for 60 months of imprisonment, to be followed by three years of supervised release. El–Zoubi appeals his conviction * * *. We affirm his conviction * * *.

"In May of 1991 El–Zoubi purchased the Almadafa International Market, also known as the Holy Land Market (the market), in Arlington, Texas. The next month, after obtaining fire insurance for the market, El–Zoubi paid his 20 year old nephew, Adel Ahmad Saliem Alzoubi (Adel), to burn it down. The fire occurred around 9:30 p.m. on June 14. A trail of footprints burned into the market's tile floor led fire fighters to Adel's body. Predictably, examiners determined the cause of death to be smoke inhalation, carbon monoxide poisoning, and extensive burns. The fire caused about $200,000 of damage to the strip mall in which the market was located.

"We initially consider El–Zoubi's conviction. First, he argues that the evidence was insufficient to support his conviction. Second, he contends that the trial court erroneously admitted hearsay testimony offered by the government. * * *

* * *

"We summarize below the evidence on which the government relies to support El–Zoubi's conviction on the counts referred to above. El–Zoubi was in dire financial straits: his checking account at the Federal Savings Banc had just been closed because of excessive insufficient funds checks; he owed over $500 on a Visa credit card that had just been canceled; he had been denied a bank loan; he had to borrow $300 to cover a bad check he had written; and his wife had just filed for divorce. Moreover, the business was failing: lease payments had fallen behind by $6,625; inventory was low; and business was poor—the day of the fire, the market made only a four dollar sale.

"On June 7, El–Zoubi applied for $50,000 of fire insurance, representing that sales at the market amounted to $300 a day. In the following days, he asked his insurance agent three times if the application had been approved. Two days before the fire, the application was approved. The next day, El–Zoubi paid the premium, and sought assurances that any insurance proceeds would be paid to him. That day El–Zoubi told another shop keeper in the same strip shopping center, 'we got our insurance.' "

"The day of the fire, El–Zoubi asked Rami Ghanem, an acquaintance whose business had burned, whether he had any difficulties with fire investigators or the insurance and also told him, referring to the market, 'I'm going to knock it down today.' The fire was reported at 9:22 p.m. The fire fighters found all doors locked, even though the business was scheduled to be open until 10:00 p.m. Inside they found Adel's body. Investigators found that the fire was intentionally set and of an incendiary nature. In Adel's truck, investigators found a $5,000 check to Adel, signed by El–Zoubi and postdated to June 30. At the time of the fire, the balance in El–Zoubi's account was $261.16.

"The fire caused $200,000 of damage to the shopping center structure. The market and neighboring businesses were closed. El–Zoubi concedes that the market was used in an activity affecting interstate commerce. This evidence amply supports the jury's apparent conclusion that El–Zoubi paid Adel to burn the market in order to fraudulently collect fire insurance proceeds, and that he used the mails to further this scheme.

"El–Zoubi next argues that the district court erroneously admitted testimony about a conversation between Adel and Salif Alahmad (Alahmad), who owns a photo business in the strip shopping center that housed the market. According to Alahmad, four days before the fire, Adel said that he was 'sick and tired of [the market]' and was going to 'burn it down and get out of Arlington.' The government concedes that the statement constituted hearsay, but argues that it was admissible under Fed.R.Evid. 801(d)(2)(E), the coconspirator exception to the hearsay rule.

"In order to fit the coconspirator exception, a statement must have been made (1) by a coconspirator of a party, (2) during the course of the conspiracy, and (3) in furtherance of the conspiracy. Although the evidence supports a finding that Adel and El–Zoubi were coconspirators, it does not support a conclusion that Adel's statement was made in furtherance of the conspiracy. The government argues that Adel's statement was made in furtherance of the conspiracy because it identified his role in the conspiracy. 'Ordinarily, a statement that identifies the role of one coconspirator to another is in furtherance of the conspiracy.' United States v. Lechuga, 888 F.2d 1472, 1480 (5th Cir.1989). However 'mere conversation between conspirators' does not fit within this exception. The statement in question was not made to a coconspirator. Moreover, the record does not allow the inference that Adel thought the conspiracy would be more likely to succeed if Alahmad knew of Adel's intent to burn the market. Therefore it was error to admit Adel's statement under the coconspirator exception to the hearsay rule.

"Nevertheless, the error was harmless. In determining whether the admission of hearsay evidence was harmless, we must consider the other evidence in the case, and then decide if the inadmissible evidence actually contributed to the jury's verdict. We will find such testimony harmful and reverse a conviction only if it had a 'substantial impact' on the jury's verdict. The statement is probative of Adel's intent to burn down the market. Yet, as we have already explained, the physical evidence overwhelmingly established this fact. Thus, viewing the evidence as a whole, we conclude that the statement had no effect on the verdict."

5. Justice Jackson's attack on the conspiracy offense focuses on the "conduct" requirement for crimes. What is the criminal conduct that must be proven to convict a person of conspiracy? Do you agree with Justice Jackson that the conspiracy charge allows conviction without sufficient proof of criminal conduct on the part of the accused, or do you believe that the corroboration supplied by the required overt acts overcomes this alleged deficiency?

6. Justice Jackson refers to some of the practical difficulties a defendant must overcome in defending against a conspiracy charge. Which of these do you think presents the greatest problem?

7. As you contemplate Justice Jackson's critique of the conspiracy offense, consider the following excerpt from *Developments in the Law, Criminal Conspiracy*, 72 *Harv.L.Rev.* 920, 923–25 (1959)[i] which sets forth the rationale for the conspiracy offense. With whom do you agree—the authors of this article, or Justice Jackson?

i. Reprinted with permission from Note, *Developments in the Law, Criminal Conspiracy*, 72 Harv.L.Rev. 923–25. Copyright © 1959 by the Harvard Law Review Association.

"The heart of the rationale for the conspiracy offense lies in the fact—or at least the assumption—that collective action toward an antisocial end involves a greater risk to society than individual action toward the same end. Primarily, the state is concerned with punishing conduct that has actually resulted in antisocial consequences. It is reluctant to intervene as long as the actor can still withdraw and as long as his conduct is still consistent with the absence of any criminal intent. However, as action toward a criminal end nears execution, a point is reached at which the increasing risk to society is thought to outweigh the diminishing likelihood of a change of heart or of a misreading of intent, and at this point mere 'preparation' becomes punishable as 'attempt.' When the defendant has chosen to act in concert with others, rather than to act alone, the point of justifiable intervention is reached at an earlier state. In this situation the reasons for which the law is reluctant to intervene are considerably weaker. The agreement itself, in theory at least, provides a substantially unambiguous manifestation of intent; it also reduces the probability that the defendant can stop the wheels he has set in motion, since to restore the status quo would now require the acquiescence and co-operation of other wills than his own. More important, the collaboration magnifies the risk to society both by increasing the likelihood that a given quantum of harm will be successfully produced and by increasing the amount of harm that can be inflicted. A conspirator who has committed himself to support his associates may be less likely to violate this commitment than he would be to revise a purely private decision. Moreover, the encouragement and moral support of the group strengthens the perseverance of each member. Furthermore, the existence of numbers both facilitates a division of labor which promotes the efficiency with which a given object can be pursued, and makes possible the attainment of objects more elaborate and ambitious than would otherwise be attainable. The notion of increased social risk also provides a possible rationale for the punishment of agreements to engage in certain types of conduct that would not otherwise be criminal, since the absence of any specific prohibition against such conduct may be due to the fact that the likelihood that a single person will engage in it is small, or that its harmful impact when engaged in by a single person is slight. A further rationale may be that reliance on social pressure alone to deter certain forms of antisocial conduct becomes unwarranted when this pressure is countered by that of the conspiratorial group itself.

"The antisocial potentialities of a conspiracy, unlike those of an attempt, are not confined to the objects specifically contemplated at any given time. The existence of a grouping for criminal purposes provides a continuing focal point for further crimes either related or unrelated to those immediately envisaged. Moreover, the uneasiness produced by the consciousness that such groupings exist is in itself an important antisocial effect. Consequently, the state has an interest in stamping out conspiracy above and beyond its interest in preventing the commission of any specific substantive offense."

C. THE *PINKERTON* DOCTRINE

In his concurring opinion in *Krulewitch supra*, Justice Jackson singled out the next case as a prime example of the Court's willingness to expand the conspiracy offense. What do you think about the scope of criminal liability sanctioned in *Pinkerton* ?

PINKERTON v. UNITED STATES

United States Supreme Court, 1946.
328 U.S. 640.

DOUGLAS, JUSTICE.

Walter and Daniel Pinkerton are brothers who live a short distance from each other on Daniel's farm. They were indicted for violations of the Internal Revenue Code. The indictment contained ten substantive counts and one conspiracy count. The jury found Walter guilty on nine of the substantive counts and on the conspiracy count. It found Daniel guilty on six of the substantive counts and on the conspiracy count. Walter was fined $500 and sentenced generally on the substantive counts to imprisonment for thirty months. On the conspiracy count he was given a two year sentence to run concurrently with the other sentence. Daniel was fined $1,000 and sentenced generally on the substantive counts to imprisonment for 30 months. On the conspiracy count he was fined $500 and given a two year sentence to run concurrently with the other sentence. The judgments of conviction were affirmed by the Circuit Court of Appeals. The case is here on a petition for a writ of certiorari which we granted, because one of the questions presented involved a conflict between the decision below and United States v. Sall, 116 F.2d 745, decided by the Circuit Court of Appeals for the Third Circuit.

* * *

It is contended that there was insufficient evidence to implicate Daniel in the conspiracy. But we think there was enough evidence for submission of the issue to the jury.

There is, however, no evidence to show that Daniel participated directly in the commission of the substantive offenses on which his conviction has been sustained, although there was evidence to show that these substantive offenses were in fact committed by Walter in furtherance of the unlawful agreement or conspiracy existing between the brothers. The question was submitted to the jury on the theory that each petitioner could be found guilty of the substantive offenses, if it was found at the time those offenses were committed petitioners were parties to an unlawful conspiracy and the substantive offenses charged were in fact committed in furtherance of it.

Daniel relies on United States v. Sall, 116 F.2d 745 (3d Cir.1940). That case held that participation in the conspiracy was not itself enough to sustain a conviction for the substantive offense even though it was committed in furtherance of the conspiracy. The court held that, in addition to evidence that the offense was in fact committed in further- ance of the conspiracy, evidence of direct participation in the commission of the substantive offense or other evidence from which participation might fairly be inferred was necessary.

We take a different view. We have here a continuous conspiracy. There is here no evidence of the affirmative action on the part of Daniel which is necessary to establish his withdrawal from it. As stated in Hyde v. United States, 225 U.S. 347, 369 (1911), "Having joined in an unlawful scheme, having constituted agents for its performance, scheme and agency to be continuous until full fruition be secured, until he does some act to disavow or defeat the purpose he is in no situation to claim the delay of the law. As the offense has not been terminated or accom- plished, he is still offending. And we think, consciously offending, offend- ing as certainly, as we have said, as at the first moment of his confedera- tion, and consciously through every moment of its existence." *Id.* And so long as the partnership in crime continues, the partners act for each other in carrying it forward. It is settled that "an overt act of one partner may be the act of all without any new agreement specifically directed to that act." United States v. Kissel, 218 U.S. 601, 608 (1910). Motive or intent may be proved by the acts or declarations of some of the conspirators in furtherance of the common objective. A scheme to use the mails to defraud, which is joined in by more than one person, is a conspiracy. Yet all members are responsible, though only one did the mailing. The governing principle is the same when the substantive offense is committed by one of the conspirators in furtherance of the unlawful project. The criminal intent to do the act is established by the formation of the conspiracy. Each conspirator instigated the commission of the crime. The unlawful agreement contemplated precisely what was done. It was formed for the purpose. The act done was in execution of the enterprise. The rule which holds responsible one who counsels, procures, or commands another to commit a crime is founded on the same principle. That principle is recognized in the law of conspiracy when the overt act of one partner attributable to all. An overt act is an essential ingredient of the crime of conspiracy under [the statute charged herein]. If that can be supplied by the act of one conspirator, we fail to see why the same or other acts in furtherance of the conspiracy are likewise not attributable to the others for the purpose of holding them responsible for the substantive offense.

A different case would arise if the substantive offense committed by one of the conspirators was not in fact done in furtherance of the conspiracy, did not fall within the scope of the unlawful project, or was merely a part of the ramifications of the plan which could not be reasonably foreseen as a necessary or natural consequence of the unlaw- ful agreement. But as we read this record, that is not this case.

Affirmed.

Notes

1. In reaching its decision that Daniel Pinkerton could be held liable for the substantive offenses committed by his brother, Walter, the court noted that "in the law of conspiracy * * * the overt act of one partner in crime is attributable to all." Is the court correct when it suggests that coconspirators are held liable for each other's overt acts? Or, is it more accurate to view a conspirator as liable for joining a conspiracy which is *manifested* by the overt acts of other coconspirators? Does it cast doubt upon the wisdom of the *Pinkerton* ruling if the court overstated a conspirator's liability for the overt acts committed by a coconspirator?

2. In *Pinkerton,* the court analogizes to the law of complicity by noting that, "the rule which holds responsible one who counsels, procures, or commands another to commit a crime is founded on the same principles." Do you agree that by joining a conspiracy, a conspirator provides the same level of assistance as does an individual who incurs liability as an aider and abettor for the criminal act committed by another?

3. In the following case, United States v. Smith, 934 F.2d 270 (11th Cir.1991), the United States Court of Appeals for the Eleventh Circuit reversed mail fraud convictions after finding that the *Pinkerton* test had not been met:

> "[Russell Dewey] Smith was convicted on three counts of mail fraud and one count of conspiracy to commit mail fraud after participating in a scheme that involved staging an automobile accident, feigning an injury, and collecting $450 from State Farm Insurance Company. Smith was not personally at the scene of the 'accident' but was taken to a hospital emergency room for treatment of the claimed injuries. Smith's coconspirators told police that he had been taken to the hospital by a passerby. We find that the evidence was insufficient to support the substantive convictions for mail fraud. We affirm Smith's conspiracy conviction.

> "Smith was convicted on two counts for the actions of his coconspirators in causing accounting copies of drafts to be mailed. The government did not show that Smith's coconspirators knew or should have foreseen the mailings of the accounting copies. The most the government showed was that it was foreseeable that information concerning the claim itself would have to be sent through the mails. Smith's convictions on these counts cannot stand."

4. Recall that a coconspirator's statements was admitted in *Lindemann, supra*, even though Lindemann was not charged with conspiracy. Similarly, as shown in following excerpts from United States v. Macey, 8 F.3d 462 (7th Cir.1993), it is not necessary that the government charge conspiracy for the *Pinkerton* doctrine to apply. Do you think this fact fulfills Justice Jackson's condemnation of the expansive use of conspiracy permitted by the courts?

> "[Thomas E.] Macey was the president and half-owner of Asbestos Real Estate Consultants, Inc. (ARC), a company which inspected buildings for asbestos and consulted with building owners concerning asbestos removal. When ARC discovered asbestos contamination in a building, another company, Three Way Environmental, Inc. (Three Way), was often called

to perform the actual asbestos removal. Although no formal referral agreement existed between ARC and Three Way, they had a close business relationship; ARC found asbestos problems and Three Way fixed them. Three Way's president, David Souser, was friendly with Macey, and the two often talked about going into business together. In the summer of 1989, ARC provided Three Way with office space in its building.

"Business boomed for ARC from early 1988 through the spring of 1989. Federal law required that all public schools be inspected for asbestos by April 1989. Due to the impetus of the government mandate, asbestos inspection businesses thrived. For a time, school administrators scrambled to comply with the federal law. By the spring of 1989, however, most schools had complied, and the demand for asbestos inspection services dropped off sharply.

"To accelerate its cash flow, in March 1989, ARC entered into a contract with Sunmark. Basically, Sunmark agreed to pay cash for ARC invoices. ARC would offer to sell invoices for completed work to Sunmark, which would make appropriate inquiries to confirm that the invoices were legitimate. After verifying an invoice, Sunmark would immediately pay ARC seventy percent of its value up front. The debtor who owed on the invoice was then notified that payment should be made to Sunmark. When Sunmark eventually received full payment, it would pay a portion of the remaining thirty percent to ARC. Sunmark withheld an agreed-upon portion of the thirty percent as its fee for providing this financing service.

"From April 1989 through August 1989, Sunmark purchased numerous legitimate invoices from ARC. During this time, the asbestos inspection business remained languid. ARC began having trouble paying its bills. In late August and the first week of September 1989, ARC's bank account had a negative balance. Macey then concocted a scheme to gain funds from Sunmark. Macey had his office manager, Kim Kaiser, execute an invoice in the amount of $97,000 for inspection services ARC claimed to have provided Three Way. The invoice identified three projects ARC purportedly worked on for Three Way: 'Port Clinton,' 'Olds Center, State of Michigan,' and 'Records Danville.' But, in fact, ARC had never done any of the work. Macey then had the sham invoice sent to Sunmark. When Sunmark attempted to verify it, David Souser, president of Three Way, related that ARC had provided the inspection services. Successfully duped, Sunmark paid ARC 70% of the invoice— $67,900.

"Sunmark required Three Way to make its first payment for the invoice by October 7, 1989. Three Way never made this payment and Mark Kraus, Sunmark's general manager, began to investigate. Eventually, Kraus discovered the truth about the sham invoice. He immediately stopped payments to ARC on other invoices. On September 18, 1991, a grand jury returned a 7–count indictment charging Macey with mail fraud and wire fraud, in violation of 18 U.S.C. §§ 1341 and 1343. * * *

"The jury returned a guilty verdict against Macey on six of the seven counts charged in the indictment, including count IV, involving a letter which Macey's coconspirator drafted and sent. * * *

* * *

"The district court gave a slightly modified version of this court's pattern instruction [which] basically states the legal principle enunciated in *Pinkerton*. Macey does not challenge the slight adjustments the district court made to the pattern instruction. Instead, Macey challenges the fact that the district court gave any kind of conspiracy instruction. He contends that such an instruction was inappropriate because the indictment did not charge conspiracy.

"On appeal, our review of jury instructions is limited. We must determine 'whether the instructions as a whole were sufficient to inform the jury correctly of the applicable law....' United States v. Villarreal, 977 F.2d 1077, 1079 (7th Cir.1992). We reverse only if the instruction misguides the jury so much that a litigant is prejudiced. We will not reverse if the instructions as a whole 'fairly and adequately' treat the issues.

"Macey's argument is one of law. He asserts that a person cannot be liable for the acts of coconspirators unless the indictment charges conspiracy. The Seventh Circuit Committee on Jury Instructions issued two instructions concerning *Pinkerton* liability: one to be used when the indictment charges conspiracy, and one to be used when it does not. We have long recognized that '[i]t is not essential that the indictment contain a separate count charging conspiracy in order to take advantage of the doctrines peculiar to conspiracy.' United States v. Wilson, 506 F.2d 1252, 1257 (7th Cir.1974). '[C]onspiracy doctrines apply to a multi-member mail fraud scheme even if the indictment does not charge conspiracy.' The jury instructions accurately stated the law. In a mail fraud case, a defendant is liable for the acts of his coconspirator even if the indictment did not charge conspiracy. Therefore, the district court did not err in giving the instruction."

Chapter 2

MAIL FRAUD

Flashy, powerful new federal crimes may come and go but mail fraud remains the favorite staple of a federal prosecutor's arsenal. As one former federal prosecutor explained:

"To federal prosecutors of white collar crime, the mail fraud statute is our Stradivarius, our Colt 45, our Louisville Slugger, our Cuisinart—and our true love. We may flirt with RICO, show off with 10b–5, and call the conspiracy law 'darling,' but we always come home to the virtues of 18 U.S.C. § 1341, with its simplicity, adaptability, and comfortable familiarity. It understands us and, like many a foolish spouse, we like to think we understand it. * * *.[a]

" * * * First enacted in 1872, the mail fraud statute, together with its lineal descendant, the wire fraud statute, has been characterized as the 'first line of defense' against virtually every new area of fraud to develop in the United States in the past century. Its applications, too numerous to catalog, cover not only the full range of consumer frauds, stock frauds, land frauds, bank frauds, insurance frauds, and commodity frauds, but have extended even to such areas as blackmail, counterfeiting, election fraud, and bribery. In many of these and other areas, where legislatures have sometimes been slow to enact specific prohibitory legislation, the mail fraud statute has frequently represented the sole instrument of justice that could be wielded against the ever-innovative practitioners of deceit.[b]"

The mail fraud statute is over one century old:

"The original federal mail fraud statute was enacted on June 8, 1872 as part of a 327–section omnibus act chiefly intended to revise and recodify the various laws relating to the post office. Unlike most of the other sections of the act, however, the mail fraud section,

---

a. Jed S. Rakoff, *The Federal Mail Fraud Statute (Part I)*, 18 Duq. L.Rev. 771, 771–72 (1979). Reprinted with permission. Copyright © 1979, Duquesne University. Jed S. Rakoff served as an Assistant United States Attorney in the Southern District of New York from 1973–1980. In this capacity he also served as Chief of Business and Securities Fraud Prosecutions. In 1996 Mr. Rakoff was appointed to the bench of the United States District Court, S.D.N.Y.

b. *Id.*

section 301, has no obvious precursor. In view of the novelty and breadth of this section, it is surprising that it generated no congressional debate or other legislative history explaining its origins and purpose. Looking at the broader context, however, the mail fraud statute was not unlike a host of federal legislation (both criminal and civil) enacted in the Reconstruction Period immediately following the Civil War, that extended federal authority to areas previously reserved to the states. Two impulses, in particular, seem likely to have generated such legislation as the mail fraud statute. One was the growth of a national economy, evident even before the Civil War but greatly accelerating after the war, and a concomitant growth in large-scale swindles, get-rich-quick schemes, and financial frauds. With the increase in such crimes, it 'soon became apparent that rudimentary criminal codes, conceived for rural societies and confined by state lines and local considerations, could not cope with those who saw manifold opportunities for gain in the new activities.' Goldstein, *Conspiracy to Defraud the United States*, 68 Yale L.J. 405, 405–06 (1959). Thus, there existed a perceived need for federal intervention to dispel widespread fraud.[c]

"This need was coupled with a perception of enlarged and dynamic federal power, hugely enhanced by both the exigencies of fighting a Civil War and by the fervor with which Reconstruction Republicans set about the legislative remodeling of the northern and southern states alike. One result was that, although Reconstruction statutes were passed in response to specific ills and grievances, they tended to be drawn in sweeping language appropriate to the federal government's new-found sense of power. This was particularly true where earlier, more specific legislation proved unable to cope in any coherent fashion with the multitude of upheavals and dislocations that immediately followed the end of the Civil War."[d]

The mail fraud statute reads in pertinent part as follows:

"Whoever, having devised or intending to devise any scheme or artifice to defraud, or for obtaining money or property by means of false or fraudulent pretenses, representations, or promises * * * for the purpose of executing such scheme or artifice or attempting so to do, places in any post office or authorized depository for mail matter, any matter or thing whatever to be sent or delivered by the Postal Service, or deposits or causes to be deposited any matter or thing whatever to be sent or delivered by any private or commercial

---

c. *Id.* at 779–80.

d. *Id.* at 779–80; Other scholarship discussing the mail fraud offense includes George D. Brown, *Should Federalism Shield Corruption?—Mail Fraud, State Law and Post–Lopez Analysis*, 82 Cornell L. Rev. 225 (1997); Adam H. Kurland, *The Guarantee Clause as a Basis for Federal Prosecutions of State and Local Officials*, 62 Cal. L. Rev. 367, 487–91 (1989). Williams, *Good*

Government by Prosecutorial Decree: The Use and Abuse of Mail Fraud, 32 Ariz. L.Rev. 137 (1990); Coffee, *The Metastasis of Mail Fraud: The Continuing Story of the "Evolution" of a White Collar Crime*, 21 Am.Crim.L.Rev. 19 (1983); Note, *Intracorporate Mail and Wire Fraud: Criminal Liability for Fiduciary Breach*, 94 Yale L.J. 1427 (1985).

interstate carrier or takes or receives therefrom, any such matter or thing, or knowingly causes to be delivered by mail or such carrier according to the direction thereon * * * any such matter or thing, shall be fined under this title[e] or imprisoned not more than five years, or both. If the violation affects a financial institution, such person shall be fined under this title or imprisoned not more than 30 years, or both.''[f]

A. THE MAILING

The next case, Pereira v. United States, 347 U.S. 1 (1954), exemplifies one of the more blatant frauds prosecuted pursuant to 18 U.S.C. § 1341. The defendants, Pereira and Brading, were convicted on charges of mail fraud (18 U.S.C. § 1341), interstate transportation of property obtained by fraud (18 U.S.C. § 2341), and conspiracy (18 U.S.C. § 371). The issue raised on appeal concerned the mailing, specifically, whether the petitioners "caused" the mailing.

PEREIRA v. UNITED STATES

United States Supreme Court, 1954.
347 U.S. 1.

WARREN, CHIEF JUSTICE.

* * *

On April 19, 1951, Mrs. Gertrude Joyce, a wealthy widow, fifty-six years old, and her younger half-sister, Miss Katherine Joyner, were accosted by the petitioner Brading as they were about to enter a hotel in El Paso, Texas. Mrs. Joyce and her sister had just arrived from their home in Roswell, New Mexico, and were preparing to register at the hotel. Brading identified himself, assisted them in parking their car, and invited them into the hotel bar to meet a friend of his. They accepted. The friend was petitioner Pereira, thirty-three years of age. After a few drinks, the men suggested that they all go to Juarez for dinner. The women accepted, and after dinner visited some night clubs with the petitioners. Pereira devoted himself to Mrs. Joyce, telling her that their meeting was an "epoch" in his life. He mentioned that he was getting a divorce. This same performance was repeated the following night. When Pereira said that he would like to return to Roswell with the women, Mrs. Joyce invited the two men to be her house guests, and they accepted. Pereira commenced to make love to Mrs. Joyce, and she responded to his attentions. On May 3, Pereira exhibited a telegram to Mrs. Joyce, in the presence of Brading and Miss Joyner, stating that his

e. Section 3571 of title 18, United States Code, provides that with a few exceptions individuals convicted of a felony may be fined $250,000 while organizations convicted of a felony may be fined $500,000. Individuals convicted of a Class A misde-

meanor may be fined $100,000 while organizations convicted of a Class A misdemeanor may be fined $200,000.

f. 18 U.S.C. § 1341 (West 1984, Supp. 1991).

divorce would be granted on May 27, but that he would not receive his share of the property settlement, some $48,000, for a month.

Brading represented himself as a prosperous oil man, dealing in leases, and Pereira as the owner and operator of several profitable hotels. Brading then told Mrs. Joyce that Pereira was about to lose an opportunity to share in the profits of some excellent oil leases because of the delay in the divorce property settlement, and persuaded her to lend Pereira $5,000.

Pereira suggested that he and Mrs. Joyce take a trip together to "become better acquainted." He borrowed $1,000 from her to finance the trip. Brading joined them at Wichita Falls, and the three of them continued the trip together as far as Dallas. Pereira discussed his purported hotel business in Denver during this part of the trip. He stated that he was giving two hotels to his divorced wife, but intended to reenter the hotel business in the fall. In the meantime, he was going to "play a little oil" with Brading. In Hot Springs, Arkansas, Pereira proposed marriage and was accepted. Brading reappeared on the scene, expressing great joy at the impending marriage. Pereira then told Brading, in the presence of Mrs. Joyce, that he would have to withdraw from further oil deals and get a hotel to assure himself of a steady income.

Pereira and Mrs. Joyce were married May 25, 1951, in Kansas City, Missouri. While there, Pereira persuaded Mrs. Joyce to procure funds to enable him to complete an arrangement to purchase a Cadillac through a friend. She secured a check for $6,956.55 from her Los Angeles broker, and drawn on a California bank, which she endorsed over to Pereira. The price of the car was $4,750, and she instructed Pereira to return the balance of the proceeds of the check to her. He kept the change.

From that time on, Pereira and Brading, in the presence of Mrs. Joyce, discussed a hotel which by words and conduct they represented that Pereira was to buy in Greenville, Texas. They took Mrs. Joyce—by this time Mrs. Pereira—to see it, and exhibited an option for its purchase for $78,000 through a supposed broker, "E.J. Wilson." Pereira asked his then wife if she would join him in the hotel venture and advance $35,000 toward the purchase price of $78,000. She agreed. It was then agreed, between her and Pereira, that she would sell some securities that she possessed in Los Angeles, and bank the money in a bank of his choosing in El Paso. On June 15, she received the check for $35,000 on the Citizens National Bank of Los Angeles from her brokers in Los Angeles, and gave it to Pereira, who endorsed it for collection to the State National Bank of El Paso. The check cleared, and on June 18, a cashier's check for $35,000 was drawn in favor of Pereira.

At five o'clock in the morning of June 19, Pereira and Brading, after telling their victim that they were driving the Cadillac to a neighboring town to sign some oil leases, left her at home in Roswell, New Mexico, promising to return by noon. Instead Pereira picked up the check for

$35,000 at the El Paso Bank, cashed it there, and with Brading left with the money and the Cadillac.

That was the last Mrs. Joyce saw of either petitioner, or of her money, until the trial some seven months later. She divorced Pereira on November 16, 1951.

The record clearly shows that Brading was not an oil man; that Pereira was not a hotel owner; that there was no divorce or property settlement pending in Denver; that Pereira arranged to have the telegram concerning the divorce sent to him by a friend in Denver; that there were no oil leases; that the hotel deal was wholly fictitious; and that "E.J. Wilson" was the petitioner Brading. The only true statements which the petitioners made concerned the purchase of the Cadillac, and they took that with them. Pereira and Brading contrived all of the papers used to lend an air of authenticity to their deals. In short, their activities followed the familiar pattern of the "confidence game."

* * *

Petitioners do not deny that the proof offered establishes that they planned to defraud Mrs. Joyce. Collecting the proceeds of the check was an essential part of that scheme. For this purpose, Pereira delivered the check drawn on a Los Angeles bank to the El Paso bank. There was substantial evidence to show that the check was mailed from Texas to California, in the ordinary course of business.

The elements of the offense of mail fraud under 18 U.S.C. § 1341 are (1) a scheme to defraud, and (2) the mailing of a letter, etc., for the purpose of executing the scheme. It is not necessary that the scheme contemplate the use of the mails as an essential element. Here, the scheme to defraud is established, and the mailing of the check by the bank, incident to an essential part of the scheme, is established. There remains only the question whether Pereira "caused" the mailing. That question is easily answered. Where one does an act with knowledge that the use of the mails will follow in the ordinary course of business, or where such use can reasonably be foreseen, even though not actually intended, then he "causes" the mails to be used. The conclusion that Pereira's conviction under this count was proper follows naturally from these factors.

* * * When Pereira delivered the check, drawn on an out-of-state bank, to the El Paso bank for collection, he "caused" it to be transported in interstate commerce. It is common knowledge that such checks must be sent to the drawee bank for collection, and it follows that Pereira intended the El Paso bank to send this check across state lines. The trial court charged the jury that one who "aids, abets, counsels, commands, induces, or procures" the commission of an act is as responsible for that act as if he had directly committed the act himself. * * *

* * *

Notes

1. Can you list the misrepresentations made by the defendants to Mrs. Joyce? Which of these misrepresentations are possibly contained in documents? If you were the prosecutor in this case, what records would you seek to obtain, both to show the representations made by the defendants and to show that these representations were false?

2. If you were defense counsel in this case, how would you cross examine Mrs. Joyce?

3. Although the government need not prove positive knowledge on the part of the defendant that the mails were used, only "knowledge that the use of the mails will follow in the ordinary course of business," the government must meet this standard. United States v. Hannigan, 27 F.3d 890 (3d Cir.1994) demonstrates the type of evidence the government should produce.

Hannigan, the manager of an auto body shop, and Giordano, an appraiser employed by Travelers Insurance Company, were charged with mail fraud for submitting an insurance claim which falsely represented that a car had been damaged by chemical emissions from a factory.[g] The United States Court of Appeals for the Third Circuit reversed Hannigan's mail fraud conviction finding that there was insufficient evidence that the charged mailing a check from Traveler's to Hannigan's Auto Body Shop was in fact mailed.

At the trial the government had produced a witness from Travelers who testified as to Travelers' procedures for processing claims. She testified "that Travelers usually mailed claim checks and that special procedures were required when someone wanted instead to pick up a check."[h] This witness also testified that the special procedures were not followed as to the check to Hannigan's body shop. Her testimony was corroborated by computer printouts indicating that Hannigan's check was to be mailed. However, the government did not produce, through this witness or otherwise, evidence as to the business practice or office custom within Travelers for mailing checks.[i]

The cross-examination of the government's witness, Ms. Skowronski, revealed this gap:

Q: Now, you didn't mail the checks in this case yourself, did you?

A.: No.

Q: All right. And, you didn't see them put into the mail yourself, did you?

A: No.

Q: And, can you tell the jury where they're put to be mailed or who mails them?

A: No.

Q: You don't know that?

A: I . . .

g. *Id.* at 891.

h. *Id.* at 892.

i. *Id.* at 892–93.

Q: After they're stuffed in an envelope, you don't know where the envelope goes?

A: To our mail department.

Q: Your mail department. And where is your mail department?

A: At that time, it was on, like—I think we were on the seventh floor and that was, like, on the fifth floor.

Q: The fifth floor. So, you never saw them actually put in the mail or picked up in the mail, is that right?

A: No.

Q: And, someone could go to the mail department and pick one up and you would never know it even though there was supposed to be a procedure, is that correct?

A: That's correct.

The government did not conduct redirect examination of Ms. Skowronski.

The Third Circuit found this testimony to be deficient:

"It is well-established that evidence of business practice or office custom supports a finding of the mailing element of § 1341. * * * Had the government presented some competent evidence that as a routine practice the mail room sent claims checks through the United States mail, the verdict would be sustained. However, the direct and cross examination of Skowronski reveals that she had no personal knowledge that the routine practice of Travelers was to use the Untied States mails."

What type of questions could the prosecutor have asked Ms. Skowronski to establish adequate evidence of the mailing? What if Ms. Skowronski had never ventured into the mail room at Travelers—would she still be able to give the testimony the Third Circuit deems necessary?

4. Section 1343 of title 18, United States Code, is the wire fraud "cousin" to § 1341's mail fraud offense. Section 1343, in pertinent part, provides:

Whoever, having devised or intending to devise any scheme or artifice to defraud, or for obtaining money or property by means of false or fraudulent pretenses, representations, or promises, transmits or causes to be transmitted by means of wire, radio, or television communication interstate or foreign commerce, any writings, signs, signals, pictures, or sounds for the purpose of executing such scheme or artifice, shall be fined under this title or imprisoned not more than five years, or both. If the violation affects a financial institution, such person shall be fined not more than $1,000,000 or imprisoned not more than 30 years, or both.

Note that *interstate or foreign* use of "wire, radio, or television communication" is required before a violation of § 1343 occurs. Recall that any mailing (intrastate or interstate) suffices for a violation of § 1341. As with mail fraud, the government need not prove that a defendant knew interstate wires were or would be used, only that "the Defendant act with knowledge that the use of the wires will follow in the ordinary course or business, or can be reasonably foreseen.* * * " United States v. Brandon, 50 F.3d 464, 467 (7th Cir.1995).

The next case, United States v. Sampson, 371 U.S. 75 (1962), addresses the mailing requirement and provides some guidance as to when the mailing at issue is "for the purpose of executing such scheme or artifice."

UNITED STATES v. SAMPSON
United States Supreme Court, 1962.
371 U.S. 75.

BLACK, JUSTICE.

The appellees were indicted in a United States District Court on charges that they had used the mails "for the purpose of executing" a fraudulent scheme in violation of 18 U.S.C. § 1341 and that they had conspired to so use the mails. It is clear that the allegations, if proved, would show that a fraudulent scheme existed and that the mailings charged in fact occurred. The District Court dismissed 34 of the counts, however, on the ground that the facts alleged showed that the mails were not used "for the purpose of executing" the alleged scheme, as required by the statute. The court also dismissed the conspiracy count without giving additional reasons. The case is properly here on direct appeal by the Government under 18 U.S.C. § 3731.[j] The only question we must decide with reference to the 34 substantive counts is whether the allegations in the indictment were sufficient to permit a jury to find that the mails were used "for the purpose of executing" the fraudulent scheme. Whether the indictment sufficiently charges that the mails were so used depends upon its allegations.

In brief summary, these allegations are:

The individual defendants were officers, directors and employees of a large, nationwide corporation, also a defendant, with regional offices in various States. The defendants purported to be able to help businessmen obtain loans or sell out their businesses. Although lavish promises were freely given, the defendants did not intend to and in fact did not make any substantial efforts to perform these promised services. As a part of this scheme, the defendants secured salesmen who were trained to deceive those with whom they dealt by innuendos, half-truths, and false statements.[3] These defendants, according to the allegations, were not

---

j. At the time this case was appealed, 18 U.S.C. § 3731 provided that the United States could appeal directly from the district courts to the Supreme Court in criminal cases from where there was "a decision or judgment setting aside, or dismissing any indictment * * * or any count thereof, where such decision or judgment is based upon the * * * construction of the statute upon which the indictment * * * is founded." 18 U.S.C. § 3731, 62 Stat. 844 (1948).

3. "It was a further part of the said scheme and artifice to defraud that the defendants would secure salesmen * * *

mere small-time, sporadic swindlers but rather they have deliberately planned and devised a well-integrated, long-range, and effective scheme for the use of propaganda, salesmen, and other techniques to soften up and then cheat their victims one by one. Under the plan, personal calls were made upon prospects who were urged by false and fraudulent representations to sign applications asking defendants to help them obtain loans or sell their businesses. The salesmen further urged prospects, many times successfully, to give a check for an "advance fee," all being assured that if their applications were not accepted at the regional office the "advance fee" would be refunded. Payments of the fees were promptly converted by the salesmen into cashiers' checks on local banks and then forwarded with the applications to the corporate regional offices where all applications, as a part of the plan, were accepted if signed and accompanied by a check for the right amount. The fees were immediately deposited in the defendants' bank account. Although the money had already been obtained, the plan still called for a mailing of the accepted application together with a form letter to the victims "for the purpose of lulling said victims by representing that their applications had been accepted and that the defendants would therefore perform for said victims the valuable services which the defendants had falsely and fraudulently represented that they would perform."[4] It was further a part of the scheme to compile rudimentary financial data and forward it to various lending agencies and to inform the victims of this fact in an attempt to convince them that they had not been defrauded and that the defendants were performing meaningful services on their behalves. Moreover, under the plan, defendants, while refusing to refund the fee, pretended to investigate complaints from their victims and encouraged their salesmen to deny having made false representations, all the time seeking by false and fraudulent statements to make the victims believe that the defendants had faithfully performed and would continue to perform the promised services. In short, the indictment alleged that the scheme, as originally planned by defendants and as actually carried out, included fraudulent activities both before and after the victims had actually given over their money to the defendants. Of course, none of these charges have been established by evidence, but at this stage of the proceedings the indictment must be tested by its sufficiency to charge an offense.

who would be agreeable to the use of unethical sales talks and hire and use them as field representatives, and it was a further part of the scheme to teach such salesmen that prospective victims were at a complete disadvantage and would jump and act like puppets if the salesman handled the client right, and to teach them to try and impress upon the victims that said salesman was an expert; to teach salesmen to try and confuse victims and to lead them into believing that LSC was a lending company * * * and to teach said salesmen that LSC and the de-

fendants did not care how such salesmen sold a contract to a victim and that it was perfectly all right for a salesman to use innuendos and half-truths * * *." Record, pp. 4–5.

4. * * * It was also charged that a further purpose of the mailing was to inform the victims that they could not obtain a refund of their fees, that the contract was not cancelable, and that the victim had no recourse for retrieving his money.

The use of the mails relied on in the 34 dismissed counts was the mailing by the defendants of their acceptances of the victims' applications for their services. As conceded by the Government, prior to each mailing of an acceptance to a victim the defendants had obtained all the money they expected to get from that victim. The district judge's reason for holding that these counts did not charge a federal offense was that, since the money had already been obtained by the defendants before the acceptances were mailed, these mailings could not have been "for the purpose of executing" the scheme. For this holding the court relied chiefly on Kann v. United States, 323 U.S. 88 (1944), and Parr v. United States, 363 U.S. 370 (1960).

In *Kann,* the defendants defrauded their corporate employer in matters confined to their local region. As a part of their scheme, the defendants had fraudulently obtained checks payable to them which were cashed or deposited at a bank. The use of the mails charged as a violation of the federal statute was the mailing of the checks for collection by the banks which cashed them to the banks upon which they were drawn. Prior to that mailing, the Court found, the defendants had obtained the money they sought, and as far as they were concerned their plan had reached its fruition and come to a complete rest. The scheme, as the Court viewed it, had contemplated no more. The mailing was done by outsiders, the banks, which had no connection whatsoever with the fraud. The checks were mailed for the banks' own purposes and not in any way for the furthering of the fraudulent scheme. In the Court's view it was immaterial to the consummation of the defendants' scheme how or whether the banks which had cashed the checks sought to collect them.

In *Parr,* the second case upon which the District Court relied, the defendants had obtained gasoline and other products and services for themselves by the use of the credit card of a School District which had authorized the defendants to use the card for the District's purposes only. The mailings complained of in the *Parr* case were two invoices sent by the oil company to the District and the District's check mailed back in payment. Again the Court was able to find that the mailings by the outsiders were not an integral part of the scheme as planned and executed by the defendants and that, as a matter of fact, it was completely immaterial to them what the oil company did about collecting its bill.

We are unable to find anything in either the *Kann* or the *Parr* case which suggests that the Court was laying down an automatic rule that a deliberate, planned use of the mails after the victims' money had been obtained can never be "for the purpose of executing" the defendants' scheme. Rather the Court found only that under the facts in those cases the schemes had been fully executed before the mails were used. And Court of Appeals decisions rendered both before and after *Kann* have followed the view that subsequent mailings can in some circumstances provide the basis for an indictment under the mail fraud statutes.

Moreover, as pointed out above, the indictment in this case alleged that the defendants' scheme contemplated from the start the commission of fraudulent activities which were to be and actually were carried out both before and after the money was obtained from the victims. The indictment specifically alleged that the signed copies of the accepted applications and the covering letters were mailed by the defendants to the victims for the purpose of lulling them by assurances that the promised services would be performed. We cannot hold that such a deliberate and planned use of the United States mails by defendants engaged in a nationwide, fraudulent scheme in pursuance of a previously formulated plan could not, if established by evidence, be found by a jury under proper instructions to be "for the purpose of executing" a scheme within the meaning of the mail fraud statute. For these reasons, we hold that it was error for the District Court to dismiss these 34 substantive counts.

At the time the trial court dismissed the substantive counts it also dismissed the conspiracy count without stating additional reasons. In this Court, however, it is contended that the conspiracy count duplicates the 34 substantive counts because each substantive count is in reality a conspiracy count. On this basis, it is argued that there is an unjustified pyramiding of conspiracy counts which could be used by the Government in such a way as to deny the defendants, in particular the salesmen, a fair trial. We cannot anticipate arguments that would be more appropriately addressed to the trial court should the conduct or the result of the trial deny any of the defendants their rights. Since the conspiracy count on its face, like the substantive counts on their faces, properly charges a separate offense against each of the defendants, it was also error to dismiss the conspiracy count.

Reversed.

Notes

1. Can you explain exactly what fraud was committed by the individual defendants (the officers, directors and employees of the corporate defendant)?

2. This case addressed the issue of whether the mailings were "for the purpose of executing the scheme." Do you agree that the applications and cover letters could have "lulled" the fraud victims into a sense of security and thus perpetuated the fraud? Do you believe such a "lulling" effect is sufficient to find that the mailings were "for the purpose of *executing* the scheme"?

3. Is it a credible defense that the defendants were not "fraud artists," but that they were simply unorganized and poorly skilled business persons? What types of evidence might possibly support such a defense? What evidence might a prosecutor introduce to rebut this defense theory?

Twenty-seven years after its decision in *Sampson* the Supreme Court again addressed the issue of whether mailings were sufficiently related to the scheme. In Schmuck v. United States, 489 U.S. 705 (1989), the Court reiterated its prior position and affirmed the mail fraud convictions of Wayne T. Schmuck. Note Justice Scalia's dissenting opinion. With whom do you agree: Are courts permitting federal jurisdiction to expand too much through expansive interpretations of flexible statutes such as mail fraud?

SCHMUCK v. UNITED STATES

United States Supreme Court, 1989.
489 U.S. 705.

BLACKMUN, JUSTICE.

* * * Wayne T. Schmuck, a used car distributor, was indicted in the United States District Court for the Western District of Wisconsin on 12 counts of mail fraud, in violation of 18 U.S.C. §§ 1341 and 1342.

The alleged fraud was a common and straightforward one. Schmuck purchased used cars, rolled back their odometers, and then sold the automobiles to Wisconsin retail dealers for prices artificially inflated because of the low-mileage readings. These unwitting car dealers, relying on the altered odometer figures, then resold the cars to customers, who in turn paid prices reflecting Schmuck's fraud. To complete the resale of each automobile, the dealer who purchased it from Schmuck would submit a title-application form to the Wisconsin Department of Transportation on behalf of his retail customer. The receipt of a Wisconsin title was a prerequisite for completing the resale; without it the dealer could not transfer title to the customer and the customer could not obtain Wisconsin tags. The submission of the title-application form supplied the mailing element of each of the alleged mail frauds.

* * *

[Relying on *Kann*, *Parr* and United States v. Maze, 414 U.S. 395 (1974), Schmuck] argue[d] that mail fraud can be predicated only on a mailing that affirmatively assists the perpetrator in carrying out his fraudulent scheme. The mailing element of the offense, he contends, cannot be satisfied by a mailing, such as those at issue here, that is routine and innocent in and of itself, and that, far from furthering the execution of the fraud, occurs after the fraud has come to fruition, is merely tangentially related to the fraud, and is counterproductive in that it creates a "paper trail" from which the fraud may be discovered.

[ed.-The court disagreed with Schmuck's "characterization of the mailings" and with his "description of the applicable law."] We begin by considering the scope of Schmuck's fraudulent scheme. Schmuck was charged with devising and executing a scheme to defraud Wisconsin retail automobile customers who based their decisions to purchase certain automobiles at least in part on the low-mileage readings provided by the tampered odometers. This was a fairly large-scale operation. Evidence at trial indicated that Schmuck had employed a man known only as "Fred" to turn back the odometers on about 150 different cars. Schmuck then marketed these cars to a number of dealers, several of whom he dealt with on a consistent basis over a period of about 15 years. Indeed, of the 12 automobiles that are the subject of the counts of the indictment, 5 were sold to "P and A Sales," and 4 to "Southside Auto." Thus, Schmuck's was not a "one-shot" operation in which he sold a single car to an isolated dealer. His was an ongoing fraudulent venture. A rational jury could have concluded that the success of Schmuck's venture depended upon his continued harmonious relations with, and good reputation among, retail dealers, which in turn required the smooth flow of cars from the dealers to their Wisconsin customers.

Under these circumstances, we believe that a rational jury could have found that the title-registration mailings were part of the execution of the fraudulent scheme, a scheme which did not reach fruition until the retail dealers resold the cars and effected transfers of title. Schmuck's scheme would have come to an abrupt halt if the dealers either had lost faith in Schmuck or had not been able to resell the cars obtained from him. These resales and Schmuck's relationships with the retail dealers naturally depended on the successful passage of title among the various parties. Thus, although the registration-form mailings may not have contributed directly to the duping of either the retail dealers or the customers, they were necessary to the passage of title, which in turn was essential to the perpetuation of Schmuck's scheme. As noted earlier, a mailing that is "incident to an essential part of the scheme," *Pereira*, 347 U.S. at 8, satisfies the mailing element of the mail fraud offense. The mailings here fit this description.

* * *

JUSTICE SCALIA, WITH WHOM JUSTICE BRENNAN, JUSTICE MARSHALL, AND JUSTICE O'CONNOR JOIN, DISSENTING.

The Court today affirms petitioner's mail fraud conviction under 18 U.S.C. § 1341. A jury found that petitioner had defrauded retail automobile purchasers by altering odometer readings on used cars and then selling the cars to unwitting dealers for resale. The scheme was a continuing one, and some dealers bought a number of the cars from petitioner over a period of time. When the dealers sold the cars, state law required them to submit title application forms to the appropriate state agency. The Court concludes that the dealers' compliance with this requirement by mail caused the scheme to constitute mail fraud, because "a failure in this passage of title would have jeopardized Schmuck's relationship of trust and goodwill with the retail dealers upon whose unwitting cooperation his scheme depended." In my view this is inconsistent with our prior cases' application of the statutory requirement that mailings be "for the purpose of executing" a fraudulent scheme.

The purpose of the mail fraud statute is "to prevent the post office from being used to carry [fraudulent schemes] into effect." Durland v.

United States, 161 U.S. 306, 314 (1896); Parr v. United States, 363 U.S. 370, 389 (1960). The law does not establish a general federal remedy against fraudulent conduct, with use of the mails as the jurisdictional hook, but reaches only "those limited instances in which the use of the mails *is a part of the execution of the fraud*, leaving all other cases to be dealt with by appropriate state law." Kann v. United States, 323 U.S. 88, 95 (1944) (emphasis added). In other words, it is mail fraud, not mail and fraud, that incurs liability. This federal statute is not violated by a fraudulent scheme in which, at some point, a mailing happens to occur— nor even by one in which a mailing predictably and necessarily occurs. The mailing must be in furtherance of the fraud.

In Kann v. United States, we concluded that even though defendants who cashed checks obtained as part of a fraudulent scheme knew that the bank cashing the checks would send them by mail to a drawee bank for collection, they did not thereby violate the mail fraud statute, because upon their receipt of the cash "[t]he scheme . . . had reached fruition," and the mailing was "immaterial . . . to any consummation of the scheme." *Id.* at 94. We held to the same effect in United States v. Maze, 414 U.S. 395, 400–402 (1974), declining to find that credit card fraud was converted into mail fraud by the certainty that, after the wrongdoer had fraudulently received his goods and services from the merchants, they would forward the credit charges by mail for payment. These cases are squarely in point here. For though the Government chose to charge a defrauding of retail customers (to whom the innocent dealers resold the cars), it is obvious that, regardless of who the ultimate victim of the fraud may have been, the fraud was complete with respect to each car when petitioner pocketed the dealer's money. As far as each particular transaction was concerned, it was as inconsequential to him whether the dealer resold the car as it was inconsequential to the defendant in *Maze* whether the defrauded merchant ever forwarded the charges to the credit card company.

Nor can the force of our cases be avoided by combining all of the individual transactions into a single scheme, and saying, as the Court does, that if the dealers' mailings obtaining title for each retail purchaser had not occurred then the dealers would have stopped trusting petitioner for future transactions. (That conclusion seems to me a non sequitur, but I accept it for the sake of argument.) This establishes, at most, that the scheme could not technically have been consummated if the mechanical step of the mailings to obtain conveyance of title had not occurred. But we have held that the indispensability of such mechanical mailings, not strictly in furtherance of the fraud, is not enough to invoke the statute. For example, when officials of a school district embezzled tax funds over the course of several years, we held that no mail fraud had occurred even though the success of the scheme plainly depended on the officials' causing tax bills to be sent by mail (and thus tax payments to be received) every year. *Parr*, 363 U.S. at 388–392. Similarly, when those officials caused the school district to pay by mail credit card bills—a step plainly necessary to enable their continued fraudulent use of the credit card—we concluded that no mail fraud had occurred. *Id.* at 392–393.

I find it impossible to escape these precedents in the present case. Assuming the Court to be correct in concluding that failure to pass title to the cars would have threatened the success of the scheme, the same could have been said of failure to collect taxes or to pay the credit card bills in *Parr*. And I think it particularly significant that in *Kann* the Government proposed a theory *identical* to that which the Court today uses. Since the scheme was ongoing, the Government urged, the fact that the mailing of the two checks had occurred after the defendants had pocketed the fraudulently obtained cash made no difference. "[T]he defendants expected to receive further bonuses and profits," and therefore "the clearing of these checks in the ordinary course was essential to [the scheme's] further prosecution." 323 U.S. at 95. The dissenters in *Kann* agreed. "[T]his," they said, "was not the last step in the fraudulent scheme. It was a continuing venture. Smooth clearances of the checks were essential lest these intermediate dividends be interrupted and the conspirators be called upon to disgorge." *Id.* at 96 (Douglas, J., dissenting). The Court rejected this argument, concluding that "the subsequent banking transactions between the banks concerned were merely incidental and collateral to the scheme and not a part of it." *Id.* at 95. I think the mailing of the title application forms equivalently incidental here.

What Justice Frankfurter observed almost three decades ago remains true: "The adequate degree of relationship between a mailing which occurs during the life of a scheme and the scheme is ... not a matter susceptible of geometric determination." *Parr, supra,* 363 U.S. at 397 (dissenting opinion). All the more reason to adhere as closely as possible to past cases. I think we have not done that today, and thus create problems for tomorrow.

Notes

1. With whom do you agree, the majority or the dissent? Why?

2. There is another nuance regarding the mailing element. In Parr v. United States, 363 U.S. 370 (1960), prominently mentioned in *Sampson* and *Schmuck, supra,* the Court reversed defendants' convictions for two reasons. First, as noted in *Maze* the Court found that there was an insufficient connection between the mailing and the execution of the defendant's scheme involving collection of taxes and embezzlement of receipts collected.[k] In addition, however, the Court found that state law required collection and receipt of the taxes which, in the circumstances presented, "compelled" the use of the mails.[l] This discussion in *Parr* led to a doctrine known as the "innocent mailings" or "statutory duty" exception to the mail fraud statute. This exception applies when the "mailings are both not themselves false or fraudulent and their mailing is required by law." United States v. Krenning, 93 F.3d 1257, 1263 (5th Cir.1996); *Parr,* 363 U.S. at 390–92.

k. *Parr,* 363 U.S. at 375.   **l.** *Id.*

United States v. Krenning 93 F.3d 1257 (5th Cir.1996), demonstrates an effort by defendants to use the "innocent mailings" argument. Krenning was convicted on multiple mail fraud and conspiracy counts arising from an insurance company he created and operated. Through a series of bribes, false statements about the assets in reserve, and sham transactions, Krenning obtained approval from the Louisiana Insurance Commissioner to establish and operate his company. Krenning argued that his conduct could not constitute mail fraud because he was required, by state law, to mail the policies and related documents (the mailings charged) to insureds.[m] Assuming that the mailings were factually accurate and required, the Fifth Circuit nevertheless rejected Krenning's argument on the ground that "the 'innocent mailings' exception does not apply where the legal requirement to make the mailings is triggered by the fraudulent scheme."[n] The court found this to be the case: "we conclude that none of the mailings would have occurred but for the Defendants' scheme to fraudulently disguise the insurance company's reserve deficiency."[o]

B. BREACH OF FIDUCIARY DUTY: IS IT A "SCHEME OR ARTIFICE TO DEFRAUD"?

Until 1987 courts affirmed convictions of government officials who had been convicted of mail fraud on the theory that the officials defrauded citizens when the officials represented that they were providing honest and faithful services when they were not.[p]

Similarly, until 1987 courts affirmed mail fraud convictions of private sector employees for defrauding their employers by accepting kickbacks or selling confidential information on the same theory, that the employees falsely represented they were providing honest and faithful services.

United States v. George, 477 F.2d 508 (7th Cir.1973), was one of the first cases to approve use of the "breach of fiduciary duty" theory in the private sector. Peter K. Yonan, a purchaser agent for Zenith was convicted, along with Irving H. Greensphan and Andrew George, of

m. *Id.* at 1264.

n. *Id.* at 1263.

o. *Id.* at 1264.

p. Convictions based on this theory have included:

"judges, State Governors, chairmen of state political parties, state cabinet officers, city aldermen, Congressmen ... convicted of defrauding citizens of their right to the honest services of their governmental officials. In most of these cases, the officials * * * made governmental decisions with the objective of benefitting themselves or promoting their own interests, instead of fulfilling their legal commitment to provide the citizens of the State or local government with their loyal service and honest government. Similarly, many elected officials and their campaign workers [were] convicted of mail fraud when they have used the mails to falsify votes, thus defrauding the citizenry of its right to an honest election." McNally v. United States, 483 U.S. 350, 362–63 (1987) (Stevens, J. dissenting).

devising "a scheme to defraud Zenith whereby Yonan received kickbacks on * * * sales of cabinets to Zenith."[q] Irving H. Greensphan was President of Accurate Box Corporation which supplied the cabinets to Zenith. Over a 3½ year time period, Greensphan paid in excess of $300,000 to Yonan[r] "because he was afraid he was otherwise going to lose Zenith's business."[s] There was no evidence that Greensphan increased the price of the cabinets charged to Zenith because of the payments he made to Yonan. Nor was there evidence of bid-rigging or other improprieties in the awarding of the cabinet contract to Greensphan. For these reasons, the defendants argued there was no fraud. The United States Court of Appeals for the Seventh Circuit rejected this argument:

> "Defendants contend that the evidence was insufficient to satisfy the first element—the existence of a scheme to defraud. Reduced to its essential distillation, their argument is that because the kickbacks were never shown to come out of Zenith's pockets, as opposed to Greensphan's, because Yonan was never shown to provide or secure any special services for Greensphan and his company, and because Zenith was never shown to be dissatisfied with Accurate's cabinets or prices, no fraud within the contemplation of the statute can have occurred. We reject this argument, in part because it misses the point in two respects and in part because the particular scheme shown by the evidence to defraud Zenith is, from every defendant's point of view, within the reach of the mail fraud statute.

> "Since the gravamen of the offense is a 'scheme to defraud,' it is unnecessary that the Government allege or prove that the victim of the scheme was actually defrauded or suffered a loss. If there was intent on the part of a schemer to deprive Zenith of Yonan's honest and loyal services in the form of his giving Greensphan preferential treatment, it is simply beside the point that Yonan may not have had to (or had occasion to) exert special influence in favor of Greensphan or that Zenith was satisfied with Accurate's product and prices. And it is of no moment whether or not the kickback money actually came from Zenith. Thus the district court correctly charged the jury that it was unnecessary for the Government to prove 'that anyone actually be defrauded.' Contrary to defendants' contentions, the evidence hardly shows that it was impossible for Yonan to exercise favoritism toward Greensphan. As the Court noted in Shushan v. United States, 117 F.2d 110, 115 (5th Cir.1941): 'The fact that the official who is bribed is only one of several and could not award the contract by himself does not change the character of the scheme where he is expected to have influence enough to secure the end in view.' In our view the evidence shows that Yonan did have opportunities to give Greensphan preferential

---

q. *Id.* at 510.

r. These funds were paid through Andrew George, doing business as A & G

Woodworking Co. George was the third defendant.

s. *Id.* at 514.

treatment, particularly by avoiding the solicitation of potential competitors. Of course, the actual exercise of any such opportunity by a person in Yonan's position may be practically undetectable.

"Furthermore, even if Yonan never intended to give Greensphan preferential treatment, and the Government does not argue that the evidence was sufficient to support a conclusion that he did, the defendants' argument still misses the mark. The evidence shows Yonan actually defrauded Zenith. We need not accept the Government's far-ranging argument that anytime an agent secretly profits from his agency he has committed criminal fraud. Not every breach of every fiduciary duty works a criminal fraud. But here Yonan's duty was to negotiate the best price possible for Zenith or at least to appraise Zenith that Greensphan was willing to sell his cabinets for substantially less money. Not only did Yonan secretly earn a profit from his agency, but also he deprived Zenith of material knowledge that Greensphan would accept less profit. There was a very real and tangible harm to Zenith in losing the discount or losing the opportunity to bargain with a most relevant fact before it. As Judge Learned Hand stated in a related context:

> 'A man is none the less cheated out of his property, when he is induced to part with it by fraud, because he gets a quid pro quo of equal value. It may be impossible to measure his loss by the gross scales available to a court, but he has suffered a wrong; he has lost his chance to bargain with the facts before him. That is the evil against which the statute is directed.' United States v. Rowe, 56 F.2d 747, 749 (2d Cir.).

"Here the fraud consisted in Yonan's holding himself out to be a loyal employee, acting in Zenith's best interests, but actually not giving his honest and faithful services, to Zenith's real detriment."

In a 1987 decision, McNally v. United States, 483 U.S. 350 (1987), the Supreme Court held that mail fraud did not cover breaches of fiduciary duty because the mail fraud statute did not cover losses of "intangible rights" such as the right to honest and faithful services. At issue in *McNally* were convictions of various elected and appointed public officials and a private citizen in Kentucky who awarded the state's workmen's compensation policies to insurance agencies in which these officials had a concealed ownership interest.[t] The defendants were convicted of one count of mail fraud on the theory they had devised a scheme (1) to defraud the citizens and the government of Kentucky of their right to have the Commonwealth's affairs conducted honestly, and (2) to obtain, directly and indirectly, money and other things of value by means of false pretenses and the concealment of material facts.[u]

---

t. *Id.* at 362.

u. The defendants were also convicted of conspiring "to violate the mail fraud statute through the scheme just described and conspir[ing] to defraud the United States by obstructing the collection of federal taxes." *Id.* at 354. This count was also reversed by the Supreme Court: "The Government concedes that if petitioner's substantive mail fraud convictions are reversed

Finding that the mail fraud statute was limited to "schemes or artifices to defraud * * * for obtaining *money or property* by means of false or fraudulent pretenses," the Court held that the statute did not reach schemes to deprive victims of intangible rights.[v] The Court explained:

> "Rather than construe the statute in a manner that leaves its outer boundaries ambiguous and involves the Federal Government in setting standards of disclosure and good government for local and state officials, we read § 1341 as limited in scope to the protection of property rights. If Congress desires to go further, it must speak more clearly than it has."

There was a vigorous dissent by Justice Stevens who argued that the majority was rejecting the plain language of the mail fraud statute,[w] as well as "the accumulated wisdom of the many distinguished federal judges who have thoughtfully considered and correctly answered the question this case presents."[x]

Immediately, after the *McNally* decision, Congress began hearings on how to amend the mail fraud statute to remedy the "*McNally* problem." On November 18, 1988, President Reagan signed into law an addition to the federal criminal code:

§ 1346. Definition of "scheme or artifice to defraud"

For the purposes of this chapter, the term "scheme or artifice to defraud" includes a scheme or artifice to deprive another of the intangible right of honest services.[y]

In the next case, the United States Court of Appeals for the Fifth Circuit, sitting en banc, addressed the reach of the mail fraud offense after passage of § 1346.

their conspiracy convictions should be reversed." *Id.* at 361. The defendants were convicted of an additional six counts of mail fraud where all six mailings were Seton's tax returns. Relying on *Parr's* 363 U.S. 370 (1960) "innocent mailings" doctrine, the Court of Appeals reversed these counts. The Government did not seek review of this ruling. *McNally,* 483 U.S. at 353 n.2.

v. *Id.* at 360.

w. *Id.* at 365.

x. *Id.* at 376.

y. Following the Supreme Court's decision in *McNally,* a number of public officials who had been convicted on the "intangible rights" theory sought to set aside their convictions. These defendants argued that McNally's holding should be applied retroactively. At first, the courts were split. *Cf.* United States v. Smith, 675 F.Supp. 978

(M.D.Pa.1987) *aff'd* 865 F.2d 253 (1988). (*McNally* not retroactively applied) with Ingber v. Enzor, 841 F.2d 450 (2d Cir.1988) (McNally retroactively applied). Quickly, however, the federal courts of appeal agreed that *McNally* should be applied retroactively to invalidate mail fraud convictions tried under an intangible rights theory. These courts ruled that in light of the Supreme Court's decision in *McNally,* conviction of mail fraud upon an intangible theory was "a fundamental defect which inherently result[ed] in a complete miscarriage of justice." *See, e.g.,* United States v. Shelton, 848 F.2d 1485, 1489 (10th Cir.1988). Soon thereafter, the government abandoned any argument to the contrary. United States v. Mitchell, 867 F.2d 1232, 1233 (9th Cir. 1989).

UNITED STATES v. BRUMLEY

United States Court of Appeals, Fifth Circuit, 1997.
116 F.3d 728.

Higginbotham, Circuit Judge.

Michael Bryant Brumley was convicted in a bench trial of conspiring to defraud the citizens of the State of Texas of honest services by use of interstate wire communications and the United States mail in violation of 18 U.S.C. § 371, three counts of wire fraud in violation of 18 U.S.C. § 1343, three counts of money laundering in violation of 18 U.S.C. § 1956, and two counts of making a false statement to a financial institution in violation of 18 U.S.C. § 1014. Brumley does not appeal his conviction on the last two counts of defrauding a financial institution and they are not before us.

As we will explain, Brumley's primary contention is that the government has misused federal criminal statutes to prosecute a state employee for ethical lapses. * * * First, Brumley urges that neither the plain language of § 1346 nor its legislative history expands the types of victims protected by the statute to include a state employer. Second, he insists that an ethical lapse, or at worst a state misdemeanor, is not a deprivation of honest services. Third, he argues that the Commerce Clause does not support § 1346. * * *

We reject each of these contentions and affirm the convictions. In doing so we reject the argument that Congress failed in its 1988 effort to expand the statute to cover the deprivation of honest services which the *McNally* and *Carpenter* decisions found were outside the statute's reach. *See* Carpenter v. United States, 484 U.S. 19, 25 (1987); McNally v. United States, 483 U.S. 350, 359–60 (1987). This argument has gathered strength from the Supreme Court's recent Commerce Clause decisions, but we ultimately conclude that it cannot escape the plain language of § 1346.

* * *

II

Texas' workers' compensation law was long administered by the Texas Industrial Accident Board. Under this regime the Board dealt with three groups: claimants, their lawyers, and insurance carriers insuring the employers. Brumley worked for the Board and resided in Beaumont, Texas. In 1990 the Texas legislature changed the process for resolving workers' compensation claims. The Board became the Texas Workers' Compensation Commission, and Brumley was promoted to Regional Associate Director of the new commission, and moved to the new commission's Houston office. Brumley's duties included the handling of claims arising under the old law and, according to the indictment, responsibility for "identifying attorneys and insurance carriers who failed to follow TWCC or IAB rules and regulations." Brumley's work gave him knowledge of the conduct of lawyers, the identity of unrepresented claimants, and the details of the process itself.

Brumley never seemed to be able to live within his income. As early as 1982, he began to solicit loans from lawyers representing claimants and their assistance in obtaining loans from lending institutions. In 1985 and 1986, while he was conducting prehearing conferences in cases in Lufkin, Texas, he charged and never repaid several hundred dollars to the account of a claimant's counsel at the local country club. By 1988 Brumley had borrowed money from at least eight lawyers and struck up a relationship with John M. Cely, a Lufkin attorney with a substantial workers' compensation practice. Cely and persons employed by his law firm made frequent appearances before Brumley in prehearing conferences. They began a process whereby Cely would cause wire transfers to be made from the Western Union office in Lufkin to Brumley at various locations in Texas. These wire transfers were accomplished electronically through a Western Union facility located outside of Texas. From 1987 to May of 1992, Cely made some seventy wire transfers to Brumley totaling approximately $86,730. In all, Brumley "borrowed" some $112,156 from eleven lawyers, including Cely. None of this sum was ever repaid.

The indictment charged a scheme to defraud "the citizens of the State of Texas, including the members of the Texas Industrial Accident Board . . ., an agency of the State of Texas, from receiving the intangible right to honest services."

III

Brumley contends that Congress did not intend to reach schemes to deprive an entity of state government of the intangible right of honest services in its 1988 enactment of § 1346. That statute provides:

> For the purposes of this Chapter, the term "scheme or artifice to defraud" includes a scheme or artifice to deprive another of the intangible right of honest services.

Reading § 1346 with § 1343 we have the following prohibition:

> Whoever, having devised or intending to devise any [scheme or artifice to deprive another of the intangible right of honest services], . . . transmits or causes to be transmitted by means of [interstate wires] for the purpose of executing such scheme or artifice, shall be fined under this title or imprisoned not more than five years, or both.

Brumley's present argument, taking a cue from the second panel opinion, takes two related cuts at the application of the statute to his conduct. First, he contends that "another" has the same meaning as the term "whoever" for purposes of the fraud chapter of the criminal code, specifically Chapter 63 of Title 18. And "another" cannot include his state employer or the citizens of the State of Texas. Second, invoking federalism, Brumley contends that Congress failed to state its purpose with the clarity demanded for federal incursions into state matters, at least those traveling on the commerce power.

We are persuaded that a governmental entity qualifies as "another" within the meaning of § 1346, and that "honest services" can include "honest and impartial government." The panel opinion notes that Section 1 of Title I of the U.S.Code provides that " 'person' and 'whoever' include corporations, companies, associations, firms, partnerships, and societies, and joint stock companies, as well as individuals." 79 F.3d at 1435. It "note[s] that among the meanings of the word 'whoever' in Section 1, Title I, there is nothing that could even remotely be interpreted or construed to mean 'a state,' 'a political subdivision of a state,' 'a government,' 'a governmental agency,' or 'the citizens of a state as a body politic.' "*Id.*

Brumley is himself an "individual," and we think he must qualify as a "whoever" within the meaning of the statute, in which case he can be prosecuted for depriving "another" of his intangible right of honest services. This case does not involve a prosecution of a state, state subdivision, government, or agency. Rather, it is a prosecution of an individual who abused his position as an employee of a state commission. That the mail fraud statute reaches Brumley's conduct is consistent with the proposition that the statute does not allow prosecution of a state or state agency.

Moreover, Section 1 of Title I provides that "person" and "whoever" include the listed terms. We read this to mean that "person" and "whoever" include the listed terms without deciding whether other non-mentioned entities may qualify as a "person" or a "whoever." Otherwise, Congress would have said something other than "include," such as "person" and "whoever" mean the listed terms (or consist of, or perhaps include only). In this criminal statute, "another" defines the range of victims while "whoever" defines the perpetrator; we do not think it makes sense to define the victims by reference to the definition of the perpetrator.

IV

Brumley argues that even if "another" does not modify "whoever," it does not include "citizens as the body politic." The exact thrust of this contention is uncertain, given the fact that the defendant is not a political entity but a person charged with fraudulent activity while employed by a state entity. We understand the argument to be that "another" should not be read to reach such abuses of state office. The contention is that § 1343 is at least sufficiently uncertain that it need not be so read, and traditional principles of lenity and the doctrine of clear statement counsel that it should not be. The argument points to *McNally* itself, specifically the Court's observation that:

> Rather than construe the statute in a manner that leaves its outer boundaries ambiguous and involves the Federal Government in setting standards of disclosure and good government for local and state officials, we read [the statute] as limited in scope to the protection of property rights. If Congress desires to go further, it must speak more clearly than it has.

483 U.S. at 360.

The argument fails because Congress accepted the Court's invitation and was clear in its purpose. First, we think the statutory language plainly reaches state officials such as Brumley, and thus it is unnecessary to repair to legislative history. That history is recounted by the dissent and by the panel majority, and we will not rehearse it again. There is nothing to suggest that Congress did not intend by § 1346 to overturn the Supreme Court's *McNally* decision and to insist that the fraud statutes cover deprivations of intangible rights such as those charged in the counts for which Brumley was convicted. We join the First, Fourth, and Eleventh Circuits in rejecting similar attacks on § 1343 convictions.

The dissent, worried that the text of § 1346 fails to give citizens adequate notice, accuses the majority of illicitly re-drafting a criminal statute. But we are hardly announcing a common-law crime. As the Supreme Court has recently explained, "the touchstone is whether the statute, either standing alone or as construed, made it reasonably clear at the relevant time that the defendant's conduct was criminal." United States v. Lanier, 117 S.Ct. 1219, 1225 (1997). Gauging fair notice requires an inquiry into the state of the law as a whole, not merely into the words printed on a single page of the United States Code. Constructions of a statute announced by the Supreme Court or lower courts can give citizens fair warning, even if the cases are not "fundamentally similar." *Id.* at 1226–28.

Here Brumley had notice that Congress had repudiated the Supreme Court's interpretation in *McNally*. Congress, in other words, announced that it wanted the courts to enforce the honest-services doctrine developed in the years leading up to *McNally*. Because Congress was not faced with a uniform formulation of the precise contours of the doctrine, some defendants on the outer reaches of the statute might be able to complain that they were not on notice that Congress criminalized their conduct when it revived the honest-services doctrine. But even if there are such defendants, Brumley is not among them. As we will explain, his conduct was inconsistent with his duties under Texas law. The boundaries of "intangible rights" may be difficult to discern, but that does not mean that it is difficult to determine whether Brumley in particular violated them.

V

We must next find the meaning of honest services as used in this federal statute. As we have explained, Congress has insisted that the fraud statutes cover the deprivation of intangible rights. In doing so, it reestablished the honest services doctrine. It bears emphasis that before *McNally* the doctrine of honest services was not a unified set of rules. And Congress could not have intended to bless each and every pre-*McNally* lower court "honest services" opinion. Many of these opinions have expressions far broader than their holdings.

Before *McNally*, the meaning of "honest services" was uneven. [citations omitted]

A close look at these cases uncovers two uncertainties regarding the draw by this federal statute upon state law, specifically in defining the statutory element of honest services. First, must the services be owed under state law? Second, must the breach of a duty to provide services rooted in state law violate the criminal law of the state? We decide today that services must be owed under state law and that the government must prove in a federal prosecution that they were in fact not delivered. We do not reach the question of whether a breach of a duty to perform must violate the criminal law of the state.

We begin with the plain language of the statute. There are two words—"honest" and "services." We will not lightly infer that Congress intended to leave to courts and prosecutors, in the first instance, the power to define the range and quality of services a state employer may choose to demand of its employees. We find nothing to suggest that Congress was attempting in § 1346 to garner to the federal government the right to impose upon states a federal vision of appropriate services— to establish, in other words, an ethical regime for state employees. Such a taking of power would sorely tax separation of powers and erode our federalist structure. Under the most natural reading of the statute, a federal prosecutor must prove that conduct of a state official breached a duty respecting the provision of services owed to the official's employer under state law. Stated directly, the official must act or fail to act contrary to the requirements of his job under state law. This means that if the official does all that is required under state law, alleging that the services were not otherwise done "honestly" does not charge a violation of the mail fraud statute. The statute contemplates that there must first be a breach of a state-owed duty. It follows that a violation of state law that prohibits only appearances of corruption will not alone support a violation of §§ 1343 and 1346. As the Ninth Circuit put it, "[t]o hold otherwise that illegal conduct alone [would suffice] would have the potential of bringing almost any illegal act within the province of the mail fraud statute." United States v. Dowling, 739 F.2d 1445, 1450 (9th Cir.1984), rev'd on other grounds, 473 U.S. 207 (1985).

Stated another way, "honest services" contemplates that in rendering some particular service or services, the defendant was conscious of the fact that his actions were something less than in the best interests of the employer—or that he consciously contemplated or intended such actions. For example, something close to bribery. If the employee renders all the services his position calls for, and if these and all other services rendered by him are just the services which would be rendered by a totally faithful employee, and if the scheme does not contemplate otherwise, there has been no deprivation of honest services. Thus, the mere violation of a gratuity statute, even one closer to bribery than the Texas statute, will not suffice.

Finally, the statute proscribes an actual scheme or artifice to defraud. There is nothing in the informing principles of federalism or legislative history to suggest that the scheme or artifice to defraud elements are drawn from state law. Rather, they are familiar terms of federal criminal law generating and drawing their sustenance from federal common law. These wholly federal elements, read with the jurisdictional elements of mail usage and coupled with the draw upon state law for the definition of service, allow the statute to serve federal interests without supplanting rights of core state governance. The indictment charged that Brumley used his position to assist Cely in exchange for money. Thus, the federal component of the crime was properly charged, and, as we will explain, was proved.

We pause to put aside the frequent invocations of a deprivation of citizens' rights to honest services. The reference to such "rights" of citizens has little relevant meaning beyond a shorthand statement of a duty rooted in state law and owed to the state employer. Despite its rhetorical ring, the rights of citizens to honest government have no purchase independent of rights and duties locatable in state law. To hold otherwise would offer § 1346 as an enforcer of federal preferences of "good government" with attendant potential for large federal inroads into state matters and genuine difficulties of vagueness. Congress did not use those words, and we will not supply them.

The federalism arguments that inform the definition of "honest services" under federal criminal law are powerful, and we acknowledge them in our holdings today. A sitting state official with adjudicatory authority who accepts payments from lawyers practicing in front of him and simultaneously acts for those lawyers in his official capacity contrary to his state-law duty has provided dishonest services to his employer, here the Texas Industrial Accident Board and its successor, the TWCC. As it turns out, Texas condemns such conduct by making it a criminal offense punishable by imprisonment for up to one year and a fine as large as $4,000, and this violation was part of a fraudulent scheme and conspiracy under § 1346, as found by the district court. The tension inherent in federal criminalization of conduct by state officials innocent under state law is absent here.

We have held that services under § 1346 are those an employee must provide the employer under state law. Using his office to pursue his own account and not that of his employer, Brumley violated a Texas criminal statute. This case does not then require us to decide whether the amended federal statute criminalizes conduct no part of which is criminal under state law.

Our previous cases have not made clear the use of state law we emphasize today. To the extent our prior cases are contrary, they are overruled.

VI

Having concluded that § 1343 applies to deprivations of honest services by state employees and that such services must be owed under state law, we now address Brumley's contention that his own actions did not do so. At trial, the government stipulated that it would not try to prove that any IAB award was enhanced by Brumley or that any claimant was awarded more money by Brumley or that Brumley referred any unrepresented claimant to an attorney in return for cash. Rather, the government's "position [was] that the quid pro quo [was] intangible, such as favoritism or other types of intangible matters." The government points out that Cely admitted to the trial court that the $86,780 in payments to Brumley were not "loans." And during the time period that Brumley was receiving these payments from Cely, Brumley vouched for Cely's good character when Cely was investigated by IAB and interceded to try to stop the investigation altogether. Brumley also advised Cely on the alteration of documents subpoenaed by the IAB, so as to make easy detection of wrongdoing difficult. The relationship between Cely and Brumley was so tight that when one of Cely's employees inquired into Cely's unconcerned confidence about an impending TWCC/IAB investigation of Cely, he replied "We have Brumley." Brumley also helped Cely's attempt to lease property in Lufkin to the TWCC by advising Cely how to conceal his efforts and by aggressively discouraging the TWCC from leasing from another bidder.

The district court found "ample and convincing" evidence to support each of the counts of the indictment. According to the district court, Brumley and Cely engaged in a conspiracy in which Cely would give Brumley money and Brumley would use his position with the IAB and TWCC to assist Cely's dealings with the agency. Although the district court found clear evidence of ethical violations, it did not rely on them to make its decision. Instead, the district court found a scheme to defraud that included conduct that violated Texas penal law. See Tex. Penal Code Ann. § 36.08(e) (making it a Class A misdemeanor for a public servant with judicial authority to "solicit[ ], accept [ ], or agree[ ] to accept any benefit from a person the public servant knows is interested in or likely to become interested in any matter before the public servant or [his] tribunal").

Brumley's other contentions are without merit, and we affirm the judgment of convictions.

AFFIRMED.

E. GRADY JOLLY AND DEMOSS, CIRCUIT JUDGES, WITH WHOM JERRY E. SMITH, CIRCUIT JUDGE, JOINS, DISSENTING:

We respectfully dissent from what we consider to be an issue-evasive and jurisprudentially flawed majority opinion. With little analysis, and much judicially engrafted legislation, it holds that general, undefined, vague, and ambiguous words constitute a clear statement that Congress intended for federal prosecutors and grand juries to police the conduct of state officers acting in their official state capacities. We should make clear that we do not at all suggest that the criminal statute at issue is unconstitutional or must otherwise be stricken—only that as the statute is applied in this case, the indictment and proof fails to state and prove a crime.

INTRODUCTION

First, the majority needs to be reminded that when interpreting a criminal statute, courts must apply the rule of lenity; that is, when choosing between two readings of a criminal statute, the courts must favor the narrower interpretation unless Congress has spoken to the contrary in language that is clear and definite. This is an indisputable rule of statutory construction ignored by the majority. Second, the Supreme Court has emphasized that when a statute is applied, as here, to alter the balance of federalism, congressional intent must be plain on the face of the statute—an intent that even infrared eyes cannot detect from this statute.

The words we interpret today are these few: "For the purpose of this chapter, the term 'scheme or artifice to defraud' includes a scheme or artifice to deprive another of the intangible right of honest services." For the majority to prevail, these words must clearly demonstrate that Congress intended to apply the wire fraud statute to police the integrity of state officials acting in the capacities of their offices. Moreover, these words must satisfy constitutional due process, which requires that citizens be given fair notice that specific conduct constitutes a crime.

The majority utterly fails to address these principles of statutory construction. The reason the majority opinion avoids raising these crucial matters is simple: it cannot possibly conform its conclusions with principles of statutory construction.

Principles of statutory construction are not the only obstacles to the majority's reading of the statute. The legislative history is also devastating to the majority's position that Congress has spoken clearly in § 1346 to reach the conduct of state officers acting in their official capacity. Because the statute fails on its face to make a crime of the charged conduct, this dissent need not address the matter of legislative history. The legislative history does, however, make plain beyond any doubt that § 1346 cannot be fairly construed to reflect a clear congressional intent to police the integrity of state officers. Thus, rather than deal with the legislative history, the majority pursues the only course available to it: silence.

Indeed, the only significant issue in this case that the majority squarely faces is the meaning of "honest services," a term that the majority acknowledges is ambiguous and undefined by Congress. One would think that the majority would directly acknowledge that this patent and indisputable ambiguity cripples this prosecution. But no. Instead, the majority assumes a role somewhere between a philosopher king and a legislator to create its own definitions of the terms of a criminal statute. Surely, the majority should recognize the laudatory principle to which we as a Court try scrupulously to adhere: The courts may not assume the place of Congress by writing or rewriting criminal laws pursuant to which citizens will be prosecuted. This is solely the prerogative of Congress. With great respect for the usual judgment of our colleagues, we must say that the majority opinion in this respect is hardly a judicial opinion.

The majority opinion is flawed in other respects as we shall develop more fully in this dissent. Its argument that it makes no sense to "define victims by reference to the definition of the perpetrator" is sophistry, a glib phrase giving the appearance of a truism, resorted to by the majority because it can provide no answer to otherwise define the meaning of "another" as it appears in the statute. Although it may be less than a perfect method of divining the hidden intent of Congress, we suggest that defining "another," which is otherwise completely undefined by Congress, by referring to "whoever," is an absolutely correct grammatical construction of the one-sentence statute; at least it provides some definitional meaning or limits to the term "another." The majority opinion provides no definitional limits for a key term in a criminal statute. The majority also says nothing about the due process problems of sufficient notice of what behavior has been prohibited when such key terms have no definitional limits.

In this dissent, we shall further show that the majority, without any analysis, baldly states that "another" means the citizens as the body politic. It is beyond our capacity to accept the conclusion that by using the term "another" in § 1346, Congress clearly has referred to the entire "body politic" of the State of Texas. In so concluding without analysis, the majority gives the phrase judicial chutzpa new meaning.

After the majority completes its assumed legislative task of defining honest services, it appears to have some second thoughts about the application of "another" to the body politic, and "pauses" to

> put aside the frequent invocations of a deprivation of citizens' rights to honest services. The reference to such "rights" of citizens has little relevant meaning beyond a shorthand statement of a duty rooted in state law and owed to the state employer. Despite its rhetorical ring, the rights of citizens to honest government have no purchase independent of rights and duties locatable in state law. To hold otherwise would offer § 1346 as an enforcer of federal preferences of "good government" with attendant potential for large federal inroads into state matters and genuine difficulties of vagueness. Congress did not use those words, and we will not supply them.

It is certainly true that Congress did not use those words. Indeed, that is a major point of this dissent. The indictment, however, used those words. Does the majority conclude that the indictment charges the specifics of a crime unauthorized by Congress? If for no other purpose than to remind the majority, we point out that the indictment charged Brumley with depriving "the citizens of the State of Texas ... from receiving ... honest services." Yet the majority says the term has no "purchase." No purchase? The deprivation of the "citizens of Texas rights to honest services" in this case has "purchased" a federal prison sentence for Mr. Brumley.

* * *

It is clear, of course, that, under the Supremacy Clause, the Congress may legislate in areas traditionally regulated by the States. Nevertheless, the Court has emphasized that "[t]his is an extraordinary power in a federalist system. It is a power that we must assume Congress does not exercise lightly." Gregory v. Ashcroft, 501 U.S. 452, 460 (1991). "If Congress intends to alter the usual constitutional balance between the States and the Federal Government, it must make its intention to do so unmistakably clear in the language of the statute." Id. at 460.

* * *

It is * * * incomprehensible to us that the majority can conclude, as it must in order to uphold this conviction, that the inclusion of the words "[f]or the purposes of this chapter, the term 'scheme or artifice to defraud' includes a scheme or artifice to deprive another of the intangible right of honest services," reflects a clear statement of a Congressional intention to protect the citizenry of a state from corrupt state officials. Given this certain ambiguity of statutory words, there is surely no call for us to proceed further into legislative history to demonstrate that Congress has failed to satisfy the requirements delineated in * * * Ashcroft. * * *

* * *

[ed.-After reviewing legislative history pertaining to § 1346, the dissent concluded that the] wording of § 1346 simply does not effect a change in the portion of the McNally opinion which held that the mail fraud statute does not reach "schemes to defraud citizens of their intangible rights to honest and impartial government." The legislative history reinforces this view.

The majority opinion seems to make the test of "speaking more clearly" simply Congress' evidencing an intention to overrule McNally. But overruling McNally does nothing to place in the statutory language the necessary words, phrases and language which would notify the average citizen that these statutes have been dramatically extended to include conduct and activities not previously stated therein. Clearly, when the Supreme Court decided McNally, all of the preexisting Circuit Court constructions, interpretations and applications went down the drain; the convictions of many defendants who had been prosecuted under the pre-McNally law had to be vacated, and conduct occurring prior to the effective date of § 1346 could no longer be prosecuted under the old law.

McNally placed the burden on Congress to put down in statutory form whatever expanded scope it chose to give to the fraud statutes. In effect, Congress was charged with codifying in statutory form the definitions of the conduct which would be prohibited by the concepts of "intangible rights," "honest services," and "good and honest government," and to expressly indicate whether Congress intended to extend these concepts to the conduct of state officials. The requirement imposed by the Supreme Court to speak more clearly was not for the benefit of the Circuit Courts which had, in fact, given birth to these concepts in the first place. Rather, the requirement to speak more clearly, in addition to addressing federalism concerns, was for the benefit of the public, the average citizen, the average mid-level state administrator like Brumley, who must be forewarned and given notice that certain conduct may subject him to federal prosecution. The staff of the Senate Judiciary Committee and the Department of Justice clearly understood these requirements and drafted S2793 (see addendum) which would satisfy them. This bill passed the Senate, but the House was unwilling to specifically regulate the conduct of state officials. In its place, the House substituted a one-sentence statement that did not define the word "another," did not define the term "intangible right," and did not define the term "honest services." It is difficult to understand how the majority can conclude that the statutory language of § 1346 "plainly reaches state officials such as Brumley."

* * *

Finally, we have to register our disagreement with the fundamental premise upon which the majority opinion seems to be based, i.e., that Congress can delegate to the federal courts the task of defining the key terms and coverage of a criminal statute. We have found no Supreme Court case which supports that proposition, and the majority opinion cites no authority, either constitutional, statutory or decisional, for that premise. The majority pays lip service to the principle that Congress must define the criminal conduct when it states:

> We will not lightly infer that Congress intended to leave to courts and prosecutors, in the first instance, the power to define the range and quality of services a state employer may choose to demand of its employees.

Surprisingly, the majority flatly contradicts itself when it states that the passage of § 1346 has set the Courts "back on a course of defining honest services, and we turn to that task." As stated earlier, research indicates that the term "honest services" has never been used by the United States Congress in any statute prior to its use in § 1346, and that the term is nowhere defined by Congress. Likewise, there is nothing in the words of the statute itself nor in any of the legislative history of § 1346 which would indicate any Congressional intent to delegate to the Courts the task of defining the words "honest services," even if Congress could constitutionally do so.

The majority's attempt to define "honest services" demonstrates why such ad hoc definitions cannot possibly satisfy the requirements of "fair notice" to our fellow citizens as to where the line between permitted and prohibited conduct is drawn. On the one hand, the majority says that "the statute contemplates that there must first be a breach of a state owed duty," but on the other hand, it states that "the mere violation of a gratuity statute, even one closer to bribery than the Texas statute, will not suffice." Likewise, at one point the majority states that "we do not reach the question of whether a breach of duty to perform must violate the criminal law of the state," but in another point the majority supports its evidentiary analysis by saying that "Brumley violated a Texas criminal statute." Finally, at two points the majority recognizes that the case law on "honest services" prior to *McNally* was "not a unified set of rules" and was "uneven." From its review of the pre-*McNally* cases, the majority found "two uncertainties regarding the draw by this federal statute upon state law, specifically in defining the statutory element of honest services." Maj. Op. It is obvious, therefore, that the majority has recognized that the term "honest services" has not achieved the status of a commonly accepted and recognized term of art which Congress could have been relying upon in using these words. The majority makes a labored effort to infuse some sort of meaning to these words; but in truth and in fact, the majority finds that meaning in its own subjective notions and not in the words of Congress.

CONCLUSION

Because our colleagues in the majority (1) have closed their eyes to obvious ambiguities in the text of 28 U.S.C. § 1346; (2) have chosen to completely ignore and avoid the legislative history of § 1346 which * * * undermines the majority's conclusion; (3) have concluded, without analysis or reference to any principles of statutory construction, that § 1346 "plainly reaches state officials such as Brumley;" and (4) now legislate the definition of honest services, we find ourselves in total and fundamental disagreement with the majority opinion. We therefore respectfully dissent.

Notes

1. What do you think of Brumley's federalism argument that Congress never intended to permit federal prosecutors to intrude into state political matters through prosecutions under § 1341? Recall the majority's interpretation of § 1341 ("[A] federal prosecutor must prove that conduct of a state official breached a duty respecting the provision of services owed to the official's employer *under state law*." (emphasis added)). Do you agree that § 1341 requires this? If so, does this cure the potential for the federal government imposing a federal "ethical regime" on state employees?

2. The dissent is especially strong. It describes the majority opinion as "issue-evasive," "jurisprudentially flawed," "sophistry," "glib," and "incomprehensible." Do you agree?

C.   INTENT

1.   INTENT TO HARM

In 1970, the United States Court of Appeals for the Second Circuit articulated the view that before mail fraud can be found there must exist an intent to harm. United States v. Regent Office Supply Co., 421 F.2d 1174.

In *Regent* two corporations, Regent Office Supply, Inc. (Regent) and Oxford Office Systems, Inc. (Oxford) were convicted of mail fraud because of false representations made by their sales representatives to potential purchasers of stationery supplies. The false representations included claims that the salesperson had been referred by a friend of the customer; the salesperson was a "doctor, or other professional person, who had stationery to be disposed of"; the salesperson needed to dispose of stationery because of a death and "the customer would help to relieve this difficult situation by purchasing it." *Id.* at 1176. Although not condoning the "deceitfulness" of such business practices, the court found that the defendant's conduct did not constitute mail fraud. The court explained: the salespersons "did not attempt to deceive their prospective customers with respect to the bargain they were offering; rather, they gave a false reason for being able to offer the bargain." Intent to deceive is not sufficient, according to the Second Circuit. There must be intent to defraud. Since all customers received what they bargained for, at the price agreed upon, they were not defrauded nor was there evidence of intent to defraud.

Since the decision in *Regent*, courts have examined mail fraud cases for evidence of intent to defraud. The next case demonstrates this analysis.

UNITED STATES v. D'AMATO

United States Court of Appeals, Second Circuit, 1994.
39 F.3d 1249.

WINTER, CIRCUIT JUDGE.

Armand P. D'Amato appeals from his conviction by a jury before Judge Mishler. D'Amato was convicted of seven counts of mail fraud in violation of 18 U.S.C. § 1341 and sentenced principally to a term of five months imprisonment, two years of supervised release * * * and restitution. D'Amato's conviction arises from services he provided to the Unisys Corporation ("Unisys"). The government claimed at trial that D'Amato was hired by a "rogue" Unisys employee, Charles Gardner, and that D'Amato, with Gardner's aid, defrauded Unisys in two ways. First, the government maintained that D'Amato committed mail fraud by structuring his billings to conceal from those in control of corporate funds the nature of his relationship with Unisys and the fact that his actual services involved lobbying his brother, a United States Senator and member of the Senate Appropriations Committee. We will style this theory the "right to control theory." The government maintained, second, that D'Amato committed mail fraud by contracting with Unisys to provide written reports on Senate proceedings while never intending to provide those reports. We will style this theory the "false pretenses theory."

Because the evidence of criminal intent was insufficient on either theory, we reverse the judgment of conviction and order the indictment dismissed.

BACKGROUND

* * *

D'Amato, an attorney, started a law partnership with Jeffrey Forchelli in 1976. By 1988, the two were practicing as partners of D'Amato, Forchelli, Libert, Schwartz, Mineo & Carlino ("D'Amato Forchelli"), a firm of roughly twenty lawyers based in Mineola, New York. D'Amato's brother, Alfonse D'Amato, was a United States Senator from the State of New York throughout the period of relevant events. Senator D'Amato was a member of the Senate Appropriations Committee, the Senate committee charged with oversight of defense procurement programs.

Unisys, a Fortune 100 company, maintained a Surveillance and Fire Control Systems Division ("S & FCS") in Great Neck, New York. This division manufactured radar missile control systems that were sold to the United States government. Charles Gardner served as a Unisys vice president in charge of marketing for S & FCS from the early 1980's until March 1988. Throughout the pertinent period, Gardner bribed Navy officials, made illegal campaign contributions to Congressmen, and personally profited through kickbacks. The government has stipulated, however, that none of these illegal activities involved D'Amato or Senator D'Amato, and there was no evidence that D'Amato was aware of any of Gardner's illegal activities.

Gardner first met D'Amato in spring 1984. At the time, Gardner was seeking to obtain support for the purchase of Unisys products in the Senate Appropriations Committee. Over the course of two meetings, Gardner expressed his interest in gaining Senator D'Amato's support and told Armand D'Amato that he was being hired to further that purpose. Gardner told D'Amato that he would be paid by means of a purchase order, and that these purchase orders would generally call for the production of some form of reports on Congressional proceedings. D'Amato apparently agreed to represent Unisys, although the work was to be done by Peter Iovino, who was joining D'Amato Forchelli to open a Washington, D.C. office.

In 1985, Gardner, dissatisfied with Iovino, sent Herbert Chodosh, a Unisys marketing manager, to ask D'Amato to work for Unisys personally. D'Amato agreed, and the parties discussed another purchase order arrangement, this time through Coastal Energy Enterprises ("Coastal"), a Unisys subsidiary. In a subsequent meeting with D'Amato, Gardner made clear that Unisys was hiring D'Amato to "support[ ] our programs in the Senate Appropriations Committee through [ ] Senator D'Amato's office." Gardner told D'Amato that he would receive $5,000 per month for his services and would be paid through Coastal's issuance of a purchase order calling for the production of reports on Congressional proceedings. Gardner further indicated to D'Amato that Unisys "would offer to help to do the report."

Pursuant to this agreement, in April 1986 Coastal sent D'Amato a purchase order to cover the period from June 1, 1986 to May 31, 1987. The purchase order called for D'Amato Forchelli to "[p]rovide technical services to advise Coastal on matters as specified in the attached Statement of Work." The statement of work contained directives such as "[a]nalyze matters within the purview of Coastal Energy Enterprises in such areas as Federal budgeting, legislative action, likelihood of program funding" and "[p]rovide reports to Coastal relative to performance of competitive companies' offerings of products."

Pursuant to the purchase order, D'Amato Forchelli sent monthly bills on its letterhead to Coastal seeking payment "For Professional Services Rendered: Re: Coastal Energy Enterprises, Inc. Monthly Retainer." By December 1986, Coastal had raised D'Amato Forchelli's retainer to $6,500 a month, and in May 1987 the agreement was extended for another year. In or around July 1986 and December 1987, Unisys employees asked D'Amato to transmit to Senator D'Amato's office draft letters to the Secretary of the Navy composed by Unisys employees. D'Amato apparently complied on both occasions, and letters bearing Senator D'Amato's signature were in fact sent to the Secretary of the Navy.

* * *

* * * Gardner * * * closed Coastal in 1987. Coastal's last payment to D'Amato Forchelli came in November 1987, bringing the total of payments to D'Amato Forchelli by Coastal to $88,000. Gardner decided, however, to continue to retain D'Amato's services through Unisys. Unisys internal procedures dictated that purchase orders to law firms had to be released and controlled by Unisys's law department. Gardner and Dennis Mitchell, a Unisys marketing manager, conceived the idea of circumventing this requirement by issuing the purchase order in the name of Jeffrey Forchelli, the second name on the firm's letterhead. At a subsequent meeting attended by Norm Steiger, head of the Unisys legal department at its Great Neck facility, it was mutually agreed that purchase orders would be issued in the name of Forchelli. Gardner further testified that the decision to use Forchelli's name rather than D'Amato's was "made because it was considered to be in the interest of Unisys company[ ] not to have the D'Amato name out there, because it ... could be politically embarrassing." At Gardner's direction, Mitchell called the D'Amato Forchelli firm and confirmed that the law firm would accept a check made out to Forchelli alone.

Gardner also spoke to D'Amato about the payment of D'Amato Forchelli's outstanding bills. Gardner told D'Amato that he would be issuing a purchase order directly from Unisys, and that the purchase order, like the ones before, would "use the reports as a means to the end. And we would be supplying reports or helping him do the reports."

Thereafter, in February 1988, Mitchell issued a purchase order from Unisys in the name "J. Forchelli" at D'Amato Forchelli's address. The purchase order, dated February 2, 1988, covered the period of November and December 1987, in order to compensate D'Amato for two months he was not paid due to the closing of Coastal. The purchase order provided for payment of $13,000, per the prior agreement of $6,500 per month. The purchase order required the seller to "[p]rovide technical services to produce two survey reports evaluating the proceedings of the U.S. Senate" in accordance with an attached statement of work. The statement of work read as follows:

> Provide technical services to produce two reports on senatorial proceedings. Each report is to provide a quantitative and qualitative statement of senatorial action during the period for each program of concern to Unisys. Also provide an assessment of ultimate senatorial direction and any outside or competitive actions that may adversely influence the outcome of these programs.

The purchase order also provided, "Reports and invoices to be approved by C.F. Gardner Prior to payment." Mitchell testified that he did not understand the purchase order to require that D'Amato produce the reports.

* * *

[From February through June, 1988, Unisys paid $32,500 to Forchelli upon invoices received, "For Professional Services Rendered: Re: Monthly Retainer."-ed.]

Throughout D'Amato's relationship with Unisys, he never supplied Unisys with any written reports. Gardner testified, however, that he told D'Amato that D'Amato would not be responsible for the preparation of the reports. In fact, Unisys employees prepared five brief (less than half-a-page) reports and attached them to Forchelli's bills.

In connection with the sentencing, the district court found that D'Amato spent approximately 100 hours performing lobbying services for Unisys. The court further found that D'Amato traveled three times to Washington, D.C., at least in part on behalf of Unisys. In addition, D'Amato met with Unisys employee Lynch around ten times in his office, where Lynch briefed D'Amato on Unisys's programs and needs. D'Amato also helped cause two letters by Senator D'Amato and one by Congressman Norman Lent to be sent to Navy and Commerce Department officials concerning defense contracts.

Gardner resigned from Unisys in March 1988. He was immediately rehired by Unisys, however, as a consultant, later to resign. The final payment to Forchelli was made after Gardner had resigned, the last check being issued on June 3, 1988.

A grand jury returned an indictment charging D'Amato with twenty-four counts of mail fraud. In particular, the indictment charged that twenty-four separate mailings constituted mail fraud under two separate legal theories. First, the indictment charged that the mailings were used as part of a scheme and artifice to "defraud Sperry/Unisys and its uninvolved officers, directors and shareholders, of the right to control the expenditure of corporate funds and to decide the manner and purpose of those expenditures" (the "right to control theory"). Second, the indictment charged that the mailings were part of a scheme to "obtain money and property from Sperry/Unisys, by means of false and fraudulent pretenses, representations and promises" (the "false pretenses theory"). Counts 1–17 of the indictment pertained to invoices D'Amato sent Coastal and checks he received from Coastal. Counts 18–24 pertained to invoices sent to Unisys and the two checks D'Amato received from Unisys totaling $32,500.

Prior to trial, D'Amato moved, inter alia, to dismiss the indictment principally on the grounds that it failed to allege the deprivation of a property right necessary for a mail fraud prosecution. The district court denied D'Amato's motion. * * *

The case was tried to a jury before Judge Mishler from April 19 to May 7, 1993. D'Amato was acquitted of the charges stemming from his work on behalf of Coastal (Counts 1–17), but convicted of the charges relating to his representation of Unisys (Counts 18–24).

On November 5, 1993, the district court sentenced D'Amato. After commenting that "[m]aybe one out of 100 [lawyers] would say no" to a retainer offered on the condition that the bills not disclose that lobbying was the purpose of the agreement, the district court sentenced D'Amato to five months imprisonment, five months home detention, and two years of supervised release. D'Amato was also ordered to pay $7,500 in restitution to Unisys, and a special assessment of $350. This appeal followed.

DISCUSSION

D'Amato raises a number of arguments on appeal. Because we agree that the government failed to produce legally sufficient evidence of D'Amato's criminal intent, we address only his sufficiency argument.

D'Amato of course bears a "heavy burden" in challenging his conviction on the ground of insufficiency of the evidence. * * *

Nonetheless, a conviction based on speculation and surmise alone cannot stand. * * *

The mail fraud statute criminalizes use of the mails in furtherance of a "scheme or artifice to defraud, or for obtaining money or property by means of false or fraudulent pretenses. * * *" 18 U.S.C. § 1341. Therefore, an essential element of any mail fraud prosecution is proof of a "scheme or artifice to defraud." Essential to a scheme to defraud is fraudulent intent. * * *

The scheme to defraud need not have been successful or complete. Therefore, the victims of the scheme need not have been injured. However, the government must show "that some actual harm or injury was contemplated by the schemer." *Regent Office Supply Co.*, 421 F.2d at 1180.

Because the defendant must intend to harm the fraud's victims, "[m]isrepresentations amounting only to a deceit are insufficient to maintain a mail or wire fraud prosecution." United States v. Starr, 816 F.2d 94, 98 (2d Cir.1987). "Instead, the deceit must be coupled with a contemplated harm to the victim." *Id.* In many cases, this requirement poses no additional obstacle for the government. When the "necessary result" of the actor's scheme is to injure others, fraudulent intent may be inferred from the scheme itself. Where the scheme does not cause injury to the alleged victim as its necessary result, the government must produce evidence independent of the alleged scheme to show the defendant's fraudulent intent.

1. The Right to Control Theory

a) The Elements.

We first address the right to control theory. That "theory is predicated on a showing that some person or entity has been deprived of potentially valuable economic information." United States v. Wallach, 935 F.2d, 445, 462–63 (2d Cir.1991). Thus, "the withholding or inaccurate reporting of information that could impact on economic decisions can provide the basis for a mail fraud prosecution."[4] *Id.* A person charged with mail fraud under the right to control theory must intend to injure the person or entity misled—here Unisys, its management, and/or its shareholders—and the person or entity must thus be a specific target of the inaccurate or concealed information. Mail fraud cannot be charged against a corporate agent who in good faith believes that his or her (otherwise legal) misleading or inaccurate conduct is in the corporation's best interests.

Where no rule otherwise provides, persons acting on behalf of a corporation may well find it necessary to disguise or conceal certain matters in the interests of that corporation. For example, failure to disclose the nature of a service provided or the identity of the entity performing such a service may minimize the risk of disclosure of information that would enable competitors to learn of a corporation's future activities or plans. Mining companies may thus conceal the hiring of geologists and the site of their work. Such measures may be necessary also to protect company assets. A company may thus disguise the hiring of forensic accountants in order to avoid giving warning to an undetected embezzler. The preservation of a positive public relations image is a proper corporate goal and may be pursued by a policy of concealment. Such a policy may be necessary also to prevent insider trading. Firms planning a takeover may thus wish to conceal relationships with law firms, accountants, or banks until required to disclose under the Williams Act. 15 U.S.C. §§ 78m(d), (e) & 78n(d)-(f) (1988).

The critical elements are: (i) whether corporate management has made an otherwise lawful decision, that concealment or a failure to disclose is in the corporation's best interests and (ii) whether management acted in good faith in making, and did not personally profit from,

---

4. We assume, without deciding, that the disguising of D'Amato's services was material under the Wallach test.

the decision. As we noted in *Wallach*, 935 F.2d at 464, the principle that directors and officers may act on behalf of a corporation does not extend to acts of self-enrichment. However, a good faith, unconflicted decision may not be second-guessed by the government or by the courts.

In the instant matter, of course, the defendant is not someone in corporate management but a person hired to perform services for the corporation. Such a person cannot be found to intend to harm a corporation or its shareholders through otherwise lawful misleading conduct if he or she follows the instructions of an appropriate corporate agent who appears to be unconflicted and acting in good faith. So far as the duty of a party contracting to provide ordinary business or professional services to the corporation is concerned, therefore, that party may rely upon instructions from a corporate agent with apparent authority and no ostensible conflict of interest to determine the contracting party's obligations and appropriate billing practices.

Additional considerations apply to a claim that shareholders have been deprived of their right to control. Unlike management, shareholders have no right to manage the business. *Wallach*, 935 F.2d at 462. Nevertheless, they do have property rights of which they may not be fraudulently deprived by "the withholding or inaccurate reporting of information that could impact on economic decisions." *Id.* at 463.

These property rights are defined by (i) state law concerning access to the company's books and records and the fiduciary obligations of management and (ii) the law of fraud concerning corporate information that is public. An inaccurate statement in documents that are not lawfully available for inspection by shareholders, and do not materially affect information that is available, can hardly be said, without more, to defraud, or to be intended to defraud, such shareholders. Moreover, good-faith, unconflicted business decisions of management are protected from shareholder challenge by the business judgment rule. A policy of concealment that is protected by the business judgment rule, therefore, does not deprive shareholders of anything useful, and those responsible for the inaccuracy cannot have intended to defraud shareholders. Of course, the concealment of some information may be intended to further a breach of a state law fiduciary obligation to shareholders, including a fiduciary obligation not to commit illegal acts. Where the inaccuracy is intended to conceal such a breach, both a deprivation and fraudulent intent may exist.

The otherwise lawful "withholding or inaccurate reporting of information" must thus relate to: (i) information available to shareholders as provided by the state of incorporation's laws providing access to corporate books and records (maintenance of accurate books and records is of "central importance" to preservation of shareholders' property interest); (ii) information that, if withheld or inaccurate, would result in rendering information that is public materially misleading (right to public information, required to be disclosed by law, is important component of shareholders' property rights), and (iii) information that would materially aid shareholders in enforcing management's fiduciary obligations under state law ("complete information" enables a stockholder to take "steps" to prevent corporate actions of which he or she disapproves). Where a third party acting upon instructions from a corporate agent is charged with depriving shareholders of their right to control, the government must prove that the third party knew that the concealment would involve (i), (ii), or (iii).

b) Sufficiency of the Evidence.

The government's claim that D'Amato intended to injure Unisys by depriving its management or its shareholders of their right to control was not based on legally sufficient evidence. The jury could have found that D'Amato knew that his services on behalf of Unisys were disguised. However, the government concedes that the payments to D'Amato for the purpose of gaining "access" to his brother were not illegal. From D'Amato's point of view, if such access resulted in political support from the Senator that helped Unisys's sales, Unisys and its shareholders would benefit. Also from D'Amato's point of view, it was evident that Unisys might desire to keep its source of access to the Senator confidential because the means of access could easily become controversial and self-defeating if disclosed. D'Amato thus could have intended to deprive Unisys management (or shareholders) of "valuable" information that "could impact" on economic decisions only if (i) Gardner had no authority to instruct D'Amato to disguise his services in billing Unisys and D'Amato knew it, (ii) the payments to D'Amato were otherwise unlawful and D'Amato knew it, or (iii) Gardner was personally profiting from the concealed arrangement with D'Amato and D'Amato knew it. None of these conditions has been met in the instant matter.

The government does not claim that the payments were otherwise unlawful. Nor does it claim that Gardner received kickbacks from D'Amato or otherwise profited from the concealed arrangement. Conditions (ii) and (iii) are thus not at issue. With regard to (i), there is no evidence that D'Amato complied with Unisys's request to disguise his services through Forchelli in order to further a scheme to injure Unisys rather than because he thought it was a reasonable request by his client. Gardner testified that he met with Unisys in-house lawyers and that they agreed that D'Amato should bill through Forchelli because it was "in the interest of Unisys" and otherwise could be "politically embarrassing." Likewise, D'Amato testified that he and Forchelli determined that Unisys must have decided to suppress D'Amato's name to avoid negative publicity. They thought this especially likely because Unisys was a Long Island company and Senator D'Amato was at the time receiving critical attention from the Long Island-based newspaper, *Newsday*. The government thus offered no reason why anyone in D'Amato's position would think that he or she was injuring Unisys by complying with the request to use the Forchelli invoice.

The government seems to argue that D'Amato's reliance on Gardner's instructions is unavailing because Gardner and his "cohorts" were "rogue employees." Rhetoric aside, however, there was no evidence that D'Amato knew, should have known, or could have known, that these employees had no authority to pay him to obtain access to his brother, even if that were true.[7] Gardner testified that he never told D'Amato of his payment of bribes or receipt of kickbacks in dealing with others. No Unisys employee or anyone else testified that D'Amato knew, or had reason to know, of such actions. Absent any indication of wrongdoing, D'Amato was warranted in relying on the apparent authority of these Unisys employees. Restatement (Second) of Agency §§ 8, 161. In fact, Unisys continued to pay D'Amato after Cresce's report had exposed Gardner's wrongdoing and after Gardner had been forced to resign, albeit to remain on as a consultant. (We were informed at oral argument that although Unisys was aware of Gardner's misdeeds, it continued to use his services and severed all connections with him only after "search warrants were executed.").

With regard to the shareholders' right to control, similar considerations apply. D'Amato had no reason to believe that Gardner's apparent authority to act did not bind the shareholders. Moreover, the government failed to show that Unisys shareholders were deprived of "valuable economic information" that "could impact" on any decision that was theirs to make. The government thus failed to show that shareholders had a right to such information under applicable Delaware law. It even failed to introduce Unisys's pertinent books of account, and we are thus unaware of what a shareholder would have found if a right to examine them existed. No claim is made that D'Amato's conduct affected any filing with the Securities and Exchange Commission or other public information concerning Unisys's finances. Nor can it be argued that the disguising of the payments deprived shareholders of a right to seek injunctive redress against the payments to D'Amato as a breach of a state law fiduciary obligation because the government concedes the payments were legal and neither Gardner nor any other Unisys employee profited from them.

* * *

2. The False Pretenses Theory

The false pretenses theory, simply stated, is a claim that D'Amato represented to Unisys that he would prepare reports in exchange for the fees he received, and took the money but prepared no reports. The government's false pretenses theory thus rests on the allegation that D'Amato did not perform the services that he contracted to perform for Unisys and for which he was paid.

7. Although we do not rely upon the claim of error raised—whether Unisys has waived the attorney-client privilege concerning its management's knowledge of Gardner's activities—the conclusion that Gardner was a "rogue" and not authorized by senior Unisys management is based on a flawed record. Unisys was allowed to invoke the attorney-client privilege to block defense inquiries at trial into communications concerning management's knowledge of Gardner's activities notwithstanding the government's introduction in its main case of similarly privileged material provided to it by Unisys. *See In re Steinhardt Partners*, 9 F.3d 230, 235 (2d Cir.1993) (provision of privileged materials to government agency waives privilege).

D'Amato admits that he never intended to produce any reports in exchange for the fees he received.[8] Criminal intent was not proven, however. As noted, there was no evidence that D'Amato ever believed, or even had reason to believe, that Gardner and others lacked authority to represent and bind Unisys in their dealings with D'Amato, and the record unambiguously demonstrates that Gardner told D'Amato that he did not have to prepare reports. Gardner testified that his understanding had been that Unisys employees would supply the reports. Indeed, the government in its argument stresses that Gardner, Chodosh, and other Unisys employees repeatedly told D'Amato that the reports would be written by Unisys staffers. Moreover, Dennis Mitchell, the Unisys official who issued the relevant purchase order, testified that he did not understand the purchase order to require D'Amato to produce the reports.

D'Amato could hardly have believed that he was supposed to provide written reports. From the beginning of the relationship, all the purchase orders contained roughly the same description of work. D'Amato had consistently been paid without comment by Unisys concerning his failure to submit reports. Given this consistent course of dealing, D'Amato had no reason whatsoever to believe that the most recent purchase order required him to submit a written report. There is thus no dispute that D'Amato performed all the services for Unisys that were requested of him. The government's theory was and is that D'Amato was paid for lobbying his Senator brother, concededly lawful conduct. There is no evidence that he did not perform such services. It is inconceivable on this record that Unisys could survive a motion for summary judgment in a civil suit to recover fees from D'Amato based on a false pretenses theory, even under the lower burden of proof applicable to civil cases.

Finally, the government argues that D'Amato's services were not worth what Unisys paid for them. This argument is seriously misguided. The mail fraud statute does not criminalize the charging of an allegedly excessive fee, where, as here, a corporate agent with at least apparent authority to do so agreed to the fee, received no personal benefit from the fee, and was not deceived by the payee. Retainer agreements that keep providers of services available are commonplace, and sometimes those services are not needed. We decline the government's invitation to infer fraudulent intent on the part of an attorney who accepts a retainer arrangement and is subsequently not called upon to perform services that the government or trier of fact deems worth the fee paid. Moreover, the government offered no evidence that access to the Senator was not worth the fees paid.

We vacate the conviction, and order dismissal of the indictment.

Notes

1. The uncontroverted evidence appears to show that D'Amato knew his law firm was billing, and being paid, for supplying reports when in fact

---

8. A breach of contract does not amount to mail fraud. Failure to comply with a contractual obligation is only fraudulent when the promisor never intended to honor the contract. To infer fraudulent intent from mere nonperformance, therefore, would eviscerate the distinction between a breach of contract and fraud.

his firm was not supplying reports but lobbying. Why isn't this fraud under the mail fraud statute? What was the government's theory as to why this knowledge was sufficient to find "contemplated harm to the victim"? Is there another victim of the "fraud" arranged between Gardner and D'Amato? Could charging another victim besides Unisys help overcome the finding of insufficiency of the evidence? Who might be another victim?

2. Note the brief discussion of attorney client privilege in footnote 7. What is the "flawed record" the court is referring to?

2. RELIANCE

There is a split in the circuits as to whether mail fraud exists when the misrepresentations made are such that no reasonable person would rely on them. In the next case, United States v. Brown, 79 F.3d 1550 (11th Cir.1996), the United States Court of Appeals for the Eleventh Circuit holds that this is not mail fraud. As you read this opinion determine what you think: is it appropriate to focus on the naivete of the victim rather than the intent of the perpetrator?

UNITED STATES v. BROWN

United States Court of Appeals, Eleventh Circuit, 1996.
79 F.3d 1550.

EDMONDSON, CIRCUIT JUDGE.

This appeal is one by four defendants, formerly executives with General Development Corporation ("GDC"), who were convicted of defrauding and conspiring to defraud home buyers throughout the 1980's. Their guilt was not proved: insufficient evidence was presented *[Insufficient Evidence]* that a scheme reasonably calculated to deceive persons of ordinary prudence and comprehension was devised. We reverse the convictions.

In the 1950's, GDC began buying huge tracts of undeveloped land throughout Florida. Over the years, the company created nine separate Florida communities. GDC first built the infrastructure (including over 3,700 miles of paved roads) necessary to permit residential development. Then, GDC sold lots and homes in these communities; it also permitted local businesses to build on lots purchased from GDC and to sell these lots in competition with GDC. To increase the attractiveness of the communities, GDC encouraged development; for example, the company helped persuade the New York Mets to build their spring training stadium in Port St. Lucie; GDC built and landscaped utility plants; it sold land to churches at below market value; and GDC donated land for schools. The company became the single largest developer in the entire state. Today over 250,000 people live in GDC's Florida communities.

By the 1980's, GDC was selling some of its homes at significantly higher prices than independently built homes within the same neighborhoods.[1] (For example, GDC offered a home it sold for between eighty-five

---

1. Despite these high prices, GDC consistently lost money on home sales. GDC priced homes at about $70 over its cost.

and one hundred thousand dollars as a prize on the "Dream House" game show; the home was later appraised at under fifty thousand dollars.) GDC blamed its prices on higher expenses: the testimony was that independent builders had much lower overhead costs than GDC. Whatever the cause of the price disparity, attempting to sell homes of similar quality in the same neighborhood at a much higher price proved problematic for GDC.

GDC was, however, still able to sell Florida homes to certain customers, mostly those residing in "snowbelt" states. GDC marketed their communities as a great place to own a second home.[2] "One stop shopping" was available for non-residents: GDC buyers could initially purchase just a lot and later trade in that lot, plus any "appreciation" in the price GDC charged for that lot, as a down payment on a home. And, GDC offered in-house financing through GDC, a wholly-owned subsidiary. Florida Home Finders, a property management subsidiary, was designed to help absentee owners rent and maintain Florida property. GDC did not inform its customers that they might be paying much more for these homes than they would for a largely identical one next door.

Customers intrigued by the home sales pitch, and especially those who had already purchased building lots, were encouraged to take a "Southward Ho" trip (a "SoHo").[3] On SoHo trips, GDC would pay for the customer to travel to Florida and to visit a GDC community for a few days. SoHo travelers were shepherded about Florida by the southern salesforce, who took affirmative steps to "focus" customers on GDC homes only. If the customer remained interested, GDC would have the customer enter an agreement to purchase.

GDC started prohibiting salespeople from recommending financing from entities other than GDV (the government alleged that 80 to 90 percent of buyers financed through GDV), and all financing was processed through GDV. GDV financing agreements, which were signed sometime after contracts to purchase had been made, would note that an appraisal of the property was done. This appraisal compared the home being purchased only with other homes GDC sold nationally, not those selling in the same area for less; thus, the appraisal would show GDC that the home was worth what was being paid. Never were customers shown these appraisals.

Official GDC policy forbade "investment selling," that is, encouraging people to purchase GDC homes as a way to make money as opposed to purchasing a home for use in Florida. And, official GDC literature and form agreements signed by buyers disclaimed the homes' investment potential; for example, a GDC customer "bill of rights" provided: "The

---

2. A GDC training tape encouraged salespeople to stress that Florida, with a 77 degree average temperature, was a great place for boating, swimming and golf. The instructor also told salespeople to explain that GDC communities were "pre-

planned," making the transition to a new home easier.

3. Although this prosecution involved house sales, the company also encouraged customers to visit Florida before the purchase of a lot.

land you are purchasing is being sold to you for future use and not as a business investment."

Despite this official policy, certain salesmen sometimes told purchasers that the homes were "safe investments." Some customers were told that rental income would exceed mortgage payments. Some salesmen falsely said that they, personally, owned GDC homes and were making money on them. And, they said that, if a customer would hang onto their homes for a year, the homes could be sold at a profit. Some of GDC's northern sales managers even encouraged these lies. But, salesmen violating official company policy were supposed to be disciplined or fired. In fact, few were disciplined severely; several were retrained, fined, or demoted.

Due to the price disparity, GDC homes were not "good investments." Customers discovered that rental income was sometimes less than GDC's Florida Home Finders had promised. Some owners could find no tenants at all for significant periods. And, several GDC customers found that they could only sell their homes by asking for much less than they paid. In the mid–1980s, GDC established Housing Customer Service (HSC) to deal with customer complaints. Many "value complaints" (that is, complaints that homes were not worth as much as was paid for them) were received. Some customers also claimed that official sales tactics, such as the SoHo, put "blinders" on them. And, the company received some complaints that the salesforce had lied about the investment or income potential of GDC homes. HSC sometimes negotiated settlements with complainants, especially those who had lawyers or were particularly persistent.

Several lawsuits were filed, and GDC received bad publicity. The U.S. Attorney's office began an investigation. GDC, itself, pled guilty to fraud and established a $169 million fund to pay customers; it also filed bankruptcy per Chapter 11. But, the United States also indicted the upper echelon of GDC management for fraud and conspiracy on the sale of GDC homes between 1982 and 1989. * * *

David Brown, a lawyer, was instrumental in the 1985 public offering of GDC, which had been a subsidiary of City Investing. After the offering (which was midway through the indictment period), Brown became Chairman of the Board. Bob Ehrling became president of GDC in 1980 and was ultimately responsible for GDC marketing. Tore DeBella began working for GDC in 1971 after serving as a soldier in Vietnam. By 1981 he had become Senior Vice President of Marketing and oversaw GDC's salesforce. Rick Reizen was Vice President of Housing and active in the sale of homes.

Defendants were each charged with 73 total counts of mail fraud, interstate transportation of persons in furtherance of a fraud, and conspiracy. Their trial lasted nine months. Brown was acquitted on 72 counts but was convicted on one conspiracy count. He was sentenced to 5 years in jail. Ehrling was convicted on 39 counts and sentenced to 121 months in jail. DeBella was also convicted on 39 counts and was sentenced to 97 months. Reizen was convicted on one conspiracy count and sentenced to 5 years. Each was also ordered to pay $500,000 in restitution.

* * *

[ed.-The Eleventh Circuit assumed, for purposes of appeal that "the evidence showed defendants, through their failure to discipline salespeople or otherwise, acted to authorize misrepresentations by salespeople to customers about value." *Id.* at 1555. Yet, the court reversed the convictions. It explained why:]

* * * The mail fraud statute prohibits devising a "scheme or artifice to defraud, or for obtaining money or property by means of false or fraudulent pretenses," which is furthered by use of the mails.

* * *

* * * In this circuit, mail fraud requires the government to prove that a reasonable person would have acted on the representations. See Pelletier v. Zweifel, 921 F.2d 1465, 1498–99 (11th Cir.1991). To prove a crime, the government must show the defendant intended to create a scheme "reasonably calculated to deceive persons of ordinary prudence and comprehension." *Id.* at 1498–99. The "person of ordinary prudence" standard is an objective standard not directly tied to the experiences of a specific person or persons.

In some situations, a reasonable person is always permitted to rely on the recommendations of a particular person; and, certain people must always disclose facts where nondisclosure could result in harm. This circumstance exists when there is a special relationship of trust, such as a fiduciary relationship, between people. Where a relationship "fiduciary in nature" exists between a defendant and his intended victims, the federal fraud statutes are broadly interpreted and were intended by Congress to "protect the careless and the naive from lupine predators.... " United States v. Kreimer, 609 F.2d 126, 131, 132 (5th Cir.1980).

In this case, defendants were not in some kind of legal relationship with its customers which required defendants to disclose pricing structures under every circumstance. Instead, GDC and its customers were entering into an arm's length transaction; a transaction which was of considerable financial importance to the customer.[13] Under federal law,

13. This case is materially different from Silverman v. United States, 213 F.2d 405, 406 (5th Cir.1954). In *Silverman*, the defendant sent solicitations to customers of Southern Bell; the solicitations were intended to look like routine invoices from Southern Bell. Three hundred and fifty people, thinking that they were paying Southern Bell what they owed that company, sent in a total of seven thousand dollars. A close reading of the solicitation would have revealed that the mailing was not connected with Southern Bell.

In *Silverman* the defendant tricked his victims so they did not realize they were entering an arrangement with him and did not understand the transaction's basic nature. In this case, customers were fully aware that they were negotiating with GDC for the purchase of a home. And, in *Silverman* the victims sent in an average of twenty dollars. *The small amount involved is*

GDC (and, a fortiori, these defendants) had no general affirmative obligation to disclose the sales price disparity between its houses and its competitors' houses.

We know that—under certain circumstances—a person, outside of a fiduciary relationship, can rely on representations of future wealth or investment potential. This circumstance—which is present in most mail fraud cases—arises where a reasonable jury could find that a person of ordinary prudence would not know that he should not rely on these representations.

We conclude in the case before us now that reasonable jurors could not find that a person of ordinary prudence, about to enter into an agreement to purchase a GDC home in Florida, would rely on (that is, in the words of Pelletier, "act on") the seller's own affirmative representations about the value or rental income of the GDC homes. Therefore, a "scheme to defraud" within the meaning of the federal criminal statutes has been not proved.

A "scheme to defraud" under the pertinent criminal statutes has not been proved where a reasonable juror would have to conclude that the representation is about something which the customer should, and could, easily confirm—if they wished to do so—from readily available external sources. In this case, the relevant market prices are not difficult to investigate. The essential pricing information can be obtained by nonexperts readily, for example, by a telephone call or a visit to a GDC competitor or by a look at newspaper classified ads.

* * *

"The law is a causeway upon which, so long as he keeps to it, a citizen may walk safely." Robert Bolt, "A Man For All Seasons" Act II, 89 (Vintage 1960) (speech of Sir Thomas More). To be free of tyranny in a free country, the causeway's edges must be clearly marked. The exercise of federal government power to criminalize conduct and thereby to coerce and to deprive persons, by government action, of their liberty, reputation and property must be watched carefully in a country that values the liberties of its private citizens. Never can we allow federal prosecutors to make up the law as they go along. So, we today heed the warning of the Supreme Court and "hesitate to adopt a construction making the difference between legal and illegal conduct in the field of business relations depend upon so uncertain a test as whether prices are reasonable." U.S. v. Trenton Potteries Co., 273 U.S. 392, 398 (1927).

relevant to the level of care a prudent person would invest in protecting himself. Even in 1954, reasonably prudent customers of Southern Bell could be expected to pay what appeared in the ordinary course of their business to be a legitimate bill for twenty dollars. See also, Blachly v. United States, 380 F.2d 665, 671, 672 & n. 13 (5th Cir.1967) (despite that, upon careful thought impossibility of referral selling plan would become plain, if scheme calculated to deceive reasonable person, scheme is unlawful). In this case, GDC customers were entering what they knew to be an isolated and substantial financial transaction, involving many tens of thousands of dollars.

Looking at the evidence in this case, our worry is that the criminal fraud statutes were used to convict four people simply for charging high prices—all allegations of misconduct in this case involved the price customers paid for their homes, not the physical qualities of these homes. The government tries to draw a distinction; they say these men were convicted for deceptions about these high prices. For us, at least in the context of home sales and of the openness of the Florida real estate market, this distinction is a distinction without meaning.

Construing the evidence at its worst against defendants, it is true that these men behaved badly. We live in a fallen world. But, "bad men, like good men, are entitled to be tried and sentenced in accordance with law." Green v. United States, 365 U.S. 301, 309 (1961) (Black, J. dissenting). And, the fraud statutes do not cover all behavior which strays from the ideal; Congress has not yet criminalized all sharp conduct, manipulative acts, or unethical transactions.

We might prefer that Brown, Ehrling, DeBella and Reizen would have told these customers to shop around before buying. But, "there are ... things ... which we wish that people should do, which we like or admire them for doing, perhaps dislike or despise them for not doing, but yet admit that they are not bound to do." John Stuart Mill, *Utilitarianism* 60 (O. Piest, ed., Bobbs-Merrill 1957) (1861). Although the line between unethical behavior and unlawful behavior is sometimes blurred—especially under the federal fraud statutes—we, in the absence of clear direction from Congress, conclude that the behavior established by the government's evidence in this case is not the kind that a reasonable jury could find, in fact, violated the federal fraud statutes. Likewise, no reasonable jury could find an agreement to violate the fraud statutes. Defendants' conduct does not fall plainly within the pertinent prohibitions.

* * *

Notes

The United States Courts of Appeals for the District of Columbia and First Circuit disagree with the holding in *Brown*. These courts hold that mail fraud exists even where only the "most gullible" would be deceived. United States v. Maxwell, 920 F.2d 1028, 1036 (D.C.Cir.1990); United States v. Brien, 617 F.2d 299, 311 (1st Cir.1980). The reasoning of the First Circuit provides a counterpoint to *Brown*:

> "If a scheme to defraud has been or is intended to be devised, it makes no difference whether the persons the schemers intended to defraud are gullible or skeptical, dull or bright. These are criminal statutes, not tort concepts. The only issue is whether there is a plan, scheme or artifice intended to defraud. We discern no intention on the part of Congress to differentiate between schemes that will ensnare the ordinary prudent investor and those that attract only those with lesser mental acuity." *Brien*, 617 F.2d at 311.

Judge Posner weighs in on a middle ground in United States v. Coffman, 94 F.3d 330 (7th Cir.1996). In *Coffman*, the United States Court of Appeals for the Seventh Circuit affirmed the mail fraud convictions of defendants even though the court found that their scheme to defraud Smith Barney Brokerage was preposterous and did not fool a sophisticated business such as Smith Barney. Judge Posner reasoned as follows:

"It is true that many cases, including some in this court, say that a scheme to defraud is not within the reach of the mail-or wire-fraud statutes unless a reasonable person would be deceived by the defendants' misrepresentations. But it is hard to believe that this language is intended to be understood literally, for if it were it would invite con men to prey on people of below-average judgment or intelligence, who are anyway the biggest targets of such criminals and hence the people most needful of the law's protection—and most needful or not are within its protective scope. 'Taking advantage of the vulnerable is a leitmotif of fraud.' Emery v. American General Finance, Inc., 71 F.3d 1343, 1347 (7th Cir.1995). It would be very odd for the law to protect only those who, being able to protect themselves, do not need the law's protection. In fact picking on the vulnerable normally makes your conduct more rather less culpable, earning you a heavier sentence.

"[Our decision in United States v. Biesiadecki, 933 F.2d 539, 544 (7th Cir.1991)] aligns us with those courts that hold that the mail- and wire-fraud statutes protect the gullible against frauds directed against them, yet [our decision in Spiegel v. Continental Ill. Nat'l. Bank, 790 F.2d 638, 646 (7th Cir.1986)] aligns us with those courts that define mail and wire fraud in terms of misrepresentations or omissions calculated to deceive a reasonable person. We doubt that there is real inconsistency. The 'reasonable person' language has two purposes, neither of which has anything to do with declaring open season on the people most likely to be targets of fraud. The first is to guide the jury in evaluating circumstantial evidence of fraudulent intent: that the defendants' scheme was calculated to deceive a person of ordinary prudence is some evidence that it was intended to deceive. Evidence that the scheme could fool only an idiot would not be evidence of such intent—would be, if anything, evidence against an inference of such intent—unless the scheme was aimed at an idiot. But if it were, this would make it a case of direct evidence of wrongful intent. The fact that a reasonable person would not have been deceived would be no more relevant than the fact that a murder victim would have survived had he been wearing a bulletproof vest.

"Second, the 'reasonable person' language gestures, although clumsily, toward the indistinct border zone between real fraud and sharp dealing. Almost all sellers engage in a certain amount of puffing; all buyers, even those who are rather fallible, know this; it would not do to criminalize business conduct that is customary rather than exceptional and is relatively harmless. The cases carve a safe harbor for the type of misrepresentation that, being so commonplace as to be 'normal,' is not likely to fool anyone. This is not such a case. Indeed, the defendants' argument is not that they were just puffing, but that their misrepresentations were so gross as to be unbelievable. They ask that the safe harbor for small lies be expanded to include the biggest whoppers. But there is a difference between lies so small that they are discounted in advance, as part of the language of business, and so are harmless, and lies so large that the sophisticated see through them. The latter lies are not normal. Most people who are worth nothing do not claim to a prospective lender to be worth $76 million. The extravagance of the lie may make it difficult to believe, but we saw earlier that a scheme to defraud is not excused by being unlikely to succeed."[z]

What do you think about the three views? Is the Eleventh Circuit correct in reasoning that mail fraud is not present when the misrepresentations would fool only the naive or the unreasonable since doing so makes the "difference between legal and illegal conduct in the field of business relations * * * uncertain."? *Brown, supra,* 79 F.3d at 1562. Or, is the First Circuit correct in asserting that "[t]he only issue is whether there is a plan, scheme or artifice to defraud" and that it "makes no difference [in assessing intent] whether the persons the schemers intended to defraud are gullible or skeptical, dull or bright." *Brien, supra,* 617 F.2d at 311. Or, is Judge Posner correct in suggesting that the gullibility of the intended victims of the scheme or artifice to defraud is relevant in assessing intent? Under Judge Posner's test, is mail fraud possible when the victims were gullible yet the perpetrators also had criminal intent to defraud? Is such an outcome possible under the Eleventh Circuit's view? Under the First Circuit's?

* * *

3. MAIL FRAUD AND EXISTING RELATIONSHIPS

As the Eleventh Circuit noted in *Brown,* when the parties are "in some kind of legal relationship," there is an obligation to disclose certain information. The next case, Emery v. American General Finance, Inc., 71 F.3d 1343 (7th Cir.1995), addresses this duty, albeit in the context of RICO. (RICO is discussed in the next chapter.) *Emery* also discusses the issue addressed in the last section: whether mail fraud exists when the victim becomes a victim because of her naivete, ignorance or even laziness. Does *Emery* cause you to change your view on this issue?

EMERY v. AMERICAN GENERAL FINANCE, INC.

United States Court of Appeals, Seventh Circuit, 1995.
71 F.3d 1343.

Posner, Chief Judge.

This is a suit for damages under the RICO statute. 18 U.S.C. §§ 1961 et seq. The plaintiff, Verna Emery, charges the defendant, American General Finance, a maker of small loans, with engaging in the practice of "loan flipping," a practice that the plaintiff claims is "racketeering activity" within the meaning of RICO. § 1962(c). To be such, it must involve one or more of the crimes listed in section 1961(1), * * * the only one alleged by the complaint, is mail fraud, prohibited by 18

---

z. *Coffman,* 94 F.3d at 334–35.

U.S.C. § 1341. The district judge dismissed the complaint under Fed. R.Civ.P. 12(b)(6) on the ground that the facts alleged do not violate section 1341.

Here is what is alleged. On July 14, 1992, Emery borrowed $1,983.81 from American General Finance, the loan being secured by miscellaneous personal property, including a typewriter and a television set. The finance charge, based on the 36 percent annual rate of interest charged for the loan, was $1,327.08, and the loan was for three years. Six months later, American General Finance wrote a letter to Emery. The letter, signed by a branch manager, reads as follows:

Facts

> Dear Verna:
>
> I have extra spending money for you.
>
> Does your car need a tune-up? Want to take a trip? Or, do you just want to pay off some of your bills? We can lend you money for whatever you need or want.
>
> You're a good customer. To thank you for your business, I've set aside $750.00* in your name.
>
> Just bring the coupon below into my office and if you qualify, we could write your check on the spot. Or, call ahead and I'll have the check waiting for you.
>
> Make this month great with extra cash. Call me today—I have money to loan.
>
> * Subject to our normal credit policies.

At the bottom of the letter is a coupon captioned "$750.00 Cash Coupon" made out to Verna M. Emery at her address. Her name and address are preceded by the words "$750.00 cash for:". Small print explains at the bottom, "This is not a check."

Emery wanted a loan, so she responded to the letter. When she showed up in the branch manager's office, he gave her forms for a refinancing of her existing loan with additional funds advanced. The new note which she signed was for an amount financed of $2,399.83 and a finance charge (computed at the same 36 percent interest rate) of $1,641.28, payable over three years. The monthly payment, which had been $89.47 under the original loan, jumped to $108.20 (more for the first payment) for the new loan. Had she not refinanced she would have had to pay $89.47 a month for another 30 months or so (for the refinancing took place approximately six months after the original loan was made), while with the refinancing she had to pay $108.20 for the next 36 months—and this to receive $200. The increment in cost to her came to about $1,200, paid over three years, and this is for the right to get only $200 now. The cost to her of borrowing $200 in this way was roughly three times as great as it would have been had she borrowed that amount for three years in a separate loan at the annual interest rate of 36 percent. By our calculation, the implicit interest rate that she paid for the $200 loan exceeded 110 percent per annum. This was not disclosed on the Truth in Lending Act form that Emery received because the Act treats the transaction as a reborrowing of the original amount of the loan plus $200. So much for the Truth in Lending Act as a protection for borrowers.

We have said that $200 was Emery's benefit from the loan, but the figure may be larger. The difference between the amount financed by the new loan and the amount financed by the old is more than $400. The only cash she received was a check for $200, the rest of the difference being eaten up by increased insurance and other expenses. Perhaps those expenses inured to her benefit. If so the implicit interest rate would be less than 110 percent. These are not details that can be or have to be resolved at the complaint stage.

The complaint alleges, a little less clearly than could be desired but clearly enough, that while the letter sent to Emery and other customers of American General Finance implies that the customer is being offered a separate loan, when the customer shows up to take advantage of the offer the company presents him with papers for refinancing the customer's existing loan with additional funds being advanced and does not disclose, indeed conceals the fact, that this method of obtaining additional funds is much more costly than taking out a new loan. The customers do not understand this, because American General Finance "markets its loans to working-class borrowers who generally do not understand ... the computations necessary to determine the comparative cost" of a second loan and a refinancing (with additional funds advanced) of their existing loan. This practice is alleged to be a "scheme or artifice to defraud," and one who having devised such a scheme or artifice uses the mails "for the purpose of executing such scheme or artifice or attempting so to do" violates the mail fraud statute.

The language of the mail-fraud statute is very broad, and concern has repeatedly been expressed that it not be given too vague and encompassing a scope by judicial interpretation. Since it is a purely criminal statute, unlike statutes such as the Sherman Act that authorize both civil and criminal remedies and are interpreted more liberally in cases where only the former are sought, if a narrow interpretation is appropriate to meet the concern with breadth and vagueness it would have to apply to the invocation of the statute in this civil suit.

Consistent with this concern, recent cases, at least, make clear that all the statute punishes is *deliberate* fraud, where in order to get money or something else of monetizable value from someone you make a statement to him that you know to be false, or a half truth that you know to be misleading, expecting him to act upon it to your benefit and his detriment. We emphasize the "half truth" half of this definition. United States v. Keplinger, 776 F.2d 678, 697 (7th Cir.1985), holds "that omissions or concealment of material information can constitute fraud ... cognizable under the mail fraud statute, without proof of a duty to disclose the information pursuant to a specific statute or regulation." In that case a laboratory had omitted from a report on the toxicity of a drug an opinion by a consultant that the drug had some toxic effects, and we held that the jury was entitled to find that this omission was fraudulent, given the impression, conveyed by the report, of the utter harmlessness of the drug. Plenty of cases say that "mere failure to disclose" is not, without more, mail fraud, and we certainly have no quarrel with this proposition. Whether a failure to disclose is fraudulent depends on context, to which we now turn.

We do not of course know the state of mind of the employees of American General Finance who drafted the letter to Emery and its other customers; nor can the plaintiff have more than an inkling until she has an opportunity to conduct pretrial discovery. But assume, as the complaint adequately invites us to do, that these employees, desiring to exploit the financial naivete of working-class borrowers, realizing that these borrowers do not read Truth in Lending Act disclosure forms intelligently, and hoping to trick them into overpaying disastrously for credit, drafted a letter that they believed would be effective in concealing the costs of refinancing. Read against this background of nefarious purpose, the letter is seen to be replete with falsehoods and half truths. "Dear Verna ... You're a good customer. To thank you for your business, I've set aside $750.00* in your name." She is no "Dear Verna" to them; she has not been selected to receive the letter because she is a good customer, but because she belongs to a class of probably gullible customers for credit; the purpose of offering her more money is not to thank her for her business but to rip her off; nothing has been "set aside" for her. "[W]e could write your check on the spot. Or, call ahead and I'll have the check waiting for you." Yes—along with a few forms to sign whereby for only $1,200 payable over three years at an even higher monthly rate than your present loan (and than your present loan plus a separate loan for $200, which we could have made you), you can have a meager $200 now. We were not reassured when at the oral argument American General Finance's lawyer was unable to tell us what it cost Verna Emery to obtain the $200 through a refinancing compared to what it would have cost her had the company simply made her a separate loan for that amount.

The district court thought the scheme was saved from illegality by the plaintiff's failure to allege either a violation of the Truth in Lending Act or a fiduciary relationship between the finance company and her. The points turn out to be related. A careful reader, comparing the Truth in Lending Act disclosure forms for the original loan to Emery and the refinancing-plus-additional-advance loan, would notice that the monthly payment was almost $20 a month higher under the second loan and by comparing the dates of the two forms would also realize that the second loan would require six more months of payments. But not all persons are capable of being careful readers. Suppose Emery were blind. Or retarded. Would anyone argue that shoving a Truth in Lending Act disclosure form in front of her face would be a defense to fraud? The allegation is that she belongs to a class of borrowers who are not competent interpreters of such forms *and that the defendant knows this and sought to take advantage of it.* Taking advantage of the vulnerable is a leitmotif of fraud. Competent people can protect themselves well enough against most forms of fraud. The incompetent are for that reason a frequent target of con men and other defrauders, and such targeting is, of course, unlawful, and indeed earns the criminal a longer sentence.

The district court acknowledged that if the finance company had had a fiduciary relationship with Verna Emery, it would have been guilty of fraud had it failed to disclose so material a fact as that refinancing would be a much more costly method of borrowing another $200 than borrowing it in a separate loan. A fiduciary must be as honest with the persons to whom he stands in a fiduciary relationship as he would want other people to be with him. But it is not true that if you are not a fiduciary anything goes, short of false statements. A half truth, or what is usually the same thing, a misleading omission, is actionable as fraud, including mail fraud if the mails are used to further it, if it is intended to induce a false belief and resulting action to the advantage of the misleader and the disadvantage of the misled. This is adequately alleged in the complaint.

We do not hold that "loan flipping" is fraud, because the boundaries of the term are obscure. We do not hold that American General Finance engaged in fraud, or even in "loan flipping." We do not hold that the mail fraud statute criminalizes sleazy sales tactics, which abound in a free commercial society. State of mind is crucial in a case of criminal fraud, as we have emphasized, and there is no evidence as yet concerning the state of mind of the defendant's relevant employees. We have no idea who composed the letter to Verna Emery or what the author had in mind when he composed it. All we know is that the allegations of fraud are sufficient to withstand a motion to dismiss the complaint for failure to state a claim. There is a state of facts consistent with the complaint that if proved would establish a violation of the mail fraud statute, and no more is required at this stage for the suit to continue.

* * *

REVERSED AND REMANDED.

COFFEY, CIRCUIT JUDGE, DISSENTING.

It is a truth at least as old as the Bible that "the borrower is servant to the lender." *Proverbs* 22:7. Polonius recognized this when he advised Laertes:

Neither a borrower nor a lender be; For loan oft loses both itself and friend, And borrowing dulleth th' edge of husbandry.

Hamlet, Act I, scene iii, line 75 (Riverside Shakespeare). For whatever reason, Verna Emery did not heed this wisdom and, in the words of the majority, she ended up "overpaying disastrously for credit." Emery then brought a suit under civil RICO, claiming that American General Finance, Inc. ("AGF") engaged in a pattern of racketeering activity, i.e., acts of "loan-flipping" that allegedly constitute mail fraud pursuant to 18 U.S.C. § 1341. The majority concludes that it was improper for the district court to dismiss Emery's suit on a 12(b)(6) motion. I am unable to join in this conclusion and therefore respectfully dissent.

ANALYSIS

* * *

The elements of mail fraud under 18 U.S.C. § 1341 are: "(1) the defendant's participation in a scheme to defraud; (2) defendant's commission of the act with intent to defraud; and (3) use of the mails in furtherance of the fraudulent scheme." United States v. Walker, 9 F.3d 1245, 1249 (7th Cir.1993). The district court, pursuant to Rule 12(b)(6), dismissed Emery's civil RICO claim because it failed to state a claim for mail fraud. The district court was troubled by the plaintiff's failure to "identify any specific false statement of material fact allegedly made by the defendant" and concluded, in light of AGF's compliance with state and federal consumer lending laws, that Emery could not establish a "scheme to defraud" within the meaning of 18 U.S.C. § 1341.

The gist of Emery's complaint is not that AGF outright lied to her; she cannot make such a claim because the flier distributed to her (quoted at length in the majority opinion) contained no false statements or affirmative misrepresentations. Rather, Emery argues that AGF omitted or failed to disclose material information (specifically, the fact that refinancing her existing loan would be more costly than obtaining a new loan). "Indeed," as the district court observed, "plaintiff's entire case is premised upon defendant's failure to volunteer the fact that a second loan would be cheaper than a refinancing of the first loan." *Id.*

The majority, citing United States v. Keplinger, 776 F.2d 678, 697 (7th Cir.1985), asserts that an omission or a non-disclosure *can sometimes amount to fraud* within the meaning of the mail fraud statute, even "without proof of a duty to disclose the information pursuant to a specific statute or regulation." In *Keplinger*, this court borrowed language evidently first used by the Fifth Circuit stating that "the measure of fraud is its departure from moral uprightness, fundamental honesty, fair play and candid dealings in the general life of members of society." 776 F.2d at 698; *see* Gregory v. United States, 253 F.2d 104, 109 (5th Cir.1958). However, subsequent to our decision in *Keplinger*, this court "repented" of our earlier infatuation with such broad language, calling it "hyperbole." Matter of EDC, Inc., 930 F.2d 1275, 1281 (7th Cir.1991). In an opinion authored by Chief Judge Posner, this court *explicitly warned against "extravagant rhetoric ... interpreting the federal mail fraud ... statute [ ]."* Id. (emphasis added). "Read literally," we cautioned, the " 'fair play' theory of mail and wire fraud" would *"put federal judges in the business of creating new crimes; federal criminal law would be the nation's moral vanguard."* Id. (emphasis added) . Our cases thus make clear that the mail fraud statute does not codify a strict code of honor in business dealings, but rather targets only conduct that is widely recognized as fraudulent.

Since *Keplinger*, this court has also clarified that "mere failure to disclose, absent *something more*," does not constitute mail fraud, notwithstanding the broad language used in *Keplinger* and a handful of other cases. Reynolds v. East Dyer Development Co., 882 F.2d 1249, 1252 (7th Cir.1989) (emphasis added). The cases in which this court has held that "non-disclosure" may be deemed fraudulent all involved a special circumstance of some kind.

There were no such special circumstances in this case. AGF, as Emery's creditor, was not a fiduciary. AGF did not engage in a "wide variety of deceptive actions," nor can its conduct vis-a-vis Emery be fairly described as an "elaborate attempt at concealment."

Defeating all of the potential arguments available to Emery is a simple and uncontroverted fact: AGF fully complied with the disclosure requirements of both the federal Truth in Lending Act ("TILA"), 15 U.S.C. § 1601 et seq., and the Illinois Consumer Installment Loan Act ("CILA"), 205 ILCS 670/1 et seq.

* * *

* * * [T]he majority * * * makes much of the "financial naiveté of working-class borrowers." Emery, we are told, belongs to a "class of probably gullible customers for credit." Lack of financial acumen, according to the majority, is much like blindness or mental retardation because it renders one vulnerable to "con men and defrauders." By enacting TILA, however, Congress has provided all the protection it deems appropriate for borrowers, be they financially astute or ill-informed and gullible. Moreover, notwithstanding the majority's critique of TILA, the legislation does offer extensive protection to borrowers by requiring disclosures that are easy to comprehend "so that the consumer will be able to compare more readily the various credit terms available to him and avoid the uninformed use of credit." 15 U.S.C. § 1601(a). It appears from the record before us that Verna Emery is a fully capable adult citizen suffering from no physical or mental disabilities, such as blindness, deafness, or mental incapacity. I am therefore unable to see the relevance of her susceptibility to business practices which, although arguably manipulative and unethical, fully complied with the law.

I do not condone AGF's practices, nor am I unsympathetic to Emery's plight. The conduct in the factual record before us may very well have been improper, but it violated neither statute nor case law. As a distinguished colleague on the Ninth Circuit once observed, "courts do not sit to compensate the luckless; this is not Sherwood Forest." Kern v. Levolor Lorentzen, 899 F.2d 772, 798 (9th Cir.1990) (Kozinski, J., dissenting). I must insist, as this court has in the past, that "[n]ot all conduct that strikes a court as sharp dealing or unethical conduct is a 'scheme or artifice to defraud' "within the meaning of the federal mail fraud statute. *Reynolds*, 882 F.2d at 1252.

* * *

Conclusion

I am somewhat heartened by the limited nature of the majority's holding. Wisely, my colleagues refuse to hold that "loan-flipping" is fraud, or that AGF engaged in fraud in this case. The majority also denies any intention to "criminalize[ ] sleazy sales tactics, which abound in a free commercial society." Nevertheless, the majority does hold that it was premature for the district court to dismiss the suit. I disagree. In light of AGF's compliance with TILA and the Illinois consumer lending statute, I do not believe that Emery will ever be able to establish a "scheme or artifice to defraud," much less "an elaborate attempt at concealment. . . ." Remanding the case for further proceedings at this juncture is, in my opinion, both unnecessary and a waste of judicial resources. The majority's holding sends the wrong message to district judges, who are trying desperately to manage their dockets in the face of mounting civil litigation, and will only encourage further lawsuits based on novel and expansive readings of the mail fraud statute and of RICO. For these reasons, I respectfully dissent from the majority.

Notes

What do you think? Does it make a difference in determining whether the mail fraud statute covers schemes to defraud the naive and gullible if the victim and perpetrator have a relationship such as the one which existed between Verna M. Emery and American General Finance (AGF)? Is this relationship any different than the relationship which exists in any arms length business relationship? Was there more reliance by Ms. Emery on AGF because of the prior relationship? More trust? More of a fraud? Was Ms. Emery situated any differently than the individuals who purchased land in Florida from General Development Corporation (GDC)?

Chapter 3

RACKETEER INFLUENCED AND CORRUPT ORGANIZATIONS (RICO)

A. OVERVIEW OF RICO[a]

RICO[b] can be prosecutor's powerhouse and a civil plaintiff's dream. Its breadth and penalty provisions benefit both. RICO is also a statute of "daunting complexity."[c] Passed in 1970 as part of a major crime fighting bill,[d] RICO's stated goal is to protect the public from "parties who conduct organizations affecting interstate commerce through a pattern of criminal activity."[e]

RICO has been extended to cover a wide range of conduct: organized crime,[f] white collar crime,[g] even Croation terrorists,[h] and abortion clinic protestors.[i] The Supreme Court has not been sympathetic when RICO defendants have argued that this broad application exceeds the intended scope of RICO, stating, "RICO is to be read broadly. This is the lesson not only of Congress' self-consciously expansive language and overall approach * * * but also of its express admonition that RICO is 'to be liberally construed to effectuate its remedial purposes.' "[j]

---

a. Portions of section A are reprinted with permission from Pamela H. Bucy & Steven T. Marshall, *An Overview of RICO*, 51 *Ala.Law.* 283–89 (1990). Copyright © 1990 by the Alabama State Bar.

b. 18 U.S.C. § 1961 et seq.

c. Gerald Lynch, *RICO: The Crime of Being a Criminal, Parts I and II*, 87 *Colum.L.Rev.* 661, 680 (1987); see also Lynch, *RICO: Crime of Being a Criminal, Parts III and IV*, 87 *Colum.L.Rev.* 920 (1987) [hereinafter both above-cited articles referred to as *G. Lynch*].

d. Organized Crime Control Act of 1970, Title IX, Pub.L. No. 91–452, 84 Stat. 941 (1970).

e. 115 Cong.Rec. 9568 (1969), Remarks of Senator McClellan.

f. *See, e.g.*, United States v. Local 560, 550 F.Supp. 511 (D.N.J.1982), affirmed, 780 F.2d 267 (3d Cir.1985); United States v. Gambino, 566 F.2d 414 (2d Cir.1977).

g. *See, e.g.*, United States v. Milken, 759 F.Supp. 109 (S.D.N.Y.1990) (securities fraud).

h. United States v. Bagaric, 706 F.2d 42 (2d Cir.1983).

i. Northeast Women's Center, Inc. v. McMonagle, 624 F.Supp. 736 (E.D.Pa.1985).

With few exceptions, the United States Supreme Court has consistently rejected restrictive interpretations by lower courts to limit expansive uses of RICO.[k] In construing RICO, the Court relies on the expressed legislative intent that RICO "be liberally construed to effectuate its remedial purpose."[l] Recent Supreme Court cases during the past five years are typical. The Court has reaffirmed that the "interstate commerce" requirement is to be broadly intrepreted,[m] that RICO violations do not require an "economic purpose,"[n] and that RICO forfeiture authority is expansive even in light of first amendment claims.[o]

Despite the Supreme Court's reluctance to interpret RICO restrictively, lower courts have shown consistent hostility to expansive RICO applications.[p] For example, a review of all Court of Appeals decisions concerning RICO reported during the five year period 1991–96, indicates that approximately one-third of civil RICO cases[q] were dismissed before trial. As CHART 3A on following page shows, most were dismissed for lack of standing; the next most common reason was for failure to allege sufficient "pattern of racketeering activity."

One of RICO's unique features is that it provides both criminal and civil causes of action for a violation of its provisions. Thus, the United States Department of Justice[r] may seek a criminal indictment or file a civil complaint alleging RICO violations. At the same time, private parties may file a complaint alleging the same RICO violations.[s] RICO has become renowned, in part, because of the stiff sanctions it provides: mandatory forfeiture for a criminal violation, in addition to possible imprisonment and fines;[t] treble damages and attorney fees for a civil violation.[u]

j. Sedima, S.P.R.L. v. Imrex Co., Inc., 473 U.S. 479, 497–98 (1985).

k. *See* NOW v. Scheidler, 510 U.S. 249 (1994) (rejecting a restrictive "economic purpose" requirement for standing); H. J. Inc. v. Northwestern Bell Telephone Co., 492 U.S. 229 (1989) (rejecting a restrictive "multiple scheme" requirement for "pattern"); Sedima, S.P.R.L. v. Imrex Co., 473 U.S. 479 (1985) (rejecting a judicially construed "racketeering injury" requirement for civil standing); United States v. Turkette, 452 U.S. 576 (1981) (rejecting a restrictive "legitimate organization" requirement for "enterprise"). *Cf.* Reves v. Ernst & Young, 507 U.S. 170 (1993) (imposing the most restrictive test for "participate" to section 1962(c) violations).

l. Pub. L. No. 91–452, § 904(a), 84 Stat. 947 (1970).

m. United States v. Robertson, 514 U.S. 669 (1995).

n. NOW v. Scheidler, 510 U.S. 249 (1994).

o. Alexander v. United States, 509 U.S. 544 (1993).

p. *See* Michael Goldsmith, *Judicial Immunity for White–Collar Crime*, 30 HARV. J. ON LEGIS. 1 (1993) (arguing against judicial activism by the lower courts, in the absence of Congressional reform. Goldsmith's research found that approximately 75% of RICO actions filed during six months in 1991 and six months in 1992 were dismissed prior to trial).

q. 112 out of 350.

r. *RICO Guidelines,* UNITED STATES ATTORNEY'S MANUAL § 9–110.000 et seq.

s. Cf. *Civil RICO is a Misnomer: The Need For Criminal Procedural Protections in Actions Under 18 U.S.C. § 1964,* 100 HARV.L.REV. 1288, 1298 (1987).

t. 18 U.S.C. § 1963(a).

u. *Id.* at § 1964(c).

CHART 3A

REASONS FOR PRETRIAL DISMISSAL
OF CIVIL RICO CASES

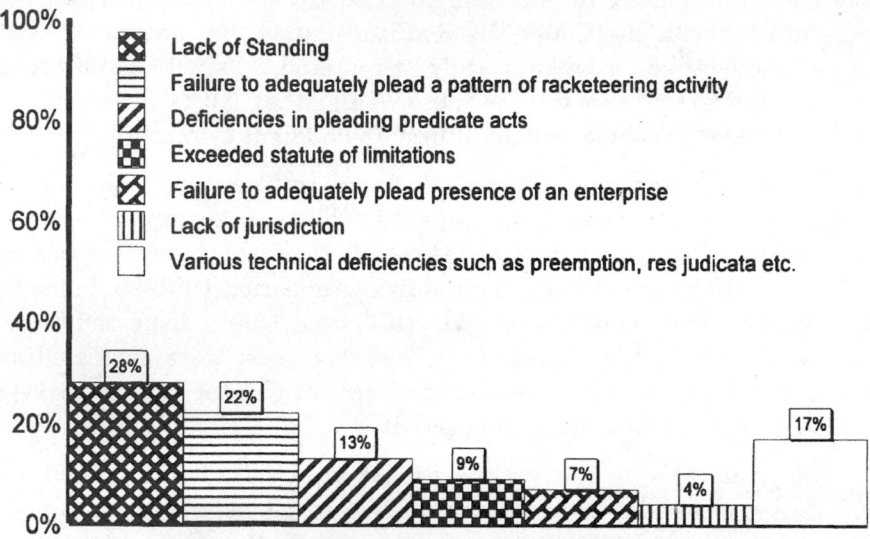

The RICO statute is organized very logically. Section 1961 sets forth definitions. Section 1962 lists the four types of conduct that constitute a RICO violation. Section 1963 sets forth the criminal penalties; Section 1964 sets forth the civil penalties. Sections 1965 through 1968 provide housekeeping details. Section 1965 deals with venue and process. Section 1966 provides for expediting certain civil RICO actions brought by the government. Section 1967 gives a court the discretion to close civil proceedings to the public. Section 1968 gives the Attorney General the authority to issue civil investigative demands for documents in certain circumstances.

There are four types of conduct prohibited by RICO. The gist of all four is using a business to commit crime. Whether the case is civil or criminal, the plaintiff must prove that the defendant committed at least one of these types of conduct. Before discussing the prohibited conduct, it is helpful to review three major RICO definitions.

The first significant definition is "racketeering activity." Section 1961(1) defines "racketeering activity" as committing any one of specifically listed crimes, often referred to as "predicate acts." The crimes listed in Section 1961(1) include some state felony offenses (murder, kidnapping, gambling, arson, robbery, bribery, extortion, obscenity and narcotics) and approximately 55 federal felony offenses. The federal offenses include those typically thought of as "racketeering" offenses, i.e., the Hobbs Act[v] (interfering with interstate commerce through violence or the threat of violence), distribution of illegal narcotics, bribery, extortion, gambling and prostitution. Also included as "racketeering activity" are many white collar crimes: mail fraud, wire fraud, labor union and pension fraud, money laundering and securities fraud.[w]

One does not commit a RICO offense simply by committing one "racketeering activity," rather, one must engage in a "pattern of racketeering activity." "Pattern of racketeering activity" is defined in Section 1961(5) as "at least two acts of racketeering activity within a ten-year time period."[x] The federal courts have struggled with this minimal definition. In 1986 the United States Court of Appeals for the Eighth Circuit gave a narrow interpretation to "pattern," holding that two counts (i.e., often just two mailings) in a mail fraud scheme were so closely related to each other that they constituted only one "racketeering activity" and not a "pattern" of racketeering activity.[y] Almost every other federal court of appeals had rejected this narrow interpretation[z] when the Supreme Court also rejected it in H.J. Inc. v. Northwestern Bell Telephone Company.[aa]

The third significant definition in RICO is "enterprise." Simply engaging in a "pattern of racketeering activity" will not constitute a RICO offense. The statute forbids engaging in a pattern of racketeering only insofar as an enterprise is involved.[bb] Section 1961(4) defines enterprise broadly as "any individual, partnership, corporation, association, or other legal entity, and any union or group of individuals associated in fact although not a legal entity."[cc] Sections 1962(a)–(d) add that the enterprise "must affect interstate or foreign commerce."[dd] This commerce requirement is minimal and easily met.[ee]

To prove the existence of an enterprise, the RICO plaintiff must first prove that there exists some type of "ongoing organization, formal or informal."[ff] Evidence of just enough organization among individuals to carry out the predicate acts could suffice to meet this burden.[gg] The RICO plaintiff must also prove that the various associates in this ongoing organization "function as a continuing unit."[hh] This "continuity" can be shown by evidence of repeated commission of the same types of acts (even if the people performing these acts change).[ii]

---

v. 18 U.S.C. § 1951, et seq.

w. *Id.* at § 1961(1).

x. *Id.* at § 1961(5).

y. Superior Oil Co. v. Fulmer, 785 F.2d 252, 257–58 (8th Cir.1986).

z. *See, e.g.,* United States v. Indelicato, 865 F.2d 1370 (2d Cir.1989).

aa. 492 U.S. 229 (1989).

bb. Bennett v. Berg, 685 F.2d 1053, 1060 (8th Cir.1982).

cc. 18 U.S.C. § 1961(4).

dd. *Id.* at § 1962(a), (b), (c), (d).

ee. R.A.G.S. Couture, Inc. v. Hyatt, 774 F.2d 1350, 1353 (5th Cir.1985); United States v. Robinson, 763 F.2d 778, 781 (6th Cir.1985).

ff. United States v. Turkette, 452 U.S. 576 (1981).

gg. See, e.g., United States v. Cagnina, 697 F.2d 915, 921–22 (11th Cir.1983); United States v. Mazzei, 700 F.2d 85 (2d Cir. 1983).

hh. *Turkette*, 452 U.S. at 583.

ii. United States v. Lemm, 680 F.2d 1193, 1199 (8th Cir.1982).

Courts also have required clear proof of a nexus between the pattern of racketeering activity and the enterprise, typically requiring "proof that the facilities and services of the enterprise were regularly and repeatedly utilized to make possible the racketeering activity."[jj] It is not necessary to go further and prove that the racketeering activities had "an effect upon the common, everyday affairs of the enterprise."[kk]

The four types of conduct prohibited by RICO are set forth in four subsections of Section 1962. Section 1962(a) makes it unlawful for any person to "use or invest" any income derived from a pattern of racketeering activity in an enterprise.[ll] United States v. Zang,[mm] provides an example of a Section 1962(a) offense. Zang and Porter were partners who owned oil refining and related businesses. They falsified information about the oil they were processing, used the mails to do so, and were found to have committed the racketeering activity of mail fraud.[nn] A Section 1962(a) violation occurred because Zang and Porter ("persons") funneled the profits they made from their mail fraud scheme ("pattern of racketeering activity") into one of the businesses ("enterprise") they owned. The portion of this business attributable to the ill-gotten profits was forfeitable property under RICO.[oo]

Section 1962(b) makes it unlawful for any person to acquire or maintain control of any enterprise through a pattern of racketeering activity. United States v. Local 560,[pp] provides an example of a Section 1962(b) action. In this case, the United States brought a civil RICO action against 12 individuals, Local 560 of the International Brotherhood of Teamsters, and Local 560's Welfare Fund and Severance Pay Plan. A Section 1962(b) violation was alleged on the ground that the individuals ("persons") acquired an interest in and control of Local 560 ("enterprise") through extortion and murder[qq] ("pattern of racketeering activity").

Section 1962(c) makes it unlawful for any person "employed by or associated with any enterprise" to conduct the affairs of the enterprise through a pattern of racketeering activity.[rr] Section 1962(c) offenses are the most common. One study of all reported RICO cases showed that 92% of the cases charged a violation of Section 1962(c), or a conspiracy to violate Section 1962(c).[ss] Bennett v. Berg[tt] provides an example of a Section 1962(c) action. Residents of a retirement community filed a civil complaint against numerous individuals and corporations alleging that because of the defendants' fraud, the retirement community was on the

---

jj. United States v. Carter, 721 F.2d 1514, 1527 (11th Cir.1984); See e.g., Sun Savings and Loan Association v. Dierdorff, 825 F.2d 187, 195 (9th Cir.1987); United States v. Scotto, 641 F.2d 47, 54 (2d Cir. 1980); United States v. Carlock, 806 F.2d 535, 546 (5th Cir.1986); United States v. Blackwood, 768 F.2d 131, 138 (7th Cir. 1985).

kk. *Carter,* 721 F.2d at 1527.

ll. 18 U.S.C. § 1962(a).

mm. 703 F.2d 1186 (10th Cir.1982).

nn. *Id.* at 1193.

oo. *Id.* at 1195.

pp. 780 F.2d 267 (3d Cir.1985).

qq. *Id.* at 273–74.

rr. 18 U.S.C. § 1962(c).

ss. *Lynch, supra* note c at 724, 726 and 731.

tt. 685 F.2d 1053 (8th Cir.1982).

verge of bankruptcy and the residents faced the loss of the services they had paid for and been promised.[uu] The complaint alleged violations of Section 1962(c), asserting that some of the defendants ("persons") conducted the affairs of the retirement community ("enterprise") through mail and wire fraud ("pattern of racketeering activity").

Section 1962(d) makes it unlawful for any person to conspire to do any of the acts in Sections 1962(a)–(c).[vv] The usual elements of conspiracy must be proven to prevail on a Section 1962(d) action: the defendants agreed to commit at least one type of RICO conduct as specified in Section 1962(a), (b) or (c), and at least one conspirator committed at least one overt act in furtherance of the conspiracy.[ww] A RICO conspiracy requires proof of an agreement to violate *substantive* RICO provisions.[xx] The RICO plaintiff does not have to prove that each defendant also agreed to personally commit the predicate acts that make up the "pattern of racketeering activity," but the plaintiff must prove that each defendant personally agreed to the commission by someone of the predicate acts.[yy] By the same token, proof only that a defendant agreed to the commission of the predicate acts without further proof of an *agreement* to violate a substantive RICO offense is inadequate to prove a RICO conspiracy.[zz]

The following example demonstrates what proof is necessary to establish a Section 1962(d) RICO conspiracy. If a plaintiff proves that the defendants agreed to collect insurance proceeds from the arson of several businesses and that one defendant committed one overt act in furtherance of this insurance fraud, the plaintiff may have proven a conspiracy to commit mail fraud (assuming the insurance claim was mailed). However, unless the plaintiff also proves an agreement to use or invest the ill-gotten insurance proceeds in an enterprise (a Section 1962(a) action), or to acquire or maintain control of one enterprise through the insurance fraud (a Section 1962(b) action), or to conduct the affairs of an enterprise through the insurance fraud (a Section 1962(c) action), no RICO conspiracy has been proven.

If, as one court stated, the RICO statute is "constructed on the model of a treasure hunt,"[a] Sections 1963 and 1964 are the treasure. Section 1963 sets forth the criminal penalties. A criminal conviction subjects the RICO defendant to a possible sentence of imprisonment of 20 years,[b] substantial fines,[c] and forfeiture of "any interest * * * acquired or maintained" in violation of RICO.[d] Most of Section 1963 deals

---

uu. *Id.* at 1057.

vv. 18 U.S.C. § 1962(d).

ww. United States v. Carter, 721 F.2d 1514, 1528 (11th Cir.1984).

xx. *Id.* (citing United States v. Elliott, 571 F.2d 880, 902 (5th Cir.1978)).

yy. *Carter*, 721 F.2d at 1531.

zz. *Elliott*, 571 F.2d at 902–03.

a. Sutliff Inc. v. Donovan Companies, Inc., 727 F.2d 648, 652 (7th Cir.1984).

b. 18 U.S.C. § 1963(a).

c. RICO provides a maximum fine of $25,000, 18 U.S.C. § 1962(a). The Alternative Fine Provision, which applies to all Title 18 offenses, imposes a higher and more complex fine structure; 18 U.S.C. § 3571.

d. 18 U.S.C. § 1963(a).

with the forfeiture penalty. The government is given broad power to seek restraining orders or performance bonds "to preserve the availability of the property subject to forfeiture."[e] In unusual cases, such orders or bonds may be obtained before indictment, ex parte and without notice.[f] Section 1963 also sets forth the procedure a bona fide purchaser of property subject to forfeiture should follow to secure her rights to her property.[g]

Section 1964 addresses standing for civil plaintiffs and civil penalties. It confers standing to bring a civil RICO action on "any person injured in his business or property by reason of a violation of 1962"[h] and sets forth the damages recoverable: "threefold the damages [sustained] and the cost of the suit, including a reasonable attorney's fee."[i]

B. DEFINITIONS

1. ENTERPRISE

The concept of an "enterprise" is central to RICO. RICO applies only when an actor invests in an "enterprise," acquires or maintains control of an "enterprise," conducts or participates in the affairs of an "enterprise" or conspires to do any of the above assuming, of course, that all other elements of RICO are met. RICO defines "enterprise" as "any individual, partnership, corporation, association, or other legal entity, and any union or group of individuals associated in fact although not a legal entity." 18 U.S.C. § 1961(4). The next case, United States v. Console, 13 F.3d 641 (3d Cir.1993), provides a straight-forward analysis of the enterprise element.

UNITED STATES v. CONSOLE
United States Court of Appeals, Third Circuit, 1993.
13 F.3d 641.

GREENBERG, CIRCUIT JUDGE.

* * *

* * * Console and Curcio were partners in a law firm (the "firm") located in Berlin, New Jersey, and Markoff was an osteopathic physician who practiced in nearby Clementon, New Jersey. Console started the firm in 1973, and soon began hiring other associates, some of whom later became partners. Curcio joined the firm in 1978 and became a partner in 1982. Philip LiVolsi was another partner.

The firm developed a relationship with Markoff in the 1970's, which continued into the 1980's. Markoff referred accident victims to the firm for legal services, and the firm referred clients to Markoff for medical services. When treating a client of the firm, Markoff sent the client's

---

e. *Id.* at § 1963(b)–(h).

f. *Id.* at § 1963(d)(1)(B) and (2).

g. *Id.* at § 1963(i)–(m).

h. *Id.* at § 1964(c).

i. *Id.*

medical bills to the firm, which in turn sent them to the client's insurance company for the payment of the client's personal injury protection ("PIP") benefits pursuant to New Jersey's No–Fault law governing claims for injuries from automobile accidents.[1] When making a claim on behalf of a client seeking "special damages," the firm also sent the medical bills either to the client's or the defendant's insurance company to support claims for pain and suffering or other "special damages" sustained by the client. Markoff received the PIP payments corresponding to the medical bills he sent to the firm, and the firm retained a share of any recovery made for a claim.

In 1985, federal agents searched the firm, and in April 1989, a grand jury indicted Curcio and Markoff along with four codefendants: LiVolsi, the firm's legal administrator (Peter Hulmes), and two of Markoff's employees (Virginia Knowlton and Carmella Lombardi). The indictment charged the defendants with violations of the Racketeer Influenced and Corrupt Organizations Act (RICO), 18 U.S.C. § 1961 et seq., and the federal mail fraud statute, 18 U.S.C. §§ 1341–42, perpetrated in connection with a scheme to defraud insurance companies by submitting inflated medical bills on behalf of accident victims represented by the firm.

On April 24, 1990, LiVolsi agreed to plead guilty to one count of RICO and two predicate acts of mail fraud and to testify before a new grand jury. This grand jury returned a superseding indictment on August 23, 1990, charging two additional defendants, Console and Kathy Baldwin–Sabath, an employee of the firm, with the commission of offenses. Subsequently there were two jury trials in the United States District Court in this case.

Count 1 of the final superseding indictment charged the appellants and the codefendants with conducting and participating in the conduct of an enterprise consisting of the firm and Markoff's medical practice (the "Law Firm–Markoff Enterprise") through a pattern of racketeering activity involving multiple acts of mail fraud. 18 U.S.C. §§ 1962(c) and 2. Similarly, Count 2 charged the appellants and the codefendants with conspiring to conduct the affairs of the Law Firm–Markoff Enterprise through a pattern of racketeering activity. 18 U.S.C. § 1962(d). The indictment also charged each of the appellants with multiple counts of mail fraud. 18 U.S.C. §§ 1341 and 2.

* * *

The first trial began on February 26, 1991. During this trial, Knowlton agreed to plead guilty to one count of mail fraud. The jury returned its verdict in June 1991. Markoff was convicted of the RICO counts and 24 counts of mail fraud but he was acquitted of 11 mail fraud

---

1. In New Jersey, an automobile accident victim obtains PIP benefits which include medical bills, lost wages and certain "essential services" from his own insurance company. Accident victims also can insti- tute third-party suits if their medical bills exceed a threshold amount and may make claims against their own insurance companies if the other drivers are underinsured or uninsured.

counts. Console and Curcio also were acquitted of certain mail fraud counts. The jury, however, did not reach a verdict on the RICO counts and certain mail fraud counts against Console, Curcio, and Hulmes, and consequently the court declared a mistrial as to these counts. The jury acquitted Sabath and Lombardi on all counts.

* * *

Following his convictions, Markoff entered into a cooperation agreement with the government and agreed to testify against Console, Curcio, and Hulmes at a second trial. Console moved to dismiss the charges against him on double jeopardy grounds prior to the second trial, but the district court denied his motion. The district court also denied Curcio's severance motion. The second trial began on February 25, 1992, and the jury returned its verdict on May 21, 1992, convicting Console and Curcio on both RICO counts. The jury also convicted Console and Curcio of eight counts of mail fraud and four counts of mail fraud, respectively. The jury, however, acquitted Hulmes of all charges except for one which the court then dismissed.

* * *

The appellants argue that the evidence was insufficient to support their convictions for violations of 18 U.S.C. § 1962(c) and (d), because the government failed to establish the existence of a RICO "enterprise." Section 1962(c) prohibits "any person employed by or associated with any enterprise" affecting interstate or foreign commerce from conducting or participating "in the conduct of such enterprise's affairs through a pattern of racketeering activity." Section 1962(d) makes it unlawful to conspire to violate Section 1962(c) or the other substantive provisions of RICO.

RICO defines an "enterprise" as "any individual, partnership, corporation, association, or other legal entity, and any union or group of individuals associated in fact although not a legal entity." 18 U.S.C. § 1961(4). In United States v. Turkette, 452 U.S. 576, 583 (1981), the Supreme Court stated that an enterprise "is an entity separate and apart from the pattern of activity in which it engages," and that it is "proved by evidence of an ongoing organization, formal or informal, and by evidence that the various associates function as a continuing unit." In United States v. Riccobene, 709 F.2d 214, 222 (3d Cir.1983), "we construed Turkette to require proof of each of the three sub-elements referred to by the Court in this passage": (1) proof of an ongoing organization, (2) proof that the associates function as a continuing unit, and (3) proof that the enterprise is an "entity separate and apart from the pattern of activity in which it engages." Thus, although the proof used to establish the existence of an enterprise and a pattern of racketeering "may in particular cases coalesce," proof of a pattern of racketeering activity "does not necessarily" establish the existence of an enterprise.[5]

_____

5. Although proof of a pattern of racke-   teering does not "necessarily" establish the

In this case, the government alleged that the RICO enterprise was an association in fact composed of the law firm and Markoff's medical practice and designed "to enrich its members through the pursuit of personal injury business." The appellants argue, however, that the evidence did not demonstrate (1) "that there was any kind of organizational structure for decisionmaking," (2) that the appellants associated together on more than "an ad hoc basis," or (3) that the "enterprise existed separate and apart from the racketeering activity alleged." Thus, according to the appellants, "[a]ll that was shown was that the medical practice and the lawyer's office combined to commit mail fraud on an ad hoc basis."

The existence vel non of a RICO enterprise is a question of fact for the jury. In this case, both the jury that convicted Markoff of RICO violations (Trial I), and the jury that convicted Console and Curcio of RICO violations (Trial II) determined that the government established the existence of the RICO enterprise beyond a reasonable doubt. We must sustain these determinations "if there is substantial evidence, taking the view most favorable to the Government, to support [them]." [citations omitted] Thus, we must review the evidence introduced at trial, drawing all reasonable inferences in favor of the prosecution, to determine whether there is substantial evidence to support the existence of a RICO enterprise.

As we stated in *Riccobene*, 709 F.2d at 222, "[e]ach of the [three] elements enumerated by the Supreme Court describes a separate aspect of the life of the enterprise." The first element requires proof of an "ongoing organization."

> To satisfy this element, the government must show that some sort of structure exists within the group for the making of decisions, whether it be hierarchical or consensual. There must be some mechanism for controlling and directing the affairs of the group on an ongoing, rather than an ad hoc, basis.

Riccobene, 709 F.2d at 222. The government introduced ample evidence at both trials of the existence of an organizational structure within the Law Firm–Markoff Enterprise. The evidence indicates that Markoff and Console met in the early 1980's. At that meeting, Markoff agreed to inflate the bills of the law firm's clients in exchange for continued patient referrals from the firm. Following this meeting, Console and Markoff supervised the execution of this agreement. Under Markoff's supervision, his employees falsified patient bills and charts to meet the specifications communicated by Console, LiVolsi and various employees of the firm. Under Console's direction, attorneys referred clients to Markoff, specified the dates and charges that should be reflected on their bills, and coached clients to make false statements regarding the extent

existence of an enterprise, we have stated that "in the appropriate case, the enterprise can be inferred from proof of the pattern." United States v. Pelullo, 964 F.2d 193, 212 (3d Cir. 1992) (citing United States v. Perholtz, 842 F.2d 343, 363 (D.C.Cir.1988)).

of their medical treatment to support fraudulent insurance claims. Thus, at each trial the government established the existence of an ongoing organization, the first element required to prove the existence of a RICO enterprise.

The second element of the Supreme Court's definition of a RICO enterprise requires proof "that the various associates function as a continuing unit." *Turkette*, 452 U.S. at 583. To satisfy this element, the government must demonstrate "that each person perform[ed] a role in the group consistent with the organizational structure established by the first element and which furthers the activities of the organization." *Riccobene*, 709 F.2d at 223. The government also introduced sufficient evidence to satisfy this requirement at each of the trials.

The evidence indicates that between 1981 and 1985, Console, Markoff, Curcio, LiVolsi, and various employees of the firm and the Markoff practice each performed roles within the enterprise structure and through their roles advanced the scheme to defraud insurance companies through the submission of falsified records, inflated bills, and false statements by patients. Console and Markoff devised the scheme and directed its execution. Curcio referred clients to Markoff and coached them to make false statements regarding their medical treatment. LiVolsi met with Markoff and his employee in charge of billing to communicate the dates and charges that should be reflected on patient bills. Other firm employees also delivered lists of patient records requiring falsification to Markoff's office, and discussed the required changes with Markoff's employees over the phone. Employees of the Markoff practice then falsified the records, which subsequently would be submitted to the insurance companies. Thus, there is substantial evidence to support the juries' determinations "that the various associates [in the Law Firm–Markoff Enterprise] function[ed] as a continuing unit." *Turkette*, 452 U.S. at 583.

Finally, the third element of the enterprise requirement demands proof that the enterprise is an "entity separate and apart from the pattern of activity in which it engages." *Turkette*, 452 U.S. at 583.

> As we understand this last requirement, it is not necessary to show that the enterprise has some function wholly unrelated to the racketeering activity, but rather that it has an existence beyond that which is necessary merely to commit each of the acts charged as predicate racketeering offenses. The function of overseeing and coordinating the commission of several different predicate offenses and other activities on an on-going basis is adequate to satisfy the separate existence requirement.

Riccobene, 709 F.2d at 223–24. This requirement is satisfied by the evidence that both the firm and the Markoff practice coordinated the commission of multiple predicate offenses, and continued to provide legitimate services during the period in which they were engaged in racketeering activities. Thus, the evidence introduced at each trial supports the juries' determinations that the three elements of the enterprise requirement were established.

The appellants, however, also argue that the government failed to allege and establish a RICO enterprise consistent with the definition contained in Section 1961(4). Specifically, they argue that under Section 1961(4), an association in fact between two legal entities, like a law firm and a medical practice, is not a RICO enterprise. As noted above, Section 1961(4) defines an "enterprise" as "any individual, partnership, corporation, association, or other legal entity, and any union or group of individuals associated in fact although not a legal entity." 18 U.S.C. § 1961(4). According to the appellants' construction of this section, "[a]n enterprise can be either a legal entity or an association-in-fact between non-legal entities," but not an association in fact between legal entities.

As the government points out, we rejected this restrictive definition of a RICO enterprise in United States v. Aimone, 715 F.2d 822, 828 (3d Cir.1983). *Aimone* involved a challenge to an indictment alleging the existence of an enterprise composed of "a group of individuals and a corporation associated in fact." *Id.* Like the appellants in this case, the appellants in Aimone argued that an enterprise could consist of either a legal entity or an association in fact, but not both. *Id.* We held that the indictment charged "a proper statutory enterprise" because an association in fact could be composed of legal as well as non-legal entities. *Id.* * * * Accordingly, the association in fact between the law firm and Markoff's medical practice constitutes a RICO enterprise under Section 1961(4).

Notes

There is a split in the courts of appeals on the issue whether an enterprise must be an ascertainable structure separate from the pattern of racketeering activity. The majority of jurisdictions, including the Third Circuit, require that the enterprise have a distinct structure. The Second and Eleventh Circuits hold that an enterprise may consist of nothing more than the sum of the predicate acts.

Consider the following rationale for the minority view from United States v. Cagnina, 697 F.2d 915, 920–21 (11th Cir.1983). Note the reliance on the Ninth Circuit precedent.

"Cagnina claims that the evidence was insufficient to support his RICO convictions because it failed to establish the existence of an "enterprise" within the meaning of the RICO statute. He contends that a RICO "enterprise" must possess an "ascertainable structure" distinct from that inherent in the conduct of a pattern of racketeering activity, while the evidence here shows only "individuals associated together for sporadic crime."

"Both the law and the facts of this case defeat Cagnina's argument. Although the Government must prove both an enterprise and a pattern of racketeering activity, it has done both in this case. As to the law, United States v. Turkette, 452 U.S. 576 (1981), which held that a RICO enterprise could be engaged solely in illegitimate activity, discounted the argument that such a holding would fuse the enterprise with the pattern of racketeering activity. The Court stated:

> That a wholly criminal enterprise comes within the ambit of the statute does not mean that a "pattern of racketeering activity" is an "enterprise." In order to secure a conviction under RICO, the Government must prove both the existence of an "enterprise" and the connected "pattern of racketeering activity." The enterprise is an entity, for present purposes a group of persons associated together for a common purpose of engaging in a course of conduct. The pattern of racketeering activity is, on the other hand, a series of criminal acts as defined by the statute [citation omitted]. The former is proved by evidence of an ongoing organization, formal or informal, and by evidence that the various associates function as a continuing unit. The latter is proved by evidence of the requisite number of acts of racketeering committed by the participants in the enterprise. While the proof used to establish these separate elements may in particular cases coalesce, proof of one does not necessarily establish the other.

452 U.S. at 583.

"This Circuit has interpreted 'enterprise' to include an informal criminal network engaged in racketeering activity, such as the association of Cagnina and his colleagues. In United States v. Elliott, 571 F.2d 880 (5th Cir.1978), the Court held that a group of persons who had committed a variety of unrelated offenses with no agreement as to any particular crime could be convicted of a RICO offense, because they were associated for the purpose of making money from repeated criminal activity. The Court stated that RICO reaches any group of individuals 'whose association, however loose or informal, furnishes a vehicle for the commission of two or more predicate crimes.... There is no distinction, for 'enterprise' purposes, between a duly formed corporation that elects officers and holds annual meetings and an amoeba-like infra-structure that controls a secret criminal network.' 571 F.2d at 898. *Elliott* was consistently followed in this Circuit before the Supreme Court's decision in *Turkette*.

"Contrary to Cagnina's argument, *Turkette* does not prevent this Court from adhering to *Elliott*. *Elliott* has been cited with approval in this Circuit after *Turkette*. *Turkette* did not suggest that the enterprise must have a distinct, formalized structure. Instead, the Supreme Court noted that the organization may be formal or informal. Although both an enterprise and a pattern of racketeering activity must be shown, the Court noted that the proof used to establish the two elements may in particular cases coalesce.

"We recognize that the Eighth Circuit has held that a RICO enterprise must possess an 'ascertainable structure' distinct from the association necessary to conduct a pattern of racketeering activity. United States v. Anderson, 626 F.2d 1358, 1372 (8th Cir.1980). In *Anderson*, the court expressly acknowledged that its position was contrary to *Elliott*. 626 F.2d at 1372.

"Other courts have rejected the assertion that the Government must submit proof of an enterprise distinct from the evidence showing a pattern of racketeering. *See* United States v. De Rosa, 670 F.2d 889, 895–96 (9th Cir.1982) (evidence of a lengthy association between defendants, and payments for introduction to narcotics sources and for permission to distribute illegal drugs was sufficient to show enterprise); United States v. Bagnariol, 665 F.2d 877, 890–91 (9th Cir.1981) ('the government is not precluded from using the same evidence to establish the element of an enterprise and the element of a pattern of racketeering activity')."

* * *

Consider the following analysis by the Ninth Circuit in Chang v. Chen, 80 F.3d 1293 (9th Cir.1996) when it opted to follow the majority approach:

"This appeal raises the issue whether the Supreme Court's decision in United States v. Turkette, 452 U.S. 576 (1981), requires a RICO enterprise to have an ascertainable structure separate and apart from that inherent in the pattern of racketeering activity, or whether *Turkette* permits a RICO enterprise to be no more than the sum of the predicate racketeering acts. We hold that a RICO enterprise must have an ascertainable structure separate and apart from the structure inherent in the conduct of the pattern of racketeering activity.

* * *

"*Turkette* does not specify how much structure an organization must have to be an enterprise under RICO. This issue has divided the circuit courts that have considered it. Six circuits have interpreted the Supreme Court's decision in *Turkette* to require a RICO enterprise to have an ascertainable structure separate and apart from the pattern of racketeering activity in which it engages.[j]

"The six circuits that utilize this majority interpretation of the enterprise element have expressed concern that an overly broad construction of the term 'enterprise' would render that element of the offense interchangeable with the 'pattern of racketeering' element. These circuits relied, in part, on language in the *Turkette* decision to justify their interpretation. In *Turkette*, the Court stated that '[t]he 'enterprise' is not the 'pattern of racketeering activity'; it is an entity separate and apart from the pattern of activity in which it engages.' *Turkette*, 452 U.S. at 583.

"In contrast, two circuits have interpreted *Turkette* to permit the organization constituting the enterprise to be no more than the sum of the predicate racketeering acts.[k] The two circuits that adhere to this minority view of the enterprise element also relied, in part, upon

---

j. *See* United States v. Riccobene, 709 F.2d 214, 223–24 (3d Cir.1983) (as amended); United States v. Tillett, 763 F.2d 628, 632 (4th Cir.1985); Atkinson v. Anadarko Bank and Trust Co., 808 F.2d 438, 441 (5th Cir.1987) (per curiam); Richmond v. Nationwide Cassel L.P., 52 F.3d 640, 645 (7th Cir.1995); United States v. Bledsoe, 674 F.2d 647, 665 (8th Cir.1982); United States v. Sanders, 928 F.2d 940, 944 (10th Cir. 1991).

k. See United States v. Bagaric, 706 F.2d 42, 55 (2d Cir.1983); United States v. Cagnina, 697 F.2d 915, 921 (11th Cir.1983).

language in the *Turkette* decision to justify their interpretation. Specifically, in *Turkette*, the Supreme Court stated that the proof used to establish the existence of an enterprise 'may in particular cases coalesce' with the proof used to establish the pattern of racketeering activity.

"The Ninth Circuit has not yet resolved how much structure RICO's enterprise element requires.

"District courts in the Ninth Circuit, however, have been fairly consistent in applying the majority interpretation to determine whether a RICO enterprise existed.

"We now adopt the majority interpretation of the enterprise element, which requires the organization, formal or informal, to be 'an entity separate and apart from the pattern of [racketeering] activity in which it engages.' *Turkette*, 452 U.S. at 583.

"We agree with the reasons set forth by Judge Rymer in Allington v. Carpenter, 619 F.Supp. 474, 479 (C.D.Cal.1985), for rejecting the minority interpretation of the enterprise element. First, adoption of the minority approach effectively would render the enterprise element superfluous, because under that view every 'pattern of racketeering activity' becomes an 'enterprise' whose affairs are conducted through the 'pattern of racketeering activity.' Such a result would be 'incongruous given the centrality of the 'enterprise' element in the statutory scheme.'

"Second, adoption of the minority approach would strip RICO of its focus on 'organized' crime by ignoring 'the organizational nexus at the heart of the RICO scheme.' 'The statute was directed at 'organized' crime, which, unlike individual and group crime, has access to resources that pose a special threat to legitimate business.' *Id.*

"Finally, adoption of the minority approach would permit proof of a conspiracy to satisfy the enterprise element of § 1962(c). This, in turn, would render § 1962(d), which makes it unlawful to conspire to violate § 1962(c), a proscription of conspiracies to conspire. 'Because RICO does not require proof of a single agreement as in [the standard 18 U.S.C. § 371] conspiracy case, [the minority approach] creates a danger of guilt by association.' [citations omitted]

"A comparison of the severe penalties and remedies authorized by RICO with those for section 371 conspiracy indicates that RICO 'must have been directed at participation in enterprises consisting of more than simple conspiracies to perpetrate the predicate acts of racketeering.' Compare 18 U.S.C. § 1963(a) (fine up to $25,000 or imprisonment up to 20 years or both) and 18 U.S.C. § 1964(c) (allowing for treble damages and reasonable attorney's fees in civil actions) with 18 U.S.C. § 371 (prior to 1994 amendment) (5 years imprisonment and maximum fine of $10,000). Further, under the minority approach, RICO's greater punishment could only be explained by its requirement of two predicate acts. That construction would render RICO nothing more than a tool for punishing recidivists. Such could not have been Congress' intent, because RICO explicitly provided for heightened punishment of repeat offenders."

* * *

Which view do you find more persuasive?

The next case, Burdett v. Miller, 957 F.2d 1375 (7th Cir.1992), provides an apt example of why careful "lawyering" is needed in RICO cases. The United States Court of Appeals for the Seventh Circuit found that an enterprise existed but that the plaintiff had not adequately pled her case.

BURDETT v. MILLER

United States Court of Appeals, Seventh Circuit, 1992.
957 F.2d 1375.

POSNER, CIRCUIT JUDGE.

Patricia Burdett sued Robert Miller, charging a violation of the RICO statute (Racketeer Influenced and Corrupt Organizations, 18 U.S.C. § 1962) and, in a pendent count, a breach of fiduciary duty under Illinois law. After a bench trial, the district judge awarded Burdett damages in excess of $600,000 (after trebling), and later an attorney's fee of some $125,000. Miller challenges both awards.

Burdett is a sales representative for a typography firm and a highly successful salesperson, but she is unsophisticated about investing and her modest stock portfolio is managed by her stock broker. Miller is a certified public accountant, a professor of accounting at Northwestern University, and the owner of his own accounting firm. Burdett and Miller met and became friends in 1979 when Burdett enrolled in a course that Miller taught. She hired him to prepare her income tax returns. They would have lunch occasionally and discuss both business and personal matters. In 1983 Burdett's income soared to $200,000 and she asked Miller for advice on how she might minimize the tax bite. He made a number of suggestions, including that she invest in tax shelters. In the ensuing two years he steered her to a series of shelters sponsored by corporations controlled by three acquaintances of his, Mark George, Tim McDonald, and Tom Fox. When advising her to invest in the first of these ventures he did not tell her that it was the group's first venture, that investment units in it would be unmarketable, and that the two units he was urging her to buy (at $10,000 apiece) represented a third of the total investment in the project. She not only bought the two units but at his further urging executed a promissory note for $20,000 to the tax shelter, secured by a letter of credit that she obtained from a bank; he assured her that she would never be asked to make good on the letter of credit. She received no prospectus or other written information about the project. The other ventures were broadly similar, though in one Miller sold Burdett his own shares without disclosing that he was the owner. The house of cards collapsed in 1986. George, McDonald, and Fox fled to Canada. Burdett's investment in all the ventures was wiped out, and in addition she was forced to make good on the letter of credit. She lost a total of $200,000 before subtracting the tax benefits that the tax shelters generated for her and the tax savings that she obtained by being able to write off the losses from the fraud against her income.

The RICO statute forbids persons associated with an enterprise to conduct, or conspire to conduct, that enterprise's affairs through a pattern of "racketeering activity," defined as the commission of two or more violations of any of a number of specified statutes, including federal securities statutes. Burdett's complaint charged Miller with having conducted the affairs of an enterprise defined as Miller plus his accounting firm through a pattern of racketeering activity consisting of misleading statements and omissions that violated federal securities laws. The district judge found, however, that while Miller and his three associates, George, McDonald, and Fox, had indeed committed numerous violations of those laws, the accounting firm had not been involved in the shenanigans at all, so that there was no "enterprise" consisting of Miller and his firm of which it could be said that Miller had conducted the enterprise's activities through a pattern of racketeering activity. Burdett does not challenge this finding. The judge went on, however, to find that Miller plus his three associates in the fraud constituted a RICO enterprise the affairs of which Miller had conspired to conduct through a pattern of racketeering activity consisting of the securities violations.

Miller argues that there is insufficient evidence that the four individuals were leagued in an "enterprise" within the meaning of the statute. They may have conspired to defraud Burdett, but not every conspiracy is an enterprise. That is true, but there was enough evidence of structure to justify a finding of an informal enterprise. The statute is aimed not only at formal enterprises such as corporations, labor unions, and government departments controlled by racketeers (in the special sense that the statute gives this term) but also at criminal gangs, which have a less formal, a less reticulated and differentiated structure. There must be some structure, to distinguish an enterprise from a mere conspiracy, but there need not be much. Here that structure is supplied by the continuity of the informal enterprise—it was not an ad hoc affair but persisted as an identifiable entity through time—and by the differentiation of roles within it. Miller acted as the respectable front man to enlist the mark, Patricia Burdett, while the other three created and operated over a period of two years a series of tax shelters designed to separate the mark from her money. The enterprise so constituted resembled the informal enterprise between a criminal defense lawyer and local police officials that we held sufficient for RICO liability in United States v. Masters, 924 F.2d 1362, 1367 (7th Cir.1991).

But we agree with Miller that the enterprise was injected into the litigation too late. The complaint specified an enterprise consisting of Miller and his accounting firm. So did the pretrial order and the pretrial briefs. Of course much evidence came in during the trial concerning the dealings between Miller and his three associates, because Miller was charged with conspiring with them to conduct the enterprise consisting of himself and his firm through a pattern of racketeering activity. But there was no mention of an enterprise consisting of the four conspirators themselves. And no motion to amend the pleadings. Burdett moved for a directed finding of liability on the RICO count; the motion did not mention the new enterprise. The district judge did not permit closing argument or post-trial briefs, so the issue couldn't come in at that stage. In fact the enterprise was not changed until the district judge, after the trial, on her own initiative dropped a footnote to that effect in the opinion announcing her findings of fact and conclusions of law.

That was too late. It is true that when "issues not raised by the pleadings are tried by express or implied consent of the parties, they shall be treated in all respects as if they had been raised in the pleadings." Fed.R.Civ.P. 15(b). This is so even if there is no motion to amend the pleadings; indeed, that's the point of Rule 15(b). The key word, however, is "consent." The district judge inferred the parties' consent from the fact that both had presented extensive evidence concerning Miller's connection with George, McDonald, and Fox. But that presentation was not a manifestation of consent to a charge that the four were leagued in an enterprise. Miller had no warning that evidence manifestly admissible because relevant to the conspiracy charge would also be used to establish the existence of an enterprise to which no one in the course of this litigation had alluded.

Ours is an adversarial system; the judge looks to the parties to frame the issues for trial and judgment. Our busy district judges do not have the time to play the "proactive" role of a Continental European judge. True, they want to do justice as well as merely umpire disputes, and they should not be criticized when they point out to counsel a line of argument or inquiry that he has overlooked, although they are not obliged to do so and (with immaterial exceptions) they may not do so when an issue has been waived. When the unfolding evidence persuaded the district judge that the plaintiff's counsel had misidentified the RICO enterprise, she could without impropriety have invited him to shift the line of his attack, and if he had taken up the invitation the defendant could have sought to parry the attack. The judge did not do this but instead changed the plaintiff's theory of the case after the time had passed for the defendant to present contrary evidence.

Burdett argues that the error was harmless because the proof of the four-man enterprise is conclusive. It is not. So informal an enterprise as the judge found here is at the limit of RICO's reach, and Miller might have presented convincing evidence that the alleged "enterprise" lacked even the minimum structure that the judge inferred from evidence not directed to the issue because it wasn't an issue.

Burdett quite properly does not argue that if the judge erred in changing the enterprise the remedy should be a new trial rather than judgment for the defendant. Save within the dispensation of Rule 15(b) and other provisions of law not cited to us, a plaintiff who fails at trial to prove an essential element of his case may not retry the case on a different theory. Burdett does not argue that the judge was wrong to reject an enterprise consisting of Miller and his accounting firm, so that route to establishing a RICO violation is closed too.

This does not end the appeal, because the district judge also found that Miller had violated a fiduciary duty to Burdett imposed on him by Illinois law by giving her deliberately misleading investment advice. A fiduciary duty is the duty of an agent to treat his principal with the utmost candor, rectitude, care, loyalty, and good faith—in fact to treat the principal as well as the agent would treat himself. The common law imposes that duty when the disparity between the parties in knowledge or power relevant to the performance of an undertaking is so vast that it is a reasonable inference that had the parties in advance negotiated expressly over the issue they would have agreed that the agent owed the principal the high duty that we have described, because otherwise the principal would be placing himself at the agent's mercy. An example is the relation between a guardian and his minor ward, or a lawyer and his client. The ward, the client, is in no position to supervise or control the actions of his principal on his behalf; he must take those actions on trust; the fiduciary principle is designed to prevent that trust from being misplaced.

We have given two examples of categories of relations in which fiduciary duties are imposed (lawyer-client, guardian-ward), and the relation between an investment advisor and the people he advises is not a third. But fiduciary duties are sometimes imposed on an ad hoc basis. If a person solicits another to trust him in matters in which he represents himself to be expert as well as trustworthy and the other is not expert and accepts the offer and reposes complete trust in him, a fiduciary relation is established.

We have emphasized knowledge and expertise but we do not mean to suggest that every expert is automatically a fiduciary. That is not the law in Illinois or anywhere else. A fiduciary relation arises only if "one person has reposed trust and confidence in another who thereby gains influence and superiority over the other." Amendola v. Bayer, 907 F.2d 760, 763 (7th Cir.1990). One source of such an ascendancy, however—a source conspicuous in the lawyer-client relation—is that the agent has (or claims to have) expert knowledge the deployment of which the principal cannot monitor. Miller cultivated a relation of trust with Burdett over a period of years, holding himself out as an expert in a field (investments) in which she was inexperienced and unsophisticated. He knew that she took his advice uncritically and unquestioningly and that she sought no "second opinion" or even—until the end, when at last her suspicions were aroused—any documentary confirmation of the investments to which he steered her.

Miller could have protected himself from being deemed a fiduciary by explaining the character and circumstances of the investments to Burdett, by disclosing his stake in them to her, by seeing to it that she received prospectuses and other documents describing the risks of the investments, and if need be by advising her to seek additional investment counsel before staking large sums on these risky ventures. He did none of these things. It is true that he did not ask her simply to sign over all her wealth to him to be invested in his sole discretion. But the district court was entitled to find that he did the next best thing from his standpoint (and in doing so brought himself within the orbit of fiduciary duty). That was to invite her to accept his advice with no questions asked or answered, in reliance on his professional and professorial status, on his insight into the arcana of tax shelter investments—a technical area about which she was ignorant—and on a continuing business relationship shading into a social friendship.

We cannot say that in finding a fiduciary relation the district judge committed a clear error. Actually she did commit one clear error on the fiduciary count, and that was to apply the normal civil standard of preponderance of the evidence, rather than the higher standard of proof—proof by clear and convincing evidence—that Illinois requires to establish the existence of a fiduciary duty outside of the per se categories such as lawyer-client and guardian-ward. But Miller waived the error in the district court by failing to ask the judge for the higher standard. The normal standard of proof in a civil case is, of course, proof by a preponderance of the evidence, not proof by clear and convincing evidence. (Even many fraud cases are governed by the normal standard.) A federal district judge cannot be presumed to carry around in his head every esoteric rule of the law of the state in which he happens to sit. If the parties do not mention the standard of proof in a civil case, the district judge is bound to apply the normal civil standard, just as he will apply the substantive law of the forum state if the case is a diversity case and neither party argues choice of law. The preponderance standard, and the forum state's substantive law, are the default rules to be applied in such situations in the absence of objection. And that is what happened here. The parties did not mention the burden of proof in any of their filings in the district court; the pretrial order didn't mention it; so naturally the judge applied the preponderance standard.

Even in Miller's brief in this court there is no suggestion that the judge applied the wrong standard. The brief does remark in passing that the evidence for a fiduciary relation was not clear and convincing, but does not acknowledge that the judge applied a different standard. Miller's lawyer may not have believed that there was a practical difference between preponderance and clear and convincing in the circumstances of this case, although in many cases the difference is critical. Nothing in his brief save the bare mention of the clear and convincing standard indicates such a belief, and we do not think that that glancing reference was enough to preserve the issue, or to alert the other side that it must argue that the issue had indeed been waived in the district court in order to avoid being found to have waived the waiver issue. We think the parties must be taken to have consented to having the trial conducted and findings made under the usual standard. It would have been better had the judge allowed closing argument or post-trial briefs, for then Miller would have had another opportunity to point out that the judge should apply the higher standard of proof in evaluating the evidence. Yet he does not argue that he would have mentioned it. In fact it seems that the parties were oblivious to the issue throughout the trial.

* * *

The judgment is reversed with directions to enter judgment for the defendant on the RICO count, vacate the award of attorneys' fees, and conduct further proceedings consistent with this opinion on the damages to which the plaintiff is entitled for the defendant's breach of his fiduciary duty to her.

Notes

1. If you represented Burdett in the above action, exactly what would you have done differently, and when?

2. Recall rules of civil procedure: could Miller have obtained removal of the action to Illinois state courts after the District Court dismissed the RICO claim. Why or why not?

2. PATTERN

A defendant must engage in "pattern" of racketeering activity before there is a RICO offense or cause of action. The courts of appeals struggled to define "pattern," culminating in a split among the circuits. In the next case, H. J. Inc. v. Northwestern Bell Telephone Company, 492 U.S. 229 (1989), the Supreme Court resolved the split and set forth guidance as to when a "pattern" of racketeering activity is present.

H.J. INC. v. NORTHWESTERN BELL TELEPHONE COMPANY
United States Supreme Court, 1989.
492 U.S. 229.

BRENNAN, JUSTICE.

* * *

Petitioners, customers of respondent Northwestern Bell Telephone Co., filed this putative class action in 1986 in the District Court for the District of Minnesota. Petitioners alleged violations of 18 U.S.C. §§ 1962(a), (b), (c), and (d) by Northwestern Bell and the other respondents—some of the telephone company's officers and employees, various members of the Minnesota Public Utilities Commission (MPUC) and other unnamed individuals and corporations—and sought an injunction and treble damages under RICO's civil liability provisions, §§ 1964(a) and (c).

The MPUC is the state body responsible for determining the rates that Northwestern Bell may charge. Petitioners' five-count complaint alleged that between 1980 and 1986 Northwestern Bell sought to influence members of the MPUC in the performance of their duties—and in fact caused them to approve rates for the company in excess of a fair and

reasonable amount—by making cash payments to commissioners, negotiating with them regarding future employment, and paying for parties
and meals, for tickets to sporting events and the like, and for airline
tickets. Based upon these factual allegations, petitioners alleged in their
first count a pendent state-law claim, asserting that Northwestern Bell
violated the Minnesota bribery statute, *Minn.Stat.* § 609.42 (1988), as
well as state common law prohibiting bribery. They also raised four
separate claims under § 1962 of RICO. Count II alleged that, in violation
of § 1962(a), Northwestern Bell derived income from a pattern of
racketeering activity involving predicate acts of bribery and used this
income to engage in its business as an interstate "enterprise." Count III
claimed a violation of § 1962(b), in that, through this same pattern of
racketeering activity, respondents acquired an interest in or control of
the MPUC, which was also an interstate "enterprise." In Count IV,
petitioners asserted that respondents participated in the conduct and
affairs of the MPUC through this pattern of racketeering activity,
contrary to § 1962(c). Finally, Count V alleged that respondents conspired together to violate § 1962(a), (b), and (c), thereby contravening
§ 1962(d).

The District Court granted respondents' Federal Rule of Civil Procedure 12(b)(6) motion, dismissing the complaint for failure to state a
claim upon which relief could be granted. The Court found that "[e]ach
of the fraudulent acts alleged by [petitioners] was committed in furtherance of a single scheme to influence MPUC commissioners to the
detriment of Northwestern Bell's ratepayers." It held that dismissal was
therefore mandated by the Court of Appeals for the Eighth Circuit's
decision in Superior Oil Co. v. Fulmer, 785 F.2d 252 (1986), which the
District Court interpreted as adopting an "extremely restrictive" test for
a pattern of racketeering activity that required proof of "multiple illegal
schemes." The Court of Appeals for the Eighth Circuit affirmed the
dismissal of petitioners' complaint, confirming that under Eighth Circuit
precedent "[a] single fraudulent effort or scheme is insufficient" to
establish a pattern of racketeering activity, and agreeing with the
District Court that petitioners' complaint alleged only a single scheme.
Two members of the panel suggested in separate concurrences, however,
that the Court of Appeals should reconsider its test for a RICO pattern.
Most Courts of Appeals have rejected the Eighth Circuit's interpretation
of RICO's pattern concept to require an allegation and proof of multiple
schemes, and we granted certiorari to resolve this conflict. We now
reverse.

[The Court then referred to the lower courts' many attempts to
explain the "pattern" requirement and noted that interpreting this term
was "a task [the Supreme Court] must undertake in order to decide this
case." It began its analysis with the text of the RICO statute.]

We begin, of course, with RICO's text, in which Congress followed a
"pattern [of] utilizing terms and concepts of breadth." Russello v.
United States, 464 U.S. 16, 21 (1983). As we remarked in Sedima,
S.P.R.L. v. Imrex Co., 473 U.S. 479 (1985), the section of the statute

headed "definitions," 18 U.S.C. § 1961, does not so much define a pattern of racketeering activity as state a minimum necessary condition for the existence of such a pattern. Unlike other provisions in § 1961 that tell us what various concepts used in the Act "mean," 18 U.S.C. § 1961(5) says of the phrase "pattern of racketeering activity" only that it "requires at least two acts of racketeering activity, one of which occurred after [October 15, 1970] and the last of which occurred within ten years (excluding any period of imprisonment) after the commission of a prior act of racketeering activity." It thus places an outer limit on the concept of a pattern of racketeering activity that is broad indeed.

Section 1961(5) does indicate that Congress envisioned circumstances in which no more than two predicate acts would be necessary to establish a pattern of racketeering—otherwise it would have drawn a narrower boundary to RICO liability, requiring proof of a greater number of predicates. But, at the same time, the statement that a pattern "requires at least" two predicates implies "that while two acts are necessary, they may not be sufficient." *Sedima.*, 473 U.S. at 496. Section 1961(5) concerns only the minimum *number* of predicates necessary to establish a pattern; and it assumes that there is something to a RICO pattern *beyond* simply the number of predicate acts involved. The legislative history bears out this interpretation, for the principal sponsor of the Senate bill expressly indicated that "proof of two acts of racketeering activity, without more, does not establish a pattern." 115 Cong.Rec. 18940 (1970) (statement of Sen. McClellan). Section 1961(5) does not identify, though, these additional prerequisites for establishing the existence of a RICO pattern.

In addition to § 1961(5), there is the key phrase "pattern of racketeering activity" itself, from § 1962, and we must "start with the assumption that the legislative purpose is expressed by the ordinary meaning of the words used." Richards v. United States, 369 U.S. 1, 9 (1962). In normal usage, the word "pattern" here would be taken to require more than just a multiplicity of racketeering predicates. A "pattern" is an "arrangement or order of things or activity," 11 Oxford English Dictionary 357 (2d ed. 1989), and the mere fact that there are a number of predicates is no guarantee that they fall into any arrangement or order. It is not the number of predicates but the relationship that they bear to each other or to some external organizing principle that renders them "ordered" or "arranged." The text of RICO conspicuously fails anywhere to identify, however, forms of relationship or external principles to be used in determining whether racketeering activity falls into a pattern for purposes of the Act.

It is reasonable to infer, from this absence of any textual identification of sorts of pattern that would satisfy § 1962's requirement, in combination with the very relaxed limits to the pattern concept fixed in § 1961(5), that Congress intended to take a flexible approach, and envisaged that a pattern might be demonstrated by reference to a range of different ordering principles or relationships between predicates, within the expansive bounds set. For any more specific guidance as to the meaning of "pattern," we must look past the text to RICO's legislative history, as we have done in prior cases construing the Act.

The legislative history, which we discussed in *Sedima,* shows that Congress indeed had a fairly flexible concept of a pattern in mind. A pattern is not formed by "sporadic activity," and a person cannot "be subjected to the sanctions of Title IX simply for committing two widely separated and isolated criminal offenses." Instead, "[t]he term 'pattern' itself requires the showing of a relationship" between the predicates and of " 'the threat of continuing activity.' ""It is this factor of *continuity plus relationship* which combines to produce a pattern." RICO's legislative history reveals Congress' intent that to prove a pattern of racketeering activity a plaintiff or prosecutor must show that the racketeering predicates are related, and that they amount to or pose a threat of continued criminal activity.

For analytic purposes these two constituents of RICO's pattern requirement must be stated separately, though in practice their proof will often overlap. The element of relatedness is the easier to define, for we may take guidance from a provision elsewhere in the Organized Crime Control Act of 1970 (OCCA), Pub.L. No. 91–452, 84 Stat. 922, of which RICO formed Title IX. OCCA included as Title X the Dangerous Special Offender Sentencing Act, 18 U.S.C. § 3575 et seq. (now partially repealed). Title X provided for enhanced sentences where, among other things, the defendant had committed a prior felony as part of a pattern of criminal conduct or in furtherance of a conspiracy to engage in a pattern of criminal conduct. As we noted in *Sedima,* Congress defined Title X's pattern requirement solely in terms of the *relationship* of the defendant's criminal acts one to another: "[C]riminal conduct forms a pattern if it embraces criminal acts that have the same or similar purposes, results, participants, victims, or methods or commission, or otherwise are interrelated by distinguishing characteristics and are not isolated events." § 3575(e). We have no reason to suppose that Congress had in mind for RICO's pattern of racketeering component any more constrained a notion of the relationships between predicates that would suffice.

RICO's legislative history tells us, however, that the relatedness of racketeering activities is not alone enough to satisfy § 1962's pattern element. To establish a RICO pattern it must also be shown that the predicates themselves amount to, or that they otherwise constitute a threat of, *continuing* racketeering activity. As to this continuity requirement, § 3575(e) is of no assistance. It is this aspect of RICO's pattern element that has spawned the "multiple scheme" test adopted by some lower courts, including the Court of Appeals in this case. 829 F.2d at 650. ("In order to demonstrate the necessary continuity appellants must allege that Northwestern Bell 'had engaged in similar endeavors in the past or that [it was] engaged in other criminal activity.' * * * A single fraudulent effort or scheme is insufficient"). But although proof that a RICO defendant has been involved in multiple criminal schemes would certainly be highly relevant to the inquiry into continuity of the defendant's racketeering activity, it is implausible to suppose that Congress thought continuity might be shown *only* by proof of multiple schemes. The Eighth Circuit's test brings a rigidity to the available methods of proving a pattern that simply is not present in the idea of "continuity" itself; and it does so, moreover, by introducing a concept—the "scheme"—that appears nowhere in the language or legislative history of the Act. We adopt a less inflexible approach that seems to us to derive from a common sense, everyday understanding of RICO's language and Congress' gloss on it. What a plaintiff or prosecutor must prove is continuity of racketeering activity, or its threat, *simpliciter*. This may be done in a variety of ways, thus making it difficult to formulate in the abstract any general test for continuity. We can, however, begin to delineate the requirement.

"Continuity" is both a closed- and open-ended concept, referring either to a closed period of repeated conduct, or to past conduct that by its nature projects into the future with a threat of repetition. It is, in either case, centrally a temporal concept—and particularly so in the RICO context, where *what* must be continuous, RICO's predicate acts or offenses, and the *relationship* these predicates must bear one to another, are distinct requirements. A party alleging a RICO violation may demonstrate continuity over a closed period by proving a series of related predicates extending over a substantial period of time. Predicate acts extending over a few weeks or months and threatening no future criminal conduct do not satisfy this requirement: Congress was concerned in RICO with long-term criminal conduct. Often a RICO action will be brought before continuity can be established in this way. In such cases, liability depends on whether the *threat* of continuity is demonstrated.

Whether the predicates proved establish a threat of continued racketeering activity depends on the specific facts of each case. Without making any claim to cover the field of possibilities—preferring to deal with this issue in the context of concrete factual situations presented for decision—we offer some examples of how this element might be satisfied. A RICO pattern may surely be established if the related predicates themselves involve a distinct threat of long-term racketeering activity, either implicit or explicit. Suppose a hoodlum were to sell "insurance" to a neighborhood's storekeepers to cover them against breakage of their windows, telling his victims he would be reappearing each month to collect the "premium" that would continue their "coverage." Though the number of related predicates involved may be small and they may occur close together in time, the racketeering acts themselves include a specific threat of repetition extending indefinitely into the future, and thus supply the requisite threat of continuity. In other cases, the threat of continuity may be established by showing that the predicate acts or offenses are part of an ongoing entity's regular way of doing business. Thus, the threat of continuity is sufficiently established where the predicates can be attributed to a defendant operating as part of a long-term association that exists for criminal purposes. Such associations include, but extend well beyond, those traditionally grouped under the phrase "organized crime." The continuity requirement is likewise satisfied where it is shown that the predicates are a regular way of conducting defendant's ongoing legitimate business (in the sense that it is not a business that exists for criminal purposes), or of conducting or participating in an ongoing and legitimate RICO "enterprise."

The limits of the relationship and continuity concepts that combine to define a RICO pattern, and the precise methods by which relatedness and continuity or its threat may be proved, cannot be fixed in advance with such clarity that it will always be apparent whether in a particular case a "pattern of racketeering activity" exists. The development of these concepts must await future cases, absent a decision by Congress to revisit RICO to provide clearer guidance as to the Act's intended scope.

Various amici urge that RICO's pattern element should be interpreted more narrowly than as requiring a relationship and continuity in the senses outlined above, so that a defendant's racketeering activities form a pattern only if they are characteristic either of organized crime in the traditional sense, or of an organized-crime-type perpetrator, that is, of an association dedicated to the repeated commission of criminal offenses. Like the Court of Appeals' multiple scheme rule, however, the argument for reading an organized crime limitation into RICO's pattern concept, whatever the merits and demerits of such a limitation as an initial legislative matter, finds no support in the Act's text, and is at odds with the tenor of its legislative history.

* * *

The occasion for Congress' action [in passing RICO] was the perceived need to combat organized crime. But Congress for cogent reasons chose to enact a more general statute, one which, although it had organized crime as its focus, was not limited in application to organized crime. In Title IX, Congress picked out as key to RICO's application broad concepts that might fairly indicate an organized crime connection, but that it fully realized do not either individually or together provide anything approaching a perfect fit with "organized crime." ("It is impossible to draw an effective statute which reaches most of the commercial activities of organized crime, yet does not include offenses commonly committed by persons outside organized crime as well.")

It seems, moreover, highly unlikely that Congress would have intended the pattern requirement to be interpreted by reference to a concept that it had itself rejected for inclusion in the text of RICO at least in part because "it is probably impossible precisely and definitively to define." Congress realized that the stereotypical view of organized crime as consisting in a circumscribed set of illegal activities, such as gambling and prostitution—a view expressed in the definition included in the Omnibus Crime Control and Safe Streets Act, and repeated in the OCCA preamble—was no longer satisfactory because criminal activity had expanded into legitimate enterprises. Title 18 USC § 1961(1), with its very generous definition of "racketeering activity," acknowledges the breakdown of the traditional conception of organized crime, and responds to a new situation in which persons engaged in long-term criminal activity often operate *wholly* within legitimate enterprises. Congress drafted RICO broadly enough to encompass a wide range of criminal activity, taking many different forms and likely to attract a broad array of perpetrators operating in many different ways. It would be counterproductive and a mismeasure of congressional intent now to adopt a narrow construction of the statute's pattern element that would require proof of an organized crime nexus.

As this Court stressed in *Sedima,* in rejecting a pinched construction of RICO's provision for a private civil action, adopted by a lower court because it perceived that RICO's use against non-organized-crime defendants was an "abuse" of the Act, "Congress wanted to reach both 'legitimate' and 'illegitimate' enterprises." Legitimate business "enjoy neither an inherent capacity for criminal activity nor immunity from its consequences"; and, as a result, § 1964(c)'s use "against respected businesses allegedly engaged in a pattern of specifically identified criminal conduct is hardly a sufficient reason for assuming that the provision is being misconstrued." *Id.* If plaintiffs' ability to use RICO against businesses engaged in a pattern of criminal acts is a defect, we said, it is one "inherent in the statute as written," and hence beyond our power to correct. *Id.* RICO may be a poorly drafted statute; but rewriting it is a job for Congress, if it is so inclined, and not for this Court. There is no more room in RICO's "self-consciously expansive language and overall approach" for the imposition of an organized crime limitation that for the "amorphous 'racketeering injury' requirement" we rejected in *Sedima.* We thus decline the invitation to invent a rule that RICO's pattern of racketeering concept requires an allegation and proof of an organized crime nexus.

* * *

Under the analysis we have set forth above, and consistent with allegations in their complaint, petitioners may be able to prove that the multiple predicates alleged constitute "a pattern of racketeering activity," in that they satisfy the requirements of relationship and continuity. The acts of bribery alleged are said to be related by a common purpose, to influence commissioners in carrying out their duties in order to win approval of unfairly and unreasonably high rates for Northwestern Bell. Furthermore, petitioners claim that the racketeering predicates occurred with some frequency over at least a 6–year period, which may be sufficient to satisfy the continuity requirement. Alternatively, a threat of continuity of racketeering activity might be established at trial by showing that the alleged bribes were a regular way of conducting Northwestern Bell's ongoing business, or a regular way of conducting or participating in the conduct of the alleged and ongoing RICO enterprise, the MPUC.

The Court of Appeals thus erred in affirming the District Court's dismissal of petitioners' complaint for failure to plead "a pattern of racketeering activity." The judgement is reversed and the case is remanded for further proceedings consistent with this opinion.

It is so ordered.

SCALIA, J., concurring.

Four Terms ago, in Sedima, S.P.R.L. v. Imrex Co., we gave lower courts the following four clues concerning the meaning of the enigmatic term "pattern of racketeering activity" in [RICO]. First, we stated that the statutory definition of the term in 18 U.S.C. § 1961(5) implies "that while two acts are necessary, they may not be sufficient." *Sedima*. Second, we pointed out that "two isolated acts," "sporadic activity," and "proof of two acts of racketeering activity, without more" would not be enough to constitute a pattern. Third, we quoted a snippet from the legislative history stating "[i]t is this factor of *continuity plus relationship* which combines to produce a pattern." Finally, we directed lower courts' attention to 18 U.S.C. § 3575(e), which defined the term "pattern of conduct which was criminal" used in a different title of the same Act, and instructed them that "[t]his language may be useful in interpreting other sections of the Act." Thus enlightened, the District Courts and Courts of Appeals set out "to develop a meaningful concept of 'pattern,'" and promptly produced the widest and most persistent Circuit split on an issue of federal law in recent memory. Today, four years and countless millions in damages and attorney's fees later (not to mention prison sentences under the criminal provisions of RICO), the Court does little more than repromulgate those hints as to what RICO means, though with the caveat that Congress intended that they be applied using a "flexible approach."

* * *

It is, however, unfair to be so critical of the Court's effort, because I would be unable to provide an interpretation of RICO that gives significantly more guidance concerning its application. It is clear to me from the prologue of the statute, which describes a relatively narrow focus upon "organized crime," that the word "pattern" in the phrase "pattern of racketeering activity" was meant to import some requirement beyond the mere existence of multiple predicate acts. Thus, when § 1961(5) says that a pattern "requires at least two acts of racketeering activity" it is describing what is needful but not sufficient. (If that were not the case, the concept of "pattern" would have been unnecessary, and the statute could simply have attached liability to "multiple acts of racketeering activity"). But what that something more is, is beyond me. As I have suggested, it is also beyond the Court. Today's opinion has added nothing to improve our prior guidance, which has created a kaleidoscope of Circuit positions, except to clarify that RICO may in addition be violated when there is a "threat of continuity." It seems to me this increases rather than removes the vagueness. There is no reason to believe that the Courts of Appeals will be any more unified in the future, then they have in the past, regarding the content of this law.

That situation is bad enough with respect to any statute, but it is intolerable with respect to RICO. For it is not only true, as Justice Marshall commented in *Sedima*, that our interpretation of RICO has "quite simply revolutionize[d] private litigation" and "validate[d] the federalization of broad areas of state common law frauds," *id.*, (dissenting opinion), so that clarity and predictability in RICO's civil applications are particularly important; but it is also true that RICO, since it has criminal applications as well, must, even in its civil applications, possess the degree of certainty required for criminal laws. No constitutional challenge to this law has been raised in the present case, and so that issue is not before us. That the highest Court in the land has been unable to derive from this statute anything more than today's meager guidance bodes ill for the day when that challenge is presented.

However unhelpful its guidance may be, however, I think the Court is correct in saying that nothing in the statute supports the proposition that predicate acts constituting part of a single scheme (or single episode) can never support a cause of action under RICO. Since the Court of Appeals here rested its decision on the contrary proposition, I concur in the judgment of the Court reversing the decision below.

Notes

Is the Supreme Court's clarification of the "pattern" requirement helpful, or is Justice Scalia correct that the Court's effort fails to clarify this element?

2. Upon remand, the customers' RICO action was dismissed on the ground that the action was barred by the "filed rate doctrine." This doctrine:

> "forbids a regulated entity [from charging] rates for its services other than those properly filed with the appropriate federal regulatory authority. * * * The purpose of the filed rate doctrine is to: (1) preserve the regulating agency's authority to determine the reasonableness of rates; and (2) insure that the regulated entities charge only those rates that the agency has approved or been made aware of as the law may require."[l]

The plaintiffs argued that the filed rate doctrine should not apply when there has been a fraud committed on the agency. The Eighth Circuit disagreed, holding that the relevant issue was what "impact a court decision may have on agency procedures and rate determinations."[m] The Eighth Circuit found that a court's decision on the plaintiffs' claims would disrupt the ability of the Minnesota Public Utilities Commission to review and set rates. It therefore dismissed the class action.[n] What do you think about this resolution?

---

l. H. J. Inc. v. Northwestern Bell, 954
F.2d 485, 488 (8th Cir.1992).

m. *Id.* at 489.

n. *Id.*

The next three cases provide examples of applications of *H.J. Inc.* In the first case, Word of Faith World Outreach Center Church, Inc. v. Sawyer, 90 F.3d 118 (5th Cir.1996), the court found that no pattern existed. In the second case, Vild v. Visconsi, 956 F.2d 560 (6th Cir.1992), the court also found, over vigorous dissent, that no pattern existed. In the last case, Uniroyal Goodrich Tire Co. v. Mutual Trading Corp., 63 F.3d 516 (7th Cir.1995), the court found that a pattern existed. As you read these cases, see if you can get a sense of how one litigates the pattern issue. Focus especially on the facts deemed relevant.

WORD OF FAITH WORLD OUTREACH CENTER CHURCH INC. v. SAWYER

United States Court of Appeals, Fifth Circuit, 1996.
90 F.3d 118.

JONES, CIRCUIT JUDGE.

This lawsuit began as a result of critical television reports on the weekly ABC news program PrimeTime Live concerning Reverend Robert Tilton and Word of Faith World Outreach Center Church. The Church and Word of Faith World Outreach Center Church, Inc. appeal the decision of the district court dismissing their claims against ABC and others who assisted ABC in preparing the shows for violation of the RICO statute and a federal civil rights statute. We affirm.

* * *

The facts are distilled from appellants' pleadings. Word of Faith World Outreach Center Church is a Christian church based in Farmers Branch, Texas, a suburb of Dallas. Robert Tilton is the Church's head pastor, and central to the Church's beliefs is the importance of tithing and making vows to God. The Church teaches that expressions of faith as manifested by financial vows to God, through the Church, are rewarded by God with physical, spiritual, and financial prosperity. At the peak of the Church's popularity, approximately 8,000 people regularly attended services, with an additional national television audience estimated in the hundreds of thousands.

In addition to weekly services and television broadcasts, the Church on a regular basis mails items of correspondence to members who have asked that their names be placed on the Church's mailing list. Often, these mailings include materials that the member can return to the Church in an enclosed preaddressed envelope, such as a prayer cloth or prayer request, and which Reverend Tilton has promised to pray over. The Church classifies mail returned as a result of these mailings as "regular mail." The Church also routinely receives unsolicited pieces of mail, known by the Church as "white mail."

In the spring of 1991, journalists working for ABC's weekly news program PrimeTime Live ("PrimeTime") began an investigation of Tilton. PrimeTime's investigation was aided by Ole Anthony and others affiliated with the Trinity Foundation, Inc., a non-profit corporation founded by Anthony for the purpose of supporting Christ centered communication projects. Anthony is passionately opposed to some televangelists, including Tilton.

On November 21, 1991, PrimeTime broadcast a report concerning three televangelists, including Tilton, that was highly critical of Tilton and his fund-raising practices. A week later, PrimeTime broadcast a brief update reporting reactions to the November 21 broadcast. On July 9, 1992, the original November 21 program was rebroadcast, with certain minor changes, together with a follow-up report. PrimeTime's ratings, which had been low, significantly improved following the Tilton broadcast.

The theme of the broadcasts was that Tilton personally acquired millions of dollars of donations sent to the Church, and that he never prayed over thousands of prayer requests. PrimeTime's claim that Tilton failed to pray over the prayer requests derived from prayer requests purportedly found during "trash sweeps" conducted by persons affiliated with the Trinity Foundation at the direction of ABC representatives.

The Church disputes PrimeTime's claim that prayer requests where thrown away before the promised prayers by Tilton. As evidence, the Church points to its sophisticated document and financial accounting system which accounts for every piece of mail received and its contents. This system involves a bank and a mail-handling contractor, and the Church asserts that it can establish that none of the prayer requests reportedly found in the trash could have been found at the times and places claimed by those who carried out the "trash sweeps." Instead, the Church claims, the items depicted in the trash consist of: (1) Church mailings received directly by ABC operatives who had placed their names on the Church's mailing lists, and which were never mailed back to the Church; (2) items obtained from the Church by the defendants while attending worship services, and which also were never mailed back to the Church; (3) "regular mail" and other items stolen by the defendants from the bank and mail-handling contractor; and (4) "white mail" stolen from either the bank or the Church.

Following the broadcast, Church membership and financial giving dropped sharply. This, in turn, required the Church to close its television ministry and reduce its outreach ministry. Additionally, since the PrimeTime broadcasts, the Church has been investigated by numerous local, state, and federal authorities.

In November 1993, the Church brought suit on behalf of its members against Capital Cities/ABC, Inc., Diane Sawyer, co-anchor of PrimeTime, the Trinity Foundation, Ole Anthony, and several other business entities and persons associated with the broadcasts. The Church alleged that through a pattern of racketeering acts ABC and the other defendants sought to drive the Church out of business. The alleged racketeering acts included interstate transportation of stolen computer disks; theft of donations, Church mail, and other Church property by certain defendants or by bank, mail-handling, or Church employees who had been persuaded to help the defendants; wire fraud in the form of false statements made during broadcasts; a scheme to deprive the Church, its bank, its mail-handling contractor, and its law firm of the honest services of its loyal employees; and obstruction of justice. * * *

All defendants moved to dismiss for failure to state a claim upon which relief can be granted. The district court granted the motions, finding that the Church failed to plead a pattern of racketeering activity * * *. The Church appeals.

* * *

The Church alleges the defendants violated 18 U.S.C. § 1962(c) and (d) of the Racketeer Influence and Corrupt Organization Act (RICO), * * *

The central issue on appeal is whether the Church sufficiently pled a "pattern of racketeering activity." "Racketeering activity" consists of two or more predicate offenses, defined by the statute to include acts violating federal wire or mail fraud statutes. To establish a pattern of racketeering activity, the Supreme Court explained in H.J. Inc. v. Northwestern Bell Telephone Co., 492 U.S. 229 (1989), that a plaintiff "must show that the racketeering predicates are *related*, and that they amount to or pose a threat of continued criminal activity." *Id.* at 239 (emphasis added). The element of relatedness is established if the acts have the "same or similar purposes, results, participants, victims, or methods of commission." *Id.* at 240. To establish continuity, plaintiffs must prove "continuity of racketeering activity, or its threat." *Id.* at 241. This may be shown by either a closed period of repeated conduct, or an open-ended period of conduct that "by its nature projects into the future with a threat of repetition." *Id.* at 241. A closed period of conduct may be demonstrated "by proving a series of related predicates extending over a substantial period of time." *Id.* at 242. An open period of conduct involves the establishment of "a threat of continued racketeering activity." *Id.* This may be shown where there exists a "specific threat of repetition extending indefinitely into the future," or "where it is shown that the predicates are a regular way of conducting defendant's ongoing legitimate business." *Id.* at 242–43. The Court stated that in enacting RICO, Congress was concerned with "long-term criminal conduct." *Id.* at 242.

Defendants do not contest the "relatedness" element of the "pattern of racketeering" requirement. Issue is joined by the parties over the continuity of ABC's alleged conduct: the Church contends it pled both a closed period of conduct and an open period of conduct as described in H.J. Inc. We disagree, as three of this court's precedents foreclose the establishment of continuity.

In the first case, a doctor alleged that during the course of a lawsuit with an insurance company over payment of claims, the insurance company and others committed many fraudulent acts, including sending letters to other insurers to dissuade them from paying on the doctor's claims; creating a company to generate negative reviews of the doctor's methods of treatments; and "goading" government agencies into investigating the doctor. In re Burzynski, 989 F.2d 733 (5th Cir.1993). This court concluded that the doctor failed to plead the continuity element of a "pattern of racketeering":

> All of the alleged predicate acts took place as part of the *Burzynski I* litigation, which has ended. In [Delta Truck & Tractor, Inc. v. J.I. Case Co., 855 F.2d 241 (5th Cir.1988)], we affirmed the dismissal of a RICO claim where the plaintiff alleged multiple acts of fraud that were part and parcel of a single, discrete and otherwise lawful commercial transaction. In *Delta*, the lawful transaction was a merger; here, it is the defense of a lawsuit—which is now over. The conduct did not constitute or threaten long-term criminal activity.

In re Burzynski, 989 F.2d at 743.

Similarly, in Calcasieu Marine Nat'l Bank v. Grant, 943 F.2d 1453 (5th Cir.1991) the court found a lack of continuity. The plaintiff, Mrs. Grant, sued her former husband for depriving her of her community property interest in a partnership in which he had been an active member. To establish continuity, Mrs. Grant claimed a closed period of conduct. The court held, however, that

> there is no threat here of continued criminal acts. [Mr.] Grant's acts which were alleged to have deprived Mrs. Grant of a property interest were, when completed, without threat of repetition. Short-term criminal conduct is not the concern of RICO.

Calcasieu, 943 F.2d at 1464.

The earliest case that discusses the element of continuity under RICO, albeit before the Supreme Court's decision in *H.J. Inc.*, is *Delta Truck & Tractor, Inc., supra.* Delta Truck, an International Harvester dealer, alleged that International Harvester, J.I. Case Co., and Tenneco, Inc. had committed numerous predicate acts of wire and mail fraud in connection with the acquisition of International Harvester by Case and Tenneco. The district court dismissed the complaint. This court affirmed, focusing on the concept of continuity as incorporated in the enterprise element of RICO. The court stated:

> Delta has attempted to state a RICO claim by alleging multiple acts of fraud that were part and parcel of a single, discrete and otherwise lawful commercial transaction. This claim fails to state a RICO cause of action as a matter of law because the pleadings do not assert that the corporate defendants posed a continuous threat as a RICO person. Delta has alleged as a pattern of racketeering activity nothing more than numerous predicate acts which were necessary segments of an otherwise legitimate and singular commercial endeavor.

Id. at 244.

It is unnecessary to delve into the arcane concepts of closed-end or open-ended continuity under RICO. *Burzynski, Calcasieu,* and *Delta Truck* make clear that where alleged RICO predicate acts are part and parcel of a single, otherwise lawful transaction, a "pattern of racketeering activity" has not been shown. In this case, the alleged predicate acts occurred during the production and airing of PrimeTime broadcasts concerning Tilton and his Church. The alleged acts were all part of a single, lawful endeavor—namely the production of television news reports concerning a particular subject. We agree with the district court that the Church has failed to plead a "continuity of racketeering activity, or its threat." *H.J. Inc.,* 492 U.S. at 241.[4]

The Church alternatively contends that it is ABC's regular pattern of conducting business to use illegal means to further its TV production, citing to newspaper reports and to several lawsuits brought by parties dissatisfied with their portrayal in ABC news programs. However, in the case whose facts are most similar to those present here, the district court found that the plaintiff failed to establish continuity and dismissed the RICO claims. Pleading the mere existence of lawsuits is not the same as pleading the facts that demonstrate predicate illegal acts as the defendant's regular way of doing business. The Church has not in this respect sufficiently alleged a continued threat of illegal activity by ABC.

* * *

Notes

Review footnote 4: If the courts of appeal apply *H.J. Inc.* so differently, how successful was the Supreme Court in giving guidance on the "pattern" requirement?

VILD v. VISCONSI

United States Court of Appeals, Sixth Circuit, 1992.
956 F.2d 560.

WELLFORD, SENIOR CIRCUIT JUDGE.

John Vild, the plaintiff, appeals from the district court's denial of his Fed.R.Civ.P. 59(e) motion to alter or amend an earlier judgment dismissing his RICO complaint and Fed.R.Civ.P. 15(a) motion to amend his RICO complaint. The defendants, various persons involved in a series of real estate enterprises, cross-appeal from the district court's denial of their Fed.R.Civ.P. 11 motion for sanctions against the plaintiff. Put

---

4. The law in other circuits might have allowed this case to proceed further. See Shields Enterprises, Inc. v. First Chicago Corp., 975 F.2d 1290 (7th Cir.1992) (where defendant used extortion every time it wished to accomplish a goal in dealing with plaintiff, a pattern could be shown); Ticor Title Ins. Co. v. Florida, 937 F.2d 447 (9th Cir.1991) (three forgeries within thirteen month period suggests a regular way of conducting business); United States v. Busacca, 936 F.2d 232 (6th Cir.1991) (where defendant misappropriated money whenever an expense was incurred, a pattern was established); Ikuno v. Yip, 912 F.2d 306 (9th Cir.1990) (pattern requirement met with the filing of two allegedly false annual reports). The precedents of this circuit concerning continuity are consistently different from these cases.

simply, Vild tries to convince us that he has properly stated a RICO claim in his complaint or proposed amended complaint, while the defendants maintain that he failed to state a claim, and that his failure should bring about sanctions. We find that the district court did not err when it denied the plaintiff's motions under Rules 15(a) and 59(e), and therefore, we AFFIRM that portion of the decision. * * *

* * *

Plaintiff, an Ohio citizen, sued Dominic Visconsi of Ohio, C.W. and Patricia Sattenfield of Florida, Gerald Plonski of Ohio, and ten other unnamed individuals and several business entities, for alleged violations of RICO, common law fraud, intentional interference with business relationships, conversion, negligence and breach of contract. Vild's allegations arose from a failed scheme in which he was to market interests in the Longboat Bay Club (Club), a real estate resort venture.

In addition to the original complaint, the plaintiff filed, or attempted to file, three amended complaints, the details of which are necessary for a complete understanding of the controversy before us. The plaintiff alleged throughout subject matter jurisdiction under RICO and under 28 U.S.C. § 1332 (diversity of citizenship).

The original complaint alleges that in late January, 1989, defendant C.W. Sattenfield, on behalf of the other named defendants, Dominic Visconsi, Patricia Sattenfield, and Gerald Plonski, contacted the plaintiff by telephone to induce him to sign a marketing agreement to sell real estate interests in the Club. Vild contends that the defendants made material misrepresentations regarding the marketing agreement. He maintains in particular that the defendants represented that there was sufficient start-up capital to begin business operations. Allegedly due to these material misrepresentations, Vild complained that he entered into an exclusive marketing agreement and shortly thereafter signed a note for money advanced to him by defendants to initiate the venture. Vild asserts that the defendants encouraged him to establish the business so that they could later force him out and acquire the enterprise for themselves.

From the outset, the arrangement was a failure. Once the plaintiff entered into the business relationship, C.W. Sattenfield telephoned him seeking to change the terms of the marketing agreement and proposing that the defendants receive "kickbacks" on any interests sold to the public. According to Vild, C.W. Sattenfield made threats to him, his family and to ruin his reputation. When Vild did not comply with the proposed changes, the defendants allegedly refused to provide additional inventory and start-up money.[2] The original complaint also alleges that the defendants refused to compensate Vild for sales made by him under the marketing agreement. Plaintiff maintains that these threats, phone

---

2. Defendants provided $20,000 to the plaintiff, but they did not supply additional funds and inventory allegedly promised un-der an oral agreement. No reference was made to this in the written agreement.

calls, and material misrepresentations all constitute predicate acts under RICO because they are violations of mail fraud, wire fraud and extortion statutes as well as the Hobbs Act.

The original complaint also alleges other predicate acts which are separate and distinct from the previously described scheme to defraud and extort the plaintiff. Vild contends that the defendants used, and continue to use, telephones and facsimile machines to solicit customers in Ohio to purchase interests in the Club. According to Vild, these solicitations constitute wire fraud because the defendants' salespersons are not licensed and registered to do business in Ohio. The plaintiff also alleges that the defendants engaged in, and continue to engage in, mail fraud because they used, and continue to use, letters which technically violate several laws and regulations governing direct mail solicitation in Ohio. For instance, the letters do not contain, as required by law, the odds of winning prizes. They also improperly use the word "sweepstake." Vild further complains that the defendants sent similar letters to potential consumers in Indiana in violation of that state's laws. Plaintiff maintains also that the defendants violated Florida law by fraudulently using real estate contracts which did not contain a mandatory ten-day cancellation provision.

Vild amended his original complaint by introducing several additional defendants, Gerald Plonski and ten unnamed individuals, who allegedly also violated the RICO statute. The plaintiff contends that Plonski, his sales agent, refused to pay him money earned from Club sales because of "kickbacks" to the other defendants. The ten unnamed defendants were alleged officers, directors and shareholders of Sea/Mountain Resorts Inc. (Sea Mountain) established by defendants to market real estate interests in Ohio. These added individual defendants also allegedly engaged in the same type of racketeering, wire and mail fraud activities as the other defendants.

The plaintiff also attempted to file a second amended complaint, but the court denied his motion to amend. The second amended complaint alleges several new predicate acts and introduces a host of additional defendants. The new predicate acts center on the allegedly illegal status of another business entity controlled by the defendants. Vild maintains that Longboat Venture Ltd. (Longboat), the owner of the Club, was prohibited from doing business in Ohio and Florida because its general partner, DVB, Inc. (DVB), failed to maintain its legal corporate status and also failed properly to register to do business. The plaintiff maintains that any solicitations by Longboat accordingly constitute wire and mail fraud.

The second amended complaint also alleges that several new RICO defendants were a part of the illegal enterprise. Vild contends that the defendants' law firm and three lawyers representing defendants fraudulently represented DVB's corporate status and its capacity to do business. One defendant lawyer allegedly sent a letter to the state of Ohio which indicated incorrectly that DVB had good standing in Ohio. Another defendant lawyer allegedly made a similar misrepresentation to the Court of Common Pleas of Cuyahoga County stating that Longboat was a valid limited partnership. Plaintiff's contention is that Longboat was not a valid limited partnership because of DVB's status. These misrepresentations were allegedly intentionally made with knowledge that they were false.

Vild moved to file still another amended complaint, but this motion was denied. The third amended complaint adds very little to the earlier versions. Defendants further committed mail fraud by misrepresenting DVB's status to the State of Florida in order to validate its certificate to do business. The plaintiff also alleges that the defendants committed another RICO predicate act by misrepresenting DVB's status to the State of Ohio during the course of settlement negotiations.

* * *

After Vild filed his first amended complaint, the defendants moved to dismiss the action under Fed.R.Civ.P. 12(b)(6) for failure to state a claim and under Fed.R.Civ.P. 9(b) for failure to allege fraud with particularity. While these motions were pending, the plaintiff requested leave to file his second amended complaint which the court denied.

The next day, the district court granted defendants' motion to dismiss for failure to state a RICO claim because Vild did not allege "a pattern of racketeering activity," as defined by H.J. Inc. v. Northwestern Bell Telephone Co., 492 U.S. 229 (1989).

Without a valid RICO claim, the district court concluded that there was no subject matter jurisdiction. The plaintiff could not invoke 28 U.S.C. § 1332 diversity jurisdiction because he did not show that "each defendant [was] a citizen of a different State from each plaintiff."

* * *

The district court determined that the plaintiff failed to satisfy the continuity prong of the pattern requirement. Although we are prone to agree with the district court that the plaintiff has not alleged a RICO pattern, we reach this conclusion by using a slightly different analysis. The district court did not determine whether the plaintiff fulfilled the relationship prong of the test. We find it necessary to examine the relatedness issue first before arriving at the continuity prong.

The plaintiff may satisfy the relationship requirement if the predicate acts alleged "have the same or similar purposes, results, participants, victims, or methods of commission, or otherwise are interrelated by distinguishing characteristics and are not isolated events." *Id.* at 2901. This "test is not a cumbersome one for a RICO plaintiff," but it sets forth a requirement for a RICO cause of action nevertheless. Feinstein v. Resolution Trust Corp., 942 F.2d 34 (1st Cir.1991).

Here, Vild alleges two types of predicate acts to satisfy RICO's pattern requirement. The first type of conduct involves acts directed at the plaintiff by the defendants. Vild is the alleged victim of fraudulent and unlawful acts which include allegations of mail and wire fraud designed to induce him to enter into the marketing agreement plus allegations of extortion, threats and fraud in the administration of the marketing agreement. These events occurred over the course of a few months. The second type of conduct alleged in the proposed amended complaint involves improprieties by defendants directed at others including ultimate purchasers of real estate interests, the states of Florida, Ohio and Indiana, and an Ohio court. These allegations focus on wire and mail fraud resulting from technical violations of laws regulating direct mail solicitation and marketing, misrepresentations about the status of one of the defendant business entities, and the use of illegal real estate contracts in Florida. The plaintiff maintains that all of these activities, whether directly involving him or others, are related for the purpose of the pattern requirement. We do not agree. Even if the predicates within each of the two types of conduct may be somehow interrelated, the two types of alleged conduct are not related within the meaning of RICO.

Applying the *H.J., Inc.* relationship test, we find that the two types of conduct have distinct and dissimilar "purposes, results, participants, victims, or methods of commission." According to the plaintiff's third amended complaint, the defendants' conduct directed toward him had two purposes—to induce him to sign the marketing agreement and then to force him out of business. The other alleged conduct was directed at ultimate purchasers of the real estate interests. This conduct, violations of laws governing direct mail solicitation and the use of certain illegal contracts in Florida, had, in our view, separate and unrelated purposes. In the case of the direct mail solicitations, the defendants' purpose was to sell real estate interests to purchasers without the use of middlemen such as the plaintiff and to gain a marketing advantage with persons and entities beside plaintiff. None of this conduct had a similar or related purpose of inducing the plaintiff to make a contract with defendants or forcing the plaintiff out of business.

The two types of conduct also had disparate results. The first line of activities resulted in the plaintiff's association with the defendants in a marketing agreement and the eventual demise of the business venture. The second line of conduct was directed toward ultimate purchasers and resulted in unspecified individuals attending sales meetings and perhaps acquiring real estate interests in the Club, Longboat, or some other venture of defendants.

That the two types of conduct were directed at different victims indicates another critical distinction which suggests to us that the alleged illegal acts were unrelated and dissimilar. The plaintiff was the only victim of the threats, extortion and fraud perpetrated with regard to the failed marketing agreement. He alleges no activity directed against anyone in his position. In contrast, ultimate purchasers and the states of Ohio, Florida and Indiana were the alleged victims of the illegal direct mail solicitations and the invalid real estate contracts. The plaintiff was never an ultimate purchaser of real estate interests, and never sought to be a customer or owner of the Club or Longboat. Plaintiff does not come to the court as an innocent purchaser of Florida swampland who was hoodwinked by the fast-talking defendants. He cannot complain about harm to these other persons or any state agency. The plaintiff alleges that the defendants denied him the benefits of a marketing agreement which would, in actuality, have put the plaintiff in the same position as the defendants, vis-a-vis third party purchasers, if the agreement had not been breached. Vild would have been an agent of defendant sellers. The plaintiff sues the defendants because he could not sell real estate interests, as he planned and contracted to do, to ultimate purchasers, the alleged victims of the conduct which the plaintiff now cites as related predicate acts under RICO. We do not hold that a civil RICO plaintiff must necessarily be directly harmed by all the alleged predicate acts, because harm from one enumerated violation may, in certain situations, be sufficiently connected. Our conclusion merely reflects that this plaintiff, under the circumstances of this case, may not use unrelated predicate acts that allegedly may have harmed ultimate purchasers or other third parties not similarly situated to the plaintiff. When Vild complains that he was not allowed to reap the benefits of the injury-causing enterprise, of which he would have been a part, he has failed the relationship test.

* * *

Our conclusion that the two lines of conduct were unrelated is also bolstered by the different "methods of commission" used by the defendants. The allegations regarding the marketing scheme with Vild involved extortion, threats, wire and mail fraud. The other alleged conduct included only alleged mail and wire fraud in the form of illegal telephone, fax and mail communications under consumer protection laws and misrepresentations concerning DVB's corporate status. The claimed violations are technical in nature and would not necessarily preclude purchasers from enforcing contract rights. A mere allegation that the defendants used wire and mail fraud in two otherwise dissimilar schemes does not, under the circumstances, satisfy the relationship prong of the pattern test. We agree that multiple wire and mail fraud allegations "are perhaps unique among the various sorts of 'pattern of racketeering activity.' "U.S. Textiles, Inc. v. Anheuser–Busch Co., 911 F.2d 1261, 1268 (7th Cir.1990). The "number of [mail and wire fraud] offenses is only tangentially related to the underlying fraud, and can be a matter of happenstance" in some instances. We believe this description of "tangentially related" offenses applies in this case. Though the direct mail solicitations may have been part of a concerted plan, we find that the wire and mail fraud offenses perpetrated against the plaintiff during the negotiation and administration of the marketing agreement were, at best, "happenstance," and therefore, unrelated to the other alleged conduct committed against ultimate consumers.

That some of the same participants engaged in both lines of conduct does not alter our conclusion that the predicate acts in the two schemes were unrelated.

We are aware that some cases hold that the relationship test is satisfied by conduct which seems to us to be disconnected or dissimilar. *See e.g.*, Banks v. Wolk, 918 F.2d 418 (3d Cir.1990). In *Banks*, applying a very liberal version of this test, the court determined that the seven episodes were sufficiently related because, among other things, several of the allegations involved breaches of fiduciary duty and attempts to drive down the price of real estate. *Id.* at 425. We construe the relationship prong more narrowly than the Third Circuit did in *Banks*.

GUY, JR., CIRCUIT JUDGE, DISSENTING.

The court concludes that the continuity requirement is not met because the defendants' allegedly fraudulent marketing practices are not related to the conduct involving Vild. Since I believe the two types of alleged conduct are sufficiently related to constitute a pattern of racketeering activity, I respectfully dissent.

* * *

The two types of predicate acts alleged in Vild's complaint meet [*H.J. Inc.*'s] broad test of relatedness because the two schemes have the same participants. This fact distinguishes this case from Feinstein v. Resolution Trust Corp., 942 F.2d 34 (1st Cir.1991). In *Feinstein*, the court held that the two predicate schemes were unrelated as to most of the defendants because only two of the defendants participated in both schemes. However, the court stated that the two schemes were "arguably sufficient to show relatedness with regard to the actions of common participants.... "

Since both sets of Vild's allegations involve the same participants, I would find that his complaint meets the relatedness requirement. Since Vild alleges that the defendants have fraudulently marketed the condominiums to investors for several years, I would also find that the continuity requirement is met. I would therefore reverse the district court's dismissal of Vild's RICO count.

Notes

With whom do you agree, the majority or the dissent?

UNIROYAL GOODRICH TIRE CO. v. MUTUAL TRADING CORPORATION

United States Court of Appeals, Seventh Circuit, 1995.
63 F.3d 516.

BAUER, CIRCUIT JUDGE.

A jury found the defendants (collectively "MTC") liable for civil violations of the Racketeer Influenced and Corrupt Organizations Act ("RICO"), 18 U.S.C. § 1962 et seq., and for violations of various state laws. Uniroyal was also awarded its attorneys' fees and costs incurred in bringing this action. MTC appeals the verdict and the award of fees and costs. It also appeals the trial court's rejection of its counterclaims. Unpersuaded by its arguments, we affirm.

I.

Throughout most of the 1980s, MTC purchased tires from Uniroyal Goodrich ("Uniroyal") and its predecessors and resold them in Saudi Arabia. During the relevant period, Mohammad Shafiq was MTC's president and sole shareholder; John Hauper was MTC's Vice–President. Uniroyal's complaint alleges that MTC bribed a Uniroyal employee in order to induce him into providing MTC with confidential information and into assisting MTC with its plan to defraud Uniroyal. The picture presented by Uniroyal at trial illustrates how this unfolded.

A. The Detroiter Scheme

It became apparent soon after MTC began selling tires in Saudi Arabia that MTC would develop into a significant customer of Goodrich's. Consequently, Goodrich offered MTC the exclusive sale rights to a tire model known as the Detroiter. This opportunity was potentially lucrative because although MTC had two competing Goodrich distributors, it would be alone in selling the Detroiter. To the dismay of its competitors, MTC achieved a significant degree of success with the Detroiter.

In 1986, MTC informed Uniroyal that an entity named Palmer Industries had begun exporting flawed versions of the Detroiter from Mexico into Saudi Arabia. Purchasers of the flawed tires were coming to MTC for refunds, and MTC had paid them. MTC requested that Uniroyal reimburse it.

Uniroyal insisted that MTC substantiate its claim for reimbursement by supplying Uniroyal with a list of the serial numbers for the returned tires. Uniroyal also instructed MTC to hold all the returned tires for Uniroyal's inspection. MTC submitted a list of serial numbers for 4,896 tires which matched Uniroyal's records of blemished tires it had sold in Mexico, and so Uniroyal reimbursed MTC. When Uniroyal representatives went to Saudi Arabia to inspect the tires, however, they were told that the majority of the tires already had been discarded. The tires which remained were not on Uniroyal's list of blemished tires or on MTC's list submitted for reimbursement, nor were they marked with the "appearance imperfect" designation as they should have been. Uniroyal subsequently discovered that the information on MTC's reimbursement list had been compiled from information supplied to MTC by Richard Germano, a Uniroyal pricing administrator. After further investigation, Uniroyal concluded that the claim for reimbursement was fraudulent.

B. The Cooperative Advertising Scheme

Germano furthered MTC's position with Uniroyal in other ways. Uniroyal ran a cooperative advertising program under which Uniroyal would bear a portion of its customers' advertising costs. Germano administered this program for Uniroyal's international customers.

In 1988, with Uniroyal's blessing, MTC decided to enter the tire market in Nigeria. Under Nigerian law, MTC had to conduct business through a domestic entity. MTC selected a company called Multiplex Globe as its Nigerian liaison. Multiplex Globe was owned by Shafiq and MTC. MTC submitted requests for cooperative funds for the erection of several billboards and for magazine advertising. Germano approved all of these requests, reimbursing MTC for one hundred percent of its costs despite the fact that the program provided for a maximum reimbursement level of fifty percent. In total, Germano approved reimbursements close to $300,000 for MTC. Upon discovering other fraudulent activity in MTC's account, Uniroyal dispatched its own internal auditor, Martin Wynne–Brown and a subordinate, Tom Taylor, to Nigeria to inspect the billboards. Their investigation uncovered some unsettling truths. First, they obtained estimates from two advertising agencies in Lagos, Nigeria, which placed the cost of the work done at approximately $25,000. Second, they learned that the billboards they had seen had only recently been erected. This was about two years after the reimbursements had been requested.

Meanwhile, back at the Uniroyal ranch, the company's investigation was closing in on Germano. On February 29, 1990, Germano confessed to being "lenient" on MTC's advertising account. He also told company auditors that about the time he was handling the cooperative advertising payments for MTC, he had met with Hauper, MTC's Vice–President. Hauper gave Germano a plane ticket to London where Germano met Patrick Mehl, an MTC representative. Mehl gave Germano $15,000 which Germano deposited in a Gibraltar bank account. Ten months later, Germano received another $5,000 from MTC. (The two payments remained unreported in Germano's tax returns until he was deposed in this case at which time he filed an amended return reflecting the payments.)

C. The Volume Bonus Scheme

Yet another instance of fraud arose from some creative bookkeeping with respect to MTC's account. Uniroyal had an incentive program which rewarded customers annually for high volume purchases. To be included in any given year's calculation, tires had to have been shipped and paid for. In December of 1987, Germano included in MTC's account an order for 50,000 tires which had not yet been manufactured let alone purchased and delivered. Moreover, Germano did not deduct those orders from the 1988 purchase tally. In fact, Germano added 80,000 tires to MTC's account which never existed. The result of Germano's shenanigans was an unearned credit to MTC's account exceeding $230,000.

D. Other Schemes

Another scam involving Germano and MTC occurred after Germano agreed to help unload the excess inventory of a discontinued model known as the Reno tire. Germano shipped some of these to MTC but billed MTC for a cheaper type of tire, a model known as the ADV tire. Germano claimed MTC told him that the tires were ADV tires and not

Reno tires. But testimony from those who saw the tires revealed that the tires were in fact the more expensive Reno tires.

In addition to these more elaborate schemes, Germano engaged in several isolated but no less serious actions most of which involved some creative bookmaking but all of which bestowed upon MTC a healthy windfall at the expense of his employer. He often charged MTC prices well below those authorized by Uniroyal and on one occasion, in direct defiance of his superior's directions, wrote off interest charges in excess of $38,000.

Subsequent to his confession to Uniroyal's auditors, Germano resigned, and Uniroyal severed its relationship with MTC. Uniroyal then filed a twelve-count complaint consisting of five civil RICO counts and seven pendent state law counts. The defendants filed a five-count counterclaim, which alleged, among other things, that Uniroyal violated its contract by halting production of the Detroiter and by selling tires that were not as warranted.

The trial court granted Uniroyal summary judgment on some of MTC's counterclaims, and on the remainder, the trial court entered judgment as a matter of law in Uniroyal's favor at the close of the evidence. The jury then returned a verdict in Uniroyal's favor on the RICO counts and the state law claims. In total, Uniroyal was awarded approximately $2.8 million in damages. The court then assessed fees and costs against MTC in the amount of $1.4 million.

* * *

We proceed * * * to consider MTC's challenge to the finding of RICO liability. Section 1964 of RICO imposes civil liability on those found liable for deriving money through a "pattern of racketeering activity." The remedies available to a successful plaintiff are plentiful: they include provisions for treble damages, costs, and attorneys' fees. 18 U.S.C. § 1964(c). The murkiness of RICO's parameters coupled with its alluring remedies have led many plaintiffs to take garden variety business disputes and dress them up as elaborate racketeering schemes.

At issue in this case is whether this dispute truly presents a pattern of racketeering. The vagaries of the statute itself make the task of defining this requirement formidable, to say the least. * * *

In conclusory fashion, the defendants argue that the trial court erred in failing to grant their motion for judgment as a matter of law, despite the jury's verdict. They claim that the evidence failed to establish anything more than an isolated and short-lived instance of fraud in an otherwise successful business relationship.

MTC's attempt to depict this as one single fraud is understandable. Our RICO jurisprudence is replete with examples of failed attempts to dress up state fraud claims as suave RICO cases using the expansive definitions of mail and wire fraud. In Lipin Enters. v. Lee, 803 F.2d 322, 324 (7th Cir.1986), the plaintiffs alleged that a fraudulent acquisition of stock amounted to a RICO violation because it entailed a multitude of fraudulent statements and representations transmitted through the mails and wires. We rejected that assertion, holding that just because the complexity of the transaction creates the potential for a greater number of possible fraudulent acts does not mean that there is the requisite threat of continued criminal activity. "[M]ultiple acts of mail fraud in furtherance of a single episode of fraud involving one victim and relating to one basic transaction cannot constitute the necessary pattern." Jones v. Lampe, 845 F.2d 755, 757 (7th Cir.1988).

In Olive Can Co. Inc. v. Martin, 906 F.2d 1147, 1150 (7th Cir.1990), the defendants set up a sham corporation in an attempt to divert money from their own failing cookie manufacturing business and then concealed its existence from the plaintiffs who sold them supplies on credit. The district court had found that the scam was not continuous within the meaning of RICO because it was done to pay off one of the defendants' personal obligations. Hence, the fraudulent scheme had a natural ending with no threat of ongoing criminal activity. We agreed and affirmed the finding of no liability.

Lee and *Olive Can* notwithstanding, the existence of a single victim does not preclude the existence of a pattern of racketeering activity. In Liquid Air Corp. v. Rogers, 834 F.2d 1297, 1300 (7th Cir.1987), the plaintiff, Liquid Air, had leased compressed gas cylinders to the defendant, D & R. After D & R terminated operations, it was slow to return the rented equipment. *Id.* When Liquid Air began charging D & R a higher rate for the remaining 3,000 cylinders, D & R obtained the services of a Liquid Air employee, who, over the course of seven months, generated nineteen separate false invoices making it appear as if the cylinders were being returned. We were consequently faced with deciding whether a single scheme which lasted seven months and defrauded one victim established a pattern of racketeering activity. We held that it did. Crucial to our conclusion was the fact that each instance of false billing inflicted an injury separate and independent of the previous and succeeding instances of false billing. "[T]he repeated infliction of economic injury upon a single victim of a single scheme is sufficient to establish a pattern of racketeering activity for purposes of civil RICO." *Id.* at 1305.

In this circuit, we have looked to several factors in ascertaining the existence of a pattern: the number and variety of predicate acts, the length of time over which they were committed, the number of victims, the presence of separate schemes, and the occurrence of distinct injuries. Neither the presence or absence of any one of these factors is determinative, and though these factors may be helpful, the touchstones of the inquiry remain the elements of relationship and continuity. Of these factors, all but one weigh in Uniroyal's favor. The predicate acts were numerous and spread out over a period of years. Uniroyal offered proof of several different schemes, all intended to bleed money from Uniroyal. And each scheme caused a harm distinct from that caused by the others. Only the existence of a single victim, Uniroyal, favors MTC. By itself, that is not enough.

The distinctions between *Liquid Air* and *Lee* and *Liquid Air* and *Olive Can* command the outcome in this case. The potential expansiveness of RICO stems largely from the capacious definitions of mail and wire fraud. It is therefore hard to formulate a bright-line test for the pattern of racketeering activity based solely on the number of predicate acts. But from these three single-victim cases, we begin to see what distinguishes a pattern. In *Lee* and *Olive Can*, there was an interdependence amongst the predicate acts, and each act was not responsible for a discrete injury. The various fraudulent representations made in *Lee* did not inflict separate harms; rather they were all necessary to perpetrate one large fraud. Similarly, the predicate acts in *Olive Can* were all related to the perpetration of one scam which would have ended on its own. On the other hand, in *Liquid Air*, each false invoice on its own deprived the plaintiffs of a specific amount of revenue. Each invoice represented a discrete attempt to defraud Liquid Air and had little to do with the previous or subsequent false invoices.

If this case is in any way distinguishable from *Liquid Air*, it is that it presents a stronger case for liability; the facts of this case put it squarely within RICO's ambit. Taken in a light most favorable to Uniroyal, proven at trial were the existence of at least four separate schemes all of which were designed to swindle money from Uniroyal and all of which utilized the mails and wires to further their ends. The existence of several schemes strengthens the support for the jury's verdict and satisfies the dictates in *Sedima* and *H.J. Inc.* The various predicates of mail and wire fraud occurred repeatedly over a period as long as three years and each scheme, though inflicted upon the same victim, caused separate and distinct injuries like those caused in *Liquid Air*.

* * *

Notes

1. What do you think about the decisions in *Word of Faith*, *Vild* and *Uniroyal*? Note the Seventh Circuit's description in *Uniroyal* of RICO when the predicate acts are mail fraud or wire fraud: "The potential expansiveness of RICO stems largely from the capacious definitions of mail and wire fraud." Does this view dictate an expansive reading of pattern?

2. Consider the following analysis of *H. J. Inc.*'s practical impact:

"The threshold question in determining if the pattern requirement[61] has been met is whether the alleged, related RICO predicate acts have ceased or are continuing. If the alleged acts relate to a single objective in connection with a single completed transaction, the alleged scheme is

---

61. As formulated by the courts, the specific legal elements necessary to prove the pattern requirement are, (1) a person who engages in (2) a pattern of racketeering activity that amounts to or poses a threat of continued activity (3) connected to the acquisition, establishment, conduct or control of an enterprise, and (4) direct injury proximately caused by elements (1), (2), and (3). Holmes v. Securities Investor Protection Corp., 503 U.S. 258 (1992); Calcasieu Marine Nat'l Bank v. Grant, 943 F.2d 1453, 1461, 1463 (5th Cir.1991).

closed-ended. Accordingly, in a civil case, when the activity is closed-ended, of short durations, and ends voluntarily before suit is filed, the continuity element is not satisfied as a matter of law.

"A paradigm of this type of closed-end scheme is illustrated by Thompson v. Paasche,[64] Paasche subdivided a scenic property into ten lots and sold them to various buyers over a period of less than six months. The buyers alleged that Paasche falsely represented that reservation of mineral rights in favor of Paasche in protective covenants was to protect the land from exploitation, when in fact he planned to enter into an oil and gas lease on the property. Once Paasche had sold all of the lots, the scheme was over because he had no more land to sell. Thus, as a matter of law the six-month scheme did not constitute a RICO pattern.

"The issue in a closed-ended situation is relatively simple: What is the length of time necessary to establish a RICO pattern? *H.J. Inc.* set imprecise parameters on the requisite length of time: A "few" weeks or months is insufficient, but six years is sufficient. Since *H.J. Inc.*, the courts have almost universally held that racketeering activity lasting less than one year will not satisfy the pattern requirement. A leading example of this simple duration analysis is contained in Johnston v. Wilbourn,[71] in which the alleged predicate acts consisted of bank directors purchasing bank shares from individuals in order to gain majority control of the bank without disclosing a plan to merge the bank with another bank. The alleged acts occurred over a period of approximately nine months. The *Johnston* plaintiffs argued that the phrase "few weeks or months" used by the Supreme Court in *H.J. Inc.* to identify time periods that are too short to satisfy the continuity requirement implied that activity lasting almost one year must be sufficient. The district court rejected any such implication from *H.J. Inc.* and concluded, as a matter of law, that the pattern requirement was unsatisfied because the alleged scheme involved only one objective, was short-lived, and carried no threat of repetition. *Johnston* surveyed every reported case decided in the wake of *H.J. Inc.* and found no case in which predicate acts spanning less than one year satisfied the continuity requirement. In fact, the cases in which the pattern was found sufficient to satisfy the continuity requirement ranged from a minimum of three years to the statutory maximum of ten years. Apparently, these cases represent the "common sense approach," mandated by *H.J. Inc.*, that RICO cases much involve actual or potential long-term criminal activity.

"Of course, if the activity ceased 'independently of discovery' by plaintiffs, the threat of continuity is nonexistent. At least one court has suggested that RICO liability is never appropriate for single-scheme, single-victim conduct threatening no future harm, regardless of its duration, even if the alleged scheme continued for well beyond one year.

"Finally, the seriousness of the alleged predicate acts is not a determinative factor in closed-ended schemes. In Fowler v. Burns International Security Services, Inc.[81] the alleged RICO predicate acts included acts of

---

64. 950 F.2d 306 (6th Cir.1991).
71. 760 F.Supp. 578 (S.D.Miss.1991).

81. 763 F.Supp. 862 (N.D.Miss.1991), aff'd, 979 F.2d 1534 (5th Cir.1992).

alleged extortion of sexual favors amounting to kidnapping and rape in exchange for continued employment. Although the court found that these alleged acts did not actually constitute extortion, it went on to hold that because they occurred over a short period of time (nine months), the pattern requirement could not be established.

* * *

"If the plaintiff files suit before enough time has elapsed to establish continuity in a closed-end situation (i.e., before the activity has continued for at least one year), the threat of continued racketeering activity typically will not exist. Plaintiffs often contend, however, that the only reason that the alleged RICO activity ceased was because the defendant was caught. In these instances, plaintiffs must establish a "specific" threat that the RICO activity would "continue indefinitely" into the future. In the ordinary civil case, this threat often cannot be demonstrated without covering a single episode into more than it is by tacking other innocuous business activity onto the alleged RICO activity or by combining the alleged RICO activity of multiple defendants.

"Mere allegations that the alleged RICO activity might have continued, without specific factual support, are wholly insufficient to meet the plaintiffs' burden of pleading a RICO claim. There must be a genuine threat of continued activity. Plaintiffs have the burden of demonstrating a "realistic prospect of continuity over an open-ended period yet to come."[89] In the case of ordinary businesses, this burden should be nearly insurmountable: Most activities have a foreseeable end and thus cannot extend indefinitely into the future.

"Consequently, as Justice Scalia observed in his concurrence in *H.J. Inc.*, a few months of racketeering activity 'is generally for free.'[91] Regardless of whether this grace period should exist in the case of archetypical gangster activity, it is, as Justice Scalia recognized, a 'safe harbor' for alleged racketeering activity that 'does not last too long, no matter how many different crimes and different schemes are involved.' "[92]

C. CONDUCT

1. USE OR INVEST

There are four types of RICO conduct. Section 1962(a) prohibits any person from using or investing any income derived from a pattern of racketeering activity in an enterprise. The next case exemplifies a § 1962(a) RICO action.

89. Feinstein v. Resolution Trust Corp., 942 F.2d 34, 45 (1st Cir.1991).

91. H.J. Inc. v. Northwestern Bell Tel. Co., 492 U.S. 229, 254 (1989).

92. *Id.* William E. Marple, *"Pattern" Requirement Renders RICO Inapplicable to* *Ordinary Business Disputes*, 14 REV. LITIGATION 343, (1995). Published originally in 14 THE REVIEW OF LITIGATION 343 (1995). Copyright © 1995 by the University of Texas at Austin School of Law Publications, Inc. Reprinted by permission.

UNITED STATES v. ZANG

United States Court of Appeals, Tenth Circuit, 1982.
703 F.2d 1186.

SETH, CHIEF JUDGE.

The defendants, W. Darrell Zang and Louis Porter, were convicted by a jury of one count of conspiracy (18 U.S.C. § 371), six counts of mail fraud (18 U.S.C. § 1341 and § 2), eight counts of wire fraud (18 U.S.C. § 1343 and § 2), and one count of racketeering (18 U.S.C. § 1962(a), § 1963, and § 2). The court sentenced each of the defendants to five years on each count to be served concurrently, a total fine of $49,000, and ordered the forfeiture, pursuant to 18 U.S.C. § 1963(a)(1), of the defendants' respective interests in Dalco Investments, which included an interest in the Dalco Building.

The facts leading up to their indictment and conviction concern the purchase and resale of crude oil. The government alleged that from approximately December of 1976 through September of 1978 the appellants fraudulently miscertified over one million barrels of lower tier priced controlled crude oil as higher tier crude oil resulting in an illegal profit of nearly 7.5 million dollars.

Mr. Porter owned, among other businesses, a company known as Dalco Petroleum, Inc. which had as one of its wholly owned subsidiaries, Dalco Crude, Inc. (Dalco). In 1976 he formed Dalco Crude, Inc. to operate a crude oil and natural gas liquids trading business. Mr. Porter hired Mr. Zang to run the enterprise. Mr. Zang had previously been the vice president and regional manager of Western Crude Oil, Inc. (Western). As the manager of Dalco Crude, Mr. Zang received an annual salary and an interest in the profits. Later in January of 1978 Dalco Crude, Inc. was succeeded by Dalco, Inc., a company owned jointly by Mr. Porter and Mr. Zang.

In December of 1976 Dalco negotiated with Cities Services (Cities) for the purchase of 310,000 barrels of low tier crude oil. Under that contract Dalco would pay Cities' acquisition cost which was based on posted prices for crude oil, the gathering charges or pipeline fees, plus 24 cents per barrel. Dalco simultaneously resold the crude to Western. Under the contract with Western Dalco received an acquisition cost based on posted prices, plus 19 cents per barrel.

The basis for the indictment was that Dalco recertified the lower tier crude oil from Cities as high tiered crude oil and thus a higher priced crude, when it was resold to Western. The then prevailing price control regulations required the producer to certify the tier of the oil sold and each reseller was required to certify the crude to its purchaser to be of the same tier as the certification it received. The certification was usually typed on the reseller's invoice. As a reseller Dalco was thus required to pass onto Western the same tier designation it had received for the oil. Because of the fraud perpetrated through miscertification the government alleged that Dalco overcharged Western $7,482,837.

Similar arrangements were negotiated between Cities and Western through July of 1978. Dalco negotiated for the purchase of resale of about 15,000 barrels per day, and over a fifteen-month period 7,629,442 barrels were traded in this manner.

* * *

The appellants * * * contend that the evidence is insufficient to prove that they conspired to defraud the United States. The indictment charged the defendants with fraud against the United States in its Entitlements Program under the Emergency Petroleum Allocation Act (EPAA).

The Entitlements Program was a method of equalizing the acquisition costs of a refiner's crude oil. Under the program refiners who purchased and processed lower priced "old" oil in excess of the national average were required to compensate by cash payment the refiners who purchased and processed more expensive "new" oil. The tier designations enable the government to determine the entitlement. If lower tiered crude oil is miscertified as higher tiered crude then the entitlement is deflated.

The government introduced evidence that barrels of crude purchased by Western from Dalco were later sold to Gulf Oil and OKC. Mr. Mills of Western so testified. Tom Fagan and John Madden of Gulf Oil and OKC testified that their respective companies brought crude from Western. OKC was a refiner. Gulf reported its tier information at its refineries to DOE. Reviewing the evidence in the light most favorable to the government, it is reasonable for a jury to infer and find that the miscertification of lower tier crude oil impacted upon and disrupted the Entitlements Program administered by DOE. Where there is sufficient evidence to show that a federal program has been disrupted, the evidence is sufficient to support the finding of fraud against the United States.

The appellants next contend that the evidence is insufficient to support their convictions of mail fraud. They argue that the mailings were not sufficiently related to the alleged scheme to defraud, and thus their conduct was not within the mail fraud statute.

To warrant a conviction under the mail fraud statute the government must prove that a scheme to defraud exists and that a mailing was made for the purpose of that scheme. The appellants argue that the indictment charged them with fraudulent miscertification of crude oil tiers on the invoices. They contend that the method of delivering the invoices was irrelevant to the legality of the transaction.

The mail fraud statute requires that the mails be an integral part of the scheme to defraud. This means that the item mailed be an integral part of the execution of the scheme. In this way the use of the mails becomes "incident to an essential part of the scheme." Clearly the scheme to defraud depended upon the invoices stating the tier certification. Mailing those invoices was necessary and an integral part of the scheme. Thus the mail fraud counts are supported by the evidence.

The appellants claim several errors with respect to the application of the Racketeer Influenced and Corrupt Organizations (RICO) statute, 18 U.S.C. §§ 1961–1968. In Count 16 of the indictment Mr. Zang and Mr. Porter were charged with receiving monies from a pattern of racketeering and willfully investing that income to acquire an interest in violation of 18 U.S.C. § 1962(a). The racketeering activity alleged consisted of the acts of mail and wire fraud also alleged in the indictment. The indictment further contended that Mr. Zang and Mr. Porter transferred to Dalco Investments approximately $1,067,576 of the profit obtained from the Cities–Western transaction. The government sought forfeiture of the appellants' respective interests in Dalco Investments, including its sole asset, the Dalco Building, pursuant to § 1963(a)(1).

Under RICO the government must prove both the existence of an enterprise and a connected pattern of racketeering activity. United States v. Turkette, 452 U.S. 576, 101 S.Ct. 2524, 69 L.Ed.2d 246. Mr. Porter and Mr. Zang each owned a 50% interest in a partnership called Dalco Investments. The partnership received a handling fee for the Cities–Western crude oil transactions. This constituted an ongoing association for the purpose of engaging in interstate commerce. It was a separate element proved by the government. Thus Dalco Investments was an "enterprise" within the meaning of the RICO statute. As the Court said in *Turkette:*

> "RICO also proscribes the investment of income derived from racketeering activity in an enterprise engaged in or which affects interstate commerce * * *."

The pattern of racketeering activity is a series of criminal acts as defined by the statute. In the case before us racketeering activity was the alleged wire and mail fraud. To prove a pattern, the government must establish two or more predicate offenses which are related to the activities of the enterprise. The jury found the appellant guilty on all counts of mail and wire fraud. Those predicate acts concerned the fraudulent miscertification of crude oil tiers in the Cities–Western transactions. As such they were sufficiently related to the appellants' enterprise of selling crude oil to support the conviction under § 1962.

The appellants claim error in the trial court's instruction to the jury concerning the "pattern of racketeering." The court instructed the jury that to find "a pattern of racketeering activity the law requires at least two acts of racketeering activity." The appellants argue that the trial court's instruction should have also specifically stated that the two acts had to be related to constitute a pattern.

On review we must consider the trial court's instructions as a whole. The trial court instructed the jury that an activity of racketeering includes any act which constitutes a violation of the mail or wire fraud statutes. The court further stated that if the government proved at least two of the wire and mail fraud counts then the pattern of racketeering activity would also be sufficiently proven. Any two of the counts of mail and wire fraud alleged in the indictment were sufficiently related to the enterprise to constitute a violation of RICO. Based on the instructions as a whole, there was no need to explain specifically the required relationship.

* * *

The appellants also contend that the forfeiture of their interests in Dalco Investments, particularly the Dalco Building, was not supported by the weight of the evidence. The government sought forfeiture under 18 U.S.C. § 1963(a)(1) which provides that any person found in violation of § 1962 shall forfeit any interest acquired or maintained in violation of § 1962. Even though the "interest" is not specifically defined by the statute, its meaning can be derived from the activities barred by § 1962. The section proscribed three types of activities. The defendants were charged with violating § 1962(a), which prohibits the use or investment of racketeering income to acquire an interest in any enterprise. Thus the interest subject to forfeiture in this case is any interest in an enterprise acquired or maintained through racketeering income.

The enterprise at issue is Dalco Investments, a partnership equally held by Mr. Zang and Mr. Porter. Under the evidence adduced at trial the partnership's sole asset is the Dalco Building. Mr. Porter had transferred a half-interest in the building to Mr. Zang for value. They each contributed their share in the building to the partnership. The partnership received over a million dollars from the Cities–Western transactions, which was in turn used to pay the mortgage on the building.

The appellants' interest in Dalco Investments which was acquired by tainted funds is subject to forfeiture. Merely contributing the building to a partnership is not prohibited by § 1962. Thus the entire building is not necessarily subject to forfeiture. However, the partnership's interest in the building which was acquired by racketeering funds is subject to forfeiture under § 1963.

The government presented precise, uncontroverted evidence as to the amount of racketeering income funneled into Dalco Investments. It totaled $1,067,576. The untainted interests which may exist and the interest of innocent third parties should be protected. Thus we remand this issue to the district court to establish terms and conditions of the forfeiture under its authority described in 18 U.S.C. § 1963(c).

Notes

1. In approaching a RICO case, or a potential RICO case, one should first list the elements of the RICO offense. Each violation of §§ 1962(a), (b), (c), or (d) will be a separate offense; because the conduct in each section is different, the elements for each offense will vary. Next, one should list exactly what evidence has been produced (or available, when evaluating the strength of a potential RICO offense) to prove each element in *Zang*.

To that end, can you list the elements of § 1962(a) and ascertain the evidence that was produced to prove each element?

2. Note that the defendants' interest in the assets of Dalco Investments (i.e., the Dalco Building) was subject to forfeiture. Recall that 18 U.S.C. § 1963(a) provides that in addition to possible imprisonment and criminal fines, any person convicted of criminal violations of RICO "shall forfeit to the United States * * * any property * * * derived from any proceeds which the person obtained, directly or indirectly, from racketeering activity * * * in violation of section 1962."

Section 1963(a) also requires forfeiture of "any interest the person acquired or maintained in violation of section 1962" and "any interest in * * * any enterprise which the person has established, operated, controlled, conducted, or participated in the conduct of, in violation of section 1962 * * *."

The remainder of § 1963 specifies procedures third parties must pursue to protect their interest in property subject to forfeiture, and procedures available to the government, both before and after indictment, to protect property possibly subject to forfeiture under RICO.

_____

2. ACQUIRE OR MAINTAIN

Section 1962(b) makes it unlawful for any person to acquire or maintain control of any enterprise through a pattern of racketeering activity.

The next case is a civil RICO action brought by the government. In addition to RICO, this opinion also discusses a "Hobbs Act"[o] violation. While the Hobbs Act is covered in greater detail in Chapter 7, you can begin to get a feel for it with this case. *Local 560* also addresses the issue of "intangible property" and exemplifies the government's use of expert testimony. The thrust of the opinion is devoted to RICO, however. As you read this opinion, observe what constitutes the "pattern of racketeering activity" and how the court's interpretation of the enterprise differs from the enterprise as identified in the complaint.

UNITED STATES v. LOCAL 560

United States Court of Appeals, Third Circuit, 1985.
780 F.2d 267.

GARTH, CIRCUIT JUDGE:

This appeal culminates a lengthy and complex civil action brought pursuant to the Racketeer Influenced and Corrupt Organizations ("RICO") Act, 18 U.S.C. §§ 1961, et seq., by the United States against several defendants who allegedly acquired an interest in, and effectively dominated, Local 560 of the International Brotherhood of Teamsters

o. 18 U.S.C. § 1951, et seq.

("Local 560"). The district court, concluding that Local 560 was a "captive labor organization," enjoined certain defendants from any future contacts with Local 560, and removed the current members of the Local 560 Executive Board, replacing the Executive Board with a temporary trusteeship until free elections could be held. * * * The district court stayed its injunction pending appeal to this Court. We affirm.

On March 9, 1982, the government filed its civil complaint naming as defendants twelve individuals, Local 560 and Local 560's Welfare Fund and Severance Pay Plan. The government alleged that five of the named defendants: Anthony Provenzano, Nunzio Provenzano, Steven Andretta, Thomas Andretta and Gabriel Briguglio, were members of an ongoing criminal confederation—the Provenzano Group—which, through acts of extortion and murder,[p] effectively acquired an interest in, and control of, Local 560, an enterprise within the meaning of RICO, in violation of 18 U.S.C. § 1962(b). The government also charged these defendants, as the Provenzano Group, with unlawfully participating, directly and indirectly, in the conduct of Local 560's affairs through a

---

p. The "acts of extortion and murder" included: "(1) the June 1961 murder of Anthony Castellitto; (2) the August 1961 appointment of Salvatore Provenzano to the position of Trustee formerly occupied by Castellitto; (3) the September 1961 appointment of Salvatore Briguglio—the alleged murderer of Castellitto—to the position of Business Agent; (4) the February 1963 appointment of Nunzio Provenzano to the position of Business Agent following his January 1963 conviction for extortion; (5) the May 1963 murder of Walter Glockner; (6) the 1964 appointment of Robert A. Luizzi to the position of Business Agent in spite of a record of criminal convictions; (7) the May 1967 appointment of Luizzi to the position of Trustee; (8) the February 1969 appointment of Salvatore Briguglio to position of Business Agent following completion of a term of imprisonment for extortion; (9) the April 1969 appointment of Nunzio Provenzano to the position of clerk following completion of a term of imprisonment for extortion; (10) the 1970 appointment of Nunzio Provenzano to the position of Business Agent; (11) the 1971 appointment of Thomas Reynolds, Sr. to the position of Business Agent in spite of a record of criminal activity; (12) the 1972 appointment of Nunzio Provenzano to the position of Fund Trustee; (13) the 1972 appointment of Salvatore Briguglio to the position of Fund Trustee; (14) the allowance of frequent visitations by Armand Faugno and Thomas Andretta to the offices of Local 560; (15) the January 1963 appointment of Nunzio Provenzano to the position of Secretary-Treasurer; (16) the 1973 appointment of Reynolds to the position of Fund Trustee; (17) the 1974 resumption of duties as Business Agent by Salvatore Briguglio following completion of a term of imprisonment for counterfeiting; (18) the 1974 appointment of Luizzi to the position of Fund Trustee; (19) the November 1975 appointments of Anthony and Nunzio Provenzano to the positions of Secretary–Treasurer and President, respectively, in spite of a record of convictions for extortion; (20) the February 1977 appointment of Reynolds to the position of Trustee; (21) the July 1978 appointment of Josephine Provenzano to the position of Secretary–Treasurer following Anthony Provenzano's conviction for the Castellitto murder; (22) the July 1981 appointment of Salvatore Provenzano to the position of President following Nunzio Provenzano's forced resignation as a condition of bail on a labor racketeering conviction; (23) the Executive Board's failure to recover monies wrongfully converted by Anthony Provenzano; (24) the retention of Marvin Zalk as Fund Administrator in spite of payments accepted by him from an insurance company representative during the 1950's; (25) the retention of Ralph Torrace as the Fund's independent certified public accountant in spite of his federal indictment for systematically overbilling the Fund; (26) the extortion of contributions to the defense funds of the Provenzanos and Michael Sciarra from union members; (27) the 1981 appointment of Luizzi to the position of Business Agent; and (28) associations by some the defendants with Frank 'Funzi' Tieri and Matteo Alfredo Ianniello, reputed to be organized crime members." 780 F.2d at 271.

pattern of racketeering activity in violation of 18 U.S.C. § 1962(c) and with conspiring to violate the above two provisions of RICO (§§ 1962(b) and (c)) in contravention of 18 U.S.C. § 1962(d).

Finally, the government charged the remaining seven individual defendants: Salvatore Provenzano, Joseph Sheridan, Josephine Provenzano, J.W. Dildine, Thomas Reynolds, Michael Sciarra and Stanley Jaronko, who, at the time the suit was brought, constituted the Executive Board of Local 560, with aiding and abetting the Provenzano Group in violating 18 U.S.C. § 1962(b) and (d).

* * *

In its demand for relief, the government sought only injunctive and equitable remedies. The government asked that the district court * * * enjoin [various individual defendants] from having any dealings, directly or indirectly, with any officer or employee of the Local 560 enterprise or any other labor organization or employee benefit plan; * * * enjoin [other individual defendants] from acting in any official capacity for or on behalf of Local 560 or its funds; * * * appoint one or more trustees to discharge all duties and responsibilities of the Executive Board of Local 560 until such time as free elections can be held; and * * * after the membership participation in a free election, permanently enjoin all individual defendants from having any future dealings of any nature whatsoever, directly or indirectly, with any officer, agent, representative, or employee of Local 560 or any other labor organization.

* * *

On January 25, 1983, the bench trial of this cause commenced. The trial lasted until May 17, 1983, comprising 51 days of testimony. On March 16, 1984, the district court entered its final order, granting the government's requested injunctive relief in all respects.

At the same time, the district court withheld the appointment of a trustee because it stayed its order pending appeal. All of the defendants except alleged Provenzano Group members Stephen Andretta and Gabriel Briguglio filed timely notices of appeal.

* * *

We address first the issue which concerns both the Provenzano Group defendants and the Executive Board defendants: namely, whether the district court properly found a violation of section 1962(b) of the RICO Act. The district court held that the Provenzano Group members, aided and abetted by the Executive Board, acquired an interest in and control of Local 560 through a pattern of racketeering activity.

Central to the district court's section 1962(b) analysis is its finding that the Provenzano Group and the Executive Board extorted the membership's LMRDA rights to democratic participation in their union's affairs. LMRDA rights apply to every member of a labor organization. These rights include the right to nominate Union leaders; to vote in union elections; to meet and assemble freely with other members; and to express any views, arguments, or opinions at union meetings.

* * *

[The court reviewed the trial testimony of a government witness, Professor Summers, who specialized in labor law for approximately forty years:] * * * According to Professor Summers, a significant proportion of Local 560's rank and file were induced by fear of the Provenzano Group to surrender their membership rights. Summers' conclusion that the membership did not feel free to criticize openly the policies and practices of the Local 560 leadership (and, thus, were fearful of exercising their union democratic rights) was based primarily on the observation that, throughout the history of Local 560, incidents which should have raised criticism of Local 560's leadership among its membership, did not. Among the incidents which Summers' believed should have spurred membership reaction were: the murder of Walter Glockner [a union member] the morning after his public display of opposition at a union meeting; the many convictions of union officials on union-related offenses; the failure of the Executive Board to take any action when an official was indicted; the appointment and reappointment of persons who had been convicted of union-related offenses; the payment of salary increases to Anthony Provenzano; the appointment of Anthony's daughter, Josephine Provenzano, to the office of Secretary–Treasurer of the union following Anthony's incarceration; and the proposal to pay Anthony Provenzano a one-half salary pension despite his conviction for the murder of Anthony Castellitto. As Professor Summers testified, "[I]t is beyond belief that 10,000 members would sit by and watch these things done and never utter a peep," unless a substantial number of the membership were fearful for their lives or their jobs.

The district court accepted Summers' testimony as convincing, and we agree. There seems to be no other plausible explanation for the silence of Local 560's membership in the face of repeated outrageous events. The district court, placing an emphasis on Summers' testimony, found that the silence was due to the repressive atmosphere of Local 560, an atmosphere created and maintained by the Provenzano Group and the Executive Board. We cannot characterize such a finding as clearly erroneous.

In addition to the testimony of Professor Summers, the district court, in determining that the membership's rights had been extorted, also relied on the testimony of August Muller. Muller, an employee of Maislin Brothers Trucking Company and a member of Local 560, testified at trial that, at a general membership meeting in 1983, he heard Salvatore Provenzano state that Maislin would soon be out of business because the International Brotherhood of Teamsters would insist that Maislin repay certain monies which Teamster employees had loaned the company. After hearing Salvatore Provenzano's warning, Muller testified that Local 560 Business Agent Stanley Jaronko went to the Maislin terminal to hold a meeting and speak to the drivers. At this meeting,

Muller challenged Jaronko about the statements Salvatore Provenzano had made earlier at the general membership's meeting. The exchange between Muller and Jaronko became increasingly heated, and Jaronko ultimately struck Muller, sending him into a wall. It was after this altercation that Muller recalled the shooting death of Walter Glockner, which occurred the morning after Glockner had voiced opposition to Local 560's leadership at a general meeting.

At trial, Muller was called to testify about the incident. The district court observed that: "Throughout his direct and cross-examination, Muller's demeanor evinced the precise attributes of a man in the *grip of extreme fear or even sheer terror* because of what he was being compelled to say publicly." (Emphasis added). Professor Summers' testimony indicated that Muller's feelings and fears were shared by a large percentage of Muller's compatriots. As the district court noted, Muller's testimony dramatically illustrated the climate of fear within Local 560 and served to support and reinforce Professor Summers' conclusion that the membership's LMRDA rights to democratic participation in Local 560 were extorted through intimidation and fear.

Accordingly, we believe that the district court was not clearly erroneous in finding that the Provenzano Group and the Executive Board had extorted the LMRDA rights of a substantial number of Local 560 members.

* * *

The district court not only found by a preponderance of the evidence that the Provenzano Group and the Executive Board extorted the membership's LMRDA rights, but also concluded that such extortions constituted predicate acts for purposes of section 1962(b) of the RICO Act. Section 1962(b) makes it unlawful for any person to maintain an interest in, or control of, any enterprise through a pattern of "racketeering activity." Section 1961(1) of the RICO Act, in relevant part, defines "racketeering activity" as "any act which is indictable under * * * [the Hobbs Act]" * * *. Thus, in the instant case, the question is whether the extortion of the membership's LMRDA rights constitutes a Hobbs Act violation so as to satisfy the predicate act requirement of section 1962(b) of the RICO Act.

The Hobbs Act, 18 U.S.C. § 1951,[q] prohibits the obstruction or interference with commerce by use of threats or extortion. This court

---

q. § 1951. Interference with commerce by threats or violence

(a) Whoever in any way or degree obstructs, delays, or affects commerce or the movement of any article or commodity in commerce, by robbery or extortion or attempts or conspires so to do, or commits or threatens physical violence to any person or property in furtherance of a plan or purpose to do anything in violation of this section shall be fined not more than $10,000 or imprisoned not more than twenty years, or both.

(b) As used in this section—

* * *

(2) The term "extortion" means the obtaining of property from another, with his consent, induced by wrongful use of actual or threatened force, violence, or fear, or under color of official right.

* * *

has held that the primary elements of a Hobbs Act violation are (1) that the defendants induce their victims to part with property; (2) that the defendants do so through the use of fear; and (3) that, in so doing, the defendants adversely affect interstate commerce.

The defendants initially argue that the membership's LMRDA rights are intangible property rights, and as such, cannot be the basis for a claim of extortion under the Hobbs Act. Defendants maintain that only the extortion of tangible property (i.e., physical items or possessions) can be cognizable as a Hobbs Act violation.

However, the language of the Hobbs Act makes no such distinction between tangible and intangible property. Section 1951(b)(2) broadly defines "extortion" as "the obtaining of property from another, with his consent, induced by wrongful use of actual or threatened force * * *." Moreover, other circuits which have considered this question are unanimous in extending the Hobbs Act to protect intangible, as well as tangible, property.

Moreover, at least one court has expressly addressed the question of whether rights incident to union membership are protectable property interests. In Dusing v. Nuzzo, 177 Misc. 35, 29 N.Y.S.2d 882 (Sup.Ct. Ulster County), modified on other grounds and aff'd, 263 A.D. 59, 31 N.Y.S.2d 849 (1941), the court held that such rights are "as real and as needful of equitable protection, surely, as money or chattels."

"The right to membership in a union is empty if the corresponding right to an election guaranteed with equal solemnity in the fundamental law of the union is denied. If a member has a 'property right' in his position on the roster, I think he has an equally enforceable property right in the election of men who will represent him in dealing with his economic security and collective bargaining where that right exists by virtue of express contract in the language of a union constitution."

This holding is significant because the Hobbs Act's definition of extortion was closely modelled on that in the New York statute and Congress intended that extortion as used in the Hobbs Act reflect the common understanding of the states. Thus, we conclude that the membership's intangible property right to democratic participation in the affairs of their union is properly considered extortable "property" for purposes of the Hobbs Act.

* * *

Having thus far determined that the district court did not err in concluding that the membership's rights to democratic participation in Local 560 were extorted by the Provenzano Group and the Executive Board in violation of § 1962(b) of the RICO Act, the question remains whether the Provenzano Group was properly characterized by the district court as a "person" for purposes of section 1962(b) and an "enterprise" for purposes of section 1962(c) of the RICO Act. As stated earlier, section 1962(b) of the RICO Act prohibits any "person" from acquiring an interest in and control of any "enterprise" through a pattern of racketeering activity. 18 U.S.C. § 1962(b).[26] Section 1962(c) makes it unlawful for any "person" to conduct or participate in the affairs of an "enterprise" through a pattern of racketeering activity. Referring to section 1962(b), the district court determined that the Provenzano Group was a "person," and that Local 560 was the "enterprise"[27] in which the Provenzano Group acquired an interest. The district court, then referring to section 1962(c), held that the named Provenzano Group defendants—as individuals—were "persons" for purposes of that section, and that the Provenzano Group, as a separate entity, represented an "enterprise."

The defendants, relying primarily on Haroco, Inc. v. American National Bank and Trust Co., 747 F.2d 384 (7th Cir.1984), aff'd, 473 U.S. 606 (1985) (per curiam opinion), argue that the Provenzano Group cannot be properly characterized as a "person" under section 1962(b) of the RICO Act. Section 1961(3) of the RICO Act defines "person" as "any individual or entity capable of holding a legal or beneficial interest in property." 18 U.S.C. § 1961(3). The defendants cite to dicta in the Seventh Circuit's *Haroco* opinion, which states that:

> "Where persons associate 'in fact' for criminal purposes, each person may be held liable under RICO for his, her or its participation in conducting the affairs of the association in fact through a pattern of racketeering activity. But the nebulous association in fact does not itself fall within the RICO definition of 'person.' * * * In the association in fact situation, each participant in the enterprise may be a 'person' liable under RICO, but the association itself cannot be."

Id. at 401.

In the instant case, however, the district court did not treat the Provenzano Group as a "nebulous association in fact." Rather, the district court, as the government suggests, regarded the Provenzano Group as representing a conspiracy of seven identifiable, culpable individuals. As we read and understand the district court's discussion, the term "Provenzano Group" was utilized by the district court as simply a convenient appellation for the collective defendants and was not meant to represent, in itself, a "person" for purposes of Section 1962(b). Indeed, the individual conspirators in question were included as named defendants in the government's complaint and were identified by name in the district court opinion. Moreover, the district court held that *"the culpability of the individual associates of the Provenzano Group under § 1962(b) * * * has been established by their own conduct."* (Emphasis added). Thus, while the district court might have been more explicit in

---

26. In Hirsch v. Enright, 751 F.2d 628, 633–34 (3d Cir.1984), this court held that for purposes of a single violation of § 1962(b), the same entity cannot be both a "person" and an "enterprise." In so holding, *Hirsch* recognized that the district court in this case had not committed that error. Accordingly, *Hirsch* distinguished the *Hirsch* situation from the reasoning and holding of the district court in United States v. Local 560, 581 F.Supp. 279 (D.N.J. 1984). See *Hirsch*, 751 F.2d at 634.

27. The defendants do not dispute that Local 560 is properly an "enterprise" under 18 U.S.C. § 1962(b).

its holding, it is the individual Provenzano Group defendants who are the "persons" for purposes of 1962(b) and not the Provenzano Group as a separate entity.[29]

The district court also held, and the defendants hotly contested, that the Provenzano Group is an "enterprise" for purposes of section 1962(c) of the RICO Act. Section 1961(4) of the RICO Act broadly defines an "enterprise" as including "any individual, partnership, corporation, association, or other legal entity, and any union or group of individuals associated in fact although not a legal entity." 18 U.S.C. § 1961(4).

In United States v. Riccobene, 709 F.2d 214, 221 (3d Cir.1983), this court limited the definition of "enterprise," holding that, to establish an enterprise as defined by Section 1961(4), the government must demonstrate "evidence of an ongoing organization, formal or informal, and evidence that the various associates function as a continuing unit. In addition, the enterprise must be shown to have an existence 'separate and apart from the pattern of activity in which it engages.' " [Citations omitted.]

In the instant case, the district court applied the *Riccobene* standard and found that the individuals forming the Provenzano Group as well as the Provenzano Group itself have "maintained an ongoing organizational structure in the form of a hierarchy and protocol during approximately the past thirty-five years." The court then held the Provenzano Group to be an "enterprise" for purposes of its analysis under section 1962(c), and concluded that the individual Provenzano Group associates had conducted the affairs of the enterprise through a pattern of racketeering activity.

The defendants take issue with this holding on two separate grounds: 1) that the district court changed the theory of the government, which originally regarded Local 560 as the section 1962(c) enterprise, and 2) that the court was clearly erroneous in finding that the Provenzano Group had continued vitality. We find no merit in either contention.

First, although the district court's analysis may have taken a somewhat different tack than that originally presented in the government's complaint, the district court correctly found that the defendants were on notice of this alternative theory and that it was fully litigated with the implied consent of the defendants. Moreover, the complaint itself specifically charges that the Provenzano Group defendants "associated together in fact as an enterprise (the Provenzano Group) within the meaning of Section 1961 of Title 18 of the United States Code." The question of whether the Provenzano Group was an "enterprise" was therefore properly before the district court, and it was not prejudicial to the defendants for the court to base its holding in part on this finding.

---

29. As noted, the government argued that the Provenzano Group itself could be a person, and the district court so held. We cannot say that the district court's holding was in error, although in light of our discussion respecting the individual Provenzano Group defendants, we need not rely on that point.

The defendants further argue, however, that even if this theory was properly before the district court, the court's finding was irrelevant to the relief sought and granted with respect to Local 560; the only relevant question, argue defendants, was whether the individual Provenzano defendants conducted the affairs of *Local 560* through a pattern of racketeering activity such as to justify the relief granted. Irrespective of the labels applied, however, the district court's findings amply supported a holding under section 1962(c). * * * The district court, in reaching its conclusion, relied heavily on the testimony of Salvatore Sinno. Sinno, an early associate of Anthony Provenzano and a member of the Provenzano Group, is one of only two Provenzano Group members to turn state's evidence. Sinno, who assisted in the murder of Anthony Castellitto, was one of the chief witnesses against Anthony Provenzano and others at the Castellitto murder trial.

Sinno testified at the instant trial about the formation of the Provenzano Group in the late 1940's and that Group's niche within the Genovese crime family of New York—headed for a time by "Lucky" Luciano. According to Sinno, Anthony Provenzano was a "made member" ("button man" or "soldier") of the Genovese organization in addition to being the leader of the Provenzano Group. Members of the Provenzano Group in the early 1960s included Nunzio Provenzano, Sinno, and Salvatore Briguglio. Sinno stated that the Genovese family permitted the Provenzano Group during this time to participate in certain criminal activities (such as illegal gambling and labor racketeering) but prohibited the Group from engaging in other crimes (such as narcotics, prostitution, and counterfeiting).

Sinno's testimony indicates that, from the early 1940's to 1961 (when Sinno disassociated himself from the Provenzano Group), the Provenzano Group was a continuing criminal organization which was affiliated with an even larger criminal confederation.

The district court also regarded the many criminal convictions of Provenzano group members over the past thirty years—(convictions, which also represented RICO predicate acts for purposes of sections 1962(b) and (c))—as a strong indication that the Provenzano Group is still an ongoing criminal organization. These offenses, which include [murders and extortion] all implicate the same core of individuals, and illustrate the insular nature of the Provenzano Group. The defendants maintain that these crimes do not represent evidence of an "enterprise" but rather should be regarded as "disparate events, spread over two decades, and involving numerous people." However, considering these crimes in conjunction with Sinno's testimony, as we observed earlier, we cannot say that the district court was clearly erroneous in finding that the Provenzano Group was an "enterprise" under section 1962(c), even though such a finding was unnecessary in light of the district court's contemporaneous finding that the Provenzano Group defendants were individually culpable under that section. We observe that the district court also took note of the fact that, over the 30 year history of the Provenzano Group, only two associates (Sinno and Picardo) have defected. To the district court, this indicated an impressive degree of "internal discipline, loyalty, and perseverance."

Against this backdrop of continued criminal activity, it is difficult to accept the defendants' argument that the Provenzano Group is now defunct.

* * *

[The court affirmed the district court's holdings that sections 1962(b) and (c) had been violated. After briefly addressing the defendants' liability for conspiring to violate RICO, under section 1962(d), the court also affirmed that conviction.]

Notes

1. In Local 560, decided two years before the Supreme Court's decision in *McNally, supra*, Chapter Two, the Third Circuit held that extortion of intangible property rights was cognizable under the Hobbs Act, 18 U.S.C. § 1951. After reviewing the Supreme Court's decision in *McNally* and the policy arguments advanced therein for narrowing the federal government's power to prosecute certain conduct, do you believe the Third Circuit correctly interpreted the Hobbs Act? Does the language of the Hobbs Act, unlike the language of the mail fraud statute, justify a more expansive interpretation?

2. Note the expert testimony of Professor Summers which was admitted pursuant to Fed.R.Evid. 702. Fed.R.Evid. 702 provides for generous use of expert witnesses:

"If scientific, technical, or other specialized knowledge will assist the trier of fact to understand the evidence or to determine a fact in issue, a witness qualified as an expert by knowledge, skill, experience, training, or education, may testify thereto in the form of an opinion or otherwise."

In the trial of white collar criminal cases, expert witnesses can be especially helpful because the legal issues and facts are complex and often, more abstract, than in most cases.

Do you think that Professor Summers' opinion testimony in the *Local 560* trial was appropriate and helpful to the jury in its quest to assess something as abstract as intimidation of union voting rights? Or, do you believe that admission of Professor Summer's testimony inappropriately allowed the government to communicate its theory of the case to the jury through a witness cloaked with the credibility and impartiality of an expert?

3. Can you list some of the predicate acts for the § 1962(b) and § 1962(c) violations committed by the defendants in *Local 560?* Begin by listing the elements of 1962(b) and (c). Determine how the various Hobbs Act violations become the predicate acts, that is, the "racketeering activity" for purposes of §§ 1962(b) and 1962(c)? How do these individual racketeering acts show "a pattern of racketeering activity?"

4. *Local 560* provides a fascinating discussion of the RICO concept of "enterprise."

How did the government characterize the "persons" and "enterprise" for the § 1962(b) offense? How did the district court alter the government's characterization of "persons" for this offense?

How did the government characterize the "person" and "enterprise" for the § 1962(c) offense? How did the district court alter the government's characterization of "enterprise"? Did this alteration significantly change the government's theory? Is it a strength or weakness of the RICO statute that it allows for this type of flexibility in applying the statute?

---

3. PARTICIPATE OR CONDUCT

Section 1962(c) makes it unlawful for any person "employed by or associated with any enterprise" to conduct the affairs of the enterprise through a pattern of racketeering. The next case provides a straightforward application of § 1962(c).

UNITED HEALTHCARE CORPORATION v. AMERICAN TRADE INSURANCE CO., LTD.

United States Court of Appeals, Eighth Circuit, 1996.
88 F.3d 563.

BEAM, CIRCUIT JUDGE.

Edmund Benton (Benton) appeals from the district court's entry of judgment on a jury verdict awarding United HealthCare Corporation (UHC) damages for Benton's violation of the Racketeer Influenced and Corrupt Organizations Act, 18 U.S.C. § 1962(c) (RICO). * * *

In the 1980s, Congress responded to a perceived crisis in certain insurance markets by passing the Liability Risk Retention Act, 15 U.S.C. §§ 3901–06 (Act). The Act loosened previous restrictions on the ability of non-traditional insurers to provide liability insurance through "risk retention groups" and "purchase groups."[1] Under the Act and its subsequent amendments, risk retention groups and purchase groups are exempt from state laws prohibiting their operation or regulating their membership. 15 U.S.C. §§ 3902 & 3903.

UHC is the parent company of United HealthCare Management Corporation (United HealthCare Management), a management company which owns and manages a number of Health Maintenance Organizations (HMOs) across the United States.[2] According to its management

---

1. The Act defines a risk retention group as any corporation or limited liability association chartered or licensed as a liability insurance company under the laws of a state "whose primary activity consists of assuming and spreading all, or any portion, of the liability exposure of its group members." 15 U.S.C. § 3901(a)(4)(A)-(C). A pur-chase group includes a group domiciled in any state which "has as one of its purposes the purchase of liability insurance on a group basis." 15 U.S.C. § 3901(a)(5)(A).

2. United HealthCare Management operated several HMOs in which it had either a full or partial ownership interest. It also

agreements, United HealthCare Management is responsible for obtaining liability insurance coverage for these HMOs. In 1987, United HealthCare Management sought this coverage from Healing Arts National Association (HANA), a purchase group formed to take advantage of the exemptions provided by the Act. Over the next two years, UHC, through its subsidiary, paid nearly $300,000 in premiums to the HANA program to obtain insurance coverage on behalf of the HMOs it owned or managed.

During the period at issue in this case, HANA insureds were to be covered by master insurance policies provided by either Diversified Insurers Corporation (Diversified) or Victoria Insurance Company (Victoria). After purchasing insurance through HANA for two years, however, UHC discovered that the insurance premiums it had paid had never in fact reached these insurance companies and that the policies purporting to provide insurance coverage were worthless. UHC instigated this lawsuit, naming over 40 individuals and entities as defendants. Originally, UHC focused its litigation efforts on the recovery of costs associated with defending lawsuits brought against one of its HMOs, Physician's Health Plan of Arizona, which was to be insured through the HANA program. By the time of trial, however, UHC had abandoned this course of action and elected, instead, to seek reimbursement of insurance premiums. Most of the defendants either defaulted or settled with UHC, leaving only defendant Benton and one of Benton's corporations, BFT Management, in the litigation at the time of trial.

At trial, UHC traced the premiums it paid to HANA through various entities, including several owned by Benton. The premiums were initially sent to IMACO, an insurance brokerage company. That company would deduct its commission and forward the remaining premium to Robis International, a re-insurance intermediary. Robis would subtract its commission and wire the premium balance to Comtell, a defendant corporation which began its association with HANA in 1986. Benton was Comtell's vice president and a signator on Comtell's bank accounts. Benton also owned approximately twenty-five percent of Comtell through one of his corporations.

Comtell provided "administrative services" to HANA, and thus was responsible for securing insurance coverage for the HANA members, forwarding premiums to the participating insurers, and issuing insurance certificates. By 1987, however, two other companies, SUMI, Inc. and Purchase Group Management (PGM), were established to assume some of Comtell's responsibilities. Both of these companies were owned and controlled by Benton. With the establishment of these entities, Comtell was no longer responsible for forwarding premiums to the insurance companies. Instead, Comtell transmitted the premiums it received to PGM to forward on to the insurers.

Despite this arrangement, the evidence demonstrated that neither Victoria nor Diversified received premiums from either Comtell or PGM. Financial records and bank statements showed that after the premiums

managed HMOs in which it had no financial interest.

reached Comtell and PGM, approximately $600,000 went into brokerage accounts controlled by Benton, several hundred thousand dollars worth of checks were made out to "cash" and individual defendants, including Benton, and over one million dollars of premium monies disappeared and remain untraceable.

After UHC completed its case, Benton and BFT Management moved for judgment as a matter of law. The court granted the motion as to all counts except UHC's RICO claims, brought under 18 U.S.C. § 1962(a)-(d). Benton and BFT Management then presented their defense, claiming that Benton was merely a computer consultant to Comtell and challenging UHC's basic premise that, because none of the premiums reached Victoria and Diversified, UHC's HMOs were never, in fact, insured. After presentation of their defense, Benton and BFT Management renewed their requests for judgment as a matter of law. The district court granted BFT's motion and dismissed it from the case, and granted Benton's motion as to all of UHC's claims except its claim under 18 U.S.C. § 1962(c). The court allowed this claim to go to the jury, and the jury returned a verdict for UHC in the amount of $188,426.80. The court trebled the damage award as required by 18 U.S.C. § 1964(c) and entered judgment in the amount of $565,280.40.

After trial, the district court considered Benton's renewed motion for judgment as a matter of law and UHC's petition for attorney's fees and costs. The district court denied Benton's motion and UHC's request for fees and costs, and both parties appeal.

* * * Benton * * * argues that judgment as a matter of law should have been granted because UHC failed to establish the elements required to prove a RICO violation under 18 U.S.C. § 1962(c). * * *

* * *

Benton asserts that UHC failed to present adequate evidence of each of RICO's required elements, and therefore the district court should have granted Benton's motion for judgment as a matter of law. * * *

UHC's surviving RICO claim was predicated on 18 U.S.C. § 1962(c), which states:

> It shall be unlawful for any person employed by or associated with any enterprise engaged in, or the activities of which affect, interstate or foreign commerce, to conduct or participate, directly or indirectly, in the conduct of such enterprise's affairs through a pattern of racketeering activity or collection of unlawful debt.

In order to demonstrate a violation of this section, therefore, a plaintiff must establish (1) the existence of an enterprise; (2) defendant's association with the enterprise; (3) defendant's participation in predicate acts of racketeering; and (4) defendant's actions constitute a pattern of racketeering activity. In addition, the plaintiff must demonstrate that "he has been injured in his business or property by the conduct constituting the violation," a requirement equivalent to a showing of proximate causation and damages. [citations omitted] We address each element in turn.

1. ENTERPRISE

Benton argues that UHC failed to establish the existence of an "enterprise." Under RICO, an "enterprise" includes "any individual, partnership, corporation, association, or other legal entity, and any union or group of individuals associated in fact although not a legal entity." 18 U.S.C. § 1961(4). The enterprise must be distinct from the person named as the RICO defendant. Moreover, the enterprise must be distinct from the alleged pattern of racketeering activity. In other words, as the Supreme Court explained, an enterprise is not established merely by proof of a series of racketeering acts. Instead, an enterprise must exhibit three characteristics: "(1) a common or shared purpose; (2) some continuity of structure and personnel; and (3) an ascertainable structure distinct from that inherent in a pattern of racketeering." [citations omitted]

UHC's evidence met these standards. UHC demonstrated that HANA and its affiliated "service" companies, including Comtell, PGM, and SUMI, Inc., operated as a continuing business unit. This association of corporations exhibited continuity in both structure and personnel in its insurance sales and marketing activities. Despite Benton's involvement in many of the corporations which comprised the enterprise, the enterprise and Benton were not identical. See id. (defendant's membership in the enterprise does not eliminate distinction between the enterprise and the culpable person). Further, the record shows that the enterprise engaged in some legitimate functions and maintained a discrete existence beyond that necessary to perform acts of mail and wire fraud. Thus, the enterprise was sufficiently distinct from the predicate acts of racketeering activity to meet the requirements set forth in *Turkette* and *Atlas Pile*. Accordingly, UHC adduced sufficient evidence for a jury to determine that an "enterprise" existed for purposes of its RICO claim.

2. ASSOCIATION WITH AND PARTICIPATION IN THE CONDUCT OF THE ENTERPRISE'S AFFAIRS

A RICO defendant must "conduct or participate, directly or indirectly, in the conduct of such enterprise's affairs." 18 U.S.C. § 1962(c). Here, UHC presented ample evidence of Benton's participation in the enterprise. Several witnesses attested to Benton's involvement in Comtell, PGM, and SUMI, Inc. Benton himself admitted he was a computer consultant to Comtell and received payments from that entity through his corporation, BFT Management. Therefore, UHC has satisfied this element.

3. RACKETEERING ACTIVITY

To prevail under RICO, UHC was also required to demonstrate, at a minimum, two predicate offenses listed in 18 U.S.C. § 1961(1)(B). In this case, UHC alleged predicate offenses of mail fraud and wire fraud. Mail and wire fraud are established through proof of: "(1) a scheme to defraud; (2) intent to defraud; (3) reasonable foreseeability that the mails (or wires) would be used; and (4) use of the mails (or wires) in furtherance of the scheme." [citations omitted] Each of these elements was satisfied in this case.[5]

We have held that a scheme to defraud requires "some degree of planning by the perpetrator." [citations omitted] Here, such a plan is evidenced by an examination of the money trail, which consistently made its way to various corporations and accounts controlled by Benton rather than to the intended insurance companies. From Benton's systematic siphoning of premium funds, a jury could reasonably find that Benton had the intent to defraud UHC and other HANA members. Thus, UHC established the first and second elements of mail and wire fraud.

With respect to the third element, we conclude that it was foreseeable that the mails and wires would be used in carrying out the intended scheme. There can be little doubt that Benton understood a scheme to defraud UHC would require at least the appearance of a legitimate insurance purchase group with supporting services. Cultivating this appearance would require the wire transfer of premium funds and the mailing of premium checks and insurance certificates. Therefore, it was almost certain that the mails and wires would be used in carrying out the scheme to defraud.

Finally, UHC provided sufficient evidence to satisfy the fourth element, actual use of the mails and wires in furtherance of the scheme. Several witnesses at trial described both mail and wire transfers of premiums. For example, Mark Robis, the insurance intermediary who introduced IMACO to the HANA program, made repeated references to wire transfers from his office to Comtell. Mitzi King, co-founder of Comtell, testified that after premiums were received by Comtell, insurance certificates purporting to verify insurance coverage were mailed by Comtell to the HANA insureds. UHC's accounting expert Arthur Cobb also testified, based on his analysis of check registers and other bank documents, that premium funds were wire-transferred into accounts controlled by Benton. Although Benton contends these mailings were not fraudulent and were not a part of his scheme to defraud but were merely "incidental" to the operation of Comtell, this argument is to no avail. We have held that even a routine mailing (or wire use), or one sent for a legitimate business purpose may satisfy the "actual use" requirement "so long as it assists ... in carrying out the fraud." Therefore, we conclude that UHC presented sufficient evidence to establish the predicate acts of racketeering.

4.   PATTERN OF RACKETEERING ACTIVITY

Although UHC clearly presented sufficient evidence to sustain the jury's finding of predicate offenses, RICO's language specifically requires that a plaintiff establish a "pattern" of racketeering activity. This language "implies 'that while two acts are necessary, they may not be

---

5. Benton contends that UHC was required to demonstrate its detrimental reliance upon a misrepresentation or omission made by Benton. This contention lacks merit, as it is well settled that such a showing is not required to prove mail or wire fraud.

sufficient' ''to constitute a pattern of racketeering activity. H.J. Inc. v. Northwestern Bell Tel., 492 U.S. 229, 237. Instead, to prove a pattern of racketeering activity, a plaintiff must show that ''the racketeering predicates are related, and that they amount to or pose a threat of continued criminal activity." *Id.* at 239. The Court has stated that the ''relatedness'' element of this test embraces '' 'criminal acts that have the same or similar purposes, results, participants, victims or methods of commission, or otherwise are interrelated by distinguishing characteristics and are not isolated events.' '' *Id.* at 240. ''Continuity," the Court has held, is essentially a temporal concept, and may refer ''either to a closed period of repeated conduct, or to past conduct that by its nature projects into the future with a threat of repetition." *Id.* at 241.

Applying these principles to the evidence in the record, we find that UHC has adequately shown that Benton's racketeering activities manifested both relatedness and continuity. The record indicates that Benton's racketeering activities in the enterprise were undertaken for the common purpose of defrauding HANA insureds, and that these activities were accomplished by a common method—the systematic diversion of incoming premium moneys. Each of the acts deprived HANA insureds of the coverage they believed they were purchasing. These activities were undertaken regularly during Benton's lengthy association with HANA and therefore clearly demonstrate ''continuity." Accordingly, UHC's evidence was sufficient for the jury to determine that Benton's predicate acts constituted a ''pattern'' of racketeering activity under RICO.

* * *

Notes

There is a split in the courts of appeals on the issue of whether a corporation may be both the enterprise and the ''person'' charged under § 1962(c) as a defendant. All circuits, except the Third and Eleventh, hold that a corporation cannot be both the enterprise and the ''person'' charged with violating § 1962(c).[r] The courts following this approach focus on the language of RICO. Whereas as § 1962(a) and (b) specify that ''any person'' may engage in the conduct outlined in these sections, § 1962(c) specifies that only ''a person employed by or associated with an enterprise'' may violate § 1962(c). These courts reason that this difference is significant and was intended to prevent an enterprise from qualifying as a defendant (logically,

---

r. *See*: Doyle v. Hasbro, 103 F.3d 186, 190 (1st Cir.1996); United HealthCare Corp. v. American Trade Ins. Co., 88 F.3d 563, 570 (8th Cir.1996); Discon, Inc. v. NYNEX Corp., 93 F.3d 1055, 1063 (2d Cir. 1996); Richmond v. Nationwide Cassel L.P., 52 F.3d 640, 646 (7th Cir.1995); Davis v. Mutual Life Ins. Co., 6 F.3d 367, 377 (6th Cir.1993); Ashe v. Corley, 992 F.2d 540, 544 (5th Cir.1993); Bd. of County Commissioners v. Liberty Group, 965 F.2d 879, 885 (10th Cir.1992); Busby v. Crown Supply Inc., 896 F.2d 833, 840 (4th Cir.1990); Yellow Bus Lines, Inc. v. Drivers, Chauffeurs & Helpers Local Union 639, 839 F.2d 782, 791 (D.C.Cir.1988); Wilcox v. First Interstate Bank, 815 F.2d 522, 529 (9th Cir. 1987);

But See: Jaguar Cars v. Royal Oaks, 46 F.3d 258, 265 (3d Cir.1995) (overruling its prior ''distinction'' requirement); United States v. Hartley, 678 F.2d 961, 988 (11th Cir.1982).

an enterprise cannot be "employed by or associated with" itself).[s] The courts following this approach acknowledge the injustice of this position when the corporation is the perpetrator of the RICO offense, however, they suggest that charging the RICO violation under § 1962(a) rather than § 1962(c) would alleviate the problem. The Seventh Circuit articulated this view in Haroco v. American Nat. B. & T. Co.:[t]

"We are persuaded * * * that section 1962(c) requires separate entities as the liable person and the enterprise which has its affairs conducted through a pattern of racketeering activity. * * * [W]e focus our attention on the language in section 1962(c) requiring that the liable person be 'employed by or associated with any enterprise' which affects interstate or foreign commerce. The use of the terms 'employed by' and 'associated with' appears to contemplate a person distinct from the enterprise. * * *

"At the policy level of the dispute, there are several significant competing arguments. The Eleventh Circuit [has] argued * * * that where the defendant corporation is the central figure in a criminal scheme, as it was in that case, Congress could not have meant to let the central perpetrator escape RICO liability while subjecting only the sidekicks to RICO's severe penalties. Similarly, plaintiffs here argue that Congress intended to make a 'deep pocket' (in the person to the corporation) liable where corporate agents engage in a pattern of racketeering activity redounding to the benefit of the corporation. * * *

"In our view, the RICO provisions have already taken into account these competing policies in different situations, and a careful parsing of section 1962 reveals a sensible balance among these policies. * * *

"In our view, the tensions between these policies may be resolved sensibly and in accord with the language of section 1962 by reading subsection (c) together with subsection (a). As we read subsection (c), the 'enterprise' and the 'person' must be distinct. However, a corporation-enterprise may be held liable under subsection (a) when the corporation is also a perpetrator. As we parse subsection (a), a 'person' (such as a corporation-enterprise) acts unlawfully if it receives income derived directly or indirectly from a pattern or racketeering activity in which the person has participated as a principal within the meaning of 18 U.S.C. § 2, and if the person uses the income in the establishment or *operation* of an enterprise affecting commerce. Subsection (a) does not contain any of the language in subsection (c) which suggests that the liable person and the enterprise must be separate. Under subsection (a), therefore, the liable person may be a corporation using the proceeds of a pattern of racketeering activity in its operations. This approach to subsection (a) thus makes the corporation-enterprise liable under RICO when the corporation is actually the direct or indirect beneficiary of the pattern of racketeering activity, but not when it is merely the victim, prize, or passive instrument of racketeering. This result is in accord with the primary purpose of RICO, which, after all, is to reach those who ultimately profit from racketeering, not those who are victimized by it."

s. Securitron Magnalock Corp. v. Schnabolk, 65 F.3d 256 (2d Cir.1995).

t. 747 F.2d 384, 400–02 (7th Cir.1984).

Jaguar Cars, Inc. v. Royal Oak Motor Car Co., demonstrates the minority view. In *Jaguar Cars*, the Third Circuit abandoned its adherence to the majority rule and held that RICO did not prevent charging an enterprise as defendant.[u] A Jaguar car manufacturer obtained a judgment under section 1962(c) against Royal Oak Motors, a family-owned car dealership, for a systematic scheme of submitting fraudulent warranty claims to Jaguar Cars. Under the scheme, Royal Oak Motors submitted thousands of warranty claims for repairs that were either unnecessary or never actually performed. The court acknowledged that the dealership, as the RICO enterprise, was the "person" charged but rejected defendant's argument that this required dismissal. After analyzing recent Supreme Court cases, the Third Circuit rejected the "distinction" requirement on the ground that it could not survive Supreme Court precedent which made clear that in some circumstances the enterprise could be the "person" in § 1962(c) actions.[v]

Which view do you find more compelling?

4. CONSPIRACY

Section 1962(d) makes it unlawful to conspire to violate §§ 1962(a), (b), or (c). The next case provides a straight-forward application of § 1962(d). As interesting side points, note the forfeiture ordered and the discussion of *Pinkerton*.

UNITED STATES v. JENSEN

United States Court of Appeals, Fifth Circuit, 1994.
41 F.3d 946.

BENAVIDES, CIRCUIT JUDGE.

Paul Arlin Jensen (Jensen) appeals his convictions on 18 counts stemming from a fraudulent scheme which lead [sic] to the failure of certain savings and loan institutions. We affirm.

I. FACTS AND PROCEDURAL HISTORY

In 1982, Jensen, Van Zinnis, and William Tar were partners in a California mortgage brokerage company called Mountain West. The company was seeking borrowers through an advertisement. Clifton Brannon, a builder in the Dallas area, answered the ad. As a result, Jensen flew to Dallas and met with Brannon. Jensen introduced himself as a medical doctor with an impressive business career and told Brannon that he wanted larger projects than the one presented by Brannon. He further stated that he and his employer at Mountain West were interested in acquiring a savings and loan. Brannon introduced Jensen to Weldon Hays, who owned Lancaster First Federal Savings and Loan (Lancaster) in Colony, Texas. Jensen met with Hays' father, James Hays, to discuss the purchase of that institution.

u. Jaguar Cars v. Royal Oaks, 46 F.3d 258, 265 (3d Cir.1995).

v. *Id.* at 266 (referring to the Supreme Court's decisions in National Organization for Women v. Scheidler, 510 U.S. 249 (1994); Reves v. Ernst & Young, 507 U.S. 170 (1993)).

Brannon also introduced Jensen to David Faulkner, a real estate developer, and Jim Toler, a real estate developer and former mayor of the City of Garland. Those two men were involved in the development of real estate projects in an area known as the I–30 corridor in Dallas, Texas. To attract participants for the various projects, Faulkner would arrange elaborate Saturday morning breakfast meetings where high profile individuals and dignitaries would meet with the investors and developers. Faulkner and Toler bought large tracts of land and sold them to "investors," "builder-investors," or "builder-developers" at inflated prices. United States v. Faulkner, 17 F.3d 745, 752 (5th Cir.1994). The property would then change hands in a series of "land flips" which were frequently on the same day. *Id.*

After meeting with Faulkner and Toler, Jensen moved to Texas and became involved in funding the loans for the projects in the I–30 corridor. Jensen set up an office in Dallas, and employed Tim Jensen, Bjornar Fredricksen, loan processors Ellen Burns and Kateland Curly, and accountant Jay Housley. Additionally, Jensen operated several entities which obtained financing for the I–30 corridor projects, including Antum Financial Corporation, Mountain West Mortgage, Snowball Investment Corporation, and Helaman Investment Corporation.

The loans made in connection with the I–30 development were provided by federally insured institutions: Lancaster and Bell Savings (which were controlled by Jensen); and Empire Savings and Loan (which was controlled by Spencer Blain). The borrowers, however, did not necessarily have to be financially qualified to take out these loans.

Faulkner referred individuals to Clifford Sinclair to put together loan packages for the condominium deals. Sinclair and Mike Faldmo[2] were associated with a company called Kitco. Kitco would put together these packages for the borrowers. Faldmo testified that Toler and Faulkner would acquire the land and then decide how much money needed to be made out of a transaction. The personnel at Kitco would calculate the valuation amount of the land necessary to generate the cash requested. The Kitco employees would contact the appraisers and advise them of the needed amount per square foot. The personnel at Kitco would assist the borrowers in preparing the financial statement. The personnel would use false tax returns to insure the borrowers would qualify for the loans. The borrowers would receive "rebates" or "kickbacks" at closing. Frequently, the properties would undergo "land flips" on the closing date among intermediate buyers and others who were designated to make money on the ultimate loan taken by the last purchaser. Faldmo testified that the deals were not driven by market demand but rather, they were based on the amount available to be loaned.

Lancaster Savings and Loan

To obtain control of Lancaster, Jensen purchased the resignations of the board of directors for $150,000 pursuant to an agreement. The board

---

2. Faldmo testified for the government   and had previously plead guilty.

members signed undated letters of resignation, which Jensen never exercised. Jensen was named chairman of the board, and Hays introduced Jensen to the employees of Lancaster as the new boss. After acquiring control of Lancaster, Jensen and his companies continued brokering loans to Lancaster. Jensen also taught the Lancaster personnel how to obtained brokered funds.[3] Jensen testified that the brokers were anxious to do business with Lancaster because it was federally insured. Jensen instructed Carole Harris, Hays' secretary, "how much money" to order on a certain day and "how high to negotiate rates." Numerous such brokered funds transactions were conducted from out of state using wire transfers to Lancaster in $100,000 increments. Jensen hired Charles Brizius as executive vice-president of Lancaster in November 1982. Brizius was an experienced savings and loan executive and was to implement policies and procedures. Brizius testified that he examined the loan files and discovered that the loans were poorly underwritten and much documentation was missing. Brizius also noticed that fees were being paid to companies affiliated with Jensen, and so Brizius confronted Jensen and informed him that there was a conflict of interest for the institution to fund loans with fees paid to entities controlled and owned by Jensen. Brizius further explained that affiliated party transactions required approval of the Federal Home Loan Bank Board. Jensen expressed surprise and indicated that he was not aware of the regulation on conflicts of interest. Brizius testified that Jensen's surprise appeared sincere. As a result of this conversation, Jensen resigned as chairman of the board of Lancaster. Jensen was made an advisory director.[4] Brizius further recommended that no further loans be funded until he returned from his Christmas vacation. Contrary to that advice, Lancaster funded the Oates Corners project, a multi-million dollar transaction, in Brizius' absence.

During Lancaster's annual audit in 1982, Kenneth Stein, an auditor, noticed that the assets had grown at an "unusual" and "very fast" rate: from $17,000,000 (August) to $55,000,000 (September) to $105,000,000 (December). Stein and the other auditors became very concerned about: loans in apparent violation of the limit to individual borrowers; potential conflicts of interest; concentrations of credit in the I–30 corridor; the validity of appraisals made in such a short period of time prior to purchase; and whether the transactions were at arms' length.

In December of 1982, the Federal Home Loan Bank Board conducted an examination of Lancaster. An examiner asked Jensen about the brokerage fees received by companies owned by Jensen. Jensen responded that after he learned that such an affiliation was inappropriate, he

---

3. A "brokered funds" transaction was described at trial as follows. "If I had a million dollars I would break my million dollars up into ten $100,000 investments. And rather than myself calling to savings and loans and banks all around the country, I would call a local brokerage house who would, in turn, know who was paying the best interest rates at banks and savings and loans for me to invest my money and they would invest it for me for a commission." A brokered funds transactions in and of itself was legal.

4. Jensen testified that initially he was not aware that the board had made him an advisory director.

separated himself from those institutions and resigned as chairman of the board at Lancaster. Jensen wrote a letter stating that he had no interest in either Snowball or Helaman. The evidence, however, showed that Jensen did receive proceeds from Snowball and Helaman. Jensen testified that his attorney drafted that letter and that, according to his attorney's advice, he understood that he had no conflict of interest because he was not an officer or a director.

In early 1983, a meeting was held to discuss the conversion of Lancaster from a mutual institution to a stock institution. During that meeting, Jensen revealed that he had purchased the resignation of the board of directors. Brizius was concerned because no application for change of control had been filed with the Federal Home Loan Bank Board. The Federal Home Loan Bank Board was then notified, and Lancaster's board was neutralized by bringing in outside directors. Jensen was then removed as an advisory director.

BELL COUNTY FEDERAL SAVINGS AND LOAN

In September 1982, Jensen met with Kenneth Law, a lawyer and the president of Bell Savings and Loan, to discuss the acquisition of Bell. Jensen again represented that he was a medical doctor. An oral agreement was reached in which Jensen, James Hays, and Weldon Hays would purchase Bell's outstanding stock subject to the approval of the Federal Home Loan Bank Board.

While the application for change of control was pending, Law requested that Jensen buy some stock that certain Bell shareholders wanted to sell. Law advised Jensen that he could not put the stock in his own name so Jensen bought the stock in the name of other persons. Jensen told Law that he was interested in funding some loans in the five to ten million dollar range, and Law informed him that Bell did not have that amount of money to loan. Jensen responded that was not a problem and suggested brokering funds. Jensen then ran an ad for Bell offering rates on jumbo certificates of deposit and instructed the personnel how to offer brokered funds. Jensen indicated to personnel at Bell the amount of money needed for a project, and they would receive the money through brokered funds transactions. Law testified that Bell had no reason to take these brokered funds except to fund the large loans brought by Jensen.

Law examined the loan documents and found them to be incomplete. Law advised Jensen of the problem and Jensen responded that his people would take care of it. Certain remarks Jensen had made gave Law the impression that Jensen owned or was connected with a company that received proceeds funded by Lancaster. Consequently, Law told Jensen that, as an owner of a savings and loan, he could not receive money other than the brokerage fees. Jensen assured Law that he understood and that it would not happen at Bell.

Subsequently, Law began to suspect that Jensen was secretly taking money from the projects. Because of those suspicions, Law and Brizius went to the scheduled closing of a project named Tiffany Cove. Jensen was out of state at the time, and Fredricksen represented him at the closing. None of the borrowers appeared at the closing. Law and Brizius then called the borrowers involved in the Tiffany Cove project to determine whether they were to receive money from the deal. They also talked to the Dallas Title Company to determine whether the property was changing hands. As a result of these conversations, Law and Brizius called Jensen and told him that they "were satisfied that he lied to us," and they were not going to fund the transaction. They also told Jensen that Fredricksen admitted that he was to receive $150,000 of the proceeds, that the loan was going through three or four different hands, and that the borrowers were to receive cash from the proceeds. This information had been concealed because it was not on the borrower's statement, it was on another disclosure statement.

In March 1983, the board of directors of Bell terminated the agreement in which Jensen, Weldon Hays, and James Hays were to acquire the Bell stock. Law and others borrowed the money to buy back the stock Jensen had purchased.

In his defense, Jensen testified that he did not realize he was violating any regulation or law. He was relying on the advice of his attorneys and other individuals who he believed had more expertise in the area of savings and loans.

RESULT OF LOANS

During 1982 and 1983, loans totaling over 300 million dollars were made on the real estate projects in the I–30 corridor. Of that amount, Jensen received approximately $25,000,000.[5] The Federal Deposit Insurance Corporation suffered financial losses totaling $327,942,431, in connection with the above scheme. As a result of the above activities, an 88–count indictment was filed charging Jensen and seven other defendants with numerous offenses. Ultimately, Jensen was severed from the other defendants and tried on 18 counts of the indictment. The jury found him guilty on all the following 18 counts: count 1, conspiracy (18 U.S.C. § 371); counts 7, 15, 22, 24, 27, and 36, fraudulent participation in loan monies and false entries (18 U.S.C. § 1006); counts 14, 16, 21, and 23, fraudulent misapplication of bank funds (18 U.S.C. § 657); counts 52, 53, 65, and 66, wire fraud (18 U.S.C. § 1343); counts 84 and 85, interstate transportation of property taken by fraud (18 U.S.C. § 2314); and count 88, RICO conspiracy (18 U.S.C. § 1962(d)).

The court sentenced Jensen to: 5 years on count 1; 5 years on counts 7, 15, 22, 24, 27, and 36 (concurrent to each other but consecutive to count 1); 5 years on counts 14, 16, 21, and 23 (concurrent with each other and the preceding group, but consecutive to count 1); 5 years on counts 52, 53, 65, and 66 (concurrent with each other and the preceding two groups, but consecutive to count 1); 10 years on counts 84 and 85 (concurrent to each other and concurrent with the preceding three

5. In one real estate transaction, Jensen received a $4,000,000 mansion for what he termed as "equity participation."

groups but consecutive to count 1); and 20 years on count 88 (concurrent with all counts). The court, pursuant to the jury's finding, entered an order of forfeiture against Jensen in the amount of $23,000,000.

* * *

To prove a conspiracy, the government must show that an agreement existed between two or more persons to violate the law, that the defendant had knowledge of the agreement, and that the defendant voluntarily participated in the conspiracy. Each element of a conspiracy may be inferred from circumstantial evidence. *Id.* The agreement may be inferred from a "concert of action." "Once the government has produced evidence of a conspiracy, only slight evidence is needed to connect an individual to that conspiracy." "Knowledge of a conspiracy and voluntary participation in a conspiracy may be inferred from a collection of circumstances." [internal quotation marks and citations omitted]

The evidence at trial was largely undisputed. In fact, it was undisputed that Jensen received approximately $25,000,000 in a matter of months from the transactions at issue. From the beginning of trial, the defense focused the jury on the issue of whether Jensen had the intent to commit the charged offenses. During opening statement, defense counsel argued as follows:

> Now, I don't mean to imply and I don't want to mislead you. I'm not trying to tell you that the things that Paul did were all right. Paul Jensen took some money. He took a lot of money out of these savings and loans, out of these deals that were—that he took in violation of laws and regulations. He should not have taken that money. There is no question about that. That is not the issue of this case. Don't—don't waste one second worrying about that because we can set that aside right now. Paul Jensen took money that he should not have taken.

> As I said before, that's not what this case is about. The question is: Did he know that he was taking money he should not have taken.…

* * *

> The Government's evidence is going to show, and this is another thing that is totally uncontested, there was a conspiracy. The conspiracy involved Faulkner, Toler, Blain, Clifford Sinclair and others. And this was a conspiracy that was going on long before Paul Jensen ever came to Dallas. It is a conspiracy that continued after he left Dallas. That is not an issue in the case. These people were engaged in illegal activity. There is no question about that.

> The question is: Did Paul [Jensen] willfully and knowingly engage in illegal activity with those people? The answer to that is no. So don't worry about trying to decide whether there's something illegal going on. Faulkner, Toler, Blain, Sinclair, they're all doing things that are illegal. That's not the question for this trial.

Jensen was a central figure in this scheme. As the government asserts, Jensen personally participated in the planning of the deals when he negotiated the high points for his mortgage companies and instructed the personnel at Lancaster and Bell how to obtain brokered funds to have money available to loan on the various real estate projects. He purchased the resignation of the board of directors at Lancaster to gain control of that institution. Jensen gained control of both Lancaster and Bell to finance these projects. Without the funding Jensen organized, the scheme would not have been possible or at least not on such a grand scale. In addition, his actions were accompanied by deceit and misrepresentations. For instance, although Jensen still received proceeds from Snowball and Helaman, he represented to the Federal Home Loan Bank Board that he had no interest in either company. Jensen knew that the mortgage companies were receiving high points without the proper underwriting, that buyers were receiving "upfront" money or "kickbacks," and that the property would undergo a series of "land flips" at inflated prices on the day of closing. As a result of these intermediate transactions, Jensen received millions of dollars in loan proceeds.

Although Jensen testified at length regarding his lack of intent to defraud, the jury obviously did not believe him. Intent to defraud was properly before the jury for a factual determination. After a review of the record, we conclude that a rational jury could have inferred Jensen's knowledge of and participation in the conspiracy beyond a reasonable doubt.

Jensen also blanketly contends that the evidence is insufficient to demonstrate that he had the requisite intent regarding the substantive counts. However, "under the Pinkerton [v. United States, 328 U.S. 640 (1946)] rule '[a] party to a conspiracy may be held responsible for a substantive offense committed by a coconspirator in furtherance of a conspiracy, even if that party does not participate in or have any knowledge of the substantive offense.' " [citations omitted] Accordingly, because we have determined that Jensen's conspiracy conviction should stand, Jensen may be held responsible for any substantive offenses committed by coconspirators in furtherance of the conspiracy regardless whether he had knowledge of or participated in the substantive offenses.

Jensen does not challenge any element of the substantive convictions except for his requisite mental state. Again, Jensen's intent was a question for the fact finder. We find there is sufficient evidence to support the jury's conclusion that Jensen had the requisite mental state to commit the substantive offenses.

* * *

Jensen claims the government failed to prove that one conspiracy existed as charged in the indictment. He claims that the evidence introduced demonstrated multiple conspiracies rather than the single overarching conspiracy alleged in count one, resulting in a material variance that prejudiced his substantial rights.

When reviewing a claim of fatal variance, we will reverse only if the evidence at trial varied from what the indictment alleged, and the variance prejudiced the defendant's substantial rights. The following factors are considered to determine whether one or multiple conspiracies existed: (1) a common goal; (2) the nature of the scheme; and (3) an overlapping of participants in the various transactions.

Jensen has not set forth with any specificity the facts necessary to support his claim that more than one conspiracy existed or that there was a material variance between what was charged and the facts adduced at trial. Nevertheless, as in *Faulkner*, the evidence at Jensen's trial demonstrated that the defendants "shared a common goal of enriching themselves by profiting from the leveraged selling and reselling of real estate along I–30." Likewise, "[t]he nature of the scheme was such that different participants played different but important functions necessary to its success." As for the third factor, Jensen implicitly acknowledges that there were overlapping participants in the various transactions when he states that the existence of common participants does not demonstrate only one conspiracy. [citations omitted]

Assuming arguendo that more than one conspiracy existed, Jensen is not entitled to relief. In *Faulkner*, we concluded "that where the indictment alleges a single conspiracy and the evidence established each defendant's participation in at least one conspiracy a defendant's substantial rights are affected only if the defendant can establish reversible error under general principles of joinder and severance." 17 F.3d at 762. Jensen was tried separately, and thus, the jury could not have been confused as to compartmentalizing evidence against other defendants. Jensen has not shown improper joinder or severance.

* * *

Jensen was convicted of conspiring to violate the RICO statute, 18 U.S.C. § 1962(d), as alleged in Count 88 of the indictment. Jensen claims insufficiency of the evidence, contending that the law of this Circuit requires the government to prove that a RICO conspirator, and thus Jensen himself, agreed to personally commit two racketeering acts.

The court below instructed the jury that the evidence must show beyond a reasonable doubt:

> That at the time the Defendant knowingly and wilfully agreed to join in such conspiracy, he did so with the specific intent either to personally participate in the commission of two "racketeering acts," as elsewhere defined in these instructions, or that he specifically intended to otherwise participate in the affairs of the enterprise with the knowledge and intent that *other members* of the conspiracy would commit two or more "racketeering acts" as a part of a "pattern of racketeering activity."

(emphasis added).[6]

The government argues that we have not definitely resolved the personal agreement argument presented by Jensen, and urges us to

6. Additionally, the court below instructed the jury that it was not to find

resolve it in favor of the majority of the Circuits that require only that there is evidence of an agreement that members of the conspiracy will commit two proscribed acts.

Faulkner controls the disposition of this insufficiency claim. There, we held that regardless whether the conviction for conspiracy to violate RICO required the defendant to agree to personally commit two predicate acts or only that he agree with the other conspirators that two predicate acts be committed pursuant to the conspiracy, the RICO conviction was supported by the jury's finding that each had committed the requisite predicate acts. Likewise, in this case, the jury found Jensen guilty of four counts of wire fraud (counts 52, 53, 65, and 66). There is sufficient evidence to support the wire fraud convictions, which are racketeering acts. Jensen is not entitled to relief on this claim, and we need not resolve the personal agreement argument presented by Jensen.

* * *

Notes

1. The court was able to avoid the RICO conspiracy question raised by *Jensen* (whether the government must prove that a defendant personally agreed to commit the predicate acts or simply agreed that a conspirator commit the predicate acts). How would you decide this issue?

2. What do you think about the role played by the attorney, Kenneth Law? Would you have done anything differently?

3. Can you determine exactly what charges Jensen was convicted of under *Pinkerton*?

D. ISSUES UNIQUE TO CIVIL RICO

1. IN GENERAL

Although passed in 1970, RICO was used relatively little until the 1980s. One of the reasons for the change was the Supreme Court's decision in the next case, Sedima, S.P.R.L. v. Imrex Company, Inc., 473 U.S. 479 (1985). This decision "opened the floodgates" for RICO civil action. As you read *Sedima*, note the number of major issues concerning RICO that were unresolved at the time of the decision. Note also Justice Marshall's dissent. It remains one of the most eloquent arguments against "private attorney general" actions such as RICO.

SEDIMA, S.P.R.L. v. IMREX COMPANY, INC.
United States Supreme Court, 1985.
473 U.S. 479.

WHITE, JUSTICE.

The Racketeer Influenced and Corrupt Organizations Act (RICO), 18 U.S.C. §§ 1961–1968, provides a private civil action to recover treble

Jensen guilty unless it unanimously agreed
that he committed at least two particular
racketeering acts.

damages for injury "by reason of a violation of" its substantive provisions. 18 U.S.C. § 1964(c). The initial dormancy of this provision and its recent greatly increased utilization[1] are now familiar history.[2] In response to what it perceived to be misuse of civil RICO by private plaintiffs, the court below construed § 1964(c) to permit private actions only against defendants who had been convicted on criminal charges, and only where there had occurred a "racketeering injury." While we understand the court's concern over the consequences of an unbridled reading of the statute, we reject both of its holdings.

I

RICO takes aim at "racketeering activity," which it defines as any act "chargeable" under several generically described state criminal laws, any act "indictable" under numerous specific federal criminal provisions, including mail and wire fraud, and any "offense" involving bankruptcy or securities fraud or drug-related activities that is "punishable" under federal law. Section 1962, entitled "Prohibited Activities," outlaws the use of income derived from a "pattern of racketeering activity" to acquire an interest in or establish an enterprise engaged in or affecting interstate commerce; the acquisition or maintenance of any interest in an enterprise "through" a pattern of racketeering activity; conducting or participating in the conduct of an enterprise through a pattern of racketeering activity; and conspiring to violate any of these provisions.

Congress provided criminal penalties of imprisonment, fines, and forfeiture for violation of these provisions. In addition, it set out a far-reaching civil enforcement scheme, including the following provision for private suits:

> "Any person injured in his business or property by reason of a violation of section 1962 of this chapter may sue therefor in any appropriate United States district court and shall recover threefold the damages he sustains and the cost of the suit, including a reasonable attorney's fee." § 1964(c).

In 1979, petitioner Sedima, a Belgian corporation, entered into a joint venture with respondent Imrex Co. to provide electronic components to a Belgian firm. The buyer was to order parts through Sedima; Imrex was to obtain the parts in this country and ship them to Europe. The agreement called for Sedima and Imrex to split the net proceeds. Imrex filled roughly $8 million in orders placed with it through Sedima.

---

1. Of 270 District Court RICO decisions prior to this year, only 3% (nine cases) were decided throughout the 1970's, 2% were decided in 1980, 7% in 1981, 13% in 1982, 33% in 1983, and 43% in 1984. Report of the Ad Hoc Civil RICO Task Force of the ABA Section of Corporation, Banking and Business Law 55 (1985) (hereinafter ABA Report); see also id. at 53a (table).

2. For a thorough bibliography of civil RICO decisions and commentary, see Milner, *A Civil RICO Bibliography,* 21 *C.W.L.R.* 409 (1985).

Sedima became convinced, however, that Imrex was presenting inflated bills, cheating Sedima out of a portion of its proceeds by collecting for nonexistent expenses.

In 1982, Sedima filed this action in the Federal District Court for the Eastern District of New York. The complaint set out common-law claims of unjust enrichment, conversion, and breach of contract, fiduciary duty, and a constructive trust. In addition, it asserted RICO claims under § 1964(c) against Imrex and two of its officers. Two counts alleged violations of § 1962(c), based on predicate acts of mail and wire fraud. A third count alleged a conspiracy to violate § 1962(c). Claiming injury of at least $175,000, the amount of the alleged overbilling, Sedima sought treble damages and attorney's fees.

The District Court held that for an injury to be "by reason of a violation of section 1962," as required by § 1964(c), it must be somehow different in kind from the direct injury resulting from the predicate acts of racketeering activity. 574 F.Supp. 963 (1983). While not choosing a precise formulation, the District Court held that a complaint must allege a "RICO-type injury," which was either some sort of distinct "racketeering injury," or a "competitive injury." It found "no allegation here of any injury apart from that which would result directly from the alleged predicate acts of mail fraud and wire fraud," *id.*, and accordingly dismissed the RICO counts for failure to state a claim.

A divided panel of the Court of Appeals for the Second Circuit affirmed. 741 F.2d 482 (1984). After a lengthy review of the legislative history, it held that Sedima's complaint was defective in two ways. First, it failed to allege an injury "by reason of a violation of section 1962." In the court's view, this language was a limitation on standing, reflecting Congress' intent to compensate victims of "certain specific kinds of organized criminality," not to provide additional remedies for already compensable injuries. *Id.* Analogizing to the Clayton Act, which had been the model for § 1964(c), the court concluded that just as an antitrust plaintiff must allege an "antitrust injury," so a RICO plaintiff must allege a "racketeering injury"—an injury "different in kind from that occurring as a result of the predicate acts themselves, or not simply caused by the predicate acts, but also caused by an activity which RICO was designed to deter." *Id.* Sedima had failed to allege such an injury.

The Court of Appeals also found the complaint defective for not alleging that the defendants had already been criminally convicted of the predicate acts of mail and wire fraud, or of a RICO violation. This element of the civil cause of action was inferred from § 1964(c)'s reference to a "violation" of § 1962, the court also observing that its prior-conviction requirement would avoid serious constitutional difficulties, the danger of unfair stigmatization, and problems regarding the standard by which the predicate acts were to be proved.

The decision below was one episode in a recent proliferation of civil RICO litigation within the Second Circuit and in other Courts of Appeals. In light of the variety of approaches taken by the lower courts and the importance of the issues, we grant certiorari. We now reverse.

II

As a preliminary matter, it is worth briefly reviewing the legislative history of the private treble damages action. RICO formed Title IX of the Organized Crime Control Act of 1970, Pub.L.No. 91–452, 84 Stat. 922. The civil remedies in the bill passed by the Senate, S 30, were limited to injunctive actions by the United States and became §§ 1964(a), (b), and (d). Previous versions of the legislation, however, had provided for a private treble-damages action in exactly the terms ultimately adopted in § 1964(c).

During hearings on S 30 before the House Judiciary Committee, Representative Steiger proposed the addition of a private treble-damages action "similar to the private damage remedy found in the anti-trust laws * * *. [T]hose who have been wronged by organized crime should at least be given access to a legal remedy. In addition, the availability of such a remedy would enhance the effectiveness of Title IX's prohibitions." Hearings on S 30, and Related Proposals, before Subcommittee No. 5 of the House Committee on the Judiciary, 91st Cong., 2d Sess., 520 (1970) (hereinafter House Hearings). The American Bar Association also proposed an amendment "based upon the concept of Section 4 of the Clayton Act." *Id.*

Over the dissent of three members, who feared the treble-damages provision would be used for malicious harassment of business competitors, the Committee approved the amendment. In summarizing the bill on the House floor, its sponsor described the treble-damages provision as "another example of the antitrust remedy being adapted for use against organized criminality." 116 Cong.Rec. 35295 (1970). The full House then rejected a proposal to create a complementary treble-damages remedy for those injured by being named as defendants in malicious private suits. Representative Steiger also offered an amendment that would have allowed private injunctive actions, fixed a statute of limitations, and clarified venue and process requirements. The proposal was greeted with some hostility because it had not been reviewed in Committee, and Steiger withdrew it without a vote being taken. The House then passed the bill, with the treble-damages provision in the form recommended by the Committee.

The Senate did not seek a conference and adopted the bill as amended in the House. The treble-damages provision had been drawn to its attention while the legislation was still in the House, and had received the endorsement of Senator McClellan, the sponsor of S 30, who was of the view that the provision would be "a major new tool in extirpating the baneful influence of organized crime in our economic life."

III

The language of RICO gives no obvious indication that a civil action can proceed only after a criminal conviction. The word "conviction" does not appear in any relevant portion of the statute. To the contrary, the predicate acts involve conduct that is "chargeable" or "indictable," and "offense[s]" that are "punishable," under various criminal statutes. As defined in the statute, racketeering activity consists not of acts for which the defendant has been convicted, but of acts for which he could be. See also S.Rep. No. 91–617, p. 158 (1969): "a racketeering activity * * * must be an act in itself subject to criminal sanction." Thus, a prior-conviction requirement cannot be found in the definition of "racketeering activity." Nor can it be found in § 1962, which sets out the statute's substantive provisions. Indeed, if either § 1961 or § 1962 did contain such a requirement, a prior conviction would also be a prerequisite, nonsensically, for a criminal prosecution, or for a civil action by the Government to enjoin violations that had not yet occurred.

The Court of Appeals purported to discover its prior-conviction requirement in the term "violation" in § 1964(c). However, even if that term were read to refer to a criminal conviction, it would require a conviction under RICO, not of the predicate offenses. That aside, the term "violation" does not imply a criminal conviction. It refers only to a failure to adhere to legal requirements. This is its indisputable meaning elsewhere in the statute. § 1962 renders certain conduct "unlawful," § 1963 and § 1964 impose consequences, criminal and civil, for "violations" of § 1962. We should not lightly infer that Congress intended the term to have wholly different meanings in neighboring subsections.[7]

The legislative history also undercuts the reading of the court below. The clearest current in that history is the reliance on the Clayton Act model, under which private and governmental actions are entirely distinct. The only specific reference in the legislative history to prior convictions of which we are aware is an objection that the treble-damages provision is too broad precisely because "there need not be a conviction under any of these laws for it to be racketeering." 116 Cong.Rec. 35342 (1970). The history is otherwise silent on this point and contains nothing to contradict the import of the language appearing in the statute. Had Congress intended to impose this novel requirement, there would have been at least some mention of it in the legislative history, even if not in the statute.

The Court of Appeals was of the view that its narrow construction of the statute was essential to avoid intolerable practical consequences.[9]

---

7. When Congress intended that the defendant have been previously convicted, it said so. Title 18 U.S.C. § 1963(f) (1982 ed., Supp. III) states that "[u]pon conviction of a person under this section," his forfeited property shall be seized. Likewise, in Title X of the same legislation Congress explicitly required prior convictions, rather than prior criminal activity, to support enhanced sentences for special offenders. See 18 U.S.C. § 357(e).

9. It is worth bearing in mind that the holding of the court below is not without problematic consequences of its own. It arbitrarily restricts the availability of private actions, for lawbreakers are often not apprehended and convicted. Even if a conviction has been obtained, it is unlikely that a private plaintiff will be able to recover for all of the acts constituting an extensive "pattern," or that multiple victims will all be able to obtain redress. This is because criminal convictions are often limited to a small portion of the actual or possible charges. The decision below would also create peculiar incentives for plea bargaining

First, without a prior conviction to rely on, the plaintiff would have to prove commission of the predicate acts beyond a reasonable doubt. This would require instructing the jury as to different standards of proof for different aspects of the case. To avoid this awkwardness, the court inferred that the criminality must already be established, so that the civil action could proceed smoothly under the usual preponderance standard.

We are not at all convinced that the predicate acts must be established beyond a reasonable doubt in a proceeding under § 1964(c). In a number of settings, conduct that can be punished as criminal only upon proof beyond a reasonable doubt will support civil sanctions under a preponderance standard. There is no indication that Congress sought to depart from this general principle here. That the offending conduct is described by reference to criminal statutes does not mean that its occurrence must be established by criminal standards or that the consequences of a finding of liability in a private civil action are identical to the consequences of a criminal conviction. But we need not decide the standard of proof issue today. For even if the stricter standard is applicable to a portion of the plaintiff's proof, the resulting logistical difficulties, which are accepted in other contexts, would not be so great as to require invention of a requirement that cannot be found in the statute and that Congress, as even the Court of Appeals had to concede, did not envision.

The court below also feared that any other construction would raise severe constitutional questions, as it "would provide civil remedies for offenses criminal in nature, stigmatize defendants with the appellation 'racketeer,' authorize the award of damages which are clearly punitive, including attorney's fees, and constitute a civil remedy aimed in part to avoid the constitutional protections of the criminal law." We do not view the statute as being so close to the constitutional edge. As noted above, the fact that conduct can result in both criminal liability and treble damages does not mean that there is not a bona fide civil action. The familiar provisions for both criminal liability and treble-damages under the antitrust laws indicate as much. Nor are attorney's fees "clearly punitive." Cf. 42 U.S.C. § 1988. As for stigma, a civil RICO proceeding leaves no greater strain than do a number of other civil proceedings. Furthermore, requiring conviction of the predicate acts would not protect against an unfair imposition of the "racketeer" label. If there is a problem with thus stigmatizing a garden variety defrauder by means of a civil action, it is not reduced by making certain that the defendant is

to non-predicate-act offenses so as to ensure immunity from a later civil suit. If nothing else, a criminal defendant might plead to a tiny fraction of counts, so as to limit future civil liability. In addition, the dependence of potential civil litigants on the initiation and success of a criminal prosecution could lead to unhealthy private pressures on prosecutors and to self-serving trial testimony, or at least accusations thereof. Problems would also arise if some or all of the convictions were reversed on appeal. Finally, the compelled wait for the completion of criminal proceedings would result in pursuit of state claims, complex statute of limitations problems, or the wasteful splitting of actions, with resultant claim and issue preclusion complications.

guilty of fraud beyond a reasonable doubt. Finally, to the extent an action under § 1964(c) might be considered quasi-criminal, requiring protections normally applicable only to criminal proceedings, the solution is to provide those protections, not to ensure that they were previously afforded by requiring prior convictions.

Finally, we note that a prior-conviction requirement would be inconsistent with Congress' underlying policy concerns. Such a rule would severely handicap potential plaintiffs. A guilty party may escape conviction for any number of reasons—not least among them the possibility that the Government itself may choose to pursue only civil remedies. Private attorney general provisions such as § 1964(c) are in part designed to fill prosecutorial gaps. This purpose would be largely defeated, and the need for treble damages as an incentive to litigate unjustified, if private suits could be maintained only against those already brought to justice.

In sum, we can find no support in the statute's history, its language, or considerations of policy for a requirement that a private treble-damages action under § 1964(c) can proceed only against a defendant who has already been criminally convicted. To the contrary, every indication is that no such requirement exists. Accordingly, the fact that Imrex and the individual defendants have not been convicted under RICO or the federal mail and wire fraud statutes does not bar Sedima's action.

IV

In considering the Court of Appeals' second prerequisite for a private civil RICO action—"injury * * * caused by an activity which RICO was designed to deter"—we are somewhat hampered by the vagueness of that concept. Apart from reliance on the general purposes of RICO and a reference to "mobsters," the court provided scant indication of what the requirement of racketeering injury means. It emphasized Congress' undeniable desire to strike at organized crime, but acknowledged and did not purport to overrule Second Circuit precedent rejecting a requirement of an organized crime nexus. The court also stopped short of adopting a "competitive injury" requirement; while insisting that the plaintiff show "the kind of economic injury which has an effect on competition," it did not require "actual anticompetitive effect."

The court's statement that the plaintiff must seek redress for an injury caused by conduct that RICO was designed to deter is unhelpfully tautological. Nor is clarity furnished by a negative statement of its rule: standing is not provided by the injury resulting from the predicate acts themselves. That statement is itself apparently inaccurate when applied to those predicate acts that unmistakably constitute the kind of conduct Congress sought to deter. The opinion does not explain how to distinguish such crimes from the other predicate acts Congress has lumped together in § 1961(1). The court below is not alone in struggling to define "racketeering injury," and the difficulty of that task itself cautions against imposing such a requirement.

We need not pinpoint the Second Circuit's precise holding, for we perceive no distinct "racketeering injury" requirement. Given that "racketeering activity" consists of no more and no less than commission of a predicate act, § 1961(1), we are initially doubtful about a requirement of a "racketeering injury" separate from the harm from the predicate acts. A reading of the statute belies any such requirement. Section 1964(c) authorizes a private suit by "[a]ny person injured in his business or property by reason of a violation of § 1962." Section 1962 in turn makes it unlawful for "any person"—not just mobsters—to use money derived from a pattern of racketeering activity to invest in an enterprise, to acquire control of an enterprise through a pattern of racketeering activity, or to conduct an enterprise through a pattern of racketeering activity. §§ 1962(a)–(c). If the defendant engages in a pattern of racketeering activity in a manner forbidden by these provisions, and the racketeering activities injure the plaintiff in his business or property, the plaintiff has a claim under § 1964(c). There is no room in the statutory language for an additional, amorphous "racketeering injury" requirement.

A violation of § 1962(c), the section on which Sedima relies, requires (1) conduct (2) of an enterprise (3) through a pattern[14] (4) of racketeering activity. The plaintiff must, of course, allege each of these elements to state a claim. Conducting an enterprise that affects interstate commerce is obviously not in itself a violation of § 1962, nor is mere commission of the predicate offenses. In addition, the plaintiff only has standing if, and can only recover to the extent that, he has been injured in his business or property by the conduct constituting the violation. As the Seventh Circuit has stated, "[a] defendant who violates section 1962 is not liable for treble damages to everyone he might have injured by

---

14. As many commentators have pointed out, the definition of a "pattern of racketeering activity" differs from the other provisions in § 1961 in that it states that a pattern "requires at least two acts of racketeering activity," § 1961(5), not that it "means" two such acts. The implication is that while two acts are necessary, they may not be sufficient. Indeed, in common parlance two of anything do not generally form a "pattern." The legislative history supports the view that two isolated acts of racketeering activity do not constitute a pattern. As the Senate Report explained: "The target of [RICO] is thus not sporadic activity. The infiltration of legitimate business normally requires more than one 'racketeering activity' and the threat of continuing activity to be effective. It is this factor of *continuity plus relationship* which combines to produce a pattern." S.Rep. No. 91–617, p. 158 (1969) (emphasis added). Similarly, the sponsor of the Senate bill,

after quoting this portion of the Report, pointed out to his colleagues that "[t]he term 'pattern' itself requires the showing of a relationship * * *. So, therefore, proof of two acts of racketeering activity, without more, does not establish a pattern * * *." 116 Cong.Rec. 18940 (1970) (statement of Sen. McClellan). See also id. at 35193 (statement of Rep. Poff) (RICO "not aimed at the isolated offender"); House Hearings at 665. Significantly, in defining "pattern" in a later provision of the same bill, Congress was more enlightening: "[C]riminal conduct forms a pattern if it embraces criminal acts that have the same or similar purposes, results, participants, victims, or methods of commission, or otherwise are interrelated by distinguishing characteristics and are not isolated events." 18 U.S.C. § 3575(e). This language may be useful in interpreting other sections of the Act. *Cf.* Iannelli v. United States, 420 U.S. 770 (1975).

other conduct, nor is the defendant liable to those who have not been injured."

But the statute requires no more than this. Where the plaintiff alleges each element of the violation, the compensable injury necessarily is the harm caused by predicate acts sufficiently related to constitute a pattern, for the essence of the violation is the commission of those acts in connection with the conduct of an enterprise. Those acts are, when committed in the circumstances delineated in § 1962(c), "an activity which RICO was designed to deter." Any recoverable damages occurring by reason of a violation of § 1962(c) will flow from the commission of the predicate acts.

This less restrictive reading is amply supported by our prior cases and the general principles surrounding this statute. RICO is to be read broadly. This is the lesson not only of Congress' self-consciously expansive language and overall approach, see United States v. Turkette, 452 U.S. 576, 586–87, 101 S.Ct. 2524, 69 L.Ed.2d 246 (1981), but also of its express admonition that RICO is to "be liberally construed to effectuate its remedial purposes," Pub.L. No. 91–452, § 904(a), 84 Stat. 947. The statute's "remedial purposes" are nowhere more evident than in the provision of a private action for those injured by racketeering activity. Far from effectuating these purposes, the narrow readings offered by the dissenters and the court below would in effect eliminate § 1964(c) from the statute.

RICO was an aggressive initiative to supplement old remedies and develop new methods for fighting crime. While few of the legislative statements about novel remedies and attacking crime on all fronts, were made with direct reference to § 1964(c), it is in this spirit that all of the Act's provisions should be read. The specific references to § 1964(c) are consistent with this overall approach. Those supporting § 1964(c) hoped it would "enhance the effectiveness of Title IX's prohibitions" and provide "a major new tool." Its opponents, also recognizing the provision's scope, complained that it provided too easy a weapon against "innocent businessmen" and would be prone to abuse. It is also significant that a previous proposal to add RICO-like provisions to the Sherman Act had come to grief in part precisely because it "could create inappropriate and unnecessary obstacles in the way of * * * a private litigant [who] would have to contend with a body of precedent—appropriate in a purely antitrust context—setting strict requirements on questions such as 'standing to sue' and 'proximate cause.' "In borrowing its "racketeering injury" requirement from antitrust standing principles, the court below created exactly the problems Congress sought to avoid.

Underlying the Court of Appeals' holding was its distress at the "extraordinary, if not outrageous," uses to which civil RICO has been put. 741 F.2d at 487. Instead of being used against mobsters and organized criminals, it has become a tool for everyday fraud cases brought against "respected and legitimate 'enterprises.' " Id. Yet Congress wanted to reach both "legitimate" and "illegitimate" enterprises.

The former enjoy neither an inherent incapacity for criminal activity nor immunity from its consequences. The fact that § 1964(c) is used against respected businesses allegedly engaged in a pattern of specifically identified criminal conduct is hardly a sufficient reason for assuming that the provision is being misconstrued. Nor does it reveal the "ambiguity" discovered by the court below. "[T]he fact that RICO has been applied in situations not expressly anticipated by Congress does not demonstrate ambiguity. It demonstrates breadth."

It is true that private civil actions under the statute are being brought almost solely against such defendants, rather than against the archetypal, intimidating mobster.[16] Yet this defect—if defect it is—is inherent in the statute as written, and its correction must lie with Congress. It is not for the judiciary to eliminate the private action in situations where Congress has provided it simply because plaintiffs are not taking advantage of it in its more difficult applications.

We nonetheless recognize that, in its private civil version, RICO is evolving into something quite different from the original conception of its enactors. Though sharing the doubts of the Court of Appeals about this increasing divergence, we cannot agree with either its diagnosis or its remedy. The "extra-ordinary" uses to which civil RICO has been put appear to be primarily the result of the breadth of the predicate offenses, in particular the inclusion of wire, mail, and securities fraud, and the failure of Congress and the courts to develop a meaningful concept of "pattern." We do not believe that the amorphous standing requirement imposed by the Second Circuit effectively responds to these problems, or that it is a form of statutory amendment appropriately undertaken by the courts.

V

Sedima may maintain this action if the defendants conducted the enterprise through a pattern of racketeering activity. The questions whether the defendants committed the requisite predicate acts, and whether the commission of those acts fell into a pattern, are not before us. The complaint is not deficient for failure to allege either an injury separate from the financial loss stemming from the alleged acts of mail and wire fraud, or prior convictions of the defendants. The decision below is accordingly reversed, and the case is remanded for further proceedings consistent with this opinion.

It is so ordered.

JUSTICE MARSHALL, WITH WHOM JUSTICE BRENNAN, JUSTICE BLACKMUN, AND JUSTICE POWELL JOIN, DISSENTING.

16. The ABA Task Force found that of the 270 known civil RICO cases at the trial court level, 40% involved securities fraud, 37% common law fraud in a commercial or business setting, and only 9% "allegations of criminal activity of a type generally associated with professional criminals." ABA Report, at 55–56. Another survey of 132 published decisions found that 57 involved securities transactions and 38 commercial and contract disputes, while no other category made it into double figures. American Institute of Certified Public Accountants, The Authority to Bring Private Treble–Damage Suits Under "RICO" Should be Removed 13 (Oct. 10, 1984).

The Court today recognizes that "in its private civil version, RICO is evolving into something quite different from the original conception of its enactors." The Court, however, expressly validates this result, imputing it to the manner in which the statute was drafted. I fundamentally disagree both with the Court's reading of the statute and with its conclusion. I believe that the statutory language and history disclose a narrower interpretation of the statute that fully effectuates Congress' purposes, and that does not make compensable under civil RICO a host of claims that Congress never intended to bring within RICO's purview.

I

The Court's interpretation of the civil RICO statute quite simply revolutionizes private litigation; it validates the federalization of broad areas of state common law of frauds, and it approves the displacement of well-established federal remedial provisions. We do not lightly infer a congressional intent to effect such fundamental changes. To infer such intent here would be untenable, for there is no indication that Congress even considered, much less approved, the scheme that the Court today defines.

The single most significant reason for the expansive use of civil RICO has been the presence in the statute, as predicate acts, of mail and wire fraud violations. Prior to RICO, no federal statute had expressly provided a private damages remedy based upon a violation of the mail or wire fraud statutes, which make it a federal crime to use the mail or wires in furtherance of a scheme to defraud. Moreover, the Courts of Appeals consistently had held that no implied federal private causes of action accrue to victims of these federal violations. The victims normally were restricted to bringing actions in state court under common-law fraud theories.

Under the Court's opinion today, two fraudulent mailings or uses of the wires occurring within 10 years of each other might constitute a "pattern of racketeering activity," § 1961(5), leading to civil RICO liability. The effects of making a mere two instances of mail or wire fraud potentially actionable under civil RICO are staggering, because in recent years the Courts of Appeals have "tolerated an extraordinary expansion of mail and wire fraud statutes to permit federal prosecution for conduct that some had thought was subject only to state criminal and civil law." United States v. Weiss, 752 F.2d 777, 791 (2d Cir.1985) (Newman, J., dissenting). In bringing criminal actions under those statutes, prosecutors need not show either a substantial connection between the scheme to defraud and the mail and wire fraud statutes, or that the fraud involved money or property.

[Discussion of mail fraud cases omitted.-ed.]

* * *

The only restraining influence on the "inexorable expansion of the mail and wire fraud statutes" has been the prudent use of prosecutorial discretion. Prosecutors simply do not invoke the mail and wire fraud provisions in every case in which a violation of the relevant statute can be proved. See United States Attorney's Manual § 9–43.120 (Feb. 16, 1984). For example, only where the scheme is directed at a "class of persons or the general public" and includes "a substantial pattern of conduct," will "serious consideration * * * be given to [mail fraud] prosecution." In all other cases, "the parties should be left to settle their differences by civil or criminal litigation in the state courts." *Id.*

The responsible use of prosecutorial discretion is particularly important with respect to criminal RICO prosecutions—which often rely on mail and wire fraud as predicate acts—given the extremely severe penalties authorized by RICO's criminal provisions. Federal prosecutors are therefore instructed that "[u]tilization of the RICO statute, more so than most federal criminal sanctions, requires particularly careful and reasoned application." *Id.*, § 9–110.200 (Mar. 9, 1984). The Justice Department itself recognizes that a broad interpretation of the criminal RICO provisions would violate "the principle that the primary responsibility for enforcing state laws rests with the state concerned." *Id.* Specifically, the Justice Department will not bring RICO prosecutions unless the pattern of racketeering activity required by 18 U.S.C. § 1962 has "some relation to the purpose of the enterprise." United States Attorney's Manual § 9–110.350 (Mar. 9, 1984).

Congress was well aware of the restraining influence of prosecutorial discretion when it enacted the criminal RICO provisions. It chose to confer broad statutory authority on the Executive fully expecting that this authority would be used only in cases in which its use was warranted. Moreover, in seeking a broad interpretation of RICO from this Court in *Turkette,* the Government stressed that no "extreme cases" would be brought because the Justice Department would exercise "sound discretion" through a centralized review process.

In the context of civil RICO, however, the restraining influence of prosecutors is completely absent. Unlike the Government, private litigants have no reason to avoid displacing state common-law remedies. Quite the contrary, such litigants, lured by the prospect of treble damages and attorney's fees, have a strong incentive to invoke RICO's provisions whenever they can allege in good faith two instances of mail or wire fraud. Then the defendant, facing a tremendous financial exposure in addition to the threat of being labeled a "racketeer," will have a strong interest in settling the dispute. The civil RICO provision consequently stretches the mail and wire fraud statutes to their absolute limits and federalizes important areas of civil litigation that until now were solely within the domain of the States.

In addition to altering fundamentally the federal-state balance in civil remedies, the broad reading of the civil RICO provision also displaces important areas of federal law. For example, one predicate offense under RICO is "fraud in the sale of securities." 18 U.S.C.A. § 1961(1) (1982 ed., Supp. III 1985). By alleging two instances of such fraud, a plaintiff might be able to bring a case within the scope of the civil RICO provision. It does not take great legal insight to realize that such a plaintiff would pursue his case under RICO rather than do so solely under the Securities Act of 1933 or the Securities Exchange Act of 1934, which provide both express and implied causes of action for violations of the federal securities laws. Indeed, the federal securities laws contemplate only compensatory damages and ordinarily do not authorize recovery of attorney's fees. By invoking RICO, in contrast, a successful plaintiff will recover both treble damages and attorney's fees.

More importantly, under the Court's interpretation, the civil RICO provision does far more than just increase the available damages. In fact, it virtually eliminates decades of legislative and judicial development of private civil remedies under the federal securities law. Over the years, courts have paid close attention to matters such as standing, culpability, causation, reliance, and materiality, as well as the definitions of "securities" and "fraud." All of this law is now an endangered species because plaintiffs can avoid the limitations of the securities laws merely by alleging violations of other predicate acts.

* * *

The dislocations caused by the Court's reading of the civil RICO provision are not just theoretical. In practice, this provision frequently has been invoked against legitimate businesses in ordinary commercial settings. As the Court recognizes, the ABA Task Force that studied civil RICO found that 40% of the reported cases involved securities fraud, 37% involved common-law fraud in a commercial or business setting. Many a prudent defendant, facing ruinous exposure, will decide to settle even a case with no merit. It is thus not surprising that civil RICO has been used for extortive purposes, giving rise to the very evils that it was designed to combat.

Only 9% of all civil RICO cases have involved allegations of criminal activity normally associated with professional criminals. The central purpose that Congress sought to promote through civil RICO is now a mere footnote.

In summary, in both theory and practice, civil RICO has brought profound changes to our legal landscape. Undoubtedly, Congress has the power to federalize a great deal of state common law, and there certainly are no relevant constraints on its ability to displace federal law. Those, however, are not the questions that we face in this case. What we have to decide here, instead, is whether Congress in fact intended to produce these far-reaching results.

Established canons of statutory interpretation counsel against the Court's reading of the civil RICO provision. First, we do not impute lightly a congressional intention to upset the federal-state balance in the provision of civil remedies as fundamentally as does this statute under the Court's view.

* * *

In this case, nothing in the language of the statute or the legislative history suggests that Congress intended either the federalization of state common law or the displacement of existing federal remedies. Quite to the contrary, all that the statute and the legislative history reveal as to these matters is what Judge Oakes called a "clanging silence." 741 F.2d at 492.

Moreover, if Congress had intended to bring about dramatic changes in the nature of commercial litigation, it would at least have paid more than cursory attention to the civil RICO provision. This provision was added in the House of Representatives after the Senate already had passed its version of the RICO bill; the House itself adopted a civil remedy provision almost as an afterthought; and the Senate thereafter accepted the House's version of the bill without even requesting a Conference. Congress simply does not act in this way when it intends to effect fundamental changes in the structure of federal law.

* * *

Notes

1.   Note the Court's discussion of the burden of proof which the civil RICO plaintiff must bear. The Court noted that the government, which is the plaintiff in a criminal RICO action, must prove all elements beyond a reasonable doubt. The Court then hinted that the civil plaintiff must prove the RICO elements by a preponderance standard. Subsequent Courts of Appeals opinions have assumed, from this hint, that preponderance is the standard of proof in civil RICO actions.[w] It is important to note what is implicit in this discussion: the plaintiff in a criminal RICO case and the plaintiff in a civil RICO case will always prove the same elements and, it is likely, will prove these elements with the same facts. Thus, the difference in the criminal and civil cases may be only the degree by which the plaintiff must prove these elements.

2.   The Second Circuit ruled that a civil RICO action could proceed only after a criminal conviction. This view was rejected by the Supreme Court in the foregoing opinion. What were the reasons for the Second Circuit's view? What are some of the policy and practical problems in adhering to this view? What are the problems caused by the Supreme Court's rejection of this view?

3.   The Supreme Court also rejected the Second Circuit's effort to limit racketeering acts to injuries "caused by activity which RICO was designed to deter." According to the Supreme Court, what are the problems with such an interpretation? Do you agree?

———

As *Sedima* discussed, there are some differences in criminal and civil RICO causes of action. Criminal actions are brought only by the United

w.   *See, e.g.*, Fleischhauer v. Feltner, 879 F.2d 1290 (6th Cir.1989); Liquid Air Corp.   v. Rogers, 834 F.2d 1297 (7th Cir.1987).

States Department of Justice; are punishable by a term of imprisonment, fine and forfeiture; and, all elements must be proven beyond a reasonable doubt. Civil actions may be brought by any party who qualifies for standing under 18 U.S.C. § 1964(c); equitable relief as well as awards of treble damages, attorneys fees and costs are available; and, all elements must be proven only by a preponderance of evidence rather than beyond a reasonable doubt. Otherwise, with few exceptions, the prosecutor in the criminal action and the plaintiff in the civil action prove the same case. The case below, Chisolm v. TranSouth Financial Corporation, 95 F.3d 331 (4th Cir.1996), demonstrates one of these exceptions. *Chisolm* refers briefly to Holmes v. Securities Investor Protection Corporation, 503 U.S. 258 (1992) which is discussed in the next subsection.

CHISOLM v. TRANSOUTH FINANCIAL CORPORATION

United States Court of Appeals, Fourth Circuit, 1996.
95 F.3d 331.

HALL, CIRCUIT JUDGE.

The appellants are three of four plaintiffs who filed a putative class action against appellee TranSouth Financial Corporation and others, seeking redress under the Racketeer Influenced and Corrupt Organizations Act (RICO), 18 U.S.C. § 1961 et seq., for damages they sustained as victims of a "revolving repossession" scheme. The district court entered a final judgment dismissing the action as to TranSouth under Fed.R.Civ.P. 12(b)(6), because the plaintiffs had failed to allege in their complaint that, following the repossession of their vehicles, they had relied to their detriment on the written notices of sale mailed to them by TranSouth.

In the wake of the judgment, the plaintiffs moved to amend their complaint, but the district court denied the motion because it believed that the plaintiffs could prove no set of facts establishing that they had relied on the mailings. We hold that the district court's denial of the plaintiffs' motion to amend was an abuse of its discretion; we thus vacate the court's judgment and remand with instructions to permit the amendment.

* * *

According to the complaint, TranSouth conspired with Charlie Falk's Auto Wholesale, Inc., and JB Collection Corporation, both of Norfolk, Virginia, to effect an automobile "churning" or revolving repossession scheme. Falk's sold used vehicles at inflated prices, offering to arrange financing at interest rates as high as thirty percent. Under the terms of the financing contracts, Falk's retained a security interest in the vehicles pending full repayment of the loan by the borrower. Falk's then assigned the secured notes to TranSouth, agreeing to buy back the notes for a fixed price—usually $1,000 to $1,500—in the event of the borrower's default.

If a borrower missed a payment, TranSouth had the vehicle repossessed.[1] It then mailed a "Notice of Private Sale," giving the borrower an opportunity to redeem the vehicle. Any vehicles that were not redeemed were retransferred, with the accompanying notes, to Falk's for the prearranged consideration.

Upon repurchasing the notes, Falk's assigned them to JB, its wholly-owned subsidiary. JB then demanded payment from the borrowers for the "deficiency" between the loan balance and the price obtained by the "sale" of the vehicle, i.e., the retransfer price. If the borrower failed to pay, JB filed a deficiency action in state court for the stated amount. On occasion, JB also claimed attorney fees of twenty-five percent, notwithstanding that it had filed suit without the assistance of counsel.

While JB was trying to collect from the borrowers, Falk's resold the repossessed vehicles for about the same price as (or even more than) it had previously, starting the process all over again. The original borrowers were never notified of these subsequent, legitimate sales; the amount of the purchase price was not credited to the deficiencies, and the borrowers were not paid any resultant surplus.[4]

* * *

On June 17, 1993, four victims of the scheme filed a complaint in the district court against Falk's, JB, and TranSouth. The complaint alleged that the three had violated various provisions of RICO, and that JB had failed to comply with the Fair Debt Collection Act, 15 U.S.C.A. § 1692 *et seq*. The plaintiffs also asserted state law claims against each defendant for violations of Virginia's Consumer Protection Act and its version of the Uniform Commercial Code, and for common law fraud and conspiracy.

The matter was referred by the district court to a magistrate judge to conduct hearings and make proposed findings. The magistrate judge issued his report and recommendation on November 19, 1993, wherein he concluded that the RICO claims should be dismissed (as to TranSouth) or judgment granted on the pleadings (as to Falk's and JB).

* * *

1. TranSouth usually employed a subsidiary of Falk's to repossess the automobiles, and the vehicles were frequently taken to a lot leased from Falk's by TranSouth.

4. The case of plaintiff Starlette Seamster illustrates the effect of the scheme on its victims. On August 21, 1987, Seamster purchased a 1984 Dodge Aries on credit from Falk's for $6,492. Falk's assigned the loan to TranSouth, agreeing to buy back the note for $1,500 in the event of Seamster's default, which indeed occurred about fourteen months later. TranSouth repossessed the car and mailed its "Notice of Private Sale" to Seamster, who failed to respond. Falk's repurchased the loan, and JB demanded payment of the $2,743 "deficiency" between the $1,500 repurchase price and the outstanding loan balance; in March 1989, with no payment forthcoming, JB filed suit. On May 20, 1989, Falk's resold the Aries for $6,300, only $192 less than what Seamster had paid for it almost two years earlier, and $2,057 more than the balance of her loan. Notwithstanding this windfall, JB neither remitted any of the surplus to Seamster nor withdrew its lawsuit.

The appellants maintain that TranSouth was more than just an unwitting participant in the scheme, and that its actions violated two distinct provisions of RICO: 18 U.S.C. §§ 1962(a) and (d). * * * The appellants assert that TranSouth committed mail fraud each time that it notified a defaulting borrower that his or her repossessed vehicle would, if not redeemed, be disposed of at a private "sale." According to the appellants, the notice was intentionally misleading because TranSouth knew that a transfer of collateral under a repurchase agreement was not a "sale" at all.

* * *

The elements of mail fraud are (1) a scheme disclosing an intent to defraud, and (2) the use of the mails in furtherance of the scheme. See Pereira v. United States, 347 U.S. 1, 8 (1954). Although the crime of common law fraud requires the intended victim to have justifiably and detrimentally relied on the defendant's misrepresentation, no such "reliance" element must be proved to obtain a conviction for mail fraud. Thus, assuming that TranSouth, through its agents, mailed the notice letters with the intent to defraud the borrowers by facilitating the churning scheme, it committed mail fraud. By mailing many such letters, it may have engaged in a pattern of activity sufficient to establish one or more RICO violations.

The difficulty in this case lies in § 1964(c)'s requirement that, in order to recover damages in a civil action, a person be injured in his business or property "by reason of" a § 1962 violation. The statute is not so broad as it first seems:

> This language can of course be read to mean that a plaintiff is injured "by reason of" a RICO violation, and therefore may recover, simply on showing that the defendant violated § 1962, the plaintiff was injured, and the defendant's violation was a "but for" cause of plaintiff's injury. This conclusion is hardly compelled, however, and the very unlikelihood that Congress meant to allow all factually injured plaintiffs to recover persuades us that the Act should not get such an expansive reading.

Holmes v. Securities Investor Protection Corp., 503 U.S. 258, 265–66 (1992). Consequently, it is not enough that a civil RICO plaintiff prove that, but for the defendant's violation, he would not have been injured; he must also show that the violation *proximately* caused the harm. *Id.* at 268; Brandenburg v. Seidel, 859 F.2d 1179, 1189 (4th Cir.1988). The pertinent inquiry in determining the existence of proximate, or "legal" cause, is "whether the conduct has been so significant and important a cause that the defendant should be held responsible." *Brandenburg* at 1189.

In *Brandenburg*, depositors of an insolvent Maryland savings and loan association brought civil RICO claims against former officers and directors of the equally insolvent Maryland Savings–Share Insurance Corporation (MSSIC), a quasi-public entity established by the state legislature to regulate S & Ls and insure their deposits. The depositors asserted, among other things, that MSSIC's print advertisements and promotional materials, touting the security of the deposits that it insured, persuaded them to deposit their funds in member institutions. In addition, newspaper advertisements carrying the MSSIC seal, but placed by the savings and loan itself, were said to have encouraged the deposit of more funds than MSSIC could safely insure. MSSIC's advertisements and promotional literature were alleged to have intentionally conveyed the misleading impression that it was a state agency and that its depositors' accounts were insured by the state. The depositors maintained that the deceptive materials violated the federal mail fraud statute.

We held, *inter alia*, that the depositors had failed to allege a sufficient causal connection between their losses and MSSIC's purported crimes. Although we acknowledged that the agency's representations might have induced deposits beyond its capacity to insure them, and thus may have been a cause-in-fact of the insolvency, we concluded that the depositors' losses were proximately caused by the saving and loan's failure to maintain adequate reserves, in conjunction with MSSIC's negligent dereliction of its oversight responsibilities. Because any injury suffered by the depositors to their property was not "by reason of" any racketeering activity proscribed by § 1961(1), we affirmed the district court's dismissal of the RICO claims against MSSIC.

* * *

Our decision in *Brandenburg* essentially bifurcated the "by reason of" analysis. We said that, where the predicate act giving rise to civil liability under RICO was alleged to have been mail fraud, prospective plaintiffs must, in order to demonstrate their standing to sue, plausibly allege both that they detrimentally relied in some way on the fraudulent mailing, and that the mailing was a proximate cause of the alleged injury to their business or property. Though our decision focused primarily on the depositors' inability to allege proximate cause, we also noted that their supposed reliance on certain representations made by MSSIC was not justifiable.

When we decided in *Brandenburg* to impose a reliance requirement in the civil RICO context, we were fully aware that no analogous rule existed in criminal RICO prosecutions involving mail fraud. As we made clear in Caviness v. Derand Resources Corp., 983 F.2d 1295 (4th Cir. 1993), a showing of reliance on the predicate act of fraud ensures the existence of a "direct relation between the injury asserted and the injurious conduct alleged." *Id.* at 1305, quoting *Holmes*, 503 U.S. at 268.

The appellants here contend that our pleading requirement is too rigid, contrary both to Congress's intent that RICO be liberally construed, and the Supreme Court's admonition that strict requirements of standing or proximate cause not be erected as obstacles to private RICO litigants. *See Sedima*, 473 U.S. at 498–99. The appellants insist that § 1964(c)'s "by reason of" language contemplates that a civil RICO suit may be maintained, not only in mail fraud cases where the deceitful mailing is the blade rushing down toward the guillotine victim, but also in cases involving more grandiose schemes to cheat, where the mailing is but part of the frame that holds the blade.

We have never held otherwise. Inasmuch as an injury may have more than one proximate cause, our rule that reliance be shown in civil RICO fraud actions does not also dictate that the fraud be the sole legal cause of the plaintiff's injury, so long as it is a legal cause. The only caveat is that, where fraud is alleged as a proximate cause of the injury, the fraud must be a "classic" one. In other words, the plaintiff must have justifiably relied, to his detriment, on the defendant's material misrepresentation.

* * *

The complaint filed in this matter adequately alleges injury. The appellants allege that their vehicles were repossessed and "sold" at a price substantially below market value. The vehicles were later resold legitimately, but the appellants were never informed of those transactions. Hence, not only were excess funds generated by the "sale" of the collateral illegally withheld, but the appellants also ostensibly remained obligated to pay phantom deficiencies. Consequently, the appellants suffered injury to their property.

The complaint also adequately alleges proximate cause. In order for the scheme to succeed, the appellants needed to be convinced that the "private sales" referenced in the TranSouth notices were legitimate. Had an appellant's suspicion been aroused, she might have inquired further or—worse—retained a lawyer to investigate the matter. ("To further the scheme, Transouth issues false and deceptive notices of private sale which are intended to and which do mislead the public about their repossession and redemption rights."). Indeed, concealment of the nature of the "private sales" was the very linchpin of the scheme.

As we have noted, "the legal cause determination is properly one for the court, taking into consideration such factors as the foreseeability of the particular injury, the intervention of other independent causes, and the factual directness of the causal connection." *Brandenburg*, 859 F.2d at 1189. If we accept, as we must for now, the appellants' allegation that TranSouth acted in concert with Falk's and JB in a unified scheme, it is readily apparent that all of the *Brandenburg* factors militate strongly in favor of holding TranSouth responsible for its actions.

It is equally obvious, though, that the appellants have failed to allege that they actually relied on the TranSouth mailings to inform them of their rights and to assure them that these rights were being protected. Inasmuch as the appellants did not specifically plead reliance, we can hardly fault the district court for faithfully applying our precedents and dismissing the complaint.

* * *

We see no reason, however, to deprive the appellants of the opportunity to amend their complaint, if they can, to allege reliance. No discovery has yet been conducted, and the complaint has not previously been substantively amended, at least as far as TranSouth is concerned.[9] Although TranSouth has filed its answer, the rules provide that leave to amend "shall be freely given when justice so requires." Fed.R.Civ.P. 15(a).

Here, the district court apparently believed that the appellants were incapable of pleading reliance on TranSouth's notice mailings; thus, granting them leave to amend would be a fruitless act. The magistrate judge's report, appended to the district court's opinion, makes the point:

> [The] plaintiffs' argument concedes that they would not have redeemed the cars even if they had known that the process was a sham and concedes further that the plaintiffs cannot make such an allegation. In short, plaintiffs did not, and can not, allege that they acted in reliance on the TranSouth mailings.

851 F.Supp. at 757 (citation to record omitted).

In our view, the magistrate judge's conclusion misconstrues the role of the notice letter in the overall scheme. If the appellants' theory of the case prove to be true, TranSouth did not mail the notices to prevent the defaulting borrowers from exercising their redemption rights, but only to assure them that the liquidation of the collateral was proceeding legally and legitimately, thus influencing them to accept the process without question, and depriving them of a meritorious defense to JB's deficiency suit. As the magistrate judge noted in the very next sentence of his opinion:

> Plaintiffs' "reliance" argument amounts to no more than a general complaint that TranSouth participated in a massive fraud, an illegal and profitable scam, that took advantage of the innocent plaintiffs' reliance on the apparent legitimacy and legality of the operation.

Id. (emphasis supplied). We could scarcely say it more clearly. The only difficulty with the appellants' approach so far is that they have argued reliance without first pleading it. We therefore vacate the district court's judgment of dismissal and remand the case with instructions for it to give the appellants an opportunity to correct this defect.

* * *

2. STANDING

As Chart 3A, *supra,* demonstrated, a significant number of civil RICO claims are dismissed by the courts for lack of standing. The seminal case on standing is Holmes v. Securities Investor Protection Corporation.

---

9. Two amendments of the complaint have been allowed, but only for the purpose of effectuating the settlement agreement negotiated with Falk's and JB.

HOLMES v. SECURITIES INVESTOR PROTECTION CORPORATION

United States Supreme Court, 1992.
503 U.S. 258.

Souter, Justice.

Respondent Securities Investor Protection Corporation (SIPC) alleges that petitioner Robert G. Holmes, Jr., conspired in a stock-manipulation scheme that disabled two broker-dealers from meeting obligations to customers, thus triggering SIPC's statutory duty to advance funds to reimburse the customers. The issue is whether SIPC can recover from Holmes under the Racketeer Influenced and Corrupt Organizations Act (RICO), 18 U.S.C. §§ 1961–1968 (1988 ed. and Supp. II). We hold that it cannot.

I

A

The Securities Investor Protection Act of 1970 (SIPA), 84 Stat. 1636, as amended, 15 U.S.C. §§ 78aaa–78lll, authorized the formation of SIPC, a private nonprofit corporation, of which most broker-dealers registered under § 15(b) of the Securities Exchange Act of 1934, § 78o(b), are required to be "members." Whenever SIPC determines that a member "has failed or is in danger of failing to meet its obligations to customers," and finds certain other statutory conditions satisfied, it may ask for a "protective decree" in federal district court. Once a court finds grounds for granting such a petition, it must appoint a trustee charged with liquidating the member's business.

After returning all securities registered in specific customers' names, the trustee must pool securities not so registered together with cash found in customers' accounts and divide this pool ratably to satisfy customers' claims. To the extent the pool of customer property is inadequate, SIPC must advance up to $500,000 per customer to the trustee for use in satisfying those claims.[3]

B

On July 24, 1981, SIPC sought a decree from the United States District Court for the Southern District of Florida to protect the customers of First State Securities Corporation (FSSC), a broker-dealer and SIPC member. Three days later, it petitioned the United States District Court for the Central District of California, seeking to protect the customers of Joseph Sebag, Inc. (Sebag), also a broker-dealer and SIPC member. Each court issued the requested decree and appointed a trustee, who proceeded to liquidate the broker-dealer.

---

3. To cover these advances, SIPA provides for the establishment of a SIPC Fund. SIPC may replenish the fund from time to time by levying assessments, which members are legally obligated to pay.

Two years later, SIPC and the two trustees brought this suit in the United States District Court for the Central District of California, accusing some 75 defendants of conspiracy in a fraudulent scheme leading to the demise of FSSC and Sebag. Insofar as they are relevant here, the allegations were that, from 1964 through July 1981, the defendants manipulated stock of six companies by making unduly optimistic statements about their prospects and by continually selling small numbers of shares to create the appearance of a liquid market; that the broker-dealers bought substantial amounts of the stock with their own funds; that the market's perception of the fraud in July 1981 sent the stocks plummeting; and that this decline caused the broker-dealers' financial difficulties resulting in their eventual liquidation and SIPC's advance of nearly $13 million to cover their customers' claims. The complaint described Holmes' participation in the scheme by alleging that he made false statements about the prospects of one of the six companies, Aero Systems, Inc., of which he was an officer, director, and major shareholder; and that over an extended period he sold small amounts of stock in one of the other six companies, the Bunnington Corporation, to simulate a liquid market. The conspirators were said to have violated § 10(b) of the Securities Exchange Act of 1934, 15 U.S.C. § 78j(b), Securities and Exchange Commission (SEC) Rule 10b–5, 17 CFR § 240.10b–5 (1991), and the mail and wire fraud statutes, 18 U.S.C. §§ 1341, 1343 (1988 ed., Supp. II). Finally, the complaint concluded that their acts amounted to a "pattern of racketeering activity" within the meaning of the RICO statute, 18 U.S.C. §§ 1962, 1961(1), and (5) (1988 ed. and Supp. II), so as to entitle the plaintiffs to recover treble damages, § 1964(c).

After some five years of litigation over other issues, the District Court entered summary judgment for Holmes on the RICO claims, ruling that SIPC "does not meet the 'purchaser-seller' requirements for standing to assert RICO claims which are predicated upon violation of Section 10(b) and Rule 10b–5," and that neither SIPC nor the trustees had satisfied the "proximate cause requirement under RICO." Although SIPC's claims against many other defendants remained pending, the District Court under Federal Rule of Civil Procedure 54(b) entered a partial judgment for Holmes, immediately appealable. SIPC and the trustees appealed.

The United States Court of Appeals for the Ninth Circuit reversed and remanded after rejecting both of the District Court's grounds. The Court of Appeals held first that, whereas a purchase or sale of a security is necessary for entitlement to sue on the implied right of action recognized under § 10(b) and Rule 10b–5, the cause of action expressly provided by § 1964(c) of RICO imposes no such requirement limiting SIPC's standing. Second, the appeals court held the finding of no proximate cause to be error, the result of a mistaken focus on the causal relation between SIPC's injury and the acts of Holmes alone; since Holmes could be held responsible for the acts of all his co-conspirators, the Court of Appeals explained, the District Court should have looked to

the causal relation between SIPC's injury and the acts of all conspirators.[6]

Holmes' ensuing petition to this Court for certiorari presented two
issues, whether SIPC had a right to sue under RICO,[7] and whether
Holmes could be held responsible for the actions of his co-conspirators.
We granted the petition on the former issue alone, and now reverse.[8]

II

A

RICO's provision for civil actions reads that

"[a]ny person injured in his business or property by reason of a
violation of section 1962 of this chapter may sue therefor in any
appropriate United States district court and shall recover threefold
the damages he sustains and the cost of the suit, including a
reasonable attorney's fee." 18 U.S.C. § 1964(c).

This language can, of course, be read to mean that a plaintiff is
injured "by reason of" a RICO violation, and therefore may recover,
simply on showing that the defendant violated § 1962, the plaintiff was
injured, and the defendant's violation was a "but for" cause of plaintiff's
injury. This construction is hardly compelled, however, and the very
unlikelihood that Congress meant to allow all factually injured plaintiffs
to recover persuades us that RICO should not get such an expansive
reading. Not even SIPC seriously argues otherwise.

The key to the better interpretation lies in some statutory history.
We have repeatedly observed, that Congress modeled § 1964(c) on the
civil-action provision of the federal antitrust laws, § 4 of the Clayton
Act, which reads in relevant part that

"any person who shall be injured in his business or property by
reason of anything forbidden in the antitrust laws may sue therefor
. . . and shall recover threefold the damages by him sustained, and
the cost of suit, including a reasonable attorney's fee." 15 U.S.C.
§ 15.

* * *

We may fairly credit the 91st Congress, which enacted RICO, with
knowing the interpretation federal courts had given the words earlier
Congresses had used first in § 7 of the Sherman Act, and later in the
Clayton Act's § 4. It used the same words, and we can only assume it

---

6. For purposes of this decision, we will
assume without deciding that the Court of
Appeals correctly held that Holmes can be
held responsible for the acts of his co-conspirators.

7. The petition phrased the question as
follows: "Whether a party which was neither a purchaser nor a seller of securities,
and for that reason lacked standing to sue
under Section 10(b) of the Securities Exchange Act of 1934 and Rule 10b–5 there-

under, is free of that limitation on standing
when presenting essentially the same
claims under the Racketeer Influenced and
Corrupt Organizations Act ('RICO')."

8. Holmes does not contest the trustees'
right to sue under § 1964(c), and they took
no part in the proceedings before this Court
after we granted certiorari on the first
question alone.

intended them to have the same meaning that courts had already given them. Proximate cause is thus required.

B

Here we use "proximate cause" to label generically the judicial tools used to limit a person's responsibility for the consequences of that person's own acts. At bottom, the notion of proximate cause reflects "ideas of what justice demands, or of what is administratively possible and convenient." Accordingly, among the many shapes this concept took at common law, was a demand for some direct relation between the injury asserted and the injurious conduct alleged. Thus, a plaintiff who complained of harm flowing merely from the misfortunes visited upon a third person by the defendant's acts was generally said to stand at too remote a distance to recover.

Although such directness of relationship is not the sole requirement of Clayton Act causation, it has been one of its central elements, for a variety of reasons. First, the less direct an injury is, the more difficult it becomes to ascertain the amount of a plaintiff's damages attributable to the violation, as distinct from other, independent, factors. Second, quite apart from problems of proving factual causation, recognizing claims of the indirectly injured would force courts to adopt complicated rules apportioning damages among plaintiffs removed at different levels of injury from the violative acts, to obviate the risk of multiple recoveries. And, finally, the need to grapple with these problems is simply unjustified by the general interest in deterring injurious conduct, since directly injured victims can generally be counted on to vindicate the law as private attorneys general, without any of the problems attendant upon suits by plaintiffs injured more remotely.

We will point out in Part III–A below that the facts of the instant case show how these reasons apply with equal force to suits under § 1964(c).

III

As we understand SIPC's argument, it claims entitlement to recover, first, because it is subrogated to the rights of those customers of the broker-dealers who did not purchase manipulated securities, and, second, because a SIPA provision gives it an independent right to sue. The first claim fails because the conspirators' conduct did not proximately cause the nonpurchasing customers' injury, the second because the provision relied on gives SIPC no right to sue for damages.

A

As a threshold matter, SIPC's theory of subrogation is fraught with unanswered questions. In suing Holmes, SIPC does not rest its claimed subrogation to the rights of the broker-dealers' customers on any provision of SIPA. SIPC assumes that SIPA provides for subrogation to the customers' claims against the failed broker-dealers, but not against third parties like Holmes. As against him, SIPC relies rather on "common law rights of subrogation" for what it describes as "its money paid to

customers for customer claims against third parties." At oral argument
in this Court, SIPC narrowed its subrogation argument to cover only the
rights of customers who never purchased manipulated securities. But
SIPC stops there, leaving us to guess at the nature of the "common law
rights of subrogation" that it claims, and failing to tell us whether they
derive from federal or state common law, or, if the latter, from common
law of which State. Nor does SIPC explain why it declines to assert the
rights of customers who bought manipulated securities.

It is not these questions, however, that stymie SIPC's subrogation
claim, for even assuming, arguendo, that it may stand in the shoes of
nonpurchasing customers, the link is too remote between the stock
manipulation alleged and the customers' harm, being purely contingent
on the harm suffered by the broker-dealers. That is, the conspirators
have allegedly injured these customers only insofar as the stock manipulation first injured the broker-dealers and left them without the where-
withal to pay customers' claims. Although the customers' claims are
senior (in recourse to "customer property") to those of the broker-
dealers' general creditors, the causes of their respective injuries are the
same: The broker-dealers simply cannot pay their bills, and only that
intervening insolvency connects the conspirators' acts to the losses
suffered by the nonpurchasing customers and general creditors.

As we said, however, in Associated General Contractors of Cal., Inc.
v. Carpenters, 459 U.S. 519, 534 (1983), quoting Justice Holmes, "The
general tendency of the law, in regard to damages at least, is not to go
beyond the first step" and the reasons that supported conforming
Clayton Act causation to the general tendency apply just as readily to the
present facts, underscoring the obvious congressional adoption of the
Clayton Act direct-injury limitation among the requirements of
§ 1964(c). [internal quotation marks and citations omitted] If the nonpurchasing customers were allowed to sue, the district court would first
need to determine the extent to which their inability to collect from the
broker-dealers was the result of the alleged conspiracy to manipulate, as
opposed to, say, the broker-dealers' poor business practices or their
failures to anticipate developments in the financial markets. Assuming
that an appropriate assessment of factual causation could be made out,
the district court would then have to find some way to apportion the
possible respective recoveries by the broker-dealers and the customers,
who would otherwise each be entitled to recover the full treble damages.
Finally, the law would be shouldering these difficulties despite the fact
that those directly injured, the broker-dealers, could be counted on to
bring suit for the law's vindication. As noted above, the broker-dealers
have in fact sued in this case, in the persons of their SIPA trustees
appointed on account of their insolvency. Indeed, the insolvency of the
victim directly injured adds a further concern to those already expressed,
since a suit by an indirectly injured victim could be an attempt to
circumvent the relative priority its claim would have in the directly
injured victim's liquidation proceedings. See Mid–State Fertilizer Co. v.
Exchange National Bank of Chicago, 877 F.2d 1333, 1336 (7th Cir.1989).

As against the force of these considerations of history and policy, SIPC's reliance on the congressional admonition that RICO be "liberally construed to effectuate its remedial purposes," does not deflect our analysis. There is, for that matter, nothing illiberal in our construction: We hold not that RICO cannot serve to right the conspirators' wrongs, but merely that the nonpurchasing customers, or SIPC in their stead, are not proper plaintiffs. Indeed, we fear that RICO's remedial purposes would more probably be hobbled than helped by SIPC's version of liberal construction: Allowing suits by those injured only indirectly would open the door to "massive and complex damages litigation[, which would] not only burde[n] the courts, but [would] also undermin[e] the effectiveness of treble-damages suits." *Associated General Contractors*, 459 U.S., at 545.

In sum, subrogation to the rights of the manipulation conspiracy's secondary victims does, and should, run afoul of proximate-causation standards, and SIPC must wait on the outcome of the trustees' suit. If they recover from Holmes, SIPC may share according to the priority SIPA gives its claim.

* * *

Notes

What did you find most persuasive in the Court's opinion? Why do you think SIPC brought suit after those directly injured, the broker-dealers, had also sued?

———

In the next case, Mid Atlantic Telecom, Inc. v. Long Distance Services, Inc., 18 F.3d 260 (4th Cir.1994), the United States Court of Appeals for the Fourth Circuit applied *Holmes* and found that the RICO plaintiff had standing. As you read *Mid Atlantic*, determine whether you agree with the Fourth Circuit or the district court, which held that the plaintiff had no standing.

MID ATLANTIC TELECOM, INC. v. LONG DISTANCE SERVICES, INC.

United States Court of Appeals, Fourth Circuit, 1994.
18 F.3d 260.

SPROUSE, SENIOR CIRCUIT JUDGE.

Mid Atlantic Telecom, Inc. (Mid Atlantic) instituted this civil action against Long Distance Services, Inc. (LDS), charging LDS and its president, Richard Rice, with violations of the Racketeer Influenced and Corrupt Organizations Act (RICO), 18 U.S.C. §§ 1962(a) and (c), and conspiracy to violate those sections under § 1962(d). Mid Atlantic also brought state law claims of unfair competition and tortious interference with its contracts and business relationships. After LDS filed a motion to dismiss Mid Atlantic's complaint, Mid Atlantic submitted an amended complaint. Without allowing the plaintiff the opportunity to engage in discovery, the district court granted summary judgment in favor of the defendants. In a revised order, the district court declined to exercise jurisdiction over the plaintiff's state law claims and dismissed them without prejudice. Mid Atlantic appeals the grant of summary judgment, complaining particularly about the court's decision to grant summary judgment prior to discovery.

I

Mid Atlantic and LDS are resellers of long-distance telecommunications services in the mid-Atlantic region of the United States. As resellers, they purchase time wholesale on the transmission lines of common carriers, such as AT & T, Sprint, and MCI, and then sell that time to customers. Because resellers are able to purchase time from common carriers at a rate below tariff, they can offer customers lower rates and can develop specialized services and rate plans for their clients. The market shares for regional resellers are limited, and Mid Atlantic and LDS have less than one percent of the long-distance market in their region.

Resellers, like other long-distance telephone service providers, charge their customers on a per minute basis. The rate may fluctuate according to the time of day during which calls are placed or the distance between callers. In order to register this information, telephone companies rely on complicated switching equipment and billing software. During one weekend in 1986, an employee of defendant LDS neglected to turn on certain switching equipment. As a result, LDS was unable to record any data regarding use of its transmission lines. When the error was discovered, Richard Rice, the president of LDS, instructed Henry Luken, an employee of the firm, to develop a program to recoup the losses. Luken created a computer program that randomly added minutes to the calls of LDS customers. By artificially inflating the lengths of calls, LDS was able to charge excessive prices and recover its losses from the weekend in 1986.

Mid Atlantic asserts that LDS did not eliminate the fraudulent billing scheme after it had compensated itself for the losses of the one weekend. Instead, Rice allegedly insisted that LDS employees continue to use the inflated billing program to offer artificially lower rates to new customers and entice Mid Atlantic customers to sign up with LDS.[1] In practical effect, however, the quoted rates were not lower, since additional minutes were randomly and artificially added to the lengths of telephone calls. The fraudulent billing scheme apparently ceased in 1991 when the Federal Bureau of Investigation served a search warrant on LDS's offices.

---

1. At oral argument, counsel for LDS conceded, for purposes of this appeal, that LDS fraudulently solicited customers by randomly assigning more time to telephone calls made through LDS.

In its amended complaint filed on April 13, 1992, Mid Atlantic alleged that LDS and its president violated §§ 1962(a) and (c) of RICO and conspired to violate those sections in contravention of § 1962(d) of RICO. In support of these claims, Mid Atlantic accused LDS and Rice of engaging in a pattern of racketeering activity by fraudulently using the mails and telephone wires to solicit customers of Mid Atlantic in violation of 18 U.S.C. §§ 1341 and 1343. According to the complaint, LDS's billing scheme enabled it to offer artificially low rates which forced Mid Atlantic to match LDS's low rates or lose its customers. Because of these lost revenues and customers, Mid Atlantic claims that it meets the injury requirement of § 1964(c) of RICO and has standing to sue.

The district court first ruled as a matter of law that LDS and its president Rice did not enter into a conspiracy. This ruling is not contested on appeal. The court then, without allowing discovery, granted summary judgment in favor of LDS on the ground that the activities conducted by LDS could not have been the proximate cause of Mid Atlantic's injuries under the Supreme Court's ruling in Holmes v. Securities Investor Protection Corp., 503 U.S. 258, 112 S.Ct. 1311 (1992). Mid Atlantic consequently pursued this appeal.

II

Our review of a district court's grant of a motion for summary judgment is de novo, employing the same standards applied by the district court. Under those standards, the non-movant, in order to prevail, must produce sufficient evidence to create a genuine issue of material fact. The district court's decision denying Mid Atlantic's request to conduct discovery is subject to review under the abuse of discretion standard.

In *Holmes*, 503 U.S. at 259, the Supreme Court addressed the causation requirements of § 1964(c) of RICO. It held that the same causation principles discussed in Associated Gen. Contractors of Cal., Inc. v. Carpenters, 459 U.S. 519 (1983), are implicated in § 1964(c). In *Associated Gen. Contractors*, the Supreme Court examined the causation requirements of section 4 of the Clayton Act. Under that statute, "any person who shall be injured in his business or property by reason of anything forbidden in the antitrust laws may sue therefor.... " 15 U.S.C. § 15(a). The Court concluded that the appropriate inquiry to determine whether a plaintiff was injured "by reason of" a violation of the antitrust laws was the same as the common law test for determining proximate causation. *Associated Gen. Contractors*, 459 U.S. at 535–36.

Confronting the identical "by reason of" language in the RICO context, however, the *Holmes* Court cautioned against an overly expansive view of proximate cause: "[A] plaintiff who complained of harm flowing merely from the misfortunes visited upon a third person by the defendant's acts [is] generally said to stand at too remote a distance to recover." *Holmes*, 503 U.S. at 268. In *Holmes*, the Securities Investor Protection Corp. ("SIPC") had sued the perpetrators of a stock manipulation scheme to satisfy the claims of customers of broker-dealer firms that had failed in the wake of their purchase of the manipulated stocks. The Court refused to find that the scheme operators' actions were the proximate cause of the investors' injuries: "The broker-dealers simply cannot pay their bills, and only that intervening insolvency connects the conspirators' acts to the losses suffered by the nonpurchasing customers and general creditors." *Id.*

In *Holmes*, the Court was particularly concerned with the assertion of the rights of the directly injured targets of the RICO conspiracy by plaintiffs who had only been indirectly injured. The Court reasoned that the broker-dealers were the targets of the stock manipulators' scheme and could be counted on to vindicate their rights. In contrast, the injuries suffered by the broker-dealers' customers were merely derivative of the injuries suffered by the investment firms themselves. "Allowing suits by those injured only indirectly would open the door to 'massive and complex damages litigation [which would] not only burde[n] the courts, but also undermin[e] the effectiveness of treble-damages suits.' "*Id.*

In Brandenburg v. Seidel, 859 F.2d 1179, 1187 (4th Cir.1988), we pointed out that the "by reason of" language in § 1964(c) "requires the plaintiff to make two closely related showings: (1) that he has suffered injury to his business or property; and (2) that this injury was caused by the predicate acts of racketeering activity that make up the violation of § 1962." The plaintiffs in *Brandenburg* sued, among others, the former officers and directors of Maryland Savings–Share Insurance Corporation (MSSIC) for losses they suffered when the deposit insurance system collapsed. The depositors claimed they were injured by reason of MSSIC mailings that contained misrepresentations about the stability of the Maryland savings and loan industry. We found that the plaintiffs had alleged an attenuated cause-in-fact connection between the defendants' conduct and their injury.

In affirming the grant of summary judgment in favor of the defendants, we noted that "[s]uch a cause-in-fact connection, standing alone, does not suffice to establish liability. Civil RICO is, of course, a statutory tort remedy—simply one with particularly drastic remedies. Causation principles generally applicable to tort liability must be considered applicable." *Id.* at 1189. In *Brandenburg*, the causal connection was considered too tenuous, and the plaintiffs' theory ignored the more immediate causes of their injuries (i.e., duplicity by the management of savings and loans and failure of MSSIC to prevent those depredations). Where the injuries were more appropriately attributable to intervening causes that were not predicate acts under RICO, the RICO action could not lie. *Id.* at 1190.

LDS and Rice argue that *Holmes* and *Brandenburg* compel the result reached by the district court. Mid Atlantic does not allege that it received mail or telephone solicitations offering artificially low rates, merely that its customers did. LDS and Rice contend that their customers were the only victims of the alleged fraud and only those customers can assert their rights. They further maintain that any injury to Mid Atlantic stemmed from the independent intervening acts of Mid Atlantic customers after LDS's solicitations. It follows, the appellees argue, that the solicitations could not have been the proximate cause of Mid Atlantic's injuries.

We are unable to agree. In *Brandenburg*, it was recognized that "the legal cause determination is properly one of law for the court, taking into consideration such factors as the foreseeability of the particular injury, the intervention of other independent causes, and the factual directness of the causal connection." Brandenburg also explained that proximate causation requires a nexus between the proscribed acts and the injuries. We did not, however, intend to establish a rule that only injuries suffered by the immediate victim of a predicate act satisfied the "by reason of" requirement of § 1964(c). In conducting the traditional common-law proximate cause analysis, therefore, courts should focus on the temporal and circumstantial relationship between the defendant's conduct and the injury suffered by the plaintiff, and the foreseeability that intervening events would cause injury to the plaintiff.

In its amended complaint, Mid Atlantic alleges that LDS engaged in fraudulent use of the mails and telephone wires to entice customers away from Mid Atlantic and to eliminate Mid Atlantic as a competitor. Taking the complaint at face value, it cannot be said that we are confronted with circumstances similar to those presented in *Brandenburg*, where the intervening acts were wholly independent of the alleged predicate acts. LDS customers, of course, were the direct victims of the defendants' scheme to fraudulently inflate their telephone bills. Given the opportunity to engage in discovery, however, Mid Atlantic may be able to show that while the scheme was initially aimed only at defrauding LDS customers, Rice broadened the sweep of the intrigue to include Mid Atlantic as a direct target (i.e., to obtain an unfair competitive advantage in recruiting Mid Atlantic customers). Discovery might or might not reveal that the artificially low billings were purposefully devised to lead to harm to Mid Atlantic.

A finding of proximate cause in such a situation would not be at odds with the Supreme Court's holding in *Holmes*, since Mid Atlantic is not seeking to vindicate the rights of its former customers who may have been offered fraudulently low rates. Furthermore, Mid Atlantic's injuries, as alleged, are not derivative of any losses suffered by its former customers. Rather, it claims distinct and independent injuries: lost customers and lost revenue due to the necessity of offering lower rates to match LDS's fraudulent ones. At this point, these claims are not established, but they are alleged in the complaint, and the plaintiff should have the opportunity to develop support for its claims through discovery. The district court, after discovery, will be in a better position to consider "such factors as the foreseeability of the particular injury, the intervention of other independent causes, and the factual directness of the causal connection." *Brandenburg*, 859 F.2d at 1189.

LDS and Rice argue that summary judgment is appropriate on an alternative ground. They contend that Mid Atlantic was aware of LDS's use of the fraudulent billing program and how that program enabled LDS to offer artificially low rates; therefore, Mid Atlantic could not have relied on LDS's proffered lower rates in setting its own rates. Absent reliance, Mid Atlantic could not bring a RICO claim under § 1964(c). This argument is predicated on *Brandenburg* where we stated: "[W]hile . . . it is not necessary to establish detrimental reliance by the victim in order to make out a violation of the federal mail fraud statute, such reliance is necessary to establish injury to business or property 'by reason of' a predicate act of mail fraud within the meaning of § 1964(c)." 859 F.2d at 1188 n. 10. Because the district court based its proximate cause determination on the Supreme Court's decision in *Holmes*, it did not resolve the reliance issue. In light of the factual uncertainties surrounding Mid Atlantic's allegations of solicitation of its customers, resolution of the reliance issue should be deferred until completion of discovery on remand.

In sum, we hold that the district court abused its discretion in denying Mid Atlantic's request for discovery to establish support for its claim that it was an intended target of LDS's fraudulent scheme. Summary judgment is vacated and the case is remanded for action consistent with the views expressed in this opinion.

Notes

1.   Do you think Mid Atlantic's argument—that as a competitor of LDS it was injured by having to raise its rates to keep pace with LDS's artificially high rates—was sufficient standing to bring a RICO action?

2.   After you have studied the False Claims Act (FCA), 31 U.S.C. § 3129, in Chapter 10, return to this case. Is there a potential FCA action in the LDS conduct?

The next case, Manson v. Stacescu, 11 F.3d 1127 (2d Cir.1993), tests the logic of *Holmes*. As you read this case, note the potential harm the Mansons are facing: how could this not be sufficient for standing?

MANSON v. STACESCU

United States Court of Appeals, Second Circuit, 1993.
11 F.3d 1127.

TIMBERS, CIRCUIT JUDGE.

David Manson and Mark Manson (the Mansons) appeal from a judgment entered in the District of Connecticut, Warren W. Eginton, District Judge, 823 F.Supp. 76, dismissing their action which sought relief under the Racketeer Influenced and Corrupt Organizations Act (RICO), 18 U.S.C. §§ 1961–68 (1988). The court held that the Mansons do not have standing to commence an action under RICO and denied the Mansons' motion for leave to amend their complaint to allege additional facts relating to standing. On appeal, the Mansons contend that the court erred in holding that they do not have standing under RICO and that the court abused its discretion in denying their motion for leave to amend their complaint.

We reject the Mansons' claims. We affirm the district court's judgment in all respects.

We summarize only those facts and prior proceedings believed necessary to an understanding of the issues raised on appeal.

The Mansons commenced this RICO action against twenty-six defendants for alleged abuses against the Stavola–Manson Electrical Construction Company, Inc. (the Company). David Manson is a director, president, and fifty percent shareholder of the Company. Appellee Anca Stacescu is the other fifty percent shareholder. David Manson and Mark Manson are personal obligors on a $450,000 loan to the Company.

The Mansons allege that appellees, who include persons both inside and outside the Company, engaged in a pattern of racketeering activity through a criminal enterprise masterminded by the other director of the Company, Jay Stavola. Appellees allegedly committed various felonious acts, including bribery of a labor union official, attempted extortion, money laundering, threatened murder, credit card fraud, bankruptcy fraud, obstruction of justice, mail fraud, and conspiracy in violation of RICO. These acts allegedly were part of a scheme through which appellees looted the Company to the point of bankruptcy in order to enrich themselves.

In 1988, after the Company had sustained heavy losses, David Manson petitioned for chapter eleven bankruptcy relief and filed a derivative action on behalf of the Company. The Mansons allege that David Fitzpatrick, the attorney for Jay Stavola and several other appellees, manufactured evidence and submitted it to the bankruptcy court in order to persuade the court to dismiss the petition. After the court dismissed the petition, Fitzpatrick asked the court to appoint Richard Winter as the receiver for the Company and he was. Fitzpatrick allegedly selected Winter with the understanding that Winter either would not seek to recover debts owed to the Company by Fitzpatrick's clients or would settle debts for substantially less than the amounts owed.

Since being appointed receiver, Winter allegedly has failed to act in the best interests of the Company. Winter has pursued only two actions on behalf of the Company and settled both for substantially less than the amount owed. When David Manson inquired about these settlements, Jay Stavola and others allegedly threatened him with financial ruin and murder if he refused to "back off". The Mansons also allege that Winter is covering up appellees' fraudulent scheme by intentionally failing to pursue the derivative action filed by David Manson. The Mansons further allege that as a result they cannot obtain relief under state law.

The Mansons claim that appellees' acts injured them personally. David Manson claims that he has lost earnings and profits in the Company and has sustained injury to his reputation and business credit. In addition, he and Mark Manson claim that they have sustained damages by virtue of their personal liability on the Company's $450,000 loan.

On March 23, 1993, the district court held that the case should be dismissed for want of standing. The court held that the Mansons do not have standing as creditors of the Company and that David Manson does not have standing either as a shareholder or as an employee of the Company. The Mansons subsequently moved for leave to amend their complaint to allege additional facts relating to standing. The court denied the Mansons' motion for leave to amend their complaint on the ground that it was moot. On April 27, 1993, the court entered an order dismissing the action as to all appellees.

On appeal, the Mansons contend that * * * the court erred in holding that the Mansons do not have standing to commence an individual RICO action regarding the looting of a company to which the Mansons are personal obligors on a loan and in which David Manson is a fifty percent shareholder and employee * * *.

* * *

The standing provision of RICO provides that "[a]ny person injured in his business or property by reason of a violation of section 1962 of this chapter may sue therefor ... and shall recover threefold the damages he sustains". 18 U.S.C. § 1964(c) (1988). The Supreme Court has interpreted this language as limiting standing to plaintiffs whose injuries were caused proximately by the RICO predicate acts. Holmes v. Securities Investor Protection Corp., 503 U.S. 258 (1992). A central element of proximate cause is a showing of some "direct relation between the injury asserted and the injurious conduct alleged". *Id.*

The district court reasoned that the Company was the primary victim of the RICO conspiracy alleged by the Mansons and that the Mansons' injuries in their capacities as creditors, shareholder, and employee were derivative of the Company's injuries. The court held, therefore, that the Mansons' injuries were not caused proximately by the alleged conduct and that the Mansons do not have standing to seek relief under RICO. Our standard of review of the district court's holding, which is a ruling of law, is de novo.

* * *

The Mansons claim that they have standing as obligors on a $450,-000 loan to the Company. Since the Company allegedly cannot pay its loan obligations, the Mansons are responsible personally for the repayment of this loan and have become creditors of the Company. Creditors of a bankrupt corporation, however, generally do not have standing under RICO. The creditor generally sustains injury only because he has a claim against the corporation. The creditor's injury is derivative of that of the corporation and is not caused proximately by the RICO violations.

We have recognized a narrow exception to the general rule denying creditors standing. We held that creditors of a bankrupt company had standing to bring an individual RICO action when they had sustained a direct injury. Specifically, the creditors in *Bankers Trust* were forced to defend against frivolous lawsuits filed to harass them and to cause them monetary loss over and above that caused by the company's bankruptcy. Furthermore, the defendants in *Bankers Trust* had made a fraudulent conveyance for the direct purpose of insulating the corporation from its creditors.

Unlike the plaintiffs in *Bankers Trust*, the Mansons do not allege a direct injury. The alleged looting of the Company only harmed the Mansons indirectly. Furthermore, since the Mansons are personal obligors on a corporate bank loan and not primary creditors of the Company, the Mansons did not become liable until the looting of the Company rendered the corporation unable to pay its debts. If the Company were to recover its assets, the Mansons' injuries would be cured. The Mansons' injuries are even further down the chain of causation than those sustained by primary creditors.

We hold that the Mansons do not have standing in their capacities as obligors.

The Mansons claim that David Manson has standing to sue as a fifty percent shareholder of the Company. A shareholder generally does not have standing to bring an individual action under RICO to redress injuries to the corporation in which he owns stock. This is true even when the plaintiff is the sole shareholder of the injured corporation. Since the shareholder's injury, like that of the creditor, generally is derivative of the injury to the corporation, the shareholder's injury is not related directly to the defendant's injurious conduct.

The Mansons claim that, by looting the Company, appellees violated their fiduciary duties to David Manson in his capacity as a shareholder. The Mansons assert that such a claim states a personal, not a derivative, cause of action. The district court, however, held that the Mansons' complaint did not allege a breach of fiduciary duty and denied the Mansons' motion for leave to amend their complaint specifically to allege such a breach.

Even if the court had permitted the Mansons to amend their complaint to include such an allegation, David Manson would not have standing to assert a federal RICO claim. We recognized a special duty exception in the context of RICO actions in Ceribelli v. Elghanayan, 990 F.2d 62, 63–65 (2d Cir.1993), but we suggested that that exception is limited to cases in which the shareholder sustains an injury that is separate and distinct from the injury sustained by the corporation.

In *Ceribelli*, the defendants fraudulently failed to disclose material information prior to the shareholders' purchase of their shares. Unlike

David Manson, the shareholder in *Ceribelli* was able to allege a breach of an independent duty owed to him in his capacity as a securities purchaser. We reasoned that, if the fraudulent activity had taken place after the purchase of the shares, at which point the shareholder would not have been owed an independent duty as a securities purchaser, a direct action by the shareholder would have been "doubtful". Since the Mansons do not allege that any appellee owed David Manson an independent duty that is distinguishable from the duty owed to the corporation, the special duty exception that we recognized in *Ceribelli* does not apply to this case.

Furthermore, the Mansons cannot claim that any appellees owed David Manson a duty that was separate and distinct from the duty owed to the other shareholder. Courts have recognized an exception to the general rule of not recognizing a shareholder's individual claim where the injury sustained by the shareholder is separate and distinct from that sustained by other shareholders. *E.g.*, Sax v. World Wide Press, Inc., 809 F.2d 610, 614 (9 Cir.1987). Here, however, the other shareholder, Anca Stacescu, also sustained losses in the value of her shares. Even though Stacescu is alleged to have participated in some of the wrongdoing, she and David Manson have sustained the same injury with respect to the value of their shares and both would be made whole by a derivative action. *Id.* at 614 ("Even if the [majority shareholders] depleted [the corporation's] assets with the sole purpose of decreasing the value of [the minority shareholder's] stock and destroying his return on his investment, the action would nonetheless be derivative."). Even if we were to recognize such an exception, David Manson would not have standing.

The Mansons rely heavily on Yanow v. Teal Industries, Inc., 178 Conn. 262, 422 A.2d 311 (1979). This Connecticut Supreme Court decision concerning standing to assert a state law claim, however, does not control the instant case, which involves the interpretation of a federal statute and raises important questions of federal policy. There are sound reasons for limiting standing under RICO to plaintiffs whose injuries are personal and directly caused by the RICO violations, particularly when the primary victim of the RICO conspiracy is a corporation.

The proximate cause requirement serves the interests of judicial economy by allowing courts to determine in a derivative action one damage award that will restore the corporation and, therefore, its shareholders, creditors, and employees. "[R]ecognizing claims of the indirectly injured would force courts to adopt complicated rules apportioning damages among plaintiffs removed at different levels of injury from the violative acts, to obviate the risk of multiple recoveries". *Holmes*, 503 U.S. at 268.

Furthermore, the standing requirement prevents some claimants from diverting the corporation's assets from other creditors whose claims have priority. This is a particularly important concern in the context of a RICO action brought by a shareholder, where a treble damage award under RICO would impair the rights of prior claimants to the corporation's assets.

These important policy concerns counsel strongly against a holding that would ease the requirements for standing under RICO. The Mansons essentially claim that the Company was looted, thereby causing the value of David Manson's shares to decline.

Since there is no claim that David Manson sustained injuries that are distinct from those sustained by the corporation or the other shareholder, we hold that David Manson does not have standing as a shareholder.

* * *

The Mansons claim that David Manson has standing to sue as president and director of the Company. Employees of a bankrupt corporation, however, like creditors and shareholders, generally do not have standing under RICO. The employee's injury generally is derivative of that of the corporation and does not satisfy RICO's proximate cause requirement.

For example, in Willis v. Lipton, 947 F.2d 998, 1000–01 (1st Cir. 1991), a chief executive officer of a bankrupt corporation claimed that the defendants' RICO conspiracy caused the loss of his employment, damage to his reputation, and legal expenses. The court held that the chief executive officer did not have standing under RICO because his injuries were the indirect result of RICO violations that were aimed at the corporation by which he was employed. *Id.* Similarly, David Manson's loss of income as president and director is an indirect result of the conspiracy and subsequent bankruptcy of the Company.

The Mansons also assert that David Manson was injured by appellees' threats, which were made to intimidate him and to stop him from investigating the alleged scheme. These threats were directed at David Manson because of his positions of employment with the Company. The threats, however, were part of a RICO scheme that was directed at the Company, not David Manson. There is no claim that these threats caused David Manson to sustain any direct injury. To the extent that these threats allowed the alleged conspiracy to succeed, only the Company sustained direct injury, and any injury sustained by David Manson as an employee was an indirect result of the Company's injuries.

We hold that David Manson does not have standing as an employee.

Notes

If true, the Mansons are victims of a pattern of crimes which left the company of which David Manson was director, president and fifty percent shareholder, bankrupt. Not only did David Manson lose his job and the value of his stock, but he and his brother will have to pay $450,000 because they personally guaranteed a loan to the company. To the Mansons, these injuries must appear direct. Yet, as the Second Circuit notes, there are strong policy reasons for holding that parties such as the Mansons do not have standing (allows manipulation of the otherwise established order of creditors). If you were a judge on the Second Circuit, how would you decide this case?

Chapter 4

MONEY LAUNDERING OVERVIEW

A. OVERVIEW

"Money laundering is the concealment of the existence, nature or illegal source of illicit funds in such a manner that the funds will appear legitimate if discovered."[a]

Although most people think of money launderers as drug dealers, white collar defendants increasingly are being prosecuted for money laundering. This enthusiasm of prosecutors for including money laundering offenses in white collar criminal cases may be due to the sentencing guidelines promulgated by the United States Sentencing Commission. The guidelines escalate the punishment that individual or corporate defendants receive if their convictions include money laundering offenses.[b]

There are two types of money laundering offenses. The reporting offenses, most of which were passed in 1970 as part of the Bank Secrecy Act (BSA)[c], require reporting of cash transactions. There are three major reporting statutes: 31 U.S.C. § 5313 which requires a domestic financial institution involved in a cash transaction of $10,000 or more to file a report on the transaction; 31 U.S.C. § 5324 which prohibits structuring financial transactions (as in breaking the transactions into small transactions) for the purpose of evading reporting requirements; and 26 U.S.C. § 6050I which requires "all persons engaged in a trade or business" to report cash transactions over $10,000.

Until recently the major anti-money laundering strategy in the United States was heavy reliance on reporting by financial institutions.[d] However, because there are more than 250,000 American financial

a. *Business Community's Compliance With Federal Money Laundering Statutes: Hearing Before the Subcomm. on Oversight of House Comm. on Ways And Means, 101st Cong., 2d Sess. 142 (1990)* (statement of Michael J. Murphy, Senior Deputy Comm'r, Internal Revenue Service).

b. United States Sentencing Guidelines, §§ 251.1–3.

c. Pub. L. No. 91–508, Titles I, II, 84 Stat. 1114 (Codified as amended in scattered sections of titles 12, 18, 26, and 31, United States Code).

d. GENERAL ACCOUNTING OFFICE (GAO), MONEY LAUNDERING: A FRAMEWORK FOR UNDERSTANDING U.S. EFFORTS OVERSEAS (May 4, 1996).

institutions subject to BSA rules,[e] monitoring the reports generated has been overwhelming.

The second type of money laundering offenses are the "transportation" offenses which forbid moving illegally-obtained money into, out of, or among bank accounts, or moving legally-obtained money out of or among bank accounts to avoid tax or reporting obligations.[f] The transportation offenses were passed as part of the Money Laundering Control Act of 1986(MLCA).[g] Until passage of the MLCA, money laundering itself was not illegal.

The reporting statutes contain both civil and criminal penalties for "willful" violations.[h] The transportation statutes, 18 U.S.C. §§ 1956, 1957, impose criminal liability only.

Forfeiture of property "involved" in a money laundering offense or "traceable" to a money laundering offense is almost certain. Conviction under either the reporting or transportation statutes carries mandatory forfeiture of assets involved in the offense. Thus, for example, if the government convicts a physician of false billing and demonstrates that the physician's clinic was involved in the false billing, the clinic automatically is forfeited under 18 U.S.C. § 982. Proof supporting a § 982 forfeiture will always be beyond a reasonable doubt since the forfeiture is part of the criminal action.

Civil forfeiture of property "involved" in a reporting or transportation offense is also possible.[i] In civil forfeiture proceedings the government must simply show that probable cause exist to believe that an offense has been committed. Thus, for example, by filing a civil forfeiture suit against a physician's clinic, rather than convicting the physician, the government will be able to obtain forfeiture simply by demonstrating probable cause to believe that the clinic was "involved in" the false billing and that the proceeds from such billings were not reported as required or were "laundered" in violation of Section 1956 or Section 1957.

The Office of Technology Assessment of the United States Congress provides the following overview of money laundering enforcement in the United States:[j]

e. OFFICE OF TECHNOLOGY ASSESSMENT, UNITED STATES CONGRESS, MONEY LAUNDERING (1995).

f. 18 U.S.C. §§ 1956, 1957.

g. Pub. L. 99–570, Title I, Subtitle H, 100 Stat. 3207–18 (Codified as amended in scattered sections of titles 12, 18, and 31, United States Code).

h. Section 5321, title 31, United States Code, imposes a civil penalty for violations of the reporting statutes. Section 5322, title 31, U.S.C., imposes a criminal penalty of a five year maximum term of imprisonment, a fine of not more than $250,000, or both, for willful violations of the reporting statutes. Section 5324, title 31, U.S.C., which prohibits structuring financial transactions includes its own criminal provision. All violations of § 5324 are criminal; there is no civil sanction counterpart and proof of willfulness is not required to obtain a criminal conviction. 31 U.S.C. § 5134(c).

i. 18 U.S.C. § 981.

j. UNITED STATES CONGRESS, OFFICE OF TECHNOLOGY ASSESSMENT, MONEY LAUNDERING 3–13 (1995).

"Federal agencies estimate that as much as $300 billion is laundered annually, worldwide. From $40 billion to $80 billion of this may be drug profits made in the United States. A multinational Financial Action Task Force estimated that about $85 billion per year could be available for laundering from drug proceeds alone. However, this and other estimates of the scale of money laundering must be viewed skeptically. The official estimates are derived from a mix of experience, extrapolation, and intuition; the hard evidence to support them is limited. No one can be sure how much money is laundered.

* * *

"Money laundering is not, however, limited to drug trafficking. It is associated with nearly all kinds of 'crime for profit,' including organized crime and white collar crimes, such as the real estate fraud and savings and loan abuses that marked the last decade. One economist lists a number of other reasons (not all of them criminal) for wishing to hide money:

- to prevent the erosion of business and personal asset values through legal means (such as law suits or divorce proceedings);
- tax evasion, either personal or corporate;
- capital flight from one country to other countries, triggered by adverse changes in economic, political, and social conditions;
- securities law violations, especially insider trading;
- government undercover activities such as spying and support for "freedom fighters";
- smuggling of contraband.

* * *

"Law enforcement officials describe three steps in money laundering:

- placement–introducing cash into the banking system, or into legitimate commerce;
- layering–separating the money from its criminal origins by passing it through several financial transactions, for example, transferring it into and then out of several bank accounts, or exchanging it for travelers' checks or a cashier's check;
- integration–aggregating the funds with legitimately obtained money or providing a plausible explanation for its ownership.

* * *

"One way of getting money into the banking system, more subtle and sophisticated than smurfing, is to provide a rationale or cover for its existence as cash. Money launderers may use a legitimate business as a front, or they may use "shell companies" (corporations that exist only on paper), often chartered in another country. In choosing a legitimate business to serve as a front, money launderers usually look for businesses with high cash sales and high turnover. The size of the business is a consideration; a news stand or Laundromat that deposits tens of thousands of dollars a day will soon attract suspicion. Once the illegal proceeds have been mixed with other money flows, they are extremely difficult to find. This is the step in money laundering described above as 'layering,' or passing the money through a number of transactions to confuse its trail.

"International money launderers also use false invoicing. Greatly overpricing goods being imported into the United States can explain large amounts of money being wire transferred abroad. Researchers at Florida International University developed an analytical computer program to identify "irregularities" in government trade data–such as the pricing of the drug erythromycin at $1,694 a gram for imports, as compared with eight cents a gram for exports. Their results indicate frequent use of inflated invoices. A federal grand jury in 1994 indicted five importers of medical devices on 50 counts of money laundering involving wire transfers of $1.3 million (by wire) to Pakistan.

"Money laundering is associated with all categories of 'crimes for profit' (as contrasted with 'crimes of passion'), but to differing extents. Drug traffickers and other kinds of organized crime such as gambling and prostitution must struggle to get large volumes of small denomination bills to safety. The traditional American crime families, however, are thought to keep most of the money in the United States and to invest it in domestic assets; the South American cartels attempt to get the lion's share of the profits out of this country. 'White collar' crimes (embezzlement, fraud, tax evasion) seldom require the placement of cash. Typically, in fraud cases, money extracted from the victims under false pretenses is in the form of their personal checks, which the perpetrator accumulates in one or more bank accounts and then wire transfers to an account in a country with strong bank secrecy laws. In real estate fraud, developers may take out huge loans, wire the money out of the country, and then declare bankruptcy. With terrorism and illegal arms trades, the intent may be to conceal the intended destination and use of funds as well as their origin. There may be other significant differences in the characteristics of money laundering associated with different crimes, which further complicate attempts to define a profile or pattern by which money laundering can be recognized.

"Law enforcement agents believe that organized crime lords and money launderers are highly flexible and agile at shifting among these various modes of money laundering, responding to changes and improvements in law enforcement initiatives. This is another factor that complicates efforts to lay out a "profile" of characteristics of money laundering that could be used to design other artificial-intelligence-based monitoring system.

* * *

"Money launderers are increasingly sophisticated in manipulating financial systems and instruments. Professionals who have become white collar criminals provide 'the link between the underworld and limitless commercial and financial opportunities in the legitimate sector' of the economy. These are often lawyers or accountants.' "

B.   REPORTING STATUTES

Since 1970 federal law has required financial institutions to report cash transactions. Today, financial institutions must report these transactions by filing Treasury Form 4789, "Currency Transaction Report," (CTR), with the Internal Revenue Service. (Appendix A to this chapter.) Since originally passing this reporting requirement, Congress has strengthened it in three major ways.

Congress' first effort to strengthen the reporting requirement was passage of 31 U.S.C. § 5324. Soon after the reporting statutes were passed, it became clear that some customers of financial institutions were avoiding reporting requirements by dividing their deposits into amounts less than $10,000, a process nicknamed "smurfing." Section 5324 closes this loophole by prohibiting the structuring of financial transactions for the purpose of evading reporting requirements.[k] Willful structuring of financial transactions to avoid the filing of a CTR is punishable by imprisonment of not more than 5 years, a fine of not more than $250,000, or both.[l] The first case in this section, Ratzlaf v. United States, 510 U.S. 135 (1994), involves a structuring offense under § 5324.

The second change in the reporting requirement for cash transactions expanded the group of persons who must report. Originally only a narrowly defined group of "financial institutions" was required to report cash transactions over $10,000. In 1984, Congress enacted § 6050I of Title 26, which requires "all persons engaged in a trade or business" to report cash transactions over $10,000. This report must be filed with the Internal Revenue Service on a Form 8300. (Appendix B to this chapter.) Willful failure to file a Form 8300 is punishable by imprisonment of up

---

k. Title 31 U.S.C. § 5324 (West 1984 & Supp.1991) provides as follows: "No person shall for the purpose of evading the reporting requirements of section 5313(a) with respect to such transaction—

  (1) cause or attempt to cause a domestic financial institution to fail to file a report required under section 5313(a);

  (2) cause or attempt to cause a domestic financial institution to file a report required under section 5313(a) that contains a material omission or misstatement of fact; or

  (3) structure or assist in structuring, or attempt to structure or assist in structuring, any transaction with one or more domestic financial institutions."

For an excellent discussion of § 5324 see Welling, *Smurfs, Money Laundering and the Federal Criminal Law: The Crime of Structuring Transactions,* 41 FLA.L.REV. 287 (1989).

l.   31 U.S.C. § 5322.

to five years, or a fine of up to $250,000, or both.[m] Ironically, willful filing of a false Form 8300 is punishable by imprisonment of up to three years and a fine of up to $250,000, or both.[n]

The third change in the reporting requirements expands the type of information banks are required to report. Since 1988, financial institutions have been required to report "suspicious transactions" by customers as well as qualifying "financial transactions." The current form for such reporting is the "Suspicious Activity Report," included as Appendix C to this chapter.[o]

The next case, Ratzlaf v. United States, 510 U.S. 135 (1994), involves an alleged structuring offense. The Supreme Court's ruling on what the government must prove when a criminal offense contains a mens rea element of "willfully" has had a far-reaching impact. As you will see in other chapters[p] a *"Ratzlaf"* defense is now raised in almost every white collar case. As you read the case now, however, focus on the discussion of the reporting statutes. Two of the three statutes, summarized *supra*, are at issue in *Ratzlaf*: 31 U.S.C. §§ 5313 and 5324.

RATZLAF v. UNITED STATES

United States Supreme Court, 1994.
510 U.S. 135.

GINSBURG, JUSTICE.

Federal law requires banks and other financial institutions to file reports with the Secretary of the Treasury whenever they are involved in a cash transaction that exceeds $10,000. 31 U.S.C. § 5313; 31 CFR § 103.22(a) (1993). It is illegal to "structure" transactions—i.e., to break up a single transaction above the reporting threshold into two or more separate transactions—for the purpose of evading a financial institution's reporting requirement. 31 U.S.C.§ 5324. "A person willfully violating" this antistructuring provision is subject to criminal penalties. § 5322. This case presents a question on which Courts of Appeals have divided: Does a defendant's purpose to circumvent a bank's reporting obligation suffice to sustain a conviction for "willfully violating" the antistructuring provision? We hold that the "willfulness" requirement mandates something more. To establish that a defendant "willfully

---

m. 26 U.S.C. § 7203. If financial institutions file a CTR pursuant to 31 U.S.C. § 5313, they are exempt from filing a Form 8300. Treasury Reg. § 1.60501–1(d). Some entities designated as "financial institutions" in 31 U.S.C. § 5312(a)(2), such as car dealerships or realtors, are not included in the regulations implementing the CTR requirement, and thus are not required to file CTRs, 31 C.F.R. § 103.11(g). These businesses must, therefore, file Form 8300.

n. 26 U.S.C. § 7206(1).

o. 31 CFR § 103.20 (1996); SAR/CTR EXEMPTION LIST MIGHT EMERGE March 1, http://www.newsnet.com/libiss/fizz.html#2.

p. *See, e.g.,* Chapter 10, Section C. (Hanlester Network v. Shalala).

violat[ed]" the antistructuring law, the Government must prove that the defendant acted with knowledge that his conduct was unlawful.[1]

I

On the evening of October 20, 1988, defendant-petitioner Waldemar Ratzlaf ran up a debt of $160,000 playing blackjack at the High Sierra Casino in Reno, Nevada. The casino gave him one week to pay. On the due date, Ratzlaf returned to the casino with cash of $100,000 in hand. A casino official informed Ratzlaf that all transactions involving more than $10,000 in cash had to be reported to state and federal authorities. The official added that the casino could accept a cashier's check for the full amount due without triggering any reporting requirement. The casino helpfully placed a limousine at Ratzlaf's disposal, and assigned an employee to accompany him to banks in the vicinity. Informed that banks, too, are required to report cash transactions in excess of $10,000, Ratzlaf purchased cashier's checks, each for less than $10,000 and each from a different bank. He delivered these checks to the High Sierra Casino.

Based on this endeavor, Ratzlaf was charged with "structuring transactions" to evade the banks' obligation to report cash transactions exceeding $10,000; this conduct, the indictment alleged, violated 31 U.S.C. §§ 5322(a) and 5324(3). The trial judge instructed the jury that the Government had to prove defendant's knowledge of the banks' reporting obligation and his attempt to evade that obligation, but did not have to prove defendant knew the structuring was unlawful. Ratzlaf was convicted, fined, and sentenced to prison.[2]

Ratzlaf maintained on appeal that he could not be convicted of "willfully violating" the antistructuring law solely on the basis of his knowledge that a financial institution must report currency transactions in excess of $10,000 and his intention to avoid such reporting. To gain a conviction for "willful" conduct, he asserted, the Government must prove he was aware of the illegality of the "structuring" in which he engaged. The Ninth Circuit upheld the trial court's construction of the legislation and affirmed Ratzlaf's conviction. We granted certiorari, and now conclude that, to give effect to the statutory "willfulness" specification, the Government had to prove Ratzlaf knew the structuring he undertook was unlawful. We therefore reverse the judgment of the Court of Appeals.

1. *Compare, e.g.*, United States v. Scanio, 900 F.2d 485, 491 (C.A.2 1990) ("proof that the defendant knew that structuring is unlawful" is not required to satisfy § 5322's willfulness requirement), *with* United States v. Aversa, 984 F.2d 493, 502 (C.A.1 1993) (en banc) (a "willful action" within the meaning of § 5322(a) "is one committed in violation of a known legal duty or in consequence of a defendant's reckless disregard of such a duty").

2. Ratzlaf's wife and the casino employee who escorted Ratzlaf to area banks were codefendants. For convenience, we refer only to Waldemar Ratzlaf in this opinion.

II

A

Congress enacted the Currency and Foreign Transactions Reporting Act (Bank Secrecy Act) in 1970, Pub.L. 91–508, Tit. II, 84 Stat. 1118, in response to increasing use of banks and other institutions as financial intermediaries by persons engaged in criminal activity. The Act imposes a variety of reporting requirements on individuals and institutions regarding foreign and domestic financial transactions. The reporting requirement relevant here, § 5313(a), applies to domestic financial transactions. Section 5313(a) reads: "When a domestic financial institution is involved in a transaction for the payment, receipt, or transfer of United States coins or currency (or other monetary instruments the Secretary of the Treasury prescribes), in an amount, denomination, or amount and denomination, or under circumstances the Secretary prescribes by regulation, the institution and any other participant in the transaction the Secretary may prescribe shall file a report on the transaction at the time and in the way the Secretary prescribes.... "[3]

To deter circumvention of this reporting requirement, Congress enacted an antistructuring provision, 31 U.S.C. § 5324, as part of the Money Laundering Control Act of 1986 Section 5324, which Ratzlaf is charged with "willfully violating," reads:

"No person shall for the purpose of evading the reporting requirements of section 5313(a) with respect to such transaction—

. . . . .

(3) structure or assist in structuring, or attempt to structure or assist in structuring, any transaction with one or more domestic financial institutions."

The criminal enforcement provision at issue, 31 U.S.C. § 5322(a), sets out penalties for "[a] person willfully violating," inter alia, the antistructuring provision. Section 5322(a) reads: "A person willfully violating this subchapter [31 U.S.C. § 5311 et seq.] or a regulation prescribed under this subchapter (except section 5315 of this title or a regulation prescribed under section 5315) shall be fined not more than $250,000, or imprisoned for not more than five years, or both."

B

Section 5324 forbids structuring transactions with a "purpose of evading the reporting requirements of section 5313(a)." Ratzlaf admits that he structured cash transactions, and that he did so with knowledge of, and a purpose to avoid, the banks' duty to report currency transactions in excess of $10,000. The statutory formulation (§ 5322) under which Ratzlaf was prosecuted, however, calls for proof of "willful[ness]"

---

3. By regulation, the Secretary ordered reporting of "transaction[s] in currency of more than $10,000." 31 CFR § 103.22(a) (1993). Although the Secretary could have imposed a report-filing requirement on "any ... participant in the transaction," 31 U.S.C. § 5313(a), the Secretary chose to require reporting by the financial institution but not by the customer. 31 CFR § 103.22(a) (1993).

on the actor's part. The trial judge in Ratzlaf's case, with the Ninth Circuit's approbation, treated § 5322(a)'s "willfulness" requirement essentially as surplusage—as words of no consequence. Judges should hesitate so to treat statutory terms in any setting, and resistance should be heightened when the words describe an element of a criminal offense. *See* Pennsylvania Dept. of Public Welfare v. Davenport, 495 U.S. 552, 562 (1990) (expressing "deep reluctance" to interpret statutory provisions "so as to render superfluous other provisions in the same enactment")

"Willful," this Court has recognized, is a "word of many meanings," and "its construction [is] often . . . influenced by its context." Spies v. United States, 317 U.S. 492, 497. Accordingly, we view §§ 5322(a) and 5324(3) mindful of the complex of provisions in which they are embedded. In this light, we count it significant that § 5322(a)'s omnibus "willfulness" requirement, when applied to other provisions in the same subchapter, consistently has been read by the Courts of Appeals to require both "knowledge of the reporting requirement" and a "specific intent to commit the crime," i.e., "a purpose to disobey the law." [citations omitted]

Notable in this regard are 31 U.S.C. § 5314,[8] concerning records and reports on monetary transactions with foreign financial agencies, and § 5316,[9] concerning declaration of the transportation of more than $10,000 into, or out of, the United States. Decisions involving these provisions describe a "willful" actor as one who violates "a known legal duty." [citations omitted]

A term appearing in several places in a statutory text is generally read the same way each time it appears. We have even stronger cause to construe a single formulation, here § 5322(a), the same way each time it is called into play. See United States v. Aversa, 984 F.2d 493, 498 (1st Cir.1993) (en banc) ("Ascribing various meanings to a single iteration of § 5322(a)'s willfulness requirement"—reading the word differently for each code section to which it applies—would open Pandora's jar. If courts can render meaning so malleable, the usefulness of a single penalty provision for a group of related code sections will be eviscerated and . . . almost any code section that references a group of other code sections would become susceptible to individuated interpretation.).

The United States urges, however, that § 5324 violators, by their very conduct, exhibit a purpose to do wrong, which suffices to show "willfulness":

---

8. Section 5314 provides that "the Secretary of the Treasury shall require a resident or citizen of the United States or a person in, and doing business in, the United States, to keep records, file reports, or keep records and file reports, when the resident, citizen, or person makes a transaction or maintains a relation for any person with a foreign financial agency."

9. Section 5316 requires the filing of reports prescribed by the Secretary of the Treasury when "a person or an agent or bailee of the person . . . knowingly (1) transports, is about to transport, or has transported, monetary instruments of more than $10,000 at one time" into, or out of, the United States.

"On occasion, criminal statutes—including some requiring proof of 'willfulness'—have been understood to require proof of an intentional violation of a known legal duty, i.e., specific knowledge by the defendant that his conduct is unlawful. But where that construction has been adopted, it has been invoked only to ensure that the defendant acted with a wrongful purpose.

* * *

"The anti-structuring statute, 31 U.S.C. § 5324, satisfies the 'bad purpose' component of willfulness by explicitly defining the wrongful purpose necessary to violate the law: it requires proof that the defendant acted with the purpose to evade the reporting requirement of Section 5313(a)."

" '[S]tructuring is not the kind of activity that an ordinary person would engage in innocently,' " the United States asserts. It is therefore "reasonable," the Government concludes, "to hold a structurer responsible for evading the reporting requirements without the need to prove specific knowledge that such evasion is unlawful." [citations omitted]

Undoubtedly there are bad men who attempt to elude official reporting requirements in order to hide from Government inspectors such criminal activity as laundering drug money or tax evasion.[11] But currency structuring is not inevitably nefarious. Consider, for example, the small business operator who knows that reports filed under 31 U.S.C. § 5313(a) are available to the Internal Revenue Service. To reduce the risk of an IRS audit, she brings $9,500 in cash to the bank twice each week, in lieu of transporting over $10,000 once each week. That person, if the United States is right, has committed a criminal offense, because she structured cash transactions "for the specific purpose of depriving the Government of the information that Section 5313(a) is designed to obtain."[12] Nor is a person who structures a currency transaction invariably motivated by a desire to keep the Government in the dark. But under the Government's construction an individual would commit a felony against the United States by making cash deposits in small doses, fearful that the bank's reports would increase the likelihood of burglary,[13] or in an endeavor to keep a former

11. On brief, the United States attempted to link Ratzlaf to other bad conduct, describing at some length his repeated failure to report gambling income in his income tax returns. Ratzlaf was not prosecuted, however, for these alleged misdeeds. Nor has the Government ever asserted that Ratzlaf was engaged in other conduct Congress sought principally to check through the legislation in question—not gambling at licensed casinos, but laundering money proceeds from drug sales or other criminal ventures.

12. At oral argument, the United States recognized that, under its reading of the legislation, the entrepreneur in this exam-

ple, absent special exemption, would be subject to prosecution.

13. See United States v. Dollar Bank Money Market Account No. 1591768456, 980 F.2d 233, 241 (C.A.3 1992) (forfeiture action under 18 U.S.C. § 981(a)(1)(A) [involving a cash gift deposited by the donee in several steps to avoid bank's reporting requirement]; court overturned grant of summary judgment in Government's favor, noting that jury could believe donee's "legitimate explanations for organizing his deposits in amounts under $10,000," including respect for donor's privacy and fear that information regarding the donor—an "eccentric old woman [who] hid hundreds of

spouse unaware of his wealth.[14]

Courts have noted "many occasions" on which persons, without violating any law, may structure transactions "in order to avoid the impact of some regulation or tax." This Court, over a century ago, supplied an illustration: "The Stamp Act of 1862 imposed a duty of two cents upon a bank-check, when drawn for an amount not less than 20 dollars. A careful individual, having the amount of twenty dollars to pay, pays the same by handing to his creditor two checks of ten dollars each. He thus draws checks in payment of his debt to the amount of twenty dollars, and yet pays no stamp duty.... While his operations deprive the government of the duties it might reasonably expect to receive, it is not perceived that the practice is open to the charge of fraud. He resorts to devices to avoid the payment of duties, but they are not illegal. He has the legal right to split up his evidences of payment, and thus to avoid the tax." United States v. Isham, 84 U.S. (17 Wall.) 496 (1873).

In current days, as an amicus noted, countless taxpayers each year give a gift of $10,000 on December 31 and an identical gift the next day, thereby legitimately avoiding the taxable gifts reporting required by 26 U.S.C. § 2503(b).[15]

In light of these examples, we are unpersuaded by the argument that structuring is so obviously "evil" or inherently "bad" that the "willfulness" requirement is satisfied irrespective of the defendant's knowledge of the illegality of structuring. Had Congress wished to dispense with the requirement, it could have furnished the appropriate instruction.[16]

C

In § 5322, Congress subjected to criminal penalties only those "willfully violating" § 5324, signaling its intent to require for conviction proof that the defendant knew not only of the bank's duty to report cash transactions in excess of $10,000, but also of his duty not to avoid triggering such a report. There are, we recognize, contrary indications in the statute's legislative history. But we do not resort to legislative history to cloud a statutory text that is clear. Moreover, were we to find § 5322(a)'s "willfulness" requirement ambiguous as applied to § 5324, we would resolve any doubt in favor of the defendant.

thousands of dollars in her house"—might lead to burglary attempts).

14. See *Aversa*, 984 F.2d, at 495 (real estate partners feared that "paper trail" from currency transaction reports would obviate efforts to hide existence of cash from spouse of one of the partners).

15. The statute provides that "[i]n the case of gifts ... made to any person by [a] donor during [a] calendar year, the first $10,000 of such gifts to such person shall not ... be included in the total amount of gifts made during such year." 26 U.S.C. § 2503(b).

16. Congress did provide for civil forfeiture without any "willfulness" requirement in the Money Laundering Control Act of 1986. See 18 U.S.C. § 981(a) (subjecting to forfeiture "[a]ny property, real or personal, involved in a transaction ... in violation of section 5313(a) or 5324(a) of title 31 ..."); see also 31 U.S.C. § 5317(a) (subjecting to forfeiture any "monetary instrument ... being transported [when] a report on the instrument under section 5316 of this title has not been filed or contains a material omission or misstatement").

We do not dishonor the venerable principle that ignorance of the law generally is no defense to a criminal charge. In particular contexts, however, Congress may decree otherwise. That, we hold, is what Congress has done with respect to 31 U.S.C. § 5322(a) and the provisions it controls. To convict Ratzlaf of the crime with which he was charged, violation of 31 U.S.C. §§ 5322(a) and 5324(3), the jury had to find he knew the structuring in which he engaged was unlawful.[19] Because the jury was not properly instructed in this regard, we reverse the judgment of the Ninth Circuit and remand this case for further proceedings consistent with this opinion.

It is so ordered.

JUSTICE BLACKMUN, WITH WHOM THE CHIEF JUSTICE, JUSTICE O'CONNOR, AND JUSTICE THOMAS JOIN, DISSENTING.

On October 27, 1988, petitioner Waldemar Ratzlaf[1] arrived at a Nevada casino with a shopping bag full of cash to pay off a $160,000 gambling debt. He told casino personnel he did not want any written report of the payment to be made. The casino vice president informed Ratzlaf that he could not accept a cash payment of more than $10,000 without filing a report.

Ratzlaf, along with his wife and a casino employee, then proceeded to visit several banks in and around Stateline, Nevada, and South Lake Tahoe, California, purchasing separate cashier's checks, each in the amount of $9,500. At some banks the Ratzlafs attempted to buy two checks—one for each of them—and were told that a report would have to be filed; on those occasions they canceled the transactions. Ratzlaf then returned to the casino and paid off $76,000 of his debt in cashier's checks. A few weeks later, Ratzlaf gave three persons cash to purchase additional cashier's checks in amounts less than $10,000. The Ratzlafs themselves also bought five more such checks in the course of a week.

A jury found beyond a reasonable doubt that Ratzlaf knew of the financial institutions' duty to report cash transactions in excess of $10,000 and that he structured transactions for the specific purpose of evading the reporting requirements.

The Court today, however, concludes that these findings are insufficient for a conviction under 31 U.S.C. §§ 5322(a) and 5324(3), because a defendant also must have known that the structuring in which he engaged was illegal. Because this conclusion lacks support in the text of the statute, conflicts in my view with basic principles governing the

---

19. The dissent asserts that our holding "largely nullifies the effect" of § 5324 by "mak[ing] prosecution for structuring difficult or impossible in most cases." See post, at 669–670. Even under the dissent's reading of the statute, proof that the defendant knew of the bank's duty to report is required for conviction; we fail to see why proof that the defendant knew of his duty to refrain from structuring is so qualitative-

ly different that it renders prosecution "impossible." A jury may, of course, find the requisite knowledge on defendant's part by drawing reasonable inferences from the evidence of defendant's conduct.

1. For convenience, I follow the majority and refer only to Waldemar Ratzlaf in this opinion.

interpretation of criminal statutes, and is squarely undermined by the evidence of congressional intent, I dissent.

I

"The general rule that ignorance of the law or a mistake of law is no defense to criminal prosecution is deeply rooted in the American legal system." Cheek v. United States, 498 U.S. 192, 199 (1991). The Court has applied this common-law rule "in numerous cases construing criminal statutes." [citations omitted]

Thus, the term "willfully" in criminal law generally "refers to consciousness of the act but not to consciousness that the act is unlawful." *Cheek*, 498 U.S., at 209.

As the majority explains, 31 U.S.C. § 5322(a), originally enacted in 1970, imposes criminal penalties upon "person[s] willfully violating this subchapter." The subchapter (entitled "Records and Reports on Monetary Instruments Transactions") contains several different reporting requirements, including § 5313, which requires financial institutions to file reports for cash transactions over an amount prescribed by regulation; § 5314, which requires reports for transactions with foreign financial agencies; and § 5316, which requires reports for transportation of more than $10,000 into or out of the United States. In 1986, Congress added § 5324 to the subchapter to deter rampant evasion by customers of financial institutions' duty to report large cash transactions. The new section provides: "No person shall for the purpose of evading the reporting requirements of section 5313(a) ... (3) structure ... any transaction with one or more domestic financial institutions."

Unlike other provisions of the subchapter, the antistructuring provision identifies the purpose that is required for a § 5324 violation: "evading the reporting requirements." The offense of structuring, therefore, requires (1) knowledge of a financial institution's reporting requirements, and (2) the structuring of a transaction for the purpose of evading those requirements. These elements define a violation that is "willful" as that term is commonly interpreted. The majority's additional requirement that an actor have actual knowledge that structuring is prohibited strays from the statutory text, as well as from our precedents interpreting criminal statutes generally and "willfulness" in particular.

The Court reasons that the interpretation of the Court of Appeals for the Ninth Circuit, and that of nine other circuits, renders § 5322(a)'s willfulness requirement superfluous. This argument ignores the generality of § 5322(a), which sets a single standard—willfulness—for the subchapter's various reporting provisions. Some of those provisions do not themselves define willful conduct, so the willfulness element cannot be deemed surplusage. Moreover, the fact that § 5322(a) requires willfulness for criminal liability to be imposed does not mean that each of the underlying offenses to which it applies must involve something less than willfulness. Thus, the fact that § 5324 does describe a "willful" offense, since it already requires "the purpose of evading the reporting requirements," provides no basis for imposing an artificially heightened scienter requirement.

The majority also contends that § 5322(a)'s willfulness element, when applied to the subchapter's other provisions, has been read by the courts of appeals to require knowledge of and a purpose to disobey the law. In fact, the cases to which the majority refers stand for the more subtle proposition that a willful violation requires knowledge of the pertinent reporting requirements and a purpose to avoid compliance with them.[4] Consistent with and in light of that construction, Congress' 1986 enactment prohibited structuring "for the purpose of evading the reporting requirements." The level of knowledge imposed by the term "willfully" as it applies to all the underlying offenses in the subchapter on reporting requirements is "knowledge of the reporting requirements."[5]

The Court next concludes that its interpretation of "willfully" is warranted because structuring is not inherently "nefarious." It is true that the Court, on occasion, has imposed a knowledge-of-illegality requirement upon criminal statutes to ensure that the defendant acted with a wrongful purpose. I cannot agree, however, that the imposition of such a requirement is necessary here. First, the conduct at issue— splitting up transactions involving tens of thousands of dollars in cash for the specific purpose of circumventing a bank's reporting duty—is hardly the sort of innocuous activity involved in cases such as Liparota, in which the defendant had been convicted of fraud for purchasing food

4. The dominant formulation of the standard for a willful violation of the related provisions demands "proof of the defendant's knowledge of the reporting requirement and his specific intent to commit the crime." United States v. Granda, 565 F.2d 922, 926 (C.A.5 1978). The term "specific intent" does not, as the majority appears to assume, import the notion of knowledge of illegality. Rather, that term generally corresponds to the concept of "purpose," and it does not add to the requisite knowledge, which is specified in the first prong of the standard. The majority correctly notes that courts in a few instances have referred to a willful violation of the reporting provisions as involving violation of a "known legal duty." Those courts, however, either applied the standard from *Cheek*, 498 U.S., at 200, despite this Court's restriction of that standard's application to the tax context, or were referring simply to the reporting requirements as the "law" that one must know and actually applied the dominant standard from *Granda*. This understanding is supported by *Granda's* statement that "the proper instruction would include some discussion of the defendant's ignorance of the law since the defendant's alleged ignorance of the reporting requirements goes to

the heart of his or her denial of the specific intent necessary to commit the crime." 565 F.2d, at 926 (emphasis added).

5. "Knowledge of the reporting requirements" is easily confused with "knowledge of illegality" because, in the context of the other reporting provisions—s 5313, § 5314, and § 5316—the entity that can "willfully violate" each provision is also the entity charged with the reporting duty; as a result, a violation with "knowledge of the reporting requirements" necessarily entails the entity's knowledge of the illegality of its conduct (that is, its failure to file a required report). In contrast, § 5324 prohibits a customer from purposefully evading a bank's reporting requirements, so knowledge of the reporting requirements does not collapse into actual knowledge that the customer's own conduct is prohibited. Under the cases interpreting the statute as well as fundamental principles of criminal law, it is one's knowledge of the reporting requirements, not "knowledge of the illegality of one's conduct," that makes a violation "willful." Moreover, as explained below, Congress in 1992 rejected the majority's construction when it enacted a parallel anti-structuring provision for attempts to evade § 5316's reporting requirements.

stamps for less than their face value. Further, an individual convicted of structuring is, by definition, aware that cash transactions are regulated, and he cannot seriously argue that he lacked notice of the law's intrusion into the particular sphere of activity. By requiring knowledge of a bank's reporting requirements as well as a "purpose of evading" those requirements, the antistructuring provision targets those who knowingly act to deprive the Government of information to which it is entitled. In my view, that is not so plainly innocent a purpose as to justify reading into the statute the additional element of knowledge of illegality.[6] In any event, Congress has determined that purposefully structuring transactions is not innocent conduct.

In interpreting federal criminal tax statutes, this Court has defined the term "willfully" as requiring the "voluntary, intentional violation of a known legal duty." *Cheek*, 498 U.S., at 200. Our rule in the tax area, however, is an "exception to the traditional rule," applied "largely due to the complexity of the tax laws." *Cheek*, 498 U.S., at 200. The rule is inapplicable here, where, far from being complex, the provisions involved are perhaps among the simplest in the United States Code.[8]

* * *

III

The petitioner in this case was informed by casino officials that a transaction involving more than $10,000 in cash must be reported, was informed by the various banks he visited that banks are required to report cash transactions in excess of $10,000, and then purchased

---

6. The question is not whether structuring is "so obviously 'evil' or inherently 'bad' that the 'willfulness' requirement is satisfied irrespective of the defendant's knowledge of the illegality of structuring." The general rule is that "willfulness" does not require knowledge of illegality; the inquiry under exceptional cases such as *Liparota* is whether the statute criminalizes "a broad range of apparently innocent conduct," 471 U.S., at 426 at 2088, such that it requires no element of wrongfulness. The majority expresses concern about the potential application of the antistructuring law to a business operator who deposits cash twice each week to reduce the risk of an IRS audit. First, it is not at all clear that the statute would apply in this situation. If a person has legitimate business reasons for conducting frequent cash transactions, or if the transactions genuinely can be characterized as separate, rather than artificially structured, then the person is not engaged in "structuring" for the purpose of "evasion." Even if application of § 5324 were theoretically possible in this extreme situation, the example would not establish prohibition of a "broad range of apparently innocent conduct" as in *Liparota*, 471 U.S., at 426, and

it would not justify reading into the statute a knowledge-of-illegality requirement.

8. The majority offers examples of tax "avoidance" as further evidence of the apparent "innocence" of structuring transactions to evade the reporting requirements. These examples are inapposite because Congress specifically has prohibited the structuring of transactions to evade the reporting requirements. Indeed, its use of the word "evading" in § 5324 reveals that Congress deemed the intent to circumvent those requirements a "bad purpose." Moreover, the analogy to the tax field is flawed. Tax law involves a unique scheme consisting of myriad categories and thresholds, applied in yearly segments, designed to generate appropriate levels of taxation while also influencing behavior in various ways. Innocent "avoidance" is an established part of this scheme, and it does not operate to undermine the purposes of the tax law. In sharp contrast, evasion of the currency transaction reporting requirements completely deprives the Government of the information that those requirements are designed to obtain, and thus wholly undermines the purpose of the statute.

$76,000 in cashier's checks, each for less than $10,000 and each from a different bank. Petitioner Ratzlaf, obviously not a person of limited intelligence, was anything but uncomprehending as he traveled from bank to bank converting his bag of cash to cashier's checks in $9,500 bundles. I am convinced that his actions constituted a "willful" violation of the antistructuring provision embodied in 31 U.S.C. § 5324. As a result of today's decision, Waldemar Ratzlaf—to use an old phrase—will be "laughing all the way to the bank."

The majority's interpretation of the antistructuring provision is at odds with the statutory text, the intent of Congress, and the fundamental principle that knowledge of illegality is not required for a criminal act. Now Congress must try again to fill a hole it rightly felt it had filled before. I dissent.

Notes

1. The majority held that because breaking one large financial transaction into numerous smaller financial transactions is not inherently evil, the government must prove that a defendant engaged in such transactions with knowledge that such conduct is unlawful. The dissent would hold that the government has met its burden simply by proving that a defendant structured financial transactions with knowledge of the reporting requirements. The facts in *Ratzlaf* demonstrate the difference in the positions well. The jury "found * * * that Ratzlaf knew of financial institutions' duty to report cash transactions in excess of $10,000 * * *." (This would suffice, in the dissent's view.) The Court held, however, that the government must prove more, that Ratzlaf also knew "that the structuring in which he engaged was illegal." With whom do you agree, the majority or the dissent? Why?

2. The majority found persuasive instances where individuals may structure financial transactions for reasons other than a desire to hide transactions from the government (i.e., fear of burglaries; a wish to hide assets from a spouse; structuring gifts to reap tax benefits). If these activities are not crimes, the Court reasoned, Ratzlaf's activity was not a crime, unless the government demonstrates criminal intent. Do you find this reasoning persuasive? Did Ratzlaf have any motive for his actions other than avoiding the reporting of his transaction to the IRS? Does it matter what one's motive may be for structuring financial transactions?

3. Upon remand, Ratzlaf's case was set for trial. On the eve of trial, the court granted the government's motion for dismissal of all charges.[q]

4. Note the different approaches in statutory analysis followed by the majority and dissent. Recall that the majority looked to how lower courts had interpreted the term "willfully" in other provisions of the same statute; disregarded the legislative history ("we do not resort to legislative history to cloud a statutory text that is clear"); and, relied on the general rule of statutory construction which requires resolving any statutory ambiguity in favor of the defendant. The dissent relied on a general rule in criminal law

q. July 17, 1997, Telephone Interview   Nevada.
with Criminal Docketing Clerk, District of

that ignorance of the law is not an excuse; found that the stated purpose of § 5324 provides guidance as to the meaning of willfulness for § 5324 offenses; looked to the legislative history which it found conclusive on the intent requirement; and, accused the majority of misreading lower courts' interpretations of willfully in other provisions of the statute. Which approach do you find more persuasive? Why?

5. Consider the following facts about currency transaction reports, the form Ratzlaf avoided filing.

"Between 1970 and April 1983, there were 49.8 million Currency Transaction Reports (CTRs) filed; thereafter, the rate greatly increased, growing by nearly 13 percent per year from 1987 to the present. (Note that inflation averaged 3.3 percent). In 1994, there were 10,765,000 CTRs filed. Until mid–1993, the volume of CTRs filed far overwhelmed any attempt to investigate all of them and made it difficult to locate specific records needed to complete an investigation or to provide evidence in prosecutions. Now, the Financial Crime Enforcement Network (FinCEN), a law enforcement support unit in the U.S. Department of the Treasury, uses the FinCEN Artificial Intelligence System (FAIS) to process every CRT. By relating this information to other BSA records, suspicious subjects can be targeted for investigation.

* * *

"Over 98 percent of CTRs are filed by banks, although other financial institutions, such as money exchangers, are also required by law to file. The banking industry maintains that this imposes a heavy and unnecessary burden on banks. In 1993, reportedly, the 368 largest banks (those with assets of over \$1 billion) filed 4.5 million CTRs, and this compliance was estimated to have cost the banks \$72 million dollars. The American Bankers Association says that it costs a bank from \$3 to \$15 to file a CTR, depending on the size of the bank, its overhead, and whether its system is manual or automatic. The IRS says it costs the federal government \$2 to process and store each one.

"Ninety percent of the businesses that are the subjects of CTRs are involved in 50 or fewer CTRs a year, or about one a week, while just over half of one percent filed 400 to 1000 CTRs a year, or better than one a day. About 30 to 40 percent of the currency transactions are regular and routine deposits by well-known retail stores or chains. Banks have the power to establish exemptions for regular customers of this kind, and so eliminate many of these routine filings, but most do not. Banks say that they are reluctant to use their exemption power for fear of penalties if they err on the side of exemptions. Also, most large banks have automated the CTR filing in such a way that exercising the exemption is more expensive (for the bank) than filing the CTR.

"The CTRs are sent to six federal and state law enforcement or regulatory agencies and are processed in two databases: one maintained by the Internal Revenue Service in Detroit and one maintained by the U.S. Customs Service in Virginia. Because of the huge volume of CTRs, access to these data is cumbersome. The data can be used in building a case or as prosecutorial evidence more easily than in identifying money laundering activities not already under active investigation."[r]

6.   Because of the recent growth in the number of casinos in the United States, they have received close scrutiny from government officials concerned about money laundering. According to a 1996 General Accounting Office (GAO) report:

"Legalized gaming is expanding rapidly across the United States. Currently, 48 states permit some form of legalizing gaming—lotteries; charitable bingo; card room gaming; pari-mutual wagering; and games of chance, such as roulette, craps, slot machines, and blackjack, that take place at casinos. Casino gaming is among the fastest growing forms of gaming, and new casinos are continuing to open across the country. Two areas of notable growth are river boat casino gaming and Indian gaming, which includes casino and bingo operations. Since 1991, close to 60 river boat casinos have started operations, and in the last decade, Indian gaming operations have grown from very few to about 237 separate operations—119 of which were tribal casinos—as of March 1995.

"The amount of cash wagered annually in casinos, as estimated by International Gaming and Wagering Business, a gaming industry trade publication, has growth from about $117 billion in 1984 to about $407 billion in 1994. Casino gaming accounts for more than 80 percent of the amounts wagered in gaming activities around the country. The proliferation of casinos, together with the rapid growth of the amounts wagered, may make these operations highly vulnerable to money laundering.

* * *

"According to IRS' Criminal Investigation Division, casinos are particularly vulnerable to the initial stage of money laundering, called the "placement" stage, in which money from illegal activities is introduced into the financial system through banks or cash-intensive businesses. Casinos are also vulnerable to money launderers because of the fast-paced nature of the games and because casinos can provide their customers with many financial services nearly identical to those generally provided by banks."[s]

The following case, United States v. Simon, 85 F.3d 906 (2d Cir. 1996), provides an interesting application of *Ratzlaf*.

UNITED STATES v. SIMON

United States Court of Appeals, Second Circuit, 1996.
85 F.3d 906.

MESKILL, CIRCUIT JUDGE.

* * *

---

r. CONGRESS OF THE UNITED STATES, OFFICE OF TECHNOLOGY ASSESSMENT, MONEY LAUNDERING 17 (1995).

s. GAO, Money Laundering: Rapid Growth of Casinos Makes Them Vulnerable (January 4, 1996). We recommend that the Secretary of the Treasury consider the costs and benefits of an amendment to BSA to allow for the prohibition, as Nevada does, of certain cash transactions in casinos that may lend themselves to money laundering.

Between July 18, 1989 and July 25, 1989, Simon, a licensed stock-broker, deposited more than $130,000 in cash into one account through 14 deposits at eight Citibank branches located throughout Brooklyn, Nassau County and Suffolk County, New York. More specifically, on Tuesday, July 18, 1989, he made two deposits of $9,730 and $9,620, respectively, at Plainview, Long Island and Melville, Long Island Citibank branches. On Wednesday, July 19, 1989, he made two deposits of $9,000 and $8,800, respectively, at Hicksville, Long Island and Garden City, Long Island Citibank branches. On Thursday, July 20, 1989, he made four deposits of $9,900, $9,900, $9,920 and $9,900, respectively, at 13th Avenue, Brooklyn, 18th Avenue, Brooklyn, Shore Parkway, Brooklyn and Plainview, Long Island Citibank branches. On Monday, July 24, 1989, he made four deposits of $9,900, $9,700, $9,600 and $9,920, respectively, at 13th Avenue, Brooklyn, 18th Avenue, Brooklyn, Shore Parkway, Brooklyn, and Plainview, Long Island Citibank branches. On Tuesday, July 25, 1989, he made two deposits of $9,920 and $5,400, respectively, at Avenue J, Brooklyn and Plainview, Long Island Citibank branches.

Internal Revenue Service Agent Anthony Curieri arrested Simon on March 3, 1992. At trial, Agent Curieri testified that, after Simon signed a waiver of his Fifth Amendment rights, he questioned Simon about the 1989 cash deposits. According to Curieri's testimony, the defendant admitted that "he structured these deposits to conceal the monies from the government and to avoid having, in his words, [the] special $10,000 form filled out."

At trial, the defendant, who did not testify, conceded, through his counsel, that he structured the cash deposits, as described, with the purpose of avoiding the currency reporting requirements. He denied, however, any knowledge that his conduct was illegal. In other words, he conceded knowledge of bank reporting requirements, but denied any knowledge that it was illegal for him to structure transactions with the purpose of avoiding such requirements.

In her charge to the jury, the district judge made it clear that the jury could not convict the defendant unless the jury found beyond a reasonable doubt that the defendant knew that his conduct was illegal. More specifically, she charged the jury as follows:

> The first element of the offense that the government must prove beyond a reasonable doubt is that the defendant knew that Citibank had a duty to report currency transactions in excess of $10,000 and also knew that it was unlawful for the defendant to structure his currency transactions in order to avoid causing such a report to be filed. The act of structuring without knowledge that structuring is unlawful is not a crime.

Similarly, both the prosecution and the defense reminded the jury in summation that the only issue in dispute was whether the defendant knew that his conduct was illegal. The jury convicted.

* * *

Federal law requires financial institutions to file reports with the Treasury Department of any cash transaction exceeding $10,000. 31 U.S.C. § 5313. Federal law also makes it illegal to structure a transaction for the purpose of evading a financial institution's reporting requirement. 31 U.S.C. § 5324. A person who "willfully" violates the structuring prohibition is subject to criminal prosecution. 31 U.S.C. § 5322.

The Supreme Court recently held that conduct is not "willful" within the meaning of section 5322 unless the defendant knows that his own conduct is unlawful. *Ratzlaf*, 510 U.S. at 138. The *Ratzlaf* Court reasoned that because section 5324 itself prohibited purposeful structuring and section 5322 authorized prosecution only for willful structuring, a prosecution under section 5322 required more than a purpose to circumvent the reporting obligation. More specifically, the Court reasoned that to avoid rendering the willfulness requirement of section 5322 mere surplusage, section 5322 must be interpreted to require proof that the defendant acted with knowledge that his structuring was unlawful. Because the district court in *Ratzlaf* had instructed the jury that the government did not have to prove that the defendant acted with knowledge that structuring was unlawful, the Court reversed and remanded for further proceedings consistent with its opinion.

Thus, "*Ratzlaf* dealt with an abstract jury instruction in yes or no terms; and in its wake, courts and juries must try to answer more concrete questions," such as what type and quantum of proof is sufficient to support a reasonable inference of willfulness. In *Ratzlaf* itself, the dissenters opined that the majority's knowledge requirement would make structuring prosecutions "difficult or impossible." The majority responded with the unremarkable suggestion that knowledge of illegality can be inferred from evidence of the defendant's conduct. [citations omitted]

Courts directly and indirectly addressing this issue in the wake of *Ratzlaf* have concluded that general consciousness of illegality, the method of structuring, and the status of the defendant can support a reasonable inference of knowledge of illegality.

We recognize that currency structuring is not so "obviously 'evil' or inherently 'bad' " that the act of structuring itself satisfies the willfulness requirement. However, we also recognize that the method of structuring can provide circumstantial evidence of willfulness. As the majority noted in *Ratzlaf*, "[a] jury may, of course, find the requisite knowledge on defendant's part by drawing reasonable inferences from the evidence of defendant's conduct." [citations omitted]. And as we have noted repeatedly, a jury may infer "the state of a man's mind from the things he says and does."

In other words, when the method of structuring suggests a significant effort not only to avoid the bank reporting requirements but to conceal the currency structuring itself from the authorities, Ratzlaf 's requirement of "something more" is satisfied. Although such conduct may support more than one reasonable inference, the trier of fact may choose between reasonable inferences. In reviewing a claim that the government did not present legally sufficient evidence of willfulness, we need only determine if "any rational trier of fact could have found" knowledge of illegality. [citations omitted]

Moreover, as we have noted in other contexts, "the trier of fact may properly consider the general educational background and expertise of the defendant as bearing on the defendant's ability to form the requisite wilful intent." A jury may infer knowledge of the law from a defendant's education and expertise. [citations omitted]

We conclude that the evidence presented at trial was sufficient to sustain the defendant's conviction for currency structuring. There was sufficient circumstantial evidence for a rational jury to find that the defendant comprehended the unlawfulness of his structuring.

First, and most importantly, we emphasize that this is not a case like *Ratzlaf*, where the court improperly instructed the jury on willfulness. The district court here instructed the jury that the government was required to prove knowledge of illegality. The government and the defense reminded the jury of that requirement.

Second, the defendant's conduct in this case suggests not only knowledge of the reporting requirements and an intent to circumvent those requirements, but knowledge of illegality as well. Here, the undisputed evidence of the defendant's structuring—of his method of structuring—supports a reasonable inference that the defendant was attempting to conceal not only his deposits, but also his acts of structuring.
* * *

In structuring his deposits of more than $130,000 in cash, the defendant went to eight different branches of Citibank in Brooklyn, Nassau County and Suffolk County on 14 different occasions over a seven day period. On two separate days, Simon went to four different Citibank branches located throughout two different counties. Simon's decision to make all his deposits in different branches of the same bank rather than in different banks may have been made out of carelessness or convenience or lack of knowledge of how branches assemble information for reporting purposes. The extensive effort Simon did take in structuring these deposits amply supports a reasonable inference that he was attempting to hide his structuring activities because he knew that his conduct was unlawful.

Finally, we note that this defendant is not an unsophisticated person. He was a licensed stockbroker, and he himself was required, as a stockbroker, to file currency transaction reports with the Treasury Department. The jury reasonably could have inferred that this defendant possessed the knowledge and sophistication to understand that his own conduct was unlawful.

To the extent that defense counsel suggests, as he did at trial, that the defendant was attempting to avoid filling out the reporting forms himself, the jury logically could reject that explanation, reasoning that the defendant's structuring conduct entailed considerably more effort in time and travel than what is entailed in completing a currency transaction report. To the extent that defense counsel argues that the defendant was merely attempting to avoid scrutiny of his deposits by the IRS, we observe that he would have had a better chance of achieving this objective if he had used different banks or different account names. The defendant's attempts to conceal his activities amply support a reasonable inference that the defendant knew that his own conduct was unlawful.

* * *

WINTER, CIRCUIT JUDGE, DISSENTING:

Respectfully, I disagree with my colleagues as to the sufficiency of the evidence that Simon knew that structuring cash deposits to avoid reporting requirements was illegal. I therefore dissent.

The parties and all members of the panel are in agreement that Simon triggered the obligation of Citibank to report cash transactions exceeding $10,000. Indeed, Citibank duly reported Simon's transactions. We also agree that Simon knowingly made separate deposits of under $10,000 in an attempt to evade the daily reporting requirements. Simon concedes that he wanted to conceal the aggregate size of the transactions from the government. He readily admitted to that purpose when arrested. What is at issue is whether Simon knew that the structuring of deposits to avoid reporting requirements itself was illegal.

The government paints Simon as a sophisticated stockbroker with knowledge of reporting requirements for currency transactions in excess of $10,000. In its view, Simon conceived of a clever scheme to make separate cash deposits of slightly under that amount at different Citibank branches on the days in question. The very nature of the scheme, the government argues, supports an inference of Simon's knowledge that structuring was illegal.

The scheme was anything but clever, however, and Simon's understanding of the laws regarding the reporting of cash transactions was hardly sophisticated. Simon's fourteen deposits were all made to a single account in his own name. For Simon to have expected that daily deposits totaling over $10,000 would not be detected—the government's, and evidently the jury's, view of his purpose—he must have been ignorant of the elementary fact that banks tally all deposits during and at the end of the day in order to determine the balance in an account. In short, the government's position is that Simon's sophistication extended to knowledge of the illegality of structuring but did not include a familiarity with bank statements. Discovery of the fact that he had made cash deposits in excess of $10,000 on each of the days in question was thus as inevitable as the sunset. Indeed, the total of the daily cash deposits was reported by the bank, and the government conceded at oral argument that the reports were precisely what caused Simon's arrest. Far from being a nascent Professor Moriarty, Simon might as well have faxed his deposit receipts to the United States Attorney.

Simon's status as a licensed stockbroker adds nothing to the proof regarding his knowledge of the laws regulating structuring. The government's evidence was only that financial institutions, including stockbrokers, must file reports concerning cash transactions in excess of $10,000. The government offered no evidence as to whether Simon ever received cash from a client, ever filled out such a report, or ever received training as to pertinent statutory or regulatory requirements. The government's proof, in short, was the law itself.

The government's entire case thus rests on inferences to be drawn from Simon's conduct. What is lacking, however, is an explanation of why someone who knew that structuring deposits was illegal would make several cash deposits on the days in question—on one day totaling over $39,000—into a single account in his own name, whether or not separate branches were used.

Simon's conduct is at least as consistent with the lack of knowledge of the illegality of structuring as with that knowledge. Given that his conduct made his arrest inevitable, it is far more consistent with lack of knowledge. When asked at oral argument how Simon's behavior differed from that of a person lacking knowledge of the illegality of structuring, the government speculated that such a person might make separate deposits at the same branch but at different times during the day. However, such a person might also anticipate that a teller at that branch might recognize the depositor as a repeat customer and ask him to fill out a currency transaction report. Indeed, Simon's post-arrest statement suggested exactly that fear.

My colleagues suggest that the jury could have logically rejected the inference that Simon hoped through his efforts only to avoid having to fill out currency transaction forms himself because structuring "entailed considerably more effort in time and trouble" than filling out the reports. I may misunderstand my colleagues' reasoning, but it seems to me unresponsive. Someone who is ignorant of the illegality of structuring but wants to avoid making a currency transaction report might well spend time and effort in going to different branches to achieve that goal.

I realize that Simon's behavior is more than highly suspicious. He had access to large amounts of cash during very brief periods of time, and the likelihood of some kind of past or future serious criminal activity looms large. However, *Ratzlaf*, in overruling our precedents, requires proof beyond a reasonable doubt that Simon knew that structuring was illegal. The government's proof failed to meet this standard. Simon's conduct, the sole evidence offered to show such knowledge, demonstrates at best a belief that form—deposits just under $10,000 at separate branches—would prevail over substance—the aggregate deposits in one day—for purposes of the currency transaction rules. This is not an unreasonable or uncommon belief given our tax or regulatory laws. For example, splitting a large monetary gift between two tax years alters the tax consequences, as does the use of relatively meaningless trusts for estate purposes.

Finally, it ill behooves the government to seek a conviction based on flimsy inferences regarding a defendant's knowledge of the details of currency reporting and structuring laws. The government has refused to adopt proposals that the requirements of these laws be posted in banks. Such ignorance is presumably fostered in order to identify the depositors and to put them under surveillance in order to locate the sources of cash. The government's failure to post such requirements is surely no defense. Nevertheless, the lack of such notices undermines any assumption that the details of the laws are widely known.

I respectfully dissent.

Notes

With whom do you agree: the majority or the dissent?

It appears that Simon was up to something (fraud upon his clients? fraud his employer? trying to avoid paying income taxes?). If so, is this not exactly what the crime of structuring is designed for? Or, is this stretching the criminal law too far?

The next case, United States v. Gertner, 65 F.3d 963 (1st Cir.1995), concerns the reporting requirement imposed by 26 U.S.C. § 6050I on persons engaged in a trade or business to report any cash transaction (or two or more related transactions) in excess of $10,000. This case provides some insight into complications which arise when the trade or business is a law firm. It also provides a helpful discussion of the procedure involved when a trade or business refuses to disclose all required information. As you read this opinion, look for the strategic errors committed by the government. If you represented the government, what would you have done differently?

UNITED STATES v. GERTNER

United States Court of Appeals, First Circuit, 1995.
65 F.3d 963.

Selya, Circuit Judge.

This controversy features an old-fashioned tug of war. Pulling in one direction is the Internal Revenue Service (IRS) which, for easily understandable reasons, is intent on learning the identity of persons who pay large legal fees in cash. Pulling in the opposite direction is a consortium consisting of two lawyers and three bar associations (appearing as amici curiae) which, for equally understandable reasons (fearing inter alia that disclosure may spur prosecution), is intent on safeguarding the identity of clients who pay in cash. In this case, the parties' positions hardened and a stalemate developed. The district court resolved matters in the lawyers' favor, refusing to enforce IRS summonses designed to obtain "client identity" information pursuant to section 6050I of the Internal Revenue Code (I.R.C.), 26 U.S.C. § 6050I. The government appeals. We affirm (albeit on more circumscribed grounds than those enumerated by the lower court).

* * *

Federal law, specifically I.R.C. § 6050I and its implementing regulations, requires a person who receives more than $10,000 in cash during a single trade or business transaction to file a form (IRS Form 8300) reporting the name, address, occupation, and social security number of the payor, along with the date and nature of the transaction and the amount involved. At various times in 1991 and 1992, respondents Nancy Gertner and Jody Newman, then partners in a Boston law firm, filed forms reflecting four successive payments of hefty cash fees to the firm by a single client. Each of the forms was essentially complete except for the name of the client. The respondents advised the IRS that they were withholding the client's identity on the basis of ethical obligations, attorney-client privilege, and specified constitutional protections.

These filings sparked a lengthy course of correspondence between the law firm and the IRS. In that exchange, members of the firm attempted on at least three occasions to determine whether the IRS wanted the omitted information as part of an investigation focused on the firm or to learn more about the unnamed client. The IRS did not deign to answer these inquiries.

The parties remained deadlocked and the IRS issued summonses purporting to direct the respondents to furnish certain records and testimony anent the client's identity. The respondents declined to comply. The government then brought an enforcement action pursuant to I.R.C. §§ 7402(a) & 7604(a), claiming that it wanted the information in connection with an investigation of the law firm's tax liability. On April 20, 1994, after perusing the complaint and the declaration of Revenue Agent Sophia Ameno, the district court issued an order directing the respondents to show cause why they should not be compelled to honor the summonses.

The court permitted the client to intervene pseudonymously. Thereafter, the respondents and the intervenor mounted two lines of defense. First, they asseverated that the IRS's alleged investigation of the lawyers was merely a pretext disguising its real objective—learning more about the client—and that the government therefore should be required to follow the statutory procedure for issuing summonses affecting unidentified third parties.[1] See I.R.C. § 7609(f). Second, in concert with the amici

---

1. Such a summons is known colloquially as a "John Doe" summons. The IRS cannot issue a John Doe summons—defined by statute as a summons "which does not identify the person with respect to whose liability the summons is issued"—without

they insisted that various privileges and protections allow lawyers to shield their client's identity from the reach of such summonses. The IRS joined issue, asserting that it had employed the appropriate procedure; that the respondents had failed to show either that the supposed investigation of the law firm was a sham or that an improper motive tainted the summonses; and, finally, that no special protection of any kind attached to the desired information.

When the day of decision dawned, the respondents asked the district court to take live testimony. The government opposed the request. The court eschewed the evidentiary hearing that the respondents sought but nevertheless refused to enforce the summonses. It found as a fact that the IRS's purported probe of the law firm's tax-related affairs was a hoax, and that the IRS should have complied with I.R.C. § 7609(f) prior to serving the summonses. Nor did the court stop there; it proceeded to hold that, under the circumstances here obtaining, the attorney-client privilege thwarted the IRS's demand for information concerning client identity. This appeal ensued.

* * *

We split our analysis into three segments. First, we limn the framework for determining whether the federal judiciary's imprimatur should be impressed upon an IRS summons. Next, we mull the district court's finding on the pretext issue under the deferential standard of review that pertains in this context. Lastly, we explain why the IRS's failure to comply with I.R.C. § 7609(f) effectively ended the case.

* * *

The IRS has broad authority to issue summonses under I.R.C. §§ 7602 & 7604. Enforcement proceedings are designed to be summary, and the court's role is simply to ensure that the IRS is using its broad authority in good faith and in compliance with the law. Thus, when a challenge to a summons is lodged, the IRS must only satisfy the court that (1) its investigation is being conducted pursuant to a proper purpose, (2) the information sought in the summons is (or may be) relevant to that purpose, (3) the information is not already within the IRS's possession, and (4) all legally required administrative steps have been followed. See United States v. Powell, 379 U.S. 48, 57–58 (1964).

In determining whether to enforce IRS summonses under these substantive standards, we do not write on a pristine page. This court has constructed a three-tiered framework for expediting such determinations. To mount the first tier, the IRS must make a prima facie showing that it is acting in good faith and for a lawful purpose. This burden is not taxing, so to speak. Courts repeatedly have confirmed that an

first securing court approval. I.R.C. § 7609(f). The reason for requiring such approval is obvious: in the John Doe context, the court in effect "takes the place of the affected taxpayer" who, being un-named, cannot herself be expected to know about—let alone to oppose—the summons even if it is irregular. Tiffany Fine Arts, Inc. v. United States, 469 U.S. 310, 321, (1985). We discuss the mechanics of the preapproval process *infra*.

affidavit of the investigating agent attesting to satisfaction of the four *Powell* elements is itself adequate to make the requisite prima facie showing.

Once this minimal showing surfaces, the burden shifts to the taxpayer to rebut the good-faith presumption that arises in consequence of the government's prima facie case. The taxpayer is not at this stage required to disprove the government's profession of good faith. She must, however, shoulder a significant burden of production: in order to advance past the first tier, the taxpayer must articulate specific allegations of bad faith and, if necessary, produce reasonably particularized evidence in support of those allegations. This showing does not demand that the taxpayer conclusively give the lie to the prima facie case, but only that she create a "substantial question in the court's mind regarding the validity of the government's purpose." [citations omitted] To reach this goal, it is not absolutely essential that the taxpayer adduce additional or independent evidence; she may hoist her burden either by citing new facts or by bringing to light mortal weaknesses in the government's proffer.

If the taxpayer satisfies this burden of production, the third tier beckons. At this stage, the district court weighs the facts, draws inferences, and decides the issue. To do so, the court frequently will proceed to an evidentiary hearing, taking testimony and exhibits from both sides. But there is no hard-and-fast rule compelling an evidentiary hearing. A district court may, in appropriate circumstances, forgo such a hearing and decide the issues on the existing record.

A question lingers at the third tier as to the continuing viability of the original presumption in favor of the IRS. The case law seems to suggest that the presumption endures and serves at this stage to saddle the taxpayer with the burden of persuading the judge, qua factfinder, that at least one of the *Powell* elements is missing. The [court's] treatment of presumptions * * * is consistent with the basic principle, codified in the Federal Rules of Evidence: In all civil actions and proceedings not otherwise provided for by Act of Congress or by these rules, a presumption imposes on the party against whom it is directed the burden of going forward with evidence to rebut or meet the presumption, but does not shift to such party the burden of proof in the sense of the risk of nonpersuasion, which remains throughout the trial upon the party on whom it was originally cast. Fed.R.Evid. 301.

We are hard-pressed to fathom why IRS enforcement proceedings should diverge from this principle. It is the IRS, not the taxpayer, that seeks to invoke the processes of the court; and, in a related vein, the court is instructed to grant the requested relief only when "sufficient proof is made." I.R.C. § 7604(b). Though it certainly can be argued that "strong reasons of public policy" justify a burden-shifting scheme, it would seem that the IRS's legitimate interest in obtaining summary enforcement is satisfactorily addressed by the particularized burden of production imposed on the taxpayer, without going the whole hog.

While this point is intellectually interesting, we defer a definitive decision on it to a different day. After all, the respondents concede that the district court tacitly required them to prove improper purpose by a preponderance of the evidence, and they accepted the burden of proof without any objection. Consequently, we proceed on the assumption that the lower court's resolution of the issue will prevail only if the record suffices for a finding that the respondents carried the devoir of persuasion.

* * *

With this structure in mind, we turn to the district court's determination that the IRS's stated purpose for issuing the summonses—its avowed desire to investigate the respondents' law firm—was merely a pretext to enable it to learn more about the intervenor.

At the outset, we are constrained to note that the remarkably thin prima facie case established by Agent Ameno's declaration provides a shallow foundation for a presumption in favor of the government. While the declaration touches the requisite bases—it contains the bareboned allegations needed for the government's prima facie showing—it is utterly devoid of specifics. Though a conclusory affidavit is enough to satisfy the government's burden at the first tier of the framework, it can come back to haunt the proponent if it is not later supplemented by more hearty fare once the challenger succeeds in scaling the second tier.

At any rate, the government effectuated its prima facie showing with little room to spare. The burden then shifted to the respondents to produce evidence and/or allegations of sufficient force and exactitude to warrant further inquiry. To meet this burden, the respondents argued that the summonses should be shelved because the government's professed purpose—linking the summonses to an investigation into the law firm's tax liability—was pretextual.

Contrary to the government's dismissive suggestion, the respondents did not simply level the charge. In support of it, they submitted two affidavits. One affidavit incorporated the extensive correspondence between the firm and the IRS. The second affidavit chronicled the firm's meticulous attention to income reporting requirements, and asserted that the IRS already had the data it needed to determine whether the firm had fully complied with its tax-related obligations. In addition, the respondents documented several public statements which seem to imply that the IRS's purpose in issuing summonses to attorneys for the records of large cash-paying clients is designed less to monitor lawyers' compliance with the tax laws, and more to address money laundering, narcotics distribution, and kindred criminal activity on the part of lawyers' clients.

The lower court concluded on this chiaroscuro record that the government's supposed investigation of the law firm was a pretext for an anticipated investigation of John Doe. On appeal, the IRS rides two horses into the breach. First, it maintains that the district court erred in stabling the summonses without holding an evidentiary hearing. Second, it posits that, in all events, the court's ultimate finding of pretext, based on the record before it, is unsupportable. Both steeds are lame.

* * * The government's first question is easily answered. The decision whether to hold an evidentiary hearing in a given case generally rests within the sound discretion of the trial court. This discretion remains fully intact when the business of the day is the enforcement of an IRS summons. Appellate review is, therefore, deferential; we will interfere with a district court's bottom-line decision to conduct or withhold an evidentiary hearing in a summons enforcement proceeding only if the appellant demonstrates an abuse of the trial court's substantial discretion.

We discern no abuse in this situation. At no time during the proceedings below did the IRS request an evidentiary hearing. Rather, it vigorously (and successfully) opposed the respondents' request for such a hearing. In other words, the government chose to roll the dice, apparently confident that Agent Ameno's conclusory declaration would withstand the respondents' allegations and evidence. Having gambled and lost, the government is in a perilously poor position to pursue the point. In any event, "[w]e regularly turn a deaf ear to protests that an evidentiary hearing should have been convened but was not, where, as here, the protestor did not seasonably request such a hearing in the lower court." [citations omitted]

* * * The remaining question is whether the district court's finding of pretextual purpose is supportable. Determining the IRS's purpose in conducting an investigation is, like most motive-oriented explorations, a predominantly factbound enterprise. It follows that, absent a mistake of law, an appellate tribunal should disturb the district court's determination only if it is clearly erroneous. This means, of course, that if there are two or more plausible interpretations of the evidence, the district court's choice among them must hold sway.

Here, no clear error looms. The government's case for enforcing the summonses depended entirely on Agent Ameno's self-serving declaration (which, as we have previously indicated, is a web of unsubstantiated conclusions). In contrast, the respondents fashioned a sufficient evidentiary infrastructure to support an inference that the IRS's sole purpose in pursuing the summonses was to gain information about the lawyers' unnamed client. The law firm's affidavit, if credited, indicates that the IRS had no apparent reason to suspect it of any tax-related impropriety. And, moreover, the IRS's use of a generic affidavit, devoid of particularization, suggests that the IRS never really suspected the firm of any questionable activity. The IRS's stonewalling—its unexplained refusal to answer the firm's repeated inquiries as to whether it was in fact under investigation—points in the same direction. These facts, taken in light of the IRS's self-proclaimed practice of using information gleaned from attorneys' Form 8300 filings as a vehicle for investigating clients who pay counsel fees in cash, make the district court's conclusion that the IRS's interest lay only in the unidentified client seem quite plausible. We conclude, therefore, that notwithstanding any presumption which may have accompanied the IRS's prima facie showing, the court below reasonably could have found that a preponderance of the evidence favored the respondents' claim of pretext.

The government argues that the decision in United States v. Tiffany Fine Arts, Inc., 718 F.2d 7 (2d Cir.1983), should propel us toward the opposite conclusion. There, the Second Circuit upheld a summons issued for the dual purpose of investigating both a designated taxpayer and a John Doe, and the Supreme Court affirmed. The government tries to shoehorn this case into the Tiffany last. The fit, however, is imperfect.

In *Tiffany*, unlike here, the district court ascertained as a matter of fact that the IRS had a dual purpose, that is, an actual interest in the investigation of both the taxpayer and the John Doe. In this case, the district court ascertained, also as a matter of fact, that the IRS did not have an actual interest in the investigation of the taxpayer (the respondents' law firm), but only in learning more about John Doe. Thus, the two cases are not fair congeners except to the extent that, given Judge Brody's supportable factual finding that the summonses at issue here were not dual purpose summonses, the Supreme Court's opinion in *Tiffany* clearly indicates that we should respect that finding. And, once the judge determined as a matter of fact that the government's actual purpose in issuing the summonses was to further an investigation of the unnamed client, the follow-on conclusion that the government should have complied with the procedure for issuing John Doe summonses becomes irresistible.[7]

We take no pleasure in upholding a finding that government actors constructed a pretext to avoid due compliance with statutorily prescribed requirements. But the court below did not reach this conclusion lightly and the record, carefully examined, does not give rise to a firm conviction that the court's judgment is wide of the mark. Accordingly, the finding of pretextual purpose must stand.

* * *

Notes

The respondent-appellee in the above case, Nancy Gertner, was confirmed as a federal judge for the District of Massachusetts while this case was pending.[t]

7. At oral argument in this court, the government belatedly contended that the summonses should be enforced simply to effectuate compliance with the reporting requirements of section 6050I itself. This nascent contention materialized out of thin air; prior to oral argument, the government had attempted to justify the summons solely as a means of investigating whether the law firm had reported all the income required to be reported. Since the record reveals beyond hope of contradiction that the government's newly minted contention was not made below in any coherent fashion, we will not entertain it here.

t. *Federal Court Holds Drug Defendant's Identity Protected*, ABA JOURNAL, 28 (April, 1995).

Because of the way it resolved United States v. Gertner, the First Circuit had no need to address the attorney client privilege issue, which often arises in 8300 cases involving law firms, or the Fifth Amendment privilege, which arises in reporting cases. The Ninth Circuit addressed both of these issues in the next case.

UNITED STATES v. BLACKMAN

United States Court of Appeals, Ninth Circuit, 1995.
72 F.3d 1418.

NELSON, CIRCUIT JUDGE.

[Marc D. Blackman, personally and as a partner in the law firm of Ransom, Blackman and Weil of Portland, Oregon, appealed a District Court order granting the IRS's petition to enforce a summons served on Blackman. The IRS sought information to complete four 8300 forms filed by Blackman. Blackman omitted information on the forms identifying the client who paid cash to the firm, and the nature of services rendered by Blackman or his firm in exchange for the cash. Blackman argued that supplying the information violated the attorney client privilege and his fifth amendment privilege.-ed.]

* * *

We review *de novo* the district court's rulings on the scope of the attorney-client privilege as they involve mixed questions of law and fact. The burden of proof is on the party seeking to establish that the privilege applies. The district court correctly noted that "since the adoption of the Federal Rules of Evidence, courts have uniformly held [in adjudication of federal law] that federal common law of privilege, not state law applies." [citations omitted]

Blackman argues that the issue is not just one of privilege, however, but also of duty. According to Blackman, Oregon Revised Statute § 9.460(5), in effect at all relevant times, not only codifies the attorney-client privilege, but also imposes a positive duty upon the lawyer to avoid disclosure of his client's confidences and "secrets."[2]

This argument is specious. Because the attorney-client privilege protects the client, not the attorney, it necessarily entails a duty by the attorney to keep his client's confidences, or secrets, as the (former) Oregon statute provides. Oregon law's explicit spelling out of this duty did not thereby create an exception to the federal common law of privilege.

The Eighth Circuit recently considered a similar argument and concluded that "Congress cannot have intended to allow local rules of

---

2. Section 9.460(3) provided (prior to amendment in September 1991): "An attorney shall ... maintain inviolate the confidence, and at every peril to the attorney, preserve the secrets of the clients of the attorney."

professional ethics to carve out fifty different privileged exemptions to the reporting requirements of 26 U.S.C. § 6050I." United States v. Sindel, 53 F.3d 874, 877 (8th Cir.1995). We agree with this conclusion and accordingly consider Blackman's claims under the federal common law of privilege.

As a general rule, client identity and the nature of the fee arrangement between attorney and client are not protected from disclosure by the attorney-client privilege. However, we have recognized limited exceptions to this rule where disclosure would compromise confidential communications between attorney and client or constitute the "last link" in an existing chain of evidence likely to lead to the client's indictment.

As there is no evidence that any of Blackman's clients who may be implicated in this dispute are currently the subject of ongoing investigation, the district court correctly found that the last link doctrine does not apply. As the district court went on to observe, the exception to the general rule that fee arrangements and fee-payer identity are not privileged has had a somewhat tortuous history in the jurisprudence of this circuit. The earliest case to consider the exception is Baird v. Koerner, 279 F.2d 623 (9th Cir.1960), applying California rather than federal law regarding attorney-client privilege, and finding client identity to be within the privilege where it tends to implicate the client in the very offenses for which he sought legal advice. *Id.* at 633.

In United States v. Hodge & Zweig, 548 F.2d 1347, 1353 (9th Cir.1977), this court proposed that the exception as stated in *Baird* "also reflects federal law." Blackman relies heavily on these two cases, and their suggestion that identity information is privileged where it tends to "implicate" the fee-payer. However, as the district court noted, this definition of the exception has since been discredited within our circuit. We have repeatedly held that the attorney-client privilege does *not* apply where disclosure might incriminate the client or fee-payer, but *only* where it would convey information tantamount to a confidential communication. [citations omitted]

In deciding whether * * * Blackman had met his burden in establishing the applicability of the exception, the district court questioned whether it was appropriate to consider the *in camera* affidavits. In spite of its reservations, the court proceeded to review them. As a threshold matter, we observe that it was appropriate for the court to review these documents.

With reference to Blackman * * *, the district court found, based in part on its review of the sealed affidavits, that the identity, fee arrangement and purpose information sought by the IRS was not privileged. * * *

The district court specifically considered in its order Blackman's argument that two of the questioned transactions in his case did not involve fee arrangements. The court found as to the first non-fee related transaction that Blackman "has failed to establish that the transfer of funds related in any direct way to the purpose for which respondent was retained." As to the second, the court found that Blackman "has failed to establish that the temporary transfer of funds to his account constitutes a 'confidential' communication."

Based on his reading of *Baird* and progeny, Blackman argues that the district court misapplied the law. He states that because his receipt of the funds was "inextricably linked to the legal service his firm was retained to provide," the identity of the fee-payers and the services are privileged. Blackman is mistaken. As we stated in Ralls v. United States, 52 F.3d 223, 225 (9th Cir.1995). "The correct test [ ] is whether the fee-payer's identity and the fee arrangements are so intertwined with confidential communications that revealing either ... would be tantamount to revealing a privileged communication." 52 F.3d at 226.

Attorney Ralls was subpoenaed to provide information concerning the identity of a fee-payer who retained him to defend a third party, where the fee-payer had advised Ralls of his involvement in the crime with which the defendant was charged. We held that the fee arrangements and fee-payer's identity were therefore "inextricably intertwined with confidential communications" and protected by the attorney-client privilege.[4] No such fact pattern exists here.

The Second and Eleventh Circuits have held that, absent extraordinary circumstances, § 6050I does not conflict with traditional attorney-client privilege. We agree. As several courts have remarked, clients wishing to avoid disclosure are free to pay their counsel in some manner other than cash. Attorneys should inform clients proffering cash in excess of $10,000 for fees that they will normally be obliged to disclose fee-payer identity and the nature of the fee arrangement in filing Form 8300.

The [Second Circuit] further suggested that even if a communication might technically fall within the scope of the attorney-client privilege, the privilege must yield where it "collides head on with a federal statute that implicitly precludes its application." We need not consider whether § 6050I "trumps" the attorney-client privilege, as the Government argues these cases hold. Our case law spells out the narrow circumstances under which fee-payer identity and fee arrangements may be protected by the attorney-client privilege. Only in the extremely rare case will the receipt of cash for fees be so intertwined with the subject of the representation as to obviate compliance with § 6050I. We are hard pressed to imagine such a case, and decline to provide an illustration.

We hold that Blackman has failed to establish that the circumstances involving the clients whose identities are at stake here are such that disclosure of the information sought in conjunction with § 6050I would be "tantamount to [the revelation of] a confidential professional communication." [citations omitted]

* * *

4. We distinguished cases where the lawyer acts as a "mere conduit for the transfer of money," even where the fee-payer also sought the attorney's legal advice. *Ralls*, 52 F.3d at 226.

Courts have rejected the argument that completion by an attorney of Form 8300 violates the client's Fifth Amendment rights.[u] The privilege against self-incrimination is personal, and applies only to compulsion of the individual holding the privilege.

Blackman argues that his own Fifth Amendment rights are implicated, however, because he is the one being investigated. He avers the district court was mistaken in stating that only documents and not testimony is required of him, because the IRS petition refers to testimony as well as records. Blackman argues that under Curcio v. United States, 354 U.S. 118, 123–24 (1957), a custodian of records may not be compelled to condemn himself by his own oral testimony. He further claims, citing Fisher v. United States, 425 U.S. 391 (1976) and United States v. Doe, 465 U.S. 605, 613 (1984), that even if testimony is not required, the very act of producing documents in this case would be incriminating because it would show that he had withheld information that was actually available to him. Blackman does not argue here that the contents of the records are privileged under the Fifth Amendment.

Insofar as Blackman may be required to testify orally at a hearing pursuant to enforcement of the summons, his Fifth Amendment argument is premature. United States v. Rendahl, 746 F.2d 553, 555 (9th Cir.1984) (a petitioner cannot invoke the privilege in appeal of summons enforcement order, but must wait until he appears before the IRS and raise the privilege with respect to questions asked or documents sought). Given the district court's denial of the IRS's request for " '[a]ny other identifying date for the individual(s) or organization(s) who conducted the transaction(s) or for whom the transaction(s) was conducted,' "Blackman will likely be asked to testify for the limited purpose of identifying the records sought by the IRS. Under these circumstances, *Curcio* will not help him.

As the Supreme Court explained in Braswell v. United States, while *Curcio* drew a line between "oral testimony and other forms of incrimination" in holding that a custodian of records cannot be compelled to condemn himself by his own oral testimony in the absence of a grant of prosecutorial immunity, it distinguished "those cases in which a corporate officer was required to produce corporate records and merely identify them by oral testimony." *Braswell*, 487 U.S. 99, 114–15 (1988). " 'Requiring the custodian to identify or authenticate the documents for admission in evidence merely makes explicit what is implicit in the production itself.' "*Id.* (quoting *Curcio* v. United States, 354 U.S. 118, 125 (1957)).

As for the documentary information sought by the IRS, the "collective-entity" rule preserved in *Braswell* nullifies Blackman's Fifth Amendment argument. *Id.* 487 U.S. at 109. Partners in a law firm are included within the collective entity "which declares simply that corpo-

---

u. The Fifth Amendment issues raised by Blackman are also discussed in Chapter 6, *supra.*

rate records are not private and therefore are not protected by the Fifth Amendment." *Id.* 487 U.S. at 109. A corporate custodian cannot claim a Fifth Amendment privilege with regard to corporate records, even if the records or the act of producing them might incriminate him personally. *Id.* at 111–12.

Because Blackman may not rely upon the privilege to avoid producing records belonging to his law firm, we hold that the Fifth Amendment does not preclude enforcement of the IRS summons.

* * *

Attorneys have raised a number of constitutional arguments in addition to the Fifth Amendment. The following case raised some of these. As you read it, note the different resolution of the attorney client privilege issue than was reached in *Blackman*. Why was the outcome different?

UNITED STATES v. SINDEL

United States Court of Appeals, Eighth Circuit, 1995.
53 F.3d 874.

ARNOLD, CIRCUIT JUDGE.

Attorney Richard Sindel of Sindel & Sindel, P.C., appeals a district court order requiring him to disclose information about two clients, intervenors John Doe and Jane Doe, on Internal Revenue Service Form 8300. These forms, which are used to report cash transactions in excess of $10,000 pursuant to 26 U.S.C. § 6050I, request the name, address, tax identification number, and other information about each payor and each person on whose behalf payment is made. Sindel argues that completion of the forms would violate his own ethical duties and the First, Fifth, and Sixth Amendment rights of his clients. After considering the circumstances surrounding each client, we affirm the district court order with respect to John Doe and reverse it with respect to Jane Doe.

I.

During 1990 and 1991, Sindel received a cash payment of $53,160 for John Doe and two cash payments of $10,000 each for Jane Doe for legal services rendered. Sindel reported each of these transactions using the August, 1988, version of IRS Form 8300, but omitted any identifying information regarding the payors or the persons on whose behalf payments were made. In an attachment to each form, Sindel claimed that disclosure would "violate ethical duties owed said client, and constitutional and/or attorney-client privileges that the reporting attorney is entitled or required to invoke," and that the client had not authorized release of the information. At the request of the IRS, Sindel later withdrew the two forms reporting payments on behalf of Jane Doe and consolidated them using the January, 1990, version of Form 8300, again omitting any identifying information. This later version of Form 8300 asks the reporting party to check a box if the payment is a "suspicious transaction." The instructions accompanying the January, 1990, version of Form 8300 define a suspicious transaction as "[a] transaction in which it appears that a person is attempting to cause this report not to be filed or a false or incomplete report to be filed; or where there is an indication of possible illegal activity." Sindel left the box blank.

After filing these forms, Sindel was served with an IRS summons requesting the missing information. The government then brought an enforcement action, and the district court ordered Sindel to show cause why the summons should not be enforced. The district court divided the ensuing proceedings into two parts, one held in open court and the other an ex-parte hearing held in camera. During the in-camera portion of the proceedings, Sindel presented evidence regarding his clients' special circumstances. The district court ordered enforcement of the summons, but stayed its order pending this appeal.

II.

In order, if possible, to avoid deciding constitutional questions not essential to disposition of the case, we consider first Sindel's claims under the federal common law of attorney-client privilege and the Missouri Rules of Professional Conduct. Although the federal common law of attorney-client privilege protects confidential disclosures made by a client to an attorney in order to obtain legal representation, it ordinarily does not apply to client identity and fee information. The various Circuit Courts have, however, identified certain circumstances under which the privilege protects even client identity and fee information. One court has categorized these overlapping "special-circumstance" exceptions as the legal advice exception, the last link exception, and the confidential communications exception. The legal advice exception protects client identity and fee information when "there is a strong probability that disclosure would implicate the client in the very criminal activity for which legal advice was sought." The last link exception, as its name implies, prevents disclosure of client identity and fee information when it would incriminate the client by providing the last link in an existing chain of evidence. The confidential communications exception, which we have recognized on another occasion, protects client identity and fee information "if, by revealing the information, the attorney would necessarily disclose confidential communications." Our decision regarding Sindel's claim of attorney-client privilege therefore must rest upon a determination of whether the information requested by IRS Form 8300 is protected in this case by one of the special-circumstance exceptions. After examining Sindel's in-camera testimony about his clients' special circumstances, we conclude that he could not release information about the payments on behalf of Jane Doe without revealing the substance of a confidential communication. We do not find any similar constraints upon the disclosure of information about the payments on behalf of John Doe.

The Missouri Rules of Professional Conduct appear on their face to extend somewhat broader protection to client identity and fee information than does the federal common law of attorney-client privilege. Rule 1.6 provides that a "lawyer shall not reveal information relating to representation of a client unless the client consents after consultation." Rules Governing the Mo. Bar and Judiciary 4, 1.6 (1986). Even assuming arguendo that Rule 1.6 would prohibit disclosure of the information required to complete an IRS Form 8300, Congress cannot have intended to allow local rules of professional ethics to carve out fifty different privileged exemptions to the reporting requirements of 26 U.S.C. § 6050I. Thus the Missouri Rules of Professional Conduct do not expand the scope of the exemption beyond what is established by the federal common law of attorney-client privilege.

III.

As we do not believe that the information regarding payments on behalf of John Doe is protected from disclosure to the IRS by the federal common law of attorney-client privilege or the Missouri Rules of Professional Conduct, we necessarily undertake a consideration of Sindel's constitutional claims.

Sindel * * * argues that application of 26 U.S.C. § 6050I to an attorney violates the client's Sixth Amendment right to counsel by inhibiting the ability to retain counsel, discouraging communication between attorney and client, forcing the attorney to act as an agent for the government, and disqualifying counsel of choice. As the Second Circuit accurately points out in United States v. Goldberger & Dubin, 935 F.2d 501, 504 (2d Cir.1991), the statutory reporting requirements do not prevent a would-be client from hiring counsel. Not only are cash payments not automatically forfeit, but a client is also free to pay counsel in some other manner to avoid being reported to the IRS. Similarly, a client is not prevented from communicating with an attorney at will merely because the attorney must report large cash transactions. By contrast, we recognize the serious Sixth Amendment implications of Sindel's claim that an attorney becomes a de facto agent for the government when compelled to offer an opinion as to whether a particular cash payment was a "suspicious transaction," a question added to the January, 1990, version of Form 8300. Sindel used this later version of Form 8300 to consolidate his reporting of the payments made on behalf of Jane Doe. Because we have already determined that the federal common law of attorney-client privilege excuses Sindel from reporting any additional information regarding the Jane Doe payments, however, the constitutionality of the January, 1990, version of Form 8300 is not at issue in this case. Sindel's speculative claim that the reporting requirements of 26 U.S.C. § 6050I would disqualify counsel by allowing prosecutors to subpoena a reporting attorney to testify against a client is likewise not ripe for adjudication. There is thus no Sixth Amendment bar to enforcement of the IRS summons against Sindel.

* * *

Sindel's final constitutional claim is that completion of Form 8300 constitutes "compelled speech" and thus violates both his own and his clients' First Amendment rights. It is true that "the right of freedom of thought protected by the First Amendment against state action includes both the right to speak freely and the right to refrain from speaking at all." Wooley v. Maynard, 430 U.S. 705, 714 (1977). A First Amendment protection against compelled speech, however, has been found only in the context of governmental compulsion to disseminate a particular political or ideological message. There is no right to refrain from speaking when "essential operations of government may require it for the preservation of an orderly society,—as in the case of compulsion to give evidence in court." West Virginia State Board of Education, 319 U.S. at 645, 63 S.Ct. at 1189 (Murphy, J., concurring). The IRS summons requires Sindel only to provide the government with information which his clients have given him voluntarily, not to disseminate publicly a message with which he disagrees. Therefore, the First Amendment protection against compelled speech does not prevent enforcement of the summons.

For the foregoing reasons, we vacate the district court's order with respect to Jane Doe and affirm the order with respect to John Doe

Notes

1. As noted in the above opinion, the 1990 version of the Form 8300 required a trade or business to indicate whether the transaction it was reporting qualified as a "suspicious transaction." In excusing Sindel from completing this form, the Eighth Circuit recognized the threat to the attorney-client privilege presented by this requirement. As can be seen in the appendices to this chapter, neither the current Form 8300 nor the current Form 4789 (CTR) inquires about suspicious transactions. Instead, there is a new form to be completed only by banks whenever the following conditions apply:

- a transaction is "conducted or attempted by, at, or through [a] bank,"

- the transaction "involves or aggregates at least $5,000 in funds or other assets," and

- "the bank knows, suspects or has reason to suspect that (i) the transaction involves funds derived from illegal activities or is intended or conducted in order to hide or disguise funds or assets derived from illegal activities * * *;" (ii) the transaction is designed to evade reporting requirements under the Bank Secrecy Act, or (iii) "The transaction has no business or apparent lawful purpose or is not the sort in which the particular customer would normally be expected to engage, and the bank knows of no reasonable explanation for the transaction after examining the available facts, including the background and possible purpose of the transaction."[v]

Note how broad the third condition is and the "policing" duty it imposes on banks. Is this wise public policy? Is it necessary?

v. 31 C.F.R. § 103.20 (1996). A copy of the "Suspicious Activity Report" is includ- ed in Appendix C to this Chapter.

2. Note that the *Sindel* court recognized another exception, besides the "last link" exception which justifies withholding information on a client identity and fee amount. According to the court, "the confidential communications exception * * * protects client identity and fee information, 'if, by revealing the information, the attorney would necessarily disclose confidential communications.' " How would an attorney attempt to prove the applicability of this exception—without disclosing the confidential communication?

C. SECTIONS 1956 AND 1957

The next case, United States v. Jackson, 935 F.2d 832 (7th Cir. 1991), is one of the earliest prosecutions under § 1956. Note that the prosecutors were somewhat unfamiliar with the statute and its elements.

UNITED STATES v. JACKSON

United States Court of Appeals, Seventh Circuit, 1991.
935 F.2d 832.

FLAUM, CIRCUIT JUDGE.

* * * Joseph Davis * * * was indicted and convicted of * * * three counts of money laundering in violation of 18 U.S.C. § 1956(a). * * * We affirm * * *.

The Reverend Joseph Davis describes himself as "a small-time, hellfire and brimstone country preacher." The evidence at trial, however, presented a more complete view of Mr. Davis' talents. It showed how he repaired a run-down East St. Louis church and revitalized its congregation, helping to restore the social fabric of a community in distress. Sadly, it also showed that Davis devoted his considerable skills to a variety of schemes that ranged from shady to down-right illegal. One of these schemes was the ongoing distribution of late-twentieth century America's counterpart to brimstone, crack cocaine.

Davis became the preacher at the 15th Street Baptist Church in the mid–1980s. Shortly thereafter he began to sell drugs, and by mid–1987 was actively selling crack from two houses, the first at 735 Wabashaw and the second at 1479 Belmont. * * *

Davis deposited some of the cash he collected from the houses in bank accounts maintained in the name of the 15th Street Baptist Church Development Corporation ("Development Corporation account") and the 15th Street Baptist Church ("Church account") at Illinois Federal, a local savings and loan. Also deposited in the Development Corporation accounts were funds that Davis and the Corporation obtained from other activities. One of Davis' other activities was steering his parishioners and others to used-car outlets in the East St. Louis area in return for commissions from the dealers, a practice known as "bird-dogging." Davis would secure consumer credit for the cars and other purchases he helped to arrange through Sam Bennett, a loan officer at Jefferson Bank & Trust in St. Louis. Bennett, it is alleged, would turn a blind eye to the inability of many of the borrowers Davis sent his way to repay their obligations to Jefferson. In return, he and Davis would split the fees they received for arranging these loans. Davis also deposited in the Church and the Development Corporation accounts funds he received from more legitimate activities, including a contract for the Corporation to demolish a building in East St. Louis.

Davis could write checks on these accounts. Some of these checks were made out to cash, which Davis diverted to his personal use. Others were made out to local vendors who provided services such as beepers and mobile telephones. Still others were made out to the landlord who owned the Swanson, Illinois, residence where Davis lived. Davis also purchased numerous cars, spending over $79,000 on a variety of vehicles for personal and church use between October 1987 and November 1988.

* * *

[During the investigation,] Davis was searched and was found to be carrying over $1,000 in cash. A search of his home uncovered a precision scale, * * * guns, and numerous plastic sandwich bags, some of which contained traces of cocaine. The office at the Fifteenth Street Baptist Church was also searched, yielding another precision scale and records of the Church and Development Corporation bank accounts. These records revealed that from October 1987 to February 1989, over $191,000 had been deposited in the Development Corporation account. Of this amount, over $100,000 was deposited in cash.

* * * Davis was charged with four counts of laundering funds derived from drug activities in violation of 18 U.S.C. § 1956(a)(1). One count was based on a series of checks drawn on the Development Corporation account and made out to providers of cellular telephone and paging services. Another was based on checks drawn on the same account and made out to Davis' landlord. A third was based on a series of Development Corporation checks that Davis or the church secretary presented at the savings and loan in return for cash. The last count was based on Davis' use of $5,500 in cash derived in part from his drug activities to purchase a car.

* * *

We first discuss Davis' argument that the money laundering statute under which he was convicted in counts three through five, 18 U.S.C. § 1956(a)(1), violates his constitutional right to due process because it is impermissibly vague. The government responds that as applied to Davis the statute gave ample notice that the conduct he engaged in was prohibited.

In evaluating a vagueness challenge, it is not enough to conclude "that Congress might, without difficulty, have chosen '[c]learer and more precise language' equally easily." United States v. Powell, 423 U.S. 87, 94 (1975). Rather, "the void-for-vagueness doctrine requires only that a penal statute define the criminal offense with sufficient definiteness that ordinary people can understand what conduct is prohibited and in a manner that does not encourage arbitrary and discriminatory enforcement." Kolender v. Lawson, 461 U.S. 352, 357 (1983). The second of these two aspects is more important than the first, and bars criminal statutes "of such a standardless sweep [as to] allow[ ] policemen, prosecutors, and juries to pursue their personal predilections." Smith v. Goguen, 415 U.S. 566, 575 (1974). "Vagueness challenges to statutes not threatening First Amendment interests are examined in light of the facts of the case at hand; the statute is judged on an as-applied basis." Maynard v. Cartwright, 486 U.S. 356, 361 (1988).

As applied to Davis, we conclude that § 1956 is not unconstitutionally vague. The two provisions of 18 U.S.C. § 1956 under which Davis was charged provide, in relevant part, that:

"(a)(1) Whoever, knowing that the property involved in a financial transaction represents the proceeds of some form of illegal activity, conducts or attempts to conduct such a financial transaction which in fact involves the proceeds of specified unlawful activity—

(A)(i) with the intent to promote the carrying on of specified unlawful activity; or

* * *

(B) knowing that the transaction is designed in whole or in part—

(i) to conceal or disguise the nature, the location, the source, the ownership, or the control of the proceeds of specified unlawful activity.

* * *

shall be sentenced to a fine of not more than $500,000 or twice the value of the property derived in the transaction, whichever is greater, or imprisonment for not more than twenty years, or both."

We first note that this provision requires the government to prove that a defendant charged with participating in the financial transaction identified in the indictment knew that it involved the proceeds of unlawful activities. In a case brought under § 1956(a)(1)(A)(i), the government must also prove that the defendant intended to promote the carrying on not just of any criminal activity, but rather the limited number of activities identified in § 1956(c)(7), which defines the term "specified unlawful activity." In a case brought under § 1956(a)(1)(B)(i), the government must prove that the transaction was designed to conceal one or another of the enumerated attributes of the proceeds involved. See United States v. Sanders, 928 F.2d 940, 946 (10th Cir.1991). These requirements of intent and knowledge "do[ ] much to destroy any force in the argument that application of the [statute] would be so unfair that it must be held invalid," Boyce Motor Lines v. United States, 342 U.S. 337, 342 (1952), "especially with regard to the adequacy of notice to the complainant that his conduct is proscribed." Village of Hoffman Estates v. Flipside, Hoffman Estates, Inc., 455 U.S. 489, 499 (1982).

Tuesday

418-427; 435-448

881-889; 471-480

March 30, 2004
  - Computer Crime●
Class on Wednesday March 24,
                              2004
          2:40-3:30

Student Services - Thursday

Turning to the second prong of the vagueness test, the specific and detailed definitions given to numerous terms used in the statute, such as "specified unlawful activity," see 18 U.S.C. § 1956(c)(7), "financial transaction," *see id.*, § 1956(c)(4), and "transaction," *see id.*, § 1956(c)(3), suggest that in drafting this statute, Congress hardly abdicated its "responsibilities for setting the standards of the criminal law," *Goguen,* 415 U.S. at 575, 94 S.Ct. at 1248. Law enforcement officers are not free to apply the money laundering statute guided solely by their likes and dislikes. Rather, Congress has limited their discretion by describing with particularity "what a suspect must do in order to satisfy the statute." *Id.* As is discussed more fully below, the evidence established Davis' knowing and intentional use of a bank account controlled by his employer to promote his continued narcotics activities and to hide the source of his tainted gains in an account containing both drug profits and legitimate income. As applied to these facts, the money laundering statute is sufficiently definite to survive a vagueness challenge.

* * *

Davis next asserts that the evidence the jury heard was insufficient to convict him of laundering funds derived from his narcotics activities. Davis points to his various other sources of income, including the money he made bird-dogging cars, arranging purchase-money loans, and demolishing buildings, all of which produced revenue which was deposited into the Development Corporation account. He argues that no rational juror could decide beyond a reasonable doubt that the individual checks and transactions enumerated in counts three through five of the indictment involved money derived from drug activities. The government responds that the testimony of Internal Revenue Service Agent James Wehrheim established that Davis earned approximately $102,500 from non-drug sources during the period of the drug conspiracy charged in the indictment. During the same period, over $200,000 was deposited in the two church accounts to which Davis had access. In light of the other evidence presented at trial, it argues, jurors could rationally infer that the difference was attributable to drug activities. Second, it contends that the money laundering statute does not require the prosecution to prove that the funds used in the various transactions listed in the indictment came exclusively from drug activities, but only that some of it was derived from these activities.

Though Davis styles this argument in terms of the sufficiency of the evidence, we believe that it involves a preliminary question of statutory construction. The question posed is whether a defendant can be convicted under either 18 U.S.C. § 1956(a)(1)(A)(i) or (a)(1)(B)(i) where the transaction that forms the basis of the indictment involves the proceeds of both "specified unlawful activity" as defined in § 1956(c)(7), and other conduct, either innocent or criminal, but not among the enumerated criminal activities that may serve as a predicate for a money laundering conviction.

Both of the money laundering provisions Davis was charged with under § 1956(a)(1)(A)(i) and (a)(1)(B)(i), require only that a transaction "involved" in this case is itself suggestive of a design to hide the source of ill-gotten gains that the government must prove under § 1956(a)(1)(B)(i).

The risk that this reading of the statute will have unduly harsh consequences is mitigated by the requirements imposed upon the government by other parts of the statute. To convict under § 1956(a)(1)(i), the government bears the burden of proving beyond a reasonable doubt that the party engaged in the transaction knew that the funds used represented, in whole or in part, proceeds of an unlawful activity and intended the transaction to promote one of the varieties of criminal conduct identified in § 1956(c)(7). In a case under (a)(1)(B)(i), the government must also prove that the transaction was carried out in whole or in part with the design of concealing "the nature, the location, the source, the ownership, or the control" of the proceeds of one of the forms of criminal conduct enumerated in § 1956(c)(7). It will be a rare case in which these requirements will be satisfied without proof that the funds used in the charged transaction were derived in substantial measure from "specified unlawful activities" rather than from other legal or illegal conduct.

Having concluded that § 1956(a)(1)(A)(i) and (a)(1)(B)(i) allow for convictions where the funds involved in the transaction are derived only in part from "specified unlawful activities," we move to the question of whether the evidence at trial was sufficient to convict Davis of violating these provisions when he wrote the various checks identified in the money laundering counts of the indictment. A defendant challenging the sufficiency of the evidence supporting his conviction faces a "formidable" burden

> "as we must affirm as long as 'any rational trier of fact could have found the essential elements of the crime beyond a reasonable doubt.' In making this determination we look to all of the evidence and draw all reasonable inferences from that evidence in the light most favorable to the government. We must affirm unless the record is barren of any evidence, regardless of weight, from which the trier of fact could find guilt beyond a reasonable doubt."

United States v. Atterson, 926 F.2d 649, 655 (7th Cir.1991).

We have already set out the elements of a conviction under § 1956(a)(1)(A)(i) and (a)(1)(B)(i). We think that a rational juror could find that the government sustained its burden of proving these elements beyond a reasonable doubt as to the transactions charged in counts three through five of the indictment. As to the elements set out in § 1956(a)(1) and common to both (a)(1)(A)(i) and (a)(1)(B)(i), the proof that Davis knew that money derived from his drug organization was deposited in the church account was established, first, by the testimony of Davis' church secretary, who testified that Davis would give her cash to deposit into the Development Corporation bank account. Second, Agent Wehrheim testified as to Davis' sources of cash and established that Davis and the Development Corporation made bank deposits equal to approximately twice the amount that could be accounted for out of legitimate sources of income. Over half the total amount of these deposits was in cash.

The evidence at trial also established that Davis had access to large amounts of cash. For example, Marcie Rupert testified she had helped him count approximately $35,000 in currency. Pierre Manley, who worked as a runner transporting cash from the Wabashaw house to Davis, testified that he would often pick up $1500 a day from the house. Reasonable jurors could certainly infer that the cash contained in the deposits Davis made or ordered to be made were derived to a large extent from Davis' drug operations and that Davis knew this. The jury was also entitled to conclude, as it did in deciding that Davis was guilty under count one of the indictment, that Davis' drug-derived funds were the proceeds of a drug operation involving a continuing series of narcotics distributions, composed of five or more other persons, and from which Davis derived substantial income. These findings, taken together, established that Davis was guilty of operating a continuing criminal enterprise within the meaning of 21 U.S.C. § 848(c), one of the "specified unlawful activit[ies]" that may serve as a predicate act under the money laundering statute. 18 U.S.C. § 1956(c)(7)(C). Writing a check, whether for cash or to a vendor who has provided services, falls within the definition of a "financial transaction" contained in § 1956(c)(4)(B) because it involved Illinois Federal, a "financial institution * * * the activities of which affect[ ] interstate * * * commerce." Writing a check drawn on an account maintained in such an institution is also a "transaction" falling within the "very broad[ ]" definition given to that term under the money laundering statute.

Turning to the elements set out in subsections (a)(1)(A)(i) and (a)(1)(B)(i) as applied to the conduct charged in the three money laundering counts contained in the indictment, count three charged Davis with issuing seven Development Corporation checks to vendors providing beeper services and mobile telephone services. Pierre Manley testified that Davis gave him a beeper when he began to serve as one of Davis' runners, and that Davis would call Manley's beeper to tell him to contact Davis. When Manley called back, Davis instructed him to drive to the Wabashaw house to make pickups. This and other evidence of the use of beepers as an integral part of Davis' conduct of his continuing criminal enterprise suffice to establish that the use of the funds derived from Davis' drug activities to purchase beepers was intended to promote this activity, establishing a violation of § 1956(a)(1)(A)(i).

We are, however, unable to view the mobile phone purchases that comprise the remainder of count 3, the rental payments alleged in count 4, or the checks written to cash charged in count 5 as intended to promote the continued operations of Davis' continuing criminal enterprise under § 1956(a)(1)(A)(i). The government did not prove that the cellular phones played the same role—or indeed, any role—in Davis' drug operations as the beepers. Likewise the rental payments and the checks written to cash; certainly these expenditures maintained Davis' lifestyle, but more than this is needed to establish that they promoted his drug activities. These transactions, however, do fall within the second money laundering provision under which Davis was charged, § 1956(a)(1)(B)(i). The conversion of cash into goods and services as a way of concealing or disguising the wellspring of the cash is a central concern of the money laundering statute. This is not to say that "the money laundering statute should be interpreted to broadly encompass all transactions, however ordinary on their face, which involve the proceeds of unlawful activity." *Sanders,* 928 F.2d at 946. To convict under § 1956(a)(1)(B)(i) the government must prove not just that the defendant spent ill-gotten gains, but that the expenditures were designed to hide the provenance of the funds involved.

We believe that the government met this burden. Davis chose to place the proceeds of his drug sales not in a personal bank account but in bank accounts ostensibly maintained by the 15th Street Baptist Church and the 15th Street Baptist Church Development Corporation. He nevertheless treated the funds in these accounts as his own, using them to pay for cellular telephones he installed in his many cars and vans, his rent, and his credit card and home phone bills. The jury could reasonably infer that the use of the church accounts was an attempt to hide the ownership and source of Davis' drug money while preserving his ready access to the funds in the accounts, which were as close as the church's checkbook. Moreover, the evidence also established that Davis frequently removed himself still further from the funds in the church accounts by using the church secretary to present Development Corporation checks made out to cash at Illinois Federal. She would then hand over cash she received to Davis. A rational juror could certainly conclude that these maneuvers were designed to conceal the source of Davis' ample store of tainted cash, bringing Davis squarely within the ambit of § 1956(a)(1)(B)(i). That the deception was ultimately unsuccessful, and even that it was relatively easy for investigators to pierce, does not mean that it falls beyond the statute's reach.

Because the money laundering statute is a relatively recent addition to the government's arsenal, and because this case raises unsettling questions about the breadth of its application, we pause to note that the government in its indictment, and the district court in its jury instructions, erroneously read the statute as requiring the government to prove that the transactions charged were both intended to promote Davis' continuing criminal enterprise under § 1956(a)(1)(A)(i), and were designed to conceal the source of the funds used in the transactions under § 1956(a)(1)(B)(i). The statute, however, only requires proof of one or the other. The fact that the government imposed an additional burden on itself does not warrant a reversal. That being said, we are unable to agree with the jury's apparent conclusion that the checks to cellular telephone providers, to Davis' landlord, and to cash, promoted his ongoing sales of crack in any direct way.

The error in the indictment and the jury charge does point to another question, however, namely the relationship between § 1956(a)(1)(A)(i) and (a)(1)(B)(i). These two provisions are aimed at different activities, the first at the practice of plowing back proceeds of "specified unlawful activity" to promote that activity, the second at hiding the proceeds of the activity. The different aims suggest that the prosecution in a money laundering case will generally make its case under one provision or the other; only in the unusual case will the government be able to prove that a single transaction was intended to both promote an illegal activity *and* conceal the origin of the funds used in that activity. This suggests that the government should advise the district court and defense counsel whether it is proceeding under the former, the latter, or both, and that the jury be charged accordingly. The potential breadth of the statute, and the risk that juries will confuse money laundering with money spending, persuades us that their inquiry should be channeled by more specific instructions than the one given in this case.

Notes

1. Should the fact that the government apparently misinterpreted the statutory elements of § 1956 affect the Seventh Circuit's conclusion that § 1956 is not unconstitutionally vague?

2. Were you persuaded that the evidence sufficiently demonstrated that Davis was laundering drug proceeds? If so, what was the most persuasive evidence?

3. Do you agree with the Seventh Circuit's conclusion that a person can be convicted for violating § 1956 when the funds allegedly laundered are derived only in part from specific unlawful activities?

The next case, United States v. Sanders, 929 F.2d 1466 (10th Cir.1991), is another early use of § 1956. It addresses the mens rea element in § 1956.

UNITED STATES v. SANDERS
United States Court of Appeals, Tenth Circuit, 1991.
929 F.2d 1466.

SAFFELS, DISTRICT JUDGE.

Renee Armstrong Sanders, defendant-appellant herein, was convicted in the United States District Court for the Western District of Oklahoma of violating 18 U.S.C. §§ 1962(c) [RICO], 1962(d) [conspiracy to violate RICO], 1956(a)(1)(B)(i) [money laundering] and 21 U.S.C. § 846 [conspiracy to distribute heroin]. * * *

* * *

* * * [D]efendant Sanders argues that her money laundering convictions based upon two car purchases should be overturned because the

evidence was insufficient to establish that these purchases were designed to conceal or disguise drug proceeds. * * *

* * *

* * * [Section 1956, in pertinent part,] provides:

Whoever, knowing that the property involved in a financial transaction represents the proceeds of some form of unlawful activity, conducts or attempts to conduct such a financial transaction which in fact involves the proceeds of specified unlawful activity—

(B) knowing that the transaction is designed in whole or in part—

(i) to conceal or disguise the nature, the location, the source, the ownership, or the control of the proceeds of specified unlawful activity; * * *

shall be sentenced to a fine * * * or imprisonment for not more than twenty years, or both.

Sanders' convictions under the money laundering statute were based upon two car purchases: the November 6, 1986 purchase of a Volvo and the April 24, 1987 purchase of a Lincoln. Defendant argues that these car purchases were ordinary commercial transactions and that the evidence at trial failed to establish that these transactions were designed to conceal or disguise proceeds from the sale of drugs.

The 1986 Volvo, which formed the basis for Count 14 of the superseding Indictment, was ordered by the Sanderses for Mrs. Sanders on October 18, 1986, less than one month after the Sanders' marriage, using Mrs. Sanders' 1981 Volvo as a trade-in. The Sanderses paid a $500 cash deposit at the time the order was placed. When the Volvo was delivered on November 6, 1986, the Sanderses paid for the car by a combination of $3,535 in cash, which was received from Mr. Sanders, and a $10,000 credit union bank draft. At the time of the Volvo purchase, Mrs. Sanders was employed by the Oklahoma State Tax Commission and she took out the $10,000 loan from her credit union to purchase the Volvo. The Sanderses personally handled the transaction to purchase the Volvo and were readily identified by the salesperson with whom they dealt. The salesperson described the approximately $3,500 cash payment as a "normal cash transaction."

Defendant's second money laundering conviction is based upon the purchase of a Lincoln. On April 24, 1987, the Sanderses went to a Lincoln/Mercury dealership and traded in an old Lincoln for a new one, tendering $11,400 in cash for the trade-in difference. Mr. Sanders told the salesman that the car was to be titled in the name of his daughter, Denise Sanders. Mr. Sanders testified that he titled the car in his daughter's name to obtain lower insurance rates. Approximately ten minutes thereafter, Denise Sanders arrived at the car lot. In the meantime, Mrs. Sanders had signed Denise's name as purchaser. All three of the Sanderses were readily identified by the Lincoln salesperson with whom they had dealt. Both the Volvo and the Lincoln were conspicuously used by the Sanderses.

In this appeal, defendant argues that there is insufficient evidence that these car purchase transactions were designed to conceal the identity of the participants to sustain her convictions for violating the money laundering statute. Defendant argues that a necessary element of a violation of the money laundering statute is knowledge that the transaction in question is designed at least in part to conceal or disguise the nature, the source, the ownership, or the control of the proceeds of unlawful activities. Specifically, defendant contends that the undisputed fact that she and her husband were personally present when the cars were purchased and that the Sanderses used the cars conspicuously after they were purchased undermine the element of concealment. Defendant further argues that although the Lincoln was titled in Mr. Sanders' daughter's name, there remains insufficient evidence of a design to conceal her identity as the source of the proceeds because all three Sanderses, including the daughter, were present when the car was purchased and that, because Denise shared the family's last name, her connection to Mr. and Mrs. Sanders would be obvious. She also argues that the money laundering law was not intended to apply to "ordinary commercial transactions" (albeit by alleged drug dealers) but rather was directed toward transactions designed to conceal the identity of the participants to a transaction (including for example, those transactions where third parties are used to make purchases).

The government essentially presents no arguments to counter defendant's contentions with respect to the Volvo purchase. With respect to the purchase of the Lincoln, the government argues that the design of concealment is evidenced by several facts: that the Sanderses paid $11,400 in cash for the car, and that the Sanderses titled the car in the name of Mr. Sanders' daughter, that Mrs. Sanders signed the purchase agreement for the car as "Denise Sanders," and that Denise Sanders was never observed driving the car. The government's basic position, however, is that the money laundering statute should be broadly interpreted to include all purchases made by persons with knowledge that the money used for the transaction represents the proceeds of illegal activity.

We reject the government's argument that the money laundering statute should be interpreted to broadly encompass all transactions, however ordinary on their face, which involve the proceeds of unlawful activity. To so interpret the statute would, in the court's view, turn the money laundering statute into a "money spending statute." This interpretation would be contrary to Congress' expressly stated intent that the transactions being criminalized in the statute are those transactions "designed to conceal or disguise the nature, the location, the source, the ownership, or the control of the proceeds of specified unlawful activity." 18 U.S.C. § 1956(a)(1)(B)(i). Thus, by the express terms of the statute, a design to conceal or disguise the source or nature of the proceeds is a necessary element for a money laundering conviction. In other words, the purpose of the money laundering statute is to reach commercial transactions intended (at least in part) to disguise the relationship of the item purchased with the person providing the proceeds and that the proceeds used to make the purchase were obtained from illegal activities.

Further, we agree with defendant that the evidence of a design to conceal the nature or source of the proceeds used to purchase the cars was insufficient to support her convictions. Clearly, the transaction involving the purchase of the Volvo, and to a slightly lesser extent the purchase of the Lincoln, differ from what could be described as a "typical money laundering transaction" in the Sanderses' failure to use a third party to make the car purchases and thereby conceal the buyers' identities. * * * As outlined above, both defendant and her husband, Johnny Lee, were present at these purchases and were readily identified by the respective salespersons involved. Further, both cars were conspicuously used by the Sanderses, making the association of these vehicles with the Sanderses obvious to law enforcement.

Although the Lincoln purchase clearly presents a closer case in favor of conviction than the Volvo purchase, we hold that the evidence in connection with the Lincoln purchase was also insufficient to support defendant's conviction. Although Mr. Sanders titled the Lincoln in his daughter's name, and Mrs. Sanders signed the daughter's name to the car purchase agreement, we conclude that the daughter's presence in person at the car lot during or somewhat subsequent to the transaction, the fact that the daughter shared the family last name, and defendant's and her husband's conspicuous use of the car after the purchase, undermine the government's argument (based in large part upon the titling of the car in the daughter's name), that the Lincoln purchase involved the requisite design of concealment.

Therefore, because on this record we hold that there was insufficient evidence of concealment in defendant's car purchases to support her convictions under the statute, defendant's convictions for money laundering will be reversed.[w]

* * *

Notes

1. After reading this case, how would you describe the mens rea element of § 1956?

2. Both Sanders and Davis (United States v. Jackson, *supra*) were prosecuted under 18 U.S.C. § 1956(a)(1)(B)(i) which makes it a crime to conduct a financial transaction that involves the proceeds of specified unlawful activity knowing that the property represents the proceeds of some form of illegal activity and "knowing that the transaction is designed * * * to

---

w. The court then held that "[b]ecause of our holding * * * that defendant's convictions under the money laundering statute should be vacated, defendant's substantive conviction for RICO under 18 U.S.C. § 1962(c) must also be vacated because this conviction is no longer supported by two racketeering acts." 929 F.2d at 1473. The court next concluded that "defendant's single conviction for conspiracy to distribute heroin is insufficient to support her conviction for conspiracy to commit RICO." *Id.*

conceal or disguise the nature, the location, the source, the ownership, or the control of the proceeds of specified unlawful activity."

Do you believe Sanders could have been convicted of § 1956(a)(1)(B)(i) if the prosecutor had used the same approach that was employed to convict Davis? Recall that the government proved that Davis' legitimate sources of income were insufficient to account for the amount of money deposited into Davis' accounts, leaving the inference that the excess amount came from illegal sources. Would Sanders have been convicted if the government had been able to prove that Sanders did not have adequate income from legitimate sources to purchase the automobiles in question? Exactly what evidence would the government need if it is going to use this theory?

3. Both the *Sanders* and *Jackson* cases involved violations of § 1956(a)(1). Section 1956(a)(2) focuses on international transportation and contains the following elements:

(1) transporting, transmitting, transferring, or attempting to transport, transmit, or transfer,

(2) a monetary instrument or funds,

(3) in or out of the United States,

(4) with at least one of the following specific intents:

(a) The intent to promote the carrying on of specified unlawful activity, or

(b) Knowing that the monetary instrument or funds involved in the transportation represents the proceeds of some form of unlawful activity *and* knowing that such transportation is designed, in whole or part to:

(i) conceal or disguise the nature, location, source, ownership or control of the proceeds of the specified unlawful activity, or

(ii) to avoid a transaction reporting requirement under State or Federal law.

The crime prohibited in § 1956(a)(2) is narrower in four respects than the crime specified in § 1956(a)(1). First, § 1956(a)(2) applies only to transactions going *in or out of the United States* while § 1956(a)(1) applies to transactions occurring solely within the borders of the United States. Second, the conduct prohibited in § 1956(a)(2), (transports, transmits, or transfers) is narrower than that prohibited in § 1956(a)(1) (engaging in a financial transaction). Even so, § 1956(a)(2)'s reach is quite broad, covering "all means of transporting funds or monetary instruments, including wire transmissions, electronic fund transfers, etc." Third, § 1956(a)(2) covers only transactions concerning "monetary instruments," whereas § 1956(a)(1) covers any "financial transaction." A "monetary instrument" is "coin or currency of the United States or of any other country, travelers' checks, personal checks, bank checks, and money orders, or investment securities or negotiable instruments, in bearer form." Thus, § 1956(a)(2) is restricted to concrete transactions whereas § 1956(a)(1) covers tangibles such as loans and pledges. Lastly, the specific intent element of § 1956(a)(2) is not as comprehensive as than that in § 1956(a)(1): § 1956(a)(2) does not include the intent to engage in tax fraud or evasion, which is listed in § 1956(a)(1).

The last offense in § 1956 (§ 1956(a)(3)) covers the situation where an actor engages in conduct specified in § 1956(a)(1) with "property *represented* to be the proceeds of specified unlawful activity * * *." (emphasis added). Thus, this section applies in undercover situations where law enforcement agents falsely represent that property is proceeds of specified unlawful activity.

4.   Section 1956 is an unusual criminal statute because it includes two intent requirements. Recall that § 1956(a)(1) requires proof of *knowledge* "that the property involved in a financial transaction represents the proceeds of some form of unlawful activity" *and* one of the following *specific intents*:

• intent to promote the carrying on of specified unlawful activity; or

• intent to engage in tax fraud; or

• knowledge that the transaction is designed in whole or in part to conceal or disguise the nature, the location, the source, the ownership, or the control of the proceeds of specified unlawful activity; or

• knowledge that the transaction is designed in whole or in part to avoid a transaction reporting requirement under State or Federal law.

3.   The *Sanders'* holding that "concealment" sufficient for a money laundering conviction cannot be shown when the suspect conducted financial transactions openly and without deceit, remains alive and well. Consider the following opinion by the Fifth Circuit in United States v. Dobbs, 63 F.3d 391 (5th Cir.1995). Dobbs was a cattle farmer and rancher in Texas who was convicted of fraudulently disposing of cattle pledged to the Farmers Home Administration (FmHA) (in violation of 18 U.S.C. § 658), bank fraud (in violation of 18 U.S.C. § 1344) and money laundering (in violation of 18 U.S.C. § 1956). The Fifth Circuit affirmed Dobbs' convictions for fraud upon the FmHA and for bank fraud but set aside the money laundering convictions. Do you agree with the decision in *Dobbs*?

"Dobbs contends that there is insufficient evidence in the record to convict him of money laundering.

"The government must prove that the specific transactions in question were designed, at least in part to launder money. It is necessary to show a desire to create the appearance of legitimate wealth or otherwise to conceal the nature of funds so that it might enter the economy as legitimate funds. The purpose of the money laundering statute is to reach commercial transactions intended (at least in part) to disguise the relationship of the item purchased with the person providing the proceeds and that the proceeds used to make the purchase were obtained from illegal activities.

"One of the money laundering counts charges that Dobbs deposited approximately $4500 of the cattle sale proceeds into his wife's bank account. The Dobbses had decided to use the account as their main operational account. The money was used to pay the ordinary expenses of the ranch and household. The other money laundering count charges that Dobbs converted a cattle sale check for approximately $37,000 into a cashiers check for $37,000 and then converted the cashiers check into four separate cashier's checks. These smaller cashiers checks were then used to pay for ranch and family expenses. The government concedes that Dobbs' records reflected use of the funds to pay ranch and family expenses. These transactions were open and notorious—at least as much as the typical bank transactions can be. Dobbs also did not use any third parties to make purchases or otherwise hide his identity when making the transactions.

"In United States v. Sanders, 929 F.2d 1466 (10th Cir.1991) the defendant had been convicted of money laundering for purchasing two cars. On the first car purchase, the defendant and her husband paid a $500 cash deposit when ordering the car. When the car was delivered, Sanders paid $3535 in cash and $10,000 by credit union bank draft. On the second car purchase, the defendant traded an old Lincoln for a new one with $11,400 in cash for the trade-in difference. The defendant had the salesman put the car in her daughter's name and signed the daughter's name to the purchase agreement. The cars were conspicuously used by the defendant and her husband making the association of the vehicles with the Sanderses obvious to law enforcement.

"The court [in United States v. Sanders, 929 F.2d 1466, 1472 (10th Cir.1991)] held that the very purpose of the statute was to reach commercial transactions intended at least in part to disguise the relationship of the item purchased with the person providing the illegally obtained proceeds. The court found that the fact the defendant and her husband were present at the car purchases and were readily identified by the respective sales person plus the fact that the cars were used in a conspicuous manner provided an insufficient basis to support a conviction for money laundering. Similarly in this case where the use of the money was not disguised and the purchases were for family expenses and business expenses is not disputed, there is also insufficient evidence to support the money laundering conviction.

"The government argues that evidence in the record showing that Dobbs did not disclose these transactions to the bank or to his bankruptcy attorney provides a reasonable basis for the jury to find that the transactions were designed to conceal the origins of the funds. We disagree. This evidence in the record only provides a basis for showing that the defendant was engaged in some type of fraud. There is no link between this evidence of fraud and these specific transactions, or that the transactions were done to disguise the relationship between Dobbs and the proceeds. As stated by the Tenth Circuit in United States v. Garcia–Emanuel, 14 F.3d 1469, 1474 (10th Cir.1994) '[m]erely engaging in a transaction with money whose nature has been concealed through other means is not in itself a crime.' "

Other defendants have not been as successful with a *Sanders* argument. In United States v. Tencer, 107 F.3d 1120 (5th Cir.1997), for example, the defendant unsuccessfully argued that because he opened bank accounts in his own name, there was insufficient evidence, under § 1956, of his intent to conceal any activity. The Fifth Circuit rejected his argument, focusing on the location of the accounts and falsehoods Tencer told bank employees about his future plans. The Fifth Circuit explained:

"Steven Tencer and Ronald Lazar [were convicted] * * * on multiple counts related to their scheme to submit fraudulent claims to insurance companies and obtain proceeds for unperformed chiropractic services.

* * *

"Tencer * * * challenges the sufficiency of the evidence supporting his conviction for money laundering * * *.

* * *

"Between May 1989 and April 1992, Tencer opened bank accounts in various banks across the country and deposited checks drawn on his personal account at Fidelity Homestead and on the Allied Clinic account at Whitney National Bank. On July 9, 1992, a little more than a week after federal agents had executed a search warrant at Allied Clinic, Tencer faxed instructions to several of the regional banks where he had accounts. He directed those banks to transmit his funds on deposit by mailing cashiers checks by Federal Express to an Algiers, Louisiana, address at which Tencer neither worked nor resided. On July 13, 1992, Tencer opened an account at California Federal Bank in Las Vegas, Nevada, using some of the cashiers checks; his initial deposit totaled $662,637.06. He told employees at the Las Vegas bank that he was moving into the area and needed cash to buy a business. He also directed banks that had not yet mailed cashiers checks to the Algiers address to wire funds totaling $312,297.89 to the account at California Federal Bank. The next day, Tencer deposited an $89,832.10 cashiers check into the account and withdrew $9,900.[3] Later that day, Tencer arranged to have the entire balance in the account—roughly $1,055,-000—delivered to him in cash at a local airport. Before the funds could be picked up by a security company and delivered to Tencer, a seizure warrant was executed on the California Federal account.

"Tencer argues that the government has presented no evidence that he sought to conceal the nature, source, ownership, or control of the funds. He contends that when he opened the regional accounts initially and later transferred those balances to the California Federal account, he used his own name and handled his own transactions. No third parties were used, and a paper trail clearly connected Tencer to both the regional and California Federal accounts.

"The government counters that the use of a false identity is not essential to a money laundering conviction. It contends that Tencer's request that funds be sent to an address at which he neither worked nor resided, his use of a Las Vegas bank hundreds of miles away from his home and business to consolidate funds, and his false statements to bank employees about his plans to move to the area demonstrated his intent to conceal.

---

3. Withdrawals of more than $10,000 in cash require the completion of a Currency Transaction Report; according to a bank official, withdrawals slightly below the regulated amount are not unusual.

"We reject as overly narrow Tencer's view that § 1956's concealment element is satisfied only by an attempt to disguise the defendant's identity.

* * *

" * * * Tencer endeavored to consolidate illicit funds in a city that was hundreds of miles from his home and where large cash transactions are commonplace. He asked regional banks to wire funds to an address to which he had no connection. His false statements to bank officials showed an intent to minimize attention to the transactions. Based on the evidence in the record, a jury could infer that Tencer was attempting to conceal the nature of the funds and facilitate laundering of the proceeds of his fraudulent activities

4. The Tenth Circuit has provided a helpful list of factors to consider in determining whether there is sufficient evidence of concealment:

"As we [have] noted * * *, separating money laundering from mere money spending is often a formidable task. In ascertaining whether the requisite intent to disguise or conceal was present, we consider a variety of types of evidence including: statements by a defendant probative of intent to conceal; unusual secrecy surrounding the transaction; structuring the transaction to avoid attention; depositing illegal profits in the bank account of a legitimate business; highly irregular features of the transaction; using third parties to conceal the real owner; a series of unusual financial moves cumulating in the transaction; and expert testimony on practices of criminals. Of course, this is not an exclusive list of factors for a court to consider when determining whether a defendant possessed the intent to disguise or conceal.ˣ"

Do you think these factors will apply more or less often to defendants accused of white collar crimes than to defendants routinely prosecuted for money laundering (drug dealers)? Is this a problem or is this exactly the type of harm at which the money laundering statutes are aimed?

———

The next case, United States v. Johnson, 971 F.2d 562 (10th Cir.1992), involves a prosecution under both §§ 1956 and 1957. It addresses three issues regarding money laundering. The first concerns intent and is, essentially, an application of *Jackson, supra*. This issue is pertinent in a § 1956 or a § 1957 prosecution. The second issue is unique to § 1957: whether the crime which generates the "criminally derived property" referred to in § 1957 must be completed at the time of the monetary transaction. The third issue arises in both § 1956 and § 1957 cases and was initially addressed in by the Tenth Circuit in *Jackson, supra*. It concerns the extent to which the funds in question must be traced to specific criminal acts when legitimately obtained and illegitimately obtained funds have been co-mingled. As you will see in the Notes and cases which follow *Johnson*, other circuits tend to follow the

x. United States v. Contreras, 108 F.3d 1255 (10th Cir.1997).

Tenth Circuit on the second issue. On the third issue, however, the courts are developing several approaches.

UNITED STATES v. JOHNSON

United States Court of Appeals, Tenth Circuit, 1992.
971 F.2d 562.

BROWN, CIRCUIT JUDGE.*

The defendant-appellant Robert Johnson was charged in a sixty-three count indictment with various violations of the Money Laundering Control Act of 1986 (18 U.S.C. §§ 1956 & 1957). A jury found him guilty on all but one count. Appellant was sentenced by the district court to 405 months imprisonment. On appeal, Johnson raises several challenges to the propriety of the convictions and the sentence.

The government alleged that the defendant masterminded a "peso scheme" which defrauded investors out of millions of dollars. According to the government, the defendant convinced investors that he was buying Mexican pesos at a discount rate and then reselling the pesos for their market value in American dollars. Johnson told potential investors that he had served in the war in Vietnam with a man from Mexico whose father was highly placed in the Mexican government. Johnson said that through this contact he had access to Mexican citizens and businesses that wanted to exchange pesos for dollars. The Mexicans wanted to convert their money to dollars, Johnson explained, because the peso was rapidly losing its value and the Mexicans preferred to hold a more stable currency. The defendant told investors that, depending on the number of trades he could make in a day, an investor could realize anywhere from fifteen to twenty-five per cent profit per week.[1]

Several individuals who sent money to the defendant for investment in the peso scheme testified at the defendant's trial. They each testified that they began by giving relatively small amounts of money to the defendant for investment in the peso deal. At the defendant's request, they transferred money they wanted to invest in the deal by means of a wire transfer from their own bank to the defendant's account at the Sooner Federal Savings & Loan in Broken Arrow, Oklahoma. Shortly thereafter, the defendant would wire back the amount of "profit" supposedly made by the investor from the purchase and sale of pesos. The amount wired back by the defendant was often fifteen to twenty per cent of the initial investment. The huge "profits" being made by investors apparently convinced them to invest heavily in the scheme and numerous individuals wired a steady stream of money to the defendant. Several of the investors who testified at trial sent upwards of half a million dollars to the defendant. The defendant managed to gain their complete confidence.

* The Honorable Wesley E. Brown, United States Senior District Judge for the District of Kansas, sitting by designation.

1. A black market in the exchange of pesos apparently sprang up in reaction to attempts by the Mexican government in 1982 to regulate transfers of that currency.

An Internal Revenue Service agent who had examined the defendant's bank records determined that about five and a half million dollars were deposited into the defendant's account in shortly over a year's time. The agent further determined that approximately $1.8 million of that amount was withdrawn out of the account and was used by the defendant to purchase various items, including a house, a car, and assorted cashier's checks. Approximately $1.3 million worth of liquid assets was seized from the defendant when he was arrested. The remainder of the money had been intermittently wired back to investors in the form of "profits."

We find it unnecessary for purposes of this opinion to fully recount the evidence presented by the government relating to the defendant's involvement in the peso scheme; we simply observe that the evidence overwhelmingly supported a conclusion that the scheme was fraudulent and that the defendant was not using the investors' money to purchase and resell pesos.

Counts two and three of the indictment charged the defendant with violations of 18 U.S.C. § 1956(a)(1)(A)(i). That section provides:

§ 1956. Laundering of monetary instruments

(a)(1) Whoever, knowing that the property involved in a financial transaction represents the proceeds of some form of unlawful activity, conducts or attempts to conduct such a financial transaction which in fact involves the proceeds of specified unlawful activity—

(A)(i) with the intent to promote the carrying on of specified unlawful activity. . . .

shall be sentenced to, . . . imprisonment for not more than twenty years. . . .

The "specified unlawful activity" alleged in the indictment was wire fraud in violation of 18 U.S.C. § 1343. Count two of the indictment alleged that Johnson used the proceeds of a wire fraud to pay off the mortgage on his house in Tulsa in the amount of $122,796. Count three alleged that Johnson used wire fraud proceeds to purchase a 1989 Mercedes automobile.

Appellant's first argument is that the evidence was insufficient to support his conviction on counts two and three. Our standard of review on this issue is well established: "In judging the sufficiency of the evidence, we are bound to view the proof presented in the light most favorable to the government to ascertain if there is sufficient substantial proof, direct and circumstantial, together with reasonable inferences to be drawn therefrom, from which a jury might find a defendant guilty beyond a reasonable doubt." United States v. Sullivan, 919 F.2d 1403, 1431 (10th Cir.1990).

Appellant contends that the evidence did not show that the payment of the mortgage on his home was done "with the intent to promote the carrying on" of the wire fraud. He argues that there was no evidence to support a conclusion that he paid off the mortgage in order to further the wire fraud activity. In response, the government points out that the defendant maintained an office in the home which he used to carry out much of the fraudulent activity.

Direct evidence of a defendant's intent is seldom available. Intent can be proven, however, from surrounding circumstances. We find that the evidence, when viewed in the light most favorable to the government, is sufficient to support the conviction on count two. The evidence clearly showed that the defendant used the office in his home to carry out the fraudulent scheme. In addition, the defendant's aura of legitimacy was bolstered in the minds of investors who saw the defendant's house. The circumstances give rise to an inference that the defendant paid the mortgage on the house so that he could continue using the office in furtherance of the fraudulent scheme. Although, as appellant points out, he could have retained the use of the office simply by continuing to make monthly mortgage payments, the fact is that he did not do so. Instead, he used wire fraud proceeds to retire the outstanding balance on the loan secured by the mortgage. Paying off the loan gave him the right to continue using the office and the home. The jury could legitimately infer that paying off the mortgage with wire fraud proceeds was done with the intent to promote the carrying on of the unlawful activity.

The evidence similarly supports the conviction on count three of the indictment. The evidence suggests that the defendant used the Mercedes described in count three to impress investors. The jury could conclude from the evidence that appellant purchased the car to promote the carrying on of his fraudulent scheme. Appellant argues that he had two Mercedes automobiles and that evidence was lacking to show that the one described in count three was used by him in furthering the peso scheme. He contends that the Mercedes described in count three was purchased for his wife. The defendant in fact told one of the investors that he had purchased this car for his wife. But the record contains some evidence that contradicts this assertion. Testimony indicated that the defendant used this particular car both before and after he was separated from his wife. Also, after the defendant talked about the car with the same investor mentioned above, the investor went and talked to the auto dealer who sold the car to the defendant. The dealer spoke very highly of the defendant, who had put a down payment of approximately $66,000 on the car. After speaking with the auto dealer and others about the defendant, the investor was persuaded that the defendant was a legitimate businessman. This evidence suggests that the defendant used the car to persuade investors to invest in his scheme. His use of the car in this manner further tends to show that he purchased the car with that purpose in mind. *Cf.* United States v. Jackson, 935 F.2d 832, 841 (7th Cir.1991) (No evidence that cellular phones purchased by the defendant played any role in his drug operation; evidence was therefore insufficient to show that their purchase was intended to promote his drug activities.) Taken as a whole, the evidence supports the jury's finding that the defendant engaged in the financial transaction of purchasing the car with the intent to promote the carrying on of the wire fraud activity.

Appellant's next argument is that the evidence was insufficient to support the convictions on counts four through sixty-three of the indictment. These counts were brought under 18 U.S.C. § 1957, which provides in part:

§ 1957. Engaging in monetary transactions in property derived from specified unlawful activity

(a) Whoever, ... knowingly engages or attempts to engage in a monetary transaction in criminally derived property that is of a value greater than $10,000 and is derived from specified unlawful activity, shall be punished as provided in subsection (b).

* * *

(f) As used in this section—

(1) the term "monetary transaction" means the deposit, withdrawal, transfer, or exchange, in or affecting interstate or foreign commerce, of funds or a monetary instrument ... by, through, or to a financial institution. ...

(2) the term "criminally derived property" means any property constituting, or derived from, proceeds obtained from a criminal offense; ...

Counts four through thirty-one of the indictment against the defendant alleged violations of § 1957 based on twenty-eight separate wire transfers of funds from investors to the defendant's account in Tulsa, Oklahoma. Counts thirty-two through fifty-seven were based upon wire transfers of funds from the defendant's account to individual investors. The final charges in the indictment, counts fifty-eight through sixty-three, were based upon withdrawals by the defendant from his account in the form of cashier's checks. The funds involved in all of the transactions were alleged to be the proceeds of wire fraud.

Appellant's primary argument pertains to counts four through thirty-one. He argues that the transfer of funds from the investors to his account did not violate § 1957 because those transfers were not monetary transactions in "criminally derived property." Although appellant's argument is characterized as a challenge to the sufficiency of the evidence, it raises a question concerning the proper scope of § 1957 and it requires us to interpret the language of the statute. Appellant's brief sets forth two basic arguments in support of his contention that the funds transferred to him were not "criminally derived property." First, he argues that the funds could not be considered the proceeds of a wire fraud until the wire fraud was completed. "Proceeds," according to appellant, are funds from a previous and completed criminal activity. Second, appellant contends that § 1957 requires that the proceeds of an offense be "obtained" before a defendant can engage in a monetary transaction with those proceeds. He points to the definition of criminally derived property, which is "any property constituting ... proceeds obtained from a criminal offense." § 1957(f)(2). He argues that he did not obtain the proceeds of the wire fraud until they were credited to his account. Thus, he maintains, the transaction in which those funds were wired to him did not involve "criminally derived property." * * * The government's response is that "it was not necessary for these funds to have been received by appellant in order to acquire their denomination as 'criminally derived property.' "

Under § 1957, "criminally derived property" means any property constituting, or derived from, proceeds obtained from a criminal offense. § 1957(f)(2). Because there is no other "property" at issue here, we are only concerned with the funds transferred by the investors to the defendant. We agree with appellant that under the facts presented here, the transfer of funds from the investors to the defendant's account did not constitute violations of § 1957.

Both the ordinary meaning of the word "obtained" and the legislative history behind § 1957 suggest that this section was not intended to apply to transactions of the type alleged in counts four through thirty-one. We turn first to the language of the statute. The statute itself defines criminally derived property in terms of proceeds "obtained" from a criminal offense. "A fundamental canon of statutory construction is that, unless otherwise defined, words will be interpreted as taking their ordinary, contemporary, common meaning." Perrin v. United States, 444 U.S. 37, 42 (1979). "Obtain" most commonly means "to gain or attain possession or disposal of usually by some planned action or method." Webster's Third New International Dictionary, 1559 (1961). This suggests that Congress viewed a violation of § 1957 as occurring only after the individual involved in the specified criminal activity gained possession or disposal of the proceeds generated by the criminal activity.

When the plain language of a statute does not unambiguously reveal its meaning, we turn to the legislative history. The legislative history behind the Money Laundering Control Act of 1986 is fairly sparse. No committee reports were submitted by Congress with the Act. Two reports related to the Act contain some discussion of the purpose behind § 1956 and § 1957. Neither of the reports sheds much light on the question before us, however. The examples of money-laundering activity discussed throughout these reports show that Congress had in mind the "classic" case of laundering drug money—that is, where a drug trafficker collects large amounts of cash from drug sales and, acting with the complicity of a banker or other person in a financial institution, deposits the drug proceeds in a bank under the guise of conducting a legitimate business transaction. The Act appears to be part of an effort to criminalize the conduct of those third persons—bankers, brokers, real estate agents, auto dealer and others—who have aided drug dealers by allowing them to dispose of the profits of drug activity, yet whose conduct has not been considered criminal under traditional conspiracy law. It must be noted, however, that the Act itself prohibits a much broader range of conduct than just the "classic" example of money laundering.

* * *

It is possible to construe the phrase "proceeds obtained from a criminal offense" more broadly than this. One might logically infer that Congress could have intended § 1957 to apply when the underlying criminal activity occurs simultaneously with a monetary transaction with the proceeds of the activity. In this case, the result achieved by causing the investors to wire the funds directly into the defendant's account was no different than if the defendant had first obtained the funds and then deposited them himself. This latter transaction would clearly have violated § 1957. It would be logical, then, to assume that the former transaction would also be proscribed by the statute. Yet, both the plain language of § 1957 and the legislative history behind it suggest that Congress targeted only those transactions occurring after proceeds have been obtained from the underlying unlawful activity. At the very least, the statute is ambiguous on this point because, after examining all the relevant material which might aid us in construing its provisions, a reasonable doubt persists as to the statute's intended scope. Accordingly, the "rule of lenity" requires that we adopt the more lenient interpretation.

The underlying criminal activity in this case was wire fraud, which the defendant accomplished by causing the investors to wire funds to his account. Whether or not the funds that were wired to the defendant were "criminally derived property" depends upon whether they were proceeds obtained from a criminal offense at the time the defendant engaged in the monetary transaction. We find they were not. Section 1957 appears to be drafted to proscribe certain transactions in proceeds that have already been obtained by an individual from an underlying criminal offense. The defendant did not have possession of the funds nor were they at his disposal until the investors transferred them to him. The defendant therefore cannot be said to have obtained the proceeds of the wire fraud until the funds were credited to his account. Thus, the transfers alleged in counts four through thirty-one of the indictment were not transactions in criminally derived property and the defendant's convictions on those counts are reversed.

Appellant's next argument is that the evidence was insufficient as to counts thirty-two through sixty-three of the indictment. These counts alleged violations of § 1957 based on transfers of funds from the defendant's account to the investors in the peso scheme. Appellant argues that the government did not show that the funds that he wired out of his account were the proceeds of wire fraud, stating "It is entirely possible that the funds paid out . . . came from sources other than the investors."

We find that the evidence here was sufficient for the jury to conclude that these funds were in fact derived from specified unlawful activity. The evidence showed that over five and a half million dollars were deposited into the defendant's account at the Sooner Federal

Savings & Loan. The government presented evidence that at least $2.4 million of this amount was from specific instances of wire fraud. The testimony and the defendant's bank records indicated that most of the remainder, about $3 million, came from other investors in the peso scheme. The source of approximately 1.2% of the funds deposited in the defendant's account could not be determined. The amount of funds withdrawn from the defendant's account in the transactions set forth in counts thirty-two through sixty-three was approximately $1.8 million. An examination of the defendant's bank records gave no indication that the funds in the defendant's account came from any source other than investors in the alleged peso trades. Under the circumstances, the evidence was sufficient for the jury to find that the funds withdrawn were derived from the specified unlawful activity.

The government had the burden of showing that the criminally derived property used in the monetary transactions was in fact derived from specified unlawful activity. This does not mean, however, that the government had to show that funds withdrawn from the defendant's account could not possibly have come from any source other than the unlawful activity. Once proceeds of unlawful activity have been deposited in a financial institution and have been credited to an account, those funds cannot be traced to any particular transaction and cannot be distinguished from any other funds deposited in the account. The "tainted" funds may be commingled with "untainted" funds, with the result being simply a net credit balance in favor of the depositor. The credit balance gives the depositor a claim against the bank and allows him to withdraw funds to the extent of the credit. In the context of a withdrawal, the portion of § 1957 requiring a showing that the proceeds were in fact "derived from specified unlawful activity" could not have been intended as a requirement that the government prove that no "untainted" funds were deposited along with the unlawful proceeds. *Cf.* United States v. Jackson, 935 F.2d 832, 840 (7th Cir.1991). Such an interpretation would allow individuals to avoid prosecution simply by commingling legitimate funds with proceeds of crime. *Id.* This would defeat the very purpose of the money-laundering statutes.

* * *

Notes

1.   Johnson's peso scam was a classic "Ponzi scheme". Now used as a term of art, "Ponzi scheme" arose from the antics of Charles Ponzi. In the words of the First Circuit, Charles Ponzi experienced a "remarkable criminal financial career":

> "With capital of $150, Ponzi began the business of borrowing money on his promissory notes. He spread the false tale that he was engaged in buying international postal coupons in foreign countries and selling them in other countries at a 100 percent profit. He claimed that this was made possible by excessive differences in the rates of exchange.

"With a written promise to pay $150 in ninety days for every $100 he borrowed, Ponzi induced thousands to lend to him. Within eight months he took in over $9,500,000, for which he issued notes for over $14,000,-000. He made no investments of any kind. All the money he had at any time resulted solely from loans made to him under his scheme. When notes became due, they were paid off with money from new investors. Ever since, investments in which early investors are paid off with monies from new investors are characterized as Ponzi schemes."[y]

2. The Tenth Circuit found sufficient "intent to promote the carrying on" of wire fraud in Johnson's purchase of a Mercedes and the paying off of his home mortgage on the ground that both the Mercedes and Johnson's home added an "aura of legitimacy" to Johnson, helping impress investors. Recall the evidence that Johnson used his home to carry out the fraud (he had an office at home). The most the government was able to show about the Mercedes, however, was that an investor happened to speak with a Mercedes dealer about the cost of the defendant's Mercedes and, arguably, this helped persuade the investor of the defendant's legitimacy. Do you agree with this reasoning? What if a defendant purchased an inexpensive compact car instead of a Mercedes? Would such a purchase cease to be money laundering?

3. Counts 2 and 3 involved purchases (of a house and a car) with the proceeds of a "specified unlawful activity" (wire fraud resulting from the pesos scheme). Counts 4–63 involved wire transfers between victims and the defendant. Note that Counts 2 and 3 of the indictment charged violations of § 1956 and Counts 4–63 charged violations of § 1957. Why the difference? The answer may lie in the distinction between a "financial transaction" (§ 1956) and a "monetary transaction" (§ 1957). A "financial transaction" within § 1956 is quite broad: it covers any transaction between private individuals as long as the transaction "in any way or degree affects interstate or foreign commerce."[z] A "monetary transaction" within § 1957, however, must be "by, through, or to a financial institution."[aa]

There are other differences in § 1956 and § 1957. Whereas § 1956 applies regardless of the amount of money involved, § 1957 applies only when $10,000, or more, is involved. Whereas § 1956 requires proof of knowledge that the property at issue represents the proceeds of some form of unlawful activity, *plus* a specific intent or knowledge, § 1957 contains no specific intent or knowledge requirement. To convict on § 1957 the government must simply prove that the defendant knew that the proceeds were from some form of criminal activity.

4. Recall that the Tenth Circuit rejected Johnson's argument that Counts 32–63 of the indictment should be reversed. Johnson had argued that the government failed to show that funds at issue were proceeds of the alleged fraud since the funds had been commingled. In the defendant's words: "It is entirely possible that the funds paid out * * * came from sources other than investors." Note the proof the government presented to

---

y. Robert Grafton & Clyde Posey, *Tax Implications of Fraudulent Income Earning Schemes: Ponzi and Others*, 27 Am. Bus. L.J. 599, 600, 601 (1990); Cunningham v. Merchant's Nat. Bank, 4 F.2d 25 (1st Cir. 1925).

z. 18 U.S.C. § 1957(f)(1).

aa. 18 U.S.C. § 1957(f)(1).

overcome this argument (tracing the source of all but 1.2% of the funds in the $5.4 million account). How do you think the government developed such evidence?

5. The issue for which the *Johnson* case is cited most frequently is that on which the defendant won. The Tenth Circuit reversed the defendant's § 1957 convictions on Counts 4–31 which were wire transfers of funds from investors to the defendant's account in Tulsa, Oklahoma. Note the court's reasoning: that the defendant had not "obtained" the proceeds of his specified unlawful activity (wire fraud) until the funds were credited to his account. Do you think the Government could have saved these counts by charging, as the "monetary transaction" in each count, the *deposit* into the defendant's account of the investors' wire transfers rather than the *sending* of the wire transfer by the investors to the defendant? Consider the definition of "monetary transaction":

> "the term 'monetary transaction' means the deposit, withdrawal, transfer, or exchange, in or affecting interstate or foreign commerce, of funds or a monetary instrument * * * by, through, or to a financial institution* * *."[bb]

Many courts have struggled with the question of whether the property is "obtained" at the time of the monetary transaction (i.e. whether it is criminally derived property instead of on its way to being criminally derived). Three cases follow: United States v. Piervinanzi, 23 F.3d 670 (2d Cir.1994), United States v. Kennedy, 64 F.3d 1465 (10th Cir.1995), and United States v. Allen, 76 F.3d 1348 (5th Cir.1996). As you read these cases, see if you can predict each court's decision. If not, is it because the *Johnson* analysis provides insufficient guidance? Can you think of a better approach?

UNITED STATES v. PIERVINANZI

United States Court of Appeals, Second Circuit, 1994.
23 F.3d 670.

MAHONEY, CIRCUIT JUDGE.

* * *

From 1982 to 1988, Lorenzo DelGiudice was an auditor and computer operations specialist for Irving Trust. DelGiudice was responsible for monitoring and improving the security of the bank's wire transfer procedures to prevent unauthorized transfers. In March 1988, Anthony Marchese told DelGiudice that he and [Michael] Piervinanzi were planning to rob an armored car. DelGiudice suggested a less violent alternative—an unauthorized wire transfer of funds from Irving Trust into an overseas account. DelGiudice explained that he could use his position at Irving Trust to obtain the information necessary to execute such a

bb. 18 U.S.C. § 1957(f)(1).

transfer. DelGiudice also explained that it would be necessary to obtain an overseas bank account for the scheme to succeed, because (1) United States banking regulations made the rapid movement of proceeds difficult, and (2) a domestic fraudulent transfer could, if detected, be readily reversed.

* * *

In July 1988, in a move unrelated to the attempted bank fraud, DelGiudice left his job at Irving Trust and accepted a "better position" at Morgan Guaranty as audit manager. His first assignment at Morgan Guaranty was to perform an audit of the bank's wire transfer department. During the autumn of 1988, DelGiudice, Marchese, and Piervinanzi began planning a fraudulent wire transfer from Morgan Guaranty. DelGiudice agreed to acquire the necessary information for the transfer; Marchese and Piervinanzi took responsibility for arranging other aspects of the scheme, such as locating an overseas bank account to receive the stolen funds, recruiting a "caller" to initiate the wire transfer, and arranging for the distribution of the proceeds. * * *

Marchese and Piervinanzi contacted Philip Wesoke, a self-styled "financial consultant" who had previously invested (and lost) money for Piervinanzi. Marchese and Piervinanzi told Wesoke that they represented individuals who wanted to invest $14 to $20 million discreetly in a liquid, unregistered asset. Marchese and Piervinanzi told Wesoke that the investment could be "settled" overseas, and Piervinanzi mentioned the Cayman Islands, saying that he and Marchese had recently completed a transaction there. Having learned from the aborted Irving Trust scheme that correspondent bank information was necessary to transfer funds out of the country, Piervinanzi told Wesoke to provide the identity of a correspondent bank.

Wesoke recommended, and Piervinanzi and Marchese agreed, that they invest in diamonds. Wesoke accordingly arranged for a syndicate of Israeli diamond dealers to assemble a portfolio of diamonds for the conspirators. Wesoke also provided Piervinanzi with the necessary account and correspondent bank information for the planned recipient bank.

DelGiudice had selected an account of Shearson Lehman Hutton, Inc. ("Shearson") at Morgan Guaranty as his target, and compiled the necessary information for the transfer. Piervinanzi gave DelGiudice the information that Wesoke had provided concerning the recipient bank and its American correspondent bank. DelGiudice then met with Robin Piervinanzi [Michael's brother], who * * * was chosen to make the call that would trigger the fraudulent transfer. DelGiudice provided Robin with the appropriate Morgan Guaranty telephone number, dictated a script for him to use, and told him when to make the call.

On February 23, 1989, Robin telephoned Morgan Guaranty and, purporting to be Shearson employee William Cicio, directed a wire transfer of $24 million to the selected account in London, with Bankers

Trust Company in New York ("Bankers Trust") serving as the correspondent bank. Although Robin supplied all the information needed to complete the transfer, Morgan Guaranty's clerk became suspicious because she had spoken with Cicio previously, and discerned that the voice on the telephone was not Cicio's. The clerk processed the transfer, but reported her suspicions to a supervisor. Either the supervisor or the clerk then contacted Shearson and learned that the transaction had not been authorized. Although the $24 million had already reached Bankers Trust, the wire transfer was stopped and reversed.

* * *

Count seven charged that Piervinanzi violated § 1957 by fraudulently causing the transfer of approximately $24 million from Morgan Guaranty. Piervinanzi argues that the language of the statute only encompasses transactions in which a defendant first obtains "criminally derived property," and then engages in a monetary transaction with that property. Because the funds transferred from Morgan Guaranty were not yet property derived from the wire fraud and bank fraud scheme, Piervinanzi contends, his actions did not come within the purview of § 1957. The government does not dispute this reading of the statute, and joins Piervinanzi's request to vacate his conviction on this count.

"[T]he starting point for interpreting a statute is the language of the statute itself." Thus, the first canon of statutory construction is that "a legislature says in a statute what it means and means in a statute what it says there." [citations deleted] * * *

The language of § 1957 supports Piervinanzi's interpretation of that statute. The ordinary meaning of the word "obtained" entails possession of a thing. See Webster's Third New International Dictionary 1559 (1986). Similarly, the word "property" implies ownership, or the "exclusive right to possess, enjoy, and dispose of a thing." Id. at 1818. The use of such language demonstrates a congressional intent that the proceeds of a crime be in the defendant's possession before he can attempt to transfer those proceeds in violation of § 1957. See United States v. Johnson, 971 F.2d 562, 569 (10th Cir.1992) ("both the plain language of § 1957 and the legislative history behind it suggest that Congress targeted only those transactions occurring after proceeds have been obtained from the underlying unlawful activity").

Piervinanzi and his colleagues succeeded in transferring $24 million from Morgan Guaranty to Bankers Trust, but these funds never came into the possession or under the control of the conspirators. Thus, Piervinanzi was improperly convicted of money laundering in violation of § 1957, and we reverse his conviction on count seven.

* * *

UNITED STATES v. KENNEDY

United States Court of Appeals, Tenth Circuit, 1995.
64 F.3d 1465.

EBEL, CIRCUIT JUDGE.

Defendant–Appellant William R. Kennedy, Jr. ("Kennedy") was charged in a 109–count indictment for a massive scheme to defraud precious metals investors. * * *

In 1979, Kennedy helped found Western Monetary Consultants, Inc. ("WMC"). He served as WMC's president from the corporation's inception through his indictment in this case. WMC marketed itself as a large scale seller of precious metals and coins. Through various literature mailings and a series of seminars, referred to as "war colleges," WMC advocated the purchase of tangible precious metals as a hedge against inflation caused by certain world events. Investors could purchase the metals from WMC either through cash transactions or through cash down-payments coupled with bank-financed loans.

When an investor agreed to purchase a certain quantity of metal from WMC, a WMC consultant would quote the investor an approximate price. The consultant would then contact the WMC trading department, which would locate the best price for the metal from one of its dealers. The consultant would then inform the investor of the exact price, which was to be "locked-in" at that point in time, and the investor would then transfer funds to WMC via check, often supplemented with funds from a bank loan. If WMC did not in turn provide the dealer with the purchase price within 48 hours of ordering, the dealer typically nullified the contract with WMC, requiring WMC to reorder at a new price.

Between 1984 and 1987, WMC increased its sales rapidly and began to experience serious cash shortages. Kennedy nevertheless continued to promote sales to new investors, without informing them that WMC was between ten to thirteen million dollars behind in filling backlogged orders. * * *

In July of 1992, after a five year investigation of WMC's practices, the government indicted Kennedy and numerous other WMC participants. The 109–count indictment against Kennedy alleged a massive Ponzi scheme to defraud numerous precious metals investors. The government alleged that when WMC "locked-in" a price for an investor, it did so under the false pretenses that it would purchase the investor's metal immediately. However, rather than purchasing immediately, the government alleged that WMC frequently delayed purchases or failed to fill orders altogether. Specifically, the government alleged that WMC diverted many investors' funds to other uses, including speculating in futures markets, operating the Conservative Digest magazine, and financing personal endeavors.

* * *

Kennedy's [argues] is that the indictment included legally inadequate allegations of the "proceeds" element of all seven money laundering convictions.

* * *

The government indicted Kennedy for the specific money laundering violations set forth in 18 U.S.C. § 1956. * * * The government alleged that Kennedy violated this statute by depositing checks or foreign currency from various investors into a WMC account. Each separate count represented a particular deposit involving a different named investor's funds. The government claimed that each of these deposits constituted financial transactions "involving the proceeds of specified unlawful activity"—namely, the proceeds of the mail fraud scheme described above.

Kennedy argues that these deposits cannot violate § 1956 because § 1956 only covers transactions that occur after a defendant has taken complete control of the funds from the predicate crime. Relying on United States v. Johnson, 971 F.2d 562 (10th Cir.1992), Kennedy suggests that to state a § 1956 money laundering violation, the indictment would have had to allege another transaction, subsequent to his taking possession of the funds by depositing them into a WMC account. We disagree. All that is required to violate § 1956 is a transaction meeting the statutory criteria that takes place after the underlying crime has been completed. Thus, the central inquiry in a money laundering charge is determining when the predicate crime became a "completed" offense—and it is that inquiry that distinguishes this case from *Johnson*.

In *Johnson*, the defendant was charged with money laundering under a companion statute, 18 U.S.C. § 1957. Section 1957 prohibits "knowingly engag[ing] or attempt[ing] to engage in a monetary transaction in criminally derived property," which is defined as "any property constituting, or derived from, proceeds obtained from a criminal offense." 18 U.S.C. § 1957(a), (f)(2). Each count against the defendant in *Johnson* was based on a wire transfer of funds from an investor's account directly into the defendant's account. Thus, the predicate crimes were the use of the wires in violation of 18 U.S.C. § 1343. Significantly, however, the only wirings that were alleged to support the predicate wire fraud crimes in *Johnson* were the very transfers of funds identified in the money laundering transactions. Based on that fact, we held that the wirings could not also be used to support convictions for § 1957 money laundering crimes.

Kennedy's case is thus distinguishable in one important and dispositive respect.[14] As noted, the only use of the wires alleged in *Johnson* to prove the predicate wire fraud crimes were the very wire transfers that allegedly involved "criminally derived property" under the money laundering statute. In Kennedy's case, in contrast, the government alleged

---

14. There are also some differences in the language of § 1956 and § 1957, but we need not address those differences here, as we distinguish *Johnson* on other grounds.

many prior mailings to prove the predicate mail fraud crimes, which occurred before the monetary transactions that formed the basis of his money laundering counts. Thus, unlike in *Johnson*, the illegal mailings in this case involved discrete, earlier mailings by Kennedy, rather than the receipt of funds by Kennedy from his victims. It was the subsequent and distinct transfers of funds that were alleged as the separate transactions involving "proceeds of specified unlawful activity" which constituted the alleged money laundering under § 1956.[15]

This factual difference is important because Congress clearly intended the money laundering statutes to punish new conduct that occurs after the completion of certain criminal activity, rather than simply to create an additional punishment for that criminal activity. The "completion" of both wire and mail fraud occurs when any wiring or mailing is used in execution of a scheme; there is no requirement that the scheme actually defraud a victim into investing money for the crime to be complete. Thus, because the money deposits in Kennedy's case occurred after other mailings had already completed the predicate mail fraud crime, those transfers properly could be construed as new transactions involving the proceeds of mail fraud. In contrast, because the specific wire fraud violations alleged in *Johnson* were not complete until the wires were used to transfer the funds, those transfers could not be construed as new transactions to support a money laundering offense. Accordingly, we reject Kennedy's contention that his money laundering convictions must be set aside for failure to allege the "proceeds" element of those crimes.

UNITED STATES v. ALLEN

United States Court of Appeals, Fifth Circuit, 1996.
76 F.3d 1348.

HIGGINBOTHAM, CIRCUIT JUDGE.

This case involves an elaborate series of interlocking schemes to defraud various banks, particularly First City National Bank of Houston, of substantial sums of money. A grand jury returned a 34–count indictment against Frank Cihak, Lloyd Swift, and Willia Allen. After an eight week trial, the district court dismissed one of the counts and submitted the remaining 33 to the jury. The jury found the defendants guilty on all counts.

The activities of defendant Frank Cihak lie at the center of this case. In the early 1980s, Cihak was a Chicago banker. Through holding companies, he controlled or owned a substantial interest in several Illinois banks, including Worth Bank & Trust, Mount Greenwood Bank, and First National Bank of Danville. Cihak held high-level management or board positions at many of these banks and maintained offices at most

---

15. In fact, the parties stipulated to the fact that "the financial transactions alleged in the indictment occurred following mailings from Western Monetary Consultants, Inc. to persons who did not receive their precious metals orders."

of them. Late in the 1980s, Cihak became involved in the recapitalization of the failed First City National Bank of Houston, the largest of a number of banks owned by a holding company called First City Bancorporation. The principal figure in the First City recapitalization was Robert Abboud. Cihak organized the nuts and bolts of the recapitalization and assumed the number two position at First City Bancorporation and Bank upon its completion.

Joseph Fahy was a New York City securities dealer. Throughout the 1980s, he operated several businesses, including STS Holding Corp. and Fahy & Co., which attempted to generate funds through municipal securities and automobile loan transactions. Although Fahy testified for the United States at trial under a subpoena, a grant of immunity did not improve his poor memory of the events involved.

David Lucterhand was a Chicago businessman who began as a dealer on the Chicago Board of Options Exchange. In the 1980s, Lucterhand operated businesses called the Lucterhand Group, Inc. and L.L. Chandos Co. Lucterhand initially attempted several business deals with Fahy. In desperate financial straits as a result of these deals, he turned to Cihak for help in finding a way to generate funds. Cihak eventually arranged for First City Bank to hire Lucterhand as a consultant. Lucterhand testified on behalf of the United States at trial as part of a plea bargain.

Defendant Lloyd Swift was a horse breeder with a farm in Missouri. He ran a horse trading operation and other businesses including Swift Thoroughbred, Swift Farms, and Swift Implement Co. Swift also possessed considerable knowledge of automobile sale and loan transactions. In the late 1970s and early 1980s, the market for thoroughbreds crashed, and Swift's financial situation deteriorated. Cihak eventually arranged for First City to hire Swift as a consultant on automobile matters.

Defendant Willia Allen was an accountant who owned and operated her own accounting firm, Allen & Associates. Allen was not a CPA. Together with another individual, Allen bought a company called Shepherd Fleets, which eventually held Dollar Rent–A–Car franchises in at least three cities. Allen also owned a construction firm called Combined General Contractors. Allen possessed some knowledge of bank obligations under the Community Reinvestment Act, a federal statute designed to encourage banks to lend funds to lower income businesses and individuals in the banks' communities. Cihak arranged for First City to hire Allen as a consultant on CRA matters.

The Cochonours were a wealthy Chicago family. Two Cochonour brothers, Don and Robert, had extensive dealings with Swift's horse businesses. At one time, the two brothers also owned a percentage in Tri–Star Cablevision, Inc.; Cihak claimed an interest in this company as well.

According to the government, Cihak used two principal methods to divert funds from First City bank to his own use. In the first method, Cihak used his position at First City to have that entity hire Lucterhand,

Swift, and Allen as consultants. Cihak had these consultants bill First City for substantial sums of money in consulting fees. Cihak approved the invoices, and First City paid them. In order to avoid the watchful eyes of First City auditors, the consultants normally transferred the proceeds of these fees from accounts in their names at First City to accounts in their names at one of Cihak's Chicago banks. Once the funds were out of Houston, the consultants transferred a portion of their fees to Cihak. These kickbacks occurred either when a consultant wrote a check to Cihak or authorized an internal transfer, or when Cihak used his position at the Chicago banks to transfer the funds to himself on his own.

In the second method of defrauding the First City entities, Cihak used his position to arrange for First City Bank to fund various loans to Lucterhand, Swift, and Shepherd Fleets. Cihak then either diverted the funds generated to his own use or received bribes from the borrowers. In Lucterhand's case, Cihak used the funds generated from the consulting fee kickbacks to pay back these loans.

* * *

[A]ll three defendants * * * [contend] that their convictions for money laundering to conceal the proceeds of unlawful activity may not stand because the funds at issue were not yet proceeds at the time they were laundered. This attack concerns counts 28–33 of the indictment. It is without merit.

Counts 28–31 all involved the kickback of the consultant fees from Lucterhand, Swift, and Allen. In each of the transactions corresponding to these counts, the consultant invoiced First City Bank, Cihak approved the invoice, the Bank issued a check, and the consultant deposited the check into an account at First City Bank in the name of either the consultant or one of the consultant's businesses. The consultant then transferred the money from the First City Bank account into an account at Worth. From the Worth accounts, the consultant kicked a portion of the funds back to Cihak. The defendants argue that the illegality of the transaction stemmed from their failure to disclose to First City that a portion of fees charged in the invoice was to benefit Cihak. Therefore, the defendants argue, the money could not constitute proceeds of a misapplication or fraud until the moment Cihak received the benefit of the funds. Since the transactions specified in the indictment took place before this moment, they could not constitute laundering of the proceeds of illegal activity.

Counts 32 and 33 concerned the First City Bank loan of $1,800,000 to Lucterhand, which Cihak used for his own purposes. After First City Bank funded a portion of this loan, Cihak had Lucterhand transfer $300,000 of the money from Lucterhand's account at First City Bank to the Worth Lucterhand trust account. Cihak used his position at Worth to transfer this $300,000 through his personal account at Citibank to Citibank in repayment of his $1,600,000 loan. In June, 1990, a payment on the First City Bank loan came due. Lucterhand notified Cihak, then invoiced the bank for a consulting fee. After Cihak had approved the invoice, Lucterhand deposited the resulting First City Bank check into his account at the bank. Lucterhand ended up transferring $112,515.84 of this fee to the bank as a payment on the loan. Count 32 alleged that the transfer of the $300,000 from Lucterhand's First City Bank account to the Worth Lucterhand trust account constituted money laundering. Count 33 recited an identical charge in the transfer of the $112,515.84 from Lucterhand's account at First City Bank to the bank in repayment of the loan.

Defendants' contentions fail because the funds at issue in each of the transactions became proceeds at the moment the money left the control of First City Bank and was deposited into an account of a consultant or borrower. Suppose, for example, a consultant and a bank officer agree to an invoice and kickback scheme, but the consultant decides to cheat by keeping all the money and making no kickback. The two would have perpetrated a fraud against the bank. The bank officer in this example participated in the scheme by approving the invoice with intent to defraud. The dishonor among thieves is not relevant, certainly not to the bank.[4]

As this hypothetical illustrates, the fraudulent scheme produces proceeds at the latest when the scheme succeeds in disgorging the funds from the victim and placing them into the control of the perpetrators. Had Swift, Lucterhand, and Allen refused to kick back money to Cihak, they nonetheless would have been guilty. Accordingly, the money produced from the defendants' fraud became proceeds when it left the control of First City Bank and came into the possession of one of the consultants. The jury could infer, from the circuitous nature of the subsequent transactions as well as the other evidence in the case, that the flow of funds recited in the indictment was designed to conceal the fact that these funds were proceeds of fraud from First City Bank internal auditors and from federal regulators.

For similar reasons, the defendants' implication that First City Bank did not overpay the consultants, who performed valuable services for the bank and First City Bancorporation, is beside the point. If, as the jury found, the defendants perpetrated a kickback scheme, then by definition the consultants were willing to perform these tasks for less money than they actually charged. The bank, not Cihak, should have been the beneficiary of the consultants' willingness to do the job for less.

Nothing in our resolution of this case conflicts with United States v. Johnson, 971 F.2d 562, 567–70 (10th Cir.1992). In *Johnson*, the defendant convinced several investors to dedicate millions of dollars to a nonexistent currency exchange business. Some of the investors wired their

---

4. The only problem created by a refusal to kick back is evidentiary, not legal. The government might have more difficulty convincing a jury that a bank officer approved the invoice with intent to defraud when the bank officer never received the benefit of the alleged scheme. If the government were able to solve this evidentiary problem, for instance, by taping conversations between the consultant and the bank officer, no legal principle would bar a conviction of fraud or misapplication.

funds from their own bank accounts to that of the defendant. The indictment charged a violation of 18 U.S.C. § 1957, which renders unlawful the knowing execution of a transaction involving more than $10,000 of the proceeds of illegal activity, alleging that the deposit of the funds from the investors into the defendant's account as a result of the wire transfer violated the statute. The Tenth Circuit reversed the defendant's convictions under section 1957, holding that the wire transfers did not involve proceeds of criminal activity because the money did not become proceeds until the wire transfers, which did constitute wire fraud, were completed.

The difference between *Johnson* and this case is in the timing of the wire transfers. The *Johnson* court held, in essence, that the money at issue did not become proceeds until it left the account of the victims and reached the account of the defendant. The wire transfers were the means by which the funds made this journey and thus occurred too early to form the basis of a money laundering conviction. In this case, the consultant fees and loans left the control of First City Bank and reached the accounts of the conspirators before the wire transfers occurred. The charged transactions distributed the proceeds among the various defendants and helped hide the fraud from First City auditors and federal regulators.

* * *

In *Johnson*, *supra*, the Tenth Circuit held that it is not necessary, in a § 1957 case, for the government to trace each and every dollar of the monetary transaction to specified unlawful activity. The Ninth Circuit disagrees as shown in the next case, United States v. Rutgard, 116 F.3d 1270 (9th Cir.1997). With whom do you agree, the Ninth Circuit or the Tenth Circuit?

UNITED STATES v. RUTGARD

United States Court of Appeals, Ninth Circuit, 1997.
116 F.3d 1270.

NOONAN, CIRCUIT JUDGE.

* * *

[Jeffrey Jay Rutgard, an opthalmologic surgeon, was convicted on numerous counts of mail fraud, in violation of 18 U.S.C. § 1341; submitting false claims to Medicare, in violation of 18 U.S.C. § 287; and money laundering, in violation of 18 U.S.C. § 1957. Judgment of forfeiture in the amount of $7.5 million, pursuant to 18 U.S.C. § 982, was ordered, as was restitution in the amount of $16 million pursuant to the Victim Witness Protection Act, 18 U.S.C. § 3663(a)(2). The convictions, forfeiture and order of restitution arose from Rutgard's medical practice between 1988 and April, 1992 in LaJolla, California.

Rutgard worked 6 1/2 days per week, 16 hours per day, taking trips for medical meetings but no vacations. Rutgard staffed two offices as well as an ambulatory surgery center. Rutgard made a lot of money: between 1988 and May, 1992, Medicare (which was 80% of his practice) paid him over $15.5 million.

During the five month trial, the government sought to prove that Rutgard falsely represented to Medicare that cataract and eye lid surgeries he performed on Medicare patients were necessary; misrepresented to Medicare the procedures he performed on Medicare patients; and made false statements about patient diagnoses.

On March 15, 1995, the jury found Rutgard guilty on 132 counts. The jury also found that transactions in the amounts of $5,629,220.74 and $1,935,220.48 were monies derived from Rutgard's Medicare fraud. Because these amounts were transferred by wire, in violation of 18 U.S.C. § 1957, they were forfeitable under 18 U.S.C. § 982(a)(1). On appeal, the Ninth Circuit affirmed Rutgard's convictions on 109 counts and reversed his convictions on 23 counts. The Ninth Circuit also reversed the judgment of forfeiture. Lastly, the court remanded for a recalculation of restitution. Among the counts reversed were Rutgard's convictions under 18 U.S.C. § 1957 for money laundering.-ed.]

Was Rutgard's Entire Medical Practice a Fraud? * * * [T]he government undertook to prove that Rutgard's entire practice was a fraud on the insurers * * * to prove the § 1957 monetary transaction counts * * *. As the prosecution told the jury, "The scheme to defraud was to treat every eye covered by insurance as a profit center and to do whatever was necessary to milk that eye for as much money as [Rutgard] could possibly get. The scheme was conducted with a total disregard for medical necessity." * * *

At the core of the government's proof of its contention was the testimony of fourteen ex-employees of Rutgard, insiders who testified for the government. Nurse Sigrid Thordin, who worked for Rutgard from October, 1991 to April, 1992, testified that 90 to 95 percent of the photos taken for ptosis and ectropion surgery did not accurately represent the true condition of the patient's eyelid. Berta Todor, a technician in Rutgard's employ from 1987 to 1989, testified that suture removals were routinely misbilled as the removal of a foreign body from the eye, that cortisone injections were misbilled as if rendered to the back of the eyeball, and that the BAT [Brightness Acuity Test] was routinely set on "high" in order to justify surgery. Billing clerk Jean Havel testified about Rutgard's regular EKG misbillings to Medicare and that the W–5 modifier [a code which justifies higher reimbursement] was "vastly overused". Nancy Biagioni, who worked as a technician for Rutgard from 1988 until April, 1992, testified that she was told to fill out patient complaint forms by circling certain standard complaints without seeing the patient. She also testified that, as a result of discussing with Rutgard the problem of what to do with patients who needed pre-surgery authorization from an insurer for ptosis surgery but had automatic visual field scores "too good" to get the authorization, she used fake field tests. Jesse Del Valle, Rutgard's office administrator in 1988, did a review with Rutgard of all patient charts in anticipation of a possible Medicare audit. Del Valle testified: "Any time there was no reason to have done surgery, or any time I saw some surgeries that were not documented, I would put a note on the section that needed to be amended." Del Valle would then hand the chart to Rutgard, and Rutgard would make the needed entry with his own hands, making up the information that was missing. George Butera, Rutgard's office administrator from 1988 to 1991, was asked by the prosecutor: "While you were administrator, could you be sure of the accuracy of the information about a patient's condition and treatment in any chart at Jeff Rutgard's practice?" Butera answered: "I would say No. I came to believe No.". Butera testified in particular that visual fields which at Rutgard's direction he inserted in patients' charts which CMRI[cc] was to review were in fact "fictitious," i.e. not based on actual observation but drawn to justify ptosis surgery that had already occurred. He also testified that Rutgard paid $10,000 to a former employee who threatened to report Rutgard to Medicare.

These questionable practices took place in an ophthalmologic practice where around 10,000 patient visits occurred each year, where patients were often herded through examinations, where frequently Rutgard himself spent no more than two minutes examining a patient, and where profit making was the focus of the physician.

* * *

The government did not, however, provide sufficient evidence that Rutgard's entire medical practice was an insurance fraud. * * * [T]he ex-employee witnesses presented themselves at trial as doing honest work, only occasionally doing recording or billing against their honest judgment because of Rutgard's overriding directions. The inescapable inference is that a fair amount of recording and billing in the Rutgard practice was performed without fraud.

* * *

* * * [Also] there are portions of Rutgard's practice where no fraud was suggested. He had some small number of cash patients, who were not insured. He did some work with glaucoma—how much is not clear, but reference is made at trial to diagnosis of glaucoma and to treatment of glaucoma by laser surgery. It would be surprising in any ophthalmology practice where a high percentage of patients are over 65 that glaucoma was not a complaint of some patients. * * * [But] no fraud was charged as to glaucoma patients. Some of his patients also must have had retina problems, which nationally accounted for 14% of Medicare eye visits in 1991. But fraud as to the retina was not charged. It was the

---

cc. CMRI (California Medical Review of Insurance) was hired by Medicare to review the medical necessity and quality of services provided by medicare providers. *Rutgard*, 108 F.3d at 1058.

burden undertaken by the government, not the defense, to show that 100 percent of Rutgard's medical practice was fraudulent.

* * *

In the light of this analysis we * * * [turn to the § 1957 charges].

* * * In May, 1992 after the government's search of Rutgard's office, his wife Linda, at his direction, made two wire transfers to the National Westminster Bank on the Isle of Man, one of $5,629,220.74 on May 5 and one of $1,935,220.48 on May 6. The transfers were made from the Rutgard Family Trust, whose accounts were at the Imperial Trust Company in San Diego.

The government's accounting expert noted $15.8 million paid by Medicare to Rutgard entities between the beginning of 1988 and April, 1992. He testified that Rutgard deposited $3,754,056 derived from these entities into the family trust account during this period and deposited $1.9 million in municipal bonds so that a total of $5,654,056 entered this account from October 29, 1990, when Rutgard opened the account with a personal check for $560,000, to May, 1992. He testified that the balance of the account came from municipal bonds delivered to the trust account at unspecified times. On appeal the government argues that the jury could take into account the first year, 1987, when insurance fraud began, and come to the conclusion that the entire amount transferred by wire transfers on May 5 and 6 was the proceeds of insurance fraud.

To prove this contention the government advanced the theory that all of Rutgard's practice was a fraud. If the government had succeeded in this proof, it would have properly convicted him of the monetary transaction counts. But we have just determined that the government's proof was deficient. The government, as we have also held, established Rutgard's guilt of particular counts of fraud. The proceeds of that fraud come to over $46,000. Can the convictions under § 1957 be sustained on the theory that at least $20,000 of fruits of fraud were incorporated in the wire transfers of May 6 and 7? To answer that question requires a consideration of the terms and purpose of § 1957 and a close look at the companion statute, § 1956.

These statutes govern monetary transactions in criminally derived property. The standard money laundering statute is 18 U.S.C. § 1956. The other statute, the one under which Rutgard was convicted, is 18 U.S.C. § 1957. In construing § 1956, we referred to § 1957 as "a companion money laundering statute," United States v. Garcia, 37 F.3d 1359, 1365 (9th Cir.1994), without having occasion to mark the differences between the two. We now have occasion to mark those differences.

Section 1956, alone at issue in *Garcia*, bears the title "Laundering of monetary instruments." It punishes by imprisonment of up to 20 years and a fine a defendant who:

knowing that *the property involved* in a financial transaction represents the proceeds of some form of unlawful activity, conducts or attempts to conduct such a financial transaction which in fact involves the proceeds of specified unlawful activity—

> (A)(i) with the intent to promote the carrying on of specified unlawful activity; or

> (ii) with intent to engage in conduct constituting a violation of section 7201 or 7206 of the Internal Revenue Code of 1986; or

> (B) knowing that the transaction is designed in whole or in part—

> (i) to conceal or disguise the nature, the location, the source, the ownership, or the control of the proceeds of specified unlawful activity; or

> (ii) to avoid a transaction reporting requirement under State or Federal law.

18 U.S.C. § 1956(a)(1). For present purposes, five elements of § 1956 differentiate it from § 1957, the statute at issue here—its title, its requirement of intent, its broad reference to "the property involved," its satisfaction by a transaction that "in part" accomplishes the design, and its requirement that the intent be to commit another crime or to hide the fruits of a crime already committed.

Section 1957 has a different heading: "Engaging in monetary transactions in property derived from specified unlawful activity." It punishes by up to ten years' imprisonment and a fine anyone who:

> knowingly engages or attempts to engage in a monetary transaction in criminally derived property that is of a value greater than $10,000 and is derived from specified unlawful activity.

18 U.S.C. § 1957(a). The description of the crime does not speak to the attempt to cleanse dirty money by putting it in a clean form and so disguising it. This statute applies to the most open, above-board transaction. See 18 U.S.C. § 1957(f)(1) (broadly defining "monetary transaction"). The intent to commit a crime or the design of concealing criminal fruits is eliminated. These differences make violation of § 1957 easier to prove. But also eliminated are references to "the property involved" and the satisfaction of the statute by a design that "in part" accomplishes the intended result. These differences indicate that proof of violation of § 1957 may be more difficult.

Section 1957 could apply to any transaction by a criminal with his bank. * * *

Section 1957 was enacted as a tool in the war against drugs. It is a powerful tool because it makes any dealing with a bank potentially a trap for the drug dealer or any other defendant who has a hoard of criminal cash derived from the specified crimes. If he makes a "deposit, withdrawal, transfer or exchange" with this cash, he commits the crime; he's forced to commit another felony if he wants to use a bank. This draconian law, so powerful by its elimination of criminal intent, freezes the proceeds of specific crimes out of the banking system. As long as the underlying crime has been completed and the defendant "possesses" the funds at the time of deposit, the proceeds cannot enter the banking system without a new crime being committed. A type of regulatory crime has been created where criminal intent is not an element. See Morissette v. United States, 342 U.S. 246, 252–56 (1952). Such a powerful instrument of criminal justice should not be expanded by judicial invention or ingenuity. We "should not enlarge the reach of enacted crimes by constituting them from anything less than the incriminating components contemplated by the words used in the statute." Id. at 263.

For these reasons we do not find helpful in interpreting § 1957 the cases applying § 1956, which speaks of design "in whole or in part" and of "a financial transaction involving property." Other circuits, however, have used the § 1956 precedents to eliminate any tracing of funds in a § 1957 case. See United States v. Moore, 27 F.3d 969, 976–77 (4th Cir.1994); United States v. Johnson, 971 F.2d 562 (10th Cir.1992). They have reasoned that otherwise § 1957 could be defeated by a criminal mingling innocently-obtained funds with his ill-gotten moneys.

This reasoning rests on the fungibility of money in a bank. That fungibility, destroying the specific identity of any particular funds, makes the commingling of innocent funds with criminal funds an obvious way to hide the criminal funds. If § 1956 required tracing of specific funds, it could be wholly frustrated by commingling. For that reason, the statute not only proscribes any transaction whose purpose is to hide criminal funds but reaches any funds "involved" in the transaction. Neither the same reasoning nor the same language is present in § 1957, the statute here applied.

The monetary transaction statute cannot be made wholly ineffective by commingling. To prevail, the government need show only a single $10,000 deposit of criminally-derived proceeds. Any innocent money already in the account, or later deposited, cannot wipe out the crime committed by the deposit of criminally-derived proceeds. Commingling with innocent funds can defeat application of the statute to a withdrawal of less than the total funds in the account, but ordinarily that fact presents no problem to the government which, if it has proof of a deposit of $10,000 of criminally-derived funds, can succeed by charging the deposit as the crime; or the government may prevail by showing that all the funds in the account are the proceeds of crime. Commingling will frustrate the statute if criminal deposits have been kept under $10,000. But that is the way the statute is written, to catch only large transfers. Moreover, if the criminal intent was to hide criminal proceeds, as would presumably be the case any time criminally derived cash was deposited with innocently derived funds to hide its identity, § 1956 can kick in and the depositor of amounts under $10,000 will be guilty of a § 1956 crime.

The government did not take its possible course of charging Rutgard with deposits of over $10,000 of fraudulent proceeds. The government had the means of doing so because its accounting expert identified the large deposits Rutgard made. But as Rutgard was neither charged nor convicted of deposits in violation of § 1957, we cannot uphold his convictions on that basis.

Rutgard's convictions may be upheld if he transferred out of the account all the funds that were in it or if there was a rule or presumption that, once criminally-derived funds were deposited, any transfer from the account would be presumed to involve them for the purpose of applying § 1956. Rutgard did not transfer all the funds in the family trust account, however. The government showed that the account held $8.5 million on April 2, 1992 and $13,901 on July 2, 1992, the dates of the quarterly bank statements. But so far as evidence at trial goes, more than $46,000 remained in the account after the May 5 and 6 transfers. These transfers therefore did not necessarily transfer the $46,000 of fraudulent proceeds.

The alternative way of sustaining the convictions depends on a presumption, which the Fourth Circuit created in *Moore*, 27 F.3d at 976–77, but which we decline to create. The statute does not create a presumption that any transfer of cash in an account tainted by the presence of a small amount of fraudulent proceeds must be a transfer of these proceeds. Unlike § 1956, § 1957 does not cover any funds "involved." To create such a presumption in order to sustain a conviction under § 1957 would be to multiply many times the power of that draconian law. It would be an essay in judicial lawmaking, not an application of the statute. As the government did not prove that any fraudulently-derived proceeds left the account on May 5 or May 6, 1992, the monetary transfer counts, Counts 216 and 217, were not proved beyond a reasonable doubt.

* * *

Notes

1. As summarized in *Johnson* and *Rutgard* there are four possible approaches when a suspect allegedly conducts a monetary transaction in "criminally derived property" from a commingled account. It may help in discussing these choices to use the following hypothetical: Allan Adams, a physician, bills Medicare for services not rendered, and falsely represents that the services were rendered. Adams receives $5 million because of these false claims and deposits this $5 million, in increments of less than $10,000, into his business account. During this same time period Adams receives $5 million from other insurers on legitimate claims. Adams makes 2 withdrawals: a $2 million withdrawal and a $4 million withdrawal. Are these withdrawals monetary transactions which violate § 1957?

a. The *Johnson* approach: The government need not show that "the funds withdrawn from the defendant's account could not possibly have come from any source other than the unlawful activity." The government must present sufficient evidence "for the jury to find that the funds withdrawn were derived from specified unlawful activity." If you were the prosecutor, would you charge Adams with violations of 18 U.S.C. § 1957 for one deposit? both deposits? If you were a juror, would you vote to convict? on either deposit?

b. The *Rutgard* approach. The government must show that each withdrawal consisted of "criminally deprived property." As prosecutor, is there any way to charge Adams if you are in the Ninth Circuit? For either withdrawal?

c. The *Moore* approach (referred to by the Ninth Circuit in *Rutgard*). The Fourth Circuit upheld Jerry A. Moore's convictions for bank fraud (in violation of 18 U.S.C. § 1344), conspiracy (in violation of 18 U.S.C. § 371), filing false tax returns (in violation of 18 U.S.C. § 26 U.S.C. § 7206(1)), and making false statements (in violation of 18 U.S.C. § 1957).[dd] All charges arose from several schemes by Moore to obtain real estate loans from a bank by supplying the bank with false financial information. Moore argued that the evidence was insufficient to support his money laundering conviction because the government had been unable to exclude the possibility that the monetary transactions at issue did not entirely consist of legitimately obtained funds. The Fourth Circuit dismissed Moore's argument with the following presumption:

> "Money is fungible, and when funds obtained from unlawful activity have been combined with funds from lawful activity into a single asset, the illicitly-acquired funds and the legitimately-acquired funds * * * cannot be distinguished from each other * * *. As a consequence, it may be presumed in such circumstances, as the language of section 1957 permits, that the transacted funds, at least up to the full amount originally derived from crime, were the proceeds of the criminal activity or derived from that activity."[ee]

What do you think about the Fourth Circuit's approach? Is the presumption it articulates permitted "by the language of section 1957," as the Court states? How, exactly, is the Fourth Circuit approach different from the Tenth Circuit's approach? As a prosecutor in the Fourth Circuit, would you seek a grand jury indictment charging Adams with money laundering as to either deposit?

d. The undercover approach. Assume there is an undercover agent who has ingratiated himself to Adams and become his confidant on banking matters. Is there a problem with the agent suggesting to Adams that Adams should save a few checks from Medicare and deposit them all at the end of the week, rather than daily? (Recall that § 1957 requires a $10,000 minimum per transaction.)

Among the *Johnson*, *Rutgard* and *Moore* approaches, which do you think is more consistent with § 1957?

2. Recall the Ninth Circuit's statement in *Rutgard* about § 1957: "This draconian law, so powerful by its elimination of criminal intent * * *." Take a look at the language of § 1957. Does § 1957 eliminate the criminal intent requirement? What could the Ninth Circuit mean?

────────

The next two cases, United States v. Aramony, 88 F.3d 1369 (4th Cir.1996) and United States v. Ripinsky, 109 F.3d 1436 (9th Cir.1997),

dd. United States v. Moore, 27 F.3d 969   **ee.** *Id.* at 977.
(4th Cir.1994).

address the interstate commerce element in § 1957. They also demonstrate a practical point about effective appellate advocacy.

UNITED STATES v. ARAMONY

United States Court of Appeals, Fourth Circuit, 1996.
88 F.3d 1369.

HAMILTON, CIRCUIT JUDGE.

After a jury trial, the appellants, William Aramony, Thomas Merlo, and Stephen Paulachak, were convicted of numerous violations of federal laws [including violations of 18 U.S.C. § 1957] for participating in a scheme to defraud the United Way of America (UWA).[ff] * * * The district court sentenced Aramony to eighty-four months' imprisonment, Merlo to fifty-five months' imprisonment, and Paulachak to thirty months' imprisonment. Additionally, pursuant to 18 U.S.C. §§ 853 & 982, the district court ordered Aramony and Merlo to forfeit $552,188.97 because of their convictions under 18 U.S.C. § 1957.

I

UWA is a nonprofit organization that acts as a service organization for local United Way organizations located throughout the United States. Aramony became the chief executive officer of UWA in 1970, and he held that position until he was fired in March 1992. Merlo, a certified public accountant and close friend of Aramony, began performing accounting services for UWA on a consulting basis in the 1970s. In July 1989, Merlo became UWA's interim chief financial officer, and approximately six months later, he took the job on a permanent basis. Paulachak began working for UWA in the 1970s. In 1988, he left UWA to become the president of Partnership Umbrella, Inc. (PUI).[9]

ff. More specifically, Aramony was convicted of conspiracy to defraud the United States by impeding the lawful functions of the IRS, see 18 U.S.C. § 371; six counts of mail fraud, see 18 U.S.C. § 1341; two counts of wire fraud, see 18 U.S.C. § 1343; nine counts of engaging in the interstate transportation of fraudulently acquired property, see 18 U.S.C. § 2314; two counts of engaging in monetary transactions in the proceeds of specified unlawful activity, see 18 U.S.C. § 1957; three counts of filing false tax returns, see I.R.C. § 7206(1); and two counts of aiding the filing of false tax returns, see I.R.C. § 7206(2). Merlo was convicted of conspiracy to defraud the United States by impeding the lawful functions of the IRS, one count of mail fraud, one count of wire fraud, four counts of interstate transportation of fraudulently acquired property, three counts of engaging in monetary transactions in property derived from specified unlawful activity, three counts of filing false tax returns, and four counts of aiding in the filing of false tax

returns. Paulachak was convicted of conspiracy to defraud the United States by impeding the lawful functions of the IRS, one count of wire fraud, and six counts of filing false tax returns. Additionally, the jury acquitted Aramony on two counts of engaging in monetary transactions in the proceeds of specified unlawful activity, acquitted Merlo on one count of aiding in the filing of a false tax return, and acquitted Paulachak on one count of interstate transportation of fraudulently acquired property and three counts of aiding the filing of false tax returns. 88 F.3d at 1373.

9. The UWA Board of Directors established PUI as a for-profit organization in December 1986 to ensure UWA's continued 501(c)(3) status (charitable status). PUI was designed to act as a support organization for charities and "to aid and assist not-for-profit organizations to secure the economic and related benefits of volume purchasing through development and management of national purchasing programs on

From the mid–1980s to the early 1990s, the appellants improperly used UWA money for personal gain. The nature of the scheme was primarily to use UWA money to assist Aramony in furthering his relationships with various women. However, UWA money was also used to pay a variety of Aramony's other personal expenses. For example, when Aramony visited New York, he often used the chauffeuring service of Charles Harrison. From 1988 to 1990, Aramony incurred over $100,000 in bills due to his use of Harrison's service. * * *

Although the government's arsenal of information of Aramony's wrongdoing was extensive, the government's case at trial basically focused on Aramony's use of UWA funds to further his relationships with various women, especially Lori Villasor and Anita Terranova. From December 1986 to July 1990, Aramony had a personal relationship with Lori Villasor. From late 1988 to mid–1990, Aramony traveled to Gainesville, Florida, Villasor's hometown, at least once a month to visit Villasor, and he had UWA pay for these trips. On some of his trips to Gainesville, Aramony used UWA money to pay for rental cars. The billing of Aramony's flights to Gainesville to UWA and the billing of his rental cars in Gainesville to UWA formed the basis of two of Aramony's convictions for mail fraud.

Aramony also used UWA money to help pay for taking Villasor with him on UWA business trips and vacations. In December 1988, Aramony took Villasor to London and Paris for her birthday. In December 1989, he took her on a two-week trip to London and Cairo. And in April 1990, Aramony used UWA money to fly Villasor to London, England to be with him while he and Paulachak attended a board meeting of Charities Fund Transfer (CFT), like PUI a "spin-off" corporation established with the approval of the UWA Board of Directors. Merlo gave Laura Shifflet, one of Aramony's assistants, his UWA corporate credit card number so that she could use it to charge Villasor's airline tickets. In addition, Paulachak arranged for $50,000 of CFT's money to be transferred to his Diner's Club card, and part of this money ($4,529.94) was used to pay the chauffeuring bill that Villasor incurred while in London. These events formed the basis for Aramony's convictions of three counts of mail fraud, two counts of wire fraud, and one count of engaging in the interstate transportation of fraudulently acquired property. The $50,000 wire transfer of CFT's money to Paulachak's Diner's Club card formed the basis for his conviction of one count of wire fraud.

The government also introduced evidence that Aramony used Merlo to provide Villasor with money. From 1988 to 1991, Merlo received over $300,000 in consulting fees from PUI despite doing no work for the money. Merlo, in turn, paid Villasor a total of $89,000 over this period. One manner of getting Villasor this money was to have Merlo pay her a monthly salary despite Villasor doing, at the most, only a day or two of

behalf of such organizations." (Joint Appendix (J.A.) 643). Additionally, PUI was designed to use its income "for purposes consistent with those of United Way['s] domestic and international activities," and PUI's property was "irrevocably dedicated to charitable purposes.... " Id. at 670.

work. One transaction involving a $25,000 bonus from UWA to Merlo, $5,000 of which was a reimbursement to Merlo for a previous wire transfer to Villasor, formed the basis of one of Aramony's and Merlo's convictions for engaging in the interstate transportation of fraudulently acquired property.

Terranova lived in Florida and had a long history with Aramony. As with Villasor, Aramony often traveled to Florida at UWA expense to visit her. Importantly, Aramony bought a condominium in Florida to meet Terranova. The money for this apartment came from a donation that Mutual of America (MOA)—an insurance company that did business with UWA—made to UWA. In 1987, MOA decided to donate the interest from a $1 million fund to the William Aramony Initiatives in Voluntarism Fund (WAIF), a restricted fund at UWA, intending that the money be used "to support the expansion of the nation's voluntary sector." On December 10, 1987, the UWA Board passed a resolution that gave Aramony wide discretion to use the money that MOA contributed to WAIF. Under this authority, Aramony caused the MOA money to be transferred from WAIF to Voluntary Initiatives America (VIA), a Florida 501(c)(3) corporation.

VIA was formed in April 1990, with Aramony as its chairman, his son as its president, and Merlo as its secretary/treasurer. On the same day that VIA was formed, Merlo caused a UWA check drawn upon the MOA donation to be issued for $125,576.92 to VIA. Several days later Aramony used the money from this check to buy the condominium in Florida for him and Terranova. UWA funds, namely, $10,000, were used to furnish this condominium. In June 1991, the condominium was sold to PUI for approximately $125,000. The acquisition, furnishing, and sale of the Florida condominium formed the basis of Aramony's and Merlo's convictions for one count of mail fraud, two counts of engaging in the interstate transportation of fraudulently acquired property, and one count of engaging in monetary transactions in the proceeds of specified unlawful activity.

* * *

* * * Aramony and Merlo take issue with * * * the district court's instruction on the elements necessary for conviction under 18 U.S.C. § 1957. Aramony was convicted of two counts, and Merlo three, under § 1957.

Before the trial, Aramony and Merlo objected to the government's proposed instruction concerning whether the government had to prove an effect on interstate commerce. Specifically, they stated that "the government must show some effect on interstate commerce." In instructing the jury on the elements of § 1957, the district court stated:

> It is *not necessary for the Government to show* that the defendant actually intended or anticipated an effect on foreign or interstate commerce or *that commerce was actually affected*. All that is necessary is that the natural and probable consequences of the defen-

dant's action would be to affect interstate or for [sic] foreign commerce no matter how minimal.

Id. at 1585 (emphasis added).

Following the district court's jury charge, Aramony and Merlo objected to the district court's failure to instruct the jury that it had to make a finding that Aramony's and Merlo's activities had affected interstate commerce. The district court rejected this contention, concluding that the jury was properly instructed. * * * [W]e review the district court's instruction de novo because Aramony and Merlo contend that the district court incorrectly instructed the jury on the statutory elements necessary for conviction under 18 U.S.C. § 1957.

On appeal, Aramony and Merlo seek reversal of their § 1957 convictions on the ground that the district court violated their rights under the Fifth and Sixth Amendments to have a jury make every factual finding essential to their conviction by instructing the jury that it did not need to find that their actions had actually affected interstate commerce. According to Aramony and Merlo, the finding of at least a minimal effect on interstate commerce is an essential element that the government must prove beyond a reasonable doubt in order to convict a defendant of violating § 1957.

The government admits that an effect on interstate commerce is an element of a § 1957 offense. Nonetheless, the government argues that the jury did not have to make a finding that the acts of Aramony and Merlo had an effect on interstate commerce because that element is not an essential element of the crime.

Although our circuit precedent does not specifically answer whether an effect on interstate commerce is an essential element of a § 1957 violation, it does answer a nearly indistinguishable question in the affirmative. In United States v. Peay, 972 F.2d 71, 74 (4th Cir.1992) we concluded that proof of a *de minimis* effect on interstate commerce is essential to show a violation of 18 U.S.C. § 1956. 972 F.2d 71, 74 (4th Cir.1992). We cannot conceive of a rational reason to hold differently in the context of § 1957, which is "the sister provision of 18 U.S.C. § 1956." Accordingly, we hold a de minimis effect on interstate commerce is an essential element of a § 1957 violation.

* * *

In this case * * * [t]he jury was required to determine a question of historical fact: Did Aramony and Merlo engage in a monetary transaction that involved criminally derived property having a value greater than $10,000? The ultimate question, at least for present purposes, is whether such activities would affect interstate commerce. Because the answer to the ultimate question involves an application of the law to the facts, the jury was required to make a finding on the interstate commerce element.

The district court's instruction did not require the jury to make a finding on the interstate commerce element. Because this is an essential element of the crime, the district court's instruction stating otherwise constituted a failure to instruct the jury on an essential element necessary for a conviction under § 1957. Therefore, the district court's instruction was a constitutional error.

Despite the erroneous instruction, the government argues that we should affirm the convictions of Aramony and Merlo under § 1957, contending that the error in the district court's instruction was harmless. Under certain circumstances, the type of error involved here is harmless. *See* United States v. Johnson, 71 F.3d 139, 144 (4th Cir.1995). For example, if a jury is erroneously instructed that a mandatory presumption arose as to one element if it found certain predicate facts, but " 'no rational jury could find the predicate acts but fail to find the fact presumed,' " *id.*, then the error is harmless. Another example is when the reviewing court can be satisfied that the jury actually made an equivalent or identical finding pursuant to another instruction.

Because neither of these situations is present here, the error in the district court's instruction is not amenable to harmless-error analysis. Consideration of the instruction given to the jury reveals that the jury simply did not make an independent finding that the actions of Aramony and Merlo as charged in the § 1957 counts had a *de minimis* effect on interstate commerce. A finding that the natural and probable consequences of their actions would be to affect interstate or foreign commerce is not an equivalent or identical finding. Furthermore, the fact that the jury was presented with evidence that each conviction involved a substantial check that had actually traveled in interstate commerce is of no moment. A verdict of guilty must rest on an actual jury finding of guilty. Speculation about the probable finding that the jury would have made in view of the evidence before it had it been properly instructed does not satisfy this requirement.

In sum, we hold that the district court erred by instructing the jury that it did not have to find that the actions of Aramony and Merlo as charged in the § 1957 counts had a de minimis effect on interstate commerce. Furthermore, we hold the error is not subject to harmless error analysis. Accordingly, we vacate the convictions of Aramony and Merlo for engaging in the interstate transportation of fraudulently acquired property.[11]

UNITED STATES v. RIPINSKY

United States Court of Appeals, Ninth Circuit, 1997.
109 F.3d 1436.

WALLACE, CIRCUIT JUDGE.

* * *

The indictment under which Ripinsky and Kingston were convicted alleged that they defrauded Independence Bank of Encino, California, by

---

11. Because the forfeiture order is predicated on these convictions, we vacate the forfeiture order as to Aramony and Merlo as well.

taking undisclosed finder's fees in connection with the purchase of real estate properties by six real estate ventures in which they and Independence Bank were jointly involved. Ripinsky and Kingston received equity interests in return for managing the ventures. They were convicted of defrauding Independence Bank and other lenders by causing payment of up-front finder's fees for locating the properties Ripinsky and Kingston themselves controlled.[gg] * * *

* * *

We now address Ripinsky's interrelated contentions that the district court lacked subject matter jurisdiction over the section 1957 counts and deprived him of a jury determination of the jurisdictional element of the offense.

Section 1957(f) requires that the monetary transaction be "in or affecting interstate commerce." It also provides, however, that this requirement is met by any transaction that would be a "financial transaction" within the meaning of section 1956(c)(4)(B), which in turn defines "financial transaction" to include "a transaction involving the use of a financial institution which is engaged in, or the activities of which affect, interstate or foreign commerce in any way or degree."

We hold that section 1957's jurisdictional requirement is an essential element of the offense that must be determined by the jury beyond a reasonable doubt. The government concedes that a nexus with interstate commerce is a jurisdictional requirement that must be proved by sufficient evidence. The government argues, however, that we should follow the Tenth Circuit and conclude that while a nexus with interstate commerce is a jurisdictional "requirement" under section 1957, it is not an "element" of the offense. See United States v. Lowder, 5 F.3d 467, 472 (10th Cir.1993) (Lowder). We do not have that luxury because we are bound by our prior holdings that such requirements constitute essential elements that must be found by the factfinder.

Our conclusion that section 1957's jurisdictional requirement constitutes an essential element of the offense leads us to United States v. Lopez, 514 U.S. 549 (1995), where the Court reiterated that Congress may regulate three broad categories of activity under its Commerce Clause powers: (1) the use of the channels of interstate commerce; (2) the instrumentalities of interstate commerce or persons or things in interstate commerce; and (3) those activities having a substantial relation to or that substantially affect interstate commerce. Furthermore, the Court has explained that these three branches of its commerce power are analytically distinct. When Congress regulates the use of the channels of interstate commerce, or protects the instrumentalities of interstate commerce or persons or things in interstate commerce, it may do so without showing that the regulated activity substantially affects interstate commerce. The corollary of this is that a finding that the transaction was "in" interstate commerce or utilized the instrumentalities of

gg. This case is discussed more fully in Chapter 9, *infra*.

interstate commerce is sufficient to satisfy section 1957's jurisdictional element. Accord United States v. Kunzman, 54 F.3d 1522, 1526 (10th Cir.1995) (checks drawn on federally insured banks and services purchased from out-of-state company sufficient); United States v. Lovett, 964 F.2d 1029, 1038 (10th Cir.1992) (transfer of funds across state lines and purchase of goods in interstate commerce with funds traceable to the transactions sufficient). Only if the transaction was purely intrastate must the government show that it had some effect on interstate commerce. Moreover, because the regulated activity here—making financial transactions—is commercial in nature, the government need only prove that the individual transactions in this case each had a minimal effect on interstate commerce that, through repetition by others similarly situated, could have a substantial effect on interstate commerce.

Before we proceed further, it is important to explain that the issue is not really whether the district court had subject matter jurisdiction (it did), but whether the jury was properly instructed concerning the "jurisdictional" element of the offense. Because Ripinsky failed to object to the jury instructions, we can review them only for plain error. * * *

We recently held in United States v. Turman, 104 F.3d 1191 (9th Cir.1997), that whether an error is "plain" should be judged as of the time of trial.

> Plain error, as we understand that term, is error that is so clear-cut, so obvious, a competent district judge should be able to avoid it without benefit of objection. When the state of the law is unclear at trial and only becomes clear as a result of later authority, the district court's error is perforce not plain; we expect district judges to be knowledgeable, not clairvoyant.

Id. at 1194.

* * *

The district court instructed the jury that "the deposit of a check constitutes a monetary transaction." Standing alone, this instruction was inadequate, but our review is limited to plain error. As explained earlier, we evaluate whether an error was "plain" as of the time of trial. In addition, we will exercise our discretion to correct an error under such circumstances only if the error "seriously affect[s] the fairness, integrity, or public reputation of judicial proceedings." United States v. Olano, 507 U.S. 725, 736.

We will not order a new trial. There is no dispute that the deposits in this case involved financial institutions engaged in interstate activities. Indeed, some of the deposits were made at large, well-known institutions such as Wells Fargo Bank. Ripinsky made no objection to the instructions given. The error was not plain and it did not "seriously affect the fairness, integrity or public reputation of judicial proceedings." *Id.* Under such circumstances we will not reverse the district court.

Notes

1. Both the Fourth Circuit in *Aramony* and the Ninth Circuit in *Ripinsky* held that the trial courts committed error by failing to instruct their respective juries that the jury must find that the monetary transactions at issue affected interstate commerce. Aramony obtained a reversal because of this error; Ripinsky did not. Note the reason for the difference. Aramony's attorney objected to the jury charge before the District Court and before the instructions were given. Ripinsky's attorney did not object at the trial court stage. When an issue is not raised before the trial court, an appellate court may reverse only if the error "seriously affect[ed] the fairness, integrity, or public reputation of judicial proceedings." Ripinsky was unable to meet this high standard.

2. The Ninth Circuit referred to United States v. Lopez, 514 U.S. 549 (1995), which is discussed more fully in Chapter Eighteen. In *Lopez* the Supreme Court held that Congress exceeded its authority "[t]o regulate commerce ... among the several states" (U.S. Const. Art. I, § 8, cl.3) by passing the Gun–Free School Zones Act of 1990. By 5–4, the Court found that the conduct prohibited by the Act did not "substantially affect interstate commerce." *Id. Lopez* is widely viewed as challenging the long held assumption that an effect on interstate commerce is easily shown. It is not clear what impact *Lopez* will have but a *"Lopez* defense" is now commonly raised in many federal criminal cases.

3. Although excerpted from the Fourth Circuit's opinion above for purposes of this chapter, the court relied heavily upon United States v. Gaudin, 515 U.S. 506 (1995), in reaching its conclusion that the interstate commerce issue should have been submitted to the jury. In *Gaudin*, the Supreme Court held that all elements of a crime should be decided by the jury, not by the court. The Court explained:

> "The Constitution gives a criminal defendant the right to demand that a jury find him guilty of all the elements of the crime with which he is charged; one of the elements in the present case is materiality; respondent therefore had a right to have the jury decide materiality."

Id. at 522–23.[hh] A difficulty sometimes encountered in applying *Gaudin* is determining the exact elements of the crime. As the discussion in *Aramony* and *Riplinsky* demonstrates there are gradations: an issue may be an element, a "jurisdictional requirement," or "an essential element." According to *Gaudin*, only the latter must be presented to a jury.

hh. *Gaudin* is discussed more fully in Chapter 10.

APPENDIX A

Form **4789**	**Currency Transaction Report**	
(Rev. October 1995)	▶ Use this 1995 revision effective October 1, 1995.	
Department of the Treasury Internal Revenue Service	▶ For Paperwork Reduction Act Notice, see page 3. ▶ Please type or print. *(Complete all parts that apply—See instructions)*	OMB No. 1545-0183

1 Check all box(es) that apply:

a ☐ Amends prior report   **b** ☐ Multiple persons   **c** ☐ Multiple transactions

Part I Person(s) Involved in Transaction(s)

Section A—Person(s) on Whose Behalf Transaction(s) Is Conducted

2 Individual's last name or Organization's name			**3** First name		**4** M.I.
5 Doing business as (DBA)			**6** SSN or EIN		
7 Address (number, street, and apt. or suite no.)			**8** Date of birth	M M D D Y Y	
9 City	**10** State	**11** ZIP code	**12** Country (if not U.S.)	**13** Occupation, profession, or business	

14 If an individual, describe method used to verify identity:

a ☐ Driver's license/State I.D.   **b** ☐ Passport   **c** ☐ Alien registration   **d** ☐ Other ....

e ☐ Issued by: **f** Number:

Section B—Individual(s) Conducting Transaction(s) (if other than above).

If Section B is left blank or incomplete, check the box(es) below to indicate the reason(s):

a ☐ Armored Car Service   **b** ☐ Mail Deposit or Shipment   **c** ☐ Night Deposit or Automated Teller Machine (ATM)

d ☐ Multiple Transactions   **e** ☐ Conducted On Own Behalf

15 Individual's last name			**16** First name		**17** M.I.
18 Address (number, street, and apt. or suite no.)			**19** SSN		
20 City	**21** State	**22** ZIP code	**23** Country (if not U.S.)	**24** Date of birth	M M D D Y Y

25 If an individual, describe method used to verify identity:

a ☐ Driver's license/State I.D.   **b** ☐ Passport   **c** ☐ Alien registration   **d** ☐ Other ....

e ☐ Issued by: **f** Number:

Part II Amount and Type of Transaction(s). Check all boxes that apply.

		26 Date of Transaction	M M D D Y Y
26 Cash In $ _____ .00	**27** Cash Out $ _____ .00		

29 ☐ Foreign Currency _____ (Country)   **30** ☐ Wire Transfer(s)   **31** ☐ Negotiable Instrument(s) Purchased

32 ☐ Negotiable Instrument(s) Cashed   **33** ☐ Currency Exchange(s)   **34** ☐ Deposit(s)/Withdrawal(s)

35 ☐ Account Number(s) Affected (if any):   **36** ☐ Other (specify)

Part III Financial Institution Where Transaction(s) Takes Place

37 Name of financial institution	Enter Federal Regulator or BSA Examiner code number from the instructions here. ▶ [ ]
38 Address (number, street, and apt. or suite no.)	**39** SSN or EIN
40 City	**41** State	**42** ZIP code	**43** MICR No.

Sign Here ▶	**44** Title of approving official	**45** Signature of approving official	**46** Date of signature	M M D D Y Y
	47 Type or print preparer's name	**48** Type or print name of person to contact	**49** Telephone number ( )	

Cat. No. 42004W   Form **4789** (Rev. 10-95)

Form 4789 (Rev. 10-95)   Page **2**

Multiple Persons

(Complete applicable parts below if box 1b on page 1 is checked.)

Part I   Person(s) Involved in Transaction(s)

Section A—Person(s) on Whose Behalf Transaction(s) Is Conducted

2 Individual's last name or Organization's name	3 First name	4 M.I.
5 Doing business as (DBA)	6 SSN or EIN	
7 Address (number, street, and apt. or suite no.)	8 Date of birth M M D D Y Y	

9 City	10 State	11 ZIP code	12 Country (if not U.S.)	13 Occupation, profession, or business

14 If an individual, describe method used to verify identity:
a ☐ Driver's license/State I.D.   b ☐ Passport   c ☐ Alien registration   d ☐ Other ------------------
e Issued by: f Number:

Section B—Individual(s) Conducting Transaction(s) (if other than above).

15 Individual's last name	16 First name	17 M.I.
18 Address (number, street, and apt. or suite no.)	19 SSN	

20 City	21 State	22 ZIP code	23 Country (if not U.S.)	24 Date of birth M M D D Y Y

25 If an individual, describe method used to verify identity:
a ☐ Driver's license/State I.D.   b ☐ Passport   c ☐ Alien registration   d ☐ Other ------------------
e Issued by: f Number:

~~~~~~

Part I   Person(s) Involved in Transaction(s)

Section A—Person(s) on Whose Behalf Transaction(s) Is Conducted

2 Individual's last name or Organization's name	3 First name	4 M.I.
5 Doing business as (DBA)	6 SSN or EIN	
7 Address (number, street, and apt. or suite no.)	8 Date of birth M M D D Y Y	

9 City	10 State	11 ZIP code	12 Country (if not U.S.)	13 Occupation, profession, or business

14 If an individual, describe method used to verify identity:
a ☐ Driver's license/State I.D.   b ☐ Passport   c ☐ Alien registration   d ☐ Other ------------------
e Issued by: f Number:

Section B—Individual(s) Conducting Transaction(s) (if other than above).

15 Individual's last name	16 First name	17 M.I.
18 Address (number, street, and apt. or suite no.)	19 SSN	

20 City	21 State	22 ZIP code	23 Country (if not U.S.)	24 Date of birth M M D D Y Y

25 If an individual, describe method used to verify identity:
a ☐ Driver's license/State I.D.   b ☐ Passport   c ☐ Alien registration   d ☐ Other ------------------
e Issued by: f Number:

Form 4789 (Rev. 10-95) Page **3**

Paperwork Reduction Act Notice.—The requested information has been determined to be useful in criminal, tax, and regulatory investigations and proceedings. Financial institutions are required to provide the information under 31 U.S.C. 5313 and 31 CFR Part 103. These provisions are commonly referred to as the Bank Secrecy Act (BSA) which is administered by the U.S. Department of the Treasury's Financial Crimes Enforcement Network (FinCEN).

The time needed to complete this form will vary depending on individual circumstances. The estimated average time is 19 minutes. If you have comments concerning the accuracy of this time estimate or suggestions for making this form simpler, we would be happy to hear from you. You can write to the **Internal Revenue Service,** Attention: Tax Forms Committee, PC:FP, Washington, DC 20224. **DO NOT** send this form to this office. Instead, see **When and Where To File** below.

Suspicious Transactions

This Currency Transaction Report (CTR) should NOT be filed for suspicious transactions involving $10,000 or less in currency OR to note that a transaction of more than $10,000 is suspicious. Any suspicious or unusual activity should be reported by a financial institution in the manner prescribed by its appropriate federal regulator or BSA examiner. (See Item 37.) If a transaction is suspicious and in excess of $10,000 in currency, then both a CTR and the appropriate referral form must be filed.

Should the suspicious activity require immediate attention, financial institutions should telephone 1-800-800-CTRS. An Internal Revenue Service (IRS) employee will direct the call to the local office of the IRS Criminal Investigation Division (CID). This toll-free number is operational Monday through Friday, from approximately 9:00 am to 6:00 pm Eastern Standard Time. If an emergency, consult directory assistance for the local IRS CID Office.

General Instructions

Who Must File.—Each financial institution (other than a casino, which instead must file Form 8362 and the U.S. Postal Service for which there are separate rules), must file Form 4789 (CTR) for each deposit, withdrawal, exchange of currency, or other payment or transfer, by, through, or to the financial institution which involves a transaction in currency of more than $10,000. Multiple transactions must be treated as a single transaction if the financial institution has knowledge that (1) they are by or on behalf of the same person, and (2) they result in either currency received (Cash In) or currency disbursed (Cash Out) by the financial institution totaling more than $10,000 during any one business day. For a bank, a business day is the day on which transactions are routinely posted to customers' accounts, as normally communicated to depository customers. For all other financial institutions, a business day is a calendar day.

Generally, financial institutions are defined as banks, other types of depository institutions, brokers or dealers in securities, money transmitters, currency exchangers, check cashers, issuers and sellers of money orders and traveler's checks. Should you have questions, see the definitions in 31 CFR Part 103.

When and Where To File.—File this CTR by the 15th calendar day after the day of the transaction with the IRS Detroit Computing Center, ATTN: CTR, P.O. Box 33604, Detroit, MI 48232-5604 or with your local IRS office. Keep a copy of each CTR for five years from the date filed.

A financial institution may apply to file the CTRs magnetically. To obtain an application to file magnetically, write to the IRS Detroit Computing Center, ATTN: CTR Magnetic Media Coordinator, at the address listed above.

Identification Requirements.—All individuals (except employees of armored car services) conducting a reportable transaction(s) for themselves or for another person must be identified by means of an official document(s).

Acceptable forms of identification include a driver's license, military, and military/dependent identification cards, passport, state issued identification card, cedular card (foreign), non-resident alien identification cards, or any other identification document or documents, which contain name and preferably address and a photograph and are normally acceptable by financial institutions as a means of identification when cashing checks for persons other than established customers.

Acceptable identification information obtained previously and maintained in the financial institution's records may be used. For example, if documents verifying an individual's identity were examined and recorded on a signature card when an account was opened, the financial institution may rely on that information. In completing the CTR, the financial institution must indicate on the form the method, type, and number of the identification. Statements such as "known customer" or "signature card on file" are not sufficient for form completion.

Penalties.—Civil and criminal penalties are provided for failure to file a CTR or to supply information or for filing a false or fraudulent CTR. See 31 U.S.C. 5321, 5322 and 5324.

For purposes of this CTR, the terms below have the following meanings:

Currency.—The coin and paper money of the United States or any other country, which is circulated and customarily used and accepted as money.

Person.—An individual, corporation, partnership, trust or estate, joint stock company, association, syndicate, joint venture or other unincorporated organization or group.

Organization.—Person other than an individual.

Transaction in Currency.—The physical transfer of currency from one person to another. This does not include a transfer of funds by means of bank check, bank draft, wire transfer or other written order that does not involve the physical transfer of currency.

Negotiable Instruments.—All checks and drafts (including business, personal, bank, cashier's and third-party), money orders, and promissory notes. For purposes of this CTR, all traveler's checks shall also be considered negotiable instruments. All such instruments shall be considered negotiable instruments whether or not they are in bearer form.

Specific Instructions

Because of the limited space on the front and back of the CTR, it may be necessary to submit additional information on attached sheets. Submit this additional information on plain paper attached to the CTR. Be sure to put the individual's or organization's name and identifying number (items 2, 3, 4, and 6 of the CTR) on any additional sheets so that if it becomes separated, it may be associated with the CTR.

Item 1a. Amends Prior Report.—If this CTR is being filed because it amends a report filed previously, check Item 1a. Staple a copy of the original CTR to the amended one, complete Part III fully and only those other entries which are being amended.

Item 1b. Multiple Persons.—If this transaction is being conducted by more than one person or on behalf of more than one person, check Item 1b. Enter information in Part I for one of the persons and provide information on any other persons on the back of the CTR.

Item 1c. Multiple Transactions.—If the financial institution has knowledge that there are multiple transactions, check Item 1c.

PART I - Person(s) Involved in Transaction(s)

Section A **must** be completed. If an individual conducts a transaction on his own behalf, complete Section A; leave Section B BLANK. If an individual conducts a transaction on his own behalf and on behalf of another person(s), complete Section A for each person; leave Section B BLANK. If an individual conducts a transaction on behalf of another person(s), complete Section B for the individual conducting the transaction, and complete Section A for each person on whose behalf the transaction is conducted of whom the financial institution has knowledge.

Section A. Person(s) on Whose Behalf Transaction(s) is Conducted.—See instructions above.

Items 2, 3, and 4. Individual/Organization Name.—If the person on whose behalf the transaction(s) is conducted is an individual, put his/her last name in Item 2, first name in Item 3 and middle initial in Item 4. If there is no middle initial, leave Item 4 BLANK. If the transaction is conducted on behalf of an organization, put its name in Item 2 and leave Items 3 and 4 BLANK.

Item 5. Doing Business As (DBA).—If the financial institution has knowledge of a separate "doing business as" name, complete Item 5. For example, Johnson Enterprises DBA PJ's Pizzeria.

Item 6. Social Security Number (SSN) or Employer Identification Number (EIN).—Enter the SSN or EIN of the person identified in Item 2. If none, write NONE.

Items 7, 9, 10, 11 and 12. Address.—Enter the permanent street address including zip code of the person identified in Item 2. Use the Post Office's two letter state abbreviation code. A P.O. Box should not be used by itself and may only be used if there is no street address. If a P.O. Box is used, the name of the apartment or suite number, road or route number where the person resides must also be provided. If the address is outside the U.S., provide the street address, city, province, or state, postal code (if known), and the name of the country.

Item 8. Date of Birth.—Enter the date of birth. Six numerals must be inserted for each date. The first two will reflect the month of birth, the second two the calendar day of birth, and the last two numerals the year of birth. Zero (0) should precede any single digit number. For example, if an individual's birth date is April 3, 1948, Item 8 should read 04 03 48.

Item 13. Occupation, Profession, or Business.—Identify fully the occupation, profession or business of the person on whose behalf the transaction(s) was conducted. For example, secretary, shoe salesman, carpenter, attorney, housewife, restaurant, liquor store, etc. Do not use non-specific terms such as merchant, self-employed, businessman, etc.

Item 14. If an Individual, Describe Method Used To Verify.—If an individual conducts the transaction(s) on his/her own behalf, his/her identity must be verified by examination of an acceptable document (see **General Instructions**). For example, check box a if a driver's license is used to verify an individual's identity, and enter the state that issued the license and the number in items e and f. If the transaction is conducted by an individual on behalf of another individual not present or an organization, enter N/A in item 14.

Section B. Individual(s) Conducting Transaction(s) (if other than above).—Financial institutions should enter as much information as is available. However, there may be instances in which Items 15-25 may be left BLANK or incomplete.

If Items 15-25 are left BLANK or incomplete, check one or more of the boxes provided to indicate the reason(s).

Example: If there are multiple transactions that, if only when aggregated, the financial institution has knowledge the transactions exceed the reporting threshold, and therefore, did not identify the transactor(s), check box d for Multiple Transactions.

Items 15, 16, and 17. Individual(s) Name.—Complete these items if an individual conducts a transaction(s) on behalf of another person. For example, if John Doe, an employee of XYZ Grocery Store makes a deposit to the store's account, XYZ Grocery Store should be identified in Section A, and John Doe should be identified in Section B.

Items 18, 20, 21, 22, and 23. Address.—Enter the permanent street address including zip code of the individual. (See Items 7, 9, 10, 11, and 12.)

Item 19. SSN.—If the individual has an SSN, enter it in Item 19. If the individual does not have an SSN, enter NONE.

Item 24. Date of Birth.—Enter the individual's date of birth. See the instructions for item 8.

Item 25. If an Individual, Describe Method Used To Verify.—Enter the method by which the individual's identity is verified (see **General Instructions** and Item 14).

PART II - Amount and Type of Transaction(s)

Complete Part II to identify the type of transaction(s) reported and the amount(s) involved.

Items 26 and 27. Cash In/Cash Out.—In the spaces provided, enter the amount of currency received (Cash In) or disbursed (Cash Out) by the financial institution. If foreign currency is exchanged, use the U.S. dollar equivalent on the day of the transaction.

If less than a full dollar amount is involved, increase that figure to the next highest dollar. For example, if the currency totals $20,000.05, show the total as $20,001.00.

Item 28. Date of Transaction.—Six numerals must be inserted for each date. (See Item 8.)

Determining Whether Transactions Meet the Reporting Threshold

Only cash transactions that, if alone or when aggregated, exceed $10,000 should be reported on the CTR. Transactions shall not be offset against one another.

If there are both Cash In and Cash Out transactions that are reportable, the amounts should be considered separately and not aggregated. However, they may be reported on a single CTR.

If there is a currency exchange, it should be aggregated separately with each of the Cash In and Cash Out totals.

Example 1: A person deposits $11,000 in currency to his savings account and withdraws $3,000 in currency from his checking account.

The CTR should be completed as follows: Cash In $11,000 and no entry for Cash Out. This is because the $3,000 transaction does not meet the reporting threshold.

Example 2: A person deposits $11,000 in currency to his savings account and withdraws $12,000 in currency from his checking account.

The CTR should be completed as follows: Cash In $11,000, Cash Out $12,000. This is because there are two reportable transactions. However, one CTR may be filed to reflect both.

Example 3: A person deposits $6,000 in currency to his savings account and withdraws $4,000 in currency from his checking account. Further, he presents $5,000 in currency to be exchanged for the equivalent in French francs.

The CTR should be completed as follows: Cash In $11,000 and no entry for Cash Out. This is because in determining whether the transactions are reportable, the currency exchange is aggregated with each of the Cash In and the Cash Out amounts. The result is a reportable $11,000 Cash In transaction. The total Cash Out amount is $9,000 which does not meet the reporting threshold; therefore, it is not entered on the CTR.

Example 4: A person deposits $6,000 in currency to his savings account and withdraws $7,000 in currency from his checking account. Further, he presents $5,000 in currency to be exchanged for the equivalent in French francs.

The CTR should be completed as follows: Cash In $11,000, Cash Out $12,000. This is because in determining whether the transactions are reportable, the currency exchange is aggregated with each of the Cash In and Cash Out amounts. In this example, each of the Cash In and Cash Out totals exceed $10,000 and must be reflected on the CTR.

Item 29. Foreign Currency.—If foreign currency is involved, check Item 29 and identify the country. If multiple foreign currencies are involved, identify the country for which the largest amount is exchanged.

Items 30-33.—Check the appropriate item(s) to identify the following type of transaction(s):

30. Wire Transfer(s)

31. Negotiable Instrument(s) Purchased

32. Negotiable Instrument(s) Cashed

33. Currency Exchange(s)

Item 34. Deposits/Withdrawals.—Check this item to identify deposits to or withdrawals from accounts, e.g., demand deposit accounts, savings accounts, time deposits, mutual fund accounts or any other account held at the financial institution. Enter the account number(s) in item 35.

Item 35. Account Numbers Affected (if any).—Enter the account numbers of any accounts affected by the transaction(s) that are maintained

at the financial institution conducting the transaction(s). If necessary, use additional sheets of paper to indicate all of the affected accounts.

Example 1: If a person cashes a check drawn on an account held at the financial institution, the CTR should be completed as follows: Indicate Negotiable Instrument(s) Cashed and provide the account number of the check.

If the transaction does not affect an account, make no entry.

Example 2: A person cashes a check drawn on another financial institution. In this instance, Negotiable Instrument(s) Cashed would be indicated, but no account at the financial institution has been affected. Therefore, item 35 should be left BLANK.

Item 36. Other (specify).—If a transaction is not identified in Items 30-34, check Item 36 and provide an additional description. For example, a person presents a check to purchase "foreign currency".

Part III - Financial Institution Where Transaction(s) Takes Place

Item 37. Name of Financial Institution and Identity of Federal Regulator or BSA Examiner.—Enter the financial institution's full legal name and identify the federal regulator or BSA examiner, using the following codes:

FEDERAL REGULATOR OR BSA EXAMINER	CODE
Comptroller of the Currency (OCC)	1
Federal Deposit Insurance Corporation (FDIC)	2
Federal Reserve System (FRS)	3
Office of Thrift Supervision (OTS)	4
National Credit Union Administration (NCUA)	5
Securities and Exchange Commission (SEC)	6
Internal Revenue Service (IRS)	7
U.S. Postal Service (USPS)	8

Items 38, 40, 41, and 42. Address.—Enter the street address, city, state, and ZIP code of the financial institution where the transaction occurred. If there are multiple transactions, provide information on the office or branch where any one of the transactions has occurred.

Item 39. EIN or SSN.—Enter the financial institution's EIN. If the financial institution does not have an EIN, enter the SSN of the financial institution's principal owner.

Item 43. MICR Number.—If a depository institution, enter the Magnetic Ink Character Recognition (MICR) number.

Signature

Items 44 and 45. Title and Signature of Approving Official.—The official who reviews and approves the CTR must indicate his/her title and sign the CTR.

Item 46. Date the Form Was Signed.—The approving official must enter the date the CTR is signed. (See Item 8.)

Item 47. Preparer's Name.—Type or print the full name of the individual preparing the CTR. The preparer and the approving official may not necessarily be the same individual.

Items 48 and 49. Contact Person/Telephone Number.—Type or print the name and telephone number of an individual to contact concerning questions about the CTR.

Form 8300

(Rev. August 1997)

Department of the Treasury
Internal Revenue Service

**Report of Cash Payments Over $10,000
Received in a Trade or Business**

▶ See instructions for definition of cash.
▶ Use this form for transactions occurring after July 31, 1997.
Please type or print.

OMB No. 1545-0892

1 Check appropriate box(es) if: **a** ☐ Amends prior report; **b** ☐ Suspicious transaction.

Part I   Identity of Individual From Whom the Cash Was Received

2 If more than one individual is involved, check here and see instructions . . . . ▶ ☐

3 Last name	4 First name	5 M.I.	6 Taxpayer identification number

7 Address (number, street, and apt. or suite no.)	8 Date of birth . ▶ (see instructions)	M M D D Y Y Y Y

9 City	10 State	11 ZIP code	12 Country (if not U.S.)	13 Occupation, profession, or business

14 Document used to verify identity: **a** Describe identification ▶ ....
b Issued by _____ **c** Number _____

Part II   Person on Whose Behalf This Transaction Was Conducted

15 If this transaction was conducted on behalf of more than one person, check here and see instructions . . . . . ▶ ☐

16 Individual's last name or Organization's name	17 First name	18 M.I.	19 Taxpayer identification number

20 Doing business as (DBA) name (see instructions)	Employer identification number

21 Address (number, street, and apt. or suite no.)	22 Occupation, profession, or business

23 City	24 State	25 ZIP code	26 Country (if not U.S.)

27 Alien identification: **a** Describe identification ▶ ....
b Issued by _____ **c** Number _____

Part III   Description of Transaction and Method of Payment

28 Date cash received M M D D Y Y Y Y	29 Total cash received $ .00	30 If cash was received in more than one payment, check here . . . ▶ ☐	31 Total price if different from item 29 $ .00

32 Amount of cash received (in U.S. dollar equivalent) (must equal item 29) (see instructions):

a U.S. currency $ _____ .00 (Amount in $100 bills or higher $ _____ .00)
b Foreign currency $ _____ .00 (Country ▶ _____)
c Cashier's check(s) $ _____ .00 } Issuer's name(s) and serial number(s) of the monetary instrument(s) ▶ ....
d Money order(s) $ _____ .00
e Bank draft(s) $ _____ .00
f Traveler's check(s) $ _____ .00

33 Type of transaction

a ☐ Personal property purchased
b ☐ Real property purchased
c ☐ Personal services provided
d ☐ Business services provided
e ☐ Intangible property purchased
f ☐ Debt obligations paid
g ☐ Exchange of cash
h ☐ Escrow or trust funds
i ☐ Bail bond
j ☐ Other (specify) ▶

34 Specific description of property or service shown in 33. (Give serial or registration number, address, docket number, etc.) ▶ ....

Part IV   Business That Received Cash

35 Name of business that received cash	36 Employer identification number

37 Address (number, street, and apt. or suite no.)	Social security number

38 City	39 State	40 ZIP code	41 Nature of your business

42 Under penalties of perjury, I declare that to the best of my knowledge the information I have furnished above is true, correct, and complete.

Signature of authorized official _____   Title of authorized official _____

43 Date of signature M M D D Y Y Y Y	44 Type or print name of contact person	45 Contact telephone number ( )

For Paperwork Reduction Act Notice, see page 4.   Cat. No. 62133S   Form **8300** (Rev. 8-97)

Form 8300 (Rev. 8-97) Page **2**

Multiple Parties
(Complete applicable parts below if box 2 or 15 on page 1 is checked)

Part I **Continued—Complete if box 2 on page 1 is checked**

3 Last name	**4** First name	**5** M.I.	**6** Taxpayer identification number

7 Address (number, street, and apt. or suite no.)	**8** Date of birth ▶ (see instructions)	M M D D Y Y Y Y

9 City	**10** State	**11** ZIP code	**12** Country (if not U.S.)	**13** Occupation, profession, or business

14 Document used to verify identity: **a** Describe identification ▶ ....
b Issued by **c** Number

3 Last name	**4** First name	**5** M.I.	**6** Taxpayer identification number

7 Address (number, street, and apt. or suite no.)	**8** Date of birth ▶ (see instructions)	M M D D Y Y Y Y

9 City	**10** State	**11** ZIP code	**12** Country (if not U.S.)	**13** Occupation, profession, or business

14 Document used to verify identity: **a** Describe identification ▶ ....
b Issued by **c** Number

Part II **Continued—Complete if box 15 on page 1 is checked**

16 Individual's last name or Organization's name	**17** First name	**18** M.I.	**19** Taxpayer identification number

20 Doing business as (DBA) name (see instructions)	Employer identification number

21 Address (number, street, and apt. or suite no.)	**22** Occupation, profession, or business

23 City	**24** State	**25** ZIP code	**26** Country (if not U.S.)

27 Alien identification: **a** Describe identification ▶ ....
b Issued by **c** Number

16 Individual's last name or Organization's name	**17** First name	**18** M.I.	**19** Taxpayer identification number

20 Doing business as (DBA) name (see instructions)	Employer identification number

21 Address (number, street, and apt. or suite no.)	**22** Occupation, profession, or business

23 City	**24** State	**25** ZIP code	**26** Country (if not U.S.)

27 Alien identification: **a** Describe identification ▶ ....
b Issued by **c** Number

Item You Should Note

Clerks of Federal or State courts must now file Form 8300 if more than $10,000 in cash is received as bail for an individual(s) charged with certain criminal offenses. For these purposes, a clerk includes the clerk's office or any other office, department, division, branch, or unit of the court that is authorized to receive bail. If a person receives bail on behalf of a clerk, the clerk is treated as receiving the bail.

If multiple payments are made in cash to satisfy bail and the initial payment does not exceed $10,000, the initial payment and subsequent payments must be aggregated and the information return must be filed by the 15th day after receipt of the payment that causes the aggregate amount to exceed $10,000 in cash. In such cases, the reporting requirement can be satisfied either by sending a single written statement with an aggregate amount listed or by furnishing a copy of each Form 8300 relating to that payer. Payments made to satisfy separate bail requirements are not required to be aggregated. See Treasury Regulations section 1.6050I-2.

Casinos must file Form 8300 for nongaming activities (restaurants, shops, etc.).

General Instructions

Who must file.—Each person engaged in a trade or business who, in the course of that trade or business, receives more than $10,000 in cash in one transaction or in two or more related transactions, must file Form 8300. Any transactions conducted between a payer (or its agent) and the recipient in a 24-hour period are related transactions. Transactions are considered related even if they occur over a period of more than 24-hours if the recipient knows, or has reason to know, that each transaction is one of a series of connected transactions.

Keep a copy of each Form 8300 for 5 years from the date you file it.

Voluntary use of Form 8300.—Form 8300 may be filed voluntarily for any suspicious transaction (see **Definitions**), even if the total amount does not exceed $10,000.

Exceptions.—Cash is not required to be reported if it is received:

● By a financial institution required to file **Form 4789,** Currency Transaction Report.

● By a casino required to file (or exempt from filing) **Form 8362,** Currency Transaction Report by Casinos, if the cash is received as part of its gaming business.

● By an agent who receives the cash from a principal, if the agent uses all of the cash within 15 days in a second transaction that is reportable on Form 8300 or on Form 4789, and discloses all the information necessary to complete Part II of Form 8300 or Form 4789 to the recipient of the cash in the second transaction.

● In a transaction occurring entirely outside the United States. See **Pub. 1544,** Reporting Cash Payments Over $10,000 (Received in a Trade or Business),

regarding transactions occurring in Puerto Rico, the Virgin Islands, and territories and possessions of the United States.

● In a transaction that is not in the course of a person's trade or business.

When to file.—File Form 8300 by the 15th day after the date the cash was received. If that date falls on a Saturday, Sunday, or legal holiday, file the form on the next business day.

Where to file.—File the form with the Internal Revenue Service, Detroit Computing Center, P.O. Box 32621, Detroit, MI 48232, or hand carry it to your local IRS office.

Statement to be provided.—You must give a written statement to each person named on a required Form 8300 on or before January 31 of the year following the calendar year in which the cash is received. The statement must show the name, telephone number, and address of the information contact for the business, the aggregate amount of reportable cash received, and that the information was furnished to the IRS. Keep a copy of the statement for your records.

Multiple payments.—If you receive more than one cash payment for a single transaction or for related transactions, you must report the multiple payments any time you receive a total amount that exceeds $10,000 within any 12-month period. Submit the report within 15 days of the date you receive the payment that causes the total amount to exceed $10,000. If more than one report is required within 15 days, you may file a combined report. File the combined report no later than the date the earliest report, if filed separately, would have to be filed.

Taxpayer identification number (TIN).—You must furnish the correct TIN of the person or persons from whom you receive the cash and, if applicable, the person or persons on whose behalf the transaction is being conducted. **You may be subject to penalties for an incorrect or missing TIN.**

The TIN for an individual (including a sole proprietorship) is the individual's social security number (SSN). For certain resident aliens who are not eligible to get an SSN and nonresident aliens who are required to file tax returns, it is an IRS Individual Taxpayer Identification Number (ITIN). For other persons, including corporations, partnerships, and estates, it is the employer identification number.

If you have requested but are not able to get a TIN for one or more of the parties to a transaction within 15 days following the transaction, file the report and attach a statement explaining why the TIN is not included.

Exception: You are not required to provide the TIN of a person who is a nonresident alien individual or a foreign organization if that person does not have income effectively connected with the conduct of a U.S. trade or business **and** does not have an office or place of business, or fiscal or paying agent, in the United States. See Pub. 1544 for more information.

Penalties.—You may be subject to penalties if you fail to file a correct and complete Form 8300 on time and you cannot show that the failure was due to reasonable cause. You may also be subject to penalties if you fail to furnish timely a correct and complete statement to each person named in a required report. A minimum penalty of $25,000 may be imposed if the failure is due to an intentional disregard of the cash reporting requirements.

Penalties may also be imposed for causing, or attempting to cause, a trade or business to fail to file a required report; for causing, or attempting to cause, a trade or business to file a required report containing a material omission or misstatement of fact; or for structuring, or attempting to structure, transactions to avoid the reporting requirements. These violations may also be subject to criminal prosecution which, upon conviction, may result in imprisonment of up to 5 years or fines of up to $250,000 for individuals and $500,000 for corporations or both.

Definitions

Cash.—The term "cash" means the following:

● U.S. and foreign coin and currency received in any transaction.

● A cashier's check, money order, bank draft, or traveler's check having a face amount of $10,000 or less that is received in a **designated reporting transaction** (defined below), or that is received in any transaction in which the recipient knows that the instrument is being used in an attempt to avoid the reporting of the transaction under section 6050I.

Note: Cash does not include a check drawn on the payer's own account, such as a personal check, regardless of the amount.

Designated reporting transaction.—A retail sale (or the receipt of funds by a broker or other intermediary in connection with a retail sale) of a consumer durable, a collectible, or a travel or entertainment activity.

Retail sale.—Any sale (whether or not the sale is for resale or for any other purpose) made in the course of a trade or business if that trade or business principally consists of making sales to ultimate consumers.

Consumer durable.—An item of tangible personal property of a type that, under ordinary usage, can reasonably be expected to remain useful for at least 1 year, and that has a sales price of more than $10,000.

Collectible.—Any work of art, rug, antique, metal, gem, stamp, coin, etc.

Travel or entertainment activity.—An item of travel or entertainment that pertains to a single trip or event if the combined sales price of the item and all other items relating to the same trip or event that are sold in the same transaction (or related transactions) exceeds $10,000.

Exceptions.—A cashier's check, money order, bank draft, or traveler's check is not considered received in a designated reporting transaction if it constitutes the proceeds of a bank loan or if it is received as a payment on certain promissory notes, installment sales contracts, or down payment plans. See Pub. 1544 for more information.

Person.—An individual, corporation, partnership, trust, estate, association, or company.

Recipient.—The person receiving the cash. Each branch or other unit of a person's trade or business is considered a separate recipient unless the branch receiving the cash (or a central office linking the branches), knows or has reason to know the identity of payers making cash payments to other branches.

Transaction.—Includes the purchase of property or services, the payment of debt, the exchange of a negotiable instrument for cash, and the receipt of cash to be held in escrow or trust. A single transaction may not be broken into multiple transactions to avoid reporting.

Suspicious transaction.—A transaction in which it appears that a person is attempting to cause Form 8300 not to be filed, or to file a false or incomplete form. The term also includes any transaction in which there is an indication of possible illegal activity.

Specific Instructions

You must complete all parts. However, you may skip Part II if the individual named in Part I is conducting the transaction on his or her behalf only.

Item 1.—If you are amending a prior report, check box 1a. Complete the appropriate items with the correct or amended information only. Complete all of Part IV. Staple a copy of the original report to the amended form.

To voluntarily report a suspicious transaction (see **Definitions**), check box 1b. You may also telephone your local IRS Criminal Investigation Division or call 1-800-800-2877.

Part I

Item 2.—If two or more individuals conducted the transaction you are reporting, check the box and complete Part I for any one of the individuals. Provide the same information for the other individual(s) on the back of the form. If more than three individuals are involved, provide the same information on additional sheets of paper and attach them to this form.

Item 6.—Enter the taxpayer identification number (TIN) of the individual named. See **Taxpayer identification number (TIN)** under **General Instructions** for more information.

Item 8.—Enter eight numerals for the date of birth of the individual named. For example, if the individual's birth date is July 6, 1960, enter 07 06 1960.

Item 13.—Fully describe the nature of the occupation, profession, or business (for example, "plumber," "attorney," or "automobile dealer"). Do not use general or

nondescriptive terms such as "businessman" or "self-employed."

Item 14.—You must verify the name and address of the named individual(s). Verification must be made by examination of a document normally accepted as a means of identification when cashing checks (for example, a driver's license, passport, alien registration card, or other official document). In item 14a, enter the type of document examined. In item 14b, identify the issuer of the document. In item 14c, enter the document's number. For example, if the individual has a Utah driver's license, enter "driver's license" in item 14a, "Utah" in item 14b, and the number appearing on the license in item 14c.

Part II

Item 15.—If the transaction is being conducted on behalf of more than one person (including husband and wife or parent and child), check the box and complete Part II for any one of the persons. Provide the same information for the other person(s) on the back of the form. If more than three persons are involved, provide the same information on additional sheets of paper and attach them to this form.

Items 16 through 19.—If the person on whose behalf the transaction is being conducted is an individual, complete items 16, 17, and 18. Enter his or her TIN in item 19. If the individual is a sole proprietor and has an employer identification number (EIN), you must enter both the SSN and EIN in item 19. If the person is an organization, put its name as shown on required tax filings in item 16 and its EIN in item 19.

Item 20.—If a sole proprietor or organization named in items 16 through 18 is doing business under a name other than that entered in item 16 (e.g., a "trade" or "doing business as (DBA)" name), enter it here.

Item 27.—If the person is **NOT** required to furnish a TIN (see **Taxpayer identification number (TIN)** under **General Instructions)**, complete this item. Enter a description of the type of official document issued to that person in item 27a (for example, "passport"), the country that issued the document in item 27b, and the document's number in item 27c.

Part III

Item 28.—Enter the date you received the cash. If you received the cash in more than one payment, enter the date you received the payment that caused the combined amount to exceed $10,000. See **Multiple payments** under **General Instructions** for more information.

Item 30.—Check this box if the amount shown in item 29 was received in more than one payment (for example, as installment payments or payments on related transactions).

Item 31.—Enter the total price of the property, services, amount of cash exchanged, etc. (for example, the total cost

of a vehicle purchased, cost of catering service, exchange of currency) if different from the amount shown in item 29.

Item 32.—Enter the dollar amount of each form of cash received. Show foreign currency amounts in U.S. dollar equivalent at a fair market rate of exchange available to the public. **The sum of the amounts must equal item 29.** For cashier's check, money order, bank draft, or traveler's check, provide the name of the issuer and the serial number of each instrument. Names of all issuers and all serial numbers involved must be provided. If necessary, provide this information on additional sheets of paper and attach them to this form.

Item 33.—Check the appropriate box(es) that describe the transaction. If the transaction is not specified in boxes a–i, check box j and briefly describe the transaction (for example, car lease, boat lease, house lease, aircraft rental).

Part IV

Item 36.—If you are a sole proprietorship, you must enter your SSN. If your business also has an EIN, you must provide the EIN as well. All other business entities must enter an EIN.

Item 41.—Fully describe the nature of your business, for example, "attorney," "jewelry dealer." Do not use general or nondescriptive terms such as "business" or "store."

Item 42.—This form must be signed by an individual who has been authorized to do so for the business that received the cash.

Paperwork Reduction Act Notice

The requested information is useful in criminal, tax, and regulatory investigations, for instance, by directing the Federal Government's attention to unusual or questionable transactions. Trades or businesses are required to provide the information under 26 U.S.C. 6050I.

You are not required to provide the information requested on a form that is subject to the Paperwork Reduction Act unless the form displays a valid OMB control number. Books or records relating to a form or its instructions must be retained as long as their contents may become material in the administration of any Internal Revenue law. Generally, tax returns and return information are confidential, as required by Code section 6103.

The time needed to complete this form will vary depending on individual circumstances. The estimated average time is 21 minutes. If you have comments concerning the accuracy of this time estimate or suggestions for making this form simpler, you can write to the Tax Forms Committee, Western Area Distribution Center, Rancho Cordova, CA 95743-0001. DO NOT send this form to this office. Instead, see **Where To File** on page 3.

	1

Suspicious Activity Report

FRB:	FR 2230	OMB No. 7100-0212
FDIC:	6710/06	OMB No. 3064-0077
OCC:	8010-9,8010-1	OMB No. 1557-0180
OTS:	1601	OMB No. 1550-0003
NCUA:	2362	OMB No. 3133-0094
TREASURY: TD F 90-22.47		OMB No. 1506-0001

ALWAYS COMPLETE ENTIRE REPORT

Expires September 30, 1998

1 Check appropriate box:
a ☐ Initial Report   b ☐ Corrected Report   c ☐ Supplemental Report

Part I   Reporting Financial Institution Information

2 Name of Financial Institution

3 Primary Federal Regulator
a ☐ Federal Reserve   d ☐ OCC
b ☐ FDIC   e ☐ OTS
c ☐ NCUA

4 Address of Financial Institution

5 City   6 State   7 Zip Code   8 EIN or TIN

9 Address of Branch Office(s) where activity occurred   10 Asset size of financial institution $ .00

11 City   12 State   13 Zip Code   14 If institution closed, date closed (MMDDYY) ___ / ___ / ___

15 Account number(s) affected, if any
a _____
b _____

16 Have any of the institution's accounts related to this matter been closed?
a ☐ Yes   b ☐ No   If yes, identify _____

Part II   Suspect Information

17 Last Name or Name of Entity   18 First Name   19 Middle Initial

20 Address   21 SSN, EIN or TIN (as applicable)

22 City   23 State   24 Zip Code   25 Country   26 Date of Birth (MMDDYY) ___ / ___ / ___

27 Phone Number - Residence (include area code) ( )   28 Phone Number - Work (include area code) ( )

29 Occupation

30 Forms of Identification for Suspect:
a ☐ Driver's License   b ☐ Passport   c ☐ Alien Registration   d ☐ Other _____
e Number _____   f Issuing Authority _____

31 Relationship to Financial Institution:
a ☐ Accountant   d ☐ Attorney   g ☐ Customer   j ☐ Officer
b ☐ Agent   e ☐ Borrower   h ☐ Director   k ☐ Shareholder
c ☐ Appraiser   f ☐ Broker   i ☐ Employee   l ☐ Other _____

32 Is insider suspect still affiliated with the financial institution?
a ☐ Yes   If no, specify { c ☐ Suspended   e ☐ Resigned
b ☐ No   { d ☐ Terminated

33 Date of Suspension, Termination, Resignation (MMDDYY) ___ / ___ / ___

34 Admission/Confession
a ☐ Yes   b ☐ No

Part III   Suspicious Activity Information   2

35 Date of suspicious activity (MMDDYY)   36 Dollar amount involved in known or suspicious activity
    ___ / ___ / ___ $ .00

37 Summary characterization of suspicious activity:

a ☐ Bank Secrecy Act/Structuring/ Money Laundering	g ☐ Counterfeit Check		m ☐ False Statement	
b ☐ Bribery/Gratuity	h ☐ Counterfeit Credit/Debit Card		n ☐ Misuse of Position or Self-Dealing	
c ☐ Check Fraud	i ☐ Counterfeit Instrument (other)			
d ☐ Check Kiting	j ☐ Credit Card Fraud		o ☐ Mortgage Loan Fraud	
e ☐ Commercial Loan Fraud	k ☐ Debit Card Fraud		p ☐ Mysterious Disappearance	
f ☐ Consumer Loan Fraud	l ☐ Defalcation/Embezzlement		q ☐ Wire Transfer Fraud	

    r ☐ Other _____

38 Amount of loss prior to recovery (if applicable) $ .00	39 Dollar amount of recovery (if applicable) $ .00	40 Has the suspicious activity had a material impact on or otherwise affected the financial soundness of the institution? a ☐ Yes b ☐ No

41 Has the institution's bonding company been notified?

    a ☐ Yes   b ☐ No

42 Has any law enforcement agency already been advised by telephone, written communication, or otherwise?
    If so, list the agency and local address.
    Agency _____

43 Address	
44 City	45 State	46 Zip Code

Part IV   Witness Information

47 Last Name	48 First Name	49 Middle Initial
50 Address		51 SSN
52 City	53 State	54 Zip Code	55 Date of Birth (MMDDYY) ___ / ___ / ___
56 Title	57 Phone Number (include area code) ( )	58 Interviewed a ☐ Yes b ☐ No

Part V   Preparer Information

59 Last Name	60 First Name	61 Middle Initial
62 Title	63 Phone Number (include area code) ( )	64 Date (MMDDYY) ___ / ___ / ___

Part VI   Contact for Assistance (If different than Preparer Information in Part V)

65 Last Name	66 First Name	67 Middle Initial
68 Title	69 Phone Number (include area code) ( )	
70 Agency (If applicable)		

| Part VII | Suspicious Activity Information Explanation/Description | 3 |

Explanation/description of known or suspected violation of law or suspicious activity. This section of the report is critical. The care with which it is written may make the difference in whether or not the described conduct and its possible criminal nature are clearly understood. Provide below a chronological and complete account of the possible violation of law, including what is unusual, irregular or suspicious about the transaction, using the following checklist as you prepare your account. If necessary, continue the narrative on a duplicate of this page.

a **Describe** supporting documentation and retain for 5 years.
b **Explain** who benefited, financially or otherwise, from the transaction, how much, and how.
c **Retain** any confession, admission, or explanation of the transaction provided by the suspect and indicate to whom and when it was given.
d **Retain** any confession, admission, or explanation of the transaction provided by any other person and indicate to whom and when it was given.

e **Retain** any evidence of cover-up or evidence of an attempt to deceive federal or state examiners or others.
f **Indicate** where the possible violation took place (e.g., main office, branch, other).
g **Indicate** whether the possible violation is an isolated incident or relates to other transactions.
h **Indicate** whether there is any related litigation; if so, specify.
i **Recommend** any further investigation that might assist law enforcement authorities.
j **Indicate** whether any information has been excluded from this report; if so, why?

For Bank Secrecy Act/Structuring/Money Laundering reports, include the following additional information:

k **Indicate** whether currency and/or monetary instruments were involved. If so, provide the amount and/or description.
l **Indicate** any account number that may be involved or affected.

Suspicious Activity Report
Instructions

Safe Harbor Federal law (31 U.S.C. 5318(g)(3)) provides complete protection from civil liability for all reports of suspected or known criminal violations and suspicious activities to appropriate authorities, including supporting documentation, regardless of whether such reports are filed pursuant to this report's instructions or are filed on a voluntary basis. Specifically, the law provides that a financial institution, and its directors, officers, employees and agents, that make a disclosure of any possible violation of law or regulation, including in connection with the preparation of suspicious activity reports, "shall not be liable to any person under any law or regulation of the United States or any constitution, law, or regulation of any State or political subdivision thereof, for such disclosure or for any failure to notify the person involved in the transaction or any other person of such disclosure."

Notification Prohibited Federal law (31 U.S.C. 5318(g)(2)) requires that a financial institution, and its directors, officers, employees and agents who, voluntarily or by means of a suspicious activity report, report suspected or known criminal violations or suspicious activities may not notify any person involved in the transaction that the transaction has been reported.

In situations involving violations requiring immediate attention, such as when a reportable violation is ongoing, the financial institution shall immediately notify, by telephone, appropriate law enforcement and financial institution supervisory authorities in addition to filing a timely suspicious activity report.

WHEN TO MAKE A REPORT:

1. All financial institutions operating in the United States, including insured banks, savings associations, savings association service corporations, credit unions, bank holding companies, nonbank subsidiaries of bank holding companies, Edge and Agreement corporations, and U.S. branches and agencies of foreign banks, are required to make this report following the discovery of:

   a. **Insider abuse involving any amount.** Whenever the financial institution detects any known or suspected Federal criminal violation, or pattern of criminal violations, committed or attempted against the financial institution or involving a transaction or transactions conducted through the financial institution, where the financial institution believes that it was either an actual or potential victim of a criminal violation, or series of criminal violations, or that the financial institution was used to facilitate a criminal transaction, and the financial institution has a substantial basis for identifying one of its directors, officers, employees, agents or other institution-affiliated parties as having committed or aided in the commission of a criminal act regardless of the amount involved in the violation.

   b. **Violations aggregating $5,000 or more where a suspect can be identified.** Whenever the financial institution detects any known or suspected Federal criminal violation, or pattern of criminal violations, committed or attempted against the financial institution or involving a transaction or transactions conducted through the financial institution and involving or aggregating $5,000 or more in funds or other assets, where the financial institution believes that it was either an actual or potential victim of a criminal violation, or series of criminal violations, or that the financial institution was used to facilitate a criminal transaction, and the financial institution has a substantial basis for identifying a possible suspect or group of suspects. If it is determined prior to filing this report that the identified suspect or group of suspects has used an "alias," then information regarding the true identity of the suspect or group of suspects, as well as alias identifiers, such as drivers' licenses or social security numbers, addresses and telephone numbers, must be reported.

   c. **Violations aggregating $25,000 or more regardless of a potential suspect.** Whenever the financial institution detects any known or suspected Federal criminal violation, or pattern of criminal violations, committed or attempted against the financial institution or involving a transaction or transactions conducted through the financial institution and involving or aggregating $25,000 or more in funds or other assets, where the financial institution believes that it was either an actual or potential victim of a criminal violation, or series of criminal violations, or that the financial institution was used to facilitate a criminal transaction, even though there is no substantial basis for identifying a possible suspect or group of suspects.

   d. **Transactions aggregating $5,000 or more that involve potential money laundering or violations of the Bank Secrecy Act.** Any transaction (which for purposes of this subsection means a deposit, withdrawal, transfer between accounts, exchange of currency, loan, extension of credit, purchase or sale of any stock, bond, certificate of deposit, or other monetary instrument or investment security, or any other payment, transfer, or delivery by, through, or to a financial institution, by whatever means effected) conducted or attempted by, at or through the financial institution and involving or aggregating $5,000 or more in funds or other assets, if the financial institution knows, suspects, or has reason to suspect that:

i. The transaction involves funds derived from illegal activities or is intended or conducted in order to hide or disguise funds or assets derived from illegal activities (including, without limitation, the ownership, nature, source, location, or control of such funds or assets) as part of a plan to violate or evade any law or regulation or to avoid any transaction reporting requirement under Federal law;

ii. The transaction is designed to evade any regulations promulgated under the Bank Secrecy Act; or

iii. The transaction has no business or apparent lawful purpose or is not the sort in which the particular customer would normally be expected to engage, and the financial institution knows of no reasonable explanation for the transaction after examining the available facts, including the background and possible purpose of the transaction.

The Bank Secrecy Act requires all financial institutions to file currency transaction reports (CTRs) in accordance with the Department of the Treasury's implementing regulations (31 CFR Part 103). These regulations require a financial institution to file a CTR whenever a currency transaction exceeds $10,000. If a currency transaction exceeds $10,000 and is suspicious, the institution must file both a CTR (reporting the currency transaction) and a suspicious activity report (reporting the suspicious or criminal aspects of the transaction). If a currency transaction equals or is below $10,000 and is suspicious, the institution should only file a suspicious activity report.

2. A financial institution is required to file a suspicious activity report no later than 30 calendar days after the date of initial detection of facts that may constitute a basis for filing a suspicious activity report. If no suspect was identified on the date of detection of the incident requiring the filing, a financial institution may delay filing a suspicious activity report for an additional 30 calendar days to identify a suspect. In no case shall reporting be delayed more than 60 calendar days after the date of initial detection of a reportable transaction.

3. This suspicious activity report does not need to be filed for those robberies and burglaries that are reported to local authorities, or (except for savings associations and service corporations) for lost, missing, counterfeit or stolen securities that are reported pursuant to the requirements of 17 CFR 240.17f-1.

HOW TO MAKE A REPORT:

1. Send each completed suspicious activity report to:

   FinCEN, Detroit Computing Center, P.O. Box 33980, Detroit, MI 48232

2. For items that do not apply or for which information is not available, leave blank.

3. Complete each suspicious activity report in its entirety, even when the suspicious activity report is a corrected or supplemental report.

4. Do not include supporting documentation with the suspicious activity report. Identify and retain a copy of the suspicious activity report and all original supporting documentation or business record equivalent for 5 years from the date of the suspicious activity report. All supporting documentation must be made available to appropriate authorities upon request.

5. If more space is needed to complete an item (for example, to report an additional suspect or witness), a copy of the page containing the item should be used to provide the information.

6. Financial institutions are encouraged to provide copies of suspicious activity reports to state and local authorities, where appropriate.

Chapter 5

ASSET FORFEITURE

Forfeiture is "the divestiture without compensation of property used in a manner contrary to the laws of the sovereign."[a] The rapidly growing legal specialty of asset forfeiture epitomizes the hybrid civil/criminal nature of white collar crime. Forfeiture may be ordered after a criminal conviction or ordered in a civil proceeding separate from the criminal action. However, even civil forfeiture requires proof that property has been involved in criminal activity or is the proceeds of criminal activity. Whether the forfeiture proceeds criminally or civilly, however, knowledge of business and property law is necessary to prosecute or defend the forfeiture of commercial enterprises.[b]

Criminal forfeiture has developed fairly recently. The RICO[c] and Continuing Criminal Enterprise (CCE) statutes,[d] passed in 1970, were the first criminal forfeiture statutes.[e] More recently Congress has passed the Money Laundering Control Act of 1986 which includes forfeiture provisions found at 18 U.S.C. §§ 981 and 982.[f] Criminal forfeiture is an "in personam" action in which the government must prove, beyond a reasonable doubt, that an individual, or group of individuals, has committed a crime and that property was sufficiently involved in the criminal activity to meet all elements of forfeiture.[g]

There are three major statutes pertaining to criminal forfeiture. All require a trial court to order forfeiture upon conviction of certain crimes. Section 853 of title 21, United States Code, pertains to drug offenses, and requires forfeiture of property constituting or derived from drug offenses or used to commit or facilitate the commission of drug offenses.

a. U.S. Dept. of Justice, Asset Forfeiture Office, 1 Asset Forfeiture: Law, Practice and Policy 1 (1988) citing United States v. Eight (8) Rhodesian Stone Statues, 449 F.Supp. 193 (C.D.Cal.1978).

b. *Id.* at Preface.

c. 18 U.S.C. § 1963.

d. 21 U.S.C. §§ 848, 853.

e. David B. Smith, 1 Prosecution and Defense of Forfeiture Cases §§ 1.01, 13.01

(1993) [hereinafter Smith on Forfeiture] (Smith's treatise is an excellent source on asset forfeiture law.)

f. Relevant provisions of the Act are codified at 18 U.S.C. §§ 981 & 982 (1994).

g. Arthur W. Leach & John G. Malcolm, *Solution to the Debate*, 10 Ga.St.U.L.Rev. 241, 264 (1994) [hereinafter *Solution to the Debate*].

This section will be discussed very little in this casebook. RICO, discussed in Chapter 3, requires forfeiture upon conviction of property acquired or maintained in violation of RICO. Section 982, of title 18, United States Code, requires forfeiture of property involved in or traceable to a specific offense.[h]

When forfeiture is sought as a part of a criminal prosecution, the issues raised by the forfeiture often are intertwined with other issues in the criminal prosecution. Thus, criminal forfeiture issues are addressed primarily in other chapters of this casebook, such as money laundering. This chapter focuses on issues arising in the context of civil forfeiture.

Civil forfeiture has been available to prosecutors since the founding of the United States. Almost all civil forfeiture statutes are "in rem," which means that the object of the lawsuit is the property. To prevail, the government must prove that "the property * * * was used during the commission of a crime or [that] the property constitutes proceeds from a crime."[i] In the 1800's, civil forfeiture statutes were used to protect the neutrality of the United States by seizing and obtaining forfeiture of hostile ships in United States waters.[j] Early civil forfeiture statutes also were used to raise revenue by enforcing payments of customs duties.[k] Because of this early use, civil forfeiture law adopted and still retains many of the procedures of admiralty and customs law.[l]

The government's use of civil forfeiture has been widely criticized. Its critics point to the following aspects of the civil forfeiture process as unfair: (1) the allocation of the burden of proof, (2) the relation back doctrine, and (3) the potential infringement on the Fifth Amendment privilege against self incrimination.

The first criticism arises because the government must simply prove that probable cause exists to believe that property is subject to forfeiture in order to obtain forfeiture under civil statutes. Hearsay evidence may

---

h. Section 982 parallels its civil counterpart, 18 U.S.C. § 981, in some respects. There is a notable difference, however, beyond the fact that § 981 provides for civil forfeiture and § 982 provides for criminal forfeiture. The violations activating forfeiture under § 982 are broader than those under § 981. Although § 982 requires a conviction and § 981 simply requires a violation, both are activated by money laundering offenses, currency transaction reporting offenses; offenses involving the structuring of transactions to avoid reporting requirements; and, offenses involving financial institutions. Section 982 goes further, however, extending forfeiture to conviction of twenty-four enumerated crimes in the federal criminal code (title 18, United States Code). Some of these are white collar crimes: for example §§ 471–481, 485–88, 510 (regarding the counterfeiting securities or currency of the United States); §§ 501–502 (regarding forgery of postage stamps); §§ 542, 545, 842 (customs violations);

§ 1028 (fraud involving identification documents); § 1029 (fraud involving access devices); § 1030 (computer fraud) and various crimes (mail fraud, for example) involving the sale of assets held by FDIC, etc. It is interesting to note that the more widely used white collar crimes in the federal code (such as mail fraud, false statements, false claims) are not included in this list.

i. *Solution to the Debate, supra*, note g at 246.

j. SMITH ON FORFEITURE, *supra*, note e at § 2.01.

k. Arthur W. Leach & John G. Malcolm, *Solution to the Debate, supra* note g at 248–49.

l. Steven L. Schwarcz & Alan E. Rothman, *Civil Forfeiture: A Higher Form of Commercial Law*, 62 FORDHAM L. REV. 287, 291 n.25 (1993) [hereinafter *Higher Form of Commercial Law*].

be used to meet this burden. Once the government has shown probable cause, the burden switches to the party seeking to retain the property. This party must prove, by a preponderance of the evidence, that the property is not subject to forfeiture. Hearsay is not admissible at this stage. If the claimant meets this burden, the government has another chance to demonstrate probable cause, but must use non-hearsay evidence.[m]

The second criticism is directed at the "relation back" doctrine, which describes the government's right of forfeiture as of the time of the illegal act rather than at the time the government initiates or prevails on the forfeiture action.

The third criticism of civil forfeiture focuses on the right against self-incrimination. Critics argue that the government by-passes the fifth amendment's protection against self-incrimination by employing civil forfeiture.[n] Many claimants seeking to protect their property against forfeiture are potential defendants in criminal actions. Anything the claimant asserts in the civil forfeiture action could be used against her in a subsequent prosecution; for this reason a claimant may wish to assert her fifth amendment privilege in the forfeiture proceedings. Doing so, however, risks losing the forfeiture action, since it is permissible in a civil action to draw adverse inferences against a witness who invokes the fifth amendment privilege.[o]

There are a large number of civil forfeiture statutes in American federal law.[p] One of the most commonly used civil forfeiture statutes is 21 U.S.C. § 881. Section 881 forfeitures will be discussed very little in this casebook because they concern property involved in controlled substance offenses. Of more relevance to white collar crime is 18 U.S.C. § 981, the civil counterpart to § 982. Section 981, like § 982, provides for forfeiture of property involved in a transaction or attempted transaction in violation of money laundering offenses, currency transaction reporting offenses, or structuring of transactions to avoid reporting requirements.[q]

m. *Id.* at 254–56.

n. *Id.* at 242.

o. *Id. See* Baxter v. Palmigiano, 425 U.S. 308 (1976) (Although parties to non-criminal proceedings may assert their Fifth Amendment privilege against self-incrimination, *id.* at 316, "the Fifth Amendment does not forbid adverse inferences against parties in civil actions when they refuse to testify in response to probative evidence offered against them. . . . " *id.* at 318).

p. *See e.g.,* 8 U.S.C. § 1324 (regarding forfeitures of conveyances used in offenses involving undocumented aliens); 18 U.S.C. § 981 (regarding forfeitures for money laundering offenses and other offenses affecting financial institutions); 18 U.S.C.

§ 3681–3682 (requiring forfeiture of proceeds from a book, movie, etc. in which otherwise would go to a defendant convicted of a federal crime involving physical harm to an individual); 21 U.S.C. § 881 (regarding drug offenses); 26 U.S.C. § 7302 (property used in violation of the internal revenue laws or regulations); 31 U.S.C. § 5317(c) (forfeiture of property involved for failure to file customs report).

q. None of these offenses must affect a financial institution; however § 981, unlike § 982, specifies that additional violations (of statutes such as 18 U.S.C. §§ 1341, 1343) must affect a financial institution before § 981 is activated.

A. STANDING

The three cases in this section all address standing primarily but also provide helpful examples of how the burden of proof is allocated in civil forfeiture actions. Section B of this chapter will discuss the burden of proof issue in more detail. The first case, United States v. $3,000 in Cash, 906 F.Supp. 1061 (E.D.Va.1995), also introduces the "innocent owner" defense which is discussed more extensively in Section D of this chapter. As you read these cases note the way issues in property and commercial law arise in forfeiture actions.

UNITED STATES v. $3,000 IN CASH

Unites States District Court, Eastern District of Virginia, 1995.
906 F.Supp. 1061.

ELLIS, DISTRICT JUDGE.

This 18 U.S.C. § 981 civil forfeiture action presents two questions concerning who qualifies as an "owner" so as to have standing to invoke the innocent-owner provision of § 981(a)(2). The first is whether one who is at once a victim and a participant in a fraud is barred by the doctrine of unclean hands from asserting an equitable interest in the money he paid in connection with the fraud. The second question is whether one who gives an associate money in connection with a planned commercial real estate venture, knowing that the money will be commingled with the associate's other funds in bank accounts, is a bailor with standing to challenge the forfeiture of the associate's accounts, or merely a general creditor without such standing.

The matter is now before the Court on plaintiff's motion for summary judgment and claimants' various cross-motions for summary judgment. For the reasons that follow, plaintiff's motion is granted and claimants' motions are denied.

This is a tale of audacious international fraud. It serves as a striking reminder that avarice fueled by the lure of easy money can overwhelm good judgment, with costly consequences.

In April 1994, Kurt Moylan, a Guam businessman and former Lieutenant Governor of Guam, was contacted by a person identifying himself as Dr. Benjamin Okafor from Nigeria. Okafor represented himself to be a member of the Nigerian royal family and the second-in-command of the Nigerian National Petroleum Corporation ("NNPC"), a state-owned enterprise. Okafor told Moylan that the predecessor government of Nigeria had "over-invoiced" a construction project by $20 million. Specifically, he explained that a foreign contractor had performed certain construction work for NNPC, and although the firm had billed and been fully paid $30 million, the Nigerian government had already earmarked or released a total of $50 million for the project. According to Okafor, the excess $20 million was being held in an account at the Central Bank of Nigeria ("CBN") and because the money had been designated for payment of a foreign firm, the current Nigerian government could not directly access the funds. For this reason, Okafor explained to Moylan, the current Nigerian government needed the assistance of a foreign firm to retrieve the funds. And this is where Moylan, as the operator of a foreign firm, could help the Nigerian government and, not incidentally, himself. The specifics of the deal, Okafor told Moylan, were that the Nigerian government was willing to pay 40% of the $20 million to Moylan if Moylan would provide an invoice for work done to NNPC in the amount of $20 million and a bank account outside of Nigeria into which the funds could be transferred.

Moylan agreed to the proposal and submitted the requested false invoice on April 20, 1994. This invoice for $20 million stated that his company, Home Financial Corp., had erected "super propylene for Monax axial flow turbine pipes" at a Nigerian refinery, even though, as Moylan admitted in his deposition, none of his companies had ever performed such work. After submission of the false invoice, all that remained, it seemed, was for Moylan to complete the "formal application" for the funds. To this end, Moylan agreed to meet Okafor in Hong Kong in late May 1994 so that Okafor could guide him through the technicalities of the Nigerian formal application documents. In Hong Kong, for the first time, Okafor told Moylan that he would have to pay administrative fees and taxes totaling $1,350,000 before CBN would release the money. Moylan, although initially reluctant, ultimately agreed to pay the requested amount. Okafor said the payments would have to be made to an official Nigerian "money exchanger" and identified Ihedi Uzodinma in Woodbridge, Virginia as such an official. Thereafter, Moylan wired $500,000 from Guam to Uzodinma's account at NationsBank in Virginia in two installments. At Okafor's direction, Moylan wired the remaining $850,000 to an account in England in the name of another money exchanger, George Oxford. On learning the account in England was closed, Moylan wired the $850,000 to Uzodinma in Virginia.

As a result of the large transfers to Uzodinma, an agent of the Federal Bureau of Investigation ("FBI") contacted Moylan on June 20 and inquired about the transfers. In a ten minute conversation with the agent, Moylan outlined the transaction and expressed no concern regarding its legitimacy. At the time, Moylan still believed he would receive the $8 million on June 21. On the morning of June 21, Moylan received a call from Okafor who asked whether he had been contacted about the deal. Because this call followed closely on the heels of the FBI visit, Moylan began to suspect that something was amiss. That afternoon, at 3:45 p.m. in Guam, Moylan received a call from a purported employee of the National Reserve Bank in New York telling him that his money was coming. Rather than soothing Moylan's anxieties, the call further aroused his suspicions because he recognized that the call had to have been made at 1:45 a.m. New York time, a time when Federal Reserve Bank employees were unlikely to be at work. By this time, Moylan had begun to believe he had fallen victim to a fraud. He attempted to recover the money through his local banks and when those efforts failed, he contacted the FBI.

The FBI, as a result of its investigation, arrested Uzodinma in Virginia, and in June 1994 seized $1,291,128.89 in cash and bank accounts related to the fraud. The government has alleged two bases for the forfeiture of this cash. Count I alleges that Okafor used wire communications in a scheme to defraud Moylan, and that after Uzodinma received these proceeds of wire fraud, he engaged in unlawful financial transactions with them in amounts greater than $10,000, thereby rendering the money forfeitable for violations of 18 U.S.C. § 1957. Count II alleges that by wiring the $1,350,000 to Uzodinma to promote a wire fraud against NNPC, Moylan transferred or attempted to transfer the money internationally, thereby rendering it forfeitable for a violation of 18 U.S.C. § 1956(a)(2).

There are three claimants to the funds: Uzodinma, Moylan, and Victor Mbakpuo. Mbakpuo, who for purposes of these motions was wholly unaware of the fraud on Moylan, had given Uzodinma $55,000 in anticipation of joining with him in a commercial real estate joint venture. Uzodinma deposited this sum in various accounts: $30,000 in an account with First Virginia Bank, Fairfax, Virginia and $20,000 in a Third Federal Savings and Loan account in Cleveland, Ohio, both of which accounts were seized by the government, and the remaining $5,000 in an account with Ameribanc, Annandale, Virginia, which account was not seized.

II

The funds in this case were seized pursuant to 18 U.S.C. § 981. Under § 981, the government bears the burden of demonstrating probable cause that a substantial connection exists between the property seized and the underlying criminal activity. This showing can be made on the basis of otherwise inadmissible hearsay. The burden then shifts to the claimant to establish, by a preponderance of the evidence, either that the property was not involved in illegal activity, thereby rebutting the government's showing of probable cause, or that claimant did not know about or consent to the illegal activity, pursuant to the so-called "innocent-owner defense" of 18 U.S.C. § 981(a)(2).[2] But before the innocent-owner defense can be asserted, the claimant "first must demonstrate a sufficient interest in the property to give him Article III standing; otherwise there is no 'case or controversy' in the constitutional sense, capable of adjudication in the federal courts." United States v. $38,000 in United States Currency, 816 F.2d 1538, 1543 (11th Cir.1987). To establish the requisite standing, the claimant must offer some evidence that he is an owner of the seized property.

---

2. The innocent-owner provision states that: No property shall be forfeited under this section to the extent of the interest of an owner or lienholder by reason of any act or omission established by that owner or lienholder to have been committed without the knowledge of that owner or lienholder. 18 U.S.C. § 981(a)(2).

Congress has indicated that the "term 'owner' should be broadly interpreted to include any person with a recognizable legal or equitable interest in the property seized." Even one who merely possessed the seized property might qualify as an "owner." [citations omitted] But despite its liberal interpretation, "owner" does not encompass those with an undefined interest in the seized property. Specifically, an unsecured creditor generally lacks standing to challenge a forfeiture because, while that person may have an interest in the property of the debtor from whom assets were seized, she cannot show that she held an interest in the specific property forfeited. Finally, it is important to note that because the forfeiture statute "contains no rule for determining the scope of property rights, 'it is appropriate to refer to state law in determining the nature of the property interest' involved in a forfeiture proceeding." United States v. Smith, 966 F.2d 1045, 1054 n. 10 (6th Cir.1992).

It now remains to apply these principles to the facts of the case at bar.

III

The government contends Moylan has no standing to invoke the innocent owner provision of 18 U.S.C. § 981(a)(2) because he is merely a general, unsecured creditor and is therefore not an "owner or lienholder" as required by the statute. For his part, Moylan argues, first, that he holds both legal and equitable title to the money and thus is more than a general creditor, and second, that even if he is only a general creditor, he is still an owner for purposes of the statute.

Moylan did not retain legal title to the money he transferred to Uzodinma's accounts. It is well-settled that legal title to money passes with delivery to a person who acquires it in good faith and for valuable consideration. Here, the $1,350,000 was transferred to Uzodinma's NationsBank account. NationsBank accepted the transfers without knowledge of the international fraud and gave valuable consideration for the money in that it became indebted to Uzodinma for the deposited amounts. NationsBank, and not Moylan, therefore held legal title to the seized funds.

Moylan next argues that he holds equitable title to the funds he gave to Uzodinma because he is the beneficiary of a constructive trust. Although not yet decided in this circuit, other circuits have held that claimants have standing to challenge a forfeiture on the theory that they hold equitable title to the property as a result of a constructive trust. Moylan contends that because he was the victim of a fraud, he should be deemed to be the beneficiary of a constructive trust consisting of the money he gave to Uzodinma.[8] This argument fails, for the equitable

---

8. Moylan cites United States v. Benitez, 779 F.2d 135, 140 (2d Cir.1985), as an example of a court creating a constructive trust for the benefit of a fraud victim in a non-forfeiture context. Because the definition of "owner" for purposes of the federal forfeiture statutes incorporates state property law, it would first be necessary to determine which state's law applied here: Virginia's, Guam's, or perhaps some other

remedy of a constructive trust is unavailable to Moylan because he has unclean hands.

A constructive trust arises "by construction of law, being fastened upon the conscience of him who has the legal estate, in order to prevent what would otherwise be a fraud." In re Prime Construction Corp., 156 B.R. 176, 179 (Bankr.E.D.Va.1993). As an equitable doctrine, it is subject to the requirement that "[h]e who comes into equity for relief must come with clean hands." Everett v. Bodwell, 185 Va. 405, 38 S.E.2d 319, 320 (1946). It is well settled that courts "will not permit anyone to reap the benefits of a contract or an agreement, the carrying out of which involves his complicity in any fraudulent act, or any conduct inhibited by sound public policy." Dye v. Dye, 128 W.Va. 754, 39 S.E.2d 98, 107 (1946). Courts will not enforce a constructive trust in order to enable a person "to enforce a right which had grown out of a fraudulent transaction." Ford v. Buffalo Eagle Colliery Co., 122 F.2d 555, 563 (4th Cir.1941).

Here, the undisputed facts in the record reflect that Moylan's hands were far from clean in this transaction.[9] It is undisputed that Moylan provided Okafor with a $20 million invoice for work that Moylan and his firm did not do in order to cause the $20 million to be released. The invoice purported to be from Home Financial Corp., one of Moylan's companies, and sought payment for the construction of super propylene for axial flow turbines for the NNPC. None of Moylan's companies had in fact done any such work, nor had they done any business at all in Nigeria. Even if Moylan believed that Okafor represented the Nigerian government, the false document was clearly intended to deceive someone. Indeed, at the hearing on this matter, counsel for Moylan conceded that the document was meant to deceive certain members of the former Nigerian regime who were still employed by the new government. Regardless of how Moylan might characterize or attempt to justify his decision, the undisputed fact remains that he submitted a false invoice in order to receive $8 million. Submitting that false invoice was no more honest than forging an $8 million check. By any measure, this constitutes unclean hands.

Nor is this the full extent of Moylan's unclean hands. In addition to providing a fraudulent invoice, Moylan provided Okafor with his corporate seal for Okafor to use in "authenticating" a forged signature purporting to be Moylan's. Moylan contends that he did not believe that his signature would be forged, but rather that CBN officials would decide

state's. Second, Moylan would have to prove that the elements necessary for the creation of a constructive trust are met here.

9. Moylan argues that the government has essentially admitted his ownership under Count I because there the government alleges that Moylan was defrauded by Uzodinma, that he was a victim, and that it alleged no wrongdoing on Moylan's part. This argument is unpersuasive. In Count I,

the government lays claim to Uzodinma's money on the theory that the money was involved in a money laundering scheme perpetrated by Okafor. Moylan's culpability is wholly irrelevant to such a theory and the absence of any allegation of wrongdoing by Moylan in Count I does not constitute an admission on the part of the government.

whether the document was sufficient to consummate the transaction with the corporate seal alone. In his deposition, however, he testified to the contrary. * * * Moylan anticipated that his signature would be forged, and he provided Okafor with his seal so that the forgery could be "authenticated." Participation in the forgery bars Moylan from seeking equitable relief.

These undisputed facts demonstrate that Moylan cannot seek equity for he has not "done equity."[11] Accordingly, he cannot be deemed to have an equitable interest in the seized funds.

The remaining question with respect to Moylan is whether he has standing as a general creditor to challenge the forfeiture. In general, an unsecured creditor does not have standing to challenge a forfeiture by way of the innocent-owner provision. Yet, this circuit has indicated the existence of a narrow exception to this general proposition. In United States v. Reckmeyer, 836 F.2d 200, 205–06 (4th Cir.1987), the panel addressed whether a general unsecured creditor may qualify as a third-party claimant under the continuing criminal enterprise forfeiture provision of 21 U.S.C. § 853(n)(2). The panel noted that unsecured creditors hold a legal interest in the debtor's property, but that they typically face a substantial hurdle in making the necessary showing that they possess an interest in the specific property forfeited. Nonetheless, the unanimous panel, speaking through Judge Phillips, held that the petitioner in that case had overcome the hurdle because it was undisputed that all of the debtor's assets had been forfeited. Thus, because petitioner's interest necessarily lay within the estate, petitioner had an interest in the forfeited property.

The government seeks to distinguish *Reckmeyer* on the ground that it involved an *in personam* criminal forfeiture whereas this is a civil *in rem* proceeding. The government makes much of this distinction, but, in this context, it is a distinction without a difference, as the panel itself apparently recognized in relying on civil forfeiture cases in support of its holding. The heart of *Reckmeyer* is that because the debtor's entire estate was forfeited, it was certain that the general creditor's interest was within the forfeited property. That principle would seem to apply equally to both civil and criminal forfeitures, provided a debtor's entire estate has been forfeited.

Moylan argues that *Reckmeyer* is not limited to situations where the debtor's entire estate is forfeited. The point of *Reckmeyer*, Moylan contends, is that where it is possible to link the creditor's interest to the seized property, the creditor has standing to challenge the forfeiture. In *Reckmeyer*, that link was possible because the debtor's entire estate was

---

11. The government also argues that as a matter of public policy Moylan should not be held to have standing to claim any portion of the seized funds. In the government's view, Moylan's position is analogous to that of one who, in an attempt to further an unlawful scheme, gives money to a person whom the first believes to have the same illicit goal, only to find that the recipient is a government agent who has confiscated his money. The government cites several cases for the proposition that, in such circumstances, the payor cannot obtain a refund of the money that was seized.

forfeited. Here, Moylan argues, he can link his claim to the seized assets either by tracing the money he gave Uzodinma into the various seized accounts, or by reasoning that, pursuant to Count I of the Complaint, the assets are subject to forfeiture because of the fraud on Moylan, so Moylan has an interest in all seized funds.

This expansive reading of *Reckmeyer* must be rejected. In no reported case has an unsecured creditor been allowed to challenge a forfeiture apart from showing a legal, equitable, or possessory interest in the seized property. Specifically, no unsecured creditor has been permitted to trace the loaned funds to a particular seized asset. In considering Moylan's suggested expansive reading, it is also important to note that other circuits have rejected *Reckmeyer,* either more or less explicitly. Given this criticism, and that *Reckmeyer* has not been explicitly reaffirmed in light of that criticism, it would seem prudent to limit *Reckmeyer* to its particular facts.

Thus, if Uzodinma were shown to have forfeited his entire estate, *Reckmeyer* might provide Moylan standing to challenge the forfeiture pursuant to 18 U.S.C. § 981(a)(2). It is undisputed, however, that Uzodinma still retains numerous assets: bank accounts and property in Nigeria, a house in Cleveland, and a car, at least. *Reckmeyer*, then, does not save the day for Moylan, and as a general creditor, he is without standing to challenge the forfeiture of the seized assets. Moylan must pursue other means of recovering his money. He may, for example, have a cause of action in tort against Uzodinma. Also, if he believes that as a victim of the fraud he deserves the money seized from Uzodinma, he may file a petition for remission of forfeited property with the Attorney General.

IV

Also at issue is the standing of Mbakpuo. It is undisputed that Mbakpuo gave Uzodinma a total of $55,000 in anticipation of their joint commercial real estate venture. The government contends that the transfer is properly characterized as a loan and Mbakpuo is therefore nothing more than an unsecured creditor, without standing to claim the seized money. Mbakpuo argues that he is a bailor of the funds and that he therefore retained title to the money and should be allowed to trace his payments to the seized funds.

Whether Mbakpuo should be considered a bailor or a creditor turns on the intent of Mbakpuo and Uzodinma in entering into the transaction, as manifested by their conduct and statements and any other relevant evidence. This principle, coupled with a review of the record as a whole, points convincingly to the conclusion that Mbakpuo is a creditor, not a bailor.

First, deposition testimony of Mbakpuo and Uzodinma indicates that the two viewed Mbakpuo as a creditor rather than a bailor. Thus, Mbakpuo stated that he did not know into which account or accounts Uzodinma would deposit the money, nor did it seem to matter to Mbakpuo. In other words, Mbakpuo expected that the money would be commingled with Uzodinma's money, not segregated as in a bailment. In Mbakpuo's own words, "Money is money, you know, and he can deposit money from several sources into one account, you know." Moreover, Mbakpuo apparently viewed himself as a creditor of Uzodinma, with the latter being indebted to him in the amount of $55,000. When asked whether he placed any restrictions on Uzodinma regarding what he could do with the money, Mbakpuo replied, "No, I did not place any restrictions. As far as I know—well, let me answer the question that you did ask. I mentioned before, I knew that he had a home in Cleveland. All I have to do is drag his behind in Court and sell the realty off.... I knew that on demand I would get it.... " Mbakpuo Dep. at 31–32. Uzodinma's deposition testimony similarly reflects that he saw himself as indebted to Mbakpuo for $55,000 and that he did not identify any particular monies as belonging to Mbakpuo. Rather, when Mbakpuo demanded the money, he intended simply to repay Mbakpuo from whatever account or accounts he deemed convenient.

Second, the conclusion that Mbakpuo is a creditor rather than a bailor comports with cases regarding the deposit of money in a bank. In those cases, the presumption is that "funds deposited in a general account immediately become the property of the bank and the bank becomes a debtor of the depositor." Alexander & Jones v. Sovran Bank (In re Nat Warren Contracting Co.), 905 F.2d 716 (4th Cir.1990). A depositor may be a bailor if the deposit is a "special" one, which requires that the money be kept in a separate account and not commingled with other funds. Here, Mbakpuo neither intended nor expected to have returned to him the very same money he transferred to Uzodinma. Indeed he could not have had this intention or expectation since he paid by check. Nor was the money kept in a special account. Rather, the money was deposited in various of Uzodinma's personal accounts and was commingled with Uzodinma's other money, including—unfortunately for Mbakpuo—money from Moylan. Giving Uzodinma money to hold was tantamount to depositing the funds in a bank, making Mbakpuo a creditor rather than a bailor.

Finally, Mbakpuo claims he gave the money to Uzodinma in anticipation of a joint commercial real estate venture. In so doing, he merely made a business investment, not a bailment. Unless that investment matured into some form of legal or equitable interest in some property, Mbakpuo cannot be an owner of any specific property.

In sum, because Mbakpuo is a creditor rather than a bailor, he lacks standing to claim any portion of the seized assets and his claim must be dismissed. At oral argument, Mbakpuo recited an African saying that when two elephants fight, the grass suffers. Mbakpuo likened himself to the grass in this fight between the government and the fraud participants. Even though Mbakpuo is not entitled to assert the innocent-owner defense, the grass may yet survive the trampling it has suffered: Uzodinma appears to be indebted to Mbakpuo in the amount of $55,000, and Mbakpuo must seek repayment from Uzodinma directly.

An appropriate order will issue.

Notes

1. Note that the government sought civil forfeiture of $1,291,128.89 in cash and bank accounts pursuant to 18 U.S.C. § 981 on the ground that these assets were "proceeds traceable to a violation of section 1343 [wire fraud]" and forfeitable as "property involved in a transaction . . . in violation of . . . section 1956 [and] 1957 [money laundering]." Thus, the blending of criminal and civil law: the government must prove by a preponderance of the evidence that crimes (wire fraud and money laundering) were committed.

2. Moylan offered two theories as to why he retained a sufficient interest in the $1,291,128.89 to challenge its forfeiture: that he was the beneficiary of a constructive trust and/or that he was a general creditor. Mbakpuo claimed that as a bailor of $55,000, he had standing to challenge the forfeiture, at least to the $55,000. All arguments were rejected. Recall the following from property law:

● A "constructive trust" is a device used by courts of equity to compel one who unfairly holds a property interest to convey it to another.[r] In other words, if a party obtains a property interest unlawfully or unjustly, equity will take that interest away and return it to the wronged party.[s]

● A "general creditor" is one to whom money is owed. (This compares to a secured creditor which is a creditor whose rights are protected by the legally enforceable promise of delivery of collateral upon failure to repay. Thus, if a debtor refuses to repay a debt owed to a secured creditor, the secured creditor has more protection under the law than does an unsecured or general creditor.[t]) As the court noted a secured creditor is recognized as possessing standing for purposes of challenging forfeiture. Do you see why the court recognizes the narrow exception noted in *Reckmeyer*?

● A "bailor" is one who delivers to another (the "bailee") a thing on condition that "it be restored to the bailor in accordance with his directions as soon as the purpose for which it was bailed is satisfied."[u]

Do you agree with the court that beneficiaries of a constructive trust, a general creditor and a bailor have insufficient interest in property to establish standing to challenge forfeiture of the property?

In the next case, United States v. Contents of Accounts, 971 F.2d 974 (3d Cir. 1992), the government is seeking forfeiture of two brokerage

---

r. GEORGE GLEASON BOGERT & GEORGE TAYLOR BOGERT, THE LAW OF TRUSTS AND TRUSTEES, § 471 (revised 2d ed. 1978).

s. *Id.*

t. *See generally*, UNIFORM COMMERCIAL CODE, Article 9; PETER F. COOGAN ET AL., SECURED TRANSACTIONS UNDER THE UNIFORM COMMERCIAL CODE, § 2.02[3] (1997); *see also* U.C.C. §§ 1–201(12) & (37); Thomas M. Quinn, Quinn's Uniform Commercial Code Commentary and Law Digest ¶ 1–201[A][12] (2d ed. 1991).

u. GEORGE GLEASON BOGERT & GEORGE TAYLOR BOGERT, THE LAW OF TRUSTS AND TRUSTEES, § 11 n.5 (Supp. 1996) (*quoting* Temple v. McCaughen & Burr, 839 S.W.2d 322, 326 (Mo.App.1992)).

accounts held with Merrill, Lynch, Pierce, Fenner & Smith in the name of Friko Corporation (Friko). The government is proceeding under 18 U.S.C. § 981, alleging that the proceeds in two accounts resulted from financial transactions designed to avoid currency transaction reporting requirements.

UNITED STATES v. CONTENTS OF ACCOUNTS

United States Court of Appeals, Third Circuit, 1992.
971 F.2d 974.

HUTCHINSON, CIRCUIT JUDGE.

* * *

Following a criminal indictment filed in the United States District Court for the District of New Jersey alleging money laundering against, *inter alia*, Julio Montes Cardona (Cardona), [Johnny] Daccarett, Friko, and Quasil International Corporation (Quasil), the government filed an amended complaint for civil forfeiture in rem against Friko's accounts 3034504504 (the credit card account) and 144–07143 (the brokerage account) (collectively "the accounts") at Merrill, Lynch, Pierce, Fenner & Smith (the broker) in New York, New York on May 14, 1990 in the United States District Court for the District of New Jersey. A seizure warrant for the arrest of the brokerage account was then served on the broker in the United States District Court for the Southern District of New York. The credit card account had already been arrested.

* * *

This forfeiture is part of the government's efforts to halt money laundering by drug dealers in the United States. According to the government, after drug dealers in the United States with suppliers in South America collect the cash proceeds of their illicit sales they face the problem of transferring money back to South America to pay the suppliers. Our federal banking laws are structured to minimize the use of our banking system to channel these illegal cash proceeds to South America.

Accordingly, any time a financial institution is involved in an all cash transaction that exceeds an amount specified by a banking regulation, it must be reported by the financial institution involved. See 31 U.S.C.A. § 5313 (West 1983). Current regulations require cash transactions exceeding $10,000.00 to be reported. See 31 C.F.R. § 103.22(a)(1) (1991). If the reporting requirement is not observed, criminal penalties are imposed. 31 U.S.C.A. § 5322 (West Supp.1992). It is also illegal to structure transactions intentionally to avoid the financial institution's reporting requirement. Id. § 5324 (West Supp.1992). Thus, systematic cash deposits in an amount less than $10,000.00 that are made for the purpose of avoiding section 5313's bank reporting requirement subjects the depositor to that section's criminal penalties. Purchasing money orders and then depositing the money orders in a bank account in order to avoid the section 5313 reporting requirement also subjects the depositor to section 5324's penalties.

Friko was formed in September of 1980. Its principal directors and corporate officers were all members of the Daccarett family. Jorge Daccarett, Friko's Secretary, has signed an authorization that allows Johnny and Delia Daccarett to obligate the company. Friko opened the accounts in question in Panama in October of 1983 and believed them to be located there. In fact, the brokerage account is held in New York, while certain free credit balances are held in the United Kingdom.[2]

The indictment charged that Cardona ran a money laundering operation in New Jersey and that Friko, Daccarett and Quasil, a Panamanian company owned by Daccarett, inter alia, participated in that operation. The investigation uncovered evidence that substantial sums passed between the accounts of Quasil[v] and Friko. Quasil's Florida accounts show deposits from the Cardona money laundering operation of 351 money orders of small denominations totaling $224,000.00 over an eight-month period, many of which were sequentially numbered. Moreover, a $41,000.00 check from Friko's brokerage account was used to open a New York savings account by Luis Saad, who also had dealings with the Cardona operation and another Quasil account in Panama. The government states that its investigation has not uncovered any business activities for Friko or Quasil except for a series of transactions in various bank accounts on which they are shown as holders of legal title.

Friko "present[s] itself as a money exchanger in Colombia['s] parallel market." In support it presented an affidavit of Mohammad Haris Jafri, an economist formerly with the International Money Fund. Jafri stated that South American businesses frequently hold dollars in American banks as a hedge against the volatility of South American currencies. Saad also filed an affidavit on Friko's behalf. He stated that he worked for his father's textile business and went regularly to New York to buy textiles. Saad says he had no cash to buy the textiles because his money was all tied up in certificates of deposit, when Daccarett, a friend of Saad's father, helped him out by giving him $41,000.00 for the purpose of buying textiles. The $41,000.00 was Saad's initial deposit in his New York account. Saad said he has repaid Daccarett.

Friko and Daccarett were named as defendants in the Cardona indictment. While Daccarett himself did not enter an appearance, he signed a corporate resolution that authorized an appearance for Friko as a defendant in the Cardona criminal case. The government subsequently chose to dismiss Friko from the criminal case on October 19, 1990 but continued to proceed on its civil forfeiture action against the accounts

2. The parties do not tell us how these free credit balances arose, the nature of the rights they evidence or the persons entitled to those rights. In any event, the "free credit balances," like the accounts, are not located in New Jersey. If they are located in the United Kingdom, we leave to the dis- trict court any question concerning its subject matter jurisdiction over them. * * *

v. The government alleged that Quasil was a Panamanian company owned by Daccarett.

Friko claims it owns. At the time the accounts were seized, Friko says they had a balance totaling more than $1,700,000.00.

After the district court held that Friko was a straw man for Daccarett and struck its claim, Friko, in support of its motion for reargument, submitted an affidavit from Isidoro Rodriguez (Rodriguez), a member of the Virginia bar as well as Friko's lawyer in Colombia. Rodriguez stated that Daccarett is the "Legal Representative" for two of Colombia's one-hundred largest exporters and that the combined trans-actions of these two exporters totaled over $9,000,000.00 in the first half of 1990. Rodriguez also swore that Friko was formed to help facilitate these transactions and that Friko's initial capitalization came from the sale of another Daccarett-family-owned business. Finally, he represented that Friko "is capable of presenting documentation to establish its legal and equitable interest in the property seized."

* * *

In forfeiture, as elsewhere, we must distinguish between standing conferred by statute and the standing requirements of Article III to the Constitution. Article III standing requires the claimant to show an interest in the property sufficient to create a "case or controversy," while statutory standing requires claimants to comply with certain procedures. Friko maintains that it has fulfilled both the statutory and constitutional prerequisites for standing. It again relies on the Supple-mental Rules and contends they provide the only statutory prerequisite for standing is the filing of a claim.[7] If so, when Friko filed its claim to obtain standing, it has complied with the only formality required.[8] Friko goes on to assert that it also has Article III standing because it holds legal title to the accounts.

The government does not dispute Friko's statutory standing under Supplemental Rule C(6). Thus, we are left with the question whether Friko had Article III standing.

The government concedes Friko's legal title but then questions its legal existence as an entity apart from Daccarett, as if Daccarett, masked and cloaked in the garments of Friko, had stolen, incognito, onto our shores. According to the government, it is Daccarett's standing that is in question, and the government contends that he has none because he is a fugitive whose access to court is precluded by the fugitive disentitlement doctrine.

Article III standing is commonly associated with an inquiry into injury-in-fact, causation, redressability and other prudential factors, see, e.g., Warth v. Seldin, 422 U.S. 490, 498–502 (1975), but the inquiry is more focused in forfeiture cases. Courts generally do not deny standing

7. Supplemental Rule C(6) requires that "[t]he claimant of property that is the sub-ject of an action in rem shall file a claim." Supp.R. C(6).

8. Even though this is not an admiralty or maritime claim, the Supplemental Rules apply to this action because the forfeiture statutes provide an action analogous to a maritime action in rem.

to a claimant who is either the colorable owner of the res or who has any colorable possessory interest in it. We see little analytic difference between *Warth's* approach and the owner-possessor approach in forfeiture cases. An owner or possessor of property that has been seized necessarily suffers an injury that can be redressed, at least in part, by return of the seized property.

* * *

Though it is undisputed that Friko had legal title to the seized account, "courts have uniformly rejected standing claims put forward by nominal or straw owners. Thus, even possession of legal title to the res may be insufficient to establish standing to contest the forfeiture." Case law is in accord * * *. In United States v. One 1981 Datsun 280ZX, 563 F.Supp. 470 (E.D.Pa.1983), the court disregarded a car's legal title and denied a father standing because it was his son who stood "to suffer from the Datsun's forfeiture." Id. at 475. The court relied on evidence that the car was referred to as the son's, that the son frequently drove the car but the father did not, that the car was "turbocharged and capable of great speed" but the father was 72 years old and suffered from a heart condition and that the father did not pay for the car. *Id.* Thus, though the car was kept at the father's house and the father held legal title to it, the district court held the father did not have standing to contest the forfeiture because the son exercised dominion and control over the car. *Id.* at 476.

* * *

In this case, the district court was faced with a subtly different issue. The government not only argued that Daccarett actually exercised dominion and control over the money in Friko's accounts, it also argued that Daccarett was, for all intents and purposes, Friko. That distinction does not change our analysis.

Once the government made out a *prima facie* case, Friko had the burden of establishing its independent power to control the accounts. The government's evidence persuaded the district court that the New York accounts in Friko's name were linked to money laundering. It noted that Friko's directors were all members of Daccarett's family and that it was Daccarett himself who had authorized Friko to file its claim while he remained in Colombia, safe from prosecution. This evidence was enough to meet the government's initial burden and shift to Friko the burden of coming forward with some evidence to show that it had independent existence and could exercise dominion and control over the account independent of Daccarett.

Friko's efforts to rebut the government's evidence that Daccarett, not it, actually owned and controlled the accounts were feeble. It relied in large part on Jafri's affidavit describing the parallel market for dollars in Colombia and his assertion that Colombian businessmen customarily hold dollars in United States banks. Jafri's affidavit tells us nothing about Friko's identity vis-a-vis Daccarett; it only describes the practice of Colombian businessmen in transactions exchanging foreign currencies for dollars. Friko also offered the affidavit of accountant H. Charles Hess (Hess), to rebut the government's evidence on Friko's lack of existence apart from Daccarett. Hess merely attested to Friko's incorporation and the opening of the accounts in question. His affidavit said nothing about Friko or Daccarett's operations in the business world. Saad's affidavit, the final piece of evidence Friko submitted before entry of the order striking its claim, asserts only that Daccarett was in the textile business. Saad says nothing about Friko's business. Friko's documentary evidence verifies its formation as a corporation, its power to open the seized accounts and to litigate this claim, but it does not tend to show that Friko itself conducts any kind of trade or business beyond holding legal title to various accounts, nor to establish Friko's existence independent of Daccarett.

If Friko had an independent existence, it should have presented evidence of legitimate business dealings in its own right. For example, if Friko were engaged in exchanging pesos for dollars in the parallel market, it should have been able to produce evidence of transactions with currency traders other than those the record shows as linked to the laundering of drug proceeds. Under the circumstances, the district court's finding that Friko was a straw owner of accounts owned and controlled by Daccarett was not clearly erroneous. Therefore, it did not err in entering the order of April 8, 1991, striking Friko's claim for lack of standing to contest the seizure.[9]

Notes

1. Note, once again, the interplay of criminal and civil law. The government has brought a civil suit in which it must prove its case by a preponderance of the evidence, but part of what the government must prove is that the property it seeks to forfeit was involved in certain crimes (here, structuring financial transactions so as to avoid currency transaction reporting requirements).

Note also that all of the significant players in the structuring offense which serves as the basis for forfeiture were also indicted. Immediately following indictment, the complaint for civil forfeiture against the brokerage accounts was filed, pursuant to 18 U.S.C. § 981. As noted in the introducto-

---

9. Once the district court determined Friko was a straw man for Daccarett, it applied the fugitive disentitlement doctrine since Daccarett had not appeared for his criminal proceeding. The district court declared he was a fugitive who could not challenge the forfeiture. On appeal, the parties continue to dispute the application of the fugitive disentitlement doctrine in the forfeiture context. We do not need to reach this question because Daccarett has not filed a claim pursuant to Supplemental Rule C(6) and he therefore lacks statutory standing. However, even if we were presented with the issue, we believe the holding of the United States Court of Appeals for the Second Circuit that fugitive disentitlement does apply in forfeiture proceedings is persuasive.

ry comments to this chapter, under 18 U.S.C. § 982, the government would obtain forfeiture of these accounts if it prevailed in its criminal case. A major advantage of proceeding under § 982 rather than § 981 is consolidation of everything—the criminal case and the forfeiture—into one proceeding. Given this advantage, why do you think the government filed the civil forfeiture complaint?

2. Both *$3,000 in Cash* and *Contents of Accounts* demonstrate how the burden of proof works in civil forfeiture actions: the government must present probable cause to believe that a substantial connection exists between property seized and the underlying criminal activity. The burden then shifts to the claimant to demonstrate, by a preponderance of the evidence, that the property was not involved in illegal activity or that the claimant was an "innocent owner" of the property. Before the claimant may raise either of these arguments, however, the claimant must prove that it has standing. This can be done only by offering evidence that the claimant is an "owner," for civil forfeiture purposes. As the court in *$3,000 in Cash* noted, Congress has indicated that "owner" should be interpreted broadly in the civil forfeiture context. However, the courts in the above opinions held that general unsecured creditors, beneficiaries of constructive trusts and bailors have no standing (*$3,000 in Cash*); nor does the holder of legal title in the property (*All Accounts*). Do you agree that the claimants have an inadequate interest to qualify for standing? Are the above decisions consistent with Congress' admonition that "owner" should be interpreted broadly in the civil forfeiture action?

B. THE GOVERNMENT'S BURDEN

As discussed in *United States v. $3,000 in Cash*, *supra*, the government bears the burden of "demonstrating probable cause that a substantial connection exists between the property seized and the underlying criminal activity." Once the government has shown this, the property is ordered forfeited unless the claimant comes forward and defeats the government's showing of probable cause or demonstrates that the claimant is an "innocent owner." The next two cases discuss these burdens. In the first case, *In re Seizure of All Funds*, 887 F.Supp. 435 (E.D.N.Y. 1995), the government failed to meet its burden. As a side point, when you read *Seizure of All Funds*, note the interplay between the on-going criminal investigation and the civil forfeiture action. In the second case, *United States v. $448,342.85*, the government successfully proved "a substantial connection * * * between the property seized and the underlying criminal activity," albeit in a circumstantial manner. As you read both cases note the strategy of the claimants. What pre-trial investigation would help them pursue their strategy?

IN RE THE SEIZURE OF ALL FUNDS IN ACCOUNTS IN THE NAMES REGISTRY PUBLISHING

United States District Court, Eastern District of New York, 1995.
887 F.Supp. 435.

SPATT, DISTRICT JUDGE.

The methods of contemporary telemarketing have become sophisticated in the "information age," relying a great deal on demographic statistics and public opinion surveys. One popular method used in telemarketing is selecting potential customers from mailing list data bases that have been refined to delineate their addressees by any number of possible criteria and characteristics. Indeed, such lists are so fundamental and useful in direct mail advertising or contribution solicitation that they are bought and sold through brokers in an open market, much like other commodities.

Moreover, to survive in today's competitive business environment some businesses utilize aggressive telemarketing techniques. The character of such techniques, often accompanied by bodacious hyperbole, at times borders on deceit and creates a shady area between sharp sales practice and criminal fraud.

In the present case, the Court is asked to determine whether a business using refined mailing lists to aggressively solicit customers for inclusion in its version of a "Who's Who" registry crossed the hazy line from sharp sales practice to criminal fraud. The Government contends that the line was crossed, and has seized certain of the companies' bank accounts, totalling an estimated $511,731. On the other hand, the companies contend that at the worst their conduct constituted sales "puffery," but not criminal fraud. They move to dismiss the *in rem* seizure warrant on the ground that no crime has been committed, and cry foul at the Government's *ex parte* seizure of their bank accounts, which they contend has virtually destroyed their business.

* * *

The companies involved in this case are Who's Who Worldwide Registry, Inc. ("Worldwide"), Sterling Who's Who, Inc. ("Sterling"), Who's Who Executive Club, Who's Who Worldwide Communications, Tribute Magazine, Registry Publishing, Inc., Publishing Ventures, Inc., Who's Who of Retailers, and William's Who's Who (collectively the "Companies").

Bruce Gordon ("Gordon") founded the Companies with investment capital supplied by his brother and sister-in-law (Gordon and the Companies are also collectively referred to as the "Petitioners"). Gordon does not own the Companies, but he does control them. The Companies are not affiliated in any way with the entity that originally published the "Who's Who" directory in the United States, Marquis Who's Who, which is presently owned and published by Reed Elsevier, Inc. ("Reed Elsevier"). Indeed, because of Gordon's use of the term "Who's Who" in his companies' names, Reed Elsevier commenced a civil action against Worldwide under section 43(a) of the Lanham Act, 15 U.S.C. § 1125(a) for trademark infringement and false designation of origin. That case was tried by consent of the parties before former United States Magistrate Judge David F. Jordan, who issued a decision on March 31, 1994 finding that Reed Elsevier's mark was infringed, and among other things awarding $1,649,000 in damages to Reed Elsevier. As a result of not being able to satisfy the judgment Worldwide filed a petition for Chapter 11 bankruptcy protection. Judge Jordan's decision is presently being appealed to the United States Court of Appeals for the Second Circuit.

Gordon incorporated Worldwide in November, 1989. The business originally entailed publishing "Who's Who Worldwide Registry" ("Worldwide Registry"), and soliciting customers to purchase a membership in the registry. Customers designated for solicitation were selected by using various mailing lists of corporate executives and other professional people. Described in more detail later in this opinion, the solicitation process used by Gordon consists of sending a letter to the potential customer, informing them that they had been "nominated" for inclusion in the registry, and that their inclusion in the registry has been confirmed by Worldwide's officers. The letter also states, among other things, that (i) the Worldwide Registry is a leading publication of accomplished individuals, (ii) inclusion in the registry is limited to exceptional people who are prominent or successful in their field, and (iii) that inclusion in the registry is without cost or obligation to the customer. The solicitation letter also includes a biographical questionnaire for the customer to complete and return, if they wish to be considered for inclusion in the registry.

After receiving the biographical information, the company contacts the customer and aggressively solicits them to purchase a membership in the registry. Membership includes receiving a copy of the bound volume of Worldwide Registry, which lists all of the members and certain biographical information in coded form. The salesperson making the membership solicitation to the customer reiterates that membership in the Worldwide Registry is selective and prestigious. Networking among Worldwide Registry members is also stressed as a unique aspect of membership. In order to make the purchase more attractive, members are also offered a commemorative plaque and camera ready art as part of a membership purchase.

Customers can purchase lifetime, five-year, three-year, corporate or associate membership. Listing in a registry is classified according to the type of membership bought. A typical entry in the Executive Club Registry is as follows:

MORALES, J.M. President & Principal, Micro–Bac International Inc., 9607 Gray Boulevard, Austin, Tx Bus: Biotechnology, P/S: Para–Bac Oil Field Products, Org: Research & Development, MA:

Worldwide, Exp: Degradation of Substance, FM: Forbes, FV: Mexico, H/S: Traveling/Football. Who's Who Executive Club Registry 1994–1995, at 101.

A listing of codes at the beginning of the registry explains that "Bus" refers to type of business, "P/S" to major product or service, "Org" to type of organization, "MA" to marketing area, "Exp" to expertise, "FM" to favorite magazine, "FV" to favorite vacation place, and "H/S" to favorite hobbies and sports.

In addition to receiving a free registry, wall plaque and camera ready art, Gordon's Companies offered members a host of other support services, such as a subscription to a magazine entitled Tribute, a Gold MasterCard, public relations services, discounts on telephone service, and airborne express service. Gordon used two offices for his business operations; one in Lake Success, New York and on Lexington Avenue in Manhattan, New York.

* * *

Based on complaints regarding the Companies' business practices received from, among others, the New York State Department of Law, the New York State Consumer Protection Board and the Better Business Bureau, the United States Postal Inspection Service ("Postal Service") commenced an investigation of Gordon and his companies in July, 1994.* * *

The investigation culminated in a 115 page complaint and affidavit ("Complaint"), sworn to by Postal Inspector Martin T. Biegelman ("Biegelman") and dated March 22, 1995. The Complaint concludes that based on the Postal Service's investigation, the Companies' business operations constituted a "telemarketing boiler room" operation using "high pressure telephone sales pitches that misrepresent the identity of the Company and the nature of the products in order to defraud customers into purchasing one of the Company's 'Who's Who' directories and other products." According to Biegelman, since 1989 Gordon and the Companies have defrauded customers of approximately $22 million dollars. The Complaint charges that the Companies' use of the mail and telephones to make the solicitations was in furtherance of a scheme to defraud people, and constitutes a violation of the mail and wire fraud statute, 18 U.S.C. §§ 1341 and 1343.

* * *

Grounded upon Biegelman's Complaint, on March 22, 1995, United States Magistrate Judge Joan M. Azrack signed warrants for the arrest of Gordon and twenty nine of the Companies' salespersons. On March 29, 1995, the United States obtained an ex parte warrant of seizure pursuant to Rule 41 of the Federal Rules of Criminal Procedure from Judge Azrack, authorizing the seizure of funds on deposit in certain of the Companies' bank accounts. According to the affidavit in support of the seizure warrant, sworn to by Biegelman, the funds on deposit in the accounts are controlled by Gordon, and contain the proceeds of his alleged fraud scheme. The Government contends that these funds are subject to forfeiture pursuant to 18 U.S.C. §§ 981(a)(1)(A) and (C), because they are, respectively, transactions or attempted transactions at money laundering, and are the proceeds of mail and wire fraud.

* * *

On April 10, 1995, Gordon and his Companies brought an Order to Show Cause challenging the legality of the seizure, and seeking the return of the seized property pursuant to Fed.R.Civ.P. 41(e). The essential contention of the Petitioners' motion is that the criminal Complaint should be dismissed and the seized property be released because no crimes were committed. According to the Petitioners, there is no probable cause for believing that mail and wire fraud were committed, and, therefore, the accounts are not forfeitable and thus not subject to seizure.

* * *

The Petitioners contend that, even if, arguendo, some fraud was committed, it was limited to a small amount of customers. In the Petitioners' view, the proceeds traceable to such a minuscule amount of fraud does not warrant a seizure of the magnitude conducted by the Government in this case. Moreover, the Petitioners contend that some seized funds should be released to allow the Petitioners to continue their business and pay counsel fees. If release of funds is not granted expeditiously, the Petitioners maintain that the Companies will be forced out of business.

* * *

In addition, the Petitioners claim that a letter sent to members of the Worldwide and Sterling Registries by Biegelman after the arrests on March 30 and March 31, 1995, which announces the arrests on charges of mail and wire fraud and includes a five-page questionnaire regarding the member's experience with the Companies, is premature, reckless, and has irreparably damaged the Companies' business. The Petitioners also challenge an administrative complaint filed by the Postal Service against Gordon, Worldwide and Sterling, which seeks the issuance of orders that would prevent delivery of mail to the Companies and forbid the Postmaster General to pay any money orders drawn on the Companies. According to the Petitioners, these actions by the Postal Service are part of a deliberate and concerted effort to destroy the Companies' business prior to any determination of the merits of the criminal charges.

The Petitioners' motion seeks the following relief: (1) an order directing the Government to return all bank accounts and other property seized, or alternatively, an immediate hearing or the propriety of the seizure and/or release of part of the funds for the Companies' ordinary and necessary business and counsel expenses; (2) an order directing the Government, and the United States Postal Inspectors, to cease contacting and sending questionnaires to members and customers of Who's Who Worldwide and Sterling Who's Who, and to cease disseminating information to the public about arrests and charges relating to Gordon's Companies; * * * and (3) an order directing an accounting for damages incurred by reason of the alleged improper Government conduct.

On the other hand, the Government contends that fraud has indeed been committed, because the Companies have knowingly made false and misleading statements during solicitations in order to fraudulently induce customers to purchase their Who's Who registries. According to the Government, the Companies misrepresent, among other things, the selectivity, uniqueness and quality of the registries they publish, and the benefits of membership in such registries. The Government argues that probable cause exists to believe the accounts are the proceeds of mail and wire fraud.

* * *

Because an indictment has not been filed in the related criminal actions, the Government further contends that the Petitioners are not entitled to a probable cause hearing with respect to the necessity of obtaining some of the seized money in order to pay for their counsel. * * *

* * *

In order for property to be seized, the government must have probable cause to believe that the seized property is subject to forfeiture. Property is subject to forfeiture if it is the fruit or proceeds of illegal activity. To demonstrate probable cause, the government must prove a nexus between the property and the illegal activity.

Despite their interconnectedness, seizure and forfeiture remain two distinct statutory events. While each event requires the government to have probable cause, different consequences for each event flow from the government's failure to establish probable cause. Failure of the government to establish that there was probable cause at the time of the seizure only results in suppression of evidence gained from the improper seizure in later proceedings. The defendant property, however, itself is immune from suppression and remains subject to forfeiture. On the other hand, failure by the government to establish probable cause on the forfeiture issue, namely, failure to establish probable cause that the property is connected to illegal activity, will result in dismissal of the forfeiture action.

Generally, the government is not required to demonstrate probable cause for seizing property until the forfeiture trial. However, if a claimant challenges the validity of a seizure, as the Petitioners have done here, then the merits of the forfeiture trial are expedited and the government must establish probable cause for the forfeiture prior to the forfeiture trial. Accordingly, the Government must demonstrate here that it had probable cause to believe that the accounts seized are subject to forfeiture.

A hearing requiring the Government to show probable cause is also triggered in certain situations prior to the filing of an indictment when funds are sought from the seized res in order to pay counsel fees for the criminal case underlying the seizure and forfeiture. The standards governing such a hearing were set forth by the Second Circuit in U.S. v. Monsanto, 924 F.2d 1186 (2d Cir.1991): We conclude that (1) the fifth and sixth amendments, considered in combination, require an adversary, post-restraint, pre-trial hearing as to probable cause that (a) the defendant committed the crimes that provide the basis for forfeiture, and (b) the properties specified as forfeitable in the indictment are properly forfeitable, to continue a restraint of assets (i) needed to retain counsel of choice and (ii) ordered ex parte ... (2) ... the Court may receive and consider at such a hearing evidence and information that would be inadmissible under the Federal Rules of Evidence; and (3) grand jury determinations of probable cause may be reconsidered in such a hearing. *Id.* at 1195, 1203. *Monsanto's* holding has been extended to require a probable cause hearing in a civil forfeiture case, where the claimant is also a defendant in the related criminal matter.

As mentioned previously, in order to establish probable cause, the government must demonstrate a nexus between the seized property and the illegal activity. To demonstrate such a nexus when the res seized is a bank account, the government must establish that there is probable cause to believe the funds represent proceeds traceable to the illegal activity. The government is not required to link the bank account to a particular illegal activity. Rather, "[p]robable cause is established if the government can show that it has reasonable grounds, more than mere suspicion, to believe that the property is subject to forfeiture," namely, that the funds represent the proceeds of criminal activity. *See* Marine Midland Bank, N.A. v. U.S., 11 F.3d 1119, 1126 (2d Cir.1993).

Moreover, particularly in cases involving bank accounts, a finding of probable cause may be based on hearsay, including hearsay from confidential informants or circumstantial evidence. In addition, great deference is paid to the probable cause determinations of magistrate judges and judges who issue warrants. Any doubts are resolved in favor of upholding the warrant, and all of the evidence is construed in a light most favorable to the government.

Finally, after the government establishes probable cause, the burden shifts to the claimant to demonstrate by a preponderance of the evidence that the property is not subject to forfeiture, because it was not used unlawfully or because the illegal use was without the claimant's knowledge or consent. If the res is a bank account, the claimant bears the burden of proving that the account does not contain proceeds traceable to the criminal activity, but "rather represents legitimate funds."

The Court wishes to pause at this point in order to highlight several matters. First, the bank accounts at issue in this case were seized pursuant to a seizure warrant issued by [Magistrate] Judge Azrack under Fed.R.Civ.P. 41(c)(1), on a determination of probable cause based on the contents of Biegelman's affidavit and Complaint. Interestingly, a forfeiture action has not yet been commenced by the Government. Moreover, a grand jury investigation into the criminal allegations continues and there have not been any indictments of the persons arrested in connection with the Companies' operations. As stated above, one such person arrested has pleaded guilty to an information, pursuant to a cooperation agreement.

Second, the Petitioners challenge the validity of the seizure under Fed.R.Civ.P. 41(e), and have requested that counsel fees be released from the seized accounts to pay for Gordon's defense in the related criminal proceedings.

Accordingly, in this Court's view, a hearing in which the Government is obligated to show that it had probable cause to believe the accounts seized are subject to forfeiture is required, under the rule of both *Marine Midland*, 11 F.3d at 1125, and *Monsanto*, 924 F.2d at 1203.

In the present case, the Petitioners rely on two grounds to assert that the Government lacks probable cause to believe that the seized proceeds are connected to the alleged mail and wire fraud. First, the Petitioners contend that any misrepresentations contained in the solicitation letters or made by the salespersons in telephone calls constitute "mere puffing," and do not give rise to a violation of the mail fraud or wire fraud statutes. Second, they contend that, even assuming a violation of these statutes, the payments made by the alleged victims of the fraud cannot be traced to the seized bank accounts.

Because the elements of mail and wire fraud are essentially the same, the Court will conduct its analysis of probable cause under the mail fraud statute.

* * *

The federal mail fraud statute provides in relevant part that a person is guilty of mail fraud, if, having devised or intending to devise any scheme or artifice to defraud, or for obtaining money or property by means of false or fraudulent pretenses, representations, or promises ... for the purpose of executing such scheme or artifice or attempting so to do, [the person] places in any post office or authorized depository for mail matter, any matter or thing whatever to be sent or delivered by the Postal Service, or takes or receives therefrom, any such thing[.] 18 U.S.C. § 1341.

The elements of mail fraud necessary to establish the offense are (1) a scheme or artifice to defraud, (2) for the purpose of obtaining money or property, or of depriving another of an intangible right of honest services, and (3) use of the mails in furtherance of the scheme.

A "scheme or artifice to defraud" under the statute is interpreted broadly, and includes everything designed to defraud by representations as to the past or present, or suggestions and promises as to the future. The scheme to defraud need not have been successful or complete, and the victims need not have been injured. Rather, "the government must show 'that some actual harm or injury was *contemplated* by the schemer.' " U.S. v. D'Amato, 39 F.3d 1249, 1257 (2d Cir.1994).

In order for the statute to be violated in the context of solicitations to purchase a product, the alleged fraud must concern facts material to the bargain the potential customer is induced to enter through the seller's representations. The seminal case in this regard is United States v. Regent Office Supply Co., 421 F.2d 1174, 1180 (2d Cir.1970).

* * *

In attempting to delineate the boundary line between puffing and fraud, the Second Circuit in *Regent* first explained that in discerning whether a particular practice constitutes fraud or an aggressive sales tactic, courts were to consider the realities of the market and contemporary business sales practice. The court then explained that mail fraud can only exist when the seller's representations mislead the buyer as to the quality or effectiveness of the product, or as to the advantages or future benefits accruing to the purchaser when such benefits cannot realistically be ascertained:

> The most nearly analogous cases sustaining convictions for mail fraud have involved sales tactics and representations which have tended to mislead the purchaser, or prospective purchaser, *as to the quality or effectiveness of the thing being sold, or to mislead him with regard to the advantages of the bargain which should accrue to him. Thus claims or statements in advertising may go beyond mere puffing and enter the realm of fraud where the product must inherently fail to do what is claimed for it. And promotion of an inherently useful item may also be fraud when the scheme of promotion is based on claims of additional benefits to accrue to the customer, if the benefits as represented are not realistically attainable by the customer.*

Regent, 421 F.2d at 1180 (emphasis supplied).

Moreover, the *Regent* court rejected the government's contention that, even though the purchasers received what they bargained for, the sales tactics by the defendants' agents constituted a fraudulent scheme because the customers struck a bargain without knowledge of all of the facts.* * *

Ultimately, the court in *Regent* concluded that the defendants had not conducted a scheme to defraud within the meaning of the mail fraud statute. Although the Court determined that the agents' misrepresentations were intended to deceive their customers, they were not intended to defraud them, because

> the falsity of their representations was not shown to be capable of affecting the customer's understanding of the bargain nor of the influencing his assessment of the value of the bargain to him, and thus no injury was shown to flow from the deception. *Id.* at 1182.

The Petitioners [in the present case] contend that the Companies' representations concerning the "nomination" of the customer being solicited for membership, the "selectivity" of the nomination process, the reputation and quality of the Companies, and value of the registries and membership for business networking, the representations in the pitch sheets, and the many other representations cited by the government are not fraudulent within the meaning of the mail fraud statute. In the Petitioners' view, most of these representations are not false. In other cases, the representations are puffery and are a way of securing the attention of the customer, similar in all respects to the representations in *Regent* that were held not to constitute a basis for mail fraud. According to the Petitioners, the representations in this case cannot provide a basis for probable cause to seize the accounts, because the elements of the underlying crimes of mail and wire fraud—which require a scheme to defraud—cannot be established as a matter of law.

The Government disagrees, and contends that the representations are false, and in violation of the mail and wire fraud statutes. According to the Government, the Companies' false representations are directed at the quality, adequacy and price of the products being sold. Moreover, the Government contends that the alleged victim is made to bargain without facts that are essential in deciding whether he or she should enter into the transaction and purchase a membership. The Government believes that, based on the Complaint and hearing testimony, it has "more than amply" demonstrated probable cause.

Before discussing the allegations raised in the Government's Complaint, the Court believes it is necessary to state exactly what the "bargain" is in this case. The underlying transactions occur in the following sequence: a person, usually selected from a mailing list, is first contacted by a letter stating, among other things, that he or she has been "nominated" for inclusion in one of the registries by a member of the registry or by some other process, and that the nomination has been approved by some official committee, usually pending receipt of the biographical data form the nominee is asked to return. If the person responds by sending in the biographical data form, they are then solicited by telephone to purchase a membership. If they decline to purchase a membership, they may still be listed in the registry as a "Listee," provided there is space. The actual monetary transaction that would constitute the basis for a mail fraud claim, however, occurs when the membership is purchased.

The Court believes that the membership purchase transaction is the "bargain"—the exchange of mutual promises and consideration—that the customer enters into with the Company. In addition, the Court is of the view that this bargain entails not only purchasing membership in a registry that the member will be listed in and which will be sent to the member. A membership purchase also includes the availability of other services or products that either accompany the purchase free of charge, such as camera ready art with the Worldwide logo and a personalized plaque, or services that are extended to the member under the auspices of the Companies for a cost, such as a Gold MasterCard, a subscription to Tribute magazine, overnight airborne express at discount rates, telephone service at discount rates, media/public relations services at discount rates, and use of a business center for networking. The Government acknowledges that these additional services were made available to members. Thus, any analysis of what is material to the "bargain" in this case must also consider the services and products represented as available to members.

* * *

[ed. The Court reviewed each of the allegations of fraud in the government's complaint. Typical of the court's analysis is the following:] It is the Court's view that the representations regarding nomination of members do not implicate matters that are material to the bargain. Rather, like the representations regarding prestige and membership selectivity, these representations are a tactic to gain the immediate attention of the customer.* * *

* * *

The solicitation letters generally include a sentence stating that "since the majority of new candidates who are nominated are not accepted for inclusion, we wish to extend our congratulations for this coveted event." In the Court's view, this statement, although misleading, is pure sales hyperbole, directed at gaining the customers' attention. [T]he Court does not believe that the representation is fraudulent in any way that is material to the bargain.

[The complaint alleges that] the Company falsely represents to customers that its directories are invaluable tools for networking among members. In truth, the directory does not contain home or work telephone numbers nor zip codes, which makes it virtually useless for any networking purposes.

The Court finds this allegation by the government to be superficial and troublesome. In the Court's view, the allegation is Inspector Biegelman's opinion, and inappropriately replaces the membership purchaser's estimate of the value of a membership with the Government's own estimate of that value.

Contrary to the Government's contention, the absence of telephone numbers and zip codes does not make the registry "virtually useless." The are valid business reasons for excluding someone's home and business phone from the listing, and the absence of a zip code from an address will not necessarily prevent a letter from being delivered. The registry lists the member's business address, and it is a relatively simple exercise to dial directory assistance and obtain the phone number. Moreover, the CD ROM version of the directory contains the zip codes.

Another misconception in the Government's understanding of the networking usefulness of the registry is in its belief that networking involves only the ability to contact someone. According to Inspector

Biegelman, "the importance of networks is to contact other people" and "[t]he easiest way to contact other people is to pick up a phone and call somebody." However, knowing whom to contact is as important in today's business networking as is making the contact. The registries at issue provide more utility with regard to this aspect of networking, than perhaps they do with actually making the contact, because they list professional and biographical data of the member. The Government may not credit this information, but to the creative entrepreneur seeking to contact a specific audience, knowing, for example, where executives in a certain industry prefer to vacation or what their favorite hobbies are can lead to a wealth of business opportunities. A creative mind can discover many marketing applications in the biographical data accompanying the member listing, and, contrary to the Government's conclusion, there are many networking possibilities arising from the information provided in the registries.

In addition, there are other services provided by the Company conducive to networking that the Government apparently overlooked in this regard, such as Tribute magazine, cocktail parties, and the availability of the registry on CD ROM. The Government admits that these services were made available to members. In the Court's view, the registries and accompanying services offered by the Company clearly establish that there are real, viable business networking opportunities incident to membership in the Company's registries. This conclusion is further supported by the affidavits of several members who attest to the networking value and usefulness of the registry and other services provided by the Company for members.

What is particularly troublesome to the Court about this allegation, however, is how the Government can commence a criminal prosecution and seize assets with devastating pecuniary effects, in part, merely on its opinion that the networking opportunities offered by the Company is fraudulent. That opinion is based on nothing more than the Government's estimate that the value of the services offered by the Company is worthless.* * *

The Court also believes that different kinds of "value" other than networking opportunities can be derived from membership, and that the Government has also overlooked this value in its somewhat subjective and superficial estimation of the value of a registry listing. For example, a member, or even a Listee, can derive value just from being listed in a registry. This value can arise from the ability to put on their resume that they are listed in Who's Who Worldwide, or from prominently displaying the registry plaque for all who enter their office to see. This Court cannot say that some prominent business executives may not find value in making the $400 dollar investment to purchase a five-year membership or $250 to purchase an associate membership and be listed in a registry, on the possibility that it may lead to a contact and a subsequent lucrative business opportunity.

* * *

Based on the above reasons and findings, it is the Court's determination that the Government has not established probable cause that the bank accounts at issue are subject to forfeiture. On the facts and evidence presented to the Court, even construed in the favorable light required, the Government has not shown anything other than mere suspicion that the elements of mail and wire fraud exist in this case. The representations made by the salespersons that form the crux of the Government's Complaint do not constitute a scheme or artifice to defraud, either singly or in the aggregate, and the Government has failed to meet its burden that the representations can be reasonably construed to constitute such a scheme.

In the Court's view the representations cannot be equated with an intent to defraud. To begin with, some of the alleged representations set forth in the Complaint are not false. With regard to other alleged statements, although false or deceiving, the representations are not material to the bargain struck between the membership purchaser and the Company. These representations, even when taken in the totality of the circumstances, are mainly directed at obtaining the customer's interest and gaining his or her immediate attention. They are not directed at "the quality, adequacy or price of the goods," nor do they concern facts "essential in deciding whether to enter the bargain." *Regent*, 421 F.2d at 1182.

* * *

In effect, what the Government did in this case was to take every minute transgression and ambiguous statement by a salesperson attempting to sell a registry membership, and combine such statements into a Complaint that unfairly exaggerates the Companies' conduct. In their totality, the number of misleading statements can be construed to superficially resemble a criminal fraud, and the Court can easily understand how the Magistrate Judge, presented only with the Government's Complaint and contentions on an ex parte and expedited basis, could have believed that there was probable cause that mail and wire fraud were committed. A closer look at the evidence however, after a hearing, reveals otherwise. The fact that the Companies' sales approach generally involved grandiose and misleading statements, innuendo and puffery, does not warrant the conclusion that they committed criminal fraud. The court in *Regent* explained that "courts cannot dwell in their ivory towers without descending occasionally into the market place," to observe the day to day practices of merchants. *Regent*, 421 F.2d at 1178. Regretfully, a descent into today's telemarket world reveals that sharp sales techniques exist and caveat emptor is still the rule.

For the reasons stated above, the warrant of seizure must be vacated, and the Petitioners' funds in the seized bank accounts must be immediately released. Having decided that the Government has failed to establish probable cause, and indeed, that the crimes of mail and wire fraud have not been committed, the remaining issues raised by the parties need not be addressed. If the Petitioners wish to pursue a claim for damages against the Government, they must commence a new action.

* * *

Notes

1. In addition to vacating the warrant of seizure, the District Court ordered

> "that the Assistant United States Attorneys involved in this case and all other counsel who have appeared in the related criminal cases are directed to appear before the Court for a status conference on Tuesday, June 6, 1995 at 9:00 a.m., in order to discuss the disposition of the pending criminal cases related to this forfeiture."

What do you think will happen at this status conference?

2. What went wrong for the government in *Seizure of All Funds*? If you were a prosecutor planning to seize property in the Eastern District of New York after the above opinion, what would you do to try to ensure that your case did not meet the same fate?

3. What evidence did the claimant's attorney present? If you represented the claimants in *Seizure of All Funds*, how would you go about gathering such evidence? Can you think of additional evidence you would seek to gather?

The above decision in *Seizure of All Funds* was rendered on May 30, 1995. The government immediately moved for a stay of the release of the $511,000 seized. The District Court granted a temporary stay, but on June 9, 1995, released $220,000 of the seized funds. On June 26, 1995, the United States Court of Appeals for the Second Circuit denied the government's motion for a stay of the release of the funds pending appeal. The appeal of the above decision was argued before the Second Circuit on August 31, 1995. On October 17, 1995, the Second Circuit remanded and reversed in the decision set forth below. As you read the Second Circuit's opinion, determine with which court—if either—you agree. As a side point, what do you think the government will obtain through forfeiture, if it is ultimately successful in proving mail fraud? Should the courts have granted the government's motion for a stay of the release of the funds? Why or why not?

IN RE SEIZURE OF ALL FUNDS IN ACCOUNTS IN THE NAMES REGISTRY PUBLISHING

United States Court of Appeals, Second Circuit, 1995.
68 F.3d 577.

POLLACK, CIRCUIT JUDGE.

* * *

Since the district court's May 30, 1995 vacatur of the TRO, the government has redesigned its questionnaire in order to generate from the registry members information regarding the materiality of the misrepresentations. The government now has mailed over 49,000 questionnaires to the members, and has received approximately 7000 responses. The government has moved in this court for permission to supplement the record with the responses to these questionnaires or, in the alternative, for remand to allow the district court to consider whether its order should be modified in light of these questionnaires.

* * *

In order to seize property under 18 U.S.C. § 981, the government must demonstrate that there was probable cause to believe that the property is subject to forfeiture. [The government has alleged that the funds at issue are subject to forfeiture pursuant to 18 U.S.C. § 981 because they are the proceeds of mail and wire fraud and transactions or attempted transactions at money laundering.-ed.]

Whether probable cause exists must be determined on the basis of the totality of the circumstances. In the context of civil forfeiture proceedings, these circumstances are not limited to evidence presented to the magistrate who issued the warrant. United States v. 4492 South Livonia Rd., 889 F.2d 1258, 1268 (2d Cir.1989) ("Once a forfeiture proceeding is brought, if further evidence is legally obtained to justify [a finding of probable cause], there is no persuasive reason to bar its use."). The findings supporting a district court's determination as to probable cause are reviewed for clear error, but the determination itself is a conclusion of law reviewed de novo.

* * *

An essential element of mail fraud, and the element that is in dispute here, is intent to defraud. In order to establish that the defendant acted with an intent to defraud, the government "must show that some actual harm or injury was contemplated by the schemer." United States v. D'Amato, 39 F.3d 1249, 1257 (2d Cir.1994) (internal quotations omitted).

In United States v. Regent Office Supply Co., 421 F.2d 1174 (2d Cir.1970), we stated that an intent to defraud could be found in sales tactics that misrepresent the usefulness of an item. *Id.* at 1180. We asserted that: * * * "in order for sales tactics to rise to the level of mail fraud, misrepresentations must be material to the bargain that the customer is induced to enter into with the company." *See id.* at 1182.

* * *

In the present case, the government contends that the Companies' misrepresentations likewise were material to the bargain between the members and the Companies. The government argues that networking and the financial opportunities that networking might generate were the principal purposes for which the members had joined the Companies' registries. According to the government, the value of the networking, and hence the value of the membership, largely was dependent on the selection criteria and processes used to choose the members. Since the Companies misrepresented these criteria and processes, the government argues, the false claims were material to the nature of the bargain between the members and the Companies, and therefore constituted mail fraud.

The district court, however, found that the misrepresentations of the Companies did not rise to the level of mail fraud. The court stated that the bargain between the Companies and the members entailed both 1) the purchase of "membership in a registry that the member will be listed in," and 2) the Companies' making available "other services or products that either accompany the purchase free of charge" or are available to the members for a cost. In evaluating whether the Companies' sales tactics were material to this bargain, the court examined separately each of the nineteen misrepresentations allegedly made by the Companies. The court concluded that the misrepresentations did "not constitute a scheme or artifice to defraud, either singly or in the aggregate."

In making this determination, the district court largely relied on our description of fraudulent sales tactics in *Regent*, and found that the sales tactics used by the Companies did not amount to mail fraud. Although the court determined that some of the Companies' representations were "false or deceiving," it found that these representations were "not material to the bargain struck between the membership purchaser and the Company." The court stated that the representations were "not directed at 'the quality, adequacy or price of the goods,' nor [did] they concern facts 'essential in deciding whether to enter the bargain.'" Furthermore, the court found that the members "received exactly what [they] paid for when they purchased a membership," and that there was not a "discrepancy between benefits reasonably anticipated because of the misleading statements and the actual benefits which the defendant delivered, or intended to deliver." Accordingly, the court determined that the government had not shown that it had probable cause to believe that the Companies had committed mail or wire fraud.

Although the court concluded that the Companies' misrepresentations were not material to the bargain between the Companies and the members, we think that the court did not fully evaluate the true nature of the bargain. The members had bargained with the Companies to join exclusive registries that would provide opportunities for networking among a prominent group of individuals. Although the members did obtain membership in "selective" registries, they had bargained to join registries of a more exclusive nature than ones whose members merely were culled from mailing lists. As a result, this may be a different situation than that presented in *Regent*, where the consumers received the products for which they had bargained. In the present case, membership in the registries may not have provided the members with the full networking capability that they expected to receive from the Companies.

On remand, the district court should re-examine, with the benefit of the information provided by the new questionnaires, the nature of the bargain and the inducements that impelled the members to join and whether any misrepresentations were material to the bargain.

* * *

The injunction ordered by the district court enjoined the government from mailing additional questionnaires to obtain further evidence of probable cause. This injunction was improper. In United States v. Burzynski Cancer Research Inst., 819 F.2d 1301 (5th Cir.1987) the Fifth Circuit held that "[a]s an incident to the separation of powers founded in the Constitution, the courts are not to interfere with the free exercise of the discretionary powers of the attorneys of the United States in their control over criminal prosecutions." 819 F.2d at 1312. We agree. In the present case, the injunction especially resulted in improper interference because * * *, the government may use post-seizure evidence at a probable cause hearing.

On remand, the district court should allow the government to continue collecting questionnaires. We note that, after the vacatur of the injunction, the government redesigned its questionnaires in order to generate from the registry members information regarding the materiality of the misrepresentations. The district court, on remand, should consider the responses to these questionnaires, along with the evidence previously introduced, and reconsider whether the Companies' misrepresentations were material to the bargain between the Companies and the members. The totality of the circumstances should inform the district court's determination of probable cause.

* * *

For the foregoing reasons, we vacate the order of the district court and remand for further findings and reconsideration in accordance with the foregoing.

Notes

Do you find the decision of the District Court or the Second Circuit more appealing? Why? Did the Second Circuit's opinion cause you to re-think your prior views?

––––––––

As the next case demonstrates, in forfeiture actions the government must not only prove that the property was involved in illegal activity but must also prove that "a substantial connection exists between the property seized and the underlying criminal activity." Note how the government met this burden in *United States v. $448,342.85.*

UNITED STATES v. $448,342.85 ET AL.

United States Court of Appeals, Seventh Circuit, 1992.
969 F.2d 474.

EASTERBROOK, CIRCUIT JUDGE.

Competition among sellers, coupled with bargain-hunting by buyers, leads to prices that protect ignorant, lazy, or busy customers. Comparison shopping by even a fairly small portion of potential customers drives prices to the level reflecting full information about goods of their quality. Because buyers know this effect, if only hazily, sellers try to persuade them that they need not shop. "Look what knowledgeable people pay!" is the sales pitch. All to the good, if the claim be true; sometimes, however, the come-on is too good to be true.

Brothers Gary, Thomas, Robert, and Ray Sophie teamed up with Thomas McGough to exploit customers' belief that any price less than savvy people pay is a bargain. McGough and the Sophies formed Network Sound, Inc., to make, and Westmont Corporation and J.M. Distributors to sell, stereo speakers in the United States, Canada, and Australia. Although Network Sound manufactured the speakers for about $36 per pair, Westmont and J.M. were able to unload them for between $200 and $500 to gullible souls, raking in some $24 million during 1988 and half of 1989. Network Sound packed the speakers in unmarked boxes. Then Westmont or J.M. loaded them into unmarked trucks, which driver-salesmen took cruising in search of marks. After pulling into a driveway or parking lot, the drivers would feign delivery of speakers to nearby stores or taverns. To onlookers, the drivers would explain that the warehouse had mistakenly loaded too many of these fancy speakers into the trucks. Anyone who seemed interested in taking the "excess" off the drivers' hands would be shown literature touting the quality of the speakers or "power invoices" purporting to show actual sales at high prices. Some customers must have been impressed with the glowing verbal descriptions, others with the invoices seeming to show what commercial buyers at ritzy establishments had paid, and still others must have concluded that unmarked boxes in unmarked vans were stolen and hence deeply discounted. Buyers paid cash, received trash, and had no clue where to complain.

Salesmen deposited the money in the organization's local bank accounts, where it was pooled for transfer to other accounts, often via cashiers' checks of less than $10,000. Further transfers routed the money to the three corporations at the pinnacle, which filed few currency transaction reports despite receiving millions in currency. Eventually the Sophies, McGough, and the three corporations pleaded guilty to conspiring to commit mail and wire fraud and "launder" the proceeds. The United States froze the balances in the corporations' principal accounts—about $750,000 in the name of Network Sound, $450,000 for J.M. Distributors, and $205,000 for Westmont. Invoking 18 U.S.C. § 981, the United States demanded forfeiture of these sums, which it depicted as proceeds of the fraud. The district court granted summary judgment against J.M. and Westmont, entering a partial final judgment under Fed.R.Civ.P. 54(b).

Section 981(a)(1)(A) provides that "[a]ny property . . . involved in a transaction or attempted transaction in violation of . . . section 1956 . . . of this title, or any property traceable to such property" is forfeit, unless the claimant satisfies the "innocent owner" defense of § 981(a)(2). Section 1956(a)(1) in turn makes it criminal when a person, "knowing that the property involved in a financial transaction represents the proceeds of some form of unlawful activity, conducts or attempts to conduct such a financial transaction which in fact involves the proceeds of specified unlawful activity—(A)(i) with the intent to promote the carrying on of specified unlawful activity; or . . . (B) knowing that the transaction is designed in whole or in part—(i) to conceal or disguise the nature, the location, the source, the ownership, or the control of the proceeds of specified unlawful activity; or (ii) to avoid a transaction reporting requirement under State or Federal law". Finally, § 1956(c)(7)(D) defines "specified unlawful activity" to include mail and wire fraud. Counsel for the government submits that the money it seized represents proceeds of the fraud and that Westmont and J.M. Distributors used their accounts with both the forbidden intent (§ 1956(a)(1)(A)(i)) and the prohibited designs (§ 1956(a)(1)(B)(i) and (ii)).

Westmont and J.M. Distributors concede this much—concede, indeed, that their guilty pleas establish it—but deny that sums seized in September 1989 can be traced to a fraudulent scheme that they insist ended late in 1988. Although the three corporations had no business other than the manufacture and sale of speakers, they say that their 1989 sales were honest. The indictment to which they pleaded guilty charged that the conspiracy lasted through August 1989, but a judgment based on a guilty plea forecloses only those issues necessarily determined. The terminal date of the conspiracy was not a necessary element of their convictions. When pleading guilty, the Sophies and McGough said that they cleaned up their acts by early 1989. Because the pleas do not settle the issue, the claimants contend, there must be a trial in the forfeiture action.

Shooting for the moon, the United States insists that it matters not whether the balances in the accounts may be traced to "specified unlawful activity". The accounts were "involved in" the fraud during 1988, and that is that. This approach treats the accounts as the criminals, taking the concept of deodands one step further (an account is not even a tangible object). Bank accounts do not commit crimes; people do. It makes no sense to confiscate whatever balance happens to be in an account bearing a particular number, just because proceeds of crime once passed through that account. Suppose Westmont abandoned the speaker business at the end of 1988, sent the balance to the victims as restitution, and used the same account (replenished from an untainted source) to buy and sell Treasury bills. That the "account" had been "involved" in the fraud would be irrelevant; the government confiscates the funds, not the account. Recall that § 981 authorizes forfeiture of "[a]ny property ... involved in a transaction or attempted transaction in violation of ... section 1956" (emphasis added). An "account" is a name, a routing device like the address of a building; the money is the "property". Once we distinguish the money from its container, it also follows that the presence of one illegal dollar in an account does not taint the rest—as if the dollar obtained from fraud were like a drop of ink falling into a glass of water.

Only property used in or traceable to the "specified unlawful activity" is forfeit. Money need not be derived from crime to be "involved" in it; perhaps a particular sum is used as the bankroll facilitating the fraud. That is not the United States' theory here, however; it treats these balances as proceeds. It is easy to imagine difficult problems in associating proceeds with crime. The law of trusts supplies an elaborate set of tracing rules, but rules designed to adjust accounts between (apparently) honest persons are not suited to frauds in which funds have been shuffled at least in part for the purpose of disguising their source. Section 981(d) incorporates the provisions of the customs laws, including the rule that a showing of probable cause shifts the burden to the claimant. Probable cause to believe that the proceeds of the fraud exceed the balance of the account at the time of seizure justifies calling on the claimant to identify sums derived from lawful activities.

Even if the fraud stopped at the end of 1988, the criminal proceeds vastly exceed the sums on deposit at the time of the seizure. J.M. Distributors and Westmont had only one line of business: selling speakers. Although eleven affidavits filed in this case assert that by the end of 1988 the Sophies had told their salesmen to phase out the use of "power invoices", and another three that power invoices were not used during 1989, none of the affiants says that the firms barred the other fraudulent sales techniques (or, for that matter, that the claimants started making complete currency transaction reports). Abandoning one deceitful device among a large repertory does not make the operation lawful. Drawing all inferences in favor of the persons opposing the motion for summary judgment does nothing to help these claimants. Details of tracing are accordingly irrelevant; the United States is entitled to the entire balances.

Notes

1. Once again, note how the above cases, *In re Seizure of All Funds* and *United States v. $448,342.85*, blend criminal and civil law. As is true in most civil forfeiture cases, *Seizure of All Funds* arose during the investigation of crimes. After receiving complaints from various state agencies and the Better Business Bureau, the United States Postal Service began investigating possible mail fraud violations. Upon completion of this investigation the government filed a Complaint and an Affidavit with a United States Magistrate seeking arrest warrants for thirty individuals. Although arrested,

none of these individuals had been indicted two months later when the District court rendered the above opinion.

2. At the same time that the government obtained arrest warrants, it obtained an ex parte warrant of search and seizure pursuant to Rule 41 of the Federal Rules of Criminal Procedure, which provides, in relevant part:

> "A warrant may be issued * * * to search for and seize any * * * property that constitutes evidence of the commission of a criminal offense; or * * * property designed or intended for use or which is or has been used as the means of committing a criminal offense * * * ."

As can be seen, to obtain a warrant under FRCrP 41, the government must prove, by probable cause, that the property constitutes, "evidence of the commission of a criminal offense or [that the] property [is] designed or intended for use [or is or has been used] as the means of committing a criminal offense." Because the complaint and affidavit were presented to the Magistrate ex parte, as permitted in Rule 41, Gordon and his associate received a big surprise between March 29–31, 1995. Not only were they arrested on felony charges of mail fraud, wire fraud and money laundering, they also saw all of the funds in the *Who's Who* business accounts seized. Ten days later Gordon and his associates brought an Order to Show Cause challenging the seizure. They proceeded under Rule 41(e), which provides:

> "A person aggrieved by an unlawful search and seizure or by the deprivation of property may move the district court for the district in which the property was seized for the return of the property on the ground that such person is entitled to lawful possession of the property."

Note that unlike the civil forfeiture cases studied thus far, which are governed largely by the Supplemental Rules for Certain Admiralty and Maritime Claims, Gordon and his associates proceeded under the Federal Rules of Criminal Procedure. They did so because their corporate bank account was initially seized as evidence in a pending criminal investigation.

C. EX PARTE SEIZURES

As noted in the discussion of *FirstRock Stock*, in some forfeiture cases the government may seize property after making an ex parte showing of probable cause to believe the property is involved in illegal activity. The Supplemental Rules for Certain Admiralty and Maritime Claims, which govern most civil forfeiture proceedings, provide for "forthwith" seizure and sale of property potentially subject to forfeiture "if the ends of justice require." 19 U.S.C. §§ 1604, 1612(a). Criminal forfeiture statutes also provide for seizure of property prior to the filing of criminal charges if there is a "substantial probability" that the government will prevail on the forfeiture action and the court determines that seizure is necessary to preserve the availability of the property.[aa]

---

aa. *See,* *e.g.,* 18 U.S.C. § 1963(d)(1)(B)(RICO), 21 U.S.C. 853(f) (governs drug forfeitures, CCE forfeitures) (21 U.S.C. § 848) and forfeitures pursuant

Although statutory provisions authorizing ex parte, pretrial seizures do not limit such seizures to certain types of property, the Supreme Court has held that due process requires certain procedural protections be followed before pretrial seizure of some types of property. As you read the next opinion, determine whether you agree with the Court.

UNITED STATES v. JAMES DANIEL GOOD REAL PROPERTY

United States Supreme Court, 1993.
510 U.S. 43.

KENNEDY, JUSTICE.

The principal question presented is whether, in the absence of exigent circumstances, the Due Process Clause of the Fifth Amendment prohibits the Government in a civil forfeiture case from seizing real property without first affording the owner notice and an opportunity to be heard. We hold that it does.

* * *

I

On January 31, 1985, Hawaii police officers executed a search warrant at the home of claimant James Daniel Good. The search uncovered about 89 pounds of marijuana, marijuana seeds, vials containing hashish oil, and drug paraphernalia. About six months later, Good pleaded guilty to promoting a harmful drug in the second degree, in violation of Hawaii law. He was sentenced to one year in jail and five years' probation, and fined $1,000. Good was also required to forfeit to the State $3,187 in cash found on the premises.

On August 8, 1989, four and one-half years after the drugs were found, the United States filed an *in rem* action in the United States District Court for the District of Hawaii, seeking to forfeit Good's house and the four-acre parcel on which it was situated. The United States sought forfeiture under 21 U.S.C. § 881(a)(7), on the ground that the property had been used to commit or facilitate the commission of a federal drug offense.[1]

to 18 U.S.C. § 982 (see § 982(b)(1)(A)); F.R.Cr.P. 41.

1. Title 21 U.S.C. § 881(a)(7) provides:
"(a) The following shall be subject to forfeiture to the United States and no property right shall exist in them:

* * *

"(7) All real property, including any right, title, and interest (including any leasehold interest) in the whole of any lot or tract of land and any appurtenances or improvements, which is used, or intended to be used, in any manner or part, to commit, or to facilitate the commission of, a violation of this subchapter punishable by more than one year's imprisonment, except that no property shall be forfeited under this paragraph, to the extent of an interest of an owner, by reason of any act or omission established by that owner to have been

On August 18, 1989, in an ex parte proceeding, a United States Magistrate Judge found that the Government had established probable cause to believe Good's property was subject to forfeiture under § 881(a)(7). A warrant of arrest *in rem* was issued, authorizing seizure of the property. The warrant was based on an affidavit recounting the fact of Good's conviction and the evidence discovered during the January 1985 search of his home by Hawaii police.

The Government seized the property on August 21, 1989, without prior notice to Good or an adversary hearing. At the time of the seizure, Good was renting his home to tenants for $900 per month. The Government permitted the tenants to remain on the premises subject to an occupancy agreement, but directed the payment of future rents to the United States Marshal.

Good filed a claim for the property and an answer to the Government's complaint. He asserted that the seizure deprived him of his property without due process of law * * *. The District Court granted the Government's motion for summary judgment and entered an order forfeiting the property.

The Court of Appeals for the Ninth Circuit affirmed in part, reversed in part, and remanded for further proceedings. The court was unanimous in holding that the seizure of Good's property, without prior notice and a hearing, violated the Due Process Clause.

* * *

We granted certiorari, to resolve a conflict among the Courts of Appeals on the constitutional question presented. We now affirm the due process ruling * * *.

The Due Process Clause of the Fifth Amendment guarantees that "[n]o person shall ... be deprived of life, liberty, or property, without due process of law." Our precedents establish the general rule that individuals must receive notice and an opportunity to be heard before the Government deprives them of property.

The Government does not, and could not, dispute that the seizure of Good's home and four-acre parcel deprived him of property interests protected by the Due Process Clause. By the Government's own submission, the seizure gave it the right to charge rent, to condition occupancy, and even to evict the occupants. Instead, the Government argues that it afforded Good all the process the Constitution requires. * * *. [The Government] argues that the seizure of real property under the drug forfeiture laws justifies an exception to the usual due process requirement of preseizure notice and hearing. * * *.

* * *

Whether *ex parte* seizures of forfeitable property satisfy the Due Process Clause is a question we last confronted in Calero–Toledo v.

committed or omitted without the knowl-   edge or consent of that owner."

Pearson Yacht Leasing Co., 416 U.S. 663 (1974), which held that the Government could seize a yacht subject to civil forfeiture without affording prior notice or hearing. Central to our analysis in *Calero-Toledo* was the fact that a yacht was the "sort [of property] that could be removed to another jurisdiction, destroyed, or concealed, if advance warning of confiscation were given." Id., at 679. The ease with which an owner could frustrate the Government's interests in the forfeitable property created a " 'special need for very prompt action' "that justified the postponement of notice and hearing until after the seizure. *Id.*, at 678.

We had no occasion in *Calero-Toledo* to decide whether the same considerations apply to the forfeiture of real property, which, by its very nature, can be neither moved nor concealed. In fact, when *Calero-Toledo* was decided, both the Puerto Rican statute, and the federal forfeiture statute upon which it was modeled, authorized the forfeiture of personal property only. It was not until 1984, ten years later, that Congress amended § 881 to authorize the forfeiture of real property.

The right to prior notice and a hearing is central to the Constitution's command of due process. "The purpose of this requirement is not only to ensure abstract fair play to the individual. Its purpose, more particularly, is to protect his use and possession of property from arbitrary encroachment—to minimize substantively unfair or mistaken deprivations of property . . . ." Fuentes v. Shevin, 407 U.S.67, 80–81 (1972).

We tolerate some exceptions to the general rule requiring predeprivation notice and hearing, but only in "extraordinary situations where some valid governmental interest is at stake that justifies postponing the hearing until after the event." *Id.*, at 82. Whether the seizure of real property for purposes of civil forfeiture justifies such an exception requires an examination of the competing interests at stake, along with the promptness and adequacy of later proceedings. The three-part inquiry set forth in Mathews v. Eldridge, 424 U.S. 319 (1976), provides guidance in this regard. The *Mathews* analysis requires us to consider the private interest affected by the official action; the risk of an erroneous deprivation of that interest through the procedures used, as well as the probable value of additional safeguards; and the Government's interest, including the administrative burden that additional procedural requirements would impose.

Good's right to maintain control over his home, and to be free from governmental interference, is a private interest of historic and continuing importance. The seizure deprived Good of valuable rights of ownership, including the right of sale, the right of occupancy, the right to unrestricted use and enjoyment, and the right to receive rents. All that the seizure left him, by the Government's own submission, was the right to bring a claim for the return of title at some unscheduled future hearing.

In *Fuentes*, we held that the loss of kitchen appliances and household furniture was significant enough to warrant a predeprivation hearing. And in Connecticut v. Doehr, 501 U.S. 1 (1991), we held that a state statute authorizing prejudgment attachment of real estate without prior notice or hearing was unconstitutional, in the absence of extraordinary circumstances, even though the attachment did not interfere with the owner's use or possession and did not affect, as a general matter, rentals from existing leaseholds.

The seizure of a home produces a far greater deprivation than the loss of furniture, or even attachment. It gives the Government not only the right to prohibit sale, but also the right to evict occupants, to modify the property, to condition occupancy, to receive rents, and to supersede the owner in all rights pertaining to the use, possession, and enjoyment of the property.

The Government makes much of the fact that Good was renting his home to tenants, and contends that the tangible effect of the seizure was limited to taking the $900 a month he was due in rent. But even if this were the only deprivation at issue, it would not render the loss insignificant or unworthy of due process protection. The rent represents a significant portion of the exploitable economic value of Good's home. It cannot be classified as *de minimis* for purposes of procedural due process. In sum, the private interests at stake in the seizure of real property weigh heavily in the *Mathews* balance.

The practice of *ex parte* seizure, moreover, creates an unacceptable risk of error. Although Congress designed the drug forfeiture statute to be a powerful instrument in enforcement of the drug laws, it did not intend to deprive innocent owners of their property. The affirmative defense of innocent ownership is allowed by statute. See 21 U.S.C. § 881(a)(7) ("[N]o property shall be forfeited under this paragraph, to the extent of an interest of an owner, by reason of any act or omission established by that owner to have been committed or omitted without the knowledge or consent of that owner").

The *ex parte* preseizure proceeding affords little or no protection to the innocent owner. In issuing a warrant of seizure, the magistrate judge need determine only that there is probable cause to believe that the real property was "used, or intended to be used, in any manner or part, to commit, or to facilitate the commission of" a felony narcotics offense. *Ibid.* The Government is not required to offer any evidence on the question of innocent ownership or other potential defenses a claimant might have. Nor would that inquiry, in the *ex parte* stage, suffice to protect the innocent owner's interests. "[F]airness can rarely be obtained by secret, one-sided determination of facts decisive of rights.... No better instrument has been devised for arriving at truth than to give a person in jeopardy of serious loss notice of the case against him and opportunity to meet it." Joint Anti-Fascist Refugee Committee v. McGrath, 341 U.S. 123, 170–172 (1951) (Frankfurter, J., concurring).

The purpose of an adversary hearing is to ensure the requisite neutrality that must inform all governmental decisionmaking. That protection is of particular importance here, where the Government has a direct pecuniary interest *in the* outcome of the proceeding.[2] Moreover, the availability of a postseizure hearing may be no recompense for losses caused by erroneous seizure. Given the congested civil dockets in federal courts, a claimant may not receive an adversary hearing until many months after the seizure. And even if the ultimate judicial decision is that the claimant was an innocent owner, or that the Government lacked probable cause, this determination, coming months after the seizure, "would not cure the temporary deprivation that an earlier hearing might have prevented." [citation omitted]

This brings us to the third consideration under *Mathews*, "the Government's interest, including the function involved and the fiscal and administrative burdens that the additional or substitute procedural requirement would entail." 424 U.S. at 335. The governmental interest we consider here is not some general interest in forfeiting property but the specific interest in seizing real property before the forfeiture hearing. The question in the civil forfeiture context is whether *ex parte* seizure is justified by a pressing need for prompt action. We find no pressing need here.

This is apparent by comparison to *Calero-Toledo*, where the Government's interest in immediate seizure of a yacht subject to civil forfeiture justified dispensing with the usual requirement of prior notice and hearing. Two essential considerations informed our ruling in that case: first, immediate seizure was necessary to establish the court's jurisdiction over the property, and second, the yacht might have disappeared had the Government given advance warning of the forfeiture action.

Because real property cannot abscond, the court's jurisdiction can be preserved without prior seizure. It is true that seizure of the res has long been considered a prerequisite to the initiation of in rem forfeiture proceedings. Justice Story, writing for the Court in The Brig Ann, 13 U.S. (9 Cranch) at 291, explained the justification for the rule as one of fixing and preserving jurisdiction: "[B]efore judicial cognizance can attach upon a forfeiture *in rem*, ... there must be a seizure; for until seizure it is impossible to ascertain what is the competent forum." But when the res is real property, rather than personal goods, the appropriate judicial forum may be determined without actual seizure.

As *The Brig Ann* held, all that is necessary "[i]n order to institute and perfect proceedings *in rem*, [is] that the thing should be actually or constructively within the reach of the Court." *Ibid.* * * * In the case of real property, the res may be brought within the reach of the court

---

2. The extent of the Government's financial stake in drug forfeiture is apparent from a 1990 memo, in which the Attorney General urged United States Attorneys to increase the volume of forfeitures in order to meet the Department of Justice's annual budget target:

"We must significantly increase production to reach our budget target.

" ... Failure to achieve the $470 million projection would expose the Department's forfeiture program to criticism and undermine confidence in our budget projections. Every effort must be made to increase forfeiture income during the remaining three months of [fiscal year] 1990." Executive Office for United States Attorneys, U.S. Dept. of Justice, 38 United States Attorney's Bulletin 180 (1990).

simply by posting notice on the property and leaving a copy of the process with the occupant. In fact, the rules which govern forfeiture proceedings under § 881 already permit process to be executed on real property without physical seizure:

> "If the character or situation of the property is such that the taking of actual possession is impracticable, the marshal or other person executing the process shall affix a copy thereof to the property in a conspicuous place and leave a copy of the complaint and process with the person having possession or the person's agent."

Rule E(4)(b), Supplemental Rules for Certain Admiralty and Maritime Claims.

Nor is the *ex parte* seizure of real property necessary to accomplish the statutory purpose of § 881(a)(7). The Government's legitimate interests at the inception of forfeiture proceedings are to ensure that the property not be sold, destroyed, or used for further illegal activity prior to the forfeiture judgment. These legitimate interests can be secured without seizing the subject property.

Sale of the property can be prevented by filing a notice of *lis pendens* as authorized by state law when the forfeiture proceedings commence. If there is evidence, in a particular case, that an owner is likely to destroy his property when advised of the pending action, the Government may obtain an *ex parte* restraining order, or other appropriate relief, upon a proper showing in district court. The Government's policy of leaving occupants in possession of real property under an occupancy agreement pending the final forfeiture ruling demonstrates that there is no serious concern about destruction in the ordinary case. Finally, the Government can forestall further illegal activity with search and arrest warrants obtained in the ordinary course.

In the usual case, the Government thus has various means, short of seizure, to protect its legitimate interests in forfeitable real property. There is no reason to take the additional step of asserting control over the property without first affording notice and an adversary hearing.

Requiring the Government to postpone seizure until after an adversary hearing creates no significant administrative burden. A claimant is already entitled to an adversary hearing before a final judgment of forfeiture. No extra hearing would be required in the typical case, since the Government can wait until after the forfeiture judgment to seize the property. From an administrative standpoint it makes little difference whether that hearing is held before or after the seizure. And any harm that results from delay is minimal in comparison to the injury occasioned by erroneous seizure.

* * *

The constitutional limitations we enforce in this case apply to real property in general, not simply to residences. That said, the case before us well illustrates an essential principle: Individual freedom finds tangible expression in property rights. At stake in this and many other forfeiture cases are the security and privacy of the home and those who take shelter within it.

Finally, the suggestion that this one petitioner must lose because his conviction was known at the time of seizure, and because he raises an as applied challenge to the statute, founders on a bedrock proposition: fair procedures are not confined to the innocent. The question before us is the legality of the seizure, not the strength of the Government's case.

In sum, based upon the importance of the private interests at risk and the absence of countervailing Government needs, we hold that the seizure of real property under § 881(a)(7) is not one of those extraordinary instances that justify the postponement of notice and hearing. Unless exigent circumstances are present, the Due Process Clause requires the Government to afford notice and a meaningful opportunity to be heard before seizing real property subject to civil forfeiture.[3]

To establish exigent circumstances, the Government must show that less restrictive measures—*i.e.*, a *lis pendens*, restraining order, or bond— would not suffice to protect the Government's interests in preventing the sale, destruction, or continued unlawful use of the real property. We agree with the Court of Appeals that no showing of exigent circumstances has been made in this case, and we affirm its ruling that the *ex parte* seizure of Good's real property violated due process.

* * *

JUSTICE O'CONNOR, CONCURRING IN PART AND DISSENTING IN PART.

Today the Court declares unconstitutional an act of the Executive Branch taken with the prior approval of a federal magistrate in full compliance with the laws enacted by Congress. On the facts of this case, however, I am unable to conclude that the seizure of Good's property did not afford him due process. I agree with the Court's observation in an analogous case more than a century ago: "If the laws here in question involved any wrong or unnecessary harshness, it was for Congress, or the people who make congresses, to see that the evil was corrected. The remedy does not lie with the judicial branch of the government." Springer v. United States, 102 U.S. 586, 594, 26 L.Ed. 253 (1881).

* * *

My first disagreement is with the Court's holding that the Government must give notice and a hearing before seizing any real property prior to forfeiting it. That conclusion is inconsistent with over a hundred years of our case law. We have already held that seizure for purpose of forfeiture is one of those "extraordinary situations," Fuentes v. Shevin,

---

3. We do not address what sort of procedures are required for preforfeiture seizures of real property in the context of criminal forfeiture. *See, e.g.*, 21 U.S.C. § 853; 18 U.S.C. § 1963 (1988 ed. and Supp. IV). We note, however, that the federal drug laws now permit seizure before entry of a criminal forfeiture judgment only where the Government persuades a district court that there is probable cause to believe that a protective order "may not be sufficient to assure the availability of the property for forfeiture." 21 U.S.C. § 853(f).

407 U.S. 67, 82 (1972). Calero–Toledo v. Pearson Yacht Leasing Co., 416 U.S. 663, 676–680 (1974). As we have recognized, *Calero-Toledo* "clearly indicates that due process does not require federal [agents] to conduct a hearing before seizing items subject to forfeiture." United States v. $8,850, 461 U.S. 555, 562, n. 12 (1983). Those cases reflect the common-sense notion that the property owner receives all the process that is due at the forfeiture hearing itself.

The distinction the Court tries to draw between our precedents and this case—the only distinction it *can* draw—is that real property is somehow different than personal property for due process purposes. But that distinction has never been considered constitutionally relevant in our forfeiture cases. Indeed, this Court rejected precisely the same distinction in a case in which we were presented with a due process challenge to the forfeiture of real property for back taxes:

> "The power to distrain personal property for the payment of taxes is almost as old as the common law. . . . Why is it not competent for Congress to apply to realty as well as personalty the power to distrain and sell when necessary to enforce the payment of a tax? It is only the further legitimate exercise of the same power for the same purpose." *Springer, supra*, 102 U.S. at 593–594.

There is likewise no basis for distinguishing between real and personal property in the context of forfeiture of property used for criminal purposes. The required nexus between the property and the crime—that it be used to commit, or facilitate the commission of, a drug offense—is the same for forfeiture of real and personal property. Forfeiture of real property under similar circumstances has long been recognized.

The Court attempts to distinguish our precedents by characterizing them as being based on "executive urgency." But this case, like all forfeiture cases, also involves executive urgency. Indeed, the Court in *Calero-Toledo* relied on the same cases the Court disparages:

> "[D]ue process is not denied when postponement of notice and hearing is necessary to protect the public from contaminated food; . . . or to aid the collection of taxes, or the war effort," [citations omitted].

The Court says that there is no "plausible claim of urgency today to justify the summary seizure of real property under § 881(a)(7)." But we said precisely the opposite in *Calero-Toledo*: "The considerations that justified postponement of notice and hearing in those cases are present here." 416 U.S. at 679. The only distinction between this case and *Calero-Toledo* is that the property forfeited here was realty, whereas the yacht in *Calero-Toledo* was personalty.

It is entirely spurious to say, as the Court does, that executive urgency depends on the nature of the property sought to be forfeited. The Court reaches its anomalous result by mischaracterizing *Calero-Toledo*, stating that the movability of the yacht there at issue was "[c]entral to our analysis." What we actually said in *Calero-Toledo*, however, was that "preseizure notice and hearing might frustrate the interests served by [forfeiture] statutes, since the property seized—as here, a yacht—will *often be of a sort* that could be removed to another jurisdiction, destroyed, or concealed, if advance warning of confiscation were given." 416 U.S. at 679 (emphasis added). The fact that the yacht could be sunk or sailed away was relevant to, but hardly dispositive of, the due process analysis. In any event, land and buildings are subject to damage or destruction. Moreover, that was just one of the three justifications on which we relied in upholding the forfeiture in *Calero-Toledo*. The other two—the importance of the governmental purpose and the fact that the seizure was made by government officials rather than private parties—are without a doubt equally present in this case * * *.

My second disagreement is with the Court's holding that the Government acted unconstitutionally in seizing *this* real property for forfeiture without giving Good prior notice and an opportunity to be heard. I agree that the due process inquiry outlined in *Mathews v. Eldridge*, 424 U.S. 319, 335 (1976)—which requires a consideration of the private interest affected, the risk of erroneous deprivation and the value of additional safeguards, and the Government's interest—provides an appropriate analytical framework for evaluating whether a governmental practice violates the Due Process Clause notwithstanding its historical pedigree. But this case is an as *applied* challenge to the seizure of Good's property; on these facts, I cannot conclude that there was a constitutional violation.

The private interest at issue here—the owner's right to control his property—is significant. Yet the preforfeiture intrusion in this case was minimal. Good was not living on the property at the time, and there is no indication that his possessory interests were in any way infringed. Moreover, Good's tenants were allowed to remain on the property. The property interest of which Good was deprived was the value of the rent during the period between seizure and the entry of the judgment of forfeiture—a monetary interest identical to that of the property owner in $8,850, *supra*, in which we stated that preseizure notice and hearing was not required.

The Court emphasizes that people have a strong interest in their homes. But that observation confuses the Fourth and the Fifth Amendments. The "sanctity of the home" recognized by this Court's cases, is founded on a concern with governmental *intrusion* into the owner's possessory or privacy interests—the domain of the Fourth Amendment. Where, as here, the Government obtains a warrant supported by probable cause, that concern is allayed. The Fifth Amendment, on the other hand, is concerned with *deprivations* of property interests; for due process analysis, it should not matter whether the property to be seized is real or personal, home or not. The relevant inquiry is into the governmental interference with the owner's interest in whatever property is at issue, an intrusion that is minimal here.

Moreover, it is difficult to see what advantage a preseizure adversary hearing would have had in this case. There was already an *ex parte* hearing before a magistrate to determine whether there was probable cause to believe that Good's property had been used in connection with a drug trafficking offense. That hearing ensured that the probable validity of the claim had been established. The Court's concern with innocent owners is completely misplaced here, where the warrant affidavit indicated that the property owner had already been convicted of a drug offense involving the property.

At any hearing—adversary or not—the Government need only show probable cause that the property has been used to facilitate a drug offense in order to seize it; it will be unlikely that giving the property owner an opportunity to respond will affect the probable-cause determination. And we have already held that property owners have a due process right to a prompt *post*seizure hearing, which is sufficient to protect the owner's interests.

The Government's interest in the property is substantial. Good's use of the property to commit a drug offense conveyed all right and title to the United States, although a judicial decree of forfeiture was necessary to perfect the Government's interest. Seizure allowed the Government to protect its inchoate interest in the property itself.

Seizure also permitted the Government "to assert *in rem* jurisdiction over the property in order to conduct forfeiture proceedings, thereby fostering the public interest in preventing continued illicit use of the property and in enforcing criminal sanctions." *Calero-Toledo*, 416 U.S. at 679. In another case in which the forfeited property was land and buildings, this Court stated:

> "Judicial proceedings *in rem*, to enforce a forfeiture, cannot in general be properly instituted until the property inculpated is previously seized by the executive authority, as it is the preliminary seizure of the property that brings the same within the reach of such legal process." *Dobbins' Distillery*, 96 U.S. at 396, citing The Brig Ann, 13 U.S. (9 Cranch) 289, 3 L.Ed. 734 (1815).

The Government in *Dobbins' Distillery* proceeded almost exactly as it did here: The United States Attorney swore out an affidavit alleging that the premises were being used as an illegal distillery, and thus were subject to forfeiture; a federal judge issued a seizure warrant; a deputy United States Marshal seized the property by posting notices thereon admonishing anyone with an interest in it to appear before the court on a stated date; and the court, after a hearing at which Dobbins claimed his interest, ordered the property forfeited to the United States. The Court noted that "[d]ue executive seizure was made in this case of the distillery and of the real and personal property used in connection with the same." 96 U.S. at 396.

The Court objects that the rule has its origins in admiralty cases, and has no applicability when the object of the forfeiture is real property. But Congress has specifically made the customs laws applicable to drug forfeitures, regardless of whether the Government seeks to forfeit real or personal property. Indeed, just last Term, we recognized in a case involving the seizure and forfeiture of real property that "it long has been understood that a valid seizure of the res is a prerequisite to the *initiation* of an *in rem* civil forfeiture proceeding." Republic Nat. Bank of Miami v. United States, 506 U.S. 80, 84, (1992).

Finally, the burden on the Government of the Court's decision will be substantial. The practical effect of requiring an adversary hearing before seizure will be that the Government will conduct the full forfeiture hearing on the merits before it can claim its interest in the property. In the meantime, the Government can protect the important federal interests at stake only through the vagaries of state laws. And while under the current system only a few property owners contest the forfeiture, the Court's opinion creates an incentive and an opportunity to do so, thus increasing the workload of federal prosecutors and courts.

For all these reasons, I would reverse the judgment of the Court of Appeals. I therefore respectfully dissent from Part II of the opinion of the Court.

Notes

With whom do you agree: the majority or the dissent? Why?

D. INNOCENT OWNER DEFENSE

As noted in other cases in this chapter a number of forfeiture statutes specifically establish a defense for "innocent owners": those who own property without knowledge or consent of the illegal activity activating the forfeiture.[bb] As discussed in Section E of this chapter, there are substantial constitutional reasons for allowing an innocent owner defense to any forfeiture, whether statutorily specified or not.

There are three cases in this section. The first case, United States v. 5709 Hillingdon Road, 919 F.Supp. 863 (W.D.N.C.1996), is a straightforward example of a party attempting to assert an innocent owner defense. The second case, United States v. 92 Buena Vista Ave., 507 U.S. 111 (1993), discusses the "relation back" doctrine in the context of the innocent owner defense. The third case, United States v. One 1990 Lincoln Town Car, 817 F.Supp. 1575 (N.D.Ga.1993), applies *Buena Vista* to a different forfeiture statute. *Lincoln Town Car* also shows what can happen when there are competing innocent owners.

As you read *Hillingdon Road*, determine whether there may have been a different outcome if the claimant had been a waitress at her husband's nightclub, instead of the club's accountant. Should this make a difference?

---

bb. *See e.g.,* 21 U.S.C. § 881(a)(6) (civil forfeiture); 18 U.S.C. § 981(a)(2) (civil forfeiture); *cf.* 18 U.S.C. § 1963(c) (RICO, criminal forfeiture statute providing similar protection for bona fide purchasers of the property).

UNITED STATES v. 5709 HILLINGDON ROAD

United States District Court, Western District, North Carolina, 1996.
919 F.Supp. 863.

POTTER, DISTRICT JUDGE.

This matter is before the Court on the Motion of the United States for Summary Judgment and the cross-motion of Claimant Karen T. Leak for Summary Judgment. For the reasons stated herein, the Government's Motion will be granted, and Ms. Leak's Motion will be denied.

I. BACKGROUND

Curtis J. Leak owns a nightclub called "Side Effects" * * * in Charlotte. His wife, Karen T. Leak, graduated with an accounting degree *summa cum laude*, is an accountant for Duke Power Company, and she has acted as the accountant for the corporation that owns her husband's night-club (he controls the corporation). The Leaks own the real and personal property that is the subject matter of this dispute. Essentially, the Government seeks forfeiture of this property because of its connection with the structuring of financial transactions to avoid the currency transaction reporting requirements.

The facts underlying the Government's case took place over January 17–18, 1991, when thirty-three deposits, all less than $10,000, were made into accounts owned or controlled by Curtis James Leak or Karen T. Leak. The deposits, which totaled $152,000, were made into three different institutions. More specifically, $51,100 was deposited into Wachovia Bank & Trust, $50,700 was deposited into Southern National Bank, and $50,800 was deposited into First Citizens Bank.

This deposit spree that occurred on January 17–18, 1991, took the following form. Eleven cash deposits, totalling $51,100.00 were made into a personal checking account of Curtis J. Leak, at Wachovia Bank, checking account No. 186155579. The deposits were made at ten (10) separate branches and the depositor(s) utilized eleven (11) different tellers. The deposit amounts were as follows: one (1) deposit I/A/O [in the approximate amount of] $5,200.00; eight (8) deposits I/A/O $5,000.00; one (1) deposit I/A/O $3,000.00; and, one (1) deposit I/A/O $2,900.00. Also, eleven (11) cash deposits, totalling $50,700.00, were made into a personal checking account of Curtis James Leak, checking account no. 251209540, at Southern National Bank. The deposits were made at five (5) different branches and the depositor(s) utilized eleven (11) different tellers. The amounts of the deposits were as follows: nine (9) deposits I/A/O $5,000.00; one (1) deposit I/A/O $3,200.00; and, one (1) deposit I/A/O $2,500.00. Finally, eleven (11) cash deposits totalling $50,800.00 were made into a personal checking account of Karen T. Leak, checking account no. 0137099514, at First Citizens Bank. The deposits were made at seven (7) separate branches and the depositor(s) utilized eleven (11) different tellers. The amounts of the deposits were as follows: nine (9) deposits I/A/O $5,000.00; one (1) deposit I/A/O $3,000.00; and, one (1) deposit I/A/O $2,500.00.[1]

Twenty-two of these deposits were made into accounts held in the name of Curtis J. Leak, eleven of these deposits were made into the account of Karen T. Leak, the Claimant still before this Court.[2] According to Ms. Leak, she cannot remember exactly how many deposits she made during this two-day deposit spree in January of 1991, but admits to making at least a couple. We know too that a Ford Taurus registered in her name was identified and connected with several of these deposits, that one assistant manager at a Southern National Bank branch positively identified Karen Leak as a depositor, and that several other tellers gave descriptions of a depositor that closely resemble Ms. Leak.

We also know how the Leaks used the money provided by these deposits and we know that Ms. Leak participated in the disbursement of those funds. For on the day *before* the depositing spree began, three checks were drawn on these three accounts as follows: One check was drawn on the account of Curtis J. Leak from his account at Wachovia Bank. That check, number 940, was drawn in the amount of $50,680.54, bears the signature "Curtis J. Leak" and the lower left corner of the check bears the note: "#033634–7 1 of 3." A second check was drawn on the account of Curtis J. Leak from his account at Southern National Bank. That check, number 577, was in the amount of $50,680.54, bears the signature "Curtis J. Leak" and the lower left corner of the check bears the note: "#033634–7 3 of 3." The third check was drawn on the account of Karen T. Leak from her account at First Citizens Bank. That check, number 337, was drawn in the amount of $50,680.54, bears the signature Karen T. Leak, and the lower left corner of the check bears the note: "#033634–7 2 of 3." The Government has offered proof that Ms. Leak actually signed each of the three checks noted earlier, and Ms. Leak has not denied or otherwise rebutted the Government's evidence on this point. And we know that the number "033634–7" is the loan number for the mortgage on the property at Hillingdon Road, and as a result of their two-day deposit spree, the Leaks retired their mortgage on the defendant property by drafting three checks, one from each account, for a total of $152,041.62.[3]

---

1. Later in May there were a similar series of deposits totalling some fifty thousand dollars. These transactions serve to confirm that the Leaks were deliberately avoiding the reporting requirements, but they are not directly relevant to the claims here, and therefore, they will not be discussed at length.

2. The Court has already granted the Government's motion for summary judgment as to the claim of Mr. Leak and his corporation, TKC, Inc., because there was no genuine dispute concerning his knowl-

edge of, and attempts to avoid, the currency transaction reporting requirement. As noted in this Court's earlier ruling, a bank teller had previously explained that requirement to a very irate Mr. Leak before the deposit spree at issue.

3. While the checks are dated January 16, 1991, prior to the deposits, the accounts did not contain sums sufficient to honor these checks prior to the deposits at issue, and none of the checks were presented until after the deposits were completed.

II. Disposition

The Government and Ms. Leak have filed cross-motions for summary judgment. According to the Government, there is no genuine dispute concerning whether Ms. Leak was aware of, and participated in efforts to evade, the currency transaction reporting requirements. According to Ms. Leak, there is no evidence from which a reasonable juror could find that she had any knowledge of the reporting requirement, and therefore, she is entitled to her interest as an innocent owner as a matter of law.

A. *Probable Cause, Substantial Connection and Structuring.*

Both parties seek summary judgment pursuant to Fed.R.Civ.Proc. 56. "Under Rule 56(c), summary judgment is proper 'if the pleadings, depositions, answers to interrogatories, and admissions on file, together with the affidavits, if any, show that there is no genuine issue as to any material fact and that the moving party is entitled to judgment as a matter of law.' "Celotex Corp. v. Catrett, 477 U.S. 317, 321.

As with any summary judgment motion, "the court must draw any permissible inference from the underlying facts established in the record in the light most favorable to the non-moving party." Austin v. Clark Equipment Co., 48 F.3d 833, 835 (1995).

In a civil forfeiture action in rem brought pursuant to 21 U.S.C. § 881 or 18 U.S.C. § 981, the United States has the burden to "show probable cause that a substantial connection exists between the property forfeited and the criminal activity defined by the statute." U.S. v. $95,945.18 United States Currency, 913 F.2d 1106, 1110 (4th Cir.1990). The probable cause determination "requires the court to make a practical common-sense decision whether, given all the circumstances set forth … there is a fair probability that the properties to be forfeited" have a substantial connection to the specified criminal activity. U.S. v. Thomas, 913 F.2d 1111, 1114 (4th Cir.1990). Like the probable cause inquiry, the "substantial connection" requirement must be applied with common sense, and the Court is required to determine whether the property has more than an "incidental or fortuitous" connection with criminal activity. U.S. v. Schifferli, 895 F.2d 987, 990 (4th Cir.1990).

Upon a finding of probable cause, the burden shifts to the claimant to show by a preponderance of the evidence that he or she owned the defendant property and the property was neither used nor intended to be used unlawfully. A claimant can also avoid forfeiture of their interest by proving, by a preponderance of the evidence, that he or she neither consented to nor had knowledge of the illegal use and took reasonable steps necessary to prevent the property's illegal use. Recognizing that the substantive law and standard of proof shapes the summary judgment inquiry, the Fourth Circuit has held that once the Government has made a showing of probable cause, the burden shifts to the claimant who cannot rest on mere allegations or denial but must come forward with specific facts showing that there is not a substantial connection between property at issue and the criminal activity outlined in the Government's complaint. Thus, while the Court is obliged to draw reasonable inferences in favor of the nonmoving party, those inferences must be reasonable in light of competing inferences to the contrary. So if the claimant does not produce evidence sufficient to create a genuine issue of material fact, the unrebutted showing of probable cause is sufficient to support a forfeiture.

As noted, 18 U.S.C. § 981(a)(1)(A) provides for the forfeiture of any real or personal property involved in a transaction in violation of 31 U.S.C. §§ 5313(a) or 5324(c) or any property traceable to such property. In this case, the Government seeks the forfeiture of the property at Hillingdon Road and the Ford Taurus because they were involved in, facilitated, or represent the proceeds of the deposits structured to avoid the currency reporting requirement. Essentially, the Government argues that Curtis and Karen Leak committed multiple violations of 31 U.S.C. §§ 5313(a) & 5324 by causing three financial institutions to fail to complete the Currency Transaction Reports ("CTRs") as required by law and by structuring the case transactions with three separate financial institutions to avoid the reporting requirements. And the Fourth Circuit has held that a violation of Section 5324 is established by evidence that an individual knew of the reporting requirements and took steps to avoid them. U.S. v. Wollman, 945 F.2d 79, 81 (4th Cir.1991).

The Government and Ms. Leak have filed cross-motions for summary judgment. According to the Government, there is no genuine dispute concerning whether Ms. Leak was aware of, and participated in efforts to evade, the currency transaction reporting requirements, and therefore, she has not satisfied her burden of establishing that she is an innocent owner within the meaning of § 981(a)(2). According to Ms. Leak, there is no evidence from which a reasonable juror could find that she had any knowledge of the reporting requirement, and therefore, she is entitled to summary judgment on her innocent owner defense as a matter of law.

The argument raises an interesting question about the nature of the innocent owner defense. By its terms, § 981(a)(2) which creates the "innocent owner" defense that Ms. Leak relies [sic], provides that no property shall be forfeited "to the extent of the interest of an owner or lienholder by reason of any act or omission established by that owner or lienholder to have been committed without knowledge of that owner or lienholder." 18 U.S.C. § 981(a)(2). Read literally, the section merely requires the Government to show that the claimant knew about the act or omission that gave rise to liability—here the series of deposits less than $10,000—in order to forfeit the claimant's interest; and it does not require the Government to show that the claimant knew the acts are illegal, in order to rebut a properly supported claim under § 981(a)(2). This Court has found two courts that appear to read the statute this way. See U.S. v. 105,800 Shares of Common Stock, 830 F.Supp. 1101, 1131 (N.D.Ill.1993) (innocent owner within the meaning of § 981(a)(2) "refers to lack of knowledge of the illegal transaction, not lack of knowledge of the transaction's illegality."); U.S. v. 316 Units of Mun. Securities, 725 F.Supp. 172, 180 (S.D.N.Y.1989).

* * *

This Court finds the reasoning [in these cases] persuasive. But ultimately, this Court need not decide whether Ms. Leak must show that she was unaware of the deposits at issue, or unaware that the deposits were unlawful, or unaware that the deposits at issue were made for the purpose of avoiding the currency transaction reporting requirement, because she has failed to meet her burden of rebuttal under any standard. After all, Ms. Leak signed three checks from the very accounts into which the illegal deposits would be made within the next two days on the very day *before* the deposit spree occurred. She also annotated the checks to indicate the purpose for which the deposits were made, and her notations establish her knowledge that the checks were a part (a one third part) of a common scheme to pay off the mortgage on the Hillingdon Road property. Also, there is no doubt that her husband knew about the reporting requirement, that she made at least one and probably several of the deposits at issue, and that her car was used to make the deposits. She has also acted as the accountant for her husband's nightclub, which she now claims is the (legitimate) source of the funds that were deposited in the accounts owned or controlled by the Leaks.[5] Under these circumstances, Ms. Leak's claim that she was unaware of her husband's structuring scheme is untenable.

Ms. Leak's effort to explain away her participation in the structuring scheme is also untenable. According to Ms. Leak, the money she and her husband deposited between January 17 and 18, 1991 is legitimate income from her husband's nightclub (although she earlier filed tax returns which stated that the nightclub's income was only $96,693). Ms. Leak also argue[s] that and [sic] what appears to be a transparent structuring scheme is really her husband's effort to ensure privacy and security by making small deposits in many banks for the purpose of avoiding theft. In short, Ms. Leak would have this Court believe that in order to avoid being robbed, she and her husband rode around Charlotte with some $152,000 in the car, even bringing large amounts of money to the same banks on the same days, in order to avoid theft so that no one would notice their large transactions (which is obviously not the case). Further, she implicitly asks this Court to believe that it is just a coincidence that all of the thirty-three transactions were below the $10,000 threshold for filing a CTR. Finally, Ms. Leak maintains that these deposits were consistent with her husband's effort to ensure the security and privacy of his bank deposits, but she has produced no evidence that he utilized this strategy at any time during the many years when he operated the nightclub. For these reasons, Ms Leak's bare assertion that there was another legitimate purpose for the two-day

---

5. The Leaks are currently being prosecuted for income tax evasion and related offenses.

deposit spree is incredible as a matter of law, and so is her effort to make out an innocent ownership claim. Therefore, the Government's Motion for Summary Judgment will be granted.

Notes

1. If you represented Ms. Leak and she was a waitress at the nightclub rather than the club's accountant, what would you argue?

2. Note the court's holding that to defeat Ms. Leak's innocent owner defense, the government need not prove that Ms. Leak knew that structuring of funds was illegal, only that structuring occurred. Do you agree?

Prior to reading the next case, it may be helpful to review the "relation back" doctrine. This doctrine is set forth in various forfeiture statutes and provides that the government's right to the property which is subject to forfeiture dates from the time of the illegal act rather than from the date the government initiates or prevails in the forfeiture action. Section 981(f) of title 18, United States Code, for example, provides:

> "All right, title, and interest in property [subject to forfeiture pursuant to this section] shall vest in the United States upon commission of the act giving rise to forfeiture under this section."

As you read the next case, consider the three options as to *when* title to property subject to forfeiture could vest in the government: (1) when the property is used illegally, (2) when the property is seized for forfeiture, or (3) when judgment of forfeiture is entered.[cc] Are you persuaded that the Court adopted the correct option?

UNITED STATES v. 92 BUENA VISTA AVE.

United States Supreme Court, 1993.
507 U.S. 111.

STEVENS, JUSTICE; joined by BLACKMUN, O'CONNOR, and SOUTER, JUSTICES.

The question presented is whether an owner's lack of knowledge of the fact that her home had been purchased with the proceeds of illegal drug transactions constitutes a defense to a forfeiture proceeding under The Comprehensive Drug Abuse Prevention and Control Act of 1970, § 511(a), 84 Stat. 1276, as amended, 21 U.S.C. § 881(a)(6).[1]

---

cc. DAVID B. SMITH, PROSECUTION AND DEFENSE OF FORFEITURE CASES, § 3.05[2]. Smith's treatise is an excellent resource on the law of forfeiture.

1. The statute provides:

"The following shall be subject to forfeiture to the United States and no property right shall exist in them:

* * *

"(6) All moneys, negotiable instruments, securities, or other things of value furnished or intended to be furnished by any

On April 3, 1989, the Government filed an *in rem* action against the parcel of land in Rumson, New Jersey, on which respondent's home is located. The verified complaint alleged that the property had been purchased in 1982 by respondent with funds provided by Joseph Brenna that were "the proceeds traceable to an [unlawful] exchange for a controlled substance," App. 13, and that the property was therefore subject to seizure and forfeiture under § 881(a)(6). *Id.*, at 15.[2]

On April 12, 1989, in an *ex parte* proceeding, the District Court determined that there was probable cause to believe the premises were subject to forfeiture, and issued a summons and warrant for arrest authorizing the United States Marshal to take possession of the premises. Respondent thereafter asserted a claim to the property, was granted the right to defend the action, and filed a motion for summary judgment.

During pretrial proceedings, the following facts were established. In 1982, Joseph Brenna gave respondent approximately $240,000 to purchase the home that she and her three children have occupied ever since. Respondent is the sole owner of the property. From 1981 until their separation in 1987, she maintained an intimate personal relationship with Brenna. There is probable cause to believe that the funds used to buy the house were proceeds of illegal drug trafficking, but respondent swears that she had no knowledge of its origins.

Among the grounds advanced in support of her motion for summary judgment was the claim that she was an "innocent owner" within the meaning of § 881(a)(6). The District Court rejected this defense for two reasons: First it ruled that "the innocent, owner defense may only be invoked by those who can demonstrate that they are bona fide *purchasers for value*" (emphasis in original). Second, the court read the statute to offer the innocent owner defense only to persons who acquired an

---

person in exchange for a controlled substance in violation of [21 U.S.C. §§ 801–904], all proceeds traceable to such an exchange, and all moneys, negotiable instruments, and securities used or intended to be used to facilitate any violation of this subchapter, except that no property shall be forfeited under this paragraph, to the extent of the interest of an owner, by reason of any act or omission established by that owner to have been committed or omitted without the knowledge or consent of that owner."

2. See n. 1, *supra*. The complaint also alleged that the property had been used in 1986 to facilitate the distribution of proceeds of an illegal drug transaction, and was therefore subject to forfeiture pursuant to § 881(a)(7), which provides:

"The following shall be subject to forfeiture to the United States and no property right shall exist in them:

"(7) All real property, including any right, title, and interest (including any leasehold interest) in the whole of any lot or tract of land and any appurtenances or improvements, which is used, or intended to be used, in any manner of part, to commit, or to facilitate the commission of, a violation of this subchapter punishable by more than one year's imprisonment, except that no property shall be forfeited under this paragraph, to the extent of an interest of an owner, by reason of any act or omission established by that owner to have been committed or omitted without the knowledge or consent of that owner."

No issue concerning the Government's claim under subparagraph (7) is presented before us.

* * *

interest in the property before the acts giving rise to the forfeiture took place.

* * *

The decision by Congress in 1978 to amend the Comprehensive Drug Abuse Prevention and Control Act of 1970, 84 Stat. 1236, to authorize the seizure and forfeiture of proceeds of illegal drug transactions, * * * marked an important expansion of governmental power.[16] Before that amendment, the statute had authorized forfeiture of only the illegal substances themselves and the instruments by which they were manufactured and distributed. * * * *

* * * * The statute, after its 1978 amendment * * * contains an express and novel protection for innocent owners * * * .

* * *

"[N]o property shall be forfeited under this paragraph, to the extent of the interest of an owner, by reason of any act or omission established by that owner to have been committed or omitted without the knowledge or consent of that owner." 21 U.S.C. § 881(a)(6).

* * *

That the funds respondent used to purchase her home were a gift does not, therefore, disqualify respondent from claiming that she is an owner who had no knowledge of the alleged fact that those funds were "proceeds traceable" to illegal sales of controlled substances. Under the terms of the statute, her status would be precisely the same if, instead of having received a gift of $240,000 from Brenna, she had sold him a house for that price and used the proceeds to buy the property at issue.

* * *

Although the Government does not challenge our interpretation of the statutory term "owner," it insists that respondent is not the "owner" of a house she bought in 1982 and has lived in ever since. Indeed, it contends that she never has been the owner of this parcel of land because the statute vested ownership in the United States at the moment when the proceeds of an illegal drug transaction were used to pay the purchase price. In support of its position, the Government relies on both the text of the 1984 amendment to the statute and the common-law relation back doctrine. We conclude, however, that neither the amendment nor the common-law rule makes the Government an owner of property before forfeiture has been decreed.

---

16. A precedent for this expansion had been established in 1970 by the Racketeer Influenced and Corrupt Organizations Act (RICO), see 18 U.S.C. § 1963(a). Even RICO, however, did not specifically provide for the forfeiture of "proceeds" until 1984, when Congress added § 1963(a)(3) to re-solve any doubt whether it intended the statute to reach so far. See S. Rep. No. 98–225, pp. 191–200 (1983), U.S. Code Cong. & Admin. News pp. 3182, 3374–3383; *Russello v. United States*, 464 U.S. 16, 104 S. Ct. 296, 78 L. Ed. 2d 17 (1983).

In analyzing the Government's relation back argument, it is important to remember that respondent invokes the innocent owner defense against a claim that *proceeds* traceable to an illegal transaction are forfeitable. The Government contends that the money that Brenna received in exchange for narcotics became Government property at the moment Brenna received it and that respondent's house became Government property when that tainted money was used in its purchase. Because neither the money nor the house could have constituted forfeitable proceeds until after an illegal transaction occurred, the Government's submission would effectively eliminate the innocent owner defense in almost every imaginable case in which proceeds could be forfeited. It seems unlikely that Congress would create a meaningless defense. Moreover, considering that a logical application of the Government's submission would result in the forfeiture of property innocently acquired by persons who had been paid with illegal proceeds for providing goods or services to drug traffickers, the burden of persuading us that Congress intended such an inequitable result is especially heavy.

* * *

Chief Justice Marshall explained that forfeiture does not automatically vest title to property in the Government:

"It has been proved, that in all forfeitures accruing at common law, nothing vests in the government until some legal step shall be taken for the assertion of its right, after which, for many purposes, the doctrine of relation carries back the title to the commission of the offence." *United States v. Grundy*, 3 Cranch 337, 350–351, 2 L.Ed. 459 (1806).

* * *

If the Government wins a judgment of forfeiture * * * the vesting of its title in the property relates back to the moment when the property became forfeitable. Until the Government does win such a judgment, however, someone else owns the property. That person may therefore invoke any defense available to the owner of the property before the forfeiture is decreed.

In this case a statute allows respondent to prove that she is an innocent owner.

* * *

Therefore, when Congress enacted this innocent owner defense, and then specifically inserted this relation back provision into the statute, it did not disturb the common-law rights of either owners of forfeitable property or the Government. The common-law rule had always allowed owners to invoke defenses made available to them *before* the Government's title vested, and after title *did* vest, the common-law rule had always related that title back to the date of the commission of the act that made the specific property forfeitable. Our decision denies the Government no benefits of the relation back doctrine. The Government cannot profit from the common-law doctrine of relation back until it has obtained a judgment of forfeiture.

Notes

The Government's argument that the relation back doctrine should prevail and that title should vest in the government at the time the property is used illegally is twofold: (1) that all right, title and interest in property obtained by criminals through illicit means vest in the United States upon commission of the act giving rise to forfeiture, and (2) a property owner cannot give good title to property which is subject to forfeiture because the owner does not have good title. Do you find this argument persuasive? Do you agree with the Supreme Court in *Buena Vista* that the above argument must be rejected if the "innocent owner" defense is to remain viable? If the relation back doctrine is inherently inconsistent with the innocent owner defense, how could the courts ever have applied the relation back doctrine to innocent owner claims?

In the next case, United States v. One 1990 Lincoln Town Car, 817 F.Supp. 1575 (N.D.Ga.1993), the District Court has little trouble extending *Buena Vista's* holding regarding the civil forfeiture drug statute (21 U.S.C. § 881), to the more general civil forfeiture statute (18 U.S.C. § 981). Note the adverse positions taken by the competing "innocent owners."

UNITED STATES v. ONE 1990 LINCOLN TOWN CAR

United States District Court, Northern District of Georgia, 1993.
817 F.Supp. 1575.

SHOOB, SENIOR DISTRICT JUDGE.

This action is before the Court on * * * several summary judgment motions. For the reasons stated below, the Court * * * grants claimant Eastwood Yarn Corporation's motion for summary judgment against the Government, and denies Eastwood's motion for summary judgment against claimant Mitsubishi International Corporation.

In August 1991, the Government filed this civil forfeiture action under 18 U.S.C. § 981 against the defendant properties. The Government seized the defendant properties after showing that Joseph Smith, Raymond Lippincott III, and Mary Ellen Lee defrauded Mitsubishi International Corporation from November 1988 to June 1991 and used the money to purchase the defendant properties. The Government settled with various claimants to the defendant properties, and the only remaining defendant property in this action is the real property and improvements at a processing plant at 100 Sun Industrial Boulevard in Talladega County, Alabama ("Sun Fibres property"), formerly operated by Sun Fibres, Inc. The only claimants to the Sun Fibres property are the Government, Mitsubishi, Eastwood Yarn Corporation, the Independent Bank of Oxford, and the City of Talladega Industrial Development Board. In August 1992, the Government and Mitsubishi entered into a consent agreement in which the Government recognized Mitsubishi's right to the Sun Fibres property and made Mitsubishi substitute custodian of the property.

The Court must determine whether the Sun Fibres property may be forfeited to the Government or whether one of the claimants * * * has a superior right to the property. Eastwood claims to have a superior right to the Sun Fibres property because it obtained a judgment lien on the property when it recorded its judgment against Sun Fibres, Inc., on August 22, 1991, at 8:41 a.m., in the Office of the Probate Judge of Talladega County, Alabama. Mitsubishi also claims to have a superior right to the Sun Fibres property because it has a constructive trust on the property, which arose when the fraudulent acts were committed in November 1988. Mitsubishi argues that its *lis pendens* notices filed on August 16, 22, and 26, 1991, in the Office of the Probate Judge of Talladega County, gave Eastwood notice of Mitsubishi's constructive trust on the property, though Eastwood claims that the only *lis pendens* notice which could have been effective against Eastwood, the August 16 *lis pendens*, was defective. Mitsubishi further claims that Eastwood had notice of Mitsubishi's constructive trust since its attorney took the deposition of Joseph Smith, one of the perpetrators of the fraud, on August 12, 1991, and since newspapers of general circulation in Alabama and Georgia carried stories about the fraud.

* * *

In its motion for summary judgment against the Government, Eastwood argues that, as a judgment lienholder on the Sun Fibres property, it is an innocent lienholder under 18 U.S.C. § 981(a)(2) and its interest in the Sun Fibres property is not subject to forfeiture. In response, the Government argues that Eastwood never acquired an interest in the Sun Fibres property because the relation back doctrine of § 981(f) caused the property to immediately vest in the Government when the fraudulent acts were committed in November 1988.

The Money Laundering Control Act of 1986, 18 U.S.C. § 981, allows property seized in violation of money laundering statutes to be forfeited to the United States. 18 U.S.C. § 981(a)(1). Section 981 applies only to property that is "subject to forfeiture," which does not include the interest so-called innocent owners or lienholders have in the property.[2] The relation back doctrine of § 981 is set forth in subsection (f), which states that "[a]ll right, title, and interest in property described in subsection (a) of this section shall vest in the United States upon

---

2. Section 981(a)(2) provides in part:
"No property shall be forfeited under this section to the extent of the interest of an owner or lienholder by reason of any act or omission established by that owner or lienholder to have been committed without the knowledge of that owner or lienholder ..."

commission of the act giving rise to forfeiture under this section." *Id.* § 981(f).

The crux of the dispute between Eastwood and the Government is not merely whether Eastwood is an innocent owner under § 981(a)(2) but whether the relation back doctrine of § 981(f) applies to property under the innocent owner or lienholder defense. The Court concludes that the relation back doctrine of § 981(f) applies only to property that is subject to forfeiture under § 981(a) and not to property that is not subject to forfeiture under the innocent owner or lienholder defense of § 981(a)(2).

The plain language of § 981 supports this conclusion. Section 981(a)(1) defines what property is subject to forfeiture, and section (a)(2) exempts certain property from forfeiture to the extent of an innocent owner or lienholder's interest in the property. Logically, the relation back doctrine of § 981(f) can apply only to property that is subject to forfeiture and cannot apply to property exempt from forfeiture under the innocent owner defense; otherwise, the innocent owner defense of § 981(a)(2) would serve no purpose. Thus, the relation back doctrine applies only when a claimant fails to make out an innocent owner defense.

Cases interpreting an analogous forfeiture statute, 21 U.S.C. § 881, which with small exception contains the same innocent owner defense as § 981, support the Court's conclusion that the relation back doctrine of § 981(f) does not apply to property not subject to forfeiture under the innocent owner defense of § 981(a)(2). Most recently, the Supreme Court held that the relation back doctrine in § 881(h) does not make the Government an owner of seized property before a court has decreed a forfeiture. United States v. A Parcel of Land, Buildings, Appurtenances and Improvements, Known as 92 Buena Vista Avenue, 507 U.S. 111, (1993). As at common law, the Court noted, § 881 allows an owner to invoke the innocent owner defense of § 881(a)(6) before the Government's title vests in the property, and after the Government's title vests, the title relates back to the date of the acts giving rise to the forfeiture.

Having concluded that the relation back doctrine of § 981(f) does not apply to property that is not subject to forfeiture under § 981(a)(2), the Court now addresses whether Eastwood has established the innocent owner or lienholder defense and whether a genuine issue of material fact exists to defeat Eastwood's motion for summary judgment.

Under § 981(a)(2), property is not subject to forfeiture to the extent of an owner or lienholder's interest in the property if the owner or lienholder shows that she lacked knowledge of the act or omission giving rise to the forfeiture. * * *[A]n owner must have actual, not constructive, knowledge of the act or omission giving rise to the forfeiture. Since the case law interpreting the innocent owner defense of § 981(a)(2) is scant, the Court concludes that, as under § 881(a)(7), if Eastwood had actual knowledge of the fraud giving rise to this forfeiture action, it would not be an innocent owner or lienholder and its interest in the Sun Fibres property would be subject to forfeiture under § 981(a)(1).

Eastwood argues that it is an innocent judgment lienholder under § 981(a)(2) because it lacked actual knowledge of the fraud giving rise to this forfeiture action. Therefore, Eastwood argues, its interest in the Sun Fibres property is not subject to forfeiture. The Government fails to produce evidence sufficient to create a genuine issue of material fact on whether Eastwood had actual knowledge of the criminal acts giving rise to this action when Eastwood obtained its judgment against Sun Fibres, Inc.

Instead, the Government focuses on the argument that the relation back doctrine of § 981(f) caused the property to vest in the Government in November 1988, and does not offer evidence to refute Eastwood's showing that there is an absence of evidence indicating that Eastwood lacked actual knowledge of the criminal acts giving rise to this forfeiture action.[4] Summary judgment for Eastwood against the Government is therefore appropriate since the Government has failed to meet its burden of producing evidence on this issue. *Anderson*, 477 U.S. at 248. For these same reasons, the Court denies the Government's motion for summary judgment.[5]

Eastwood also moves for summary judgment against claimant Mitsubishi. Eastwood argues that Mitsubishi is not an innocent owner under § 981(a)(2); that Mitsubishi is not an exceptionally innocent owner under Calero–Toledo v. Pearson Yacht Leasing Co., 416 U.S. 663 (1974); that Eastwood's recorded judgment lien is superior to Mitsubishi's constructive trust on the Sun Fibres property; and that even if Mitsubishi's constructive trust were deemed superior to Eastwood's recorded judgment lien, Mitsubishi is equitably estopped from asserting its claim against Eastwood. In response, Mitsubishi argues that its constructive trust is superior to Eastwood's judgment lien on the Sun Fibres property, that Mitsubishi is the innocent owner of the Sun Fibres property, and that there are genuine issues of material fact which preclude summary judgment.

Initially, the Court notes that it must apply Alabama law in this forfeiture action. District courts must apply the conflict of law rules of their forum state. In cases involving real property, Georgia courts generally follow the traditional conflict of law rule of lex loci rei sitae, that is, the law of the place where the thing is. Here the real property and improvements that comprise the Sun Fibres property are located in Alabama; therefore, Alabama law applies.

4. Claimant Mitsubishi argues on behalf of the Government that Eastwood had knowledge of the criminal acts giving rise to this forfeiture action and points to the reports of these acts in newspapers of general circulation in Georgia and Alabama. These facts, however, show only that Eastwood may have had constructive knowledge of the criminal acts.

5. The Court concludes that, as a judgment lienholder which has filed a claim on the Sun Fibres property, Eastwood has both Article III and statutory standing to bring its claim under 18 U.S.C. § 981. Therefore, the Court denies the Government's motion for summary judgment on its argument that Eastwood lacks standing in this action.

Assuming that Mitsubishi is an innocent owner under § 981(a)(2),[6] the Court addresses the central issue presented: whether Eastwood's recorded judgment lien on the Sun Fibres property is superior in right to any constructive trust the Court may impose on the property on behalf of Mitsubishi. Alabama is a title theory state, which means that Alabama follows the general rule of first in time, superior in right, that is, if a party is first in time, then the party is first in right. Ala.Code § 35–4–90 (1991).

The Court must next examine Alabama law to determine when a court should impose a constructive trust, when a constructive trust may have arisen, and when a judgment lienholder can prevail over a constructive trust. Under Alabama law, a court may impose a constructive trust on property on behalf of one who is entitled to the property when another holds title to the property by fraud, commission of a wrong, abuse of a confidential relationship, or any other form of unconscionable conduct. In essence, a constructive trust is not a real trust at all but an equitable remedy that operates to prevent unjust enrichment.

Once a court concludes that a constructive trust should be imposed, the beneficiary of the constructive trust has an equitable interest in the property, and the constructive trust is deemed to have arisen when the wrongful acts giving rise to the trust were committed.[7] The issue of whether a constructive trust in land exists is an issue of fact, and the burden of proof is on the party asserting the trust.

Most states recognize that only a bona fide purchaser who takes property without notice of the facts giving rise to a constructive trust can prevent a constructive trust from arising, that is, cut off the trust. Alabama law, however, not only protects a bona fide purchaser but also a creditor who has a lien on the property and lacks knowledge of the facts giving rise to the trust. "No such trusts [those concerning land, see Ala.Code § 35–4–255], whether implied by law or created or declared by the parties, can defeat the title of creditors or purchasers for a valuable consideration without notice." Ala.Code § 35–4–256 (1991). The Alabama courts have long held that section 35–4–256 protects a creditor with a lien acquired after the trust arose only as long as the creditor had no notice of the trust when her judgment lien was created.

6. The Court concludes that a genuine issue of material fact exists on whether Mitsubishi is an innocent owner under 18 U.S.C. § 981(a)(2). Mitsubishi has produced evidence sufficient to create a jury issue on whether, by virtue of its constructive trust, Mitsubishi is an owner and on whether Mitsubishi lacked actual knowledge of the fraud leading to this forfeiture action.

7. Contrary to Mitsubishi's assertion, the person committing the fraud still has good title to the property gained by the fraud. "The fact that a court of equity will decree a constructive trust in property obtained by fraud or purchased with funds obtained by fraud does not mean that the title of the owner is defective or his possession tortious. A constructive trust is not a title or lien upon property but a mere remedy to which equity resorts in granting relief against fraud; and it does not exist so as to affect the property held by a wrongdoer until it is declared by a court of equity as a means of affording relief." International Refugee Organization v. Maryland Drydock Co., 179 F.2d 284, 287 (4th Cir.1950).

While no Alabama court has expressly held that section 35–4–256 applies to constructive trusts, the Alabama Supreme Court has recently stated that this is the case. See McClure v. Moore, 565 So.2d 8, 11 (Ala.1990). Further, the Alabama courts have applied section 35–4–256 to resulting trusts and to other equitable estates. Finally, the language of section 35–4–256 states that the statute applies to trusts "implied by law." Ala.Code § 35–4–256.

The general rule with regard to notice of a constructive trust is that

[a] person has notice of facts giving rise to a constructive trust where he has actual knowledge of these facts or where he should know them, [though] the circumstances under which a person should know of the existence of an express trust may be different from those under which he should know of the existence of a constructive trust. Moreover, in the case of land the matter is affected by the existence and scope of recording statutes. An express trust of land ordinarily must be recorded, whereas constructive trusts ordinarily fall outside the scope of the recording statutes.[8]

The standard for determining whether a person has actual or constructive notice of the facts giving rise to a constructive trust is the subjective standard of honesty, not the objective standard of negligence.

In this action, Eastwood argues that its judgment lien against the Sun Fibres property is superior to any constructive trust the Court might impose on Mitsubishi's behalf. Specifically, Eastwood claims that it lacked notice of Mitsubishi's constructive trust because Mitsubishi failed to file an adequate *lis pendens*. Eastwood's judgment lien was recorded at 8:41 a.m. on August 22, 1991, in Talladega County, Alabama, where the Sun Fibres property is. Although Mitsubishi recorded a lis pendens in Talladega County on August 16, 1991, Eastwood argues that this notice was defective under Alabama law because it did not include a description of any real estate in Talladega County, a description of the defendants, and a description of the Sun Fibres property, all of which are required under Alabama law. Therefore, Eastwood argues that it lacked notice of a constructive trust that might be imposed for Mitsubishi over the Sun Fibres property. While Mitsubishi refiled its *lis pendens* notice on August 22, 1991, at 4:15 p.m., and again on August 26, 1991, Eastwood argues that it had no obligation to check for lis pendens notices after recording its judgment and that these filings were also inadequate.

In response, Mitsubishi argues that the Court should impose a constructive trust on its behalf over the Sun Fibres property because the Sun Fibres property was purchased with money fraudulently obtained from Mitsubishi. Mitsubishi argues that this constructive trust should be

---

8. [AUSTIN W. SCOTT, 5 THE LAW OF TRUSTS § 476 at 3457–58.] Thus, in contrast to the actual notice required under 18 U.S.C. § 981, see United States v. Real Property and Improvements at 5000 Palmetto Drive, 928 F.2d 373, 375 (11th Cir.1991) (actual notice required under 21 U.S.C. § 881(a)(7)), a creditor with a lien or a bona fide purchaser cannot cut off a constructive trust if the creditor or purchaser knew or should have known of the facts giving rise to the constructive trust.

deemed to have arisen in November 1988 when the fraudulent acts began. Mitsubishi also claims that its *lis pendens* notices were not defective and put Eastwood on constructive notice that the Sun Fibres property was subject to pending litigation.

Applying the first in time, superior in right principle to these facts, if the Court were to impose a constructive trust on behalf of Mitsubishi,[10] Mitsubishi would, at first glance, have the superior right to the Sun Fibres property since Mitsubishi's constructive trust arose in November 1988, long before August 22, 1992, when Eastwood recorded its judgment. As a creditor with a lien, however, Eastwood would be protected under Alabama law from any constructive trust imposed on behalf of Mitsubishi if Eastwood lacked actual or constructive knowledge of the facts giving rise to the trust at the time Eastwood obtained its lien on the property.

The Court then must determine whether Eastwood had, at the time of its judgment, either actual or constructive knowledge of the facts giving rise to any constructive trust that might be imposed on Mitsubishi's behalf. The Court agrees with the late Professor Scott that the circumstances under which a person would have actual or constructive knowledge of the existence of a constructive trust are indeed limited. Nonetheless, the Court concludes that a person could have actual or constructive knowledge of the facts giving rise to a constructive trust through any means by which a person gains constructive knowledge of any facts or through state recording statutes.[12]

The Court concludes that Mitsubishi has created a genuine issue of fact on whether Eastwood had constructive, and perhaps actual, knowledge of the facts giving rise to the constructive trust at the time of Eastwood's judgment. Mitsubishi presents evidence that Eastwood may have had actual knowledge of Mitsubishi's constructive trust since Eastwood deposed Joseph Smith as part of discovery in obtaining its judgment lien. Mitsubishi also presents evidence that Eastwood may have had constructive knowledge of the trust since Smith had confessed his fraud to Government agents by the time he conducted business with Eastwood and since newspapers of general circulation carried news of Smith's arrest and fraud. On these facts, summary judgment for Eastwood against Mitsubishi is inappropriate.

Likewise, the Court concludes that genuine issues of material fact preclude summary judgment in favor of Eastwood against Mitsubishi on

---

10. As noted above, since the question of whether a constructive trust should be imposed is an equitable issue, the question is essentially a question of fact, and the Alabama courts consistently require a jury to decide whether a constructive trust should be imposed. See, e.g., Rhyne v. Martin, 292 Ala. 163, 290 So.2d 650, 651 (1974).

12. The Court disagrees with Eastwood's claims that actual notice is required and that constructive trusts must comply with state recording statutes under Alabama law. Since a constructive trust can be imposed only by a court of equity and since the beneficiary of a constructive trust may not know of the trust's existence, filing a record of a constructive trust under state recording statutes would be impossible in most cases, though, as in this action, the party asserting a constructive trust may file a lis pendens to notify third parties that property is subject to pending litigation.

Eastwood's argument that Mitsubishi is equitably estopped from asking the Court to impose a constructive trust on the Sun Fibres property. While the Court agrees with Eastwood that, under Alabama law, "[w]henever one of two innocent persons must suffer by the acts of a third, he who has enabled such third person to occasion the loss must sustain it," H.C. & W.B. Reynolds Co. v. Reynolds, 67 So. 293, 296 (1914), the Court still finds that a genuine issue of material fact exists on whether Mitsubishi was in a position to detect and prevent the fraud giving rise to this forfeiture action. Therefore, summary judgment for Eastwood is also inappropriate on this ground.

Notes

1. Note the blending of civil and criminal law, federal and state law, and forfeiture and property law in the above case.

2. Ultimately, the parties settled the above case.

3. The District Court rendered the above decision in *Lincoln Town Car* on March 28, 1993. The Supreme Court decided *Buena Vista* on February 24,1993. If you were the government attorney in *Lincoln Town Car* what would you have done on February 25, 1993?

E.   CONSTITUTIONAL CONSIDERATIONS

The Supreme Court recently considered two major constitutional challenges to forfeiture, ruling that the Fifth Amendment's protection against double jeopardy is not activated by forfeiture, but that the Eighth Amendment's protection against excessive fines is activated.

The next case, United States v. Ursery, 518 U.S. 267, (1996), is a consolidation, on appeal, of two cases. It addresses the Fifth Amendment question. As you read it, determine whether you agree that forfeiture of properties belonging to Ursery, Arlt and Wren was remedial, not punitive. If you represented the claimants, what additional argument would you have made?

UNITED STATES v. URSERY; UNITED STATES v. $405,089.23 IN UNITED STATES CURRENCY

United States Supreme Court, 1996.
518 U.S. 267.

REHNQUIST, CHIEF JUSTICE.

In separate cases, the United States Court of Appeals for the Sixth Circuit and the United States Court of Appeals for the Ninth Circuit held that the Double Jeopardy Clause prohibits the Government from both punishing a defendant for a criminal offense and forfeiting his property for that same offense in a separate civil proceeding. We consolidated those cases for our review, and now reverse. These civil forfeitures (and civil forfeitures generally), we hold, do not constitute "punishment" for purposes of the Double Jeopardy Clause.

I

No. 95–345: Michigan Police found marijuana growing adjacent to respondent Guy Ursery's house, and discovered marijuana seeds, stems, stalks, and a growlight within the house. The United States instituted civil forfeiture proceedings against the house, alleging that the property was subject to forfeiture under 84 Stat. 1276, as amended, 21 U.S.C. § 881(a)(7) because it had been used for several years to facilitate the unlawful processing and distribution of a controlled substance. Ursery ultimately paid the United States $13,250 to settle the forfeiture claim in full. Shortly before the settlement was consummated, Ursery was indicted for manufacturing marijuana, in violation of § 841(a)(1). A jury found him guilty, and he was sentenced to 63 months in prison.

The Court of Appeals for the Sixth Circuit by a divided vote reversed Ursery's criminal conviction, holding that the conviction violated the Double Jeopardy Clause of the Fifth Amendment of the United States Constitution. 59 F.3d 568 (1995). The court based its conclusion in part upon its belief that our decisions in United States v. Halper, 490 U.S. 435 (1989), and Austin v. United States, 509 U.S. 602 (1993), meant that any civil forfeiture under § 881(a)(7) constitutes punishment for purposes of the Double Jeopardy Clause. Ursery, in the court's view, had therefore been "punished" in the forfeiture proceeding against his property, and could not be subsequently criminally tried for violation of 21 U.S.C. § 841(a)(1).

No. 95–346: Following a jury trial, Charles Wesley Arlt and James Wren were convicted of: conspiracy to aid and abet the manufacture of methamphetamine, in violation of 21 U.S.C. § 846; conspiracy to launder monetary instruments, in violation of 18 U.S.C. § 371; and numerous counts of money laundering, in violation of § 1956. The District Court sentenced Arlt to life in prison and a 10–year term of supervised release, and imposed a fine of $250,000. Wren was sentenced to life imprisonment and a 5–year term of supervised release.

Before the criminal trial had started, the United States had filed a civil in rem complaint against various property seized from, or titled to, Arlt and Wren, or Payback Mines, a corporation controlled by Arlt. The complaint alleged that each piece of property was subject to forfeiture both under 18 U.S.C. § 981(a)(1)(A), which provides that "[a]ny property . . . involved in a transaction or attempted transaction in violation of" § 1956 (the money-laundering statute) "is subject to forfeiture to the United States"; and under 21 U.S.C. § 881(a)(6), which provides for the forfeiture of (i) "[a]ll . . . things of value furnished or intended to be furnished by any person in exchange for" illegal drugs, (ii) "all proceeds traceable to such an exchange," and (iii) "all moneys, negotiable instruments, and securities used or intended to be used to facilitate" a federal drug felony. The parties agreed to defer litigation of the forfeiture action during the criminal prosecution. More than a year after the conclusion of the criminal trial, the District Court granted the Government's motion for summary judgment in the civil forfeiture proceeding.

Arlt and Wren appealed the decision in the forfeiture action, and the Court of Appeals for the Ninth Circuit reversed, holding that the forfeiture violated the Double Jeopardy Clause. 33 F.3d 1210 (1994). The court's decision was based in part upon the same view as that expressed by the Court of Appeals for the Sixth Circuit in Ursery's case—that our decisions in *Halper, supra,* and *Austin, supra,* meant that, as a categorical matter, forfeitures under § 981(a)(1)(A) and § 881(a)(6) always constitute "punishment."

We granted the Government's petition for certiorari in each of the two cases, and we now reverse.

II

The Double Jeopardy Clause provides: "[N]or shall any person be subject for the same offence to be twice put in jeopardy of life or limb." U.S. Const., Amdt. 5. The Clause serves the function of preventing both "successive punishments and ... successive prosecutions." United States v. Dixon, 509 U.S. 688, 696 (1993). The protection against multiple punishments prohibits the Government from "punishing twice, or attempting a second time to punish criminally for the same offense." [citation omitted]

In the decisions that we review, the Courts of Appeals held that the civil forfeitures constituted "punishment," making them subject to the prohibitions of the Double Jeopardy Clause. The Government challenges that characterization of the forfeitures, arguing that the courts were wrong to conclude that civil forfeitures are punitive for double jeopardy purposes.

A

Since the earliest years of this Nation, Congress has authorized the Government to seek parallel *in rem* civil forfeiture actions and criminal prosecutions based upon the same underlying events. And, in a long line of cases, this Court has considered the application of the Double Jeopardy Clause to civil forfeitures, consistently concluding that the Clause does not apply to such actions because they do not impose punishment.

* * *

[The Court reviewed a number of its prior cases then concluded:] Our cases reviewing civil forfeitures under the Double Jeopardy Clause adhere to a remarkably consistent theme. * * * [T]he conclusion was the same in each case: in rem civil forfeiture is a remedial civil sanction, distinct from potentially punitive in personam civil penalties such as fines, and does not constitute a punishment under the Double Jeopardy Clause.

In the case that we currently review, the Court of Appeals for the Ninth Circuit recognized as much, concluding that after United States v. One Assortment of 89 Firearms, 465 U.S. 354 (1984) "the law was clear that civil forfeitures did not constitute 'punishment' for double jeopardy purposes." 33 F.3d, at 1218. Nevertheless, that court read three of our decisions to have "abandoned" *89 Firearms* and the oft-affirmed rule of *Various Items*. According to the Court of Appeals for the Ninth Circuit, through our decisions in United States v. Halper, 490 U.S. 435 (1989), Austin v. United States, 509 U.S. 602 (1993), and Department of Revenue of Mont. v. Kurth Ranch, 511 U.S. 767 (1994), we "changed [our] collective mind," and "adopted a new test for determining whether a nominally civil sanction constitutes 'punishment' for double jeopardy purposes." 33 F.3d, at 1218–1219. The Court of Appeals for the Sixth Circuit shared the view of the Ninth Circuit, though it did not directly rely upon *Kurth Ranch*. We turn now to consider whether *Halper*, *Austin*, and *Kurth Ranch* accomplished the radical jurisprudential shift perceived by the Courts of Appeals.

In *Halper*, we considered "whether and under what circumstances a civil penalty may constitute 'punishment' for the purposes of double jeopardy analysis." *Halper, supra*, at 436. Based upon his submission of 65 inflated Medicare claims, each of which overcharged the Government by $9, Halper was criminally convicted of 65 counts of violating the false-claims statute, as well as of 16 counts of mail fraud, and was sentenced to two years in prison and fined $5,000. Following that criminal conviction, the Government successfully brought a civil action against Halper under 31 U.S.C. § 3729. The District Court hearing the civil action determined that Halper was liable to the Government for over $130,000 under § 3729, which then provided for liability in the amount of $2,000 per violation, double the Government's actual damages, and court costs. The court concluded that imposing the full civil penalty would constitute a second punishment for Halper's already-punished criminal offense, however, and therefore reduced Halper's liability to double the actual damages suffered by the Government and the costs of the civil action. The Government directly appealed that decision to this Court.

This Court agreed with the District Court's analysis. We determined that our precedent had established no absolute and irrebuttable rule that a civil fine cannot be "punishment" under the Double Jeopardy Clause. Though it was well established that "a civil remedy does not rise to the level of 'punishment' merely because Congress provided for civil recovery in excess of the Government's actual damages," we found that our case law did "not foreclose the possibility that in a particular case a civil penalty ... may be so extreme and so divorced from the Government's damages and expenses as to constitute punishment." Emphasizing the case-specific nature of our inquiry, we compared the size of the fine imposed on Halper, $130,000, to the damages actually suffered by the Government as a result of Halper's actions, estimated by the District Court at $585. Noting that the fine was more than 220 times greater than the Government's damages, we agreed with the District Court that "Halper's $130,000 liability is sufficiently disproportionate that the sanction constitutes a second punishment in violation of double jeopardy." We remanded to the District Court so that it could hear evidence regarding the Government's actual damages, and could then reduce Halper's liability to a nonpunitive level. [citations omitted]

In *Austin*, we considered whether a civil forfeiture could violate the Excessive Fines Clause of the Eighth Amendment to the Constitution, which provides that "[e]xcessive bail shall not be required, nor excessive fines imposed.... " U.S. Const., Amdt. 8. Aware that Austin had sold two grams of cocaine the previous day, police searched his mobile home and body shop. Their search revealed small amounts of marijuana and cocaine, a handgun, drug paraphernalia, and almost $5,000 in cash. Austin was charged with one count of possessing cocaine with intent to distribute, to which he pleaded guilty. The Government then initiated a civil forfeiture proceeding against Austin's mobile home and auto shop, contending that they had been "used" or were "intended for use" in the commission of a drug offense. See 21 U.S.C. §§ 881(a)(4) and (a)(7). Austin contested the forfeiture on the ground of the Excessive Fines Clause, but the District Court and the Court of Appeals held the forfeiture constitutional.

We limited our review to the question "whether the Excessive Fines Clause of the Eighth Amendment applies to forfeitures of property under 21 U.S.C. §§ 881(a)(4) and (a)(7)." We began our analysis by rejecting the argument that the Excessive Fines Clause was limited solely to criminal proceedings: The relevant question was not whether a particular proceeding was criminal or civil, we determined, but rather was whether forfeiture under §§ 881(a)(4) and (a)(7) constituted "punishment" for the purposes of the Eighth Amendment. In an effort to answer that question, we briefly reviewed the history of civil forfeiture both in this country and in England, taking a categorical approach that contrasted sharply with *Halper*'s case-specific approach to determining whether a civil penalty constitutes punishment. Ultimately, we concluded that "forfeiture under [§§ 881(a)(4) and (a)(7)] constitutes 'payment to a sovereign as punishment for some offense,' and, as such, is subject to the limitations of the Eighth Amendment's Excessive Fines Clause." [citations omitted]

In Department of Revenue of Mont. v. Kurth Ranch, 511 U.S. 767 (1994), we considered whether a state tax imposed on marijuana was invalid under the Double Jeopardy Clause when the taxpayer had already been criminally convicted of owning the marijuana which was taxed. We first established that the fact that Montana had labeled the civil sanction a "tax" did not end our analysis. We then turned to consider whether the tax was so punitive as to constitute a punishment subject to the Double Jeopardy Clause. Several differences between the marijuana tax imposed by Montana and the typical revenue-raising tax were readily apparent. The Montana tax was unique in that it was conditioned on the commission of a crime and was imposed only after the taxpayer had been arrested: thus, only a person charged with a criminal offense was subject to the tax. We also noted that the taxpayer did not own or possess the taxed marijuana at the time that the tax was imposed. From these differences, we determined that the tax was motivated by a "penal and prohibitory intent rather than the gathering of revenue." Concluding that the Montana tax proceeding "was the functional equivalent of a successive criminal prosecution," we affirmed the Court of Appeals' judgment barring the tax.

We think that the Court of Appeals for the Sixth Circuit and the Court of Appeals for the Ninth Circuit misread *Halper*, *Austin*, and *Kurth Ranch*. None of those decisions purported to overrule the well-established teaching of [our prior cases]. *Halper* involved not a civil forfeiture, but a civil penalty. That its rule was limited to the latter context is clear from the decision itself, from the historical distinction that we have drawn between civil forfeiture and civil penalties, and from the practical difficulty of applying *Halper* to a civil forfeiture.

* * *

It is difficult to see how the rule of *Halper* could be applied to a civil forfeiture. Civil penalties are designed as a rough form of "liquidated damages" for the harms suffered by the Government as a result of a defendant's conduct. The civil penalty involved in *Halper*, for example, provided for a fixed monetary penalty for each false claim count on which the defendant was convicted in the criminal proceeding. Whether a "fixed-penalty provision" that seeks to compensate the Government for harm it has suffered is "so extreme" and "so divorced" from the penalty's nonpunitive purpose of compensating the Government as to be a punishment may be determined by balancing the Government's harm against the size of the penalty. Civil forfeitures, in contrast to civil penalties, are designed to do more than simply compensate the Government. Forfeitures serve a variety of purposes, but are designed primarily to confiscate property used in violation of the law, and to require disgorgement of the fruits of illegal conduct. Though it may be possible to quantify the value of the property forfeited, it is virtually impossible to quantify, even approximately, the nonpunitive purposes served by a particular civil forfeiture. Hence, it is practically difficult to determine whether a particular forfeiture bears no rational relationship to the nonpunitive purposes of that forfeiture. Quite simply, the case-by-case balancing test set forth in *Halper*, in which a court must compare the harm suffered by the Government against the size of the penalty imposed, is inapplicable to civil forfeiture.

We recognized as much in *Kurth Ranch*. In that case, the Court expressly disclaimed reliance upon Halper, finding that its case-specific approach was impossible to apply outside the context of a fixed civil-penalty provision. Reviewing the Montana marijuana tax, we held that because "tax statutes serve a purpose quite different from civil penalties, . . . Halper's method of determining whether the exaction was remedial or punitive simply does not work in the case of a tax statute." * * *

* * *

In sum, nothing in *Halper*, *Kurth Ranch*, or *Austin*, purported to replace our traditional understanding that civil forfeiture does not constitute punishment for the purpose of the Double Jeopardy Clause. Congress long has authorized the Government to bring parallel criminal proceedings and civil forfeiture proceedings, and this Court consistently has found civil forfeitures not to constitute punishment under the Double Jeopardy Clause. It would have been quite remarkable for this Court both to have held unconstitutional a well-established practice, and to have overruled a long line of precedent, without having even suggested that it was doing so. *Halper* dealt with *in personam* civil penalties under the Double Jeopardy Clause; *Kurth Ranch* with a tax proceeding under the Double Jeopardy Clause; and *Austin* with civil forfeitures under the Excessive Fines Clause. None of those cases dealt with the subject of this case: in rem civil forfeitures for purposes of the Double Jeopardy Clause.

* * *

We turn now to consider the forfeitures in these cases under the teaching of * * * *89 Firearms*. Because it provides a useful analytical tool, we conduct our inquiry within the framework of the two-part test used in *89 Firearms*. First, we ask whether Congress intended proceedings under 21 U.S.C. § 881, and 18 U.S.C. § 981, to be criminal or civil. Second, we turn to consider whether the proceedings are so punitive in fact as to "persuade us that the forfeiture proceeding[s] may not legitimately be viewed as civil in nature," despite Congress' intent. *89 Firearms*, 465 U.S. at 366.

There is little doubt that Congress intended these forfeitures to be civil proceedings. As was the case in *89 Firearms*, "Congress' intent in this regard is most clearly demonstrated by the procedural mechanisms it established for enforcing forfeitures under the statute[s]." 465 U.S. at 363. Both 21 U.S.C. § 881 and 18 U.S.C. § 981, which is entitled "Civil forfeiture," provide that the laws "relating to the seizure, summary and judicial forfeiture, and condemnation of property for violation of the customs laws ... shall apply to seizures and forfeitures incurred" under § 881 and § 981. Because forfeiture proceedings under the customs laws are *in rem*, it is clear that Congress intended that a forfeiture under § 881 or § 981, like the forfeiture reviewed in *89 Firearms*, would be a proceeding *in rem*. Congress specifically structured these forfeitures to be impersonal by targeting the property itself. "In contrast to the *in personam* nature of criminal actions, actions *in rem* have traditionally been viewed as civil proceedings, with jurisdiction dependent upon seizure of a physical object." *89 Firearms*, 465 U.S. at 363.

* * *

Moving to the second stage of our analysis, we find that there is little evidence, much less the "clearest proof" that we require, see *89 Firearms, supra*, at 365, suggesting that forfeiture proceedings under 21 U.S.C. §§ 881(a)(6) and (a)(7), and 18 U.S.C. § 981(a)(1)(A), are so punitive in form and effect as to render them criminal despite Congress' intent to the contrary. The statutes involved in this case are, in most significant respects, indistinguishable from those reviewed, and held not to be punitive, in * * *.

Most significant is that § 981(a)(1)(A), and §§ 881(a)(6) and (a)(7), while perhaps having certain punitive aspects, serve important nonpunitive goals. Title 21 U.S.C. § 881(a)(7), under which Ursery's property was forfeited, provides for the forfeiture of "all real property ... which is used or intended to be used, in any manner or part, to commit, or to facilitate the commission of" a federal drug felony. Requiring the forfeiture of property used to commit federal narcotics violations encourages property owners to take care in managing their property and ensures that they will not permit that property to be used for illegal purposes.

The forfeiture of the property claimed by Arlt and Wren took place pursuant to 18 U.S.C. § 981(a)(1)(A), and 21 U.S.C. § 881(a)(6). Section 981(a)(1)(A) provides for the forfeiture of "any property" involved in illegal money-laundering transactions. Section 881(a)(6) provides for the forfeiture of "[a]ll ... things of value furnished or intended to be furnished by any person in exchange for" illegal drugs; "all proceeds traceable to such an exchange"; and "all moneys, negotiable instruments, and securities used or intended to be used to facilitate" a federal drug felony. The same remedial purposes served by § 881(a)(7) are served by § 881(a)(6) and § 981(a)(1)(A). Only one point merits separate discussion. To the extent that § 881(a)(6) applies to "proceeds" of illegal drug activity, it serves the additional nonpunitive goal of ensuring that persons do not profit from their illegal acts.

Other considerations that we have found relevant to the question whether a proceeding is criminal also tend to support a conclusion that § 981(a)(1)(A) and §§ 881(a)(6) and (a)(7) are civil proceedings. First, in light of our decisions in * * * and *89 Firearms*, and the long tradition of federal statutes providing for a forfeiture proceeding following a criminal prosecution, it is absolutely clear that *in rem* civil forfeiture has not historically been regarded as punishment, as we have understood that term under the Double Jeopardy Clause. Second, there is no requirement in the statutes that we currently review that the Government demonstrate *scienter* in order to establish that the property is subject to forfeiture; indeed, the property may be subject to forfeiture even if no party files a claim to it and the Government never shows any connection between the property and a particular person. Though both § 881(a) and § 981(a) contain an "innocent owner" exception, we do not think that such a provision, without more indication of an intent to punish, is relevant to the question whether a statute is punitive under the Double Jeopardy Clause. Third, though both statutes may fairly be said to serve the purpose of deterrence, we long have held that this purpose may serve civil as well as criminal goals.

We hold that these *in rem* civil forfeitures are neither "punishment" nor criminal for purposes of the Double Jeopardy Clause. The judgments of the Court of Appeals for the Sixth Circuit, in No. 95–345, and of the Court of Appeals for the Ninth Circuit, in No. 95–346, are accordingly reversed.

It is so ordered.

JUSTICE STEVENS, CONCURRING IN THE JUDGMENT IN PART AND DISSENTING IN
PART.

The question the Court poses is whether civil forfeitures constitute
"punishment" for purposes of the Double Jeopardy Clause. Because the
numerous federal statutes authorizing forfeitures cover such a wide
variety of situations, it is quite wrong to assume that there is only one
answer to that question. For purposes of analysis it is useful to identify
three different categories of property that are subject to seizure: proceeds, contraband, and property that has played a part in the commission of a crime. The facts of these two cases illustrate the point.

In No. 95–346 the Government has forfeited $405,089.23 in curren-
cy. Those funds are the proceeds of unlawful activity. They are not
property that respondents have any right to retain. The forfeiture of
such proceeds, like the confiscation of money stolen from a bank, does
not punish respondents because it exacts no price in liberty or lawfully
derived property from them. I agree that the forfeiture of such proceeds
is not punitive and therefore I concur in the Court's disposition of No.
95–346.

None of the property seized in No. 95–345 constituted proceeds of
illegal activity. Indeed, the facts of that case reveal a dramatically
different situation. Respondent Ursery cultivated marijuana in a heavily
wooded area not far from his home in Shiawassee County, Michigan. The
illegal substance was consumed by members of his family, but there is no
evidence, and no contention by the Government, that he sold any of it to
third parties. Acting on the basis of the incorrect assumption that the
marijuana plants were on respondent's property, Michigan police officers
executed a warrant to search the premises. In his house they found
marijuana seeds, stems, stalks, and a growlight. I presume those items
were seized, and I have no difficulty concluding that such a seizure does
not constitute punishment because respondent had no right to possess
contraband. Accordingly, I agree with the Court's opinion insofar as it
explains why the forfeiture of contraband does not constitute punishment for double jeopardy purposes.

The critical question presented in No. 95–345 arose, not out of the
seizure of contraband by the Michigan police, but rather out of the
decision by the United States Attorney to take respondent's home. There
is no evidence that the house had been purchased with the proceeds of
unlawful activity and the house itself was surely not contraband. Nonetheless, 21 U.S.C. § 881(a)(7) authorized the Government to seek forfeiture of respondent's residence because it had been used to facilitate the
manufacture and distribution of marijuana.[1] Respondent was then himself prosecuted for and convicted of manufacturing marijuana. In my
opinion none of the reasons supporting the forfeiture of proceeds or

---

1. The contraband found on the premises was evidence that the building had been
used to facilitate the commission of a violation of Title 21 punishable by more than
one year's imprisonment. To justify that
forfeiture, the Government assumed the
burden of proving (a) that respondent had
committed such an offense, and (b) that the
property had played some part in it. * * *

contraband provides a sufficient basis for concluding that the confiscation of respondent's home was not punitive.

* * *

In recent years, both Congress and the state legislatures have armed their law enforcement authorities with new powers to forfeit property that vastly exceed their traditional tools. In response, this Court has reaffirmed the fundamental proposition that all forfeitures must be accomplished within the constraints set by the Constitution. This Term the Court has begun dismantling the protections it so recently erected. In Bennis v. Michigan, 516 U.S. ___ (1996), the Court held that officials may confiscate an innocent person's automobile. And today, for the first time it upholds the forfeiture of a person's home. On the way to its surprising conclusion that the owner is not punished by the loss of his residence, the Court repeatedly professes its adherence to tradition and time-honored practice. * * *

The recurrent theme of the Court's opinion is that there is some mystical difference between *in rem* and *in personam* proceedings, such that only the latter can give rise to double jeopardy concerns. The Court claims that "[s]ince at least *Various Items*," we have drawn this distinction for purposes of applying relevant constitutional provisions. That statement, however, is incorrect. We have repeatedly rejected the idea that the nature of the court's jurisdiction has any bearing on the constitutional protections that apply at a proceeding before it. "From the relevant constitutional standpoint, there is no difference between a man who 'forfeits' $8,674 because he has used the money in illegal gambling activities and a man who pays a 'criminal fine' of $8,674 as a result of the same course of conduct." United States v. Coin & Currency, 401 U.S., 715, 718. Most recently, in our application of *Halper's* definition of punishment, we stated that "[w]e do not understand the Government to rely separately on the technical distinction between proceedings *in rem* and proceedings *in personam*, but we note that any such reliance would be misplaced." *Austin*, 509 U.S. at 615.

* * *

The pedantic distinction between *in rem* and *in personam* actions is ultimately only a cover for the real basis for the Court's decision: the idea that the property, not the owner, is being "punished" for offenses of which it is "guilty." Although the Court prefers not to rely on this notorious fiction too blatantly, its repeated citations to *Various Items* make clear that the Court believes respondent's home was "guilty" of the drug offenses with which he was charged. On that rationale, of course, the case is easy. The *owner* of the property is not being punished when the Government confiscates it, just the *property*. The same sleight-of-hand would have worked in *Austin*, too: The owner of the property is not being excessively fined, just the property itself. Despite the Government's heavy reliance on that fiction in *Austin*, we did not allow it to stand in the way of our holding that the seizure of property may punish the owner.

Even if the point had not been settled by prior decisions, common sense would dictate the result in this case. There is simply no rational basis for characterizing the seizure of this respondent's home as anything other than punishment for his crime. The house was neither proceeds nor contraband and its value had no relation to the Government's authority to seize it. Under the controlling statute an essential predicate for the forfeiture was proof that respondent had used the property in connection with the commission of a crime. * * * As we unanimously recognized in *Halper*, formalistic distinctions that obscure the obvious practical consequences of governmental action deserve the " 'humane interests' "protected by the Double Jeopardy Clause. 490 U.S. at 447. Fidelity to both reason and precedent dictates the conclusion that this forfeiture was "punishment" for purposes of the Double Jeopardy Clause.

Notes

With whom do you agree, the majority or dissent? Does Justice Stevens have a point that from the property owner's perspective, forfeiture of one's home is punishment? On the other hand, if Justice Stevens' view had prevailed and civil forfeiture was found to constitute punishment, what would happen to criminals who had been convicted after a related civil forfeiture? Would their convictions be overturned on grounds of double jeopardy? Do you believe this consideration was a factor in the majority's decision? Should it be a factor?

In the next case, the Supreme Court held that forfeiture may violate the Eighth Amendment's protection against excessive fines. Note the Court's conclusion that "forfeiture serves, at least in part, to punish the owner." Recall the Court's conclusion in *Ursery* that "civil forfeiture does not constitute punishment for the purpose of the Double Jeopardy Clause."[dd] Are these positions consistent?

AUSTIN v. UNITED STATES

United States Supreme Court, 1993.
509 U.S. 602.

BLACKMUN, JUSTICE.

In this case, we are asked to decide whether the Excessive Fines Clause of the Eighth Amendment applies to forfeitures of property under 21 U.S.C. §§ 881(a)(4) and (a)(7). We hold that it does and therefore remand the case for consideration of the question whether the forfeiture at issue here was excessive.

dd. 518 U.S. 267, ____, 116 S.Ct. 2135, 2147.

On August 2, 1990, petitioner Richard Lyle Austin was indicted on four counts of violating South Dakota's drug laws. Austin ultimately pleaded guilty to one count of possessing cocaine with intent to distribute and was sentenced by the state court to seven years' imprisonment. On September 7, the United States filed an *in rem* action in the United States District Court for the District of South Dakota seeking forfeiture of Austin's mobile home and auto body shop under 21 U.S.C. §§ 881(a)(4) and (a)(7).[1] Austin filed a claim and an answer to the complaint.

On February 4, 1991, the United States made a motion, supported by an affidavit from Sioux Falls Police Officer Donald Satterlee, for summary judgment. According to Satterlee's affidavit, Austin met Keith Engebretson at Austin's body shop on June 13, 1990, and agreed to sell cocaine which he sold to Engebretson. Austin left the shop, went to his mobile home, and returned to the shop with two grams of cocaine which he sold to Engebretson. State authorities executed a search warrant on the body shop and mobile home the following day. They discovered small amounts of marijuana and cocaine, a .22 caliber revolver, drug paraphernalia, and approximately $4,700 in cash. App. 13. In opposing summary judgment, Austin argued that forfeiture of the properties would violate the Eighth Amendment.[2] The District Court rejected this argument and entered summary judgment for the United States.

The United States Court of Appeals for the Eighth Circuit "reluctantly agree[d] with the government" and affirmed. * * *

Austin contends that the Eighth Amendment's Excessive Fines Clause applies to *in rem* civil forfeiture proceedings. We have had occasion to consider this Clause only once before. In Browning–Ferris Industries v. Kelco Disposal, Inc., 492 U.S. 257 (1989), we held that the Excessive Fines Clause does not limit the award of punitive damages to a private party in a civil suit when the government neither has prosecuted the action nor has any right to receive a share of the damages. The Court's opinion and JUSTICE O'CONNOR'S opinion, concurring in part and dissenting in part, reviewed in some detail the history of the Excessive Fines Clause. The Court concluded that both the Eighth Amendment and § 10 of the English Bill of Rights of 1689, from which it derives,

---

1. These statutes provide for the forfeiture of:

"(4) All conveyances, including aircraft, vehicles, or vessels, which are used, or are intended for use, to transport, or in any manner to facilitate the transportation, sale, receipt, possession, or concealment of [controlled substances, their raw materials, and equipment used in their manufacture and distribution]

         * * *

"(7) All real property, including any right, title and interest (including any leasehold interest) in the whole of any lot or tract of land and any appurtenances or improvements, which is used, or intended to be used, in any manner or part, to commit, or to facilitate the commission of, a violation of this subchapter punishable by more than one year's imprisonment. . . ."

Each provision has an "innocent owner" exception. See §§ 881(a)(4)(C) and (a)(7).

2. "Excessive bail shall not be required, nor excessive fines imposed, nor cruel and unusual punishments inflicted." U.S. Const. Amdt. 8.

were intended to prevent *the government* from abusing its power to punish, and therefore "that the Excessive Fines Clause was intended to limit only those fines directly imposed by, and payable to, the government."

We found it unnecessary to decide in *Browning-Ferris* whether the Excessive Fines Clause applies only to criminal cases. The United States now argues that

"any claim that the government's conduct in a civil proceeding is limited by the Eighth Amendment generally, or by the Excessive Fines Clause in particular, must fail unless the challenged governmental action, despite its label, would have been recognized as a *criminal* punishment at the time the Eighth Amendment was adopted." Brief for United States 16 (emphasis added).

It further suggests that the Eighth Amendment cannot apply to a civil proceeding unless that proceeding is so punitive that it must be considered criminal under Kennedy v. Mendoza-Martinez, 372 U.S. 144 (1963), and United States v. Ward, 448 U.S. 242 (1980). We disagree.

Some provisions of the Bill of Rights are expressly limited to criminal cases. The Fifth Amendment's Self–Incrimination Clause, for example, provides: "No person ... shall be compelled in any criminal case to be a witness against himself." The protections provided by the Sixth Amendment are explicitly confined to "criminal prosecutions." See generally *Ward*, 448 U.S. at 248. The text of the Eighth Amendment includes no similar limitation.

* * *

The purpose of the Eighth Amendment, putting the Bail Clause to one side, was to limit the government's power to punish. The Cruel and Unusual Punishments Clause is self-evidently concerned with punishment. The Excessive Fines Clause limits the Government's power to extract payments, whether in cash or in kind, "as *punishment* for some offense." *Id.*, at 265 (emphasis added). "The notion of punishment, as we commonly understand it, cuts across the division between the civil and the criminal law." United States v. Halper, 490 U.S. 435, 447–448 (1989). "It is commonly understood that civil proceedings may advance punitive and remedial goals, and, conversely, that both punitive and remedial goals may be served by criminal penalties." *Id.*, at 447. Thus, the question is not, as the United States would have it, whether forfeiture under §§ 881(a)(4) and (a)(7) is civil or criminal, but rather whether it is punishment.

In considering this question, we are mindful of the fact that sanctions frequently serve more than one purpose. We need not exclude the possibility that a forfeiture serves remedial purposes to conclude that it is subject to the limitations of the Excessive Fines Clause. We, however, must determine that it can only be explained as serving in part to punish. We said in *Halper* that "a civil sanction that cannot fairly be said solely to serve a remedial purpose, but rather can only be explained as also serving either retributive or deterrent purposes, is punishment, as we have come to understand the term." 490 U.S. at 448. We turn, then, to consider whether, at the time the Eighth Amendment was ratified, forfeiture was understood at least in part as punishment and whether forfeiture under §§ 881(a)(4) and (a)(7) should be so understood today.

* * *

[The Court reviewed the history of forfeiture and the Courts' prior precedents in forfeiture cases. ed.]

In sum, even though this Court has rejected the "innocence" of the owner as a common-law defense to forfeiture, it consistently has recognized that forfeiture serves, at least in part, to punish the owner. See *Peisch v. Ware*, 4 Cranch, 347, 364 (1808) ("the act punishes the owner with a forfeiture of the goods"); *Dobbins' Distillery*, 96 U.S. 395, 404 (1878) ("The acts of violation as to the penal consequences to the property are to be considered just the same as if they were the acts of the owner"); *Goldsmith-Grant Co.*, 254 U.S. 505, 511 (1921) ("such misfortunes are in part owing to the negligence of the owner, and therefore he is properly punished by the forfeiture"). More recently, we have noted that forfeiture serves "punitive and deterrent purposes," *Calero-Toledo*, 416 U.S. 663, 686 (1974) and "impos[es] an economic penalty," *id.*, at 687. We conclude, therefore that forfeiture generally and statutory *in rem* forfeiture in particular historically have been understood, at least in part, as punishment.

* * *

Fundamentally, even assuming that §§ 881(a)(4) and (a)(7) serve some remedial purpose, the Government's argument must fail. "[A] civil sanction that cannot fairly be said *solely* to serve a remedial purpose, but rather can only be explained as also serving either retributive or deterrent purposes, is punishment, as we have come to understand the term." *Halper*, 490 U.S. at 448 (emphasis added). In light of the historical understanding of forfeiture as punishment, the clear focus of §§ 881(a)(4) and (a)(7) on the culpability of the owner, and the evidence that Congress understood those provisions as serving to deter and to punish, we cannot conclude that forfeiture under §§ 881(a)(4) and (a)(7) serves solely a remedial purpose. We therefore conclude that forfeiture under these provision constitutes "payment to a sovereign as punishment for some offense," *Browning-Ferris*, 492 U.S. at 265, and, as such, is subject to the limitations of the Eighth Amendment's Excessive Fines Clause.

* * *

Notes

1. Does the Supreme Court's opinion in *Austin* blur or clarify the line between criminal and civil law?

2. What if Lyle Austin was married and his wife, as joint owner of the mobile home, contested the forfeiture as an innocent owner? Or, similarly, what if Lyle Austin lived with his parents who owned the mobile home: would his parents have much luck contesting the forfeiture as innocent owners? Recognizing that such inquiries are highly fact specific, consider the thoughts of Professor Guerra.[ee]

"The civil asset forfeiture laws turn our *laissez faire* system of justice on its head. Ordinarily, citizens rely on the police to investigate crimes, conduct searches and make arrests, and the law imposes no duties on private individuals to perform the work of police officers. The forfeiture laws, however, single out property owners and require them, under threat of punishment, to police their property for illegal use. The law subjects property owners' actions to heightened scrutiny and holds them responsible for the illegal acts of others if they fail to report the offenses or fail to take other steps to prevent illegal activity on the premises.

* * *

"The application of civil forfeiture law within the family is a new legal development. For the first time, this system imposes duties on family members to act as police officers in their own homes. Parents and spouses are expected to report their relatives' violations to the police, search their relatives' possessions for contraband, evict their children or divorce their spouses, and otherwise cooperate with the authorities. By requiring family members to police each other or risk the loss of the family's assets, the law eliminates other options family members may have for dealing with relatives who have gone astray.

* * *

"In the family context, the forfeiture laws have the effect of transferring decisionmaking authority regarding family life from individual family members to the judiciary and the law enforcement establishment. Unlike other explicit attempts to regulate family life, the asset forfeiture laws do not focus on family members per se; the effect on the family is incidental. Nevertheless, many federal courts have not trod lightly in this area; they have, to the contrary, brought the full force of federal confiscation power to bear on family members who have not fulfilled the perceived duties of citizenship imposed on them by the courts via the "reasonable steps" test.

* * *

"The practice of visiting the sins of one family member on another sacrifices the interests of the uninvolved person for the societal good of deterring wrongdoing. It threatens the special bond of love and loyalty that exists between family members. The failure to make an exception for family situations in the application of civil forfeiture laws ignores those important emotional and psychological bonds. It also ignores the moral, cultural, and religious beliefs that may require family members

ee. Sandra Guerra, *Family Values: The Family As An Innocent Victim of Civil Drug Asset Forfeiture*, 81 CORNELL L. REV. 343 (1996). Copyright ©. All rights reserved. Reprinted with permission from Sandra Guerra and Cornell Law Review.

to give shelter and protection to each other in the face of government pressure to betray them.

"In a family setting, the forfeiture rules can have a detrimental impact on family relationships and on the long-term development of individuals within the family. The spousal property cases demonstrate a callous indifference to gender-related issues of power and authority. The Eleventh Circuit's decision in *Sixty Acres* epitomizes the cruelty of the forfeiture regime, dispossessing an uninvolved wife because she had failed to report her husband to the police, even though she reasonably believed that had she done so, her husband would have retaliated against her, inflicting serious bodily harm or even killing her. In the words of the Third Circuit, the forfeiture cases "defy marital reality" by expecting wives, who may be responsible for young children and financially dependent on their husbands for support, to either report their spouses to the police or file for divorce.

"The parent-child cases likewise disregard the reality of family life by encouraging the parents of teenage or young adult children via the "reasonable steps" test to (1) search their children's possessions; (2) report their children's illegal activity to the police; or (3) evict their children from the home. Parents may oppose random searches because they may reasonably believe in the need to respect their older children's privacy. They may, in other words, view establishing and maintaining trust between themselves and their children as they key to effective parenting.

"Parents may also oppose the second and third options, preferring, when they discover illegal activity in the home, to take measures that fall short of reporting their children to the authorities or evicting them. Parents may believe that through stern, caring discussions, intrafamily discipline, and demonstrated faith in the ability of their children to improve, the family stands a better chance at rehabilitating the errant children.

"Some parents may, in fact, choose to call the police only as a last resort when and if their children's behavior reaches the point at which it threatens the health and peace of the entire family. In certain situations, parents may, depending on their assessment of their children in relation to the family unit, determine police intervention to be necessary. They may even believe that spending a short time in jail would have a certain "shock" value to their children, helping to steer them in the right direction. Parents make such choices with the best long-term interests of their children and the entire family in mind.

"It is a question of conflicting goals: The asset forfeiture law seeks to enforce the anti-drug laws and calls on property owners to make valiant efforts toward that end. Parents, on the other hand, seek to achieve the long-term goal of guiding family members away from drugs and encouraging productive, law-abiding behavior. Most parents will attempt to spare their children the potentially devastating impact of criminal conviction and incarceration. Parents may also reasonably believe that policing their children in the manner required by the courts will destroy the parent-child relationship.

"The third option—requiring parents to throw their children out of the house—poses another set of problems. First, for working class parents, the suggestion that they evict their children may mean literally putting their children out on the street. If they fear loss of the home to forfeiture, they cannot in good conscience send their children to live with other relatives or friends because doing so would simply transfer the risk of forfeiture to them.

"Second, many of the children in forfeiture cases have drug addiction problems. Although institutionalization in a residential treatment facility would be an ideal solution for the family at risk of forfeiture, this form of treatment may be prohibitively expensive for working class families, who may not have medical insurance coverage for this service or the fund to pay for it outright. In addition, they may not have access to public rehabilitation programs because of unavailability or because they may not meet the indigency requirements for such programs.

"The eviction option thus presents a cruel irony of the forfeiture rules as applied to families. Hard working, working-class people who do well enough to buy a home for their family, but who are not wealthy, cannot afford to send their children away for residential treatment like a wealthy person can and even a poor person might. Working-class parents thus occupy the most vulnerable position when faced with forfeiture of the family home. If a wealthy person's home is forfeited, he or she will simply buy another. If a poor person who rents an apartment or house is evicted, he or she can usually rent another. Those in between these two extremes—usually single mothers who may have struggled for years to stay above the poverty line—lose everything they have invested in their homes and cannot likely afford comparable housing.

"What, then can lawmakers do to eliminate the unfairness of civil asset forfeiture laws? * * * Congress could, for example, enact an exception for the primary residences of family members who are not themselves guilty of any drug offense. At a minimum, lawmakers could give standing to innocent minor children whose homes become subject to forfeiture.

"To protect innocent spouses, Congress should amend the forfeiture laws to prohibit the partition of marital real property so that uninvolved spouses are not penalized for the wrongdoing of their husbands or wives. Such a rule would not protect the ill-gotten gains of drug dealers since the cases suggest that the homes confiscated under the civil asset forfeiture laws are not purchased with drug proceeds. Nor would guilty spouses avoid punishment; they would be subject to criminal prosecution for their offenses.

"Even absent legislative change, however, the courts could reexamine precedent on what steps are "reasonable," when one or more family members become involved in the drug trade. The case law demonstrates a lack of awareness of important gender and class issues created by the forfeiture rules. Courts should emulate those cases that have contextualized the "reasonableness" analysis, considering factors such as educational background, work schedule, and total number of dependents, which may affect a parent's ability to supervise the use of his or her property. Furthermore, courts should recognize the value of preserving the family, and of showing maternal concern for young children, as legitimate factors in evaluating the reasonableness of a parent's response to drug offenses on his or her property. In spousal property cases, the courts should similarly recognize the reality of married life and the importance of maintaining marital bonds. No woman should be required by law to either report her husband to the police, or divorce him, because he has violated drug laws. In cases of violent oppression by an abusive husband, the courts should not expect a woman to take any measures that would endanger her or her family. No woman should have to sacrifice her safety or that or her children to further the government's war on drugs."

* * *

Do you agree with Professor Guerra that forfeiture laws impose an unacceptable obligation on family members? Would you agree if the family was non-traditional: a couple living together for years as a single family unit? living together for weeks? living together sporadically?

F.   LOCATING ASSETS

Suppose the government wins a judgment of forfeiture but is having a difficult time locating the defendant's assets. This problem would be more likely to arise, of course, after an award of forfeiture in a criminal case since with civil forfeiture the property itself is served. As the next case demonstrates, the government may be able to look in some interesting places for information about seizable assets.

UNITED STATES v. SACCOCCIA

United States District Court, District of Rhode Island, 1995.
898 F.Supp. 53.

TORRES, DISTRICT JUDGE.

Stephen A. Saccoccia, Donna Saccoccia, and Vincent "Mickey" Hurley (the "defendants") have been convicted of various money laundering offenses and of a RICO conspiracy to launder money derived from the illegal sale of narcotics. The judgments entered pursuant to their convictions require them to forfeit the sum of $136,344,231.87, which represents the proceeds of their racketeering activity.

The Government, relying on 18 U.S.C. § 1963(k) and 21 U.S.C. § 853(m) as incorporated by 18 U.S.C. § 982(b)(1)(A), has applied for an order authorizing it to depose several attorneys who represented the defendants at various stages of the criminal prosecution and further requiring the production of unspecified documents for the purpose of identifying and locating assets of the defendants that may be used to satisfy the forfeiture judgment. The principal questions presented are whether allowing the Government to depose counsel with respect to the fee arrangements between them and their clients would violate the attorney-client privilege, the Fifth Amendment's privilege against self-incrimination and/or the defendants' Sixth Amendment right to counsel. For reasons stated below, I find that the answer to each of these questions is, no.

* * *

The forfeiture order constitutes a money judgment against the defendants and may be satisfied either from the proceeds of their racketeering activity, property derived from those proceeds or, if such proceeds or property have been concealed, from any other property belonging to the defendants. 18 U.S.C. §§ 1963(a)(1), (3) and (m). The Government seeks to depose counsel because only a portion of the amount declared forfeited has been recovered and because the number of attorneys they have employed suggests that the defendants may have considerable sums of money at their disposal.

When the Government filed its application, appeals by all of the defendants were pending and Stephen Saccoccia was awaiting trial in California on related conspiracy and money laundering charges.

* * *

The time for decision, now, has arrived. The Court of Appeals for the First Circuit has affirmed the convictions and forfeiture orders against all of the defendants.[ff]

* * *

The defendants and their counsel urge that the Government's application should be denied for a variety of reasons.

Attorney-Client Privilege

The purpose of the attorney-client privilege is to encourage the client to make full disclosure of all pertinent facts to the attorney so that the attorney may render informed legal advice with respect to the matters about which the attorney is consulted. Fisher v. U.S., 425 U.S. 391, 403 (1976). The privilege is based on the concern that if damaging information communicated in confidence to an attorney later might be revealed to third parties, the client would be deterred from making a full disclosure. Although the privilege occasionally may deprive the Government of evidence necessary to convict a criminal, that is the price extracted by a system of justice that places a premium on an individual's right to the effective assistance of counsel.

However, because the privilege may cause relevant information to be withheld from the fact finder, it applies only to the extent necessary to achieve its purpose. Consequently, the privilege does not necessarily extend to all information imparted to an attorney during the course of representing a client. The privilege "protects only those disclosures

---

ff. *Saccoccia*, 58 F.3d 754; United States v. Hurley, 63 F.3d 1 (1st Cir.1995).

necessary to obtain informed legal advice which might not have been made absent the privilege." *Fisher*, 96 S.Ct. at 1577. To put it another way, communications by the client are privileged only if they are both confidential and made in order to obtain effective legal assistance.

Moreover, with respect to criminal matters, the privilege applies only if the advice sought relates to past conduct. The "crime/fraud" exception renders the privilege inapplicable to information provided for the purpose of obtaining advice about ongoing criminal activity or plans to commit criminal acts in the future. The crime/fraud exception comes into play even if the attorney is unaware of the client's purpose. Seeking advice in order to further an ongoing or future criminal activity constitutes an abuse of the attorney-client relationship and, in such cases, the purpose of the privilege is not served by preventing disclosure.

The party invoking the attorney-client privilege has the burden of establishing that it applies. However if the Government claims that the "crime/fraud" exception applies, it has the burden of making a *prima facie* showing to that effect.

Generally speaking, neither the identity of a client nor information regarding fee arrangements is protected by the attorney-client privilege. The reason for excluding fee information is that, ordinarily, such information does not constitute a confidential communication relating to the advice sought. In the words of the Second Circuit, "While consultation with an attorney, and payment of a fee, may be necessary to obtain legal advice, their disclosure does not inhibit the ordinary communication necessary for an attorney to act effectively, justly, and expeditiously." In re Grand Jury Subpoena Served Upon Doe, 781 F.2d 238, 247–248 (2d Cir.1986).

However, there may be exceptional cases in which fee information is so intertwined with the matter about which counsel is consulted that the threat of disclosure would deter the client from communicating information necessary to obtain informed legal advice. The case law reflects considerable confusion with respect to the criteria to be applied in determining when those circumstances exist. Some decisions seem to suggest that fee information is protected when it is likely to incriminate the client with respect to the matter about which he consulted counsel. That notion, commonly referred to as the "legal advice" exception, often is attributed to the Ninth Circuit's decision in Baird v. Koerner, 279 F.2d 623 (9th Cir.1960). Thus in *Hodge and Zweig* the Court required disclosure of the fee information at issue but cited *Baird* for the proposition that " ... the nature of [a] client's fee arrangement may be privileged where the person invoking the privilege can show that a strong probability exists that disclosure of such information would implicate that client in the very criminal activity for which legal advice was sought." *Hodge and Zweig*, 548 F.2d at 1353.

However, the Ninth Circuit since has repudiated any suggestion that *Baird* should be read as automatically making fee information privileged merely because it may be incriminating. It has focused, instead, on whether the information reveals confidential attorney-client communications. That view is shared by those circuits that most recently have addressed the issue.

The First Circuit has not yet ruled on the specific question of whether the possibility of incrimination is, by itself, sufficient to render fee information privileged. In U.S. v. Strahl, 590 F.2d 10, 11 (1st Cir.1978), the Court, citing *Baird*, did recognize that the identity of a client may be privileged when identification "amount[s] to the prejudicial disclosure of a confidential communication." The Court distinguished *Baird* on the ground that, in *Baird* "disclosure of [the identity] of the client would [have] implicate[d] that client in the very criminal activity for which legal advice was sought." *Strahl*, 590 F.2d at 11. However, the Court determined that, in a prosecution for counterfeiting stolen treasury notes, an attorney who had previously represented the defendant with respect to unrelated matters could be required to identify the defendant as the man who had tendered stolen treasury notes in payment for the past legal services. The *Strahl* Court held that the payments at issue in that case were not privileged because there was "no indication that [the defendant] went to [the attorney] for legal advice concerning his counterfeiting activities and disclosed confidential information to him" and because preventing disclosure of "a fraudulent act as well as a convenient means of unloading highly incriminating evidence, possession of which was itself a crime" did not further the policies underlying the attorney-client privilege. *Strahl*, 590 F.2d at 11–12.

Strahl was decided long before the Ninth Circuit clarified its holding in *Baird*. Nevertheless, a close reading of *Strahl* indicates that, in order to fall within the "legal advice" exception, fee information must amount to or reveal confidential communications regarding the advice sought from the attorney. In short, the fee information must satisfy the requirements of the attorney-client privilege and does not become privileged simply because it might incriminate the client.

In this case, the defendants have failed to establish that information regarding the amount, form or source of the legal fees paid should be treated as confidential attorney-client communications necessary to obtain legal advice with respect to their money laundering activities. Although payment of a fee undoubtedly was a prerequisite to retaining the services of counsel, the defendants presumably had the option to determine the form of payment and whether or not to divulge the sources. Furthermore, the mere fact that the amount of fees paid may constitute evidence of unexplained wealth that arguably could have been derived from criminal activity is insufficient to invoke the attorney-client privilege.

Moreover, even if the possibility of incrimination, alone, were sufficient to satisfy the "legal advice" exception, the exception would have no application to this case. As already noted, all of the defendants now stand convicted of the offenses with which they were charged and their appeals from those convictions have been exhausted. Consequently, disclosure of information regarding the fees they paid can no longer implicate them in those offenses.

Finally, to the extent the defendants are suggesting that the fee information is confidential because the amounts paid were derived from the money laundering activities about which they consulted counsel, their claim of privilege would be defeated by the crime/fraud exception. Such payments would constitute continued laundering of illicitly-derived proceeds. See 18 U.S.C. §§ 1956 and 1957.

II. THE STATUTES AUTHORIZING DISCOVERY

The defendants correctly observe that the Court has discretion to decide whether the Government should be permitted to depose counsel pursuant to 18 U.S.C. § 1963(k) and/or 21 U.S.C. § 853(m). Both statutes provide that:

> " ... the Court *may*, upon application of the United States, order that the testimony of any witness relating to the property forfeited be taken by deposition ..." [emphasis added]

The defendants argue that, in this case, the application should be denied because the Government has failed to demonstrate a sufficient need for deposing counsel and there is a risk that such action may "drive a 'chilling wedge' between the attorney and client, create conflicts of interest, undermine an attorney's ability to represent his client and potentially lead to disqualification of the attorney." In support of their argument, the defendants point to [local] Rule 3.8(f), which, as already noted, requires a prosecutor to obtain Court approval before issuing subpoenas that would compel lawyers to provide evidence concerning their clients that was obtained as a result of the attorney-client relationship.

The short answer to that argument is that the concerns underlying Rule 3.8(f) are not implicated in this case. The overriding purpose of the rule is to ensure that subpoenas do not become instruments of abuse that infringe on the attorney-client privilege, deprive a defendant of the Sixth Amendment right to effective assistance of counsel or otherwise unjustifiably interfere with the defendant's legal representation. Here, those matters are no longer factors warranting consideration. There is no risk that counsel will be disqualified from continuing to represent their clients in this case or that such representation will be undermined by their testimony because the case has been terminated.

Furthermore, Rule 3.8(f) does not require the Government to demonstrate any greater need for information in order to obtain or enforce a subpoena directed to counsel than it would for any other subpoena. Rather, it provides a mechanism for determining, in advance, whether the Government should be precluded from seeking the information on the ground that it is protected by the attorney-client privilege or that issuance of the subpoena infringes on a defendant's Sixth Amendment rights or otherwise constitutes an abuse of the process.

In this case, there is ample reason for permitting the depositions of counsel pursuant to § 1963(k). As already noted, more than $136 million was laundered by these defendants and, to date, only a portion of the proceeds has been recovered or accounted for. Furthermore, the fact that the defendants have employed and continue to employ numerous attorneys provides reason to believe that they possess considerable assets. Whether those assets are "proceeds" of criminal activity or "substitute assets," they are subject to forfeiture. Since information regarding the amount, form and sources of any fees paid by the defendants to their counsel is likely to provide information that may be helpful in locating those assets, and since that information no longer implicates any of the concerns underlying Rule 3.8(f), the requirements of §§ 1963(k) and 853(m) have been satisfied.

III.   SIXTH AMENDMENT RIGHT TO COUNSEL

Like most of their other arguments, the defendants' argument that granting the Government's application would violate their Sixth Amendment rights has been blunted by intervening events.

The Sixth Amendment protects against unwarranted interference with defense counsel's trial preparation and prevents unjustifiably placing defense counsel in a position that might result in disqualification. The prospect of disqualification looms especially large when an attorney is subpoenaed to testify regarding dealings with a client who is being investigated or prosecuted for a criminal offense. However, that does not mean that counsel never may be subpoenaed when criminal charges are pending against the client.

In any event, the concerns underlying the Sixth Amendment no longer are implicated in this case. The defendants' trials are over. Consequently, the depositions sought by the Government will neither interfere with counsel's trial preparation nor create any risk that counsel will be disqualified from continuing to represent their clients with respect to criminal charges for which they were prosecuted. Indeed, the defendants' Sixth Amendment rights are no longer applicable because their appeals have been exhausted.

The mere possibility that counsel might represent the defendants in some future prosecution does not alter matters. To begin with, there is no indication that any future prosecution is contemplated. More importantly, the defendants' Sixth Amendment rights with respect to any possible future prosecution have not yet attached.

IV.   FIFTH AMENDMENT PRIVILEGE AGAINST SELF-INCRIMINATION

The defendants and some of their attorneys argue that granting the Government's application would violate their Fifth Amendment privileges against self-incrimination with respect to the money laundering activities at issue in this case.

A.   *Defendants' Fifth Amendment Rights*

The defendants' claims are unfounded for two reasons. First, once a defendant's conviction becomes final, he no longer is in danger of incriminating himself with respect to the crime charged and, therefore, the privilege against self-incrimination ceases to apply.

Furthermore, the Fifth Amendment protects a *defendant* from being compelled to bear witness against himself. See U.S. Const. amend. V. A defendant's Fifth Amendment rights are not violated by a subpoena directed to his attorney because such a subpoena does not compel the defendant, himself, to do anything.

Consequently, any impediment to making inquiry of the attorney must be found in the attorney-client privilege, the Sixth Amendment right to counsel and/or the rules applicable to subpoenas, in general.

B. The Attorneys' Self-incrimination Rights

Counsel's rather surprising assertion of *their* privilege against self-incrimination presents different questions that are not as easily answered.

A party claiming the privilege against self-incrimination must establish that the testimony being compelled creates a "substantial and real" as opposed to a "trifling and imaginary" risk of criminal prosecution. Marchetti v. United States, 390 U.S. 39, 53 (1968). In this case, counsel assert that their testimony would subject them to possible prosecution for money laundering based on charges that they knowingly took tainted funds as payment for their services. The Court finds that argument unpersuasive for several reasons.

First, among other things, conviction under the money laundering statutes requires proof that a defendant engaged in a monetary transaction involving the proceeds of unlawful activity and that the defendant knew that the money came from illegal sources. See 18 U.S.C. §§ 1956(a)(1), 1956(a)(2)(B), and 1957. Here, counsel do not even allege that they are under suspicion or investigation for money laundering. They argue that a possibility of prosecution exists because the Government apparently believes that the defendants used tainted funds to pay their legal fees. However, even assuming that the Government's belief is well-founded, counsel have provided no reason for inferring either that counsel knew that the money paid to them came from illegal sources or that their testimony would assist the Government in establishing such knowledge.

On the contrary, such an inference would be inconsistent with counsels' argument that the information sought is protected by the attorney-client privilege. Any use of tainted funds to pay the defendants' legal fees would have constituted a continuation of their money laundering efforts. As already noted, the crime/fraud exception renders the privilege inapplicable to communications regarding continuing or future criminal activity. Therefore, by arguing that the fee information at issue falls within the attorney-client privilege, counsel have implicitly represented that there was no reason for them to believe that any amounts paid to them were derived from illegal activities.

CONCLUSION

For all of the foregoing reasons, I find that the Government should be permitted to depose counsel and require the production of relevant documents for the purpose of determining the amount, form and source of payments made to counsel in connection with their representation of the defendants. However, absent any showing that the defendants sought advice for the purpose of engaging in continuing criminal activity, the Government should not be permitted to compel counsel to reveal the substance of communications with their clients relating to non-fee matters that may qualify for protection under the attorney-client privilege.

Notes

Which, if any, of the attorneys' arguments did you find most persuasive? What did you think of the attorneys' argument that enforcing the subpoenas "may drive a chilling wedge" between the attorney and client, create conflicts of interest, undermine an attorney's ability to represent his client and potentially lead to disqualification of the attorney? Even if some of these problems are moot in the above case since the clients have been convicted and the representation is over, what will decisions like *Saccoccia* do to communication between client and counsel in future cases? Is there another solution?

Chapter 6

CRIMINAL PROCEDURE*

Unlike the investigation of most street crimes, the investigation of most white collar crimes involves extensive use of the grand jury.[a] It is not uncommon for a grand jury to spend years investigating a single case. One result of this extensive use of the grand jury is that different criminal procedure issues often arise with regard to white collar crimes than are traditionally raised by the investigation of street crimes.

Prior to reading these cases, it may be helpful to review, briefly, the purpose and powers of a grand jury. According to the Supreme Court, "[t]he grand jury is an integral part of our constitutional heritage which was brought to this country with the common law. * * * Its historic office has been to provide a shield against arbitrary or oppressive action, by insuring that serious criminal accusations will be brought only upon the considered judgment of a representative body of citizens acting under oath and under judicial instruction and guidance." United States v. Mandujano, 425 U.S. 564, 571 (1976). "Traditionally the grand jury has been accorded wide latitude to inquire into violations of criminal law. No judge presides to monitor its proceedings. It deliberates in secret and may determine alone the course of its inquiry. The grand jury may compel the production of evidence * * * and its operation generally is unrestrained by the technical, procedural and evidentiary rules governing the conduct of criminal trials." United States v. Calandra, 414 U.S. 338, 343 (1974). A witness appearing before the grand jury may not refuse to respond to a subpoena or refuse to answer questions on the grounds of relevance, or because he feels testifying may result in physical harm. A witness must respond to a grand jury subpoena even if her compliance results in hardship or inconvenience. A witness appearing before the grand jury may invoke applicable privileges (self-incrimination, attorney-client, spousal, etc.), but the exclusionary rule does not apply. Thus, evidence seized in violation of a defendant's constitutional rights may be used in a grand jury investigation. The grand jury has the

---

* Professor Melissa Harrison joins as co-author in portions of Sections C, D, and E of this chapter.

a. For an excellent resource on the law regarding grand juries, see Beale & Bryson, *Grand Jury Law and Practice* (1986).

power to subpoena physical evidence in addition to testimony. Such subpoenas are called "subpoenas duces tecum." In white collar criminal investigations, voluminous documents are usually subpoenaed with a subpoena duces tecum. Grand jury subpoenas duces tecum may be quashed or modified if compliance would be unreasonable or oppressive. Fed.R.Crim.P. 17(c). A typical subpoena duces tecum addressed to a company requests the following types of documents for a specified period of time, usually spanning several years:

> [R]eceipts and disbursement journals; general ledger and subsidiaries; accounts receivable/accounts payable ledgers, cards, and all customer data; bank records of savings and checking accounts, including statements, checks, and deposit tickets; contracts, invoices—sales and purchase—conveyances, and correspondence; minutes and stock books and ledgers; loan disclosure statements and agreements; liability ledgers; and retained copies of Forms 1120, W–2, W–4, 1099, 940 and 941.[b]

The methods for selecting grand jurors vary from jurisdiction to jurisdiction. The federal system, and many state systems, randomly select grand jurors from various lists such as registered voters, licensed drivers, and in Alaska, licensed hunters. Some states use a "key person" form of selection in which a small group of individuals is given power to select grand jurors. See, e.g., *Ark.Code Ann.* §§ 39–205.1, 39–217.1; *Official Code Ga.Ann.* § 15–12–40(a). In the federal system a grand jury consists of twenty-three persons, sixteen of whom must be present to constitute a quorum. Fed.R.Crim.P. 6(a). The required size of a grand jury varies considerably among the states, ranging from five to twenty-three persons. In the federal system a regular grand jury sits for up to eighteen months, usually convening four to six days per month although additional sitting days may be added. Special grand juries may sit for up to thirty-six months. The terms of state grand juries vary from ten days to eighteen months, with extensions possible.

A. GRAND JURY POWERS IN GENERAL

In the following case, the Supreme Court reviews the power of the grand jury.

UNITED STATES v. R. ENTERPRISES, INC.

United States Supreme Court, 1991.
498 U.S. 292.

O'CONNOR, JUSTICE.[*]

This case requires the Court to decide what standards apply when a party seeks to avoid compliance with a subpoena duces tecum issued in connection with a grand jury investigation.

---

b. Braswell v. United States, 487 U.S. 99, 101 n. 1, 108 S.Ct. 2284, 2286 n. 1, 101 L.Ed.2d 98, 104 (1988).

* Justice Scalia joins in all but Part III–B of this opinion.

I

Since 1986, a federal grand jury sitting in the Eastern District of Virginia has been investigating allegations of interstate transportation of obscene materials. In early 1988, the grand jury issued a series of subpoenas to three companies—Model Magazine Distributors, Inc. (Model), R. Enterprises, Inc., and MFR Court Street Books, Inc. (MFR). Model is a New York distributor of sexually oriented paperback books, magazines, and videotapes. R. Enterprises, which distributes adult materials, and MFR, which sells books, magazines, and videotapes, are also based in New York. All three companies are wholly owned by Martin Rothstein. The grand jury subpoenas sought a variety of corporate books and records and, in Model's case, copies of 193 videotapes that Model had shipped to retailers in the Eastern District of Virginia. All three companies moved to quash the subpoenas, arguing that the subpoenas called for production of materials irrelevant to the grand jury's investigation and that the enforcement of the subpoenas would likely infringe their First Amendment rights.

The District Court, after extensive hearings, denied the motions to quash. As to Model, the court found that the subpoenas for business records were sufficiently specific and that production of the videotapes would not constitute a prior restraint. As to R. Enterprises, the court found a "sufficient connection with Virginia for further investigation by the grand jury." The court relied in large part on the statement attributed to Rothstein that the three companies were "all the same thing, I'm president of all three." Additionally, the court explained in denying MFR's motion to quash that it was "inclined to agree" with "the majority of the jurisdictions," which do not require the Government to make a "threshold showing" before a grand jury subpoena will be enforced. Even assuming that a preliminary showing of relevance was required, the court determined that the Government had made such a showing. It found sufficient evidence that the companies were "related entities," at least one of which "certainly did ship sexually explicit material into the Commonwealth of Virginia." The court concluded that the subpoenas in this case were "fairly standard business subpoenas" and "ought to be complied with." Notwithstanding these findings, the companies refused to comply with the subpoenas. The District Court found each in contempt and fined them $500 per day, but stayed imposition of the fine pending appeal.

The Court of Appeals for the Fourth Circuit upheld the business records subpoenas issued to Model, but remanded the motion to quash the subpoena for Model's videotapes. In re Grand Jury 87-3 Subpoena Duces Tecum, 884 F.2d 772 (1989). Of particular relevance here, the Court of Appeals quashed the business records subpoenas issued to R. Enterprises and MFR. In doing so, it applied the standards set out by this Court in United States v. Nixon, 418 U.S. 683, 699–700 (1974). The court recognized that *Nixon* dealt with a trial subpoena, not a grand jury subpoena, but determined that the rule was "equally applicable" in the grand jury context. Accordingly, it required the Government to clear the three hurdles that *Nixon* established in the trial context—relevancy, admissibility, and specificity—in order to enforce the grand jury subpoenas. The court concluded that the challenged subpoenas did not satisfy the *Nixon* standards, finding no evidence in the record that either company had ever shipped materials into, or otherwise conducted business in, the Eastern District of Virginia. The Court of Appeals specifically criticized the District Court for drawing an inference that, because Rothstein owned all three businesses and one of them had undoubtedly shipped sexually explicit materials into the Eastern District of Virginia, there might be some link between the Eastern District of Virginia and R. Enterprises or MFR. It then noted that "any evidence concerning Mr. Rothstein's alleged business activities outside of Virginia, or his ownership of companies which distribute allegedly obscene materials outside of Virginia, would most likely be inadmissible on relevancy grounds at any trial that might occur," and that the subpoenas therefore failed "to meet the requirements [*sic*] that any documents subpoenaed under [Federal] Rule [of Criminal Procedure] 17(c) must be admissible as evidence at trial." *Id.* at 777. The Court of Appeals did not consider whether enforcement of the subpoenas *duces tecum* issued to respondents implicated the First Amendment.

We granted certiorari to determine whether the Court of Appeals applied the proper standard in evaluating the grand jury subpoenas issued to respondents. We now reverse.

II

The grand jury occupies a unique role in our criminal justice system. It is an investigatory body charged with the responsibility of determining whether or not a crime has been committed. Unlike this Court, whose jurisdiction is predicated on a specific case or controversy, the grand jury "can investigate merely on suspicion that the law is being violated, or even just because it wants assurance that it is not." United States v. Morton Salt Co., 338 U.S. 632, 642–43 (1950). The function of the grand jury is to inquire into all information that might possibly bear on its investigation until it has identified an offense or has satisfied itself that none has occurred. As a necessary consequence of its investigatory function, the grand jury paints with a broad brush. "A grand jury investigation 'is not fully carried out until every available clue has been run down and all witnesses examined in every proper way to find if a crime has been committed.'" Branzburg v. Hayes, 408 U.S. 665 (1972).

A grand jury subpoena is thus much different from a subpoena issued in the context of a prospective criminal trial, where a specific offense has been identified and a particular defendant charged. "[T]he identity of the offender, and the precise nature of the offense, if there be one, normally are developed at the conclusion of the grand jury's labors, not at the beginning." Blair v. United States, 250 U.S. 273, 282 (1919). In short, the Government cannot be required to justify the issuance of a grand jury subpoena by presenting evidence sufficient to establish probable cause because the very purpose of requesting the information is to ascertain whether probable cause exists.

This Court has emphasized on numerous occasions that many of the rules and restrictions that apply at a trial do not apply in grand jury proceedings. This is especially true of evidentiary restrictions. The same rules that, in an adversary hearing on the merits, may increase the likelihood of accurate determinations of guilt or innocence do not necessarily advance the mission of a grand jury, whose task is to conduct an *ex parte* investigation to determine whether or not there is probable cause to prosecute a particular defendant. In Costello v. United States, 350 U.S. 359 (1956), this Court declined to apply the rule against hearsay to grand jury proceedings. Strict observance of trial rules in the context of a grand jury's preliminary investigation "would result in interminable delay but add nothing to the assurance of a fair trial." In United States v. Calandra, 414 U.S. 338 (1974), we held that the Fourth Amendment exclusionary rule does not apply to grand jury proceedings. Permitting witnesses to invoke the exclusionary rule would "delay and disrupt grand jury proceedings" by requiring adversarial hearings on peripheral matters, and would effectively transform such proceedings into preliminary trials on the merits. The teaching of the Court's decisions is clear: A grand jury "may compel the production of evidence or the testimony of witnesses as it considers appropriate, and its operation generally is unrestrained by the technical, procedural and evidentiary rules governing the conduct of criminal trials." *Id.* at 343.

This guiding principle renders suspect the Court of Appeals' holding that the standards announced in *Nixon* as to subpoenas issued in anticipation of trial apply equally in the grand jury context. The multi-factor test announced in *Nixon* would invite procedural delays and detours while courts evaluate the relevancy and admissibility of documents sought by a particular subpoena. We have expressly stated that grand jury proceedings should be free of such delays. "Any holding that would saddle a grand jury with minitrials and preliminary showings would assuredly impede its investigation and frustrate the public's interest in the fair and expeditious administration of the criminal laws." United States v. Dionisio, 410 U.S. 1, 17 (1973). Additionally, application of the *Nixon* test in this context ignores that grand jury proceedings are subject to strict secrecy requirements. *See* Fed.R.Crim.P. 6(e). Requiring the Government to explain in too much detail the particular reasons underlying a subpoena threatens to compromise "the indispensable secrecy of grand jury proceedings." United States v. Johnson, 319 U.S. 503, 513 (1943). Broad disclosure also affords the targets of investigation far more information about the grand jury's internal workings than the Rules of Criminal Procedure appear to contemplate.

III

A

The investigatory powers of the grand jury are nevertheless not unlimited. Grand juries are not licensed to engage in arbitrary fishing expeditions, nor may they select targets of investigation out of malice or an intent to harass. In this case, the focus of our inquiry is the limit imposed on a grand jury by Federal Rule of Criminal Procedure 17(c), which governs the issuance of subpoenas *duces tecum* in federal criminal proceedings. The Rule provides that "the court on motion made promptly may quash or modify the subpoena if compliance would be unreasonable or oppressive."

This standard is not self-explanatory. As we have observed, "what is reasonable depends on the context." New Jersey v. T.L.O., 469 U.S. 325, 337 (1985). In *Nixon*, this Court defined what is reasonable in the context of a jury trial. We determined that, in order to require production of information prior to trial, a party must make a reasonably specific request for information that would be both relevant and admissible at trial. But, for the reasons we have explained above, the *Nixon* standard does not apply in the context of grand jury proceedings. In the grand jury context, the decision as to what offense will be charged is routinely not made until after the grand jury has concluded its investigation. One simply cannot know in advance whether information sought during the investigation will be relevant and admissible in a prosecution for a particular offense.

To the extent that Rule 17(c) imposes some reasonableness limitation on grand jury subpoenas, however, our task is to define it. In doing so, we recognize that a party to whom a grand jury subpoena is issued faces a difficult situation. As a rule, grand juries do not announce publicly the subjects of their investigations. A party who desires to challenge a grand jury subpoena thus may have no conception of the Government's purpose in seeking production of the requested information. Indeed, the party will often not know whether he or she is a primary target of the investigation or merely a peripheral witness. Absent even minimal information, the subpoena recipient is likely to find it exceedingly difficult to persuade a court that "compliance would be unreasonable." As one pair of commentators has summarized it, the challenging party's "unenviable task is to seek to persuade the court that the subpoena that has been served on [him or her] could not possibly serve any investigative purpose that the grand jury could legitimately be pursuing." S. Beale & W. Bryson, Grand Jury Law and Practice § 6:28 (1986).

Our task is to fashion an appropriate standard of reasonableness, one that gives due weight to the difficult position of subpoena recipients but does not impair the strong governmental interests in affording grand juries wide latitude, avoiding minitrials on peripheral matters, and preserving a necessary level of secrecy. We begin by reiterating that the law presumes, absent a strong showing to the contrary, that a grand jury acts within the legitimate scope of its authority. Consequently, a grand jury subpoena issued through normal channels is presumed to be reasonable, and the burden of showing unreasonableness must be on the recipient who seeks to avoid compliance. Indeed, this result is indicated by the language of Rule 17(c), which permits a subpoena to be quashed only "on motion" and "if *compliance* would be unreasonable" (emphasis added). To the extent that the Court of Appeals placed an initial burden on the Government, it committed error. Drawing on the principles articulated above, we conclude that where, as here, a subpoena is challenged on relevancy grounds, the motion to quash must be denied unless the District Court determines that there is no reasonable possibility that the category of materials the Government seeks will produce information relevant to the general subject of the grand jury's investigation. Respondents did not challenge the subpoenas as being too indefinite nor did they claim that compliance would be overly burdensome. The Court of Appeals accordingly did not consider these aspects of the subpoenas, nor do we.

B

It seems unlikely, of course, that a challenging party who does not know the general subject matter of the grand jury's investigation, no matter how valid that party's claim, will be able to make the necessary showing that compliance would be unreasonable. After all, a subpoena recipient "cannot put his whole life before the court in order to show that there is no crime to be investigated," Marston's Inc. v. Strand, 560 P.2d 778, 788 (1977) (Gordon, J., specially concurring in part and dissenting in part). Consequently, a court may be justified in a case where unreasonableness is alleged in requiring the Government to reveal the general subject of the grand jury's investigation before requiring the challenging party to carry its burden of persuasion. We need not resolve this question in the present case, however, as there is no doubt that respondents knew the subject of the grand jury investigation pursuant to which the business records subpoenas were issued. In cases where the recipient of the subpoena does not know the nature of the investigation, we are confident that district courts will be able to craft appropriate procedures that balance the interests of the subpoena recipient against the strong governmental interests in maintaining secrecy, preserving investigatory flexibility, and avoiding procedural delays. For example, to ensure that subpoenas are not routinely challenged as a form of discovery, a district court may require that the Government reveal the subject of the investigation to the trial court *in camera,* so that the court may determine whether the motion to quash has a reasonable prospect for success before it discloses the subject matter to the challenging party.

IV

Applying these principles in this case demonstrates that the District Court correctly denied respondents' motions to quash. It is undisputed that all three companies—Model, R. Enterprises, and MFR—are owned by the same person, that all do business in the same area, and that one of the three, Model, has shipped sexually explicit materials into the Eastern District of Virginia. The District Court could have concluded from these facts that there was a reasonable possibility that the business records of R. Enterprises and MFR would produce information relevant to the grand jury's investigation into the interstate transportation of obscene materials. Respondents' blanket denial of any connection to Virginia did not suffice to render the District Court's conclusion invalid. A grand jury need not accept on faith the self-serving assertions of those who may have committed criminal acts. Rather, it is entitled to determine for itself whether a crime has been committed.

Both in the District Court and in the Court of Appeals, respondents contended that these subpoenas sought records relating to First Amendment activities, and that this required the Government to demonstrate that the records were particularly relevant to its investigation. The Court of Appeals determined that the subpoenas did not satisfy Rule 17(c) and thus did not pass on the First Amendment issue. We express no view on this issue and leave it to be resolved by the Court of Appeals.

The judgment is reversed insofar as the Court of Appeals quashed the subpoenas issued to R. Enterprises and MFR, and the case is remanded for further proceedings consistent with this opinion.

It is so ordered.

JUSTICE STEVENS, with whom JUSTICES MARSHALL and BLACKMUN join, concurring in part and concurring in the judgment.

Federal Rule of Criminal Procedure 17(c) authorizes a Federal District Court to quash or modify a grand jury subpoena *duces tecum* "if compliance would be unreasonable or oppressive." This rule requires the district court to balance the burden of compliance, on the one hand, against the governmental interest in obtaining the documents on the other. A more burdensome subpoena should be justified by a somewhat higher degree of probable relevance than a subpoena that imposes a minimal or nonexistent burden. Against the procedural history of this case, the Court has attempted to define the term "reasonable" in the abstract, looking only at the relevance side of the balance. Because I believe that this truncated approach to the Rule will neither provide adequate guidance to the district court nor place any meaningful constraint on the overzealous prosecutor, I add these comments.

The burden of establishing that compliance would be unreasonable or oppressive rests, of course, on the subpoenaed witness. * * *

The moving party has the initial task of demonstrating to the Court that he has some valid objection to compliance. This showing might be made in various ways. Depending on the volume and location of the requested materials, the mere cost in terms of time, money, and effort of responding to a dragnet subpoena could satisfy the initial hurdle. Similarly, if a witness showed that compliance with the subpoena would intrude significantly on his privacy interests, or call for the disclosure of trade secrets or other confidential information, further inquiry would be required. Or, as in this case, the movant might demonstrate that compliance would have First Amendment implications.

The trial court need inquire into the relevance of subpoenaed materials only after the moving party has made this initial showing. And, as is true in the parallel context of pretrial civil discovery, a matter also committed to the sound discretion of the trial judge, the degree of need sufficient to justify denial of the motion to quash will vary to some extent with the burden of producing the requested information. For the reasons stated by the Court, in the grand jury context the law enforcement interest will almost always prevail, and the documents must be produced. * * *

I agree with the Court that what is "unreasonable or oppressive" in the context of a trial subpoena is not necessarily unreasonable or oppressive in the grand jury context. Although the same language of Rule 17(c) governs both situations, the teaching of United States v. Nixon is not directly applicable to the very different grand jury context. Thus, I join in Parts I and II of the Court's opinion, and I am in accord with its decision to send the case back to the Court of Appeals. I also agree that the possible First Amendment implications of compliance should be considered by that court. I would only add that further inquiry into the possible unreasonable or oppressive character of this subpoena should also take into account the entire history of this grand jury investigation, including the series of subpoenas that have been issued to the same corporations and their affiliates during the past several years.

Notes

1. At issue in R. Enterprises were subpoenas duces tecum which called for the production of physical evidence. A subpoena that merely directs a person to appear before the grand jury to testify is a *subpoena ad testificandum*. The typical subpoena ad testificandum states, "You are hereby commanded to attend before the Grand Jury of said Court on _____, the _____ day of _____, 19__, at _____ o'clock __.m. to testify." The subpoena duces tecum will add, "You are also commanded to bring with you the following document(s) or object(s)." All such items will be listed on the subpoena or on attachments to the subpoena.

If a person served with a grand jury subpoena believes there is some reason he should not be required to comply with the subpoena, he should file a Motion to Quash the Subpoena. The district court handling grand jury matters generally is the court to rule upon such a motion. The above case began when Model Magazine Distributors, Inc., R. Enterprises, Inc., and MFR Court Street Books, Inc. received a grand jury subpoena and chose to file a motion to quash rather than comply. Failure to comply with a grand jury subpoena without filing a Motion to Quash, or after losing on a Motion to Quash, is contempt of court which may be punishable by imprisonment and/or fines.

In the federal system and most state systems, the prosecutor has the authority to decide which witnesses to call to a grand jury and which records or objects to request for production. A few states, however, require that subpoenas be issued at the request of the grand jury. *See e.g., Miss.Code 1972*, § 13–5–63 (foreman has power to subpoena witness); *Tenn.R.Crim.P.* 6(i)(2) (clerk shall issue subpoenas upon application of the grand jury). One controversial practice is the prosecutor's custom of instructing a subpoenaed witness to appear at the prosecutor's office prior to his grand jury appearance. Critics claim that this practice turns the grand jury subpoena into a prosecutor's "office subpoena" and gives the prosecutor unfair access to grand jury witnesses. Holderman, *Preindictment Prosecutorial Conduct in the Federal System,* 71 *J.Crim.L. & Criminology* 1, 7 (1980). Prosecutors maintain that this practice is necessary to allow the grand jury witness an opportunity to preview the documents or transactions he will be asked about in the grand jury. Such a preview is needed, prosecutors suggest, out of fairness to the witness and to make the often tedious, and lengthy, testimony in the grand jury proceed more efficiently.

2. In *R. Enterprises,* the Court ruled that while a grand jury subpoena duces tecum must comply with Federal Rule of Criminal Procedure 17(c), and cannot be "unreasonable or oppressive," reasonableness is to be judged in the context of the grand jury process, not in the context of a trial which has become focused on a particular individual and charges. This scope of reasonableness is broad indeed, for as the Court noted in United States v. Morton Salt Co., 338 U.S. 632, 642–43 (1950), the grand jury "can investigate merely on suspicion that the law is being violated, or even just because it wants assurance that it is not." What do you see as the hazards—and benefits—of vesting such power in grand juries and prosecutors?

The Supreme Court again addressed the role of the grand jury in United States v. Williams. In a 5–4 decision, the Court held that the government was not obliged to disclose "substantial exculpatory evidence" in its possession to the grand jury.

UNITED STATES v. WILLIAMS

United States Supreme Court (1992).
504 U.S. 36.

SCALIA, JUSTICE.

The question presented in this case is whether a district court may dismiss an otherwise valid indictment because the Government failed to disclose to the grand jury "substantial exculpatory evidence" in its possession.

I

On May 4, 1988, respondent John H. Williams, Jr., a Tulsa, Oklahoma, investor, was indicted by a federal grand jury on seven counts of "knowingly making [a] false statement or report . . . for the purpose of influencing . . . the action [of a federally insured financial institution]," in violation of 18 U. S. C. § 1014. According to the indictment, between September 1984 and November 1985 Williams supplied four Oklahoma banks with "materially false" statements that variously overstated the value of his current assets and interest income in order to influence the banks' actions on his loan requests.

Williams' misrepresentation was allegedly effected through two financial statements provided to the banks, a "Market Value Balance Sheet" and a "Statement of Projected Income and Expense." The former included as "current assets" approximately $6 million in notes receivable from three venture capital companies. Though it contained a disclaimer that these assets were carried at cost rather than at market value, the Government asserted that listing them as "current assets"—i. e., assets quickly reducible to cash—was misleading, since Williams knew that none of the venture capital companies could afford to satisfy the notes in the short term. The second document—the Statement of Projected Income and Expense—allegedly misrepresented Williams' interest income, since it failed to reflect that the interest payments received on the notes of the venture capital companies were funded entirely by Williams' own loans to those companies. The Statement thus falsely implied, according to the Government, that Williams was deriving interest income from "an independent outside source."

Shortly after arraignment, the District Court granted Williams' motion for disclosure of all exculpatory portions of the grand jury transcripts. *See* Brady v. Maryland, 373 U.S. 83 (1963). Upon reviewing this material, Williams demanded that the District Court dismiss the indictment, alleging that the Government had failed to fulfill its obligation under the Tenth Circuit's prior decision in United States v. Page, 808 F.2d 723, 728 (1987), to present "substantial exculpatory evidence" to the grand jury (emphasis omitted). His contention was that evidence which the Government had chosen not to present to the grand jury—in particular, Williams' general ledgers and tax returns, and Williams' testimony in his contemporaneous Chapter 11 bankruptcy proceeding— disclosed that, for tax purposes and otherwise, he had regularly accounted for the "notes receivable" (and the interest on them) in a manner consistent with the Balance Sheet and the Income Statement. This, he contended, belied an intent to mislead the banks, and thus directly negated an essential element of the charged offense.

The District Court initially denied Williams' motion, but upon reconsideration ordered the indictment dismissed without prejudice. It found, after a hearing, that the withheld evidence was "relevant to an essential element of the crime charged," created " 'a reasonable doubt about [respondent's] guilt,' " and thus "rendered the grand jury's decision to indict gravely suspect". Upon the Government's appeal, the Court of Appeals affirmed the District Court's order, following its earlier decision.

* * *

"[R]ooted in long centuries of Anglo–American history," Hannah v. Larche, 363 U.S. 420, 490 (1960) (Frankfurter, J., concurring in result), the grand jury is mentioned in the Bill of Rights, but not in the body of the Constitution. It has not been textually assigned, therefore, to any of the branches described in the first three Articles. It " 'is a constitutional fixture in its own right.' " United States v. Chanen, 549 F.2d 1306, 1312 (CA9). [Citations omitted]. In fact the whole theory of its function is that it belongs to no branch of the institutional Government, serving as a kind of buffer or referee between the Government and the people.

Although the grand jury normally operates, of course, in the courthouse and under judicial auspices, its institutional relationship with the Judicial Branch has traditionally been, so to speak, at arm's length. Judges' direct involvement in the functioning of the grand jury has generally been confined to the constitutive one of calling the grand jurors together and administering their oaths of office.

The grand jury's functional independence from the Judicial Branch is evident both in the scope of its power to investigate criminal wrongdoing and in the manner in which that power is exercised. "Unlike [a] court, whose jurisdiction is predicated upon a specific case or controversy, the grand jury 'can investigate merely on suspicion that the law is being violated, or even because it wants assurance that it is not.'" United States v. R. Enterprises, Inc., 498 U.S. 292, 297 (1991). It need not identify the offender it suspects, or even "the precise nature of the offense" it is investigating. Blair v. United States, 250 U.S. 273, 282 (1919). The grand jury requires no authorization from its constituting court to initiate an investigation, nor does the prosecutor require leave of court to seek a grand jury indictment. And in its day-to-day functioning, the grand jury generally operates without the interference of a presiding judge. It swears in its own witnesses, Fed. Rule Crim. Proc. 6(c), and deliberates in total secrecy.

True, the grand jury cannot compel the appearance of witnesses and the production of evidence, and must appeal to the court when such compulsion is required. And the court will refuse to lend its assistance when the compulsion the grand jury seeks would override rights accorded by the Constitution, or even testimonial privileges recognized by the common law. Even in this setting, however, we have insisted that the grand jury remain "free to pursue its investigations unhindered by external influence or supervision so long as it does not trench upon the legitimate rights of any witness called before it." United States v. Dionisio, 410 U.S. 1, 17–18 (1973). Recognizing this tradition of independence, we have said that the Fifth Amendment's "constitutional guarantee *presupposes* an investigative body 'acting independently of either prosecuting attorney or *judge*'...." *Id.* at 16 (emphasis added).

No doubt in view of the grand jury proceeding's status as other than a constituent element of a "criminal prosecution," U. S. Const., Amdt. 6, we have said that certain constitutional protections afforded defendants in criminal proceedings have no application before that body. The Double Jeopardy Clause of the Fifth Amendment does not bar a grand jury from returning an indictment when a prior grand jury has refused to do so. We have twice suggested, though not held, that the Sixth Amendment right to counsel does not attach when an individual is summoned to appear before a grand jury, even if he is the subject of the investigation. And although "the grand jury may not force a witness to answer questions in violation of [the Fifth Amendment's] constitutional guarantee" against self-incrimination, our cases suggest that an indictment obtained through the use of evidence previously obtained in violation of the privilege against self-incrimination "is nevertheless valid." [citation omitted]

Given the grand jury's operational separateness from its constituting court, it should come as no surprise that we have been reluctant to invoke the judicial supervisory power as a basis for prescribing modes of grand jury procedure. Over the years, we have received many requests to exercise supervision over the grand jury's evidence-taking process, but we have refused them all, including some more appealing than the one presented today. In United States v. Calandra, 414 U.S. 338 (1974), a grand jury witness faced questions that were allegedly based upon physical evidence the Government had obtained through a violation of the Fourth Amendment; we rejected the proposal that the exclusionary rule be extended to grand jury proceedings, because of "the potential injury to the historic role and functions of the grand jury." [citation omitted]

These authorities suggest that any power federal courts may have to fashion, on their own initiative, rules of grand jury procedure is a very limited one, not remotely comparable to the power they maintain over their own proceedings. * * *

* * *

It is axiomatic that the grand jury sits not to determine guilt or innocence, but to assess whether there is adequate basis for bringing a criminal charge. That has always been so; and to make the assessment it has always been thought sufficient to hear only the prosecutor's side. As Blackstone described the prevailing practice in 18th-century England, the grand jury was "only to hear evidence on behalf of the prosecution[,] for the finding of an indictment is only in the nature of an enquiry or accusation, which is afterwards to be tried and determined." 4 W. Blackstone, Commentaries 300 (1769). According to the description of an early American court, three years before the Fifth Amendment was ratified, it is the grand jury's function not "to enquire ... upon what foundation [the charge may be] denied," or otherwise to try the suspect's defenses, but only to examine "upon what foundation [the charge] is made" by the prosecutor. Respublica v. Shaffer, 1 U.S. (1 Dall.) 236. As a consequence, neither in this country nor in England has the suspect under investigation by the grand jury ever been thought to have a right to testify or to have exculpatory evidence presented.

Imposing upon the prosecutor a legal obligation to present exculpatory evidence in his possession would be incompatible with this system. If a "balanced" assessment of the entire matter is the objective, surely the first thing to be done—rather than requiring the prosecutor to say what he knows in defense of the target of the investigation—is to entitle the target to tender his own defense. To require the former while denying (as we do) the latter would be quite absurd. It would also be quite pointless, since it would merely invite the target to circumnavigate the system by delivering his exculpatory evidence to the prosecutor, whereupon it would have to be passed on to the grand jury—unless the prosecutor is willing to take the chance that a court will not deem the evidence important enough to qualify for mandatory disclosure.

* * *

* * * For the reasons set forth above, however, we conclude that courts have no authority to prescribe such a duty pursuant to their inherent supervisory authority over their own proceedings. The judgment of the Court of Appeals is accordingly reversed, and the cause is remanded for further proceedings consistent with this opinion.

So ordered.

JUSTICE STEVENS, with whom JUSTICE BLACKMUN and JUSTICE O'CONNOR join, and with whom JUSTICE THOMAS joins [in part], dissenting.

* * *

Like the Hydra slain by Hercules, prosecutorial misconduct has many heads.

* * *

Justice Sutherland's identification of the basic reason why that sort of misconduct is intolerable merits repetition:

"The United States Attorney is the representative not of an ordinary party to a controversy, but of a sovereignty whose obligation to govern impartially is as compelling as its obligation to govern at all; and whose interest, therefore, in a criminal prosecution is not that it shall win a case, but that justice shall be done. As such, he is in a peculiar and very definite sense the servant of the law, the twofold aim of which is that guilt shall not escape or innocence suffer. He may prosecute with earnestness and vigor—indeed, he should do so. But, while he may strike hard blows, he is not at liberty to strike foul ones. It is as much his duty to refrain from improper methods calculated to produce a wrongful conviction as it is to use every legitimate means to bring about a just one." Berger v. United States, 295 U.S. 78, 88 (1935).

It is equally clear that the prosecutor has the same duty to refrain from improper methods calculated to produce a wrongful indictment. Indeed, the prosecutor's duty to protect the fundamental fairness of judicial proceedings assumes special importance when he is presenting evidence to a grand jury. As the Court of Appeals for the Third Circuit recognized, "the costs of continued unchecked prosecutorial misconduct" before the grand jury are particularly substantial because there

"the prosecutor operates without the check of a judge or a trained legal adversary, and virtually immune from public scrutiny. The prosecutor's abuse of his special relationship to the grand jury poses an enormous risk to defendants as well. For while in theory a trial provides the defendant with a full opportunity to contest and disprove the charges against him, in practice, the handing up of an indictment will often have a devastating personal and professional impact that a later dismissal or acquittal can never undo. Where the potential for abuse is so great, and the consequences of a mistaken indictment so serious, the ethical responsibilities of the prosecutor, and the obligation of the judiciary to protect against even the appearance of unfairness, are correspondingly heightened." United States v. Serubo, 604 F.2d 807, 817 (1979). * * *

* * *

In an opinion that I find difficult to comprehend, the Court today repudiates the assumptions underlying these cases and seems to suggest that the court has no authority to supervise the conduct of the prosecutor in grand jury proceedings so long as he follows the dictates of the Constitution, applicable statutes, and Rule 6 of the Federal Rules of Criminal Procedure. The Court purports to support this conclusion by invoking the doctrine of separation of powers and citing a string of cases in which we have declined to impose categorical restraints on the grand jury. Needless to say, the Court's reasoning is unpersuasive.

* * *

Although the Court recognizes that it may invoke its supervisory authority to fashion and enforce privilege rules applicable in grand jury proceedings and suggests that it may also invoke its supervisory authority to fashion other limited rules of grand jury procedure, it concludes that it has no authority to prescribe "standards of prosecutorial conduct before the grand jury," because that would alter the grand jury's historic role as an independent, inquisitorial institution. I disagree.

We do not protect the integrity and independence of the grand jury by closing our eyes to the countless forms of prosecutorial misconduct that may occur inside the secrecy of the grand jury room. After all, the grand jury is not merely an investigatory body; it also serves as a "protector of citizens against arbitrary and oppressive governmental action." * * *

* * *

It blinks reality to say that the grand jury can adequately perform this important historic role if it is intentionally misled by the prosecutor—on whose knowledge of the law and facts of the underlying criminal investigation the jurors will, of necessity, rely.

Unlike the Court, I am unwilling to hold that countless forms of prosecutorial misconduct must be tolerated—no matter how prejudicial they may be, or how seriously they may distort the legitimate function of the grand jury—simply because they are not proscribed by Rule 6 of the Federal Rules of Criminal Procedure or a statute that is applicable in grand jury proceedings.

What, then, is the proper disposition of this case? I agree with the Government that the prosecutor is not required to place all exculpatory evidence before the grand jury. A grand jury proceeding is an ex parte investigatory proceeding to determine whether there is probable cause to believe a violation of the criminal laws has occurred, not a trial. Requiring the prosecutor to ferret out and present all evidence that could be used at trial to create a reasonable doubt as to the defendant's guilt would be inconsistent with the purpose of the grand jury proceeding and would place significant burdens on the investigation. But that does not mean that the prosecutor may mislead the grand jury into believing that there is probable cause to indict by withholding clear evidence to the contrary.

* * *

More importantly, because I am so firmly opposed to the Court's favored treatment of the Government as a litigator, I would dismiss the writ of certiorari as improvidently granted.

Notes

1. Is the major problem in requiring prosecutors to present exculpatory evidence to the grand jury a practical one? How would a court or a defendant know whether exculpatory evidence has been withheld? Would it be necessary to invade the secrecy of grand jury proceedings to monitor prosecutors' presentation of exculpatory evidence?

2. Brady v. Maryland, 373 U.S. 83 (1963), referred to in the *Williams* opinion, held that failure to provide material, favorable evidence to a defendant who requests it violates due process, regardless of the good or bad faith of the prosecutor. Grand jury testimony may need to be disclosed under *Brady*, as might rough notes of investigating agents.

United States v. Agurs, 427 U.S. 97 (1976) sets forth three situations that could arise under *Brady*: (1) if the prosecutor suppressed favorable material evidence, the conviction will be set aside if the defendant shows there is "any reasonable likelihood" that the verdict could have been affected. (2) If the prosecutor fails to respond to a defendant's specific request for information, the conviction will be set aside if the defendant shows the non-produced evidence "might have affected the outcome." (3) If the defendant fails to request favorable evidence or requests it only generally, the conviction will be set aside only if the defendant proves that the undisclosed information "creates a reasonable doubt as to guilt that did not otherwise exist." *Id.* at 103–112.

3. The *Brady* motion is just one type of pretrial motion typically filed. Other pretrial motions routinely filed in white collar criminal cases include a Motion for Discovery and Motions to Suppress Statements or evidence (depending on facts). Some cases may call for other pretrial motions such as a motion to Release on Bail, motion for Bill of Particulars, or Request for Competency Hearing.

In criminal cases, unlike civil cases, there are no opportunities for interrogatories or, except in highly unusual circumstances, depositions. FRCrP 15. Police and investigative reports and statements of witnesses not otherwise discoverable are specifically exempted from discovery, FRCrP

16(a)(2). Rule 16 specifies that the following are discoverable: statements of defendant, the prior criminal records of defendant, documents and tangible objects in the government's possession which are material to the defense or intended for use as exhibits; reports of physical or mental examinations, scientific tests and summaries of expert testimony, FRCrP 16(a). The defendant must provide similar items as reciprocal discovery, FRCrP 16(b).

In a complex case, how would a prosecutor ensure that he or she had provided all favorable evidence to the defendant when the prosecutor is not sure what the defense theory(ies) will be and what evidence may be relevant to such a theory(ies)?

4. In complex cases where there are multiple defendants, there are advantages for the defendants of joint preparation and presentation of the defense. Early in a case such cooperation may help the defense better learn where the government is going in its investigation. As the case progresses, joint defense efforts can help strengthen the defense case.

There are substantial hazards, however, when one attorney represents multiple defendants. Even when the clients are willing to waive their sixth amendment right to effective (and thus conflict-free) counsel, courts may order disqualification of attorneys. For example, in United States v. RMI, 467 F.Supp. 915 (W.D.Pa.1979), counsel representing both the company and employees was disqualified from representing the employees even though both the company and the employees waived their right to effective assistance of counsel. Although the employees had been immunized, the parties and their attorney asserted that they accepted the truth of the employees' grand jury testimony. *Id.* at 921. Nevertheless, the court held:

"This puts the witnesses and the corporation in an adversary posture.

"There is . . . the continuing possibility that, in seeking counsel's advice in the course of testifying at trial, the witness will disclose information to counsel that will prevent probing of an important area on cross-examination for fear of jeopardizing the position of the witness. . . . The Court is unaware of how counsel would harmonize their dual loyalties if faced with testimony by any of the three witnesses that is ambiguous and possibly contradicts his or her statements before the grand jury.

* * *

"In addition to its duty to protect the constitutional right to effective assistance of counsel, this Court also has a responsibility 'to supervise the conduct of the members of its bar' and 'to maintain public confidence in the legal profession.' "

Id. at 921–922. Ethical rules also forbid multiple representation when representation of one client is "directly adverse" to that of another client. Model Rule 1.7; Model Code D.R. 5–105. Especially in cases of complex facts, it may be difficult to determine that a conflict exists until the case has progressed to the point that disqualification is the only remedy available.

Joint defense agreements offer a way of obtaining some of the advantages of multiple representation without the risks. Parties subject to possible criminal liability in connection with the same transactions, but represented by separate counsel, may enter into an agreement to pursue a joint defense effort, the communications of which become privileged. The United States Court of Appeals for the Second Circuit discussed joint defense agreements, and the accompanying privilege:

> "The joint defense privilege, more properly identified as the 'common interest rule' has been described as 'an extension of the attorney client privilege.' It serves to protect the confidentiality of communications passing from one party to the attorney for another party where a joint defense effort or strategy has been decided upon and undertaken by the parties and their respective counsel. Only those communications made in the course of an ongoing common enterprise and intended to further the enterprise are protected."

United States v. Schwimmer, 892 F.2d 237, 243–44 (2d Cir.1989).

Do you see problems with joint defense agreements? Would you, as a prosecutor, feel comfortable initiating or maintaining confidential communications (regarding cooperation, for example) with a defendant who participated in a joint defense agreement? If you were a low level employee, targeted in a grand jury investigation along with your corporate employer and high level officers and directors, would you participate in a joint defense effort? By participating you could save legal costs by sharing trial preparation expenses and expertise. If your corporate employer is paying for your legal fees, would you feel obligated to participate? Would you be in the best position to cooperate with the government and save yourself from criminal liability if you participated? Could participating in a joint defense agreement keep the government from extending to you an offer of cooperation? Would participation in a joint defense keep you from accepting such an offer, even if it was in your best interest? Returning to the discovery issue: how might joint defense agreements affect discovery obligations?

B.   THE FIFTH AMENDMENT

The fifth amendment privilege not to incriminate oneself is a prime example of the unique criminal procedure issues that arise in white collar criminal cases. With street crimes, the usual inquiry when a statement has been provided to investigators, is whether the statement was made voluntarily. To assess the voluntariness of a statement, the analysis usually focuses on Miranda v. Arizona, 384 U.S. 436 (1966), and issues such as whether *Miranda* rights should have been given to the suspect; whether *Miranda* rights were given; and whether the suspect waived his *Miranda* rights. With white collar crimes, however, the inquiry more often concerns who (or what) is entitled to assert the fifth amendment privilege and how far this privilege extends. Two cases in this section, United States v. Doe, 465 U.S. 605 (1984), and Braswell v. United States, 487 U.S. 99 (1988), address these issues.

UNITED STATES v. DOE
United States Supreme Court, 1984.
465 U.S. 605.

Powell, JUSTICE.

The case represents the issue whether, and to what extent, the Fifth Amendment privilege against compelled self-incrimination applies to the business records of a sole proprietorship.

I

Respondent is the owner of several sole proprietorships. In late 1980, a grand jury, during the course of an investigation of corruption in the awarding of county and municipal contracts, served five subpoenas on respondent. The first two demanded the production of the telephone records of several of respondent's companies and all records pertaining to four bank accounts of respondent and his companies. The subpoenas were limited to the period between January 1, 1977, and the dates of the subpoenas. The third subpoena demanded the production of a list of virtually all the business records of one of respondent's companies for the period between January 1, 1976, and the date of the subpoena. The fourth subpoena sought production of a similar list of business records belonging to another company. The final subpoena demanded production of all bank statements and canceled checks of two of respondent's companies that had accounts at a bank in the Grand Cayman Islands.

II

Respondent filed a motion in Federal District Court seeking to quash the subpoenas. The District Court for the District of New Jersey granted his motion except with respect to those documents and records required by law to be kept or disclosed to a public agency. In reaching its decision, the District Court noted that the Government had conceded that the materials sought in the subpoena were or might be incriminating. The court stated that, therefore, "the relevant inquiry is * * * whether the *act* of producing the documents has communicative aspects which warrant Fifth Amendment protection." In re Grand Jury Empanelled March 19, 1980, 541 F.Supp. 1, 3 (1981) (emphasis in original). The court found that the act of production would compel respondent to "admit that the records exist, that they are in his possession, and that they are authentic." While not ruling out the possibility that the Government could devise a way to ensure that the act of turning over the documents would not incriminate respondent, the court held that the Government had not made such a showing.

The Court of Appeals for the Third Circuit affirmed. It first addressed the question whether the Fifth Amendment ever applies to the records of a sole proprietorship. After noting that an individual may not assert the Fifth Amendment privilege on behalf of a corporation, partnership, or other collective entity under the holding of Bellis v. United States, 417 U.S. 85 (1974),[4] the Court of Appeals reasoned that the owner of a sole proprietorship acts in a personal rather than a representative capacity. As a result, the court held that respondent's claim of the privilege was not foreclosed by the reasoning of *Bellis*.

---

4. *Bellis* defined a "collective entity" as "an organization which is recognized as an independent entity apart from its individual members."

The Court of Appeals next considered whether the documents at issue in this case are privileged. The court noted that this Court held in Fisher v. United States, 425 U.S. 391 (1976), that the contents of business records ordinarily are not privileged because they are created voluntarily and without compulsion. The Court of Appeals nevertheless found that respondent's business records were privileged under either of two analyses. First, the court reasoned that, notwithstanding the holdings in *Bellis* and *Fisher*, the business records of a sole proprietorship are no different from the individual owner's personal records. Noting that Third Circuit cases had held that private papers, although created voluntarily, are protected by the Fifth Amendment the court accorded the same protection to respondent's business papers. Second, it held that respondent's act of producing the subpoenaed records would have "communicative aspects of its own." The turning over of the subpoena documents to the grand jury would admit their existence and authenticity. Accordingly, respondent was entitled to assert Fifth Amendment privilege rather than produce the subpoenaed documents.

The Government contended that the court should enforce the subpoenas because of the Government's offer not to use respondent's act of production against respondent in any way. The Court of Appeals noted that no formal request for use immunity under 18 U.S.C. §§ 6002 and 6003 had been made. In light of this failure, the court held that the District Court did not err in rejecting the Government's attempt to compel delivery of the subpoenaed records.

We granted certiorari to resolve the apparent conflict between the Court of Appeals holding and the reasoning underlying this Court's holding in *Fisher*. We now affirm in part, reverse in part, and remand for further proceedings.

III

A

The Court in *Fisher* expressly declined to reach the question whether the Fifth Amendment privilege protects the contents of an individual's tax records in his possession.[7] The rationale underlying our holding in that case is, however, persuasive here. As we noted in *Fisher*, the Fifth Amendment protects the person asserting the privilege only from *compelled* self-incrimination. Where the preparation of business records is voluntary, no compulsion is present.[8] A subpoena that demands

---

7. In *Fisher*, the Court stated: "Whether the Fifth Amendment would shield the taxpayer from producing his own tax records in his possession is a question not involved here; for the papers demanded" here are not his private papers. We note that in some respects the documents sought in *Fisher* were more "personal" than those at issue here. The *Fisher* documents were accountant's workpapers in the possession of the taxpayer's lawyers. The workpapers related to the taxpayer's individual personal returns. To that extent, the documents were personal, even though in the possession of a third party. In contrast, each of the documents sought here pertained to respondent's businesses.

8. Respondent's principal argument is that the Fifth Amendment should be read as creating a "zone of privacy which protects an individual and his personal records from compelled production." This argument derives from language in Boyd v. United

production of documents "does not compel oral testimony; nor would it ordinarily compel the taxpayer to restate, repeat, or affirm the truth of the contents of the documents sought." *Fisher,* 425 U.S. at 396. Applying this reasoning in *Fisher,* we stated:

> "[T]he Fifth Amendment would not be violated by the fact alone that the papers on their face might incriminate the taxpayer, for the privilege protects a person only against being incriminated by his own compelled testimonial communications. The accountant's work-papers are not the taxpayer's. They were not prepared by the taxpayer, and they contain no testimonial declarations by him. Furthermore, as far as this record demonstrates, the preparation of all of the papers sought in these cases was wholly voluntary, and they cannot be said to contain compelled testimonial evidence, either of the taxpayer or of anyone else. The taxpayer cannot avoid compliance with the subpoena merely by asserting that the item of evidence which he is required to produce contains incriminating writing, whether his own or that of someone else." *Fisher,* 425 U.S. at 409–10, 96 S.Ct. 1569.

This reasoning applies with equal force here. Respondent does not contend that he prepared the documents involuntarily or that the subpoena would force him to restate, repeat, or affirm the truth of their contents. The fact that the records are in respondent's possession is irrelevant to the determination of whether the creation of the records was compelled. We therefore hold that the contents of those records are not privileged.

B

Although the contents of a document may not be privileged, the act of producing the document may be. A government subpoena compels the holder of the document to perform an act that may have testimonial aspects and an incriminating effect. As we noted in *Fisher:*

> "Compliance with the subpoena tacitly concedes the existence of the papers demanded and their possession or control by the taxpayer. It also would indicate the taxpayer's belief that the papers are those described in the subpoena. The elements of compulsion are clearly present, but the more difficult issues are whether the tacit averments of the taxpayer are both 'testimonial' and 'incriminating' for purposes of applying the Fifth Amendment. These questions perhaps do not lend themselves to categorical answers; their resolution may instead depend on the facts and circumstances of particular cases or classes thereof." *Fisher,* 425 U.S. at 410, 96 S.Ct. 1569.

States, 116 U.S. 616, 630 (1886). This Court addressed substantially the same argument in *Fisher:*

> "Within the limits imposed by the language of the Fifth Amendment, which we necessarily observe, the privilege truly serves privacy interests; but the Court has never on any ground, personal priva-

cy included, applied the Fifth Amendment to prevent the otherwise proper acquisition or use of evidence which in the Court's view, did not involve compelled testimonial self-incrimination of some sort."

* * *

In *Fisher,* the Court explored the effect that the act of production would have on the taxpayer and determined that the act of production would have only minimal testimonial value and would not operate to incriminate the taxpayer. Unlike the Court in *Fisher,* we have the explicit finding of the District Court that the act of producing the documents would involve testimonial self-incrimination.[11] The Court of Appeals agreed. The District Court's finding essentially rests on its determination of factual issues. Therefore, we will not overturn that finding unless it has no support in the record. Traditionally, we also have been reluctant to disturb findings of fact in which two courts below have concurred. We therefore decline to overturn the findings of the District Court in this regard, where, as here, it has been affirmed by the Court of Appeals.

IV

The Government, as it concedes, could have compelled respondent to produce the documents listed in the subpoena. Title 18 U.S.C. §§ 6002 and 6003 provide for the granting of use immunity with respect to the potentially incriminating evidence. The Court upheld the constitutionality of the use immunity statute in Kastigar v. United States, 406 U.S. 441 (1972).

The Government did state several times before the District Court that it would not use respondent's act of production against him in any way. But counsel for the Government never made a statutory request to the District Court to grant respondent use immunity. We are urged to adopt a doctrine of constructive use immunity. Under this doctrine, the courts would impose a requirement on the Government not to use the incriminatory aspects of the act of production against the person claiming the privilege even though the statutory procedures have not been followed.

We decline to extend the jurisdiction of courts to include prospective grants of use immunity in the absence of the formal request that the statute requires. As we stated in Pillsbury Co. v. Conboy, 459 U.S. 248 (1983), in passing the use immunity statute, "Congress gave certain officials in the Department of Justice exclusive authority to grant immunities. * * * Congress foresaw the courts as playing only a minor role in the immunizing process * * *." The decision to seek use immunity necessarily involves a balancing of the Government's interest in obtaining information against the risk that immunity will frustrate the Government's attempts to prosecute the subject of the investigation.

---

11. The District Court stated:

"With few exceptions, enforcement of the subpoenas would compel [respondent] to admit that the records exist, that they are in his possession, and that they are authentic. These communications, if made under compulsion of a court decree, would violate [respondent's] Fifth Amendment rights * * *. The govern- ment argues that the existence, possession and authenticity of the documents can be proved without [respondent's] testimonial communication, but it cannot satisfy this court as to how that representation can be implemented to protect the witness in subsequent proceedings." 541 F.Supp. at 3.

Congress expressly left this decision exclusively to the Justice Department. If, on remand, the appropriate official concludes that it is desirable to compel respondent to produce his business records, the statutory procedure for requesting use immunity will be available.

V

We conclude that the Court of Appeals erred in holding that the contents of the subpoenaed documents were privileged under the Fifth Amendment. The act of producing the documents at issue in this case is privileged and cannot be compelled without a statutory grant of use immunity pursuant to 18 U.S.C. §§ 6002 and 6003. The judgment of the Court of Appeals is, therefore, affirmed in part and reversed in part, and the case is remanded to the District Court for further proceedings consistent with this opinion.

It is so ordered.

Notes

In Doe, the Supreme Court reaffirmed prior rulings that the content of business records is not protected by the fifth amendment. According to the Court, the rationale for this position has three steps: (1) At the time they are created, business records (such as invoices, ledgers, letters, etc.) are created voluntarily, so as to conduct business. (2) The fifth amendment prohibits only *compelled* self incrimination; it does not prohibit voluntary incrimination. (3) Therefore, the fifth amendment does not apply to business records, even those that may prove to be incriminating. Do you agree with this reasoning?

In *Doe,* the Court also held that, at least for the sole proprietor at issue, the *act* of producing these same business records may be protected. To understand this holding, it may be helpful to review the process by which records are produced to the grand jury.

Often, when a person receives a grand jury subpoena to produce records, this person's appearance before the grand jury is not deemed necessary and the prosecutor will inform the person that, in lieu of appearing before the grand jury, the records may be simply turned over to an investigative agent who will accept the records on behalf of the grand jury. A mutually convenient time is arranged, all records are turned over to the agent, and the agent informs the grand jury that the records have been received. The person receiving the subpoena never appears before the grand jury.

On other occasions, however, the person receiving the subpoena is required to appear before the grand jury. When this is so, the prosecutor and the witness will appear in the grand jury. Defense counsel will not be permitted inside the grand jury room although defense counsel may wait outside and the witness may leave to consult with counsel. After the person is sworn as a witness the prosecutor asks this witness to identify herself, whether she is present pursuant to a grand jury subpoena, and whether she has brought with her records requested in this subpoena. At this point, the prosecutor usually goes through the list of records requested in the subpoena and, document by document, ascertains from the witness whether she is producing each record requested. As the witness produces and identifies each record, it is marked with a grand jury exhibit number. Often, questions during this "production" process also establish the witness's basis of knowledge as to each record.

In this manner, a witness who produces records before the grand jury may well provide detailed testimony about the existence and identification of specific records. In cases built on documents, such as white collar criminal cases, such testimony may be crucial in actually proving guilt or innocence. For example, a witness who produces certain income ledgers for the grand jury may incriminate herself by demonstrating her knowledge that such ledgers exist and what they contain. If a tax fraud prosecution results from the investigation against this witness (now defendant) for failure to report this income, this defendant would have difficulty credibly asserting that she did not know or understand that this income existed. Simply identifying records could also incriminate a witness in crimes involving a double set of books. Such crimes include tax fraud, bank fraud, false statements to the government—in other words, any offense wherein the defendant allegedly reported one amount of income or expenses, when in fact she had a different amount of income or expenses, as reflected in the second set of books.

Given such scenarios, do you agree with the Court that the act of producing documents may independently incriminate the person producing documents? Do you see any problems in protecting the *act* of producing records when the *content* of the same records is not protected?

———

In the next case, Braswell v. United States, 487 U.S. 99, the Court began to address the nuances of its *Doe* ruling when a corporation, rather than a sole proprietor, sought to invoke the fifth amendment privilege against self incrimination as to the *act* of producing records. Prior to reaching its holding, the Court provides a helpful summary of relevant case law.

BRASWELL v. UNITED STATES

United States Supreme Court, 1988.
487 U.S. 99.

REHNQUIST, CHIEF JUSTICE.

This case presents the question whether the custodian of corporate records may resist a subpoena for such records on the ground that the act of production would incriminate him in violation of the Fifth Amendment. We conclude that he may not.

From 1965 to 1980, petitioner Randy Braswell operated his business—which comprises the sale and purchase of equipment, land, timber, and oil and gas interests—as a sole proprietorship. In 1980, he incorporated Worldwide Machinery Sales, Inc., a Mississippi corporation, and began conducting the business through that entity. In 1981, he formed a second Mississippi corporation, Worldwide Purchasing, Inc., and funded that corporation with the 100 percent interest he held in Worldwide Machinery. Petitioner was and is the sole shareholder of Worldwide Purchasing, Inc.

Both companies are active corporations, maintaining their current status with the State of Mississippi, filing corporate tax returns, and keeping current corporate books and records. In compliance with Mississippi law, both corporations have three directors, petitioner, his wife, and his mother. Although his wife and mother are secretary-treasurer and vice-president of the corporations, respectively, neither has any authority over the business affairs of either corporation.

In August 1986, a federal grand jury issued a subpoena to "Randy Braswell, President Worldwide Machinery, Inc. [and] Worldwide Purchasing, Inc.," requiring petitioner to produce the books and records of the two corporations. The subpoena provided that petitioner could deliver the records to the agent serving the subpoena, and did not require petitioner to testify. Petitioner moved to quash the subpoena, arguing that the act of producing the records would incriminate him in violation of Fifth Amendment privilege against self-incrimination. The District Court denied the motion to quash, ruling that the "collective entity doctrine" prevented petitioner from asserting that his act of producing the corporations' records was protected by the Fifth Amendment. The court rejected petitioner's argument that the collective entity doctrine does not apply when a corporation is so small that it constitutes nothing more than the individual's alter ego.

The United States Court of Appeals for the Fifth Circuit affirmed, citing Bellis v. United States, 417 U.S. 85, 88 (1974), for the proposition that a corporation's records custodian may not claim a Fifth Amendment privilege no matter how small the corporation may be. The Court of Appeals declared that Bellis retained vitality following United States v. Doe, 465 U.S. 605 (1984), and therefore, "Braswell, as custodian of corporate documents, has no act of production privilege under the fifth amendment regarding corporate documents." We granted certiorari to resolve a conflict among the Courts of Appeals. We now affirm.

* * *

Had petitioner conducted his business as a sole proprietorship, *Doe* would require that he be provided the opportunity to show that his act of production would entail testimonial self-incrimination. But petitioner has operated his business through the corporate form, and we have long recognized that for purposes of the Fifth Amendment, corporations and other collective entities are treated differently from individuals. This doctrine—known as the collective entity rule—has a lengthy and distinguished pedigree.

* * *

[The Court reviewed numerous cases discussing the rights of collective entities—ed.]

The plain mandate of these decisions is that without regard to whether the subpoena is addressed to the corporation, or as here, to the individual in his capacity as a custodian, a corporate custodian such as petitioner may not resist a subpoena for corporate records on Fifth Amendment grounds.

* * *

We note further that recognizing a Fifth Amendment privilege on behalf of the records custodians of collective entities would have a detrimental impact on the Government's efforts to prosecute "white-collar crime," one of the most serious problems confronting law enforcement authorities. "The greater portion of evidence of wrongdoing by an organization or its representatives is usually found in the official records and documents of that organization. Were the cloak of the privilege to be thrown around these impersonal records and documents, effective enforcement of many federal and state laws would be impossible." United States v. White, 322 U.S. 694, 700 (1944). If custodians could assert a privilege, authorities would be stymied not only in their enforcement efforts against those individuals but also in their prosecutions of organizations. In Bellis v. United States, 417 U.S. 85, 88 (1974), the Court observed: "In view of the inescapable fact that an artificial entity can only act to produce its records through its individual officers or agents, recognition of the individual's claim of privilege with respect to the financial records of the organization would substantially undermine the unchallenged rule that the organization itself is not entitled to claim any Fifth Amendment privilege, and largely frustrate legitimate governmental regulation of such organizations." *Id.* at 90.

Petitioner suggests, however, that these concerns can be minimized by the simple expedient of either granting the custodian statutory immunity as to the act of production, or addressing the subpoena to the corporation and allowing it to chose [sic] an agent to produce the records who can do so without incriminating himself. We think neither proposal satisfactorily addresses these concerns. Taking the last first, it is no doubt true that if a subpoena is addressed to a corporation, the corporation "must find some means by which to comply because no Fifth Amendment defense is available to it." The means most commonly used to comply is the appointment of an alternate custodian. But petitioner insists he cannot be required to aid the appointed custodian in his search for the demanded records, for any statement to the surrogate would itself be testimonial and incriminating. If this is correct, then petitioner's "solution" is a chimera. In situations such as this—where the corporate custodian is likely the only person with knowledge about the demanded documents—the appointment of a surrogate will simply not ensure that the documents sought will ever reach the grand jury room; the appointed custodian will essentially be sent on an unguided search.

This problem is eliminated if the Government grants the subpoenaed custodian statutory immunity for the testimonial aspects of his act of production. But that "solution" also entails a significant drawback. All of the evidence obtained under a grant of immunity to the custodian may of course be used freely against the corporation, but if the Government has any thought of prosecuting the custodian, a grant of act of production immunity can have serious consequences. Testimony obtained pursuant to a grant of statutory use immunity may be used neither directly nor derivatively. Kastigar v. United States, 406 U.S. 441 (1972). And "[o]ne raising a claim under [the federal immunity] statute need only show that he testified under a grant of immunity in order to shift to the government the heavy burden of proving that all of the evidence it proposes to use was derived from legitimate independent sources." *Id.* at 461–62. Even in cases where the Government does not employ the immunized testimony for any purpose—direct or derivative—against the witness, the Government's inability to meet the "heavy burden" it bears may result in the preclusion of crucial evidence that was obtained legitimately.

Although a corporate custodian is not entitled to resist a subpoena on the ground that his act of production will be personally incriminating, we do think certain consequences flow from the fact that the custodian's act of production is one in his representative rather than personal capacity. Because the custodian acts as a representative, the act is deemed one of the corporation and not the individual. Therefore, the Government concedes, as it must, that it may make no evidentiary use of the "individual act" against the individual. For example, in a criminal prosecution against the custodian, the Government may not introduce into evidence before the jury the fact that the subpoena was served upon and the corporation's documents were delivered by one particular individual, the custodian. The Government has the right, however, to use the corporation's act of production against the custodian. The Government may offer testimony—for example, from the process server who delivered the subpoena and from the individual who received the records—establishing that the corporation produced the records subpoenaed. The jury may draw from the corporation's act of production the conclusion that the records in question are authentic corporate records, which the corporation possessed, and which it produced in response to the subpoena. And if the defendant held a prominent position within the corporation that produced the records, the jury may, just as it would had someone else produced the documents, reasonably infer that he had possession of the documents or knowledge of their contents. Because the jury is not told that the defendant produced the records, any nexus between the defendant and the documents results solely from the corporation's act of production and other evidence in the case.

Consistent with our precedent, the United States Court of Appeals for the Fifth Circuit ruled that petitioner could not resist the subpoena for corporate documents on the ground that the act of production might tend to incriminate him. The judgment is therefore affirmed.

JUSTICE KENNEDY, WITH WHOM JUSTICE BRENNAN, JUSTICE MARSHALL, AND JUSTICE SCALIA JOIN, DISSENTING.

Our long course of decisions concerning artificial entities and the Fifth Amendment served us well. It illuminated two of the critical foundations for the constitutional guarantee against self-incrimination: first, that it is an explicit right of a natural person, protecting the realm of human thought and expression; second, that it is confined to governmental compulsion.

It is regrettable that the very line of cases which at last matured to teach these principles is now invoked to curtail them, for the Court rules that a natural person forfeits the privilege in a criminal investigation directed against him and that the Government may use compulsion to elicit testimonial assertions from a person who faces the threat of criminal proceedings. A case that might have served as the paradigmatic expression of the purposes served by the Fifth Amendment instead is used to obscure them.

The Court today denies an individual his Fifth Amendment privilege against self-incrimination in order to vindicate the rule that a collective entity which employs him has no such privilege itself. To reach this ironic conclusion, the majority must blur an analytic clarity in Fifth Amendment doctrine that has taken almost a century to emerge. After holding that corporate employment strips the individual of his privilege, the Court then attempts to restore some measure of protection by its judicial creation of a new zone of immunity in some vaguely defined circumstances. This exercise admits what the Court denied in the first place, namely that compelled compliance with the subpoena implicates the Fifth Amendment self-incrimination privilege.

The majority's apparent reasoning is that collective entities have no privilege and so their employees must have none either. The Court holds that a corporate agent must incriminate himself even when he is named in the subpoena and is a target of the investigation, and even when it is conceded that compliance requires compelled, personal, testimonial, incriminating assertions. I disagree with that conclusion; find no precedent for it; maintain that if there is a likelihood of personal self-incrimination the narrow use immunity permitted by statute can be granted without frustrating the investigation of collective entities; and submit that basic Fifth Amendment principles should not be avoided and manipulated, which is the necessary effect of this decision.

* * *

There is some common ground in this case. All accept the longstanding rule that labor unions, corporations, partnerships, and other collective entities have no Fifth Amendment self-incrimination privilege; that a natural person cannot assert such a privilege on their behalf; and that the contents of business records prepared without compulsion can be used to incriminate even a natural person without implicating Fifth Amendment concerns. Further, all appear to concede or at least submit the case to us on the assumption that the act of producing the subpoenaed documents will effect personal incrimination of Randy Braswell, the individual to whom the subpoena is directed.

The petitioner's assertion of the Fifth Amendment privilege against the forced production of documents is based not on any contention that their contents will incriminate him but instead upon the unchallenged premise that the act of production will do so. * * *

* * *

The heart of the matter, as everyone knows, is that the Government does not see Braswell as a mere agent at all; and the majority's theory is difficult to square with what will often be the Government's actual practice. The subpoena in this case was not directed to Worldwide Machinery Sales, Inc., or Worldwide Purchasing, Inc. It was directed to "Randy Braswell, President, Worldwide Machinery Sales, Inc., Worldwide Purchasing, Inc." and informed him that "[y]ou are hereby commanded" to provide the specified documents. The Government explained at oral argument that it often chooses to designate an individual recipient, rather than the corporation generally, when it serves a subpoena because "[we] want the right to make that individual comply with the subpoena." This is not the language of agency. By issuing a subpoena which the Government insists is "directed to petitioner personally," it has forfeited any claim that it is simply making a demand on a corporation that, in turn, will have to find a physical agent to perform its duty. What the Government seeks instead is the right to choose any corporate agent as a target of its subpoena and compel that individual to disclose certain information by his own actions.

The majority gives the corporate agent fiction a weight it simply cannot bear. In a peculiar attempt to mitigate the force of its own holding, it impinges upon its own analysis by concluding that, while the Government may compel a named individual to produce records, in any later proceeding against the person it cannot divulge that he performed the act. But if that is so, it is because the Fifth Amendment protects the person without regard to his status as a corporate employee; and once this be admitted, the necessary support for the majority's case has collapsed.

Perhaps the Court makes this concession out of some vague sense of fairness, but the source of its authority to do so remains unexplained. It cannot rest on the Fifth Amendment, for the privilege against self-incrimination does not permit balancing the convenience of the Government against the rights of a witness, and the majority has in any case determined that the Fifth Amendment is inapplicable. If Braswell by his actions reveals information about his state of mind that is relevant to a jury in a criminal proceeding, there are no grounds of which I am aware for declaring the information inadmissible, unless it be the Fifth Amendment.

In *Doe I* we declined expressly to do what the Court does today. Noting that there might well be testimonial assertions attendant upon the production of documents, we rejected the argument that compelled production necessarily carried with it a grant of constructive immunity. We held that immunity may be granted only by appropriate statutory proceedings. The Government must make a formal request for statutory use immunity under 18 U.S.C. §§ 6002, 6003 if it seeks access to records in exchange for its agreement not to use testimonial acts against the individual. Rather than beginning the practice of establishing new judicially created evidentiary rules, conferring upon individuals some partial use immunity to avoid results the Court finds constitutionally intolerable, I submit our precedents require the Government to use the only mechanism yet sanctioned for compelling testimony that is privileged: a request for immunity as provided by statute.

II

The majority's abiding concern is that if a corporate officer who is the target of a subpoena is allowed to assert the privilege, it will impede the Government's power to investigate corporations, unions, and partnerships, to uncover and prosecute white-collar crimes, and otherwise to enforce its visitatorial powers. There are at least two answers to this. The first, and most fundamental, is that the text of the Fifth Amendment does not authorize exceptions premised on such rationales. Second, even if it were proper to invent such exceptions, the dangers prophesied by the majority are overstated.

Recognition of the right to assert a privilege does not mean it will exist in many cases. In many instances, the production of documents may implicate no testimonial assertions at all. In Fisher v. United States, 425 U.S. 391 (1976), for example, we held that the specific acts required by the subpoena before us "would not itself involve testimonial self-incrimination" because, in that case, "the existence and location of the papers [were] a foregone conclusion and the taxpayer adds little or nothing to the sum total of the Government's information by conceding that he in fact has the papers." Whether a particular act is testimonial and self-incriminating is largely a factual issue to be decided in each case. In the case before us, the Government has made its submission on the assumption that the subpoena would result in incriminating testimony. The existence of a privilege in future cases, however, is not an automatic result.

Further, to the extent testimonial assertions are being compelled, use immunity can be granted without impeding the investigation. Where the privilege is applicable, immunity will be needed for only one individual, and solely with respect to evidence derived from the act of production itself. The Government would not be denied access to the records it seeks, it would be free to use the contents of the records against everyone, and it would be free to use any testimonial act implicit in production against all but the custodian it selects. In appropriate cases the Government will be able to establish authenticity, possession, and control by means other than compelling assertions about them from a suspect.

In one sense the case before us may not be a particularly sympathetic one. Braswell was the sole stockholder of the corporation and ran it himself. Perhaps that is why the Court suggests he waived his Fifth Amendment self-incrimination rights by using the corporate form. One does not always, however, have the choice of his or her employer, much less the choice of the business enterprise through which the employer conducts its business. Though the Court here hints at a waiver, nothing in Fifth Amendment jurisprudence indicates that the acceptance of employment should be deemed a waiver of a specific protection that is as basic a part of our constitutional heritage as is the privilege against self-incrimination.

The law is not captive to its own fictions. Yet, in the matter before us the Court employs the fiction that personal incrimination of the employee is neither sought by the Government nor cognizable by the law. That is a regrettable holding, for the conclusion is factually unsound, unnecessary for legitimate regulation, and a violation of the Self–Incrimination Clause of the Fifth Amendment of the Constitution. For these reasons, I dissent.

C. GRAND JURY SECRECY

The grand jury operates in secret. Grand jurors, attorneys appearing before the grand jury, stenographers who record grand jury proceedings, and court personnel who may have access to information about grand jury proceedings are prohibited from disclosing information about the grand jury. Only grand jury witnesses may disclose their experience before the grand jury. This strict rule of secrecy arises because of the broad power of the grand jury to investigate. Recall the Court's statement in *R. Enterprises, supra,* that the grand jury "can investigate merely on suspicion that the law is being violated, or even just because it wants assurance that it is not."

Reputations could be ruined if word about an investigation leaked to the public, only to have the investigation later closed without the bringing of criminal charges. In addition, if word about ongoing investigations becomes public, witnesses' lives could be jeopardized, evidence destroyed, and future testimony compared, discussed and possibly "cleaned up" by potential witnesses. For all of these reasons, grand jury secrecy is crucial.

The cases in this section discuss the issue of grand jury secrecy. Be sure to study Federal Rule of Procedure 6(e), quoted in footnote 7 of the next case, United States v. Sells Engineering, Inc., 463 U.S. 418 (1983).

UNITED STATES v. SELLS ENGINEERING, INC.

United States Supreme Court, 1983.
463 U.S. 418.

BRENNAN, JUSTICE.

The question in this case is under what conditions attorneys for the Civil Division of the Justice Department, their paralegal and secretarial staff, and all other necessary assistants, may obtain access to grand jury materials, compiled with the assistance and knowledge of other Justice Department attorneys, for the purpose of preparing and pursuing a civil suit. * * *

I

Respondents Peter A. Sells and Fred R. Witte were officers of respondent Sells Engineering, Inc. That company had contracts with the United States Navy to produce airborne electronic devices designed to interfere with enemy radar systems. In 1974, a Special Agent of the Internal Revenue Service began a combined criminal and civil administrative investigation of respondents. The Agent issued administrative summonses for certain corporate records of Sells Engineering. When the corporation refused to comply, the Agent obtained a district court order enforcing the summonses. Enforcement was stayed, however, pending appeal.

While the enforcement case was pending in the Court of Appeals, a federal grand jury was convened to investigate charges of criminal fraud on the Navy and of evasion of federal income taxes. The grand jury subpoenaed, and respondents produced, many of the same materials that were the subject of the IRS administrative summonses.[1] The grand jury indicted all three respondents on two counts of conspiracy to defraud the United States[2] and nine counts of tax fraud.[3] Respondents moved to dismiss the indictment, alleging grand jury misuse for civil purposes. Before the motion was decided, however, the parties reached a plea bargain. The individual respondents each pleaded guilty to one count of conspiracy to defraud the Government by obstructing an IRS investigation. All other counts were dismissed, and respondents withdrew their charges of grand jury misuse.

Thereafter, the Government moved for disclosure of all grand jury materials to attorneys in the Justice Department's Civil Division, their paralegal and secretarial assistants, and certain Defense Department experts, for use in preparing and conducting a possible civil suit against respondents under the False Claims Act, 31 U.S.C. § 231 et seq.[4]

---

1. The Court of Appeals, upon learning this, remanded the summons enforcement action for reconsideration. The Government did not pursue the matter further, and the suit was dismissed for want of prosecution.

2. 18 U.S.C. § 371.

3. 26 U.S.C. § 7206(2).

4. Although the Government has always contended that the Civil Division attorneys are entitled to disclosure without any court order, the Government chose to request permission for disclosure from the District

Respondents opposed the disclosure, renewing their allegations of grand jury misuse. The District Court granted the requested disclosure, concluding that attorneys in the Civil Division are entitled to disclosure as a matter of right under Rule 6(e)(3)(A)(i). The Court also stated that disclosure to Civil Division attorneys and their non-attorney assistants was warranted because the Government had shown particularized need for disclosure. The Court of Appeals vacated and remanded, holding that Civil Division attorneys could obtain disclosure only by showing particularized need under Rule 6(e)(3)(C)(i), and that the District Court had not applied a correct standard of particularized need. We now affirm.

II

A

The grand jury has always occupied a high place as an instrument of justice in our system of criminal law—so much so that it is enshrined in the Constitution. It serves the "dual function of determining if there is probable cause to believe that a crime has been committed and of protecting citizens against unfounded criminal prosecutions." Branzburg v. Hayes, 408 U.S. 665, 686–687 (1972). It has always been extended extraordinary powers of investigation and great responsibility for directing its own efforts:

> Traditionally the grand jury has been accorded wide latitude to inquire into violations of criminal law. No judge presides to monitor its proceedings. It deliberates in secret and may determine alone the course of its inquiry. The grand jury may compel the production of evidence or the testimony of witnesses as it considers appropriate, and its operation generally is unrestrained by the technical procedural and evidentiary rules governing the conduct of criminal trials. "It is a grand inquest, a body with powers of investigation and inquisition, the scope of whose inquiries is not to be limited narrowly by questions of propriety or forecasts of the probable result of the investigation, or by doubts whether any particular individual will be found properly subject to an accusation of crime."

United States v. Calandra, 414 U.S. 338, 343 (1974).

These broad powers are necessary to permit the grand jury to carry out both parts of its dual function. Without thorough and effective investigation, the grand jury would be unable either to ferret out crimes deserving of prosecution, or to screen out charges not warranting prosecution.

The same concern for the grand jury's dual function underlies the "long-established policy that maintains the secrecy of the grand jury proceedings in the federal courts." United States v. Procter & Gamble, 356 U.S. 677, 681 (1958).

Court. It stated that it thought no order necessary, but requested an order in the alternative.

We consistently have recognized that the proper functioning of our grand jury system depends upon the secrecy of grand jury proceedings. In particular, we have noted several distinct interests served by safeguarding the confidentiality of grand jury proceedings. First, if pre-indictment proceedings were made public, many prospective witnesses would be hesitant to come forward voluntarily, knowing that those against whom they testify would be aware of that testimony. Moreover, witnesses who appeared before the grand jury would be less likely to testify fully and frankly, as they would be open to retribution as well as to inducements. There also would be the risk that those about to be indicted would flee, or would try to influence individual grand jurors to vote against indictment. Finally, by preserving the secrecy of the proceedings, we assure that persons who are accused but exonerated by the grand jury will not be held up to public ridicule.

Douglas Oil Co. v. Petrol Stops Northwest, 441 U.S. 211, 218–219 (1979). Grand jury secrecy, then, is "as important for the protection of the innocent as for the pursuit of the guilty." [citation omitted] Both Congress and this Court have consistently stood ready to defend it against unwarranted intrusion. In the absence of a clear indication in a statute or Rule, we must always be reluctant to conclude that a breach of this secrecy has been authorized.

B

Rule 6(e) of the Federal Rules of Criminal Procedure codifies the traditional rule of grand jury secrecy:

Paragraph 6(e)(2) provides that grand jurors, Government attorneys and their assistants, and other personnel attached to the grand jury are forbidden to disclose matters occurring before the grand jury. Witnesses are not under the prohibition unless they also happen to fit into one of the enumerated classes. Paragraph 6(e)(3) sets forth four exceptions to this nondisclosure rule.[7]

---

7. Rules 6(e)(2) and (3), as presently in force, provide as follows:

"(e) Recording and Disclosure of Proceedings

* * *

"(2) General Rule of Secrecy.—A grand juror, an interpreter, a stenographer, an operator of a recording device, a typist who transcribes recorded testimony, an attorney for the government, or any person to whom disclosure is made under paragraph (3)(A)(ii) of this subdivision shall not disclose matters occurring before the grand jury, except as otherwise provided for in these rules. No obligation of secrecy may be imposed on any person except in accordance with this rule. A knowing violation of Rule 6 may be punished as a contempt of court.

"(3) Exceptions.

"(A) Disclosure otherwise prohibited by this rule of matters occurring before the grand jury, other than its deliberations and the vote of any grand juror, may be made to—

"(i) an attorney for the government for use in the performance of such attorney's duty; and

"(ii) such government personnel as are deemed necessary by an attorney for the government to assist an attorney for the government in the performance of such attorney's duty to enforce federal criminal law.

"(B) Any person to whom matters are disclosed under subparagraph (A)(ii) of this paragraph shall not utilize that

Subparagraph 6(e)(3)(A) contains two authorizations for disclosure as a matter of course, without any court order. First, under subparagraph 6(e)(3)(A)(i), disclosure may be made without a court order to "an attorney for the government for use in the performance of such attorney's duty" (referred to hereinafter as "(A)(i) disclosure"). "Attorney for the government" is defined in Rule 54(c) in such broad terms as potentially to include virtually every attorney in the Department of Justice. Second, under subparagraph 6(e)(3)(A)(ii), grand jury materials may likewise be provided to "government personnel * * * [who] assist an attorney for the government in the performance of such attorney's duty to enforce federal criminal law" ("(A)(ii) disclosure"). Subparagraph 6(e)(3)(B) further regulates (A)(ii) disclosure, forbidding use of grand jury materials by "government personnel" for any purpose other than assisting an attorney for the Government in his enforcement of criminal law, and requiring that the names of such personnel be provided to the district court.

Subparagraph 6(e)(3)(C) also authorizes courts to order disclosure. Under subparagraph 6(e)(3)(C)(i), a court may order disclosure "preliminarily to or in connection with a judicial proceeding" (a "(C)(i) order"). Under subparagraph 6(e)(3)(C)(ii), a court may order disclosure under certain conditions at the request of a defendant.

The main issue in this case is whether attorneys in the Justice Department may obtain automatic (A)(i) disclosure of grand jury materials for use in a civil suit, or whether they must seek a (C)(i) court order for access. If a (C)(i) order is necessary, we must address the dependent question of what standards should govern issuance of the order.

III

The Government contends that all attorneys in the Justice Department qualify for automatic disclosure of grand jury materials under (A)(i), regardless of the nature of the litigation in which they intend to use the materials. * * *

grand jury material for any purpose other than assisting the attorney for the government in the performance of such attorney's duty to enforce federal criminal law. An attorney for the government shall promptly provide the district court, before which was impaneled the grand jury whose material has been so disclosed, with the names of the persons to whom such disclosure has been made.

"(C) Disclosure otherwise prohibited by this rule of matters occurring before the grand jury may also be made—

"(i) when so directed by a court preliminarily to or in connection with a judicial proceeding; or

"(ii) when permitted by a court at the request of the defendant, upon a showing that grounds may exist for a motion to dismiss the indictment because of matters occurring before the grand jury.

"If the court orders disclosure of matters occurring before the grand jury, the disclosure shall be made in such manner, at such time, and under such conditions as the court may direct."

A fifth exception has been created this Term in an amendment to Rule 6(3), to take effect August 1, 1983. 461 U.S. 1121 (1983). The amendment adds a new subparagraph 6(e)(3)(C)(iii), permitting disclosure "when the disclosure is made by an attorney for the government to another federal grand jury." The Advisory Committee's Note points out that secrecy is not thereby compromised, since the second grand jury is equally under Rule 6's requirement of secrecy.

A

The Government correctly contends that attorneys for the Civil Division of the Justice Department are within the class of "attorneys for the government" to whom (A)(i) allows disclosure without a court order. Rule 54(c) defines the phrase expansively, to include "authorized assistants to the Attorney General"; 28 U.S.C. § 515(a) provides that the Attorney General may direct any attorney employed by the Department to conduct "any kind of legal proceeding, civil or criminal, including grand jury proceedings . * * * " *See also* § 518(b). In short, as far as Rules 6 and 54 are concerned, it is immaterial that certain attorneys happen to be assigned to a unit called the Civil Division, or that their usual duties involve only civil cases. If, for example, the Attorney General (for whatever reason) were to detail a Civil Division attorney to conduct a criminal grand jury investigation, nothing in Rule 6 would prevent that attorney from doing so; he need not secure a transfer out of the Civil Division. [I]t does not follow, however, that any Justice Department attorney is free to rummage through the records of any grand jury in the country, simply by right of office. Disclosure under (A)(i) is permitted only "in the performance of such attorney's duty." The heart of the primary issue in this case is whether performance of duty, within the meaning of (A)(i), includes preparation and litigation of a civil suit by a Justice Department attorney who had no part in conducting the related criminal prosecution.

Given the strong historic policy of preserving grand jury secrecy, one might wonder why government attorneys are given any automatic access at all. The draftsmen of the original Rule 6 provided the answer: "Government attorneys are entitled to disclosure of grand jury proceedings, other than the deliberations and the votes of the jurors, inasmuch as they may be present in the grand jury room during the presentation of evidence. The rule continues this practice." Advisory Committee's Notes on Federal Rule of Criminal Procedure 6(e), 18 U.S.C.App., p. 1411. This is potent evidence that Rule 6(e) was never intended to grant free access to grand jury materials to attorneys not working on the criminal matters to which the materials pertain. The Advisory Committee's explanation strongly suggests that automatic access to grand jury materials is available only to those attorneys for the Government who would be entitled to appear before the grand jury. But government attorneys are allowed into grand jury rooms, not for the general and multifarious purposes of the Department of Justice, but because both the grand jury's functions and their own *prosecutorial* duties require it. As the Advisory Committee suggested, the same reasoning applies to disclosure of grand jury materials outside the grand jury room.

The purpose of the grand jury requires that it remain free, within constitutional and statutory limits, to operate "independently of either prosecuting attorney or judge." [citation omitted] Nevertheless, a modern grand jury would be much less effective without the assistance of the prosecutor's office and the investigative resources it commands. The prosecutor ordinarily brings matters to the attention of the grand jury and gathers the evidence required for the jury's consideration. Although the grand jury may itself decide to investigate a matter or to seek certain evidence, it depends largely on the prosecutor's office to secure the evidence or witnesses it requires.[13] The prosecutor also advises the lay jury on the applicable law. The prosecutor in turn needs to know what transpires before the grand jury in order to perform his own duty properly. If he considers that the law and the admissible evidence will not support a conviction, he can be expected to advise the grand jury not to indict. He must also examine indictments, and the basis for their issuance, to determine whether it is in the interests of justice to proceed with prosecution.

None of these considerations, however, provides any support for breaching grand jury secrecy in favor of government attorneys *other than prosecutors*—either by allowing them into the grand jury room, or by granting them uncontrolled access to grand jury materials. An attorney with only civil duties lacks both the prosecutor's special role in supporting the grand jury, and the prosecutor's own crucial need to know what occurs before the grand jury.[15]

Of course, it would be of substantial help to a Justice Department civil attorney if he had free access to a storehouse of evidence compiled by a grand jury; but that is of a different order from the prosecutor's need for access. The civil lawyer's need is ordinarily nothing more than a matter of saving time and expense. The same argument could be made for access on behalf of any lawyer in another government agency, or indeed, in private practice. We have consistently rejected the argument that such savings can justify a breach of grand jury secrecy. In most cases, the same evidence that could be obtained from the grand jury will be available through ordinary discovery or other routine avenues of investigation. If, in a particular case, ordinary discovery is insufficient for some reason, the Government may request disclosure under a (C)(i) court order.

Not only is disclosure for civil use unjustified by the considerations supporting prosecutorial access, but it threatens to do affirmative mischief. The problem is threefold.

First, disclosure to government bodies raises much the same concerns that underlie the rule of secrecy in other contexts. Not only does disclosure increase the number of persons to whom the information is available (thereby increasing the risk of inadvertent or illegal release to others), but it renders considerably more concrete the threat to the willingness of witnesses to come forward and to testify fully and candid-

---

13. Not only would the prosecutor ordinarily draw up and supervise the execution of subpoenas, but he commands the investigative forces that might be needed to find out what the grand jury wants to know. *See also, e.g.,* 18 U.S.C. § 6003 (United States Attorney to request order granting use immunity).

15. This case involves only access by Civil Division attorneys who played no part in the criminal prosecution of respondents. It does not present any issue concerning continued use of grand jury materials, in the civil phase of a dispute, by an attorney who himself conducted the criminal prosecution. We decline to address that problem in this case.

ly. If a witness knows or fears that his testimony before the grand jury will be routinely available for use in governmental civil litigation or administrative action, he may well be less willing to speak for fear that he will get himself into trouble in some other forum.

Second, because the Government takes an active part in the activities of the grand jury, disclosure to government attorneys for civil use poses a significant threat to the integrity of the grand jury itself. If prosecutors in a given case knew that their colleagues would be free to use the materials generated by the grand jury for a civil case, they might be tempted to manipulate the grand jury's powerful investigative tools to root out additional evidence useful in the civil suit, or even to start or continue a grand jury inquiry where no criminal prosecution seemed likely. Any such use of grand jury proceedings to elicit evidence for use in a civil case is improper per se. *Procter & Gamble*, 356 U.S., at 683–684. We do not mean to impugn the professional characters of Justice Department lawyers in general; nor do we express any view on the allegations of misuse that have been made in this case. Our concern is based less on any belief that grand jury misuse is in fact widespread than on our concern that, if and when it does occur, it would often be very difficult to detect and prove.

Third, use of grand jury materials by government agencies in civil or administrative settings threatens to subvert the limitations applied outside the grand jury context on the Government's powers of discovery and investigation. While there are some limits on the investigative powers of the grand jury, there are few if any other forums in which a governmental body has such relatively unregulated power to compel other persons to divulge information or produce evidence. Other agencies, both within and without the Justice Department, operate under specific and detailed statutes, rules, or regulations conferring only limited authority to require citizens to testify or produce evidence. Some agencies have been granted special statutory powers to obtain information and require testimony in pursuance of their duties. Others (including the Civil Division) are relegated to the usual course of discovery under the Federal Rules of Civil Procedure. In either case, the limitations imposed on investigation and discovery exist for sound reasons— ranging from fundamental fairness to concern about burdensomeness and intrusiveness. If government litigators or investigators in civil matters enjoyed unlimited access to grand jury material, though, there would be little reason for them to resort to their usual, more limited avenues of investigation. To allow these agencies to circumvent their usual methods of discovery would not only subvert the limitations and procedural requirements built into those methods, but would grant to the Government a virtual ex parte form of discovery, from which its civil litigation opponents are excluded unless they make a strong showing of particularized need. In civil litigation as in criminal, "it is rarely justifiable for the [Government] to have exclusive access to a storehouse of relevant fact." Dennis v. United States, 384 U.S. 855, 873 (1966). We are reluctant to conclude that the draftsmen of Rule 6 intended so remarkable a result.

In short, if grand juries are to be granted extraordinary powers of investigation because of the difficulty and importance of their task, the use of those powers ought to be limited as far as reasonably possible to the accomplishment of the task. The policies of Rule 6 require that any disclosure to attorneys other than prosecutors be judicially supervised rather than automatic.

* * *

We conclude, then, that Congress did not intend that "attorneys for the government" should be permitted free civil use of grand jury materials. Congress was strongly concerned with assuring that prosecutors would not be free to turn over grand jury materials to others in the Government for civil uses without court supervision, and that statutory limits on civil discovery not be subverted—concerns that apply to civil use by attorneys within the Justice Department as fully as to similar use by persons in other government agencies. Both the Advisory Committee Notes and the testimony of the Justice Department's own representative suggested that even under the old Rule such disclosure for civil use would not have been permissible; indeed, the latter gave a hypothetical illustration closely similar to this very case. The express addition of a "criminal-use" limitation in (A)(ii) appears to have been prompted by an abundance of caution, owing to Congress's special concern that non-attorneys were the ones most likely to pose a danger of unauthorized use.

IV

Since we conclude that the Government must obtain a (C)(i) court order to secure the disclosure it seeks in this case, we must consider what standard should govern the issuance of such an order.

Rule 6(e)(3)(C)(i) simply authorizes a court to order disclosure "preliminarily to or in connection with a judicial proceeding." Neither the text of the Rule nor the accompanying commentary describes any substantive standard governing issuance of such orders. We have consistently construed the Rule, however, to require a strong showing of particularized need for grand jury materials before any disclosure will be permitted. We described the standard in detail in *Douglas Oil*:

> "Parties seeking grand jury transcripts under Rule 6(e) must show that the material they seek is needed to avoid a possible injustice in another judicial proceeding, that the need for disclosure is greater than the need for continued secrecy, and that their request is structured to cover only material so needed. * * *.

> "It is clear from *Procter & Gamble* and *Dennis* that disclosure is appropriate only in those cases where the need for it outweighs the public interest in secrecy, and that the burden of demonstrating this balance rests upon the private party seeking disclosure. It is equally clear that as the considerations justifying secrecy become less rele-

vant, a party asserting a need for grand jury transcripts will have a lesser burden in showing justification. In sum, * * * the court's duty in a case of this kind is to weigh carefully the competing interests in light of the relevant circumstances and the standards announced by this Court. And if disclosure is ordered, the court may include protective limitations on the use of the disclosed material . * * *"

441 U.S. at 222–223.

* * *

V

The Court of Appeals correctly held that disclosure to government attorneys and their assistants for use in a civil suit is permissible only with a court order under Rule 6(e)(3)(C)(i), and that the District Court did not apply correctly the particularized need standard for issuance of such an order. Accordingly, the judgment of the Court of Appeals is Affirmed.

CHIEF JUSTICE BURGER, WITH WHOM JUSTICE POWELL, JUSTICE REHNQUIST, AND JUSTICE O'CONNOR JOIN, DISSENTING.

The Court today holds that attorneys within the Department of Justice who are not assigned to the grand jury investigation or prosecution must seek a court order on a showing of particularized need in order to obtain access, for the purpose of preparing a civil suit, to grand jury materials already in the Government's possession. In my view, this holding is contrary not only to the clear language but also to the history of Rule 6(e)(3)(A)(i) of the Federal Rules of Criminal Procedure. In addition, the Court's decision reflects an erroneous assessment of the relevant policies, and provides the courts and the Department of Justice with precious little guidance in an area of great importance. I believe that, when a grand jury is validly convened and conducted on the request of the Government for criminal investigatory purposes, it is proper and entirely consistent with the Federal Rules of Criminal Procedure for any attorney in the Department of Justice to have access to grand jury materials in pursuing inquiry into civil claims involving the same or related matters. I therefore dissent.

* * *

The Court * * * asserts that a blanket rule against access to grand jury materials for civil purposes is needed to prevent the possibility that the grand jury will be used improperly as a tool for civil discovery. I fully agree with the Court that use of grand jury proceedings for the purpose of obtaining evidence for a civil case is improper. But the mere *potential* for such abuse does not justify this Court's precluding Department of Justice attorneys from reviewing grand jury materials in assessing and prosecuting civil actions in the vast majority of cases where the grand jury has been convened and conducted for valid criminal investigatory purposes. As the Court recognized in *Procter & Gamble, supra*, the proper approach to the danger of abuse is not to adopt an across-the-board ban on civil use of grand jury materials by those not assigned to the criminal investigation, but rather for a District Court to impose appropriate sanctions if it turns out that the grand jury process has been abused to elicit evidence for a civil case. In *Procter & Gamble*, this Court indicated that one available remedy for abuse would be compensating disclosure to civil defendants. In other cases it might prove appropriate to prohibit the Government from making any use of grand jury materials in prosecuting its civil case. And in egregious cases it might be proper to hold certain individuals in contempt. Here, however, the District Court found no grand jury abuse.

* * * [T]he Court argues that civil use of grand jury materials would subvert the limitations on civil discovery and investigation that would otherwise apply. As the basis for this contention, the Court relies primarily on the Civil Division's access to the discovery provisions of the Federal Rules of Civil Procedure. The Court argues that the need for and limitations on this discovery method would be undermined by allowing government attorneys automatic access to grand jury materials for use in civil actions. This argument rests on the assumption that the civil discovery provisions of the Federal Rules of Civil Procedure were designed with but a single Division of the Justice Department in mind. Plainly that is untrue. The Federal Rules of Civil Procedure govern virtually all civil actions, the vast majority of which involve only private litigants. The civil discovery provisions were undoubtedly designed with these private litigants in mind, and the Civil Division of the Department has simply been relegated by the Court to the civil discovery provisions for lack of a better alternative.[12] Of course, if attorneys for the Justice Department are considering a civil action, they may not institute a grand jury in order to develop evidence for that civil case, but must make use of the available means for civil investigations. When a valid grand jury investigation has taken place, however, nothing in the Federal Rules of Civil Procedure precludes attorneys in the Justice Department from making use of the grand jury materials in preparing for and prosecuting civil suits.

Besides greatly overstating the interests that would be served by a blanket rule prohibiting attorneys from examining grand jury materials for possible civil prosecution, the Court also has given very short shrift

---

12. In my view, the civil discovery provisions of the Federal Rules are wholly insufficient for the Department of Justice to carry out its responsibilities to pursue fraud claims effectively. Under the Federal Rules, discovery may not normally take place until *after* a complaint has been filed. Yet *before* filing a complaint, an attorney must satisfy himself that to the best of his knowledge "there is good ground to support it." Fed. Rules Civ.Proc. 11. In a typical action between private parties, the parties themselves will have sufficient personal knowledge to determine whether an action is warranted. Civil Division attorneys seldom have actual personal knowledge of the underlying facts, however, and frequently must undertake additional investigation before they will be able to ascertain whether litigation is appropriate. If limited to voluntary cooperation or the civil discovery provisions, therefore, those attorneys will be unable to pursue many frauds against the public. These same concerns led Congress to enact legislation authorizing the Antitrust Division to issue civil investigative demands, 15 U.S.C. § 1312. The Civil Division has not been provided with similar authority to issue civil investigative demands.

to the public interests that are served by allowing government attorneys access to grand jury materials for the full range of their responsibilities. The Court dismisses these interests as "nothing more than a matter of saving time and expense." This cavalier comment overlooks the vital importance of time and money in the proper functioning of any system. The unwarranted burdens that the Court's rule imposes upon the Department of Justice will not mean simply that the Government must pay more to keep the system operating. Rather, the additional time and expense will result in a substantial decrease in the Government's ability to enforce important laws in meritorious civil actions—thus striking a severe blow to the public interest.[13]–

Notes

1.   What do you think? Is the majority correct in restricting grand jury access to Civil Division attorneys? Or, is the dissent more persuasive in arguing that Civil Division attorneys need greater discovery to properly perform their functions and that sanctions exist for abuses?

From reading both opinions, one gets the impression that within the Department of Justice (DOJ), Civil Division attorneys are separate from Criminal Division attorneys. This is true at "Main Justice," the DOJ headquarters in Washington, D.C. and at many larger U.S. Attorneys' Offices. However, at smaller U.S. Attorneys' offices, one attorney may handle both criminal and civil matters. Even more significant is the trend toward "global" investigations where fraud is investigated by a team of attorneys and investigators who specialize in criminal, civil, and administrative matters. It may not be until the end of the investigation that a decision is made whether to pursue the matter criminally, civilly, administratively or simultaneously on all fronts. This investigative strategy is especially prevalent in complex regulatory areas like health care. Does *Sells* address the problem of attorneys wearing "two hats" or the problems posed by joint investigations by teams of civil and criminal attorneys and investigators?

2.   Note footnote 12 in the dissenting opinion. Justice Burger makes the argument that "the civil discovery provisions of the Federal Rules are wholly insufficient for the Department of Justice to carry out its responsibilities to pursue fraud claims effectively." *Sells* was decided in 1983. In 1986, Congress gave the Department of Justice authority to issue civil investigative demands (CIDs) in fraud cases as part of its major overall of the False Claims Act. Section 3733, title 31, United States Code, provides:

---

13. It bears note, moreover, that not just the Government's time and money are at stake. Witnesses who have testified fully before the grand jury may have their schedules disrupted again for civil investigations. In many civil cases, a number of witnesses would undoubtedly be deposed in any event; but other witnesses will be forced to undergo the burden of appearing for testimony that would be unnecessary if government attorneys had access to the grand jury materials. In addition, witnesses may die, their memories may fade, records may be lost, and statutes of limitations may run. Presumably, even under the Court's approach, government attorneys could gain access to the grand jury materials through a court order in the first three of those situations— if the attorneys learned that the witnesses had testified before the grand jury or produced the relevant records. Where the statute of limitations has run, however, there would be no such relief.

"Whenever the Attorney General has reason to believe that any person may be in possession, custody, or control of any documentary material or information relevant to a false claims law investigation, the Attorney General may, before commencing a civil proceeding under section 3730 or other false claims law, issue in writing and cause to be served upon such person, a civil investigative demand requiring such person—

(A) to produce such documentary material for inspection and copying,

(B) to answer in writing written interrogatories with respect to such documentary material or information,

(C) to give oral testimony concerning such documentary material or information, or

(D) to furnish any combination of such material, answers, or testimony."

How might this increased CID authority affect the *Sells* holding?

3. The Court delivered its opinion in United States v. Baggot, 463 U.S. 476 (1983), simultaneously with its opinion in *Sells*. At issue in *Baggot* was Federal Rule of Criminal Procedure 6(e)(3)(C)(i) [referred to by the court as "(C)(i)"], which provides that disclosure of matters appearing before the grand jury may be made "when so directed by a court preliminarily to or in connection with a judicial proceeding." James E. Baggot was the target of a grand jury investigation into certain commodity futures transactions on the Chicago Board of Trade. He was not indicted but pleaded guilty to two misdemeanor counts of violating the Commodity Exchange Act, 7 U.S.C. § 6c(a)(A). After his plea of guilty, the Government filed a (C)(i) motion for disclosure of grand jury materials to the IRS for use in an audit of Baggot. The Supreme Court held that such an investigation was not preliminary to or in connection with a judicial proceeding:

"It follows that disclosure is not appropriate for use in an IRS audit of civil tax liability, because the purpose of the audit is not to prepare for or conduct litigation, but to assess the amount of tax liability through administrative channels. Assuming arguendo that this audit will inevitably disclose a deficiency on Baggot's part, there in no particular reason why that must lead to litigation, at least from the IRS's point of view. * * * The IRS need never go into court to assess and collect the amount owed; it is empowered to collect the tax by non-judicial means (such as levy on property or salary, 26 U.S.C. §§ 6331, 6332), without having to prove to a court the validity of the underlying tax liability. Of course, the matter may end up in court if Baggot chooses to take it there, but that possibility does not negate the fact that the primary use to which the IRS proposes to put the materials it seeks is an extrajudicial one— the assessment of a tax deficiency by the IRS. The Government takes countless actions that affected citizens are permitted to resist or challenge in court. The fact that judicial redress may be sought, without more, does not mean that the Government's action is 'preliminarily to a judicial proceeding.' Of course, it may often be loosely said that the Government is 'preparing for litigation,' in the sense that frequently it will be wise for an agency to anticipate the chance that it may be called upon to defend its actions in court. That, however, is not alone enough to bring an administrative action within (C)(i). Where an agency's action does not require resort to litigation to accomplish the agency's present goal, the action is not preliminary to a judicial proceeding for purposes of (C)(i)." 463 U.S. at 480–82.

Again, Justice Burger dissented, arguing:

"The Court today holds that administrative agencies may not inspect grand jury materials unless the "primary purpose of disclosure" is "to assist in preparation or conduct of a judicial proceeding. * * * " This holding is not compelled by either the language or history of Rule 6(e), and it ignores the vital public interest in effective law enforcement in noncriminal cases.

"Rule 6(e)(3)(C)(i), Fed. Rules Crim. Proc., provides that a District Court may in its discretion order disclosure of grand jury materials *'preliminarily to* or in connection with the judicial proceeding.' (Emphasis added.) It is evident from the language of the rule that disclosure prior to the actual filing of a complaint was contemplated by the Congress. Disclosure 'in connection with a judicial proceeding' encompasses those situations where a suit is pending or about to be filed. The words 'preliminary to' necessarily refer to judicial proceedings not yet in existence, where, for example, a claim is under study. The Court's interpretation of this language effectively reads the words 'preliminary to' out of the Rule. The Court interprets the Rule to apply only to cases where the 'actual use' of the materials sought is to prepare for or conduct litigation. If this were indeed Congress' intent, then it would have sufficed to allow disclosure 'in connection with judicial proceedings' without the added words permitting disclosure 'preliminary to' judicial proceedings. As the Court now interprets the Rule, disclosure prior to the filing of a complaint will only rarely be permitted.

* * *

"In focusing on the 'actual use' of the grand jury materials, the Court attempts in a crude and rigid way to reconcile the conflicting policies at issue. I believe a better balance is struck by holding that the threshold test for disclosure under Rule 6(e)(3)(C)(i) is satisfied so long as there is a possibility that the agency's action, should it ultimately act, would be subject to judicial review. In this respect, it makes no difference whether the judicial review would be de novo, as here, or more limited; nor does it matter that the party adversely affected by agency action might choose to forego judicial review. This king of broad interpretation of the language 'preliminary to * * * a judicial proceeding' clearly enlarges the potential for aiding civil law enforcement. If this standard is met—as it often would be—the questions for the court would be whether the prosecutor has shown that grand jury has not been used primarily for civil discovery purposes, and whether the agency's need for the materials outweighs the need for grand jury secrecy. * * * The result will be to enhance civil law enforcement interests while reducing the risk of abuse.

"The Court is proceeding on an assumption that government agencies, with the assistance of prosecutors, will subvert the grand jury into a tool of civil discovery whenever possible. Accordingly, the Court erects a rigid barrier restricting agency access on the theory that this will remove the incentive for abuse. The fundamental flaw in this analysis is the idea that abuse of the grand jury is a common phenomenon, which, of course, it is not. Few cases of grand jury abuse have ever been reported, and even fewer since this Court made clear in *United States v. Procter & Gamble Co.*, 356 U.S. 677, 683 (1958), that the Government's use of 'criminal procedures to elicit evidence in a civil case * * * would be flouting the policy of the law.' Moreover, the tremendous pressure on Government prosecutors to investigate the federal crimes in their jurisdictions—crimes which today are both more numerous and complex than ever before—reduces the likelihood that prosecutors will be swayed from their primary tasks or violate professional ethical standards at the behest of agency personnel. Finally, there is no reason to think that the courts are incapable of policing such occasional abuses as might occur. On the contrary, the reported cases show the sensitivity of the courts to the risks of grand jury abuse, and their readiness to act to ensure the integrity of the grand jury.

"In its battle against a largely phantom, 'strawman' threat, the Court fails to account for the substantial costs its rule will impose on the public. In investigating complex financial crimes, federal prosecutors often seek assistance from such agencies as the Securities Exchange Commission and the IRS. Agency personnel may devote countless thousands of lawyer hours assisting in the investigation of a criminal case. To force the agencies to duplicate these investigations is not only a waste of resources; the result may be that some meritorious administrative actions will never be brought. I cannot believe that Congress intended or would approve such a result." *Id.* at 483–89.

Are you becoming more or less persuaded by Chief Justice Burger's argument for more open access to grand jury proceedings? For years, defense attorneys have called for grand jury reforms such as: permitting defense counsel to accompany clients into a grand jury proceeding; opportunities for defense counsel to present exculpatory evidence to the grand jury (or that prosecutors be required to present exculpatory evidence); and, greater access to information considered by grand juries. If Chief Justice Burger's view prevails, do you believe there would be a stronger momentum for such reforms? Would these changes (greater access to grand jury proceedings by civil DOJ attorneys and government agencies, coupled with reforms favored by the defense bar) be a good or bad thing for the grand jury process?

Four years after its decisions in *Sells* and *Baggot*, the Court revisited the grand jury secrecy issue in the following case, United States v. John Doe, Inc. I, 481 U.S. 102 (1987). Note that the civil investigative demands discussed *supra*, are at issue in *Doe I*. Note also who is writing the dissent in *Doe I*.

UNITED STATES v. JOHN DOE, INC. I

United States Supreme Court, 1987.
481 U.S. 102.

STEVENS, JUSTICE.

In United States v. Sells Engineering, Inc., 463 U.S. 418 (1983), we held that attorneys for the Civil Division of the Justice Department may not automatically obtain disclosure of grand jury materials for use in a civil suit, but must instead seek a court order of disclosure, available upon a showing of "particularized need." We explicitly left open the "issue concerning continued use of grand jury materials, in the civil phase of a dispute, by an attorney who himself conducted the criminal prosecution." *Id.*, at 431, n. 15. Today, we decide that open question. In addition, for the first time, we review a concrete application of the "particularized need" standard to a request for disclosure to Government attorneys.

I

In March 1982, attorneys in the Antitrust Division of the Department of Justice were authorized to conduct a grand jury investigation of three American corporations suspected of conspiring to fix the price of tallow being sold to a foreign government and financed by the Department of State's Agency for International Development. After subpoenaing thousands of documents from the three corporate respondents, and taking the testimony of numerous witnesses, including the five individual respondents, the Department of Justice conferred with some of respondents' attorneys and concluded that although respondents had violated § 1 of the Sherman Act, 15 U.S.C. § 1, criminal prosecution was not warranted under the circumstances. In early June 1984, the grand jury was discharged without returning any indictments.

On June 28, 1984, the attorneys who had been in charge of the grand jury investigation served Civil Investigative Demands (CID's), pursuant to the Antitrust Civil Process Act, 15 U.S.C. §§ 1311–1314, on approximately two dozen persons and entities, including the corporate respondents, calling for the production of various documents. The Antitrust Division advised each respondent that it could comply with the CID by certifying that the requested documents had already been furnished to the grand jury. Two of the corporate respondents refused to do so, and also refused to furnish any additional copies of the documents.

After further investigation, the Antitrust Division attorneys came to the tentative conclusion that respondents had violated the False Claims Act, 31 U.S.C. §§ 3729–3731, and the Foreign Assistance Act, 22 U.S.C. §§ 2151–2429 (1982 ed. and Supp. III), as well as the Sherman Act. Because the Civil Division of the Department of Justice has primary responsibility for enforcing the False Claims Act, the Antitrust Division deemed it appropriate to consult with lawyers in the Civil Division before initiating a civil action. Additionally, because of the venue of the contemplated civil action, the Antitrust Division felt it necessary to consult with the United States Attorney for the Southern District of New York. Accordingly, the Antitrust Division lawyers filed a motion in the District Court for the Southern District of New York requesting an order under Federal Rule of Criminal Procedure 6(e) allowing them to disclose grand jury material to six named Government attorneys and such associates as those attorneys might designate. After an *ex parte* hearing, the District Court granted the motion, based on its finding that the Government's interest in coordinating fair and efficient enforcement of the False Claims Act, and obtaining the Civil Division's and United States Attorney's expert consultation, constituted a particularized need for the requested disclosure.

On March 6, 1985, the Government advised respondents that the Rule 6(e) order had previously been entered and that a civil action would be filed against them within two weeks. Respondents immediately moved to vacate the Rule 6(e) order and, additionally, to enjoin the Government from using the grand jury information in "preparing, filing, or litigating" the anticipated civil action. The District Court denied both forms of relief. Respondents immediately appealed, and also moved for immediate interim relief from the Court of Appeals for the Second Circuit. The Court of Appeals granted partial relief, allowing the Government to file a complaint, but ordering that it be filed under seal.

After expedited consideration, The Court of Appeals reversed both aspects of the District Court's order. First, the court examined the issue left open in *Sells*, and agreed with respondents that, because the attorneys who had worked on the grand jury investigation were now involved only in civil proceedings, the attorneys were forbidden from making continued use of grand jury information without first obtaining a court order. Nonetheless, the Court of Appeals took no action with respect to the complaint that had been filed, because the court concluded that the complaint disclosed nothing about the grand jury investigation. With respect to the District Court's order allowing disclosure to the six attorneys for consultation purposes, the Court of Appeals held that the order was not supported by an adequate showing of "particularized need." We granted certiorari and now reverse.

II

The "General Rule of Secrecy" set forth in Federal Rule of Criminal Procedure 6(e) provides that certain persons, including attorneys for the Government, "shall not disclose matters occurring before the grand jury, except as otherwise provided for in these rules." Unlike our previous decisions in this area, which have primarily involved exceptions to the general rule, this case involves a more preliminary question: what constitutes disclosure? The Court of Appeals acknowledged that "to characterize [attorneys'] continued access in the civil phase to the materials to which they had access in the criminal phase as disclosure within the meaning of rule 6(e) seems fictional at first glance." But the Court of Appeals reasoned that the attorneys could not possibly remember all the details of the grand jury investigation and therefore the use of grand jury materials "to refresh their recollection as to documents or testimony to which they had access in the grand jury proceeding is tantamount to a further disclosure."

Contrary to the Court of Appeals' conclusion, it seems plain to us that Rule 6(e) prohibits those with information about the workings of the grand jury from revealing such information to other persons who are not authorized to have access to it under the Rule. The Rule does not contain a prohibition against the continued use of information by attorneys who legitimately obtained access to the information through the grand jury investigation. The Court of Appeals' reasoning is unpersuasive because it stretches the plain meaning of the Rule's language much too far. It is indeed fictional—and not just "at first glance"—to interpret the word "disclose" to embrace a solitary re-examination of material in the privacy of an attorney's office. For example, it is obvious that the prohibition against disclosure does not mean that an attorney who prepared a legal memorandum (which happens to include some information about matters related to the workings of the grand jury) for his file, is barred from looking at the memorandum once the grand jury investigation terminates. As the Court of Appeals for the Eighth Circuit recently concluded, "[f]or there to be a disclosure, grand jury matters must be disclosed to someone." [citation omitted]

Because we decide this case based on our reading of the Rule's plain language, there is no need to address the parties' arguments about the extent to which continued use threatens some of the values of grand jury privacy identified in our cases[18] * * *. While such arguments are relevant when language is susceptible of more than one plausible interpretation, we have recognized that in some cases [w]e do not have before us a choice between a 'liberal' approach toward [a Rule], on the one hand, and a 'technical' interpretation of the Rule, on the other hand. The choice, instead, is between recognizing or ignoring what the Rule provides in plain language. We accept the Rule as meaning what it says.

Schiavone v. Fortune, 477 U.S. 21, 30 (1986). As for the policy arguments, it suffices to say that, as the Court of Appeals recognized, the implications of our construction are not so absurd or contrary to Congress' aims as to call into question our construction of the plain meaning of the term "disclosure" as used in this Rule.

Respondents urge in the alternative that Rule 6(e) prohibits attorneys' continued use of grand jury materials because the filing of a civil

---

18. In *Procter & Gamble*, the Court listed the following reasons for grand jury secrecy: " '(1) To prevent the escape of those whose indictment may be contemplated; (2) to insure the utmost freedom to the grand jury in its deliberations, and to prevent persons subject to indictment or their friends from importuning the grand jurors; (3) to prevent subornation of perjury or tampering with the witnesses who may testify before grand jury and later appear at the trial of those indicted by it; (4) to encourage free and untrammeled disclosures by persons who have information with respect to the commission of crimes; (5) to protect innocent accused who is exonerated from disclosure of the fact that he has been under investigation, and from the expense of standing trial where there was no probability of guilt.' " 356 U.S., at 681, n.6.

complaint itself discloses grand jury materials to outsiders. Respondents argue that such disclosure is inevitable because a civil complaint's factual allegations will invariably be based on information obtained during the grand jury investigation. This hypothetical fear is not substantiated by the record in this case. The Court of Appeals stated that the Government's complaint "does not quote from or refer to any grand jury transcripts or documents subpoenaed by the grand jury, and does not mention any witnesses before the grand jury, or even refer to the existence of a grand jury." Nor do respondents identify anything in the complaint that indirectly discloses grand jury information. We have no basis for questioning the accuracy of the Court of Appeals' conclusion that the filing of the complaint did not constitute a prohibited disclosure. A Government attorney may have a variety of uses for grand jury material in a planning stage, even though the material will not be used, or even alluded to, in any filing or proceeding. In this vein, it is important to emphasize that the issue before us is only whether an attorney who was involved in a grand jury investigation (and is therefore presumably familiar with the "matters occurring before the grand jury") may later review that information in a manner that does not involve any further disclosure to others. Without addressing the very different matter of an attorney's disclosing grand jury information to others, inadvertently or purposefully, in the course of a civil proceeding, we hold that Rule 6(e) does not require the attorney to obtain a court order before refamiliarizing himself or herself with the details of a grand jury investigation.

* * *

In *Sells* we noted that Rule 6(e) itself does not prescribe the substantive standard governing the issuance of an order pursuant to Rule 6(e)(3)(C)(i) and that the case law that had developed in response to requests for disclosure by private parties had consistently required "a strong showing of particularized need" before disclosure is permitted. Although we held that this same standard applies where a court is asked to order disclosure to a government attorney, we made it clear that the concerns that underlie the policy of grand jury secrecy are implicated to a much lesser extent when the disclosure merely involves Government attorneys.

* * *

In this case, the disclosures were requested to enable the Antitrust Division lawyers who had conducted the grand jury investigation to obtain the full benefit of the experience and expertise of the Civil Division lawyers who regularly handle litigation under the False Claims Act, and of the local United States Attorney who is regularly consulted before actions are filed in his or her district. The public purposes served by the disclosure—efficient, effective, and evenhanded enforcement of federal statutes—are certainly valid and were not questioned by the Court of Appeals. Particularly because the contemplated use of the material was to make a decision on whether to proceed with a civil action, the disclosure here could have had the effect of saving the Government, the potential defendants, and witnesses the pains of costly and time-consuming depositions and interrogatories which might have later turned out to be wasted if the Government decided not to file a civil action after all. To be sure, as we recognized in *Sells*, not every instance of "saving time and expense" justifies disclosure. The question that must be asked is whether the public benefits of the disclosure in this case outweigh the dangers created by the limited disclosure requested.

In *Sells* we recognized three types of dangers involved in disclosure of grand jury information to Government attorneys for use related to civil proceedings. First, we stated that disclosure not only increases the "number of persons to whom the information is available (thereby increasing the risk of inadvertent or illegal release to others), but also it renders considerably more concrete the threat to the willingness of witnesses to come forward and to testify fully and candidly." *Id.* at 432. Neither of these fears is well founded with respect to the narrow disclosure involved in this case. The disclosure of a summary of a portion of the grand jury record to named attorneys for purposes of consultation does not pose the same risk of a wide breach of grand jury secrecy as would allowing unlimited use of the material to all attorneys in another division—the disclosure involved in *Sells*. Moreover, the fact that the grand jury had already terminated mitigates the damage of a possible inadvertent disclosure. Finally, because the disclosure authorized in this case would not directly result in any witness' testimony being used against him or her in a civil proceeding, there is little fear that the disclosure will have any effect on future grand jury testimony.

The second concern identified in *Sells* is the threat to the integrity of the grand jury itself. We explained that if "prosecutors in a given case knew that their colleagues would be free to use the materials generated by the grand jury for a civil case, they might be tempted to manipulate the grand jury's powerful investigative tools to root out additional evidence useful in the civil suit, or even to start or continue a grand jury inquiry where no criminal prosecution seemed likely." *Id.*, at 432. The discussion of this concern in *Sells* dealt with whether the Civil Division should be given unfettered access to grand jury materials. We think the concern is far less worrisome when the attorneys seeking disclosure must go before a court and demonstrate a particularized need prior to any disclosure, and when, as part of that inquiry, the district court may properly consider whether the circumstances disclose any evidence of grand jury abuse. In this case, for example, one of the Government attorneys involved in the criminal investigation submitted an affidavit attesting to the Department's good faith in conducting the grand jury investigation, and there has been no evidence or allegation to the contrary. The fact that a court is involved in this manner lessens some of the usual difficulty in detecting grand jury abuse. Moreover, we think the fear of abuse is minimal when the civil use contemplated is simply consultation with various Government lawyers about the prudence of proceeding with a civil action.

The final concern discussed in *Sells* is that "use of grand jury materials by Government agencies in civil or administrative settings threatens to subvert the limitations applied outside the grand jury context on the Government's powers of discovery and investigation." *Id.* at 433. We continue to believe that this is an important concern, but it is not seriously implicated when the Government simply wishes to use the material for consultation. Of course, when the Government requests disclosure for use in an actual adversarial proceeding, this factor (as well as the others) may require a stronger showing of necessity. We have explained that "as the considerations justifying secrecy become less relevant, a party asserting a need for grand jury [material] will have a lesser burden in showing justification." *Douglas Oil*, 441 U.S. at 223.

Although it recognized that the disclosure in this case did not seriously threaten the values of grand jury secrecy, the Court of Appeals nonetheless concluded that the request for disclosure should have been denied because virtually all of the relevant information could have been obtained from respondents through discovery under the Antitrust Civil Process Act. The Court of Appeals believed that the delay and expense that would be caused by such duplicative discovery was not a relevant factor in the particularized need analysis.

While the possibility of obtaining information from alternative sources is certainly an important factor, we believe that the Court of Appeals exaggerated its significance in this case. Even if we assume that all of the relevant material could have been obtained through the civil discovery tools available to the Government,[10] our precedents do not establish a *per se* rule against disclosure. Rather, we have repeatedly stressed that wide discretion must be afforded to district court judges in evaluating whether disclosure is appropriate. The threat to grand jury secrecy was minimal in this context, and under the circumstances, the District Court properly considered the strong "public interests served" through disclosure. As we noted in *Sells*, the governing standard is "a highly flexible one, adaptable to different circumstances and sensitive to the fact that the requirements of secrecy are greater in some situations than in others." *Id.*, at 445. The District Court correctly examined the relevant factors and we cannot say that it abused its discretion in determining that the equities leaned in favor of disclosure.[11]

---

10. It is far from clear that this assumption is accurate. Only in 1986 did Congress amend the False Claims Act so as to allow the use of CID's for investigations of violations of that Act. *See* Pub.L. 99–562, 100 Stat. 3153. In addition, the Government's opportunity to proceed with civil discovery before deciding whether to file a civil complaint was significantly hampered by the fact that the statute of limitations on one of the claims was to run shortly after the grand jury was dismissed.

11. Based on his assumption that any complaint filed would necessarily disclose grand jury information, JUSTICE BRENNAN concludes that there could be no legitimate justification for disclosure to the Civil Division lawyers and the United States Attorney for consultation purposes. This argument misses two points. First, the Antitrust Division may have wanted the attorneys' advice on the matter even if they would not have been able to disclose the actual grand jury materials in a subsequent civil proceeding. *See* n. 6, *supra*. Second, in the event that the consultations confirmed the position that a civil suit was appropriate, the Antitrust Division attorneys may have planned on eventually seeking a second

The judgment of the Court of Appeals is

Reversed.

JUSTICE BRENNAN, WITH WHOM JUSTICE MARSHALL AND JUSTICE BLACKMUN JOIN, DISSENTING.

* * * [T]he Court today holds that an attorney's past connection with that body makes grand jury material automatically available to that attorney for the purpose of determining whether a civil complaint should be filed. The Court reaches this result only by adopting a severely restricted construction of the word "disclosure" in Rule 6(e). Because this construction ignores the substantive concerns of that Rule and is flatly inconsistent with the reasoning in *Sells*, I dissent.

The issue of automatic access by an attorney who earlier assisted the grand jury was not presented in *Sells*, and we did not reach it. *Id.*, at 431, n. 15. As the above language indicates, however, *Sells* makes clear that the automatic availability of grand jury information is determined not by the identity of the attorney who seeks to use the material, but by the use to which the material would be put. Thus, it is irrelevant whether an attorney *once* worked with the grand jury—what matters is whether that attorney *now* does.

* * *

The Court today evades this logic by finding that no "disclosure" under Rule 6(e) occurs when an attorney who assisted the grand jury uses grand jury material in determining whether a civil suit should be filed. The premise of this conclusion is that Rule 6(e) prohibits only "those with information about the workings of the grand jury from revealing such information to *other persons* who are not authorized to have access to it under the Rule." The Court declares that it need not inquire whether its construction of Rule 6(e) is consistent with the Rule's purposes, since the Court derives that construction from its "reading of the Rule's plain language."

Before addressing the Court's "plain language" argument, it is important to make clear just how seriously the Court's interpretation of the Rule is at odds with the Rule's underlying purposes.

The first interest furthered by the secrecy imposed by Rule 6(e) is encouragement of witnesses to testify fully and candidly. The Court's construction of the term "disclosure" directly conflicts with this interest, for "[i]f a witness knows or fears that his testimony before the grand jury will be routinely available for use in governmental civil litigation or administrative action, he may well be less willing to speak for fear that he will get himself into trouble in some other forum." *Sells, supra*, 463 U.S. at 432. The fact that the attorney utilizing this testimony received it directly from the grand jury, rather than from an attorney who

court order that would allow them to disclose the material in a civil suit. *See* post, at 1670 (Government may, of course, seek court order permitting disclosure in civil case). The purpose of the consultation, therefore, was not necessarily intertwined with any disclosure that JUSTICE BRENNAN believes is prohibited.

worked with the grand jury, will hardly be relevant to a witness. It is the *substance* of the witness' testimony that will expose him or her to civil liability, not the identity of the Government attorney who employs it for this purpose. The Court's narrow construction of the term "disclosure" thus creates exactly the disincentive that Rule 6(e)'s restriction on disclosure is intended to prevent.

A second major interest served by Rule 6(e) is protection of the integrity of the grand jury. The automatic availability of grand jury material for civil use creates a temptation to utilize the grand jury's expansive investigative powers to generate evidence useful in civil litigation. In our society, the inquisitorial character of the grand jury is an anomaly that can be justified only if that body's powers are used in service of its unique historical function. Governmental appropriation of grand jury information for civil use thus diminishes public willingness to countenance the grand jury's far-reaching authority. Furthermore, circumvention of normal restrictions on the Government's civil discovery methods "would grant to the Government a virtual *ex parte* form of discovery, from which its civil litigation opponents are excluded unless they make a strong showing of particularized need." *Sells*, 463 U.S. at 434.

* * *

The Court's construction of Rule 6(e) undercuts such objectives. The fact that there may be no expansion of the group of persons who possess grand jury information is simply irrelevant to a concern that the Government may seek to use the grand jury for civil purposes. If anything, there is even more motivation for such misuse when the prospective beneficiary in the civil context would be the prosecutor, as opposed to some other Government civil attorney. The Court's decision today creates an incentive for the Government to use prosecutors rather than civil attorneys to prepare and file civil complaints based on grand jury information, a practice directly at odds with Congress' intention to minimize the opportunity for using such information outside the grand jury context.[5] This temptation to employ the grand jury as a civil investigative unit is clearly inconsistent with the intention that Rule 6(e)

---

5. Contrary to the Court's assumption, there can be little doubt that grand jury information was used as the basis for the complaint in this case. The grand jury investigation produced some 250,000 pages of subpoenaed documents and transcripts of the testimony of "dozens of witnesses." In re Grand Jury Investigation, 774 F.2d 34, 40 (C.A.2 1985). Two of the three respondents refused to certify in response to a Civil Investigative Demand (CID) by the Government that all documents requested by the CID had been submitted to the grand jury. These respondents furnished no documents in response to the CID's, nor did the Government attempt to enforce such demands. At least as to these two corpora- tions, therefore, grand jury material is the *only* information that could have served as the basis for the civil complaint. The prominent role of grand jury material in preparing the complaint against respondents is underscored by the Antitrust Division's request for a Rule 6(e) order authorizing disclosure to the Civil Division and the United States Attorney's Office. As the Government stated in that request, "The Antitrust Division currently is considering whether to bring a civil action, *based on the evidence obtained in the course of its grand jury investigation*, alleging violations of [the Sherman, False Claims, and Foreign Assistance Acts]." App. 10 (emphasis added).

operate to impede the use of grand jury information for civil purposes.[6] It is far more consonant with that intention to find that matters occurring before the grand jury are "disclosed" any time they are put to use outside the grand jury context, whether or not the attorney who uses them assisted the grand jury at an earlier time. There was "disclosure" in this case under that standard.

Notes

With which view do you agree: is Rule 6(e) plain on its face and flexible enough to resolve the "one attorney, two hats" problem as well as permit consultation with other attorneys? Or, is the Court undercutting *Sells* and ignoring the plain meaning of Rule 6(e)?

D. THE SCOPE OF THE ATTORNEY–CLIENT PRIVILEGE AND WORK PRODUCT DOCTRINE

UPJOHN COMPANY v. UNITED STATES

United States Supreme Court, 1981.
449 U.S. 383.

REHNQUIST, JUSTICE.

We granted certiorari in this case to address important questions concerning the scope of the attorney-client privilege in the corporate context and the applicability of the work-product doctrine in proceedings to enforce tax summonses. With respect to the privilege question the parties and various *amici* have described our task as one of choosing between two "tests" which have gained adherents in the courts of appeals. We are acutely aware, however, that we sit to decide concrete cases and not abstract propositions of law. We decline to lay down a broad rule or series of rules to govern all conceivable future questions in this area, even were we able to do so. We can and do, however, conclude that the attorney-client privilege protects the communications involved in this case from compelled disclosure and that the work-product doctrine does apply in tax summons enforcement proceedings.

I

Petitioner Upjohn Co. manufactures and sells pharmaceuticals here and abroad. In January 1976 independent accountants conducting an audit of one of Upjohn's foreign subsidiaries discovered that the subsidiary made payments to or for the benefit of foreign government officials in order to secure government business. The accountants, so informed petitioner, Mr. Gerard Thomas, Upjohn's Vice President, Secretary, and

---

6. It is true that any given grand jury investigation may be challenged on the ground that it is intended to generate information for a civil suit. United States v. Procter & Gamble, Co., 356 U.S. 677, 683–684, 78 S.Ct. 983, 986–87, 2 L.Ed.2d 1077 (1958). However, the need for a prophylactic rule against automatic disclosure rests on recognition of the fact that "if and when [grand jury misuse] does occur, it would often be very difficult to detect and prove." *Sells*, 463 U.S., at 432, 103 S.Ct., at 3142.

General Counsel. Thomas is a member of the Michigan and New York Bars, and has been Upjohn's General Counsel for 20 years. He consulted with outside counsel and R. T. Parfet, Jr., Upjohn's Chairman of the Board. It was decided that the company would conduct an internal investigation of what were termed "questionable payments." As part of this investigation the attorneys prepared a letter containing a questionnaire which was sent to "All Foreign General and Area Managers" over the Chairman's signature. The letter began by noting recent disclosures that several American companies made "possibly illegal" payments to foreign government officials and emphasized that the management needed full information concerning any such payments made by Upjohn. The letter indicated that the Chairman had asked Thomas, identified as "the company's General Counsel," "to conduct an investigation for the purpose of determining the nature and magnitude of any payments made by the Upjohn Company or any of its subsidiaries to any employee or official of a foreign government." The questionnaire sought detailed information concerning such payments. Managers were instructed to treat the investigation as "highly confidential" and not to discuss it with anyone other than Upjohn employees who might be helpful in providing the requested information. Responses were to be sent directly to Thomas. Thomas and outside counsel also interviewed the recipients of the questionnaire and some 33 other Upjohn officers or employees as part of the investigation.

On March 26, 1976, the company voluntarily submitted a preliminary report to the Securities and Exchange Commission on Form 8–K disclosing certain questionable payments.[1] A copy of the report was simultaneously submitted to the Internal Revenue Service, which immediately began an investigation to determine the tax consequences of the payments. Special agents conducting the investigation were given lists by Upjohn of all those interviewed and all who had responded to the questionnaire. On November 23, 1976, the Service issued a summons pursuant to 26 U.S.C. § 7602 demanding production of:

> All files relative to the investigation conducted under the supervision of Gerard Thomas to identify payments to employees of foreign governments and any political contributions made by the Upjohn Company or any of its affiliates since January 1, 1971 and to determine whether any funds of the Upjohn Company had been improperly accounted for on the corporate books during the same period.

> The records should include but not be limited to written questionnaires sent to managers of the Upjohn Company's foreign affiliates, and memorandums or notes of the interviews conducted in the United States and abroad with officers and employees of the Upjohn Company and its subsidiaries.

1. On July 28, 1976, the company filed an amendment to this report disclosing fur-   ther payments.

The company declined to produce the documents specified in the second paragraph on the grounds that they were protected from disclosure by the attorney-client privilege and constituted the work product of attorneys prepared in anticipation of litigation. On August 31, 1977, the United States filed a petition seeking enforcement of the summons under 26 U.S.C. §§ 7402(b) and 7604(a) in the United States District Court for the Western District of Michigan. That court adopted the recommendation of a Magistrate who concluded that the summons should be enforced. Petitioners appealed to the Court of Appeals for the Sixth Circuit which rejected the Magistrate's finding of a waiver of the attorney-client privilege, but agreed that the privilege did not apply "[t]o the extent that the communications were made by officers and agents not responsible for directing Upjohn's actions in response to legal advice * * * for the simple reason that the communications were not the 'client's.' " The court reasoned that accepting petitioners' claim for a broader application of the privilege would encourage upper-echelon management to ignore unpleasant facts and create too broad a "zone of silence." Noting that Upjohn's counsel had interviewed officials such as the Chairman and President, the Court of Appeals remanded to the District Court so that a determination of who was within the "control group" could be made. In a concluding footnote the court stated that the work-product doctrine "is not applicable to administrative summonses issued under 26 U.S.C. § 7602."

II

Federal Rule of Evidence 501 provides that "the privilege of a witness * * * shall be governed by the principles of the common law as they may be interpreted by the courts of the United States in light of reason and experience." The attorney-client privilege is the oldest of the privileges for confidential communications known to the common law. Its purpose is to encourage full and frank communication between attorneys and their clients and thereby promote broader public interests in the observance of law and administration of justice. The privilege recognizes that sound legal advice or advocacy serves public ends and that such advice or advocacy depends upon the lawyer's being fully informed by the client. As we stated last Term in *Trammel v. United States*, 445 U.S. 40, 51 (1980): "The lawyer-client privilege rests on the need for the advocate and counselor to know all that relates to the client's reasons for seeking representation if the professional mission is to be carried out." And in *Fisher v. United States*, 425 U.S. 391, 403 (1976), we recognized the purpose of the privilege to be "to encourage clients to make full disclosure to their attorneys." This rationale for the privilege has long been recognized by the Court. Admittedly complications in the application of the privilege arise when the client is a corporation, which in theory is an artificial creature of the law, and not an individual; but this Court has assumed that the privilege applies when the client is a corporation. *United States v. Louisville & Nashville R. Co.*, 236 U.S. 318, 336 (1915), and the Government does not contest the general proposition.

The Court of Appeals, however, considered the application of the privilege in the corporate context to present a "different problem," since the client was an inanimate entity and "only the senior management, guiding and integrating the several operations, * * * can be said to possess an identity analogous to the corporation as a whole." The first case to articulate the so-called "control group test" adopted by the court below, reflected a similar conceptual approach:

> Keeping in mind that the question is, Is it the corporation which is seeking the lawyer's advice when the asserted privileged communication is made?, the most satisfactory solution, I think, is that if the employee making the communication, of whatever rank he may be, is in a position to control or even to take a substantial part in a decision about any action which the corporation may take upon the advice of the attorney, * * * then, in effect, *he is (or personifies) the corporation* when he makes his disclosure to the lawyer and the privilege would apply. (Emphasis supplied.)

Such a view, we think, overlooks the fact that the privilege exists to protect not only the giving of professional advice to those who can act on it but also the giving of information to the lawyer to enable him to give sound and informed advice. * * *

In the case of the individual client the provider of information and the person who acts on the lawyer's advice are one and the same. In the corporate context, however, it will frequently be employees beyond the control group as defined by the court below-"officers and agents * * * responsible for directing [the company's] actions in response to legal advice"-who will possess the information needed by the corporation's lawyers. Middle-level—and indeed lower-level—employees can, by actions within the scope of their employment, embroil the corporation in serious legal difficulties, and it is only natural that these employees would have the relevant information needed by corporate counsel if he is adequately to advise the client with respect to such actual or potential difficulties. This fact was noted in *Diversified Industries, Inc. v. Meredith*, 572 F.2d 596 (C.A.8 1977) (en banc):

> In a corporation, it may be necessary to glean information relevant to a legal problem from middle management or non-management personnel as well as from top executives. The attorney dealing with a complex legal problem is thus faced with a Hobson's choice. If he interviews employees not having the very highest authority, their communications to him will not be privileged. If, on the other hand, he interviews only those employees with the very highest authority, he may find it extremely difficult, if not impossible, to determine what happened. [internal quotation marks omitted]

The control group test adopted by the court below thus frustrates the very purpose of the privilege by discouraging the communication of relevant information by employees of the client to attorneys seeking to render legal advice to the client corporation. The attorney's advice will also frequently be more significant to noncontrol group members than to those who officially sanction the advice, and the control group test makes it more difficult to convey full and frank legal advice to the employees who will put into effect the client corporation's policy.

The narrow scope given the attorney-client privilege by the court below not only makes it difficult for corporate attorneys to formulate sound advice when their client is faced with a specific legal problem but also threatens to limit the valuable efforts of corporate counsel to ensure their client's compliance with the law. In light of the vast and complicated array of regulatory legislation confronting the modern corporation, corporations, unlike most individuals, "constantly go to lawyers to find out how to obey the law," particularly since compliance with the law in this area is hardly an instinctive matter. The test adopted by the court below is difficult to apply in practice, though no abstractly formulated and unvarying "test" will necessarily enable courts to decide questions such as this with mathematical precision. But if the purpose of the attorney-client privilege is to be served, the attorney and client must be able to predict with some degree of certainty whether particular discussions will be protected. An uncertain privilege, or one which purports to be certain but results in widely varying applications by the courts, is little better than no privilege at all. The very terms of the test adopted by the court below suggest the unpredictability of its application. The test restricts the availability of the privilege to those officers who play a "substantial role" in deciding and directing a corporation's legal response. Disparate decisions in cases applying this test illustrate its unpredictability.

The communications at issue were made by Upjohn employees[11] to counsel for Upjohn acting as such, at the direction of corporate superiors in order to secure legal advice from counsel. As the Magistrate found, "Mr. Thomas consulted with the Chairman of the Board and outside counsel and thereafter conducted a factual investigation to determine the nature and extent of the questionable payments *and to be in a position to give legal advice to the company with respect to the payments.*" (Emphasis supplied.) Information, not available from upper-echelon management, was needed to supply a basis for legal advice concerning compliance with securities and tax laws, foreign laws, currency regulations, duties to shareholders, and potential litigation in each of these areas. The communications concerned matters within the scope of the employees' corporate duties, and the employees themselves were sufficiently aware that they were being questioned in order that the corporation could obtain legal advice. The questionnaire identified Thomas as "the company's General Counsel" and referred in its opening sentence to the possible illegality of payments such as the ones on which information was sought. A statement of policy accompanying the questionnaire

11. Seven of the eighty-six employees interviewed by counsel had terminated their employment with Upjohn at the time of the interview. Petitioners argue that the privilege should nonetheless apply to communications by these former employees concerning activities during their period of employment. Neither the District Court nor the Court of Appeals had occasion to address this issue, and we decline to decide it without the benefit of treatment below.

clearly indicated the legal implications of the investigation. The policy statement was issued "in order that there be no uncertainty in the future as to the policy with respect to the practices which are the subject of this investigation." It began "Upjohn will comply with all laws and regulations," and stated that commissions or payments "will not be used as a subterfuge for bribes or illegal payments" and that all payments must be "proper and legal." Any future agreements with foreign distributors or agents were to be approved "by a company attorney" and any questions concerning the policy were to be referred "to the company's General Counsel." This statement was issued to Upjohn employee worldwide, so that even those interviewees not receiving a questionnaire were aware of the legal implications of the interviews. Pursuant to explicit instructions from the Chairman of the Board, the communications were considered "highly confidential" when made, and have been kept confidential by the company. Consistent with the underlying purposes of the attorney-client privilege, these communications must be protected against compelled disclosure. [citations omitted]

* * *

Needless to say, we decide only the case before us, and do not undertake to draft a set of rules which should govern challenges to investigatory subpoenas. Any such approach would violate the spirit of Federal Rule of Evidence 501. While such a "case-by-case" basis may to some slight extent undermine desirable certainty in the boundaries of the attorney-client privilege, it obeys the spirit of the Rules. At the same time we conclude that the narrow "control group test" sanctioned by the Court of Appeals, in this case cannot, consistent with "the principles of the common law as * * * interpreted * * * in the light of reason and experience," Fed. Rule Evid. 501, govern the development of the law in this area.

III

Our decision that the communications by Upjohn employees to counsel are covered by the attorney-client privilege disposes of the case so far as the responses to the questionnaires and any notes reflecting responses to interview questions are concerned. The summons reaches further, however, and Thomas has testified that his notes and memoranda of interviews go beyond recording responses to his questions. To the extent that the material subject to the summons is not protected by the attorney-client privilege as disclosing communications between an employee and counsel, we must reach the ruling by the Court of Appeals that the work-product doctrine does not apply to summonses issued under 26 U.S.C. § 7602.

The Government concedes, wisely, that the Court of Appeals erred and that the work-product doctrine does apply to IRS summonses. This doctrine was announced by the Court over 30 years ago in Hickman v. Taylor, 329 U.S. 495 (1947). In that case the Court rejected "an attempt, without purported necessity or justification, to secure written statements, private memoranda and personal recollections prepared or

formed by an adverse party's counsel in the course of his legal duties."
Id. at 510. The Court noted that "it is essential that a lawyer work with
a certain degree of privacy" and reasoned that if discovery of the
material sought were permitted

> much of what is now put down in writing would remain unwritten.
> An attorney's thoughts, heretofore inviolate, would not be his own.
> Inefficiency, unfairness and sharp practices would inevitably develop
> in the giving of legal advice and in the preparation of cases for trial.
> The effect on the legal profession would be demoralizing. And the
> interests of the clients and the cause of justice would be poorly
> served. *Id.* at 511.

* * *

As we stated last Term, the obligation imposed by a tax summons
remains "subject to the traditional privileges and limitations." *United
States v. Euge*, 444 U.S. 707, 714 (1980). Nothing in the language of the
IRS summons provisions or their legislative history suggests an intent
on the part of Congress to preclude application of the work-product
doctrine. Rule 26(b)(3) codifies the work-product doctrine, and the Federal Rules of Civil Procedure are made applicable to summons enforcement proceedings by Rule 81(a)(3). While conceding the applicability of
the work-product doctrine, the Government asserts that it has made a
sufficient showing of necessity to overcome its protections. The Magistrate apparently so found. The Government relies on the following
language in *Hickman*:

> We do not mean to say that all written materials obtained or
> prepared by an adversary's counsel with an eye toward litigation are
> necessarily free from discovery in all cases. Where relevant and
> nonprivileged facts remain hidden in an attorney's file and where
> production of those facts is essential to the preparation of one's case,
> discovery may properly be had * * *. And production might be
> justified where the witnesses are no longer available or can be
> reached only with difficulty. 329 U.S. at 511.

The Government stresses that interviewees are scattered across the
globe and that Upjohn has forbidden its employees to answer questions
it considers irrelevant. The above-quoted language from *Hickman*, however, did not apply to "oral statements made by witnesses * * * whether
presently in the form of [the attorney's] mental impressions or memoranda." *Id.* at 512. As to such material the Court did "not believe that
any showing of necessity can be made under the circumstances of this
case so as to justify production * * *. If there should be a rare situation
justifying production of these matters petitioner's case is not of that
type." *Id.* at 512–513. Forcing an attorney to disclose notes and memoranda of witnesses' oral statements is particularly disfavored because it
tends to reveal the attorney's mental processes.

Rule 26 accords special protection to work product revealing the
attorney's mental processes. The Rule permits disclosure of documents

and tangible things constituting attorney work product upon a showing of substantial need and inability to obtain the equivalent without undue hardship. This was the standard applied by the Magistrate. Rule 26 goes on, however, to state that "[i]n ordering discovery of such materials when the required showing has been made, the court shall protect against disclosure of the mental impressions, conclusions, opinions or legal theories of an attorney or other representative of a party concerning the litigation." Although this language does not specifically refer to memoranda based on oral statements of witnesses, the *Hickman* court stressed the danger that compelled disclosure of such memoranda would reveal the attorney's mental processes. It is clear that this is the sort of material the draftsmen of the Rule had in mind as deserving special protection.

Based on the foregoing, some courts have concluded that no showing of necessity can overcome protection of work product which is based on oral statements from witnesses. Those courts declining to adopt an absolute rule have nonetheless recognized that such material is entitled to special protection.

We do not decide the issue at this time. It is clear that the Magistrate applied the wrong standard when he concluded that the Government had made a sufficient showing of necessity to overcome the protections of the work-product doctrine. The Magistrate applied the "substantial need" and "without undue hardship" standard articulated in the first part of Rule 26(b)(3). The notes and memoranda sought by the Government here, however, are work product based on oral statements. If they reveal communications, they are, in this case, protected by the attorney-client privilege. To the extent they do not reveal communications, they reveal the attorneys' mental processes in evaluating the communications. As Rule 26 and *Hickman* make clear, such work product cannot be disclosed simply on a showing of substantial need and inability to obtain the equivalent without undue hardship.

While we are not prepared at this juncture to say that such material is always protected by the work-product rule, we think a far stronger showing of necessity and unavailability by other means than was made by the Government or applied by the Magistrate in this case would be necessary to compel disclosure. Since the Court of Appeals thought that the work-product protection was never applicable in an enforcement proceeding such as this, and since the Magistrate whose recommendations the District Court adopted applied too lenient a standard of protection, we think the best procedure with respect to this aspect of the case would be to reverse the judgment of the Court of Appeals for the Sixth Circuit and remand the case to it for such further proceedings in connection with the work-product claim as are consistent with this opinion.

Accordingly, the judgment of the Court of Appeals is reversed, and the case remanded for further proceedings.

It is so ordered.

Notes

Serving as corporate counsel requires a working understanding of *Up-john*, especially in the event wrongdoing is suspected by corporate employees and an internal investigation is undertaken. In this regard, consider the following:

"Once it appears that fraud has occurred in a business, some sort of internal investigation should be conducted. There are several advantages to conducting an internal investigation:

- fulfilling the Board of Directors' fiduciary duty to investigate allegations of fraud and corruption within an organization;[c]

- discovering, before the government or a potential whistleblower makes the discovery, whether fraud has been committed;

- remedying the problem so that any fraud ceases and does not recur;

- discouraging possible prosecution; and

- minimizing punishment if there is a conviction.

"How extensive of an investigation should be undertaken depends upon the size and resources of the business, the suspected extent of the fraud, the difficulty in determining what happened, the severity of the consequences that could befall the business because of the fraud, and the goals of the investigation.

"Care must also be taken to preserve the attorney client privilege during internal investigations or when responding to the government inquiries or subpoenas. Communications between attorney and client in the presence of third parties are not privileged. Thus, counsel may cause the attorney-client privilege to lapse if, while representing the corporation or certain individuals, counsel discloses otherwise privileged material to individuals whom counsel does not represent. This may include disclosures to corporate officers or employees. It may also include disclosures to the government. For example, in United States v. Billmyer,[d] the court held that disclosure to the government of the results of an internal investigation waived the attorney-client privilege.[e] In this case Honda Motor Company, Inc. (Honda) had undertaken an internal investigation to uncover evidence of bribery by some of Honda employees (Billmyer and others). At a subsequent criminal trial of some of the Honda employees where one of the defendant-employees sought the information revealed to the government, the court held that the factual allegations uncovered during the investigation and disclosed to the government were not privileged and must be turned over. Commentary by counsel on the legal implications of the factual assertions was not subject to disclosure, however.[f] The court reasoned that '[a] risk of unfairness is evident where information is provided to one side in a case

---

c. Block, Barton & Radin, *The Business Judgment Rule: Fiduciary Duties of Corporate Directors* 127 (3d ed/1989).

d. United States v. Billmyer, 57 F.3d 31 (1st Cir.1995).

e. *Id.*, 57 F.3d at 36.

f. *Id.*, 57 F.3d at 37.

(here, the United States) and then an inquiry into its origin is shielded by a claim of privilege.'[g]

"To avoid waiving the attorney-client privilege during an internal investigation, counsel should take care to clearly identify who counsel represents; avoid conflicts of interest in representing clients; designate material that is privileged and instruct those who have access to it of its privileged nature; disseminate privileged material on a 'need to know' basis; and, provide only legal advice. Business advice is not privileged, so combining legal and business advice risks losing the attorney-client privilege.

"Prior to producing documents or testimony pursuant to requests, subpoenas or demands, counsel should ensure that one person reviews all material allegedly protected under the attorney-client privileges. This person should make the final decision as to whether the material is privileged. This will avoid inconsistencies that may waive the privilege. If documents or testimony is to be produced pursuant to subpoenas, the 'privilege' person should review all material prior to its production.

"To ensure that actions taken during the internal investigation do not jeopardize an otherwise applicable work product privilege, counsel should clearly designate reports or summaries that are work product. Counsel should also take care to integrate counsel's impressions, views, and strategies into reports or summaries of documents or interviews. Prior to producing documents or testimony pursuant to requests, subpoenas or demands, counsel should ensure that one person reviews all material allegedly protected under the attorney-client or work product privileges. This person should make the final decision as to whether the material is privileged. This will avoid inconsistencies that may waive the privilege. If documents or testimony is to be produced pursuant to subpoenas, the 'privilege' person should review all material prior to its production."[h]

E. PROSECUTING THE IMMUNIZED WITNESS

Immunity for witnesses often is necessary in complex cases to acquire testimony of insiders. The next case, United States v. North, 910 F.2d 843 (D.C.Cir.1990), is one of the more high profile immunity cases in twentieth century American jurisprudence. As you read this opinion, note especially footnote 1, which contains the federal immunity statute.

UNITED STATES v. NORTH
United States Court of Appeals, District of Columbia, 1990.
910 F.2d 843.

PER CURIAM:

g. *Id.*, 57 F.3d at 37.

h. Pamela H. Bucy, HEALTH CARE FRAUD: CRIMINAL, CIVIL AND ADMINISTRATIVE LAW, § 8.01, § 8.07 (1996). Reprinted with permission from HEALTH CARE FRAUD: CRIMINAL, CIVIL AND ADMINISTRATIVE LAW, published by Law Journal Seminars Press, 345 Park Avenue, New York, New York, 10010. Copyright ©. All rights reserved.

INTRODUCTION

In November of 1986, a Lebanese newspaper reported that the United States had secretly sold weapons to Iran. Two months later, Congress established two committees charged with investigating the sales of arms to Iran, the diversion of proceeds therefrom to rebels (or "Contras") fighting in Nicaragua, and the attempted cover-up of these activities (controversial events popularly known as "the Iran/Contra Affair"). In July of 1987, Lieutenant Colonel Oliver L. North, a former member of the National Security Council ("NSC") staff, testified before the Iran/Contra congressional committees. North asserted his Fifth Amendment right not to testify before the committees, but the government compelled his testimony by a grant of use immunity pursuant to 18 U.S.C. § 6002. North testified for six days. His testimony was carried live on national television and radio, replayed on news shows, and analyzed in the public media.

Contemporaneously with the congressional investigation, and pursuant to the Independent Counsel statute, 28 U.S.C. §§ 591–599, the Special Division of this Court appointed Lawrence E. Walsh as Independent Counsel ("IC") and charged him with the investigation and prosecution of any criminal wrongdoing by government officials in the Iran/Contra events. As a result of the efforts of the IC, North was indicted and tried on twelve counts arising from his role in the Iran/Contra Affair. After extensive pretrial proceedings and a twelve-week trial, North was convicted in May of 1989 on three counts: aiding and abetting an endeavor to obstruct Congress in violation of 18 U.S.C. §§ 1505 and 2 ("Count 6"); destroying, altering, or removing official NSC documents in violation of 18 U.S.C. § 2071 ("Count 9"); and accepting an illegal gratuity, consisting of a security system for his home, in violation of 18 U.S.C. § 201(c)(1)(B) ("Count 10"). North now appeals his convictions on these counts.

* * *

* * * [We hold that] the District Court erred in failing to hold a full hearing as required by Kastigar v. United States, 406 U.S. 441 (1972), to ensure that the IC made no use of North's immunized congressional testimony. North's convictions on all three counts are therefore vacated and remanded to the District Court for a *Kastigar* proceeding consistent with this opinion.

* * *

No person * * * shall be compelled in any criminal case to be a witness against himself * * *. U.S. Const. amend. V.

North argues that his Fifth Amendment right against self-incrimination was violated, asserting that the District Court failed to require the IC to establish independent sources for the testimony of witnesses before the grand jury and at trial and to demonstrate that witnesses did not in any way use North's compelled testimony. North further argues that his Fifth Amendment right was violated by the District Court's failure to determine whether or not the IC made "nonevidentiary" use of the immunized testimony.

North's argument depends on the long-recognized principle that a predicate to liberal constitutional government is the freedom of a citizen from government compulsion to testify against himself:

> And any compulsory discovery by extorting the party's oath, or compelling the production of his private books and papers, to convict him of crime, or to forfeit his property, is contrary to the principles of free government. It is abhorrent to the instincts of an Englishman; it is abhorrent to the instincts of an American. It may suit the purposes of despotic power; but it cannot abide the pure atmosphere of political liberty and personal freedom.

Boyd v. United States, 116 U.S. 616, 631–32 (1886). This rule has been established in England at least since 1641.

* * *

Because the privilege against self-incrimination "reflects many of our fundamental values and most noble aspirations," [citation omitted] and because it is "the essential mainstay of our adversary system," the Constitution requires "that the government seeking to punish an individual produce the evidence against him by its own independent labors, rather than by the cruel, simple expedient of compelling it from his own mouth." Miranda v. Arizona, 384 U.S. 436, 460 (1966).

The prohibition against compelled testimony is not absolute, however. Under the rule of Kastigar v. United States, 406 U.S. 441 (1972), a grant of use immunity under 18 U.S.C. § 6002[1] enables the government to compel a witness' self-incriminating testimony. This is so because the statute prohibits the government both from using the immunized testimony itself and also from using any evidence derived directly or indirectly therefrom. Stated conversely, use immunity conferred under the statute is "coextensive with the scope of the privilege against self-incrimination, and therefore is sufficient to compel testimony over a claim of the privilege * * *. [Use immunity] prohibits the prosecutorial authorities from using the compelled testimony in *any* respect * * *." *Kastigar*, 406 U.S. at 453 (emphasis in original).

---

1. The federal use immunity statute, 18 U.S.C. § 6002, provides as follows:

Whenever a witness refuses, on the basis of his privilege against self-incrimination, to testify or provide other information in a proceeding before or ancillary to—

(1) a court or grand jury of the United States,

(2) an agency of the United States, or

(3) either House of Congress, a joint committee of the two Houses, or a committee or a subcommittee of either House,

and the person presiding over the proceeding communicates to the witness an order issued under this part, the witness may not refuse to comply with the order on the basis of his privilege against self-incrimination; but no testimony or other information compelled under the order (or any information directly or indirectly derived from such testimony or information) may be used against the witness in any criminal case, except a prosecution for perjury, giving a false statement, or otherwise failing to comply with the order.

When the government proceeds to prosecute a previously immunized witness, it has "the heavy burden of proving that all of the evidence it proposes to use was derived from legitimate independent sources." *Kastigar*, 406 U.S. at 461–62. The Court characterized the government's affirmative burden as "heavy." Most courts following *Kastigar* have imposed a "preponderance of the evidence" evidentiary burden on the government. The Court analogized the statutory restrictions on use immunity to restrictions on the use of coerced confessions, which are inadmissible as evidence but which do not prohibit prosecution. The Court pointed out, however, that the "use immunity" defendant may "be in a stronger position at trial" than the "coerced confession" defendant because of the different allocations of burden of proof.

A trial court must normally hold a hearing (a "*Kastigar* hearing") for the purpose of allowing the government to demonstrate that it obtained all of the evidence it proposes to use from sources independent of the compelled testimony. As this Court pointed out in United States v. De Diego, 511 F.2d 818, 823–24 (D.C.Cir.1975), a trial court may hold a *Kastigar* hearing pre-trial, post-trial, mid-trial (as evidence is offered), or it may employ some combination of these methods. A pre-trial hearing is the most common choice.

Whenever the hearing is held, the failure of the government to meet its burden can have most drastic consequences. One commentator has stated that "[i]f the tainted evidence was presented to the grand jury, the indictment will be dismissed; when tainted evidence is introduced at trial, the defendant is entitled to a new trial. [Defendants] are afforded similar protections against nonevidentiary uses of immunized testimony." [citation omitted]

Dismissal of the indictment or vacation of the conviction is not necessary where the use is found to be harmless beyond a reasonable doubt.

A district court holding a *Kastigar* hearing "must make specific findings on the independent nature of this proposed [allegedly tainted] evidence." Because the burden is upon the government, the appellate court "may not infer findings favorable to it on these questions." A district court's determination that the government has carried its burden of showing independent sources is a factual finding that is subject to review under the "clearly erroneous" standard. [citations omitted]

Before North's trial, the District Court held a "preliminary" *Kastigar* inquiry and issued an order based thereon which it subsequently adopted as final (with certain changes) without benefit of further proceedings or hearings.

After reviewing the relevant factual and statutory background, the District Court made four findings concerning the government's alleged use of immunized testimony before the grand jury. First, "[d]efendants' immunized testimony was not submitted to the grand jury in any form." Second, "[t]he grand jurors were effectively warned not to read about or look at or listen to this immunized testimony and it played no part in the grand jury's unanimous decision to indict." Third, "[t]he grand jury transcript and exhibits reflect solid proof and ample probable cause to indict on each and every count." Fourth, "[n]one of the testimony or exhibits presented to the grand jury became known to the prosecuting attorneys on Independent Counsel's staff or to him personally either from the immunized testimony itself or from leads derived from the testimony, directly or indirectly."

In reaching these conclusions, the District Court noted that the "Independent Counsel's legitimate independent leads to every significant witness were carefully documented," that the grand jury heard many witnesses before the immunity order issued, *id.* at 308; that North's testimony was undertaken and concluded while the grand jury was in recess, *id.*; and that the "grand jurors were specifically, repeatedly and effectively instructed to avoid exposure to any immunized testimony." The District Court provided examples of various warnings given to grand jurors, and to grand jury witnesses. The District Court also noted that Associate Independent Counsel were "apparently careful to avoid broad, rambling questions," and that "written materials from Independent Counsel demonstrat[ed] that all the prosecutor's substantive witnesses were known to him before the first immunity grant."

Addressing what it referred to as nonevidentiary problems, the District Court noted that "[w]itnesses, probably a considerable number of them, have had their memories refreshed by the immunized testimony," but because of its belief that "there is no way of determining, except possibly by a trial before the trial, whether or not any defendant was placed in a substantially worse position by the possible refreshment of a witness' memory through such exposure," the District Court concluded that "[i]f testimony remains truthful the refreshment itself is not an evidentiary use."

ANALYSIS

1. NONEVIDENTIARY USE

North's primary *Kastigar* complaint is that the District Court failed to require the IC to demonstrate an independent source for each item of evidence or testimony presented to the grand jury and the petit jury, and that the District Court erred in focusing almost wholly on the IC's leads to witnesses, rather than on the content of the witnesses' testimony. North also claims that the IC made an improper nonevidentiary use of the immunized testimony (as by employing it for purposes of trial strategy), or at least that the District Court failed to make a sufficient inquiry into the question. North also protests that his immunized testimony was improperly used to refresh the recollection of witnesses before the grand jury and at trial, that this refreshment caused them to alter their testimony, and that the District Court failed to give this question the careful examination it deserved. In our discussion here, we first consider alleged nonevidentiary use of immunized testimony by the IC. We will then proceed to consider the use of immunized testimony to refresh witnesses' recollections. Finally, we will address the distinction between use of immunized testimony as a lead to procure witnesses and use insofar as it affects the substantive content of witnesses' testimony.

* * *

This Circuit has never squarely addressed the question of whether or not *Kastigar* encompasses so-called nonevidentiary use of immunized testimony. The federal use immunity statute does not speak in terms of "evidence," but rather provides that "no testimony *or other information* compelled under the order (*or any information directly or indirectly derived from such testimony or other information*) may be used against the witness in any criminal case * * *." 18 U.S.C. § 6002 (emphasis supplied). *Kastigar* does not define, except perhaps by implication, what nonevidentiary use of compelled testimony might be nor does it expressly discuss the permissible scope of such use.

* * *

In the present appeal, the record is extensive and the District Court's findings are thorough as to precautions taken by the IC to prevent untoward exposure or use by his staff. The record is clear and the findings are not clearly erroneous. Without significant exposure, the IC could not have made significant nonevidentiary use, permissible or impermissible. Thus, even assuming without deciding that a prosecutor cannot make nonevidentiary use of immunized testimony, in the case before us the IC did not do so. We do not reach the precise question, therefore, of the permissible quantum of nonevidentiary use by prosecutors, or indeed whether such use is permissible at all. Our concern is the use of immunized testimony by witnesses before the grand jury and at trial.

We cannot agree with the District Court that the use of immunized testimony to refresh the memories of witnesses is a nonevidentiary matter and that therefore refreshment should not be subject to a *Kastigar* hearing because "[n]o court has ever so required, nor did *Kastigar* suggest anything of the kind." In our view, the use of immunized testimony by witnesses to refresh their memories, or otherwise to focus their thoughts, organize their testimony, or alter their prior or contemporaneous statements, constitutes indirect evidentiary not nonevidentiary use. This observation also applies to witnesses who studied, reviewed, or were exposed to the immunized testimony in order to prepare themselves or others as witnesses.

Strictly speaking, the term *direct evidentiary use* may describe only attempts by the prosecutors to offer the immunized testimony directly to the grand jury or trial jury, as by offering the testimony as an exhibit. But the testimony of other witnesses is also evidence that is to be considered by the grand jury or the trial jury. When the government puts on witnesses who refresh, supplement, or modify that evidence with compelled testimony, the government uses that testimony to indict and convict. The fact that the government violates the Fifth Amendment in a circuitous or haphazard fashion is cold comfort to the citizen who has been forced to incriminate himself by threat of imprisonment for contempt. The stern language of *Kastigar* does not become lenient because the compelled testimony is used to form and alter evidence in oblique ways exclusively, or at a slight distance from the chair of the immunized witness. Such a looming constitutional infirmity cannot be dismissed as merely nonevidentiary. This type of use by witnesses is not only evidentiary in any meaningful sense of the term; it is at the core of the criminal proceeding.

In summary, the use of immunized testimony—before the grand jury or at trial—to augment or refresh recollection is an evidentiary use and must be dealt with as such.

2. REFRESHMENT

Both the trial and the grand jury proceedings involved "a considerable number" of witnesses who had "their memories refreshed by the immunized testimony," a use of compelled testimony that the District Court treated as nonevidentiary. The District Court stated that "[t]here is no way a trier of fact can determine whether the memories of these witnesses would be substantially different if it had not been stimulated by a bit of the immunized testimony itself" and that "there is no way of determining, except possibly by a trial before the trial, whether or not any defendant was placed in a substantially worse position by the possible refreshment of a witness' memory through such exposure." The District Court found that such taint occurs in the "natural course of events" because "[m]emory is a mysterious thing that can be stirred by a shaggy dog or a broken promise."

This observation, while likely true, is not dispositive of the searching inquiry *Kastigar* requires. The fact that a sizable number of grand jury witnesses, trial witnesses, and their aides apparently immersed themselves in North's immunized testimony leads us to doubt whether what is in question here is simply "stimulation" of memory by "a bit" of compelled testimony. Whether the government's use of compelled testimony occurs in the natural course of events or results from an unprecedented aberration is irrelevant to a citizen's Fifth Amendment right. *Kastigar* does not prohibit simply "a whole lot of use," or "excessive use," or "primary use" of compelled testimony. It prohibits *"any* use," direct or indirect. From a prosecutor's standpoint, an unhappy byproduct of the Fifth Amendment is that *Kastigar* may very well require a trial within a trial (or a trial before, during, or after the trial) if such a proceeding is necessary for the court to determine whether or not the government has in any fashion used compelled testimony to indict or convict a defendant.

We readily understand how court and counsel might sigh prior to such an undertaking. Such a *Kastigar* proceeding could consume substantial amounts of time, personnel, and money, only to lead to the conclusion that a defendant—perhaps a guilty defendant—cannot be prosecuted. Yet the very purpose of the Fifth Amendment under these circumstances is to prevent the prosecutor from transmogrifying into the inquisitor, complete with that officer's most pernicious tool—the power of the state to force a person to incriminate himself. As between the clear constitutional command and the convenience of the government, our duty is to enforce the former and discount the latter.

The District Court ruled that "[i]f testimony remains truthful the refreshment itself is not an evidentiary use." But *Kastigar* addresses "use," not "truth." If the government uses immunized testimony to refresh the recollection of a witness (or to sharpen his memory or focus his thought) when the witness testifies before a grand jury considering the indictment of a citizen for acts as to which the citizen was forced to testify, then the government clearly has used the immunized testimony. Even if "truthfulness" were the focus of the *Kastigar* inquiry, the present record does not disclose the basis for the determination that the testimony of any witness was "truthful," nor does it indicate how we might review such a determination.

The IC attempts to meet North's refreshment argument by relying on United States v. Apfelbaum, 445 U.S. 115, 124–27 (1980), for the proposition that *Kastigar* "prohibits use [of immunized testimony] by the prosecution, not by others." The IC misreads *Apfelbaum*, which is concerned with how immunized testimony may or may not be used rather than with who may or may not use it. In *Apfelbaum*, the Supreme Court stated that it had never held that the Fifth Amendment precludes all use of immunized testimony because "[s]uch a requirement would be inconsistent with the principle that the privilege does not extend to consequences of a *noncriminal* nature, such as threats of liability in civil suits, disgrace in the community, or loss of employment." *Apfelbaum*, 445 U.S. at 125 (emphasis supplied). North does not contend that the government violated his Fifth Amendment right because he received bad press as a result of his immunized testimony, or that he has been unable to find employment. Rather, he protests that the government used his immunized testimony to secure his indictment and subsequent conviction as a federal felon. Because North appeals a judgment that apparently violates his Fifth Amendment privilege by the imposition of criminal sanctions, we find *Apfelbaum* inapplicable to this case.

The IC further relies on Monroe v. United States, 234 F.2d 49, 56–57 (D.C.Cir.1956), for the proposition that recollection may be refreshed with inadmissible evidence even when the government violated the Fourth and Fifth Amendments to obtain the evidence. In *Monroe*, this Court allowed an undercover police officer to refresh his recollection with recordings of conversations between himself and the defendants. The recordings were not in evidence. The refreshment was permissible because, inasmuch as the conversations were his own, the "connection between any possible violation of the statute and his testimony had 'become so attenuated as to dissipate the taint' in its relation to admissibility." *Monroe*, 234 F.2d at 57. Thus, the officer's "testimony was not itself the product of an illegal interception; he repeated on the stand what he himself had heard." *Id.* The IC analogizes the officer in *Monroe* to the witnesses here, claiming that "the testimony of witnesses about matters they had personally heard or observed is the product of their own memory, not of immunized testimony they might have seen or read."

We cannot agree. As an initial matter, *Monroe* nowhere hints that a violation of the Fourth or Fifth Amendments was at issue. In *Monroe*, this Court concluded that refreshed testimony was not "publication" within the meaning of section 605 of the Federal Communications Act. Here, what the federal use immunity statute prohibits is "use" of the immunized testimony. The IC would have us adopt a parallel rule: as refreshment was not "publication," so now refreshment is not "use." But, the immunity statute is constitutional only because it is coextensive with the Fifth Amendment. The clear language of the Constitution, coupled with the Supreme Court's sweeping approach in *Kastigar*, requires us to define "use" more broadly than we defined "publication" for purposes of the Federal Communications Act and prevents the sort of parallelism that the IC urges upon us. Because we conclude that refreshment is "use" within the meaning of *Kastigar* and the statute, the *Monroe* rule is inapplicable.

Indeed, the fact that immunized testimony has entered the consciousness of someone other than the immunized witness does not lessen the heavy burden upon the government to show that it has made no use, directly or indirectly, of the compelled testimony. The following hypothetical illustrates the weakness of the IC's argument. A prosecutor locates a witness known to have observed certain events, seemingly inconsequential at the time but later critical to a criminal prosecution. The witness has absolutely no recollection of those events. The prosecution then arranges to procure the immunized testimony of the defendant. The forgetful witness sits in the gallery and listens to that immunized testimony. Under the IC's theory, that witness could then be brought forward to relate the events he had previously forgotten. It would require a curiously strained use of language and learning to hold that in such a case no "use" of the immunized testimony had been made against the defendant.

The IC offers no logical distinction between that hypothetical and the dangers of use in the case at bar. It may be that it is possible in the present case to separate the wheat of the witnesses' unspoiled memory from the chaff of North's immunized testimony, but it may not. There at least should be a *Kastigar* hearing and specific findings on that question. If it proves impossible to make such a separation, then it may well be the case that the prosecution cannot proceed. Certainly this danger is a real one in a case such as this where the immunized testimony is so broadly disseminated that interested parties study it and even casual observers have some notion of its content. Nevertheless, the Fifth Amendment requires that the government establish priorities before making the immunization decision. The government must occasionally decide which it values more: immunization (perhaps to discharge institutional duties, such as congressional fact-finding and information-dissemination) or prosecution. If the government chooses immunization, then it must understand that the Fifth Amendment and *Kastigar* mean that it is taking a great chance that the witness cannot constitutionally be indicted or prosecuted.

* * *

3. "IDENTITY OF WITNESS" VS. "CONTENT OF TESTIMONY"

The refreshment of witnesses' recollections is indicative, but not exhaustive, of the *Kastigar* questions left unanswered on the present record. The District Court's disposition of the "identity-of-witness" issue, does not dispose of the "content-of-testimony" *Kastigar* problem: the District Court inquired as to whether the names of witnesses were derived independently of the immunized testimony, but it made no determination of the extent to which the substantive content of the witnesses' testimony may have been shaped, altered, or affected by the immunized testimony.

A central problem in this case is that many grand jury and trial witnesses were thoroughly soaked in North's immunized testimony, but no effort was made to determine what effect, if any, this extensive exposure had on their testimony. Papers filed under seal indicate that officials and attorneys from the Department of Justice, the Central Intelligence Agency, the White House, and the Department of State gathered, studied, and summarized North's immunized testimony in order to prepare themselves or their superiors and colleagues for their testimony before the investigating committees and the grand jury. A few examples will suffice.

* * *

The testimony of Robert C. McFarlane, the National Security Advisor to President Reagan, is especially troubling and is indeed emblematic of both the weakness of the IC's position and the necessity of further *Kastigar* inquiry. Although McFarlane completed his grand jury testimony before North gave his immunized testimony, McFarlane was a key government witness at trial. He testified before the investigating committees prior to North's immunized testimony, but then specifically requested and was granted a second appearance after North testified in order to respond to North's testimony. (Citations omitted.) In his second appearance on Capitol Hill, McFarlane revised his earlier testimony in light of North's testimony, and directly responded to North's testimony at certain points. He also apparently managed to recall items that he had not remembered in his prior testimony. McFarlane subsequently testified at North's trial. No effort was made to determine what use—if any—this government witness made of North's testimony in his trial testimony.

* * *

The core purpose of the immunity statute, 18 U.S.C. §§ 6001–6005, is to allow the prosecution of an immunized witness while preventing use of his compelled testimony. One forbidden use of the immunized testimony is the identification of a witness, but other uses of a citizen's immunized testimony—as by presenting the testimony of grand jury or trial witnesses that has been derived from or influenced by the immunized testimony—are equally forbidden. * * *

The District Court relied on United States v. Rinaldi, 808 F.2d 1579, 1583–84 (D.C.Cir.1987) (per curiam), for its conclusion that the IC's independent discovery of witnesses was dispositive of the invalidity of North's *Kastigar* claim. We read *Rinaldi* otherwise.

In *Rinaldi*, the defendant pled guilty to a count of conspiracy to import heroin. He appealed the district court's denial of his motion to suppress certain testimony that he alleged was known to the government only through his immunized testimony. A codefendant who had been present during some of Rinaldi's immunized testimony later testified to the grand jury. Her grand jury testimony was elicited in part by leading questions from the government attorney. The government argued that the codefendant knew all the important details, that the government had developed her as a witness independently of the immunized testimony, and that its discovery of her testimony was inevitable, but the trial court made no specific findings to that effect on the record before it. The government had provided no independent basis for the leading questions. This Court therefore remanded for further evidentiary hearings and specific findings.

In *Rinaldi* we pointed out that "[a]s the government bore the burden of proving that Reardon's *testimony was free of taint and independently derived*, we may not infer findings favorable to it on these questions." *Rinaldi*, 808 F.2d at 1583 (emphasis supplied). The emphasized portion of this statement directs us to two inquiries: the taint of the testimony and the *derivation* of the testimony. The District Court in the present case concentrated only on the independence of the leads to witnesses, rather than on the substance of their testimony.... Although a methodology based on derivation is a sound starting point for a *Kastigar* inquiry, such an approach is incomplete. On the record, it is clear that the District Court focused solely on the derivation of the witnesses' testimony while dealing with that testimony's substantive content only by invoking other devices, such as the IC's "warnings" to grand jury witnesses.

* * *

The assertion that there was "solid proof and ample probable cause to indict," *Id.* at 315, even if true, cannot replace a *Kastigar* inquiry. Coerced confessions and compelled testimony may often supply proof and cause, but that fact does not diminish their constitutional offensiveness in virtually all uses.

The District Court also stated that "[t]he grand jurors were specifically, repeatedly and effectively instructed to avoid exposure to any immunized testimony * * *. Many more warnings were given during the course of the grand jury's tenure." *Id.* at 309. There is no evidence that the warnings to the grand jurors were effective, however, because grand jury deliberations are not transcribed and therefore could not have been part of the record reviewed by the Court. These concerns underscore our conclusion as expressed above that the present convictions cannot stand. We are not persuaded, however, to extend our holding and require an unprecedented *Kastigar*-type hearing concerning possible exposure of individual grand jurors through the media.

Nonetheless, as to witness exposure, such a hearing is required.

The convictions are vacated and the case is remanded to the District Court. On remand, if the prosecution is to continue, the District Court must hold a full *Kastigar* hearing that will inquire into the *content* as well as the *sources* of the grand jury and trial witnesses' testimony. That inquiry must proceed witness-by-witness; if necessary, it will proceed line-by-line and item-by-item. For each grand jury and trial witness, the prosecution must show by a preponderance of the evidence that no use whatsoever was made of any of the immunized testimony either by the witness or by the Office of Independent Counsel in questioning the witness. This burden may be met by establishing that the witness was never exposed to North's immunized testimony, or that the allegedly tainted testimony contains no evidence not "canned" by the prosecution before such exposure occurred. Unless the District Court can make express findings that the government has carried this heavy burden as to the content of all of the testimony of each witness, that testimony cannot survive the *Kastigar* test. We remind the prosecution that the *Kastigar* burden is "heavy" not because of the evidentiary standard, but because of the constitutional standard: the government has to meet its proof only by a preponderance of the evidence, but any failure to meet that standard must result in exclusion of the testimony.

If the District Court finds that the government has failed to carry its burden with respect to any item or part of the testimony of any grand jury or trial witness, it should then consider whether that failure is harmless beyond a reasonable doubt. If the District Court concludes that the government's failure to carry its burden with respect to that particular witness or item is harmless beyond a reasonable doubt, the District Court should memorialize its conclusions and rationales in writing. If the government has in fact introduced trial evidence that fails the *Kastigar* analysis, then the defendant is entitled to a new trial. If the same is true as to grand jury evidence, then the indictment must be dismissed.

* * *

WALD, CHIEF JUDGE, DISSENTING [IN PART].

Oliver North's was a case of epic proportions, massively publicized, for many weeks engaging the rapt attention and emotions of the nation. The panel today reverses his convictions on three separate grounds, including a remand for an "item-by-item, line-by-line" hearing on whether any bit of evidence, as yet unidentified, may have reflected exposure to North's immunized testimony before Congress.

After studying for months the thousands of pages of transcripts and hundreds of documents produced for the grand jury and trial, I, on the other hand, am satisfied that North received a fair trial—not a perfect one, but a competently managed and a fair one. As in all trials of this magnitude, a few errors were made, but in analyzing and researching North's claims, including the three grounds on which the Per Curiam reverses, I do not find, singly or cumulatively, that any of them rose to the status of reversible error. I am convinced that the essentials of a fair trial were accorded North, and that his conviction on the three Counts of which the jury found him guilty should be affirmed.

* * *

I dissent from the majority's dismissal of North's conviction on the ground that his fifth amendment right not to incriminate himself was violated by the grand jury and trial proceedings. According to my colleagues, *Kastigar* compels a "witness-by-witness[,] if necessary, * * * line-by-line and item-by-item" inquiry into every piece of testimony presented to the grand and petit juries to insure that the prosecution in no way employed or relied on North's immunized congressional testimony in obtaining his conviction, a process that would have consumed countless extra weeks or months of trial to little or no avail. In my view, a careful analysis of the *Kastigar* inquiry that Judge Gesell actually undertook demonstrates that North received all of the constitutional protections to which he was entitled.

* * *

The Per Curiam's insistence on a "line-by-line, item-by-item" *Kastigar* hearing represents an overblown interpretation of the *Kastigar* case that is totally unnecessary to protect North's constitutional rights. Requiring a new and comprehensive "*Kastigar* hearing" this late in the game ignores the many other reasonable avenues used by Judge Gesell to protect North from any aftereffects from his congressional immunization, including his review of the prodigious efforts by prosecutors and grand and petit jurors to avoid exposure, his comparison of the substance of grand jury and trial transcripts, and his attention to the actual sources of prosecution leads and interviews with key witnesses obtained before North's immunized testimony. The majority effectively cuts off the trial judge's discretion in choosing the most practical means of ensuring a defendant's *Kastigar* rights, and in so doing it makes a subsequent trial of any congressionally immunized witness virtually impossible.

While national television coverage should not be allowed to impinge on North's statutory and constitutional rights, neither does it entitle North to escape zealous but fair prosecution. *Kastigar's* strictures must be applied in a manner that protects a defendant's constitutional rights, but also preserves the public's interest in conducting prosecutions of officials whose crimes have far-flung implications for national policy. We require trial judges to conduct fair trials, not perfect ones. North has failed to identify a single suspected *Kastigar* violation in the thousands of pages of grand jury and trial testimony, other than the misguided efforts of in-house Justice Department officials to use his immunized testimony to brief witnesses who essentially corroborated his own version of events, and who swore under oath that their ultimate testimony was derived from personal recollection only. When an "ex parte review in appellate chambers," yields a clear result that is entirely consistent with the trial court's own findings, a remand for further lengthy hearings is unjustified. I cannot conclude that Judge Gesell's prodigious and conscientious efforts to protect North's fifth amendment rights were in any way so ineffectual as to require a reversal on the formalistic grounds that the majority advances.

I can find no basis for vacating North's conviction on self-incrimination grounds.

Notes

1. On September 16, 1991, United States District Court Judge Gerhard A. Gesell dismissed all criminal charges then pending against retired Marine Lieutenant Colonel Oliver North. Iran–Contra Independent Counsel Lawrence Walsh determined that he could not meet the strict standards set forth by the court in the above opinion.

2. In United States v. Poindexter, 951 F.2d 369 (D.C.Cir.1991), the Court of Appeals for the District of Columbia reversed the convictions of John M. Poindexter for the same reasons as in the *North* case above. The Court of Appeals held that the testimony of many of the prosecution's witnesses including that of North himself was influenced by the witnesses' exposure to Poindexter's immunized testimony for purposes of refreshment. See Michael Gilbert, Note, *The Future of Congressional Use Immunity After United States v. North*, 30 Am. Crim. L. Rev. 417 (1993). In *Poindexter*, the court found that it would be useless to remand the case back to the district court because "the I.C. has not suggested any other way in which he might meet his burden if we were to remand this case for further hearings regarding taint at trial." *See Poindexter*, 951 F.2d at 376. This prompted the dissent to state that "In United States v. North, this court changed the standards the special prosecutor had to meet; today we refuse to let him try to meet them." 951 F.2d at 388 (Mikva, dissenting).

3. In United States v. Koon and Powell, 34 F.3d 1416 (9th Cir.1994), the Ninth Circuit expressly rejected the *North* standard. The Court stated the Ninth Circuit rule as "the prosecutor's *Kastigar* burden is met if the substance of the exposed witness's testimony is based on a legitimate source that is independent of the immunized testimony." 34 F.2d at 1432.

4. What do you think? Is *Kastigar*, as applied in *North*, too strict?

Chapter 7

PUBLIC CORRUPTION*

Allegedly corrupt public officials are prosecuted federally for using their public offices to illegally obtain benefits primarily under four statutes: Hobbs Act (18 U.S.C. § 1951), Mail Fraud (18 U.S.C. § 1341), RICO (18 U.S.C. § 1961) and Conspiracy (18 U.S.C. § 371). Other federal statutes also used, but not as frequently, include making a false statement to the government (18 U.S.C. § 1001) and tax offenses (26 U.S.C. §§ 7201, 7206(1)).

The Hobbs Act provides, in pertinent part, as follows:

"Whoever in any way or degree obstructs, delays, or affects commerce or the movement of any article or commodity in commerce, by robbery or extortion or attempts or conspires so to do * * * shall be fined not more than $10,000 or imprisoned not more than twenty years, or both." 18 U.S.C. § 1951(a).

The statute defines "commerce" as

[c]ommerce within the District of Columbia, or any Territory or Possession of the United States; all commerce between any point in a State, Territory, Possession, or the District of Columbia and any point outside thereof; all commerce between points within the same State through any place outside such State; and all other commerce over which the United States has jurisdiction." 18 U.S.C. § 1951(b)(3).

and "extortion" as

[t]he obtaining of property from another with his consent, induced by wrongful use of actual or threatened force, violence, or fear, or under color of official right. 18 U.S.C. § 1951(b)(2).

———

The next case discusses the meaning of the term, "induced by wrongful use of actual force, violence or fear."

* Professor Melissa Harrison joins as co-author in portions of this chapter.

UNITED STATES v. CAPO

United States Court of Appeals, Second Circuit, 1987.
817 F.2d 947.

PRATT, CIRCUIT JUDGE.

Defendants were convicted in the United States District Court for the Western District of New York, * * * for conspiring to violate and for substantive violations of the Hobbs Act, 18 U.S.C. § 1951, as well as for various false statement, witness tampering, and obstruction of justice counts. A divided panel of this court affirmed those convictions, United States v. Capo, 791 F.2d 1054 (2d Cir.1986), and, following a poll of the active judges of the court, the Hobbs Act convictions were reheard in banc. The point of demarcation between the panel majority and dissent concerned the applicability of the Hobbs Act to the facts of this case. While the panel majority held that the underlying job-selling scheme fell within the bounds of traditional Hobbs Act jurisprudence, it is the majority position upon rehearing that, without sufficient evidence to establish the requisite elements of extortion by wrongful use of fear of economic loss, defendants were improperly convicted under the federal extortion statute.

While this rehearing of the Hobbs Act counts bears little practical consequence for defendants—they remain convicted of the false statement, witness tampering, and obstruction of justice counts, for which their sentences are concurrent with their Hobbs Act sentences—we nonetheless must exercise our responsibility to ensure that federal criminal statutes are not enforced in a manner inconsistent with congressional intent. Because congress did not intend federal intervention in this factual setting, we vacate the decision of the panel majority on the Hobbs Act counts, and reverse defendants' Hobbs Act convictions.

BACKGROUND

The Eastman Kodak Company ("Kodak"), which has its headquarters in Rochester, New York, is a major economic force in upstate New York. The job-selling scheme underlying these convictions took place at Kodak's Elmgrove plant, one of the company's primary manufacturing facilities, where approximately 13,000 people were employed at all times relevant to this appeal. Early in 1981, John Baron, an unindicted co-conspirator, was hired as an employment counselor in Kodak's Industrial Relations Department. One of Baron's first responsibilities was to hire a group of permanent production employees. As directed, Baron initially hired approximately 1,400 people who had previously been laid off at Kodak, after which he followed standard Kodak procedure for hiring the remainder of the needed permanent production employees.

The primary tool at a Kodak employment counselor's disposal consisted of an accumulated file containing approximately 55,000 applications. The hiring process was designed so that when a job requisition was filed, the counselor would review the relevant applications and hire, based upon, among other considerations, prior experience, prior service with Kodak, and length of time the application had been on file. In reality, however, the hiring that gave rise to these prosecutions did not, and probably could not, follow this carefully considered format; in addition to the turnover caused by normal attrition in a large work force, employment counselors at Kodak were called upon episodically to conduct "supplemental" hirings.

In 1982, Kodak announced the supplemental hiring of approximately 2,300 people needed to commence production of the company's new "disc camera." According to Baron, the standard application system, which at its best was inefficient, collapsed under the dramatic demand to hire these new, temporary employees immediately. Baron's boss, Mr. Seils, testified that, in addition to the standard application system, Kodak had long used an internal job referral system through which department heads and other supervisors would submit lists of names of prospective applicants they wished to see hired. Seils further testified that, in the rush to satisfy the hiring needs created by the disc camera production, the referral system became the primary means of hiring, as it was far more efficient than the standard application mechanism. Indeed, even with the referral system, Baron characterized the disc-camera supplemental hiring as "out of control," indicating that people could have walked off the street without previously applying and nevertheless been hired.

It was in this hectic setting of the disc-camera supplemental hiring that the instant job-selling scheme took hold. Baron's friend, Kodak supervisor Stanford Forte, Sr., referred several people to Baron, including defendant Tadeusz Snacki ("Ted"), and Ted's wife and nephew. For hiring them, Baron was rewarded with a leather coat and a color TV. Thereafter, Forte gave Baron a VCR and asked Baron to hire three other people. When Baron again complied, Forte shared $1,500 with Baron that Forte had received from the three referrals. The following month, Forte prevailed upon Ted to help Baron move, and during the move, Baron agreed to hire Ted's son. One month later, Ted, who had not known Baron before Forte introduced them, gave Baron a wedding gift of $400.

At the same time these deals were being made, the job-peddling scheme spread to others. Ted's brother, Walter Snacki ("Walter"), an employee of another company, Rochester Products, embarked upon a string of referrals for money, all of which resulted in Kodak employment for the payors. Walter passed the word to a number of co-workers at Rochester Products that he could assure that they or their relatives or friends would be hired at Kodak for the payment of $500, or, in one case, of $600.

For example, Walter was overheard by a co-worker, Josephine Kane, discussing with another fellow employee his connection at Kodak. Kane asked Walter if he would get her husband, William, a job. Walter told her that he would see, and sometime later told Kane he could do it for $500.

Kane gave Walter her husband's application, on which she had been instructed to leave the date blank, but said she would not pay until William had been hired. Shortly thereafter, her husband was offered a job. Even though William Kane turned down that first offer of employment, Walter was able to secure for him a second offer some months later after William had reconsidered, although on that occasion Walter demanded that the money be paid in advance.

The exchange upon which the panel majority placed greatest emphasis transpired between Walter and Paul Kelso, another Rochester Products co-worker and Walter's friend. Kelso wanted to separate from his wife, Marjorie Ann, but with two children and his wife unemployed, it was not then economically feasible. Although Marjorie Ann previously had applied to Kodak on her own, she had not been successful. Walter informed Kelso that he could get a job for Marjorie Ann for $500. When Kelso balked at having to pay, Walter responded: "You want her to get a job, don't you." Once Kelso agreed to pay, Marjorie Ann was hired.

Through the Snackis' connection with Baron, Walter secured employment at the Elmgrove plant not only for William Kane and Marjorie Ann Miller–Kelso but also for several other relatives of Rochester Products employees. Among these were Rita La Delfa and Vivian Pfund, two daughters of Antonina La Delfa, a janitor at Rochester Products, both of whom paid $500 to Walter and both of whom were subsequently hired. Similarly, Peter Riccardi's and Robert Drelick's wives were both hired at Kodak after Walter received $500 and $600, respectively. Josephine Kane again invoked Walter's assistance on behalf of her sister, Carmella Angora; however, although Josephine paid Walter $600, Angora was never hired because by that time news had leaked that the FBI was investigating job-selling at Kodak.

In addition to obtaining jobs for his own family members through the job-selling network, Ted, through his daughter, also received two $500 checks from Joseph Scavo to secure employment for Michelle Sofia, Scavo's friend, and Dawn Himmelsbach, Scavo's sister. Both women ultimately were hired. In addition, Scavo borrowed $500 to secure Joe Pascente a job at Kodak through Ted's connection.

The Snackis' job-selling network branched out to encompass Robert Capo, a local barber who was Ted's friend. Capo let it be known that he had a connection at Kodak, and, over time, used his influence to help several of his customers get jobs, including Robert Frechette, for $1,000; Peter Iascone, for $800; Iascone's friend, Sam DeLeo, for $1,000; Bernard Gauthier, for $800; and Bernard's son, Brian, also for $800. The evidence at trial also established that Capo got jobs for Joan Adams, the wife of his friend, James, for $700; Joseph Licata, for $1,000; and Daniel Boerst, the son of an acquaintance, for $1,000.

Because defendants' subsequent actions in attempting to derail the investigation are not involved in this in banc rehearing, the details of their activities concerning false statements, witness tampering, and obstruction of justice need not be recounted here. With respect to the extortion counts, all three defendants were convicted on one count of conspiring to violate the Hobbs Act; additionally, Walter was convicted on six substantive Hobbs Act counts and acquitted on one other, Ted was convicted on two and acquitted on one substantive Hobbs Act count, and Capo was convicted on five substantive Hobbs Act violations and acquitted on three others. Although indicted along with defendants, Forte pled guilty before trial, and unindicted co-conspirator John Baron testified for the government at trial.

The question before this en banc court is whether defendants' conduct, although likely a violation of state law, constitutes federal extortion. We conclude that it does not.

DISCUSSION

The term "extortion" means the obtaining of property from another, with his consent, induced by wrongful use of actual or threatened force, violence, or fear, or under color of official right. 18 U.S.C. § 1951(b)(2).

The government successfully prosecuted these defendants under the theory that their activities amounted to extortion by wrongful use of fear—specifically, fear of economic loss. *See, e.g.*, United States v. Rastelli, 551 F.2d 902, 904 (2d Cir.1977). In response, defendants do not contend that a job-selling scheme could never constitute extortion under the Hobbs Act. Rather, they protest that the money they received was not extorted from their "victims" because the "victims" were not induced to pay by fear of economic loss, but, instead, by hope—the hope of obtaining employment. In substance, defendants claim that the government cannot demonstrate wrongful use of fear of economic loss absent proof either that defendants threatened to impair the "victims'" prospects for employment at Kodak if they did not pay, or that the "victims" otherwise reasonably believed their chances for employment would be impaired for nonpayment. Thus, defendants argue that, unless we are willing to accept a melding of federal extortion and state-law commercial bribery, we must recognize the insufficient evidence of fear of economic loss on these facts.

* * *

"The cases interpreting the Hobbs Act have repeatedly stressed that the element of 'fear' required by the Act can be satisfied by putting the victim in fear of economic loss." United States v. Brecht, 540 F.2d 45, 52 (2d Cir.1976). Instructing the jury in this case, the district judge charged:

It is not necessary that the Government prove that the fear of economic loss was the consequence of a direct threat made by the defendant. Nor is it necessary for the Government to prove that the defendant actually created the fear in the minds of his victims, or was responsible for creating that fear. However, it must be proved that the defendant intended to exploit the fear of the alleged victim. The fear of economic loss must be a reasonable one. The mere voluntary payment of money or delivery of property, unaccompanied by any fear of economic loss, would not constitute extortion.

In other words, if you find that any defendant asked for the payment of money as a pre-condition to his using his influence with officials at Kodak to obtain a job for someone, that alone is not extortion. To find the defendant guilty of extortion, you must also find that the victim reasonably believed that the defendant had the power and influence with officials at Kodak to hurt the victim's prospects of obtaining employment at Kodak, even if that fear was not caused by a direct threat by the defendant, and that the victim was in fear of not obtaining a job, or of seriously reducing his chances of obtaining a job, unless he gave money to the defendant.

As the panel majority and dissent agreed on the propriety of this instruction, the issue on rehearing is whether there was sufficient evidence as a matter of law to establish the Hobbs Act violations.

* * *

The absence or presence of fear of economic loss must be considered from the perspective of the victim, not the extortionist; the proof need establish that the victim *reasonably* believed: first, that the defendant had the power to harm the victim, and second, that the defendant would exploit that power to the victim's detriment. *See Rastelli*, 551 F.2d at 905. Here, although there is at least a serious question whether it would have been reasonable for the "victims" to believe defendants had the power to harm them, there is no evidence at all to suggest that it would have been reasonable for the "victims" to believe that if they did not pay, the defendants would exploit any such power to diminish their employment opportunities.

This circuit's case law on extortion by wrongful use of fear of economic loss is comprised of cases in which the evidence was plain that nonpayment would result in preclusion from or diminished opportunity for some existing or potential economic benefit. For instance, in *Brecht*, the evidence established that the defendant was the manager of Westinghouse's technical publications group, which position afforded him discretion to award outside subcontracts for the production of Westinghouse's technical manuals. At a meeting with a subcontractor's representative, the defendant "*demanded* a $1,000 kickback *as a condition for the award* of the contract to [the subcontractor]." 540 F.2d at 47 (emphasis added). We affirmed defendant's conviction for extortion by wrongful use of fear of economic loss "since the evidence showed that he obtained the $1,000 by the use of fear, attempting to convince the victim that he *would be denied any chance* to obtain a contract *unless he paid*." *Id*. at 52 (emphasis added).

Likewise, in United States v. Margiotta, 688 F.2d 108 (2d Cir.1982), we affirmed the conviction of a county political figure for extortion by wrongful use of fear of economic loss for exploiting the fear of an insurance agency that it would lose its position as broker of record for the county if certain kickbacks were not forthcoming. We rejected a challenge to the sufficiency of the evidence "[i]n light of the *overwhelming evidence that* the principals of the * * * [a]gency understood *the [a]gency would lose its position* as Broker of Record for Town and County *if it ceased making the payments specified"*. *Id.* at 133 (emphasis added)

* * *

The panel majority concluded that "[t]he evidence was adequate to allow a rational juror to find beyond a reasonable doubt that the victims reasonably feared economic loss if they did not make the payments demanded by the defendants." *Capo,* 791 F.2d at 1065. Recognizing the strict standard for viewing evidentiary sufficiency—that the evidence must be viewed in the light most favorable to the government—we disagree and hold that the evidence of fear of economic loss was insufficient here as a matter of law. First, there was no evidence that any defendant did, in fact, negatively influence any hiring decision or even attempt to do so. When defendants did intervene in Kodak's hiring it was only to assist these "victims."

Furthermore, review of the trial transcript reveals that not one witness testified to any fear that nonpayment would result in one of the defendants adversely affecting his or her chances for a job at Kodak; indeed, most of the "victims" testified that they had no such fear, while the others simply were not asked. Instead, the evidence establishes that these "victims" were willing participants seeking to improve their chances. As Robert Frechette testified, after Capo offered to help him at Kodak for $1,000, he

> thought about it for a while. Went home; talked it over with my wife. And I said, "Seemed like a good deal." I mean, I was working through agencies anyways [sic] off and on and I was paying them, too.

Trial trans. at 386. Thus, the second part of the *Rastelli* test—that the victim reasonably believed that the defendant would exploit his power to the victim's detriment—is not satisfied here.

Further representative of the trial testimony of these "victims" is an exchange between Josephine Kane and counsel for Walter Snacki. Kane's husband, William, had applied to Kodak prior to the time Josephine approached Walter about arranging a job for William. Walter's counsel asked Josephine:

> "[D]id he [Walter] ever say to you in connection with your husband's [prior] application at Eastman Kodak Company that if you didn't pay him the $500 that he was going to see someone at Kodak and be sure that your husband's application would never be processed? Did he ever say that to you?
>
> A. No, he did not."

Trial trans. at 200. Similarly, Bernard Gauthier, another "victim" was asked: "Bob [Capo] never told you that unless you paid this money for these jobs that any applications you had at Kodak would be destroyed, and you'd never get in?" A. "No." *Id.* at 331. Likewise, Joseph Scavo, who paid Ted to get jobs for Joe Pascente, Dawn Himmelsbach, and Michelle Sofia, testified:

> "Q. You were not concerned, were you, if Mr. Snacki had to give you your money back that there would be any problem with Joe Pascente, Michelle [Sofia] or Dawn Himmelsbach applying through the routine channels at Eastman Kodak Company to obtain the job?
>
> A. Right."

Id. at 640. Carmella Angora, Annie La Delfa, and James Adams also stated that they felt no pressure to pay Walter Snacki. *See id.* at 209, 226, 428. These reactions are understandable given the absence of any evidence of detrimental action for nonpayment combined with the undisputed fact that the normal hiring channels remained open at Kodak at all relevant times.

Perhaps the best example of all, however, of the absence of any fear of economic loss on the part of these "victims" is the story of Brian Gauthier. After Bernard Gauthier, Brian's father, paid $800 to Bob Capo and was hired at Kodak, he approached Capo about a job for Brian. Bernard gave Capo another $800 along with Brian's completed application; however, shortly thereafter, Brian got an interview through an application he had earlier filed at Kodak on his own. Bernard then called Capo and told him not to put through Brian's paid-for application in order to give Brian an opportunity to be hired through the normal hiring process. Capo agreed and did not process that application until Brian learned that he had not been hired. Given the go-ahead, Capo then submitted Brian's application, which was soon granted. Certainly, if Capo were threatening to impair hiring prospects, or even implying that he would impair the prospects of applicants who did not pay, he would not have acted as he did. Conversely, if either of the Gauthiers in any way feared a reprisal by Capo they would not likely have felt comfortable asking him to hold Brian's application; indeed, most probably they would not even have told Capo about it.

The evidence relied upon most heavily by the panel majority was a statement that one witness, Paul Kelso, recounted had been made by Walter. Kelso confided in Walter that he and his wife, Marjorie Ann, were experiencing marital difficulties and told Walter that it would be easier for them to separate if Marjorie Ann could get a job. As noted earlier, Walter told Paul that he could get his wife a job at Kodak, but it would cost $500. Paul "questioned the fact of why would it have to cost something. He [Walter] says, '[Y]ou want her to get a job, don't you.' "

The panel majority read the latter statement as establishing fear of economic loss because it demonstrated that the "victims" paid because they thought that was their only chance of being hired at Kodak. *Capo,* 791 F.2d at 1064–65. While that assumption undoubtedly is true for

Marjorie Ann Miller–Kelso and several others, it is not enough to establish extortion by wrongful use of fear of economic loss. Without evidence that the "victims" feared that defendants would impair their prospects of being hired, all the panel majority's observation shows is that they were unqualified, or were subjected to difficult economic circumstances, or for some other reason were unlikely to succeed through Kodak's normal hiring channels.

Walter's statement supports the conclusion that Paul Kelso paid $500 for his wife's job, not out of fear that Walter would otherwise impair her prospects for employment at Kodak, but, rather, to achieve a result she had been unable to attain on her own. In fact, Kelso later testified that "[b]efore all this came about I know my wife had put other applications into Kodak, and it was just a matter of waiting for [Kodak] to call. So when this situation arose I figured it would just better our chances or better her chances to get a job." Trial trans. at 88. Walter's statement to Paul Kelso is devoid of any suggestion of adverse action for nonpayment; fairly interpreted, all it connotes is that Walter would step in to help if, but only if, payment was made.

> In short, what happened here is no more than what Judge Telesca expressly charged the jury did *not* constitute extortion; namely, "if you find that any defendant asked for the payment of money as a precondition to his using his influence with officials at Kodak to obtain a job for someone, that alone is not extortion."

Capo, 791 F.2d at 1072 (Pratt, J., dissenting in part) (emphasis in original).

II. EXTORTION AND COMMERCIAL BRIBERY.

Although the Travel Act, 18 U.S.C. § 1952, may provide a federal jurisdictional base for prosecuting state-law bribery, commercial bribery is not within the reach of the Hobbs Act. Because these "victims" faced no increased risk if they did not pay, but, rather, stood only to improve their lots by paying defendants, this case is a classic example of bribery. While bribery and extortion are not neatly separable, *see* United States v. Hathaway, 534 F.2d 386, 395 (1st Cir.), *cert. denied*, 429 U.S. 819, 97 S.Ct. 64, 50 L.Ed.2d 79 (1976), they are distinct crimes. Both the payor and the recipient of a bribe are guilty of a crime, while under extortion statutes, only the extortionist has broken the law. *See* Ruff, *Federal Prosecution Of Local Corruption: A Case Study In The Making Of Law Enforcement Policy*, 65 Geo.L.J. 1171, 1190 (1977). Without evidence that the payor feared some negative intervention for nonpayment, the payment is solely intended to secure an otherwise unsecured result. That exemplifies bribery. In *Brecht*, we

> recognize[d] that the line between "solicitation" of a commercial bribe and extortion of a payment is thin, as is the line between bribery and extortion. Yet if the defendant purports to have the power to hurt the victim in economic terms and fear is induced, the solicitation becomes an extortionate demand.

540 F.2d at 51 n. 11. We must recognize and respect that distinction if we are to avoid judicially subsuming state-law commercial bribery within the federal extortion statute.

This certainly is not the first time a defendant charged with violating the Hobbs Act has pleaded that his conduct constituted bribery and not extortion. The arguments in those cases, however, were rejected because the victims there did in fact face a threat of suffering some economic disadvantage. For instance in United States v. DeMet, 486 F.2d 816, 819–20 (7th Cir.1973), the defendant, a Chicago police officer indicted for extortion of a bar owner by wrongful use of fear of economic loss, argued that he only received bribes and was not guilty of extortion. The court upheld the defendant's Hobbs Act conviction, finding sufficient evidence that the bar owner reasonably feared that defendant would exploit his position to harass and harm his business. "[T]he jury could reasonably infer from all the circumstances, including defendant's official position, that [the bar owner] was in fear of harm to his business, his fear was reasonable, and defendant exploited it to extort money and liquor." *Id.* at 820.

As we have noted, there is no evidence in the instant case that the "victims" were coerced or threatened by defendants, and all the evidence points to the conclusion that they paid voluntarily to improve their chances to get jobs they had not been able to obtain on their own. Therefore, defendants' conduct, while not constituting extortion by wrongful use of fear of economic loss, may well fall within the proscription of New York's commercial bribery statute, which provides:

> An employee, agent or fiduciary is guilty of commercial bribe receiving in the second degree when, without the consent of his employer or principal, he solicits, accepts or agrees to accept any benefit from another person upon an agreement or understanding that such benefit will influence his conduct in relation to his employer's or principal's affairs.

N.Y. Penal Law § 180.05 (McKinney Supp.1986). As employees of Kodak, it appears that Baron and Ted might have been prosecuted directly under section 180.05, while Walter and Capo, non-Kodak employees, might have been reached as aiders and abettors. *See id.* § 20.00 (McKinney 1975). However, we cannot and need not resolve those questions here; it is sufficient for our purposes to conclude that, whatever state violations may have occurred, defendants' conduct did not constitute a violation of the Hobbs Act.

Presumably, a prosecutorial determination was made that the interstate-commerce federal jurisdictional base, *see* 18 U.S.C. § 1952(a), needed for a Travel Act bribery prosecution, *see id.* § 1952(b)(2), could not be proved here, and, therefore, that this situation could not be prosecuted federally unless it were made to fit under the Hobbs Act. Nevertheless, our extortion precedents do not stretch that far.

It is the sensitive duty of federal courts to review carefully the enforcement of our federal criminal statutes to prevent their injection into unintended areas of state governance. *See* Miner, *Federal Courts, Federal Crimes, and Federalism*, 10 HARV.J.L. & PUB. POL'Y 117, 128 (1987). Exercising that duty, we find it necessary to nullify this attempted application of the Hobbs Act to circumstances it was never meant to reach. Incremental extensions of federal criminal jurisdiction arguably present a more pernicious hazard for our federal system than would a bold accretion to the body of federal crimes. At a minimum, a clear extension of federal responsibility is likely to be sufficiently visible to provoke inquiries and debate about the propriety and desirability of changing the state-federal balance. Less abrupt, more subtle expansions, however, such as nearly occurred here, are less likely to trigger public debate, and, yet, over time cumulatively may amount to substantial intrusions by federal officials into areas properly left to state enforcement. By holding that the Hobbs Act does not encompass state-law commercial bribery, we seek to demarcate a point beyond which congress intended federal prosecutors not to pass.

CONCLUSION

Because defendants' activities were not properly reached under the Hobbs Act, that portion of the panel majority's decision addressing defendants' Hobbs Act convictions is vacated, the judgments of conviction under the Hobbs Act are reversed, and the Hobbs Act counts in the indictment are dismissed.

KEARSE, CIRCUIT JUDGE, JOINED BY TIMBERS, CIRCUIT JUDGE, DISSENTING:

While I agree with much of the en banc majority's opinion as to the proper interpretation of the Hobbs Act, I dissent because the result it reaches depends on the majority's own interpretations of the evidence that are contrary to permissible inferences apparently drawn by the jury.

As the majority points out, we all agree that the instructions given to the jury were correct. The dividing point in this case is the proper factual inferences to be drawn from the evidence adduced at trial. Of that evidence, summarized in the panel majority opinion, the most overt statement by a defendant that the jury could have interpreted as inducing fear on the part of the victims that they would be "denied any chance to obtain [Kodak employment] unless [they] paid," United States v. Brecht, 540 F.2d 45, 52 (2d Cir.1976), was Walter Snacki's response to a question from Paul Kelso as to why Walter must be paid in order for Kelso's wife to get a job at Kodak. Walter asked, "You want her to get a job, don't you[?]" Further, though Walter may not have come right out and made the same statement to others, he nonetheless apparently managed to convey the impression that defendants had the power to withhold Kodak jobs unless the demanded payments were made. Josephine Kane, who made or arranged payments for four people to get jobs, testified as follows:

"Q. [Cross-examination by Ted Snacki's lawyer] Now, it is true, Mrs. Kane, is it not, that on none of these four occasions did Walter Snacki tell you that if you didn't pay him the money none of those people would get employed—would ever get employed at Eastman Kodak Company, correct?

A.　No. He did not come out and say that, no."

. . . .

"Q. [Redirect examination by the government] Mrs. Kane, Mr. Palmiere just asked you whether in your conversations with Mr. Snacki regarding these jobs he ever told you that these individuals wouldn't get a job if they didn't pay, and I believe your answer was he didn't come right out and say that.

Was there something that led you to believe that that might be the case?

A.　Well, when he said that, you know, if he had the right amount of money he could get him the job. So I automatically figured they weren't going to get a job, you know, unless they got the money. But he didn't come out and say it."

The jury, properly instructed that it could not return a verdict of guilty on any Hobbs Act count unless it found that the victim reasonably feared that the defendant could and would impede his chances of getting a Kodak job, found the defendants guilty of most of the Hobbs Act charges against them. The en banc majority reaches the conclusion that the evidence was insufficient to support these verdicts by giving its own "fair[ ] interpret[ation]," to Walter's statement to Kelso, and by making its own finding that other evidence "supports the conclusion," that payments were made "voluntarily" and not out of any fear that defendants could or would impede the victims' being hired at Kodak. Were I the factfinder, I might agree. But because the factfinder was the jury and our province is to review its findings by taking the evidence and drawing all inferences in the light most favorable to the government, I dissent.

Notes

1.　Is there a difference in paying to increase one's chance of getting a job and paying because of fear that without payment, there will be no job?

2.　Consider the following case: A local real estate developer is seeking a zoning variance in order to develop some property. He has tried and failed to obtain the variance. He is told that he should approach the local sheriff for help. The sheriff lives in the vicinity of the proposed development and also is a county "political boss." The developers ask the sheriff for help in influencing the decisionmakers on the variance. Later, the developers are approached by a "middleman" who tells them the sheriff will help them for a substantial payment of money. Extortion or bribery?

What if the following is added? The developer asks what will happen if he does not pay. The "middleman" replies, "You want your variance, don't you?"

What if the middleman says, "Without the sheriff's help, you will never get your variance"?[a]

The next case concerns the Hobbs Act's requirement that property be obtained "under color of official right."[b]

MCCORMICK v. UNITED STATES

United States Supreme Court, 1991.
500 U.S. 257.

WHITE, JUSTICE.

This case requires us to consider whether the Court of Appeals properly affirmed the conviction of petitioner, an elected public official, for extorting property under color of official right in violation of the Hobbs Act, 18 U.S.C. § 1951. We also must address the affirmance of petitioner's conviction for filing a false income tax return.

I

Petitioner Robert L. McCormick was a member of the West Virginia House of Delegates in 1984. He represented a district that had long suffered from a shortage of medical doctors. For several years, West Virginia had allowed foreign medical school graduates to practice under temporary permits while studying for the state licensing exams. Under this program, some doctors were allowed to practice under temporary permits for years even though they repeatedly failed the state exams. McCormick was a leading advocate and supporter of this program.

In the early 1980's, following a move in the House of Delegates to end the temporary permit program, several of the temporarily licensed doctors formed an organization to press their interests in Charleston. The organization hired a lobbyist, John Vandergrift, who in 1984 worked for legislation that would extend the expiration date of the temporary permit program. McCormick sponsored the House version of the proposed legislation and a bill was passed extending the program for another year. Shortly thereafter, Vandergrift and McCormick discussed the possibility of introducing legislation during the 1985 session that would grant the doctors a permanent medical license by virtue of their years of experience. McCormick agreed to sponsor such legislation.

During his 1984 reelection campaign, McCormick informed Vandergrift that his campaign was expensive, that he had paid considerable sums out of his own pocket, and that he had not heard anything from

---

a. These facts are taken from United States v. Thomas, 749 F.Supp. 847 (M.D.Tenn.1990).

b. For excellent discussions of "the under color of official right" portion of the Hobbs Act, see James Lindgren, *The Elusive Distinction Between Bribery and Extortion: From the Common Law to the Hobbs Act*, 35 U.C.L.A. L. REV. 815 (1988); James

Lindgren, *The Theory, History and Practice of the Bribery-Extortion Distinction*, 141 U.PA. L. REV. 1695 (1993), and Steven C. Yarbrough, *The Hobbs Act in the Nineties: Confusion or Clarification of the Quid Pro Quo Standard in Extortion Cases Involving Public Officials*, 31 TULSA L.J. 781 (1996).

the foreign doctors. Vandergrift told McCormick that he would contact the doctors and see what he could do. Vandergrift contacted one of the foreign doctors and later received from the doctors $1,200 in cash. Vandergrift delivered an envelope containing nine $100 bills to McCormick. Later the same day, a second delivery of $2,000 in cash was made to McCormick. During the fall of 1984, McCormick received two more cash payments from the doctors. McCormick did not list any of these payments as campaign contributions nor did he report the money as income on his 1984 federal income tax return. And although the doctors' organization kept detailed books of its expenditures, the cash payments were not listed as campaign contributions. Rather, the entries for the payments were accompanied only by initials or other codes signifying that the money was for McCormick.

In the spring of 1985, McCormick sponsored legislation permitting experienced doctors to be permanently licensed without passing the state licensing exams. McCormick spoke at length in favor of the bill during floor debate and the bill ultimately was enacted into law. Two weeks after the legislation was enacted, McCormick received another cash payment from the foreign doctors.

Following an investigation, a federal grand jury returned an indictment charging McCormick with five counts of violating the Hobbs Act, by extorting payments under color of official right * * *. At the close of a 6–day trial, the jury was instructed that to establish a Hobbs Act violation the Government had to prove that McCormick induced a cash payment and that he did so knowingly and willfully by extortion. As set out in the margin, the court defined "extortion" and other terms and elaborated on the proof required with respect to the extortion counts.[3]

---

3. The following are the relevant portions of the instructions discussing the extortion charges:

"Now, a definition of some of the terms used.

* * *

"As to inducement, the United States must prove that the defendant induced the person or persons described in the indictment to part with property, a term which includes money. It is charged that the defendant did so under color of official right.

"In proving this element, it is enough that the government prove beyond a reasonable doubt that the benefactor transferred something of significant value, here alleged to be money, to the public official with the expectation that the public official would extend to him some benefit or refrain from some harmful action, and the public official accepted the money knowing it was being transferred to him

with that expectation by the benefactor and because of his office.

* * *

"And so, inducement can be in the overt form of a demand, or in a more subtle form such as custom or expectation such as might have been communicated by the nature of the defendant's prior conduct of his office, if any.

"As to color of official right, in this case the government has charged that extortion was committed under color of official right, in that the defendant is charged with committing extortion by virtue of his office as a member of the West Virginia House of Delegates.

"Extortion under color of official right means the obtaining of money by a public official when the money obtained was not lawfully due and owing to him or to his office. * * * The mere voluntary payment of money, however, does not constitute extortion.

* * *

The next day the jury informed the court that it "would like to hear the instructions again with particular emphasis on the definition of extortion under the color of official right and on the law as regards the portion of moneys received that does not have to be reported as income." The court then reread most of the extortion instructions to the jury, but reordered some of the paragraphs and made the following significant addition:

> "Extortion under color of official right means the obtaining of money by a public official when the money obtained was not lawfully due and owing to him or to his office. Of course, extortion does not occur where one who is a public official receives a legitimate gift or a voluntary political contribution even though the political contribution may have been made in cash in violation of local law. Voluntary is that which is freely given without expectation of benefit."

It is also worth noting that with respect to political contributions, the last two paragraphs of the supplemental instructions on the extortion counts were as follows:

> "It would not be illegal, in and of itself, for Mr. McCormick to solicit or accept political contributions from foreign doctors who would benefit from this legislation.

> "In order to find Mr. McCormick guilty of extortion, you must be convinced beyond a reasonable doubt that the payment alleged in a given count of the indictment was made by or on behalf of the doctors with the expectation that such payment would influence Mr. McCormick's official conduct, and with knowledge on the part of Mr. McCormick that they were paid to him with that expectation by virtue of the office he held."

The jury convicted McCormick of the first Hobbs Act count (charging him with receiving the initial $900 cash payment) * * * but could not reach verdicts on the remaining four Hobbs Act counts. The District Court declared a mistrial on those four counts.

"In order to find Mr. McCormick guilty of extortion, you must first be convinced beyond a reasonable doubt that the payment alleged in a given count in the indictment was made by or on behalf of the doctors with the expectation that such payment would influence Mr. McCormick's official conduct, and with the knowledge on the part of Mr. McCormick that they were paid to him with that expectation by virtue of the office he held.

* * *

"Many public officials receive legitimate political contributions from individuals who, the official knows, are motivated by a general gratitude toward him because of his position on certain issues important to them, or even in the hope that the good will generated by such contributions will make the official more receptive to their cause.

"The mere solicitation or receipt of such political contributions is not illegal.

* * *

"So it is not necessary that the government prove that the defendant committed or promised to commit a quid pro quo, that is, consideration in the nature of official action in return for the payment of the money not lawfully owed. Such a quid pro quo may, of course, be forthcoming in an extortion case or it may not. In either event it is not an essential element of the crime."

* * *

The Court of Appeals affirmed, observing that non-elected officials may be convicted under the Hobbs Act without proof that they have granted or agreed to grant some benefit or advantage in exchange for money paid to them and that elected officials should be held to the same standard when they receive money other than "legitimate" campaign contributions. 896 F.2d 61 (4th Cir.1990) After stating that McCormick could not be prosecuted under the Hobbs Act for receiving voluntary campaign contributions, the court rejected McCormick's contention that conviction of an elected official under the Act requires, under all circumstances, proof of a *quid pro quo, i.e.,* a promise of official action or inaction in exchange for any payment or property received. Rather, the court interpreted the statute as not requiring such a showing where the parties never intended the payments to be "legitimate" campaign contributions. After listing seven factors to be considered in making this determination and canvassing the record evidence, the court concluded:

> "Under these facts, a reasonable jury could find that McCormick was extorting money from the doctors for his continued support of the 1985 legislation. Further, the evidence supports the conclusion that the money was never intended by any of the parties to be a campaign contribution. Therefore, we refuse to reverse the jury's verdict against McCormick for violating the Hobbs Act." *Id.,* at 67.

* * *

Because of disagreement in the Courts of Appeals regarding the meaning of the phrase "under color of official right" as it is used in the Hobbs Act, we granted certiorari. We reverse and remand for further proceedings.

II

McCormick's challenge to the judgment below affirming his conviction is limited to the Court of Appeals' rejection of his claim that the payments made to him by or on behalf of the doctors were campaign contributions, the receipt of which did not violate the Hobbs Act. * * * In two respects, however, we agree with McCormick that the Court of Appeals erred.

A

First, we are quite sure that the Court of Appeals affirmed the conviction on legal and factual grounds that were never submitted to the jury. Although McCormick challenged the adequacy of the jury instructions to distinguish between campaign contributions and payments that are illegal under the Hobbs Act, the Court of Appeals' opinion did not examine or mention the instructions given by the trial court. The court neither dealt with McCormick's submission that the instructions were too confusing to give adequate guidance to the jury, nor, more specifically, with the argument that although the jury was instructed that voluntary campaign contributions were not vulnerable under the Hobbs Act, the word "voluntary" as used "in several places during the course of these instructions," was defined as "that which is freely given without expectation of benefit." Neither did the Court of Appeals note that the jury was not instructed in accordance with the court's holding that the difference between legitimate and illegitimate campaign contributions was to be determined by the intention of the parties after considering specified factors.[7] Instead, the Court of Appeals, after announcing a rule of law for determining when payments are made under color of official right, went on to find sufficient evidence in the record to support findings that McCormick was extorting money from the doctors for his continued support of the 1985 legislation, and further that the parties never intended any of the payments to be a campaign contribution.

It goes without saying that matters of intent are for the jury to consider. It is also plain that each of the seven factors that the Court of Appeals thought should be considered in determining the parties' intent present an issue of historical fact. Thus even assuming the Court of Appeals was correct on the law, the conviction should not have been affirmed on that basis but should have been set aside and a new trial ordered. If for no other reason, therefore, the judgment of the Court of Appeals must be reversed and the case remanded for further proceedings.

B

We agree with the Court of Appeals that in a case like this it is proper to inquire whether payments made to an elected official are in fact campaign contributions, and we agree that the intention of the parties is a relevant consideration in pursuing this inquiry. But we cannot accept the Court of Appeals' approach to distinguishing between legal and illegal campaign contributions. The Court of Appeals stated that payments to elected officials could violate the Hobbs Act without proof of an explicit *quid pro quo* by proving that the payments "were never intended to be *legitimate* campaign contributions." This issue, as we read the Court of Appeals' opinion, actually involved two inquiries; for after applying the factors the Court of Appeals considered relevant, it arrived at two conclusions: first, that McCormick was extorting money for his continued support of the 1985 legislation and "[f]urther", that the money was never intended by the parties to be a campaign contribution at all. The first conclusion, especially when considered in light of the second, asserts that the campaign contributions were illegitimate, extortionate payments.

This conclusion was necessarily based on the factors that the court considered, the first four of which could not possibly by themselves

---

7. "Some of the circumstances that should be considered in making this determination include, but are not limited to, (1) whether the money was recorded by the payor as a campaign contribution, (2) whether the money was recorded and reported by the official as a campaign contribution, (3) whether the payment was in cash, (4) whether it was delivered to the official personally or to his campaign, (5) whether the official acted in his official capacity at or near the time of the payment for the benefit of the payor or supported legislation that would benefit the payor, (6) whether the official had supported similar legislation before the time of the payment, and (7) whether the official had directly or indirectly solicited the payor individually for the payment." 896 F.2d 61, 66 (1990).

amount to extortion. Neither could they when considered with the last three more telling factors, namely, whether the official acted in his official capacity at or near the time of the payment for the benefit of the payor; whether the official had supported legislation before the time of the payment; and whether the official had directly or indirectly solicited the payor individually for the payment. Even assuming that the result of each of these seven inquiries was unfavorable to McCormick, as they very likely were in the Court of Appeals' view, we cannot agree that a violation of the Hobbs Act would be made out, as the Court of Appeals' first conclusion asserted.

Serving constituents and supporting legislation that will benefit the district and individuals and groups therein is the everyday business of a legislator. It is also true that campaigns must be run and financed. Money is constantly being solicited on behalf of candidates, who run on platforms and who claim support on the basis of their views and what they intend to do or have done. Whatever ethical considerations and appearances may indicate, to hold that legislators commit the federal crime of extortion when they act for the benefit of constituents or support legislation furthering the interests of some of their constituents, shortly before or after campaign contributions are solicited and received from those beneficiaries, is an unrealistic assessment of what Congress could have meant by making it a crime to obtain property from another, with his consent, "under color of official right." To hold otherwise would open to prosecution not only conduct that has long been thought to be well within the law but also conduct that in a very real sense is unavoidable so long as election campaigns are financed by private contributions or expenditures, as they have been from the beginning of the Nation. It would require statutory language more explicit than the Hobbs Act contains to justify a contrary conclusion.

This is not to say that it is impossible for an elected official to commit extortion in the course of financing an election campaign. Political contributions are of course vulnerable if induced by the use of force, violence, or fear. The receipt of such contributions is also vulnerable under the Act as having been taken under color of official right, but only if the payments are made in return for an explicit promise or undertaking by the official to perform or not to perform an official act. In such situations the official asserts that his official conduct will be controlled by the terms of the promise or undertaking. This is the receipt of money by an elected official under the color of official right within the meaning of the Hobbs Act.

This formulation defines the forbidden zone of conduct with sufficient clarity. As the Court of Appeals for the Fifth Circuit observed in United States v. Dozier, 672 F.2d 531, 537 (1982):

> "A moment's reflection should enable one to distinguish, at least in the abstract, a legitimate solicitation from the exaction of a fee for a benefit conferred or an injury withheld. Whether described familiarly as a payoff or with the Latinate precision of *quid pro quo*, the

prohibited exchange is the same: a public official may not demand payment as inducement for the promise to perform (or not to perform) an official act."

The United States agrees that if the payments to McCormick were campaign contributions, proof of a *quid pro quo* would be essential for an extortion conviction, and quotes the instruction given on this subject in 9 Department of Justice Manual § 9–85A.306, p. 9–1938.134 (Supp.1988–2): "campaign contributions will not be authorized as the subject of a Hobbs Act prosecution unless they can be proven to have been given in return for the performance of or abstaining from an official act; otherwise any campaign contribution might constitute a violation."

We thus disagree with the Court of Appeals' holding in this case that a *quid pro quo* is not necessary for conviction under the Hobbs Act when an official receives a campaign contribution.[10] By the same token, we hold, as McCormick urges, that the District Court's instruction to the same effect was error.

III

The Government nevertheless insists that a properly instructed jury in this case found that the payment at issue was not a campaign contribution at all and that the evidence amply supports this finding. The instructions given here are not a model of clarity, and it is true that the trial court instructed that the receipt of voluntary campaign contributions did not violate the Hobbs Act. But under the instructions a contribution was not "voluntary" if given with *any* expectation of benefit; and as we read the instructions, taken as a whole, the jury was told that it could find McCormick guilty of extortion if any of the payments, even though a campaign contribution, was made by the doctors with the expectation that McCormick's official action would be influenced for their benefit and if McCormick knew that the payment was made with that expectation. It may be that the jury found that none of the payments was a campaign contribution, but it is mere speculation that the jury convicted on this basis rather than on the impermissible basis that even though the first payment was such a contribution, McCormick's receipt of it was a violation of the Hobbs Act.

* * *

V

* * *

[McCormick was also convicted on a tax charge for failing to report, as income, the money he received from the foreign doctors. The Court remanded the case to determine McCormick's criminal liability on that offense in light of its opinion herein.]

---

10. As noted previously, McCormick's sole contention in this case is that the payments made to him were campaign contributions. Therefore, we do not decide whether a quid pro quo requirement exits in other contexts, such as when an elected official receives gifts, meals, travel expenses, or other items of value.

JUSTICE SCALIA, CONCURRING.

I agree with the Court's conclusion and, given the assumption on which this case was briefed and argued, with the reasons the Court assigns. If the prohibition of the Hobbs Act, 18 U.S.C. § 1951, against receipt of money "under color of official right" includes receipt of money from a private source for the performance of official duties, that ambiguously described crime assuredly need not, and for the reasons the Court discusses should not, be interpreted to cover campaign contributions with anticipation of favorable future action, as opposed to campaign contributions in exchange for an explicit promise of favorable future action.

I find it unusual and unsettling, however, to make such a distinction without any hint of a justification in the statutory text: § 1951 contains not even a colorable allusion to campaign contributions or *quid pro quos*. I find it doubly unsettling because there is another interpretation of § 1951, contrary to the one that has been the assumption of argument here, that would render the distinction unnecessary. While I do not feel justified in adopting that interpretation without briefing and argument, neither do I feel comfortable giving tacit approval to the assumption that contradicts it. I write, therefore, a few words concerning the text of this statute, and the history that has produced the unexamined assumption underlying our opinion.

* * *

When, in the 1960s, it first occurred to federal prosecutors to use the Hobbs Act to reach what was essentially the soliciting of bribes by state officials, courts were unimpressed with the notion. They thought that public officials were not guilty of extortion when they accepted, or even when they requested, *voluntary* payments designed to influence or procure their official action. Not until 1972 did any court apply the Hobbs Act to bribery. * * * While [this application was] debated in academic writing, the Courts of Appeals accepted the expansion with little disagreement, and this Court has never had occasion to consider the matter.

It is acceptance of the assumption that "under color of official right" means "on account of one's office" that brings bribery cases within the statute's reach, and that creates the necessity for the reasonable but textually inexplicable distinction the Court makes today. That assumption is questionable. "The obtaining of property * * * under color of official *right*" more naturally connotes some false assertion of official *entitlement* to the property. This interpretation might have the effect of making the § 1951 definition of extortion comport with the definition of "extortion" at common law. One treatise writer, describing "extortion by a public officer," states: "At common law it was essential that the money or property be obtained under color of office, that is, under the pretense that the officer was entitled thereto by virtue of his office. The money or thing received must have been claimed or accepted in right of office, and the person paying must have yielded to official authority." 3 R. Anderson, Wharton's Criminal Law and Procedure 790–791 (1957).

* * *

Finally, where the United States Code explicitly criminalizes conduct such as that alleged in the present case, it calls the crime bribery, not extortion—and like all bribery laws I am aware of (but unlike § 1951 and all other extortion laws I am aware of) it punishes not only the person receiving the payment but the person making it. McCormick, though not a federal official, is subject to federal prosecution for bribery under the Travel Act, 18 U.S.C. § 1952, which criminalizes the use of interstate commerce for purposes of bribery—and reaches, of course, both the person giving and the person receiving the bribe.

I mean only to raise this argument, not to decide it, for it has not been advanced and there may be persuasive responses. But unexamined assumptions have a way of becoming, by force of usage, unsound law. Before we are asked to go further down the road of making reasonable but textually unapparent distinctions in a federal "payment for official action" statute—as we unquestionably will be asked—I think it well to bear in mind that the statute may not exist.

JUSTICE STEVENS, with whom JUSTICE BLACKMUN and JUSTICE O'CONNOR join, dissenting.

An error in a trial judge's instructions to the jury is not ground for reversal unless the defendant has made, and preserved, a specific objection to the particular instruction in question. Rule 30 of the Federal Rules of Criminal Procedure provides, in part:

"No party may assign as error any portion of the charge or omission therefrom unless party objects thereto before the jury retires to consider its verdict, stating distinctly the matter to which that party objects and the grounds of the objection."

This Court's disapproval of portions of the reasoning in the Court of Appeals' opinion, is not a sufficient ground for reversing its judgment. It is perfectly clear that the indictment charged a violation of the Hobbs Act, 18 U.S.C. § 1951, and that the evidence presented to the jury was adequate to prove beyond a reasonable doubt that petitioner knowingly used his public office to make or imply promises or threats to his constituents for purposes of pressuring them to make payments that were not lawfully due him. Apart from its criticism of the Court of Appeals' opinion, the Court's reversal of petitioner's conviction, in the final analysis, rests on its view that the jury instructions were incomplete because they did not adequately define the concept of "voluntary" contribution in distinguishing such contributions from extorted payments, and because the instructions did not require proof that petitioner made an "explicit" promise (or threat) in exchange for a campaign contribution. In my opinion the instructions were adequate and, in any event, to the extent that they were ambiguous, petitioner failed to preserve a proper objection.

In the Court of Appeals, petitioner argued that his conviction under the Hobbs Act was not supported by sufficient evidence. In reviewing such a contention, the appellate court must, of course, view the evidence in the light "most favorable to the Government." Glasser v. United States, 315 U.S. 60, 80 (1942). So viewed, it is perfectly clear that petitioner could properly have been found by the jury to be guilty of extortion.

Petitioner's crime was committed in two stages. Toward the end of May 1984, petitioner held an "unfriendly" conversation with Vandergrift, the representative of the unlicensed doctors, which the jury could have interpreted as an implied threat to take no action on the licensing legislation unless he received a cash payment as well as an implicit promise to support the legislation if an appropriate cash payment was made. Because the statute applies equally to the wrongful use of political power by a public official as to the wrongful use of threatened violence, that inducement was comparable to a known thug's offer to protect a storekeeper against the risk of severe property damage in exchange for a cash consideration. Neither the legislator nor the thug needs to make an explicit threat or an explicit promise to get his message across.

The extortion was completed on June 1, 1984, when Vandergrift personally delivered an envelope containing nine $100 bills to petitioner. The fact that the payment was not reported as a campaign contribution, as required by West Virginia law, or as taxable income, as required by federal law, together with other circumstantial evidence, adequately supports the conclusion that the money was intended as a payment to petitioner personally to induce him to act favorably on the licensing legislation. His covert acceptance of the cash—indeed, his denial at trial that he received any such payment—supports the conclusion that petitioner understood the payers' intention and that he had implicitly (at least) promised to provide them with the benefit that they sought.

As I understand its opinion, the Court would agree that these facts would constitute a violation of the Hobbs Act if the understanding that the money was a personal payment rather than a campaign contribution had been explicit rather than implicit and if the understanding that, in response to the payment, petitioner would endeavor to provide the payers with the specific benefit they sought had also been explicit rather than implicit. In my opinion there is no statutory requirement that illegal agreements, threats, or promises be in writing, or in any particular form. Subtle extortion is just as wrongful—and probably much more common—than the kind of express understanding that the Court's opinion seems to require.

Nevertheless, to prove a violation of the Hobbs Act, I agree with the Court that it is essential that the payment in question be contingent on a mutual understanding that the motivation for the payment is the payer's desire to avoid a specific threatened harm or to obtain a promised benefit that the defendant has the apparent power to deliver, either through the use of force or the use of public office. In this sense, the crime does require a *"quid pro quo."* Because the use of the Latin term *"quid pro quo"* tends to confuse the analysis, however, it is important to clarify the sense in which the term was used in the District Court's instructions.

As I have explained, the crime of extortion was complete when petitioner accepted the cash pursuant to an understanding that he would not carry out his earlier threat to withhold official action and instead would go forward with his contingent promise to take favorable action on behalf of the unlicensed physicians. What he did thereafter might have evidentiary significance, but could either undo a completed crime or complete an uncommitted offense. When petitioner took the money, he was either guilty or not guilty. For that reason, proof of a subsequent *quid pro quo*—his actual support of the legislation—was not necessary for the Government's case. And conversely, evidence that petitioner would have supported the legislation anyway is not a defense to the already completed crime. The thug who extorts protection money cannot defend on the ground that his threat was only a bluff because he would not have smashed the shopkeeper's windows even if the extortion had been unsuccessful. * * *

This Court's criticism of the District Court's instructions focuses on this single sentence:

"Voluntary is that which is freely given without expectation of benefit."

The Court treats this sentence as though it authorized the jury to find that a legitimate campaign contribution is involuntary and constitutes extortion whenever the contributor expects to benefit from the candidate's election. In my opinion this is a gross misreading of that sentence in the context of the entire set of instructions.

In context, the sentence in question advised the jury that a payment is voluntary if it is made without the expectation of a benefit that is specifically contingent upon the payment. An expectation that the donor will benefit from the election of a candidate who, once in office, would support particular legislation regardless of whether or not the contribution is made, would not make the payment contingent or involuntary in that sense; such a payment would be "voluntary" under a fair reading of the instructions, and the candidate's solicitation of such contributions from donors who would benefit from his or her election is perfectly legitimate. If, however, the donor and candidate know that the candidate's support of the proposed legislation is contingent upon the payment, the contribution may be found by a jury to have been involuntary or extorted.

In my judgment, the instructions, read as a whole, properly focused the jury's attention on the critical issue of the candidate's and contributor's intent at the time the specific payment was made. But even if they were ambiguous, or subject to improvement, they certainly do not provide a basis for reversing the conviction when the petitioner failed to advise the District Court of an error this Court now believes it has detected.

* * *

Given that the District Court's instructions to the jury largely tracked the instructions requested by petitioner at trial, I can see no legitimate reason for this Court now to find these instructions inadequate. Because I am convinced that the petitioner was fairly tried and convicted by a properly instructed jury, I would affirm the judgment of the Court of Appeals. * * *

Notes

1. Do you believe this "quid pro quo" requirement will render the Hobbs Act ineffective against the "subtle" extortion, which, according to Justice Stevens, is "probably much more common?"

2. Do you agree with Justice Scalia that although the majority's holding is reasonable, the language of the Hobbs Act does not justify the Court's rationale in reaching its conclusion?

3. The year after its decision in *McCormick*, the Court decided Evans v. United States, 504 U.S. 255 (1992), to "resolve a conflict in the Circuits over the question whether an affirmative act of inducement by a public official, such as a demand, is an element of the offense of extortion 'under color of official right' prohibited by the Hobbs Act. . . ." *Id.* at 256.

"[Evans] was an elected member of the Board of Commissioners of DeKalb County, Georgia. During the period between March 1985 and October 1986, as part of an effort by the Federal Bureau of Investigation (FBI) to investigate allegations of public corruption in the Atlanta area, particularly in the area of rezonings of property, an FBI agent posing as a real estate developer talked on the telephone and met with petitioner on a number of occasions. Virtually all, if not all, of those conversations were initiated by the agent and most were recorded on tape or video. In those conversations, the agent sought petitioner's assistance in an effort to rezone a 25–acre tract of land for high-density residential use. On July 25, 1986, the agent handed petitioner cash totaling $7,000 and a check, payable to petitioner's campaign, for $1,000. Petitioner reported the check, but not the cash, on his state campaign-financing disclosure form; he also did not report the $7,000 on his 1986 federal income tax return. Viewing the evidence in the light most favorable to the Government, as we must in light of the verdict, see Glasser v. United States, 315 U.S. 60, 80 (1942), we assume that the jury found that petitioner accepted the cash knowing that it was intended to ensure that he would vote in favor of the rezoning application and that he would try to persuade his fellow commissioners to do likewise. Thus, although petitioner did not initiate the transaction, his acceptance of the bribe constituted an implicit promise to use his official position to serve the interests of the bribegiver.

"In a two-count indictment, petitioner was charged with extortion in violation of 18 U. S. C. § 1951 and with failure to report income in violation of 26 U. S. C. § 7206(1). He was convicted by a jury on both counts. With respect to the extortion count, the trial judge gave the following instruction:

'The defendant contends that the $8,000 he received from agent Cormany was a campaign contribution. The solicitation of campaign contributions from any person is a necessary and permissible form of political activity on the part of persons who seek political office and persons who have been elected to political office. Thus, the acceptance by an elected official of a campaign contribution does not, in itself, constitute a violation of the Hobbs Act even though the donor has business pending before the official.'

'However, if a public official demands or accepts money in exchange for [a] specific requested exercise of his or her official power, such a demand or acceptance does constitute a violation of the Hobbs Act regardless of whether the payment is made in the form of a campaign contribution.'

"In affirming petitioner's conviction, the Court of Appeals noted that the instruction did not require the jury to find that petitioner had demanded or requested the money, or that he had conditioned the performance of any official act upon its receipt. 910 F.2d 790, 796 (C.A.11 1990). The Court of Appeals held, however, that 'passive acceptance of a benefit by a public official *is* sufficient to form the basis of a Hobbs Act violation if the official knows that he is being offered the payment in exchange for a specific requested exercise of his official power. The official need not take any specific action to induce the offering of the benefit.' *Ibid.* (emphasis in original)."[1]

The court held that the instruction satisfied the *quid pro quo* requirement of *McCormick* "because the offenses completed at the time when the public official receives a payment in return for his agreement to perform specific official acts." *Id.* at 268.

The dissent argued that:

"The Court's construction of the Hobbs Act is repugnant not only to the basic tenets of criminal justice reflected in the rule of lenity, but also to basic tenets of federalism. Over the past 20 years, the Hobbs Act has served as the engine for a stunning expansion of federal criminal jurisdiction into a field traditionally policed by state and local laws—acts of public corruption by state and local officials."

* * *

"I have no doubt that today's opinion is motivated by noble aims. Political corruption at any level of government is a serious evil, and, from a policy perspective, perhaps one well suited for federal law enforcement. But federal judges are not free to devise new crimes to meet the occasion. Chief Justice Marshall's warning is as timely today as

---

1. The Court of Appeals explained its conclusion as follows:

"[T]he requirement of inducement is *automatically* satisfied by the power connected with the public office. Therefore, once the defendant has shown that a pub-

lic official has accepted money in return for a requested exercise of official power, no additional inducement need be shown. 'The coercive nature of the official office provides all the inducement necessary.' " 910 F.2d at 796–797 (footnote omitted).

ever: "It would be dangerous, indeed, to carry the principle, that a case which is within the reason or mischief of a statute, is within its provisions, so far as to punish a crime not enumerated in the statute, because it is of equal atrocity, or of kindred character, with those which are enumerated." United States v. Wiltberger, 18 U.S. (5 Wheat.), at 96."

* * *

In *Evans* and *McCormick*, the Supreme Court struggled with the fact of modern campaigning: public officials need a lot of money to run for and remain in office. Much of this money comes from people whose livelihood may be affected by the decisions made by public officials. Thus, the dilemma of drawing the line between legitimate campaign contributions and illegal bribes and extortion. Do you believe *McCormick* and *Evans* are appropriate resolutions of this dilemma?

4. Justice Stevens, who dissented in *McCormick*, wrote the majority opinion in *Evans*. Recall that *McCormick* held that receipt of contributions by a public official violates the Hobbs Act "only if the payments are made in return for an explicit promise or undertaking by the official to perform or not to perform an official act." In *Evans*, the Court held that this require- ment of a *quid pro quo* is satisfied when "a public official receives a payment in return for his agreement to perform specific official acts.... " The *Evans* Court then rejected two of the defendant's arguments: (1) that *McCormick*'s *quid pro quo* requirement is fulfilled only with proof "of duress such as a demand," and (2) that an "affirmative step," or inducement by the public official, is an element of extortion "under color of official right." The *Evans* Court held "that the Government need only show that a public official has obtained a payment of which he was not entitled, knowing that the payment was made in return for official acts."

Is *Evans* departing from *McCormick*'s holding? Is the *Evans* test more realistic given modern day campaigning? How would you apply *Evans* to a situation where there is a *quid pro quo* between elected official and contribu- tor but no corruption, i.e., the elected official accepts the contribution after agreeing to contact the contributor before voting on a particular matter but specifically states that she won't promise how she will vote on the matter?

Chapter 8

FRAUD UPON EMPLOYEE BEN-EFIT PLANS AND LABOR ORGANIZATIONS

A. FRAUD UPON A BENEFIT PLAN

A Texas prosecutor said it well: "Nothing could be more cruel than to steal the money set aside by employers and employees for workers compensation and health benefits."[a] The case of Denny McLain and 250 families in Detroit typifies the tragedy of fraud upon benefit plans. McLain was a Detroit Tigers pitcher from 1963 to 1970; he was the last player to win 30 or more games in a major league season.[b] He also stole $2.5 million from the employees who put their savings in the Peet Packing Company Pension fund. Convicted on charges of embezzlement, fraud and money laundering, McLain, at age 52, is serving an eight year prison sentence.[c] Years earlier, when the Peet meatpacking plant was having financial difficulties, Denny McLain and his business partner took over the company and vowed to save it. Instead, they looted the employees' pension plan to pay personal and business debts. In 1997, after 110 years in business when Peet Packing Company failed, its pension fund was looted.[d]

Many Americans enjoy participation in benefit plans through their employers. These plans include pension, health care, even "cafeteria" plans which provide a menu of benefits from which employees may choose, such as child care, dental care, educational expenses, etc. In 1974, Congress enacted the Employee Retirement Income Security Act (ERISA), which introduced numerous new federal safeguards to protect plans and their participants against mismanagement of plan assets,

a. *Feds in Texas Begin Crackdown on Employee Benefits Plan Fraud*, Corporate Crime Reporter 3 (Apr. 10, 1995) [hereinafter *Feds Action*].

b. Charlie Vincent, *McLain's Pitch Worked, But Landed Him in Jail*, Detroit Free Press, Metro Section, P.1F (May 8, 1997) [hereinafter *McLain's Pitch*]

c. David Ashenfelter, *Judge Goes Easy on Peet Witness*, Detroit Free Press, P.3B (May 14, 1997).

d. David Cay Johnston, *Who's Been Eating My Nestegg?*, New York Times 3A (Nov. 26, 1995). *McLain's Pitch*, *supra* note 6 at 1F.

including fraud. Part of the protection is the Pension Benefit Guaranty Corporation (PBGC), which was created by ERISA. The PBGC insures many private sector "defined benefit" pension plans. If a PBGC insured plan fails without sufficient assets to pay benefits due, the PBGC guarantees payment of monthly benefits.[e]

Beginning in the mid–1980's, however, several changes occurred which have made employee benefit plans more vulnerable to fraud. First, for a variety of reasons, health care fraud is increasing,[f] including fraud upon employee health care plans. Second, the amount of money invested in benefit plans, especially pension plans, is staggering: in 1996, for example, over $4 trillion was invested in public and private pension funds.[g] Even if a small percentage of this was lost to fraud, the amount would be substantial. Third, in response to changes in the federal tax laws, American workers have changed the way they save.

The major change has been a huge growth in "401(k)" plans, which allow eligible employees new options for saving money.[h] Today there is more than $500 billion invested in 401(k) plans, which is about one-fourth of all private retirement plan assets.[i] Because of certain characteristics of 401(k) plans, they are particularly susceptible to fraud. Most significantly, 401(k) plans, known as "defined contribution" pension plans[j] are not as strictly regulated as "defined benefit" pension plans.[k] Also, 401(k) plans are particularly attractive to small companies where fraud is less likely to be caught.[l] According to one expert: "[A]s growing numbers of Americans go to work for small companies, the misappropriation of 401(k) money will become more common and the Government will find it harder to police misconduct."[m] By contrast, fraud within large companies is rare: "big companies are easier to police; less likely to dip into workers' funds and more likely to be able to replace the money if

e. For example, for a plan terminating in 1995, the PBGC generally will guarantee an age 65 single-life annuity benefit up to $2,642.05 per month. OFFICE OF THE FEDERAL REGISTER, THE UNITED STATES GOVERNMENT MANUAL, 647 (1996).

f. See Chapter 10 *infra*.

g. Lester B. Snyder & Marianne Gallegos, *Redefining the Role of the Federal Income Tax: Taking the Tax Law "Private" Through the Flat Tax and Other Consumption Taxes*, 13 AM.J.TAX POL'Y 1, 22 n.85 (1996).

h. STEVEN J. FRANZ, JOAN C. McDONAGH, JOHN MICHAEL MAIER, WILLIAM C. KALKE, 401(K) ANSWER BOOK 1–1 (1997).

i. *Id.* at vii.

j. A "defined contribution plan" is one in which every employee has an individual account. The employer's contributions are divided up among the employees' account, according to a set formula. The accounts are then invested. The employee's benefit

(assuming full vesting) is whatever is in the employee's account at any given time. In a defined contribution plan, investment risk and reward belong to the employee. Defined contribution plans are *not* covered by the Pension Benefits Guaranty Corporation. NORMAN STEIN, PENSION AND PROFIT-SHARING PLANS, ¶. 1.03 (Tax Advisors Planning Series, No. 24,1994).

k. A "defined benefit pension plan" is one in which no employee has an account or rights to particular assets. Instead the plan promises a specific benefit, usually a life annuity. The plan pays benefits due through collective plan assets. In a defined benefit plan, the employer bears the investment risk. Most defined benefit plans are covered by the Pension Benefit Guaranty Corporation. *Id.*

l. With 401(k) plans, employers do not have to contribute as much for employes who do not want to participate in the plan. *Id.* at 18.

m. *Nestegg, supra* note d at 6.

they do.''[n] In addition, there is less regulation of communications between employer and employee regarding 401(k) contributions than with defined benefit plans. This makes it easier for employers to supply false or incomplete information.

Compounding the above factors are the Department of Labor's limited investigative resources, inadequate education of fiduciaries, the difficulty of obtaining attorneys fees under ERISA (which makes private enforcement of fiduciary rules less likely), and fear by employees of job retaliation making less likely their reporting of fraud or exercise of private causes of actions to enforce benefit rights.[o]

For all of these reasons, it is easier for employers to "dip into the till." As former Labor Secretary Robert B. Reich explained: "It should not be surprising that some employers, feeling squeezed, may delay making a payment into a 401(k) plan or may stop making payments and use the money to pay bills. Unless business improves quickly * * * they are often unable to come up with the funds, and their trips to the till quickly turn into full blown frauds.''[p]

Those charged or convicted often see their raids on the assets of 401(k) plans as in their employees' interest. As one defense attorney explained about his clients who were convicted for diverting $294,000 of pension assets: "It's not like they reached into the plan and took money out. They used the money to keep the business going so people kept their jobs a little longer.''[q] A company owner sanctioned by the Labor Department for diverting employees' contributions similarly explained, "We had run into financial difficulties, and I was unable to get a loan. * * * It's not something that I'm proud of. But when you've got to pay your light bill and make your payroll and your bank is telling you to find some other form of financing, you don't have a lot of alternatives.''[r] Indeed, the temptation for businesses, especially fledgling small businesses, to raid funds earmarked for employee benefits to other corporate purposes, "can be overwhelming.''[s]

In short, the world of benefit plans, savings, retirement and pensions has changed. As one experienced insurance agent stated: "In the old days, you worked 20 years for a company, retired at 60 or so, and knew exactly what percentage of your salary you would receive as a pension. Today, you retire and keep your fingers crossed that the value of your plan is sufficient to give you a return you can live on.''[t]

n. *Nestegg, supra* note d at 3.

o. Interview with Norman Stein, Douglas Arant Professor of Law, University of Alabama School of Law, September 15, 1997.

p. *Nestegg, supra* note d at 3 (Money & Business).

q. *Nestegg, supra* note d at 6. This may have been defense counsel spin. The evidence in the case revealed that in the years the $294,000 was taken, the defendants "rented luxury cars, remodeled a home and paid themselves six-figure salaries." *Id.*

r. *Nestegg, supra* at 6; Kathy M. Kristof, *Troubled Firms Seen Misusing Pension Funds,* L.A. Times (Jan. 11, 1994). [hereinafter *Troubled Funds*]

s. *Troubled Firms, supra* note n.

t. *Fed Action, supra* note a.

To help monitor fraud in this changed world are five major federal statutes which pertain to fraud upon benefit programs:

- Section 664 of title 18, United States Code, makes it a criminal offense, punishable by a maximum term of imprisonment of five years, to steal or embezzle from an employee benefit plan.

- Section 666, of title 18, United States Code, is similar to § 664. It makes it a crime to embezzle, steal, or obtain by fraud the property of an organization which receives federal funds. Before § 666 applies, it must be shown that the organization received at least $10,000 "under a Federal program involving a grant, contract, subsidy, loan, guarantee, insurance, or other form of Federal assistance," in any one year time period. While state and local governmental organizations will almost always qualify under this provision, private organizations may also if they have received requisite federal financial assistance. According to the legislative history of § 666, this provision was enacted "to augment the ability of the United States to vindicate significant acts of theft, fraud, and bribery involving Federal monies that are disbursed to private organizations or state and local governments pursuant to a Federal program."[u]

- Violations of section 1027, title 18, United States Code often accompany violations of §§ 664 or 666 when a plan covered by ERISA is involved. Section 1027 of title 18, United States Code, also punishable by a maximum term of imprisonment of five years, makes it an offense to make a false statement or representation on a document required to be kept by ERISA.

- Section 501(c) of Title 29, United States Code, punishable by a maximum term of imprisonment of five years, makes it a crime for certain officials associated with labor organizations to embezzle, steal, unlawfully abstract or convert assets of the labor organization (such as benefit plans) to their own use.

- Lastly, 18 U.S.C. § 1954 makes it a criminal offense for an administrator, officer, trustee, custodian, counsel, agent or employee of any employee welfare benefit plan to receive or agree to receive or solicit a fee, kickback or thing of value.

The cases in this section focus on the most commonly used statute in this area, 18 U.S.C. § 664. Congress passed § 664 to help ensure that welfare and pension funds remain solvent and available for their intended beneficiaries. Title 18, United States Code, Section 664, provides:

"Any person who embezzles, steals, or unlawfully and willfully abstracts or converts to his own use or the use of another, any of the moneys, funds, securities, premiums, credits, property, or other assets of any employee welfare benefit plan or employee pension

u. S. Rep. No. 225, 98th Cong., 2d Sess.   3182, 3510.
369 (1984) *reprinted* in 1984 U.S.C.C.A.N.

benefit plan, or any fund connected therewith, shall be fined not more than $10,000 or imprisoned not more than five years, or both.''

An important issue in most cases involving alleged fraud from a benefit plan or labor organization is authorization for the action in question. It is difficult to prove criminal fraud if the money or assets at issue were taken with the consent of the "victims," i.e., the members of the benefit plan or labor organization. Because of the manner in which benefit plans and labor organizations conduct business, authorization for the acts in question often is present—either through ratification by the general membership or by delegation of the decision-making authority. Thus the question becomes, how can the conduct at issue be criminal if it was done with the consent of the "victims"? The next case, United States v. Butler, 954 F.2d 114 (2d Cir.1992), discusses this issue.

UNITED STATES v. BUTLER

United States Court of Appeals, Second Circuit (1992).
954 F.2d 114.

McLaughlin, Circuit Judge:

A grand jury in the Northern District of New York indicted Walter J. Butler, a union official and trustee of several employee benefit funds, for various financial improprieties. Butler was convicted, after a jury trial, on four counts in the indictment: racketeering (18 U.S.C. § 1962(c) (RICO)); causing false representations to be made in ERISA documents (18 U.S.C. § 1027); embezzlement of union funds (29 U.S.C. § 501(c)); and mail fraud (18 U.S.C. § 1341). The jury, however, acquitted Butler on the remaining six counts in the indictment. The district court for the Northern District of New York (Munson, Judge) then sentenced Butler to 21 months of imprisonment, a $30,000 fine, and ordered defendant to forfeit $29,295.79. * * *

Butler now challenges his convictions, principally on the ground of insufficient evidence. * * * For the following reasons, we affirm the convictions * * *.

Background

As a union official, Walter J. Butler wore a number of related hats. For almost thirty-five years, Butler served as president of Local 200, General Service Employees International Union ("Local 200"), representing over 16,000 employees in the Upstate New York region. He was also a trustee of four employee benefit funds affiliated with Local 200. In 1979, defendant became a vice president of Service Employees International Union ("International"). Additionally, from 1981–1988, Butler acted as secretary-treasurer of Local 362, a Florida-based union which, like Local 200, was under the umbrella of the International.

The employee benefit funds were managed by trustees. Half the trustees were either full-time employees of Local 200 (as was defendant) or rank-and-file members of Local 200; the other half were appointed by whatever employer participated in the fund. Before the enactment of

ERISA,[1] the benefit funds paid the trustees a fixed expense allowance for attending trustee meetings. ERISA changed this practice by making it unlawful for trustees of employee benefit funds, who are also full-time employees of either the participating employer or union, to receive fixed expense allowances from the funds; instead, benefit funds can reimburse such trustees only for actual expenses. The benefit funds for which defendant was a trustee thereafter agreed to reimburse their trustees for actual expenses.

At a meeting of Local 200's Executive Board, defendant announced that because of the changes mandated by ERISA, "there will probably be no expenses paid to the union and employer trustees of our pension and welfare funds." Because ERISA does not prevent a union from paying out of its own treasury—as distinct from the benefit funds—a fixed expense allowance to a trustee of a benefit fund, defendant urged that the Executive Board of the union resolve to pay fixed expense allowances to union trustees out of Local 200's treasury. The Executive Board passed such a resolution for the benefit of all the union trustees.

The Executive Board initially fixed the payments to union trustees at $50 per meeting attended for each individual fund. Some time later, defendant unilaterally increased this amount to $75, and later again to $100. In requesting these expense allowances from Local 200, defendant never told the Executive Board that the benefit funds were also paying the trustees for their actual expenses. By concealing this, defendant was able to double dip on expense payments.

Defendant's course of conduct also involved his son, W. James Butler ("Jimmy"). Jimmy worked for Local 200 as a part-time, summer employee from 1974 until he graduated from law school in 1981. In 1981, Jimmy became a full-time employee of Local 200, and, later, he also became an employee of the Central New York Welfare Fund, one of the Local 200 benefit funds.

Prior to 1978, Christmas bonuses and vacation pay were awarded to part-time employees in the discretion of Local 200's president (defendant) and its secretary-treasurer. In 1978, however, the Executive Board of Local 200 removed this discretion by passing a bonus and vacation pay schedule that limited such payments to full-time employees. Ignoring the resolution, defendant ordered that his son be paid Christmas bonuses and vacation pay for the summers Jimmy worked for Local 200. And after his son graduated to a full-time employee of both Local 200 and the Central New York Welfare Fund, defendant ordered that Jimmy be paid bonuses and vacation pay that exceeded the amount fixed in the schedule approved by the Executive Board.

Defendant's union activities also carried him to Florida, where, from 1981–1988, he served as secretary-treasurer to both Local 362, another affiliate of the International, and the Florida State Council, a loosely-

1. The Employee Retirement Income §§ 1001–1461.
Security Act of 1974, codified at 29 U.S.C.

knit association of Florida-based union locals. From August 1986 through July 1987, both Local 362 and Florida State Council made monthly payments to Butler to maintain a condominium in Dania, Florida, ostensibly as an office for Local 362.

In July 1987, Florida State Council decided to stop making the condominium payments. Then, Local 362's Executive Board also decided not to make any more rent payments for the condominium. To make up the shortfall, Butler asked Local 362 to pay him an expense allowance for his activities on its behalf without reminding anyone that he was already receiving reimbursement for actual expenses incurred while performing services for Local 362. In making his "request" for an expense allowance, defendant threatened any Board member who questioned his expenses with sanctions by the International. Not surprisingly, a resolution was thereafter passed providing an expense allowance to defendant, which he received on a monthly basis from August 1987 through April 1988. After this resolution was passed, defendant performed no further services for Local 362.

There is one final thread in this tapestry. As president of Local 200, defendant hired and set the compensation for Local 200's officers and employees. For their retirement, Local 200 employees were covered by the Service Employees International Union Affiliates Officers and Employees Pension Plan ("the Plan"). Local 200 was obligated to contribute 14% of each employee's gross compensation to the Plan. The Plan excluded from the definition of gross compensation "expenses paid or reimbursed to the Covered Persons."

Defendant split each employee's compensation into two checks, one denominated "salary" and the other, "expenses". However, defendant assured the employees that both components would constitute their gross compensation, and that whatever actual expenses they incurred would be reimbursed separately. When defendant completed the Plan's monthly remittance forms, he reported thereon only that portion of each employee's compensation that he had previously denominated as "salary." This underreporting of employees' actual compensation obviously reduced the contributions that Local 200 had to make to the Plan. The government suggested, at oral argument, that this savings allowed defendant to continue to loot the treasury of Local 200 to fund his other schemes.

* * *

DISCUSSION

* * *

Butler argues that the evidence was insufficient to support his convictions. To succeed in a challenge to the jury's verdict, defendant must bound some high hurdles. The evidence must be viewed in the light most favorable to the government and all permissible inferences must flow towards the jury's verdict. When we review the sufficiency of the evidence we need not be "convinced of guilt beyond a reasonable doubt."

Rather, where "any rational trier of fact could have found the essential elements of the crime beyond a reasonable doubt," we will not disturb the jury's verdict.

*　*　*

As to the charges that Butler embezzled funds from Locals 200 and 362 and from the employee benefit funds, defendant claims there was insufficient evidence to prove his fraudulent intent. We reject defendant's challenge.

Authorization from and benefit to the union are the controlling lodestars to determine whether a defendant acted with the fraudulent intent to deprive the union of its money. Accordingly, we have held that a union official charged with embezzling union funds, pursuant to 29 U.S.C. § 501(c), lacks the requisite criminal intent when the evidence establishes that he had a good-faith belief both that the funds were expended for the union's benefit and that the expenditures were authorized (or would be ratified) by the union.[2] To phrase it in the negative, authorization by the union or the trustees of a fund will not absolve a union official or fund trustee from criminal liability where that individual, acting with the intent to deprive the union of its property, lacks a good-faith belief that the expenditure is for the benefit of the union. Whether the defendant harbored a good-faith belief that an expenditure was for the benefit of the union is, of course, a jury question.

Defendant argues that, because all his expenditures were either authorized or would have been ratified, the only jury question was whether he had a good-faith belief that the expenditures were for the benefit of the unions or the funds. As to this issue, he claims the evidence was insufficient.

We cannot join defendant in his facile assumption that the expenditures were or would have been properly approved. In selling to Local 200's Executive Board his plan that union trustees should receive fixed expense payments for attending trustee meetings, defendant concealed from the Board that the union trustees were already being fully compensated for actual expenses. An authorization obtained without disclosure of such material information is obviously a nullity. To compound matters, the evidence indicated that defendant later increased the per-meeting payments from the Board "authorized" amount of $50, first to $75, and later to $100—all without Board approval.

As to the payments to defendant's son, the record makes clear that these payments were not authorized. After 1978, defendant had no authorization to pay vacation pay or Christmas bonuses to anyone but full-time employees. Yet, defendant continued to extend this largesse to his son, even though Jimmy did not become a full-time employee until

---

2. We have applied a similar standard when determining the criminal intent of a trustee of an employee benefit fund who is charged with embezzlement from such a fund under 18 U.S.C. § 664. *See* United States v. Snyder, 668 F.2d 686, 690–91 (2d Cir.1982).

1981. And, once Jimmy became a full-time employee, the payments made to him exceeded the amounts approved by Local 200's Executive Board in the bonus and vacation pay schedule.

Finally, as to the expense payments from Local 362, there was sufficient evidence for the jury to find that defendant used strong-arm tactics to obtain such authorization. We find it difficult to fathom that such authorization can be deemed to have been properly obtained; and the jury certainly could have found that defendant lacked a good-faith belief that these expenditures were *properly* authorized or would have been ratified, as the union "presumably would have objected if it had been able to speak freely." United States v. Silverman, 430 F.2d 106, 127 (2d Cir.1970).

Even accepting at face value defendant's argument that all these payments were authorized or would have been ratified, the evidence was still sufficient to establish his fraudulent intent. The record bristles with evidence that defendant lacked a good-faith belief that these expenditures would benefit the unions or the funds. We need cite only a few portions of the record.

When George Kennedy, assistant to the president of Local 200, eventually confronted defendant about the amounts he was receiving as fixed trustee meeting expense allowances—in addition to reimbursement for actual expenses—defendant stated, "George, I can't change my lifestyle." It was also proper for the jury to conclude that defendant lacked a good-faith belief that payments to his son—who, for a significant period of time, provided no services and yet received bonuses and vacation pay—were for the benefit of the union or the fund. Finally, as to Local 362, there was evidence that after defendant obtained "authorization" for a monthly expense allowance, he performed no services for Local 362, but simply collected his checks.

For the foregoing reasons, we hold that the evidence was sufficient to establish defendant's fraudulent intent.

* * *

Butler challenges the sufficiency of the evidence to establish that he knowingly made false statements in ERISA documents. We find the evidence sufficient.

The Plan required the union treasury to contribute 14% of each union employee's "Gross Compensation," which was defined to exclude "expenses paid or reimbursed" to the covered employee. Butler, as President of Local 200, had to file monthly remittance reports indicating each employee's gross compensation, and, based thereon, the amount Local 200 was required to contribute per employee.

The evidence established that defendant paid each employee with two checks, one denominated as "salary" and the other as "expenses." The "expenses" check, however, bore no relation to any expense, as all employees were separately reimbursed for their actual expenses. Rather, the "expenses" check amounted to straight compensation under another name. When George Kennedy asked defendant how this arrangement would affect his pension, defendant stated that, at some future date, the two checks ("salary" and "expenses") would be combined, and contributions to the Plan would then be based on the combined amount. And, defendant stated, so long as the contributions for the last three years of an employee's career were based on the combined amount, there would be no adverse effect on the employee's pension.

The jury could reasonably find that this artificial split in compensation was merely an artifice designed by defendant to reduce the amount that the Local 200 treasury was required to contribute to the Plan. Defendant's very own witness—who was called to testify that it is standard union practice not to make contributions based on expense allowances—admitted on cross-examination that contributions are not made on expense allowances only if those allowances are furnished with the intent that they will be spent on business expenses. Such clearly was not the case here. The jury was properly instructed as to the requirement that defendant knowingly made these misrepresentations, see United States v. Tolkow, 532 F.2d 853, 858–59 (2d Cir.1976), and found that the statements were made knowingly. We see no reason to disturb this conclusion.

[The court considered and rejected the defendant's remaining arguments, affirming all counts.]

Notes

1. In *Butler*, the court found that the payments at issue had not been authorized. Lack of authorization may be proven when the defendants simply fail to obtain requisite authorization. Or, even if authorization is present, it may be suspect, either because it was coerced, or as in *Butler*, because not all necessary information was provided to those individuals authorizing the expenditure.

As with most benefit plans, those at issue in *Butler* were governed by a group of trustees, some of whom were selected by management while others were selected by the Local's membership. Do you believe that authorization is present if these trustees (in lieu of the full membership) approve expenditures in question? That such authorization was given is a common, and sometimes appropriate, defense invoked by defendants who are accused of embezzling or misappropriating assets of a benefit plan or union. What facts and circumstances would support such a theory? What facts and circumstances would rebut it?

2. In *Butler* the Second Circuit held that even if the conduct at issue had been authorized, the government still proved its case under § 664 by showing that the expenditures did not benefit the fund. In this manner, lack of benefit becomes an additional element the government must prove once authorization is present. How might benefit be shown in *Butler*? Could it be argued, for example, that adequate compensation (including the payments at issue) is needed to attract qualified persons to serve as trustees, and that the "compensation plan" Butler arranged met this need? Does the disparity

between benefits earned by plan beneficiaries and by trustees pursuant to this arrangement undercut this argument in *Butler*?

3. Note the Second Circuit's reliance on 29 U.S.C. § 501(c) (regarding embezzlement from a union) when interpreting 18 U.S.C. § 664. In United States v. Andreen, 628 F.2d 1236 (9th Cir.1980), the United States Court of Appeals for the Ninth Circuit provided a helpful discussion of § 664 and its relationship to § 501(c):

"By enacting § 664 in 1962, Congress made it a federal crime to embezzle, steal, or willfully and unlawfully convert or abstract assets of an employee welfare or pension benefit plan. The legislative history indicates that the intended purpose of § 664 was to preserve welfare and pension funds for the protection of those entitled to their benefits. The statute [prohibits embezzlement from an employee welfare benefit plan.]

" 'Embezzlement' * * * encompasses the fraudulent appropriation of the property of another by one in lawful possession thereof. The concept of unlawful conversion encompasses the use of property, placed in one's custody for a limited purpose, in an unauthorized manner or to an unauthorized extent.

"The statute goes beyond traditional concepts of embezzlement, however, and imposes liability for an intentional breach of special fiduciary duties imposed by other regulatory statutes or governing instruments. The statute defines an offense 'the common thread [of which] is that the defendant, at some stage of the game, has taken another person's property or caused it to be taken, knowing that the other person would not have wanted that to be done.' United States v. Silverman, 430 F.2d 106, 126–27 (2d Cir.1970). The essence of the crime is theft and in the context of union funds or pension plans the offense includes a taking or appropriation that is unauthorized, if accomplished with specific criminal intent. In this respect lack of authorization may be shown if the diversion is substantially inconsistent with the fiduciary purposes and objectives of the union funds or pension plan, as set forth by statutes, bylaws, charters or trust documents which govern uses of the funds in question. Whatever imprecision attends this definition is remedied substantially by the requirement of scienter, which is an essential element of the crime. The act to be criminal must be willful, which means an act done with a fraudulent intent or a bad purpose or an evil motive.

"The decided cases interpreting section 664 are few, but a number of opinions have addressed the meaning of a like statute, which prohibits embezzlements from union funds. Parallel language was used in 29 U.S.C. § 501(c) and 18 U.S.C. § 664. Furthermore, Congress passed the two statutes for a similar purpose: to preserve the designated funds for those entitled to their benefits."

In *Andreen*, authorization was present and fully informed but unwise. The Ninth Circuit invalidated the authorization for this reason. "[L]ack of authorization may be shown if the diversion is substantially inconsistent with the fiduciary purposes and objectives of the union funds or pension plan * * *." Is this approach the equivalent of examining whether the expenditures benefitted the fund? If so, is this going too far, especially when criminal liability is at issue? After all, if the appropriate parties approved an expenditure, however imprudent their decision may be, is it appropriate for a prosecutor or a jury to second-guess the authorization?

As in most white collar prosecutions, some of the elements in a § 664 action can be quite technical. As you review the next two cases, United States v. Bell, 22 F.3d 274 (11th Cir.1994) and United States v. Grizzle, 933 F.2d 943 (11th Cir.1991), decide what you think: are technical cases appropriate for criminal prosecutions or do such actions more properly belong in civil or administrative arenas?

UNITED STATES v. BELL

United States Court of Appeals, Eleventh Circuit (1994).
22 F.3d 274.

CLARK, SENIOR CIRCUIT JUDGE.

Defendant-appellant Ronnie A. Bell pled guilty to charges of embezzlement, making false statements, mail fraud, and conspiracy to commit these crimes. After his guilty plea but before his sentencing, Bell filed with the district court a motion to dismiss certain counts of the indictment and a motion to withdraw his guilty plea. The district court denied both motions. We agree with Bell that several counts of the indictment, including some counts to which he pled guilty, fail to state an offense as alleged. Accordingly, we vacate Bell's convictions and remand the case for further proceedings.

BACKGROUND FACTS

Bell and his co-defendant, James E. Cushion,[1] were the administrator and assistant administrator, respectively, of two funds established for the benefit of members of the International Longshoremen's Association (the "ILA"). The first fund, known as the Welfare and Pension Fund (the "Pension Fund"), was established to provide retirement income and health benefits to eligible members of the ILA in Jacksonville, Florida. The Pension Fund is an employee welfare benefit plan and an employee pension benefit plan within the meaning of and subject to the provisions of title I of the Employee Retirement Income Security Act of 1974 ("ERISA").[2] The second fund, known as the Container Royalty Fund (the "Royalty Fund"), was established to provide supplemental income to eligible members of the ILA in Jacksonville. This fund consists of the accumulated royalty payments made by the Jacksonville Maritime Association for each container that passes through the Jacksonville port. These royalty payments are distributed at the end of each taxable year to eligible members of the ILA. The Royalty Fund is a legally separate

---

1. Cushion has not appealed his conviction; this appeal involves Bell only.

2. 29 U.S.C. §§ 1001–1145.

entity from the Pension Fund and is not subject to the provisions of ERISA.

The charges against Bell and Cushion arose out of their alleged unauthorized issuance of checks, made out to themselves and others, written on accounts of the Pension Fund and the Royalty Fund. The superseding indictment against Bell and Cushion contains 36 counts. Count 1 charges Bell and Cushion with conspiracy to embezzle funds from the Pension Fund and from the Royalty Fund, to make false statements in connection with documents required to be filed under title I of ERISA, and to commit mail fraud, all in violation of 18 U.S.C. § 371. Counts 2–22 charge Bell and Cushion with embezzlement from the Pension Fund, and counts 23–30 charge them with embezzlement from the Royalty Fund, all in violation of 18 U.S.C. § 664. Counts 31–33 charge Bell and Cushion with making false statements in relation to documents required to be filed under ERISA, in violation of 18 U.S.C. § 1027. Finally, counts 34–36 charge Bell and Cushion with mail fraud, in violation of 18 U.S.C. § 1341.

Pursuant to a written plea agreement with the government, Bell pled guilty to counts 1 (conspiracy), counts 19 and 20 (embezzlement from the Pension Fund), counts 29 and 30 (embezzlement from the Royalty Fund), count 32 (making false statements in relation to documents required to be filed under ERISA), and count 36 (mail fraud). Prior to his sentencing, however, Bell filed a motion to withdraw his guilty plea. He also filed a motion to dismiss certain counts of the indictment, arguing that several counts of the indictment failed to charge an offense; specifically, he argued that his alleged embezzlement from the Royalty Fund did not constitute a violation of 18 U.S.C. § 664 because the Royalty Fund was not subject to the provisions of ERISA. The district court denied both motions and, subsequently, sentenced Bell to 30 months in prison. Bell filed this appeal.

DISCUSSION

Bell contends that the district court erred in declining to dismiss those counts of the indictment charging him with embezzlement from the Royalty Fund and in declining to permit him to withdraw his guilty plea. He seeks vacation of his convictions and an opportunity to have his case tried before a jury.

* * *

Bell was charged with embezzling from the Royalty Fund in violation of 18 U.S.C. § 664, which provides as follows:

> Any person who embezzles, steals, or unlawfully and willfully abstracts or converts to his own use or to the use of another, any of the moneys, funds, securities, premiums, credits, property, or other assets of any employee welfare benefit plan or employee pension benefit plan, or of any fund connected therewith, shall be fined not more than $10,000, or imprisoned not more than five years, or both.

As used in this section, the term "any employee welfare benefit plan or employee pension benefit plan" means any employee benefit plan subject to any provision of title I of the Employee Retirement Income Security Act of 1974.

It is undisputed that the Royalty Fund is not an employee benefit plan subject to the provisions of ERISA. The government relies on the "fund connected therewith" language. The government points out that the Royalty Fund and the Pension Fund were both established for the benefit of ILA members in Jacksonville and that the two funds shared a common administrator; thus, the government argues, the two funds are sufficiently "connected" to bring the Royalty Fund within the purview of § 664.

The parties have not cited and we have not located any case law construing the "fund connected therewith" language of § 664. The broad reading urged upon us by the government would render two funds "connected" merely because they share common beneficiaries and administrators. We have reviewed the legislative history of § 664, and we find nothing in that history to indicate that Congress intended such a broad reading of the "fund connected therewith" language. To the contrary, the legislative history refers to § 664 as "a provision making it a crime to embezzle, steal, or unlawfully and willfully abstract or convert to his own use or to the use of another any of the assets of an employee welfare or pension benefit plan." There is no reference in the legislative history to the "fund connected therewith" language and no indication that § 664 was intended to apply to any funds other than those governed by ERISA. The Container Royalty Fund is not governed by ERISA and is not subject to the provisions of § 664.

We reject the government's broad reading of the "fund connected therewith" language, and we hold that two funds are not "connected" for purposes of § 664 merely because they share common beneficiaries and administrators. We need not and do not decide what sort of relationship would render two funds "connected" within the meaning of the statute. We only hold that common beneficiaries and administrators, without more, is insufficient.

Thus, to the extent the indictment in this case charges Bell with embezzlement from the Royalty Fund in violation of § 664, it fails to state an offense. * * *

UNITED STATES v. GRIZZLE

United States Court of Appeals, Eleventh Circuit, 1991.
933 F.2d 943.

DUBINA, CIRCUIT JUDGE.

Appellants, Douglas Richard Grizzle ("Grizzle") and Grizzle Insulation Company (the "Company"), were convicted of violating 18 U.S.C. § 662 (receiving stolen property) and § 664 (embezzlement from employee benefit plan). Grizzle was also convicted of violating 18 U.S.C.

§§ 1001 and 1002 (making false statements to any department or agency of the United States). For the reasons which follow, we affirm the appellants' convictions.

I. FACTS

Grizzle was the president of the Company, which employed members of International Association of Heat and Frost Insulation and Asbestos Workers Local #48 ("Local 48") to perform insulation work. The Company was a member of the Insulation Contractors Association ("ICA") of Atlanta, Georgia, an employers' association, which negotiated collective bargaining agreements with Local 48 regarding the terms and conditions governing wages, working conditions and fringe benefits, including vacation benefits, of its members. Under the terms of the collective bargaining agreements, Grizzle agreed to withhold from each employee's wages $1.00 per hour worked and to contribute these funds to the Local 48 Vacation Fund (the "Vacation Fund") as directed by the Vacation Fund trustees.

The Vacation Fund was established by Local 48 and the ICA of Atlanta on December 1, 1981, pursuant to a declaration and agreement of trust. The Vacation Fund was to be funded solely by employee contributions of after tax income and was essentially a savings plan whereby the money would be invested in interest-bearing accounts with disbursements to employee participants paid out twice a year. The parties stipulated that the Vacation Fund was an employee benefit plan subject to Title I of the Employee Retirement Income Security Act of 1974, 29 U.S.C. § 1001, et seq. ("ERISA").

Three representatives of the ICA and three representatives of Local 48 were designated as trustees of the Vacation Fund and were responsible for directing the administration of the Vacation Fund through Light and Associates ("L & A"). As administrator, L & A monitored the incoming contributions, which employers forwarded directly to the Vacation Fund's interest-bearing checking account, calculated the benefits due each employee and made payments to employees twice a year of the vacation monies accrued on their behalf. Each month the Company received from L & A blank remittance forms which were to be returned with the calculations of the month's Vacation Fund contributions deducted from employees' wages and paid to the Vacation Fund. L & A directed Grizzle to remit contributions directly to the Vacation Fund's bank account.

From December 1985 through May 1987, Grizzle and his son did not make timely returns of the monthly remittance forms to L & A or timely payments of employee contributions to the Vacation Fund's bank account. During this period, delinquency notices for the nonpayment of employee contributions were sent each month to Grizzle. An audit of the Vacation Fund revealed that from October 1986 to May 1987, Grizzle withheld $11,808.50 from employees' paychecks as Vacation Fund contributions, which were not forwarded to the Vacation Fund's bank account although they were due and payable to the Vacation Fund on a monthly basis.

In May 1987, Local 48 stopped supplying union members to work for the Company. Later that month, Grizzle and his son formed a new company, G & G, which performed work as a subcontractor at a number of federal construction/renovation sites. G & G eventually went out of business.

The United States Department of Labor requires that certified payrolls be submitted for all work done on federal job sites to ensure that a certain wage scale is being met. Employers are required to list employee names, social security numbers and pay rates as well as taxes, gross wages, fringe benefits, union dues and vacation pay withheld from pay checks. Grizzle admitted authorizing his son to complete and sign the certified payrolls or forms which are the subject of the indictment. Grizzle's son admitted that he certified on each payroll that union dues and vacation funds had been or would be paid to the appropriate programs. At the time of trial, both Grizzle and his son admitted that the funds were collected and were due and payable to the Vacation Fund.

II. Procedural Background

Grizzle, his son, and the Company were indicted by a federal grand jury on charges that they embezzled ERISA funds and on charges of making false statements on forms required by the United States Department of Labor. After an eight-day jury trial, Douglas Grizzle was convicted on all counts, the Company was convicted of embezzling ERISA funds and Gregory Grizzle was acquitted on all counts.

Grizzle and the Company filed their notice of appeal in which they raise the following issues for appellate review: (1) whether employee contributions to the Vacation Fund, which were withheld from employees' paychecks but not delivered to the fund, were fund moneys or assets as specified in 18 U.S.C. § 664; (2) whether a conviction under 18 U.S.C. § 664 requires proof of a fiduciary relationship; * * * .

III. Discussion

A. Fund moneys or assets

Grizzle and the Company were convicted of embezzling and converting moneys and funds of an employee welfare benefit plan under 18 U.S.C. § 664, which provides:

Any person who embezzles, steals or unlawfully and willfully abstracts or converts to his own use or to the use of another, any of the moneys, funds, securities, premiums, credits, property, or other assets of any employee welfare benefit plan [subject to Title I of the Employee Retirement Income Security Act of 1974] or of any fund connected therewith, shall be fined not more than $10,000, or imprisoned for not more than five years, or both.[2]

2. Specifically, Grizzle and the Company were charged and convicted, under Count I of the indictment, of the "embezzlement and unlawful and willful conversion to their

Grizzle and the Company contend that the evidence at trial showed that the money they are accused of embezzling never became a part of the Vacation Fund. They argue that fund money is money received by the administrators on behalf of the trustees, and since Grizzle never delivered the money to the administrators, the money could not have been taken from the "fund."

The government maintains that assets of employee benefit plans subject to ERISA include employee contributions to benefit plans which are withheld from employees' paychecks by employers though not yet delivered to the benefit plan. See Pension Benefit Guaranty Corporation v. Solmsen, 671 F.Supp. 938 (E.D.N.Y.1987). In *Solmsen*, an employer who had assumed the duty to forward employee contributions to the benefit plan but allocated the monies to corporate expenses rather than to the employee benefit plan, was held liable for the misuse of plan assets. The *Solmsen* court squarely rejected the defendant's argument that the employee contributions were not "plan assets" until they were contributed to the plan. *Id.* at 946.

Subsequent to *Solmsen*, the Department of Labor issued a regulation which clarified that "plan assets" for purposes of Title I of ERISA include employee contributions. See 29 C.F.R. § 2510.3–102 (1989). This regulation states:

> ... [T]he assets of the plan include amounts ... that a participant ... has withheld from his wages by an employer, for contribution to the plan as of the earliest date on which such contributions can reasonably be segregated from the employer's general assets, not to exceed 90 days from the date on which such amounts ... would otherwise have been payable to the participant in cash (in the case of amounts withheld by an employer from the participant's wages).[3]

Thus, the assets of employee benefit plans subject to ERISA include employee contributions to benefit plans which are withheld from employees' paychecks and for deposit into their benefit plans, even though the contributions have not actually been delivered to the benefit plan.

In the present case, the special duties imposed by ERISA, federal regulations, the collective bargaining agreements and the Declaration and Agreement of Trust regarding employee contributions to the Vacation Fund indicate that the funds withheld from the employees are plan assets entrusted to Grizzle to be accounted for by him until such time as they are remitted to the Vacation Fund. Grizzle's argument that these employee contributions are not specifically identified as moneys of the

own use the sum of $11,808.50, moneys and funds of the Vacation Trust Fund of the Asbestos Workers Local Number 48, Fringe Benefit Fund, an employee welfare benefit fund as defined in Title I of the Employee Retirement Income Security Act of 1974 (ERISA)."

3. Although this regulation was not passed until after Grizzle and the Company

had committed the actions for which they were convicted, the regulation was based on and is consistent with the provisions of ERISA which require that plan assets be held in trust and that "plan assets shall never inure to the benefit of an employer." 29 U.S.C. § 1103.

Vacation Trust in the Agreement and Declaration of Trust is misleading, as the Declaration of Trust does not purport to set forth an exhaustive definition of assets and moneys of the "Trust Fund."[4] Instead we are persuaded that the employee contributions to the Local 48 Vacation Fund were moneys and funds of an employee benefit plan subject to Title I of ERISA.

B.   FIDUCIARY RELATIONSHIP

After the government rested its case, Grizzle filed a motion for judgment of acquittal on the basis that there was no evidence he was a fiduciary of the Vacation Trust. He argues that his motion should have been granted because he was not a fiduciary or a trustee whose job is to receive, hold and administer the funds. Thus, he claims he could not be convicted under § 664 because he was not a fiduciary. Whether a fiduciary relationship is required for conviction under 18 U.S.C. § 664 is a legal issue subject to de novo review by this court.

Criminal culpability under § 664 does not require that a defendant hold any particular status in relation to an employee benefit plan or fund connected with a plan or that he or she act as a fiduciary with respect to an employee welfare benefit plan transaction. Congress intended the statute to be read broadly to include any person who misuses or misappropriates contributions intended for deposit in an employee welfare benefit plan. We find that the language "any person" in § 664 includes an employer who agrees to withhold wages from employees' paychecks for deposit in a welfare benefit plan.

Additionally, the government presented evidence at trial that Grizzle was a de facto fiduciary of the Vacation Fund to the extent that he exercised authority or control over the employee contributions by withholding those contributions from employees' paychecks. A fiduciary is defined by ERISA as follows:

> ... [A] person is a fiduciary with respect to a plan to the extent (i) he exercises any discretionary authority or discretionary control respecting management of such plan or exercises any authority or control respecting the management or disposition of its assets.

29 U.S.C. § 1002(21)(A). The evidence at trial showed that Grizzle withheld employee contributions to the Vacation Fund pursuant to collective bargaining agreements and the Declaration and Agreement of Trust for the Vacation Fund. Grizzle and his son both admitted that they received approximately $11,808.50 from their employees that was to be delivered to the Vacation Fund. This amount is still due the Fund.

The record demonstrates that Grizzle exercised discretionary authority and control respecting the disposition of the employees' contributions. Accordingly, we agree with the government that Grizzle was a de

---

4. Article I, Section 8 of the Declaration and Agreement of Trust states: " 'Trust,' 'Trust Fund,' and 'Fund,' as used herein, shall mean the entire trust estate of the Asbestos Workers #48 Vacation Fund as it may from time to time be constituted, including but not limited to, all funds received in the form of contributions, together with all contracts. . . . ''

facto fiduciary; however, a fiduciary relationship is not required for conviction under § 664. The statute clearly states that "*any person* who embezzles . . ." any moneys or funds of an employee welfare benefit plan is subject to conviction. (emphasis added).

* * *

Notes

1. As the *Bell* and *Grizzle* cases indicate, the complexity of white collar crimes presents special hurdles for prosecutors, and opportunities for defendants. As the excerpts from the three cases included in this Note demonstrate, it is not only the federal prosecutor who utilizes § 664 and must master its technicalities. Section 664 regularly is included as a predicate act in civil RICO actions.

A. Sometimes the federal government brings the civil RICO action. In 1995, for example, the United States sought injunctive relief against Mason Tenders District Council of Greater New York, 1995 ("Mason Tenders") and individual members of a reputed organized crime family in a civil RICO action which alleged racketeering activity encompassing §§ 664 and 1341 (mail fraud). The government alleged that:

> "La Cosa Nostra is so intimately linked with the activity of the District Council and its affiliates, and that it wields such control, that the District Council leadership ultimately represents the interests of organized crime—particularly of the Genovese Family— rather than those of its members. * * * La Cosa Nostra generally controlled and detrimentally affected the District Council and its related activities through acts of extortion, lack of oversight, breach of fiduciary obligations, no-show jobs, kickbacks from service providers, corruption by the Trust Funds Administrator, and corruption by Employer Trustees."[v]

The 110 alleged acts of racketeering activity included claims of conversion of union trust funds through payment for a "no-show" job.[w] The government sought to enjoin the individual defendants from associating with labor unions, employee benefit funds and the construction and asbestos industries.[x] The District Court granted most of the relief requested by the government.

B. Private parties also make use of § 664 as a predicate act of "racketeering activity" under civil RICO. For example, participants in a health insurance plan offered by Blue Cross and Blue Shield of Ohio (BCBSO) brought suit under RICO alleging violations of § 664[y] due to BCBS's failure to pass discounts negotiated with providers on to participants. The court dismissed the suit, following similar reasoning to that in *Bell*, *supra*, that the property at issue was not an asset belonging to an employee welfare benefit plan or to a "fund connected therewith:"

---

v. United States v. Mason Tenders District Council of Greater New York, 1995 WL 679245 (S.D.N.Y.1995).

w. *Id.*

x. *Id.*

y. Everson v. Blue Cross and Blue Shield of Ohio, 898 F.Supp. 532, 542 (N.D.Ohio 1994).

"[T]he amended complaint also alleges conversion of employee welfare benefit fund assets in violation of 18 U.S.C. § 664. Section 664 imposes liability on any person who "embezzles, steals, or unlawfully and willfully abstracts or converts to his own use or to the use of another, any of the moneys, funds, . . . or other assets of any employee welfare benefit plan . . . or of any fund connected therewith. . . . " 18 U.S.C. § 664.

"Thus, to assert a § 664 violation, plaintiffs must allege not only that defendant has converted money, funds, or other assets, but also that the misappropriated assets belonged to an employee welfare benefit plan or to a "fund connected therewith." *Id.* Nowhere in the amended complaint do plaintiffs allege that BCBSO converted assets of an employee welfare benefit plan or that it converted moneys or assets of any fund connected with an employee benefit plan. Nor can plaintiffs make these allegations. An insurance policy is the plan's only asset and plaintiffs do not allege that defendants converted it. Furthermore, there is no "fund" connected with this employee benefit plan that has been brought to the court's attention.

"Although plaintiffs attempt to track the 'fund connected therewith' language of § 664, the complaint merely alleges conversion of 'monies and assets connected with employee welfare benefit plans in which plaintiffs . . . are and were participants.' As stated earlier in this opinion, although the standard in ruling on a 12(b)(6) motion is decidedly liberal, it requires more than the bare assertion of legal conclusions. A 'complaint must contain either direct or inferential allegations respecting all the material elements to sustain a recovery under some legal theory.' *Id.* Plaintiffs did not allege the existence of a fund connected with the employee plan. Other allegations in the complaint assert only that BCBSO failed to pay enough money to health care providers and that, as a result, plaintiffs were required to pay higher copayments than they otherwise should have paid. The only moneys involved were those which belonged to plaintiffs themselves. Although this practice may or may not be a crime, it is not a violation of § 664 upon which a RICO claim can be based."

C.   In Young v. West Coast Industrial Relations Assn., 763 F.Supp. 64 (D.Del.1991) private parties tried again, also unsuccessfully, to use § 664 in a civil RICO action. A Teamsters Local Union and employee members of the union brought suit under RICO against their employers alleging racketeering activity under § 1341 (mail fraud) and § 664 (embezzlement from a pension fund). The plaintiffs also alleged tortious interference with contract rights under the Labor Management Relations Act. Once again, difficulty lay in the technicalities of § 664, in particular whether the defendants' conduct was "embezzlement" within § 664.

"In paragraph 49 of the amended complaint, Plaintiffs allege that Defendants WCIRA [West Coast Industrial Relations Association, Inc., a labor relations consultant] and the Tiganis, J. Paul Tigani,

James Tigani, Sr., James Tigani, Jr., and Robert Tigani, officers, agents and/or representatives of the various wine, spirits and beverage distributors, on two or more occasions, knowingly induced and caused the Employers to refuse to make Pension and Health and Welfare contributions as required by the collective bargaining agreements. Plaintiffs contend that Defendants' conduct constitutes embezzlement within the meaning of 18 U.S.C. § 664 and thus are 'predicate acts' of racketeering activity as defined in Section 1961(1) of RICO.

"The elements of a Section 664 embezzlement claim include: (1) the unauthorized; (2) taking or appropriation; (3) of union benefit plan funds; (4) with specific criminal intent. United States v. Andreen, 628 F.2d 1236, 1240–41 (9th Cir.1980). In order to have specific criminal intent, 'the criminal act must have been willful, which means an act done with a fraudulent intent or bad purpose or an evil motive.' Andreen, 628 F.2d at 1241 * * *.

"While the Court is aware that Section 664 'goes beyond the traditional concepts of embezzlement', Andreen, 628 F.2d at 1241, the Court finds the specifics of Plaintiffs' rather novel theory of embezzlement somewhat troubling. In the amended complaint, the Plaintiffs describe the basis of their legal theory in the following manner:

> 'The contracts involved in the instant case create an obligation to contribute to various employee benefit funds upon the employees' performance of services. Upon performance of the services, the obligation to contribute immediately arises. Additionally, at the same time the obligation to contribute arises, the amounts owed immediately become fund assets. Hence, the failure to remit the contributions constitutes embezzlement squarely within the scope of § 664.'

"The Court notes, however, that the reported caselaw is silent as to whether the failure to remit monies to an employee benefit fund constitutes embezzlement. Rather, all of the relevant cases address the unauthorized theft, abstraction or conversion of assets already paid into the benefit fund. Accordingly, the linchpin of Plaintiffs' legal analysis is the proposition that unpaid employer contributions to an employee benefit fund constitute assets of that fund not only when those contributions are paid into the fund but also at the moment when the contributions are due and owing.

"In Galgay v. Gangloff, 677 F.Supp. 295 (M.D.Pa.1987), the court confronted an analogous situation where defendants had failed to contribute to an employee benefit fund in accordance with a collective bargaining agreement. The plaintiffs alleged that because the unpaid contributions were assets of the fund, the defendants were fiduciaries of that fund who had breached their fiduciary duties. The plaintiffs grounded their argument upon statutory language in ERISA which provides that 'a person is a fiduciary with respect to plan to the extent (i) he exercises ... any authority or control respecting management or disposition of its assets.... ' 29 U.S.C.

§ 1002(21)(A). The plaintiffs reasoned that because the defendants retained for their own benefit contributions owed to the fund, the defendants failed to act "solely in the interest of the participants and beneficiaries" thus breaching their fiduciary duties to the fund.

"The *Galgay* court noted that the primary issue with respect to the plaintiffs' allegations was whether employer contributions purportedly owed to the benefit fund constituted assets under the circumstances alleged. Finding the statute and the scant caselaw to be of no assistance, the court turned to the language of the collective bargaining agreement. The wage agreement, to which all the defendants were allegedly either directly or indirectly a party, provided 'Title to all the monies paid into and/or due and owing said fund shall be vested in and remain exclusively in the trustees of the fund. . . .' *Id.* (emphasis added). Finding the unambiguous language of the wage agreement critical, the *Galgay* court held that by virtue of the wage agreement any delinquent employer contribution became a vested asset of the employee benefit fund when it was due and owing. *Id.*

"In the instant case, the Court must also turn to the express language of the collective bargaining agreement as it is unable to find assistance in the embezzlement statute or the relevant caselaw. Article 48, the provision which governs the terms of the Employer's contributions to the employee pension fund, makes no reference as to when monies paid into the fund vest. The provision merely states that the 'Employer shall contribute into the Pension Fund' and that failure to contribute as specified shall render the employer liable for 'all arrears in payment' as well as attorney fees, court costs, other damages and ten percent in liquidated damages. *Id.*

"The above language leads the Court to believe that the delinquent contributions are to be treated as a debt owed to the benefit fund and not as a vested asset. Accordingly, the Court cannot find that Defendants, by allegedly inducing the Employers not to pay the purported delinquent contributions, embezzled those contributions within the meaning of Section 664.

"While the Court does not want to be understood as endorsing a general rule that unpaid contributions may never constitute a benefit fund asset, the unusual circumstances in the instant case counsel against extending the reach of Section 664 in the manner urged by the Plaintiffs. Otherwise any time one party to a contract failed to remit monies or property in accordance with the terms of that contract, they could be held liable for embezzlement or conversion and, in the case of union funds, be subjected to RICO's harsh sanctions. Accordingly, the portions of Counts I and II which allege that Defendants violated 18 U.S.C. § 664 are dismissed."

    2. Another nuance in applying § 664 is whether the defendant must hold the assets at issue as a fiduciary before becoming liable under § 664. Section 664 does not explicitly require such a relationship. It simply criminalizes embezzlement of assets of any "employee welfare benefit plan or employee pension benefit plan or any fund connected therewith. * * *."

However, § 664 applies only to funds protected by ERISA and ERISA confers 'fiduciary' status on any person who exercises any discretionary authority respecting management of the plan. Thus, there are two questions: First, is it necessary that a defendant be in a position to exercise 'discretionary authority' over plan assets before becoming liable under ERISA? (If so, is the low-level clerk who has no such authority but steals thousands from a benefit plan immune from prosecution under § 664?) Second, if discretionary authority over plan assets is a requirement, what is needed to satisfy this requirement? In excerpts from the next case, United States v. Panepinto, 818 F.Supp. 48 (E.D.N.Y.1993), the court assumed there was such a requirement but found it satisfied fairly easily. Do you agree with this court's approach?

"Defendants say they did not 'embezzle' assets from the Funds but at worst merely breached their contract with the Union.

"Were the Agreement an ordinary contract for the payment of wages, perhaps defendants could be held only in a civil action. But here the amounts agreed upon as destined for the Funds were held in trust by the defendants for the benefit of others. Moreover, in order to preserve the pension and welfare benefit assets of employees and recognizing the potential for fraud where employers act as intermediaries between employees and welfare benefit funds, Congress has chosen pervasively to regulate benefit plans, and those who hold assets under them, by enacting the Employee Retirement Security Act of 1974 (ERISA), 29 U.S.C. §§ 1001–1461.

"A central figure of ERISA is to make a person 'a fiduciary with respect to a plan' if that person 'exercises any discretionary authority or discretionary control respecting management of such plan or exercises any authority or control respecting management or disposition or its assets.' 29 U.S.C. § 1002(21)(A)(i).

"Once the defendants knowingly failed to make required contributions to the Funds, they exercised control respecting the disposition of the assets of an employee welfare benefit plan. They held those funds as fiduciaries, and under 29 U.S.C. § 1104(a)(1), they were required to discharge their duty 'solely in the interest of the participants and beneficiaries' of the Funds.

"The indictment alleges that defendants conspired to convert and did convert these funds which had been entrusted to their care by nonparticipating manufacturers. Such conversion by one to whom assets have been entrusted constitutes embezzlement within the meaning of 18 U.S.C. § 664. The indictment alleges the requisite elements in Counts One and Two."

B. FRAUD UPON A LABOR ORGANIZATION

Title 29, United States Code, § 501(c), is the primary statutory authority used to prosecute those who embezzle from labor organizations. Note that unlike § 664, which allows for prosecution of "any person," § 501(c) allows for prosecution of only certain persons who violate its terms. Section 501(c) provides: "any person who embezzles, steals, or unlawfully and willfully abstracts or converts to his own use, or the use of another, any of the moneys, funds, securities, property, or other assets of a labor organization of which he is an officer, or by which he is employed, directly or indirectly, shall be fined not more than $10,000 or imprisoned for not more than five years, or both."

The purpose of § 501(c) is "to protect general union membership from the corruption, however novel, of union officers and employees."[z] However, the same question arises in § 501(c) cases as with § 664 cases: is there a violation when the union, either through its leadership or by vote of rank and file members, authorizes the use of union funds challenged as illegal? The next two cases, United States v. Stockton, 788 F.2d 210 (4th Cir.1986), and United States v. Floyd, 882 F.2d 235 (7th Cir.1989), discuss this issue. As you read these cases, note the different approaches taken by the two courts.

UNITED STATES v. STOCKTON

United States Court of Appeals, Fourth Circuit, 1986.
788 F.2d 210.

MURNAGHAN, CIRCUIT JUDGE.

Ellison Stockton appeals from his conviction of embezzlement of the assets of a labor union in violation of 29 U.S.C. § 501(c). Stockton makes four arguments: (1) that the district court's instructions to the jury incorrectly stated the elements of the statutory violation; (2) that there was insufficient evidence to support the jury's verdict; (3) that certain testimony claimed to be prejudicial should not have been admitted; and (4) that a new trial should have been granted on the basis of newly discovered evidence.

At the time of the events in question here, Ellison Stockton was the president of Local 239 of the United Automobile, Aerospace, and Agricultural Implement Workers of America (UAW), a labor organization with over 5,000 active members in the Baltimore area. Stockton was first elected to the presidency of the local in 1961, and remained in office until 1967. In 1969, he was reelected to the presidency, an office he retained until the time of his conviction.

The building housing the union's offices was owned and managed by an affiliated corporation called the Local 239 Holding Company. The union's Executive Board also served as the board of directors of the Holding Company, and Stockton acted as chairman of the Holding Company board. The Holding Company board met approximately once each year. Stockton apparently had great influence over the other Holding Company directors. Members of the Holding Company board who testified at trial could recall no instance in which the board had defeated a proposal made by Stockton.

z. United States v. Sullivan, 498 F.2d   146, 150 (1st Cir.1974).

Members of the Holding Company board also testified that the board had effectively delegated to Stockton the authority to make decisions concerning the day-to-day cleaning and maintenance of the building. Their testimony indicated that the members of the board did not inquire into such matters as long as things were running smoothly.

In late 1976, the union contracted with Herbert Branch Janitorial Service, Inc. for cleaning the union offices. Branch's monthly charge was $694.00, plus $291.00 for an initial cleaning. Branch submitted monthly invoices and was paid by checks sent through the mail. After only two months, the union terminated its contract with Branch. Stockton notified his office staff that he had engaged the M. Woods Janitorial Service to perform maintenance services at the union offices. Stockton instructed his secretary to draw checks payable to M. Woods in the amount of $200.00 per week. The checks were co-signed by the vice-president of the local, Rodney Trump, and left on Stockton's desk to be picked up by M. Woods.

The government's evidence tended to show that the M. Woods Janitorial Service was fictitious. Stockton never provided his staff or other members of the Holding Company board with an address or telephone number for M. Woods. No written contract was signed, and the office staff never prepared any forms or records relating to the janitorial service. There was no telephone listing for an M. Woods Janitorial Service in the greater Baltimore area. No corporate charter was registered under the name with the Maryland Department of Assessments and Taxation. No witness ever observed a vehicle or other equipment bearing the name "M. Woods Janitorial Service." One union member's grand jury testimony, which was introduced at trial, indicated that, to her knowledge, the M. Woods Janitorial Service was a "joke," and that the cleaning was being done by union members. The prosecution also established that all of the checks drawn to the order of the M. Woods Janitorial Service were deposited in one of Stockton's three bank accounts. There was expert testimony that at least one of the "M. Woods" endorsements was written by Stockton's wife, Mildred. Mildred Stockton had used the surname Woods before her marriage.

The evidence indicated that regular cleaning of the union offices was performed by someone. However, there was testimony that the level of cleaning during the tenure of the M. Woods Janitorial Service was not always satisfactory.

In December, 1978, Stockton told the Holding Company directors that the janitorial service had asked for an advance payment to finance the purchase of new equipment. The board authorized Stockton to issue an advance in an amount somewhere between two and three thousand dollars. Stockton made other "advances" to the janitorial service which were not cleared by the board. When the union vice-president, Rodney Trump, questioned Stockton about several checks payable to M. Woods in large amounts, he was told that the checks were advances to the janitorial company for the purchase of equipment. Each of the large "advance" checks was deposited into one of Stockton's bank accounts. In almost every instance, Stockton drew on the deposit immediately to pay personal expenses.

In August, 1982, Stockton terminated the union's arrangement with the M. Woods Janitorial Service. Genevieve Kruhl, the mother of a union member, was hired to clean the offices at $200.00 per week.

Stockton's version of the facts differed in several respects. He testified that there was indeed an M. Woods who performed cleaning services. He stated that Woods' first name was Mark, and provided a physical description of him. Stockton testified that Woods had been recommended to him by a former union official who had died in 1981. He claimed that the checks had been deposited to his accounts because he had cashed the checks and paid Woods in cash.

On February 16, 1984, Stockton was indicted on eleven counts of embezzlement of the assets of a labor union in violation of 29 U.S.C. § 501(c). The case was tried before a jury.

* * *

* * * On May 4, 1984, the jury found Stockton guilty on all counts. The court sentenced Stockton to concurrent prison terms of one year and one day for the first six counts. For the remaining counts, the court gave Stockton a suspended sentence and placed him on probation for five years. As a condition of his probation, Stockton was required to make restitution to the labor union in the amount of the lesser of $23,250 (the aggregate amount of the embezzlement charged in the indictment) or fifteen percent of his income over the five-year period.

We have not previously had occasion to address the interpretation of 29 U.S.C. § 501(c) as it applies to cases like the one presently before us. The courts that have considered the issue have adopted a variety of approaches, from which emerges a complicated and at times confusing pattern. Because for the purposes of the present case, at least, we are persuaded that the answer to the problem is simpler than application of broad principles may make it appear, we pursue an independent analysis of § 501(c).

* * *

The traditional concept of embezzlement is readily applicable in the context of misconduct by union officials. One point, however, seems to have given the courts trouble, namely, the notion of authorization. Some courts have concluded that if what was clearly a misuse of union funds was expressly approved by a superior union official, the appropriation or expenditure must be considered to have been "authorized" by the union. Courts which have done so, however, have then proceeded to construct other theories to serve as the basis for upholding convictions. We do not see the need to construct a pitfall and then ingeniously to escape it. We are not prepared to attribute so great an effect to approval from a superior who, himself, in the first place was not authorized to give it. It bears repeating that the conversion of property that lies at the core of embezzlement must be without the permission of *the owner,* and contrary to the wishes of *the owner.* In the context of Section 501(c), the owner of the property is the union itself—its collective membership—not individual union officials who are not vested with power to dissipate union funds in the manner currently before the court. An appropriation or expenditure of union funds is therefore unauthorized if it is done without the permission of *the union,* even if it is approved by a superior union official. The permission of the union is lacking if the appropriation or expenditure is outside the scope of the fiduciary trust placed in the defendant by the union as a whole and outside the scope of the powers of any superior union official on whose permission the defendant has sought to rely.

* * *

We turn to Stockton's contention that the district court erred in denying his motions for a judgment of acquittal. In reviewing the denial of a judgment of acquittal, we must determine whether there is no substantial evidence in the record to support the jury's finding that the defendant is guilty beyond a reasonable doubt. In doing so, we must construe the evidence in the light most favorable to the prosecution. We find that there is ample evidence to support Stockton's conviction.

First, the evidence strongly indicates that Stockton converted the union's funds to his own use. Bank records revealed that all of the checks charged in the indictment were deposited into one of Stockton's bank accounts, and that many of the deposits were quickly followed by payments to Stockton's creditors. Stockton's acts in depositing and spending the money clearly amounted to an exercise of control or dominion sufficient to constitute a conversion.

It is also clear that Stockton's appropriation of union funds was unauthorized and contrary to the wishes of the union. It is true that the testimony of Holding Company board members indicated that the board delegated decision-making authority concerning building maintenance to Stockton, and even suggested that the board might have approved Stockton's cleaning arrangements *had he told them honestly* that he himself, his wife, or his associates intended to perform the cleaning services.[10] Nevertheless, Stockton did not honestly seek the union's authorization for his arrangements. The union, acting through the Holding Company board, and altogether unaware of a close connection between M. Woods and Stockton, authorized the disbursement of funds

---

10. For example, one Holding Company board member testified as follows:

Q. And it is fair to say that the Board as a whole didn't care who cleaned the Union Hall as long as it was cleaned.

A. Basically, that is true. As long as we were getting the work for the money being put out.

Q. You didn't care if Mr. Stockton did it himself, did you?

A. It never came to me that point, but I don't know. It shouldn't make any difference. The only thing I can say is as long as the work was done, if he chooses to do it or if you chose to do it or anybody that desired it. If the place wasn't cleaned up, it would be a different situation.

to the M. Woods Janitorial Service, not to Stockton. By approving the payments to M. Woods, the union effectively denied permission to Stockton's appropriation of the same funds.

The other elements of embezzlement were also present here. The union's funds were already in Stockton's lawful possession, in his capacity as union president, at the time the checks were drawn. In addition, the evidence indicates that Stockton exhibited the required mental state. He knew that his appropriation of union money was unauthorized, because it was flatly inconsistent with the union's authorization of payment to a different recipient, the M. Woods Janitorial Service, which the union believed to be in existence. Moreover, Stockton's deliberate misrepresentation of his activities indicates that he feared the union's disapproval had it known the truth.

Finally, Stockton emphasizes that the union received full value for its money because the offices were in fact cleaned. It is true that the evidence showed that cleaning services were performed by someone, although there was testimony that the quality of the cleaning was not always satisfactory. Even assuming a high level of quality, however, Stockton has not made out a defense sufficient to overturn the verdict. Embezzlement is not excused by restitution of goods or services of equivalent value. We conclude that the motion for a judgment of acquittal was properly denied.

* * *

Accordingly, we affirm Stockton's conviction for embezzlement of union assets in violation of 29 U.S.C. § 501(c).

Affirmed.

———

In contrast to the Fourth Circuit's approach in *Stockton* of requiring authorization by "the union," rather than by a union official (apparently, even when the official had all pertinent information), are a variety of approaches outlined by the Seventh Circuit in *Floyd*.

UNITED STATES v. FLOYD
U.S. Court of Appeals, Seventh Circuit, 1989.
882 F.2d 235.

WOOD, CIRCUIT JUDGE.

William A. Floyd appeals from his convictions of embezzling union property in violation of 29 U.S.C. § 501(c) and of conspiring to embezzle union property in violation of 18 U.S.C. § 371.

William A. Floyd ("Floyd") admits the following facts. In 1984, Floyd served as both a business representative and trustee of Teamster Local 705 ("Local 705"). At the time, Louis Peick ("Peick") served as Secretary–Treasurer (the chief officer) of Local 705, a position he had held consecutively since 1957.

In August 1984, Peick informed Floyd that he (Peick) had a problem with a union car, the 1983 Cadillac Sedan DeVille which the union had assigned to Floyd. Peick told Floyd to "dump" the car. Floyd did not ask Peick why he wanted the car dumped nor did Floyd question Peick's authority to issue the order. Floyd contacted his cousin, Kenneth Floyd, and asked him to find someone to take the car.

Kenneth Floyd approached Otto Bremer and offered him the car. Unbeknownst to Kenneth Floyd, Otto Bremer was a government informant. Floyd subsequently gave his car keys to Kenneth Floyd so that a duplicate set could be made. On August 28, 1984, Floyd parked the car in the parking lot of a shopping center in Kankakee, Illinois where Bremer later arranged to "steal" it. Floyd then notified the Kankakee police department that the car had been stolen.

Several weeks later, Bremer met with Floyd to return the two-way radio which had been in the trunk of the car. Floyd informed Bremer that Peick had been "raising hell" with him for allowing the radio to be seized. Soon after, Floyd telephoned Peick and read off its serial numbers. After apparently checking these numbers against some records, Peick directed Floyd to get rid of the radio. Floyd threw the radio into the Kankakee River.

Floyd obtained the police report on the stolen car and gave it to Peick; Peick sent the report to the union's insurance carrier to receive reimbursement for the vehicle. The United States Fidelity & Guaranty Insurance Company subsequently issued a check for $12,850.00 to the union for the loss of the car. The insurance company also paid the union a small sum to partially defray the cost of a rental car.

In November 1985, two special investigators from the United States Department of Labor interviewed Floyd at his home about his role in the staged theft. In April 1985, a grand jury investigated union evidence relating to the taking of the car. The grand jury issued a subpoena to Peick in July 1986. On July 23, 1986, Peick's attorney, responding to the subpoena, stated that Peick had suffered a heart attack earlier that year and that he was unable to consult with counsel due to continued illness. Peick's counsel further stated that his client intended to invoke his fifth amendment privilege if he were called to testify. Peick died in November 1986.

Floyd was indicted on November 20, 1987. The indictment charged Floyd with conspiracy to commit mail fraud and to embezzle union property in violation of 18 U.S.C. § 371 (Count 1), embezzlement of union property in violation of 29 U.S.C. § 501(c) (Count 2), and mail fraud in violation of 18 U.S.C. § 1341 (Counts 3, 4, 5, 6, 7 and 8). The defendant moved to dismiss the charges against him on the ground that he was prejudiced by preindictment delay. Floyd pointed out that although the government had initiated its investigation in November 1985, he was not indicted for another two years. He argued that Peick's death in the interim precluded him from presenting a cogent defense.

The court rejected Floyd's motion to dismiss for several reasons. The court noted that the death of a material witness does not, in itself, establish prejudice. Indeed, it was not clear that Peick would have testified at trial even had he lived. The court pointed out that Peick, in his counsel's response to the grand jury subpoena, expressed an intent to invoke his fifth amendment privilege against self-incrimination. Accordingly, it was unlikely that Peick would have risked implicating himself by taking the stand at Floyd's trial. The court also remarked upon Floyd's failure to attempt to preserve Peick's testimony as a means of avoiding any prejudicial effect. Finally, the court stated that Floyd had not demonstrated how Peick's testimony could have exculpated him.

On October 3, 1988, Floyd pleaded guilty to the two counts of mail fraud (Counts 3 and 8), and to that portion of Count 1 which dealt with conspiracy to commit mail fraud. In exchange for Floyd's guilty plea on those counts, the government moved to dismiss Counts 4 through 7. Floyd waived his right to a jury trial on the charges of conspiracy to embezzle (Count 1) and embezzlement of union property (Count 2).

During the bench trial, the government established its case-in-chief primarily through stipulated evidence. The prosecution introduced portions of the constitution and bylaws of Local 705 that described the expected duties of union officers. The by-laws specified that officers owed a fiduciary duty to the union and were expected to carry out union objectives through lawful methods.

The government also introduced evidence that in May 1984, Local 705 was involved in a prolonged labor dispute with a freight company, Overnite Transportation. During the strike, Overnite's employees were threatened and several of its vehicles were damaged. Union members frequently followed Overnite drivers in their cars, a practice known as "tailgating."[1] Overnite employees reported these occurrences and, when able, recorded the license plate numbers of cars involved in tailgating. The prosecution introduced a report which indicated that Floyd's car had been involved in a tailgating incident in June 1984.

Floyd testified at trial. He explained that Peick ordered him to dump the car. Floyd conceded that, at the time the order was issued, he suspected the car might have been involved in wrongdoing related to the Overnite dispute. However, Floyd stated that he never asked Peick why he wanted the car taken away. He also testified that Peick had not spelled out how he wanted this task accomplished.

Floyd admitted to arranging for the "theft" and destruction of the automobile. Floyd defended on the ground that he lacked the scienter to be held guilty of embezzling and conspiring to embezzle the car because Peick had granted him the authority to dispose of the property.

---

1. Evidently, the union members would closely follow the trucks in order to determine which companies had hired Overnite Transportation; the union would then picket these organizations.

In support of his contention, Floyd submitted portions of the union's constitution and by-laws indicating that Local 705 was controlled by its principal executive officer, the Secretary–Treasurer. Floyd also presented testimony from John Navigato, a union board member and president of the union, and from Michael O'Grady, a former board member. Navigato and O'Grady testified that Peick ran Local 705 with "an iron fist." According to Navigato and O'Grady, Peick issued orders instead of asking for recommendations. Peick would often scream and yell at union personnel and, if a staff member disobeyed his orders, Peick would harshly reprimand, demote, or perhaps fire that worker. Peick called executive board meetings at his whim. At these meetings, other board members would generally agree to whatever Peick recommended. Peick often referred to the local as "his union."

Navigato, O'Grady, and the defendant testified that Peick exerted sole authority over the use and disposition of union cars. Moreover, the local's by-laws empowered the principal executive officer to "sell, exchange or lease automobiles or arrange financing therefor in behalf of the Local Union." Peick arranged for insurance on the cars and he alone determined who would receive the cars, and if and when the cars needed to be replaced.

The district court was not persuaded by Floyd's defense that he lacked the requisite criminal intent to embezzle union property or to conspire to embezzle. On November 4, 1988, the court found him guilty of both charges. Floyd was sentenced to two years imprisonment on Counts 1, 2, and 3, to run concurrently. The court suspended sentence on Count 8 and ordered Floyd to five years probation, conditioned on his performing 600 hours of community service and paying restitution to both the insurance company and to Local 705. Pursuant to 18 U.S.C. § 3013, Floyd was also ordered to pay a special assessment of $200.00. This appeal followed.

Floyd * * * argues that there was insufficient evidence to support his conviction under 29 U.S.C. § 501(c) and the conspiracy to embezzle conviction under 18 U.S.C. § 371 because the government failed to show that he had the requisite scienter.

Floyd contends that the government failed to prove that he willfully violated a provision of the Labor–Management Reporting and Disclosure Act, 29 U.S.C. § 501(c). In assessing a challenge to the sufficiency of the evidence, we review the evidence in the light most favorable to the prosecution to determine whether any rational trier of fact could find the defendant guilty beyond a reasonable doubt.

This Court has not previously considered what standard applies to § 501(c) criminal cases. Several different tests have been formulated by other circuits. For example, the District of Columbia Circuit, in United States v. Boyle, 482 F.2d 755 (D.C.Cir.1973), held that the use of union funds for an illegal purpose is a *per se* violation of § 501(c). Most other circuits have rejected the *per se* approach, however, favoring instead to apply varying analyses, dependent on the facts.

For example, where there is evidence of union authorization, some courts require the prosecution to show that the defendant specifically intended to deprive the union of its property and lacked a good faith belief that the appropriation would benefit the union. On the other hand, if the union did not authorize the appropriation, the government need only prove lack of authorization and the defendant's fraudulent intent.

The Second Circuit holds that a defendant should be acquitted if the evidence shows that he or she had a good faith belief that the appropriation was for union purposes and that the union had either authorized the act or would do so.

Proof of union benefit is less important in the First and Fourth Circuits. Those courts will find a § 501(c) violation if the defendant appropriated union property in the absence of either actual union authorization or a good faith belief that the action was authorized.

A common thread running through all these tests is whether the defendant acted with fraudulent intent. For this reason, the Eighth and Ninth Circuits focus on whether, at the time of the alleged appropriation, the wrongdoer acted with fraudulent intent. To determine fraudulent intent, the courts consider the totality of the circumstances. Under this analysis, authorization (or lack of) for the act is but one factor bearing on intent, as is proof that the union reaped no benefit from the act. It is this approach which the parties urge us to adopt.

We had occasion to review the legislative history and policy behind the enactment of § 501 in McNamara v. Johnston, 522 F.2d 1157, 1163–65 (7th Cir.1976), although the union officers in that case were defendants in a civil suit, not a criminal proceeding. We recognized that Congress incorporated principles from the common law of agency into § 501, and under agency law, "an agent cannot be insulated from criminal liability by the fact that his principal authorized his conduct." *Id.* at 1165. We believe that the agency principle discussed in *McNamara* has application in § 501(c) criminal proceedings as well. A union officer cannot be absolved of wrongdoing by saying that the act was done with union authorization. However, authorization or lack thereof is pertinent to a determination of the defendant's intent, as is whether the defendant possessed a good faith belief that the union would benefit from the appropriation. For these reasons, we adopt the totality of the circumstances approach to ascertain fraudulent intent. We next address whether fraudulent intent has been demonstrated in this case.

Floyd presents several reasons why his conviction should be overturned, all in support of his assertion that the prosecution failed to show that he acted with fraudulent intent. He first claims that he committed no embezzlement since he held a good faith belief that the appropriation of the car was authorized. He points to the fact that he took the car at Peick's direction as proof that he acted with the owner's assent.

We reject this argument. As the court in *Stockton, supra,* noted, a higher ranking union official's express approval of an appropriation is of little import to § 501(c) cases because the true owner of union property is the collective membership, not individual union officers:

The permission of the union is lacking if the appropriation or expenditure is outside the scope of the fiduciary trust placed in the defendant by the union as a whole and outside the scope of the powers of any superior union official on whose permission the defendant has sought to rely.

Although he acknowledges that the union members were the true owners of the car, Floyd insists that the membership vested Peick with both apparent and actual authority over the disposition of union cars. Floyd claims that he believed, in good faith, that Peick had issued his directive with the tacit or explicit approval of the union. We are unpersuaded by this contention. While the union may have given Peick a certain degree of administrative control, Peick's authority did not extend to the destruction of union property. Indeed, the union's by-laws mandated that union business be carried out through lawful methods. For this reason, Floyd's contention that he held a good faith belief that the union had authorized Peick's order is without merit.

Floyd contends that even if Peick's order was issued in contravention of his authority, it does not follow that Floyd acted with § 501(c) criminal intent. He argues that Peick ordered him merely to "dump" the car, not to stage a theft, a distinction he believes is an important one. Floyd claims that he is only guilty of exercising poor judgment in the method he used to execute Peick's order; this is why he admitted his guilt for the mail fraud charges. He therefore asserts that the method he used for disposing of the car is irrelevant to the § 501(c) issue. We disagree. It is well established that more than one category of offense can arise from the same factual context.

Floyd stresses that he received no money from either Bremer or Kenneth Floyd. He claims that absence of a personal benefit to him evinces his lack of fraudulent intent. The government counters that Floyd did benefit from the disposal of the car. The prosecution notes that because his car had been tied to incidents at Overnite Delivery, Floyd had an interest in the car's destruction.

Regardless of whether Floyd personally stood to gain from the theft, the more important issue is whether he believed that the appropriation would somehow benefit the union. It is clear that Floyd could not have held such a belief, because the union gained nothing. Floyd maintains that the union benefitted because it received the insurance proceeds in recompense for the loss of the car, an argument we find unavailing. Indeed, "[e]mbezzlement is not excused by restitution of goods or services of equivalent value." *Stockton*, 788 F.2d at 219.

All of these factors, taken in the light most favorable to the government, support the district court's findings that Floyd conspired to embezzle and embezzled union property. We therefore affirm his convictions on these counts.

* * *

AFFIRMED.

Notes

1. If you were a prosecutor, how would you approach a case of alleged benefit plan embezzlement after reading the § 501(c) and § 664 cases on authorization?

2. In *Stockton*, evidence was admitted under Federal Rule of Evidence 404(b). Such evidence can be most helpful to any party attempting to prove intent to defraud. Federal Rule of Evidence 404(b) provides:

> Evidence of other crimes, wrongs, or acts is not admissible to prove the character of a person in order to show that he acted in conformity therewith. It may, however, be admissible for other purposes, such as proof of motive, opportunity, intent, preparation, plan, knowledge, identity, or absence of mistake or accident. Provided that upon request by the accused, the prosecution in a criminal case shall provide reasonable notice in advance of trial, or during trial if the court excuses pretrial notice on good cause shown, of the general nature of any such evidence it intends to introduce at trial.

Proof of other "wrongs" need not be *crimes* for which the defendant has been convicted, or even arrested. Moreover, proof of other "wrongs" need not meet the stringent standard of proof beyond a reasonable doubt. Instead it may be proven by the lesser standard, "clear and convincing."[aa] Evidence admissible under Fed.R.Evid. 404(b) often is readily available in white collar criminal cases and can be extremely important. It is readily available because the business transaction at issue in the criminal case often forms the basis of related civil lawsuits already filed against the defendant. Or, the defendant may be embroiled in controversies with business associates who are only too eager to cooperate with the government in its prosecution of the defendant. If the prosecutor is able to lay the appropriate foundation through Fed.R.Evid. 404(b), the details of these civil lawsuits or disagreements may be introduced in the criminal action.

Fed.R.Evid. 404(b) evidence is especially powerful in fraud cases based on documentary evidence because 404(b) evidence assists the government in proving the most elusive of elements to the crime: intent. When transactions are memorialized in documents there is usually little question that the conduct alleged occurred. Often in such cases, the only issue in controversy is intent. Not surprisingly, it becomes much easier to prove intent when the defendant is shown to have engaged in a pattern of conduct over a period of time, rather than in one isolated incident. Thus, with 404(b) evidence, the government can charge the defendant with an isolated incident, yet prove criminal intent as to the incident by introducing evidence of a pattern of conduct, none of which is charged or proven beyond a reasonable doubt.

aa. 2 *D. Louisell & Mueller, Federal Evidence* § 140 (1985). For a discussion of the common law tradition of introducing other wrongs, see M.C. Slough & J. William Knightly, *Other Vices, Other Crimes,* 41 Iowa L.Rev. 325 (1956).

In *Stockton*, the following evidence allegedly qualifying under Fed. R.Evid. 404(b) was admitted:

"During the trial, the government called as a witness Sandra Simmons, a union member and longtime acquaintance of Stockton and his wife. Before the grand jury, Simmons had testified that she had been aware that the M. Woods Janitorial Service was a 'joke' and that the cleaning of the offices was being done by union members. Her testimony was otherwise at trial and unsatisfactory from the government's point of view. The government sought to impeach her trial testimony by introducing into evidence her prior contradictory statements before the grand jury. Simmons' earlier testimony further indicated that she had been threatened by associates of Stockton at the time of the grand jury proceedings. She had testified that a union member had removed the battery from her car on the day she was scheduled to testify before the grand jury, and that Mildred Stockton had told her that a 'bodyguard' would 'take care of anyone' who harmed Stockton in connection with the grand jury investigation. The court carefully instructed the jury that the grand jury testimony was admitted solely for the purpose of impeaching the credibility of Simmons' trial testimony, and added that the evidence should not be considered 'for the purpose in any way of connecting Mr. Stockton with any such statements, because there is absolutely no evidence that if any such statements were made that Mr. Stockton had anything whatsoever to do with them.' "[bb]

Stockton claimed that admission of this testimony was error, in part because it was not properly admissible under Fed.R.Evid. 404(b). The Fourth Circuit rejected Stockton's argument and affirmed the District Court's admission of such evidence.

"Stockton * * * argues that Simmons' grand jury testimony was inadmissible under Rule 404(b) * * *. Stockton contends that the government's real purpose in introducing the testimony was to link him with the threats made to Simmons, in an effort to show his bad character, and thereby to persuade the jury that he was capable of embezzlement. The government offered the evidence, however, for a genuine 'other purpose,' and the district judge emphasized that the jury was not to utilize the testimony in the manner of which Stockton complains. Although impeachment of a witness is not among the 'other purposes' explicitly listed in Rule 404(b) by way of example, that list is not exhaustive, and impeachment qualifies as a permissible purpose for the introduction of other crimes. Where a legitimate 'other purpose' is shown, the district court must proceed to weigh the probative value and the potential prejudicial effect of the evidence under Rule 403."

Was Simmons' grand jury testimony properly admitted under 404(b)? Perhaps not. There was nothing in Simmons' grand jury testimony that linked Stockton to the "wrong" of intimidating Simmons when she was to appear as a grand jury witness.

United States v. Roe, 670 F.2d 956 (11th Cir.1982), presents an example of FRE 404(b) evidence more appropriately admitted. The defendants, Neil

bb.   788 F.2d at 214.

Roe and Ray Tietjen, were convicted on charges of conspiracy, wire fraud and interstate travel to execute a fraudulent scheme. Their convictions arose from a business they operated, Deltron, that allegedly sold franchises that manufactured automobile hood scoops. The evidence demonstrated that the defendants made numerous false representations to induce purchases of the franchises. Their false representations concerned the timing and type of supplies Deltron would provide for the franchisee and the extent of Deltron's obligation to purchase the hood scoops produced.[cc] During its case in chief, the government was allowed to introduce evidence of defendant Tietjen's prior involvement with Stylefoam, a company that operated similarly to Deltron.[dd] The Eleventh Circuit affirmed the admission of this evidence. Its discussion demonstrates the limits placed on the admission of the 404(b) evidence by the District Court.

"The defendants * * * argue that the Stylefoam testimony permitted by the district court was inadmissible under Fed.R.Evid. 404(b). Only two witnesses testified as to Tietjen's association with Stylefoam. One was a Deltron investor who answered a Stylefoam advertisement and eventually was put in contact with Tietjen, a salesman for Stylefoam at the time. Although Tietjen made a sales pitch for Stylefoam, Tietjen then told the investor that Tietjen was starting Deltron, a corporation 'very similar in style' to Stylefoam, but with different products, primarily hood scoops. The investor did not testify as to any details of Stylefoam's operation. Instead, he concentrated on the vision of Deltron's organization that Tietjen described. The other witness who testified on Stylefoam, [a consultant hired by Deltron,] also gave no details of Stylefoam's practices. He testified that he developed the Deltron advertisements using 'information' derived from Stylefoam, which had the 'same general format' as Deltron. He also said that he developed part of the Deltron packet, which was given to prospective investors, from the Stylefoam packet. Some of the Stylefoam packet was used 'verbatim.' We conclude that this testimony was admissible to demonstrate that the defendants had some knowledge and experience of how to run a business like Deltron.

"A district court's decision on the admissibility of extrinsic offense evidence under Fed.R.Evid. 404(b) is reviewable only for abuse of discretion. Extrinsic offense evidence is admissible only if (1) the evidence is relevant to an issue other than the defendant's character, and (2) the probative value of the evidence is not substantially outweighed by undue prejudice. Relevancy under the first step includes (1) an adequate showing that the defendant actually committed the extrinsic offense, and (2) a similarity between the extrinsic and the charged offense that is significant for the purpose for which the extrinsic offense is introduced. The balance required under the second step includes consideration of the government's need for the evidence, the degree of similarity between the extrinsic and the charged offense, and the closeness in time of the two.

cc. Id. at 960.   **dd.** Id. at 965.

"The Stylefoam testimony satisfied the two-step predicate for admissibility under Fed.R.Evid. 404(b). Tietjen was employed by Stylefoam and had access to the materials given to prospective Stylefoam investors, showing that he 'committed' the extrinsic activity. On the similarity issue, we consider it important that the government did not introduce the Stylefoam testimony in order to establish that the defendants were sophisticated businessmen in the franchising field. The government's purpose was only to show that the defendants had some prior knowledge and experience of how to run a business like Deltron, which was relevant to negate the defendants' argument that they were innocent bumblers. For this limited purpose, the general similarity of Stylefoam and Deltron shown by the government was sufficient. Also, Tietjen's involvement with Deltron began at least immediately after he ended his association with Stylefoam, if not before. In our view, the probative value of the Stylefoam evidence was not substantially outweighed by any undue prejudice. Indeed, in our view, the prejudice was minimal. Accordingly, we hold that the district court did not abuse its discretion under Fed.R.Evid. 404(b) in admitting the Stylefoam testimony."

Section 501(c) is an embezzlement offense. As the Fourth Circuit in *Stockton* discussed, embezzlement has a highly specific meaning:

"The specific question presented * * * is the proper construction of the statutory concept of embezzlement. Although § 501(c) reaches other theft offenses as well, it is clear that embezzlement is the statute's primary concern. * * * Unlike other theft crimes, embezzlement presupposes that the appropriated property was already lawfully in the defendant's possession at the time of its appropriation. * * *

* * *

"The central element of the traditional concept of embezzlement is the conversion of property belonging to another. Conversion involves an act of control of dominion over the property that seriously interferes with the owner's rights. It is important to note that the act of dominion or appropriation must be without authorization from the owner of the property. The notion that the act of dominion or appropriation is contrary to the wishes of the owner, or at least without clear permission from the owner, is inherent in the concept of conversion. There can, of course, be no interference with the owner's rights to the property if the owner has given permission to the act in question. The mental state required for conversion is purely and simply a specific intent to appropriate the property. Knowledge that the property belongs to another, or that the appropriation is unauthorized by the owner, is not necessary."

The next two cases, United States v. Vandenbergen, 969 F.2d 338 (7th Cir.1992), and United States v. Boyle, 482 F.2d 755 (D.C.Cir.1973), discuss the conversion element of embezzlement. With which court do you agree?

UNITED STATES v. VANDENBERGEN

United States Court of Appeals, Seventh Circuit, 1992.
969 F.2d 338.

EASTERBROOK, CIRCUIT JUDGE.

Dorothy Johnson, Mayor of Appleton, Wisconsin, finished second in the multi-party primary election in 1988. Jack Voight, who finished first and was her opponent in the general election, soon led the city council in rejecting contracts between the City and some of its unionized workers. Labor favored Johnson but could not add to her war chest, for Wisconsin limits giving by unions. Wis.Stat. § 11.38(1)(a). Dennis Vandenbergen, secretary-treasurer of Teamsters Local 563, who joined the Mayor's reelection committee, hatched a scheme to evade the state's law. The seven members of the union's executive board voted themselves bonuses of $300 apiece. All donated this money to Johnson's campaign. To ensure that there was no diversion, Vandenbergen instructed the union's secretary not to release any board member's bonus check until she received a check for $300 made out to Johnson's campaign fund. Vandenbergen collected and delivered these to Johnson personally. She was reelected.

Wisconsin could have prosecuted Vandenbergen and the other members of the board. Wis.Stat. § 11.61. Instead the United States indicted Vandenbergen under 29 U.S.C. § 501(c) * * *.

The indictment charged Vandenbergen with "converting" the union's money. At trial Vandenbergen and the other members of the board testified that the bonuses were for extra work and had nothing to do with Johnson's campaign. It was mere coincidence, they asserted, that seven union officials, five of whom had never before made political contributions exceeding $100, simultaneously gave $300 apiece to a single candidate. The jury was unmoved and convicted; the judge concluded that Vandenbergen's testimony was shot through with lies, amounting to obstruction of justice. The sentence: six months' imprisonment, followed by another six months in a halfway house and a year of supervised release, plus a fine of $5,000 and restitution of $2,100. The conviction also disqualifies Vandenbergen from holding union office for five years.

Local 563 could have paid each board member an extra $300 for extra work, or just because it thought compensation for ordinary work deficient. The executive board so voted. Because neither the bylaws nor the constitution of the union is in the record, we must assume that authorization by the board alone was sufficient. According to the prosecutor, these payments are a federal crime because funneling cash to candidates for local office is illegal under state law and the board disguised the purpose of the disbursements. Yet § 501(c) is not written as a piggyback statute, turning state offenses into federal felonies. (The maximum sentence for a violation of Wis.Stat. § 11.38 is three years, two years less than the maximum under § 501(c).) Although the cock-and-bull story about extra work, coupled with Vandenbergen's conceded knowledge of Wisconsin's ban on contributions by unions, may show that he acted "willfully", it does not show that the scheme "converted" the union's money.

The prosecutor argues that all knowingly illegal uses of union money violate § 501(c). That may be the law in one circuit, see United States v. Boyle, 482 F.2d 755, 764–66 (D.C.Cir.1973), but it is not the law in ours, for we have expressly rejected Boyle's holding. It is essential to distinguish the mental element of § 501(c) from the forbidden acts— embezzlement, theft, and conversion. This list does not include all violations of other laws but only the three named sins, which collectively denote acts that enrich the officers (or their friends) at the expense of the union. "[T]he common thread is that the defendant ... has taken another person's property or caused it to be taken, knowing that the other person would not have wanted that to be done." United States v. Silverman, 430 F.2d 106, 126–27 (2d Cir.1970).

This record does not support a conclusion that Vandenbergen and friends feathered their own nests to the detriment of the union. To the contrary, it shows that the executive board did what it thought necessary to promote the reelection of a mayor considerably more sympathetic to labor's interests than was her opponent. Once the city council rejected the contracts, the union was entitled to arbitrate. Vandenbergen esti-mated (without contradiction) that arbitration would have cost the union at least $24,000—and it might have lost. With Johnson as Mayor, the union achieved its ends without that cost, and there would be other contracts to negotiate during her term. The union and its members were better off. They "would have wanted that to be done"—the benefit to unions of making political contributions is precisely why Wisconsin made them unlawful. The state was not trying to protect labor from *wasteful* expenditures!

Is every application of funds in violation of state law "conversion"? When choosing the language "embezzles, steals, or unlawfully and willfully abstracts or converts to his own use" Congress named private wrongs. Conversion is an unauthorized assumption of the incidents of ownership; authority comes from the owner, not from the state. The distinction between theft and salary is permission: a manager who draws a $10,000 check as his salary does not embezzle, steal, or convert funds, although an unauthorized check in the same amount is theft. If the manager neglects a rule of securities law obliging him to disclose to investors the full amount of his stipend, that failure would not make the cashing of the check "theft" or "conversion," although the United States could prosecute for securities fraud. So too with labor: an *authorized* diversion of funds to an illegal end violates the substantive law restricting that outlay, but it does not annul the authorization and so add "conversion" to the list of offenses.

We can imagine cases in which formally authorized expenditures violate § 501(c). United States v. Welch, 728 F.2d 1113 (8th Cir.1984), is a good example. Union officers with power to approve expenditures poured its treasury directly into their pockets. The court concluded that expenditures conferring no possible benefit on the union's members, coupled with fraudulent intent, violated the statute. An expenditure that injures the members of the union, who have a power to disapprove outlays even though officers run the local day-to-day, fits within customary ideas of conversion. *Welch* is consistent with our understanding that § 501(c) protects the members from the officers, and not the public from the union. United States v. Thordarson, 646 F.2d 1323, 1334–37 (9th Cir.1981), cannot be reconciled with this approach, for it holds that an authorized expenditure for the purpose of damaging the employer's property violates § 501(c). Although *Thordarson*, like our later opinion in *Floyd*, rejects the approach of *Boyle* under which all expenditures violating a substantive norm also violate § 501(c), it ends up in much the same place as *Boyle*, and we disapprove its holding for the same reason we rejected *Boyle's*.

One could say that a state law in the form "no union shall ..." prevents it from acting, rendering any improper outlay "unauthorized" as well. This is a variation on the theme that state law is part of every contractual relation, so that the powers of Local 563's executive board are as fettered by rules of law as they are by *Robert's Rules of Order*. Taken to its limits, this approach crushes all distinction between public and private assent. General Motors Corp. v. Romein, 503 U.S. 181 (1992), among many other cases, shows that incorporation of public law into private contract is not taken to its limit; the Court held that state rules for workers' compensation are not part of the contract between a firm and its workers. Neither the text nor anything we could find in the history of § 501(c) shows that it was designed as a multiplier for other statutes, creating second punishments for all expenditures that violate substantive restrictions. Criminal statutes should be read narrowly, so that they give clear notice of what they forbid. Stretching § 501(c) to create a federal penalty for all expenditures that violate state law would extend it far beyond the private-law connotations of "conversion." There is no federal interest in enforcing Wisconsin's rules about campaign contributions—no reason why Vandenbergen's acts would be a federal crime in Wisconsin but not in another state that permitted unions to make direct donations instead of requiring them, as Wisconsin does, to donate through political action committees.

Vandenbergen violated Wisconsin's law if, as the jury concluded, the bonuses for "extra work" were disguised political contributions. He violated federal law if, as the district judge concluded, he committed perjury at his trial. But he did not violate 29 U.S.C. § 501(c). Wisconsin may treat a union's political contribution as an offense without initiating a bootstrap by which the same acts become a federal felony.

REVERSED.

UNITED STATES v. BOYLE

United States Court of Appeals, District of Columbia Circuit, 1973.
482 F.2d 755.

WILKEY, CIRCUIT JUDGE.

Appellant W. A. Boyle is the former president of the United Mine Workers of America. Convicted on thirteen counts as an officer of the UMW of having (1) consented to unlawful contributions of labor union funds to the campaigns of candidates for federal office, (2) unlawfully converting union funds for the purpose of making such a contribution, and (3) conspired with others to commit these two offenses, appellant seeks reversal under a number of theories. We conclude that appellant's conviction on all charges was proper and affirm the District Court.

I. FACTS

Labor's Non–Partisan League (League) was created in 1936 by the Congress of Industrial Organizations (CIO) to act as its legislative and lobbying arm. In 1940 the UMW left the CIO to become a separate entity. At that time the League as originally constituted disbanded, only to be immediately reconstituted as the lobbying and information branch of the UMW alone.

In persons and in property the League and the UMW have been closely identified. Since 1940 the president of the League and the current president of the UMW have been one and the same. From the time of the separation in 1940 until the time of the indictment in this case the League received all but a small portion of its funds from the UMW's general treasury.[5]

In 1963 appellant Boyle became president of the UMW and automatically chairman of the League. In 1966 the UMW began again to be solicited for contributions by candidates for federal office, chiefly those who had recently discovered the "testimonial dinner" as a fountain of funds. Boyle knew of and authorized contributions which were made out of the League's treasury for this purpose, as the trial jury found.

Robert Howe, director of the League for a part of the time in question, testified that he was concerned that contributions by the League might violate 18 U.S.C. § 610, which makes it "unlawful ... for any labor organization to make a contribution" to a federal campaign.[ee]

---

5. There is actually no evidence in the record that the League's funds came from any source other than the UMW general treasury. The Government, however, was unable to prove the origin of a relatively small portion of the League's funds during the period of 1942 to the time of the offenses in this case. Thus, we do not know that all of the League's funds came from the UMW treasury. Appellant attempts to make much of this inability to prove the source of this small portion of the League's funds. This inability is, however, irrelevant * * *.

ee. The defendant was also convicted for violating 18 U.S.C. § 610, which at the time of Boyle's indictment provided:

It is unlawful for any national bank, or any corporation organized by authority of

He testified that he and James Kmetz, another employee and Howe's successor as director, sought to hide the source of these funds by having checks on the League's account made out to cash, depositing the proceeds in their personal accounts, and then making the contributions with a personal check. The evidence is sufficient to permit a conclusion that Boyle knew and approved of this practice, that he knew of Howe's fears that the contributions were illegal, and that he knew and approved of efforts to conceal the source of the funds involved.

Monthly statements of these transactions were prepared. Appellant's executive secretary, Suzanne Richards, instructed that only one copy of this be sent to Boyle's office and that no copies be kept in the files of the League. Richards also instructed Howe to destroy any evidence that might incriminate Boyle or the UMW.

In the spring of 1969 the League's treasury was depleted. At the request of Kmetz, Boyle authorized a transfer of $5,000, which he characterized as a "loan," from the UMW treasury to the League. The jury concluded that this amount was actually transferred to facilitate the making of a political contribution by the League.[8] This transfer was ratified by the International Executive Board of the UMW over two years after the "loan" in question.

* * *

Appellant allegedly violated 29 U.S.C. § 501(c) (1970), which provides that:

> any person who embezzles, steals, or unlawfully and willfully abstracts or converts to his own use, or the use of another, any of the

any law of Congress, to make a contribution or expenditure in connection with any election to any political office, or in connection with any primary election or political convention or caucus held to select candidates for any political office, or for any corporation whatever, or any labor organization to make a contribution or expenditure in connection with any election at which Presidential and Vice Presidential electors or a Senator or Representative in, or a Delegate or Resident Commissioner to Congress are to be voted for, or in connection with any primary election or political convention or caucus held to select candidates for any of the foregoing offices, or for any candidate, political committee, or other person to accept or receive any contribution prohibited by this section.

Every corporation or labor organization which makes any contribution or expenditure in violation of this section shall be fined not more than $5,000; and every officer or director of any corporation, or officer of any labor organization, who consents to any contribution or expendi-

ture by the corporation or labor organization, as the case may be, and any person who accepts or receives any contribution, in violation of this section, shall be fined not more than $1,000 or imprisoned not more than one year, or both; and if the violation was willful, shall be fined not more than $10,000 or imprisoned not more than two years, or both.

For the purposes of this section "labor organization" means any organization of any kind, or any agency or employee representation committee or plan, in which employees participate and which exist for the purpose, in whole or in part, of dealing with employers concerning grievances, labor disputes, wages, rates of pay, hours of employment, or conditions of work.

8. Count XIII of the indictment charged appellant with violating 29 U.S.C. § 501 (c) (1970), by transferring the $5,000 from the UMW to the League account. Count XII of the indictment charged appellant with violating 18 U.S.C. § 610 (1970) by authorizing this $5,000 to be used as a campaign contribution.

moneys, funds, securities, property, or other assets of a labor organization of which he is an officer ... [will be subject to fine or imprisonment].

The jury found that appellant violated this law by ordering the transfer of the $5,000 "loan" described above from the UMW general treasury to the League treasury with the knowledge and for the purpose of making a political contribution. Appellant does not contest that the transfer was a conversion of union funds to "the use of another." Rather, appellant argues that for two reasons this conversion was not unlawful.

First, relying on the Second Circuit's opinion in United States v. Silverman,[24] appellant argues that such a transfer violates § 501(c) only if the jury finds that (1) the conversion was made without a bona fide authorization by the union, or (2) that the union derived no benefit from the transfer. Appellant's reliance upon the *Silverman* rationale is misplaced. The use to which the money was converted in that case, support of a candidate for state office, was not unlawful. The court stressed that there was no legal bar to the use *if* the transfer was properly authorized by the union.[25]

Regardless of the validity of the Second Circuit's analysis in situations where the use is lawful, the holding in *Silverman* has no relevance here. In the instant case the use to which the money was converted could not have been lawful. As we have seen, the contribution of the $5,000 constituted a violation of § 610. Neither authorization by any union officer or body, nor any resulting benefit to the union, would have rendered lawful the transfer of general union funds to a federal political campaign. * * *

Thus, approval or benefit cannot make the conversion to "the use of another" in this case any less unlawful. If the use to which the money is knowingly transferred is unlawful, then the transfer constitutes a violation of § 501(c). The jury was properly instructed that this was the applicable standard, that it had to find the appellant authorized the transfer knowingly for the purpose of making indirectly a political contribution, and there was sufficient evidence to support its conclusion.

Second, appellant seems to argue that § 501(c) was intended to punish union officials only if the jury finds that the officer did not have at the time a "bona fide belief in the legality of his action ..." The argument is that the statute is intended to punish only *knowingly* illegal or *ultra vires* expenditures, and that union officials will be granted great latitude in forming their bona fide beliefs as to whether an expenditure is within the legal objectives of the union organization. Under this reading, § 501(c) would never punish for a transfer, even if the official knew that the money was to be used for an unlawful purpose, if the official could have reasonably believed that the transfer was authorized under the union's constitution, bylaws, and procedure. Appellant con-

---

24.   430 F.2d 106 (2d Cir.1970).   **25.**   Id. at 112.

tends that he was prejudiced by the court's refusal to permit him to argue as a defense that he believed the transfer was authorized.

This interpretation is founded upon passages in the Congressional debates on the statute in which individual Congressmen discussed, in general terms, the Labor–Management Reporting and Disclosure Act of 1959, of which § 501(c) is a small part. The thrust of the dialogue relied upon is that the Act will not punish an officer for an expenditure

> [i]f it is made in accordance with, and for a purpose permitted by, the constitution, bylaws or regularly adopted resolutions of the union's constitutional governing bodies, the officer or employee will not be required at his peril to determine whether or not the constitution, bylaws or resolution goes beyond the legitimate purposes and objectives of the organization.

The relevance of this language in this context is at best ambiguous, and the remarks by individual Congressmen made during a floor debate are not the most persuasive form of legislative history. We believe, in any case, that the remarks relied upon do not support appellant's reading of the statute. The passage simply says that a transfer will not be deemed unlawful merely because it is made for a purpose that is *ultra vires* what the court determines to be the legitimate functions of a union.

As we have noted, however, the transfer in this case was not for a purpose that was *ultra vires*, but rather for a purpose that was itself a crime. There is no hint in either the statute or its legislative history that indicates a Congressional intent to excuse from the ambit of § 501(c) transfers for a criminal purpose. No officer or union governing body could in all logic believe that a transfer for a criminal purpose was for a legitimate union purpose, was authorized by the union constitution or bylaws, or was for the union's benefit.

* * *

Notes

With which court do you agree? In both *Vandenbergen* and *Boyle*, the defendants authorized the use of union funds for illegal purposes, but in both cases the expenditures were fully authorized by all necessary parties after full disclosure. The Seventh Circuit held that such conduct was not within § 501(c); the Circuit for the District of Columbia held that it was. Is it significant that the expenditure in *Vandenbergen* violated state law while the expenditure in *Boyle* violated federal law?

———

In addition to applying only to certain conduct (embezzlement), § 501(c) applies only to certain individuals: the person(s) who may be charged under § 501(c) must be an officer, or employee (directly or indirectly) of the labor organization at issue. Can a non-officer or employee still be liable under § 501(c) as an aider and abettor? Consider the next case, United States v. Coleman, 940 F.Supp. 15 (D.D.C.1996). Do you agree with the court?

UNITED STATES v. COLEMAN

United States District Court, District of Columbia, 1996.
940 F.Supp. 15.

SPORKIN, DISTRICT JUDGE.

This matter is before the Court on defendants' motions for: * * * dismissal of the indictment in whole or in part.

The defendants are accused in a multi-count indictment with participating in a scheme of fraud, embezzlement and money laundering, and conspiracy to commit such acts. Defendant Coleman, along with defendant Gjerset, is alleged to have devised a scheme to embezzle and launder funds belonging to the United Food and Commercial Workers Union (UFCW), Coleman's employer. Defendants Arnone and Whitaker, owners of various building companies, are alleged to have assisted Coleman and Gjerset in the scheme by laundering some funds through bank accounts belonging to their companies, accepting such funds as payment for building work, and receiving loans from the UFCW that were improperly authorized by Coleman. The defendants have all pleaded not guilty.

* * *

Defendants Whitaker, Arnone and Gjerset claim that they cannot be properly charged in counts two through ten of the indictment of aiding and abetting a violation of 29 U.S.C. § 501(c). * * *

The Government concedes that defendants Whitaker, Arnone and Gjerset are not officers or employees of the UFCW. However, counts two and ten also charge defendants under 18 U.S.C. § 2, which imposes punishment on an aider or abettor as if he or she were a principal to the particular crime charged. Defendants contend that 18 U.S.C. § 2 does not apply to 29 U.S.C. § 501(c), because by its very terms, § 501(c) applies only to persons who are officers or employees, directly or indirectly, of a labor organization. They claim that to charge non-labor organization persons as aiders and abettors would circumvent the language and purpose of § 501(c).

The parties agree there is no Court holding on this issue. The Government does cite Judge Friendly's dissent in United States v. Capanegro, 576 F.2d 973 (2d Cir.1978). The majority in *Capanegro* found that the defendants in question were union employees and therefore did not reach the question of aiding and abetting. Judge Friendly disagreed with his colleagues' analysis, but noted that "[i]f the Government had procured an indictment charging that [the union employee co-defendant] had violated 29 U.S.C. § 501(c) and that [defendant] had aided and abetted him, *[he] would have no hesitation in affirming a conviction.*" *Capanegro*, 576 F.2d at 980 (emphasis added).

Section 18 U.S.C. § 2 is the most basic provision of the U.S. Criminal Code. In simple language it states in part:

Whoever commits an offense against the United States or aids, abets, counsels, commands, induces or procures its commission, is punishable as a principal.

18 U.S.C. § 2(a).

There are no exceptions to the reach of the provision. Thus whatever limitations on its application would have to emanate from the particular criminal provision with respect to which a defendant has been alleged to have aided and abetted in its violation. The precise words of 29 U.S.C.§ 501(c) provide no comfort to the defendants. There is nothing in the provision that would in anyway suggest 18 U.S.C. § 2 does not apply to those who aid and abet violations of 29 U.S.C § 501(c). The fact that 18 U.S.C. § 2 and 29 U.S.C. § 501(c) are in different sections of the criminal code does not advance defendants position. It is clear that 18 U.S.C. § 2 is not confined to only other violations of Title 18. It applies across the board.

In this case, Coleman is the alleged principal. She is an insider at the union who is alleged to have committed financial crimes against her employer. Gjerset, Arnone and Whitaker are not employees of the union. Nevertheless, they are alleged to have assisted Coleman in committing a crime from the "inside." Clearly, they can be charged as aiders and abettors.

* * *

Notes

1. *Other Remedies in § 501.* A large number of collateral issues arise in § 501(c) cases. One reason is that § 501(b) sets forth a civil cause of action for damages available to any member of a labor organization "to recover damages or secure an accounting or other appropriate relief for the benefit of the labor organization" for breach of fiduciary duty against those persons listed in Section 501(a).

Council 49 v. Reach, 843 F.2d 1343 (11th Cir.1988), demonstrates a § 501(b) action. Members of Council 49, an affiliate of the American Federation of State, County and Municipal Employees, AFLBCIO, (AFSCME) brought an action against former union officers for breach of fiduciary duty. After a bench trial, damages were awarded the plaintiffs on their claims. Affirming the judgment in all but one respect[ff] the Eleventh Circuit reviewed the facts:

"In late 1979, the Executive Board of Council 49 appointed Harold Reach to assume the position of Executive Director. Shortly thereafter, in early 1980, Jimmy Gosa was elected President of the Council. In early 1981, Ruth Boshell and Larry Trammel were elected Treasurer and Secretary, respectively. At the time Reach, Boshell, Gosa, and Trammel assumed control of Council 49, it was operating without financial difficulty and its financial records had been meticulously kept. Under the defendants' control, however, the Council rapidly deteriorated into a

ff. The appellate court affirmed the judgment on two of the three allegedly improper expenditures and remanded the case for new assessment of damages.

state of financial disaster. For example, Boshell and Gosa frequently signed blank checks and checks made out to cash, making it impossible to account for large amounts of the Council's funds. Moreover, Boshell, with Gosa's approval, often disbursed Council funds to Debbie Reach, Harold Reach's wife, who worked part-time as the office secretary. In April, 1984, for instance, $2,105.94 in Council funds was disbursed to Mrs. Reach, who was entitled to a salary of only $100 per month for her secretarial work. Boshell and Gosa also wrote checks on the Council's account to pay Reach's personal bills, such as his power and grocery bills.[33] In addition, the Board overpaid Reach by approximately $10,000 over the course of his employment. To make matters worse, many checks were drawn on insufficient funds, adding overdraft charges to the list of Council expenses.

"The Council's financial problems, however, were not limited to the defendants' freewheeling use of the Council 49 checkbook. Since early 1981 Boshell had not withheld payroll taxes from Reach's salary, resulting in unpaid taxes, interest, and penalties of $40,740.55 by the time this suit was filed in September, 1985. In addition, in 1979, William Thomason, an attorney, began representing the Council. Although he was never paid in full for his services, Thomason continued to represent the Council and accrue fees that the Council could not afford to pay. In January of 1983, Thomason obtained a default judgment against the Council for $85,000, for services rendered from March, 1979 through October, 1982. Even after obtaining the judgment, Thomason continued to represent the Council. Boshell did not report the default judgment, or the IRS tax liability, on the Council's monthly balance sheets.

"By early 1985, AFSCME International, the parent organization, became aware of Council 49's financial troubles and placed it under administratorship. Leamon Hood, AFSCME International's area director, was appointed administrator. Shortly thereafter, on April 4, 1985, Reach resigned as Executive Director and requested that Hood pick up the Council's files from Reach's home, where they were being stored. The files consisted of canceled checks, receipts, financial reports, and minutes of Board meetings. Apparently Hood did not immediately respond to this request, and by a letter dated May 10, 1985, Reach informed Hood that he had placed the Council's files 'on the side of the nearest public thru-fare to my residence' and that Hood would have to pick them up there if he wanted them. After making a diligent search of the area, however, Hood was unable to find the files, and they have not turned up since. Consequently, the evidence at trial consisted of the few Council records that Reach had not left by the roadside and copies of checks provided by the Council's bank."

The Eleventh Circuit ultimately affirmed the judgement obtained by the plaintiffs on two of the three expenditures at issue. In reaching its conclusion, the court discussed the § 501(b) civil cause of action. Note that the same issues regarding authorization arise in a civil suit for damages brought

---

33. According to their trial testimony, the Reaches did not maintain their own personal checking account during Harold Reach's tenure as Executive Director.

under § 501(b) by private parties as arise in criminal prosecutions under 501(c).

"Section 501(a) of the Labor Management Reporting and Disclosure Act, 29 U.S.C. § 501, provides that union officers 'occupy positions of trust in relation to [the union] and its members as a group.' Accordingly, section 501 requires each officer 'to hold [the organization's] money and property solely for the benefit of the organization and its members and to manage, invest, and expend the same in accordance with its constitution and bylaws and any resolutions of the governing bodies adopted thereunder * * *.' Section 501 stresses that in carrying out his or her duty, a union officer should take 'into account the special problems and functions of a labor organization.'

"In drafting section 501, Congress did not intend to give courts a license to interfere broadly in internal union affairs. Section 501 is not an invitation for courts to substitute their judgment on how a union should be managed for that of the union officers. Accordingly, where decisions regarding the use of union funds have been authorized in accordance with the union's constitution, by-laws, or other applicable governing provisions, 'a court will typically not have cause to review the reasonableness of the [decision].' Ray v. Young, 753 F.2d 386, 390 (5th Cir.1985).

"Authorization, however, is not a complete defense to an accusation of breach of fiduciary duty under section 501. Because section 501 was adopted primarily to address the problem of corruption among union officials, it has been 'given its strongest reading in [cases] involving a union officer's diversion of union funds or property into his own hands.' Ray v. Young, 753 F.2d 386, 390 (5th Cir.1985).

Where a union officer personally benefits from union funds, a court in a section 501 suit may determine whether the expenditure of funds, notwithstanding its authorization, is so manifestly unreasonable as to evidence a breach of fiduciary duty. Thus, the rule of judicial deference does not apply if an expenditure of union funds is unauthorized, or if it is authorized but bestows a direct, personal benefit on a union official. In either of these instances, courts are free to determine whether an expenditure was so unreasonable as to constitute a breach of fiduciary duty under section 501."

The Eleventh Circuit found the amount of damages awarded to the plaintiffs to be unreasonable and remanded for further consideration as to the amount of damages:

"On cross-appeal, the plaintiffs argue that the district court was clearly erroneous in awarding them only $3,000 in damages to compensate for the defendants' overpayment to Reach. We agree. The district court did not explain how it arrived at the figure of $3,000 as adequate compensation for the plaintiffs. It merely stated that this damage figure was 'no more than the court's best judgment based on poor records.' Although the records in this case were inadequate, the plaintiffs, using the only available records, estimate Reach's overpayment to be more than $10,-000 and have convinced us that the district court's award of $3,000 was clearly erroneous. In calculating Reach's overpayment, the plaintiffs relied on the Council's September, 1983, October, 1983, and February, 1984 financial reports, the only one available, and on copies of bank statements and canceled checks provided by the Council's bank. Although we offer no opinion on whether the exact amount of damages, $10,893.00, calculated the plaintiffs is correct, we endorse their method of calculation, which relies to an extent on estimates and averages based on the available records. As the defendants are responsible for the dearth of evidence making it impossible to determine damages in a more exact fashion, the plaintiffs' method of calculating damages seems especially fair. Accordingly, we remand for the district court to reconsider, based on the available evidence, the amount of damages due the plaintiffs as a result of Reach's overpayment."

* * *

Section 504, of title 29, United States Code, provides another penalty which may be imposed on persons convicted of defrauding a labor organization or benefit plan. Section 504 prohibits any person convicted of violating 29 U.S.C. § 501(c) or 18 U.S.C. § 664, or comparable state offenses, from serving as an officer, director, consultant, or in any decision making position, for a labor organization for thirteen years after such conviction or after the end of imprisonment.

2. *Employment Issues*: Another reason for the large number of collateral lawsuits which arise when there has been a prosecution under § 501(c) is that most defendants in such cases are employees of the labor organization they are accused of defrauding. Thus, improper discharge, discrimination, retention of benefits and other employment related lawsuits often parallel the criminal prosecution. In the next case, the Supreme Court addressed the issue of whether a defendant convicted under § 501(c) is entitled to pension benefits earned through his employment with the union from which he was found to have stolen money and which thereafter secured a civil judgment against him. In Guidry v. Sheet Metal Workers National Pension Fund, 493 U.S. 365 (1990), the Court held that the defendant was entitled to his pension benefits. As you read the following excerpts from the opinion, determine what, if anything, the prosecutor could have done to prevent this outcome.

"Petitioner Curtis Guidry pleaded guilty to embezzling funds from his union. The union obtained a judgment against him for $275,000. The District Court imposed a constructive trust on Guidry's pension benefits, and the United States Court of Appeals for the Tenth Circuit affirmed that judgment. Petitioner contends that the constructive trust violates the statutory prohibition on assignment or alienation of pension benefits imposed by the Employee Retirement Income Security Act of 1974 (ERISA), 88 Stat. 829, as amended, 29 U.S.C. § 1001 et seq. (1982 ed.).[1]

"From 1964 to 1981, petitioner Guidry was the chief executive officer of respondent Sheet Metal Workers International Association, Local 9

---

1. Section 206(d)(1), 29 U.S.C. § 1056(d)(1) (1982 ed.) of ERISA states: "Each pension plan shall provide that bene-fits provided under the plan may not be assigned or alienated."

(Union). From 1977 to 1981 he was also a trustee of respondent Sheet Metal Workers Local No. 9 Pension Fund. Petitioner's employment made him eligible to receive benefits from three union pension funds.[2]

"In 1981, the Department of Labor reviewed the Union's internal accounting procedures. That review demonstrated that Guidry had embezzled substantial sums of money from the Union. This led to petitioner's resignation. A subsequent audit indicated that over $998,-000 was missing. In 1982, petitioner pleaded guilty to embezzling more than $377,000 from the Union, in violation of § 501(c) of the Labor–Management Reporting and Disclosure Act of 1959 (LMRDA), 73 Stat. 536, 29 U.S.C. § 501(c) (1982 ed.). Petitioner began serving a prison sentence. In April 1984, while still incarcerated, petitioner filed a complaint against two of the plans in the United States District Court for the District of Colorado, alleging that the plans had wrongfully refused to pay him the benefits to which he was entitled.[4] The Union intervened, joined the third pension plan as a party, and asserted six claims against petitioner.[5] On the first five claims, petitioner and the Union stipulated to the entry of a $275,000 judgment in the Union's favor. Petitioner and the Union agreed to litigate the availability of the constructive trust remedy requested in the sixth claim.

"Petitioner previously had negotiated a settlement with the Local No. 9 Pension Fund. The other two plans, however, contended that petitioner had forfeited his right to receive benefits as a result of his criminal misconduct. In the alternative those plans contended that, if petitioner were found to have a right to benefits, those benefits should be paid to the Union rather than to Guidry.

"The District Court therefore was confronted with three different views regarding the disbursement of petitioner's pension benefits. Petitioner contended that the benefits should be paid to him. The two funds argued that the benefits had been forfeited. The Union asserted that the benefits had not been forfeited, but that a constructive trust should be imposed so that the benefits would be paid to the Union rather than to petitioner.

"The District Court first rejected the funds' claim that petitioner had forfeited his right to benefits. The court relied on § 203(a) of ERISA, 29 U.S.C. § 1053(a) (1982 ed.) which declares that '[e]ach pension plan shall provide that an employee's right to his normal retirement benefit

2. In addition to the Local No. 9 Pension Fund, petitioner was eligible to receive benefits from respondent Sheet Metal Workers National Pension Fund and from respondent Sheet Metal Workers Local Unions and Councils Pension Fund.

4. The complaint alleged that petitioner was eligible to receive benefits of $577 per month from the Sheet Metal Workers Local Unions and Councils Pension Fund, and $647.51 per month from the Sheet Metal Workers National Pension Fund. App. 5.

5. The first claim alleged that Guidry had breached his fiduciary duty to the Un-

ion in violation of § 501(a) of the LMRDA, 29 U.S.C. § 501(a) (1982 ed.). The second through fifth claims asserted state common-law claims under theories of conversion, fraud, equitable restitution, and negligence. The sixth claim, asserted against petitioner and the three pension funds, did not set forth a substantive ground for relief. Rather, it asserted that the District Court "must restrain and enjoin the Pension Funds from paying any further pension benefits to Plaintiff Guidry until the completion of this action and thereafter until [the Union] is made whole for its losses."

is nonforfeitable' if the employee meets the statutory age and years of service requirements. The court noted other District Court and Court of Appeals decisions holding that pension benefits were not forfeitable even upon a showing of the covered employee's misconduct.

"The court concluded, however, that the prohibition on assignment or alienation of pension benefits contained in ERISA's § 206(d)(1), 29 U.S.C. § 1056(d)(1) (1982 ed.) did not preclude the imposition of a constructive trust in favor of the Union. The court appeared to recognize that the anti-alienation provision generally prohibits the garnishment of pension benefits as a means of collecting a judgment. The court, nevertheless, stated: 'ERISA must be read in pari materia with other important federal labor legislation.' 641 F.Supp., at 362. In the Labor Management Relations Act, 1947, 61 Stat. 136, as amended, 29 U.S.C. § 141 et seq. (1982 ed.), and in the LMRDA, Congress sought to combat corruption on the part of union officials and to protect the interests of the membership. Viewing these statutes together with ERISA, the District Court concluded: 'In circumstances where the viability of a union and the members' pension plans was damaged by the knavery of a union official, a narrow exception to ERISA's anti-alienation provision is appropriate.' 641 F.Supp., at 363. The court therefore ordered that benefits payable to petitioner from all three funds should be held in constructive trust until the Union's judgment and interest thereon were satisfied.

"The United States Court of Appeals for the Tenth Circuit affirmed. 856 F.2d 1457 (1988). The court concluded that ERISA's anti-alienation provision could not be invoked to protect a dishonest pension plan fiduciary whose breach of duty injured the beneficiaries of the plan. The court deemed it 'extremely unlikely that Congress intended to ignore equitable principles by protecting individuals such as [petitioner] from the consequences of their misconduct.' *Id.*, at 1460. The court concluded that 'the district court's imposition of a constructive trust on [petitioner's] pension benefits both accorded with ... principles of trust law and was well within its discretionary power as defined by the common law and ERISA.' *Id.*, at 1461.

"Because Courts of Appeals have expressed divergent views concerning the availability of exceptions to ERISA's anti-alienation provision, we granted certiorari.

"Both the District Court and the Court of Appeals presumed that § 206(d)(1) of ERISA erects a general bar to the garnishment of pension benefits from plans covered by the Act. This Court, also, indicated as much, although in dictum, in Mackey v. Lanier Collection Agency & Service, Inc., 486 U.S. 825. In *Mackey* the Court held that ERISA does *not* bar the garnishment of welfare (e.g., vacation) benefits. In reaching that conclusion, it noted that § 206(d)(1) proscribes the assignment or alienation of *pension* plan benefits, but that no comparable provision applies to ERISA *welfare* benefit plans. It reasoned that 'when Congress was adopting ERISA, it had before it a provision to bar the alienation or garnishment of ERISA plan benefits, and chose to impose that limitation only with respect to ERISA pension benefit plans, and *not* ERISA welfare benefit plans.' *Id.*, at 837 (emphasis in original). The view that the statutory restrictions on assignment or alienation of pension benefits apply to garnishment is consistent with applicable administrative regulations, with the relevant legislative history, and with the views of other federal courts. It is also consonant with other statutory provisions designed to safeguard retirement income. We see no meaningful distinction between a writ of garnishment and the constructive trust remedy imposed in this case. That remedy is therefore prohibited by § 206(d)(1) unless some exception to the general statutory ban is applicable.

"The Court of Appeals, in holding that 'the district court's use of a constructive trust to redress breaches of ERISA was proper,' 856 F.2d, at 1460, indicated that an exception to the anti-alienation provision can be made when a pension plan fiduciary breaches a duty owed to the plan itself. The court relied on § 409(a) of ERISA, 29 U.S.C. § 1109(a) (1982 ed.), which provides that a faithless pension plan fiduciary 'shall be personally liable to make good to such plan any losses to the plan resulting from each such breach, ... and shall be subject to such other equitable or remedial relief as the court may deem appropriate.' 856 F.2d, at 1459. We need not decide whether the remedial provisions contained in § 409(a) supersede the bar on alienation in § 206(d)(1), since petitioner has not been found to have breached any fiduciary duty *to the pension plans*. Respondents contend that, due to the nature of petitioner's scheme, there exists continuing uncertainty as to how much money was stolen from the Union and how much was taken from the pension funds. It is clear, however, that petitioner was convicted of stealing money only from the Union. Moreover, petitioner has negotiated a settlement with the fund of which he was a fiduciary, and only the Union has a judgment against him. Respondents' argument plays on the natural tendency to blur the distinctions between a fund and its related union (since an injury to either will hurt the union's membership). Respondents, however, cannot avoid the fact that the funds here and the Union are distinct legal entities. (Indeed, at an earlier stage of the litigation these parties took inconsistent positions: the funds argued that petitioner's benefits were subject to forfeiture, while the Union contended that petitioner retained his right to benefits but that the benefits should be placed in constructive trust). Although petitioner's actions may have harmed the Union's members who are the beneficiaries of the funds, petitioner has not been found to have breached any duty to the plans themselves. In our view, therefore, the Court of Appeals erred in invoking § 409(a)'s remedial provisions.

"Recognizing the problem with the Court of Appeals' approach, respondents, like the District Court, rely principally on the remedial provisions of the LMRDA. Section 501(a), 29 U.S.C. § 501(a) (1982 ed.) of that Act states that a union's officers 'occupy positions of trust in relation to such organization and its members as a group' and therefore have a duty 'to hold its money and property solely for the benefit of the organization and its members.' Section 501(b), 29 U.S.C. § 501(b) (1982 ed.) provides, under certain conditions, a private right of action 'to recover damages or secure an accounting or other appropriate relief for the benefit of the labor organization.' We assume, without deciding, that the statutory provision for 'other appropriate relief' may authorize, in some circumstances, the imposition of a constructive trust. The question is whether that authorization may override ERISA's prohibition on the alienation of pension benefits.

Respondents point to § 514(d) of ERISA, 29 U.S.C. § 1144(d) (1982 ed.). It states: "Nothing in this title shall be construed to alter, amend, modify, invalidate, impair, or supersede any law of the United States ... or any rule or regulation issued under any such law." In respondents' view, application of ERISA's anti-alienation provision to preclude a remedy that would otherwise be available would "modify, impair or supersede" the LMRDA. We do not believe, however, that the LMRDA will be modified, impaired, or superseded by our refusal to allow ERISA pension plans to be used to effectuate the remedial goals of the LMRDA. Were we to accept respondents' position, ERISA's anti-alienation provision would be inapplicable whenever a judgment creditor relied on the remedial provisions of a federal statute. Such an approach would eviscerate the protections of § 206(d), and we decline to adopt so broad a reading of § 514(d).

"It is an elementary tenet of statutory construction that '[w]here there is no clear intention otherwise, a specific statute will not be controlled or nullified by a general one....' Morton v. Mancari, 417 U.S. 535, 550–551 (1974). We do not believe that congressional intent would be effectuated by reading the LMRDA's general reference to 'other appropriate relief' as overriding an express, specific congressional directive that pension benefits not be subject to assignment or alienation. In our view, the two statutes are more persuasively reconciled by holding that the LMRDA determines what sort of judgment the aggrieved party may obtain, while ERISA governs the narrow question whether that judgment may be collected through a particular means—a constructive trust placed on the pension.

"Nor do we think it appropriate to approve any generalized equitable exception—either for employee malfeasance or for criminal misconduct—to ERISA's prohibition on the assignment or alienation of pension benefits. Section 206(d) reflects a considered congressional policy choice, a decision to safeguard a stream of income for pensioners (and their dependents, who may be, and perhaps usually are, blameless), even if that decision prevents others from securing relief for the wrongs done them. If exceptions to this policy are to be made, it is for Congress to undertake that task.

"As a general matter, courts should be loath to announce equitable exceptions to legislative requirements or prohibitions that are unqualified by the statutory text. The creation of such exceptions, in our view, would be especially problematic in the context of an antigarnishment provision. Such a provision acts, by definition, to hinder the collection of a lawful debt. A restriction on garnishment therefore can be defended only on the view that the effectuation of certain broad social policies sometimes takes precedence over the desire to do equity between particular parties. It makes little sense to adopt such a policy and then to refuse enforcement whenever enforcement appears inequitable. A court attempting to carve out an exception that would not swallow the rule would be forced to determine whether application of the rule in particular circumstances would be "especially" inequitable. The impracticability of defining such a standard reinforces our conclusion that the identification of any exception should be left to Congress.

"Understandably, there may be a natural distaste for the result we reach here. The statute, however, is clear. In addition, as has been noted above, the malefactor often is not the only beneficiary of the pension.

"The judgment of the Court of Appeals is reversed, and the case is remanded for further proceedings consistent with this opinion.

"It is so ordered."

––––––––

What do you think about this opinion? Do you agree that § 501(c) will not "be modified, impaired, or superseded by [the Court's] refusal to allow ERISA plans to be used to effectuate the remedial goals of * * * [501(c)]"?

Chapter 9

FRAUD UPON FINANCIAL INSTITUTIONS

A. INTRODUCTION

There are three major types of financial institutions participating in the American economy: banks, thrifts (which include savings & loan institutions and mutual savings banks), and credit unions. Substantial fraud in or upon any of these is prosecuted almost exclusively by federal authorities. A brief background may be helpful before reviewing the statutory authority for prosecuting fraud in financial institutions.

In 1996, there were approximately 9,528 commercial banks, 1,924 thrifts (which are made up of savings and loan institutions and mutual savings banks, etc.) and 11,392 credit unions in the United States.[a] A "bank" is a financial institution that provides services such as checking accounts, and pays interest to depositors to leave their money with the bank. Banks make business and consumer loans and invest in government and commercial paper. Deposits to banks up to $100,000 are insured by the Federal Deposit Insurance Corporation (FDIC).[b] "Thrifts" were originally established to loan money for residential mortgages. With deregulation in the 1980s, thrifts began to diversify their activities beyond residential lending.[c] Until recently, most thrifts were "Savings and Loans" (S & L's). About half of the S & L's were federally chartered; the remainder were state chartered. Most S & L's were mutually owned (owned by depositors) and most were insured by the Federal Savings and Loan Insurance Corporation (FSLIC). The non-FSLIC S & Ls were insured by state sponsored private insurance.[d] Most "Savings Banks" were located in the northeast, state-chartered, mutually owned, and insured by the FDIC. Credit unions are owned by depositors,

---

a. L. WHITE, THE S & L DEBACLE, 15 (Table 2–1) (1991). American Bankers Assn., http://www.aba.com/abatool/showme_rel.html?location=BankFacts.htm (Sept. 4, 1997).

b. 12 U.S.C. § 1811.

c. *Problems of the Federal Savings & Loan Insurance Corporation (FSLIC): Hear-ing Before the Senate Comm. on Banking, Housing & Urban Affairs,* 101st Cong., 1st Sess., Pt. III, 165 (1989) (Testimony of Barney R. Beeksma, Chairman, U.S. League of Savings Institutions).

d. L. WHITE, THE S & L DEBACLE, *supra,* note a at 13 (1991).

usually all of whom share a common employer. Deposits are insured by a Credit Union Insurance Fund[e] and lending activity usually is restricted to consumer loans.

In the late 1980's and early 1990's, a financial crisis engulfed the American economy. Over 1400 banks and 700 savings institutions failed between 1982 and 1992[f] costing taxpayers over $500 billion.[g] The financial impact of this is enormous. According to one expert,

> "The federal government's bailout of depositors in America's failed thrifts will cause a massive shift in wealth between 37 states and Washington, D.C. and the 13 states where the failed thrifts are concentrated."[h]

Prosecution of financial institutions has been profoundly affected by this savings and loan crisis. It is estimated that anywhere from 25–75% of the total loss is the result of fraud.[i] One response by Congress has been to strengthen statutes criminalizing fraud upon a financial institution and to intensify efforts to prosecute those who have committed such fraud. This effort, as well as substantial reorganization of the entire thrift industry, started in 1989 when Congress passed the Financial Institutions Reform, Recovery, and Enforcement Act of 1989 (FIRREA).[j] FIRREA made many substantial changes in addition to strengthening criminal and civil penalties for fraud upon a financial institution, such as creating new regulatory and insurance structures for the thrift institutions; imposing new limits on loans, investments and activities of thrifts; and establishing more stringent requirements for capital standards. Significantly, FIRREA abolished the FSLIC, giving the FDIC responsibility for insuring the deposits of thrifts.[k]

e. 12 U.S.C. § 1782 (West 1989).

f. Bank Failures in 1994, http://www.fdic.gov/consumer/closings.html (Sept. 4, 1997). "Interestingly, there was only 5 commercial bank failures in 1996, compared to 6 in 1995; 11 in 1994; 42 in 1993 and 100 in 1992." FDIC QUARTERLY BANKING PROFILE, http://www.aba.com/aba-tool/showme_rel.html?location=BankFacts.htm (Sept. 4, 1997).

g. *Savings and Loan Crisis: Hearing Before Senate Judiciary Comm.* 101st Cong., 2d Sess. at 2 (Opening Statement of Senator Metzenbaum) and at 126 (statement of Professor Edward W. Hill). (1990) Other experts suggest that this figure may be inflated. *L. White, The S & L Debacle* at 196–97.

h. *Savings & Loan Crisis: Hearing Before Senate Judiciary Comm.* 101st Cong., 2d Sess. 121 (Statement of Professor Edward W. Hill).

i. *Id.* at 3 (statement of Senator Kohl). It should be noted that estimates of the loss attributable to fraud vary, see, e.g., id. at 6 (statement of Robert E. Litan, Senior Fel-

low, The Brookings Institution); see also KATHLEEN DAY, S & L HELL, 387 C.W.W. Norton & Co. 1994).

j. Pub.L. No. 101–73, 103 Stat. 183 (1989), codified at scattered sections of title 12, United States Code.

k. Important Banking Legislation, http://www.fdic.gov/publish/banklaws. (Sept. 4, 1997). The FDIC insurance fund created to cover thrifts was named the Savings Association Insurance Fund (SAIF), while the fund covering banks was called the Bank Insurance Fund (BIF). *Id.* The FSLIC, charged with insuring deposits in savings and loan institutions was abolished by FIRREA in 1989 with a deficit of $87 billion. Its successor, the Resolution Trust Corporation (RTC) was created by FIRREA to assume the FSLIC's duties, including disposing of insolvent thrifts, and their assets. The Savings Association Insurance Fund (SAIF) was created in 1989 as a separate fund within the FDIC insuring thrifts formerly insured by the FSLIC. Another separate fund with the FDIC, the Bank Insurance Fund (BIF) was created to insure

There are ten major federal statutes that criminalize conduct regarding financial institutions. As will be seen, some statutes apply only to conduct at a bank, others apply only to conduct at savings institutions, others generically apply to all financial institutions. Likewise, some statutes can be violated only by insiders at various financial institutions; others may be violated by "any person."

• **Section 215** of title 18, United States Code, ("bribery") makes it a crime to give, or promise to give, anything of value to an officer, director, employee or agent of a financial institution, with intent to influence any transaction of the institution. Section 215 also makes it a crime for any of these persons to receive such a thing of value.

• **Section 225** of title 18, United States Code, ("continuing financial crimes enterprise" or "CFCE") makes it a crime to organize, manage or supervise a "continuing financial crimes enterprise" in which the defendant receives $5 million or more in gross receipts from such enterprise in a 24–month period. A "continuing financial crimes enterprise" requires at least 4 persons "working in concert" to violate at least one of eleven specified federal crimes relating to a financial crime.

• **Sections 656 and 657** of title 18, United States Code ("embezzlement"), make it a crime for certain insiders (officers, directors, agents or employees, of the institution) to "embezzle, abstract, purloin or willfully misapply" funds or assets of the financial institution. Section 656 applies to insiders of banks, section 657 applies to insiders at lending, credit and insured institutions (formerly including those insured by FSLIC and currently including those under the supervision of the Office of Thrift Supervision (OTS) and Resolution Trust Corporation (RTC)).

• **Sections 1005 and 1006** of title 18, United States Code ("false statement"), make it a crime for certain insiders of financial institutions to make, or cause to be made, false statements in the books of records of the financial institution. Section 1005 applies to bank insiders; Section 1006 applies to insiders at federal credit institutions (formerly including FSLIC and currently including OTS and RTC).

• **Section 1007** of title 18, United States Code makes it a crime for anyone to make a false statement to the FDIC.

thrifts formerly insured by the FDIC. The Office of Thrift Supervision (OTS) was created in 1989 to take over the supervision of federally chartered thrifts from the Federal Home Loan Bank Board, which was abolished with the passage of FIRREA. For an excellent summary of the creation of these agencies see L. White, *The S & L Debacle* (1991).

For two excellent summaries of FIRREA see Clark, Murtagh and Corcoran, *Regulation of Savings Association's Under the Fi-*

nancial Institutions Reform, Recovery, and Enforcement Act of 1989, 45 Bus.Law. 1013 (1990) and Gail & Norton, *A Decade's Journey From "Deregulation" to "Supervisory Regulation": The Financial Institutions Reform, Recovery, and Enforcement Act of 1989,* 45 Bus.Law. 1103 (1990). For a more policy-oriented discussion of the reasons for the savings and loan crisis and FIRREA's effectiveness in resolving these problems see L. White, *The Savings and Loan Debacle.*

• **Section 1014** of title 18, United States Code, makes it a crime for anyone to make a false statement, for the purpose of influencing the action of a financial institution upon any application submitted to the financial institution.

• **Section 1032** ("concealment of assets") makes it a crime for any person to conceal assets from the conservator, receiver or liquidating agent of a financial institution.

• **Section 1344** is a mail fraud analog—without the mailing requirement. This section makes it a crime to execute or attempt to execute a scheme or artifice to defraud a financial institution. Section 1344 is a "racketeering activity" for purposes of RICO, 18 U.S.C. § 1961(1).

The CFCE offense carries the stiffest sentence: a maximum term of imprisonment of life. The rest of the offenses, except § 1032, bear stiff penalties: possible imprisonment of thirty years and fines of $1,000,000, or both.[l] Violations of section 1032 are punishable by possible imprisonment of five years and a fine of $250,000 (for individuals), $500,000 (for corporations).[m] In addition to these punishments, property "involved in," "constituting, derived from, or traceable to any proceeds" of crimes upon financial institutions, is subject to forfeiture.[n]

In addition to the above offenses which are specifically aimed at the fraud in the financial industry, § 1341 and § 1343 of title 18, the mail fraud and wire fraud provisions (which are also "racketeering offenses" for purposes of RICO, 18 U.S.C. § 1961(1)), often are used to prosecute crimes involving financial institutions.[o]

---

l. Sections 656 and 657 also provide for misdemeanor sentences (possible imprisonment of one year or a fine of $1000, or both)—if the amount embezzled abstracted, purloined or misapplied is $100 or less.

m. 18 U.S.C. § 3571.

n. 18 U.S.C. §§ 981, 982. *See* Chapter 5 *infra*.

o. These provisions can be summarized as follows:

18 U.S.C. § 215 (West 1969, Supp.1991) (Receipt of gifts or commissions for procuring loans.)

18 U.S.C. § 656 (West 1969, Supp.1991) (Theft, embezzlement or misapplication by bank officer or employee.)

18 U.S.C. § 657 (West 1969, Supp.1991) (Embezzlement, abstracting, purloining or willful misapplication by officer, agent or employee of certain lending agencies or associations.)

18 U.S.C. § 1005 (West 1969, Supp.1991) (False entry in bank entries, reports or unauthorized transactions.)

18 U.S.C. § 1006 (West 1969, Supp.1991) (False entry in bank entries, reports or unauthorized transactions at certain lending agencies or associations.)

18 U.S.C. § 1007 (West 1969, Supp.1991) (False statement to FDIC to obtain loan, acceptance or release.)

18 U.S.C. § 1014 (West 1969, Supp.1991) (False statement or report to certain lending agencies or associations.)

18 U.S.C. § 1032 (West 1969, Supp.1991) (Concealing assets from the FDIC, RTC or other on conservator, receiver or liquidating agent of a financial institution.)

18 U.S.C. § 1341 (West 1969, Supp.1991) (Obtaining money from a financial institution by means of false or fraudulent pretenses by use of the mails)

18 U.S.C. § 1343 (West 1969, Supp.1991) (Obtaining money or property from a financial institution by false or fraudulent means or representations by means of wire, radio or television communications in interstate commerce.)

18 U.S.C. § 1344 (West 1969, Supp.1991) (Defrauding financial institution.)

Substantial civil and administrative consequences may also flow from the conduct at issue in the criminal case. These consequences include suspension or termination of federal insurance,[p] civil penalties of up to $1 million per day for violation of orders imposed on a financial institution by regulatory agencies[q] and prohibitions against certain individuals from future affiliations with the thrift industry.[r]

The FBI has described five types of criminal conduct involving financial institutions:

> **"Nominee Loans.**—Loans obtained by one person on behalf of an undisclosed person. The nominee or 'straw borrower' typically has no involvement in the loan transaction other than to pose as the borrower.

> **"Double Pledging of Collateral.**—Loans obtained at two or more different financial institutions by pledging the same property as collateral. The combined amount of the loans exceeds the value of the property and the borrower does not disclose the pledging of the property as collateral to a previous loan.

> **"Reciprocal Loan Arrangements.**—Loans made to insiders of a financial institution or sold to the financial institution itself based upon an agreement with insiders of another financial institution to reciprocate in future loan transactions. This arrangement results in less than arms-length transactions between insiders of the two financial institutions and has been used previously to conceal loans from * * * [Federal agency] examiners.

> **"Land Flip.**—Transfers of land between related parties to fraudulently inflate the value of the land. The land is used as collateral for loans based on the inflated or fraudulent valuation. Loan amounts typically greatly exceed the actual value of the land.

> **"Linked Financing.**—The practice of depositing money into a financial institution with the understanding that the financial institution will make a loan conditioned upon receipt of the deposits."[s]

According to the FBI, the greatest dollar losses from criminal conduct involve commercial or real estate loans where an insider is participating in a loan.[t] For this reason, it may be appropriate that half of the statutes outlined above target criminal activity by insiders (18 U.S.C. §§ 215(a)(2), 656, 657, 1005, 1006). As will be seen from the cases in this section, one form of criminal conduct is often prosecuted as a violation of a number of different statutes.

p. 12 U.S.C. § 1818(a)(7) and § 1818(a)(8)(B) (West 1989).

q. 12 U.S.C. § 1786(e) and § 1818(b), (s)(3) (West 1989, Supp.1991).

r. 12 U.S.C. § 1818(e) (West 1989).

s. *Adequacy of Federal Efforts to Combat Fraud, Abuse, and Misconduct in Federally Insured Financial Institutions: Hearing before Subcomm. on Commerce, Consumer and Monetary Affairs of House Comm. on Government Operations,* 100th Cong., 1st Sess. at 605 (Nov. 19, 1987).

t. Id.

B. SECTIONS 1005 AND 1014: FALSE STATE-MENTS, FALSE ENTRIES IN BANK BOOKS AND FALSE STATEMENTS TO A FINANCIAL INSTITUTION

1. SECTION 1014: FALSE STATEMENTS TO A FINANCIAL INSTITUTION

Section 1014, United States Code, Title 18 provides, in relevant part:

> "Whoever knowingly makes any false statement or report, or willfully overvalues any land, property or security, for the purpose of influencing in any way the action of * * any institution the accounts of which are insured by the Federal Deposit Insurance Corporation * * * shall be fined not more than $1,000,000 or imprisoned not more than 30 years, or both."

Although the above statute appears to be straightforward, as the next two cases demonstrate, it is more difficult than it would seem for the government to prove all elements of § 1014. As you read the next two cases, United States v. Jobe, 101 F.3d 1046 (5th Cir.1996) and United States v. Williams, 12 F.3d 452 (5th Cir.1994), assess the strategies employed by the prosecutors and defense counsel.

UNITED STATES v. JOBE

United States Court of Appeals, Fifth Circuit, 1996.
101 F.3d 1046.

JONES, CIRCUIT JUDGE.

Appellants Billie Mac Jobe ("Billie Mac"), Stanley Pruet Jobe ("Stanley"), Stephen Taylor, Philip Mark Sutton and Fernando Novoa were convicted by a jury of various offenses undertaken to organize, conduct, and maintain an elaborate and expanded check-kiting scheme through El Paso banks for over a year and a half. * * *

* * *

Billie Mac was a 1/3 owner, officer and director of Jobe Concrete Products, Inc., in El Paso, Texas. He also owned the Jobe Bar Track Ranch and was a part owner, officer and director of Cal–Tex Spice Co. He and his son, Stanley, owned a 40% share of First Park National Bank ("FPNB") of Livingston, Montana, a federally insured financial institution. Billie Mac maintained checking accounts at FPNB as well as at El Paso State Bank ("EPSB"), a federally insured, state chartered bank in El Paso; Jobe Concrete Products and Cal–Tex Spice had checking accounts at EPSB. Billie Mac was a shareholder of EPSB.

Stanley, Billie Mac's son, was president and a 1/3 owner of Jobe Concrete Products, Inc., a partial owner and director of Cal–Tex Spice Co. and a shareholder and director of EPSB. At FPNB in Montana, Stanley maintained a checking account and sat on the board of directors.

The remaining appellants are employees of some of the financial institutions involved. Taylor was the president of EPSB. Novoa, as a cashier and officer of EPSB, approved significant wire transfer transactions involving Billie Mac. After leaving his employment with EPSB, Novoa became president of Cal–Tex Spice and performed various financial and administrative work for Jobe Concrete Products. Sutton was the president of another federally insured bank used in the kite, Continental National Bank ("CNB").

The scope of the expanded check kite was uncovered essentially by FBI special agent Randy Wolverton ("Wolverton"), whose analysis is of the activity in several Jobe checking accounts from December of 1989 through July of 1991, revealed that a large kite was underway involving Billie Mac and Stanley and their checking accounts at CNB, TCB, FNPB, and EPSB.

In order to manipulate and maximize the float, or lag time between transactions in the banking system, Billie Mac and his cohorts inflated his account balances artificially by making countless wire transfers based on uncollected funds, by writing checks against uncollected or nonexistent funds, and by consummating fraudulent loans that were camouflaged by false entries or statements in bank records. As a result of these machinations, very large checks were routinely paid in full despite the actual insufficiency of funds to cover them. Billie Mac's check kite was remarkably efficient; unlike the vast majority of check kites, this one not only stayed constantly ahead of the lag but never did self-destruct. Evidence at trial demonstrated that none of the checks written by Billie Mac was ever dishonored or returned for insufficient funds, and all of the loans used to commence the kiting scheme were paid in full and with interest to the lenders.

Further evidence of the "success" of the check-kiting is revealed by the vast sums of money floated. Wolverton testified that bank records for December 1, 1989 through March 12, 1990, created the impression that $150,000,000 had been deposited into the Jobe accounts, although less than 15% of that figure, or approximately $20,000,000, was actually present in these accounts. Similarly, from April through June of 1991, Wolverton explained that although bank records indicated that $58,000,-000 was deposited into these accounts, "77% of those, or about $44,000,-000 worth of those deposits, were nothing more than checks and wire transfers being exchanged with each other through these accounts, thereby artificially inflating the accounts." Only $13,000,000 was actually deposited into the accounts.

Profits from the scheme were used to finance business ventures for Billie Mac and Stanley. For example, in late 1989, Cal–Tex Spice Co., co-owned by Billie Mac, purchased a spice plant from the Baltimore Spice Co. for nearly $3,500,000. Austin Hale ("Hale"), the credit manager and eventually vice-president of Jobe Concrete Products, testified that neither Jobe Concrete Products nor Billie Mac had enough liquidity to fund these purchases. Hale further testified that Stanley concurred and expressed his concern to Hale that the company needed cash not only to finance its investment and business activities, but also so that his father, who was "overly stressed about the situation", would not need to work as hard.

Billie Mac commenced the kite by opening a checking account for the Jobe Bar Track Ranch at CNB. Before it was officially opened, Billie Mac wrote himself a check from the new account or starter booklet for $990,000, endorsed this check, and deposited it at EPSB. The opening balance of the CNB checking account was, however, only $1,000. Sutton was the account officer at CNB supervising the Jobe Bar Track Ranch checking account.

After the CNB check was deposited at EPSB, EPSB issued a cashier's check for $3,536,347 to Billie Mac signed by Taylor, the bank president. Although standard banking practice would require EPSB to post an entry in its books or records indicating that the cashier's check had been issued, no such entry was made in EPSB records that day; in fact, no entry was made into EPSB records until several days later on January 4, 1990. Nearly a week earlier, on the same afternoon that he obtained the EPSB check, Billie Mac used this cashier's check to purchase the spice plant.

When the original $990,000 CNB check was presented for payment at that bank, Martha Karlsruher ("Karlsruher"), a senior vice president and bank cashier, noticed that this large check had been written on the Jobe Bar Track Ranch account before it had opened and that the balance in the account was merely $1,000. She immediately advised Sutton of her findings, but he authorized forced payment of the check nonetheless, explaining that a pending loan from CNB to Billie Mac would provide the necessary funds.

As Sutton had explained, CNB did lend Billie Mac $925,000, its legal lending limit, on January 8, 1990 and back-dated this loan to January 5. The loan's stated purpose was to "[r]eplenish personal liquidity utilized in the purchase of Baltimore Spice of Texas." However, the loan did not replenish Billie Mac's personal liquidity, but was rather deposited directly into the Jobe Bar Track Ranch checking account, so that the $990,000 check that had been presented for payment could clear. Karlsruher further explained that because the bank's management and loan committee were "in a hurry to fund the loan [and] disburse the monies to the customer," they did not review Billie Mac's loan application before approving it.

* * *

Sutton's actions began to breach standard banking practice or policy. He occasionally extended CNB's closing deadline in order to give Billie Mac sufficient time to deposit or wire funds to cover overdrafts. Karlsruher testified that Billie Mac was virtually the only customer who received such specialized treatment. Further, despite express warnings from Karlsruher that kiting was going on and that a criminal referral should be filed regarding Billie Mac's activities, Sutton continued to approve forced payment of countless checks written by Billie Mac far in excess of the balance in the Jobe Bar Track Ranch account at CNB. Although Karlsruher could have filed a criminal referral regarding the activity, she explained that she did not do so because she was "provided a copy of a board resolution that ordered management not to file this referral."

* * *

Indeed, loan activity at CNB involving the Jobes continued. On May 21, 1990, with Sutton acting as the bank's loan officer, CNB funded a $750,000 loan to Deer Creek Spice Co., guaranteed by Stanley. In a loan presentation form, an internal document prepared by bank employees, the purpose of the Deer Creek Spice loan was described as acquisition of inventory, and the loan principals were listed as Stanley and Frank Owen IV. Although the size of the Deer Creek Spice loan mandated review by CNB's management loan committee, no such review occurred.

On the very day that the Deer Creek Spice loan was authorized, Stanley endorsed the check for the proceeds and turned it over to Billie Mac who, in turn, deposited it into the cashier's checking account at EPSB. The proceeds of the Deer Creek Spice loan were used to pay for cashier's checks that Billie Mac had obtained from EPSB earlier in the day. These cashier's checks had been deposited at CNB to allow a $750,000 check written against the Jobe Bar Track Ranch account to clear; not surprisingly, the $750,000 check had been written by Billie Mac and was payable to him.

* * *

Stanley Jobe was convicted under Counts 5 and 6 of making false statements on a loan application, in violation of 18 U.S.C. § 1014, * * *. Stanley argues insufficient evidence. In these instances, we agree with the contention. To prove a violation of 18 U.S.C. § 1014, the government must demonstrate beyond a reasonable doubt that "(1) the defendant made a false statement to a financial institution; (2) the defendant made the false statement knowingly; (3) he did so for the purpose of influencing the financial institution's action; and (4) the statement was false as to a material fact." United States v. Thompson, 811 F.2d 841, 844 (5th Cir.1987). Stanley is also charged in Count 6 with aiding and abetting Philip Sutton to make false entries in the bank records concerning the same application, which was made, as the indictment charges, "by Stanley Pruet Jobe." After reviewing the evidence and the reasonable inferences therefrom in the light most favorable to the government, this court concludes that the government has failed to prove that Stanley Jobe made a false statement to a financial institution or that he made a loan application concerning the Deer Creek Spice loan. As a result, Stanley Jobe's convictions are not supported by sufficient evidence.

Under Counts 5 and 6, the government's theory of false statement and aiding and abetting is that Stanley Jobe misrepresented that the purpose of the Deer Creek Spice loan was to finance the acquisition of inventory. The government further suggests that this intentional misrepresentation was entered on a "loan application" made by Stanley Jobe at CNB, dated May 18, 1990. CNB was allegedly influenced by the false statement because this statement was relied upon by bank officers in the bank's loan approval committee. Under the government's theory and indictment of Counts 5 and 6, because Stanley Jobe knowingly misrepresented the purpose of the loan and also aided and abetted Philip Sutton in making material false bank entries at CNB, he is guilty. The record does not, however, support the government's assertion that Stanley Jobe made a false statement on a loan application at CNB or communicated with Philip Sutton in any way to assist Sutton in making false bank records concerning the loan. It is undisputed that Stanley made no direct representations concerning the loan.[22] He was neither the borrower nor the payee of the proceeds, although he was a guarantor. Moreover, Stanley Jobe did not sign any loan application at CNB on May 18, 1990;[23] in fact, there was no formal loan application whatsoever, but rather a loan presentation form that was compiled by CNB employees and used by Sutton but unsigned by Stanley. At no time during trial did the government introduce into evidence a loan application on which Stanley Jobe made a false statement. Because the government's evidence at trial was insufficient to allow a reasonable juror to conclude that Stanley made false statements on a loan application or aided and abetted Sutton, his Counts 5 and 6 convictions are reversed.

Notes

According to the Fifth Circuit, Stanley Jobe guaranteed the $750,000 loan to Deer Creek Spice Company; Stanley Jobe was listed as a principal of the loan; Stanley Jobe endorsed the check for the loan proceeds and turned the proceeds over to his father who used the proceeds to keep the check kite afloat; profits from the check kite "were used to finance business ventures for Billie Mac and Stanley." Given these facts, what further evidence might have been available to the government to prove that Stanley Jobe did in fact make the false statements to CNB about the Deer Creek Spice loan?

UNITED STATES v. WILLIAMS

United States Court of Appeals, Fifth Circuit, 1994.
12 F.3d 452.

WISDOM, CIRCUIT JUDGE.

The appellant/defendant, Lynn Williams, originally was indicted on August 7, 1991, on charges of conspiracy to embezzle funds belonging to

---

22. The record demonstrates that bank examiners investigating this loan at CNB did not suspect Stanley Jobe of criminal activity.

23. The promissory note was actually signed by Frank Owen.

a labor union pension plan under 18 U.S.C. § 371 and embezzlement of those pension funds under 18 U.S.C. § 664. A series of superseding indictments additionally charged him with making false statements to a federally insured bank under 18 U.S.C. § 1014. * * *

Williams was charged along with several co-defendants, all of whom pleaded guilty. He refused to do so, presumably because his participation in the criminal enterprise consisted only of lending his friends money and, on two fateful occasions, signing documents that they presented to him. A jury nonetheless found Williams guilty of one count of conspiracy and three counts under § 1014; the jury found him not guilty on the two pension fund theft counts. After denying Williams's motion for judgment of acquittal or for a new trial, the district judge sentenced Williams to 21 months in prison. Williams appeals from that conviction. We AFFIRM his conviction for conspiracy but VACATE his convictions under § 1014.

I. BACKGROUND

Although the charges against Williams are not particularly complex, some background on the other defendants's relationships and business ventures is helpful to understand their context. Eugene Sykes, of Baton Rouge, Louisiana, owned and operated Morning Treat Coffee Co. for two years until it filed for bankruptcy in 1985. In July of that year, Charles Sykes (Eugene's brother) formed Southern Coffee Co. as a distinct successor to Morning Treat; Southern bought the remaining assets of Morning Treat. Although Charles owned 100% of Southern Coffee, he made Eugene president. Eugene spent his time handling the day-to-day affairs of Southern Coffee while Charles continued his main vocation, practicing law and representing labor unions along the Gulf Coast in Mississippi.

In April 1986, Eugene sought additional funding for Southern Coffee. He applied for a loan of two million dollars to the Louisiana Imports and Exports Trust Authority (LIETA), an organization designed to aid small businesses in Louisiana in gaining access to the import and export markets. During this time, Williams, an attorney in Baton Rouge, maintained an ongoing personal and business relationship with Eugene. For example, Williams accompanied Eugene when he went to New Orleans to address the LIETA Board and, further, applied to a bank for a letter of credit for Eugene to pledge as collateral. When that application was rejected, Williams personally borrowed $50,000 and lent the money to Eugene.

Always the entrepreneur, Eugene decided to get into the marble cutting business. In particular, he started China Marble of America, Inc., and sought to buy the Columbus Marble Works of Columbus, Mississippi (with a quarry in Alabama) for $460,000. Eugene told his brother Charles, the attorney, about his interest in the marble venture and enlisted his help in securing funding. Eugene knew that Charles was extremely influential with the unions he represented and might have access to money in their pension funds.

Eventually Eugene gave Charles documents outlining a proposal for the marble venture and proposing plans to build a Morning Treat Coffee plant in Mississippi. The proposal sought interim funding until a loan of one million dollars from LIETA could be consummated. Charles passed the proposal to co-defendants Wilson Evans and Robert Matthews, two trustees of the Gulfport Steamship Company–International Longshoremen's Association Pension Fund ("Fund").[3]

Evans and Matthews may have been blinded by wishful naivete: the proposal came when jobs were scarce. They doubtless saw the marble cutting venture as the source of some much-needed local employment opportunities. The reality, unfortunately, was quite different. The proposal was but a means of misappropriating pension money to secure loans for Eugene's various ventures. In addition, LIETA would never have given money to a venture in Mississippi (the organization was founded to aid small businesses in Louisiana, as the "L" in LIETA indicated). Evans and Matthews wrote Eugene a letter telling him that the Fund would pledge one million dollars in certificates of deposit to secure the LIETA loan. When no LIETA money was forthcoming, Eugene and Charles applied to two banks in Mississippi, using the pension's certificates of deposit as collateral. On the strength of the pledged collateral, the banks approved the loans. Eugene used the bank loans for the purchase of the marble equipment and for operating expenses for his other ventures.

When his businesses failed, Eugene's loans went into default. The banks exercised their rights over the certificates of deposit against the Fund. The pension fund lost the money represented by the certificates of deposit.

II.   FACTS PERTINENT TO THE SECTION 1014 CHARGES AGAINST WILLIAMS

In the course of arranging the bank loans, Charles prepared three form resolutions, a standard component of a loan application. Eugene then presented these forms to Williams who signed them. By signing both of the loan applications and, accordingly, attesting to the veracity of the information contained there, Williams allegedly made two statements that formed the basis for his convictions. First, the forms listed him as the treasurer, secretary, and certifying officer of Southern Coffee. Second, the resolutions stated that approval for the loans had been given at a meeting of the board of directors of Southern Coffee.

The government contended that Williams had never been elected to those positions or served in those capacities and, similarly, that the board of directors had not formally approved the resolution. The jury agreed and convicted Williams of making false statements to a federally insured bank.

III.   MATERIALITY UNDER SECTION 1014

It is illegal under 18 U.S.C. § 1014 to make a false, material statement to a federally insured banking institution. To sustain a

---

3. Williams also was a business associate of Evans and Matthews.

conviction under this statute, the government must prove that: (1) the defendant made a false statement to a financial institution; (2) the defendant knew the statement was false when he made it; (3) he made it for the purpose of influencing the financial institution's action; and (4) the statement was false as to a material fact.[6]

The defendant challenges that the statements were false, that he knew they were false, and that they were material. He concedes that the statements were made to influence the bank's decision on Eugene and Charles's loan application. We need not address whether the statements were false or whether Williams knew of their falsity for we hold that the statements were not material. As a result, the government failed to meet its burden and we must vacate Williams's convictions under § 1014.

Statutes imposing criminal penalties for making false statements long have required materiality as an essential element. Section 1014 is no exception: the government must prove that the false statement matters.

Statutes like section 1014 and section 1001 (the statute that makes it illegal to make a false statement to a government department or agency) are "highly penal" and, thus, require that the materiality element be taken seriously. In United States v. Beer,[9] we emphasized that the severe penalties flowing from a conviction for making a false statement require the government to "make a reasonable showing of the potential effects of the statement". In the present case, the government failed to do so.

* * *

A false statement is material if it is shown to be capable of influencing a decision of the institution to which it was made.[14] Moreover, the statements must be analyzed in the particular context in which they were made. In the context of the present matter, our inquiry is limited to whether the statements at issue—the loan application forms listing Williams as secretary and treasurer and attesting that the board of directors formally approved the loan—were capable of influencing the bank's decision to loan the Sykes brothers money. We hold that these statements were not capable of influencing the bank's decision one way or the other and, as such, fail to meet the materiality requirement.

The United States urges that we adopt the broadest possible definition of materiality, relying on United States v. Lueben, 838 F.2d 751, 755 (5th Cir.1988) for the proposition: "[I]f these statements were immaterial, why were they required by the lending institution in each of the transactions?" This dictum was intended as a rhetorical guidepost, not a bright line rule. Otherwise, the law of materiality would change every time that a bank printed up a new loan application form. We need

---

6. United States v. Thompson, 811 F.2d 841, 844 (5th Cir.1987).

9. 518 F.2d 168 (5th Cir.1975).

14. *Id.* at 754. The statement need not actually influence a decision provided that it is capable of doing so. Reliance is irrelevant. [citation omitted]

not resort to these short-hand approaches, however, for the standard we are to apply is clear: If Williams's statements were capable of influencing the bank's decision, they are material.

The government marshaled evidence showing that the banks would not have made the loans if they had known that these statements were false. In actuality, the bank officers merely testified that they would not have approved the loans if they had discovered that the applicant had lied. That does not make the lies themselves material, however. This is a crucial distinction. Aided by hindsight, the banks undoubtedly would not have made these loans. Any bank would be understandably reluctant to lend money to a corporation when its officers lie on the loan application. In sum, the government's evidence demonstrates only that the banks maintain a policy that warns against loaning money to entities which do not tell the truth; it is no way probative of the materiality of these particular statements.

Williams, in contrast, urges that we limit the parameters of materiality by looking to the purpose of the loan application. He argues that the fact that a board of directors meeting may not have taken place or that Williams was not actually secretary or treasurer did not matter to the bank in its evaluation of the loan application. He asserts instead that the only material fact elicited by the forms was that Charles, as sole director and shareholder of Southern Coffee, had authorized his brother Eugene to act for and bind the corporation when dealing with the banks. Williams presented evidence that the purpose of a corporate resolution in this context is to identify the person who has the power to bind the corporation. As to these loans, that person was primarily Eugene and, secondarily, Charles. Hence, Williams argues, he was but an unnecessary (and immaterial) bystander.

We agree that an examination of the purpose of the loan forms is appropriate when defining the boundaries of materiality. The loan application includes standard forms used to verify the identity of those persons legally authorized to sign corporate checks and indorse instruments payable to the corporation. Moreover, the forms identify the persons capable of borrowing money from the bank in the corporations's name or of paying notes to the bank. * * *

The forms clearly identify those people as Eugene Sykes, the president, and C.T. (Charles) Sykes, the agent. In the light of this purpose, the fact that Williams was or was not secretary and treasurer or the question of whether the board met is of no consequence.

When we look to the purpose of the bank forms, we are asking whether reliance on the false statements would have changed the outcome. In the *Beer* case, for example, we held that the defendant's failure to include a loan to which he was accommodated on an FDIC form was immaterial. We explained that one way of determining whether the statements were capable of influencing a bank's decision is to extrapolate from the facts and ask, "If the bank had relied on the defendant's statements, would it have made any difference?" Similarly, the Weinstock court held that inaccurate information about the name of an organization on particular dates was not material for, if relied on, it would not have influenced any decision made by the agency to which it was directed.

From that point of view, the cases upon which the government relies are distinguishable. This is not a case like United States v. Lueben, 838 F.2d 751, 754 (5th Cir.1988) where the defendant lied about his income to make his financial position look more attractive to the bank. Nor is it like United States v. Puente, 982 F.2d 156, 159 (5th Cir.1993) where the defendant lied about his previous felony conviction in an effort to whitewash his past. In those circumstances, it is clear why a bank or federal institution, armed with the truth, would have arrived at a different decision on a pending application.

Section 1014 was not designed to convict on a technicality. More is required. Williams merely signed the resolutions based upon the representations of Eugene and Charles. Williams's signature reflected Charles's designation of a secretary and treasurer, if only for the purposes of procuring the loan money. The banks wanted to know who was responsible for these loans. Eugene and Charles were; Williams was not. We hold that Williams's statements were not material and, accordingly, we vacate his convictions under § 1014.

IV. THE CONSPIRACY COUNT

Williams was charged under 18 U.S.C. § 371 with conspiracy to convert to one's own use securities of a pension fund. Although the jury acquitted Williams of the substantive crime of embezzling pension funds, it convicted him of conspiracy. Upon appeal, he charges that the evidence was not sufficient to sustain that verdict.

* * *

To sustain a conviction for conspiracy, the government had to prove that: (1) two or more persons agreed to commit a crime; (2) the defendant knew of the agreement and voluntarily became a part of it; and (3) at least one of the conspirators committed an act in furtherance for the conspiracy. Williams contends that the government failed to meet its burden with respect to the second prong. He argues that the evidence is insufficient to show that he possessed the requisite knowledge of the conspiracy and voluntarily participated in it.

Although we will not conjecture as to what weight the jury accorded any particular piece of evidence, some evidence stands out for its probative worth. For example, the government demonstrated that on at least two occasions discussions took place in Williams's presence outlining the conspiracy to use the pension fund certificates as collateral for the loans. The pension fund certificates were identified specifically as Longshoreman Pension Fund CD's. In addition, the government properly introduced circumstantial evidence of guilt, including the defendant's presence at discussions and associations with the co-conspirators.

The government cast doubt on Williams's contention that he never knew that the pension fund CD's were pledged as collateral for the loans. Williams maintained close business relationships with his co-defendants. He knew that Southern Coffee was in some financial trouble, for he had lent Eugene Sykes large sums of money to keep the company afloat. Williams knew that Eugene needed $435,000 to procure the marble cutting business (the purchase price of $460,000 less the $25,000 that Williams had lent him). Accordingly, Williams knew that Eugene would be going to Mississippi banks for that money. Similarly, the certificates were used to secure loans well in excess of the $460,000 that Williams knew was needed for the marble cutting venture. In fact, the loan from People's Bank alone amounted to $600,000, leaving an unexplained surplus.

Williams is a trained attorney and no stranger to the world of business. A reasonable jury could have concluded that Williams understood the intent of his friends and, more, knew that Eugene had appropriated the pension funds's CD's to finance his various ventures.

Although Williams's false statements on the bank forms were not material, he was by no means an innocent bystander in the overall criminal scheme. While his co-defendants plotted the enterprise, Williams helped them achieve their aims. Williams did introduce some exculpatory testimony, but the jury apparently elected to accord it little credibility. While no one piece of evidence may be patently sufficient, in the aggregate the quantum of evidence introduced was enough to allow a jury to reach a guilty verdict. We affirm his conspiracy conviction.

Notes

1.   Recall the two false statements on the loan application at issue: that Williams was treasurer, secretary and certifying officer of Southern Coffee Company, and that the Southern Coffee Board of Directors had approved seeking the loan in question. Do you agree with the court's materiality analysis? Note the question posed by the prosecutor to the bank officers: "Would the bank have made the loans if they had known that these statements were false?" When the officers answered "no," the Fifth Circuit drew the conclusion that the officers were testifying only that the bank would not make a loan if the officers knew the loan applicant had lied on the application. Can you think of a way the prosecutor could have asked the materiality question differently, so that a negative answer (assuming the answer was still negative) clearly demonstrated materiality?

2.   Note the grounds on which the court affirmed Williams' conviction on conspiracy charges: Williams was present when details of the pension fund embezzlement were discussed and, "Williams is a trained attorney * * *; [a] reasonable jury could have concluded that Williams understood [the embezzlement]." What do you think about this evidence of conspiracy?

Not only is § 1014 often difficult to prove but its fairly straight-forward terms have generated a fair amount of legal controversy. The next two Supreme Court cases, Williams v. United States, 458 U.S. 279 (1982) and United States v. Wells, 519 U.S. ___, 117 S.Ct. 921 (1997), demonstrate this. In *Williams,* the Court, voting 5–4, held that conduct long prosecuted under § 1014 was not within the statute. Like McNally v. United States, 483 U.S. 350 (1987), *supra,*[u] *Williams* demonstrates how difficult it can be in white collar cases to determine whether conduct is a crime.

WILLIAMS v. UNITED STATES

United States Supreme Court, 1982.
458 U.S. 279.

BLACKMUN, JUSTICE.

In this case we must decide whether the deposit of a "bad check" in a federally insured bank is proscribed by 18 U.S.C. § 1014.

I

In 1975, petitioner William Archie Williams purchased a controlling interest in the Pelican State Bank in Pelican, Louisiana, and appointed himself president. The bank's deposits were insured by the Federal Deposit Insurance Corporation.

Among the services the bank provided its customers at the time of petitioner's purchase was access to a "dummy account," used to cover checks drawn by depositors who had insufficient funds in their individual accounts. Any such check was processed through the dummy account and paid from the bank's general assets. The check was then held until the customer covered it by a deposit to his own account, at which time the held check was posted to the customer's account and the dummy account was credited accordingly. As president of the bank, petitioner enjoyed virtually unlimited use of the dummy account, and by May 2, 1978, his personal overdrafts amounted to $58,055.44, approximately half the total then covered by the account.

On May 8, 1978, federal and state examiners arrived at the Pelican bank to conduct an audit. That same day, petitioner embarked on a series of transactions that seemingly amounted to a case of "check kiting."[1] He began by opening a checking account with a deposit of

---

u. *See* Chapter 2.

1. As the government explains, a check-kiting scheme typically works as follows:

"The check kiter opens an account at Bank A with a nominal deposit. He then writes a check on that account for a large sum, such as $50,000. The check kiter then opens an account at Bank B and deposits the $50,000 check from Bank A in that account. At the time of deposit, the check is not supported

by sufficient funds in that account at Bank A .. However, Bank B, unaware of this fact, gives the check kiter immediate credit on his account at Bank B. During the several-day period that the check on Bank A is being processed for collection from that bank, the check kiter writes a $50,000 check on his account at Bank B and deposits it into his account at Bank A. At the time of the deposit of that check, Bank A gives the check kiter immediate credit on

$4,649.97 at the federally insured Winn State Bank and Trust Company in Winnfield, Louisiana. The next day, petitioner drew a check on his new Winn account for $58,500—a sum far in excess of the amount actually on deposit at the Winn Bank—and deposited it in his Pelican account. Pelican credited his account with the face value of the check, at the same time deducting from petitioner's account the $58,055.44 total of his checks that previously had been cleared through the dummy account. At the close of business on May 9, then, petitioner had a balance of $452.89 at the Pelican Bank.

On May 10, petitioner wrote a $60,000 check on his Pelican account—again, a sum far in excess of the account balance—and deposited it in his Winn account. The Winn Bank immediately credited the $60,000 to petitioner's account there, and Pelican cleared the check through its dummy account when it was presented for payment on May 11. The Winn Bank routinely paid petitioner's May 9 check for $58,500 when it cleared on May 12.

Petitioner next attempted to balance his Pelican account by depositing a $65,000 check drawn on his account at yet another institution, the Sabine State Bank in Many, Louisiana. Unfortunately, the balance in petitioner's Sabine account at the time was only $1,204.81. The Sabine Bank therefore refused payment when Pelican presented the check on May 17. On May 23, petitioner settled his Pelican account by depositing at the Pelican Bank a $65,000 money order obtained with the proceeds from a real estate mortgage loan.

The bank examiners, meanwhile, had been following petitioner's activities with considerable interest. Their scrutiny ultimately led to petitioner's indictment, in the United States District Court for the Western District of Louisiana, on two counts of violating 18 U.S.C. § 1014.[2] The provision makes it crime to

> "knowingly mak[e] any false statement or report, or willfully over-valu[e] any land, property or security, for the purpose of influencing in any way the action of [certain enumerated financial institutions, among them banks whose deposits are insured by the Federal Deposit Insurance Corporation], upon any application, advance, discount, purchase, purchase agreement, repurchase agreement, commitment, or loan * * *."

The first of the counts under § 1014 was directed at the May 9, 1978, check drawn on the Winn Bank, and charged that petitioner "did knowingly and willfully overvalue * * * a security, that is a check * * *

his account there, and on the basis of that grant of credit pays the original $50,000 check when it is presented for collection.

"By repeating this scheme, or some variation of it, the check kiter can use the $50,-000 credit originally given by Bank B as an interest-free loan for an extended period of time. In effect, the check kiter can take advantage of the several-day period re-quired for the transmittal, processing, and payment of checks from accounts in different banks * * *.

2. Petitioner also was charged—and thereafter convicted—with one count of misapplying bank funds, in violation of 18 U.S.C. § 656. The validity of that conviction, which was affirmed on appeal, is not before us.

for the purpose of influencing the Pelican State Bank * * * a bank the deposits of which are insured by the Federal Deposit Insurance Corporation, upon an advance of money and extension of credit." The other § 1014 used virtually identical language to indict petitioner for depositing in his Winn account the May 10 check drawn on the Pelican Bank.[3]

At petitioner's trial the court charged the jury that "[a] check is a security for purposes of Section 1014." The court then explained that "[t]he Government charges that Mr. Williams was involved in check-kiting—a scheme whereby false credit is obtained by the exchange and passing of worthless checks between two or more banks." To convict petitioner, the court continued, the jury had to find as to each count that "the defendant * * * did knowingly and willfully make a false statement of a material fact," that the statement "influence[d] the decision of the [bank] officers or employees," and that "the defendant made the false statement with fraudulent intent to influence the [bank] to extend credit to the defendant. * * * The crucial question in check-kiting," the court concluded, "is whether the defendant intended to write checks which he could not reasonably expect to cover and thereby defraud the bank, or whether he was genuinely involved in the process of depositing funds and then making legitimate withdrawals against them." The jury convicted petitioner on both counts, and he was sentenced to six months' incarceration on the second § 1014 count. For the first § 1014 count he was placed on five years' probation, to begin upon his release from confinement.

Among other things, petitioner argued on appeal that the indictment did not state a violation of § 1014. The Court of Appeals rejected this contention, however, concluding that petitioner's actions "constitute classic incidents of check kiting." 639 F.2d at 1319. In line with its earlier decision in United States v. Payne, 602 F.2d 1215 (5th Cir.1979), the court found such action proscribed by the statute.

We granted certiorari * * * in order to resolve a conflict concerning the reach of § 1014.

To obtain a conviction under § 1014, the Government must establish two propositions: it must demonstrate (1) that the defendant made a "false statement or report," or "willfully overvalue[d] any land, property, or security," and (2) that he did so "for the purpose of influencing in any way the action of [a described financial institution] upon any application, advance * * * commitment, or loan." We conclude that petitioner's convictions under § 1014 cannot stand, because the Government has failed to meet the first of these burdens.

3. Neither of the § 1014 counts of the indictment expressly charged petitioner with making a "false statement." The first count, however, did allege that he "presented said check for deposit at pelican State bank * * * and represented and caused to be represented to said bank that said check was of a value equal to the face amount of the check, when in truth and fact, as the [petitioner] then well knew, there were no sufficient funds in the account of W.A. Williams at the Winn State Bank and Trust Company, to cover said check." Similar language was employed in the second § 1014 count.

A

Although petitioner deposited several checks that were not supported by sufficient funds, that course of conduct did not involve the making of a "false statement," for a simple reason: technically speaking, a check is not a factual assertion at all, and therefore cannot be characterized as "true" or "false." Petitioner's bank checks served only to direct the drawee banks to pay the face amounts to the bearer, while committing petitioner to make good the obligations if the banks dishonored the drafts. Each check did not, in terms, make any representation as to the state of petitioner's bank balance. As defined in the Uniform Commercial Code, 2 U.L.A. 17 (1977), a check is simply "a draft drawn on a bank and payable on demand," § 3–104(2)(b), which "contain[s] an unconditional promise or order to pay a sum certain in money," § 3–104(1)(b). As such, "[t]he drawer engages that upon dishonor of the draft and any necessary notice of dishonor or protest he will pay the amount of the draft to the holder." § 3–413(2), 2 U.L.A. 424 (1977). The Code also makes clear, however, that "[a] check or other draft does not of itself operate as an assignment of any funds in the hands of the drawee available for its payment, and the drawee is not liable on the instrument until he accepts it." § 3–409(1), 2 U.L.A. 408 (1977). Louisiana, the site of petitioner's unfortunate banking career, embraces verbatim each of these definitions.

For similar reasons, we conclude that petitioner's actions cannot be regarded as "overvalu[ing]" property or a security. Even assuming that petitioner's checks were property or a security as defined by § 1014, the value legally placed upon them was the value of petitioner's obligation; as defined by Louisiana law, that is the only meaning actually attributable to a bank check. In a literal sense, then, the face amounts of the checks were their "values."

The foregoing description of bank checks is concededly a technical one, and the Government therefore argues with some force that a drawer is generally understood to represent that he "currently has funds on deposit sufficient to cover the face value of the check." If the drawer has insufficient funds in his account at the moment the check is presented, the Government continues, he effectively has made a "false statement" to the recipient. While this broader reading of § 1014 is plausible, we are not persuaded that it is the preferable or intended one. It "slights the wording of the statute," United States v. Enmons, 410 U.S. 396, 399 (1973), for, as we have noted, a check is literally not a "statement" at all. In any event, whatever the general understanding of a check's function, "false statement" is not a term that, in common usage, is often applied to characterize "bad checks." And, when interpreting a criminal statute that does not explicitly reach the conduct in question, we are reluctant to base an expansive reading on inferences drawn from subjective and variable "understandings."

Equally as important, the Government's interpretation of § 1014 would make a surprisingly broad range of unremarkable conduct a violation of federal law. While the Court of Appeals addressed itself only to check kiting, its ruling has wider implications: it means that any check, knowingly supported by insufficient funds, deposited in a federally insured bank could give rise to criminal liability, whether or not the drawer had an intent to defraud. Under the Court of Appeals' approach, the violation of § 1014 is not the *scheme* to pass a number of bad checks; it is the presentation of one false statement—that is, one check that at the moment of deposit is not supported by sufficient funds—to a federally insured bank. The United States acknowledged as much at oral argument. Indeed, each individual count of the indictment in this case stated only that petitioner knowingly had deposited a single check that was supported by insufficient funds, not that he had engaged in an extended scheme to obtain credit fraudulently.

Yet, if Congress really set out to enact a national bad check law in § 1014, it did so with a peculiar choice of language and in an unusually backhanded manner. Federal action was not necessary to interdict the deposit of bad checks, for, as Congress surely knew, fraudulent checking activities already were addressed in comprehensive fashion by state law. Absent support in the legislative history for the proposition that § 1014 was "designed to have general application to the passing of worthless checks," we are not prepared to hold petitioner's conduct proscribed by that particular statute.

B

[The Court reviewed the legislative history of § 1014 and concluded that the statute unambiguously excluded check-kiting.—ed.]

* * *

Given this background—a statute that is not unambiguous in its terms and that if applied here would render a wide range of conduct violative of federal law, a legislative history that fails to evidence congressional awareness of the statute's claimed scope, and a subject matter that traditionally has been regulated by state law—we believe that a narrow interpretation of § 1014 would be consistent with our usual approach to the construction of criminal statutes. The Court has emphasized that " 'when choice has to be made between two readings of what conduct Congress has made a crime, it is appropriate, before we choose the harsher alternative, to require that Congress should have spoken in language that is clear and definite.' " United States v. Bass, 404 U.S. 336, 347 (1971). To be sure, the rule of lenity does not give courts license to disregard otherwise applicable enactments. But in a case such as this one, where both readings of § 1014 are plausible, "it would require statutory language much more explicit than that before us here to lend to the conclusion that Congress intended to put the Federal Government in the business of policing the" deposit of bad checks. *Enmons*, 410 U.S. at 411.

The judgment of the Court of Appeals is reversed, and the case is remanded for further proceedings consistent with this opinion.

It is so ordered.

JUSTICE MARSHALL, with whom the CHIEF JUSTICE, JUSTICE BRENNAN, and JUSTICE WHITE join, dissenting.

The majority, after developing an overly technical "definition" of the meaning of a check—a definition which will come as quite a surprise to banks and businesses that accept checks in exchange for goods, services, or cash on the representation that the drawer has sufficient funds to cover the check—concludes that the question whether petitioner Williams' check-kiting scheme is covered by 18 U.S.C. § 1014 is ambiguous. The majority then applies its version of the rule of lenity, and decides that Williams cannot be convicted for violating this statute. Because I believe that the majority misapplies the rule of lenity, and because Williams' conduct is clearly prohibited by the statute, I respectfully dissent.

* * *

Before addressing the application of § 1014 to Williams' conduct, I think that it is helpful to set forth clearly what is *not* involved here. This is not a case in which a defendant, through careless bookkeeping, wrote checks on accounts with insufficient funds. Nor is this a case in which a defendant wrote a check on an account containing insufficient funds with the good-faith intention to deposit in that account an amount that would cover the check before it cleared in the normal course of business. Rather, this case clearly involves fraudulent conduct. Petitioner Williams engaged in an intentional check-kiting scheme. He misled the first bank into honoring his worthless, or virtually worthless, check and extending him immediate credit. This extension of credit enabled him to "play the float" and cover that check by misleading another bank into extending him credit on an equally worthless check. In effect, Williams was able to obtain interest-free extensions of credit. Williams, who was a bank president, does not, nor can he, make any credible argument that he was unaware that his conduct was wrongful. With this in mind, I turn to the question whether Williams' conduct constitutes a violation of 18 U.S.C. § 1014.

Section 1014 is a comprehensive statute designed to protect the assets of federally insured lending institutions. The Government establishes a violation of this statute by proving that the defendant "knowingly [made] *any* false statement or * * * willfully overvalue[d] *any* * * * property or security, for the purpose of influencing in *any way* the action of [any federally insured bank] upon *any* * * * *advance* * * * commitment, or loan." 18 U.S.C. § 1014. Just last Term, we reiterated that "[i]n determining the scope of a statute, we look first to its language. If the statutory language is unambiguous, in the absence of a 'clearly expressed legislative intent to the contrary, that language must ordinarily be regarded as conclusive.' " United States v. Turkette, 452 U.S. 576, 580 (1981). In my view, the plain language of § 1014 covers the check-kiting scheme practiced by Williams, and nothing in the legislative history of the statute indicates that Congress intended to exclude this type of scheme from the coverage of the statute.

A

The language of § 1014 is sweeping. It embraces numerous entities in which the federal Government has a financial interest. It proscribes, in the disjunctive, a wide variety of deceptive schemes that might impair the financial stability of these institutions. The statute refers broadly to "any false statement or report," and to overvaluation of "any" property or security. The list of transactions to which the statute applies is equally expansive—it covers "any application, advance, discount, purchase, purchase agreement, repurchase agreement, commitment, or loan, or any change or extension of any of the same, by renewal, deferment of action or otherwise, or the acceptance, release, or substitution of security therefor." 18 U.S.C. § 1014.

The broad statutory language clearly evinces its legislative purpose—Congress hoped to protect federally insured institutions from losses stemming from false statements or misrepresentations that mislead the institutions into making financial commitments, advances, or loans. The statute was intended to be broad enough "to maintain the vitality of the FDIC insurance program * * * and 'to cover all undertakings which might subject the FDIC insured bank to risk of loss.'" United States v. Pinto, 646 F.2d 833, 838 (1981).

Nothing on the face of § 1014 "suggests a congressional intent to limit its coverage" to a particular kind of transaction. Check-kiting, which threatens the assets of federally insured banks in precisely the same way as a misrepresentation in a loan application, should not be excluded from the reach of the statute simply because the terms of the statute and its legislative history do not specifically identify check kiting by name or precise description. This method of statutory construction was rejected recently in Harrison v. PPG Industries, Inc., 446 U.S. 578, 592 (1980):

> "[I]t would be a strange canon of statutory construction that would require Congress to state in committee reports or elsewhere in its deliberations that which is obvious on the face of a statute. In ascertaining the meaning of a statute, a court cannot, in the manner of Sherlock Holmes, pursue the theory of the dog that did not bark."

Unfortunately, in my view, the Court's approach to interpreting § 1014 comes dangerously close to the method we rejected in *Harrison*. Unless one accepts the Court's overly restrictive and technical "definition" of a check, check-kiting schemes clearly fall within the broad language of that statute.

B

As the majority recognizes, a violation of § 1014 is established when the Government proves two elements: that the defendant either made a "false statement or report," or "willfully overvalue[d] any * * * property or security;" and that the defendant did so "for the purpose of influencing in any way the action of [a federally insured institution] upon any application, advance commitment, or loan." After recognizing this, however, the majority's analysis jumps the track. The majority concludes that when a drawer presents a kited check to a bank with the knowledge that he does not have sufficient funds, and with the intent not to cover that check with anything other than another virtually worthless kited check, he has not made "any false statement or report," or "willfully overvalue[d] any * * *" property or security within the meaning of the statute. In my view, neither of these conclusions withstands analysis.

The basis for the Court's conclusion that Williams did not make a "false statement or report" is concededly technical and "simple:" "a check is not a factual assertion at all, and therefore cannot be characterized as 'true' or 'false.' " This argument proves too much: it would apply equally to material omissions or failures to disclose in connection with loan applications. However, the Courts of Appeals have held that the failure to disclose material information needed to avoid deception in connection with loan transactions covered by § 1014 constitutes a "false statement or report," and thus violates the statute. I assume that the majority would not disagree with this analysis, which is based on established contract principles. I am at a loss as to why the majority does not apply the same analysis to the transactions at issue in this case.

The majority's description of a check as an " 'unconditional promise or order to pay a sum certain in money,' " is unexceptionable as a conclusory description of "black-letter" law. However, this oversimplified description fails to look behind the bare technical definition of a check. Moreover, this description is not at all inconsistent with the necessary implications that a check carries. "In giving a check, the drawer impliedly represents that he has on deposit with the drawee banks funds equivalent to the face amount of the check." F. Whitney, The Law of Modern Commercial Practices § 341 (2d ed. 1965). Despite the majority's equivocation on this point, those who write or accept checks in exchange for goods, services, or cash undoubtedly understand that this implicit representation has been made. A check is accepted with the expectation that it will be paid in the normal course of collection. A banker who knew that the drawer did not have funds on deposit would not credit the check to the drawer's account or reduce it to cash. Regardless of any contractual breach also involved in check kiting, a person who writes a series of checks knowing that there are no funds to cover them has made intentional false representations within the reach of § 1014.

Any other view, including that endorsed by the Court today, would interfere with the manner in which a major portion of commercial transactions are conducted in our society today. Williams was charged with, and the jury convicted him of, making a false representation (or, more precisely, a material omission) when he presented his check to the bank with the knowledge that he did not have sufficient funds to cover the check, and with the further intent not to cover that check before it cleared with anything other than another worthless kited check. Therefore, his conviction under § 1014 should stand.

In addition to violating § 1014 by intentionally making a false statement to a federally insured bank for the purpose of obtaining credit, Williams also violated the statute for a separate and independent reason. Although Williams presented to the bank for immediate credit a check which on its face represented an amount exceeding $50,000, he well knew that in fact the check was virtually worthless. In so doing, he "willfully overvalue[d] * * * property or security" for the purpose of obtaining credit. The Court's rejection of the Government's argument with respect to this issue is startling in both its brevity and its concededly technical and "literal" interpretation of the legal value of a check which completely ignores the meaning attributed to checks in the real world.

The very essence of a check-kiting scheme is the successful overvaluation of a security or property which misleads a bank into issuing immediate credit on the assumption that the security or property is in fact valued at the amount represented on its face. A check-kiting scheme is successful only when the bank to which the check is presented assumes that the check is supported by adequate funds in the account upon which it is drawn, and that the face amount of the check is in fact its value. If the bank does not accept the valuation on the face of the check, and instead either inquires into the status of the account on which the check is drawn or waits until the check clears before paying the face amount of the check, the scheme will collapse. Of course, it would be more prudent for a bank to take such precautions just as it would be prudent for banks to inquire carefully into the accuracy of all representations made concerning the value of collateral pledged as security for conventional loans. However, this more prudent course is not always practicable. Moreover, the bank may not believe that such precautions are necessary where, as here, the person presenting the check is the president of another bank presumed to know the illegality, and the drastic adverse consequences to a bank, of a check-kiting scheme. In any event, a bank's failure to take all possible precautions does not bar prosecution under § 1014, which placed the burden of avoiding false representations, at the risk of criminal prosecution, upon the person who seeks the funds of the federally insured bank. Section 1014 forbids a person seeking such funds to make "any" false statement or to "willfully overvalue" any security or property to obtain use of the bank's funds. A kited check is "willfully overvalued" within the meaning of the statute, just as worthless securities presented as collateral for a loan are "willfully overvalued." *See* United States v. Calandrella, 605 F.2d 236 (6th Cir.1979).

The Court does not question that the second element of a § 1014 violation—that Williams presented his kited check for the purpose of influencing the bank to extend him credit in the form of a loan or an advance—is satisfied in this case. Clearly, Williams' conduct was directed at misleading a bank into extending immediate credit. Indeed, the whole purpose of Williams' kiting scheme was to obtain an immediate extension of credit by depositing a check purportedly supported by adequate funds. The banks that extended funds on the basis of Williams' worthless, and not yet collected, checks made an "advance," a "loan," and a "commitment" within the ordinary meaning of the terms.

If a worthless check is submitted to a bank for reasons other than to obtain an extension of credit, the conduct simply is not check kiting in the ordinary sense of the term, and would not fall within the prohibition of § 1014. However, if a properly instructed jury concludes that a worthless check was submitted in order to obtain immediate credit from a bank, there is no reason to regard the conduct as falling outside the reach of § 1014. The jury that convicted Williams was so instructed, and found that Williams' conduct constituted a "false representation" designed to influence the banks into extending him immediate credit.

C

The unambiguous language of § 1014 clearly proscribes conduct commonly referred to as check-kiting. This language should be given effect in the absence of clear indications in the legislative history that Congress did not intend to proscribe this conduct. There are no such indications in the legislative history. To the contrary, the legislative history makes clear that the statute was not limited to borrowers or to loan applications.

The Court finds no indication that Congress intended to exclude check-kiting schemes from the scope of the statute. The Court's brief review of the legislative history to § 1014 does suggest that the primary purpose of the statute is to prohibit misrepresentations in connection with conventional loan applications. However, neither this fact, nor the fact that most convictions under the statute involve such transactions, compels the Court to ignore the broad language and purposes of the statute by interpreting it to cover *only* these transactions. In the past, we have consistently rejected the argument that a criminal statute must be given its narrowest meaning by limiting its scope to effectuate only its primary purpose.

* * *

* * * In order to find Williams' conduct outside the scope of § 1014, the majority ignores the function of a check in today's society. The rule of lenity has never been interpreted to require this kind of result. I am at a loss to explain why the Court adopts this approach today and consequently turns the rule of lenity on its head. Accordingly, I dissent.

Notes

It was partially in response to the decision in *Williams* that Congress passed 18 U.S.C. § 1344, discussed further in the next section of this chapter. Section 1344 criminalizes any scheme to defraud a bank. According to the legislative history of § 1344:

"Recent Supreme Court decisions have underscored the fact that serious gaps now exist in Federal jurisdiction over frauds against banks and other credit institutions which are organized or operating under Federal law or whose deposits are federally insured. Clearly, there is a strong Federal interest in protecting the financial integrity of these institutions, and the legislation in this part would assure a basis for Federal prosecution of those who victimize these banks through fraudulent schemes.

"The need for Federal jurisdiction over crimes committed against federally insured and controlled financial institutions has been recognized by the Congress in its passage of statutes specifically reaching crimes of embezzlement, robbery, larceny, burglary, and false statement directed at these banks. However, there is presently no similar statute generally proscribing bank fraud. As a result, Federal prosecutions of these frauds may now be pursued only if the circumstances of a particular fraud are such that the elements of some other Federal offense are met. Thus, whether Federal interests may be properly vindicated through prosecution turns on whether the fraudulent activity constitutes a crime under some other bank statutes, such as those governing larceny or false statement (18 U.S.C. §§ 2113 and 1014), or whether the fraudulent scheme involves a use of the mails or telecommunications that would permit prosecution under the mail or wire fraud statutes (18 U.S.C. §§ 1341 and 1343).

"This approach of prosecuting bank fraud under statutes not specifically designed to reach this criminal conduct is necessarily problematic. Nonetheless, for some time the Department of Justice had considerable success in using such statutes. The most useful of these was the mail fraud offense, for not only had the statute been held to reach a wide range of fraudulent activity, but also its jurisdictional element—use of the mails—could generally be satisfied in bank fraud cases because the collection procedures of victim banks ordinarily entailed use of the mails. In 1974, however, the utility of the mail fraud statute was notably diminished by the Supreme Court decisions in United States v. Maze.[1] In *Maze*, the Court held that proof that use of the mails occurred in or was caused by a fraudulent scheme was insufficient for conviction under the mail fraud statute. Instead, proof that use of the mails played a significant part in bringing the scheme to fruition would be required. In addition to the problems of proof posed by the *Maze* decision, banks' increasing use of private courier services for collection purposes in lieu of the mails has further limited the instances in which the mail fraud statute may be used to prosecute bank fraud.

"The use of other Federal statutes to attack bank fraud as an alternative to prosecution under the mail fraud offense has also been circumscribed by recent court decisions. By virtue of the Supreme Court's decision last year in Williams v. United States,[2] the bank false statement offense, 18 U.S.C. § 1014, may no longer be applied to address one of the most pervasive forms of bank fraud, check-kiting. In *Williams*, the

---

1. 414 U.S. 395 (1974).   **2.** 458 U.S. 279 (1982).

Court concluded this form of fraud did not fall within the scope of 18 U.S.C. § 1014 because a check did not constitute a 'statement' within the meaning of the statute. As a result of this decision, the Committee has been advised by the Justice Department that it has been necessary to cease prosecution of numerous pending check-kiting cases. Similarly, there appears to be an absence of coverage with respect to some types of fraud in the general bank theft statute, 18 U.S.C. § 2113. Although the Supreme Court recently held that section 2113 is not limited to common law larceny and reaches also certain offenses involving the obtaining of property from banks by false pretenses,[3] the Court noted that, by its clear terms, section 2113 'does not apply to a case of false pretenses in which there is not a taking and carrying away' of the property. These various gaps in existing statutes, as well as the lack of a unitary provisions aimed directly at the problem of bank fraud, in the Committee's view created a plain need for enactment of the general bank fraud statute set forth in this part of title XI."

S. Rep. No. 224, 98th Cong., 2d Sess. 377–79, reprinted in 1984 U.S. Code Cong. & Admin. News 3182, 3517–19.

In United States v. Gaudin, 515 U.S. 506 (1995),[v] the Supreme Court held that materiality, an element of the offense under 18 U.S.C. § 1001, is an issue which must be decided by a jury, not by a court. Soon thereafter, in United States v. Wells, 519 U.S. ___, 117 S.Ct. 921 (1997), the Supreme Court addressed the same question, but ruled differently with regard to § 1014. Determine whether you agree with the majority or dissent:

UNITED STATES v. WELLS
United States Supreme Court, 1997.
519 U.S. ___, 117 S.Ct. 921.

SOUTER, JUSTICE.

The principal issue before us is whether materiality of falsehood is an element of the crime of knowingly making a false statement to a federally insured bank, 18 U.S.C. § 1014. We hold that it is not.

I

In 1993, the Government charged respondents, Jerry Wells and Kenneth Steele, with violating and conspiring to violate the cited statute as officers and part-owners of Copytech Systems, Inc., a lessor of office copiers for a monthly fee covering not only use of the equipment but any service that might be required. To raise cash, Copytech sold its interest in the income stream from these contracts to banks.

In Count I of the indictment, the Government charged respondents with conspiring to violate § 1014 by concealing from several banks the

---

3. Bell v. United States, 462 U.S. 356   v. See Chapter 10.
(1983).

true contractual terms. Respondents supposedly conspired to provide the banks with versions of lease contracts purporting to indicate that Copytech's customers were responsible for servicing the equipment when, in fact, secret side agreements placed that responsibility on Copytech at no further cost to the lessees. The Government alleged that respondents concealed the service obligations in order to avoid tying up needed cash in reserve accounts, which the banks might have required Copytech to maintain if they had known of the company's servicing obligations.

In Count II, respondents were charged with violating § 1014 by giving a bank forgeries of respondents' wives' signatures on personal guaranties designed to enable the bank to pursue the wives' assets if Copytech defaulted on any liability to the bank. Each count of the indictment charged respondents with submitting one or more statements that were both false and "material."

At the end of the trial, the District Court instructed the jury, at the Government's behest, that withholding a "material fact" made a statement or representation false, and defined a material fact as one "that would be important to a reasonable person in deciding whether to engage or not to engage in a particular transaction." Although there was no controversy over the law as stated in these instructions, the Government argued that materiality was for the judge to determine, while respondents said it was an issue for the jury. Following Eighth Circuit precedent then prevailing, the District Court agreed with the Government and told the jury that "[t]he materiality of the statement ... alleged to be false ... is not a matter with which you are concerned and should not be considered by you in determining the guilt or innocence of the defendant [s]," The jury convicted respondents on both counts, the court treated the statements as material, and respondents appealed. [citations omitted]

While the appeal was pending, we decided United States v. Gaudin, 515 U.S. 506 (1995), in which the parties agreed that materiality was an element of 18 U.S.C. § 1001, but disputed whether materiality was a question for the judge or jury. Applying the rule that "[t]he Constitution gives a criminal defendant the right to have a jury determine ... his guilt of every element of the crime with which he is charged," we held that the jury was entitled to pass on the materiality of Gaudin's statements. When the Court of Appeals in this case requested supplemental briefing on the applicability of *Gaudin*, respondents argued that under § 1014 materiality is an element on which they were entitled to a jury's determination; the Government argued, for the first time, that materiality is not an element under § 1014, so that no harm had been done when the judge dealt with the issue. The Court of Appeals agreed with respondents, vacated their convictions and sentences, and remanded the case for a new trial.

We granted the Government's petition for certiorari to decide whether materiality of a false statement or report is an element under

§ 1014.[3] We now vacate and remand.

* * *

* * * Section 1014 criminalizes "knowingly mak[ing] any false statement or report . . . for the purpose of influencing in any way the action" of an FDIC-insured bank "upon any application, advance, . . . commitment, or loan." 18 U.S.C. § 1014. Nowhere does it further say that a material fact must be the subject of the false statement or so much as mention materiality. To the contrary, its terms cover "any" false statement that meets the other requirements in the statute, and the term "false statement" carries no general suggestion of influential significance. Thus, under the first criterion in the interpretive hierarchy, a natural reading of the full text, materiality would not be an element of § 1014.

Nor have respondents come close to showing that at common law the term "false statement" acquired any implication of materiality that came with it into § 1014. We do, of course, presume that Congress incorporates the common-law meaning of the terms it uses if those " 'terms . . . have accumulated settled meaning under . . . the common law' " and " 'the statute [does not] otherwise dictat[e].' " [citations omitted] Respondents here, however, make no claims about the settled meaning of "false statement" at common law; they merely note that some common-law crimes involving false statements, such as perjury, required proof of materiality. But Congress did not codify the crime of perjury or comparable common-law crimes in § 1014; as we discuss next, it simply consolidated 13 statutory provisions relating to financial institutions, and, in fact, it enacted a separate general perjury provision at 18 U.S.C. § 1621.

Statutory history confirms the natural reading. When Congress originally enacted § 1014 as part of its recodification of the federal criminal code in 1948, it explicitly included materiality in other provisions involving false representations. Even more significantly, of the 13 provisions brought together by § 1014, 10 had previously contained no express materiality provision and received none in the recodification, while 3 of the 13 had contained express materiality requirements and lost them in the course of consolidation. The most likely inference in these circumstances is that Congress deliberately dropped the term "materiality" without intending materiality to be an element of § 1014.

Respondents' remaining arguments for affirmance are unavailing. They contend that Congress has ratified holdings of some of the Courts of Appeals that materiality is an element of § 1014 by repeatedly amending the statute without rejecting those decisions. But the significance of subsequent congressional action or inaction necessarily varies with the circumstances, and finding any interpretive help in congression-

3. Most, but not all, of the Federal Courts of Appeals have held that materiality is an element. [citations omitted]

al behavior here is impossible. Since 1948, Congress has amended § 1014 to modify the list of covered institutions and to increase the maximum penalty, but without ever touching the original phraseology criminalizing "false statement[s]" made "for the purpose of influencing" the actions of the enumerated institutions. We thus have at most legislative silence on the crucial statutory language, and we have "frequently cautioned that '[i]t is at best treacherous to find in congressional silence alone the adoption of a controlling rule of law.' " But even if silence could speak, it could not speak unequivocally to the issue here, since over the years judicial opinion has divided on whether § 1014 includes a materiality element and we have previously described the elements of § 1014 without any mention of materiality. It would thus be impossible to say which view Congress might have endorsed.

* * *

Respondents next urge that we follow the reasoning of some Courts of Appeals in reading materiality into the statute to avoid the improbability that Congress intended to impose substantial criminal penalties on relatively trivial or innocent conduct. But we think there is no clear call to take such a course. It is true that we have held § 1014 inapplicable to depositing false checks at a bank, in part because we thought that it would have "ma[d]e a surprisingly broad range of unremarkable conduct a violation of federal law," and elsewhere thought it possible to construe a prohibition narrowly where a loose mens rea requirement would otherwise have resulted in a surprisingly broad statutory sweep. [citations omitted] But an unqualified reading of § 1014 poses no risk of criminalizing so much conduct as to suggest that Congress meant something short of the straightforward reading. The language makes a false statement to one of the enumerated financial institutions a crime only if the speaker knows the falsity of what he says and intends it to influence the institution. A statement made "for the purpose of influencing" a bank will not usually be about something a banker would regard as trivial, and "it will be relatively rare that the Government will be able to prove that" a false statement "was ... made with the subjective intent" of influencing a decision unless it could first prove that the statement has "the natural tendency to influence the decision," Hence the literal reading of the statute will not normally take the scope of § 1014 beyond the limit that a materiality requirement would impose. [citations omitted]

* * *

The judgment of the Court of Appeals is vacated, and the case is remanded for further proceedings consistent with this opinion.

It is so ordered.

JUSTICE STEVENS, DISSENTING.

Violation of 18 U.S.C. § 1014 is a crime punishable by up to 30 years in prison, a fine of up to $1,000,000, "or both." I am convinced that Congress did not intend this draconian statute to apply to immaterial falsehoods, even when made for the purpose of currying favor with a bank's loan officer. * * *

* * *

* * * [Section] 1014 was revised at a time when a different view of statutory interpretation held sway. When Congress enacted the current version of the law in 1948, a period marked by a spirit of cooperation between Congress and the Federal Judiciary, Congress looked to the courts to play an important role in the lawmaking process by relying on common-law tradition and common sense to fill gaps in the law—even to imply causes of action and remedies that were not set forth in statutory text. It was only three years earlier that one of the greatest judges of the era—indeed, of any era—had admonished us "not to make a fortress out of the dictionary." Cabell v. Markham, 148 F.2d 737, 739 (C.A.2 1945). The Court's approach to questions of statutory construction has changed significantly since that time. The textual lens through which the Court views the work product of the 1948 revisers is dramatically different from the contemporary legal context in which they labored. In 1948, it was entirely reasonable for Congress and the revisers to assume that the judiciary would imply a materiality requirement that was a routine aspect of common-law litigation about false statements.

Indeed, subsequent history confirms the reasonableness of such an assumption: the vast majority of judges who have confronted the question have found an implicit materiality requirement in § 1014. As the Court recognizes, all but one of the Courts of Appeals have so held. Moreover, both in this case and in *Gaudin* the prosecutor initially proceeded on the assumption that a nonexplicit statute contained an implicit materiality requirement. Only after it failed to convince us in *Gaudin* that the materiality issue should be resolved by the judge rather than the jury did the Government switch its position and urge us to reject that assumption entirely.

* * *

Congress, the Court seems to recognize, could not have intended that someone spend up to 30 years in prison for falsely flattering a bank officer for the purpose of obtaining favorable treatment.[14] Yet the Court justifies its interpretation of the statute by positing that a literal reading of § 1014 will not "normally" extend the statute "beyond the limit that

---

14. Consider the following scenario. A crafty home owner in need of a mortgage, having learned that the bank's loan officer is a bow tie aficionado, purchases his first bow tie to wear at their first meeting. As expected, the loan officer is wearing such a tie, which, incidentally, the prospective borrower considers downright ugly. Nevertheless, thinking that flattery will increase the likelihood that the officer will be favorably disposed to approving the loan, the applicant swallows hard and compliments the officer on his tie; he then volunteers the information that he too always wears a bow tie. This is a lie. Under the majority's interpretation, this person could spend 30 years in federal prison. He made a "false statement." 18 U.S.C. § 1014. In fact, until that day he had never worn a bow tie. And the statement was made "for the purpose of influencing" the bank. Ibid. The applicant subjectively hoped that the loan officer—flattered and feeling a sartorial common ground—would be more likely to approve his mortgage.

a materiality requirement would impose." In making this assertion, the Court correctly avoids relying on prosecutors not to bring frivolous cases. Rather, it appears to have made an empirical judgment that false statements will not "usually" be about a trivial matter, and that the government will " 'relatively rare[ly]' "be able to prove that nonmaterial statements were made for the purpose "of influencing a decision." I am not at all sure, nor do I know how the Court determined, that attempted flattery is less common than false statements about material facts. Even if it were, the "unusual" nature of trivial statements provides scant justification for reaching the conclusion that Congress intended such peccadillos to constitute a felony.

* * *

Today the Court misconstrues § 1014, its history, and our precedents in holding that the statute does not contain a basic materiality requirement. In doing so, the Court confidently asserts that almost every court to interpret § 1014, [and] the revisers of the statute, * * * were all simply wrong. Unwarranted confidence in one's own ability to ascertain the truth has prompted many a victim of deception to make the false statement that "flattery will get you nowhere." It now appears that flattery may get you into a federal prison.

I respectfully dissent.

Notes

1. What do you think of Justice Stevens' criticism of the majority's view that without a materiality requirement the most trivial lie violates § 1014?

2. Recall the Supreme Court's decisions in Williams v. United States, 458 U.S. 279 (1982), and McNally v. United States, 483 U.S. 350 (1987). In *Wells*, the Supreme Court once again held that years of lower court interpretations of statutory coverage are wrong. What kind of due process problems does it present when the courts cannot agree on the basic elements of a statute?

---

2. SECTION 1005: FALSE ENTRIES IN BANK BOOKS

Section 1005, United States Code, Title 18 provides, in relevant part:

"Whoever makes any false entry in any book, report, or statement of such bank,[w] company, branch, agency, or organization with intent to injure or defraud such bank, company, branch, agency, or organization * * * [s]hall be fined not more than $1,000,000 or imprisoned not more than 30 years, or both."

---

w. "[A]ny federal Reserve bank, member bank, depository institution holding company, national bank, insured bank, branch or agency of a foreign bank, or organization operating under section 25 or section 25(a) of the Federal Reserve Act" 18 U.S.C. § 1005.

It has long been recognized that the following elements must be proven in a § 1005 prosecution: "(1) the entry is false; (2) the defendant either personally made the entry or caused it to be made, (3) the defendant knew the entry was false when he made it; and (4) the defendant intended that the entry injure or deceive the bank officers * * *."ˣ As noted in the next case, United States v. Harvard, 103 F.3d 412 (5th Cir.1997), courts are reassessing whether materiality is also an element. As you read *Harvard*, recall the Supreme Court's recent decision in United States v. Wells, 519 U.S. ___, 117 S.Ct. 921 (1997). Note that the Fifth Circuit rendered its opinion in *Harvard* about six weeks before the Supreme Court released its opinion in *Wells*. Does *Wells* strengthen or weaken the Fifth Circuit's decision in *Harvard*?

UNITED STATES v. HARVARD

United States Court of Appeals, Fifth Circuit, 1997.
103 F.3d 412.

JONES, CIRCUIT JUDGE.

Appellant Jack C. Harvard appeals his convictions for conspiracy, bank fraud, misapplying bank funds, causing false bank entries to be made, and receiving a bribe for a bank transaction. The most difficult question he raises on appeal is whether 18 U.S.C. § 1005, which criminalizes the act of causing false bank entries to be made, embodies a requirement of materiality for an actual misstatement. We hold that it does not and affirm Harvard's conviction on this and the other counts against him.

I. FACTUAL BACKGROUND

A detailed recitation of the facts as presented at Harvard's trial is necessary for resolution of the issues presented.

* * *

In 1983, Harvard, then vice-president at Northpark Bank of Dallas ("Northpark"), led a group of investors in borrowing $1,493,000 from Northpark to organize Willow Bend National Bank ("Willow Bend"), a federally insured bank. Harvard served as chairman of the board and chief executive officer at Willow Bend until August 1989. Willow Bend Bancshares, Inc. ("Bancshares"), a bank holding company in which Harvard became chairman of the board, was formed in 1984 to acquire Willow Bend. Bancshares also acquired Bonham State Bank ("Bonham"). Harvard was a director at Bonham from 1984 to 1989. Incidentally, Harvard served as mayor of Plano, Texas during the mid-1980s.

* * *

In 1987, Diana Cheng, a Dallas businesswoman, needed $400,000 and a $1,000,000 letter of credit in order to undertake a $2,000,000 Indonesian lumber import deal. A customer and shareholder of Willow

---

x. United States v. Harvard, 103 F.3d   412, 418 (5th Cir.1997).

Bend, Cheng had been involved in commercial real estate in the Dallas area for several years. Cheng discussed her needs for the Indonesian transaction with Thomas C. Flood, a loan officer at Willow Bend. Flood informed Cheng that Willow Bend could not grant her the loan because she had reached her borrowing limit. Nevertheless, Flood arranged a meeting among Harvard, Cheng, and himself at which Harvard informed Cheng that Willow Bend could lend the money if something was in it for him. By the end of the meeting, Cheng had agreed to give Harvard and Flood, respectively, a 10% and 5% share of the import business. At the meeting, Flood intimated that Cheng should create a real estate note to pledge as collateral for the loan. Cheng did so by creating a $395,600 note payable by her joint venture to the fictitious name of C.D. Donge (the "Donge note"). In connection with these events, Cheng pleaded guilty to conspiring to give money to Harvard and Flood and creating a false document to obtain a loan from Willow Bend. She testified against Harvard.

Harvard then asked Jay Paul Schapiro, an acquaintance through bank-related business and various civic activities, to purchase the Donge note from Willow Bend "to get it off the books."[1] Harvard told Schapiro that the note was secured by undeveloped real estate. When Schapiro stated that he could not pay off the note in the event of default, Harvard assured him that he would find a guarantor, who turned out to be Ms. Cheng. Schapiro purchased the note. Although such notes would usually be purchased at a discount, in this transaction Schapiro borrowed the face value of the note—$395,000—from Willow Bend in return for a $9,000 fee. Apparently unbeknownst to Schapiro, the actual discounted price of the note was $345,000; the remaining balance, less Schapiro's fee, went to Willow Bend. Schapiro never made any payments on the note and was told by Harvard and Flood to ignore late notices and demands for collection. In May of 1987, Flood had the deed of trust for the Donge note recorded in the county real estate records, even though the Donge note was dated December 9, 1985. Cheng gave cash payments of $15,000 to Flood and $10,000 to Harvard. Flood pleaded guilty to bank bribery.

* * *

In 1985 Harvard had a 10% interest in the Plano–Shiloh Joint Venture (the "Joint Venture"), which purchased and operated a strip mall in Plano, Texas. By March of 1986, the Joint Venture was not self-sustaining and each partner was requested to contribute additional capital. The Joint Venture experienced a loss in excess of $81,986 in 1986, and by 1987 was still losing money. When the Joint Venture decided to refinance with a different lender to reduce interest expenses, Harvard volunteered to assist in having the note refinanced at Bonham

---

1. Purchasing a note usually consists of discounting a promissory note to present value or below and then borrowing funds to purchase it. This produces a positive cash flow if the payments on the loan by the purchaser of the note are below the payments on the original note.

where, as stated earlier, he was a director. Harvard solicited John Armstrong, then a bank officer who had risen to chairman of the board by the time of trial, and assured Armstrong that the loan was performing and that the shopping center was "cash flowing." Armstrong also asked for and received assurance that an appraisal substantiating the value of the Joint Venture property would be provided.

The Board of Bonham approved the loan. Although Harvard did not vote on the loan, the directors were well aware that Harvard was the chairman of Bancshares, Bonham's holding company. Additionally, on at least one occasion, Harvard reminded Warren Jamieson—president and chief executive officer of Bonham—of Harvard's control of Bonham and his ability to replace Jamieson. In extending the loan to the Joint Venture, Bonham required personal guarantees of the individual joint venture participants. On May 29, 1987, the title company forwarded all documents for the loan, including the guarantees, to Nancy Long, Harvard's then-secretary at Willow Bend. Oddly, the guarantee agreements showed the Joint Venture to be indebted to Willow Bend, not Bonham. Harvard was aware of these defects of the guarantees.

After closing on the loan with Bonham, Brenda Brown, a one-percent participant in the Joint Venture and an employee of the Joint Venture's management company, was instructed by her boss at the managing company to write a check in the amount of $10,640 (one percent of the loan amount) payable to Harvard and to call it a "consulting fee." This payment to Harvard was not disclosed on the settlement sheet to Bonham nor was it disclosed by any of the other partners of the Joint Venture.

* * *

In 1989 Willow Bend's procedure for the issuance of cashier's checks required bank tellers, at the time that cashier's checks were issued, to collect payment of either cash or a cash equivalent. After doing so, a special machine would imprint the appropriate amount on the check along with a machine imprinted signature. Amounts in excess of $5000 required a bank officer's signature; very large amounts required the signature of Willow Bend's vice-president. The details regarding the issuance of all cashier's checks—including the date, check number, remitter, payee, and amount—were to be entered into a cashier's check log at the time of issuance.

On March 7, 1989, Harvard called Warren Jamieson, who was still president, chief executive officer, and—at this time—a director of Bonham, to borrow money from Bonham for the purchase of a house at a foreclosure sale. Harvard represented to Jamieson that he needed only interim financing for the house as he had already obtained a commitment for personal financing from Plano Savings and Loan conditioned on his becoming the successful bidder. Jamieson told Harvard that he did not have the authority to approve another $175,000 debt to Harvard, but he would seek the Board's approval, which was obtained that day. Jamieson informed Harvard, however, that the loan would not be funded until Bonham received the loan documents. The loan documents prepared at Willow Bend were faxed to Bonham the following day, March 8. On that day, Bonham wire transferred $175,000 to Harvard's personal account at Willow Bend.

On March 7, the day before the money was wired (and the same day that Harvard requested the loan from Jamieson), Janice Smith, a teller at Willow Bend, handed Harvard two blank cashier's checks. Ignoring Willow Bend's policy, she did not record in the cashier's check log the details of her parting with these checks. She knew that Harvard was the chief executive officer at Willow Bend, and she did not question him about the checks. She was also unaware that Harvard left the bank with both cashier's checks. Laura Palmer, Smith's supervisor, completed the log after Smith left for the day. Palmer entered "Farm and Home, $166,201" for one of the cashier's checks and initialed the entry; the other cashier's check was voided. Harvard ultimately completed the check by endorsing it and writing in by hand the amount of $166,201 payable to "Farm and Home Savings." This cashier's check was dated March 7, 1989, but the date stamp on the back of the check was March 8. The proof stamp on the face of the check was March 9. Neither Palmer nor Smith ever received any cash payment for either cashier's check. The cashier's check for $166,201 was used to purchase a house at a foreclosure sale on March 7. Willow Bend did not receive funds to pay for the check until June 11, 1989. As a result, Willow Bend suffered a cash loss of $117.73 in interest income it would have received from the $166,201.

* * *

After a trial to a jury, Harvard was convicted pursuant to the indictment of:

Count One—violating 18 U.S.C. § 371 by conspiring to (a) misapply monies belonging to Willow Bend, (b) make and cause to be made false entries in the books of Willow Bend, and (c) corruptly accept something of value in connection with the business of Willow Bend;

Count Two—violating 18 U.S.C. § 215 by corruptly accepting something of value in connection with the business of Willow Bend;

Count Three—violating 18 U.S.C. § 656 by misapplying monies belonging to Willow Bend;

Count Four—violating 18 U.S.C. § 1005 by making a false entry on the books of Willow Bend in connection with the Cheng/Schapiro loans;

Count Five—violating 18 U.S.C. §§ 1344 and 2 by committing and aiding and abetting in the commission of bank fraud; and

Count Fourteen—violating 18 U.S.C. §§ 1005 and 2 by misapplying monies and aiding and abetting in the misapplication of monies belonging to Willow Bend.

Harvard complains on appeal that (1) the district court erred in instructing the jury that 18 U.S.C. § 1005 does not require a finding by the jury of materiality regarding the false entries * * *.

II. DISCUSSION

* * *

18 U.S.C. § 1005 provides, in relevant part:

> Whoever makes any false entry in any book, report, or statement of [a] bank . . . with intent to injure or defraud such bank . . . or to deceive any officer of such bank . . . [s]hall be fined . . . or imprisoned . . . or both.

18 U.S.C. § 1005 (West Supp.1996).

In regard to this § 1005 offense charged against Harvard, the court instructed the jury, in relevant part:

> An entry may be false if it omits material information. An entry may also be false when it contains a half truth or when it conceals a material fact, and a statement that is technically true may be false if the transaction it reports is a sham or mere formality. An omission of material information as well as affirmative representations also constitutes a false statement.

> You are instructed that these entries are material within the meaning of the statute, and you are not to concern yourselves with the issue of materiality.

Harvard asserts that because of the Supreme Court's recent decision in United States v. Gaudin, 515 U.S. 506 (1995), this instruction was in error because it did not require the jury to make a finding of materiality. * * *

In *Gaudin*, the Court held that, where materiality of a false statement is an element of the offense charged, the defendant has the right to have the jury decide the issue of materiality. On that basis, the Court affirmed reversal of Gaudin's conviction under 18 U.S.C. § 1001.[3] In United States v. Pettigrew, 77 F.3d 1500, 1510 (5th Cir.1996) we relied on *Gaudin* in ruling that a jury must make a finding of materiality in order to establish a violation of 18 U.S.C. § 1006.[4]

---

3. 18 U.S.C. § 1001 provides, in relevant part:

> Whoever . . . knowingly and wilfully falsifies, conceals or covers up by any trick, scheme or device a material fact, or makes any false, fictitious or fraudulent statements or representations, or makes or uses any false writing or document knowing the same to contain any false, fictitious or fraudulent statement or entry, shall be fined . . . or imprisoned . . . or both.

Gaudin, 515 U.S. at 509.

4. 18 U.S.C. § 1006 provides, in relevant part:

> Whoever . . . with intent to defraud any such institution or any other company, body politic or corporate, or any individual, or to deceive any officer, auditor, examiner or agent of any such institution . . . makes any false entry in any book, report or statement of or to any such institution . . . shall be fined . . . or imprisoned . . . or both.

18 U.S.C. § 1006 (West Supp.1996).

Significantly, neither in *Gaudin* nor in Pettigrew did the government contest materiality as an essential element of the offenses proscribed by §§ 1001 or 1006. In this case it is different; the parties vigorously dispute whether materiality is a required element of an offense proscribed by § 1005.[6] Perhaps somewhat at odds with its jury instruction, the district court found that "[m]ateriality is not an essential element in order to establish a violation of [§ 1005]." Therefore, unlike the procedural posture of *Gaudin* and *Pettigrew*, this case poses the issue whether materiality is an essential element of the offense before we can consider the applicability of *Gaudin*. Based on due respect for the statutory text, pertinent case law, and related legislation, we conclude that materiality is not an element of a § 1005 offense charging an actual misstatement.

First, as quoted earlier, § 1005 makes no reference to the required materiality of a criminal false bank entry.

Second, we have found no Fifth Circuit case that imported a materiality requirement into § 1005. Instead, this court has previously stated:

> The government establishes a violation of section 1005 by proving beyond a reasonable doubt that: (1) the entry is false; (2) the defendant either personally made the entry or caused it to be made; (3) the defendant knew the entry was false when he made it; and (4) the defendant intended that the entry injure or deceive the bank officers or public officers.... *An omission of material information as well as an actual misstatement qualifies as a false entry under the statute.*

United States v. Jackson, 621 F.2d 216, 219 (5th Cir.1980) (emphasis added). *Jackson* holds that the government establishes a violation of § 1005 if it proves, *inter alia*, that the defendant made either (1) an actual misstatement or (2) a *material omission* of information. Proof of an actual misstatement does not require proof of its materiality. The government is only required to prove materiality after *Jackson* when it seeks to convict a defendant pursuant to § 1005 for an *omission* of information. As Harvard was indicted and convicted under § 1005 for an actual misstatement of information, no finding of materiality was required.

Third, § 1005 does not require that the courts add an element of materiality because materiality is inherent in the statute. To convict an offender pursuant to § 1005, the jury must find that the false entry at issue was made *with intent to defraud or injure*. It is highly unlikely that the government could show—or a jury would find—that a genuinely trivial entry was made with fraudulent or injurious intent. To rule otherwise and require the government to prove materiality would reward only that individual who intended to defraud or injure a bank, but did so by making a "non-material" misstatement. Based on the text of the

---

6. The government has become more assertive in contesting implied materiality requirements in federal criminal statutes.

* * *. [*See, e.g.*, the government's appeal in United States v. Wells, 519 U.S. ___ (1997)].

statute, a more reasonable interpretation of § 1005 is that Congress intended that punishment follow culpability regardless of the "materiality" of the means chosen to effectuate the fraud or injury.

We must respect the fact that the legislature is entrusted with the responsibility of defining the elements of a criminal offense—particularly in the case of federal crimes, which are solely creatures of statute. According to the plain language of § 1005, Congress manifested the intent to punish *any* false entry made with intent to defraud. Had Congress intended to reserve punishment for only those individuals who made *material* fraudulent entries, it could easily have done so. Indeed, Congress has expressly included a materiality requirement in other false statement statutes. *See, e.g.,* 18 U.S.C. § 1621 (perjury); 18 U.S.C. § 1623 (false declaration before grand jury or court); 18 U.S.C. § 922(a)(6) (false statement on firearms application); 18 U.S.C. § 1033 (false statement on insurance application). The absence of a materiality requirement in § 1005 thus seems deliberate.

* * *

As Harvard points out, two other circuits appear to have decided, without debate, that conviction for an actual misstatement under § 1005 requires proof of materiality. *See* United States v. Rapp, 871 F.2d 957, 963 (11th Cir.1989); United States v. McGuire, 744 F.2d 1197, 1202 (6th Cir.1984). Other courts appear to require proof of materiality for false omissions, and it is uncertain whether their materiality requirement has been extended further. Bolstered by *Jackson, supra,* however, and by the foregoing analysis, we are confident that materiality is not an element of § 1005 when the government seeks, as here, to convict a defendant for an actual misstatement.

* * *

Notes

1. Does it seem odd that something as fundamental as the elements of long-standing and much used statutes (such as 18 U.S.C. §§ 1005, 1014) are still uncertain? Note the Fifth Circuit's observation that the government has become more assertive in arguing that materiality is not an element in federal criminal statutes. Could this affect the current uncertainty about the materiality element? Why might the government have become more assertive in making such arguments?

2. Note the court's distinction between § 1005 "omission" cases and "actual misstatement" cases. How might this distinction affect the materiality element?

3. Compare § 1005 and § 1014: to which type of factual patterns would each offense apply?

C. FRAUD UPON FINANCIAL INSTITUTIONS BY INSIDERS

Section 656, United States Code, Title 18 provides, in relevant part:

"Whoever, being an officer, director, agent or employee of, or connected in any capacity with any * * * bank * * * embezzles, abstracts, purloins or willfully misapplies any of the moneys, funds or credits of such bank, branch, agency or organization or holding company or any moneys, funds, assets or securities intrusted to such bank, branch, agency, or organization, or holding company * * * shall be fined not more than $1,000,000 or imprisoned not more than 30 years, or both * * *."

The next case, United States v. Adamson, 700 F.2d 953 (5th Cir.1983), focuses on the intent element in § 656 and § 1005.

UNITED STATES v. ADAMSON

United States Court of Appeals, Fifth Circuit, 1983.
700 F.2d 953.

ANDERSON, CIRCUIT JUDGE.

The appellant, John R. Adamson, III, and three others were indicted under 18 U.S.C.A. §§ 656, 1005, 1014, and 2 in connection with several loans made by the First Augusta Bank and Trust Company. After a jury trial, appellant was convicted of one count of willful misapplication of bank funds in violation of § 656, one count of making a false entry in the books, reports and statements of the bank in violation of §§ 1005 and 2, and three counts of knowingly making false statements to the bank for the purpose of influencing loan applications in violation of §§ 1014 and 2. A panel of this court affirmed the convictions under § 656 and 1014, but reversed the conviction under § 1005. United States v. Adamson, 665 F.2d 649 (5th Cir.1982). Rehearing en banc was granted, and the panel opinion vacated. 665 F.2d 660. Upon rehearing * * * the only issues presented to the en banc court relate[d] to the propriety of the jury instructions under §§ 656 and 1005. We conclude that the jury instructions improperly lowered the mens rea standard under § 656 to mere "recklessness" * * *. However, we conclude that the error did not taint the jury charge with respect to § 1005, and therefore we affirm appellant's conviction on that false entry count.

I. FACTS AND POSTURE OF THE ISSUES

This case arises out of a series of events which contributed to the failure of the First Augusta State Bank of Augusta, Georgia. The bank was insured by the Federal Deposit Insurance Corporation. During the times covered by the indictment, appellant Adamson was the president and a director of the bank. He also served as a lending officer and was a member of the bank's Loan and Investment Committee. Two of Adamson's co-defendants, Glenn Bertrand Hester and R. Eugene Holley, also were convicted on both the § 656 count and the § 1005 count. Hester was a major stockholder of the bank, a member of the bank's executive committee, and the attorney for the bank. Holley, a close friend, business associate and law partner of Hester, was also a major borrower from the bank. Hester and Holley also appealed, but both appeals subsequently were dismissed upon motions for voluntary dismissal.

The two counts presented to the en banc court involve a substantial loan which appellant Adamson authorized and which ostensibly was made to Island Summit, Inc., a corporation either wholly owned by or under the control of Hester. The actual beneficiaries of the loan were co-defendants Hester and Holley, who signed the note as guarantors. The evidence permitted a finding by the jury that the corporation was inactive and financially unable to repay the loan. Further, the defendants admitted that no one expected the corporation to repay the loan; rather, the loan was made on the strength of the net worth of the actual beneficiaries of the loan, Hester and Holley. At trial, the government's theory of the case was that appellant Adamson authorized a sham loan to a nominal corporate borrower in order to conceal an illegal and potentially unsafe concentration of bank loans to a single debtor. The evidence justified a finding that the loan would have violated the bank's legal aggregate lending and unsecured loan limits if it had been made directly to Holley. The evidence also permitted a finding that the loan was structured in a way which made detection difficult and which tended to deceive the bank and the bank examiners about the true state of affairs. The jury found appellant guilty of willful misapplication of bank funds (§ 656) and a false entry in the bank's records (§ 1005) in connection with this loan.

With respect to § 656, appellant contends that the jury instructions erroneously defined the requisite mental state that the accused must have in order to commit willful misapplication of bank funds. In particular, the appellant objects to the charge that:

> "A reckless disregard of the interest of the bank is the equivalent of the intent to injure or defraud the bank.

> * * *

> "I charge you that the element of criminal intent necessary for conviction for a willful misapplication of bank funds is not fulfilled by a mere showing of indiscretion or foolhardiness on the part of the bank officer. His conduct must amount to reckless disregard of the bank's interests

> * * *

> "The word 'willful' is also employed to characterize a thing done without ground for believing it is lawful, or conduct marked by a reckless disregard, whether or not one has the right to so act."

If the proper mens rea for § 656 is knowledge, and if the jury instructions as a whole either equate recklessness with knowledge or substitute recklessness for knowledge, then Sandstrom v. Montana, 442 U.S. 510

(1979), compels the conclusion that the charge is erroneous. Neither the government nor the dissenting judges dispute this. *Sandstrom* found error in a charge under which the requisite mens rea was merely presumed. Here there was more than a presumption; the charge actually equated the lesser recklessness mens rea with the higher mens rea of knowledge.

To resolve the issues raised by appellant, we first must determine the appropriate mens rea for a § 656 conviction (Part II). Then we must decide whether the jury instructions as a whole erroneously permitted the jury to apply a lower recklessness mens rea standard to the § 656 count (Part III) Finally, although the jury instructions regarding the § 1005 count did not include a reference to the recklessness mens rea, we must address appellant's argument that the jury instructions on § 656, which immediately preceded those on § 1005, carried over and tainted the § 1005 charge (Part IV).

II. MENS REA FOR § 656

A. *Background*

As explained in the panel opinion, a previous Fifth Circuit case, United States v. Welliver, 601 F.2d 203 (5th Cir.1979), held that a defendant's reckless disregard for the interests of the bank was sufficient to satisfy the intent requirement of § 656. If the rule as stated in *Welliver* is correct, then the instant charge which permitted a finding of guilt based on a mens rea of recklessness would not be erroneous. We brought this case en banc to reconsider *Welliver*'s § 656 holding because it is inconsistent with the Supreme Court's interpretation of the predecessor statute, because it is inconsistent with the position taken by the other circuit courts of appeal, because other Fifth Circuit cases cast some doubt on the rule, and because of the inconsistent mens rea requirement of the related statute, § 1005.

B. *The Predecessor Statute*

The predecessor to § 656 was 12 U.S.C. § 592 (Rev.Stat. 5209), which utilized language substantially the same as that of the current statute.5 The Supreme Court, the Fifth Circuit, and other circuits had held that knowledge or purpose was the required mens rea for the predecessor statute.[5] The legislative history of § 656 makes it clear that no change of substance or meaning was intended. The Reviser's Note to 18 U.S.C.A. § 656 asserts: "The original section, containing more than 500 words, was verbose, diffuse, redundant, and complicated * * *. The revised section *without changing in any way the meaning or substance of existing* law, clarifies, condenses, and combines related provisions largely rewritten in matters of style."

---

5. The primary difference is the omission in the current statute of the language "with intent to injure or defraud." However, courts almost uniformly have judicially imposed the element of intent to injure or defraud, noting that the legislative history indicates that § 656 was not intended to change the meaning or substance of the preexisting law. [citations omitted]

C. The Positions of Other Circuit Courts of Appeal

The Fifth Circuit's rule permitting a conviction under § 656 based on a reckless disregard of a bank's interest stands alone. Cases in the other circuits uniformly state that knowledge is the proper mens rea standard for § 656.

[The court discussed the development of law on this issue in each federal circuit court of appeals, then summarized its discussion:] In summary, we believe that a careful reading of the cases from other circuits reveals a uniform rule that the appropriate mens rea standard for § 656 is *knowledge*. The Eighth Circuit has explicitly rejected the lower recklessness standard. The First, Sixth and Ninth Circuits have adopted knowledge as the proper mens rea, expressly placing reckless-ness in its proper role as evidence from which intent may be inferred. The Second, Third, Fourth and Tenth Circuits have all either stated or held, without discussion, that knowledge is the proper mens rea stan-dard. Further, although imprecise language occasionally has led to confusion, courts generally recognize that the proper role of recklessness is that it may justify an inference of intent to injure or defraud. Such a reading of the case law is buttressed by the government's brief in this case which, after surveying a number of cases, states:

> "It is nowhere suggested that 'recklessness' is the standard of intent under any element of 656. Rather, reckless disregard, has always been used * * to describe the kind of activity the jury must find from the facts before considering whether to make the permissible infer-ence that such activity demonstrated an intent to injure or defraud the bank."

Thus, by the government's own admission, the Fifth Circuit's rule, as stated in the outline of cases leading up to *Welliver*, is inconsistent with the case law of the other circuits. Moreover, as discussed below, numer-ous other Fifth Circuit cases cast considerable doubt upon the rule.

D. Previous Fifth Circuit Cases

The *Welliver* court cited two former Fifth Circuit decisions, United States v. Wilson, 500 F. 2d 715 (5th Cir.1974), and United States v. Reynolds, 573 F.2d 242 (5th Cir.1978), to support its holding that recklessness is sufficient to satisfy the intent requirement of § 656. Both of the cited cases contain the following language: "[R]eckless disregard of the interest of a bank is, for the purpose of 'willful misapplication,' the equivalent of intent to injure or defraud." Although the evolution of the rule is thus understandable, we now believe that a careful examina-tion of the issues and authorities discussed in *Wilson* and *Reynolds* reveals that we erred when we held in *Welliver* that a jury is properly charged that recklessness is the equivalent of intent to injure or defraud.

In *Wilson*, the appellant sought to overturn his conviction on the ground that the term "willfully misapplied" in § 656 was unconstitu-tionally vague. The court rejected this argument, noting that courts had adequately defined the term to cover actions which, while "not covered by the technical terms 'embezzlement' or 'abstraction' " are "obviously improper and amount to the unjustified use of bank funds and which amount to more than mere bad judgment or maladministration." The court then made the statement on which *Welliver* relied: "Recent cases have held that reckless disregard of the interest of a bank is, for the purpose of 'willful misapplication,' the equivalent of intent to injure or defraud." Clearly, that statement was dictum. More importantly, the cases cited for that proposition were Logsdon v. United States, 253 F.2d 12 (6th Cir.1958), and Giragosian v. United States, 349 F.2d 166 (1st Cir. 1965), neither of which held that recklessness was the *equivalent* of willfulness or intent to defraud. Rather, both cases properly state that reckless disregard can justify an *inference* of intent.

In *Reynolds,* the second case cited in *Welliver,* the appellant challenged his conviction on the ground that there was insufficient evidence of intent and willfulness under § 656. In rejecting the appellant's argument, the court first quoted the statement from United States v. Wilson, regarding recklessness being the equivalent of intent to defraud. However, the court went on to state: "Such was the conduct of defendant Reynolds described above, and the jury was entitled to *infer intent* from these facts." 573 F.2d at 245. Like numerous other cases involving the sufficiency of the evidence, Reynolds contains what we now regard as loose language regarding recklessness; we believe that the case is best read as holding merely that reckless disregard justifies an *inference* of intent to defraud.

Although the evolution of the rule in the *Wilson-Reynolds–Welliver* line of cases represents an understandable translation of recklessness as a proper basis for inferring intent to recklessness as the equivalent of intent, we now view that translation as error. Numerous other Fifth Circuit decisions suggest, albeit without holding, that knowledge is the required mens rea for § 656 conviction.

E. Mens Rea for Companion § 1005

As noted, * ** the predecessor to § 656 was 12 U.S.C. § 592 (Rev.Stat. 5209) In 1948, Congress separated § 592 into three distinct sections:§ 334, a seldom-invoked provision which deals with the issuance and circulation of Federal Reserve Notes; 656; and § 1005, which deals with false entries in bank records and the wrongful issuance of bank obligations. The Reviser's Note accompanying § 656 indicates that the reason for the division of § 592 into separate sections was that "[t]he original section, containing more than 500 words, was verbose, diffuse, redundant, and complicated." In addition, the notes accompanying § 656 and § 1005 both state that the revision was not intended to change the "meaning or substance" of the existing law.

This historical background suggests that the mens rea standard for § 656 should be consistent with the standard for the crime of making false entries under § 1005. Both offenses derive from the same predecessor statute, and both require the government to prove that the defendant had "intent to injure or defraud" the bank. Thus, we believe it is significant that none of the circuit courts of appeals have held that a reckless disregard of the interest of a bank is the proper mens rea standard for § 1005. Moreover, two circuit courts recently have reversed convictions under § 1005 because the jury instructions permitted a guilty verdict based upon a finding of recklessness.

One of the recent cases reversing a § 1005 conviction was United States v. Welliver, the same decision which permitted a recklessness standard for § 656 violations in this circuit. The court reversed the § 1005 conviction because the trial judge had charged that "reckless disregard" was the equivalent of intent to injure or defraud under § 1005. The court stated that "[a]s pertains to § 1005, [the Fifth Circuit] has never held 'recklessness' to be sufficient to satisfy the specific intent requirement, nor do we think it should be." 601 F.2d at 210. The court went on to note that "[w]hen a trial judge in his instructions refers to 'recklessness,' no more is necessarily implied than such mere negligence, carelessness, thoughtlessness, or inadvertence as could not be regarded as the equivalent of an intentional wrong." *Id.*

Similarly, in United States v. McAnally, 666 F.2d 1116 (7th Cir. 1981), the Seventh Circuit reversed a § 1005 conviction because the trial court had instructed the jury that "[a] reckless disregard by a bank official of his bank's interest is sufficient to establish the requisite intent to defraud." *Id.* at 1118. The court held that "the false-entry offense is one of intent and not of carelessness," *id.* at 1119, and persuasively explained the strong policy reasons influencing its decision. The court stated:

> "There must be at least a hundred thousand bank officers in this country, many of them, like McAnally, young and inexperienced employees of small and unsophisticated banks. These officers make in the aggregate millions of entries in the books of their banks every day; no doubt many of those entries are inaccurate; and many of the inaccuracies are probably due to negligence, some of it gross. We do not think Congress meant to expose all of these bank employees to felony prosecutions; the danger that the heavy penalties prescribed in § 1005 would overdeter, with resulting social costs vividly described in a different context by the Supreme Court in United States v. United States Gypsum Co., 438 U.S. 422, 440–43 (1978), would be too great." *Id.*

We believe that the policy considerations which prompted the *Welliver* and *McAnally* courts to hold that recklessness is not sufficient to satisfy the specific intent requirement of § 1005 also apply to § 656. For example, the same bank employees who make entries in bank books which might result in a false entry also make loans which might constitute a misapplication. In either case, we do not believe that Congress intended that bank employees engaged in routine transactions, such as making book entries or making loans, should be exposed to felony prosecutions unless they act knowingly. Thus, we believe that the rules which courts have developed for § 1005, establishing knowledge as the proper mens rea standard and requiring that the jury instructions do not equate recklessness with intent to injure or defraud, also should be applied to § 656.

F. Conclusion: § 656 Prong of United States v. Welliver Overruled

For the reasons discussed above, we conclude that the appropriate mens rea standard for § 656 is knowledge. In order to convict a defendant for willfully misapplying funds with intent to injure or defraud a bank, the government must prove that the defendant *knowingly* participated in a deceptive or fraudulent transaction. The trier of fact may infer the required intent, i.e., knowledge, from the defendant's reckless disregard of the interest of the bank; however, jury instructions should not equate recklessness with intent to injure or defraud. Our conclusion is amply supported by the cases interpreting the predecessors to § 656, by the holdings of cases from other circuits, by Fifth Circuit cases other than the line of cases culminating in *Welliver,* by the equivalent mens rea standard of the companion § 1005, and by sound policy considerations. Accordingly, we overrule that portion of United States v. Welliver which held that the proper mens rea standard for § 656 was a reckless disregard of the interests of the bank.

III. THE § 656 JURY INSTRUCTIONS

Having determined that knowledge is the proper mens rea standard for § 656, we must decide whether the charge in this case erroneously permitted the jury to apply the lower recklessness standard to the element of willful misapplication with intent to defraud. If the jury charge did equate reckless disregard with the required higher standard of knowledge, *Sandstrom,* 442 U.S. 510 (1979), mandates a reversal of appellant's Section 656 conviction.

Appellant took exception to the jury instructions, asserting that they improperly equated recklessness with the requisite mens rea element of the crime. Appellant pointed specifically to the following charge: "A reckless disregard to the interest of the bank is the equivalent of intent to injure or defraud the bank."

The dissenting judges argue that the instructions considered as a whole fairly and accurately state the law. It is true, of course, that a jury charge must be judged as a whole. However, looking to the entire charge only compounds the problem in this case. The trial judge also charged as follows:

> "I charge you that the element of criminal intent necessary for conviction for a willful misapplication of bank funds is not fulfilled by a mere showing of indiscretion or foolhardiness on the part of the bank officer. His conduct must amount to *reckless disregard* of the bank's interests or outright abstraction of funds."

Two paragraphs later the trial judge defined "willful" in terms of the highest mens rea standard, i.e., purpose, but in the very next sentence stated that recklessness was an additional meaning: "The word 'willful' is also employed to characterize a thing done without ground for believing it is lawful, *or conduct marked by a reckless disregard,* whether or not one has the right so to act." The foregoing quotations obviously constitute clear and unequivocal instructions that the jury need find only recklessness in order to satisfy the mens rea standard of the crime.

It might be argued that the following three passages from the jury charge properly informed the jury that a higher mens rea than recklessness was required:

" '[I]ntent to defraud' means to act with intent to deceive or cheat.

"To act with intent to defraud means to act willfully and with a specific intent to deceive or cheat.

"I charge you that a thing is done willfully if it is done voluntarily and purposefully and with a specific intent to fail to do what the law requires, that is to say, with an evil motive or a bad purpose, whether to disobey or disregard the law."

We need not decide whether three correct statements will cure the three incorrect statements, because it is inescapable that the jury could reasonably have thought that, while an intent to deceive or a bad purpose would suffice, it *also* would be sufficient to find recklessness. In other words, the proper charges were not simply inconsistent with the improper charges; rather, the improper charges were made in *addition to* or the *equivalent of* the proper charges. In one instance, the jury instruction expressly states that recklessness is an *additional* meaning. The third proper charge, quoted above, is followed in the next sentence with the third improper charge, also quoted above. Together, they read as follows:

"I charge you that a thing is done willfully if it is done voluntarily and purposefully and with a specific intent to fail to do what the law requires, that is to say, with an evil motive or a bad purpose, whether to disobey or disregard the law. The word 'willful' *is also* employed to characterize a thing done without ground for believing it is lawful, or conduct marked by a *reckless disregard,* whether or not one has the right so to act."

Similarly, in another instance the proper charge is followed immediately by language further defining the quality of the required intent, including the tainted language equating recklessness with intent:

"To act with intent to defraud means to act willfully and with a specific intent to deceive or cheat.

"The requirement that the defendant intended to injure or defraud the bank may be shown by an unlawful act, voluntarily done, the natural tendency of which may have been to injure the bank. It is not necessary, however, that actual injury to the bank be shown.

"*A reckless disregard of the interest of the bank is the equivalent* of intent to injure or defraud the bank."

Considering the jury instructions as a whole, we have no doubt that a reasonable juror could have thought that mere recklessness was sufficient to satisfy the element of willful misapplication with intent to defraud.

Our conclusion is supported by the § 1005 holding of *Welliver*, a separate and distinct holding from *Welliver*'s § 656 holding which we overrule today. The § 1005 holding to which we now refer reversed a § 1005 conviction based on a jury charge containing some of the same language as the instant instructions. The paragraph of the instant charge which equates recklessness with intent to injure or defraud, the immediately preceding paragraph, and the immediately following paragraph were taken verbatim from *Welliver*. *See* 601 F.2d at 209, n. 13. The *Welliver* charge also contained the sentence stating that "[t]o act with intent to defraud means to act willfully and with a specific intent to deceive or cheat," which we noted above was the "proper" charge preceding the equivalency language. The *Welliver* court held that the charge constituted reversible error because it improperly equated recklessness with the requisite mens rea.

If the *Welliver* charge is reversible error, *a fortiori* the instant charge is. The instructions in *Welliver* included only the charge equating recklessness with intent to injure or defraud, whereas the instant charge included not only that charge verbatim, but also included the other two tainted charges quoted above, i.e., charging that the element of criminal intent for willful misapplication amounts to reckless disregard, and giving the additional definition of the word "willful" as conduct marked by reckless disregard. Moreover, the "proper" charges in Welliver were more forceful than those in the instant case, primarily because the Welliver charge did not contain the explicit indication, as here, that recklessness was an additional meaning for the mens rea terms. If those more forceful "proper" charges in Welliver were insufficient to cure the single tainted charge, then *a fortiori* the less forceful "proper" charges here cannot cure the same tainted equivalency charge plus the two additional charges which expressly articulate the erroneous recklessness standard for the element of willful misapplication.

We conclude that reasonable jurors could have interpreted, and indeed most likely did interpret, the instructions in this case to establish the erroneous recklessness mens rea standard for the element of willful misapplication with intent to injure or defraud. Accordingly, appellant's conviction on the § 656 count must be reversed.

IV. THE § 1005 JURY INSTRUCTIONS

Although appellant acknowledges that the trial court did not include the improper recklessness charge in its instructions on § 1005, he nevertheless argues that the equation of recklessness with intent to injure or defraud in the preceding instructions on § 656 spilled over and tainted the § 1005 charge. After carefully reviewing the jury instructions, we conclude that appellant's argument has no merit.

There was a clear demarcation between the court's § 656 charge and the § 1005 charge. After quoting the statute and indicating which defendants were indicted on which of the new § 1005 counts, the trial court set forth the essential elements of the § 1005 offense as follows:

"First: That the Defendant *knowingly* made a false entry concerning a material fact in a book or record of an insured bank, as charged;

"Second: That the Defendant made such entry *willfully*, with *knowledge* of its falsity and with the intent of *defrauding or deceiving* the person named in the indictment."

The court also charged the jury:

"I charge you that the crime of making false entries by an officer of a bank with intent to defraud pursuant to this statute includes any entry on the books of the bank which is *intentionally* made to represent what is not true or does not exist, with the intent either to *deceive* the bank's officers or to defraud the bank."

The § 1005 jury instructions were clear and concise, and did not themselves contain any inkling of the erroneous recklessness language. We conclude that the § 1005 charge so clearly articulated the proper mens rea standard of knowledge that we are satisfied there was no spillover taint from the improper § 656 charge.

Accordingly, appellant's conviction on the § 1005 count is affirmed.

V. CONCLUSION

Appellant's conviction on the § 656 count is reversed. His conviction on the § 1005 count and his conviction on the three § 1014 counts are affirmed.

Affirmed in part, reversed in part, and remanded.

RONEY and FAY, CIRCUIT JUDGES, with whom HILL and HATCHETT, CIRCUIT JUDGES, join dissenting in part.

Most respectfully we dissent as to the reversal of the 18 U.S.C.A. § 656 conviction for two reasons. * * * Reading the instruction as a whole, we believe the jury was not misled as to mens rea required, even under the highly technical, semantic analysis of the Court's opinion. Although the district court used the words "reckless disregard" and stated that "a reckless disregard of the interest of the bank is the equivalent of intent to injure or defraud the bank," read as a whole, we think the instruction adequately conveyed to the jury the high standard of proof of intent required and the proper options available to the jury in this case.

Second, it seems to us that with all that is said in the Court's opinion, there is a level of reckless disregard that translates immutably into the precise intent espoused by the majority, with which we have no substantial quarrel. 18 U.S.C.A. § 656 deals with a very limited special group of people. By its very terms this section deals only with officers, directors, agents or employees of covered banks. These individuals have an affirmative duty to protect the funds and assets placed in their care.

As stated by Judge Morgan in United States v. Wilson, 500 F.2d at 720: "It should be remembered above all else that this statute was enacted to preserve the FDIC from loss and to preserve and protect the assets of banks having a federal relationship."

Keeping the legislative history in mind, we have no difficulty in understanding how and why the Fifth Circuit arrived at the point where "a reckless disregard of the interest of the bank is the equivalent of the intent to injure or defraud the bank." The en banc court is now changing the law of our Circuit, so that these words cannot be used in a § 656 instruction, no matter what other words are also used. It is a subtle change, however, that in our opinion will probably make no difference in the outcome of any trial and would have made no difference in this one. If applied prospectively, we would not even dissent. We should not, however, reverse a conviction on such a technicality.

As we read the Court's opinion, it will be proper for trial judges to instruct a jury to the effect that in determining whether the defendant is guilty of a willful misapplication of bank funds, it may (or may not) infer such from a reckless disregard of the bank's interest, if such existed. Then on appeal in determining the sufficiency of the evidence and whether the government has established the necessary intent to injure or defraud the bank, a showing of conduct amounting to a reckless disregard of the bank's interest will meet this requirement. The distinction between instructing a jury that reckless disregard is the equivalent of the requisite mens rea and instructing it that the requisite mens rea may be inferred from evidence of reckless disregard is so tenuous as to be more meaningful in the classroom than the courtroom.

The Court properly holds that the appropriate mens rea is knowledge. By law a bank officer must know the applicable statutes, rules and regulations controlling the bank's operations. If such an officer (or official covered by the statute) makes a loan with the level of reckless disregard of those rules and the interests of the bank as defined in the instructions in this case, he has acted knowingly in a manner contemplated by Congress to fall within the ambit of knowing and willful misapplication of the bank's funds or credit.

This is not mere recklessness or mere disregard. Tying the two words together, coupled with the strong instructions on the intent required, properly conveyed to the jury the level of knowing and willful conduct required. It seems to us that *Welliver* was correctly decided and that the panel opinion in this matter was equally correct. When we get a case with a charge of "mere recklessness," defined as little more than negligence, then might be the time for the decision in this case. But here, the instruction was at best correct, at worst contained incorrect words that were harmless when read in context, and the jury's verdict of guilty should be affirmed.

We concur in the court's affirming the 18 U.S.C.A. § 1005 conviction.

Notes

1. What is fraudulent about making a loan, ostensibly to Island Summit, Inc., a defunct corporation, instead of to the actual borrowers, Hester and Holley? Is there harm to the bank if Hester and Holley are still shown as guarantors on the loan?

2. Generally, a court will look to statutory language to determine whether a "specific intent" requirement is present. Section 656 is one of the unusual statutes where courts have been willing to look beyond statutory language to read such a requirement into an offense. *Adamson* states the majority view that "intent to injure or defraud the bank" is an element of § 656.

3. Do you agree with the majority that the "reckless disregard" jury instruction impermissibly lowers the government's burden of proving the requisite mens rea? Or, do you agree with the dissent that the instruction is permissible because of Adamson's expertise as a bank officer?

D.   SECTION 1344: SCHEME OR ARTIFICE TO DEFRAUD A FINANCIAL INSTITUTION

As noted in Section 1 of this Chapter, 18 U.S.C. § 1344 was passed in 1990 to fill "serious gaps * * * in Federal jurisdiction over frauds against banks * * *."[y] The next case, United States v. Brandon, 17 F.3d 409 (1st Cir.1994), provides a step-by-step application of § 1344. For the sake of brevity, only the court's analysis of two of the defendants is included.

UNITED STATES v. BRANDON

United States Court of Appeals, First Circuit, 1994.
17 F.3d 409.

TORRUELLA, CIRCUIT JUDGE.

The eight defendants in this case were convicted of conspiracy to commit bank fraud under 18 U.S.C. § 371 and of a varying number of bank fraud counts under 18 U.S.C. § 1344 and § 2 following a jury trial in the district court. They now challenge their convictions and sentences on a wide variety of grounds. For the reasons set forth below, we affirm all of the convictions except for the bank fraud convictions on Counts 24 and 25 against defendant John Ward and the bank fraud convictions on Counts 23 through 26 against defendant Owen Landman, which we reverse.

I.   BACKGROUND

This case involves an alleged scheme to obtain loan financing from a federally insured bank by fraudulently representing the existence of

---

y. S. Rep. No. 225, 98th Cong., 2d Sess.   3182, 3517–19.
377–79, *reprinted* in 1984 U.S.C.C.A.N.

down payments required by the bank from the investors on whose behalf the loans were made. According to the record in this case, viewed in the light most favorable to the government, United States v. Van Helden, 920 F.2d 99, 101 (1st Cir.1990), the facts of this scheme are as follows.

On January 1, 1985, defendant Peter Brandon and two others formed a partnership called Dean Street Development ("Dean Street") for the purpose of buying, developing, and selling real estate. Specifically, Brandon planned to buy and renovate motels along the Rhode Island seashore, convert them into condominiums and then sell the individual rooms to investors as condominium units. As part of this plan, the condominium buyers would lease the units back to Dean Street and Dean Street would then manage the properties as motels. Under the "lease-back" agreement with the buyers, Dean Street would apply the income from the operation of the motels to cover the monthly mortgage, tax and insurance costs incurred by the unit buyers. Any shortfalls in operating costs would be made up by Dean Street, leaving the buyers with no monthly costs on their investment.

In addition, buyers would be allowed to use their units for two weeks out of the year. Dean Street would also guaranty them a certain level of profit at sale. Some buyers would receive rebates for each unit they purchased. In short, the buyers would be offered a sweet deal.

To make the deal even sweeter, Brandon planned to arrange all the financing for the buyers. He hoped to obtain 100% financing, that is, loans for the complete purchase price of each unit. With such financing, buyers could invest in the project without putting any money down and consequently obtain that elusive—yet apparently not uncommon for the fast-paced world of 1980s real estate—deal of "something for nothing."

In early 1987, Brandon approached Homeowner's Funding Corporation ("Homeowners"), a mortgage broker that acts as an intermediary between banks and borrowers, to obtain these "end loans" for the buyers. Homeowners' President told Brandon that 100% financing was unavailable for the project. Rather, the best Brandon could hope to find was 80% financing with a 20% down payment required from the buyers. Homeowners subsequently searched for a lender and, after approaching several banks, located Bay Loan and Investment Bank ("Bay Loan"), a financial institution insured by the Federal Deposit Insurance Corporation. Bay Loan agreed to lend buyers of Dean Street's condominium units up to 80% of the required purchase price.

Homeowners, as well as East–West Financial Corporation ("East West"), the other mortgage broker involved in this case,[2] acted as brokers and servicing agents for Bay Loan. Bay Loan was the actual lender for the Dean Street project and it financed every condominium

---

2. Toward the end of 1987, Brandon became dissatisfied with what he considered the slow pace at which Homeowners was processing the loans and, after a dispute with Homeowners, retained the services of East West to continue the project. East West continued where Homeowners left off with Bay Loan again agreeing to act as the end loan financier.

sale involved in the scheme. By prior agreement, Homeowners and East West provided the original mortgages for the buyers and then sold them to Bay Loan. Homeowners and East West would forward all the loan applications to Bay Loan for approval prior to providing the mortgages for the condominium units. The decision of whether to fund a particular mortgage rested entirely with Bay Loan and Bay Loan set the terms and conditions of each mortgage.

As Bay Loan Vice President of consumer lending, Joseph Gormley, explained to Brandon, the bank required each buyer of a condominium unit to make at least a 20% down payment to the seller, Dean Street, before Bay Loan could fund the loans. Instead of instructing buyers to provide the required down payments, however, Brandon concocted a scheme that permitted buyers to avoid the down payments altogether. As a result, he was able to pursue his original goal of obtaining 100% financing for the condominium project. The scheme was formulated during the spring and summer of 1987 when Brandon had several discussions with, among other people, his attorney, George Marderosian, and co-defendant Norman Reisch, another of Marderosian's clients, concerning ways that the 20% down payment requirement "might be satisfied by alternative methods or might be avoided." During that period, Brandon also told another person involved in the conspiracy, Claude Limoges, that the down payments would be falsified.

Brandon planned and employed three basic methods of falsifying the down payments. The first method was simply providing money to the various buyers which the buyers would then use to make the down payments to Dean Street. Usually the money came from third-party investors to whom Brandon promised a commission for each down payment they funded. Once the buyer made the down payment to Dean Street, Dean Street would return the money to the investor leaving a paper trail for a down payment that was never actually made. The second method involved obtaining down payment checks from the buyers and promising not to cash them. Copies of these nonnegotiated checks would remain in the loan file to give the appearance that real funds had actually been transferred. The third method was to provide second mortgages to the buyers to fund their down payments and then to discharge those mortgages after the closings.[4]

The first method of avoiding down payments was employed from the outset of the scheme. Co-defendants Charles Gauvin and Marvin Granoff, two clients of Marderosian, agreed with Brandon to purchase some units at the Charlestown Motor Inn. Gauvin and Granoff also agreed to provide down payment funds to other buyers for subsequent unit sales. Brandon promised them $1000 for each unit sold with their down payment funds. In August of 1987, Gauvin, Granoff and a third person each purchased four units. Marderosian conducted the closing and co-defendant Owen Landman, an attorney who shared office space with Marderosian, acted as escrow agent. During the closing, Marderosian

---

4. Brandon also falsified the loan appli-   cations of otherwise unqualified buyers.

recorded the amount of each down payment ($20,500) on the closing statements—also called the HUD settlement sheets—as "amounts paid by or in behalf of borrower."

Gauvin provided the down payment funds for these twelve purchases but no actual payment was ever made; instead, the funds were passed through Dean Street and returned to Gauvin. At the closing, Gauvin delivered twelve separate checks for $20,500 each to Marderosian, drawn on an account that only had a $6000 balance at the time, and Landman deposited the checks in his escrow account. Landman then wrote twelve corresponding checks to Marderosian who in turn wrote checks to Dean Street for identical amounts of $20,500 each. Two days later, Dean Street wrote twelve checks back to Gauvin for the same amounts of $20,500 each and Gauvin deposited the money in the original checking account to cover his initial twelve checks written as down payments to the seller.

In late August and September of 1987, Gauvin provided down payments for the purchase of units at the Charlestown Motor Inn and at the Bayside Motel by Reisch and others. As with the first purchases, Dean Street returned the down payment money within a matter of days and also paid Gauvin an additional $1000 per unit.

In the beginning of 1988, Bay Loan began requiring that down payments be made with certified funds. Gauvin and Granoff agreed to provide buyers with funds so that they could obtain certified checks before the closings. In January and February of 1988, Granoff supplied $470,000 to Marderosian who deposited the funds and began distributing the money to prospective buyers. The original intention was that Dean Street would pay back the money to Granoff a few days after each closing as it had done in the previous transactions. Brandon, however, never returned the money as planned.

With no more money coming from Gauvin and Granoff, Brandon discussed the possibility of funding buyer down payments with Reisch. Reisch had earlier supplied down payment money for a buyer and was reimbursed by Dean Street the next day. Reisch agreed to provide the money, but only if he could wire the money directly to the buyers on a transaction by transaction basis in order to avoid having large amounts outstanding. Funds were wired to buyers on several occasions and the buyers then wrote down payment checks with the money. The checks were either deposited in Landman's escrow account or endorsed directly back over to Reisch. Those funds deposited in escrow were promptly returned to Reisch.

The second method of falsifying down payments, using nonnegotiated checks, was employed less frequently. In October of 1987, co-defendants Ronald Hagopian and John Ward purchased several units at the Bayside Motel using nonnegotiated checks for their down payments. Brandon also enlisted Hagopian and Ward, both real estate brokers, to solicit other buyers for the project. Hagopian and Ward told several of the buyers they had recruited to provide down payment checks which they promised would never be cashed. These buyers proceeded to write checks to Dean Street and those checks were never negotiated.

The third method of falsifying down payments was through dischargeable mortgages. Joseph Gormley at Bay Loan approved a plan for buyers to make only 5% down payments in certified funds with the balance of a required 25% down payment to be satisfied by a second mortgage provided by Dean Street. Dean Street began providing these mortgages to the buyers, but the mortgages were promptly discharged after the closings because Dean Street never actually intended to obligate the buyers. The discharges were accomplished by a "purchase price adjustment" given to buyers after the sale to "compensate" them for promised renovations that Dean Street was suddenly unable to make. In reality, the renovations "were never going to happen" in the first place.

At the closings, some of the buyers inquired about the second mortgage documents because Brandon had promised a discharge and the buyers wanted to know when that would take place. The "purchase price adjustment" letters that discharged the mortgages were excluded from the closing documentation so the bank would not see them. During the closings, Landman gestured to several buyers that they should not mention the matter to him. Brandon's assistant at Dean Street, co-defendant Momi Kumalae, did speak to buyers about the discharges and assured them that they would be taken care of. Kumalae also signed many of the discharge letters sent to the buyers.

Despite the sale of almost 200 units, by the fall of 1988, the loan proceeds from Bay Loan's financing of unit purchases was falling well short of Dean Street's expenses and its own debt service. Dean Street quickly fell behind schedule in making the mortgage payments on all the Bay Loan condominium unit loans, and it eventually stopped making any payments by early 1989.

Between August 1987 and October 1988, Dean Street had sold 196 units to 79 different buyers, all financed by Bay Loan in 176 separate loans. The face value of the loans was $18.8 million and Bay Loan actually distributed $17.3 million to Marderosian who passed on about $16.9 million to Dean Street (the balance was retained as fees or was paid to Landman for escrow services). As of the trial, approximately $16.3 million remained outstanding on the loans.

Gormley at Bay Loan, who approved the loans, did not know that down payment funds came from sources other than the buyers, that some down payments were nonnegotiated checks, that second mortgages were being discharged, or that buyers were being paid to purchase units. Gormley testified that he would not have approved the loans if he had been aware of any of these circumstances.

On February 28, 1991, a federal grand jury sitting in the District of Rhode Island handed down a 27–count indictment charging the eight appellants and four others with defrauding Bay Loan, a federally insured financial institution, of approximately $18 million. Count 1 charged all twelve defendants with conspiracy to commit bank fraud in violation of

18 U.S.C. § 371. Counts 2 through 27 charged various defendants with individual acts of bank fraud, under 18 U.S.C. § 1344, based on individual loan transactions executed during the scheme to defraud.[8] Four of the defendants pleaded guilty and did not go to trial. Two of the four, George Marderosian and Claude Limoges, testified for the government.

After a trial in the United States District Court for the District of Rhode Island, the jury found all the defendants guilty of conspiracy and each defendant guilty on multiple counts of bank fraud. Some defendants were acquitted on individual bank fraud charges as discussed below. This appeal followed.

* * *

IV. SUFFICIENCY OF THE EVIDENCE

Seven of the eight defendants argue that the evidence introduced at trial was insufficient to support their convictions for bank fraud and conspiracy to commit bank fraud.[10] They argue, with individual variations, that they did not have the requisite knowledge and intent to defraud Bay Loan because they did not know of, or intend to violate, any down payment requirements of the bank. With the few exceptions previously noted, we disagree. Before reviewing the evidence with respect to each defendant, we must first address some issues regarding the substantive offenses charged in this case.

A. The Offenses

1. Bank Fraud

To prove bank fraud under 18 U.S.C. § 1344,[11] the prosecution must show beyond a reasonable doubt that the defendant (1) engaged in a scheme or artifice to defraud, or made false statements or misrepresentations to obtain money from; (2) a federally insured financial institution; and (3) did so knowingly. The terms "scheme" and "artifice" are defined to include "any plan, pattern or cause of action, including false and

---

8. One bank fraud count was later dismissed by the government so that 26 total counts remained for trial. Brandon was the only defendant charged in all of the counts.

Each bank fraud count charges one or more of the defendants with facilitating in some way the fraudulent representation of the required down payment for a specific loan for an individual condominium unit. Although each unit purchase allegedly involved the same fraudulent scheme, only 26 specific executions of the scheme were originally charged.

10. Brandon does not challenge the sufficiency of the evidence against him on appeal. * * *

11. At the time when the offenses occurred, 18 U.S.C. § 1344 provided:

Whoever knowingly executes, or attempts to execute, a scheme or artifice—(1) to

defraud a federally chartered or insured financial institution; or (2) to obtain any of the moneys, funds, credits, assets, securities, or other property owned by, or under the custody or control of a federally chartered or insured financial institution, by means of false or fraudulent pretenses, representations, or promises; [shall be guilty of an offense against the United States].

A technical amendment in 1989 deleted the words "federally chartered or insured" from the section leaving just "financial institution." Pub.L. No. 101–73, Title IX, § 961(k), Aug. 9, 1989, 103 Stat. 500. Apparently, no substantive change was intended by this amendment as the definition of "financial institution" for all of Title 18, now contained at 18 U.S.C. § 20, still encompasses federally chartered or insured institutions.

fraudulent pretenses and misrepresentations, intended to deceive others in order to obtain something of value, such as money, from the institution to be deceived." "The term 'scheme to defraud,' however, is not capable of precise definition. Fraud instead is measured in a particular case by determining whether the scheme demonstrated a departure from fundamental honesty, moral uprightness, or fair play and candid dealings in the general life of the community." [citations omitted]

The alleged scheme in this case is the fraudulent representation of down payments that were not actually paid in order to obtain loan financing from Bay Loan. There is little doubt that this scheme took place. Defendants argue, however, that they did not know of, or participate in, the scheme, and, to the extent that they did participate in activities related to the scheme, such actions were not illegal because the actions were not intended to deceive or defraud Bay Loan. Defendants claim they were either unaware that Bay Loan existed or else unaware that Bay Loan had a down payment requirement that prohibited the various down payment transactions in which they were involved. The central issue on appeal, therefore, is whether defendants possessed the requisite knowledge and intent.

"To act with the 'intent to defraud' means to act willfully, and with the specific intent to deceive or cheat for the purpose of either causing some financial loss to another, or bringing about some financial gain to oneself. It is a well-established principle that fraudulent intent may be established by circumstantial evidence and inferences drawn from all the evidence." [citations omitted]

Defendants argue that the government must prove that they knew that the victim of their fraud was a federally insured financial institution. We disagree. The status of the victim-institution is not a separate knowledge element of bank fraud under § 1344 but an objective fact that must be established in order for the statute to apply. The government produced evidence, and defendants do not dispute, that Bay Loan is federally insured. This is sufficient to satisfy the requirement under 18 U.S.C. § 1344 that the defrauded bank be a federally insured bank.

* * *

The defendants in this case also argue that the government must prove they knew that the end loans were provided by Bay Loan and not by some other institution, such as Homeowners or East West. In other words, there was no violation of § 1344 because the scheme to defraud was not knowingly targeted at a federally insured financial institution, but instead at the non-federally insured mortgage brokers.

Defendants overstate the government's burden. The specific intent under § 1344 is an intent to defraud a bank, that is, an intent to victimize a bank by means of a fraudulent scheme. It has been established that the government does not have to show the alleged scheme was directed *solely* toward a particular institution; it is sufficient to show that defendant knowingly executed a fraudulent scheme that exposed a federally insured bank to a risk of loss.

We hold that it is also unnecessary for the government to prove that a defendant knows which particular bank will be victimized by his fraud as long as it is established that a defendant knows that *a* financial institution will be defrauded. The bank fraud statute was "designed to provide an effective vehicle for the prosecution of frauds in which the victims are financial institutions that are federally created, controlled or insured." In creating the statute, Congress noted that "there is a strong Federal interest in protecting the financial integrity of these institutions, and the legislation in this part would assure a basis for Federal prosecution of those who victimize these banks through fraudulent schemes." Thus, Congress intended to criminalize bank frauds that harm federally insured banks, not just bank frauds directed specifically toward federally insured banks. As other courts have noted, "the legislative history supports a broad construction of the statutory language" of the bank fraud statute. [citations omitted]

Defendants are essentially seeking to sanitize their fraud by interposing an intermediary or an additional victim between their fraud and the federally insured bank. We reject this attempt to escape the reach of the bank fraud statute. Instead, we find that defendants need not have had the specific intent to defraud Bay Loan so long as they intended to defraud some financial institution. The fact that it should turn out that the financial institution actually defrauded was federally insured is a fortuitous stroke of bad luck for the defendants but does not make it any less of a federal crime. In this case, evidence beyond a reasonable doubt that defendants fraudulently evaded a known down payment requirement, whether thought to be imposed by Homeowners, East West, Bay Loan or some other financing entity, is sufficient to support a bank fraud conviction. Of course, the government must also establish that a federally insured bank, Bay Loan, was victimized or exposed to a risk of loss by the scheme to defraud. This, however, is not seriously disputed in this case.

Concerns about extending the reach of the bank fraud statute into broad new areas of financial activity stem from a misunderstanding of the nature of the statute. Financial transactions are becoming increasingly integrated and complex as more and more financial instruments are scrutinized and traded on national and global markets. Consequently, the effects of fraudulent actions against one institution are increasingly likely to spill over and detrimentally affect others. As Congress' main concern in § 1344 was to provide jurisdiction for fraudulent schemes that harmed federally chartered or insured institutions, the increased risks to the institutions should be matched by increased coverage of the statute. We are not federalizing criminal transactions previously covered only by state law so much as recognizing that those criminal transactions are becoming more federal in nature.[16]

16. We do not address whether any   scheme to defraud, regardless of its intend-

An additional argument defendants make is that the government must prove defendants knew that Bay Loan's down payment requirement specifically prohibited the funding of buyers' down payments by someone other than the buyer. Defendants claim that they thought the funding of buyer down payments was just some complex financial arrangement, "supplemental financing" or required paperwork, and they did not know the funding was designed to defraud the bank.

This misrepresents the nature of the fraud. Although Bay Loan did in fact prohibit third party funding of down payments, the key misrepresentation in this case was that the required down payments were being paid when they actually were not. Bay Loan required the buyers to make down payments to the seller, Dean Street, and the existence of the payments was represented to the bank on the closing settlement sheets. In reality, the payments were not being made, either because no funds were actually transferred or because the funds were returned by Dean Street to their source. Therefore, the government need only prove that defendants knew a down payment was required and that no real down payments were actually made. It need not establish that defendants knew all of the specifics of the down payment requirement such as restrictions on third party funding.

In sum, to prove defendants knowingly engaged in the fraud, the government must establish that each defendant knew that some financial institution was lending the money for the motel-condominium project, knew that a down payment was required for these loans, knew that a scheme of one sort or another existed to make it appear that the down payments were being made when in fact they were not, and finally, that each defendant willfully participated in that scheme.

2. *Conspiracy*

Each defendant contests the sufficiency of the evidence of his or her knowledge of the conspiracy to defraud Bay Loan and his or her level of participation in that agreed upon scheme. To prove conspiracy, the government must show the existence of an agreement between defendant and another to commit a crime, that each defendant knew of the agreement, and that each defendant voluntarily participated in the conspiracy through conduct that was interdependent with the actions of the other conspirators. The defendants must have both the intent to agree to participate in the conspiracy and an intent to commit the underlying substantive offense. The government, however, need not prove that each defendant knew all of the details and members, or

ed victim, can be prosecuted under the bank fraud statute as long as it has some detrimental effect on a federally insured bank. In this case at least, the government did prove the scheme was intended to defraud a financial institution: Homeowners or East West, if not Bay Loan itself.

We also do not address possible statutory or jurisdictional limitations on the remoteness or foreseeability of the harm or the risk of loss to federally insured financial institutions beyond which § 1344 will no longer apply. We simply note that this case presents a situation of direct harm to Bay Loan resulting from a scheme specifically designed to fraudulently avoid the requirements of that federally insured bank in order to obtain funds originating directly from Bay Loan.

participated in all of the objectives, of the conspiracy as long as it can show knowledge of the basic agreement. Such proof of knowledge and intent "may consist of circumstantial evidence, including inferences from surrounding circumstances, such as acts committed by the defendant that furthered the conspiracy's purposes."

The government must also establish defendants' participation in the conspiracy with the intent to further the aims of the conspiracy. Once a conspiracy is established, as well as defendant's intent to further it, any connection between the defendant and the conspiracy, even a slight one, will be sufficient to establish knowing participation.

In this case, the government must prove that the defendants knew there was an agreement to fraudulently represent down payments in order to get loans from Bay Loan and that they willfully participated in this scheme by taking some overt action with the intent to further the scheme's objective. Thus, the evidence must be sufficient to establish the intent to commit bank fraud as discussed above and, in addition, must also establish an intent to commit the fraud in conjunction with the broader conspiratorial agreement.

B.   The Case Against Each Defendant

* * *

1.   Marvin Granoff

Granoff was convicted of conspiracy and two counts of bank fraud in connection with his purchase of units on one occasion and with his funding of buyer down payments on another occasion. Granoff argues that the evidence in this case is insufficient to show that he was anything more than an innocent investor duped by his lawyer, Marderosian, into providing money for a project he really did not know anything about. Although the evidence against Marvin Granoff reveals a more circumscribed role than some of the other defendants, we are not prepared to overturn the jury's guilty verdict on either the conspiracy charge or on the two counts of bank fraud.

Sufficient evidence supports the jury's conclusion that Granoff knew Bay Loan was funding Dean Street's condominium project, that he knew down payments were required from the buyers and that he knowingly participated in a scheme to deceive the bank into thinking the requirement was satisfied. To begin with, Granoff bought four units on one occasion and provided down payment funds on another occasion. Both times Bay Loan financed the purchases without knowing the required down payments were not actually made. Prior to each of these transactions, Granoff attended a series of meetings with Brandon concerning the motel condominium scheme. Brandon told Granoff that down payments were required and that he needed Granoff to provide money for the down payments of other buyers.[19] Granoff agreed to do so.[20]

19. Specifically, Marderosian testified that Brandon told Gauvin and Granoff in the summer of 1987 that "Homeowners required a twenty-five percent down payment

For Granoff's purchase of units at the Charlestown Inn in August of 1987, his partner, Gauvin, provided down payments to Dean Street on Granoff's behalf in the form of checks that were not backed by sufficient funds. Copies of the checks were included in the closing files. The "payments" were returned to Gauvin two days later when Dean Street wrote identical checks back to Gauvin which Gauvin deposited in his account to cover the original down payment checks. The fact that Gauvin's checks, totaling $246,000, were drawn on an account with only $6000 at the time when they were written indicates that there was no intent on Gauvin's part to make an actual down payment in the first place.

Granoff likewise provided down payment funds for other buyers and the evidence indicates he did this knowing and expecting that the money would be returned to him after the closing. Granoff provided $470,000 for down payments on the Atlantic Inn–Westerly units in the form of two checks, one for $270,000 from Marvin Granoff Real Estate and another for $200,000 from Granoff's Eastern Wire Products Co. In turn, Brandon promised to pay Granoff $1000 for each unit sold using Granoff's down payment money.

As it turns out, Granoff was never paid back, but the evidence shows that Granoff expected and intended for this money to be promptly returned to him after the closings. A recycling arrangement had been used earlier for Granoff 's own purchase, and for subsequent purchases funded by Gauvin, under the initial agreement between Granoff, Gauvin, and Brandon. More importantly, about two weeks after the first closings involving Granoff's $470,000, Gauvin sent a letter to Marderosian, on Manchester Associates[22] letterhead, complaining that the transaction involving the $470,000 was taking too long. The letter stated that the

and while that down payment would not be required of Mr. Gauvin and Mr. Granoff, he did have the problem of the down payment with subsequent purchasers and he asked Mr. Gauvin and Mr. Granoff for their assistance in meeting that problem." Despite the offer to "waive" Gauvin and Granoff's down payments, checks representing down payments were required for their purchases.

In another meeting, Brandon asked Gauvin and Granoff if they were "willing to provide the down payment money for other purchasers" and they agreed to do so. Marderosian also testified that Brandon told Granoff at a meeting in January of 1988 that he needed someone to provide funding for the certified down payment funds required from unit buyers. Brandon asked whether Gauvin and Granoff were "interested in providing those certified funds" and they agreed.

20. Marderosian testified that Granoff agreed on several different occasions to participate in Brandon's scheme and referred several times to the "agreement Mr. Gauvin and Mr. Granoff made to provide Mr. Brandon with monies for the down payments." Despite this, Granoff argues that Marderosian's testimony indicates Granoff said little or nothing at the various meetings with Brandon and this is insufficient to establish Granoff agreed to participate in the conspiracy. The fact that Granoff provided $470,000 that was used for down payments following the meetings with Brandon in which the agreement was discussed, however, is sufficient to support the conclusion that Granoff in fact did agree and did participate in the conspiracy.

Furthermore, Granoff 's involvement in the conspiracy was more than just the provision of goods and services to an operation that he knew might use the funds illegally. * * *

22. Manchester Associates was a partnership formed by and consisting of Gauvin and Granoff.

transaction involving Granoff's $470,000 "was to take at most two to three days." Marderosian also testified that on a different occasion, Gauvin told Marderosian that Gauvin and Granoff "can make money without putting up any money." In addition, there was no promissory note or other formal documentation to indicate that the $470,000 was normal loan financing. Consequently, Granoff knew that his money was used to create the appearance that down payments were being paid when in fact they were not; they were being falsified.

The arrangement of rapidly recycling "down payment" funds through Dean Street meant that, in reality, no down payments were being made at all. A paper trail was left in the closing files indicating that the buyer had made a down payment to the seller, Dean Street, when, in fact, the seller just returned the money to its source, effectively rendering that paper trail fraudulent. Bay Loan's down payment requirement was thus avoided without the bank's knowledge. As a knowing participant in this recycling scheme, Granoff possessed the necessary intent to defraud and the requisite level of involvement in the larger conspiracy to be found guilty of the offenses charged.

Although not essential for upholding Granoff's conviction, we also find that the evidence is sufficient to show that Granoff knew Bay Loan was loaning the money for the condominium units. Granoff bought four units financed by Bay Loan and he put up nearly half a million dollars to provide down payment funds for other units to be purchased with Bay Loan financing. Homeowners furnished a letter at the closings including the closing on Granoff's purchases, which Granoff attended, stating that Homeowners had "transferred all of its rights and interests" in the mortgage to Bay Loan. Granoff had occasion to see the letter and it is not unreasonably [sic] to assume he also read it.

Granoff also attended a number of planning meetings with Brandon in which plans for closing on various units, the funding of down payments, and other details of the scheme were discussed. The evidence also indicates Granoff was continually kept abreast of various details of Brandon's scheme; details, one could infer, that included the source of the financing. In the last half of 1987, Granoff and Gauvin formed a partnership called Manchester Associates for the purpose of real estate investment. On behalf of Manchester Associates, Gauvin met several times with Brandon who discussed his overall plans to close on over 400 motel units as well as the schedule for those closings. Letters referencing these meetings were written on Manchester letterhead and one could reasonably infer that Gauvin related the substance of the meetings to his partner Granoff.[25] One such letter from Gauvin states that "it would seem that the lending institutions will be in a position to begin closing." As Homeowners and Bay Loan were the only institutions involved at the time the letter was written, the plural reference to "institutions "indi-

___

25. For example, Granoff was cc'd on a letter to Dean Street that referenced plans to close on 107 units and discussed the repayment of Granoff's $470,000.

cates that Gauvin and his partner, Granoff, were aware not only of Homeowners but of Bay Loan as well.

In sum, the evidence indicates that Granoff was aware, on a fairly detailed level, of a large real estate scheme whose only source of funding happened to be Bay Loan. With substantial sums of his own money at stake in this extensive project, Granoff was likely to become aware at some point of the source of money behind it all. It is not unreasonable to conclude, therefore, that Granoff knew of Bay Loan's involvement in the project.

* * *

Granoff challenges any inferences of criminal knowledge or intent drawn from the pool of circumstantial evidence as impermissibly based merely on Granoff's association with his co-defendants. He claims that amidst the fast-paced wheeling and dealing of the 1980s real estate market, investors did not have the ability to know all the details and purposes behind every one of their transactions. It was common for investors to entrust their money to developers and lawyers without learning any of the specifics of the various projects in which they were involved. Details such as the exact nature of a bank's down payment requirement were not, Granoff implies, important enough to be discussed between a developer and an investor. Add to these circumstances the unscrupulous and deceptive acts of Brandon and Marderosian, who allegedly got Granoff into this whole mess, and Granoff contends that we cannot help but conclude he was lied to about the true nature of the project.

While it may be true that the typical real estate investor in the 1980s would readily put up hundreds of thousands of dollars for "down payment funds," expect the money back in a few days, and still not suspect he is defrauding a bank, we are certainly not prepared, given the facts discussed above, to preclude a jury from concluding otherwise. The government need not disprove every reasonable hypothesis of innocence, provided the record in its entirety supports the jury's verdict. In this case, the record does provide the requisite support. Therefore, we affirm Granoff's convictions.

* * *

5. John Ward

Ward was convicted of conspiracy and six counts of bank fraud for purchasing a unit and for soliciting and facilitating unit sales. * * * Brandon testified that he told Ward about "his relationship" with Bay Loan. Ward also knew that down payments were required as he was involved in many of the * * * discussions with potential buyers * * *. Specifically, Ward told one buyer to give him a check "for the down payment that was required."

Ward knew down payments were not actually being made as his own down payment was not negotiated and he told one buyer, whose down payment funds were to be wired into that buyer's account, that the down payment check would be cashed the same day so that the people wiring the funds "got their money back."

We reject Ward's assertion that he thought Bay Loan approved all of the various down payment shenanigans in which he was involved. Ward contends that the down payment arrangement that he was aware of was simply a paperwork requirement and not a "real" requirement; that is, Ward only knew that some sort of paper representing down payments had to exist but thought no real funds were actually required from the buyers. We suppose Ward's contention is within the realm of the possible. However, the jury looked at the intricate down payment arrangements and the way Ward explained them to the buyers and found, quite reasonably we think, that Ward knew his actions were a "departure from fundamental honesty." [citation omitted] The common sense understanding of a down payment is the transfer of actual funds from the buyer to the seller or financier. With this in mind, it is more than reasonable for a jury to find that once a defendant learned of the structure of the down payment arrangement used in this case, with no real down payments changing hands, the defendant would be tipped off to the fact that a fraudulent transaction was contemplated. Even if we assume Brandon lied to Ward and told him that Bay Loan directed Dean Street to arrange for paper, as opposed to real, down payments, the evidence was sufficient to support a finding that Ward knew he was engaging in a sham transaction.

The evidence is also sufficient to prove Ward's willful participation in the overall conspiracy and Ward's execution of the bank fraud scheme charged in Counts 9, 15, 18, and 19. However, the evidence is not sufficient to show that Ward took any actions that would constitute the engagement in bank fraud set forth in Counts 24 and 25 of the redacted indictment.[32] Consequently we * * * reverse the verdict against Ward on the latter two counts.

* * *

The evidence is not sufficient, however, to show that Ward engaged in bank fraud with respect to the transactions in Counts 24 and 25. Although Ward was present at the closings and several of the meetings where down payment arrangements were discussed for the sales in Counts 24 and 25, there is no evidence that Ward said anything to these particular buyers or did anything to otherwise facilitate their purchases.[33] Ward did not provide the buyers in Counts 24 and 25 with rebates as an incentive to buy nor did he direct these buyers to falsify

32. Counts 24 and 25 charged Ward and four other defendants with defrauding Bay Loan by obtaining an end loan for the purchases of units at the Sandcastle Motel by Bruce Schulbaum and John Mills, III.

33. Ward was involved in running the newspaper advertisement that originally attracted the buyers to the Dean Street pro-

ject. However, that act was not necessarily directed toward these specific fraud counts and, while contributing to the fraud, was not alone sufficient to constitute an affirmative act of facilitation of the fraudulent loan transactions charged in Counts 24 and 25.

their down payments. As such, Ward neither executed nor aided the execution of the scheme to defraud in these two instances. Because we see no evidence in the record to support any reasonable finding by the jury that Ward played a role in obtaining the loans in Counts 24 and 25, we reverse his convictions for these two counts.

Notes

1. Recall the excerpt from United States v. Burnett, 10 F.3d 74 (2d Cir.1993) included in Section 1 of this chapter noting that § 1344 includes two separate offenses. In United States v. Medeles, 916 F.2d 195 (5th Cir.1990), the Fifth Circuit explained the difference in the two § 1344 offenses as follows. Note the different elements for each offense.

> "Defendant-appellant Daniel A. Medeles (Medeles) appeals his conviction for executing or attempting to execute a scheme to obtain money from a federally insured financial institution by means of false or fraudulent pretenses or representations, contrary to former 18 U.S.C. § 1344(a)(2). For the section 1344(a)(2) element of pretense or representation, the government charged and proved only that Medeles knowingly wrote insufficient funds checks on his checking account at a federally insured institution and deposited those checks in his checking accounts at other financial institutions to cover other checks he had written on the latter accounts and which, but for such deposits, would have overdrawn those accounts. Medeles contends that this does not suffice to establish that he made any misrepresentation or pretense, as the unembellished depositing of a check is to of itself a representation that the bank account on which it is drawn has a sufficient balance to cover it. We agree, and accordingly reverse.

> * * *

> "Medeles was indicted and convicted on three counts of bank fraud under former 18 U.S.C. § 1344(a), which provided:

>> "(a) Whoever knowingly executes, or attempts to execute, a scheme or artifice—

>> "(1) to defraud a federally chartered or insured financial institution; or

>> "(2) to obtain any of the moneys, funds, credits, assets, securities or other property owned by or under the custody or control of a federally chartered or insured financial institution by means of false or fraudulent pretenses, representations, or promises, shall be [punished as provided by statute.][1]

1. Former section 1344 (b) merely defined "federally chartered or insured financial institution" as used in section 1344(a). In 1989, section 1344 was amended by *inter alia*, deleting former part (b) thereof and reconstituting former part (a) simply as section 1344. Pub. L. 101–73, Title IX, § 961(k), 103 Stat. 500. As so amended, section 1344 now reads in full as follows:

"Who ever knowingly executes, or attempts to execute, a scheme or artifice—
"(1) to defraud a financial institution; or
"(2) to obtain any of the moneys, funds, credits, asserts, securities, or other property owned by, or under the custody or control of, a financial institution, by means of false or fraudulent pretenses, representations, or promises;

"Count one of the indictment alleged that, during the first fifteen days of September 1988, Medeles:

"[D]id knowingly and unlawfully devise a scheme for the purpose of obtaining moneys and property by means of false and fraudulent pretense and representations, to wit:

* * *

"As the language and structure of former section 1344(a) reflect, it establishes two different offenses, though each shares common elements (and may otherwise somewhat overlap). Each offense is one against 'a federally chartered or insured financial institution' and each has the primary element of 'knowingly executes, or attempts to execute, a scheme or artifice.' The difference between the two offenses lies in what the scheme or artifice against the institution must consist of. For the first offense, defined in clause (1), the denounced scheme or artifice has but a single required element, namely, that it be one 'to defraud' the institution. For the second offense, defined in clause (2), the proscribed scheme or artifice is not characterized as one 'to defraud' but rather is described as having two somewhat different required elements, namely: *first*, that it be 'to obtain any of the moneys, funds, credits, assets, securities or other property owned by or under the custody or control of' the institution; and *second*, that it be to do so 'by means of false or fraudulent pretenses, representations, or promises.'"

2. Recall the Supreme Court's decision in McNally v. United States, 483 U.S. 350 (1987)[z] to the effect that "the words * * * to defraud commonly refer to wronging one in his property rights by dishonest methods or schemes and usually signify the deprivation of something of value by trick, deceit, chicane or overreaching." [internal quotation omitted]. As can be seen in the following excerpts from United States v. Orr, 932 F.2d 330 (4th Cir.1991), *McNally's* interpretation of "to defraud" has been held to affect the reach of § 1344:

"On October 23, 1987, defendant, Eugene Elkins, using a false name and false driver's license for identification, opened a checking account in the name of 'Eugene Rogers' at the First Union National Bank in Weaverville, North Carolina.[1] The bank clerk has testified that in opening the account, Elkins was alone, that defendant Orr was not present. Elkins deposited $1,000 in the new account. In the next day or so, Elkins drew the account down to a negative balance.

"Defendant Edward Orr is first identified as being a participant in this matter with Elkins on Saturday, October 31, 1987, when he assisted Orr in negotiating bad checks to unsuspecting merchants for sundry merchandise. Five of the fraudulent checks were negotiated on October 31

"shall be fined [punished as provided by statute.]

As a result of Pub. L. 101–73, Title IX, § 962(e), 103 Stat. 523, the term "financial institution," as used in Title 18, is now defined in 18 U.S.C. § 20.

z. *See* Chapter 2, *supra*.

1. The record indicates that in October 1987 at the time these offenses were committed, Elkins was a fugitive on escape from federal custody on other charges. This may provide insight as to the use of the name "Rogers" in this case.

and one on November 1, 1987. The bank did not honor any of the checks, returning them all for insufficient funds.

"In time, a six-count indictment was returned, each count being based upon a separate check, charging both Elkins and Orr in each count with 'bank fraud' under 18 U.S.C. § 1344. The jury returned a verdict of guilty against Elkins on all counts, and a verdict of guilty against Orr on counts one, two and six. Orr was found not guilty on counts three, four and five.

"The indictment proceeded on bank fraud charges under 18 U.S.C. § 1344 and aiding and abetting under 18 U.S.C. § 2. No conspiracy was charged.

* * *

"Restrictive court interpretations on the breadth of earlier statutes on mail fraud (18 U.S.C. § 1341) and wire fraud (18 U.S.C. § 1343) gave impetus to the passage of this bank fraud statute (18 U.S.C. § 1344).

"Each of the charges in this case proceeds upon a separate check drawn upon the account of Eugene Rogers in the First Union National Bank. Each check was made payable to a named payee (never the bank) for goods purchased. None of the checks were accepted by the bank. Rather, all were returned unpaid to the payees by reason of insufficient funds in the Rogers account. The bank suffered no loss. The losers, of course, were the payees.

"We enter the case on the initial inquiry of whether 18 U.S.C. § 1344 was meant to establish a federal bad check law. Of course, such a law was not so intended, and the record of this case indicates that the government so agrees. Was it intended to be a basis for federal criminal prosecution if the bad check was drawn upon an account in a federally chartered bank? Again, the answer is in the negative. Lastly, the inquiry narrows down to whether federal prosecution is authorized in this case, the bad check being drawn on a bank account in the name of Eugene Rogers when in fact the account in that name was opened by Eugene Elkins? We think not.

"Under 18 U.S.C. § 1344(1) and (2), the bank has not been defrauded. In McNally v. United States, 483 U.S. 350, 358 (1986), the Court wrote, '[a]s the Court long ago stated, . . . the words . . . 'to defraud' commonly refer 'to wronging one in his property rights by dishonest methods or schemes' and usually signify the deprivation of something of value by trick, deceit, chicane or overreaching.' As a matter of fact, the bank has suffered no loss at all. No evidence has been produced to show that the use of the name 'Rogers' as opposed to 'Elkins' was done with intent to defraud the bank. The initial deposit was $1,000 in cash. The account was, albeit for a short time, an active account, traded upon in proper fashion until its funds ran out. Whether the account was in the name of Rogers, or Elkins, was not of significance to the giving of checks payable to certain payees and the return of such checks for reasons of insufficient funds.

"Here is presented a simple bad check case for criminal prosecution in the proper state court to the extent state law allows. The opening of the checking account in the name of Eugene Rogers using false identification is of no moment to the return of the checks for insufficient funds. Nor of moment is the criminal activity which might be generated by these overdrafts. Of course, emergence of Eugene Elkins as the person opening the account would certainly tag him as responsible, criminally and otherwise, for repercussions attendant to that account.

"We find it is, however, an area of 'fraudulent checking activities already ... addressed in comprehensive fashion by state law.' * * *

"The convictions are accordingly vacated and the cases are remanded to the district court with directions to dismiss the indictment."

E.   CONDUCTING A CONTINUING FINANCIAL CRIMES ENTERPRISE

On November 29, 1990, Congress passed the Continuing Financial Crimes Enterprise (CFCE) statute, 18 U.S.C. § 225. This section provides as follows:

(a) Whoever—

(1) organizes, manages, or supervises a continuing financial crimes enterprise; and

(2) receives $5,000,000 or more in gross receipts from such enterprise during any 24–month period, shall be fined not more than $10,000,000 if an individual, or $20,000,000 if an organization, and imprisoned for a term of not less than 10 years and which may be life.

(b) For purposes of subsection (a), the term "continuing financial crimes enterprise" means a series of violations under section 215, 656, 657, 1005, 1006, 1007, 1014, 1032, or 1344 of this title, or section 1341 or 1343 affecting a financial institution, committed by at least 4 persons working in concert.

As can be seen, the CFCE is aimed at large scale fraud upon financial institutions. It was passed because of the "burgeoning problems of the savings and loan industry."[aa] As noted in the House Report:

Reports of criminal activity and grossly excessive behavior that led to the dramatic decline of the savings and loan industry have proliferated. Title XXI (of the Crime Control Act of 1990) responds to the public outcry to bring to justice those who defrauded the savings and loan industry by providing Federal regulating agencies, Federal prosecutors, and law enforcement agencies with additional tools to combat fraud and abuse affecting financial institutions.[bb]

Not surprisingly, given the statutory restrictions on extremely large cases, there have been few prosecutions under CFCE. The next case, United States v. Harris, 79 F.3d 223 (2d Cir.1996), is the only reported

aa. House Report No. 101–681(I) (Sept. 5, 1990), 1990 U.S. CODE CONG. AND ADMIN. NEWS 6576.

bb. Id. at 6576–6577.

CFCE prosecution in the seven years after its passage. The court's discussion of Harris' § 1344 and money laundering convictions is also included.

UNITED STATES v. HARRIS

United States Court of Appeals, Second Circuit, 1996.
79 F.3d 223.

MINER, CIRCUIT JUDGE.

On September 9, 1992, a 24–count superseding indictment was filed charging defendant-appellant Roy William Harris with conspiracy to commit wire and bank fraud in violation of 18 U.S.C. § 371, wire fraud in violation of 18 U.S.C. § 1343, bank fraud in violation of 18 U.S.C. § 1344, money laundering in violation of 18 U.S.C. § 1956(a)(2), conducting a continuing financial crimes enterprise ("CFCE") in violation of 18 U.S.C. § 225, and making a false statement on a loan application in violation of 18 U.S.C. § 1014. The government also sought the forfeiture of Harris' assets pursuant to 18 U.S.C. § 982. Prior to trial, Harris moved to dismiss certain counts of the indictment and to sever Count 23, which charged him with making a false statement on a loan application. The district court granted Harris' motion to sever Count 23, but denied his motion to dismiss those counts charging him with wire fraud, bank fraud, and engaging in a continuing financial crimes enterprise. United States v. Harris, 805 F.Supp. 166 (S.D.N.Y.1992). On December 14, 1992, a jury found Harris guilty on all counts tried. On the same day, Harris and the government entered into a stipulation settling the forfeiture count.

On March 26, 1993, Harris filed motions for a judgment of acquittal, pursuant to Fed.R.Crim.P. 29, and for a new trial, pursuant to Fed. R.Crim.P. 33, raising many of the same claims he now raises on appeal. On July 30, 1993, the district court denied Harris' motions in their entirety. United States v. Harris, No. S1 92 Cr. 455 (CSH), 1993 WL 300052 (S.D.N.Y. July 30, 1993). On December 22, 1994, the district court sentenced Harris to a 188–month term of imprisonment, a five-year term of supervised release, and a special assessment of $1100. The district court also ordered Harris to pay $200 million in restitution.

On this appeal, Harris contends that the district court erred in: (1) failing to instruct the jury, in relation to the CFCE violation, that it must find that his conduct occurred after the CFCE statute was enacted; (2) rejecting his claim that he was wrongly convicted for money laundering under 18 U.S.C. § 1956(a)(2); (3) rejecting his contention that his bank fraud convictions were multiplicitous and thus violated the Fifth Amendment; (4) imposing a $200 million restitution order in favor of the lending banks; (5) rejecting his argument that he was wrongly convicted for a CFCE violation because the statute was not meant to apply to his conduct; * * *. For the following reasons, we affirm in part, vacate in part, and remand for further proceedings consistent with this opinion.

Background

Harris was the president, chief executive officer, and majority shareholder of Arochem Corporation ("Arochem") and Arochem International, Inc. ("International") (together, the "Arochem Companies" or "Companies"). International operated a petroleum and petrochemical refinery complex in Puerto Rico, while Arochem, which maintained its principal offices in Connecticut, traded in petroleum and petroleum products and provided management services to International. These management services included supervising the inventory and trading activities of International and marketing petrochemicals and petroleum products.

Vincent J. Dispenza was the Arochem Companies' chief financial officer. Dean Seniff, the Companies' comptroller, and Greg Holtzhauer, the Companies' accounting manager, also were involved in financial matters. Other Arochem Companies officers included Gene Sebastian, the Companies' executive vice president, and Joe Sheperd, the Companies' vice president of operations.

In January of 1990, a consortium of banks led by Chase Manhattan Bank, N.A. (the "banks") entered into a revolving credit agreement (the "agreement") with the Arochem Companies. The agreement expired in January of 1991, and was extended on six separate occasions through November 30, 1991. Under the terms of the agreement, the Companies were permitted to borrow up to $245 million as needed for their business operations. The loans covered by the agreement were to be secured by the Companies' inventory of petroleum and petroleum products and by the Companies' receivables and cash. The agreement included financial covenants that required the Companies to maintain minimum levels of working capital, net worth, and debt ratios, and precluded them from holding a net unhedged position of more than one million barrels of oil. If the Companies violated any of these covenants, the banks could either charge a "penalty" for the violation or demand immediate repayment of the loans. Finally, the agreement required the Arochem Companies to provide the banks with periodic reports known as "borrowing base reports," which listed all of the Companies' assets and trading positions.

A. The Companies' Fraudulent Practices

In the fall of 1989, the Arochem Companies began to suffer financial difficulties that continued through the beginning of 1990. At a meeting of the Companies' officers in March or April of 1990, Seniff informed Harris, Dispenza, Sebastian, and Sheperd that the Arochem Companies had a year-to-date deficit of approximately $60 to $65 million. In addition, Seniff and Dispenza informed the other officers that they would be falsifying the Companies' financial statements by overvaluing the Companies' crude oil inventory.

Also discussed at this meeting was the upcoming Ernst & Young year-end audit of the Companies' books. It was understood by the Companies' officers that unless the Companies earned "$40 or so million dollars" by the end of the fiscal year, May 31, 1990, the Companies would not pass the audit. Dispenza claims that Harris then directed

Sheperd and him to become more "creative" in assisting in the preparation of the financial statements.

In late April or early May of 1990, Harris, Dispenza, and Seniff devised a strategy for the approaching audit. It was determined that, in order to conceal the Companies' $60 to $65 million loss, Dispenza would falsify and exaggerate the value of the Companies' assets. As part of the scheme to disguise the Companies' losses, according to Dispenza, Harris provided Dispenza with an inventory contract for the purchase of two cargoes of crude oil from a company called Trieast Marketing ("Trieast"). Dispenza claims that Harris informed him that International would not take possession of the oil, but that the contract should be used for the year-end audit. Accordingly, Seniff and Dispenza created false documents, such as false warehouse receipts and warranty titles, in an effort to make it appear that the Trieast contract had been performed. This allowed the Companies to use the Trieast contract to exaggerate the value of their inventory and profits.

Even after this "creative" accounting, Seniff informed Dispenza and Harris that the Companies still showed a $25 million loss and that the only way to conceal the loss was through "outright fraud." Not to be deterred, Seniff, with Dispenza and Harris' knowledge, removed from the Companies' accounts payable register several pages that revealed that the Companies owed $25 million in payables. During the course of its audit, Ernst & Young sought evidence of payment for oil inventory valued at $25 million, and Dispenza asked Harris what should be done. According to Dispenza, Harris replied, "[D]o whatever you can." Dispenza and Seniff responded by altering documents to indicate that the $25 million in oil purchases had been paid before the end of the prior fiscal year. As a result, the Companies' year-end income was increased by $25 million.

In its 1990 year-end financials, the Arochem Companies showed retained earnings of $13 million and a profit of $3.3 million. These numbers overrepresented the Companies' financial health by approximately $60 million. In September of 1990, Ernst & Young concluded its audit and provided the Arochem Companies with an unqualified opinion of financial condition based on the incorrect information supplied by the Companies. The audit then was provided by the Companies to the banks.

From September of 1990 through November of 1990, the Companies' financial troubles continued. The Companies' officers continued to misrepresent the Arochem Companies' financial health to the banks by altering their borrowing base reports and financial statements. In November of 1990, Seniff informed the Companies' officers that the Arochem Companies had sustained losses of over $103 million during the June 1990 to November 1990 period. As a result, the altered financial statements overstated the Companies' earnings at that time by approximately $106 million.

By March of 1991, it again became apparent to the Companies' officers that the Companies were going to have difficulty passing the

1991 year-end audit because of the Companies' $60 to $65 million deficit.[1] During this time, Dispenza claims that he began to receive from Harris by e-mail fraudulent contract documents, including three sham contracts (the "sham contracts"). According to Dispenza, Harris told him that he should use the sham contracts for the 1991 audit. Dispenza included additional documents, such as copies of fictitious letters of credit, with the sham contracts, to make it appear as if the Companies had paid $48 million for oil cargoes, when, in fact, the Companies had not paid any money. The sham contracts added approximately $47 million to the assets of the Companies, and an additional $11 million was reflected as profits arising from the fictitious inventory. Relying on the false contracts, Ernst & Young again issued an unqualified opinion of financial condition to the Arochem Companies at the end of the 1991 audit. This opinion also was supplied to the banks.

B.   Violations of Financial Covenant

While the Companies were misleading the banks by providing them with false financial statements and borrowing base reports, they also were violating the agreement's financial covenant by maintaining highly speculative trading positions. The agreement between the Arochem Companies and the banks prohibited the Companies from holding a net unhedged position in oil of more than one million barrels. However, the Companies regularly violated this covenant. For instance, the Companies' net unhedged position was in excess of one million barrels approximately 80% to 85% of the time during the period January, 1990 through January, 1991. By November of 1990, the Arochem Companies were maintaining net unhedged positions of up to 10 million barrels of oil. The Companies never informed the banks that they were engaged in such highly speculative trading.

C.   Money Laundering

In October of 1990, Harris formed a new company, Arochem International, Ltd., ("Limited") in order to gain financing to support a contract that the Companies had entered into with the Nigerian government and to assist the Companies with financing when their credit became tight. The banks were aware of Limited's formation and were informed that Limited would be financed by Credit Lyonnais and Banque Paribas of Switzerland (together, the "Swiss Banks"). However, the banks required the Companies to obtain their permission before entering into financial transactions with Limited.

From October of 1990 through December of 1991, the Companies entered into numerous transactions with Limited without seeking the banks' permission. By the summer of 1991, the Swiss Banks were financing $100 to $200 million of the Companies' trading in oil markets.

---

1. The Companies' deficit had decreased from its November 1990 level of approximately $103 million because, on January 16th and 17th of 1991, under Harris' direction, the Companies made approximately $40–50 million as a result of speculative oil trading.

Dispenza testified that he and Harris discussed how such financing violated the agreement's financial covenants.

As a condition to providing financing, the Swiss Banks required a cash deposit as margin before they would issue letters of credit to finance Limited's transactions. According to Dispenza, in order to supply the cash, Dispenza and Harris decided to move money from the Companies' accounts at Chase Manhattan Bank, N.A. ("Chase") in New York to their accounts at Union Trust Company ("Union Trust") in Connecticut, and then transfer the funds to the Swiss Banks. The purpose of routing the money through Connecticut was to conceal from the banks that the financing they were supplying was being used by the Companies to acquire additional financing from the Swiss Banks. From April of 1991 through September of 1991, excluding the amount used for operating needs, $7,420,000 was moved from Chase to Union Trust, and $7,723,344.90 was then moved in the same period from Union Trust to the Swiss Banks. The Companies never informed the banks of these transactions.

D. The Companies' Collapse

In December of 1991, the banks discovered that the Companies' assets and net worth had been overstated by $40 to $60 million. On February 14, 1992, the banks filed a petition to force the Companies into bankruptcy. At this time, the Companies' deficit was about $192.8 million.

On September 9, 1992, the government filed a 24–count superseding indictment charging Harris with various financial crimes. Following a six-week jury trial, the jury returned a guilty verdict on all counts tried. Harris was sentenced on December 22, 1994, and he is currently serving his sentence.

DISCUSSION

1. Ex Post Facto Claim

Harris contends that his conviction under the CFCE statute violated the Ex Post Facto Clause of the United States Constitution because the district court's charge to the jury permitted the jury to convict Harris on the basis of conduct that occurred prior to the CFCE statute's effective date, November 29, 1990.[2]

---

2. The CFCE statute, codified at 18 U.S.C. § 225 states:

(a) Whoever—

(1) organizes, manages, or supervises a continuing financial crimes enterprise; and

(2) receives $5,000,000 or more in gross receipts from such enterprise during any 24–month period,

shall be fined not more than $10,000,000 if an individual ... and imprisoned for a term of not less than 10 years and which may be life.

(b) For purposes of subsection (a), the term "continuing financial crimes enterprise" means a series of violations under section 215, 656, 657, 1005, 1006, 1007, 1014, 1032, or 1344 of this title, or section 1341 or 1343 affecting a financial institution, committed by at least 4 persons acting in concert.

The Ex Post Facto Clause states that "[n]o ... ex post facto Law shall be passed." U.S. Const. art. I, § 9, cl. 3. The Supreme Court has interpreted this clause as prohibiting Congress from passing a law that: (1) makes an act a crime that was legal when committed; (2) makes a crime greater than it was when it was committed; (3) increases the punishment for a crime after it has been committed; or (4) deprives the accused of a legal defense that was available at the time the crime was committed. While the Ex Post Facto Clause itself is a restraint on the legislative branch, its protections have been extended to the application of judicial precedent by the courts under the Due Process Clause of the Fifth Amendment.

It is well-settled that when a statute is concerned with a continuing offense, "the Ex Post Facto clause is not violated by application of a statute to an enterprise that began prior to, but continued after, the effective date of [the statute]." United States v. Torres, 901 F.2d 205, 226 (2d Cir.1990) Because the CFCE statute is a continuing crime statute, we must determine whether it was possible for the jury, following the district court's instructions, to convict Harris *exclusively* on pre-CFCE enactment conduct. After examining the jury instructions, we think that such a scenario was impossible.

The district court instructed the jury that, in order to convict Harris under the CFCE statute, it must find beyond a reasonable doubt that: (1) Harris committed three or more violations of the bank fraud and/or wire fraud statutes affecting a financial institution;[3] (2) the three or more bank fraud and/or wire fraud violations were part of a series of violations of these laws; (3) Harris undertook to commit this series of violations in concert with three or more other persons; (4) Harris organized, managed or supervised these three or more persons in connection with this series of violations; and (5) Harris received $5 million or more in gross receipts from this series of violations during any 24–month period.

Of the nineteen counts of bank and wire fraud that the jury considered when determining whether Harris committed three or more violations, only one (Count Two) involved conduct by Harris that occurred before November 29, 1990—the effective date of the CFCE statute. Therefore, the jury must have found that two or more of the violations were based on post-CFCE enactment conduct.

Harris argues that the third and fourth elements of the jury charge, relating to the "in concert" and the "supervise[ ]" requirements, could have been satisfied completely by pre-CFCE enactment conduct. Specifically, Harris contends that the jury could have found that he acted in concert with and supervised three individuals in committing the pre-CFCE enactment conduct alleged in Count Two, but that he acted alone, and supervised no one in committing the additional violations which comprised the series.

---

3. These violations were alleged in Counts Two through Eight (the bank fraud counts) and Counts 10 through 21 (the wire fraud counts).

In support of his argument, Harris relies on this court's decision in *Torres*, a case involving the operation of a continuing criminal enterprise ("CCE"), in violation of 21 U.S.C. § 848(a) and (b). In *Torres*, the district court had failed to distinguish in its jury instructions between the defendant's pre-CCE enactment conduct and the defendant's post-CCE enactment conduct. We held that, although it was unlikely that the jury had based its findings entirely on pre-CCE enactment conduct, because such a scenario was a possibility, the defendant's conviction had to be vacated.

However, in the present case, there is no possibility that the jury relied entirely on the pre-CFCE enactment conduct in determining that the government satisfied the third and fourth elements of the district court's charge. In its instructions, the district court tied both the "in concert" and "supervise [ ]" requirements to the series of violations. The district court instructed the jury as follows:

> The third element ... is that the defendant committed the *series of violations* ... in concert with three or more other persons....
>
> ... This element is satisfied if you find beyond a reasonable doubt that the defendant acted together with a total of at least three other persons to *commit the series* of bank fraud violations and/or wire fraud violations affecting a financial institution....
>
> ....
>
> The fourth element the government must prove ... is that the defendant organized, managed or supervised the three or more persons in committing the *series of violations*....

(emphasis added). Because the series of violations must have consisted of at least two violations based entirely upon post-CFCE enactment conduct, and because there is no ex post facto violation when a conviction is based partially on pre-CFCE enactment conduct, Harris' ex post facto claim as to the third and fourth elements of the charge is meritless.

In the fifth element of the charge, the jury was instructed that, in order to find Harris guilty, it must determine that he received $5 million or more in gross receipts from the series of violations during any 24–month period. Harris contends that this element of the charge was improper because it allowed the jury to consider, as part of the $5 million in gross receipts, money legitimately obtained by Harris prior to the enactment of the CFCE statute. We reject this argument.

First, like the third and fourth elements of the jury charge, the fifth element was tied to the series of violations. Thus, the jury must have considered post-CFCE enactment conduct—that is, money obtained by Harris after the enactment of the CFCE statute—when it determined that the government had satisfied the fifth element of the jury charge. We see no reason to depart from the settled rule that there is no ex post facto violation when conduct occurring before the enactment of the continuing crime statute is considered along with conduct occurring after the enactment of the statute simply because the conduct involves the obtaining of money. Moreover, Harris' argument that the district court should not have permitted the jury to consider any pre-CFCE earned money because it was legally earned by Harris is simply wrong. Any pre-CFCE enactment money the jury considered had to have been money obtained by Harris as a result of the series of violations consisting of wire and bank fraud, and therefore, this money was not legally earned.

For these reasons, Harris' CFCE conviction did not violate the Ex Post Facto Clause.

2. Money Laundering Charge

The jury convicted Harris on Count Nine of the superseding indictment, which charged Harris with violating 18 U.S.C. § 1956(a)(2) by knowingly transferring proceeds of his bank fraud "from a place in the United States to or through a place outside the United States" in order "to conceal and disguise the nature, location, source and ownership of the proceeds."[5] Harris contends that his conviction on this count was improper because § 1956(a)(2) prohibits international transfers of funds, and the transfers he made to conceal funds were domestic.

The indictment stated that,

> in order to conceal and disguise the nature, location, source and ownership of funds, [Harris] transferred approximately $7.5 million from the Arochem Companies' accounts at Chase Manhattan Bank in New York through the Union Trust Company in Connecticut and into the accounts held by Limited at Banque Paribas (Suisse) and Credit Lyonnais (Suisse) in Geneva, Switzerland, knowing that these funds were the proceeds of frauds on financial institutions.

Harris argues that each time that funds were sent to Switzerland, two transfers took place—one from New York to Connecticut and the other from Connecticut to Switzerland. Harris maintains that it was the transfers of funds from the Companies' Chase accounts in New York to its accounts at Union Trust in Connecticut that were designed to conceal the nature, location, source, and ownership of the funds from the banks, and not the transfers of funds from Connecticut to Switzerland. Therefore, Harris argues that he should not have been convicted of violating § 1956(a)(2).

We disagree because we do not interpret the movements of funds from New York to Connecticut and then from Connecticut to Switzerland as two separate events. While the scheme was implemented in two stages, each stage was an integral part of a single plan to transfer funds

---

5. Section 1956(a)(2) of the money laundering statute states in relevant part:

Whoever transports, transmits, or transfers ... funds from a place in the United States to or through a place outside the United States ... knowing that the ... funds involved in the transportation, transmission, or transfer represent the proceeds of some form of unlawful activity and knowing that such transportation is designed in whole or in part ... to conceal or disguise the nature, the location, the source, the ownership, or the control of the proceeds of specified unlawful activity [shall be guilty of an offense].

"from a place in the United States to or through a place outside the United States."

Furthermore, the district court's charge to the jury dispels any concerns that the jury considered each transfer of funds from New York to Switzerland as two transactions rather than one. In its jury instructions, the court stated:

> To convict the defendant on this count, you must conclude that the particular movement of funds from the Arochem companies' accounts at Chase through the companies' account at the Union Trust Company and to Arochem International Ltd.'s accounts in Switzerland was contemplated and executed as one transfer which was performed in two stages. If you conclude instead that the movement was in fact two independent transfers, then you may not convict the defendant on Count 9.

Because we consider Harris' movements of funds from New York to Switzerland as single transfers that served to conceal the location of the funds from the banks, we find no basis to disturb Harris' conviction for money laundering.

3. Multiplicity

In his indictment, Harris was charged with seven counts of bank fraud (Counts Two through Eight). Count Two related to the initial credit agreement between the Companies and the banks, while Counts Three through Eight related to the six subsequent extensions of the loan agreement. Harris contends that the six bank fraud counts, which corresponded to the six extensions of the agreement, should have been charged as a single count, and therefore that the district court erred when it refused to dismiss those counts as multiplicitous.

The doctrine of multiplicity "is based upon the double jeopardy clause of the Fifth Amendment, which 'assur[es] that the court does not exceed its legislative authorization by imposing multiple punishments for the same offense.' " While we have defined a multiplicitous indictment in general as "one that charges in separate counts two or more crimes, when in fact and law, only one crime has been committed," we have not addressed the issue of multiplicity in the contexts of numerous counts of bank fraud. [citations omitted]

The bank fraud statute, codified at 18 U.S.C. § 1344, states in relevant part: "Whoever knowingly executes, or attempts to execute, a scheme or artifice—(1) to defraud a financial institution ... shall be fined not more than $1,000,000 or imprisoned not more than 30 years, or both." The circuits that have addressed multiplicity in the context of bank fraud consistently have held that the bank fraud statute "punish[es] each execution of a fraudulent scheme rather than each act in furtherance of such a scheme." We agree with these circuits that the plain language of § 1344 "punish[es] each execution of a fraudulent scheme." Accordingly, we must determine whether Harris' alleged conduct constituted the execution of six separate schemes to defraud. [citations omitted]

In determining whether acts constitute separate executions of a scheme, courts have considered whether the acts were chronologically and substantively independent from the overall scheme. In the present case, the six separate extensions of the loan agreement were chronologically and substantively independent from the initial loan agreement. Although the initial loan agreement provided the criteria for the extensions, it nevertheless was an agreement for a limited time period. At the end of the original credit agreement and at the end of each loan extension, the Companies had to ask the banks to extend the credit. In agreeing to extend the credit, the banks relied on the fraudulent monthly financial statements and borrowing base reports provided by Harris and the Companies. Accordingly, the bank fraud counts were not multiplicitous.

4. Restitution

Harris contends that the district court erred in ordering him to pay restitution to the banks in the amount of $200 million. Harris argues that the district court failed to consider his financial needs and earning potential, and that, by ordering Harris to pay such a large amount, the court placed an undue burden on Harris and his dependents.

We review a district court's order of restitution for abuse of discretion. Before imposing restitution, 18 U.S.C. § 3664(a) requires that the district court "consider the amount of the loss sustained by any victim as a result of the offense, the financial resources of the defendant, the financial needs and earning ability of the defendant and the defendant's dependents, and such other factors as the court deems appropriate." While the court is not required to set forth detailed findings as to each factor, "the record must demonstrate that the court has considered these factors in ordering restitution." [citation omitted]

In the present case, the district court based its decision to order $200 million in restitution on the fact that, although unlikely, Harris potentially could earn $200 million in the future. Thus, if the court ordered restitution in a lower amount and Harris did earn that amount of money, the banks would be foreclosed from a full recovery of their losses due to double jeopardy. The district court concluded that the banks should not have to risk not recovering simply because it was unlikely that Harris would make this amount of money.

In United States v. Khan, 53 F.3d 507 (2d Cir.1995) we held that the district court abused its discretion by failing to consider the financial resources of the defendants and the needs of the defendants' dependents before ordering the defendants to pay restitution. In Khan, the district court, in making its restitution determination, had considered only the loss occasioned by each defendant. Similarly, in the present case, the district court did not discuss Harris' obligations to his dependents. Instead, the district court focused exclusively on Harris' ability to pay and the losses incurred by the banks due to Harris' fraud.

Harris claims that, prior to his incarceration, he was providing for his two daughters, ages eight and twelve, his ex-wife, mother, and two sisters. The record does not indicate that the district court considered these alleged facts, or Harris' own financial needs, in making its restitution determination.

Although the district court properly was concerned about granting a small amount of restitution and then, due to double jeopardy, being barred from increasing the amount if Harris' financial situation subsequently improved the record must still show that "the court has considered [the statutory] factors in ordering restitution." [citation omitted] Here, the record does not indicate that the district court considered "the financial needs and earning ability of the defendant and [his] dependents." 18 U.S.C. § 3664(a). Therefore, we remand to the district court with instructions to consider all of the relevant factors in making its determination of restitution.

5. *Other Arguments*

Harris contends that he improperly was convicted for a violation of the CFCE statute because the statute was enacted for the sole purpose of prosecuting savings and loan plunderers and was not enacted to prosecute defrauders of commercial banks. However, nothing in the plain language and legislative history of the CFCE statute supports this narrow reading, and, therefore, we reject his argument.

* * *

CONCLUSION

In view of the foregoing, we affirm in part, vacate in part, and remand for further proceedings consistent with this opinion.

Notes

1. At trial, Harris challenged the constitutionality of the CFCE statute on the ground that the statute was vague. The court responded as follows in rejecting Harris' argument:

"Harris contends that the statute is unconstitutionally vague, both on its face and as applied to him.

"* * * I do not reach them. In the absence of First Amendment considerations (and there are none here), 'vagueness challenges must be evaluated based on the particular application of the statute and not 'on the ground that [the statute] may conceivably be applied unconstitutionally to others in situations not before the Court." [citations omitted]

"The question therefore is whether the continuing financial crimes enterprise statute is unconstitutionally vague as applied to the conduct of Harris as described in the superseding indictment.

"To determine whether a statute is unconstitutionally vague as applied, the Supreme Court has articulated a two-part test: the court must first determine whether the statute 'give[s] the person of ordinary intelligence a reasonable opportunity to know what is prohibited' and then consider whether the law 'provide[s] explicit standards for those who apply [it].' United States v. Schneiderman, 968 F.2d 1564, 1568 (2d Cir.1992).

"Defendant argues that § 225 is void for vagueness as applied to him because it failed to provide him 'with adequate notice that obtaining a single credit agreement and extensions of that agreement would constitute a continuing financial crimes enterprise and that this conduct would allow the government to charge him with an additional, separate crime.' Thus the main thrust of defendant's vagueness argument falls upon the definition of a 'continuing financial crimes enterprise' contained in § 225(b), namely, 'a series of violations' under specified sections of Title 18. Defendant argues:

> The indictment alleges a single scheme to defraud a consortium of banks in connection with a single credit agreement, which was extended six times during a period of less than two years. It is simply not conceivable that the defendant was on notice that the single fraudulent scheme alleged in this indictment could constitute the 'series of violations' required by [the continuing financial crimes enterprise statute.]

Id. at 24.

"The first prong of the vagueness inquiry is often surreal. It presupposes that the accused, having formulated in his mind the course of conduct described in the indictment, then reads the section of the penal law under which he is subsequently charged to determine the legality of his acts. That contemplative exercise may occur on occasion, but I doubt that it does so often, and particularly doubt that it occurred in this case. That is to say, I think it unlikely that Harris considered the terms of 18 U.S.C. § 225 and decided that his conduct would not violate it.

"Nevertheless, constitutional vagueness analysis requires the assumption that people act that way. United States v. Coonan, 938 F.2d 1553, 1562 (2d Cir.1991), contains a typical statement at 1562: 'Thus, to succeed on his vagueness challenge, Kelly must demonstrate that the statute, as applied, failed to adequately warn of the prohibited conduct.' What courts do in such cases is assume that the accused read the statute before acting, although it is most unlikely that he did. To borrow a phrase from another area of the law, the accused is considered to have constructive knowledge of the statute's prohibition, and to have that knowledge prior to the charged conduct. I also think it right to say that the accused's constructive knowledge extends to judicial interpretations of the statute. It is of course just as fanciful to suggest that the accused consulted the annotations after reading the statute; but constitutional vagueness analysis begins with the inquiry of whether the statute gives a person of ordinary intelligence a reasonable opportunity to know what is prohibited, and as a practical matter that analysis must include judicial interpretations of the statute in existence at the time of the accused's actions.

"Viewing the case in this light, I conclude that the continuing financial crimes enterprise statute gave defendant adequate warning that the charged conduct would fall within its terms. The statute reaches one who 'organizes, manages or supervises' the enterprise. § 225(a)(1). These are common words. They clearly describe defendant's role in the alleged scheme. The requirements of Section 225(a)(2), the receipt of $5,000,000 or more in gross receipts during any 24–month period, are readily understandable. As for the key definition of a 'continuing financial crimes enterprise' in § 225(b), the phrase 'means a series of violations' under a number of specified sections of Title 18, including § 1344 and § 1343.

* * *

"As for the second prong of the vagueness inquiry, I think that § 225 provides sufficient guidance to prohibit its arbitrary or discrimination [sic] by law enforcement officers. The statute requires the government to persuade a grand jury that the accused 'organizes, manages, or supervises' the enterprise. § 225(a)(1).

"These commonly used words limit the sorts of persons who may be prosecuted under the statute, as do the limitations in § 225(a)(2), which require that the accused receive $5,000,000 or more in gross receipts from the enterprise during a 24–month period.[2] § 225(b) contains a definition of 'continuing financial crimes enterprise' which limits prosecutors to cases where they can show (1) a 'series of violations' (2) under specified sections of Title 18(3) 'affecting a financial institution' and (4) committed by at least four persons acting in concert. These limitations constitute in large measure 'objective criteria against which to measure possible violations of the law.' *Schneiderman*, 968 F.2d at 1568.

"Defendant at bar professes to find these limiting phrases imprecise and indefinite. I do not agree; and it is difficult to conclude that the government is invoking § 225 in an arbitrary or discriminatory manner in the case at bar, where the chief executive officer of companies is accused of seven separate executions of a scheme to defraud a financial institution, and 12 violations of the wire fraud statute in furtherance of that scheme, during a specified twenty-four month period.

"No court appears to have considered the constitutionality of the continuing financial crimes enterprise statute, which was enacted on November 29, 1990. But the Second Circuit upheld the constitutionality of the closely analogous continuing criminal enterprise statute, 21 U.S.C. § 848(b), against a challenge for vagueness in United States v. Manfredi, 488 F.2d 588, 602–03 (2d Cir.1973). § 848(a) imposes severe penalties upon a 'person who engages in a continuing criminal enterprise.' § 848(b) defines 'a person ... engaged in a continuing criminal enterprise' as one who violates specified provisions of Title 21, where the violation 'is a part of a continuing series of violations' of that Title, undertaken by the person 'in concert with five or more other persons with respect to whom such person occupies a position of organizer, a supervisory position, or any other position of management,' and 'from which such person obtains substantial income or resources.'

2. The $5,000,000 amount and the 24–month period are elements which the government must prove at trial to obtain a conviction under the statute. To the extent that defendant at bar contends that the superseding indictment does not sufficiently allege those elements, I reject the argument.

"It will be noted that the statutory scheme of 18 U.S.C. § 225 closely
follows that of 21 U.S.C. § 848. The Second Circuit held that § 848 was
not unconstitutionally vague as applied to the drug-trafficking defendants involved in *Manfredi*:

> To sustain appellant LaCosa's position would force us to hold that
> words cannot be devised to make it an offense to engage in the
> continuous sale and trafficking in heroin with a number of other
> people and with substantial sums of money changing hands; we feel
> that not to be the case and that, as applied to the conduct with
> which Joseph LaCosa was charged, the statute is not unconstitu-
> tionally vague.

Id. at 603.

"The court of appeals briskly disposed of defendants' argument that in
other circumstances the applicability of § 848 might be questionable:
'[I]t is irrelevant that a case may be hypothesized where it is difficult to
determine whether a particular defendant were engaged in a 'continuing
criminal enterprise' under § 848. *Id.*

"Defendant at bar seeks to distinguish *Manfredi* on the basis that 'the
Second Circuit applied a lenient vagueness standard when it considered
the constitutionality of 21 U.S.C. § 848.' Defendant makes that argument on the basis of the Second Circuit's quotation in *Manfredi* of
Justice Douglas's observation on Papachristou v. City of Jacksonville,
405 U.S. 156, 162 (1972): 'In the field of regulatory statutes governing
business activities, where the acts limited are in a narrow category,
greater leeway is allowed.' The Second Circuit then observed: 'In this
respect § 848 is in a very real sense a regulation—a very severe one, to
be sure—of the business of selling drugs.' *Id.* at 602.

"I find nothing to comfort defendant in all of this. Just as 21 U.S.C.
§ 848 is a 'regulation' of the business of selling drugs, so 18 U.S.C.
§ 225 is a 'regulation' of doing business with financial institutions. In
particular, the statute is intended to 'regulate' that business by safeguarding such institutions from theft or fraud. The fact that a number
of provisions in Title 18 proscribe such conduct and are incorporated by
reference in § 225(b) does not change the nature or purpose of the
statute, or serve to distinguish *Manfredi*. The continuing criminal
enterprise statute involved in *Manfredi* incorporates by reference violations of any provision of subchapter I of Title 21, or of subchapter II the
punishment for which is a felony. § 848(b)(1). While the provisions of
these subchapters all deal generally with drugs, they include a considerable variety of prohibited conduct. The variety of conduct embraced by
§ 225(b) is not different in kind, particularly where applicability of the
statute is limited by the government's need to prove a 'series of
violations . . . affecting a financial institution . . .' The phrase 'series of
violations' in 18 U.S.C. § 225(b) also appears in 21 U.S.C. § 848(b)(2).
Neither statute further defines the phrase. That did not give rise to a
vagueness problem in *Manfredi*, at least on the proven facts of that case.
The phrase does not make for a vagueness problem in the case at bar, at
least on the facts alleged in the superseding indictment.

"Defendant observes that the four concurring justices in H.J., Inc. v. Northwestern Bell Telephone Co., 492 U.S. 229 (1989), 'explicitly invited a constitutional vagueness challenge' to the RICO statute: 'No constitutional challenge to this law has been raised in the present case, and so that issue is not before us.'

"RICO's component parts are differently worded from the continuing financial crimes enterprise statute. Arguably RICO's provisions are more vulnerable to constitutional attack for vagueness, although it must be remembered that Justice Scalia wrote for a minority of the Court in *H.J.* Justice Brennan's opinion commanded a majority of five and contained no murmurings about constitutionality. In any event, subsequent to *H.J.* the Second Circuit in *Coonan* sustained the constitutionality of the RICO statute against a vagueness challenge. 938 F.2d at 1561–62.[cc]

"Defendant's motion to dismiss Count Twenty–Two on the ground that the continuing financial crimes enterprise statute, 18 U.S.C. § 225, is unconstitutionally vague is denied."

2.   What do you think about the CFCE? Is it too draconian?

3.   Multiplicity issues in crimes such as bank fraud (18 U.S.C. § 1344) can become difficult. In contrast to *Harris*, note the discussion of multiplicity in United States v. Saks, 964 F.2d 1514 (5th Cir.1992). Note how fact-specific the multiplicity analysis must be.

"A jury convicted Doyle Spruill and David Saks on one count of conspiracy to defraud the United States, 18 U.S.C. § 371, and five counts of bank fraud, 18 U.S.C. § 1344.

* * *

"Spruill and Saks were business partners in Omni Interests, Inc., a commercial real estate development company, based in San Antonio. Omni specialized in the development of office buildings, shopping centers, and apartment projects in different locations throughout Texas. In 1983, Spruill and Saks formed a limited partnership, Omni/Corpus Christi Limited, to acquire and develop a large tract of land in Corpus Christi. They purchased the property for $3 million in 1984 as a location for a large shopping center. They had the property rezoned and began negotiations with major mall developers. By year end, however, Omni had financial problems. Spruill and Saks needing cash for the company's short term financial obligations, decided to borrow, with the Corpus Christi property as collateral.

"They approached Peoples Savings & Loan Association, where officials informed them that they would need about $14 million to pay existing debt on the property and keep their company afloat. Peoples could not handle a loan of that size, and referred them to Security Savings Association. That was a fateful day. In December of 1984, Spruill and Saks met with Cliff Brannon and Don Jones, co-chairmen of the board of Security and owners of a controlling interest in it. They asked Brannon and Jones for a loan of $14 million. They had obtained an appraisal

---

cc.   United States v. Harris, 805 F.Supp.   166 (S.D.N.Y.1992).

valuing the property at $24 million, based on its potential as a site for a regional shopping mall. Brannon and Jones listened and promised to let them know soon. The prospective lender, it seems, saw in this prospective loan a solution to its own unrelated but serious problem.

"The year before, Security had loaned Ray Stockman about $20 million to develop Chaucer Village, a condominium project in Dallas. When Saks and Spruill walked in, Chaucer Village had failed. Officials of the Federal Home Loan Bank Board had determined that the Chaucer Village loan had been 'overfunded' by about $5 million. The Board had directed Brannon and Jones either to write down the loan, that is, to establish a loss reserve against the overfunded amount, or cover it with new capital. Without an infusion of funds from some outside source, Brannon and Jones would effectively be out of business or under supervisory control, since Security's net worth would fall below the minimum regulatory requirements. They did not have the money.

"Brannon and Jones explained to Stockman that Spruill and Saks had requested a $14 million loan, but that by lending $19 million, with Stockman as a business partner, Saks and Spruill could pay Stockman $5 million of the loan proceeds. Stockman would then pass the $5 million to Security for the troubled Chaucer Village loan. Stockman's name would not appear on any loan documents, hiding from federal regulators the tied transactions. In short, the proposal was a shuffle of the $5 million debt from Stockman and the Chaucer Village project, in which the regulators were keenly interested, to Spruill and Saks and the Corpus Christi project, where there was no apparent impropriety. There would be no real infusion of capital, since the source of the funds to cover the Chaucer Village loan would originate with Security itself. The transaction would create the appearance of such an infusion, however, so as to placate the FHLBB.

"Brannon and Jones persuaded Stockman with the suggestion that he would receive no further funding absent his help. The two bankers then told Spruill and Saks that the loan came with Stockman as a partner and the $5 million added would never leave the bank but would flow through Stockman to Security. They explained the Chaucer Village loan and why Stockman could not appear on any of the paper work. Spruill and Saks objected at first, but succumbed. Spruill later said that he felt that their backs were against the wall and they would lose everything they had if they did not agree to the deal.

"So then, on January 14th of 1985, Omni/Corpus Christi borrowed $19 million from Security and two closely affiliated banks, Meridian Savings Association and Peoples Savings and Loan Association. The Corpus Christi property was pledged as collateral. Spruill and Saks signed a loan agreement reciting that the loan was for the sole benefit of the lender and borrower and was not for the benefit of any third party. Stockman's name was not on any of the closing documents. Robert Brown, Meridian's attorney and the preparer of the closing documents, later said that he was completely unaware of Stockman's role. The same day, Spruill, Saks, and Stockman formed Crosstown Joint Venture to develop the Corpus Christi property. At the insistence of Spruill and

Saks, Stockman also signed a separate guaranty of the $19 million that Omni/Corpus Christi had borrowed.

"A few days later, Spruill took $5 million of the loan proceeds and made out a cashier's check to Stockman for this amount, ostensibly for his services as an 'advisor' in Crosstown Joint Venture. Stockman rendered no such services. Spruill gave the check to Jones, who met with Stockman, gave him the check, and had him purchase a certificate of deposit in the name of his company, Condo Homes Corporation. Condo Homes then wired the money to Security to pay down the Chaucer Village loan. Security informed federal regulators that a purchaser had been found to take over Chaucer Village and pay off the loan, but did not disclose the true source of the funds. With the shuffle complete, Omni was left to carry a $19 million debt, over 25% of which it had never received.

"In 1986, Meridian sued for foreclosure on the Corpus Christi property. Spruill and Saks counterclaimed against Meridian, Security, and Peoples, asserting that the loan was usurious. They argued that part of the loan transaction was a sham, since $5 million was not in fact loaned to Omni/Corpus Christi but was diverted to Security for Stockman's debt. Crosstown Joint Venture was merely an artifice conceived by Security to hide the true nature of the relationship between Spruill, Saks, and Omni/Corpus Christi on the one hand, and Stockman on the other. Spruill and Saks signed pleadings detailing the fraudulent nature of the loan arrangement, and Spruill testified at length about the transaction in depositions. Spruill and Saks ultimately won a settlement in this lawsuit dissolving the Omni note and requiring the banks to pay them approximately $2 million.

"In 1990, the government indicted Saks and Spruill on charges of conspiracy to defraud the United States and aiding and abetting bank fraud.[3] There were two theories: first, that they defrauded federal regulators by concealing Stockman's involvement in the loan transaction, and second, that they defrauded the banks of their money. Saks testified in his defense at trial. Spruill did not but the court admitted Spruill's deposition testimony from the civil suit into evidence. The jury found both defendants guilty on five counts of bank fraud, 18 U.S.C. §§ 2, 1344, and one count of conspiracy to defraud the United States, 18 U.S.C. § 371.

* * *

"Spruill and Saks * * * argue that their conviction on several counts of bank fraud arising from a single scheme was multiplicitous. They rely on United States v. Lemons, 941 F.2d 309, 316–18 (5th Cir.1991), where we found multiplicity in defendant's bank fraud convictions because § 1344 imposes punishment only for execution of the scheme, not each act in its furtherance. The government has conceded that defendants' convictions were multiplicitous under Lemons, and we agree.

---

3. Brannon, Jones, and Ron Hertlein, the President of Security, were also indict- ed. They all pled guilty. We are not aware whether Stockman was prosecuted.

Defendants were impermissibly convicted on several counts for committing several acts in furtherance of a single scheme to defraud.

"Defendants argue further that *Lemons* requires us to reverse and dismiss all of their bank fraud convictions because the indictment does not allege an offense under § 1344. Because each individual act does not constitute a scheme for the purposes of this statute, the argument goes, each count that referred to a specific act failed to charge an offense. This argument is without merit. Defendants did not object to the indictment below. We therefore read the indictment liberally to be sufficient 'unless it is so defective that by any reasonable construction, it fails to charge an offense.' (internal quotation marks and citations omitted) Each count of the indictment alleged that Saks and Spruill knowingly executed a scheme to defraud the banks by performing an individual act in execution of the scheme. The individual acts were described in each count. This was multiplicitous, but it was sufficient to charge an offense under § 1344.

"We have explained that 'multiplicity addresses double jeopardy; and where the jury is allowed to return convictions on multiplicitous counts, the remedy is to remand for resentencing, with the government dismissing the counts that create the multiplicity.' United States v. Moody, 923 F.2d 341, 347–48 (5th Cir.1991). We accordingly remand the case and direct the government to elect the § 1344 count that it wishes to leave in effect. The court must then vacate the convictions on the remaining § 1344 counts and resentence the defendants."

Do you agree with the courts that Harris' indictment was not multiplicitous while Saks' was? What is the significant difference in the cases?

4. "Duplicity" is the mirror image to "multiplicity." Duplicity is joining in a single count two or more offenses. A duplicitous indictment presents the danger that a jury "would find a defendant guilty on a count without having reached a unanimous verdict on the commission of a particular offense."[dd] Excerpts from the next case, United States v. Bruce, 89 F.3d 886 (D.C.Cir.1996), discuss duplicity. *Bruce* also discusses an unfortunate dilemma in which defense counsel was placed. Bruce was convicted on two counts of violating 18 U.S.C. § 1344. Both counts arose from Bruce's efforts on four occasions to obtain loans from Signet Bank using false identification cards.

"Bruce was indicted on, and convicted of, one charge of knowingly executing and attempting to execute a scheme and artifice to defraud Signet Bank (Count One), and one count of possessing a forged security (Count Two).

* * *

"The first count, which Bruce challenges as duplicitous, alleges one 'scheme' to defraud Signet, and embraces the four separate loan applications each as one 'part' of that overall scheme. Arguing that each application constituted a separate 'scheme' and therefore had to be charged in an individual count, Bruce moved to dismiss the indictment. The district court denied the motion, finding that Bruce's activities

dd. United States v. UCO Oil Co., 546
F.2d 833, 835 (9th Cir.1976).

evidenced a single scheme to defraud, 'because the same victim was involved, the same bank, because the same methods were used....'

"The bank fraud statute makes each 'execution' of a fraudulent scheme punishable as a separate count. It is settled law that acts in furtherance of the scheme cannot be charged as separate counts unless they constitute separate executions of the scheme and that acts which do constitute individual executions may be charged separately. What is less clear is whether the two situations are mutually exclusive; in other words, whether an act which *can* be viewed as an independent execution of a scheme *must* be charged in a separate count in order for the charge not to be duplicitous.

"We think the sensible answer, and the one dictated by the most persuasive precedent, is that the two are *not* mutually exclusive; certain situations would justify indictment either in one count or in separate counts. Caselaw supports this conclusion. The Seventh Circuit, in United States v. Hammen, 977 F.2d 379 (7th Cir.1992), stated this proposition and explained the rationale justifying it:

> [E]ach execution need not give rise to a charge in the indictment. The indictment in this case sets forth the existence of a scheme and alleges the scheme was executed on at least one occasion. The allegations tending to demonstrate the existence of the scheme do appear to be allegations that, if worded and structured differently, might constitute additional executions. This is hardly surprising; the actions that tend to prove the existence of the scheme will often be the actions actually taken to execute the scheme.

Id. at 383.

"Following *Hammen*'s lead, the question in this case is whether Bruce's indictment was written so as 'to allege only one execution of an ongoing scheme.' *Id.* Bruce's indictment charges him with having 'knowingly executed and attempted to execute a scheme and artifice to defraud Signet Bank,' and alleges that 'it was part of the scheme to defraud' that he engaged in each act required for each of the loan transactions. In paragraph 16, however, the indictment alleges that 'On or about November 18, 1994, within the District of Columbia, for the purpose of executing and attempting to execute the above-described scheme to defraud Signet Bank, N.A., the defendant, FLOYD BRUCE, and Victor Dede received cashier's check number 00140330 ... made payable to 'David Green' in the amount of $8,000.00.' Thus, the prosecution 'has carefully crafted the indictment to allege only one execution of an ongoing scheme that was executed numerous times.' *Hammen*, 977 F.2d at 383.

* * *

"Similarly, in Bruce's case, the fraudulent loans could properly be viewed as parts of a single course of conduct and the purposes of the duplicity prohibition met. Because the specific acts in furtherance of the scheme are specified in the indictment, Bruce was on notice of the charge against him and need not worry about later being charged for the same acts. Moreover, the judge carefully instructed the jury that they must unanimously agree on the overall scheme and at least one of the specified acts in furtherance of the scheme (as well as the only act that occurred in D.C.), thereby eliminating the possibility of a nonunanimous verdict.

* * *

"Next, Bruce claims that his attorney created an actual conflict of interest when, in the middle of trial, he divulged to the court in an *ex parte* hearing that Bruce had insisted that the attorney lie to the court on Bruce's behalf. We surmise from the trial transcripts that Bruce was an uncooperative and manipulative client who put his attorney in a very difficult situation, but we conclude that the attorney exhibited an error in judgment when he decided to reveal his client's confidences to the court. Nevertheless, we reject Bruce's claim that the attorney labored under a conflict of interest that adversely affected the defense.

"During the trial, Bruce decided that he was dissatisfied with the performance of his court-appointed attorney, Mr. Rudasill. Bruce demanded that Rudasill (who had been appointed to his case earlier in the proceedings when the defendant dismissed his first court-appointed attorney) seek leave to withdraw from his representation. After a lengthy (and remarkably patient) discussion with the attorney and the defendant, the judge explained that he was not going to appoint another attorney to represent Bruce and that he was not going to delay the trial. In denying Bruce's request for new counsel, the district judge noted that the attorney was 'a very competent lawyer ... who, in my judgment, is doing a good job.' The judge then went through each of the defendant's complaints regarding Rudasill's representation of Bruce and noted that most of Bruce's objections pertained to decisions the *court* had made rather than the lawyer. * * *

"The court addressed each of the defendant's concerns in this fashion, explaining that the attorney had been fully effective, and then gave Bruce the option of proceeding *pro se* or continuing with Mr. Rudasill's representation. Bruce then announced that he wanted to be removed from the proceedings, apparently believing that the trial would have to be delayed if he were not present. The judge (again, very patiently) explained that Bruce had a right to be present, but that he could waive that right if he wished. If he remained in the courtroom, he would have to refrain from disrupting the proceedings, or the court would hold him in contempt; if he opted to have the marshals remove him from the courtroom, the trial would continue in his absence. The court then recessed for an hour and a half and instructed Bruce to discuss his options with counsel and advise the court after lunch which option he was electing.

"The alleged conflict arose after the break, when the attorney announced to the court his belief that during the recess, 'an irreconcilable difference ha[d] developed' between him and Bruce, and he requested an ex parte hearing. According to Rudasill, Bruce had insisted during his lunchtime conference with his attorney that it was the attorney's responsibility 'to do anything to pursue or advance' the client's interests. Because Bruce believed his interests would be served by new counsel, he believed the attorney should do whatever was necessary to force the judge to alter his earlier decision not to remove Rudasill from the case. Apparently Bruce then demanded that Rudasill lie to the court 'concerning the status of [the lawyer's] relationship with Mr. Bruce,' presumably by falsely informing the court that he was incapable for some reason of representing the defendant.

"In his talk with Bruce, Rudasill explained that he 'could not in good conscience' lie to the court and that he 'could not compromise [his] own personal integrity to pursue [Bruce's] aims.' Nevertheless, Bruce continued to insist that it was a 'requirement of his counsel,' to do as he requested. Rudasill informed the court that he and his client had reached an impasse:

> 'I have refused to make those representations. I believe it is inconsistent with my ethical obligations to the Court and I will not do so. And my client's insistence that my failure to do so is somehow—is demonstrative of a lack of zeal in his representation is the basis of my request [to be removed from the case].'

"The court then asked if Rudasill had discussed with Bruce whether the defendant wished to represent himself. The attorney replied that Bruce had 'indicated that he does not believe that at this point he's adequately prepared to represent himself.' *Id.*

"During this *ex parte* discussion, Bruce became angry and for a while refused to answer any questions posed to him by the attorney or the judge. Apparently Rudasill had not warned Bruce that he intended to inform on him to the judge, even though he *had* made it very clear to Bruce that he would not comply with the defendant's unethical request. * * * [Bruce threatened to disrupt the proceedings.]

* * *

"The trial continued and Bruce made good on his threats to disrupt the proceedings. Because the defendant would not exercise his right to be removed from the courtroom, the judge ordered him shackled for part of the trial. Eventually, however, the defendant settled down and the court observed that Bruce and Rudasill 'seemed to the court to have reestablished a level of communication that has made it possible for them to consult with each other and to work together in presenting a defense.' The court also noted that Bruce had participated with Rudasill in the defense, and had asked constructive questions of witnesses.

"At the end of the trial, the jury returned guilty verdicts on both counts.

[Bruce argued that his attorney's 'conflict of interest' in revealing confidential communications between client and counsel constituted ineffective assistance of counsel, requiring reversal. The court rejected Bruce's argument:]

"In holding that Bruce has failed to show a conflict of interest, we in no way mean to indicate our approval of Mr. Rudasill's decision to divulge his client's confidences to the court. In fact, our review of the American Bar Association's Model Rules of Professional Conduct suggests that the attorney might indeed have violated ethical standards in doing so. But a violation of an ethical obligation does not in itself give rise to a conflict of interest, unless it involves the attorney putting his own interests (or, of course, another client's interests) in conflict with his client's.

"Chapter 1 of the Model Rules of Professional Conduct governs the 'Client-Lawyer Relationship.' Model Rules of Professional Conduct Rule 1.1–1.17 (1995). Rule 1.6, entitled 'Confidentiality of Information' requires an attorney to guard a client's confidences under virtually all circumstances. The text of the rule reads as follows:

(a) A lawyer shall not reveal information relating to representation of a client unless the client consents after consultation, except for disclosures that are impliedly authorized in order to carry out the representation, and except as stated in paragraph (b).

(b) A lawyer may reveal such information to the extent the lawyer reasonably believes necessary:

(1) to prevent the client from committing a criminal act that the lawyer believes is likely to result in imminent death or substantial bodily harm; or

(2) to establish a claim or defense on behalf of the lawyer in a controversy between the lawyer and the client, to establish a defense to a criminal charge or civil claim against the lawyer based upon conduct in which the client was involved, or to respond to allegations in any proceeding concerning the lawyer's representation of the client.

MODEL RULES OF PROFESSIONAL CONDUCT RULE 1.6 (1995). In this case, neither of the exceptions listed in part (b) would excuse Rudasill's disclosure; Bruce had not threatened to maim or kill anybody, and no charges had been brought against Rudasill which required the attorney to defend himself.

"The next three rules in the Model Rules directly address 'conflict of interest' situations, but, significantly, none of them mentions the kind of 'conflict' created by an attorney's revelation of the client's suggestion that the lawyer commit an illegal act. Rather, the rules deal with more traditional conflicts of interest: representation of multiple parties, *id.* at Rule 1.7 cmt. [12]; representation of opposing parties, *id.* at cmt. [7]; a lawyer's implication in the same conduct as the client, *id.* at cmt. [6]; representation of a client with whom the attorney has business transactions, *id.* at Rule 1.8(a); representation by an attorney with pecuniary interests adverse to the client, *id.*; representation that would be adverse to a former client, *id.* at Rule 1.9.

"The 'conflict' between an attorney's duty to safeguard a client's confidentiality and her duty to be truthful to the court is addressed in a *different* section of the rules. Rule 3.3, entitled 'Candor Toward the Tribunal,' explains that an advocate's duty of candor to the court applies 'even if compliance requires disclosure of information otherwise protected by Rule 1.6.' *Id.* at Rule 3.3. This duty includes the obligation to avoid making a false statement to the tribunal, and to avoid assisting a criminal or fraudulent act by the client. *Id.* Thus, under the Model Rules, if disclosure of a client confidence is *necessary to* avoid assisting such an act, the attorney *must* disclose that fact, even if the disclosure would conflict with the lawyer's obligations under Rule 1.6. *Id.*

"The D.C. Rules of Professional Conduct are even more protective of a client's privacy. Rule 3.3 of the local rules prohibits a lawyer from knowingly 'offer[ing] evidence that the lawyer knows to be false,' D.C.R. OF PROF. CONDUCT 3.3(a)(4), but contains an exception and a qualification that weaken the prohibition. In the case of a *criminal defendant* who intends to give false evidence, an attorney 'shall first make a good-faith effort to dissuade the client from presenting the false evidence' and then, if the client refuses and the lawyer cannot withdraw, 'the lawyer may put the client on the stand to testify in a narrative fashion.' *Id.* at 3.3(b). The last section of the rule contains the further qualification that

> [a] lawyer who receives information clearly establishing that a fraud has been perpetrated upon the tribunal shall promptly reveal the fraud to the tribunal *unless compliance with this duty would require disclosure of information otherwise protected by rule 1.6*, in which case the lawyer shall promptly call upon the client to rectify the fraud.

Id. at 3.3(d) (emphasis added).

"Although we need not decide whether Rudasill violated the code of ethics, we think his conduct highly problematic. Even given the uncomfortable position in which Bruce left him, Rudasill most likely *could* have honored his obligations under both Rule 1.6 and Rule 3.3. When Bruce demanded that Rudasill lie to the court, Rudasill correctly advised his client that he would not honor the request. Bruce's persistence created a dilemma for Rudasill, but not one which required him to request an *ex parte* hearing.

"The wiser course of action, we think, would have been for Rudasill to tell the judge, as he did, that he and his client had reached an impasse and that he would like to be removed from the case. In describing the 'impasse,' however, the lawyer should have avoided any mention of the fact that his client had asked him to lie to the court. The judge, having explained an hour before that he absolutely would not derail this trial, would likely have asked the defendant whether he agreed that he and his attorney had reached an impasse, and if so, whether he would rather proceed alone. The same result would have been reached, but without the disclosure of damaging information."

F. TRIAL STRATEGIES IN BANK FRAUD CASES

The next case, United States v. Riddle, 103 F.3d 423 (5th Cir.1997), provides an excellent discussion of two evidentiary issues which typically arise in white collar prosecutions: use of expert witnesses and admission of "similar act" evidence. Prior to reading *Riddle*, it may be helpful to briefly review rules of evidence regarding expert testimony and "similar act" evidence.

Federal Rule of Evidence (FRE) 702 provides that

"If scientific, technical, or other specialized knowledge will assist the trier of fact to understand the evidence or to determine a fact in issue, a witness qualified as an expert by knowledge, skill, experience, training, or education, may testify thereto in the form of an opinion or otherwise."

With the exception of testifying about the mental state or condition of a defendant, which is prohibited, federal rules of evidence permit an expert to testify about the "ultimate issue to be decided by the trier of fact." FRE 704. Given the complexity of most white collar prosecutions, admission of expert testimony is fairly routine.[ee] FRE 703 describes the foundation which must be presented before expert testimony becomes admissible:

"The facts or data in the particular case upon which an expert bases an opinion or inference may be those perceived or made known to the expert at or before the hearing. If of a type reasonably relied upon by experts in the particular field in forming opinions or inferences upon the subject, the facts or data need not be admissible in evidence."

As can be seen, the rules are quite flexible in specifying the foundation which must be presented. The expert need not have personal knowledge of any facts or information upon which the expert bases his or her opinion: "facts or data * * * made known to the expert" will suffice. In addition, facts or data upon which the expert relies in reaching his or her opinion need not be admissible in evidence "[i]f of a type reasonably relied upon by experts in th[at] particular field."

Federal Rule of Evidence 404(b) provides that:

"Evidence of other crimes, wrongs, or acts is not admissible to prove the character of a person in order to show that he acted in conformity therewith. It may, however, be admissible for other purposes, such as proof of motive, opportunity, intent, preparation, plan, knowledge, identity, or absence of mistake or accident, provided that upon request by the accused, the prosecution in a criminal case shall provide reasonable notice in advance of trial, or during trial if the court excuses pretrial notice on good cause shown, of the general nature of any such evidence it intends to introduce at trial."

Proof of other "wrongs" need not be *crimes* for which the defendant has been convicted or even arrested. Moreover, proof of other "wrongs" need not meet the stringent standard of proof beyond a reasonable doubt. Instead it may be proven by the lesser standard, "clear and convincing."[ff] Evidence admissible because of Fed. R. Evid. 404(b) is often readily available in white collar criminal cases and can be extremely important. It is readily available because the business transaction at

ee. *See, e.g.,* Pamela H. Bucy, *The Poor Fit of Traditional Evidentiary Doctrine and Sophisticated Crime: An Empirical Analysis of Health Care Fraud Prosecutions,* 63 FORD. L. REV. 383 (1994).

ff. 2 D. LOUISELL & MUELLER, FEDERAL EVIDENCE § 140 (1985).

issue in the criminal case may also form the basis of related civil lawsuits already filed against the defendant. Or, the defendant may be embroiled in controversies with business associates who are only too eager to cooperate with the government in its prosecution of the defendant. If the prosecutor is able to lay the appropriate foundation through Fed. R. Evid. 404(b), the details of these civil lawsuits or disagreements may be introduced in the criminal action.

Fed. R. Evid. 404(b) evidence is especially powerful in fraud cases based on documentary evidence because it assists the government in proving the most elusive of elements to the crime—intent. When transactions are memorialized in documents there is usually little question that the conduct alleged occurred. Often in such cases the only issue in controversy is intent and it becomes much easier to prove intent when the defendant is shown to have engaged in a pattern of conduct over a period of time, rather than in one isolated incident. Thus, with 404(b) evidence, the government can charge the defendant with an isolated incident yet prove criminal intent as to this incident by introducing evidence of a pattern of conduct, none of which is charged and none of which is proven beyond a reasonable doubt.

UNITED STATES v. RIDDLE

United States Court of Appeals, Fifth Circuit, 1997.
103 F.3d 423.

HIGGINBOTHAM, CIRCUIT JUDGE.

John C. Riddle appeals his convictions for bank fraud, misapplication of bank funds, making false entries, and conspiracy. Although he argues a variety of points of error, we limit our discussion to the trial court's evidentiary rulings. We are persuaded that the cumulative and interactive effect of four rulings requires that we reverse the judgment of conviction and remand for a new trial.

I.

Riddle opened Texas National Bank–Post Oak on May 7, 1984. He was chairman of the board and co-trustee of a voting trust that controlled a majority of the shares. Because of unusually high opening day deposits totaling around $38 million, the Office of the Comptroller of the Currency ("OCC") initiated an examination of TNB–Post Oak only sixty days after the bank was launched. An OCC inspector, Gary Meier, discovered that the bank's purchases of five $800,000 loan participations violated its legal lending limit. Meier expressed to the bank his concern that it was imprudently relying on repurchase agreements without inspecting the creditworthiness of the entities that had promised to repurchase the participations if they went bad. He explained to Riddle and the bank's board that OCC regulations required banks to review loan participations as thoroughly as if the bank were initiating the loan.

In March of 1985, ten months after opening TNB–Post Oak, Riddle opened a second bank, Texas National Bank–Westheimer ("TNB–W").

The criminal charges at issue in this case arose out of Riddle's relations with this second bank. As chairman, Riddle held approximately ten percent of the bank's stock. As with TNB–Post Oak, a voting trust named Riddle as co-trustee. Riddle was not an officer, but he exercised control over various board members. The board declared that Riddle was not an executive officer. But in November of 1985, the OCC concluded that the board's declaration was ineffective because Riddle in fact controlled the bank's activities, including the activities of Victor C. Bane, the bank's president and loan officer.

The OCC inspected TNB–W in September of 1985 and found a number of problems. Its loans-to-debt ratio was an unhealthy 105 percent. The most serious problem concerned loans to insiders. On opening day, it granted a $400,000 unsecured loan to Riddle, which immediately put the bank in violation of banking regulations as well as its own policies. The next month, Riddle had Bane issue a $415,000 letter of credit to Rick Dover, Riddle's real estate development partner, to satisfy the lender behind one of Riddle's commercial real estate projects. Dover did not have to post collateral, and in exchange Riddle granted a 15 percent interest in the project to Dover. According to the OCC, the bank failed to keep proper documentation for transactions with businesses owned by bank directors. A full twenty-five percent of the bank's gross loans went to insiders or companies related to insiders. The OCC inspector discussed the loans-to-insiders violations with Riddle and the board. His report listed loans to Riddle in particular as problematic.

TNB–W lost money during its first six months. To remedy this, the board decided to pursue a strategy suggested by Bane: the bank would raise its interest rate on certificates of deposit to generate short-term assets. The strategy worked as planned, and between September 30, 1985, and December 31, 1985, TNB–W tripled its assets. To pay the interest on these certificates, the board resolved to purchase loan participations. Riddle suggested that TNB–W turn to Vernon Savings & Loan, a thrift operated primarily by Don Dixon, the chairman of Dondi Corporation, Vernon's controlling shareholder. Riddle had done personal business with Vernon and Dixon in the past. He did not disclose to the board, however, that he had a personal business interest in TNB–W's purchase of participations from Vernon.

In addition to opening banks, Riddle was involved in real estate development. In September of 1984, Riddle and Dover formed Hickory Creek Joint Venture to purchase a 1230-acre tract west of Houston called Park Green. They signed a note for $40 million. In the late spring of 1985, they bought an adjacent 230 acres with $13 million in financing. Vernon bought 35 percent of the first loan; Western Savings and Loan bought the other 65 percent. Vernon and Western also funded the second loan and took a pro rata profit participation that would take effect upon sale of the property.

By the fall of 1985, Riddle was having cash-flow problems and wanted to sell the Park Green property. Another Houston developer,

John Ballis, expressed interest in buying Park Green and proposed swapping Park Green for a piece of land known as the Superior Oil tract, which was located closer to downtown Houston and thus was more desirable for development. Ballis had deposited $1 million to obtain an option to purchase the Superior Oil tract before December 23, 1985. On September 24, Riddle and Dover signed a letter of intent to purchase the Superior Oil tract from Ballis in exchange for the Park Green property.

At the end of October of 1985, Riddle sought funding for the Superior Oil deal from Vernon and Dixon. Dixon explained, however, that regulators had imposed growth restrictions on Vernon and suggested that Riddle find another lender to buy loan participations from Vernon so that Vernon could finance Riddle's project. In October and November, Dixon and Riddle took a 3–week European vacation, during which they explored ways to structure transactions so that Vernon could fund the Superior Oil deal. At a November meeting at Dixon's office, Riddle suggested that Vernon buy 30 percent of the $78 million loan that Western would issue for the Superior Oil purchase. He explained that he would have TNB–W buy $8.5 million in loan participations from Vernon. Woody Lemons, Vernon's president, expressed concern that this would violate bank regulations governing loans to insiders. But Riddle nevertheless went forward with his proposal to the TNB–W board that it buy loan participations from Vernon. Riddle brought Bane to Dixon's office to work out the details of purchasing the loan participations.

At November and December meetings, Riddle and Bane urged the TNB–W loan committee to purchase participations from Vernon. TNB–W, however, did not have time to review the quality of the loans, and Vernon did not include sufficient documentation to support TNB–W's purchase. As it turned out, Vernon's loans were delinquent: Vernon had been paying the interest itself in order to make the loans appear sound.

Dixon and other Vernon officials were aware of Riddle's scheme and acted to see that TNB–W purchased enough participations to allow Vernon to fund the Superior transaction. On December 4, TNB–W's loan committee recommended that TNB–W purchase seven participations from Vernon. In connection with the loans, Vernon issued unconditional buyback letters, which guaranteed that Vernon would pay in case the borrowers defaulted. Both Vernon and TNB–W hid these letters from regulators because, as far as the OCC was concerned, they meant that Vernon had not really reduced its loan portfolio after all. TNB–W's board approved the purchases on December 17. At the insistence of Riddle and Bane, the board also approved the purchase of an additional $6 million in participations from Vernon.

Facing the December 23 deadline, Ballis bought the Superior Oil tract for $64 million on December 17. After forming the Regents Park Limited Partnership, Riddle and Dover agreed to buy the Superior Oil tract from Ballis for $63.1 million. The closing took place on December 23, and Ballis bought the Park Green property for $64.4 million. Vernon was to fund $23 million of the $78 million loan that Riddle and Dover needed to finance the Superior Oil purchase. But on December 24, Dixon told Riddle that Vernon would not send the money until TNB–W sent the $6 million that had been due the previous week for loan participation purchases. Bane purchased an additional 21 participations from Vernon on behalf of TNB–W without approval of the TNB–W board and wired over $9 million to Vernon during the last week of December. During that same week, Vernon wired $10.9 million to Western to buy a participation in Western's loan to Riddle and Dover.

Bill Plyler, a TNB–W executive vice president, was suspicious of Riddle's behavior and asked the OCC to audit TNB–W in late December of 1985 or January of 1986. The OCC was especially worried about the high concentration of participations purchased from Vernon and TNB–W's rapid growth from $10 million to $32 million over the course of three months. Several board members confronted Riddle, who denied that his Superior loan from Vernon had been contingent on TNB–W's purchase of participations from Vernon. In part as a result of the board's discovery of Riddle's conduct, Bane resigned in January, and Plyler replaced him as president. In the aftermath of Bane's resignation, bank officials discovered that Riddle had caused TNB–W to make a number of imprudent loans for his own or his friends' benefit. Plyler insisted that Riddle write a letter to the OCC to explain TNB–W's decisions. Riddle complied, but the government ultimately concluded that the letter contained a number of misrepresentations. In April, an OCC examiner found that 76 percent of TNB–W's outstanding loans had become delinquent and recommended that the bank be declared insolvent.

Riddle resigned as chairman on June 12, 1986. On November 13, the OCC issued a cease-and-desist order for TNB–W to stop its unsafe lending practices. After Meier conducted a May, 1987, examination, the OCC declared insolvency on May 28 and appointed the FDIC as receiver.

II.

A grand jury indicted Riddle and Bane on one count of bank fraud under 18 U.S.C. § 1344, one count of misapplication of bank funds under 18 U.S.C. § 656, three counts of making false entries in violation of 18 U.S.C. § 1005, and one count of conspiracy in violation of 18 U.S.C. § 371.

Gary Meier, the OCC examiner who prepared reports on TNB–Post Oak in 1984 and on TNB–W in 1987, was one of the prosecution's primary witnesses at trial. Although he testified as a lay witness, the prosecution elicited opinions that drew on his expertise as a bank examiner. The court admitted all four bank examinations under Fed. R.Evid. 803(8)(B) as public reports prepared as required by law from observations of officials other than law enforcement personnel. Meier read from these examinations in spite of the fact that he was not involved in the 1985 and 1986 examinations. The court explained that Meier had personal knowledge of the reports because he relied on them when he conducted the 1987 examination. The court disagreed with defense counsel's contention that Meier was testifying as an expert.

According to the district court, Meier was a "hybrid lay witness" who could offer explanations of the four relevant bank examinations under the guise of lay opinion testimony. The court admitted his statements about matters such as OCC policy and sound banking practices under the rubric of Fed.R.Evid. 701.

To counter Meier's testimony, the defense offered the testimony of Stephen Huber, an expert in banking regulation who teaches law at the University of Houston. After holding a proffer hearing, however, the court barred Huber from testifying "based primarily on Rule 403." Huber had no personal contact with Riddle or Bane, and the court found that his testimony consisted largely of legal conclusions and duplicative explanations of banking practices.

The court made a variety of other contested evidentiary rulings. It admitted as exhibits a proffer letter and sworn statement given by Dixon, who had been convicted and imprisoned for bank fraud in his dealings with Vernon. The defense read portions of these documents during cross-examination, and the court granted the government's request to admit them in their entirety as prior consistent statements under Fed.R.Evid. 801(d)(1)(B). The court also allowed the government to present evidence that Riddle and Bane violated civil banking regulations in order to show that they possessed criminal intent when they urged TNB–W to buy participations from Vernon. At trial, the defense objected to the reports of bank examiners, to the cease-and-desist order, to much of Meier's testimony, and to portions of the testimony of Woody Lemons and Bill Plyler, who served as officers at Vernon and TNB–W respectively, on the grounds that the government improperly used civil violations to establish criminal violations. Finally, the court allowed the government to introduce evidence of four unrelated loan transactions in which Riddle used his power at TNB–W for his own personal gain. The court admitted the evidence as probative of a plan or motive under Fed.R.Evid. 404(b).

After seventeen days of trial, the jury returned verdicts of guilty on all counts as to both defendants. The court sentenced Riddle to a total of ten years imprisonment and ordered him to pay four million dollars in restitution.

III.

This was a difficult trial. The government chose methods of proof that forced difficult trial rulings. We are persuaded that the trial tactics resulted in an unfair trial, despite the hard work of the able trial judge to assure the fairness our courts must deliver.

A.

Before Meier began his testimony, the parties and the court agreed that the prosecution had not designated him as an expert and that he would not be offering expert testimony. Counsel for the government told the court that "what I want this witness to talk about are the specific facts that he observed." This would include such things as accounts of

Meier's interaction with bank officials during his examinations and personal observations of bank records and practices.

With this assurance, the trial court allowed the government to proceed. However, with each new trial day the government pushed to squeeze as much as possible from this "lay witness." The result is clear, certainly now, that during Meier's two-and-a-half days on the stand, he wielded his expertise as a bank examiner in a way that is incompatible with a lay witness. In connection with his examination of TNB–Post Oak, Meier explained that "[a]ccording to 12 C.F.R. 32.5, when repayment is expected from only one source, then all of the advances must be combined, again, coming from that one source." Over the defense's objections, Meier expressed his opinion that it was not "prudent" for a bank to rely on repurchase agreements issued by banks selling participations rather than on the creditworthiness of borrowers. The next day, Meier expressed his view that bank officers should discuss OCC circulars when the bank receives them and that the OCC expects officers such as Riddle to know the contents of circulars. The defense objected at length to Meier's testimony about the OCC's position on whether a bank director may bring loans to his bank. In response, the court reminded that Meier was not an expert, but that his reports had been available for some time and that his testimony should come as no surprise to the defense. "Even if you do consider him an expert," the court noted, "it seems to me that we have satisfied the requirements of the rule."

Meier continued to draw on his specialized knowledge as a bank examiner. He testified that it was imprudent "to have the buyback letter stand separate and apart from the participation certificate itself with neither referencing the other." He asserted that TNB–W violated OCC regulations when it failed to record the fact that Riddle received proceeds from its purchase of participations. He even speculated that unsafe and unsound lending practices, including loans to insiders, caused TNB–W's failure.

Under Fed.R.Evid. 701, a lay opinion must be based on personal perception, must "be one that a normal person would form from those perceptions," and must be helpful to the jury. We have allowed lay witnesses to express opinions that required specialized knowledge. In *Soden*, a witness in charge of truck maintenance testified that, based on his experience, step brackets caused the punctures in a fuel tank that had been brought into his repair yard. We held that the district court did not abuse its discretion when it allowed the plaintiff to introduce such lay opinion testimony. "No great leap of logic or expertise was necessary for one in Lasere's position to move from his observation of holes in Freightliner fuel tanks at the location of the step brackets, and presumably caused by them, to his opinion that the situation was dangerous." Other circuits have construed Rule 701 even more broadly. [citations omitted]

Meier, however, went beyond the lay testimony in *Soden*, as well as the testimony in cases from other circuits. He did not merely draw straightforward conclusions from observations informed by his own experience. Instead, he purported to describe sound banking practices in the abstract. He told the jury how the OCC viewed certain complex transactions. And he asserted a causal relationship between Riddle's alleged wrongdoing and the ultimate failure of TNB–W. He functioned not as a witness relaying his own observations so much as a knowledgeable bank examiner who could provide the jury with an overview of banking regulations and practices and who could authoritatively condemn Riddle's actions. He did not offer testimony that a lay person would have been able to offer after conducting the examinations. The district court erred in allowing Meier's testimony under Fed.R.Evid. 701.

The government insists that Meier was nothing more than a fact witness because his review of TNB–W files and the 1985 and 1986 examinations gave him personal knowledge of their contents. It is true that "[t]he modern trend favors the admission of opinion testimony, provided that it is well founded on personal knowledge and susceptible to specific cross-examination." [citations omitted] Based on this rule, Meier could draw specific conclusions from his work on the 1984 and 1987 examinations, such as that Riddle did not heed Meier's 1984 advice on self-dealing. But latitude under Rule 701 does not extend to general claims about how banks should conduct their affairs. Meier's opinions that TNB–W operated imprudently and that its imprudence caused it to fail depend on an expert's understanding of the banking industry.

The government also contends that Meier's opinions were admissible because the prosecution identified him as a witness long before trial and provided his reports to the defense. At trial, however, the government made a point of presenting Meier as a fact witness rather than as an expert. "[A] party cannot seek to have a witness certified as an expert on appeal when the party did not seek to have the witness qualified as an expert before the district court." [citations omitted]

B.

The defense proposed to offer Stephen Huber, a professor at the University of Houston Law Center, to show that banking regulations did not require Riddle to disclose his interest in the Vernon participations and that Riddle and TNB–W adhered to industry standards when it purchased loans from other banks. The court ultimately acknowledged that Meier was mistaken when he stated that 12 C.F.R. pt. 31 required Riddle to report that the purchase of participations from Vernon would allow Vernon to finance the Superior Oil deal. As Professor Huber explained at the hearing, the regulations do not apply when a bank buys participations from a thrift.

The government, then, had to prove that Riddle knew that he was doing something wrong even though he was committing no regulatory violation. Much of Meier's testimony was an effort to convince the jury that Riddle encouraged the TNB–W board to engage in unsafe lending practices when he encouraged it to buy participations from Vernon. Had he been allowed to testify, Huber would have told the jury that TNB–W handled the Vernon participations in the way that any other bank would have handled them. According to Huber, it is difficult for banks buying small loan participations to acquire documentation from the borrower, so they routinely rely on buyback letters issued by the selling bank.

After more than two weeks of testimony, it is understandable that the court would be wary of allowing the defense to present an expert witness to testify about the proper interpretation of regulations and to make general statements about banking practices. But after giving Meier extensive leeway, the court abused its discretion in refusing to allow Huber to testify regarding Riddle's knowledge that he was doing something wrong in not making the disclaimer to the board. Testimony that other banks would have made the same decision to buy the Vernon participations would have supported Riddle's contention that any failure to disclose his interest was not deceitful or even intentional. With Huber's testimony, the defense could have countered some of the damaging opinions offered by Meier and contained in the OCC examinations. The loss of Huber's testimony handicapped the ability of the defense to tell the jury its own version of how banks operate and what precautions bankers such as Riddle know they should take.

* * *

Nine government witnesses spent at least part of their time on the stand discussing four unrelated TNB–W loans that supposedly showed that Riddle systematically withheld information from the bank in order to direct loan proceeds for his personal benefit. As required by United States v. Robinson, 700 F.2d 205, 213 (5th Cir.1983), the court conducted bench conferences on whether this evidence had probative value and whether it was unduly prejudicial. The prosecution viewed the loans as evidence of "other crimes, wrongs, or acts" that showed Riddle's "motive, opportunity, intent, preparation, plan, knowledge, identity, or absence of mistake or accident." Fed.R.Evid. 404(b). For its part, the court stated that "it's relevant to motive, to plan, the way he did business, the things he did."

In the first loan, Jim Hague borrowed $350,000 from TNB–W to buy an apartment complex that Riddle owned and wanted to sell. Regulators viewed the loan as an illegal extension of credit to Riddle, but they also concluded in the 1986 examination report that the violation was a result of a misunderstanding of regulations and thus was not willful or intentional. TNB–W also loaned $300,000 to Architects Alliance, Inc., and took an interest in accounts receivable and inventory as collateral. Riddle was the architectural firm's primary client and owed it more than $500,000. Riddle also owed thousands of dollars to Richard Weems, who had done extensive mowing and landscaping work at some of Riddle's properties. At Riddle's suggestion, Weems borrowed $20,000 from TNB–W to keep up with operating expenses while waiting for Riddle to pay his debt. A fourth extension of credit went to Rick Dover, Riddle's real estate partner, who obtained a $415,000 letter of credit as collateral on a loan issued by a Florida bank to fund the development of a shopping center.

The government explained during its closing argument that these extraneous loans showed "that this was the way that John Riddle did business. That tells you about his mental state when he was entering into the loan participations for the Superior purchase deal." In other words, the 404(b) evidence was relevant because it established that Riddle consistently withheld information from the bank that he knew he had an obligation to disclose. The government's 404(b) theory is in agreement with our analysis in United States v. Beechum, 582 F.2d 898, 911 (5th Cir.1978):

> Where the issue addressed is the defendant's intent to commit the offense charged, the relevancy of the extrinsic offense derives from the defendant's indulging himself in the same state of mind in the perpetration of both the extrinsic and the charged offenses. The reasoning is that because the defendant had unlawful intent in the extrinsic offense, it is less likely that he had lawful intent in the present offense.

The government must present enough evidence to permit a reasonable jury to conclude by a preponderance of the evidence that Riddle's intent in connection with the four extraneous loans was criminal. Riddle is charged with bank fraud, misapplication of bank funds, and false entries in the records of a bank, all of which require proof that the defendant knew he was making a misrepresentation. In this case, that means that the extraneous loans must make it more likely that Riddle intentionally kept the TNB–W board in the dark on his personal interest in having TNB–W extend credit.

Our review of the record convinces us that the government did not meet its burden. At most, the evidence suggests that Riddle took improper advantage of his position to encourage TNB–W to extend credit unwisely and for the benefit of his non-banking endeavors. The OCC itself found that any violation Riddle committed in connection with the Hague loan was unintentional. Walter Beard, a TNB–W director, offered undisputed testimony that the TNB–W board "had to know" that Architects Alliance had done extensive work for Riddle because Architects Alliance designed TNB–W's building. And the government's evidence does not reveal any deception in Riddle's role in generating the loan to Weems or the letter of credit to Dover. As far as the record is concerned, Riddle simply suggested that various business associates apply for loans at TNB–W. Some of Riddle's associates needed money because he was unable to keep up with his debts, but that does not by itself mean that Riddle intended to deceive or defraud the bank. David Hall, a partner at Architects Alliance, testified that Victor Bane instructed him to submit his firm's records of accounts receivable in a format that excluded Riddle's name because "it might reflect poorly" on Riddle if TNB–W knew that Riddle owed so much money to Architects Alliance. The insinuation, of course, is that Bane was acting under Riddle's instructions. Riddle may also have used Bane to hide his debt to Weems and his involvement in real estate ventures with Dover to convince TNB–W to extend credit. But without evidence from government witnesses, we are not willing to allow the jury to make such an attenuated inference.

The government's 404(b) evidence certainly makes Riddle out to be an irresponsible banker who paid little attention to OCC warnings. But Riddle was not on trial for irresponsibility. He was on trial for bank fraud, misapplication of bank funds, and making false entries. Even if illegal, Riddle's extraneous self-serving banking practices are irrelevant under Rule 404(b) unless they tend to show that he systematically withheld vital information from the TNB–W board. By allowing the jury to consider these four loans, the trial court made the mistake of treating general evidence of poor banking as if it were evidence of Riddle's criminal intent to mislead TNB–W's board of directors.

Even if the extraneous loans were relevant to the government's case against Riddle, they failed to meet the second prong of the *Beechum* test: "the evidence must possess probative value that is not substantially outweighed by its undue prejudice and must meet the other requirements of rule 403." *Beechum*, 582 F.2d at 911. Unduly prejudicial extraneous evidence often plays on the jury's emotions unfairly, but "[p]rejudice can result from any of the significant factors set out in Rule 403, of which inflamed passion is only one." United States v. Zabaneh, 837 F.2d 1249, 1265 (5th Cir.1988). These other factors include confusion of the issues and misleading the jury, Fed.R.Evid. 403, and they are especially troubling when they take up a significant portion of the government's case.

The court's limiting instructions can "substantially reduce" the danger of prejudice, [citations omitted] but in this case they did not counteract the prejudicial effect of allowing government witnesses to testify about the extraneous loans for a total of more than a full day. The government called James Hague, David Hall, and Richard Weems for the sole purpose of explaining how Riddle had wronged them in connection with the extraneous loans. In each instance, it was clear that the witness had a gripe against Riddle that had nothing to do with the charged offense. Rick Dover, Walter Beard, William Plyler, and bank examiner Meier also went into the details of the loans. The government analyzed each loan individually during its closing argument to remind the jury that Riddle was "manipulating people and the bank for his personal benefit." And the 1986 OCC examination contained detailed descriptions and criticisms of the Hague and Architects Alliance loans.

When extraneous activity receives such intense, unfocused attention, it is too likely that the jury will "feel that the defendant should be punished for that activity even if he is not guilty of the offense charged." *Beechum*, 582 F.2d at 914. In explaining relevance under the general category of "the way he did business, the things he did," the court itself demonstrated that the evidence of extraneous loans is powerful not so much because it tends to establish Riddle's motive or scheme, but because it paints Riddle as lacking the character of an upstanding businessman. The government's extensive and undiscriminating use of the extraneous loans was misleading to the jury, not because the jury was not discerning but because the evidence was offered in such a large and unchecked way that its permissible limited use was overwhelmed.

* * *

Looking at the cumulative effect of the errors, we are persuaded that they are not harmless and require a new trial. We express no view as to whether any one of the errors standing alone would be sufficient to justify reversal.

The judgment of conviction of John C. Riddle is reversed, and the case is remanded for a new trial.

Notes

1. In comparison to *Riddle*, note the ruling in the next case, United States v. Van Dyke, 14 F.3d 415 (8th Cir.1994), in which the trial court refused to admit expert testimony offered by the defense:

"John William Van Dyke, Jr. appeals his convictions in the United States District Court for the Northern District of Iowa. Van Dyke was found guilty of four counts of false statements to a financial institution (18 U.S.C. § 1014), three counts of bank fraud (18 U.S.C. § 1344(1)), one count of false loan documentation (18 U.S.C. § 1005), and one count of mail fraud (18 U.S.C. § 1341).

* * *

"In the early 1980's, Van Dyke became President of Toy National Bank in Sioux City, Iowa. The bank had been founded by his great grandfather, and it remained largely a family operation, both in ownership and management. The Van Dyke family also owned substantial interests in several other banks in smaller Iowa towns. Toy National experienced some problems under Van Dyke's management, which came to the attention of government regulatory officials. In 1987, Van Dyke was removed from his positions as president and director of Toy National by the Federal Reserve System's Board of Governors. * * * Toy National's assets were eventually sold to Norwest Bank Corporation.

"In addition to his bank-related responsibilities, Van Dyke served as trustee for a family trust from June 1981 to December 1988. The trust held stock in several banks, including Toy National. In December 1988 Van Dyke was replaced as trustee by Dean Meine.

"In 1992 Mr. Van Dyke was indicted, based on alleged wrongdoings that he had committed both individually and in his roles as a bank officer and trustee. * * *

* * *

"The trial court * * * intervened significantly during the testimony of the defense expert, Mary Curtin. At one point, when Ms. Curtin was attempting to explain federal-law limitations on a bank loaning money to its own officers/employees, she offered a gratuitous conclusion that Mr. Van Dyke had borrowed the maximum from Toy National Bank. The trial court responded as follows:

THE COURT: Well, we'll strike that, if you don't mind.

THE WITNESS: Oh, I'm sorry.

THE COURT: You're not trying this case. You know better than that.

THE WITNESS: I apologize, your honor.

THE COURT: You are a lawyer. You've been a lawyer for 20 years. Don't tell us what was right or wrong, Ms. Curtin.

The jury is instructed to disregard it.

"Shortly thereafter, the prosecutor made very brief cross-examination of Ms. Curtin, then indicated he was through. The prosecutor had elicited (without objection) the fact that Ms. Curtin had worked for Mr. Van Dyke in the past, and the Court again intervened:

THE COURT: Well, if you're going to start asking about Mr. Van Dyke you're doing just what I wouldn't let Mr. Scalise [defense counsel.] do.

MR. HENNING: Your Honor, I asked—just—it was just asking if she had previously worked for Mr. Van Dyke.

THE COURT: Well, if she had worked for him?

MR. HENNING: Yes.

THE COURT: Oh, I have no objection to that. I'm sure counsel doesn't either.

Did you ever work for Mr. Van Dyke?

THE WITNESS: I answered the question, Your Honor. Yes, I did. In 1987.

THE COURT: You may pursue it.

MR. HENNING: No further questions.

THE COURT: I just have one question for my own information. . . .

"The Court then, on its own initiative, directed Ms. Curtin to read lengthy provisions of the lending law she had been referring to. Defense counsel said nothing about the court's intervention, until the judge told Ms. Curtin to read the section about overdrafts. Defense counsel then objected:

MR. SCALISE: Excuse me, Your Honor. I have limited her to lending limit and—

THE COURT: This deals with overdrafts.

Mr. SCALISE: Well, I didn't inquire into that, Judge.

THE COURT: Well, you haven't, but I have because I want to know what the law is. And I want to make sure that I'm reading it correctly.

MR. SCALISE: Well, Your Honor, with all due respect to you, I'm going to object to you inquiring into this, Your Honor, because I didn't. And I have a lot of respect for you, and you know that.

THE COURT: Oh, I know that, counsel. You're just brimming with it. I know that.

"Defense counsel then attempted to clarify his position, to the effect that he had avoided the subject of overdrafts with Ms. Curtin, so he thought it was improper for the judge to make her read a code section on overdrafts.

THE COURT: Counsel, there's been evidence all over this case about overdrafts, and I think the jury is entitled to know what Regulation O says about overdrafts.

MR. SCALISE: He's not charged with the crime of overdrafting.

THE COURT: He's not?

MR. SCALISE: No, he's not.

THE COURT: I thought we had an awful lot of discussion about overdrafts in the last two weeks. If I'm wrong the jury will remember what the testimony is.

MR. SCALISE: I think you're absolutely right. We have had a lot of talk about it, and the Court has said that that has come in pursuant to Rule 404(b) of the federal rules of evidence. It's not evidence of a crime.

"Ms. Curtin then obeyed the Court and read the regulation's overdraft provisions. This series of exchanges unduly emphasized the notion that overdrafts had occurred—in a context not anticipated or invited by either counsel. It also gave the jury a perception that the trial judge had general disdain and/or disbelief for the defense witness and counsel, and it is yet again another example of the district court's extensive involvement in trying the case—perceptibly as an advocate for the prosecution.

"Closely related to the above-described treatment of Ms. Curtin, the district court essentially refused to allow her to testify as an expert. As noted above, there was substantial interplay about 'Regulation O,' a lengthy and detailed provision which governs (among other things) transactions wherein a bank lends money to one of its own officers. After establishing Ms. Curtin's qualifications as an expert on this regulation (both as its author and a practicing attorney dealing with it on a regular basis), counsel for defendant attempted to have her explain or clarify the significance of a provision which says that a loan which is sold to a second bank is deemed to be an extension of credit by that second bank—not the bank that originally made the loan to its own officer. Based in part on objections by counsel for the government, the district court refused to allow Ms. Curtin to give opinion or explanation of the regulation. Rather, her testimony was limited almost exclusively to word-for-word recitation of the regulation's provisions. In contrast, the government's first witness, FDIC bank examiner Mike Nelson, had been allowed to testify regarding Regulation O, how its insider loan limitations can be violated, and his opinion that defendant had committed violations.

"A trial court's decision to exclude expert testimony is accorded broad discretion, and will be upheld unless it is manifestly erroneous. Under the circumstances, we conclude that the district court's refusal to allow Ms. Curtin to give expert opinion was reversible error. It is well settled that an expert may express an opinion even if it embraces an ultimate issue to be decided by the fact finder. Here, we are convinced that elaboration by Ms. Curtin would clearly have assisted the jury in understanding the regulation and defendant's reasons for asserting that he had not violated its provisions. This would have especially been appropriate and fair given Mr. Nelson's prior unequivocal assertion that defendant had violated Regulation O and other laws. The district court's limitation of the scope of Ms. Curtin's testimony is particularly troubling in light of his subsequent treatment of her, as noted above. This combination in all likelihood rendered her testimony meaningless to the jury at best—or perhaps even more prosecutorial than defense-oriented.

2. In the next case, United States v. Sinclair, 74 F.3d 753 (7th Cir.1996), the defendant, an officer for Mellon Bank from 1984—1989, was convicted of accepting kickbacks in connection with the business of Mellon Bank. One of the issues Sinclair raised on appeal was that the trial court erred in refusing to admit his proffered expert testimony. The Seventh Circuit rejected Sinclair's argument. Note the court's discussion in footnote 1.

"Sinclair * * * argues that the district court erred in excluding the testimony of Alexander Wayne, an expert witness who would have testified that both the CPI program and the contractual relationship between Fortney and Transamerica were illegal. To a considerable extent, the government's case turned on the credibility of Fortney and Mellon Bank employees. Sinclair wanted Wayne to tell the jury that these witnesses had engaged in illegal conduct of their own, hoping that this showing would raise an inference that some of the crucial witnesses against him sought to shift blame away from themselves by falsely implicating him in a crime.

"The district court ruled that Sinclair could establish the bias of government witnesses without Wayne's testimony. The proposed testimony would involve legal issues raised in the civil suits against Mellon Bank and Transamerica. The district court thought that this evidence could confuse or distract the jury. Moreover, the court thought that Sinclair could raise an inference of bias in other ways. Mellon Bank's employees were arguably biased because of the $6,000,000 judgment against the bank that Sinclair had helped to engineer; Fortney could be impeached by the grant of immunity that he received in return for his testimony against Sinclair. The court ruled under Federal Rule of Evidence 403 that the prejudicial effect of Wayne's testimony would outweigh its probative value.

"Rulings on the admissibility of expert testimony are entitled to the same deference as evidentiary rulings generally. The potential for jury confusion may be substantial when the evidence refers to legal issues at the heart of other litigation; such evidence can create a distracting trial within a trial. In such cases, the trial court may exclude the evidence if the purpose for which it is offered can be accomplished through other means. Here, the district court exercised precisely this kind of discretion, concluding that Sinclair could effectively impeach the witnesses against him without offering potentially confusing testimony. Our cases tell us that we should defer to such discretionary judgment.

"Sinclair urges us to do otherwise. He contends that the Supreme Court's opinion in Daubert v. Merrell Dow Pharmaceuticals, Inc., 509 U.S. 579 (1993), has changed the way that judges should balance the probative value and prejudicial effect of expert testimony. According to Sinclair's reading of *Daubert*, the Supreme Court created a special two-part test for the admissibility of expert testimony. As Sinclair tells it, this test provides that expert testimony is always admissible if: (1) it can be appropriately validated and (2) it will assist the trier of fact in understanding an issue. This test is, of course, simply a restatement of Federal Rule of Evidence 702, but in his application of it, Sinclair seems to suggest that the second part of this special test relieves a trial court from having to apply Rule 403. In Sinclair's proposed analysis, expert testimony is necessarily more probative than prejudicial if a jury could properly evaluate or understand its impact on a relevant issue. He thinks that Wayne's prospective testimony passed this test and that the district court should have admitted it.

"Because we cannot read *Daubert* as Sinclair does, we must reject his argument. *Daubert* does not create a special analysis for answering questions about the admissibility of all expert testimony. Instead, it provides a method for evaluating the reliability of witnesses who claim scientific expertise. *Daubert*, therefore, has no direct relevance to questions about the admissibility of testimony by a witness who claims legal expertise.[1] Moreover, it does not relieve courts of the obligation to evaluate expert testimony under Rule 403. Wayne's testimony was subject to the ordinary application of Rule 403, and the district court did not abuse its discretion by applying the rule.

"Sinclair also characterizes the district court's exclusion of Wayne's testimony as depending upon a conclusion that the testimony was cumulative with other evidence about the bias of witnesses against Sinclair. He claims that Wayne's testimony would have provided the first evidence about the illegality of actions by Mellon and Fortney.

---

1. By arguing about the admissibility of Wayne's testimony, Sinclair implicitly raises a legal question that neither he, nor the government, nor the district court addressed. Because an answer to this question will not be dispositive here, we will not provide one. Nevertheless, the question itself deserves some notice.

The question is this: when can expert witnesses offer legal opinions? In addressing this question, federal courts have not provided uniform answers. Our own cases have determined that Federal Rules of Evi-

dence 702 and 704 prohibit experts from offering opinions about legal issues that will determine the outcome of a case. That is, they cannot testify about legal issues on which the judge will instruct the jury. Our cases have also indicated that there are some circumstances in which experts can offer legal opinions, but we have not exhaustively identified them. Not every court has followed this approach, however; and some of their opinions do not clearly determine when experts may and may not testify about legal issues.

Therefore he argues that the exclusion of Wayne's testimony was based upon an erroneous conclusion. We reject this argument because we think that Sinclair has misunderstood the district court's reason for the exclusion. When a district court excludes one piece of evidence because other evidence will adequately replace it, it is not necessarily deciding that the excluded evidence is cumulative. It could be ruling that the evidence's probative value is less than its harmful effects. Indeed, when the district court excluded Wayne's testimony, it did not rule that the testimony would be cumulative; it ruled that the testimony was more trouble than it was worth."

Chapter 10

FALSE CLAIMS AGAINST
THE GOVERNMENT

Tens of thousands of claims for reimbursement are made to the United States government daily. These claims range from millions of dollars to less than one dollar. The claimants include defense contractors, health care providers, welfare recipients, federal job applicants, and corporate and individual loan applicants hoping to qualify for loans under a variety of federal programs. Needless to say, the complexity of claims submitted also varies, from simple, one-sentence claims to technical, multi-volume claims.

Despite this diversity in claims and claimants, all claimants who submit a false claim to the federal government are subject to the same criminal and civil liability. This chapter addresses that liability.

A. CRIMINAL CAUSES OF ACTION

There are two major federal statutes used to criminally prosecute those who submit false claims to the government, 18 U.S.C. § 287 and 18 U.S.C. § 1001. Section 287 makes it a felony offense to submit any claim to the United States, "knowing such claim to be false, fictitious, or fraudulent." Related offenses include § 286, which makes it a felony to conspire to present false claims against the government, § 288, which applies to false claims for postal losses, and § 289, which applies to false claims for pension payments. Section 1001 makes it a felony offense to submit a false statement or conceal a material fact regarding any matter "within the jurisdiction of the executive, legislative or judicial branch of the Government of the United States."

In one sense, § 1001 is broader than § 287 because it targets submitting *any* false statement, not just a false claim, to the United States government. Originally, what are now §§ 287 and 1001 were part of the same criminal offense, 18 U.S.C. § 80 (1940). The next case, United States v. Irwin, 654 F.2d 671 (10th Cir.1981), discusses these two statutes.

UNITED STATES v. IRWIN

United States Court of Appeals, Tenth Circuit, 1981.
654 F.2d 671.

HOLLOWAY, CIRCUIT JUDGE.

This is a direct appeal by the defendant-appellant James A. Irwin, Jr., from his conviction and sentence on each count of an eight-count indictment charging him with conspiracy (Count 1) in violation of 18 U.S.C. § 371,[a] the general conspiracy statute, with making a false statement to a United States agency (Count 2) in violation of 18 U.S.C. §§ 1001[b] and 2,[c] with concealing or covering up material facts (Counts 3, 5, and 7) in violation of 18 U.S.C. §§ 1001 and 2, and with filing false claims with an agency of the United States (Counts 4, 6, and 8) in violation of 18 U.S.C. §§ 287[d] and 2.

Defendant says that the essence of his appeal is that the Government failed to prove "materiality"—it failed to show how his acts might have affected in any significant way the decisions of the Government agency involved, the Economic Development Administration (EDA). Defendant argues that the trial court erred: (1) in denying a motion for judgment of acquittal, the evidence being insufficient to support the charges; (2) in submitting the issue of materiality to the jury; (3) in instructing the jury improperly on the issue of materiality; (4) in admitting evidence concerning the eligibility for reimbursement of certain expenses under a federal grant; (5) in failing to instruct the jury on the element of trick, scheme, or device for the nondisclosure counts under § 1001; and (6) in failing to dismiss the false claim counts under § 287 due to the Government's failure to set forth in the indictment the essential elements of materiality and specific intent.

We set aside the convictions on Counts 1, 3, 5, and 7 and affirm the convictions on Counts 2, 4, 6 and 8 for reasons that follow.

a. Section 371, United States Code, Title 18 makes it a crime for "two or more persons [to] conspire either to commit any offense against the United States, or to defraud the United States * * *."

b. At the time of Irwin's conduct, section 1001, United States Code, Title 18 provided:

"Whoever, in any matter within the jurisdiction of any department or agency of the United States knowingly and willfully falsifies, conceals or covers up by any trick, scheme, or device a material fact, or makes any false, fictitious or fraudulent statements or representations, or makes or uses any false writing or document knowing the same to contain any false, fictitious or fraudulent statement or entry, shall be fined not more than $10,000 or imprisoned not more than five years or both."

c. Section 2, United States Code, Title 18 provides that whoever aids, abets, counsels, commands, induces, procures or causes the commission of any offense against the United States, is punishable as a principal.

d. Section 287, United States Code, Title 18 provides:

"Whoever makes or presents to any person or officer in the civil, military, or naval service of the United States, or to any department or agency thereof, any claim upon or against the United States, * * * knowing such claim to be false, fictitious, or fraudulent, shall be imprisoned not more than five years and shall be subject to a fine of $10,000 [currently amended to a fine of $250,000 for an individual, $500,000 for a corporation, to an alternative fine pursuant to 18 U.S.C. § 3571.]"

I.

THE FACTUAL BACKGROUND

Viewing all the evidence, together with all reasonable inferences therefrom in the light most favorable to the Government, as we must on this appeal from a guilty verdict, the evidence tended to show the following facts.

In 1974 the city of Delta, Colorado, became interested in the development of an industrial park, a project which was being promoted by a local business group called the Delta County Development Co. In February 1974 the Delta city council hired Management Services Company (MSC), a trade name used by defendant, to provide assistance in obtaining federal and state funds to finance the project. Defendant's compensation under this contract was to be based, in part, on a percentage of any Government grant or loan obtained for the city through his efforts.

After being informed by a United States Congressman that the percentage method of compensating defendant for his work was illegal, the city council entered into a second contract with defendant in June 1974. Under it, Delta was obligated to pay the defendant $150 per day for his efforts in attempting to secure federal or state funds for various projects in which Delta became involved. In addition, defendant was to be reimbursed for all reasonable costs related to the preparation of grant and loan applications and for all related travel and entertainment expenses.

Although defendant began to work for Delta under the first contract in February 1974, he apparently did not bill the city for his services and expenses until September 4, 1974. Between September 4, 1974 and April 1, 1975, Irwin submitted to Delta three separate bills which purportedly represented the services rendered and the expenses incurred under the two contracts between April 10, 1974, and March 28, 1975. These bills, which totaled approximately $21,000, were paid by Delta out of its own funds.

On October 18, 1974, defendant submitted on behalf of Delta a federal grant application to the Economic Development Administration (EDA) to secure funding for the city's industrial park project. Irwin admitted at trial that he prepared the EDA grant application with some minor help from other individuals and that he was responsible for reviewing the application for its accuracy and completeness. The evidence further indicates that when EDA officials who reviewed the application found it to be incomplete or unclear, it was defendant's responsibility to rectify the problems.

After several meetings with EDA officials in which defendant provided further documentation and clarification of the information contained in the application, EDA finally approved it and made an "offer of grant" on March 19, 1975 which the city of Delta accepted on March 28, 1975.

Count 2 of the indictment concerns one page of the grant application which was approved and accepted by EDA.

In August 1974, a few months prior to the time that defendant submitted the grant application to EDA, he met with Robert J. Adams, an unindicted coconspirator, to discuss the engineering needs for Delta's industrial park project. Although Adams and his company, A & S Consultants (A & S), had performed engineering work for the city of Delta since 1967, he did not at the time of his meeting with Irwin have a contract with Delta to be the project engineer for the industrial park project.

During this meeting Adams orally agreed that if he became project engineer for Delta's industrial park project, he would pay Irwin for services primarily related to the preparation of the EDA grant application. Sometime subsequent to this initial meeting Adams became project engineer and agreed to pay Irwin $18,000 for the work he did pursuant to their oral agreement. At the time Irwin told Adams that any payments to Irwin would be eligible costs under the EDA grant.

After EDA had made its grant offer in March 1975, it was quite apparent that some of the services for which Irwin expected payment from Adams were declared by EDA to be ineligible for payment with grant funds. Adams and Irwin still agreed, however, that Irwin would be paid $18,000 for his services despite the fact that some of those services were known to be ineligible for payment with grant funds. Adams testified that it was their intention that any payment to Irwin would be derived from the grant funds.

In May 1975, subsequent to EDA's approval of Delta's grant application, Irwin was appointed by the Delta city council to a salaried position as city manager. In this position Irwin became a central figure in the disbursement of funds for the industrial park project which was being financed in part by the EDA grant.

As city manager, Irwin was the city's receiving agent for bills and invoices that were submitted for work done on capital projects such as the industrial park. Although the city council had final authority to authorize payment on a bill, Irwin was responsible for the initial screening and review of the incoming bills. By his own testimony, Irwin had the authority to authorize payment on bills prior to the final approval by the city council.

Once the federal grant money became available for disbursement to Delta, Irwin and Adams would send to EDA a monthly itemized list of costs incurred by Delta on the industrial park project which were to be reimbursed under the EDA grant. Each monthly statement to EDA also contained a compilation of the bills received that month and the payments made by Delta. Each bill would be stamped "approved" and would bear the date and initials of both Irwin and Adams.

Between August 1975 and October 1975 Adams submitted to Irwin as Delta's city manager three separate bills on A & S stationery for professional services rendered on Delta's industrial park project. Each A & S bill contained a charge for services allegedly performed by Irwin, although there was no indication of this fact on the bill. These bills were approved by Irwin as city manager and were paid by Delta. In at least one instance, Irwin authorized payment to A & S prior to the final approval of the city council. After each A & S bill was paid by Delta, it was then submitted in a monthly statement to EDA by Irwin and Adams for approval and reimbursement under the grant. These three bills became the basis for Counts 3–8.

Shortly after each payment to A & S by Delta, Adams would give Irwin a check for an amount which corresponded to a particular item on the bill paid by Delta. Defendant ultimately received approximately $18,000 from Adams. Further evidence will be detailed as necessary in discussing Irwin's appellate contentions, to which we now turn.

II.

The Count 2 False Statement Charge

Count 2 charges that defendant violated 18 U.S.C. §§ 1001 and 2 by willfully and knowingly making or causing to be made a false statement as to material facts in the EDA grant application which he prepared and submitted on behalf of Delta. The indictment specifically alleges that Irwin stated and represented in the EDA grant application that his company, MSC, had "received no compensation for services performed in connection with the application," when in fact he knew that MSC "had received compensation from the City of Delta for these services and expected to receive additional compensation from the City of Delta for these services." Defendant contends that the evidence failed to show that a false statement was made or that it was material.

The essential elements which the Government must prove in a false statement prosecution under § 1001 are that (1) the defendant made a statement; (2) the statement was false, fictitious or fraudulent as the defendant knew; (3) the statement was made knowingly and willfully; (4) the statement was within the jurisdiction of the federal agency; and (5) the statement was material.

The page of the EDA grant application containing the alleged false statements requires the applicant to list *inter alia* the names of all persons "engaged by or on behalf of the applicant * * * for the purpose of expediting applications made to * * * [EDA] for financial assistance * * *." In addition the applicant is required to state in separate columns the "total compensation" and the "compensation already paid" to each person listed. In the event that no one is employed for the purpose of expediting the application, then the applicant is required to indicate this fact by putting the word "none" on the form.

Delta's grant application to EDA indicated that MSC had been hired as "planning and administrative consultants." Under the column marked "total compensation" a zero (0) was entered, while the column marked "compensation already paid" was left blank. At trial Irwin testified and explained that the application was prepared in different stages and that MSC had not received any payment from Delta for its services at the time this part of the application was completed. He admits, however, that by the time he submitted the grant application to EDA in October 1974, Delta had paid him in part for his work on the application and he expected further payment in the future. On this appeal he argues that he did indicate in the application that MSC was being paid for its services since he listed it as a grant expediter, that leaving the "compensation already paid" column blank is inconsistent with the alleged misrepresentation that MSC received no compensation from Delta for its services, and that the zero in the "total compensation" column concerns past compensation and only demonstrates his confusion since no listing is required where no compensation is to be paid.

We cannot agree that the evidence fails to show that a false statement was being made in Delta's grant application to EDA. "Leaving a blank is equivalent to an answer of 'none' or a statement that there are no facts required to be reported." If there are facts that should be reported, leaving a blank belies the certification on the front page of the application that the information therein is "true and correct." The testimony and exhibits clearly show that Irwin submitted MSC's first bill to Delta on September 4, 1974 for $9,404.38 for services rendered between April and August of 1974; that Delta issued a check to MSC for this same amount on October 2, 1974; and that Irwin cashed this check on October 4, 1974—approximately 14 days before he submitted the grant application to EDA on October 18, 1974. We think the jury could find beyond a reasonable doubt that a false statement was made on the grant application concerning the amount of compensation paid by Delta to MSC for expediting the application and that Irwin knowingly and willfully made the false statement or caused it to be made.

Defendant's final contention with regard to Count 2 of the indictment deals with the materiality of the false statement. Not only does he challenge the evidence as being insufficient to show that the false statement was material, but he also claims that the trial court erred in submitting the issue of materiality to the jury and in instructing the jury as to this issue.

The record reflects that Irwin requested and submitted an instruction on the issue of materiality and that the district court gave the defendant's tendered instruction, changing only a few words of it. Defendant does not cite any portion of the record, nor can we find any instance, showing that he made a timely objection to the district court's submission of the materiality issue to the jury. Under these circumstances, defendant cannot claim as error that which he invited.[8]

---

8. Even if Irwin had raised a timely objection to the district court's action, under our past cases materiality is a factual question for submission to the jury with proper instructions.

Defendant argues that the majority rule is that materiality is a question of law for the court in prosecutions under § 1001, and that the trial court erred here in submitting the issue to the jury. We are not persuaded that our procedure is wrong and remain

The district court instructed the jury, *inter alia*, that:

"The making of a false statement or the concealment of the material fact to an agency of the United States Government is not an offense unless the statement made or fact concealed is material.

"A material statement or fact is one that has a natural tendency or is capable of inducing action by the agency, in this case the * * * [EDA]."

Relying on United States v. Radetsky, 535 F.2d 556 (10th Cir.1976), Irwin objected to this instruction, claiming that the word "payment" should be used in lieu of the word "action" because the latter word was too ambiguous and permitted the jury to base its decision on trivial agency actions. On this appeal Irwin argues that the proper test for materiality is whether the statement was capable of inducing "payment" or "of influencing a determination or decision required to be made." Consequently he argues that his conviction must be reversed because the district court's instruction permitted the jury to make a finding of materiality based on some "trivial bureaucratic response" to the statement in the grant application.

In Gonzales v. United States, 286 F.2d 118 (10th Cir.1960), we held that the test for materiality is whether the falsification "has a natural tendency to influence, or was capable of influencing, the decision of the tribunal in making a determination required to be made." The form of an instruction is a matter committed to the discretion of the trial court and there is no requirement that the court adopt the exact language of a requested instruction, provided that the issues of the case are adequately covered. We are satisfied that the change was not in error and that it was not prejudicial to the defendant to use the word "action" in lieu of "payment."

We also must reject defendant's claim that the Government failed to prove the materiality of the false statement. Shirley Marshall, the senior civil engineer who reviewed Delta's application, testified in depth about the EDA review process for grant applications. Marshall was asked about the effect on EDA of an applicant's acknowledgment that someone had been paid a specific amount of money for expediting the grant application. He replied that an investigation would be conducted, that EDA would want to know who was involved and what was done to expedite the application, and that EDA would determine if any of the fees paid to the expediter were eligible for payment with grant funds. He testified that no investigation would be started if the grant applicant indicated on the application that no fees had been paid to an expediter and that EDA did not care if the grant applicant hired someone to expedite the application, so long as no grant funds were used to pay the expediter for his services.

convinced that materiality is a factual question to be submitted to the jury with proper instructions like other essential elements of the offense, unless the Court rules, as a matter of law, that no submissible case is made out by the Government on the issue of materiality.

We think the evidence amply supports a jury finding that the false statement in Delta's grant application was material and had the capacity to influence EDA's decision to offer Delta financial assistance for its industrial park project. Consequently we uphold the conviction on Count 2.

III.

THE CONCEALMENT OR COVERING UP CHARGE OF COUNTS 3, 5 AND 7

Counts 3, 5 and 7 charge that defendant violated 18 U.S.C. §§ 1001 and 2 by willfully and knowingly concealing and covering up material facts in a matter within the jurisdiction of EDA. Although each count relates to a specific item on separate A & S bills, each alleges that Irwin concealed the same material facts on the bills, to wit: (1) that MSC had received or would receive a payment from A & S for services performed on the industrial park project; (2) that MSC had already received payment from Delta for all or part of these services; and (3) that all or part of the money received by MSC from A & S was for services which EDA had previously declared ineligible for payment from Delta's federal assistance grant. Count 7 also charged Irwin with the concealment of a fourth material fact, namely, that MSC did not perform any part of the revision of design on Crawford Avenue. These material facts were allegedly concealed by the trick of billing the sums paid by A & S to MSC on the letterhead bills of A & S as part of the fee for A & S's architectural and engineering services.

Irwin argues, *inter alia,* that the Government failed to prove that there was a duty to disclose in A & S's bills to Delta the facts allegedly concealed. Specifically he points to the lack of evidence showing that any statute, EDA regulation, or form required disclosure of the facts which he now stands convicted of concealing. The Government does not deny that in a § 1001 concealment prosecution it must prove that the defendant had a duty to disclose the information which is alleged to have been concealed. Instead it basically contends that § 1001 prosecutions are not limited to those statements which are required to be made by law or regulation and that the proof sufficiently shows that Irwin and A & S had a duty to disclose the concealed information.

We agree that § 1001 prosecutions are not limited to *statements* which are required to be made by law or regulation. We think, however, that the Government's argument misses the point since we are dealing not with a false statement, but rather with the concealment or nondisclosure of material facts. We believe that it was incumbent on the Government to prove that the defendant had the duty to disclose the material facts at the time he was alleged to have concealed them. And, of course, there can be no criminal conviction for failure to disclose when no duty to disclose is demonstrated. Further support for this position is found in the district court's instructions to the jury.[9]

---

9. The charge stated in part:
An act is done willfully if done voluntarily and intentionally and *with specific intent* to do something the law forbids; that is to say with bad purpose, either to disobey or to disregard the law.

We are persuaded that it must be established by the Government that the law required disclosure of the information at the time the defendant allegedly concealed it to sustain such charges. The Government was required to show that there was a legal duty to disclose to EDA the material facts which were allegedly concealed when Irwin caused the payments to him to be billed on the letterhead bills of A & S as part of the fee for A & S's architectural and engineering services on Delta's industrial park project.

The Government attempted to show through the testimony of Shirley Marshall that A & S, as project engineer, was obligated to disclose in its billings to Delta that Irwin and MSC received or would receive a payment from A & S for services performed on the industrial park project. Marshall testified that project engineers frequently subcontract work out to others and that the subcontractors are required to submit invoices for the work performed to enable EDA to review the work and to approve it for reimbursement under the grant. He further indicated that it was customary for the project engineer to disclose in its bills to the grant recipient the names of the subcontractors and the work performed by them.

On cross-examination, however, Marshall admitted that the project engineer does not have to indicate on its bills to the grant recipient the names of every employee or subcontractor who does work on the project. The defense also introduced the testimony of Fred Van Remortel, an ex-EDA official who had been a regional director for the agency. Van Remortel testified that there was nothing wrong with the project engineer subcontracting work out to others and that he was not aware of any EDA regulation or law which required the project engineer to include in its bills the names and time of the subcontractors doing work for it. He further indicated that he was not aware of any law or regulation requiring an individual to disclose or report to the EDA that he is acting as a grant expediter and as a subcontractor on the same project. There was no contradiction of this testimony of Mr. Van Remortel and we are referred to no such statutes or regulations by the Government.

We must agree that it was not shown that there was a legal duty to disclose in A & S's bills to Delta the payments made by A & S to MSC or the other matters involved. Consequently the convictions on Counts 3, 5 and 7 cannot stand.

* * *

To cause another person to commit a criminal act, it is necessary that the accused willfully do something which * * * results in the other persons either doing something the law forbids or *failing to do something which the law requires to be done.*

Once again, an act, or a failure to act, is willfully done if done voluntarily and intentionally and with specific intent to do something which the law forbids, *or with specific intent to fail to do something which the law requires to be done;* that is to say, again, with bad purpose either to disobey or to disregard the law.

IV.

THE COUNT 1 CONSPIRACY CHARGE

Count 1 charged defendant with a violation of 18 U.S.C. § 371. More specifically, Count 1 charged that between September 1974 and September 1976 Irwin and Adams conspired: (1) to defraud the United States by depriving it of its money and property, by deceiving EDA officials assigned to administer the grant, and "by circumventing, defeating, evading, and frustrating safeguards and processes established by * * * [EDA] for the proper award and sound administration of federal grants"; and (2) to commit offenses against the United States, namely 18 U.S.C. § 1001, by using a trick, scheme, and device to falsify, conceal, and cover up material facts in matters within the jurisdiction of EDA.

Irwin argues, *inter alia,* that the conspiracy conviction on Count 1 must be set aside because materiality of nondisclosure alleged in Counts 3, 5 and 7 was not proved, and that those nondisclosures offenses may have been used by the jury to reach the conspiracy verdict by finding defendant guilty under the second part of the charge—conspiracy "to commit offenses against the United States * * *." He says that his argument on lack of proof of materiality on the § 1001 counts (Counts 3, 5 and 7) thus requires reversal of the conspiracy conviction; that materiality with respect to these nondisclosure counts was not shown because the Government failed to demonstrate that there was duty to disclose the specified facts, and how nondisclosure could affect EDA decisions; and that since it cannot be determined whether the jury may have based the conspiracy conviction on the theory of conspiracy to commit these unproven § 1001 offenses, the conspiracy conviction must be set aside.

* * * [We agree] that [because] it cannot be determined whether the jury based its conspiracy verdict on a conspiracy to commit those very offenses, the conspiracy conviction cannot stand.

Accordingly, the conviction on Count 1 is set aside.

V.

THE FALSE CLAIM CHARGES OF COUNTS 4, 6 AND 8

Counts 4, 6 and 8 charge that defendant violated 18 U.S.C. §§ 287 and 2 by presenting or causing to be presented to EDA for payment three claims for engineering services performed by A & S in connection with Delta's industrial park project, knowing the claims to be "false, fictitious, and fraudulent in that a substantial part of the work so claimed did not consist of engineering services performed by A & S * * *." Each count is based on one of three bills that were submitted by A & S to Delta for services performed on the industrial park project.

Irwin argues that each false claim count should have been dismissed by the district court because the indictment failed to set forth the essential elements of specific intent and materiality. Alternatively he claims that his motion for judgment of acquittal should have been granted because the evidence failed to show "how the claims were false, fictitious, or fraudulent and how EDA payment decisions could be potentially affected by the same."

A.   Sufficiency of the indictment

Defendant argues that the greater weight of authority supports the position that § 287 is a specific intent crime requiring an allegation and proof that the defendant acted intentionally or willfully in submitting the false claim to the Government. He relies on cases requiring a finding of specific intent before liability can attach under the civil False Claim Act, 31 U.S.C. § 231. Defendant acknowledges that the district court did instruct the jury that the Government had to prove beyond a reasonable doubt that he acted knowingly and willfully. Nevertheless he argues that an oral instruction cannot cure a defective indictment, particularly where it is given to the jury for use in its deliberations.

With respect to materiality, defendant admits that "§ 287 does not expressly set forth materiality as an essential element" and that "no cases could be found which require such construction." He argues, however, that "this court should read into § 287 a materiality requirement" as was "done judicially with respect to the second clause of § 1001." This judicial requirement is necessary, he says, to insure the reasonable application of § 287 and to exclude trivial falsehoods from its purview.

The Government responds that "willfulness" and "materiality" are not elements of a § 287 crime and that consequently there was no need to specifically allege these facts in the indictment. Support for this position is found the Government says, in the fact that Congress specifically included the elements of willfulness and materiality in the statutory language of § 1001 while omitting the terms from the language of § 287 and from the Congressionally approved Form 10, Fed.R.Crim.P.

It is fundamental that an indictment must contain the elements of the offense charged, that it fairly inform the defendant of the charge against which he must defend, and that it enable him to plead an acquittal or conviction in bar of future prosecution for the same offense. It is generally sufficient that an indictment set forth the offense in the words of the statute, as long as those words of themselves fully, directly and expressly, without any uncertainty or ambiguity, set forth all the elements necessary to constitute the offense. We think that the indictment in this case, which essentially follows the language of § 287, meets this requirement.

It is true, as defendant points out, that 18 U.S.C. §§ 287 and 1001 were originally part of the same statute and that § 1001 expressly requires willfulness. However, like the Fifth Circuit in United States v. Cook, 586 F.2d 572, 575 (5th Cir.1978), we are persuaded that the inclusion of the term "willfully" in § 1001 and the omission of the term in § 287 suggests a Congressional intent to exclude this state of mind from the essential elements of the latter offense. This construction is fortified by the fact that Congressionally approved Form 10, Fed.R.Crim. P., designed for § 287 indictments, omits willfulness as an element of the offense. Although the forms are merely illustrative, see Rule 58, Fed.R.Crim.P., we think that Form 10 is "strong evidence of what the criminal law requires." Accordingly we hold that willfulness is not an essential element of 18 U.S.C. § 287 and that the indictment is not insufficient merely because it fails to allege that the defendant acted willfully.

For similar reasons we do not read into § 287 a materiality requirement as we did with respect to the second clause of § 1001 in Gonzales v. United States, supra, 286 F.2d at 120–21. There is no indication in either the statutory language of § 287 or its legislative history that Congress intended materiality to be an essential element of a § 287 offense. Admittedly there are cases indicating that materiality is an essential element of § 287. These cases, however, do not consider the effect of Form 10, Fed.R.Crim.P., on the question. We think that Form 10 is persuasive that an indictment in such form is sufficient. Consequently we hold that materiality is not an essential element of § 287 and need not be alleged in an indictment charging a violation of that statute. Therefore the district court did not err when it refused to dismiss Counts 4, 6 and 8 on this ground.

B. Sufficiency of the evidence

Defendant also argues that the Government failed to establish that the claims were false, fictitious, or fraudulent. It appears that defendant not only challenges the sufficiency of the evidence on this point but also claims there is a variance between the allegations in the indictment and the evidence presented at trial.

Defendant correctly points out that the indictment specifically alleges that the claims submitted by A & S were false, fictitious, and fraudulent because "a substantial part of the work so claimed did not consist of engineering services performed by A & S." He admitted at trial that the services listed on A & S's bills to Delta were not performed entirely by A & S. He says, however, that this fact does not make A & S's bills false, fictitious, or fraudulent because the evidence clearly establishes that the project engineer (A & S) commonly hires other individuals to do parts of the project work and then bills the grant recipient (Delta) for these services without revealing this fact on the bills. He argues that his convictions on the false claim counts must be reversed since there is no proof that A & S's claims are false, fictitious, or fraudulent when they fail to identify specifically the work performed by subcontractors.

The Government contends that the evidence is sufficient to prove each element of the crimes charged. It argues that the three A & S bills presented to EDA by Delta as part of claims for reimbursement under the EDA grant were false, fictitious, and fraudulent "because they purportedly represented the amount due for work performed entirely by * * * A & S" when in fact some of the work had been performed by MSC or had not been performed at all.

Section 287 prohibits making or presenting a claim to any United States agency, knowing that it is "false, fictitious, or fraudulent." The disjunctive term "or" clearly indicates that making any one of the three types of proscribed claims would subject the claimant to criminal liability. Thus a claim need not be fraudulent so long as it is false or fictitious.

We must agree with the defendant that the proof is insufficient to establish that A & S's bills were false, fictitious, or fraudulent because of the failure to itemize and identify on the bills the work performed by subcontractors. However, we conclude that there was evidence tending to show that the claims submitted by Irwin to A & S, and subsequently submitted by A & S to Delta and EDA, were false because they purportedly represented the amount due for work which in fact had not been performed by or on behalf of A & S. Consequently we hold that the district court did not err when it denied Irwin's motion for judgment of acquittal on the false claim counts.

Although not specifically stated Irwin appears to argue, as he did at trial, that the convictions on the false claim counts cannot be upheld since the evidence does not show that the claims were false, fictitious, or fraudulent in the manner alleged in the indictment. As noted above, we have held that the evidence sufficiently establishes that the claims were false because A & S billed for services which were not performed. Admittedly the indictment does not specifically allege that the claims were false in this manner. Nevertheless we think that if any variance exists between the evidence and the allegations in the indictment, it clearly has not affected defendant's substantial rights.

We have consistently held that a variance between the indictment and the proof is fatal only if the defendant could not have anticipated from the allegations in the indictment what the evidence would be at trial or if a conviction based on the indictment would not bar a subsequent prosecution for the same offense. There is no showing in this record that either of these circumstances exists. Consequently any variance that may exist between the indictment and the proof is not prejudicial to the defendant and therefore may be disregarded. Rule 52(a), Fed.R.Crim.P.

VI.

Conclusion

We have examined defendant's remaining contentions, and find they are without merit and require no further discussion. Accordingly, the convictions and sentences on Counts 2, 4, 6, and 8 are affirmed; the convictions and sentences on Counts 1, 3, 5, and 7 are set aside. The cause is remanded for dismissal of Counts 3, 5, and 7 and for a new trial on Count 1.

Notes

1. List, side by side, the elements which, according to the *Irwin* opinion, the government must prove to convict on § 287 and on § 1001. Were you surprised by the court's ruling that the elements differ? Are the

differences warranted by the statutory language in each section? Assuming, as would often be the case, that one factual situation could be charged as either a violation of § 287 or § 1001, which section would a prosecutor prefer to use? Why?

2. The *Irwin* court held that the test for materiality is "whether the falsification 'has a natural tendency to influence, or was capable of influencing the decision of the tribunal in making a determination required to be made.' " Does this appear to be a stringent standard for proving materiality?

What evidence did the government introduce to prove the materiality of Delta's failure to disclose payments for expediting the grant for the industrial park? With what type of evidence did the defendant counter this testimony?

Note that in *Irwin,* the Tenth Circuit ruled that materiality is a question of fact for the jury. Nine years later, the Tenth Circuit reversed its position and joined nine of the ten other circuits in holding that materiality is a question of law for the court.[e] Only the Ninth circuit adhered to the view that materiality, in section 1001 cases, was an issue for the jury.

In 1995, however, the Supreme Court agreed with the position taken by the Ninth Circuit. United States v. Gaudin, 515 U.S. 506 (1995). Citing the Fifth Amendment's right to due process and the Sixth Amendment's right to a "speedy and public trial, by an impartial jury," the Court held that a defendant is entitled to a "jury determination that the defendant is guilty of every element of the crime with which he is charged, beyond a reasonable doubt." *Id.* at 509. Because materiality is an element of section 1001, the Court held, a "trial judge's refusal to allow the jury to pass on the materiality [element] * * * infringed that right." *Id.* at 518.

3. It appears that the Tenth Circuit's conclusion that "willfully" is an element of § 1001 but not an element of § 287 generally is followed by the other circuits, although few other courts have addressed the distinction as directly as did the Tenth Circuit. For example, in United States v. Precision Medical Laboratories, Inc., 593 F.2d 434 (2d Cir.1978), the defendant, who was convicted for violating § 287, argued that the jury instructions improperly identified the *mens rea* requirement of § 287. The trial court had instructed the jury that "willfully" was the mens rea for § 287. The Second Circuit rejected the defendant's claim of error but seemed to imply that the more stringent standard of "willfully" was not required by § 287: "If the words willfully and unlawfully, found in the indictment but not the statute, had any effect at all, it was to place a more exacting standard on what the Government had to prove." *Id.* at 444.

Similarly ambiguous is Johnson v. United States, 410 F.2d 38 (8th Cir.1969), which seems to suggest that "knowledge" and "willfulness" are synonymous. In dispelling a claim by the defendant that § 287 was unconstitutionally vague, the court discussed the mens rea requirement of § 287:

> "Generally, under our system of criminal law, an individual is only punished when he has the requisite criminal intent accompanying the performance of the act. To have this requisite intent, the individual must be aware that what he is doing is wrong. But, this is not to say

e. United States v. Daily, 921 F.2d 994, 1004 (10th Cir.1990).

that he must have exact knowledge of the relevant criminal provisions governing his conduct. The defendant here was charged with knowingly making a false claim to a government agency. Sufficient evidence was introduced to establish that the defendant was well aware of the essential requirements of the contract with the government and that he acted in complete disregard of those requirements both before and after making the claim. The jury was thoroughly instructed that they must find that the defendant intentionally made false, fictitious and fraudulent claims and statements to find him guilty. The requirement that the government prove, as an essential element of their case, that the defendant's conduct was 'willful' relieves the statute of the objection that it punished without adequate warning." *Id.* at 47–48.

4. Note that there are three different types of conduct prohibited in § 1001: (1) concealing a material fact, (2) making a false, fictitious or fraudulent statement concerning a material fact, (3) making or using any writing or document containing a false, fictitious or fraudulent statement or entry concerning a material matter. It is a crime under § 1001 to commit any of these three types of conduct.

Can you determine which type of conduct was charged in count two of the charges against Irwin? What was the false statement at issue? Counts 3, 5, and 7, which alleged § 1001 violations arising from the A & S bills submitted to Delta, were charged as which type of § 1001 conduct? What information was allegedly concealed by this billing method?

The *Irwin* court held that before a person can be found guilty of willfully and knowingly concealing material facts in violation of § 1001, the government must show that the person had a legal duty to disclose the facts in question. What type of evidence did the government introduce to prove such a duty? With what type of evidence did the defense successfully neutralize this effort by the government?

5. Irwin was convicted on conspiracy charges—and successfully won a reversal of this conviction. What were the "goals" of the alleged conspiracy for which Irwin was convicted and how were these goals relevant to the court's decision to set aside the conspiracy conviction? Were you convinced that the conspiracy conviction should be set aside?

6. After Irwin obtained reversals on the conspiracy count and three of the four § 1001 counts in the foregoing opinion, Irwin filed a petition for rehearing in which he argued that his three § 287 convictions should be set aside. The court's opinion overruling Irwin's petition for rehearing provides another opportunity to examine the importance of articulating an appropriate "theory of the case."

Before examining the court's ruling on this petition for rehearing, recall that the § 1001 counts involved A & S bills submitted to Delta, wherein A & S failed to disclose that the these bills included an amount for "professional services" which A & S paid to Irwin's Company, MSC. Recall also that the § 287 counts involved these same bills, now submitted by Delta to the government agency, EDA, to obtain reimbursement to Delta for its payments to A & S. In the prior opinion, of course, the court held that there was no violation of § 1001 for concealing of A & S's payments to MSC because the government had failed to prove that there was a duty to disclose these payments.

In his petition for rehearing Irwin argued that the jury convicted him on the § 287 counts on the basis of evidence ruled to be insufficient as a matter of law, and that the Tenth Circuit affirmed his § 287 convictions on a theory that was not tried or submitted to the jury. The Tenth Circuit responded as follows to these arguments:

"It is true that * * * [our] opinion concluded that the proof was insufficient to show that A & S's bills were false, fictitious or fraudulent because of failure to identify on the bills the work performed by subcontractors. Moreover, the indictment was furnished to the jury with the general allegations concerning false claims counts 4, 6 and 8 that the claims were 'false, fictitious and fraudulent in that a substantial part of the work so claimed did not consist of engineering services performed by A & S Consultants, Inc.' Nevertheless, as [this court] stated, there was evidence tending to show that the claims submitted by defendant Irwin to A & S, and subsequently submitted by A & S to Delta and the EDA, were false because they purportedly represented the amount due for work not in fact performed by or on behalf of A & S. This theory of the Government that such services were not performed at all or were exaggerated was argued and tried. We must disagree, therefore, with defendant's contention that '[e]ven if a jury could reasonably conclude that services billed had not been performed at all, there was virtually never any government allegation to that effect in the indictment, in pretrial hearings, in the instructions, or in the government's opening statement.'

"Instead, we note that during the pre-trial hearing on various defense motions the trial court asked the Assistant United States Attorney to explain the Government's theory behind the false claim counts. After some discussion on other points the trial court had the following colloquy with the Assistant United States Attorney:

The Court: The Government didn't get the benefit. That's what you saying?

Mr. Nottingham: That's right.

The Court: The Government's beneficiaries didn't get the benefit?

Mr. Nottingham: That's right.

The Court: So, it is as if materials were ordered, billed for and never supplied?

Mr. Nottingham: That's our position, your Honor, and I don't know how I could have made it anymore clear [sic] or any clearer * * *.

"Similarly, the same Assistant United States Attorney told the jury in his opening statement that he intended to prove, among other things, that the number of hours which A & S billed to Delta for engineering work performed on the industrial park project 'were exaggerated all out of proportion,' were 'padded,' and were 'inflated.' He further indicated that some of the services which defendant had supposedly performed had not in fact been done. In his closing argument to the jury the

Assistant United States Attorney again argued that the evidence showed the work supposedly performed by Irwin on the project which was billed to Delta through A & S was 'exaggerated' or 'wasn't done.'

"Defense counsel also recognized that the Government had attempted to prove during the trial that A & S's bills to Delta were false because they contained claims for services which had not been performed. This was admitted during argument on the mid-trial and post-trial motions for judgment of acquittal. During the hearing on the post-trial motion for judgment of acquittal, the district court noted: 'Of course, it's an issue as to whether there were any services * * *. If you construe the evidence in the light favorable to the Government, there weren't any services.'

"Thus we are satisfied that there was notice of and evidence submitted on the theory that the services were not performed at all or were exaggerated. This manner of proof was not so out of the bounds of the allegations of the indictment as to be impermissible, nor was it a prejudicial variance. We are therefore also convinced that this case does not come within the rule of Dunn v. United States, 442 U.S. 100, 99 S.Ct. 2190, 60 L.Ed.2d 743 (1979), so that reversal under it is required, as defendant argues.

"What we have said also disposes of defendant's * * * argument * * * that since one theory on the false claim counts has been held insufficient as a matter of law, and since it is impossible to determine if the jury relied on that theory, the convictions cannot stand. We feel it unrealistic to predicate this argument on the assumption that the jury relied on the unsupported theory that the A & S bills were false because they failed to itemize and identify the work performed by subcontractors. As spelled out above, the Government argues the position which the evidence did support—that the work was not performed at all or was exaggerated— along with the other theory which was not supported by the proof.

"Accordingly, the panel concludes that the petition for rehearing should be overruled."

Although the Tenth Circuit found that the government had used the "claim-for-no-work-done" theory in presenting its case against Irwin to the jury, note the potential effectiveness of this argument for the defense. Generally, how could a defendant be prejudiced when the government switches its "theory of the case" during a trial or a court rules, on appeal, on a theory that was not presented to the jury?

———

Also in 1995, the Supreme Court resolved a split in the circuits on another issue concerning section 1001: whether there is a "judicial function exception" to § 1001 liability.

HUBBARD v. UNITED STATES

United States Supreme Court, 1995.
514 U.S. 695.

STEVENS, JUSTICE.

In unsworn papers filed in a bankruptcy proceeding, petitioner made three false statements of fact. Each of those misrepresentations provided the basis for a criminal conviction and prison sentence under the federal false statement statute, 18 U.S.C. § 1001. The question we address is whether § 1001 applies to false statements made in judicial proceedings.

I

In 1985, petitioner filed a voluntary petition for bankruptcy under Chapter 7 of the Bankruptcy Code. In the course of the proceedings, the trustee filed an amended complaint and a motion to compel petitioner to surrender certain business records. Petitioner opposed the relief sought by the trustee in a pair of unsworn, written responses filed with the Bankruptcy Court. Both of his responses contained falsehoods. Petitioner's answer to the trustee's complaint falsely denied the trustee's allegations that a well-drilling machine and parts for the machine were stored at petitioner's home and in a nearby warehouse. Petitioner's response to the trustee's discovery motion incorrectly stated that petitioner had already turned over all of the requested records.

When the misrepresentations came to light, petitioner was charged with three counts of making false statements under 18 U.S.C. § 1001.[1] That statute provides:

> "Whoever, in any matter within the jurisdiction of any department or agency of the United States knowingly and willfully falsifies, conceals or covers up by any trick, scheme, or device a material fact, or makes any false, fictitious or fraudulent statements or representations, or makes or uses any false writing or document knowing the same to contain any false, fictitious or fraudulent statement or entry, shall be fined not more than $10,000 or imprisoned not more than five years, or both."

Relying on our decision in United States v. Bramblett, 348 U.S. 503 (1955), the District Court instructed the jury that a bankruptcy court is a "department of the United States" within the meaning of § 1001. The jury convicted petitioner on all three § 1001 counts, and the District Court sentenced him to concurrent terms of 24 months' imprisonment.

On appeal to the Court of Appeals for the Sixth Circuit, petitioner argued that his convictions under § 1001 were barred by the so-called "judicial function" exception. First suggested over 30 years ago in Morgan v. United States, 309 F.2d 234 (C.A.D.C.1962), this doctrine

---

1. Petitioner was also charged with, and convicted of, bankruptcy fraud and mail fraud under 18 U.S.C. §§ 152 and 1341 (1988 ed. and Supp. V). The validity of those convictions is not before us.

limits the extent to which § 1001 reaches conduct occurring in the federal courts. Under the exception, only those misrepresentations falling within a court's "administrative" or "housekeeping" functions can give rise to liability under § 1001; false statements made while a court is performing its adjudicative functions are not covered.

The Court of Appeals affirmed petitioner's convictions under § 1001. Although the judicial function exception has become entrenched over the years in a number of Circuits, the Sixth Circuit concluded, over a dissent, that the exception does not exist. That conclusion created a split in the Circuits, prompting us to grant certiorari.[2] We now reverse.

II

Section 1001 criminalizes false statements and similar misconduct occurring "in any matter within the jurisdiction of any department or agency of the United States." In ordinary parlance, federal courts are not described as "departments" or "agencies" of the Government. As noted by the Sixth Circuit, it would be strange indeed to refer to a court as an "agency." And while we have occasionally spoken of the three branches of our Government, including the Judiciary, as "department[s]," that locution is not an ordinary one. Far more common is the use of "department" to refer to a component of the Executive Branch.

As an initial matter, therefore, one might be tempted to conclude that § 1001 does not apply to falsehoods made during federal court proceedings. * * *

* * *

In the case of § 1001, there is nothing in the text of the statute, or in any related legislation, that even suggests—let alone "shows"—that the normal definition of "department" was not intended. Accordingly, a straightforward interpretation of the text of § 1001, with special emphasis on the words "department or agency," would seem to lead inexorably to the conclusion that there is no need for any judicial function exception because the reach of the statute simply does not extend to courts. Our task, however, is complicated by the fact that the Court interpreted "department" broadly 40 years ago in *Bramblett*. We must, therefore, turn our attention to that case before deciding the fate of the judicial function exception.

III

Defendant Bramblett was a former Member of Congress who had falsely represented to the Disbursing Office of the House of Representa-

---

2. The judicial function exception has been recognized in the following cases: United States v. Masterpol, 940 F.2d 760, 764–766 (C.A.2 1991); United States v. Holmes, 840 F.2d 246, 248 (C.A.4 1988); United States v. Abrahams, 604 F.2d 386, 393 (C.A.5 1979); United States v. Mayer, 775 F.2d 1387, 1390 (C.A.9 1985) (per curiam); United States v. Wood, 6 F.3d 692, 694–695 (C.A.10 1993). Although the Seventh and District of Columbia Circuits have questioned the basis of the exception, *see* United States v. Barber, 881 F.2d 345, 350 (C.A.7 1989); United States v. Poindexter, 951 F.2d 369, 387 (C.A.D.C.1991), the Sixth Circuit stands alone in unambiguously rejecting it.

tives that a particular person was entitled to compensation as his official clerk. He argued that he could not be convicted under § 1001 because his falsehood was directed to an office within the Legislative Branch. The Court rejected this argument, concluding that the word "department," as used in § 1001, "was meant to describe the executive, legislative and judicial branches of the Government." *Id.*, at 509. Although *Bramblett* involved Congress, not the courts, the text and reasoning in the Court's opinion amalgamated all three branches of the Government. Thus, *Bramblett* is highly relevant here even though its narrow holding only extended § 1001 to false statements made within the Legislative Branch.

. We think *Bramblett* must be acknowledged as a seriously flawed decision. Significantly, the *Bramblett* Court made no attempt to reconcile its interpretation with the usual meaning of "department." It relied instead on a review of the evolution of § 1001 and its statutory cousin, the false claims statute presently codified at 18 U.S.C. § 287, as providing a "context" for the conclusion that "Congress could not have intended to leave frauds such as [Bramblett's] without penalty." 348 U.S. at 509. We are convinced that the Court erred by giving insufficient weight to the plain language of §§ 6 and 1001. Although the historical evolution of a statute—based on decisions by the entire Congress— should not be discounted for the reasons that may undermine confidence in the significance of excerpts from congressional debates and committee reports, a historical analysis normally provides less guidance to a statute's meaning than its final text. * * *

* * *

What, then, of the earlier statutory history chronicled in *Bramblett*? We believe it is at best inconclusive, and that it does not supply a "context" sufficiently clear to warrant departure from the presumptive definition in 18 U.S.C. § 6.

* * *

Putting *Bramblett*'s historical misapprehensions to one side, however, we believe the *Bramblett* Court committed a far more basic error in its underlying approach to statutory construction. Courts should not rely on inconclusive statutory history as a basis for refusing to give effect to the plain language of an Act of Congress, particularly when the Legislature has specifically defined the controverted term. * * *

Whether the doctrine of stare decisis nevertheless requires that we accept Bramblett's erroneous interpretation of § 1001 is a question best answered after reviewing the body of law directly at issue: the decisions adopting the judicial function exception.

IV

Although other federal courts have refrained from directly criticizing *Bramblett*'s approach to statutory construction, it is fair to say that they have greeted the decision with something less than a warm embrace. The judicial function exception, an obvious attempt to impose limits on

Bramblett's expansive reading of § 1001, is a prime example. As the following discussion indicates, the judicial function exception is almost as deeply rooted as *Bramblett* itself.

The seeds of the exception were planted by the Court of Appeals for the District of Columbia Circuit only seven years after *Bramblett* was decided. In Morgan v. United States, 309 F.2d 234 (C.A.D.C.1962), the defendant, who had falsely held himself out to be a bona fide member of the bar, was prosecuted on three counts of violating § 1001 for concealing from the court his name, identity, and nonadmission to the bar. After first acknowledging that, but for *Bramblett*, it might well have accepted the argument that Congress did not intend § 1001 to apply to the courts, the Court of Appeals upheld the conviction. But the Court was clearly troubled by the potential sweep of § 1001. Noting that the statute prohibits "concealment" and "covering up" of material facts, as well as intentional falsehoods, the Court wondered whether the statute might be interpreted to criminalize conduct that falls well within the bounds of responsible advocacy.[9] The Court concluded its opinion with this significant comment:

> "We are certain that neither Congress nor the Supreme Court intended the statute to include traditional trial tactics within the statutory terms 'conceals or covers up.' We hold only, on the authority of the Supreme Court construction, that the statute does apply to the type of action with which appellant was charged, action which essentially involved the 'administrative' or 'housekeeping' functions, not the 'judicial' machinery of the court." *Ibid.*

* * *

Once planted, the judicial function exception began to flower in a number of other Circuits. The Ninth Circuit summarized the state of the law in 1985:

> "[T]he adjudicative functions exception to section 1001 has been suggested or recognized by appellate decisions since 1962, not long after the Supreme Court decided that section 1001 applies to matters within the jurisdiction of the judicial branch. In these twenty-three years, there has been no response on the part of Congress either repudiating the limitation or refining it. It therefore seems too late in the day to hold that no exception exists." United States v. Mayer, 775 F.2d 1387, 1390 (per curiam) (footnote omitted).

* * *

Although not all of the courts of appeals have endorsed the judicial function exception, it is nevertheless clear that the doctrine has a substantial following. Moreover, as * * * the Ninth * * * Circuit[] observed, Congress has not seen fit to repudiate, limit, or refine the

---

9. " 'Does a defendant "cover up . . . a material fact" when he pleads not guilty?' 'Does an attorney "cover up" when he moves to exclude hearsay testimony he knows to be true, or when he makes a summation on behalf of a client he knows to be guilty?' " Morgan v. United States, 309 F.2d 234, 237 (C.A.D.C.1962).

exception despite its somewhat murky borders and its obvious tension with the text of the statute as construed in *Bramblett*. On the other hand, it is also true that Congress has not seen fit to overturn the holding in *Bramblett*, despite the fact that the opinions endorsing the judicial function exception evidence a good deal of respectful skepticism about the correctness of that decision.

V

With the foregoing considerations in mind, we now turn to the difficult *stare decisis* question that this case presents. It is, of course, wise judicial policy to adhere to rules announced in earlier cases. As Justice Cardozo reminded us, "[t]he labor of judges would be increased almost to the breaking point if every past decision could be reopened in every case, and one could not lay one's own course of bricks on the secure foundation of the courses laid by others who had gone before him." B. Cardozo, The Nature of the Judicial Process 149 (1921). Adherence to precedent also serves an indispensable institutional role within the Federal Judiciary. *Stare decisis* is "a basic self-governing principle within the Judicial Branch, which is entrusted with the sensitive and difficult task of fashioning and preserving a jurisprudential system that is not based upon 'an arbitrary discretion.'" Respect for precedent is strongest "in the area of statutory construction, where Congress is free to change this Court's interpretation of its legislation." [citations omitted]

In this case, these considerations point in two conflicting directions. On one hand, they counsel adherence to the construction of § 1001 adopted in *Bramblett*; on the other, they argue in favor of retaining the body of law that has cut back on the breadth of *Bramblett* in Circuits from coast to coast. It would be difficult to achieve both goals simultaneously. For if the word "department" encompasses the Judiciary, as *Bramblett* stated, the judicial function exception cannot be squared with the text of the statute. A court is a court—and is part of the Judicial Branch—whether it is functioning in a housekeeping or judicial capacity. Conversely, *Bramblett* could not stand if we preserved the thrust of the judicial function exception—*i.e.*, if we interpreted 18 U.S.C. § 1001 so that it did not reach conduct occurring in federal court proceedings. Again, although *Bramblett* involved a false representation to an office within the Legislative Branch, the decision lumped all three branches together in one and the same breath. ("department" in § 1001 "was meant to describe the executive, legislative and judicial branches of the Government").

We think the text of § 1001 forecloses any argument that we should simply ratify the body of cases adopting the judicial function exception. We are, however, persuaded that the clarity of that text justifies a reconsideration of *Bramblett*. Although such a reconsideration is appropriate only in the rarest circumstances, we believe this case permits it because of a highly unusual "intervening development of the law," and because of the absence of significant reliance interests in adhering to *Bramblett*.

The "intervening development" is, of course, the judicial function exception. In a virtually unbroken line of cases, respected federal judges have interpreted § 1001 so narrowly that it has had only a limited application within the Judicial Branch. This interpretation has roots both deep and broad in the lower courts. Although the judicial function exception has not been adopted by this Court, our review of *Bramblett* supports the conclusion that the cases endorsing the exception almost certainly reflect the intent of Congress. It is thus fair to characterize the judicial function exception as a "competing legal doctrin[e]," that can lay a legitimate claim to respect as a settled body of law. Overruling *Bramblett* would preserve the essence of this doctrine and would, to that extent, promote stability in the law.

* * * [Moreover] the reliance interests at stake in adhering to *Bramblett* are notably modest. In view of the extensive array of statutes that already exist to penalize false statements within the Judicial Branch, see, *e.g.*, 18 U.S.C. § 1621 (perjury); § 1623 (false declarations before grand jury or court); § 1503 (obstruction of justice); § 287 (false claims against the United States), we doubt that prosecutors have relied on § 1001 as an important means of deterring and punishing litigation-related misconduct. But we need not speculate, for we have direct evidence on this point. The United States Attorneys' Manual states quite plainly that "[p]rosecutions should not be brought under 18 U.S.C. § 1001 for false statements submitted in federal court proceedings"; it instead directs prosecutors to proceed under the perjury or obstruction of justice statutes. United States Attorneys' Manual ¶ 9–69.267 (1992). Clearer evidence of nonreliance can scarcely be imagined.[15]

Similarly unimpressive is the notion of congressional reliance on *Bramblett*. The longstanding judicial function exception has, to a large extent, negated the actual application of § 1001 within the Judiciary. It is unlikely that Congress has relied on what has, for many years, been an unfulfilled promise.

In sum, although the *stare decisis* issue in this case is difficult, we conclude that there are sound reasons to correct *Bramblett*'s erroneous construction of § 1001. Although we could respect prior decisions by endorsing the judicial function exception or by adhering to *Bramblett* while repudiating that exception, we believe coherence and stability in the law will best be served in this case by taking a different course. Limiting the coverage of § 1001 to the area plainly marked by its text

---

15. The absence of significant reliance interests is confirmed by an examination of statistical data regarding actual cases brought under § 1001. The Government has secured convictions under § 1001 in 2,247 cases over the last five fiscal years, but the dissent can identify only five reported § 1001 cases in that time period brought in connection with false statements made to the Judiciary and Legislature. (At least two of the five were unsuccessful, from the Government's point of view.) This tiny handful of prosecutions does not, in our view, evidence a weighty reliance interest on the part of prosecutors in adhering to the interpretation of § 1001 set forth in *Bramblett*.

will, as a practical matter, preserve the interpretation of § 1001 that has prevailed for over 30 years and will best serve the administration of justice in the future.

VI

Bramblett is hereby overruled. We hold that a federal court is neither a "department" nor an "agency" within the meaning of § 1001. The Court of Appeals' decision is therefore reversed to the extent that it upheld petitioner's convictions under § 1001.

It is so ordered.

Justice SCALIA, with whom Justice KENNEDY joins, concurring in part and concurring in the judgment.

I concur in the judgment of the Court, and join Parts I–III and VI of Justice STEVENS' opinion. United States v. Bramblett, 348 U.S. 503 (1955), should be overruled.

The doctrine of *stare decisis* protects the legitimate expectations of those who live under the law, and, as Alexander Hamilton observed, is one of the means by which exercise of "an arbitrary discretion in the courts" is restrained. Who ignores it must give reasons, and reasons that go beyond mere demonstration that the overruled opinion was wrong (otherwise the doctrine would be no doctrine at all).

The reason here, as far as I am concerned, is the demonstration, over time, that *Bramblett* has unacceptable consequences, which can be judicially avoided (absent overruling) only by limiting *Bramblett* in a manner that is irrational or by importing exceptions with no basis in law. Unlike Justice STEVENS, I do not regard the courts of appeals' attempts to limit *Bramblett* as an " 'intervening development of the law,' " that puts us to a choice between two conflicting lines of authority. Such "intervening developments" by lower courts that we do not agree with are ordinarily disposed of by reversal. Instead, the significance I find in the fact that so many Courts of Appeals have strained so mightily to discern an exception that the statute does not contain, is that it demonstrates how great a potential for mischief federal judges have discovered in the mistaken reading of 18 U.S.C. § 1001, a potential we did not fully appreciate when *Bramblett* was decided. To be sure, since § 1001's prohibition of concealment is violated only when there exists a duty to disclose, it does not actually prohibit any legitimate trial tactic. There remains, however, a serious concern that the *threat* of criminal prosecution under the capacious provisions of § 1001 will deter vigorous representation of opposing interests in adversarial litigation, particularly representation of criminal defendants, whose adversaries control the machinery of § 1001 prosecution.

One could avoid the problem by accepting the Courts of Appeals' invention of a "judicial function" exception, but there is simply no basis in the text of the statute for that. Similarly unprincipled would be rejecting *Bramblett*'s dictum that § 1001 applies to the courts, while adhering to *Bramblett*'s holding that § 1001 applies to Congress. This would construct a bizarre regime in which "department" means the Executive and Legislative Branches, but not the Judicial, thereby contradicting not only the statute's intent (as *Bramblett* does), but, in addition, all conceivable interpretations of the English language. Neither of these solutions furthers the goal of avoiding "an arbitrary discretion in the courts"; they seem to me much more arbitrary than simply overruling a wrongly decided case.

The other goal of *stare decisis*, preserving justifiable expectations, is not much at risk here. Those whose reliance on *Bramblett* induced them to tell the truth to Congress or the courts, instead of lying, have no claim on our solicitude. Some convictions obtained under *Bramblett* may have to be overturned, and in a few instances wrongdoers may go free who could have been prosecuted and convicted under a different statute if *Bramblett* had not been assumed to be the law. I count that a small price to pay for the uprooting of this weed.

CHIEF JUSTICE REHNQUIST, with whom JUSTICE O'CONNOR and JUSTICE SOUTER join, dissenting.

The bankruptcy trustee objected to the discharge of petitioner, a voluntary bankrupt, believing that he had filed false information. The trustee filed a complaint under 11 U.S.C. § 727, alleging petitioner stored a well-drilling machine at his residence; petitioner answered by denying the allegation "for the reason that it is untrue." The trustee also alleged in a separate motion that petitioner had, despite requests, failed to turn over all the books and records relating to the bankruptcy estate. Petitioner filed a response denying the allegation, and asserting that he had produced the requested documents at the behest of a previous trustee. Petitioner was then indicted under 18 U.S.C. § 1001, and a jury found that each of these responses was a lie.

Today, the majority jettisons a 40–year-old unanimous decision of this Court, United States v. Bramblett, 348 U.S. 503 (1955), under which petitioner's conviction plainly would have been upheld. It does so despite an admission that the Court's reading of § 1001 in *Bramblett* was "not completely implausible." In replacing *Bramblett*'s plausible, albeit arguably flawed, interpretation of the statute with its own "sound" reading, the Court disrespects the traditionally stringent adherence to *stare decisis* in statutory decisions. The two reasons offered by the plurality in Part V of the opinion and the justification offered by the concurring opinion fall far short of the institutional hurdle erected by our past practice against overruling a decision of this Court interpreting an act of Congress.

The first reason is styled as an "intervening development in the law"; under it, decisions of courts of appeals that cannot be reconciled with our earlier precedent are treated as a basis for disavowing, not the aberrant court of appeals decisions, but, *mirabile dictu* our own decision! This novel corollary to the principle of *stare decisis* subverts the very principle on which a hierarchical court system is built. The second reason given is that there has been little or no reliance on our *Bramblett* decision; I believe that this ground is quite debatable, if not actually erroneous.

* * *

* * * The principle of stare decisis is designed to promote stability and certainty in the law. * * *

[I]n the present day federal court system, where review by this Court is almost entirely discretionary, a different regime prevails. We receive nearly 7,000 petitions for certiorari every Term, and can grant only a tiny fraction of them. A high degree of selectivity is thereby enjoined upon us in exercising our certiorari jurisdiction, and our Rule 10 embodies the standards by which we decide to grant review. One of the reasons contained in Rule 10.1(a) is the existence of a conflict between one court of appeals and another. The negative implication of this ground, borne out time and again in our decisions to grant and deny certiorari, is that ordinarily a court of appeals decision interpreting one of our precedents—even one deemed to be arguably inconsistent with it—will not be reviewed unless it conflicts with a decision of another court of appeals. This fact is a necessary concomitant of the limited capacity in this Court.

One of the consequences of this highly selective standard for granting review is that this Court is deprived of a very important means of assuring that the courts of appeals adhere to its precedents. It is all the more important, therefore, that no actual inducements to ignore these precedents be offered to the courts of appeals. But today's decision is just such an inducement; it tells courts of appeals that if they build up a body of case law contrary to ours, their case law will serve as a basis for overruling our precedent. It is difficult to imagine a more topsy-turvy doctrine than this, or one more likely to unsettle established legal rules which the doctrine of *stare decisis* is designed to protect.

The plurality offers a second reason in defense of its decision to overrule *Bramblett*. It points to a lack of significant reliance interests in *Bramblett*. It dispels any reliance prosecutors might have in enforcement of § 1001 by arguing that the government has expressed a preference for proceeding under alternative statutes that punish comparable behavior. U.S. Department of Justice, United States Attorneys' Manual ¶ 9–69.267 (1992). The Government offered a convincing explanation for this preference: it instructs prosecutors to proceed under alternative statutes due to the uncertain mine field posed by the judicial function exception adopted in some but not all circuits. I do not think the Government disclaims reliance by adopting a defensive litigating strategy in response to the choice of lower courts to disregard precedent favorable to the Government. And in this particular case, the perjury alternative in 18 U.S.C. § 1621 was altogether unavailable to punish petitioner's falsehoods because his statements were not verified, and the obstruction of justice alternative in 18 U.S.C. § 1503 was of dubious utility.

The additional comments set forth in the concurring opinion equally disregard the respect due a unanimous decision rendered by six justices who took the same oath of office sworn by the six justices who overrule *Bramblett* today. The doctrine of *stare decisis* presumes to reinforce the notion that justice is dispensed according to law and not to serve "the proclivities of individuals." Vasquez v. Hillery, 474 U.S. 254, 265 (1986). The opinion of one justice that another's view of a statute was wrong, even really wrong, does not overcome the institutional advantages conferred by adherence to *stare decisis* in cases where the wrong is fully redressable by a coordinate branch of government.

This, then is clearly a case where it is better that the matter be decided than that it be decided right. *Bramblett* governs this case, and if the rule of that case is to be overturned it should be at the hands of Congress, and not of this Court.

Notes

1. Note the policy reasons given by the plurality and concurring opinions in favor of the judicial function exception. Do you agree that a judicial function exception is needed in § 1001?

2. What do you think about overruling *Bramblett*? If you agree that it should be overruled, do you find the plurality's or the concurring Justices' rationale more persuasive?

3. In 1996 Congress responded to the Court's decision in *Hubbard* by revising § 1001. The current version of § 1001 is:

(a) Except as otherwise provided in this section, whoever, in any matter within the jurisdiction of the executive, legislative, or judicial branch of the Government of the United States, knowingly and willfully—

    (1) falsifies, conceals, or covers up by any trick, scheme, or device a material fact;

    (2) makes any materially false, fictitious, or fraudulent statement or representation; or

    (3) makes or uses any false writing or document knowing the same to contain any materially false, fictitious, or fraudulent statement or entry;

shall be fined under this title or imprisoned not more than 5 years, or both.

(b) Subsection (a) does not apply to a party to a judicial proceeding, or that party's counsel, for statements, representations, writings or documents submitted by such party or counsel to a judge or magistrate in that proceeding.

(c) With respect to any matter within the jurisdiction of the legislative branch, subsection (a) shall apply only to—

    (1) administrative matters, including a claim for payment, a matter related to the procurement of property or services, personnel or employment practices, or support services, or a document re-

quired by law, rule, or regulation to be submitted to the Congress or any office or officer within the legislative branch; or

(2) any investigation or review, conducted pursuant to the authority of any committee, subcommittee, commission or office of the Congress, consistent with applicable rules of the House or Senate.

———

In 1988, Congress enacted the Major Fraud Act of 1988 to "curb[] the losses taxpayers suffer as a result of major fraud in connection with million-dollar contractors."[f] It was also intended to "curb procurement fraud that can cause the loss of life of American soldiers and thereby threaten national security."[g] Codified at 18 U.S.C. § 1031, the Major Fraud Act is aimed at $1 million contracts. As the next case demonstrates, courts are split over basic elements in the major Fraud Act.

UNITED STATES v. BROOKS

United States Court of Appeals, Fourth Circuit, 1997.
111 F.3d 365.

NIEMEYER, CIRCUIT JUDGE.

This case requires us to interpret for the first time the $1 million jurisdictional amount requirement of 18 U.S.C. § 1031(a), criminalizing "major fraud" against the United States.

Defendants Edwin Brooks, his sons John and Stephen Brooks, and their company, B & D Electric Supply, Inc., were charged with several crimes in relation to two subcontracts to provide electrical components to prime contractors engaged in refitting ships for the United States Navy. All four defendants were convicted of trafficking in counterfeit goods, in violation of 18 U.S.C. § 2320(a), and of conspiracy to defraud the United States and to traffic in counterfeit goods, in violation of 18 U.S.C. § 371. Edwin Brooks, John Brooks, and B & D Electric were also convicted of "major fraud" against the United States in violation of 18 U.S.C. § 1031(a). * * * On appeal, the defendants challenge the district court's interpretation of the major fraud statute as well as several evidentiary rulings, a jury instruction, and the sufficiency of the evidence sustaining several of their convictions. Finding none of the defendants' arguments persuasive, we affirm their convictions. * * *

I

The three Brooks defendants were operators of B & D Electric Supply, Inc., a marine electrical supply business which sold electrical parts to both civilian and military customers. The majority of B & D Electric's business consisted of reselling new components produced by well-established manufacturers of electrical parts. But B & D Electric

f. S.R. 101–7, 101st Cong., 1st Sess.   **g.** *Id.*
(Mar. 13, 1989).

also sold some electrical components which it custom-assembled, often out of used parts.

The charges at issue in this case arose from supply contracts that B & D Electric had with two prime contractors engaged by the United States Navy to refit several ships. B & D Electric contracted with the Jonathan Corporation to supply fourteen shipboard motor controllers meeting military specifications for a total price of $51,544. B & D Electric itself assembled these controllers from components but affixed to the controllers trademarks of the Cutler–Hammer Company, an approved military supplier of controllers. B & D Electric also supplied Ingalls Shipbuilding, Inc., with six rotary switches for a total price of $1,470, representing the switches as new when B & D Electric actually had assembled or rebuilt them. The dollar amount of the prime contract between Jonathan Corporation and the Navy was greater than $9 million, and prime contract between Ingalls Shipbuilding and the Navy was greater than $5 million.

II

Edwin Brooks, John Brooks, and B & D Electric challenge their convictions for major fraud against the United States in violation of 18 U.S.C. § 1031(a), on the jurisdictional ground that their two subcontracts did not satisfy the $1 million value prescribed by the statute. While the government does not dispute that the defendants' subcontracts were for amounts less than $1 million, it argues that the statute's jurisdictional requirement is established so long as the prime contract with the United States or any part thereof is worth $1 million. The issue is one of first impression for us.

As with all questions of statutory interpretation, we begin with the language of the statute, which provides:

> Whoever knowingly executes, or attempts to execute, any scheme or artifice with the intent—
>
> (1) to defraud the United States; or
>
> (2) to obtain money or property by means of false or fraudulent pretenses, representations, or promises,
>
> in any procurement of property or services as a prime contractor with the United States or as a subcontractor or supplier on a contract in which there is a prime contract with the United States, *if the value of the contract, subcontract, or any constituent part thereof, for such property or services is $1,000,000 or more* shall, subject to the applicability of subsection (c) of this section, be fined not more than $1,000,000, or imprisoned not more than 10 years, or both.

18 U.S.C. § 1031(a) (emphasis added). From a straightforward reading of this statute, we conclude that regardless of its privity with the United States, any contractor or supplier involved with a prime contract with the United States who commits fraud with the requisite intent is guilty so long as the prime contract, a subcontract, a supply agreement, or any constituent part of such a contract is valued at $1 million or more.

This reading recognizes that the seriousness of this species of fraud is measured not merely by the out-of-pocket financial loss incurred on a particular subcontract, but also by the potential consequences of the fraud for persons and property. In military contracts in particular, fraud in the provision of small and inexpensive parts can have major effects, destroying or making inoperable multi-million dollar systems or equipment, injuring service people, and compromising military readiness. By extending the statute's coverage even to minor contractors and suppliers whose fraudulent actions could undermine major operations, Congress enabled prosecutors to combat effectively the severe procurement fraud problem that Congress identified.

We understand that our reading is contrary to that espoused in dictum by the Second Circuit in United States v. Nadi, 996 F.2d 548 (2d Cir.1993), the only other court to have interpreted the jurisdictional amount requirement of the major fraud statute. That court stated that for purposes of ascertaining the jurisdictional amount requirement of 18 U.S.C. § 1031(a), "the value of the contract is determined by looking to the *specific* contract upon which the fraud is based." *Id.* at 551 (emphasis added). It explained that "[t]his reading avoids the potential anomaly of small subcontractors whose subcontracts are valued at far less than $1,000,000 being prosecuted under the Act simply because the prime contract is for $1,000,000 or more." *Id.* But the jurisdictional amount requirement of the major fraud statute, like any bright line rule, dictates that some cases will fall outside of the scope of the law. We believe that our reading of the statute is no more anomalous than one which allows small subcontractors to escape prosecution under the provision, regardless of the cost of the overall project which their fraud affects, simply by ensuring that their own subcontract stays below the $1 million jurisdictional amount. The *Nadi* court's interpretation could significantly undermine the purpose of the statute because pervasive fraud on a multi-million dollar defense project would be unreachable under the statute, despite Congress' intent, if it were perpetrated in multiple separate subcontracts, each involving less than the jurisdictional amount.

The legislative history also supports our interpretation that the statute reaches fraud where any part of the prime contract or subcontract is valued at $1 million or more. In discussing the steady increase in procurement fraud losses, the Senate described its broad range of concern:

> Procurement fraud is the most costly kind of fraud, accounting for about 18 percent of total losses. The Department of Defense reports losses of $99.1 million due to procurement fraud for fiscal years 1986 and 1987.

> Prosecutions of individual companies reveal other disturbing facts:

> Two corporate officials of Spring Works, Inc., were convicted of deliberately providing defective springs for installation in critical assemblies of the CH-47 helicopters, the Cruise Missile and the F-18 and B-1 aircraft.

Two corporate officials of MKB Manufacturing were sentenced for their role in the deliberate provision of defective gas pistons for installation in the M60 machine gun. Installation of the defective part would cause the machine gun to jam.

Thus, the evidence shows that besides causing financial losses, procurement fraud could cause the loss of life of American soldiers and could threaten national security.

These facts compel a legislative response.

S.Rep.No. 100–503, at 2 (1988), *reprinted in* 1988 U.S.C.C.A.N. 5969, 5969–70 (citations omitted). The parts at issue in the Spring Works case were 21–cent springs, and the total value of the subcontract was $160.25. Yet, it was fraud like that perpetrated by Spring Works to which Congress was responding in 1988 with enactment of the major fraud statute. Undoubtedly, Congress was concerned with more than the most direct and narrow financial effects of fraud committed against the United States.

The legislative history also illuminates the meaning of the phrase in § 1031(a) at issue here, "value of the contract." In the section-by-section analysis, the Senate report states:

> Section 1031(a) applies to procurement fraud "if the value of the contract, subcontract, or any constituent part thereof . . . is $1,000,-000 or more." The phrase "value of the contract" refers to the value of the contract award, or the amount the government has agreed to pay to the provider of services whether or not this sum represents a profit to the contracting company. Furthermore, a subcontractor awarded a subcontract valued at $1,000,000 or more is covered by this section, regardless of the amount of the contract award to the contractor or other subcontractors.

S.Rep.No. 100–503, at 12 (1988), *reprinted in* 1988 U.S.C.C.A.N. 5969, 5975–76. Thus, for example, if a prime contractor had entered into three separate contracts, agreeing under each to supply the United States with $750,000 worth of equipment, but entered into a single supply contract with a subcontractor for $1 million worth of parts, the subcontractor would be covered by the Act. This Senate report explanation supports the interpretation that the statute applies to the entire procurement effort where any contractual component has a value of $1 million or more, so that a court should not confine its inquiry with regard to the jurisdictional amount of § 1031(a) to the value of the subcontract under which the fraud was perpetrated. As § 1031(a) provides, the statute applies to a government contractor, subcontractor, or supplier if "any constituent part" of the contract is worth more than $1 million.

Accordingly, the district court in this case did not err in taking into account the contract values of the Navy's prime contracts with Jonathan Corporation and Ingalls Shipbuilding.

* * *

Notes

1. Do you agree with the Fourth Circuit's view that the jurisdictional threshold amount of $1 million in § 1031 may be met by looking to the prime contract, even if the prosecution is aimed at subcontractors whose subcontract does not reach $1 million? Does the Fourth Circuit's interpretation permit a prosecution, for example, of a minor subcontractor holding a $150 subcontract but who is retained by a prime contractor holding a $1 million—plus contract? If so, is such a prosecution a good idea?

2. In 1989, Congress amended the Major Fraud Act to include a whistleblower provision rewarding "persons who furnish information relating to possible prosecution under this section." § 1031(g). The reward could reach $250,000 and is to be awarded in the discretion of the Attorney General.

B.   CIVIL CAUSES OF ACTION

The original False Claims Act was passed in 1863 to provide the federal government a way of combating the large number of fraudulent claims made against the Union Army for defective or nonexisting military supplies. This early statute provided criminal and civil penalties for presenting a false claim against the United States.[h]

This statute included a "*qui tam*" provision. "*Qui tam*" comes from the Latin phrase, "*qui tam pro domino rege quam pro se ipso in hac parte sequitur*" which means "who brings the action for the king as well as for himself."[i] The Supreme Court explained the rationale behind *qui tam* actions:

> "The [*qui tam*] statute is a remedial one. It is intended to protect the Treasury against the hungry and unscrupulous host that encompasses it on every side, and should be construed accordingly. It was passed upon the theory, based on experience as old as modern civilization, that one of the least expensive and most effective means of preventing frauds on the Treasury is to make the perpetrators of them liable to actions by private persons acting * * * under the strong stimulus of personal ill will or the hope of gain. Prosecutions conducted by such means compare with the ordinary methods as the enterprising privateer does to the slow-going public vessel."[j]

Qui tam lawsuits are brought by private parties who allege and must prove fraud against the government. If successful, these *qui tam* plaintiffs (known as "relators") collect a percentage of the recovery. The general mechanism for pursuing *qui tam* actions is as follows: An individual who believes he can prove fraud against the federal govern-

---

h. Act of Mar. 2, 1863, Ch. 67, 12 Stat. 696. The False Claims act was reenacted as Rev.Stat. §§ 3490–3494, 5438 (1875 ed.); later codified as 31 U.S.C. §§ 231–235; and finally recodified in 1982 as 31 U.S.C. §§ 3729–3731.

i. Bass Anglers Sportsman's Soc. of America v. U.S. Plywood–Champion Papers, Inc., 324 F.Supp. 302, 305 (S.D.Tex.1971).

j. United States ex rel. Marcus v. Hess, 317 U.S. 537, 63 S.Ct. 379, 87 L.Ed. 443 (1943).

ment files a civil lawsuit. The action is sealed and stayed while the federal government is notified of the lawsuit and given the opportunity to enter as a party. If the government decides to enter as a plaintiff, it pursues the lawsuit; if the government does not enter, the *qui tam* relator may continue to pursue the lawsuit. After the *qui tam* statute was passed in 1863, amendments and judicial decisions weakened *qui tam* actions, so that they were rarely and ineffectively used.[k]

In 1986, Congress amended the False Claims Act to enhance the influence of the *qui tam* relator. It did so in two major ways. First, the *qui tam* relator was allowed to remain actively involved in the case even if the federal government joined as a plaintiff. Previously, once the government decided to enter the lawsuit, the *qui tam* relator had only a minor role with no power to influence the course of the lawsuit. The significance of this change is dramatically demonstrated in a 1989 Ohio case where the government, which chose to join in a fraud suit initiated by a *qui tam* relator against General Electric, was not allowed to settle the case because the *qui tam* relator objected to the settlement amount of $234,000. Later, on the eve of trial, the case was settled, with the *qui tam* relator's consent, for $3.5 million. The *qui tam* relator received $770,000—22% of the government's recovery.[l]

The second substantial change made by the 1986 amendments concerned the amount of recovery allowed the *qui tam* relator. Prior to the 1986 amendments, if the government joined the action, the *qui tam* relator could receive no more than 10% of the recovery, and the *qui tam* relator's share depended on what the court thought was an appropriate amount. The 1986 amendments guarantee that even if the government joins the lawsuit, the *qui tam* relator gets at least 15% of any judgment or settlement and the court can award more—up to 25%. If the government does not join the lawsuit, the *qui tam* relator is guaranteed 25%. Only in cases where the evidence is based on publicly disclosed information does the *qui tam* relator get 10% or less.

The *qui tam* action, which is designed to privatize law enforcement by creating "private attorneys general" who pursue "public interest for profit,"[m] mobilizes the private bar. Before 1986, the Department of Justice (DOJ) received about 6 *qui tam* cases per year.[n] Since the 1986 amendments, more than 1,550 *qui tam* lawsuits have been brought. The government has intervened in 225 of these cases.[o]

———

Numerous challenges have been made to the constitutionality of the False Claims Act's *qui tam* provisions. Thus far these challenges have

k.　Oparil, *The Coming Impact of the Amended False Claims Act,* 22 Akron L.Rev. 525, 526 (1989); Comment, *The Constitutionality of Qui Tam Actions,* 99 Yale L.J. 341, 351 (1989).

l.　France, *The Private War on Pentagon Fraud,* 76 ABA Journal 46, 47 (Mar. 1990).

m.　Id. at 46.

n.　Id. at 48.

o.　Taxpayers Against Fraud Quarterly Review 45 (Jan. 1997).

not been successful although the Supreme Court has not ruled on this issue. The next case, United States ex rel. Truong v. Northrop Corporation, 728 F.Supp. 615 (C.D.Cal.1989), provides a helpful discussion of the constitutional arguments made.

UNITED STATES EX REL. TRUONG v. NORTHROP CORPORATION

United States District Court, Central District of California, 1989.
728 F.Supp. 615.

PFAELZER, DISTRICT JUDGE.

In this action, plaintiffs allege that the officers, employees and agents of Northrop Corporation's Advanced Systems Division conspired to obtain fraudulently, through the preparation of false records and statements and the collaborative omission and suppression of material facts, payments of false claims in connection with the design and manufacture of the "B–2" or "Stealth" bomber. The suit is brought under the False Claims Act ("the Act"), 31 U.S.C.A. §§ 3729 *et seq.*, by *qui tam* relators suing on behalf of the government. Northrop now moves to dismiss the action under Fed.R.Civ.P. 12(b)(1) on the ground that the *qui tam* provisions of the statute are unconstitutional under Article III, the separation of powers doctrine, and the Appointments Clause of Article II.

DISCUSSION

I. The Statute

The False Claims Act was originally enacted in 1863 and has been twice amended, first in 1943 and again in 1986. Under all versions of the Act, individuals have been authorized to "bring a civil action for a violation of [the Act] for the person and for the United States Government." 31 U.S.C.A. § 3730(b)(1).

Briefly stated, the statute as now amended specifies the following procedure with respect to *qui tam* actions: The plaintiff must file his complaint *in camera* where it will remain under seal for at least 60 days to allow the government sufficient time to decide whether or not to enter the action. *Id.* § 3730(b)(2). If the government decides not to join the action—as in the instant case—the action will nonetheless proceed in its behalf at the direction of the relator. *Id.* § 3730(b)(4)(B). The Government may, however, intervene at a later date upon a showing of "good cause." *Id.* § 3730(c)(3).

If the Government does intervene, it assumes primary responsibility for the prosecution, "and shall not be bound by an act of the person bringing the action." *Id.* § 3730(c)(1). The relator continues, however, to be a party to the action and his participation may be limited only by order of the court. *Id.* §§ 3730(c)(2)(C)–(D), 3730(c)(4).

Whether or not the government joins in the suit, the *qui tam* plaintiff is entitled to a portion of the proceeds if the prosecution is successful. If the government does participate, the relator will receive no less than 15 and no more than 25 percent of the bounty. *Id.* § 3730(d)(1). If the Government does not join, recovery is set at 25 to 30 percent. *Id.* § 3730(d)(2).

II. Standing

To have standing under Article III, a plaintiff must show actual or threatened injury that is likely to be redressed if the requested relief is granted. This injury must be concrete, to ensure that the litigant has a personal stake in the outcome of the litigation. The purpose of this requirement is to ensure "that concrete adverseness which sharpens the presentation of issues." Flast v. Cohen, 392 U.S. 83, 99 (1968). Vigorous litigation, however, "is the anticipated consequence of proceedings commenced by one who has been injured in fact; it is not a permissible substitute for the showing of injury itself." Valley Forge Christian College v. Americans United for Separation of Church and State, Inc., 454 U.S. 464, 486 (1982). To this end, while Congress may confer standing statutorily, it may not waive the constitutional minimum of injury in fact.

In accordance with this standard, the courts have refused to recognize the standing of private parties to seek review of the conduct of the executive branch where such individuals have failed to make a showing of personal injury.

Underlying these decisions is the concern that the judicial branch refrain from issuing advisory opinions where the plaintiff has alleged only "abstract injury in nonobservance of the Constitution." In the instant case, by contrast, the alleged injury is not abstract; the fraud which is alleged is fact specific and the damages owing to the government are readily calculable.[2] The court, moreover, is not called upon to interpret the Constitution. It simply must determine whether the statute has been violated, what damages the government has suffered, and the share of the award to which the relator is entitled.

The defendant does not dispute the existence of injury to the government, but contends that the absence of injury in fact to the *qui tam* plaintiffs denies them standing. Plaintiffs have proffered a number of arguments against the application of the injury-in-fact standard to the relator, the first of which is historical. They contend that since *qui tam* actions were authorized in a number of statutes enacted by the First Congress, it is axiomatic that the Framers did not perceive any Article III violation. Moreover, while the constitutionality of this and other *qui tam* statutes has never been squarely addressed by the Supreme Court, Justices Frankfurter and Harlan, who had a generally restrictive view of Article III, intimated that these statutes presented no problems of standing. Additionally, various federal courts have indicated, either

---

2. The complaint alleges, to this end, that Northrop fraudulently inflated production costs for the B–2 Bomber by $300 million to $700 million per unit, for a total in excess of $50 billion.

directly or impliedly, that the False Claims Act passes constitutional muster.

The Court does not find this historical argument persuasive. With the exception of Public Interest Bounty Hunters v. Board of Governors of the Federal Reserve System, 548 F.Supp. 157, 161 (N.D.Ga.1982), the cases cited by Northrop were decided prior to the evolution of modern standing doctrine. Thus, they are of limited use here. More fundamentally, the fact that *qui tam* statutes date back to the time of the First Congress is not independent evidence of their constitutionality. Marbury v. Madison, 5 U.S. 137 (1803), for example, held § 13 of the Judiciary Act, a statute passed by the First Congress, to be unconstitutional.

As an analogue to their historical argument, plaintiffs contend that today, as in 1863 when the False Claims Act was first enacted, the government has insufficient time and resources to prosecute fraud even when officials have been able to detect it. Thus, under these circumstances, Congress has determined that the best way to allocate its limited resources is to "deputize ready and able people who have knowledge of fraud against the government to play an active and constructive role through their counsel to bring to justice those contractors who overcharge the government." 132 Cong.Rec. H9388 (Oct. 7, 1986).

While the paucity of resources is a legitimate justification for authorizing private enforcement of the False Claims Act as a policy matter, it is insufficient in and of itself to confer Article III standing on a private party. Otherwise, the Government could enlist a veritable army of private deputies to enforce its rights under a variety of statutes pursuant solely to a declaration that it did not have the resources to do so itself. There is no authority under Article III for such action. The tenuousness of the historical and resource-based arguments is, however, of no practical consequence for Article III purposes in light of the very clear demonstration of injury to the government and of the relator's personal stake in the litigation.

Where, as here, the presence of injury to the government is not disputed, the application of the injury-in-fact standard to the *qui tam* plaintiff[5] would be purely mechanical. Moreover, such an application would not be consistent with the underlying purpose of Article III which, as stated, is to ensure the genuine adverseness of litigation. Where there is evidence of palpable injury to the entity on whose behalf and in whose

---

5. Plaintiffs have in fact argued that the relator is injured in three different ways. The Court finds none to be persuasive. The first, the potential denial of the statutory bounty, cannot qualify as injury in fact since there is no entitlement to the award. The remaining two, the potential jeopardy to the relator's employment status upon disclosure and the possibility of his exposure to future litigation in the event of nondisclosure, fail on two grounds. First, they lack the requisite "nexus to the substantive character of the statute," being more in the nature of ancillary or collateral concerns. Diamond v. Charles, 476 U.S. 54, 70 (1986). Second, they do not constitute "actual" or "threatened" injury but are more appropriately classified as "speculative harm," which is insufficient evidence of injury in fact.

name the suit is brought, it is superfluous to require that the relator be individually aggrieved.[7]

Whenever it takes prosecutorial action, the government is obliged to designate some party to act on its behalf. Typically, their responsibility is assigned to attorneys within the Department of Justice or to one of the executive agencies, but this is not always the case. For example, under the recently enacted Federal Debt Collections Practices Act, 31 U.S.C.A. § 3718, and Farm Credit Amendments Act, 12 U.S.C.A. § 2244(c), private citizens may be hired to augment government enforcement efforts. In these instances, as with the False Claims Act, standing is based on the existence of a clearly defined, adversarial relationship between the government and the defendant, not between the defendant and the United States' particular legal representative.

In authorizing private prosecutorial action on the government's behalf in the False Claims Act and the other statutes mentioned above, Congress is making a policy decision based on its perception of how best to serve the public interest. By adjudicating these statutory claims, the judicial branch is in essence implementing this legislative definition to the public interest. Recognition of "citizen" standing involves, by contrast, the development of causes of action for plaintiffs in consideration of what, in the courts' opinion, would best advance the public interest. While there may be differing points of view as to whether the court has engaged in policymaking in a particular case, it is certainly clear that the policymaking function is not assigned to the judicial branch. The requirement that citizen plaintiffs demonstrate injury in fact may thus be viewed as doctrine designed to preclude the judiciary from exercising what are essentially executive and legislative functions.

In the instant case, the judicial branch is not called upon to create causes of actions or make any policy determinations. There is a concrete, identifiable claim for fraud against the government the prosecution of which Congress, pursuant to its policymaking authority, has placed under the direction of the *qui tam* relator. As the court need only enforce the policy under the congressionally defined substantive law, it is unnecessary to require that the relator demonstrate injury in fact to comply with Article III. Accordingly, and in sum, Northrop's contention that the *qui tam* plaintiffs lack standing to bring the instant action is without merit.

III. Separation of Powers

Even if the amended False Claims Act satisfies Article III, Northrop contends that it violates the doctrine of separation of powers by uncon-

---

7. To the extent that the relator must have a "personal stake" in the outcome of the litigation, the bounty to which he is entitled if victorious is sufficient. This statutorily-prescribed recovery is distinguishable from attorney's fees, which the Court determined did not create a judicially cognizable interest, since the former "bears no relation to the statute whose constitutionality is at issue." Diamond v. Charles, 476 U.S. 54, 70 (1986).

stitutionally undermining the authority of the executive branch. The Court does not agree.

A. General Principles

The separation of powers doctrine does not require a "hermetic division" between the branches but is intended instead to achieve a Madisonian system of checks and balances characterized by "separateness but interdependence, autonomy but reciprocity." In short, the doctrine acts as "a self-executing safeguard against the encroachment or aggrandizement of one branch at the expense of [an]other." Buckley v. Valeo, 424 U.S. 1, 122 (1976). Thus, where the functions of two coordinate branches are commingled without encroachment or aggrandizement, there is no constitutional violation.

The recent case of Morrison v. Olson, 487 U.S. 654 (1988), indicates the extent to which litigative authority may be commingled between branches. In that case, the Supreme Court considered a separation of powers challenge to the independent counsel provisions of the Ethics in Government Act of 1978. The Act created a "Special Division" of the federal court of appeals for the District of Columbia which was empowered to appoint an independent counsel and define his prosecutorial jurisdiction.

In turning back the challenge, the Court held that the Act did not unduly concentrate authority in one branch or undermine the authority of a coordinate branch. First, since Congress retains no control or supervision of the counsel, there can be no danger of Congressional usurpation of executive power. Likewise, the judicial branch cannot be seen as encroaching on the executive since it is the Attorney General who decides whether or not to seek the appointment of an independent counsel and his decision is unreviewable; while the judicial branch is responsible for appointing the counsel and defining his jurisdiction, these powers "are not supervisory or administrative, nor are they functions that the Constitution requires be performed by officials within the Executive Branch." Id. 108 S.Ct. at 2621. Finally, the Act does not undermine the executive branch's accomplishment of its constitutionally assigned functions since the Attorney General retains significant control over the independent counsel. To this end, the Court noted (a) that the Attorney General may remove a counsel for good cause, (b) that the Attorney General controls the initiation of litigation since no counsel may be appointed absent an application made by him, and (c) a counsel's jurisdiction is determined with reference to the facts submitted by the Attorney General. Id. In light of the foregoing, the Court concluded that

> "[n]otwithstanding the fact that the counsel is to some degree 'independent' and free from Executive supervision to a greater extent than other federal prosecutors, in our view these features of the Act give the Executive Branch sufficient control over the independent counsel to ensure that the President is able to perform his constitutionally assigned duties."

Id. at 2622.

Thus, under Morrison v. Olson, for the *qui tam* provisions of the False Claims Act to pass constitutional muster, the executive branch must retain "sufficient"—as against absolute or total—control over the litigation. Therefore, the specific provisions of the Act must be examined to determine whether the executive's litigative function has been impermissible undermined or usurped by another branch. This discussion is best divided into three sections representing the three phases of the litigative process.

B. False Claims Litigation

1. Phase One: Initiating the Suit

While the statute allows suit to be brought in the government's name without its consent,[9] it can hardly be said that the Attorney General is in any way at the mercy of either the *qui tam* plaintiff or the judicial branch. The government alone has absolute discretion to join the suit. If, moreover, the Government files the action first, a relator is jurisdictionally barred from bringing any action based on the same underlying facts. 31 U.S.C.A. § 3730(e)(3). Even if the government has not filed suit but has made public the findings of an investigation, a private party may not sue unless he is an original and independent source of the information on which the complaint is based. *Id.* § 3730(e)(4)(A)–(B).

The only potential judicial involvement at the initiation of litigation occurs if the government seeks to extend the 60–day investigative period. The government's burden in showing "good cause" for the extension is not particularly onerous and, more importantly, it does not involve any encroachment on the executive function.

2. Phase Two: Conducting the Litigation

In essence, there are three areas of concern with respect to the relator's role in the conduct of the litigation: (1) If the government elects not to intervene, the *qui tam* plaintiff directs the prosecution which nonetheless proceeds in the government's name; (2) if, at a later date, the government changes its mind, it may intervene only with permission of the court pursuant to a showing of "good cause"; (3) if, moreover, a dispute arises at any time between the relator and the government as to the conduct of the suit, the government must ask the court to limit the former's participation; the Attorney General does not himself have the authority to limit the relator's role.

Realistically, some of these concerns are not very significant. While it is true that the plaintiff can continue to prosecute a case in the absence of the government—as in the instant case—the government is not precluded from later litigating the same issue with different parties or relating to different facts. In addition, even if the government chooses not to intervene at the outset, it may nonetheless elect to receive all pleadings and deposition transcripts so that it may monitor the progress

---

9. The relator's authority to sue in the name of the government distinguishes the False Claims Act from most private attor-neys general statutes where citizen plaintiffs must commence suits on their own behalf. See *infra* note 13.

of the litigation and apply for intervention in the event that it determines that the *qui tam* plaintiff is not properly handling the prosecution. 31 U.S.C.A. § 3730(c)(3). If this occurs and the court grants the application, the government then assumes full control of the prosecution. *Id.* § 3730(c)(1). This renders the need for judicial approval of any limitation of the relator's role somewhat inconsequential.

The most significant issue is the government's need to show "good cause" to intervene at a later stage of the prosecution. This differs from most "citizens' suit"[13] provisions in which governmental intervention is of right. Defendant claims that the necessity of court approval limits executive discretion and threatens the integrity of the judicial process by allowing an inexperienced or incompetent plaintiff to represent the government's interests. It is unnecessary, however, to address as a constitutional matter the merit of these fears for Morrison v. Olson makes clear the good cause requirement does not present a separation of powers problem.

In *Morrison,* the Court approved a more intrusive statutory provision which requires the Attorney General to show good cause for the removal of an independent counsel; once removed, however, the judicial branch has the authority to appoint a replacement and the executive branch is at no time authorized to take part in the litigation in any way. In the instant case, by contrast, upon a showing of good cause the government may enter and subsequently orchestrate the prosecution. If, in short, the good cause provisions of the Ethics in Government Act do not encroach impermissibly on executive authority, it is difficult to see how analogous—and more attenuated—provisions in the False Claims Act could be so construed.

3. Phase Three: Terminating the Litigation

If the government joins the suit, it may settle or dismiss it notwithstanding the objections of the relator. 31 U.S.C.A. § 3730(c)(2)(A)–(B).[15] If the government elects not to participate, it may nonetheless intervene to frustrate a settlement it finds unacceptable, provided good cause is shown for the intervention. *See id.* § 3730(c)(3). A relator may, moreover, dismiss an action only with the consent of both the court and the Attorney General. *Id.* § 3730(b)(1).

By the same token, the government also lacks the authority to dismiss an action without the court's consent. This is no cause for concern, however, in light of the wealth of precedent for this sort of requirement. The court must, for example, approve a plea bargain

---

13. In the interest of enhancing enforcement of federal statutes, Congress has authorized private citizens, acting as "private attorneys general" to sue alleged violators. *See, e.g.,* 15 U.S.C.A. § 2619 (Toxic Substances Control Act); 16 U.S.C.A. § 1540(g) (Endangered Species Act Amendments of 1982); 33 U.S.C.A. § 1365 (Clean Water Act).

15. The relator is, however, given the opportunity to voice his objections in a hearing, if he so chooses. 31 U.S.C. § 3730(c)(2)(A)–(B) (West Supp.1988). [It will be up to the court as to whether it will consider such objections in its ruling.]

offered by the government in a criminal case to effectuate the settlement. Similarly, the government may file a dismissal of an indictment, information or complaint under Fed.R.Crim.P. 48(a) only with leave of the court. Other statutory schemes likewise provide for expansive judicial oversight. *See, e.g.*, 15 U.S.C.A. § 16(e) (1982) (court may enter consent judgment proposed by government in antitrust action only if it is in public interest).

In sum, the False Claims Act grants the executive branch greater litigative control than that provided for in the Ethics in Government Act of 1978, which the Supreme Court validated in Morrison v. Olson. Accordingly, defendant's constitutional challenge based on the separation of powers doctrine will not lie.

IV. The Appointments Clause

Defendant's final argument is that the statute violates the Appointments Clause of the United States Constitution[16] by allowing government litigation to be conducted by individuals who are not appointed in one of the ways enunciated in the Clause and thus are not "officers" of the United States. The principle that only "officers" may conduct litigation on behalf of the government was forwarded in Buckley v. Valeo, 424 U.S. 1 (1976), where the Supreme Court held that the Federal Election Commission could not engage in civil law enforcement as long as Congress had a role in appointing its members; "[s]uch functions," the Court stated, "may be discharged only by persons who are 'Officers of the United States' within the language of [the Appointments Clause]." Id. at 140.

To begin with, it seems relatively clear that the relators are not "officers" within the meaning of the Clause. They enjoy limited powers, have no formal duties, hold no established office, have no prescribed tenure, and receive no federal emoluments. As such, they are more appropriately classified as "agents" for Appointments Clause purposes.

If relators are not officers, the False Claims Act seems at first blush to run headlong into Buckley v. Valeo, and thus the Appointments Clause. Upon closer scrutiny, however, it becomes apparent that *Buckley* can be distinguished from the instant case. The former concerned a standing body charged with enforcing federal laws whose members were appointed by Congress, served for a specific tenure, and drew a federal salary. Under these circumstances, the Court was concerned that Congress was encroaching impermissibly on executive branch functions; Congress could not arrogate to itself the power to "enforce [the laws] or appoint the agents charged with the duty of such enforcement."

---

16. The Clause provides, *inter alia*, that the President shall appoint Ambassadors, other public Ministers and Consuls, Judges of the supreme court, and all other Officers of the United States, whose appointments are not otherwise herein provided for, and which shall be established by Law: but Congress may vest the Appointment of such inferior Officers, as they think proper, in the President alone, in the Courts of Law, or in the Heads of Department. U.S. Const. art. II, § 2.

In the instant case, the relator is not appointed by Congress and receives no federal salary. Even more importantly, he is not invested with "primary responsibility" for enforcing the statute in question nor does he have the authority to set policy; he is merely given the right to prosecute a single case, a right which the executive branch may limit in a number of respects. Thus, the underlying rationale of Buckley v. Valeo is simply not apposite here.

Lower courts have, moreover, limited the potential reach of *Buckley,* finding the case inapplicable to private parties. "Buckley v. Valeo, does not stand for the proposition * * * that private persons may not enforce any federal laws simply because they are not Officers of the United States appointed in accordance with Article II of the Constitution." Chesapeake Bay Foundation, Inc. v. Bethlehem Steel Corp., 652 F.Supp. 620, 624 (D.Md.1987); see also NRDC v. Outboard Marine Corp., 692 F.Supp. 801, 816 (N.D.Ill.1988). In both *Chesapeake* and *Outboard Marine*, the court upheld citizen suit provisions of the Clean Water Act against constitutional challenges based on the separation of powers doctrine.

In sum, as long as private participation is not a subterfuge for Congressional control, the executive branch's Article II responsibility to execute the laws faithfully is not threatened. Accordingly, defendant's challenge based on the Appointments Clause cannot survive here.

V.   Conclusion

The False Claims Act, as most recently amended, is not violative of Articles II and III of the Constitution or of the doctrine of separation of powers. Accordingly, defendant Northrop motion to dismiss the complaint under Fed.R.Civ.P. 12(b)(1) is denied.

It is ordered.

Notes

1.   The three issues addressed by the *Northrop* court: standing, separation of powers, and the appointments clause, are the common constitutional questions raised about the *qui tam* provisions of the False Claims Act.

As the court noted, to obtain standing under Article III, "a plaintiff must show actual or threatened injury." In upholding the constitutionality of the statute, the *Northrop* court held that it did not matter whether the *qui tam* relator suffered injury in fact; rather, it was sufficient if the federal government suffered an injury.[p]

In *Comment: The Constitutionality of Qui Tam Actions,* 99 *Yale L.J.* 342 (1989), a different conceptual approach to the standing question is suggested: that the *qui tam* relator's right to share in the monetary recovery confers a sufficient stake in the lawsuit to create standing. *Id.* at 383. There is a

p. Other courts approving of this "assignment" approach include United States *ex rel.* Milam v. M. D. Anderson Cancer Center, 961 F.2d 46, 49 (4th Cir.1992); United States *ex rel.* Kelly v. Boeing, 9 F.3d 743, 748 (9th Cir.1993). See also Thomas R. Lee, *Comment, The Standing Of Qui Tam Relators Under The False Claims Act,* 57 *U.Chi.L.Rev.* 543 (1990).

potential weakness in this approach—"that the plaintiff's interest in the litigation arises from the structure of the litigation itself and not from the defendant's misconduct." *Id.* How serious is this weakness in this approach to standing?[q]

Which approach—the one proposed by the *Yale* article or the one used by the *Northrop* court—do you believe is more sound? Are there other viable theories for conferring standing on the *qui tam* relator?

2. The second constitutional challenge, that *qui tam* actions violate separation of powers because Congress has conferred prosecutive initiative (albeit civil) in "private attorneys general" who are not bound to the executive branch, was also rejected by the *Northrop* court. In reaching its conclusion, the court noted several mechanisms by which the Attorney General controls the *qui tam* relator. Do you believe that the False Claims Act confers sufficient control by the executive branch over the *qui tam* relator?

3. Assuming that the *qui tam* provisions of the False Claims Act are constitutional, is it good public policy to empower "private attorneys general" to ferret out fraud against the government? Granted, governmental prosecutive resources will never be adequate to fight all fraud and private attorneys general could supplement these governmental efforts, however, are there countervailing disadvantages? For example, is it possible that *qui tam* relators will select defendants based upon the chances of a large recovery rather than upon considerations such as deterrence, retribution, and rehabilitation? If true, does it matter? Moreover, could the *qui tam* lawsuit interfere with—or even preclude—fruitful governmental investigation? Are there other competing considerations? How should these policy concerns be resolved?

The aspect of the False Claims Act that has caused the greatest confusion is the "jurisdictional bar" provision. According to the statute, a relator is jurisdictionally barred from bringing a *qui tam* lawsuit when the information leading to the *qui tam* action has become public or is known by the government, unless when the relator is the "original source" of such information.

Since enactment of the False Claims Act in 1863, the jurisdictional bar provision of the False Claims Act has undergone two major revisions. The original False Claims Act of 1863 permitted *qui tam* relators to sue on behalf of themselves and the federal government without regard to how the relator obtained the information about the alleged fraud. During World War II, several law suits alleging defense procurement fraud appeared to be based on publicly disclosed criminal indictments. Although these suits were "parasitical" in nature, the Supreme Court held that they were not barred. United States *ex rel.* Marcus v. Hess, 317 U.S. 537 (1943). The Court noted that there were "strong arguments of

q. Courts adopting this approach include United States *ex rel.* Kreindler v. United Technologies Corp., 985 F.2d 1148, 1153 (2d Cir.1993); United States *ex rel.* Givler v. Smith, 775 F.Supp. 172, 180–81 (E.D.Pa.1991).

policy" against allowing parasitical suits, but found that the plain language of the statute allowed them. *Id.* at 546–47.

After this decision, both the House and the Senate attempted to eliminate parasitical suits, and in 1943 Congress amended the False Claims Act to allow a *qui tam* suit only if the information leading to the suit was not known to the United States when the action was brought. This jurisdictional bar provision remained in effect until United States *ex rel.* State of Wisconsin v. Dean, 729 F.2d 1100 (7th Cir.1984). In *Dean*, the State of Wisconsin brought suit as a *qui tam* relator against a physician for filing allegedly false Medicaid claims with the state of Wisconsin. The Seventh Circuit dismissed the lawsuit finding that Wisconsin was jurisdictionally barred because the United States was "in possession" of the information in the lawsuit at the time the case was filed. The United States was in possession of this information because Wisconsin provided it to a federal agency as required in Medicaid laws. Recognizing the unfairness of its decision, the Seventh Circuit concluded its opinion in *Dean* by suggesting that Congress was the appropriate body from whom relators should seek relief if they believed the 1943 jurisdictional bar provisions led to unfair results. Congress responded almost immediately by amending the jurisdictional bar provision to allow relators, to proceed with *qui tam* law suits when the relator was the "original source" of the public information available regarding the fraud. Gone from the False Claims Act was the language that a *qui tam* lawsuit was barred "when it * * * appear[ed] that such suit was based upon evidence or information in the possession of the United States." 31 U.S.C. § 232(C) (1976). In its place was a provision that barred suits "based on public disclosure * * * in a criminal, civil, or administrative hearing, in a congressional, administrative, or Government Accounting Office report * * * or from the news media," *unless the relator is an "original source" of the information.* § 31 U.S.C. 3730(e)(4)(A).

The 1986 amendments remedied the problem highlighted in *Dean* and opened the door to many relators previously barred by the 1943 amendment. However, the 1986 jurisdictional bar provision, which remains in effect today, has created interpretative difficulties for courts and litigants. The cases in this section address some of these difficulties. The first two cases, United States *ex rel.* John Doe v. John Doe Corp., 960 F.2d 318 (2d Cir.1992) and United States *ex rel.* Siller v. Becton Dickinson & Co., 21 F.3d 1339 (4th Cir.1994), address the question of whether the relator is jurisdictionally barred when some or all of the information in the *qui tam* lawsuit is publicly available but the relator did not rely upon it in bringing a *qui tam* action. Determine whether you agree with the Second or Fourth Circuit.

UNITED STATES v. JOHN DOE CORPORATION

United States Court of Appeals, Second Circuit 1992.
960 F.2d 318.

McLaughlin, Circuit Judge.

Each year, fraudulent billings by federal government contractors deplete the United States Treasury by millions, if not billions, of dollars. To combat this problem, Congress recently revamped the *qui tam* provisions of the False Claims Act, 31 U.S.C. §§ 3729–3733 (1988) ("FCA" or "the Act"), to encourage suits by private citizens who learn of fraud against the government. Because *qui tam* plaintiffs ("relators") are entitled to a portion of the proceeds of successful suits, there is the potential for parasitic lawsuits by those who learn of the fraud through public channels and seek remuneration although they contributed nothing to the exposure of the fraud. To discourage such chicanery, Congress carefully crafted a jurisdictional bar to *qui tam* claims that are based on publicly disclosed information.

We are confronted with a *qui tam* action brought by an attorney who learned of the fraud while representing a client who was being investigated in a defense contract scam. The attorney negotiated use immunity in exchange for his client's sworn testimony, then obtained a waiver of the attorney-client privilege from his client, and instituted a *qui tam* action against his client's employer. Ethical implications aside, we find the relator's complaint is based on publicly disclosed information. Accordingly, we affirm the district court's dismissal.

BACKGROUND

John Doe Corp.[1] performs services for the military under several defense contracts. In July 1989, an unidentified former employee of John Doe Corp. contacted the Federal Bureau of Investigation about certain fraudulent billing practices of defendant. A team of investigators from different branches of the government—including the FBI, the Air Force Office of Special Investigations ("OSI"), the Defense Criminal Investigative Service ("DCIS"), and the Defense Contract Audit Agency ("DCAA")—was then assembled to investigate the allegations.

OSI's responsibilities include investigating allegations of fraud in Air Force contracts, and, as here, OSI often coordinates its investigations with the Department of Justice. OSI is the sole administrative body within the Air Force authorized to enforce administrative penalties, such as suspension or debarment, against those who engage in defense contract fraud. DCIS's responsibilities include investigating accusations of fraud for the Defense Logistics Agency ("DLA"). While DLA is the agency responsible for enforcing administrative penalties for defense

---

1. The FCA obligates relators to file their complaints under seal, and they remain under seal for sixty days while the government determines whether to intervene and take over the litigation. *See* 31 U.S.C. § 3730(b)(2). Because the briefs in this appeal were also filed under seal, we will not refer to the parties by name.

contract fraud, it has no independent investigative arm, and must rely on DCIS and the FBI for those services. The DCAA audits defense contractors to determine whether to levy administrative sanctions.

By early 1990, these investigators had compiled sufficient evidence against John Doe Corp. for the Justice Department to obtain search warrants for the corporation's premises and its bank's vault. On February 15, 1990, at 8:55 a.m., government agents simultaneously executed the two warrants. Twenty-one agents from the FBI, OSI, and DCIS entered defendant's premises wearing raid jackets, sealed the building, and announced that they were executing a search warrant. Present at the time were employees and several customers of John Doe Corp. The investigators served the search warrant on defendant's president and chief executive officer, John Doe II, an individual defendant in this case. As a number of the agents seized approximately 139 boxes of documents and computerized data, others questioned John Doe Corp.'s employees. The investigators explained to the employees that they were investigating allegations that John Doe Corp. was fraudulently overcharging the government under defense contracts. Several, but not all, employees questioned knew of the overcharging by the defendant.

Acting on information from their informant, the government targeted a particular employee, Ed Meyerson, who allegedly controlled the falsified records. When Meyerson refused to cooperate, the investigators served him with a subpoena to appear before a federal grand jury on March 15, 1990.

Prior to his scheduled grand jury appearance, Meyerson retained an attorney, the relator in this action. The relator informed the Assistant United States Attorneys conducting the investigation that Meyerson intended to invoke his Fifth Amendment privilege against self-incrimination before the grand jury. The government then agreed to grant Meyerson use immunity in exchange for his sworn testimony. The government attorneys drafted an immunity letter indicating that Meyerson was not a target of the criminal probe and that if he testified truthfully his testimony would not be used against him. Meyerson and his attorney signed the immunity letter and, on March 23, 1990, Meyerson submitted to a sworn examination before the government attorneys, in lieu of appearing in front of a grand jury. Meyerson admitted that he personally falsified John Doe Corp.'s records in order to overcharge the government on defense contracts. This testimony further corroborated the information provided by the informant.

During Meyerson's testimony, the relator learned that the government had not yet instituted a civil suit under the FCA against defendants. He discussed with his client the possibility of filing a *qui tam* action against defendants and noted the likelihood of a sizeable award should the suit be successful. Meyerson apparently had no interest in pursuing a *qui tam* action, but said he would not object if the relator, himself, filed such an action. Seizing the moment, the relator says he had Meyerson sign a document waiving any interest he might have in a *qui tam* action. This document, which the relator steadfastly refused to show the government (and therefore is not part of this record), also purportedly waives the attorney-client privilege between the relator and Meyerson.

Armed with this paperwork—which no one has seen—the relator then filed this *qui tam* action on behalf of the United States seeking twenty-one million dollars in damages. The complaint alleges that John Doe Corp. and its president and chief executive officer overcharged the government under various defense contracts. Specifically, the complaint alleges that John Doe Corp. used employees without security clearance on contracts requiring such clearance and padded bills by charging the government for hours not worked.

While the complaint was still under seal, the government moved, as *amicus curiae*, to dismiss for lack of subject matter jurisdiction under the FCA. The FCA provides, in pertinent part:

> No court shall have jurisdiction over an action under this section based upon the public disclosure of allegations or transactions in a criminal, civil, or administrative hearing, in a congressional, administrative, or Government Accounting Office report, hearing, audit, or investigation, or from the news media, unless the action is brought by the Attorney General or the person bringing the action is an original source of the information.

31 U.S.C. § 3730(e)(4)(A).

Judge Mishler granted the motion to dismiss on two grounds. First, he held that, in spite of the statute's language, Congress meant to bar actions based upon information already possessed by the government when the action was filed.[2] Alternatively, Judge Mishler held that the action was barred by the express language of § 3730(e)(4)(A) of the Act because the allegations in the complaint were based upon information that had been publicly disclosed.

The relator now appeals.

Discussion

By allowing *qui tam* relators to share in any recovery, the FCA encourages those with knowledge of fraud against the government to bring that information to the fore. In the past, however, that financial incentive worked against the government's interests in exposing fraud and recouping lost money. As originally enacted, the FCA did not require that relators bring any new information to the government's attention; rather, individuals were able to bring suit based solely on information already uncovered in the government's investigation and, then, share in the award. See, e.g., United States ex rel. Marcus v. Hess, 317 U.S. 537 (1943). *Qui tam* suits by individuals seeking quick cash without assisting in exposing the fraud were aptly characterized by Attorney General Biddle, in 1943, as "parasitic" actions.

---

2. At oral argument, the government conceded that this was a distorted reading   of the legislative history. We agree. See *infra*, at 321–22.

Marcus represents the high-water mark for parasitic *qui tam* actions. There, the relator's civil complaint appeared to be copied from a criminal indictment. The Supreme Court held that nothing in the FCA barred the relator's action even if his knowledge of the fraud was solely a product of the government's investigation. Reacting to *Marcus*, Congress immediately amended the *qui tam* provisions of the FCA to bar all *qui tam* actions based on information that the government already possessed.

The "government knowledge" standard embodied in the 1943 amendment eventually worked at cross-purposes with the *qui tam* provisions of the FCA. For example, the Seventh Circuit barred a *qui tam* action by the state of Wisconsin because, before filing its *qui tam* action, Wisconsin had conducted a massive investigation and had reported the fraud to the federal government, as it was required to do by law. The Seventh Circuit held that Wisconsin's action was barred because the federal government already possessed the information upon which the complaint was based, notwithstanding that the government had acquired its knowledge only through the obligatory disclosure by Wisconsin. See United States ex rel. Wisconsin v. Dean, 729 F.2d 1100, 1102–06 (7th Cir.1984).

Qui tam actions under the FCA had gone in forty years from unrestrained profiteering to a flaccid enforcement tool. In 1986, Congress set out to reinvigorate the FCA's *qui tam* provisions. The 1986 amendments attempt to strike a balance between encouraging private citizens to expose fraud and avoiding parasitic actions by opportunists who attempt to capitalize on public information without seriously contributing to the disclosure of the fraud.

As one means of encouraging private citizens to expose fraud, Congress repealed the "government knowledge" jurisdictional bar to *qui tam* actions. And, to avoid the blatant opportunism embodied in cases like *Marcus*, Congress enacted narrowly circumscribed exceptions to *qui tam* jurisdiction.

Here, we must consider whether § 3730(e)(4)(A) bars the relator's claim.[3] Public disclosure of the allegations upon which the *qui tam* complaint rests is the bedrock of § 3730(e)(4)(A)'s jurisdictional bar. We have recently stated that allegations of fraud are publicly disclosed when they are placed in the "public domain." United States ex rel. Dick v. Long Island Lighting Co., 912 F.2d 13, 18 (2d Cir.1990). We must now consider how far into the public domain the allegations must seep before the disclosure may be considered a "public" disclosure.

* * *

3. We note that, even if a relator's claim is based upon allegations or transactions that were publicly disclosed in a manner set forth in § 3730(e)(4)(A), the action is not jurisdictionally barred if the relator is an ". 'original source' of the information." 31 U.S.C. § 3730(e)(4)(A). Because the relator here does not claim to be an "original source", as that term is defined in § 3730(e)(4)(B), we consider only whether his complaint is based upon allegations or transactions that were publicly disclosed in a manner set forth in § 3730(e)(4)(A).

[The court found that the allegations of fraud in the *qui tam* complaint had been publicly disclosed prior to the filing of the complaint.] The relator's final argument is that his complaint is not based upon allegations or transactions that were publicly disclosed in a manner provided in the statute. He claims that he became aware of the allegations of fraud solely through his representation of Meyerson. The relator's argument misses the point. The allegations in his complaint are the same as those that had been publicly disclosed prior to the filing of the *qui tam* suit. Public disclosure of the allegations divests district courts of jurisdiction over *qui tam* suits, regardless of where the relator obtained his information.

Conclusion

The relator's complaint is jurisdictionally barred by the plain language of the FCA.

AFFIRMED.

Notes

1. Note that John Doe's client, Ed Meyerson, was given immunity by the government prior to testifying, yet Meyerson admitted to personally falsifying John Doe Corporation's records so as to overcharge the government on defense contracts. Why do you think the government would give immunity to someone with obvious criminal involvement?

2. Recall the conversation John Doe had with his client, Meyerson, about "the possibility of filing a *qui tam* action against defendants and * * * the likelihood of a sizeable award should the suit be successful." Consider the following provision of the False Claims Act:

> Whether or not the Government proceeds with the action, if the court finds that the act was brought by a person who planned and initiated the violation * * * upon which the action was brought, then the court may, to the extent the court considers appropriate, reduce the share of the proceeds of the action which the person would otherwise receive * * * taking into account the role of that person in advancing the case to litigation and any relevant circumstances pertaining to the violation. If the person bringing the action is convicted of criminal conduct arising from his or her role in the violation of section 3729, that person shall be dismissed from the civil action and shall not receive any share of the proceeds of the action. Such dismissal shall not prejudice the right of the United States to continue the action, represented by the Department of Justice.

31 U.S.C. § 3730(d)(2). Do you think Meyerson would receive a "sizeable" award if he was the *qui tam* relator? Do you think § 3730 (d)(2) may be the reason Meyerson declined to go forward? If Meyerson is statutorily limited in recovering under by § 3730(d)(2) shouldn't John Doe be similarly limited since he derived his information from Meyerson?

UNITED STATES EX REL. SILLER
v. BECTON DICKINSON & CO.

United States Court of Appeals, Fourth Circuit, 1994.
21 F.3d 1339.

LUTTIG, CIRCUIT JUDGE.

Appellant David Siller, the brother and employee of a former distributor of Becton Dickinson & Company products, brought a civil *qui tam* action under 31 U.S.C. § 3730 against Becton Dickinson & Company, alleging that the company had a practice of overcharging the government. The district court * * * dismissed Siller's action under section 3730(e)(4), holding that it was "based upon" publicly disclosed allegations. For the reasons that follow, we vacate the district court's dismissal order and remand for further proceedings with * * * Siller reinstated as plaintiff[ ].

I.

From January 1986 until the filing of this lawsuit in January 1991, David Siller was employed at various times, and in various capacities by Scientific Supply, Inc. (SSI), a San Antonio, Texas, distributor of health care products whose president was Siller's brother, Ruben Siller. SSI was an authorized distributor of medical device products manufactured by Becton Dickinson & Company (BD) until BD canceled its distributorship agreement in 1987.

In 1989, SSI filed suit against BD in Texas state court, asserting various causes of action arising from BD's allegedly wrongful termination of its distributorship agreement. The thrust of SSI's complaint was that BD canceled SSI's distributorship because it feared that SSI, which was seeking to sell BD products to the federal government at prices below those quoted by BD itself, would disclose that BD was overcharging the government. BD ultimately settled with SSI in September 1989. As part of the settlement agreement, Ruben Siller agreed to keep the existence and terms of the settlement confidential. David Siller, however, Ruben's brother and employee, was not similarly bound by the settlement agreement.

David Siller filed the instant *qui tam* suit against BD in January 1991. According to Siller, he originally learned that BD overcharged the government through his employment with SSI, not as a result of SSI's suit against BD. In fact, Siller asserts, he obtained this knowledge before the SLS and SSI complaints were filed and had not read those complaints until BD filed its motion to dismiss in January 1993. Siller contends that he learned about the False Claims Act (FCA) and its *qui tam* provisions in the spring of 1990, after his brother's company's suit against BD was settled, and that he subsequently conducted his own investigation which uncovered evidence revealing how BD overcharged the government and attempted to conceal those overcharges. * * *

* * *

The district court held that Siller's action was barred under section 3730(e)(4)(A) because it was "based upon" the disclosures in the complaint filed in SSI's action against BD. Siller contends that a *qui tam* action is only "based upon" a public disclosure where the relator has actually derived from that disclosure the knowledge of the facts underlying his action. Under this reading of section 3730(e)(4)(A), Siller argues, his complaint, even if substantially similar to that in the SSI litigation, was not "based upon" the disclosures in the SSI complaint because he actually learned of BD's overcharging practices independently of the SSI complaint. BD responds that any *qui tam* complaint, such as Siller's, that "echoes" previously disclosed allegations is "based upon" those disclosures, regardless of whether those disclosures are actually the source from which the *qui tam* plaintiff derived his information.

We agree that Siller's reading of "based upon" as meaning "derived from" is the only fair construction of the statutory phrase. Section 3730(e)(4)(A)'s use of the phrase "based upon" is, we believe, susceptible of a straightforward textual exegesis. To "base upon" means to "use as a basis for." *Webster's Third New International Dictionary* 180 (1986) (definition no. 2 of verb "base"). Rather plainly, therefore, a relator's action is "based upon" a public disclosure of allegations only where the relator has actually derived from that disclosure the allegations upon which his *qui tam* action is based. Such an understanding of the term "based upon," apart from giving effect to the language chosen by Congress, is fully consistent with section 3730(e)(4)'s indisputed objective of preventing "parasitic" actions, for it is self-evident that a suit that includes allegations that happen to be similar (even identical) to those already publicly disclosed, but were not actually derived from those public disclosures, simply is not, in any sense, parasitic.

We are aware, as BD points out, that other circuits have not embraced this interpretation of the phrase, assuming instead that an action is based upon a public disclosure of allegations if its allegations are identical or similar to those already publicly disclosed. However, only one court of appeals has actually held that a relator need not have derived his knowledge from a public disclosure in order for his action to have been based upon that disclosure, and that court summoned neither reasoning nor supportive case authority in defense of its holding. In *John Doe Corp.*, the Second Circuit held that a *qui tam* plaintiff's action is "based upon" a public disclosure where the relator's allegations are "the same as those that ha[ve] been publicly disclosed.... regardless of where the relator obtained his information." 960 F.2d at 324. The court in *John Doe*, however, without a single word of analysis, merely cited two cases in support of its holding, neither provides authority for the *John Doe* holding.[8]

* * *

8. Although we reject the *John Doe* construction of the statutory text, we understand why the court was drawn toward its holding that the particular *qui tam* action at issue in that case was "based upon" a previous disclosure and therefore barred.

We recognize that other courts of appeals seem implicitly to have accepted the position, contrary to ours, that *qui tam* actions are "based upon" a public disclosure whenever the factual basis for the action has been disclosed into the public domain, regardless of whether the relator actually derived his knowledge of those facts from that disclosure. [citations omitted] None of these cases, however, actually addresses the specific question whether a *qui tam* relator need have derived his knowledge of the factual basis of his action from a public disclosure in order for his action to be "based upon" that disclosure. Rather, each of these cases addresses the question whether a *qui tam* action that is only based *in part* on publicly disclosed information should be deemed to be "based upon" the public disclosure under section 3730(e)(4)(A). The extent to which a *qui tam* action must be "based upon" a public disclosure is, of course, distinct from the analytically antecedent question of what it means for an action to be "based upon" a public disclosure. Moreover, none of these cases provides any reasoning by which to reconcile its implicit understanding of the phrase "based upon" with the phrase's plain meaning. * * * Preferring the plain meaning of the words enacted by Congress over our sister Circuits' as-yet unconsidered assumptions as to the meaning of those words, and over the Second Circuit's considered but unsupported interpretation, we hold that Siller's action was only "based upon" the disclosures in the SSI lawsuit if Siller actually derived his allegations against BD from the SSI complaint.

It is not clear to us that the district court found that Siller actually derived the allegations in his *qui tam* action from the SSI complaint. The district court found that the SSI suit publicly disclosed allegations that "derive[d] from exactly the same core of operative facts ... that form[ ] the basis for" Siller's *qui tam* complaint. J.A. at 14. That the facts that were disclosed in the SSI complaint and the facts that "form[ed] the basis for" Siller's action were the same does not, however, mean that Siller actually derived his allegations from the allegations in the SSI complaint. It is certainly possible that, as Siller contends, Siller actually learned of BD's alleged fraud entirely independently of the SSI suit, and derived his allegations from that independent knowledge. Therefore, because the district court made no finding on whether Siller actually derived his allegations from the SSI suit, a finding necessary to the conclusion that Siller's action was "based upon" that suit, we * * * vacate the portion of the district court's order dismissing Siller's action so as to enable the court to address this factual question on remand.

* * *

Notes

Note the Fourth Circuit's rejection of the Second Circuit's opinion in *John Doe*: "that court summoned neither reasoning nor supportive case

There, the *qui tam* plaintiff was an attorney who only learned of the pertinent fraud allegations through his representation of a client whose employer was being investigated for suspected fraudulent billing practices in its transactions with the Government. However, under our reading of section 3730(e)(4), which we believe is more faithful to the enacted language, the same result might well obtain.

authority in defense of its holding." What do you think: is the Second Circuit or Fourth Circuit's view more appealing?

The cases we have read thus far dealing with the jurisdictional bar provision have concerned the public disclosure hurdle. If the allegations or transactions in the *qui tam* complaint have been publicly disclosed prior to the filing of the complaint, the relator is dismissed from the lawsuit unless the relator was the "original source" of the lawsuit. The next case, United States *ex rel.* Dick v. Long Island Lighting Company, 912 F.2d 13 (2d Cir.1990), and additional excerpts from United States *ex rel.* Siller v. Becton Dickinson & Company, 21 F.3d 1339 (4th Cir.1994) (also discussed *supra*), concern the original source exception and address the question of what must be shown to find that a relator qualifies as an original source.

UNITED STATES EX REL. DICK v. LONG ISLAND LIGHTING CO.

United States Court of Appeals, Second Circuit, 1990.
912 F.2d 13.

PIERCE, SENIOR CIRCUIT JUDGE.

Herein, we examine the jurisdictional requirements of 31 U.S.C. § 3730(e)(4) of the False Claims Act. We hold that the *qui tam* plaintiffs, W. Gordon Dick and John P. Daly, Jr., appellants, did not satisfy the statute's jurisdictional requirements. Accordingly, we conclude that this suit was properly dismissed by the district court.

I.

* * *

From approximately 1979 to 1984, appellants W. Gordon Dick and John P. Daly, Jr., as employees of Stone & Webster Engineering Corp., worked as mid-level managers at the Shoreham Nuclear Power Station. By virtue of their positions, they were aware of the construction status of Shoreham. On July 1, 1988, they filed a complaint against the Long Island Lighting Co. ("LILCO"), certain of its executives (collectively, the "LILCO defendants"), and Stone & Webster Engineering Corp. under the False Claims Act, 31 U.S.C. § 3729 et seq., on behalf of the United States. The basic theory of their *qui tam* suit was that LILCO had lied to the state's Public Service Commission about the construction status of Shoreham, thereby obtaining higher rates and defrauding the United States as a ratepayer.

Almost sixteen months earlier, on March 3, 1987, the County of Suffolk ("Suffolk") had commenced a putative class action against the LILCO defendants, alleging in its complaint violations of the Racketeer Influenced and Corrupt Organizations Act, 18 U.S.C. § 1961 et seq. (1988) ("RICO") leading to the rate overcharges. This action by Suffolk was widely reported in the news media, especially in the Counties of Nassau and Suffolk. Although the appellants' later-filed complaint included some factual assertions not included in Suffolk's complaint against the LILCO defendants, taken as a whole, the *qui tam* complaint was fairly characterized by the district judge as a copy of Suffolk's earlier complaint. * * *.

It clearly appears that Suffolk's original RICO complaint was based on information derived from Suffolk's independent investigation of possible wrongdoing by LILCO and not upon information provided by Dick or Daly. Appellants concede that they "came forward [to Suffolk] *after* the original RICO complaint had been filed." Dick testified at his deposition that he became aware of Suffolk's RICO action from a newspaper article in *The New York Times* or *The Wall Street Journal*. Further, although the appellants provided some information to Suffolk after Suffolk's March 3, 1987, filing, which Suffolk incorporated into its amended RICO complaint, the information given to Suffolk by the appellants did not cause Suffolk to expand upon the fraud allegation of its original complaint; both Suffolk's original and amended RICO complaint assert the same theory of liability and seek identical amounts of damages.

* * * On April 14, 1989, the district court dismissed with prejudice appellants' *qui tam* complaint on the ground of lack of jurisdiction.

II.

The False Claims Act (the "Act"), 31 U.S.C. § 3729 *et seq.*, as amended in 1986, empowers the United States, or private citizens on behalf of the United States, to recover treble damages from those who knowingly make false claims for money or property upon the United States, or cause to be made, or who submit false information in support of such claims. Our focus here is upon those *qui tam* provisions of the Act, which, under certain conditions, allow a private citizen to bring a False Claims Act suit on behalf of the federal government. More specifically, we address whether appellants' suit is barred by § 3730(e)(4) of the Act, which provides as follows:

"(e) Certain actions barred.—

* * *

"(4)(A) No court shall have jurisdiction over an action under this section based upon the public disclosure of allegations or transactions in a criminal, civil, or administrative hearing, in a congressional, administrative, or Government Accounting Office report, hearing, audit, or investigation, or from the news media, unless the action is brought by the Attorney General or the person bringing the action is an original source of the information.

"(B) For purposes of this paragraph, 'original source' means an individual who has direct and independent knowledge of the information on which the allegations are based and has voluntarily provided the information to the Government before filing an action under this section which is based on the information."

Section 3730(e)(4) does not operate to bar a *qui tam* action unless the action is based upon publicly disclosed "allegations or transactions." In this case, there is no dispute that appellants' suit is based upon publicly disclosed "allegations or transactions." Appellants assert, however, that since they were "original sources," their suit may be maintained notwithstanding the fact that it is based upon publicly disclosed allegations. Based upon our review of the evidence presented and our interpretation of the applicable statute, we do not agree.

In assessing the pertinent language of the statute, we note that "original source" is expressly defined in § 3730(e)(4)(B). A straightforward reading of § 3730(e)(4)(B) indicates that to be an "original source" a *qui tam* plaintiff must (1) have direct and independent knowledge of the information on which the allegations are based, and (2) have voluntarily provided such information to the government prior to filing suit. A close textual analysis combined with a review of the legislative history convinces us that under § 3730(e)(4)(A) there is an additional requirement that a *qui tam* plaintiff must meet in order to be considered an "original source," namely, a plaintiff also must have directly or indirectly been a source to the entity that publicly disclosed the allegations on which a suit is based.

* * *

[The court examined the statutory language then looked to Congressional intent.—ed.]

Since our fundamental task in interpreting a statute is "to give effect to the intent of Congress," United States v. American Trucking Ass'ns, 310 U.S. 534, 542 (1940), we look to the legislative history for evidence of Congress's intent. Two legislators who appear to have been the most involved with the Act's development and passage spoke at length regarding the meaning of "original source." Representative Berman, a co-drafter of the legislation, stated that a person is an "original source" if, *inter alia,* the person "had some of the information related to the claim which he made available to the government or the news media *in advance of the false claims being publicly disclosed.*" Similarly, Senator Grassley, who introduced the legislation in the Senate, noted that the jurisdictional requirements of § 3730(e)(4) barred a person "who had not been an original source *to the entity that disclosed the allegations*" from bringing a *qui tam* claim based on publicly disclosed information. If paragraph (4)(B) contained the exclusive requirements that a *qui tam* plaintiff must satisfy to be an "original source," these legislators' statements would be somewhat inexplicable. However, their statements make much sense if paragraph (4)(A) contains an additional requirement to be considered an "original source," namely, that to be considered an "original source," one must have been a source to the entity that first publicly disclosed the information on which a suit is based. Given the foregoing, we are constrained to adopt a reading of the statute in accord with those statements.

Congress was not unfamiliar with the meaning attributed to "original source" by Representative Berman and Senator Grassley. The Senate Report to the 1986 amendments noted that in 1943 "[t]he Senate specifically provided that jurisdiction would be barred in *qui tam* suits based on information in the possession of the Government unless the relator was the original source of that information. Without explanation, the resulting conference report dropped the clause regarding original sources of allegations. * * * " S.Rep. 345, 99th Cong., 2d Sess. 12, *reprinted in* 1986 U.S.Code Cong. & Admin.News 5266, 5277 [hereinafter Senate Report]. The dropped clause would have required that *qui tam* suits be "based upon information, evidence, or sources not then in the possession of the United States, unless obtained from such person (bringing the suit) * * *." 89 Cong.Rec. 10,845 (1943). The statements of Senator Grassley and Representative Berman reflect an understanding of "original source" consistent with that alluded to by the Senate in this 1986 report, as they indicate that the 1986 amendments require that a *qui tam* suit be based on information not then publicly disclosed, unless disclosed, directly or indirectly, by the person bringing the suit.

We also note that "[t]he purpose of the *qui tam* provisions of the False Claims Act is to encourage private individuals who are aware of fraud being perpetrated against the Government to bring such information forward." H.R.Rep. No. 660, 99th Cong., 2d Sess. 22 (1986). Our interpretation is in accord with this purpose and is most likely to bring "wrongdoing to light" since, by barring those who come forward only *after* public disclosure of possible False Claims Act violations from acting as *qui tam* plaintiffs, it discourages persons with relevant information from remaining silent and encourages them to report such information at the earliest possible time. The Senate Report stressed that "changes [were] necessary to halt the so-called 'conspiracy of silence' that has allowed fraud against the government to flourish." Senate Report at 6. By requiring the reporting of information *before* public disclosure, our interpretation provides the optimum encouragement to potential plaintiffs to end the "conspiracy of silence."

In sum, for the reasons stated hereinabove, we believe that if the information on which a *qui tam* suit is based is in the public domain, and the *qui tam* plaintiff was not a source of that information, then the suit is barred. Since it has not been demonstrated that Suffolk's original complaint relied upon information disclosed by appellants prior to the filing of that complaint, appellants could not have been found to be an "original source" of the publicly disclosed information on which their suit is based. Accordingly, the jurisdictional bar of § 3730(e)(4) was applicable, and the district court acted properly in dismissing their complaint for lack of jurisdiction.

Affirmed.

Notes

According to the Second Circuit, if information ultimately contained in a *qui tam* relator's complaint was released publicly prior to the filing of the *qui tam* action, the *qui tam* relator's lawsuit is barred unless the *qui tam* relator directly or indirectly was "a source to the entity that first publicly disclosed the allegations on which a suit is based." *Long Island, supra.* Exactly what does this holding require?

Assume, for example, that Messrs. Dick and Daly, as employees of Stone and Webster, suspected their employer of submitting false claims to the government regarding the Shoreham nuclear power station. Assume further that Messrs. Dick and Daly believe it prudent to investigate, as best they can, their suspicions before taking any action or publicizing their concerns. However, Messrs. Dick and Daly are aware that the media and county officials may investigate and publicize the matter before they can complete their investigation. Realizing that publicity—of which they are not the source—may jeopardize their right to bring a *qui tam* action, Messrs. Dick and Daly abandon their cautionary instincts to investigate further and present to the media, or to the government, their suspicions.

What are the possible consequences of premature disclosure of potential wrongdoing: inaccurately disparaging good reputations? jeopardizing opportunities to fully investigate wrongdoing? Does the decision in *Long Island* encourage premature disclosure?

Determine whether you become more or less persuaded by the Second Circuit's opinion in *Long Island Lighting* as you read the next case, *Becton Dickinson*. Recall from our prior review of this case, *supra*, that David Siller had been employed in various capacities by Scientific Supply Inc (SSI) which served as a distributor of medical device products manufactured by Becton Dickinson & Company (BD). BD canceled its distributorship agreement with SSI amid SSI's allegations that BD was overcharging the federal government on medical supply products. In the portion of the case we read previously, the Fourth Circuit reversed the District Court's dismissal of Siller's *qui tam* action filed against BD. In so doing the Fourth Circuit held that the allegations or transactions in the complaint were not "publicly disclosed" within the meaning of the False Claims Act even though the allegations or transactions were publicly available if, as Siller claimed, he did not rely upon the publicly available information in preparing his *qui tam* complaint. Because the trial court had not made findings on the issue of whether Siller's complaint relied on the publicly available information, the Fourth Circuit remanded for further findings. In doing so, it also provided guidance on the issue of qualifying as an original source.

UNITED STATES EX REL. SILLER
v. BECTON DICKINSON & CO.

United States Court of Appeals, Fourth Circuit, 1994.
21 F.3d 1339.

LUTTIG, CIRCUIT JUDGE.

* * *

In addition to its holding that Siller's action was based upon previously disclosed public allegations in a civil hearing within the meaning of section 3730(e)(4)(A), the district court also held that Siller was not an "original source" within section 3730(e)(4)'s exception to its jurisdictional bar. In so holding, the court expressly adopted the standard fashioned by the Second Circuit in United States *ex rel.* Dick v. Long Island Lighting Co., 912 F.2d 13, 16 (2d Cir.1990). That standard requires that, in order to be considered an "original source," a *qui tam* plaintiff must not only have direct and independent knowledge of the information on which his allegations are based, and have provided that information to the government, but also must have "been a source *to the entity that publicly disclosed the allegations* on which a suit is based." *Long Island Lighting*, 912 F.2d at 16 (emphasis added). Finding that Siller was not a source to SSI, the "entity that publicly disclosed the allegations" on which Siller's suit was found to be based, *id.*, the district court held that Siller was not an "original source" under section 3730(e)(4).

We reject the Second Circuit's standard, and the district court's adoption of that standard, as imposing an additional, extra-textual requirement that was not intended by Congress. Reading sub-paragraph (B), as we are directed by the statute, as the definition of "original source" applicable to sub-paragraph (A), sub-paragraph (A) is properly read as providing that,

> [n]o court shall have jurisdiction over an action ... based upon the public disclosure of allegations ... in a ... civil ... hearing ... *unless* ... *the person bringing the action* ... *has direct and independent knowledge of the information on which the allegations are based and has voluntarily provided the information to the Government before filing an action* under this section which is based on the information.

31 U.S.C. § 3730(e)(4) (emphasis added). Under this reading of section 3730(e)(4), the provision unambiguously does not require, as the Second Circuit has held that it does, that a relator be a source to the original disclosing entity in order to be an "original source." Rather it requires only that the relator have direct and independent knowledge of the information underlying the allegations of a false claim and voluntarily provide the information to the government before filing his *qui tam* action.

The Second Circuit's attempt to portray its holding that a relator must also be a source *to the disclosing entity* as one derived from the provision's text is not merely unpersuasive, but implausible. The Second Circuit essentially holds that sub-paragraphs (A) and (B) each provides distinct and cumulative requirements for being an "original source." Thus, it reasons, sub-paragraph (A) requires that the relator be an original source to the entity that made the public disclosure, and sub-paragraph (B) additionally requires that the relator have direct and independent knowledge of the allegations underlying his *qui tam* action and that he provide his information to the government.

The Second Circuit's interpretation of section 3730(e)(4) to require that the putative plaintiff provide his information to the disclosing entity might at least be tenable were there not a definition of "original source" in sub-paragraph (B). But the term "original source" as it is used in sub-paragraph (A) is expressly defined in sub-paragraph (B). Sub-paragraph (B) necessarily, therefore, sets forth that which the Second Circuit holds it does not—"the exclusive requirements that a *qui tam* plaintiff must satisfy to be an 'original source.' " *Id.* at 17.

The Second Circuit's "close textual analysis," *id.* at 16, that yields this interpretation is wholly indefensible. The essence of the Second Circuit's textual reasoning is that the word "information" in sub-paragraph (A) refers to the information publicly disclosed, whereas the "information" in sub-paragraph (B) refers to the information that supplies the basis for the *qui tam* action itself. This "slight difference in meaning" between these two uses of the word "information," suggests the Second Circuit, "permits the interpretation that ¶ (4)(B) does not contain the exclusive requirements in order for one to be an 'original source' and that an additional requirement is to be found in ¶ (4)(A)." *Id.* Besides the fact that a "slight difference" between the meaning of "information" in the two paragraphs cannot justify a holding that sub-paragraph (B)'s definition of "original source" is not the entire definition of that term, the reasoning that underlies the Second Circuit's conclusion that the word "information" means something different in the two provisions is demonstrably incorrect.

First, it states, "if the word 'information' means the same in ¶ (4)(A) as it does in ¶ (4)(B), then its use in ¶ (4)(A) would be superfluous." *Id.* Because the definition of "original source" in sub-paragraph (B) references the information on which the allegations are based, inclusion of the prepositional phrase "of the information" in sub-paragraph (A) is, in the most hypertechnical sense, unnecessary. However, the phrase is not superfluous in a way or to a degree that warrants ascribing different meanings to the same word used in two successive clauses. In other words, it is so unlikely that Congress would have even noticed the technical redundancy, that no significance can reasonably be inferred from inclusion of the prepositional phrase in sub-paragraph (A).

Second, the *Long Island Lighting* court suggests that, because the word "information" in sub-paragraph (B) is accompanied by a modifying phrase while the word "information" is without modification in sub-paragraph (A), "information" must mean something different in sub-paragraph (B) than it does in sub-paragraph (A). Although it is true that "information" is modified in sub-paragraph (B) and is not in sub-paragraph (A), the modifying phrase used in sub-paragraph (B)—"on which the allegations are based"—itself confirms that the word "information" in sub-paragraph (B) has the identical meaning that the Second Circuit agrees the word has in sub-paragraph (A). "The allegations" referred to in the modifying phrase can only mean those allegations publicly disclosed, since those not only are the allegations referenced in the clause preceding the modifying phrase, but are the only allegations mentioned at all in section 3730(e)(4). Thus, "the information on which the allegations are based" in sub-paragraph (B) cannot possibly refer to anything but the information on which the publicly disclosed allegations are based, which is, as the Second Circuit agrees, the precise information referenced in sub-paragraph (A).

Finally, the Second Circuit posits, without explanation, that "the most plausible reading of ¶ (4)(B) indicates that the 'information' referred to therein is that which supplies the basis for the *qui tam* action itself." Id. As set forth above, however, the fact that sub-paragraph (B) refers to "the information *on which the allegations are based*" confirms that the only possible reference of the word "information" in sub-paragraph (B) is to the information publicly disclosed—the exact same reference of the word in sub-paragraph (A).

We believe that, in truth, the Second Circuit's conclusion that a putative plaintiff must provide his information to the disclosing entity in order to be an original source rests not upon the statutory language, but entirely upon a reading, and misreading, of the legislative history. In fact, the Second Circuit's decision is a classic example of the use of legislative history to create an ambiguity in the statute where none exists in order to justify use of that history as dispositive evidence of congressional intent.

The Second Circuit fixes on Senator Grassley's comment that "the jurisdictional requirements of § 3730(e)(4) bar[ ] a person 'who had not been an original source *to the entity that disclosed the allegations'* from bringing a *qui tam* claim based on publicly disclosed information." Id. (quoting 132 Cong.Rec. 20,536 (1986)) (emphasis added). If the provision to which this comment was directed had been enacted as it existed at the time Senator Grassley made the comment, the comment would be some evidence of a congressional intent supporting the Second Circuit's interpretation, although even then we would not permit such a statement to override statutory language as clear as that in sub-paragraph (B). In fact, however, the version of the legislation addressed by Senator Grassley[12] was changed in two significant respects.

First, Congress deleted "the media" as a party whom the original source was required to inform. Given that the media is specified in the enacted version of sub-paragraph (A) as one of the disclosing entities, Congress presumably would not have deleted the media from the "original source" definition in sub-paragraph (B) if it intended to require the plaintiff to provide his information to the disclosing entity. Second,

---

12. The language upon which Senator Grassley commented defined an "original source" as an individual who has direct and independent knowledge of the information on which the allegations are based and has voluntarily informed the Government or the news media prior to an action filed by the Government.

132 Cong.Rec. S11,240 (daily ed., Aug. 11, 1986).

Congress ultimately provided that an original source had to inform the government only "before filing [his *qui tam*] action," 31 U.S.C. § 3730(e)(4)(B), as opposed to "prior to an action filed by the Government." 132 Cong.Rec. S11,240 (daily ed. Aug. 11, 1986). It would be odd, if Congress had intended a plaintiff to be a source to the disclosing entity in order to be an "original source," for it to have allowed the plaintiff to provide his information after the public disclosure (i.e., by only requiring the provision of information before the plaintiff brings his action). These two changes suggest that, even assuming that Congress may at one point have intended a plaintiff to be a source to the disclosing entity to be an original source, which is anything but clear, it ultimately chose not to enact such a requirement into law.

* * *

We are not unmindful that, in contrast to the Second * * * Circuit[ ], which * * * largely relied on the legislative history to the 1986 amendments, some courts, out of utter frustration with the many seeming inconsistencies in the history, have sought to interpret section 3730(e)(4) instead based principally upon the overarching objectives of the legislation. For example, the Third Circuit, after noting that one can find in the legislative history of the FCA amendments "some support somewhere for almost any construction" of the statutory terms, stated that it would "look instead to what [it] [could] glean from the principal intent" of the legislation, which was "to have the *qui tam* suit provision operate somewhere between the almost unrestrained permissiveness" represented by those pre–1943 cases that had allowed plaintiffs to bring *qui tam* actions based upon allegations they had learned about by reading publicly-available criminal indictments, and those post–1943 cases that had barred even suits by plaintiffs who had initially disclosed the fraud to the government. *See, e.g., Stinson,* 944 F.2d at 1154. It strikes us as especially inappropriate (not to mention frighteningly treacherous) to attempt, as these courts have done, to distill from such broad, generalized objectives, the answers to the kind of specific statutory questions that we herein address; fine calibrations are just not possible through the use of such crude instruments. This is particularly so in this context, given that, although we can perhaps divine from these abstract purposes a congressional intention to balance the need to encourage *qui tam* actions against the need to prevent parasitic suits, we can discern virtually nothing as to precisely how Congress ultimately believed it achieved that balance. If the language of law is to have any meaning at all, then surely it must prevail over the kind of speculation that is entailed in such an enterprise as these courts have undertaken.

Accordingly, we hold that a *qui tam* plaintiff need not be a source to the entity that publicly disclosed the allegations on which the *qui tam* action is based in order to be an original source under section 3730(e)(4)(B). In addition to having direct and independent knowledge of the information on which the allegations in the public disclosure is based, he need only provide his information to the government before instituting his *qui tam* action, as the provision unambiguously states.

* * *

Notes

Does the Second Circuit's approach in *John Doe* or the Fourth Circuit's approach in *Siller* seem more reasonable to you? What is achieved by permitting a relator to pursue a *qui tam* action once the information in it has become publicly available?

———

Another substantial issue involving the jurisdictional bar provision which is in flux is whether the allegations or transactions regarding the false claims must *actually* be publicly disclosed or simply *potentially* available to the public. The next two cases, United States *ex rel.* Ramseyer v. Century Healthcare Corporation, 90 F.3d 1514 (10th Cir. 1996) and United States *ex rel.* Stinson, Lyons, Gerlin & Bustamante v. Prudential Insurance Company, 944 F.2d 1149 (3d Cir.1991), address this issue. Determine whether you agree with the Tenth or Third Circuit.

UNITED STATES EX REL. RAMSEYER v. CENTURY HEALTHCARE CORP.

United States Court of Appeals, Tenth Circuit, 1996.
90 F.3d 1514.

EBEL, CIRCUIT JUDGE.

Plaintiff Susan Ramseyer brought this action on behalf of the United States under the *qui tam* provisions of the False Claims Act ("FCA"), 31 U.S.C. § 3730(b)-(f), to recover a portion of the civil penalties and damages sought from the defendants. * * * The district court dismissed the complaint pursuant to Fed.R.Civ.P. 12(b)(1) for lack of subject matter jurisdiction, relying on the "public disclosure" jurisdictional bar of the FCA. 31 U.S.C. § 3730(e)(4). This provision bars *qui tam* suits that are based upon allegations of fraud already publicly disclosed, unless the person bringing the action qualifies as an "original source" of the information. Because we conclude plaintiff's suit was not based upon publicly disclosed information, we reverse the district court's dismissal of plaintiff's *qui tam* claim. * * *

Plaintiff alleged that from October 1991 to May 1992, she was employed as a consultant to, and then as the clinical director of, a mental health facility operated by the defendants. In those capacities, it was her responsibility to monitor compliance with applicable Medicaid requirements. Plaintiff further alleged that during her employment she became aware of widespread noncompliance with minimum program components for day treatment services at defendants' facility. Although plaintiff regularly communicated the instances of noncompliance to her superiors, the defendants continued to submit noncomplying claims to the government that ultimately were paid by Medicaid.

In the meantime, and completely independent of plaintiff's efforts, a routine audit and inspection conducted by the Oklahoma Department of Human Services ("DHS") revealed deficiencies in the defendants' day treatment program similar to those discovered by plaintiff. As a result of this audit, Roy Hughes, a DHS Programs Supervisor, prepared a report (the "Hughes Report") detailing essentially the same compliance problems that plaintiff had raised. Only three copies of the Hughes Report were made: one copy was given to the DHS programs administrator, a second copy was provided to the defendants, and the third remained in the DHS files. No copies of the Hughes Report were released to the general public, nor was this report available to the public except upon a written request for the specific record and approval from the DHS legal department.

Defendants terminated plaintiff's employment in May 1992. Six months later, plaintiff filed the present lawsuit alleging that the defendants' Medicaid billing practices gave rise to false claims redressable under the FCA. * * *

Plaintiff's suit relies upon the *qui tam* provisions of the FCA, 31 U.S.C. § 3730(b)-(f), which authorize private individuals, acting on behalf of the United States, to bring a civil action against those who defraud the government. In order to encourage individuals with knowledge of fraudulent activity against the government to come forward, the FCA provides a successful *qui tam* litigant with a cash bounty of up to 30% of the final recovery. However, because Congress sought to achieve " 'the golden mean between adequate incentives for whistle-blowing insiders with genuinely valuable information and discouragement of opportunistic plaintiffs who have no significant information to contribute of their own,' " [citations omitted] the FCA also erects a jurisdictional bar for suits based upon allegations of fraud that have already been made public. In this regard, the FCA provides that

> [n]o court shall have jurisdiction over an action under this section based upon the *public disclosure* of allegations or transactions in a criminal, civil, or administrative hearing, in a congressional, administrative, or Government Accounting Office report, hearing, audit, or investigation, or from the news media, unless the action is brought by the Attorney General or the person bringing the action is an original source of the information.

31 U.S.C. § 3730(e)(4)(A) (emphasis added). Applying this statutory provision, the district court concluded that, because plaintiff's lawsuit was based upon publicly disclosed information—specifically, the allegations contained in Hughes Report—it lacked subject matter jurisdiction to entertain the action.

* * *

The district court held that because the Hughes Report was available to the general public upon a written request, the "allegations or transactions" therein were "public[ly] disclos[ed]" within the meaning of 31 U.S.C. § 3730(e)(4)(A). On appeal, plaintiff contends that the mere existence of a report that is only "theoretically" or potentially available to the public cannot constitute public disclosure. In plaintiff's view, the public disclosure bar does not come into play here because DHS took no affirmative steps to make the "allegations or transactions" in the Hughes Report publicly known.[2]

Since 1986, when Congress amended the FCA to add the public disclosure bar, the Tenth Circuit has not had the occasion to address directly what constitutes "public disclosure" for purposes of section 3730(e)(4)(A). Moreover, our sister circuits are divided on the question whether theoretical or potential accessibility—as opposed to actual disclosure—of allegations or transactions is sufficient to bar a *qui tam* suit that is based upon such information. [citations omitted] We agree with the District of Columbia and Ninth Circuits that "public disclosure" signifies more than the mere theoretical or potential availability of information. We believe that in order to be publicly disclosed, the allegations or transactions upon which a *qui tam* suit is based must have been made known to the public through some affirmative act of disclosure.

Our interpretation of "public disclosure" is supported by the common usage and understanding of the term. To "disclose" is commonly defined as "to make known; reveal or uncover." The Random House College Dictionary 378 (Rev. ed.1980). Thus, a report which is merely potentially discoverable—such as through a Freedom of Information Act request, see Schumer, 63 F.3d at 1519–20—but not actually "made known" to the public, does not come within the ambit of public disclosure. In order to bar a *qui tam* action under section 3730(e)(4)(A), the allegations or transactions upon which the suit is based must have been affirmatively disclosed to the public.

The "affirmative disclosure" interpretation of the public disclosure bar also coheres with the twin purposes of the FCA: "(1) to encourage private citizens with first-hand knowledge to expose fraud; and (2) to avoid civil actions by opportunists attempting to capitalize on public information without seriously contributing to the disclosure of the fraud." [citation omitted]

---

2. Section 3730(e)(4)(A) bars only suits that are based upon the public disclosure of "allegations or transactions in a criminal, civil, or administrative hearing, in a congressional, administrative, or Government Accounting Office report, hearing, audit, or investigation, or from the news media.... " Accordingly, it might have been argued by plaintiff here that "[n]either the [state DHS] audit nor the [Hughes Report] was made by Congress, an administrative agen-cy, or the Government Accounting Office ... [and n]either, then, can form the basis for invocation of the section 3730(e)(4)(A) jurisdictional bar." United States ex rel. Fine v. MK–Ferguson Co., 861 F.Supp. 1544, 1550 (D.N.M.1994). We acknowledge this potential argument for the sake of clarity only and do not address it, as plaintiff passed over, and therefore waived, the point.

As to the second of these purposes, we do not believe that an actual disclosure rule will encourage parasitic lawsuits. Information to which the public has potential access, but which has not actually been released to the public, cannot be the basis of a parasitic lawsuit because the relator must base the *qui tam* suit on information gathered from his or her own investigation. If a specific report detailing instances of fraud is not affirmatively disclosed, but rather is simply ensconced in an obscure government file, an opportunist *qui tam* plaintiff first would have to know of the report's existence in order to request access to it. * * *

As to the other purpose of the Act—encouraging the exposure of fraud—the amended *qui tam* provisions seek to ensure that information bearing on potential fraud will come to light even if government officials should decide not to initiate proceedings based on information contained in government files. The previous incarnation of the Act required dismissal of a *qui tam* action once it was determined that "the action is based on evidence or information the Government had when the action was brought." 31 U.S.C. § 3730(b)(4) (1982) (superseded). The 1986 amendments changed the focus of the FCA's jurisdictional bar from information that the government simply had within its files to information or evidence which actually had been disclosed to the public. We agree with the statements made by the United States District Court for the District of New Mexico in *MK–Ferguson Co.*:

> Not requiring some positive act of disclosure would reinstate the pre-1986 jurisdictional bar based on mere "government knowledge" of information pertaining to fraud. Congress sought to replace this restrictive jurisdictional prerequisite in part because of its concern that the government was not pursuing known instances of fraud. As a consequence of the government's perceived inability or unwillingness to prosecute fraud, Congress gave private attorneys general greater access to the courts. If the mere existence of a "no action" recommendation buried in an unreleased internal audit report has the effect of foreclosing *qui tam* actions, the 1986 amendments were for naught.

861 F.Supp. at 1551. Only when there is a positive act of disclosure to the public can the government "no longer throw a cloak of secrecy" around the allegations, for at that point the information has been "irretrievably released into the public domain." United States ex rel. Doe v. John Doe Corp., 960 F.2d 318, 322 (2d Cir.1992).

* * *

Applying these principles to the present case, we believe the district court erred in concluding that the plaintiff's *qui tam* action was based upon allegations or transactions already disclosed to the public. Although plaintiff concedes that the allegations in her Complaint are similar to the information contained in the Hughes Report, the mere placement of that report in the DHS files does not constitute public disclosure. Defendants argue that any member of the general public could have obtained a copy of the Hughes Report simply by requesting the documentation relating to DHS's 1991 inspection of the medical facility in question. This argument, of course, presupposes that a member of the public both knew that DHS conducted an inspection in 1991 and understood that the documented findings resulting from that inspection were available for public review upon request. DHS did not affirmatively "disclose" either the existence or the contents of the Hughes Report; instead, DHS simply placed the report in its investigative file and restricted access to those persons clairvoyant enough to specifically ask for it.[5] We cannot agree that such conjectural or speculative "accessibility" to the information bars the plaintiff's *qui tam* action.

Allowing plaintiff's lawsuit to proceed is also consistent with Congress' desire to "encourage persons with first-hand knowledge of fraudulent misconduct to report fraud." It is undisputed that plaintiff possessed first-hand knowledge of her employer's allegedly fraudulent Medicaid billing practices. Moreover, but for plaintiff's lawsuit, defendants' fraudulent activity may have gone undetected because the evidence essentially was "hidden in files." If the mere existence of a report, as opposed to the actual disclosure of the allegations or transactions contained therein, would operate to bar plaintiff's suit, it would "prevent the utilization for enforcement purposes of allegations or transactions that may not otherwise come to the attention of the authorities." Accordingly, we reverse the district court's order dismissing plaintiff's action for lack of subject matter jurisdiction.[6]

* * *

Notes

Note the Tenth Circuit's reasoning that a contrary holding (public disclosure occurs when the "allegations or transactions" are potentially available to the public) would return to pre–1986 days when there was no financial incentive for relators to pursue cases about which the government had knowledge but was doing nothing. Do you agree? Does the reasoning in the next case, United States *ex rel.* Stinson et al. v. Prudential Insurance Company, 944 F.2d 1149 (3d Cir.1991), help you decide?

5. Mr. Hughes himself described in an affidavit the difficulty a member of the public would have in obtaining a copy of his report. First, Mr. Hughes stated that a third-party request for the report "would have to be approved by the Legal Division for DHS.... " Hughes Aff. ¶. 5, Appellant App. at 351. Second, Mr. Hughes opined that "[g]iven the vast number of records maintained by the DHS Medical Services Division, and the inability of the general public to see these records, without a written request for a specific record, approved by the Legal Department, it is extremely doubtful that a member of the general public could gain access to a copy of the [Hughes] Report without already knowing of its contents and existence." Id. ¶ 6, Appellant App. at 351.

6. Because we hold that the "allegations or transactions" upon which plaintiff's action was based were not publicly disclosed, we need not address the question whether plaintiff was an "original source of the information" for purposes of 31 U.S.C. § 3730(e)(4)(A).

UNITED STATES EX REL. STINSON ET AL. v. PRUDENTIAL INSURANCE COMPANY

United States Court of Appeals, Third Circuit, 1991.
944 F.2d 1149.

SLOVITER, CIRCUIT JUDGE.

This appeal from the district court's dismissal of a complaint for lack of subject matter jurisdiction requires us to interpret the jurisdictional bar provisions of the False Claims Act, 31 U.S.C. §§ 3729–3733 (1988) (FCA). The law firm of Stinson, Lyons, Gerlin & Bustamante, P.A. (Stinson) filed this action on behalf of the United States against Prudential Insurance Company alleging that Prudential defrauded the Government by avoiding its statutory responsibility to pay certain insurance claims as the primary insurer. The district court dismissed the complaint on the ground that it lacked subject matter jurisdiction because the action was based solely on information or allegations that had been publicly disclosed in previous litigation. * * *

I.

FACTS AND PROCEDURAL HISTORY

Stinson learned of Prudential's allegedly fraudulent activity during its representation of T. Armlon Leonard in 1983 in connection with injuries sustained by Leonard in an automobile accident. Leonard, who was 67 years old at the time of the accident, was covered by a group insurance plan provided by his employer and carried by Provident Life and Accident Insurance Company (Provident).

In the course of processing Leonard's claim against Provident, Stinson formed a suspicion that Provident's claim processing practice was in violation of federal law, specifically the Tax Equity and Fiscal Responsibility Act of 1982 (TEFRA), Pub.L. No. 97–248, § 116(b), 96 Stat. 324, 353 (1982), in which Congress shifted primary liability for benefit claims of people covered both by Medicare and employer group health plans (working seniors) from Medicare to the private group plan. Stinson believed that, notwithstanding TEFRA, Provident was avoiding its responsibility by allowing Medicare to continue to pay as the primary insurer the benefit claims of Armlon and other working seniors.

* * * Through discovery in the Leonard litigation, Stinson obtained two internal Provident memoranda, admittedly hearsay, which Stinson reads as suggesting that other insurance companies had similar claim processing practices.

In early 1988, a year and a half later, Stinson brought an action on behalf of the United States against Provident under the *qui tam* provisions of the False Claims Act (FCA). Thereafter, Stinson filed identical actions against Prudential and the other insurance companies allegedly implicated by the Provident memoranda. In each case, Stinson argued that the insurance company defrauded the government by allowing Medicare to pay as primary insurer for claims of working seniors.

* * *

The district court held that Stinson's *qui tam* action was based solely on the Provident memoranda which had been publicly disclosed for purposes of the jurisdictional bar of the FCA when they were obtained by Stinson through civil discovery. The court held that Stinson was not an "original source" because its suit was based exclusively on the information contained in the Provident memoranda, and thus its knowledge of Prudential's allegedly fraudulent practice was neither direct nor independent of the public disclosure. * * *

Stinson's principal argument on appeal challenges the district court's conclusion that the Provident memoranda which refer to Prudential were publicly disclosed when they were produced by Provident to Stinson during discovery in the *Leonard* litigation. * * *

[The court noted that there was no protective order in this case, limiting access to discovery produced.-ed.] We must assume from the absence of a protective order that the information disclosed in discovery is potentially accessible to the public. Indeed, several courts of appeals have so held, relying on the "good cause" requirement of Rule 26(c).

In this case, we need not consider whether information subject to a protective order which is either advertently or inadvertently disclosed could be considered to be received pursuant to a "public disclosure." There was no reason to shield from public access the information referring to Prudential appearing in the Provident discovery, and Stinson does not suggest any. Therefore, disclosure of discovery material to a party who is not under any court imposed limitation as to its use is a public disclosure under the FCA.

Nonetheless, Stinson draws a distinction for purposes of the FCA statute based on whether or not the discovery was filed with the court.

We do not think that it is significant, for purposes of interpreting the "public disclosure" provision of the FCA, whether the discovery has in fact been filed. Due to the large volume of discovery materials, many district courts have adopted local rules which provide that discovery materials should not be filed with the court except by order of the court. Such local rules do not generally preclude access by interested persons to nonfiled material. In fact, the Local Rules of some district courts provide that the court may order the filing of discovery materials at the request of any person who has an interest in reviewing the materials.

Fed.R.Civ.P. 5(d) continues to require filing of discovery material in the absence of a court order excusing filing. The Advisory Notes to Rule 5 explain that in 1978 the Committee considered adopting a rule that discovery materials would not be filed unless the court ordered their filing, but retained the rule requiring filing because "such materials are sometimes of interest to those who may have no access to them except by a requirement of filing, such as members of a class, litigants similarly situated, or the public generally." Fed.R.Civ.P. 5(d) advisory committee note to 1980 amendment.

Moreover, a distinction based on actual filing *vel non* would in many instances make application of the "public disclosure" provision depend upon the form of discovery. It is not uncommon for parties in districts which do not have a local rule precluding filing of discovery to file answers to interrogatories but not documents disclosed in response to a request to produce under Fed.R.Civ.P. 34. Thus, in those districts, had Stinson drafted interrogatories to Provident requesting it to set forth all references in its files to the claim practice followed by other insurance companies, the information disclosed in answer to those interrogatories when filed would be information publicly disclosed whereas the same information contained in documents produced in lieu of answers to interrogatories, see Fed.R.Civ.P. 33(c), would not be publicly disclosed. We decline to base an interpretation of the statute on the happenstance of the manner of discovery or the local rule pursuant to which discovery is made.

* * *

To recapitulate, the presumption under Rule 5(d) of public access to civil discovery that is not subject to a protective order leads us to conclude that information received as a result of such discovery should be deemed based on a "public disclosure" for purposes of the FCA jurisdictional bar. It follows that the jurisdictional bar of section 3730(e)(4)(A) for actions based on the "public disclosure" of allegations or transactions in a "civil hearing" is applicable because Stinson acquired the information upon which it based its *qui tam* complaint through the material produced by Provident in discovery.

SCIRICA, CIRCUIT JUDGE, DISSENTING.

* * *

The majority finds that "public disclosure" occurred when nonpublic documents were handed over to a private party during privately conducted discovery, holding that whenever information not subject to a protective order is obtained through discovery during civil litigation, there has been "public disclosure in a civil hearing." It therefore finds "public disclosure" regardless of whether the information is available to the public when it is disclosed. By contrast, I would find that public disclosure did not occur until the Provident memoranda were actually disclosed to the public. * * *

The majority holds that information is "publicly disclosed" within the meaning of § 3730(e)(4) whenever it is disclosed in litigation to a party who is under no court imposed limitation as to its use. It recognizes that the Provident memoranda were not publicly available when they were disclosed to Stinson. Nevertheless, it finds public disclosure because the information might have become available to the public at some later date, if it had been obtained in federal court litigation. By contrast, I would find that information has been publicly disclosed only when it has actually been disclosed to the public. The Provident memoranda were not available to the general public when Stinson obtained them, and therefore I do not believe they were "publicly disclosed" at that time. Congress believed that a *qui tam* incentive system is generally unnecessary when information is publicly available. But by permitting *qui tam* suits based upon non-public information, Congress provided incentives for private individuals to report instances of fraud which the government would not otherwise have reason to know about. I do not believe Congress intended to bar relators who obtain non-public information simply because that information might become public at a later time.

This interpretation comports with the plain language of the statute, and is supported by legislative history, case law, and sound policy concerns. * * *

* * *

The majority relies on the proposition that if the Provident memoranda had been disclosed in federal court litigation, they might have become available to the public after they were obtained by Stinson. It notes the general presumption under the Federal Rules of Civil Procedure that discovery materials will be available for public inspection at some point, and deems it irrelevant whether the materials have in fact been publicly filed at the time of disclosure. The majority also finds it unimportant that the production of the Provident memoranda was not governed by the federal rules upon which it relies. By contrast, I would determine whether there has been public disclosure by examining what actually occurred in the case. I see no indication that Congress was concerned with information that might have become public if it had been obtained elsewhere.

Traditionally, pretrial discovery is not a public event. As the Supreme Court has noted with respect to the First Amendment right of access, "pretrial depositions and interrogatories are not public components of a civil trial. Such proceedings were not open to the public at common law, and, in general, they are conducted in private as a matter of modern practice." Seattle Times Co. v. Rhinehart, 467 U.S. 20, 33 (1984). This was the case here. The majority relies on the Federal Rules of Civil Procedure, which provide that all discovery materials shall be filed with the court absent a contrary court order. *See* Fed.R.Civ.P. 5(d), 26(c). I agree that the federal system provides the public with a presumptive right of access to discovery materials. However, the general public has no real access to the information until it is publicly filed. If Stinson had obtained its information by browsing through public court files, I agree that the suit would have been based on public disclosure.

But the Provident memoranda were not produced in federal court, and had not been publicly filed when Stinson obtained them. When applying the term "public disclosure," I would examine the actual circumstances of this case, not those that might have existed had the information been produced in federal litigation. The relevant facts are those pertaining to the *Leonard* litigation, which was conducted in Florida state court. Although the meaning of "public disclosure" is a federal issue, I believe its application in a particular case must depend on the factual circumstances of the disclosure. In this case, the discovery was conducted in Florida state court. Florida state rules do not require responses to discovery requests to be filed with the court. The Provident memoranda were not filed with the court upon their production and therefore did not become a matter of public record at that time. Consequently, I believe that the information was not publicly disclosed before it was filed with the court.

* * *

Notes

In *Ramseyer* the Tenth Circuit held that only actual public disclosure qualified as "public disclosure" under the FCA. It found that such a rule furthered the FCA's goal of encouraging private citizens with first hand knowledge to come forward and expose fraud while also avoiding parasitic suits wherein the *qui tam* relator relies upon public information in bringing an FCA case. Did the Third Circuit in *Stinson* address this argument? What do you think: Is the Tenth Circuit correct?

One of the more controversial issues regarding the 1986 jurisdictional bar provision is whether government employees are barred from suing as *qui tam* relators. The next case, United States ex rel. LeBlanc v. Raytheon Company, Inc., 913 F.2d 17, (1st Cir.1990), addresses this issue.

UNITED STATES EX REL. LEBLANC v. RAYTHEON COMPANY, INC.

United States Court of Appeals, First Circuit, 1990.
913 F.2d 17.

TORRUELLA, CIRCUIT JUDGE.

This is an appeal from an order entered by the United States District Court for the District of Massachusetts dismissing for lack of jurisdiction a *qui tam* action brought under the False Claims Act, 31 U.S.C. § 3729 *et seq.*, by Roland A. LeBlanc (appellant) against Raytheon Company, Inc. (appellee). Although we agree with the result reached by the district court, we find its reasoning overly broad and conclusive.

I. FACTS

Roland LeBlanc filed this lawsuit on October 21, 1988 under the False Claims Act, 31 U.S.C. §§ 3729–3733 (1988). LeBlanc's complaint alleged that, during his employment as a Quality Assurance Specialist for the United States Government Defense Contract Administrative Service ("DCAS"), he observed fraud in the handling of government contracts by the defendant Raytheon Company, Inc. ("Raytheon").

* * *

* * * However, the district court * * * [held] that *qui tam* actions by Government employees are excluded by the False Claims Act. Here, we disagree. Although we do agree that Roland LeBlanc's action is excluded, as discussed below, not all *qui tam* actions brought by government employees are excluded by the False Claims Act.

II. DISCUSSION

From 1943 to 1986, government employees were effectively prohibited from bringing *qui tam* actions by the False Claims Act. In 1986, Congress amended the statute to "encourage more private enforcement suits." This case turns on the meaning of the 1986 amendments to the *qui tam* provisions of the False Claims Act. Basically, Congress broadened the universe of potential plaintiffs, with only four exclusions. At issue here is whether or not government employees fall under one of those exclusions, § 3730(e)(4), and are still barred from bringing suits under the Act. The False Claims act provides in relevant part:

"(e) Certain actions barred * * *

* * *

" * * * (4)(A) No court shall have jurisdiction over an action under this section based upon the public disclosure of allegations or transactions in a criminal, civil, or administrative hearing, in a congressional, administrative, or Government Accounting Office Report, hearing, audit, or investigation, or from the news media, unless the action is brought by the Attorney General or the person bringing the action is an original source of the information.

"(B) For purposes of this paragraph, 'original source' means an individual who has direct and independent knowledge of the information on which the allegations are based and has voluntarily provided the information to the Government before filing an action under this section which is based on the information."

31 U.S.C.A. § 3730(e)(4).

Erickson ex rel. United States v. American Institute of Biological Sciences, 716 F.Supp. 908 (E.D.Va.1989), the only case to discuss the issue of whether government employees can bring *qui tam* actions after the 1986 amendments, held that the language structure, legislative history and purpose of the 1986 amendments reveal a legislative intent to permit such actions. The *Erickson* court reasoned that since § 3730(b) states that "any person may bring a civil action," and because nowhere in the statute are there restrictions on the term "persons," Congress intended that "Government employees are included in the general universe of permissible *qui tam* plaintiffs unless, in the particular circumstances, they fall into one of the four specifically excluded groups." Id. at 913. *Erickson* went on to hold that government employees did not fall into the exclusion of § 3730(e)(4), which is also the exclusion at issue in this case.

The district court, while agreeing with *Erickson* that the False Claims Act was specifically amended to broaden the scope of permissible plaintiffs, concluded that government employees did indeed constitute an excluded group under § 3730(e)(4) and thus are barred from bringing *qui tam* actions. The district court found that because "government employees maintain a dual status—arms of the government while at work, private citizens while not at work—a 'public disclosure' necessarily occurs whenever a government employee uses government information he learned on the job to file a *qui tam* suit in his private capacity." Furthermore, the district court went on to conclude that all government employees are barred under the original source exception of § 3730(e)(4) as well.

The district court need not have gone so far. For this reason we take this opportunity to clarify and limit the district court's holding and analysis.

A. *Public Disclosure*

The district court's analysis of the "public disclosure" provision effectively erases a large portion of § 3730(e)(3)(4). We disagree with the district court's analysis for three reasons. First, the logical reading is that the subsection serves to prohibit courts from hearing *qui tam* actions based on information made available to the public during the course of a government hearing, investigation or audit or from the news media. It bars government employees, as well as private citizens, from bringing *qui tam* actions only if the information forming the basis of the action was acquired in the circumstances described in 31 U.S.C. § 3730(e)(4)(A). It does not prevent government employees from bringing qui tam actions based on information acquired during the course of their employment but not as the result of a government hearing, investigation or audit or through the news media.

Second, the district court's analysis of the subsection requires the assumption that government employees lead schizophrenic lives and can publicly disclose information to themselves. Even were this hypothesis physically reasonable, it totally ignores the limiting language in § 3730(e)(4)(A) which follows the term "public disclosure." That language bars jurisdiction over actions "based upon the public disclosure of allegations or transactions in a criminal, civil or administrative hearing, in a congressional, administrative, or Government Accounting Office report, hearing, audit, or investigation, or from the news media * * *." It does not deny jurisdiction over actions based on disclosures other than those specified, contrary to what the district court seemed to maintain.

Last, the district court further assumes that the filing of a *qui tam* action is itself a "public disclosure." This cannot be. Such an action is filed under seal without service on anyone other than the United States and remains non-public until the district court enters an order lifting the seal. To hold otherwise would be to render each and every filing a "public disclosure," thus barring all *qui tam* actions.

B. Original Source

The district court held that a government employee in the same position as LeBlanc cannot qualify for the "original source" exception to § 3730(e)(4)'s jurisdictional bar. We agree. It was LeBlanc's responsibility, a condition of his employment, to uncover fraud. The fruits of his effort belong to his employer—the government. Thus, LeBlanc was not someone with "independent knowledge of the information" as required by the statute. This conclusion, however, does not mean that there is no government employee who could qualify to bring a *qui tam* action under the original source exception. We decline to draft a litigation manual full of scenarios that would fall under the exception. Suffice it to say that we limit our holding to the facts.

Affirmed in result.

Notes

1. In United States ex rel. Williams v. NEC Corp., 931 F.2d 1493 (11th Cir.1991), the Eleventh Circuit held that Arthur Williams, an attorney for the United States Air Force, was not barred from filing a *qui tam* lawsuit against NEC Corp. that alleged that NEC engaged in bidrigging on bids it submitted to the government. After Williams filed his *qui tam* action, the United States filed a motion to dismiss for lack of subject matter jurisdiction, alleging "that the False Claims Act contained a jurisdictional bar against suits brought by government employees based upon information acquired in the course of their government employment." Id. at 1495. The Eleventh Circuit held that the False Claim Act contains no such bar, and reversed the District Court's grant of the government's Motion to Dismiss. In reaching its conclusion, the Eleventh Circuit looked to the statutory language and legislative history, finding in neither any indication of an absolute bar against government employees as *qui tam* relators. The Court then addressed the public policy arguments offered by the United States:

> "The United States has offered several public policy reasons for finding that Congress intended to bar government employees from initiating qui tam suits based upon information acquired in the course of their government employment. The essence of the government's public policy arguments is that the False Claims Act should not allow a personal reward to government employees for the 'parasitical' use of information obtained and developed in the course of government employment. More specifically, the United States maintains that a 'parasitical' suit brought by a government employee based upon government information while a government investigation is under way will prematurely disclose the information in the possession of the government to the defendant, and thereby prejudice the government's case. In addition, the government warns of races to the courthouse in which government employees seek to file suit as private *qui tam* relators before the Attorney General can file suit on behalf of the United States. Such races, it asserts, would force the Attorney General 'to file suits based on facts that are only in a preliminary stage of investigation, with corresponding disclosure to the potential defendant of the existence of the inquiry and undermining of the government's case.' And finally, the United States asserts that

government employees should not receive compensation via the False Claims Act for reporting fraud against the government when it is part of their duties as government employees to report such fraud notwithstanding the Act.

"We recognize that the concerns articulated by the United States may be legitimate ones, and that the application of the False Claims Act since its 1986 amendment may have revealed difficulties in the administration of qui tam suits, particularly those brought by government employees.[16] Notwithstanding this recognition, however, we are charged only with interpreting the statute before us and not with amending it to eliminate administrative difficulties. The limits upon the judicial prerogative in interpreting statutory language were well articulated by the Supreme Court when it cautioned:

> " 'Legislation introducing a new system is at best empirical, and not infrequently administration reveals gaps or inadequacies of one sort or another that may call for amendatory legislation. But it is no warrant for extending a statute that experience may disclose that it should have been made more comprehensive. The natural meaning of words cannot be displaced by reference to difficulties in administration.' Commonwealth v. Grunseit, 67 C.L.R. 58, 30 (1943). For the ultimate question is what has Congress commanded, when it has given no clue to its intentions except familiar English words and no hint by the draftsmen of the words that they meant to use them in any but an ordinary sense."

2. It is interesting to note that in 1991, when Congress created *qui tam* actions against persons committing bank fraud crimes, it clearly excluded government employees as *qui tam* relators. This statute provides that a *qui tam* action may not be brought if,

> "the declaration is filed by a current or former officer or employee of the Federal or State government agency or instrumentality who discovered or gathered the information in the declaration, in whole or in part, while acting within the course of the declarant's government employment."

12 U.S.C. § 4204(a)(1). It remains to be seen whether the interpretation taken by the First or the Eleventh Circuit will prevail, and whether Con-

---

16. We note, however, that the first two concerns articulated by the United States describe administrative difficulties that might arise when any private qui tam plaintiff files suit prior to the completion of a government investigation into the subject of the action. In addition, we note that the False Claims Act provides that the qui tam complaint filed by a private person be filed in camera and that it remain under seal for at least 60 days without disclosure to the defendant, which time may be extended for good cause upon motion by the government. 31 U.S.C. § 3730(b)(2), (3). Thus, the government may, if disclosure of information concerning the qui tam complaint to the defendant would prejudice an ongoing in-vestigation, move the court for extensions of the time during which the complaint remains under seal. See 31 U.S.C. § 3730(b)(3). Further, if the government is concerned that the private qui tam plaintiff will not satisfactorily litigate the action on behalf of the United States, the government may elect to intervene and proceed with the action itself. 31 U.S.C. § 3730(b)(2). And finally, the government may dismiss the action brought by the private qui tam plaintiff, as long as the private relator is afforded notice and opportunity for a hearing on the motion to dismiss. 31 U.S.C. § 3730(c)(2)(A). Such safeguards go a long way toward alleviating many of the government's concerns.

gress will respond by amending the False Claims Act to bar government employees from becoming *qui tam* relators.

C. HEALTH CARE FRAUD[r]

As Willie Sutton said when asked why he robbed a bank, "That's where the money is."[s] Health care consumes 15% of the United States' GNP, for a total of $884 billion in 1993.[t] Even if only a small portion of health care dollars were lost to fraud and abuse, the loss would be significant. For a variety of reasons, health care is particularly susceptible to fraud and the amount lost to fraud and abuse is large, estimated at 10% of total health care expenditures. This casebook devotes a section to health care fraud for three reasons. First, currently it has a high profile among white collar crimes. In 1997, health care fraud was the second priority of the United States Department of Justice (DOJ) and the top white collar crime priority.[u] Additional prosecutors and FBI agents have been added by DOJ to focus exclusively on health care fraud.[v] The Health Insurance Portability and Accountability Act of 1996 (HIPAA) appropriated substantial amounts of money to fight health care fraud and created a trust fund which will be continuing source of funds earmarked specifically to fight health care fraud.[w] Congress also passed five new criminal offenses aimed specifically at health care fraud and expanded the reach of civil and administrative remedies.[x] With these resources devoted exclusively to prosecuting health care fraud, it is likely that this area of white collar crime will remain extremely active for the foreseeable future.

The second reason for a separate section on health care fraud is that health care fraud epitomizes the unique characteristics of white collar crime and thus makes for a convenient "case study" of white collar crime. Most white collar crimes are difficult to investigate and prove[y]

---

r. For a fuller discussion of health care fraud, see PAMELA H. BUCY, HEALTH CARE FRAUD: CRIMINAL, CIVIL AND ADMINISTRATIVE LAW (1996). Portions of this chapter are reprinted with the permission of the publisher from HEALTH CARE FRAUD: CRIMINAL, CIVIL AND ADMINISTRATIVE LAW. Published and copyrighted by Law Journal Seminars–Press, 345 Park Avenue South, New York, New York 10010. All rights reserved.

s. Quoted by Inspector General June Gibbs Brown, Department of Health and Human Services, *Health Care Fraud, Hearing before the Senate Special Comm. on Aging*, 104th Cong., 1st Sess. 71 (Mar. 21, 1995).

t. *Id.* (Prepared statement of Thomas A. Temmerman, Director, California Bureau of Medical Fraud); Prospective Payment Assessment Comm'n, *Report and Recommendations to the Congress*, 14 (March 1, 1995).

u. Health Care Fraud: Hearing before the Senate Select Comm. on Aging, 104th Cong., 1st Sess. at (Mar. 21 1995) (Prepared Statement of FBI Director Louis J. Freeh).

v. *Id.*

w. HIPAA, Pub. L. 104–191, § 2.01.

x. HIPAA, Pub. L. 104–191, § 241 (18 U.S.C. §§ 669, 1035, 1347, 1518).

y. *White Collar Crime: Hearing before the Senate Comm. on the Judiciary*, Part 1, 99th Cong., 2d Sess. at 27 (1986) (Testimony of United States Deputy Attorney General D. Lowell Jensen); CLINARD & YEAGER, CORPORATE CRIME 95 (1980); CONKLIN, ILLEGAL BUT NOT CRIMINAL 17–18 (1977); FINN & HOFFMAN, PROSECUTION OF ECONOMIC CRIME 4 (1976); GARDINER & LYMAN, THE FRAUD CONTROL GAME 87 (1984).

because white collar crime is rarely self-evident.[z] Victims of assaults know immediately when they have been assaulted but victims of fraud may never know they have been defrauded.[aa] This failure to realize that one has been defrauded is due, in part, to the fact that the perpetrator usually is in a position of trust to the victim.[bb] Because of this relationship, a fraud victim has no reason to suspect criminal activity, even when circumstances occur that would otherwise make a crime victim suspicious. The patient-physician relationship epitomizes such trust.[cc] "Often in pain, fearful of death, the sick have a special thirst for reassurance and vulnerability to belief."[dd]

In addition to the unsuspecting naivete of victims, the fact that the crime is usually hidden in voluminous documentary materials also makes white collar crime difficult to investigate and prove.[ee] It is often necessary to follow a lengthy paper trail simply to discover what occurred. This paper trail is especially arduous in the health care field because of complex and rapidly changing regulations. As one expert noted, "The billing process itself, and the paperwork necessary to monitor numerous and complex third-party insurance contracts—with varying co-insurance, deductibles, and maximum benefit schedules and with widely varying coverage and criteria for major medical payments—boggle[s] the mind.... [I]t assuredly confuses both patients and their doctors."[ff]

While many white collar crimes involve complex statutes and regulations, the complexity of regulations in the health care industry is exacerbated by several facts unique to this industry. Health care regulations change more often than those in most fields. In addition, a single provider usually deals simultaneously with several third-party providers and is subject to the varied and often inconsistent rules and regulations promulgated by each. Because of the third-party reimbursement mechanism, all providers must utilize these voluminous, changing, inconsistent rules and regulations to obtain reimbursement for performing even a minor procedure. To prove even the smallest fraud involves tracking hundreds of such regulations.

A third reason white collar crime is difficult to investigate and prove is that it is often "hidden within an organization."[gg] This is especially

---

z. *White Collar Crime, supra* note 16, at 27 (Testimony of United States Deputy Attorney General D. Lowell Jensen); FINN & HOFFMAN, *supra* note 16, at 4.

aa. BEQUAI, WHITE COLLAR CRIME: A 20TH CENTURY CRISIS 13 (1978); SUTHERLAND, WHITE COLLAR CRIME: THE UNEXPURGATED VERSION 232 (1983); EDELHERTZ, *The Nature, Impact and Prosecution of White Collar Crime,* CRIME AT THE TOP 51 (1978).

bb. *White Collar Crime, supra* note 16, at 27 (Testimony of United States Deputy Attorney General D. Lowell Jensen).

cc. *See, e.g.,* David Mechanic, *Some Dilemmas in Health Care Policy,* 59 MILBANK MEMORIAL FUND Q. 1, 4 (1981) ("Feeling highly dependent on such relationships, the typical patient has a strong need to see [his own physician] as an ally.") [hereinafter *Dilemmas*]; T. R. Marmor, *Medical Care & Procompetitive Reform,* 34 VAND. L. REV. 1003 (1981).

dd. PAUL STARR, THE SOCIAL TRANSFORMATION OF AMERICAN MEDICINE 5 (1982).

ee. *White Collar Crime, supra* note y, at 27 (Testimony of United States Deputy Attorney General D. Lowell Jensen).

ff. David Mechanic, *Dilemmas, supra* note cc, at 7–8.

gg. *White Collar Crime, supra* note y, at 103 (Testimony of Professor Stanton Wheeler, Yale Law School).

true in the area of health care fraud as these fraud schemes have increased in "sophistication and complexity."[hh] In the 1980's, when authorities first began focusing on health care fraud, most of the cases involved "individual providers filing false claims for relatively low dollar amounts."[ii] In the past few years, however, the schemes have "changed dramatically" because "organized criminal enterprises have penetrated virtually every legitimate segment of the health care industry."[jj]

The fact that health care fraud is hidden within an organization makes it difficult to find out what went on and particularly difficult to find evidence of a defendant's intent.[kk] In the health care field, fraud often occurs when false bills are submitted for reimbursement by the provider to the third-party payer. This billing process usually involves a number of people apart from the provider, such as a receptionist, billing clerk, nurse, or computer billing service. Once the claim reaches the provider it is again processed by multiple individuals and computer services. To hold the provider responsible for the false statements in the bills requires a step-by-step analysis of the billing process and proof that the provider personally knew false information was included in the bills finally submitted.[ll]

The last reason for including a separate section on health care fraud is that among the white collar crimes, all of which are fascinating, health care fraud stands out as riveting. As you read the case in this section, see if you agree.

SIDDIQI v. UNITED STATES

United States Court of Appeals, Second Circuit, 1996.
98 F.3d 1427.

WINTER, CIRCUIT JUDGE.

Naveed Siddiqi, M.D., appeals from Judge Telesca's denial of his petition under 28 U.S.C. § 2255 to vacate his conviction and his sentence for Medicare billing fraud. Siddiqi asserts that he was convicted because of constitutionally ineffective assistance of counsel at trial. We find no merit in his ineffective assistance claim, but we nevertheless vacate his conviction and sentence. The government has, throughout this prosecution, adopted shifting theories of guilt. This inconstancy of position impeded Siddiqi's defense at trial and has severely hampered judicial

---

hh. *Health Care Fraud, Hearing before the Senate Select Comm. on Aging,* 104th Cong., 1st Sess. 70 (Mar. 21, 1995) (Prepared statement of Inspector General June Gibbs Brown, Dept. of Health and Human Services).

ii. *Id.*

jj. *Id.* at 19 (Prepared statement, FBI Director Louis J. Freeh).

kk. *White Collar Crime, supra* note y, at 103 (Testimony of Professor Stanton Wheeler, Yale Law School).

ll. *Medicare & Medicaid Frauds: Hearings before the Senate Comm. on Aging,* Pt. 1, 94th Cong., 1st Sess. 21 (1975) (Statement of Paul M. Allen, Chief Deputy Director, Michigan Department. of Social Services).

consideration of this matter. At this final stage, in order to rebut a claim of ineffective assistance, the government now embraces a theory that is legally insufficient. A miscarriage of justice having occurred, we vacate the conviction.

1. BACKGROUND

Siddiqi is an oncologist who, at pertinent times, practiced medicine in Elmira, New York. He was board-certified in internal medicine, oncology, and hematology. In 1973, he was approved to participate as a physician in Medicare, the federally funded health insurance program that provides basic medical coverage to individuals over age 65 and to other qualified individuals.

The Medicare program is overseen by the Health Care Financing Administration ("HCFA"), part of the United States Department of Health and Human Services ("HHS"). Medicare is divided into two parts, commonly known as "Part A" and "Part B." Part A covers health care services rendered primarily by hospitals, while Part B covers services rendered by physicians and other noninstitutional providers. HCFA contracts with private insurance companies across the country to process the claims submitted under Medicare. In the Elmira area, Blue Shield of Western New York ("Blue Shield") administers Part B of the Medicare program.

Participating physicians and other Medicare providers submit claims by mail or computer to Blue Shield. In submitting claims for reimbursement, providers use Blue Shield's *Doctor's Manual*, a three-inch-thick looseleaf binder containing various descriptions of medical services and five-digit numerical codes. Each provider selects from the Manual the code that most accurately describes the services rendered. After processing the claim, Medicare mails the check to the physician. A deliberately misleading use of a particular code would, of course, support a criminal fraud charge under various federal statutes.

2. THE INDICTMENT AND PRETRIAL PROCEEDINGS

In 1990, a grand jury in the Western District of New York returned an indictment charging Siddiqi with 77 counts of fraud related to his Medicare billing practices between March 11, 1988 and April 27, 1989. Each count of the indictment involved one of three separate allegedly fraudulent schemes. The jury acquitted Siddiqi on every count related to two of the schemes. It convicted on five counts involving a scheme in which Siddiqi submitted allegedly false Medicare claims for chemotherapy treatments. These counts were for mail fraud, in violation of 18 U.S.C. § 1341; theft of government property, in violation of 18 U.S.C. § 641; and false claims, in violation of 18 U.S.C. § 287.

The five counts of conviction alleged that Siddiqi defrauded the Medicare program by submitting claims for outpatient chemotherapy treatments that he prescribed for his patients and that were administered by the medical staff at St. Joseph's Hospital. The indictment stated that "no chemotherapy treatment was administered to [Siddiqi's patients] at his office on the same day that the patient received chemotherapy treatment at the hospital." It further stated that the hospital chemotherapy was "administered without [Siddiqi's] participation or supervision" and that Siddiqi "caused claims to be submitted ... for the administration of chemotherapy well knowing that chemotherapy was solely administered on that day to the patient at St. Joseph's Hospital during which time [Siddiqi] was not participating in or supervising the administration of the chemotherapy." Finally, the indictment charged that Siddiqi "knew St. Joseph's Hospital would file a claim to the Medicare program for the chemotherapy" and that Siddiqi thus "caused the duplicate claims for chemotherapy treatment ... in order to receive additional monies from Medicare."

These counts all related to claims submitted for services in connection with chemotherapy treatments administered to patients between July 12, 1988 and July 28, 1988. The parties stipulated that Siddiqi, a Moslem, was on a pilgrimage to Mecca during that time. We will, therefore, style these five counts the "Mecca counts."

3. THE TRIAL

In his opening statement, the prosecutor advanced a simple theory as to the Mecca counts: "This case is really all about Medicare fraud; phony billing, billing for services not rendered.... [t]he doctor submitted a claim to Medicare saying, in essence, 'I performed that chemo. So I'm entitled to reimbursement for the cost of the administration of that chemo, for the cost of the drug and for the cost of the actual administering the chemo.'" Siddiqi, the government asserted, was "claiming for services rendered by somebody else."

The prosecution's opening statement thus presented a simple theory of double billing: St. Joseph's billed Medicare for the cost of the drug and of administering it, while Siddiqi billed Medicare for the very same things. If proven, of course, Siddiqi would indeed be guilty of fraud no matter where he was at the time the chemotherapy was administered. Indeed, the prosecutor's opening never referred to Siddiqi's whereabouts at times pertinent to the Mecca counts.

However, the opening statement was a harbinger of the way in which this prosecution was to be conducted. The double billing theory was grand advocacy but had no basis in the evidence.

First, the Mecca counts involved Siddiqi's use of code 96500 in the Blue Shield *Doctor's Manual* to bill for the chemotherapy treatments in question. To convict Siddiqi on any of the Mecca counts, the government had to show knowing falsity in using that code. However, code 96500 does not state that it covers the cost of the chemotherapy drug itself. Siddiqi's use of that code was not a statement, therefore, that he had provided the drug and was seeking reimbursement for its cost. Moreover, there was no proof that Siddiqi billed for the cost of the chemotherapy drugs, each bill in the Mecca counts amounting to roughly $40.00, or roughly 10% of the bills submitted by the hospital for the drugs and their administration. In retrospect, it is extremely doubtful that the government ever had any evidence justifying the prosecutor's assertion that Siddiqi billed for the cost of the drugs.

Second, the opening statement was incorrect in asserting that Siddiqi claimed to have administered the drug. The 96500 code covers "[c]hemotherapy injection, intravenous, single premixed agent, administered by qualified assistant under supervision of physician or by physician; by push technique." Because code 96500 covers "supervision" of the administration of chemotherapy by a qualified assistant, Siddiqi's designation of code 96500 was not necessarily a statement that he actually administered the drug.

To prove falsity under code 96500, therefore, the government had to prove that Siddiqi knowingly did nothing that might amount to supervision of the administration of the chemotherapy by the staff at St. Joseph's. The government's main witness in this regard was Joseph Niegsch, an agent with the Health & Human Services Inspector General's office. He testified that "the government alleges in [the Mecca counts] that the hospital actually performed the chemotherapy and not Dr. Siddiqi." The fraud "relates to the submission of Medicare claims for reimbursement by Dr. Siddiqi in which he listed as his claims or services that he provided patients—he listed chemotherapy as the service he provided. All of the claims related to . . . services that were provided in the hospital. Now, Dr. Siddiqi on his claims states that he did the chemotherapy." Niegsch's testimony was of course wrong. Siddiqi's "statement" was the designation of code 96500, which includes "supervision" of the administration of chemotherapy by an assistant. Use of that code was not, therefore, a claim of having actually administered the drugs.

Niegsch impliedly filled this hole in the government's case when he later testified that Siddiqi could not have supervised or administered services for the Mecca claims because Siddiqi was out of the country at the time. He stated, "[t]he government alleges they were fraudulent claims in that the services were actually provided in the hospital, but they were not provided by Dr. Siddiqi, and in many cases he was not in the hospital when the services were actually provided." Niegsch identified for the jury the dates on which Siddiqi charged Medicare under code 96500 and then read for the jury the stipulation that Siddiqi was out of the country from July 12 through July 28, 1988. Siddiqi's whereabouts thus became relevant by implication as evidence that he could not have supervised the administration of chemotherapy on the dates in question.

On cross-examination, Niegsch stated that Siddiqi "billed for services that were actually performed by someone else." Siddiqi's attorney asked Niegsch what the term "under supervision of physician" meant in the *Doctor's Manual* code 96500. Niegsch said he had no opinion.

At some point, perhaps by stipulation, "outpatient documents" relating to patients who received chemotherapy while Siddiqi was in Mecca were introduced. One of these related to a patient named Arthur Kenny. It bore a notation, "Call Dr. Siddiqi if any problems." There was no testimony during the government's main case concerning Arthur Kenny's outpatient document or other such documents, their relevance seemingly being simply to prove the administration of chemotherapy by the hospital while Siddiqi was in Mecca.

Oncology nurse Mary Ann Baker also testified as a government witness. She was in charge of the outpatient oncology service of St. Joseph's Hospital. Baker harbored no great friendship for Siddiqi and had declined to speak with his attorney before trial. She testified that Siddiqi did not attend the chemotherapy injection sessions. However, she also stated that it was a common practice for oncologists not to attend such sessions. Nevertheless, the doctors were available if needed, and she could reach them, including Siddiqi, by pager if necessary. Siddiqi's lawyer elicited from Baker on cross-examination that it is also a common practice for "physician A to have physician B cover for him." To the question, "And Dr. Siddiqi like others would on occasion as necessary have someone cover for him ... in his absence?", she answered "yes." There was no redirect examination by the government.

Baker's testimony and cross-examination introduced issues that have since plagued this matter. First, she stated that the oncologist's absence during the administration of chemotherapy was common but that the doctor might yet be involved as being on-call if needed. Arguably, such availability might amount to "supervision" under code 96500.

Second, Baker stated that it was a common practice for another doctor to "cover" for one absent on vacation or otherwise. Whether or not the significance of coverage to the five Mecca counts was apparent at this point in the trial of the 77 counts, the government certainly gave no weight to it in bringing charges against Siddiqi. Baker had cooperated with the FBI and testified before the grand jury. In each instance, she had stated that Siddiqi usually had a Dr. Mufti cover for him when Siddiqi was away.

On the first appeal, we noted that Siddiqi presented "undisputed expert and lay testimony" that 96500 was the standard billing code for the "professional service" component of the administration of chemotherapy at the times charged in the Mecca counts and that this billing practice was recommended by the American Society of Clinical Oncologists. United States v. Siddiqi, 959 F.2d 1167, 1171 (2d Cir.1992). A Dr. Weissman testified as a defense expert. He stated that considerable confusion existed over how to bill Medicare for chemotherapy and quoted one Medicare official as describing the area as "chaos." Weissman also stated that oncologists were rarely present at the actual administration of chemotherapy. He testified on direct that, after prescribing drugs and dosages, an oncologist might bill for being available for consultation and for observing charts that monitored a patient's reaction to the drugs even though there would be no contact with the patient. On cross-examination, he was asked a series of questions concerning whether an oncologist might bill Medicare for outpatient visits even though the physician performed no services. His answers boiled down to the following: If the doctor was available but performed no services, opinions differed among doctors as to whether a bill could properly be rendered; if the doctor was away, and not covered, no bill could be properly rendered. On redirect, he was asked about coverage, but the government successfully prevented this testimony on hearsay grounds.

Siddiqi testified as follows regarding the billing for services rendered while in Mecca:

Q. Now, there are certain services that are shown in three or four counts in the indictment that involve the period of time when you were out of the country and for which some services were provided in the hospital and office setting.

Would you tell the jury the arrangements you made as far as coverage on your behalf? In other words, substitute coverage or the like.

A. Yes. I—the people who were going to the hospital, I arranged with the oncology nurses for them to receive their treatment.

So I arrange for their doses. I arrange for their schedule. I arranged for their modification of the doses if it becomes necessary. This was arranged before I left.

And actually, when I left on Tuesday most of those people I actually saw on Monday. So that week basically was seen as I had seen them anyway.

And after I arrange for their chemotherapy in the outpatient setting with their drug dosage, the schedule, the number of drugs that they were going to get, I arranged for coverage with another physician, and I went ahead and I told him that there were these people who were going to be receiving treatments and they were going to get this type of treatment; there's going to be potentially this kind of side-effect.

So that what I gave him was instructions. The patients would go say, for example, on a Monday and would get their blood count, and if their blood count was below four thousand white count or the platelet count was less than a hundred thousand, any of the oncology nurses would then contact him. Then he would arrange to adjust the dose that he had with him how to adjust the dose. [sic]

If the patient got too sick he was supposed to see them.

So all this arrangement was made with another physician for both outpatient and for the office.

Q. All right. Now, in the office context for the coverage did you inform your personnel who the physician was that would be covering?

A. Yes. I mean, obviously there are people that are getting—you're gone for twenty days. There are patients who are going to get a heart attack and the patient is going to start bleeding. The nurse has to know who to contact, sure.

Q. And in the in-hospital setting, the physician—and the physician was who?

A. Dr. Mufti.

Q. Dr. Mufti to the best of your knowledge, did he also have hospital privileges at St. Joe's?

A. Yes.

Q. And did he make daily rounds as you have described the rounds you made so far as you're aware?

A. Yes.

Q. Was that at least your intention and your belief before you left?

A. Yes.

Siddiqi was not cross-examined by the government on this phase of his testimony.

Siddiqi did not present any other evidence of Mufti's covering for him. Mufti came to the trial and was ready to testify, but Siddiqi's trial counsel did not call him. As we noted on the first appeal, this was "not surprising," because the prosecutor, while cross-examining defense witness Martin Neltner, an accountant who was a medical billing consultant, apparently conceded that Siddiqi had arranged for Mufti to cover his patients in his absence. The prosecutor said, "[W]ith respect to coverage—I don't think anybody is questioning that coverage exists in this trial, but my question relates to the method by which coverage is standardly reported in the hospital." Having stated that no one was "questioning that coverage exists in this trial"—a remark entirely consistent with the information available to the government and to the defense—the prosecutor next pursued hypotheticals concerning how the identity of a covering doctor might be made known to the nurse who was to administer the chemotherapy. The following colloquy ensued:

Q. Isn't it fair to say that whenever a doctor covers for another doctor, that doctor that is covering reports in at some time to the nurse oncologist?

A. When you say "reports in"—

Q. Has some sort of contact.

A. Has some contact. Could be by phone, could be in person.

Q. Anything.

A. That's correct.

Q. Some contact.

A. A lot of times the physician will rely on the nurse to call him—

Q. Sure.

A.—when there is a problem.

Q. Sure. So if a particular doctor—let's do it as a hypothetical. If a particular doctor is standing in for Dr. Siddiqi, and in that particular situation the nurse is supposed to reach out to the covering doctor, one would expect to see the notes on the bottom of the hospital records "If a problem call covering doctor," correct?

A. Yes.

Q. Okay.

A. I would like to see that.

Q. And it wouldn't be—

A. I would like to see that.

Q. You would like to see that?

A. Yes.

Q. If a problem call Dr. Siddiqi, but it would—if a problem call the covering doctor, correct?

A. Yes.

Q. Okay. And in that light the professional component presumes that there's a service being rendered—

A. Yes.

Q.—isn't that correct?

A. Yes.

Q. That's a given.

A. Yes.

Q. That we're not billing for services not rendered.

A. That is correct.

The questions concerning notations as to the identity of a covering doctor, posed as hypotheticals to an accountant, were the sole inquiries by the prosecutor regarding coverage during trial. However, they were sandwiched between a concession that no one was "questioning that coverage exists in this trial" and testimony at the end that seemed to confirm compensability where coverage was provided. The prosecutor's reference to a hypothetical note, "If a problem, call Dr. Siddiqi," must, in the context of what turned out to be a highly misleading concession and of otherwise helpful testimony, have seemed unimportant, although it was later the basis for a crucial part of the prosecution's summation concerning Arthur Kenny's outpatient document, as set out below.

The government's case on the Mecca counts at the close of evidence was at best confusing. Double billing had not been shown. Niegsch had no opinion on what "supervision" meant. Baker had testified that oncologists did not attend the administration of prescribed chemotherapy but were available if needed, or were covered by another doctor. Weissman had testified to disagreement over whether being available was compensable. With regard to whether Siddiqi had actually arranged for coverage, Baker had stated that Siddiqi usually had a doctor cover when he was away. Siddiqi testified that Mufti covered for him at the time of the

Mecca counts, and the government seemingly conceded that coverage in cross-examining the accountant. Nevertheless, the cross-examination of the accountant, viewed in hindsight, indicates that the prosecutor had arrived at a strategy to salvage the case.

In summation, the prosecutor expressly repudiated the double-billing theory that had loomed so large in his opening. He stated: "There's no double billing. We're not alleging a double billing. We're alleging billing for services not rendered. Pure and sweet, that's it." However, he also reversed the government's position that no one was "questioning that coverage exists":

> The coverage issue. The doctor's out of the country. Dr. Mufti's going to look after my patients. There's no reference to Dr. Mufti anywhere.

> Don't trust me. Take a look at it. Specifically take a look at Arthur Kenny. [Apparently, Arthur Kenny's outpatient document.] Arthur Kenny is in the indictment July 27th, '88, July 29th, '88.

> The reference is not "Call Dr. Mufti," and if you recall, I asked Mr. Neltner, "Shouldn't it say 'Call Dr. Mufti'?"

> The coverage—if the covering doctor's there you should say "Call Dr. Mufti," and if it didn't there probably wasn't any coverage.

> The outpatient document says call Dr. Siddiqi if any problems.

> Well, old Arthur Kenny isn't going to get too quick a response if the doctor is out of the country at the time, is he? Take a look at it.

The summation was a success. As we previously noted, the issue in the jury's mind was evidently whether Siddiqi told the truth when he said he told the hospital that Mufti would be covering for him while he was away. It determined that he did not and convicted on the Mecca counts.

4. POST-TRIAL PROCEEDINGS

The defense filed a post-trial motion for a judgment of acquittal notwithstanding the verdict, see Fed.R.Crim.P. 29(c), which the district court denied. Siddiqi was sentenced to three years' probation, 1000 hours of community service as an emergency room physician, a fine of $2000.00, $640.88 in restitution, and a $250.00 special assessment. On July 15, 1991, Siddiqi filed a notice of appeal.

On August 5, he filed a motion in the district court for a new trial based upon newly discovered evidence. See Fed.R.Crim.P. 33. The evidence was a document from St. Joseph's Hospital known as the "physicians away list." This list consisted of the names of physicians who would be out of town on certain dates and the names of other physicians who would be covering for them. It reflected that Dr. Mufti was covering for Dr. Siddiqi on the dates involved in the Mecca counts.

In response, the government argued that "the 'covering physician' [Mufti] was nowhere to be seen or heard from [at trial]" and ventured that "what was newly discovered was not the list itself but the potential relevance of the list to [Siddiqi's] defense." However, the government muddied the waters by stating that its consistent position was that "the defendant should not have billed for services he did not provide" and "billed for services he allegedly performed while he was outside of the United States on travel." These latter remarks strongly suggested that, regardless of coverage by Mufti, Siddiqi was guilty because he did not personally perform services regarding the administration of chemotherapy while he was in Mecca. The district court denied Siddiqi's motion, concluding it was "highly unlikely" that the introduction of the list at trial would have led to a different result. Siddiqi filed a second notice of appeal. The appeals from the conviction and from the denial of the Rule 33 motion were consolidated.

5. THE FIRST APPEAL

Siddiqi raised three claims on the first appeal: (i) that the evidence was insufficient to support his conviction on the five Mecca counts; (ii) that the district court erroneously failed to grant a new trial on the basis of the newly discovered physicians away list; and (iii) that the district court erred in failing to give two of Siddiqi's proffered jury instructions. The arguments supporting each of these claims emphasized the shifting nature of the government's theories of the case.

The government's brief denied any inconsistency in position but hardly settled upon a single, clear theory of Siddiqi's guilt. Although the conviction on the Mecca counts was undoubtedly based on the government's argument—and the jury's conclusion—that Siddiqi had not arranged with Mufti for coverage, the government's array of theories on appeal barely alluded to that factual issue. For example, the government's brief summarized the relevant charges as alleging that Siddiqi "billed Medicare as though he administered the chemotherapy." The focus on the actual administration of the injections—as opposed to the "supervision" of them—was seemingly a resurrection of the asserted-in-the-opening, abandoned-in-the-summation double-billing theory. The brief also claimed the evidence at trial "showed that the appellant billed Medicare for chemotherapy administered to two of his patients during a two-week period of time in which appellant was out of the country." It further asserted: "The verdict of the jury reflects their [sic] collective opinion that the appellant billed Medicare for chemotherapy he claimed he administered at a time when it is undisputed he did not." However, the government also alluded to other theories: "the decision of the jury as to the five counts of conviction was an implicit rejection of the dual defense claims that he was entitled to bill for Saint Joseph's chemotherapy since he was ultimately responsible and that another doctor covered for him while he was away."

The only substantive discussion in the government's brief of the factual issue as to whether Siddiqi had arranged for coverage by Mufti was a single paragraph in the discussion of the sufficiency of the evidence. It stated:

The appellant further stresses ... that Mary Anne Baker clearly established that the appellant was available at the hospital while his patients were receiving chemotherapy and that he provided coverage for his patients at the hospital while he was away. Nowhere in the record of Ms. Baker's testimony is there an acknowledgment that Ms. Baker could have contacted the appellant while he was on vacation or that he provided coverage while he was out of the country. To the contrary, based upon Ms. Baker's own notation, she was operating under the obviously incorrect assumption that while Arthur Kenny was receiving chemotherapy on July 25, 1988, she could have contacted the appellant if any problems occurred. GA 34. [A cite to the Arthur Kenny outpatient document]

This was a misleading description of the evidence in that Baker did in fact testify that Siddiqi was either on call or provided coverage "as necessary." Moreover, there was no evidence at trial or elsewhere that she authored the notation "Call Dr. Siddiqi if any problems" on the Kenny outpatient document. We now know that she did not.

At oral argument, the prosecutor again offered various theories. He stated, "The doctor did not administer the chemotherapy.... [H]e did not perform the service, he billed Medicare for the administration of the chemotherapy." The crime, he said, was "billing for something he did not do." These statements again appeared to invoke the double-billing theory or at least a theory under which Mufti's coverage or non-coverage and Siddiqi's whereabouts were irrelevant. Later, the prosecutor emphasized the need for Siddiqi's personal involvement in the administration of the drugs: "if [Siddiqi] wanted to get credit and bill for that service ... he should have supervised the administration of the chemo." Still later, however, he asserted "there is no evidence that Mufti came in and was covering the doctor." After that, a new theory emerged: "Dr. Mufti may have come at some particular time later on in the day after the administration was done and looked at the chart, the hospital didn't know a Dr. Mufti" was covering for Dr. Siddiqi. This theory, which played no role at trial, seemed to posit that even if Mufti was available, coverage was irrelevant if it was not communicated to the hospital. It was also quite at odds with the government's position that the physicians away list would not have affected the verdict even though it showed that notice of Mufti's coverage was given. In response to questions by the court concerning whether Siddiqi had arranged for coverage by Mufti, the government emphasized the notation on the Kenny outpatient chart, "call Dr. Siddiqi if any problems."

In our decision, we rejected the jury instruction claim and concluded that "there was, barely, sufficient evidence to support Siddiqi's convictions." This was a reference to the Kenny outpatient document, which, as interpreted by the government, tended to show that Siddiqi had not arranged for coverage. However, we held that the district court erred in rejecting the newly discovered evidence claim and remanded for proceedings to determine whether the physicians away list could have been discovered prior to or during trial through the exercise of due diligence and, if not, whether the new evidence was admissible. Id. The question regarding admissibility was in response to the government's questioning of the authenticity of the list and of its admissibility under the hearsay rule. Fed.R.Evid. §§ 801 & 802. We noted that, if available, the list would "probably" have caused the jury to acquit. Our decision contained a critical ambiguity. In stating that the list would "probably" have led to an acquittal, we hedged because the government was challenging the authenticity of the list, creating the possibility that, even if admitted, the list might have been found bogus by the jury. Left unsaid was our view that if Siddiqi had arranged for coverage, then he could not have been validly convicted.

6. PROCEEDINGS AFTER REMAND

A hearing was held in the district court on remand. At that hearing, Baker was called by Siddiqi. As noted, Baker had declined even to talk with defense counsel before trial. After the conviction, however, she had a change of heart and informed defense counsel that Siddiqi had told her that he planned to go to Mecca and that Mufti would cover for him during that time. More significantly, another nurse, Cheryl Hollenbeck, testified that she was the author of the "call Dr. Siddiqi if any problems" notation on Arthur Kenny's outpatient document. As recited above, the prosecutor had read this notation in summation to the jury as proof that there was no coverage by Dr. Mufti and stated in his brief to us that it was written by Baker. Hollenbeck testified, however, that the notation was made by her after the chemotherapy had been administered and when Kenny was being discharged. This was on July 29, after Siddiqi's return from Mecca. The notation was not, according to Hollenbeck, an instruction to the oncology nurse but to Kenny, who was to call Dr. Siddiqi if he had problems. Finally, the physician's away list was authenticated. In short, the factual basis for Siddiqi's conviction—that he had not arranged for coverage by Mufti—evaporated.

Staying within the confines of our remand, the district judge interpreted our decision as directing inquiry into whether the physicians away list "could"—not "should"—have been discovered before trial. He concluded that it could have been produced in response to a properly framed subpoena and therefore denied the motion for a new trial. Siddiqi again appealed to this court. Reviewing the district court's ruling for abuse of discretion, we affirmed the denial of a new trial because the lower court found, as a matter of fact, that Siddiqi had failed to meet the due diligence requirement. United States v. Siddiqi, 986 F.2d 500 (2d Cir.1992) (unpublished summary order).

We note, however, that the government's brief on this second appeal stated "the theory of the Government's case" as follows:

> The prosecution in this case alleged that the defendant would personally claim for chemotherapy administered by the staff of St. Joseph's Hospital in Elmira, New York. The evidence at trial showed that the appellant claimed for services performed by the staff at the Oncology Department.

The failure to arrange coverage theory having been shredded, the double-billing theory was alive and well.

7. THE SECTION 2255 PETITION

Siddiqi thereafter retained new counsel and on July 2, 1994 filed the instant proceeding to vacate his conviction pursuant to 28 U.S.C. § 2255. He claimed that his trial counsel was constitutionally ineffective in failing to discover and introduce the quite substantial evidence available to support the claim that Mufti had covered for him.

In response, the government asserted that "even if trial counsel [discovered the physicians away list and elicited witness testimony about coverage], it would not have altered the outcome." In explaining this conclusion, the government entirely abandoned the theory on which the jury convicted: that Siddiqi never arranged for Mufti to cover for him. The government's papers stated:

> The defendant was convicted for billing Medicare for services that were, in fact, never performed.... The government alleged that the defendant's 96500 billings were fraudulent, because the defendant had not performed any services in connection with the chemotherapy sessions, since all of the injections referenced in the indictment were administered by the Hospital outside of the defendant's presence.

In refuting Siddiqi's assertion that he performed a cognitive professional service in diagnosing, prescribing, and monitoring the progress of chemotherapy treatments, the government contended:

> The defendant did not personally perform professional cognitive services with respect to the injections at issue in the five counts of the indictment for which he was ultimately convicted. Those counts arose out of 96500 billings submitted for ... injections given to patients while the defendant was out of the country.

Now conceding that Siddiqi arranged for Mufti to cover for him while he was in Mecca, the government introduced an entirely new argument:

> Although Dr. Mufti agreed to be available in the event that problems arose during treatments, no problems actually arose during treatments.... Thus, Dr. Mufti did not perform any services whatsoever in connection with the chemotherapy injections that occurred during the defendant's absence.

The new theory thus conceded the fact of coverage and the hospital's awareness of it but argued that Mufti's coverage was irrelevant because Mufti never performed services. Admitting that "[t]he Hospital's knowledge of coverage arguable [sic] became an issue any [sic] closing argument when ... the issue was raised by the government for the first time," the government contended that "[t]he Hospital's awareness of Mufti's availability does not alter the simple fact that Dr. Mufti did not perform any services and, consequently, the defendant's bills were fraudulent." The government's brief concluded:

No physician performed a professional service in conjunction with the second and subsequent chemotherapy injections administered to the defendant's patients while he was out of the country.... Dr. Mufti was merely "on call" in the event an emergency occurred. Simply being available, if needed, is not a professional service reimbursable by Medicare.... [T]he defendant billed Medicare for services that were, in fact, never performed. That is a crime for which he was properly convicted.

We believe it fair to say that this theory of guilt was never before put to the jury, to the district court, or to this court.

The district court denied Siddiqi's Section 2255 petition, holding that Siddiqi failed to demonstrate constitutionally ineffective assistance of counsel because he did not establish that his lawyer's actions "fell below the prevailing professional norms," and that "a reasonable probability" existed that "absent [counsel's] unprofessional performance, the outcome would have been different." Siddiqi v. United States, No. 94–CV–6323T (W.D.N.Y. Feb. 21, 1995).

With regard to the conduct of defense counsel, the district court found that it was reasonable for him to believe that further evidence corroborating Siddiqi's testimony as to coverage by Mufti was not necessary. Cross-examination of Baker regarding coverage was self-evidently dangerous in light of her refusal even to talk with defense counsel and his consequent lack of knowledge as to what answers she might give. The court found that it was reasonable for counsel to believe that the government had conceded the existence of coverage in light of the prosecutor's remark "[no]body is questioning that coverage exists." Finally, the court noted counsel's concerns over the facts that Mufti had performed no services and that, had such services been necessary, Mufti would have billed Medicare himself.

With regard to whether the evidence in question—the physicians away list and testimony by the nurses—would have affected the outcome, the district court found that it would not have.

On this appeal the government's brief largely restates the contentions and theories it set forth in the district court, stressing that "simply being available, if needed, is not a professional service reimbursable by Medicare." However, at no time has the government ever provided a citation to any rule, regulation, case, or statute stating that being available was not compensable at pertinent times.

* * *

The government's theory of criminal conduct has been a target that moves opportunistically when confronted by contrary evidence or telling argument. The government has proffered at least four basic theories:

(A) Designation of code 96500 was a statement by Siddiqi that he administered (and, sometimes, also provided) the chemotherapy; because the hospital administered and provided the drugs and billed Medicare, Siddiqi is guilty of fraud.

(B) Designation of code 96500 was a statement that Siddiqi personally "supervised" administration of the chemotherapy; because he was in Mecca at the time, the statement is a fraud.

(C) Designation of code 96500 was a statement that Siddiqi supervised administration of the chemotherapy by arranging for Mufti to cover; because Siddiqi never arranged for Mufti to cover, Siddiqi is guilty of fraud.[2] (This was the theory on which Siddiqi was convicted.)

(D) Designation of code 96500 was a fraud because, even though Mufti actually covered for Siddiqi, being on call is not compensable unless actual services were needed and provided. (This is the government's present theory.)

As to the Mecca counts, we can in retrospect say that the trial was an ambush. The defense's selection and presentation of evidence was governed by the two government theories pursued prior to summation, (A) and (B). Under (A), coverage was irrelevant. Under (B), coverage by a doctor available if needed seemed a plausible defense, particularly after the government conceded that coverage existed. The government's summation, of course, ignored that concession by adopting (C), the theory on which the jury convicted. Theory (C) now having been entirely undermined, the government now pursues theory (D). This final theory, however, is legally inadequate for reasons stated below.

* * *

Siddiqi argues that he is caught in a Catch–22. We agree. He was convicted on a then newly-minted, now-abandoned, theory that he defrauded the government because he had not arranged coverage by Mufti. When, after the conviction, he presented evidence that proved coverage sufficiently convincing for the government now to concede it, he was denied relief on the ground that the evidence would have been available before trial had due diligence been exercised. In response to his Section 2255 petition claiming that the lack of due diligence constituted ineffective assistance of counsel, the government argues that he received effective assistance because, although there was coverage by Mufti, coverage is irrelevant. It takes no great flash of genius to conclude that something is wrong somewhere. We find the ointment's fly in the failure of the government to settle upon a single theory of guilt and, then, at this final stage, in seizing upon a theory that is inadequate as a matter of law.

Collateral review is available under Section 2255 where "the alleged error constituted a fundamental defect which inherently results in a complete miscarriage of justice." Reed v. Farley, 512 U.S. 339 (1994) (internal quotation marks omitted). We are firmly convinced that Siddiqi's trial and post-trial proceedings did not meet rudimentary demands of fair procedure, and that the defects in his conviction are so fundamen-

---

2. There is a subtheory here: Siddiqi may have arranged for coverage by Mufti but neither one told the hospital. Although this theory made a cameo appearance on the first appeal, it did not, and would not, benefit from elaboration.

tal as to constitute a miscarriage of justice. We therefore order that his conviction be vacated.

The government's theories have varied as necessary to fill the gaps in its own case, to deflect the ripostes of the defense, and to provide answers to questions from the bench. The shifting nature of the government's case—which we criticized in our first opinion—materially impeded the effective presentation of a defense during the trial by misleading defense counsel as to the government's theory of guilt. This enabled the government to obtain a conviction from the jury on a factual theory that was put forth for the first time in summation and had no foundation in fact.

* * *

We now have no choice but to hold the government to theory (D). Theory (A) had no basis in any of the evidence and should never have been proffered. Theory (C) is now known also to be baseless. Theory (B) lives on, but only if Theory (D) is correct in asserting that simply being available, whether covered or not, is not compensable.

Theory (D) being inadequate as a matter of law, we order that the conviction be vacated. We emphasize that this is not a civil billing case; it is a criminal fraud case. Each of the Mecca counts required proof that Siddiqi used code 96500 with a dishonest intent. Based on the present record, inference of such an intent cannot be drawn from use of the code. As noted, code 96500 allows billing for "supervision," a term that is, on this record, unclear. The government's principal expert on this issue was unable to provide a definition of supervision, and the government cannot be allowed to prevail on the claim that it is fraud for Siddiqi not to have anticipated the definition embodied in theory (D).

Professionals, including lawyers, sometimes bill for simply being available if needed. One may disagree with the practice because the professional may be doing other billable work at the time. However, billing is nevertheless arguably appropriate because to be available, the professional must forego the opportunity to go fishing or worship in Mecca at the same time. Absent some affirmative reason to believe that use of code 96500 does not cover being available, billing under that code is at worst an attempt to bill at the outer limits permitted, not fraud.

The government has been unable to cite to us any authority whatsoever that would have alerted someone in Siddiqi's position that being available if needed is excluded as a compensable service under code 96500. Indeed, no one who has read the trial record in this case could draw that conclusion. It may well be that arranging for coverage—a common practice among physicians—is billable under code 96500 so long as the covering doctor also did not bill for being available—and Mufti did not. We cannot say on this record, therefore, that an arrangement in which the primary doctor bills Medicare for an available covering doctor was fraud at the pertinent times. This practice may not have met Judge Cardozo's standard of "the punctilio of an honor the most sensitive,"

Meinhard v. Salmon, 249 N.Y. 458, 464, 164 N.E. 545 (1928), but it does not constitute fraud.

* * *

We are, therefore, faced with a situation in which a conviction was obtained on a theory now shown to lack a factual basis and presently defended by a theory that is legally insufficient. We are firmly convinced, moreover, that the conviction would not have occurred but for the government's shifting of theories that impaired both Siddiqi's defense and our consideration and disposition of this matter. Indeed, had the government's present theory been candidly stated on the first appeal, we would have reversed outright.

Had Siddiqi been convicted on a legal theory that was invalidated by a subsequent decision of the Supreme Court, we would vacate it under Section 2255. Here we face a situation in which subsequent events compellingly demonstrate that a conviction had no legitimate factual or legal basis and that, but for the conduct of the prosecution in adopting shifting and at times misleading positions, no conviction would have been obtained or successfully defended on appeal. We see no reason why a petitioner in Siddiqi's position should fare worse than one whose conviction was based on a legal theory invalidated by later caselaw.

We are firmly convinced that Siddiqi's trial and post-trial proceedings did not meet rudimentary demands of fair procedure, see Reed v. Farley, 512 U.S. 339 (1994), and that the defects in his conviction are so fundamental as to constitute a miscarriage of justice, *id.* We therefore order that his conviction be vacated.

Notes

1. At first glance this case probably appeared to be blatant fraud; after all Dr. Siddiqi did bill for services rendered while he was out of the country. Like most white collar crimes, however, the "devil is the detail" and according to the Second Circuit, closer examination of the applicable billing code reveals that "[t]his practice * * * does not constitute fraud." Do you see why the Second Circuit said this? Do you agree?

2. Note that the claim forms for which Dr. Siddiqi was convicted pertained to two patients who required chemotherapy while Dr. Siddiqi was out of the country. The total amount of money at issue in these claim forms was $640.88. Thus, because of a $640.88 disagreement over billing (in which Dr. Siddiqi's interpretation apparently was correct), Dr. Siddiqi became a convicted felon. Although he was not sentenced to prison, he received 3 years probation, a $2,000 fine, and was

> "ordered to serve 1,000 hours of community service and ordered to pay $640.88 in restitution, the amount at issue in the counts on which he was convicted. After conviction, Dr. Siddiqi was called before the medical licensure board of New York. He successfully defended his license, receiving a reprimand. Dr. Siddiqi was, however, was excluded from participating in Medicare and Medicaid, which closed his practice. Prior to his indictment, Dr. Siddiqi's annual income from his practice was

approximately $825,000 per year. After his conviction and exclusion, he was able to practice at a Veteran's Administration Hospital, at one-tenth of his former income. During its investigation of Dr. Siddiqi, HHS had impounded $150,000 in payments due but not yet paid to Dr. Siddiqi. * * * Dr. Siddiqi's exclusion was due to expire a few months [after the Second Circuit vacated his conviction]. The $150,000 of impounded payments was returned to Dr. Siddiqi without interest. Dr. Siddiqi is currently attempting to regain this interest, as well as the $640.88 he paid in restitution. Dr. Siddiqi was 54 years old upon his conviction and 59 years old when his conviction was vacated."[vv]

vv. *Health Care Fraud, Hearings before Senate Permanent Subcomm. on Investigations*, 105 Cong., 1st Sess. 145–47 (June 26, 1997) (Testimony and Written Statement of Pamela H. Bucy). The author of this case-book and the referenced Written Statement served as a consultant to Ross, Dixon & Masback which represented Naveed A. Siddiqi in a matter related to his conviction.

Chapter 11

CRIMINAL AND CIVIL LIABILITY OF PROFESSIONALS

As an attorney, it is unsettling to me to include this chapter in this casebook. The reality, however, is that certain professionals, primarily attorneys and accountants, are at the heart of many white collar crimes. This is true for several reasons. First, because attorneys and accountants are integral planners, preparers or executors of most business dealings, these professionals wittingly, or unwittingly, are involved when these deals turn to fraud. Second, because of the fiduciary role in which they serve, attorneys and accountants have ready access to large amounts of cash belonging to others; some succumb to the temptation to steal from unsuspecting victims. Third, attorneys and judges are the primary participants in our system of justice and are faced with unique opportunities to personally benefit through graft and corruption. Again, some cannot resist the temptation.

In addressing criminal liability of professionals, this chapter builds on chapters and crimes already covered with one exception. Obstruction of justice crimes appear for the first time in this chapter. There are three sections in this chapter: Section A focuses on crimes committed by attorneys and accountants while representing clients; Section B focuses on theft by professionals from clients; Section C addresses obstruction of justice by corrupt attorneys or judges.

A. CRIMES COMMITTED WHILE REPRESENTING CLIENTS

The next case, Reves v. Ernst & Young, 507 U.S. 170 (1993), involves liability under RICO of outside professionals who assist an organization found liable under RICO. Since the mid–1980s courts faced with RICO cases increasingly have dealt with the question of what nexus or connection must be shown to exist between the enterprise and the pattern of racketeering activity to find a violation of § 1962(c).[a] Prior to

---

a. For an excellent review of the nexus issues, *see* Melissa Harrison, *Nexus: The* *Next Test of RICO's text*, 70 DENVER U.L. REV. 69 (1992).

the Supreme Court's resolution of this issue in *Reves*, the federal courts of appeal had employed several tests to analyze nexus.[b] The *Scotto-Provenzano* test, articulated by the United States Court of Appeals for the Second Circuit, was the broadest of the tests since it did not distinguish between those who play a major or minor role.[c] It provided that a sufficient nexus exists when "(1) one is enabled to commit the predicate offenses solely by virtue of his position in the enterprise or involvement in or control over the affairs of the enterprise, or (2) the predicate offenses are related to the activities of that enterprise."[d] The most restrictive of the "nexus" tests was the "manage or operate" test, articulated by the United States Court of Appeals for the District of Columbia in Yellow Bus Lines, Inc. v. Drivers, Chauffeurs & Helpers Local Union 639, 913 F.2d 948 (D.C.Cir.1990). With this test, sufficient nexus between the enterprise and racketeering activity exists only if the plaintiff proves that the defendants exercised control over the management or operation of the enterprise.[e] Note how the Court resolved this split in the next case.

REVES v. ERNST & YOUNG

United States Supreme Court, 1993.
507 U.S. 170.

BLACKMUN, JUSTICE.

This case requires us once again to interpret the provisions of the Racketeer Influenced and Corrupt Organizations (RICO) chapter of the Organized Crime Control Act of 1970, Pub. L. 91–452, Title IX, 84 Stat. 941, as amended, 18 U.S.C. §§ 1961–1968. Section 1962(c) makes it unlawful "for any person employed by or associated with any enterprise engaged in, or the activities of which affect, interstate or foreign commerce, to conduct or participate, directly or indirectly, in the conduct of such enterprise's affairs through a pattern of racketeering activity. . . . " The question presented is whether one must participate in the operation or management of the enterprise itself to be subject to liability under this provision.

* * *

The Farmer's Cooperative of Arkansas and Oklahoma, Inc. (the Co–Op), began operating in western Arkansas and eastern Oklahoma in 1946. To raise money for operating expenses, the Co–Op sold promissory notes payable to the holder on demand. Each year, Co–Op members were elected to serve on its board. The board met monthly but delegated

---

b. As outlined in Professor Harrison, *id.* at 73–80, these tests are: the *Scotto-Provenzano* test; the *Cauble* test; the "facilitation or utilization" test; the "manage or operate" test.

c. United States v. Scotto, 641 F.2d 47, 54 (2d Cir.1980); United States v. Provenzano, 688 F.2d 194, 200 (3d Cir.1982).

d. *Scotto*, 641 F.2d at 54.

e. *Id.* at 954.

actual management of the Co–Op to a general manager. In 1952, the board appointed Jack White as general manager.

In January 1980, White began taking loans from the Co–Op to finance the construction of a gasohol plant by his company, White Flame Fuels, Inc. By the end of 1980, White's debts to the Co–Op totaled approximately $4 million. In September of that year, White and Gene Kuykendall, who served as the accountant for both the Co–Op and White Flame, were indicted for federal tax fraud. At a board meeting on November 12, 1980, White proposed that the Co–Op purchase White Flame. The board agreed. One month later, however, the Co–Op filed a declaratory action against White and White Flame in Arkansas state court alleging that White actually had sold White Flame to the Co–Op in February 1980. The complaint was drafted by White's attorneys and led to a consent decree relieving White of his debts and providing that the Co–Op had owned White Flame since February 15, 1980.

White and Kuykendall were convicted of tax fraud in January 1981. Harry Erwin, the managing partner of Russell Brown and Company, an Arkansas accounting firm, testified for White, and shortly thereafter the Co–Op retained Russell Brown to perform its 1981 financial audit. Joe Drozal, a partner in the Brown firm, was put in charge of the audit and Joe Cabaniss was selected to assist him. On January 2, 1982, Russell Brown and Company merged with Arthur Young and Company, which later became respondent Ernst & Young.[2]

One of Drozal's first tasks in the audit was to determine White Flame's fixed-asset value. After consulting with White and reviewing White Flame's books (which Kuykendall had prepared), Drozal concluded that the plant's value at the end of 1980 was $4,393,242.66, the figure Kuykendall had employed. Using this figure as a base, Drozal factored in the 1981 construction costs and capitalized expenses and concluded that White Flame's 1981 fixed-asset value was approximately $4.5 million. Drozal then had to determine how that value should be treated for accounting purposes. If the Co–Op had owned White Flame from the beginning of construction in 1979, White Flame's value for accounting purposes would be its fixed-asset value of $4.5 million. If, however, the Co–Op had purchased White Flame from White, White Flame would have to be given its fair market value at the time of purchase, which was somewhere between $444,000 and $1.5 million. If White Flame were valued at less than $1.5 million, the Co–Op was insolvent. Drozal concluded that the Co–Op had owned White Flame from the start and that the plant should be valued at $4.5 million on its books.

On April 22, 1982, Arthur Young presented its 1981 audit report to the Co–Op's board. In that audit's Note 9, Arthur Young expressed doubt whether the investment in White Flame could ever be recovered. Note 9 also observed that White Flame was sustaining operating losses averaging $100,000 per month. Arthur Young did not tell the board of its

---

2. In order to be consistent with the terminology employed in earlier judicial writings in this case, we hereinafter refer to the respondent firm as "Arthur Young."

conclusion that the Co–Op always had owned White Flame or that without that conclusion the Co–Op was insolvent.

On May 27, the Co–Op held its 1982 annual meeting. At that meeting, the Co–Op, through Harry C. Erwin, a partner in Arthur Young, distributed to the members condensed financial statements. These included White Flame's $4.5 million asset value among its total assets but omitted the information contained in the audit's Note. 9. Cabaniss was also present. Erwin saw the condensed financial statement for the first time when he arrived at the meeting. In a 5–minute presentation, he told his audience that the statements were condensed and that copies of the full audit were available at the Co–Op's office. In response to questions, Erwin explained that the Co–Op owned White Flame and that the plant had incurred approximately $1.2 million in losses but he revealed no other information relevant to the Co–Op's true financial health.

The Co–Op hired Arthur Young also to perform its 1982 audit. The 1982 report, presented to the board on March 7, 1983, was similar to the 1981 report and restated (this time in its Note 8) Arthur Young's doubt whether the investment in White Flame was recoverable. See 937 F.2d, at 1320. The gasohol plant again was valued at approximately $4.5 million and was responsible for the Co–Op's showing a positive net worth. The condensed financial statement distributed at the annual meeting on March 24, 1983, omitted the information in Note 8. This time, Arthur Young reviewed the condensed statement in advance but did not act to remove its name from the statement. Cabaniss, in a 3–minute presentation at the meeting, gave the financial report. He informed the members that the full audit was available at the Co–Op's office but did not tell them about Note 8 or that the Co–Op was in financial difficulty if White Flame were written down to its fair market value. *Ibid.*

In February 1984, the Co–Op experienced a slight run on its demand notes. On February 23, when it was unable to secure further financing, the Co–Op filed for bankruptcy. As a result, the demand notes were frozen in the bankruptcy estate and were no longer redeemable at will by the noteholders.

* * *

On February 14, 1985, the trustee in bankruptcy filed suit against 40 individuals and entities, including Arthur Young, on behalf of the Co–Op and certain noteholders. The District Court certified a class of noteholders, petitioners here, consisting of persons who had purchased demand notes between February 15, 1980, and February 23, 1984. Petitioners settled with all defendants except Arthur Young. The District Court determined before trial that the demand notes were securities under both federal and state law. The court then granted summary judgment in favor of Arthur Young on the RICO claim. The District Court applied the test established by the Eighth Circuit in Bennett v. Berg, 710 F.2d 1361, 1364 (*en banc*) that § 1962(c) requires "some participation in the operation or management of the enterprise itself." The court ruled: "Plaintiffs have failed to show anything more than that the accountants reviewed a series of completed transactions, and certified the Co–Op's records as fairly portraying its financial status as of a date three or four months preceding the meetings of the directors and the shareholders at which they presented their reports. We do not hesitate to declare that such activities fail to satisfy the degree of management required by Bennett v. Berg."

The case went to trial on the state and federal securities fraud claims. The jury found that Arthur Young had committed both state and federal securities fraud and awarded approximately $6.1 million in damages. The Court of Appeals reversed, concluding that the demand notes were not securities under federal or state law. *See* Arthur Young & Co. v. Reves, 856 F.2d 52, 55 (1988). On writ of certiorari, this Court ruled that the notes were securities within the meaning of § 3(a)(10) of the Securities Exchange Act of 1934, 48 Stat. 882, as amended, 15 U.S.C. § 78c(a)(10). Reves v. Ernst & Young, 494 U.S. 56, 70 (1990).

On remand, the Court of Appeals affirmed the judgment of the District Court in all major respects except the damages award, which it reversed and remanded for a new trial. The only part of the Court of Appeals' decision that is at issue here is its affirmance of summary judgment in favor of Arthur Young on the RICO claim. Like the district court, the court of Appeals applied the "operation or management" test articulated in Bennett v. Berg and held that Arthur Young's conduct did not "rise to the level of participation in the management or operation of the Co-op." See 937 F.2d, at 1324. The Court of Appeals for the District of Columbia Circuit also has adopted an "operation or management" test. See Yellow Bus Lines, Inc. v. Drivers, Chauffeurs & Helpers Local Union 639, 913 F.2d 948, 954 (1990). We granted certiorari to resolve the conflict between these cases and Bank of America National Trust & Savings Assn. v. Touche Ross & Co., 782 F.2d 966, 970 (C.A.11 1986) (rejecting requirement that a defendant participate in the operation or management of an enterprise).

* * * Section 1962(c) makes it unlawful "for any person employed by or associated with any enterprise ... to conduct or participate, directly or indirectly, in the conduct of such enterprise's affairs through a pattern of racketeering activity.... "

The narrow question in this case is the meaning of the phrase "to conduct or participate, directly or indirectly, in the conduct of such enterprise's affairs." The word "conduct" is used twice, and it seems reasonable to give each use a similar construction. As a verb, "conduct" means to lead, run, manage, or direct. Webster's Third New International Dictionary 474 (1976). Petitioners urge us to read "conduct" as "carry on," so that almost any involvement in the affairs of an enterprise would satisfy the "conduct or participate" requirement. * * *

* * *

Once we understand the word "conduct" to require some degree of direction and the word "participate" to require some part in that direction, the meaning of § 1962(c) comes into focus. In order to "participate, directly or indirectly, in the conduct of such enterprise's affairs," one must have some part in directing those affairs. Of course, the word "participate" makes clear that RICO liability is not limited to those with primary responsibility for the enterprise's affairs, just as the phrase "directly or indirectly" makes clear that RICO liability is not limited to those with a formal position in the enterprise, but *some* part in directing the enterprise's affairs is required. The "operation or management" test expresses this requirement in a formulation that is easy to apply.

* * *

Petitioners argue that the "operation or management" test is flawed because liability under § 1962(c) is not limited to upper management but may extend to "any person employed by or associated with [the] enterprise." We agree that liability under § 1962(c) is not limited to upper management, but we disagree that the "operation or management" test is inconsistent with this proposition. An enterprise is "operated" not just by upper management but also by lower-rung participants in the enterprise who are under the direction of upper management. An enterprise also might be "operated" or "managed" by others "associated with" the enterprise who exert control over it as, for example, by bribery.

The United States also argues that the "operation or management" test is not consistent with § 1962(c) because it limits the liability of "outsiders" who have no official position within the enterprise. The United States correctly points out that RICO's major purpose was to attack the "infiltration of organized crime and racketeering into legitimate organizations," but its argument fails on several counts. First, it ignores the fact that § 1962 has four subsections. Infiltration of legitimate organizations by "outsiders" is clearly addressed in subsections (a) and (b), and the "operation or management" test that applies under subsection (c) in no way limits the application of subsections (a) and (b) to "outsiders."[10] Second, § 1962(c) is limited to persons "employed by or associated with" an enterprise, suggesting a more limited reach than subsections (a) and (b), which do not contain such a restriction. Third, § 1962(c) cannot be interpreted to reach complete "outsiders" because liability depends on showing that the defendants conducted or participated in the conduct of the *"enterprise's* affairs," not just their *own* affairs. Of course, "outsiders" may be liable under § 1962(c) if they are "associated with" an enterprise and participate in the conduct of *its* affairs— that is, participate in the operation or management of the enterprise itself—but it would be consistent with neither the language nor the legislative history of § 1962(c) to interpret it as broadly as petitioners and the United States urge.

10. Subsection (d) makes it unlawful to conspire to violate any of the other three subsections.

In sum, we hold that "to conduct or participate, directly or indirectly, in the conduct of such enterprise's affairs," § 1962(c), one must participate in the operation or management of the enterprise itself.

* * *

In this case, it is undisputed that Arthur Young relied upon existing Co–Op records in preparing the 1981 and 1982 audit reports. The AICPA's professional standards state that an auditor may draft financial statements in whole or in part based on information from management's accounting system. It is also undisputed that Arthur Young's audit reports revealed to the Co–Op's board that the value of the gasohol plant had been calculated based on the Co–Op's investment in the plant. Thus, we only could conclude that Arthur Young participated in the operation or management of the Co–Op itself if Arthur Young's failure to tell the Co–Op's board that the plant should have been given its fair market value constituted such participation. We think that Arthur Young's failure in this respect is not sufficient to give rise to liability under § 1962(c).

The judgment of the Court of Appeals is affirmed.

It is so ordered.

JUSTICE SOUTER, with whom JUSTICE WHITE joins, dissenting.

In the word "conduct," the Court today finds a clear congressional mandate to limit RICO liability under 18 U.S.C. § 1962(c) to participants in the "operation or management" of a RICO enterprise. What strikes the Court as clear, however, looks at the very least hazy to me, and I accordingly find the statute's "liberal construction" provision not irrelevant, but dispositive. But even if I were to assume, with the majority, that the word "conduct" clearly imports some degree of direction or control into § 1962(c), I would have to say that the majority misapplies its own "operation or management" test to the facts presented here. I therefore respectfully dissent.

* * *

* * * Congress has given courts faced with uncertain meaning a clear tie-breaker in RICO's "liberal construction" clause, which directs that the "provisions of this title shall be liberally construed to effectuate its remedial purposes." We have relied before on this "express admonition" to read RICO provisions broadly and in this instance, the "liberal construction" clause plays its intended part, directing us to recognize the more inclusive definition of the word "conduct," free of any restricting element of direction or control. Because the Court of Appeals employed a narrower reading, I would reverse.

Even if I were to adopt the majority's view of § 1962(c), however, I still could not join the judgment, which seems to me unsupportable under the very "operation or management" test the Court announces. If Arthur Young had confined itself in this case to the role traditionally performed by an outside auditor, I could agree with the majority that Arthur Young took no part in the management or operation of the Co-op. But the record on summary judgment, viewed most favorably to Reves, shows that Arthur Young created the very financial statements it was hired, and purported, to audit. Most importantly, Reves adduced evidence that Arthur Young took on management responsibilities by deciding, in the first instance, what value to assign to the Co-op's most important fixed asset, the White Flame gasohol plant, and Arthur Young itself conceded below that the alleged activity went beyond traditional auditing. Because I find, then, that even under the majority's "operation or management" test the Court of Appeals erroneously affirmed the summary judgment for Arthur Young, I would (again) reverse.

* * *

Notes

1. Was the government correct in arguing that the "operation or management" test forecloses prosecution of lower level employees? What must a RICO plaintiff show to prove that a defendant's pattern of racketeering activity was sufficiently connected to the enterprise? Consider the thoughts of G. Robert Blakey, Professor of Law at Notre Dame School of Law. Professor Blakey, the principal drafter of RICO, represented Trial Lawyers for Public Justice in an amicus brief filed on behalf of the plaintiffs in the *Reves* case.

> "The bad guys wanted to get from the Court an upper management only interpretation of the word 'conduct' in RICO. Had they secured it, lower level people in licit and illicit enterprises would have gone scot-free, and most particularly accountants and lawyers who provided services to the licit or illicit enterprise would have gone scot-free. They didn't get it.
>
> "The court was very express in its holding that not only upper level people but lower level people can be responsible under RICO. They were also very clear that outsiders, who participate with insiders, at least in some degree of direction of the affairs of the enterprise, can be held responsible."[f]

2. One year after its decision in *Reves*, the Supreme Court again opted for a restrictive view of liability of outside professionals for wrongdoing by the client. In Central Bank of Denver v. First Interstate Bank of Denver, 511 U.S. 164 (1994), the Court held that aiding and abetting liability was not available under section 10(b) of the Securities Act of 1934 or under Rule 10b–5. *Id.* at 191. Focusing on the language of section 10(b), the Court rejected holdings of the eleven federal courts of appeals that aiding and abetting liability existed.

In 1995, Congress passed the Private Securities Litigation Reform Act of 1995[g] which restricts liability of outside professionals in private securities

f. CORPORATE CRIME REPORTER, 9–10 (Mar. 8, 1993).

g. § 201(a) Pub. L. No. 104–67, 109 Stat. at 760 (adding subsection

actions by providing that "defendants who do not commit knowing violations will be liable only for the portion of the damages that is attributable to their percentage of responsibility."[h]

By restricting liability of outside professionals, *Reves*, *Central Bank of Denver* and the Private Securities Litigation Reform Act of 1995 may signal a view that outside professionals, as "deep pockets," have been "shouldering too much of the burden" of business frauds. Do you agree?

The next case, In re American Continental Corporation/Lincoln Savings and Loan Securities Litigation, 794 F.Supp. 1424 (D.Ariz.1992), discusses the liability of outside professionals as aiders and abettors. The case arose from the failure of the Lincoln Savings and Loan (Lincoln). Shareholders of Lincoln brought suit against a number of parties, including law firms and accounting firms, seeking damages under RICO and alleging securities fraud as racketeering activity.

IN RE AMERICAN CONTINENTAL CORPORA-TION/LINCOLN SAVINGS AND LOAN SE-CURITIES LITIGATION

United States District Court, District of Arizona, 1992.
794 F.Supp. 1424.

BILBY, DISTRICT JUDGE.

* * *

Five separate actions are consolidated before this court [including two class actions, federal and state actions on behalf of approximately 100 individual American Continental Corporation (ACC), securities purchasers, an action by the Resolution Trust Corporation ("RTC"), as receiver for Lincoln, and an action by investors in an ACC-related limited partnership.-ed.]

These actions originate from the business dealings of Charles H. Keating, Jr. ("Keating"), former chairman of ACC. The claims at issue here were brought principally against professionals who provided services to ACC and/or Lincoln Savings. [The defendants have filed motions for summary judgment.] * * *

* * * TOUCHE ROSS & COMPANY

Touche [Ross & Company] is a defendant * * *. Claims against Touche include Section 10(b), RICO, AZRAC, fraud and misrepresentation, and violations of the California Corporations Code. In addition, * * * plaintiffs allege negligent misrepresentation and professional negligence.

21D(g)(4)(A)(ii) to the Securities Exchange Act of 1934).

h. Melissa Harrison, *The Assault on the Liability of Outside Professionals: Are Law-* *yers and Accountants Off the Hook?* 65 U. CINN. L. REV. 473, 518–19 (1997).

Touche became involved with ACC/Lincoln toward the end of its business existence in October, 1988. Touche argues it did not complete an audit, and had no duty to disclose information until the audit was completed and a report issued. Touche contends it was not named in a registration statement or prospectus, and gave no public opinions with respect to ACC/Lincoln for which it could be held liable. Touche further argues that plaintiffs did not rely on its statements, and could not have relied indirectly, as Touche made no representations in any offering documents. Finally, Touche contends there is no evidence that its conduct affected regulatory decision-making.

Plaintiffs, on the other hand, argue that by accepting the ACC/Lincoln engagement, and by continuing to work for ACC/Lincoln, Touche permitted the additional sale of millions of dollars in bonds. Plaintiffs contend that the evidence raises genuine questions as to whether Touche took and retained the engagement with knowledge of or in reckless disregard of the alleged fraud by ACC/Lincoln.

The United States Supreme Court has discussed the duties of an independent public accountant:

> Corporate financial statements are one of the primary sources of information available to guide the decisions of the investing public. In an effort to control the accuracy of the financial data available to investors in the securities markets, various provisions of the federal securities laws require publicly held corporations to file their financial statements with the Securities and Exchange Commission. Commission regulations stipulate that these financial reports must be audited by an independent certified public accountant in accordance with generally accepted auditing standards. By examining the corporation's books and records, the independent auditor determines whether the financial reports of the corporation have been prepared in accordance with generally accepted accounting principles. The auditor then issues an opinion as to whether the financial statements, taken as a whole, fairly present the financial position and operations of the corporation for the relevant period.

United States v. Arthur Young & Co., 465 U.S. 805, 810–811 (1984). Plaintiffs view such statements of an auditor's responsibilities as affirmations of the accountant's duty to the public. Touche argues that its duties are limited to the completion of the audit it was hired to perform.

An accountant is not obligated to disclose ordinary business information. Knowledge of an ongoing fraud is a different matter entirely:

> The situation is quite different, however, where the issue is disclosure of actual knowledge of fraud. Standing by while knowing one's good name is being used to perpetrate a fraud is inherently misleading. An investor might reasonably assume that an accounting firm would not permit inclusion of an audit report it prepared in a placement memo for an offering the firm knew to be fraudulent, and that such a firm would let it be known if it discovered to be fraudulent an offering with which it was associated. It is not

unreasonable to expect an accountant, who stands in a "special relationship of trust vis-a-vis the public" (citation omitted) and whose duty is to safeguard the public interest, (citation omitted) to disclose fraud in this type of circumstance, where the accountant's information is obviously superior to that of the investor, the cost to the accountant of revealing the information is minimal, and the cost to the investors of the information remaining secret potentially enormous.

Id.

This court holds that an independent public accountant who knows of or recklessly disregards a client's fraud, may be held liable for aiding and abetting that fraud where the auditor provides services which constitute substantial assistance. Whether an audit has been completed is not necessarily determinative of whether the assistance is "substantial." If an auditor is aware that an ongoing fraud is a real possibility, he or she may not act as an advocate for its wrongdoing client. Nor may the auditor stand by, knowing of a fraud, and withhold damaging information from the SEC and federal bank regulators. Nondisclosure under these circumstances may constitute substantial assistance because regulators and the public are entitled to assume that an independent public accountant would take steps—either through frank discussions with regulators, the issuance of a preliminary cautionary report, or withdrawal from the account—if the auditor is aware that its client is perpetrating an ongoing fraud. Finally, an auditor may not enjoy the pecuniary benefits of an engagement, while protecting itself by postponing the issuance of an audit opinion, or making highly qualified representations to the public or regulators.

On the other hand, the court holds that an auditor may not be held liable merely for accepting an engagement unless the auditor actually knows its prospective client is committing a fraud, and provides services which substantially assist the execution of the fraud.

In addition, an auditor may not be held liable under the securities laws for innocently or negligently failing to discover a fraud sooner than it did. The line may be difficult to discern. Based on the record, the court cannot determine, as a matter of law, that Touche's conduct was innocent or negligent.

When viewed in the light most favorable to the nonmovants, the evidence regarding Touche's acceptance of the ACC/Lincoln engagement and its ongoing services raises genuine questions concerning (1) whether Touche knew of the fraud and tacitly agreed to provide assistance in exchange for fees, and/or (2) whether Touche's conduct was such an extreme departure from the standards of ordinary care as to present a danger of misleading buyers that was either known to Touche, or so obvious that Touche must have been aware of it, and (3) whether Touche provided "substantial assistance" by agreeing to serve as auditor, advocating for its client, and by withholding material information from regulators which may have been a factor in permitting the fraud to continue.

The record contains the following evidence:

On October 13, 1988, Keating offered the ACC engagement to the Phoenix office of Coopers Lybrand, which previously had been hired for the limited purpose of reviewing a transaction involving General Oriental Investments Limited ("GOIL"). Coopers Lybrand responded that they would immediately put GOIL on hold, until the completion of its client acceptance procedures, a process which would take two to three weeks. GOIL was a pivotal transaction on which ACC proposed to book significant gain. Only days earlier, ACC's prior auditor, Arthur Young, had refused to book gain on the GOIL transaction, precipitating its withdrawal from the ACC account.

In early October 1988, Touche's Phoenix office learned that ACC and Arthur Young would part company, and on October 17, 1988, Touche delivered an unsolicited bid of $1.075 million for the ACC audit engagement. Over the next several days, private meetings were held between Jerry Mayer, head of Touche's Phoenix office, Jack Atchison, and Keating, which resulted, on October 25, 1988, in Touche preparing an engagement letter for ACC.

The events surrounding Touche's retention of ACC as a client are summarized in two lengthy file memoranda written by Touche partners Jerry Mayer and Fred Martin.

On October 19, Mayer had lunch with Jack Atchison, who had been at ACC for over six months, after having left his post as Arthur Young engagement partner for the ACC account. At the time this court rendered its summary judgment decisions, Atchison, a defendant in these proceedings, had asserted his Fifth Amendment privilege. According to Mayer's November 7th file memo, Atchison was impressed with the Touche proposal, but stated that "ACC was pretty far down the road with Coopers Lybrand." Mayer's memo states that Atchison "several times mentioned the reason for the ACC–Arthur Young disagreement, but that Atchison blamed it totally on the relationship of Arthur Young's new lead partner and members of ACC and not on any particular accounting issues in which AY and the company had disagreements." Mayer comments, "it was obvious that these disagreements did bring sharp focus to the relationship process." At his deposition, Mayer had no independent recall of the topics discussed with Atchison. Kevin O'Connell of the Federal Home Loan Bank Board ("FHLBB") testified Mayer had told him that Atchison was "feeling out firms."

On the evening of October 19, Mayer called Keating. Mayer, Keating, and Charles Keating III later met privately at the Phoenician Hotel for approximately 45 minutes. Although Touche partners Dave Martin and Fred Martin accompanied Mayer to the hotel, they did not attend the meeting. At his deposition, Mayer could not recall "what the strategy was." In his November 7 file memo, Mayer wrote that Keating told him he had intended to say ACC was pretty far along with Coopers, but that at the end of his discussions with Mayer, "he was not comfortable with that conclusion any more."

Kevin O'Connell testified Mayer told him that during a private meeting, Keating "had presented hypothetical accounting situations to him" and Mayer had professed they would "keep an open mind."

On or about October 20th, Touche asked the chief executive officer of their client, M.D.C. Holdings, Inc. ("M.D.C."), to call Keating on their behalf. At the time, M.D.C. was under SEC investigation. Touche was aware of transactions between ACC and M.D.C. Touche partner Thomas Bintinger testified that Touche had audited real estate transactions between ACC and M.D.C., but could not recall their conclusions. He testified that in the fall of 1988, Touche had concerns about the integrity of M.D.C. management.

On October 21, Mayer wrote to Judy Wischer, reassuring her that the selection of Touche as auditor could be handled in a noncontroversial way. Mayer suggested that Touche Chairman Ed Kangas meet with FHLBB Chairman Danny Wall, if necessary, to explain that Touche's selection was the result of its unsolicited proposal, rather than "a request by ACC following any reaction by Coopers Lybrand." Also on October 21, Douglas McEachern of Touche's Los Angeles office and a former FHLBB fellow, reassured Keating that he would be "a team player," who would discuss issues with regulators on ACC's behalf, and that he was not negatively predisposed to ACC—an impression Keating apparently had formed. McEachern testified that he was not concerned with management integrity at ACC because Darrell Dochow, Executive Director of the FHLBB Office of Regulatory Policy, Oversight, and Supervision had told him that ACC's directors were "honorable people." Dochow testified, however, that he did not recall making that statement, "especially during that time period."

On October 24, Keating offered the ACC engagement to Touche. Mayer testified that it was during this conversation that Keating said he wanted to discuss a transaction. Prior to this phone call, Mayer testified, although he knew that Coopers Lybrand had been auditing a transaction, he did not know which transaction it was. That same afternoon, Keating and Mayer met privately for a few minutes before a larger meeting with Fred Martin, Judy Wischer and Andrew Ligget. Mayer could not recall what was discussed at this private meeting. At the larger meeting, ACC explained GOIL and gave Martin and Mayer reports written by Lexecon and Professor Sidney Davidson. On the evening of October 24, Mayer and Martin called Robert Kay, Touche senior national technical partner, at his home to explain the GOIL transaction. They sent the Lexecon and Davidson reports to Kay by overnight mail.

On October 25, Mayer advised Keating that Touche found support in the accounting literature for ACC's position that profit should be booked on GOIL. That same day, Touche prepared an engagement letter, to examine all consolidated and separate subsidiaries' financials for the year ending December 1988. The $1.075 million audit bid was gone; the letter contained no estimated audit fee. Fred Martin testified that Keating had released Mayer from the earlier bid some time after the meeting on the evening of October 24 and before the engagement letter was prepared on October 25, although Martin was not present during the conversation. Jerry Mayer, however, could not recall why the audit fee changed, nor could he recall any discussions about audit fees.

On October 26, Mayer and Keating met privately to discuss the basis for Touche's GOIL opinion. Mayer advised Keating that because the opinion would be disputed by the SEC, he recommended that ACC obtain an SEC opinion. Also on October 26, Keating signed the Touche engagement letter, subject to Touche meeting with Arthur Young, as required by the audit rules. On or about October 26, Keating informed Coopers Lybrand that they would not receive the engagement because "the chemistry was better with Touche Ross."

On November 1, 1988, Mayer, Fred Martin and Kay met with auditors from Arthur Young. Arthur Young testified that they withheld nothing. Touche, however, disputes that Arthur Young told them anything which raised concerns about management integrity. The record reflects extensive discussion among the accountants. For example, Arthur Young partner Kenneth Kroese took notes of the meeting, which state in part:

> Touche asked about management credibility problems and Janice [Vincent] said she believed that the question they were asking was about facts which might bear on the integrity of management. Those facts might be that we believed their accounting was aggressive, that they had several transactions with follow on transactions and that they had many transactions with the same parties. Bob Kay asked what that had to do with management credibility, and Janice repeated that she felt that those were facts that could bear on management integrity. Bob Kay asked then whether we would say our firm had not concluded that we had a management credibility problem. Janice said yes (we had not concluded).

On the same day, Touche accepted the engagement.

The evidence reflects that Touche was aware of ACC's sale of subordinated debentures. On November 1, ACC issued a prospectus for an additional $300 million debt offering. At about this time, Forbes magazine published an article about ACC entitled "Trust Me," which was critical of Keating and described ACC's voluminous sales of debentures. The article was produced from Touche's files. When asked whether he was aware of the debenture sales, Mayer testified that he had a "vague recall" about subordinated debentures during this time. Martin testified that, on occasion, he looked into whether ACC could sell debt without the assistance of an independent auditor, but could not recall when or why he had done so.

On November 8, Mayer and Martin wrote their lengthy and arguably self-conscious memoranda for their files, explaining the chronology of Touche's retention and discussions of the GOIL transaction. At deposition, Mayer's recollection of the events at issue was sketchy.

On November 14, 1988, ACC filed a form 8K with the SEC, accompanied by Touche's letter agreeing with statements contained therein. The form 8K stated:

> On November 1, 1988, the registrant engaged Touche Ross as independent accountants to audit registrant's financial statements. Registrant offered the engagement to Touche Ross on October 24, 1988. Subsequent thereto and prior to accepting the engagement, in accordance with professional standards, Touche Ross discussed with the registrant and its former accountants matters relating to the engagement including the matter of disagreement concerning the non-monetary exchange of assets in September, 1988 (described in the registrant's form 8K filed with the SEC on October 28, 1988). During the course of completing its procedures, Touche Ross expressed its preliminary view that the accounting literature appeared to support the registrant's analysis of the transaction. Touche Ross accepted the engagement on November 1, 1988.

In a letter to SEC's chief accountant, Touche stated that ACC's accounting treatment of GOIL was supported by accounting literature. On November 18, Touche and ACC met with the SEC to discuss GOIL. The SEC rejected ACC's proposed profit recognition on the GOIL transaction, and a press release was issued. On November 21, 1988, ACC filed a third quarter 10Q with the SEC. Touche's name does not appear in the 10Q. The document provides that although GOIL profit "is not recognized this quarter, the company expects that it will be in the future."

On December 12, 1988, Touche met with FHLBB's Kevin O'Connell and Carol Larson at the Dallas airport. The FHLBB arranged the meeting because of its concern that Touche's retention was the result of opinion shopping on the GOIL issue. FHLBB records reflect that Touche assured the regulators there was no "meaningful" discussion of GOIL until two days after the engagement. See note 2, supra. Based on these representations, FHLBB consented to Touche's retention as auditor for Lincoln. Nevertheless, Larson informed her superiors that she was "dismayed by Touche Ross' answers to questions concerning GOIL because they show no independent investigation by Touche Ross. They were just accepting Lincoln's answers."

On December 20, 1988, FHLBB sent Touche the results of its 1988 examination of ACC. The findings included:

> Management repeatedly engaged in material violations of law and regulations regarding affiliated transactions, ESOP, Hotel Pontchartrain, and tax sharing agreement;
>
> ACC is operating Lincoln solely for its own benefit;
>
> Lincoln is severely undercapitalized;
>
> Regulators have great concerns about Lincoln's continued viability;

Lincoln due over $50 million in tax payments upstreamed to ACC.

When questioned about the report, Mayer later testified that he recalled little about the FHLBB examination findings, and that the report raised no concerns in his mind concerning management integrity. Mayer testified that he did not know, even upon reading the report at his deposition, if it was "critical of management." Fred Martin testified that his first concerns about ACC's management integrity did not develop until March 1989.

Touche was engaged in December, 1988, to perform due diligence of Lincoln's assets for Spencer Scott Group, a prospective buyer of Lincoln. Touche ultimately disassociated itself from the proposed plan of sale. Information from this due diligence team was fully available to the ACC audit team.

On December 22, the California Department of Savings and Loan issued a cease and desist order, prohibiting illegal loans.

On December 28, 1988, Touche wrote to Darrell Dochow in response to the December 20 exam findings. Touche stated "we assume (though we do not necessarily concur) that the FHLBB's substantive conclusions are correct." Touche professed that it could only address substantive issues upon completion of the audit, and took issue with certain "calculation errors". On January 3 and 30, 1989, ACC filed prospectus supplements for $50 million in additional bonds.

On January 31, 1989, Darrell Dochow, by letter to Touche, requested elaboration on statements in the December 28 letter concerning reversals of income on the Crescent and Phoenician Hotels, and raised issues as to capitalized interest, capital requirements, proper accounting for a land development called Rancho Vistoso, and recovery of lost reserves. FHLBB requested the information within ten days. On February 8, 1989, Touche informed the FHLBB that they had just received the letter and could not comply within the time frame. On February 28, FHLBB's Alvin Smuzynski noted that Touche's answer had not arrived. In an E-mail to his colleagues, Smuzynski stated, "I get the impression Touche is ducking for cover now."

Fred Martin testified that he first thought about "going concern" issues and discussed the possibility of qualifying Touche's audit opinion with Keating during March 1989. He said Keating seemed to understand, and said he would get him the necessary information to avoid a qualification, but never did. Martin testified that he had his first concerns about management integrity in March 1989, when he learned about the criminal referral and about certain real estate transactions. Touche's Robert Kay testified that he never had concerns about management integrity.

On March 23, 1989, Touche wrote to the FHLBB regarding the proper accounting treatment for the sale of Lincoln Savings. This was followed by a one-hour phone meeting with Touche, ACC, and FHLBB. FHLBB's Larson subsequently summarized the letter and meeting for

Darrell Dochow. She wrote, "Touche Ross refused to make a concise comment regarding the value of the hotels and the stock. They just repeated several times that they were not far enough into the audit to determine that yet." Larson concluded, "I do not believe Touche Ross was being totally honest with us regarding the status of the audit. They have to file something with the SEC by mid-April ... they must be closer to reaching conclusions than they were willing to admit." On March 28, Larson wrote to Dochow, stating, "I agree with your sentiment regarding holding Touche to the standard audit report deadline. They have been less than forthright in their dealings with us to date and I would like to return the favor."

On April 1, 1989, Keating wrote, and Touche accepted, a check for $2.2 million for services in anticipation of bankruptcy. On April 13, 1989, ACC filed its Chapter 11 petition. One day later, FHLBB imposed a conservatorship on ACC. On April 14, 1989, Mayer sent an intra-office memorandum to Touche's Phoenix staff, instructing, "Your only proper response [to questions about ACC] is that you are unfamiliar with ACC's situation. Refer them to Martin or me if they have further questions." (Emphasis in original.) On April 21, 1989, Carol Larson E-mailed to a colleague, "We have had quite a time with Touche Ross and I just wanted to chat with you about them before you have to start dealing with them."

Based on this and other evidence in the record, the court finds summary judgment inappropriate. The court finds that the following evidence, in particular, bears on the element of reckless scienter: credibility of certain testimony on opinion shopping and other issues, knowledge potentially acquired from Keating, Wischer or Atchison, familiarity with public skepticism about ACC, information exchanged at the meeting with Arthur Young, knowledge of M.D.C. transactions with ACC and of management integrity issues with respect to M.D.C., knowledge that ACC was selling subordinated debentures without an underwriter, involvement with SEC and 8K filings, knowledge acquired through due diligence for Spencer Scott Group, knowledge of the December FHLBB examination report, inferences that could be drawn from FHLBB reports about Touche's dealings with them, and inferences from evidence concerning fees. Accordingly, based on the disputed facts above, Touche's Motion for Summary Judgment is denied.

* * *

* * * JONES, DAY, REAVIS & POGUE

Jones Day, a defendant in Shields, Roble, RTC v. Keating, and Yahr, focuses its summary judgment motion on an individual opinion letter given in connection with a 1986 registration statement. Jones Day claims this opinion letter was neither false, nor was it written in an expert capacity. Jones Day generally claims that it has not engaged in conduct for which it could be held liable because lawyers are obligated to keep their clients' confidence and to act in a ways that do not discourage their clients from undergoing regulatory compliance reviews.

1. The Record

The record reveals the following facts concerning Jones Day's involvement with ACC and Keating.

Prior to joining Jones Day, defendant William Schilling was director of the FHLBB Office of Examinations and Supervision. In that capacity, he was directly involved in the supervision of Lincoln Savings. During the summer of 1985, he wrote at least one memorandum and concurred in another, expressing serious regulatory concerns about numerous aspects of Lincoln's operations. For example, he wrote:

> [U]nder new management, Lincoln has engaged in several serious regulatory violations. Some of these violations, such as the overvaluation of real estate and failure to comply with Memorandum R–41(b), are the same type of violations that have lead to some of the worst failures in FSLIC's history.

Later in 1985, Schilling was hired by Jones Day to augment its expertise in thrift representation. On January 31, 1986, Schilling and Jones Day's Ron Kneipper flew to Phoenix to solicit ACC's business. ACC retained Jones Day to perform "a major internal audit of Lincoln's FHLBB compliance and a major project to help Lincoln deal with the FHLBB's direct investment regulations."

During the regulatory compliance audit, which Jones Day understood to be a pre-FHLBB examination compliance review, the law firm found multiple regulatory violations. There is evidence that Jones Day knew that Lincoln had backdated files, destroyed appraisals, removed appraisals from files, told appraisers not to issue written reports when their oral valuations were too low, and violated affiliated transaction regulations. Jones Day found that Lincoln did no loan underwriting and no post-closure loan follow up to ensure that Lincoln's interests were being protected. Jones Day learned Lincoln had multiple "loans" which were, in fact, joint ventures which violated FHLBB regulations, made real estate loans in violation of regulations, and backdated corporate resolutions which were not signed by corporate officers and did not reflect actual meetings. There is evidence that Jones Day may have tacitly consented to removal of harmful documents from Lincoln files. For example, one handwritten notation on a memorandum memorializing Jones Day's advice not to remove documents from files reads, "If something *is* devastating, consider it individually." (Emphasis in original).

There is evidence that Jones Day instructed ACC in how to rectify deficiencies so that they would not be apparent to FHLBB examiners. Jones Day attorneys, including Schilling, testified that they told ACC/Lincoln personnel to provide the Jones Day-generated "to do" lists only to the attorneys responsible for rectifying the deficiencies, and to destroy the lists so that FHLB–SF would not find them in the files. For the same reason, Jones Day's regulatory compliance reports to ACC/Lincoln were oral. Jones Day paralegals testified that responsibilities for carrying out the "to do" lists were divided among Jones Day and ACC staff. Jones Day continued this work into the summer of 1986.

The evidence indicates that Jones Day may have been aware that ACC/Lincoln did not follow its compliance advice with respect to ongoing activities. There are material questions of fact concerning the procedures Jones Day used—if any—to ascertain whether their compliance advice was being heeded. The testimony suggests that Jones Day partners knew ACC/Lincoln personnel were preparing loan underwriting summaries contemporaneously with Jones Day's regulatory compliance review, even though the loan transactions had already been closed. Moreover, the evidence reveals that Jones Day attorneys participated in creating corporate resolutions to ratify forged and backdated corporate records.

On April 23, 1986, Jones Day partner Fohrman wrote:

I received Neal Millard's memo on ACC. In looking at the long list of people involved, it occurred to me that there will be times when individuals may be called upon to render legal services that might require the issuance of opinion letters from Jones, Day. As we all know, we now possess information that could affect the way we write our opinion letters and our actual ability to give a particular opinion may be severely restricted. However, this large list of individuals may not be aware of knowledge that is held by Messrs. Fein and Schilling. I would suggest that a follow up memo be issued by Ron Fein indicating that any work involving ACC which requires the issuance of opinions, must be cleared by Ron....

Also in April 1986, ACC's Jim Grogan wrote to Jones Day's Kneipper, soliciting a strategy to "sunset" the FHLBB direct investment regulation. Jones Day subsequently made multiple Freedom of Information Act requests to FHLBB in furtherance of a direct investment rule strategy, for which Lincoln was billed. In a September 12, 1986 telephone conversation, Grogan allegedly told Kneipper: "[C]omment letters were great success—FHLBB picked it up 'hook, line and sinker' ... Charlie wants to do again.... "

The record indicates that the concept of selling ACC debentures in Lincoln Savings branches may have originated at an April 9, 1986 real estate syndicate seminar given by Jones Day Defendant Ron Fein. There is evidence that Fein may have contributed to the detailed bond sales program outline, attending to details such as explaining how the sales would work, and insuring that the marketing table was far enough from the teller windows to distinguish between ACC and Lincoln Savings employees. The evidence indicates that Jones Day reviewed the debenture registration statement and prospectus, which is corroborated by Jones Day's billing records. As a result, in January 1987, ACC was able to assure the California Department of Savings & Loan that:

The process of structuring the bond sales program was reviewed by Kaye, Scholer and Jones Day to assure compliance not only with securities laws and regulations, but also with banking and FSLIC laws and regulations.

Moreover, there is evidence which suggests that political contributions were made on behalf of ACC, in exchange for ACC's consent that Jones Day could "bill liberally." On June 23, 1986, Kneipper memorialized a phone conversation:

> (1) 1:15 p.m. Ron Kessler—in past, firm has given $amt. to PAC, has premium billed, & PAC contri. to candidate; concern that we're an out of state law firm and that a $#in excess of $5,000.00 would look like an unusual move; Barnett and Kessler have done before; question re whether and how we can get some busi. from GOV. for this.
>
> (2) 3:40 p.m. Jim Grogan

Ten tickets at $1,000.00 equals $10,000.00

Barr wants limits of $5,000.00/contribution

Agreed that we could bill liberally in future in recognition of this.

At deposition, Kneipper testified that his note—"agreed could bill liberally in recognition for this,"—"is what it appears to be." Jones Day set up an Arizona Political Action Committee ("PAC") specifically for the purpose of making a contribution to an Arizona gubernatorial candidate. The PAC was opened on September 4, 1986 and closed in December, 1986, after the contribution was made.

In June 1986, Jones Day solicited additional work from ACC. Jones Day attorney Caulkins wrote, in part:

> Rick Kneipper reports that ACC is very explicit that it does not care how much its legal services cost, as long as it gets the best. He states that Keating gave him an unsolicited $250,000 retainer to start the thrift work, and sent another similar check also unsolicited in two weeks. On the down side, he reports that he has never encountered a more demanding and difficult client, . . .
>
> It appears to Rick and to me that American Continental is made for us and we for them.

On October 28, 1986, Jones Day provided an opinion letter, required by Item 601(b) of SEC regulation S–K, for inclusion in an ACC bond registration statement. Jones Day's opinion letter stated that the indenture was a valid and binding obligation under California law.

2. *Section 10(b), RICO, and Common Law Fraud*

Jones Day seeks summary judgment on Plaintiffs' claims under Section 10(b), RICO and common law fraud.

Jones Day contends that it may not be held liable for counseling its client. The line between maintaining a client's confidence and violating the securities law is brighter than Jones Day suggests, however. Attorneys must inform a client in a clear and direct manner when its conduct violates the law. If the client continues the objectionable activity, the lawyer must withdraw "if the representation will result in violation of the rules of professional conduct or other law." Ethical Rule 1.16

("ER"). Under such circumstances, an attorney's ethical responsibilities do not conflict with the securities laws. An attorney may not continue to provide services to corporate clients when the attorney knows the client is engaged in a course of conduct designed to deceive others, and where it is obvious that the attorney's compliant legal services may be a substantial factor in permitting the deceit to continue. *See* Rudolph v. Arthur Andersen, supra.

The record raises material questions about whether Jones Day knew of ACC/Lincoln's fraud, but nevertheless provided hands-on assistance in hiding loan file deficiencies from the regulators, offered detailed advice about setting up the bond sales program, carried out a lobbying strategy with respect to the direct investment rule, made political contributions on ACC's behalf, reviewed SEC registration statements and prospectuses, and lent its name to a misleading legal opinion. This evidence raises material questions concerning Section 10(b), RICO, AZRAC, common law fraud and deceit, and violations of Cal.Corp.Code §§ 25401 and 25504.1.

3. Section 11 Liability

Section 11 imposes liability for misleading statements made in connection with registration statements. * * *

Jones Day * * * contends that it cannot be held liable under Section 11 because it did not issue an "expert" opinion. Section 11 applies to misleading statements made by one "whose profession gives authority to statements made by him." 15 U.S.C. § 77k. Jones Day concedes that its October 28, 1986 opinion letter was required by SEC Regulation S–K, which provides in part:

(5) *Opinion Re Legality*—(i) An opinion of counsel as to the legality of the securities being registered, indicating whether they will, when sold, be legally issued, fully paid and non-assessable, and, if debt securities, whether they will be binding obligations of the registrant.

SEC Regulation S–K, Item 601( )(5).

The court holds that an attorney who provides a legal opinion used in connection with an SEC registration statement is an expert within the meaning of Section 11.

4. Breach of Fiduciary Duty to Lincoln

* * *

Jones Day contends that claims for breach of fiduciary duty, brought by the RTC, are [invalid].

* * *

An attorney who represents a corporation has a duty to act in the corporation's best interest when confronted by adverse interests of directors, officers, or corporate affiliates. It is not a defense that corporate representation often involves the distinct interests of affiliated entities. Attorneys are bound to act when those interests conflict. There are genuine questions as to whether Jones Day should have sought independent representation for Lincoln.

Moreover, where a law firm believes the management of a corporate client is committing serious regulatory violations, the firm has an obligation to actively discuss the violative conduct, urge cessation of the activity, and withdraw from representation where the firm's legal services may contribute to the continuation of such conduct. Jones Day contends that it would have been futile to act on these fiduciary obligations because those controlling ACC/Lincoln would not have responded. Client wrongdoing, however, cannot negate an attorney's fiduciary duty. Moreover, the evidence reveals that attorney advice influenced ACC/Lincoln's conduct in a variety of ways. Accordingly, summary judgment as to this claim is denied.

* * *

Notes

1. Lincoln Savings & Loan may be the most expensive thrift failure in American banking history, ultimately costing taxpayers $2.5 billion.[i] The accounting firm of Ernst & Young paid $63 million and the law firm of Kaye, Scholer, Fierman, Hayes & Handler paid $41 million to the Office of Thrift Supervision to settle lawsuits regarding their liability for stating that Lincoln Savings & Loan was solvent when it was not.[j] District Court Judge Bilby who presided over much of the litigation brought in the aftermath of Lincoln's collapse, asked:

> "Where were these professionals * * * when these clearly improper transactions were being consummated?

> "Why didn't any of them speak up or disassociate themselves from the transactions?

> "Where also were the outside accountants and attorneys when these transactions were effectuated?

> "What is difficult to understand is that with all the professional talent involved (both accounting and legal), why at least one professional would not have blown the whistle to stop the overreaching that took place in this case."[k]

2. The collapse of Lincoln Savings and Loan shook the financial industry. Consider the following Congressional testimony by an attorney for the Office of Thrift Supervision:

> "Lincoln is the case the epitomizes the savings and loan catastrophe. It is likely to be the most costly thrift failure * * *.

> "The thrift * * * invest[ed] most of its new brokered funds in acquisition, development and construction ("ADC") loans * * * ADC loans are

---

i. Brooks Jackson, *Thrift Examiners Say They Saw Signs of Criminal Wrongdoing at Lincoln*, WALL ST. J. (Nov. 1, 1989).

j. Melissa Harrison, *The Assault on the Liability of Outside Professionals: Are Law-*

yers and Accountants off the Hook? 65 U. CINN. L. REV. 473 (1997).

k. Lincoln Sav. & Loan Ass'n v. Wall, 743 F.Supp. 901, 920 (D.D.C.1990).

made to buy land and develop it into typically, large commercial buildings. * * *

How a Typical Bad ADC Loan is Structured

"The borrower makes no down payment. The thrift loans him the full amount necessary to acquire and develop the property *plus* the so-called 'soft costs' (i.e., fees for architects and building permits), plus in a number of cases, a development fee to the borrower. In other words, the borrower puts zero money in and walks away with money in his pocket for himself. In addition, no principal payment is due on the loan for two to five years. Better yet, the borrower does not have to pay any interest during that same period. Instead, the thrift 'pays' itself the interest due out of an "interest reserve." An example may help: Assume that a developer needs $90 million dollars in funds to build a hotel. The ADC lender will loan the borrower the $90 million, plus the developer's fee, that I will assume is $1 million, plus $5 million to cover the soft costs. So a total of $96 million in *cash* is loaned. The thrift also charges $4 million in points and fees, which it again 'pays' to itself by increasing the amount of the debt from $96 to $100 million. Assuming that the loan has a 10 percent interest rate and has to be repaid in two years, the debt is increased from $100 to $120 million and a $20 million 'interest reserve' is created. The borrower gets $96 million in cash, but signs a note requiring repayment of $120 million in two years. However, the thrift 'pays' itself back the $20 million dollars over the course of the two years (no money changes hands, this is simply an accounting game). In two years the ADC borrower has to make his first real payment. He will owe approximately $100 million at that time. * * *

"Precisely because they were so risky, conservative financial institutions would not make the kind of ADC loan I have just described. Lenders willing to take on these garbage loans were generally troubled thrifts or thrifts acquired by unscrupulous individuals and quickly became known to the type of borrowers to whom no one else would lend. * * * All that was necessary to [make this appear proper] * * * was an accommodating accountant. * * *

"[Accounting firm] Arthur Young & Co.'s * * * Dallas office [allowed] almost anything that a thrift called an ADC loan [to be remain classified as] an ADC loan. * * *

"It is a sad fact that *most* of FSLIC's worst losses were from thrifts that received 'clean' audit opinions from 'Big 8' accounting firms prior to their failure. * * * Indeed, Lincoln is proof positive any thrift in America could obtain a clean audit opinion despite being grossly insolvent.

"With the right accounting firm, an ADC loan was *guaranteed* to be highly profitable for at least two years, until the interest reserve was exhausted and the borrower had to repay the loan. * * *

"Commentators have often observed that for a thrift owner with none of his own capital at risk, there was a temptation to make risky investments under the theory that: 'heads I win, tails FSLIC loses.' With ADC loans, however, it was really: 'heads or tails I win and the FSLIC loses.' "[1]

3. Were the law and accounting firms sued in the above case so concerned about attracting and satisfying a major client that they failed to provide honest, careful advice? Currently there are about 900,000 practicing attorneys in the United States with about 32,000 students graduating from law schools every year. The "chase" for clients is likely to become even more frenzied. Will more debacles like the failed Lincoln Savings and Loan occur as the pressure to woo clients increases? Are there ways to overcome this pressure?

––––––––

The next case demonstrates the peril of attorneys who aggressively represent their clients (such as a government agency) in a matter pending before a court which disapproves of, or is unfamiliar with, permissible tactics. As you read this case determine what, if anything, the attorneys representing the Resolution Trust Corporation (RTC) could have done differently to avoid the District Court's issuance of sanctions.

RESOLUTION TRUST CORPORATION
v. H. R. "BUM" BRIGHT

United States Court of Appeals, Fifth Circuit, 1993.
6 F.3d 336.

KAZEN, DISTRICT JUDGE.

This appeal arises out of a lawsuit filed in May 1992 by the Resolution Trust Corporation ("RTC") against H.R. "Bum" Bright and James B. "Boots" Reeder, based on their alleged misconduct in connection with activities at Bright Banc Savings Association, Dallas ("Bright Banc"). Approximately two months after the suit was filed, appellees moved for a protective order and sanctions against the RTC for the manner in which its attorneys, Peter F. Lovato III and Thomas D. Graber, interviewed a former Bright Banc employee. After four days of hearings on the motion for sanctions, the district court issued an oral order on October 19, 1992, finding that the attorneys, appellants herein, impermissibly attempted to persuade the witness to sign an affidavit containing statements which the witness had not previously told appellants. The order disbarred the attorneys from practicing before the district judge and disqualified the attorneys' law firm, Hopkins & Sutter, from further representing RTC in the underlying case. In a December 28, 1992 written order, the court assessed attorneys' fees against the law

––––––––

1. *Investigation of Lincoln Savings & Loan Association,* Hearing before House Comm. on Banking, Finance and urban Affairs, 101st Cong., 1st Sess. 286–89, 292–94, 297–98 (Oct. 26, 1989) (Prepared Statement of William K. Black, Acting District Counsel, S. F. Region, Office of Thrift Supervision).

firm for costs incurred by appellees in prosecuting the sanctions motion. Appellants timely appealed the district court's decision. We reverse.

* * *

On May 14, 1992, the RTC filed suit in federal district court charging appellees Bright and Reeder, as shareholders, directors and officers of Bright Banc, with fraud, negligence, and breach of fiduciary and other duties owed to the bank's shareholders. As part of their pre-filing investigation of the case, attorneys Lovato and Graber conducted several interviews—all voluntary—with Barbara Erhart, formerly the Senior Vice President of Finance Support at Bright Banc. Erhart had worked closely with defendant Reeder and had contact with defendant Bright on "critical matters."

The primary focus of the Erhart interviews was the method Bright Banc used to calculate the amount of non-cash assets it had converted to cash for a December 1986 report on the bank's financial health to the Federal Home Loan Bank Board ("FHLBB"). The RTC attorneys, including Lovato and Graber, questioned Erhart extensively about who made and authorized the computations used in the report. At the conclusion of the third interview, Lovato and Graber asked Erhart to return to their office the next day—April 9, 1992—to review and sign an affidavit summarizing what she had told them in the course of the prior interviews.

When Erhart arrived at the office of Hopkins & Sutter on April 9th, she was not immediately given the affidavit. Instead, the attorneys questioned her again about the cash conversion calculations. As Lovato and Graber spoke to Erhart, they made some last-minute changes to the draft. The changes were incorporated into a revised draft which Graber then presented to Erhart. He warned her that it "contained a couple of things [they hadn't] discussed with [her]," but which the attorneys nevertheless believed to be true. Erhart was instructed to read the affidavit "very carefully."

Erhart made several changes to the draft affidavit. Some related only to semantical differences, while others reflected Erhart's disagreement with substantive claims in the affidavit. Lovato and Graber questioned Erhart extensively about the changes she made. During this questioning, the attorneys asked Erhart whether she could reword some of her changes to emphasize that Bright and Reeder were more directly involved in the decision to use the controversial cash conversion computations. Erhart declined because she did not have personal knowledge of the statements the attorneys wanted her to include in her affidavit. With respect to some of the statements in the affidavit, the attorneys were not content to accept Erhart's initial refusal to revise her changes. In an effort to have Erhart see things their way, Lovato and Graber described their understanding of how certain events transpired at Bright Banc, presented Erhart with independent evidence to support this interpretation of events, and aggressively challenged some of Erhart's assumptions about Bright and Reeder. After making their case for further revisions,

Lovato and Graber asked Erhart whether she believed them and whether she was now convinced that their version of certain events was correct. Erhart, unconvinced, declined to alter the initial changes she had made to the draft affidavit.

When it was clear to the attorneys that Erhart would not sign a statement agreeing with the attorneys' version of some of the disputed events at Bright Banc, they incorporated Erhart's handwritten changes into a new draft affidavit. Erhart read this draft and made a few changes which were then included in a third draft. Erhart read and approved this version of the affidavit, signed it and left the offices of Hopkins & Sutter.

Approximately one month later, Erhart told appellees' attorneys that she had given a statement to appellant-attorneys regarding some of the transactions at issue in the underlying law suit. Appellees' counsel then arranged for Erhart to give them an ex parte statement on June 12, 1992 about her meetings with Lovato and Graber. This statement was transcribed by the court reporter but never signed by Erhart. However, she later adopted portions of it during testimony before Judge Kendall on August 9, 1992.

In that testimony, Erhart stated, among other things, that she did not think Lovato and Graber were asking her to say something she did not believe but rather were trying to determine if she could see the case the way they did. She denied being harassed or intimidated and expressed the view that "they were doing their job, just like everybody else." The district court essentially disregarded this testimony, finding it contrary to Erhart's earlier ex parte statement given to appellees' attorneys, and concluding that the change must have been the result of "obvious job pressure." Erhart's earlier statement clearly has a different tone from her subsequent court testimony. For example, she earlier described Lovato as having been particularly aggressive in attempts to persuade her to agree with appellants' version of certain events, "almost like browbeating me." Nevertheless even in her ex parte statement, Erhart indicated that Lovato and Graber were not trying to have her change facts but rather to agree with a different "interpretation" or "slant" from the facts.

* * *

On July 15, 1992, Bright and Reeder moved for sanctions and a protective order against the RTC based on Lovato and Graber's conduct during the Erhart interviews. The motion alleged that the manner in which the RTC's attorneys interviewed Erhart violated Texas Disciplinary Rules of Professional Conduct 3.04, 4.01(a) and 4.04(a) and probably violated 18 U.S.C. §§ 1503, 1512. [obstruction of justice]. Appellees also called upon the court to exercise its "inherent powers" to sanction the RTC for intimidating Erhart. The motion asked the court to prevent the RTC from using any notes or statements obtained through the Erhart interviews, to order the RTC not to make any further contact with Erhart, and to award attorneys fees to Bright and Reeder for their efforts in bringing and prosecuting the motion for sanctions.

On July 20, 1992, the district court ordered that both sides refrain from contacting Erhart while the sanctions motion was pending. Hearings on the sanctions motion were held over the course of several days from August to October 1992.

* * *

The district court issued an oral ruling on the motion for sanctions on October 19, 1992. This ruling was further clarified in separate written orders issued on October 23 and December 28, 1992.

The court found that Lovato and Graber "knowingly attempted to get a key witness . . . to commit to a sworn statement that they knew contained assertions of fact she had not made or told them previously in matters highly relevant to the plaintiff's civil claim." It found that the attorneys were "going to try to talk her into" those statements. The Court was particularly troubled because the draft affidavit given to Erhart added matters only in areas "that established or buttressed the [RTC's] claims." The court characterized the attorneys' actions concerning the draft affidavit as "tampering with" or attempting to "manufacture" evidence to "cause, or aid in, Defendants' downfall."

Based on its inherent power to regulate the conduct of attorneys, Judge Kendall disbarred Lovato and Graber from practicing before him. He assessed $110,000 in attorneys fees against Hopkins & Sutter for expenses incurred by Bright and Reeder in the prosecution of the sanctions motion.[3] Pursuant to its authority under Local Rule 13.2 (N.D.Tex.),[4] the court removed Hopkins & Sutter from further representing the RTC in the underlying action. Finally, it ordered the firm not to charge the RTC for defending against the sanction motion. No sanctions were assessed against the RTC. Lovato, Graber and Hopkins & Sutter timely appealed.

The district court disbarred attorneys Lovato and Graber from practicing before it pursuant to the court's inherent powers to discipline attorneys. It is beyond dispute that a federal court may suspend or dismiss an attorney as an exercise of the court's inherent powers. However, before sanctioning any attorney under its inherent powers, the court must make a specific finding that the attorney acted in "bad faith." The United States Supreme Court has held that a court's imposition of sanctions under its inherent powers is reviewable under the abuse-of-discretion standard. A court abuses its discretion when its ruling is based on an erroneous view of the law or on a clearly erroneous

3. The court explained that the award of attorneys fees was not intended as a sanction, but that it "flows from equity in light of the Court's inherent power or the purpose of reimbursement rather than sanction." December 28, 1992 Order at 3 n. 1.

4. Local Rule 13.2 of the U.S. District Court For the Northern District of Texas states, in pertinent part,

Any member of the bar of this Court . . . who proves to be incompetent to practice before this Court because of unethical behavior . . . is subject to revocation of admission to practice in this District and to other appropriate discipline, after such hearing as the Court may direct in each particular instance.

assessment of the evidence. In the specific context of a disqualification motion, this circuit reviews fact findings for "clear error" while "carefully examining" the district court's application of relevant ethical standards. [citations omitted]

Because disbarment is a quasi-criminal proceeding, any disciplinary rules used to impose this sanction on attorneys must be strictly construed, resolving ambiguities in favor of the person charged. The Texas Disciplinary Rules of Professional Conduct do not expressly apply to sanctions in federal courts, but a federal court may nevertheless hold attorneys accountable to the state code of professional conduct.

The district court failed to make specific findings of how appellants violated the Disciplinary Rules. In its oral findings, the court concluded that Lovato and Graber engaged in "inappropriate conduct, conduct that probably violates the DRs, unethical conduct, as well as a probable violation of the obstruction of justice statutes." We shall assume that the district court's comments referred to the Disciplinary Rules invoked by Appellees in their motion for sanctions.

The sanctionable conduct found by the district court was the attorneys' inclusion of statements in draft affidavits that had not been previously discussed with Erhart, combined with the attorneys' attempts to persuade Erhart to agree with their understanding of how certain events transpired at the bank. Placing statements in a draft affidavit that have not been previously discussed with a witness does not automatically constitute bad-faith conduct. It is one thing to ask a witness to swear to facts which are knowingly false. It is another thing, in an arms-length interview with a witness, for an attorney to attempt to persuade her, even aggressively, that her initial version of a certain fact situation is not complete or accurate. Disciplinary Rules 3.04(b) and 4.01(a) concern the former circumstance, not the latter. The district court never found that appellants asked Erhart to make statements which they knew to be false. Indeed, the district court pretermitted any consideration of the truth of the draft affidavits. Appellees nevertheless argue that because appellant attorneys attempted to persuade Erhart to adopt certain statements which she had not expressly made and which she refused to adopt, the attorneys thereby were either making or urging the making of "false" statements in violation of DRs 3.04(b) and 4.01(a). We disagree. The district court characterized the attorneys' behavior as "manufacturing" evidence, but there is no indication that the attorneys did not have a factual basis for the additional statements included in the draft affidavit. On the contrary, appellants have attempted to demonstrate in a detailed chart that the contested portions of the affidavit were based either on their notes of interviews with Erhart or on evidence from other sources (e.g., internal bank memorandum).

We recognize that the Texas Disciplinary Rules are not the sole authority governing a motion to disqualify in federal court; rather, such a motion must be determined by standards developed under federal law. Our source for professional standards has been the canons of ethics developed by the American Bar Association. The district court opinion, however, makes no reference to any national canons which would add to the analysis here, nor do appellees. A court obviously would be justified in disbarring an attorney for attempting to induce a witness to testify falsely under oath, but this record does not support the conclusion that Lovato and Graber engaged in such behavior. While the attorneys were persistent and aggressive in presenting their theory of the case to Erhart, they nevertheless made sure that Erhart signed the affidavit only if she agreed with its contents. The attorneys never attempted to hide from Erhart the fact that some statements were included in draft affidavits that had not been discussed with her previously. Instead, they brought the statements to her attention and warned her to read them carefully. Additionally, Lovato and Graber never claimed to be neutral parties. Erhart knew that these attorneys were advocates for a particular position, and she was also in communication with attorneys who were advocating the contrary position. Were Erhart giving testimony at a deposition or at trial, the attorneys for either side would not be required to accept her initial testimony at face value but would be able to confront her with other information to challenge her testimony or attempt to persuade her to change it.

Appellees also alleged that RTC attorneys violated Disciplinary Rule 4.04(a), which prohibits an attorney from burdening a third party without a valid "substantial purpose" or violating a third party's legal rights. The district court findings do not reveal that Lovato and Graber committed either wrong. The attorneys' sometimes laborious interviews with Erhart were conducted with the goal of eliciting an accurate and favorable affidavit from a key witness in the underlying case. Additionally, the district court made no findings that the interviews violated Erhart's legal rights, nor does the record contain any evidence to support such a finding.

The district court ordered the firm of Hopkins & Sutter to pay $100,000 in attorneys' fees to appellees for their prosecution of the sanction motion and also restrained the firm from charging the RTC for defending against the motion. The court assessed attorneys' fees under its inherent power to do so against counsel who have conducted themselves "in bad faith." It found that Lovato and Graber acted in bad faith because they tampered with or attempted to manufacture evidence and concluded that "a law firm may not escape the consequences of misconduct committed by one of its attorneys." The Supreme Court in Chambers described three exceptions to the so-called "American Rule," which prohibits fee shifting in most cases. The exception pertinent to the instant case is that a court may assess attorney's fees when a party acts "in bad faith, vexatiously, wantonly, or for oppressive reasons." The Supreme Court compared this exception to the requirement under Rule 11, Fed.R.Civ.P., providing that the signer of a paper warrants that it is not interposed for any improper purpose, such as to harass or to cause unnecessary delay or needless increase in the cost of litigation. Id. at n. 10. We understand the district court's finding of "bad faith" to be grounded exclusively on the proposition that attorneys Lovato and Graber wrongfully tried to tamper with or manufacture evidence. Because we have already found that the record does not support that conclusion, the assessment of attorney's fees cannot be sustained.

The trial court did not elaborate, either orally or in writing, on its order restraining Hopkins & Sutter from charging the RTC for time spent defending the motion for sanctions. Neither side has specifically addressed that sanction on appeal. Nevertheless, in view of the conclusions we have heretofore announced, there would likewise be no justification for this sanction.

* * *

We conclude that the district court abused its discretion when it issued its sanctions ruling against appellants. We REVERSE and REMAND for proceedings not inconsistent with this opinion.

B. FRAUD UPON CLIENTS

The next case, United States v. Myerson, 18 F.3d 153 (2d Cir.1994), involves what is probably one of the more common types of fraud committed by unscrupulous, or simply careless, professionals. As you read the opinion, assume you are in-house counsel for Shearson Lehman Hutton, Inc. (Shearson), ICN Pharmaceuticals, Inc. ("ICN"), or the Home Insurance Company ("Home") and charged with the responsibility of retaining and supervising outside counsel, as well as approving outside counsel's bills. What, if anything, would you have done to prevent Myerson's false billing?

UNITED STATES v. MYERSON

United States Court of Appeals, Second Circuit, 1994.
18 F.3d 153.

Lay, Senior Circuit Judge.

Harvey Myerson, a New York attorney, appeals from two judgments entered against him after he was convicted by juries in two separate trials. Myerson was convicted on three counts of mail fraud, in violation of 18 U.S.C. § 1341, and on two counts of travel fraud, in violation of 18 U.S.C. § 2314,[1] for significantly overbilling his clients and fraudulently claiming that personal charges were legitimate business expenses. In a second trial, Myerson was convicted under a separate indictment of conspiracy to defraud the United States, in violation of 18 U.S.C. § 371; of making a false statement on his tax return, in violation of 26 U.S.C.

---

1. The district court dismissed both travel fraud counts for lack of sufficient evidence to sustain the convictions. The government has cross-appealed these dismissals.

§ 7206(1); and of assisting in filing a false tax return for his law partnership, in violation of 26 U.S.C. § 7206(2).[2]

* * * We affirm all judgments of conviction. On the cross-appeal, we find the district court did not err in dismissing the two travel fraud counts.

I.   THE BILLING FRAUD CASE

Myerson was charged in a fifteen count superseding indictment with defrauding six clients and his own law firm while he was a partner at the New York law firm he founded, Myerson & Kuhn ("M & K"). This fraud was based on Myerson's submitting a legal fee that overbilled his clients by millions of dollars and by his fraudulent claims that personal charges were legitimate business expenses. Following a contentious six week trial, Myerson was convicted of defrauding three of his clients: Shearson Lehman Hutton, Inc. ("Shearson"), ICN Pharmaceuticals, Inc. ("ICN"), and the Home Insurance Company ("Home"). * * *

The Shearson Fraud

The Shearson fraud was discovered when three young M & K associates found doctored timesheets and computer runs, indicating that M & K attorney hours had been inflated and that Shearson had been billed considerable sums for legal work that had never been performed. The associates delivered the timesheets to Shearson. At trial, the government's witnesses included three of Myerson's partners, various Shearson employees and others who established that Myerson defrauded Shearson, M & K's most important client, out of nearly $2,000,000 in less than one year. Myerson's partners Lloyd Clareman, Mark Segall, and Arthur Ruegger all testified pursuant to cooperation agreements with the government that Myerson "would direct what he wanted the bills to be for particular matters or clients for particular months" and that these billing levels were unrelated to the service needs of the clients. Testimony at trial reflected that Myerson would direct that the actual time reported on associates' and partners' timesheets be adjusted upward to meet Myerson's desired billing levels. Clareman testified that his secretary would first draft Shearson bills based on computer runs and then, at Myerson's direction, he and Segall would inflate attorney hours in order to hike the overall bills.

When the three M & K associates found the doctored timesheets and delivered them to Shearson, along with computer runs and other materials, Shearson performed an internal audit of M & K's bills and found that, conservatively, M & K had overcharged Shearson by $1,996,003. Shearson executives called Myerson and Clareman and confronted them with the results of the audit. Myerson disputed the overcharge and stated he had no knowledge of it. However, after further discussions,

---

2. Myerson was sentenced to a term of sixty months and two concurrent terms of ten months to run consecutively to one another for the mail fraud counts, and to three concurrent terms of thirty-three months imprisonment for the tax fraud. The separate sentences on the two judgments are being served concurrently. Each sentence required a three-year term of supervised release.

Shearson executives failed to accept Myerson's explanations and terminated M & K.

The ICN Fraud

In like fashion to the Shearson fraud, the government produced evidence that showed ICN had been repeatedly overcharged for legal services that were never actually rendered, and that Myerson billed ICN for several of his pleasure trips, including a trip to the Kentucky Derby. Myerson also obtained thousands of dollars in petty cash and charged it to ICN.

Ruegger and another M & K partner, Daniel Cooper, were the partners responsible for the ICN account. According to government witnesses Segall and Ruegger, during monthly lunch meetings at which billing targets were set for various clients, Cooper was told by Myerson to get the bills for ICN to at least $300,000 per month. Ruegger testified that, on at least one occasion, Cooper told him, "Harvey wants the bills at 300 and I can't get them there."

The Home Insurance Fraud

Testimony at trial established that Myerson charged thousands of dollars in personal expenses to Home although he did no work for the company. Among these expenses were a charter flight to Myerson's summer home in East Hampton, Long Island, and over $5,000 in twenty-three petty cash disbursements. Most of the charges were reflected in Home's "Reinsurance" case which was handled by another M & K partner, Philip Kaufman. Kaufman and Home's general counsel testified at trial that Myerson had no involvement in Home cases.

Myerson's defense at trial focused on the frauds committed by other partners (primarily Myerson's close set of proteges, Segall, Clareman and Cooper) who had either pleaded guilty to their involvement in the billing fraud or had entered into cooperation agreements with the government to escape prosecution. On appeal, Myerson does not dispute that the government, as verdict-holder, is entitled to the benefit of all favorable inferences and disputed facts, and indeed Myerson does not dispute that sufficient evidence existed for the jury to find his guilt beyond a reasonable doubt on the counts upon which he was convicted. Rather, he asserts that the district court made specific errors which severely prejudiced his defense and which require reversal of his convictions. We address each of these contentions.

A. The Missing Witness Instruction

Myerson initially claims that the district court erred in refusing to instruct the jury that it could draw an adverse inference against the government because the United States had failed to immunize the testimony of accomplice and M & K partner Daniel Cooper, whose attorney had informed the district court and Myerson that, if called, Cooper would assert his Fifth Amendment privilege against self-incrimination. Myerson argues that the district court erred further by instructing the jury instead that the jury could draw no inference from the fact that Cooper had not testified.

Cooper was the billing partner for ICN who, according to the government's theory, fraudulently inflated bills at Myerson's direction. Cooper was a participant in several lunch meetings at which Myerson exhorted his partners Clareman and Segall to inflate the bills for Shearson. Additionally, Cooper worked on and was "monitoring" certain matters for Home. Consequently, Myerson argues, Cooper figured significantly with respect to each of the counts on which Myerson was convicted.

On its direct case, the government introduced statements attributed to Cooper that directly inculpated Myerson. However, the government did not call Cooper himself, who had pleaded guilty to defrauding the UFCW, but who had not yet been sentenced. In addition to his guilty plea, Cooper had acknowledged to the government his obstruction of justice, based on his destruction of records that had been subpoenaed in connection with the grand jury investigation. Cooper also admitted his part in falsifying the ICN bills. The government informed the district court, however, that Cooper had no agreement with the government concerning his plea or possible sentence.

During his defense case, Myerson announced in the presence of the jury that he intended to call Cooper as a witness. Myerson acknowledged to the court that he had done this despite having been informed by Cooper's counsel several days earlier that, if called by either party, Cooper would invoke his Fifth Amendment privilege. Cooper's counsel appeared before the district court and confirmed that Cooper would invoke his privilege. Cooper's counsel also informed the district court that Cooper's testimony would not exculpate Myerson.

Myerson did not challenge Cooper's assertion of privilege as invalid, and does not do so in this court. Rather, Myerson asked the court to recognize "the right of the jury to at least hear the questions that were asked." Myerson complained that, among other things, because the government would not immunize Cooper, he was being precluded from testing whether or not Cooper had a "de facto deal" with the government. The district court offered Myerson the opportunity to determine whether there was such a deal, but Myerson failed to take up the offer.

The district court denied Myerson's request to compel Cooper to invoke his privilege against self-incrimination in front of the jury and refused to give an instruction which would allow the jury to draw an adverse inference against the government from its failure to call Cooper as an immunized witness. The court observed that, "I think, strategically, [Myerson] doesn't really want [Cooper] to testify." In declining to give the requested instruction, the district court stated that "the Government had sufficient reason for not calling [Cooper] and not immunizing him. And I think [Myerson] really did not want the Government to call him, nor did [Myerson] really want him to testify as a witness on [Myerson's] behalf."[6]

In instructing the jury, the district court charged:

Mr. Cooper declined to testify as a witness in this case. As a result of a hearing that was held outside of your presence, I determined that Mr. Cooper could not be compelled to testify. You should not speculate as to the reasons why Mr. Cooper refused to testify, and you should not draw any inference from the fact that Mr. Cooper did not appear in this case as a witness.

Myerson insists on appeal that the trial court erred, under the circumstances, in failing to give his requested instruction, and that the jury should have been able to draw an adverse inference against the government from its failure to call Cooper. Myerson also objects to the district court's affirmative instruction that the jury could not draw any inference from the failure of the government to call Cooper as a witness.

It is well settled that when a party has it peculiarly within its power to produce witnesses and fails to do so, "the jury may infer that 'the testimony, if produced, would be unfavorable' to that party." United States v. Torres, 845 F.2d 1165, 1169 (2d Cir.1988). However, "when a witness is equally available to both sides, 'the failure to produce is open to an inference against both parties.'" *Id.* This court has observed that "the 'availability' of a witness ... depend[s] ... on all the facts and circumstances bearing upon the witness's relation to the parties, rather than merely on physical presence or accessibility." *Id.* at 1170.

Myerson acknowledges that no "extraordinary circumstances" existed in this case, and thus the district court could not have compelled the prosecution to grant immunity to Cooper to make him available to Myerson. Moreover, the district court properly rejected Myerson's attempts to call Cooper solely for the purpose of having the jury hear his invocation of the privilege and Myerson acknowledges as much. Myerson argues, however, that the government, through its power to compel testimony through a grant of use immunity, had it peculiarly within its power to produce the testimony of Dan Cooper when Cooper asserted his Fifth Amendment privilege. As a result, Myerson argues, he was entitled to a missing witness instruction.

This circuit has never addressed the precise issue before us. Other circuits to consider the issue are unanimous, however, in holding that, despite the government's power to grant immunity, a witness invoking

---

6. As noted, Cooper's attorney informed the district court that Cooper's testimony would not help Myerson and that Cooper did not have an agreement with the government. When the district court asked the prosecutor why he did not call Cooper, he explained that Cooper was vulnerable to impeachment because he had destroyed documents under subpoena. Finally, when the district court offered to have Cooper testify outside the jury's presence to see what he would claim as privileged, Myerson turned him down.

his constitutional rights is unavailable to the government as well as the defense, and no missing witness charge need be given.

* * *

As the D.C. Circuit has explained:

> The logic underlying the missing witness rule is that where the party with peculiar or exclusive control of a witness fails to call that witness, there must be some reason for its failure. Where there are other reasons why she was not called, the failure of the party having the peculiar power to control the presence of the witness to put her on the stand does not authorize an inference, supported by an instruction, that if she testified she would have done so unfavorably to the party. That is the situation in the present case.

United States v. Norris, 873 F.2d 1519, 1522 (D.C.Cir.1989). [internal quotation marks omitted] In the case of prior sworn testimony, the unavailability of a witness gives rise to circumstances in which the prior testimony should be admitted. The content of the testimony is known to both parties and is known to be exculpatory. Such is not necessarily true when a missing witness instruction is involved. We thus find the situation in *Salerno* readily distinguishable from the present case.

In refusing to require that a missing witness charge be given in each instance that a witness asserts his Fifth Amendment privilege, appellate courts have recognized that such a requirement would unnecessarily infringe on the prosecutorial decision of whether or not to grant immunity. Moreover, a prosecutor's failure to immunize a witness does not, categorically, give rise to an inference that the witness's testimony would be unfavorable to the government.

In the present case, the district court weighed the propriety of giving a missing witness charge, and concluded that "what you want is the jury to draw some inference favorable to you that you called him and he's claiming the privilege here. And somehow that they should assume from that, that it exonerates you which is not necessarily a reasonable assumption." From our review of the record, we find that the district court did not abuse its discretion by refusing to give a missing witness charge. The representations of Cooper's counsel to the district court, the testimony of the other witnesses and Myerson's own refusal to take the district court up on its offer to have Cooper testify were clearly sufficient to give the district court reason to believe Cooper's testimony would inculpate Myerson and, thus, not to give the charge.

B. Impeachment

Myerson next argues that the district court erred by failing to admit testimony to impeach co-conspirator statements attributed to Dan Cooper. He contends that the district court's failure to admit this impeachment testimony, coupled with the prosecutor's misleading statement which allegedly led the district court to refuse admission of the evidence, denied him a fair trial.

Arthur Ruegger, one of Myerson's partners, testified during the government's case:

> One time [Cooper] came in after one of those lunches. I think he came into my office or maybe I went into his office. And he just started acting like the plant in Little Shop of [Horrors]. He kept saying 'feed me, feed me, feed me.' He might have other conversations with me where he said, Harvey wants these bills at 300 and I just can't get them there....

> He did, on one occasion, make a reference in substance or in words which said 'Harvey wants the bills at 300 and I can't get them there.'

Approximately three weeks later, during Myerson's defense case, Myerson sought to present the testimony of Douglas Stahl, a former M & K partner, under Fed.R.Evid. 806 to impeach Cooper's alleged statement.[7] In a hearing outside the presence of the jury, Stahl revealed that Cooper, prior to pleading guilty, told Stahl that Cooper had prepared bills based on his own judgment, that Myerson was not involved in the billing, and that he had not inflated the bills and did not do so at Myerson's direction. The district court stated that it would admit the evidence if Myerson could specify the statement of Cooper's that Stahl's testimony would impeach. Myerson could only recall generally that such evidence existed and neither the district court, the government nor Myerson could specify a particular statement.[8]

Myerson argues on appeal that the court's ruling excluding the evidence was error and that the government erroneously, and by implication intentionally, misled the court into excluding the evidence.[9] There is little question that the testimony was admissible under Rule 806.

As an initial point, we note that Cooper's testimony related only to the ICN count. Myerson attempts to argue that the error pervaded the whole trial. We disagree. Cooper was the billing partner for ICN and the alleged declaration by Cooper, which related to getting ICN bills above $300,000, affected only the ICN count. While Cooper was present at lunch meetings where billing targets were set for the other clients, the statement at issue related only to ICN, and did not bear on the Shearson and Home counts. Thus, we address the error only as it affects the ICN count.

The question of whether the district court's failure to admit Stahl's impeachment testimony was reversible error is clouded somewhat by

---

7. Fed.R.Evid. 806 provides: "When a hearsay statement, or a statement defined in Rule 801(d)(2), (C), (D), or (E), has been admitted in evidence, the credibility of the declarant may be attacked, and if attacked may be supported, by any evidence which would be admissible for those purposes if declarant had testified as a witness."

8. Moreover, the government affirmatively responded, "Your Honor, there is no such testimony. There's been no testimony elicited from anyone that Cooper—about Cooper's words that the defendant made him do anything."

9. Myerson points out that in closing arguments the next day, the government relied on Ruegger's recollection of what Cooper had said.

Myerson's claim of prosecutorial misconduct. Myerson points out that the district court's failure to admit the evidence was error, but rather than argue its prejudicial effect he emphasizes the government's role leading to that error, suggesting that perhaps the error itself was harmless but that the combination of the error and misconduct constitutes reversible error.

When prosecutorial misconduct occurs before the jury—for example when a prosecutor engages in improper summation—our analysis involves a determination of whether improper statements cause substantial prejudice to the defendant. In evaluating whether the government's conduct warrants reversal in such a situation, we must consider whether it resulted in substantial prejudice to the defendant's right to a fair trial, weighing "the severity of the misconduct; the measures adopted to cure the misconduct; and the certainty of conviction absent the improper statements." [citations omitted]

Here, the alleged improper conduct, the prosecution's allegedly misleading declaration to the court that no triggering coconspirator statement had been made, led only to the trial court's refusal to admit impeachment evidence. An error in excluding evidence is reversible error only if the evidence is "material"; that is, " 'if there is a reasonable probability that, had the evidence been [admitted], the result of the proceeding would have been different. A "reasonable probability" is a probability sufficient to undermine confidence in the outcome.' " [citations omitted] Consequently, even assuming, without deciding, that the prosecutor's affirmative statement was improper,[10] under these circumstances we engage in the familiar harmless error analysis that accompanies evidentiary errors.

The government urges that the impeaching testimony was de minimis, and in light of the overwhelming evidence of fraud by Myerson involving the ICN count, the error should be deemed harmless. The government points to the testimony of several witnesses, including Segall, Joan Giordano, Cooper's secretary, and Robert Mandell, an M & K associate, and argues that it overwhelmingly demonstrates Myerson's involvement with ICN bills and conclusively shows his guilt on that count.[11] * * *

---

10. We are somewhat troubled by the government's rapid change in memory. That the prosecutor could so confidently declare that no such testimony existed on one day, and then rely on that exact testimony the next is disturbing. We of course endorse our previous statement that "[t]he prosecutor has a special duty not to mislead; the government should, of course, never make affirmative statements contrary to what it knows to be the truth." United States v. Universita, 298 F.2d 365, 367 (2d Cir.1962).

11. Segall corroborated Ruegger, describing Myerson's luncheon meetings at which Myerson insisted that various client bills, including ICN's, be inflated. Giordano testified that every month Cooper would take draft ICN bills into Myerson's office, and then return the bills to her, explaining that attorney hours had to be increased and that work descriptions had to be changed. Mandel testified that ICN bills reflected his work on specific matters, and that in fact, he never worked on a matter for ICN. Finally, there was evidence of Myerson's personal expenditures billed to ICN that were unrelated to ICN's business.

We find the error in this instance to be harmless. Stahl's testimony directly contradicted Ruegger and indicated that Myerson did not urge Cooper to inflate the ICN bills. However, Cooper's alleged statement was only one sentence in a trial that lasted six weeks.[12] The testimony of the other witnesses clearly demonstrates Myerson's inflation of ICN's bills and fees. Under the circumstances, we hold that the error was not prejudicial.

* * *

II. THE TAX FRAUD CASE

In a second trial, lasting four days, Myerson was convicted on three counts of conspiracy to defraud the United States, filing a false personal tax return, and causing his law firm to file a false partnership tax return. At trial, the government produced evidence that between 1980 and 1986 Myerson charged several clients over $1 million for legal services that were never rendered. Myerson schemed to have clients, through his law firm, pay Joseph Rahn, a beverage distributor in Philadelphia and Myerson's brother-in-law, as "local counsel" for Rahn's purported legal services. Rahn was not an attorney and he never rendered any services for Myerson's clients. However, Rahn agreed to accept the payments, and then return the money to Myerson.

Rahn testified that he received $408,500 for purported legal services paid by Allegheny Beverage Co., McCrae Oil and Kelley Oil. Rahn testified that he agreed to the arrangement because Myerson told him he was having alimony problems and was trying to conceal monies from his ex-wife. Myerson arranged to have Rahn deposit the funds in Rahn's account and then return the funds by personal check to Myerson. Myerson directed Rahn to file a false 1986 personal tax return and then indicated that he would reimburse him for the tax he paid. Myerson did not report any of his illicit income on his personal tax returns for the years 1980, 1982, 1983 and 1986. The transactions with Rahn served as the basis for the three tax charges.

At trial, Myerson did not dispute that the transactions with Rahn took place. Rather, Myerson contended that he lacked the state of mind to cheat on his income taxes because he had become "irrational" by the excessive alimony demands of his ex-wife. In rebuttal to Myerson's claim, the government produced evidence of other similar acts under Federal Rule of Evidence 404(b) to show Myerson's state of mind and intent. Thomas Wyatt, an attorney, testified that although he had provided no legal services for McCrae Oil, he nevertheless received checks from Myerson's law firm, at Myerson's request and paid by McCrae Oil, and deposited them to his own account. These checks were in the amounts of $65,000 in September 1980; $78,500 in January 1982; $138,500 in October 1982; $126,500 in May 1983; and $187,500 in September 1983.

---

12. Its minimal importance is emphasized by the inability of either party, or the district court, to remember whether any such testimony had been admitted at all, let alone the exact statement.

These payments all were for purported legal services Wyatt had not rendered. Myerson had told him that lawyers for his ex-wife had subpoenaed his firm in an effort to seek increased alimony and he needed to conceal the money. Wyatt in turn gave the funds back to Myerson by personal check.

Similarly, in December 1982 and May of 1983, Richard Kammerer, a yacht salesman, received the respective sums of $90,000 and $72,400 from Myerson's firm, reimbursed by McCrae Oil and Allegheny Beverage, to be applied to Myerson's purchase of a boat. The monies were paid to Kammerer for legal fees purportedly provided by Kammerer. Like Rahn, Kammerer was not a member of the bar.

The district court admitted the above evidence as "compelling," stating that it "[spoke] volumes about [Myerson's] defense and [his] state of mind." A trial judge is given broad discretion in admitting evidence under Rule 404(b). Relevant evidence of a defendant's prior bad acts is admissible under Rule 404(b) if that evidence is offered for "a purpose other than to prove the defendant's bad character or criminal propensity," and so long as that evidence is not substantially more prejudicial than probative under Rule 403 of the Federal Rules of Evidence. On appeal, a ruling admitting evidence of other crimes may be overturned only for "a clear abuse of discretion." "To find abuse, the appellate court must conclude that the district court acted arbitrarily and irrationally." [citations omitted]

We agree with the district court that Myerson's defense bordered on absurdity. We find, as did the trial court, the 404(b) evidence was clearly admissible. Myerson's argument that the district court failed to engage in a Rule 403 balancing is clearly belied by the record. Following its ruling that Myerson could offer proof that his "crazed" state of mind caused him to want to hide money from his ex-wife, the district court found that the government's similar acts evidence "demolish[ed] the defense," was "highly probative," and was "prejudicial in the sense that evidence should be prejudicial, and not in an improper way." The district court "considered the prejudicial value," and concluded that "it's outweighed by its probative value." In no sense was the district court's admission of the Rule 404(b) evidence arbitrary, irrational or an abuse of discretion.

We note that even if the evidence were not admissible, the evidence of Myerson's money laundering and his failure to report it on his income tax was sufficiently strong to render the admission of the 404(b) evidence harmless. We affirm the judgment of conviction on the tax fraud counts.

III. Conclusion

For the reasons stated above, the judgment of the district court is affirmed with respect to all counts.

Notes

1.   What type of discussion do you think took place among the three M & K associates who delivered the altered time sheets to Shearson as the associates were deciding whether to turn over the time sheets? What factors would you consider?

2.   Do you find it strange that Shearson did not realize until it received the false time sheets, that one law firm had overbilled it by almost $2 million in one year? If you were the CEO at Shearson, what changes would you make in Shearson's procedures for employing and compensating outside counsel?

3.   Recall that the "missing witness" instruction informs the jury that "when a party has it peculiarly within its power to produce witnesses and fails to do so, the jury may infer that the testimony, if produced, would be unfavorable to that party."[m] Did Myerson blunder in how he handled the Cooper issue? Do you think Myerson was entitled to the missing witness instruction?

4.   Note the discussion of coconspirator's statements. Can you identify the coconspirator's statement at issue? Would you have ruled the same way as the court? Assuming there was no bad faith, how do you think a prosecutor could make the mistake made here during the colloquy at trial among counsel and the District Court? How can this type of mistake be avoided?

5.   Consider the following:

"OVERBILLING IS the dirty secret that most lawyers at big firms share.

"The vast majority of attorneys in a survey conducted earlier this year said they were aware of lawyers who charged for work that wasn't actually done.

* * *

"With intense pressure on lawyers to produce billable hours in today's competitive market, [y]ou either work 60 or 70 hours a week and have no personal life or you're going to synthesize those bills. Most bills [I see] are padded, whether intentional or not."[n]

C.   CORRUPTION; OBSTRUCTION OF JUSTICE

There are over twenty federal statutes addressing obstruction of justice and perjury before the various courts and tribunals which constitute our justice system. As you will see from the cases in this section, however, a variety of the generic white collar statutes, such as mail fraud, wire fraud and RICO, also are used to prosecute attorneys and judges who intentionally subvert our judicial system.

---

m.   *Myerson*, 18 F.3d at 158.

n.   Margaret A. Jacobs, *Problem of Overbilling By Many Law Firms*, WALL ST. J. B8 (Sept. 18, 1995). [internal quotation marks

omitted] Copyright © Wall Street Journal. Reprinted with permission from Wall Street Journal.

The next two cases involve judges. The first case, United States v. Castro, 89 F.3d 1443 (11th Cir.1996), demonstrates a fairly routine undercover operation in a court system where kickbacks and bribes were routine. The second case, United States v. Aguilar, 515 U.S. 593 (1995), demonstrates an obstruction of justice prosecution (ultimately unsuccessful) for more subtle wrongdoing.

As you read *Castro*, notice the breadth of the charges and legal issues presented.

UNITED STATES v. CASTRO

United States Court of Appeals, Eleventh Circuit, 1996.
89 F.3d 1443.

HACHETT, CIRCUIT JUDGE.

In this "Operation Court Broom" appeal, we affirm the appellants' convictions and sentences.

FACTS

In the late 1980s, federal and state law enforcement officials conducted "Operation Court Broom," an investigation into alleged corrupt activities occurring among judges and lawyers in the Dade County Florida Circuit Court. One of the targets of the investigation, Roy T. Gelber, took the office of circuit court judge for the Eleventh Judicial Circuit in Dade County in January 1989. Prior to becoming a circuit court judge in 1989, Gelber served as an elected county court judge for Dade County since 1987 and previously had practiced as a criminal defense attorney.

In Metropolitan Dade County, circuit court judges have the authority to appoint special assistant public defenders (SAPDs) and approve their compensation terms for which Metropolitan Dade County issues payment upon receipt of a court approved bill. Shortly after assuming the position of circuit court judge, Gelber had discussions with another circuit court judge, Alfonso C. Sepe, regarding making SAPD appointments for kickbacks. Sepe arranged to have Gelber appoint Arthur Massey, a lawyer, as an SAPD in return for kickbacks. Gelber appointed Massey to some cases and received kickbacks for those appointments. Likewise, Judge Harvey N. Shenberg arranged for Gelber to appoint Manny Casabielle and Miguel DeGrandy, lawyers, as SAPDs in return for kickback payments.

In August of 1989, state and federal law enforcement officials procured the services of Raymond Takiff, a lawyer, to act in an undercover capacity as a corrupt lawyer in the Operation Court Broom investigation. From August 1989 to June 1991, Takiff engaged in a number of corrupt activities with Gelber and other judges in the Eleventh Judicial Circuit. Most of Gelber's conversations with Takiff regarding illegal conduct were tape-recorded. Takiff enlisted Gelber and other judges in activities ranging from paying kickbacks and fixing cases to releasing the name of a confidential informant believing that the informant would be killed. Sepe, Shenberg, and Judge Philip S. Davis participated in many of the schemes.

During the relevant period, Gelber recruited his secretary to assist him in the kickback scheme. Gelber asked the secretary if she knew any lawyers who would be willing to accept appointments as SAPDs in return for paying him kickbacks. Upon her agreement, Gelber used the secretary as a conduit to lawyers agreeing to join the kickback scheme. The secretary approached Arthur Luongo, Harry Boehme, and Nancy Lechtner, all lawyers, asking them to join in the kickback scheme. All of the lawyers agreed to accept SAPD appointments in exchange for paying kickbacks.

Gelber approached William Castro, a lawyer, in the fall of 1989 about the possibility of Castro investing in Gelber's corporation. Castro did not want to invest in the corporation, but he agreed to assist Gelber financially through paying kickbacks for receiving SAPD appointments. Gelber and Castro agreed that Castro would pay Gelber twenty percent of his anticipated fees within a few days of receiving appointments. Gelber began appointing Castro to cases, and Castro paid kickbacks for those appointments. Gelber received an average kickback payment of $1,000 from Castro. A few months after Castro began paying kickbacks to Gelber, Castro convinced Gelber to bring Kent Wheeler, a lawyer, into the kickback scheme. Castro served as an intermediary between Gelber and Wheeler because Gelber did not know Wheeler well.

From October 1989 to June 8, 1991, Gelber appointed Castro to sixty-four cases and received $77,000 in kickbacks. From January 1990 to June 8, 1991, Gelber appointed Wheeler to thirty-seven cases and received $34,000 in kickbacks. Similarly, Gelber appointed Boehme to twelve cases for $13,000 in kickbacks; Lechtner to four cases for $7,000 in kickbacks; and Luongo to thirty-one cases for over $20,000 in kickbacks.

PROCEDURAL HISTORY

On May 27, 1992, a federal grand jury in the Southern District of Florida returned a superseding 106–count indictment against William Castro, Arthur Luongo, Harry Boehme, Nancy Lechtner, (appellants) and codefendants Harvey N. Shenberg, Alfonso Sepe, Phillip Davis, David Goodhart, and Arthur Massey. The indictment charged appellants with conspiracy to violate RICO in violation of 18 U.S.C. §§ 1962(d) and 1963(a), mail fraud in violation of 18 U.S.C. §§ 1341, 1346, and bribery in violation of 18 U.S.C. § 666(a)(2).[1]

Appellants moved to dismiss the RICO conspiracy count, mail fraud, and bribery counts for failure to state an offense. The district court denied these motions. In July 1992, appellants filed their first round of severance motions based on prejudicial misjoinder seeking separate trials

---

1. Gelber, an unindicted co-conspirator, pleaded guilty to RICO conspiracy and testi-   fied for the government.

from each other, codefendant Massey, and the indicted judges. The district court severed the trial of Judges Goodhart, Sepe, Shenberg, and Davis from appellants' trial, and severed Massey's trial from the appellants. The district court denied appellants' subsequent motions to sever their trials from each other. The trial began on October 25, 1993. At the close of the government's case-in-chief, appellants moved for judgment of acquittal on all counts under Rule 29 of the Federal Rules of Criminal Procedure. The district court denied the motions. Appellants renewed the motions at the conclusion of their case, and the district court again denied the motions. The jury returned guilty verdicts as to all appellants on all counts.

The district court sentenced Castro to concurrent terms of thirty-seven months imprisonment, three years supervised release, and ordered him to pay a $1,400 special assessment. The district court sentenced Luongo to thirty-seven months imprisonment, three years supervised release, and ordered him to pay $850 in fines. The district court sentenced Lechtner to concurrent terms of thirty months imprisonment, three years supervised release, and ordered her to pay a $300 special assessment. The district court sentenced Boehme to concurrent terms of twenty-four months imprisonment, two years supervised release, and ordered him to pay a $500 special assessment. This appeal followed.

CONTENTIONS

* * * [A]ppellants contend that the government failed to prove the existence of a single RICO conspiracy. Appellants assert that the government offered proof of multiple conspiracies, and that this constitutes an impermissible variance from the charge of a single conspiracy.

* * *

* * *[T]he government contends that a RICO conspiracy charge brings a defendant within the conspiracy regardless of the unrelatedness of the acts of the other members of the conspiracy as long as the government can show an agreement on an overall objective or that the defendant agreed to the commission of two or more predicate acts, individually or through others. The government contends that no material variance occurred because a reasonable trier of fact could have found beyond a reasonable doubt the existence of a single conspiracy. Also, for this reason, the government contends that the appellants were properly joined.

Second, the government contends that the appellants were convicted of a RICO conspiracy, and not a substantive RICO offense. Therefore, the government only had to allege and prove that the appellants "agreed" to affect the operation or management of the RICO enterprise, and not that the appellants actually exerted any control or direction over the RICO enterprise. Third, the government contends that when the prosecutor's summation and the district court's instructions are viewed in context, it is clear that no constructive amendment occurred. Fourth, the government contends that the evidence presented at trial was sufficient to establish that appellants intended to influence an agent of Metropolitan Dade County.

* * *

DISCUSSION

I. Material Variance and Joinder

Appellants contend that at best the government's proof at trial revealed the existence of multiple conspiracies even though the indictment only charged a single conspiracy. For this reason, appellants claim that a material variance occurred that constitutes reversible error * * *. Appellants also contend that they were improperly joined because the government failed to prove that any of them knew about other lawyers participating in the kickback scheme or whether any of them knew of the existence of a single conspiracy.

A material variance between an indictment and the government's proof at trial occurs if the government proves multiple conspiracies under an indictment alleging only a single conspiracy. In order to prove a RICO conspiracy, the government must show an agreement to violate a substantive RICO provision. Specifically, the government must prove that the conspirators agreed to participate directly or indirectly in the affairs of an enterprise through a pattern of racketeering activity.

The government may prove the existence of an "agreement" to participate in a RICO conspiracy through showing (1) the existence of an agreement on an overall objective, or (2) in the absence of an agreement, on an overall objective that the defendant agreed personally to commit two or more predicate acts. In meeting its burden of proof on showing an agreement on an overall objective, the government must offer direct evidence of an explicit agreement on an overall objective or, in the absence of direct evidence, the government must offer circumstantial evidence demonstrating "that each defendant must necessarily have known that others were also conspiring to participate in the same enterprise through a pattern of racketeering activity." [citations deleted]

In this case, the indictment charged a single RICO conspiracy, and the government presented evidence that adequately proved the existence of a single conspiracy. At trial, Gelber testified that he informed the appellants that they would not only receive appointments from him but also from another judge in the circuit court. In light of this testimony, each appellant knew that at least two circuit judges agreed to use the Circuit Court of the Eleventh Judicial Circuit to engage in a kickback scheme. In addition to Gelber's testimony, other evidence adduced at trial indicates appellants' agreement to participate in and awareness that others also participated in a single conspiracy. For example, when Gelber's secretary asked appellant Boehme to enroll in the kickback scheme, she asked him whether he wished to join the "preferred list" for court appointments. Similarly, appellant Lechtner was informed that a kickback scheme was "something that's being done" in the Circuit Court of the Eleventh Judicial Circuit. Appellant Castro actually recruited another lawyer to join the kickback scheme. In light of this evidence, we find that each appellant agreed on an overall objective and agreed personally to commit two or more predicate acts by paying kickbacks for SAPD appointments.

Additionally we note that, contrary to appellants' assertions, in proving the existence of a single RICO conspiracy, the government does not need to prove that each conspirator agreed with every other conspirator, knew of his fellow conspirators, was aware of all of the details of the conspiracy, or contemplated participating in the same related crime. In viewing the evidence in the light most favorable to the government, a jury could have reasonably concluded that one common agreement on a single overall objective existed. Consequently, we find that no material variance occurred.

In considering appellants' misjoinder claim, we recognize that the Federal Rules of Criminal Procedure prohibit joinder of defendants unless the indictment covered the same act or transaction or the same series of acts or transactions. Fed.R.Crim.P. 8(b). In this circuit we have observed that "[w]hether or not separate offenses are part of a 'series of acts or transactions' under 8(b) depends ... on the relatedness of the facts underlying each offense.... [W]hen the facts underlying each offense are so closely connected that proof of such facts is necessary to establish each offense, joinder of defendants and offenses is proper." [citations deleted]

Since more than sufficient evidence existed in this trial to support the indictment and conviction of a single conspiracy, we conclude that no misjoinder occurred.[4]

II.   Sufficiency of the Evidence

Appellants contend that the government's evidence was insufficient to establish that they conspired to participate in the "operation or management" of the RICO enterprise. Appellants argue that under Reves v. Ernst & Young, 507 U.S. 170 (1993), the government was required to produce evidence showing that appellants agreed to exercise control or direction in the management of the Circuit Court of the Eleventh Judicial Circuit. Appellants suggest that as outsiders they could not have exerted the requisite degree of control over the "operation or management" of the Circuit Court of the Eleventh Judicial Circuit to meet the requirements of Reves.

As a preliminary matter, we reject appellants' limited reading of Reves. Under Reves, section 1962(c) liability is not limited to insiders or upper management as appellants suggests. In Reves, the Supreme Court emphasized that because the statute includes the phrase "to participate directly or indirectly," RICO liability is not confined to those with a

---

4. Even where the evidence does not support proof of a single conspiracy, we will not overturn a conviction unless either (1) the proof adduced at trial was so different from the indictment so as to unfairly surprise defendants in the preparation of their defense, or (2) so many defendants exist that the jury was likely to confuse the evidence at trial among the defendants.

formal position in the enterprise. *Reves,* 507 U.S. at 178–80.[5] The language in *Reves* indicates that persons in appellants' position fall within the scope of section 1962(c)'s coverage because "an enterprise might be operated or managed by others associated with the enterprise who exert control over it as, for example, by bribery." *Reves,* 507 U.S. at 184, 113 S.Ct. at 1173 (emphasis added).

We reject the appellants' narrow reading of *Reves* and their attempt to infuse the *Reves* analysis into this case. In this case, the indictment charged the appellants with RICO conspiracy under section 1962(d), and not a substantive RICO offense under section 1962(c). This court recently decided that the *Reves* "operation or management" test does not apply to section 1962(d) convictions. Our view of the evidence in the light most favorable to the government indicates that more than sufficient evidence existed to demonstrate that appellants "agreed" to affect the operation or management of the Circuit Court of the Eleventh Judicial Circuit through paying kickbacks.

* * *

IV.   Bribery Convictions

Appellants contend that their bribery convictions must be reversed. Appellants assert that since the government charged them under 18 U.S.C. § 666(a)(2), the government was required to show that they intended to enter into a direct exchange with an agent of the organization receiving federal funds.[6] Appellants argue that the government produced no evidence showing that they intended to influence or reward anyone in the Dade County Finance Department. Moreover, appellants challenge the sufficiency of the evidence presented at trial to establish that Metropolitan Dade County received federal grants in excess of $10,000.

At trial, the appropriate inquiry was: did the government prove beyond a reasonable doubt that the appellants (1) gave or offered to give a thing of value to any person (2) with the corrupt intent to influence or reward an agent of an organization that in a one-year period received benefits in excess of $10,000 under a federal program (3) in connection with any business transaction or series of transactions of such organization, government, or agency involving anything of the value of $5,000 or more. The government presented evidence at trial establishing that the appellants (1) paid kickbacks to Judge Gelber (2) with the intent to have

---

5. In fact, the Court expressly disagreed with the District of Columbia Circuit's suggestion that section 1962(c) requires significant control over or within an enterprise. *Reves,* 507 U.S. at 176–78, 179 n. 4 (1993). Outsiders may exert control over an enterprise's affairs through illegal means sufficient to satisfy *Reves's* requirements.

6. The statute provides in relevant part: (a) Whoever, if the circumstance described in subsection (b) of this section exists—(2)

corruptly gives, offers, or agrees to give anything of value to any person with intent to influence or reward an agent of an organization or of a State, local or Indian tribal government, or any agency thereof, in connection with any business, transaction, or series of transactions of such organization, government, or agency involving anything of value of $5,000 or more....

18 U.S.C.A. § 666(a)(2) (West 1976 & Supp.1995).

Judge Gelber appoint them as SAPDs and authorize an agent of the Dade County Finance Department to issue them compensation checks (3) in connection with their rendering of legal services of a value exceeding $5,000.

We reject appellants' suggestion that the government had to show a direct quid pro quo relationship between them and an agent of the agency receiving federal funds. We believe that the appellants' narrow reading of the bribery statute would belie the statute's purpose "to protect the integrity of the vast sums of money distributed through federal programs from theft, fraud, and undue influence by bribery." It is clear from the record that the appellants knew that payments for SAPD services came from Metropolitan Dade County and not the circuit court. Moreover, appellants also knew that they could not receive payments from Metropolitan Dade County unless a circuit court judge authorized Metropolitan Dade County to pay the bill or influenced an agent in the Dade County Finance Department to issue the checks. We believe that the government proved that appellants not only intended to influence Gelber, but they also intended to influence an agent in the Dade County Finance department by having Gelber authorize the agent to issue payments for their SAPD services. Accordingly, we hold that appellants were properly convicted of bribery under 18 U.S.C. § 666(a)(2).

* * *

V.   Mail Fraud

Appellants seek to invalidate their mail fraud conviction because they claim * * * that the mail fraud statute does not extend to cover schemes whose ultimate intent is to deprive a sovereign state of intangible rights.

* * *

Appellants also suggest that Congress's enactment of section 1346 restricts section 1341's protection to nongovernmental victims. In 1988, Congress enacted section 1346 of the mail fraud statute to state an offense for the deprivation of intangible rights such as "honest services," thus overruling the Supreme Court's decision in McNally v. United States, 483 U.S. 350. Appellants assert that sections 1341 and 1346 read together seek to punish "whoever having devised or intended to devise any scheme or artifice to deprive 'another' of the intangible right of honest services ... places in any post office or authorized depository for mail matter...." Appellants argue that the term "another" cannot encompass a state. We disagree.

Neither the plain language of section 1346 nor its legislative history supports the limitation appellants urge. We find it instructive to note that prior to section 1346's enactment, similar questions arose regarding the reach of section 1341's protection. In United States v. Martinez, the Third Circuit found that the mail fraud statute protected the Commonwealth of Pennsylvania from deprivation of its property interests.

Indeed, other cases decided based upon section 1341 violations, prior to the clarifying amendment of section 1346, support our finding that the mail fraud statute does protect governmental entities such as a state. [citations omitted] We can discern no reason to read sections 1341 and 1346 as appellants suggest to exclude states, and presumably, all governmental entities from the mail fraud statute's protection. We believe that such a result would belie a clear congressional intent to construe the mail fraud statute broadly.

* * *

BARKETT, CIRCUIT JUDGE, specially concurring:

I concur fully with the majority's opinion affirming the appellants' convictions for mail fraud and bribery and Castro's conspiracy conviction under RICO, and concur in affirming Boehme's, Lechtner's, and Luongo's conspiracy convictions but for different reasons. With respect to Boehme's, Lechtner's, and Luongo's conspiracy convictions, I do not think the government proffered sufficient evidence to prove the existence of the agreement necessary to prove the single overarching conspiracy charged in the indictment. Instead, the government only proved the existence of multiple independent conspiracies each of which involved one of the defendants. However, because the variance between the allegations contained in the indictment and the proof adduced at trial did not affect defendants' substantial rights, I would affirm their convictions on the RICO conspiracy charge.

* * *

The indictment in this case charged Boehme, Lechtner, and Luongo, attorneys practicing in and associated with the Eleventh Judicial Circuit, with agreeing to participate in the affairs of the Circuit Court of the Eleventh Judicial Circuit, through a pattern of racketeering, to wit, Extortion, Conspiracy to Commit Extortion and Attempt to Commit Extortion, Bribery, Unlawful Compensation or Reward for Official Behavior, Conspiracy to Commit Murder, Mail Fraud, and Laundering of Monetary Instruments, with the object of corruptly utilizing the Circuit Court for personal financial gain. Each was charged with committing at least two predicate acts in furtherance of the conspiracy, namely, on numerous occasions paying kickbacks to judges in exchange for appointments as Special Assistant Public Defenders.

Because the nature of the kickback activities did not necessarily involve anyone other than the attorney and judge to which the kickbacks were paid, the government was required to prove that each of the defendants explicitly agreed to participate in a larger conspiracy—one that involved people outside of the individual kickback deals—to conduct the affairs of the Circuit Court through a pattern of racketeering. At trial the government proffered sufficient evidence to show that each of the charged attorneys was a participant in a conspiracy involving his/herself, Judge Gelber, Judge Davis, and Margaret Ferguson. However, the evidence was insufficient to show that Luongo, Boehme, or

Lechtner explicitly agreed to participate in a conspiracy in which others also were corruptly utilizing the Circuit Court through a pattern of racketeering. With respect to Luongo, the government did not present any evidence to suggest he was even aware that there was any other criminal activity afoot in the Circuit Court. Lechtner was advised that the payment of kickbacks on court appointments was "something that's being done." Similarly, Boehme was informed that he would be placed on the "preferred list" for court appointments. These statements alone, while possibly establishing knowledge of other criminal activity within the Circuit Court, are insufficient to establish beyond a reasonable doubt that Boehme and Lechtner explicitly agreed to accomplish anything more than the receipt of court appointments for their own monetary gain.[4] Nothing suggests that they were aware of the contours or scope of the conspiracy as charged in the indictment, or that they would be interested in or benefit from the similar activities of others. To the contrary, they were interested only in profiting from their individual, clearly-defined wrongful acts, and neither benefitted from or was dependent upon the larger conspiracy. Although conspirators need not know their fellow conspirators or be aware of all the details of a conspiracy, it is equally true that "one who embarks on a criminal venture with a circumscribed outline is not responsible for acts of his co-conspirator which are beyond the goals as the defendant understands them." [citations omitted] Therefore, I believe that there was a variance between the single conspiracy charged in the indictment and the multiple conspiracies proved at trial.

Luongo, Boehme, and Lechtner are entitled to a new trial, however, only if they can show that the variance affected their substantial rights.

* * *

In this case, there were four defendants and the government proved the existence of four similar conspiracies. This case was not so complex as to render it likely that the jury transferred guilt among the defendants. Second, evidence as to each defendant's role in the kickback schemes was distinct enough so that the jury was unlikely to use evidence of one defendant's guilt against another defendant. Although the similarities between each of the defendant's activities may have made an assertion of innocence more difficult for the jury to believe, I find that the evidence as to the underlying crimes was sufficiently distinct and separate for the jury to consider each defendant's guilt independently. Similarly, the evidence as to each defendant's involvement in the kickback activities was more than sufficient to find them guilty of the individual conspiracies.

In sum, although I believe that a variance existed between the single conspiracy charged in the indictment and the multiple conspiracies

4. Castro actually solicited the participation of new attorneys in Judge Gelber's kickback scheme, and thus a reasonable trier-of-fact could find that Castro agreed to participate in a conspiracy involving numerous participants to corruptly utilize the Circuit Court.

proved at trial, the appellants' substantial rights were not affected, and thus reversal is not required. Therefore, I would affirm their convictions on all counts.

Notes

1. Do you agree with the majority or concurring opinion as to whether there are single or multiple conspiracies? If you were Castro's attorney, what evidence would be helpful to you in proving prejudice from the variance?

2. What are the federalism concerns Castro voiced concerning his mail fraud conviction? Do you agree with the court in its resolution of Castro's argument?

3. Note that Gelber testified against the defendants. What are the advantages and disadvantages for the government in using someone like Gelber as a witness?

As opposed to the pervasive misconduct in *Castro*, the conduct in question in the next case was fairly isolated. As you read this case, determine whether you believe Judge Aguilar was more or less morally culpable than the judges and attorneys convicted in *Castro*.

UNITED STATES v. AGUILAR

United States Supreme Court, 1995.
515 U.S. 593.

REHNQUIST, CHIEF JUSTICE.

A jury convicted United States District Judge Robert Aguilar * * * of endeavoring to obstruct the due administration of justice in violation of 18 U.S.C. § 1503.

Many facts remain disputed by the parties. Both parties appear to agree, however, that a motion for post-conviction relief filed by one Michael Rudy Tham represents the starting point from which events bearing on this case unfolded. Tham was an officer of the International Brotherhood of Teamsters, and was convicted of embezzling funds from the local affiliate of that organization. In July 1987, he filed a motion under 28 U.S.C. § 2255 to have his conviction set aside. The motion was assigned to Judge Stanley Weigel. Tham, seeking to enhance the odds that his petition would be granted, asked Edward Solomon and Abraham Chalupowitz, a.k.a. Abe Chapman, to assist him by capitalizing on their respective acquaintances with another judge in the Northern District of California, respondent Aguilar. Respondent knew Chapman as a distant relation by marriage and knew Solomon from law school. Solomon and Chapman met with respondent to discuss Tham's case, as a result of which respondent spoke with Judge Weigel about the matter.

Independent of the embezzlement conviction, the Federal Bureau of Investigation (FBI) identified Tham as a suspect in an investigation of labor racketeering. On April 20, 1987, the FBI applied for authorization to install a wiretap on Tham's business phones. Chapman appeared on the application as a potential interceptee. Chief District Judge Robert Peckham authorized the wiretap. The 30 day wiretap expired by law on May 20, 1987, 18 U.S.C. § 2518(5), but Chief Judge Peckham maintained the secrecy of the wiretap under 18 U.S.C. § 2518(8)(d) after a showing of good cause. During the course of the racketeering investigation, the FBI learned of the meetings between Chapman and respondent. The FBI informed Chief Judge Peckham, who, concerned with appearances of impropriety, advised respondent in August 1987 that Chapman might be connected with criminal elements because Chapman's name had appeared on a wiretap authorization.

Five months after respondent learned that Chapman had been named in a wiretap authorization, he noticed a man observing his home during a visit by Chapman. He alerted his nephew to this fact and conveyed the message (with an intent that his nephew relay the information to Chapman) that Chapman's phone was being wiretapped. Respondent apparently believed, in error, both that Chapman's phones were tapped in connection with the initial application and that the initial authorization was still in effect. Chief Judge Peckham had in fact authorized another wiretap on Tham's phones effective from October 1987 through the period in which respondent made the disclosure, but there is no suggestion in the record that the latter had any specific knowledge of this reauthorization.

At this point, respondent's involvement in the two separate Tham matters converged. Two months after the disclosure to his nephew, a grand jury began to investigate an alleged conspiracy to influence the outcome of Tham's habeas case. Two FBI agents questioned respondent. During the interview, respondent lied about his participation in the Tham case and his knowledge of the wiretap.

[The Court of Appeals for the Ninth Circuit reversed the conviction] for the reason that the conduct was not covered by the statutory language. The [court] * * * also found that respondent had not interfered with a pending judicial proceeding under § 1503. It first noted that the grand jury had not authorized or directed the FBI investigation. It then held that merely uttering false statements does not " 'corruptly influence' "within the meaning of the statute. It drew this conclusion, in part, from 1988 amendments to 18 U.S.C. § 1512, which added a prohibition on corrupt persuasion of witnesses. The court read the corrupt persuasion prohibited by § 1512 to require an active attempt to persuade a witness to tell a false story, and used the language in § 1512 as a guide to interpret the omnibus clause of § 1503 narrowly.

* * *

Section 1503 provides:

"Whoever corruptly, or by threats or force, or by any threatening letter or communication, endeavors to influence, intimidate, or

impede any grand or petit juror, or officer in or of any court of the
United States, or officer who may be serving at any examination or
other proceeding before any United States commissioner or other
committing magistrate, in the discharge of his duty, or injures any
such grand or petit juror in his person or property on account of any
verdict or indictment assented to by him, or on account of his being
or having been such juror, or injures any such officer, commissioner,
or other committing magistrate in his person or property on account
of the performance of his official duties, or *corruptly or by threats or
force, or by any threatening letter or communication, influences,
obstructs, or impedes, or endeavors to influence, obstruct, or impede,
the due administration of justice,* shall be fined not more than
$5,000 or imprisoned not more than five years, or both." 18 U.S.C.
§ 1503 (emphasis added).

The statute is structured as follows: first it proscribes persons from
endeavoring to influence, intimidate, or impede grand or petit jurors or
court officers in the discharge of their duties; it then prohibits injuring
grand or petit jurors in their person or property because of any verdict
or indictment rendered by them; it then prohibits injury of any court
officer, commissioner, or similar officer on account of the performance of
their official duties; finally, the "Omnibus Clause" serves as a catchall,
prohibiting persons from endeavoring to influence, obstruct, or impede
the due administration of justice. The latter clause, it can be seen, is far
more general in scope than the earlier clauses of the statute. Respondent
was charged with a violation of the Omnibus Clause, to wit: with
"corruptly endeavor[ing] to influence, obstruct and impede the . . . grand
jury investigation."

The first case from this Court construing the predecessor statute to
§ 1503 was Pettibone v. United States, 148 U.S. 197 (1893). There we
held that "a person is not sufficiently charged with obstructing or
impeding the due administration of justice in a court unless it appears
that he knew or had notice that justice was being administered in such
court." *Id.*, at 206. The Court reasoned that a person lacking knowledge
of a pending proceeding necessarily lacked the evil intent to obstruct.
Recent decisions of courts of appeals have likewise tended to place metes
and bounds on the very broad language of the catchall provision. The
action taken by the accused must be with an intent to influence judicial
or grand jury proceedings; it is not enough that there be an intent to
influence some ancillary proceeding, such as an investigation independent of the Court's or grand jury's authority. Some courts have phrased
this showing as a "nexus" requirement—that the act must have a
relationship in time, causation or logic with the judicial proceedings. In
other words, the endeavor must have the " 'natural and probable effect' " of interfering with the due administration of justice. [citations
omitted] This is not to say that the defendant's actions need be successful; an "endeavor" suffices. But as in *Pettibone,* if the defendant lacks
knowledge that his actions are likely to affect the judicial proceeding, he
lacks the requisite intent to obstruct.

Although respondent urges various broader grounds for affirmance, we find it unnecessary to address them because we think the "nexus" requirement developed in the decisions of the courts of appeals is a correct construction of § 1503. We have traditionally exercised restraint in assessing the reach of a federal criminal statute, both out of deference to the prerogatives of Congress, and out of concern that "a fair warning should be given to the world in language that the common world will understand, of what the law intends to do if a certain line is passed," McBoyle v. United States, 283 U.S. 25, 27 (1931). We do not believe that uttering false statements to an investigating agent—and that seems to be all that was proven here—who might or might not testify before a grand jury is sufficient to make out a violation of the catchall provision of § 1503.

The Government did not show here that the agents acted as an arm of the grand jury, or indeed that the grand jury had even summoned the testimony of these particular agents. The Government argues that respondent "understood that his false statements would be provided to the grand jury" and that he made the statements with the intent to thwart the grand jury investigation and not just the FBI investigation. Brief for United States 18. The Government supports its argument with a citation to the transcript of the recorded conversation between Aguilar and the FBI agent at the point where Aguilar asks whether he is a target of a grand jury investigation. The agent responded to the question by stating:

> "[T]here is a Grand Jury meeting. Convening I guess that's the correct word. Um some evidence will be heard I'm ... I'm sure on this issue."

Because respondent knew of the pending proceeding, the Government therefore contends that Aguilar's statements are analogous to those made directly to the grand jury itself, in the form of false testimony or false documents.

We think the transcript citation relied upon by the Government would not enable a rational trier of fact to conclude that respondent knew that his false statement would be provided to the grand jury, and that the evidence goes no further than showing that respondent testified falsely to an investigating agent. Such conduct, we believe, falls on the other side of the statutory line from that of one who delivers false documents or testimony to the grand jury itself. Conduct of the latter sort all but assures that the grand jury will consider the material in its deliberations. But what use will be made of false testimony given to an investigating agent who has not been subpoenaed or otherwise directed to appear before the grand jury is far more speculative. We think it cannot be said to have the "natural and probable effect" of interfering with the due administration of justice.

Justice SCALIA'S dissent criticizes our treatment of the statutory language for reading the word "endeavor" out of it, inasmuch as it excludes defendants who have an evil purpose but use means that would "only unnaturally and improbably be successful." This criticism is unwarranted. Our reading of the statute gives the term "endeavor" a useful function to fulfill: it makes conduct punishable where the defendant acts with an intent to obstruct justice, and in a manner that is likely to obstruct justice, but is foiled in some way. Were a defendant with the requisite intent to lie to a subpoenaed witness who is ultimately not called to testify, or who testifies but does not transmit the defendant's version of the story, the defendant has endeavored to, but has not actually, obstructed justice. Under our approach, a jury could find such defendant guilty.

Justice SCALIA's dissent also apparently believes that any act, done with the intent to "obstruct ... the due administration of justice," is sufficient to impose criminal liability. Under the dissent's theory, a man could be found guilty under § 1503 if he knew of a pending investigation and lied to his wife about his whereabouts at the time of the crime, thinking that an FBI agent might decide to interview her and that she might in turn be influenced in her statement to the agent by her husband's false account of his whereabouts. The intent to obstruct justice is indeed present, but the man's culpability is a good deal less clear from the statute than we usually require in order to impose criminal liability.

* * *

JUSTICE SCALIA, with whom JUSTICE KENNEDY and JUSTICE THOMAS join, concurring in part and dissenting in part.

* * * I would reverse the Court of Appeals, and would uphold respondent's conviction, on the count charging violation of 18 U.S.C. § 1503.

I

The "omnibus clause" of § 1503, under which respondent was charged, provides:

> "Whoever ... corruptly or by threats or force, or by any threatening letter or communication, influences, obstructs, or impedes, or endeavors to influence, obstruct, or impede, the due administration of justice, shall be fined not more than $5,000 or imprisoned not more than five years, or both."

This makes criminal not just success in corruptly influencing the due administration of justice, but also the "endeavor" to do so. We have given this latter proscription, which respondent was specifically charged with violating, a generous reading: "The word of the section is 'endeavor,' and by using it the section got rid of the technicalities which might be urged as besetting the word 'attempt,' and it describes *any effort or essay* to accomplish the evil purpose that the section was enacted to prevent." United States v. Russell, 255 U.S. 138, 143 (1921) (emphasis added) (interpreting substantially identical predecessor statute). Under this reading of the statute, it is even immaterial whether the endeavor to obstruct pending proceedings is possible of accomplishment. In Osborn v.

United States, 385 U.S. 323, 333 (1966), we dismissed out of hand the "impossibility" defense of a defendant who had sought to convey a bribe to a prospective juror through an intermediary who was secretly working for the government. "Whatever continuing validity," we said, "the doctrine of 'impossibility' . . . may continue to have in the law of criminal attempt, that body of law is inapplicable here." *Ibid.*[1]

Even read at its broadest, however, § 1503's prohibition of "endeavors" to impede justice is not without limits. To "endeavor" means to strive or work for a certain end. Webster's New International Dictionary 844 (2d ed. 1950); 1 New Shorter Oxford English Dictionary 816 (1993). Thus, § 1503 reaches only *purposeful* efforts to obstruct the due administration of justice, *i.e.*, acts performed with that very object in mind. This limitation was clearly set forth in our first decision construing § 1503's predecessor statute, Pettibone v. United States, 148 U.S. 197, which held an indictment insufficient because it had failed to allege the intent to obstruct justice. That opinion rejected the Government's contention that the intent required to violate the statute could be found in "the intent to commit an unlawful act, in the doing of which justice was in fact obstructed"; to justify a conviction, it said, "the specific intent to violate the statute must exist." *Id.*, at 207. *Pettibone* did acknowledge, however—and here is the point that is distorted to produce today's opinion—that the specific intent to obstruct justice could be found where the defendant intentionally committed a wrongful act that had obstruction of justice as its "natural and probable consequence." *Ibid.*

Today's "nexus" requirement sounds like this, but is in reality quite different. Instead of reaffirming that "natural and probable consequence" is one way of establishing intent, it *substitutes* " ' "natural and probable effect" ' "*for* intent, requiring that factor even when intent to obstruct justice is otherwise clear. But while it is quite proper to derive an *intent* requirement from § 1503's use of the word "endeavor," it is quite impossible to derive a *"natural and probable consequence"* requirement. One would be "endeavoring" to obstruct justice if he intentionally set out to do it by means that would only unnaturally and improbably be successful. As we said in *Russell*, "any effort or essay" corruptly to influence, obstruct, or impede the due administration of justice constitutes a forbidden endeavor even, as we held in *Osborn*, an effort that is *incapable* of having that effect.

The Court does not indicate where its "nexus" requirement is to be found in the words of the statute. Instead, it justifies its holding with the assertion that "[w]e have traditionally exercised restraint in assessing the reach of a federal criminal statute, both out of deference to the prerogatives of Congress and out of concern that a fair warning should

---

1. This complete disavowal of the impossibility defense may be excessive. As Pettibone v. United States, 148 U.S. 197 (1893) acknowledged, an endeavor to obstruct proceedings that did not exist would not violate the statute. "[O]bstruction can only arise when justice is being administered." *Id.*, at 207. *See, e.g.*, United States v. Williams, 874 F.2d 968, 977 (C.A.5 1989) ("There are three core elements that the government must establish . . . : (1) there must be a pending judicial proceeding").

be given ... of what the law intends to do if a certain line is passed."
[majority opinion] But "exercising restraint *in assessing the reach* of a
federal criminal statute" (which is what the rule of lenity requires, see
United States v. Bass, 404 U.S. 336, 347–348 (1971)) is quite different
from importing extratextual requirements *in order to limit the reach* of a
federal criminal statute, which is what the Court has done here. By
limiting § 1503 to acts having the "natural and probable effect" of
interfering with the due administration of justice, the Court effectively
reads the word "endeavor," which we said in *Russell* embraced "any
effort or essay" to obstruct justice out of the omnibus clause, leaving a
prohibition of only actual obstruction and competent attempts.

II

The Court apparently adds to its "natural and probable effect"
requirement the requirement that the defendant know of that natural
and probable effect. See [majority opinion] ("[I]f the defendant lacks
knowledge that his actions are likely to affect the judicial proceeding, he
lacks the requisite intent to obstruct"). Separate proof of such knowledge is not, I think, required for the orthodox use of the "natural and
probable effect" rule discussed in *Pettibone*: Where the defendant intentionally commits a wrongful act that *in fact* has the "natural and
probable consequence" of obstructing justice, "the unintended wrong
may derive its character from the wrong that was intended." 148 U.S., at
207. Or, as we would put the point in modern times, the jury is entitled
to presume that a person intends the natural and probable consequences
of his acts.

While inquiry into the state of the defendant's knowledge seems
quite superfluous to the Court's opinion (since the act performed did not
have the requisite "natural and probable effect" anyway), it is necessary
to my disposition of the case. As I have said, I think an act committed
with intent to obstruct is all that matters; and what one can fairly be
thought to have intended depends in part upon what one can fairly be
thought to have known. The critical point of knowledge at issue, in my
view, is not whether "respondent knew that his false statement *would be
provided* to the grand jury," [see majority opinion] (emphasis added) (a
heightened burden imposed by the Court's knowledge-of-natural-and-
probable-effect requirement), but rather whether respondent knew—or
indeed, even erroneously *believed*—that his false statement *might* be
provided to the grand jury (which is all the knowledge needed to support
the conclusion that the purpose of his lie was to mislead the jury).
Applying the familiar standard of Jackson v. Virginia, 443 U.S. 307
(1979), to the proper question, I find that a rational juror could readily
have concluded beyond a reasonable doubt that respondent had corruptly
endeavored to impede the due administration of justice, *i.e.*, that he lied
to the FBI agents intending to interfere with a grand jury investigation
into his misdeeds.

Recorded conversations established that respondent knew a grand
jury had been convened; that he had been told he was a target of its

investigation; and that he feared he would be unable to explain his actions if he were subpoenaed to testify. Respondent himself testified that, at least at the conclusion of the interview, it was his "impression" that his statements to the FBI agents would be reported to the grand jury. The evidence further established that respondent made false statements to the FBI agents that minimized his involvement in the matters the grand jury was investigating. Viewing this evidence in the light most favorable to the Government, I am simply unable to conclude that no rational trier of fact could have found beyond a reasonable doubt that respondent lied specifically because he thought the agents *might* convey what he said to the grand jury—which suffices to constitute a corrupt endeavor to impede the due administration of justice. In fact, I think it would be hard for a juror to conclude otherwise.

* * *

Notes

1. With whom do you agree, the majority or dissent? Is the majority's example of a husband lying to his wife about a pending investigation persuasive? Why or why not? Do you believe that Judge Aguilar intended to disrupt a pending grand jury investigation? If not, what do you believe was his intent?

2. Aguilar was also convicted of illegally disclosing wiretap information in violation of 18 U.S.C. § 2232(c). This section makes it a crime for anyone who "having knowledge that a Federal * * * officer has been authorized or has applied for authorization * * * to intercept a wire * * * communication, in order to obstruct, impede, or prevent such interception, gives notice or attempts to give notice of the possible interception to any person." The United States Court of Appeals for the Ninth Circuit affirmed Aguilar's conviction on this offense, then reversed it after rehearing en banc. The Supreme Court reversed the Ninth Circuit on this issue, thus leaving intact Aguilar's conviction on the wiretap charge.

After the Ninth Circuit's en banc decision and prior to the Supreme Court's decision restoring the wiretap conviction, a Sacramento newspaper described Aguilar and the wiretap offense as follows:

> "One of the first Latinos named to the federal bench, Aguilar in 1989 became one of the first federal judges ever indicted.

> "A son of immigrant fruit pickers, a lawyer who never finished law school, Aguilar was appointed by former President Jimmy Carter and was embroiled in controversy almost from the start.

> "He testified on the witness stand that the charges against him stemmed from his desire to avoid being ensnared by the FBI, which was 'out to get me.'

> "He claimed that he was merely circumspect, not untruthful, in answering the bureau's questions about his dealings with Chapman, who was trying to help overturn a crony's conviction for embezzling Teamster funds.

"The defense also maintained that Aguilar mentioned the expired wiretap to a mutual relative only because he wanted to keep Chapman away from him. The self-described mobster was in the habit of visiting the judge's home with small gifts of pastry or sausages. FBI agents witnessed at least one such visit, and Aguilar caught them watching him.

"Aguilar traced his sour relationship with law enforcement to 1983. While presiding in a civil rights case against the Richmond police, he caused a storm by lecturing to civil rights lawyers on how to prepare police brutality cases.

"The same year, he got into a public fight with a federal prosecutor over his sentencing of a tax evader. He sentenced the man to teach computer skills to other probationers.

"In a 1983 case, Aguilar ordered the federal government to turn over FBI personnel documents, then dismissed an indictment when the order was disobeyed.[c]

Because a system of justice cannot function if it is presented with lies and falsehoods, attorneys, as officers of the court, are obliged by codes of ethics and criminal laws to present the truth. The next three cases present situations where attorneys presented false testimony or false evidence to courts. In the next case, United States v. Lahey, 55 F.3d 1289 (7th Cir.1995), note how one attorney's ambition prevailed over his integrity.

UNITED STATES v. LAHEY

United States Court of Appeals, Seventh Circuit, 1995.
55 F.3d 1289.

BAUER, CIRCUIT JUDGE.

Charles W. Lahey and John P. Currens were convicted by a jury of conspiring to obstruct justice by agreeing that Currens would provide false testimony to a grand jury investigating Lahey. The defendants challenge their convictions on several grounds. We affirm.

I.

Lahey is an attorney who was licensed to practice law in the State of Indiana and whose practice was based in South Bend, Indiana. In June 1989, the Internal Revenue Service ("IRS") notified Lahey and his wife, Jennifer, that their tax returns for the years 1986 and 1987 had been selected for an audit. The IRS requested that the Laheys produce several records concerning Lahey's practice during those years. In their first meeting with IRS auditor Ruth Hoyt, accountants hired by Lahey informed Hoyt that Lahey had no records of the gross receipts from his practice in 1986 and in 1987.

Lahey applied for a position as an Assistant United States Attorney for the Northern District of Indiana in November 1989. Lahey was offered the position, but the offer was contingent upon Lahey successfully resolving his tax audit.

Hoyt indirectly reconstructed the Laheys' finances by comparing their actual expenditures with reported income. Her analysis revealed discrepancies between their expenditures and reported income in 1986 and in 1987. In a letter dated January 8, 1990, Hoyt informed the Laheys that the audit had been expanded to include 1988. Hoyt met with Lahey several times in January 1990. Lahey informed Hoyt that he needed to resolve the audit quickly and without penalties so that he could accept a position with the United States Attorney's office, and offered to pay $21,000 to resolve the audit. Hoyt, however, said that the audit could not be resolved quickly because she had no records of Lahey's gross receipts. Lahey told Hoyt that in 1986 and in 1987 he and his wife would have had approximately $150 in cash on hand from all sources at any one time. Lahey also told Hoyt that he received cash from clients eight to twelve times a year without recording the income. In a later meeting, Lahey claimed to have received various amounts of cash as gifts and loan repayments in 1986 and in 1987 from several family members. Hoyt then referred the matter to the Department of Justice as a criminal investigation.

In April 1992, Lahey destroyed several client files which contained records of fee payments. The IRS served Lahey with a grand jury subpoena on May 26, 1992. The subpoena requested all records concerning the receipt of payments from clients from 1986 through 1988. Although Lahey turned over several documents, he did not produce any receipt books, client ledgers, billing statements, files, or payment cards, which were specifically requested by the subpoena. Lahey destroyed additional client files in June 1992. The IRS executed a search warrant in Lahey's office on July 10, 1992, and found some records of fee payments. Lahey's receipt books from 1986 through 1988, and hundreds of client files and payment cards, were missing.

Currens, Lahey's brother-in-law, was interviewed by two IRS agents at Currens' place of employment in San Francisco, California, on February 19, 1993, in connection with the investigation of Lahey. Currens told the agents that the Laheys had loaned him $15,000 in 1992 in the form of a check. Currens was being charged interest on the loan at the rate the Laheys had been charged to obtain the funds, and he had not yet made any repayments. Currens also told the agents that he had made several cash loans to the Laheys after 1984, but the only specific loan Currens could recall was between $3,000 and $4,000. Currens said that this was his largest loan and it was made at least two years prior to the date of the interview.

Currens testified before a grand jury investigating Lahey on March 3, 1993. Currens testified that Lahey had loaned him $10,000 in 1976 by check. Currens did not repay any portion of this interest-free loan until 1986. Currens made several cash payments to the Laheys from 1986 to 1988 totaling $25,000, including a $10,000 payment to Jennifer Lahey, Currens' sister, in 1988. As a result of these payments, the Laheys owed Currens $15,000. Lahey repaid this loan by check in the fall of 1991 or in the spring of 1992. Currens testified that there were no documents reflecting the $10,000 loan to Currens in 1976, a claimed $5,000 cash repayment by Currens to the Laheys in 1986, or Currens' subsequent $15,000 loan to the Laheys. Currens denied telling the IRS agents that the $15,000 check from Lahey was a loan to Currens on which Currens would be paying interest. Currens also testified that he did not tell the IRS agents about these transactions because they had not asked him about anything from 1986 to 1988. Currens testified that he had spoken with Lahey the night before his appearance before the grand jury but did not discuss his testimony.

The grand jury returned an indictment against Lahey and Currens on April 8, 1993. Counts One through Three of the six-count indictment charged Lahey with filing false income tax returns for the years 1986, 1987, and 1988, respectively. 26 U.S.C. § 7206(1). Count Four charged Lahey with corruptly obstructing the due administration of the internal revenue laws. 26 U.S.C. § 7212(a). Count Five charged Lahey with obstructing the due administration of justice by failing to comply with the grand jury subpoena and by destroying subpoenaed records. 18 U.S.C. § 1503 (1988). Count Six charged Lahey and Currens with conspiring to obstruct the due administration of justice by agreeing that Currens would provide false testimony to the grand jury. 18 U.S.C. §§ 371, 1503 (1988).

At the close of the government's evidence, the district court granted Lahey's motion for judgment of acquittal on Counts One through Five of the indictment. Fed.R.Crim.P. 29(a). The district court denied the defendants' motion for judgment of acquittal on Count Six. The jury convicted Lahey and Currens on this count. The defendants filed post-trial motions for judgments of acquittal and a new trial, which the district court denied.

II.

The defendants first challenge the sufficiency of the evidence to support their conspiracy convictions. In reviewing their challenge, we must determine " 'whether, after viewing the evidence in the light most favorable to the prosecution, any rational trier of fact could have found the essential elements of the crime beyond a reasonable doubt.' "United States v. Johnson, 26 F.3d 669, 684 (7th Cir.1994) * * *.

The defendants contend that the government presented insufficient evidence to prove that Currens perjured himself before the grand jury in violation of 18 U.S.C. §§ 1621[1] or 1623.[2] This argument misapprehends the government's burden of proof. The defendants were not charged with perjury or subornation of perjury under 18 U.S.C. §§ 1621, 1622,[3] or 1623; they were charged with conspiracy to obstruct justice in violation of 18 U.S.C. §§ 371[4] and 1503.[5] Although the government was required to prove that an overt act was committed in furtherance of the conspiracy by one of the coconspirators, "overt acts do not have to be substantive crimes themselves." [citations omitted] The overt acts alleged in Count Six consisted of ten instances of false testimony by Currens before the grand jury. These allegations did not transform Count Six into a substantive perjury charge.

The government presented overwhelming evidence that Currens lied to the grand jury. Currens' grand jury testimony provided the Laheys with a nontaxable source of cash during the years under investigation. According to this testimony, the Laheys loaned him $10,000 in 1976, Currens repaid $5,000 of this loan in cash in 1986, and Currens paid the Laheys $10,000 in cash in 1987 and in 1988. These payments resulted in a $15,000 loan to the Laheys which they repaid by check in the fall of 1991 or in the spring of 1992. Yet less than two weeks earlier, Currens told the IRS agents that the $15,000 check was a loan from the Laheys to him. When asked about any loans he had made to the Laheys after 1984, the largest, and only specific, loan Currens could recall was between $3,000 and $4,000. Currens did not mention any of his cash payments totaling $25,000 to the Laheys from 1986 through 1988. Currens' explanation to the grand jury for these discrepancies—that the IRS agents had not asked him about any transactions from 1986 to 1988—was contradicted by the trial testimony of the two agents.

1. Section 1621 provides in relevant part:

Whoever—

(1) having taken an oath before a competent tribunal, officer, or person, in any case in which a law of the United States authorizes an oath to be administered, that he will testify, declare, depose, or certify truly, or that any written testimony, declaration, deposition, or certificate by him subscribed, is true, willfully and contrary to such oath states or subscribes any material matter which he does not believe to be true;

* * * * * *

is guilty of perjury and shall, except as otherwise expressly provided by law, be fined under this title or imprisoned not more than five years, or both.

2. Section 1623(a) provides in relevant part:

Whoever under oath ... in any proceeding before or ancillary to any court or grand jury of the United States knowingly makes any false material declaration ... shall be fined under this title or im-

prisoned not more than five years, or both.

3. Section 1622 provides:

Whoever procures another to commit any perjury is guilty of subornation of perjury, and shall be fined under this title or imprisoned not more than five years, or both.

4. Section 371 provides in relevant part:

If two or more persons conspire either to commit any offense against the United States, or to defraud the United States, or any agency thereof in any manner or for any purpose, and one or more of such persons do any act to effect the object of the conspiracy, each shall be fined under this title or imprisoned not more than five years, or both.

5. Prior to its amendments in 1994, section 1503 provided in relevant part:

Whoever ... corruptly ... influences, obstructs, or impedes, or endeavors to influence, obstruct, or impede, the due administration of justice, shall be fined not more than $5,000 or imprisoned not more than five years, or both.

Currens' grand jury testimony was also inconsistent with his other prior representations to the IRS. Currens filed financial statements with the IRS in July 1988 and in July 1989 (in connection with an unrelated tax liability of Currens') which did not include any debts owed to or from the Laheys. Currens filed another financial statement with the IRS in July 1990 which reported that Currens owed Lahey $20,000 and that Currens had repaid $7,500 of this debt in 1988 and $7,500 in 1989. Currens' grand jury testimony was further contradicted by the trial testimony of Jennifer Lahey that Currens paid her only $2,500 in cash in 1988, rather than the $10,000 in cash to which Currens testified. Jennifer Lahey also testified at trial that the $15,000 check to Currens from the Laheys in 1991 or 1992 was a gift, not a loan repayment. Finally, Lahey told Hoyt during the IRS audit that he received a $7,500 loan repayment from Currens in 1988, not a $10,000 cash loan from Currens in 1988, and Lahey did not mention that Currens was a source of cash in 1986 and in 1987. This evidence, when viewed in the light most favorable to the government, was more than sufficient for the jury to conclude that Currens committed the overt acts charged in the indictment.[6]

The defendants contend that the government presented insufficient evidence that Lahey and Currens formed an agreement to commit a crime. Given the overwhelming evidence of the falsity of Currens' grand jury testimony, the defendants' position boils down to an assertion that the government failed to prove that Currens lied pursuant to an agreement with Lahey rather than on his own. The government's evidence supporting the existence of an agreement was, however, substantial. The government's theory of the case was that, when the grand jury began to unearth evidence that Lahey had underreported his income for the years 1986, 1987, and 1988, Currens stepped forward as the purported source of thousands of dollars in undocumented cash during those years. The jury could have readily concluded that the transactions to which Currens testified before the grand jury did not occur, and that these lies were coordinated by the defendants.

IRS revenue agent Harry Bigda testified at trial that Lahey understated the gross receipts from his law practice by at least $11,869.65 on his 1986 federal income tax return, $15,312.22 on his 1987 return, and $17,478.75 on his 1988 return. Bigda's testimony was based on an analysis of Lahey's bank deposits in his legal fees account and was consistent with Hoyt's conclusion during the audit that Lahey had underreported his income.

---

6. We note that, contrary to the defendants' position, this evidence would also have been sufficient to support a perjury conviction if Currens had been charged with that offense. 18 U.S.C. §§ 1621, 1623; United States v. Waldemer, 50 F.3d 1379, 1380 (7th Cir.1995) ("In order to convict a grand jury witness of perjury under 18 U.S.C. § 1623, the government must not only prove that the witness's testimony was false, it must also prove that the false testimony was material to a legitimate inquiry of the grand jury.").

Lahey was under pressure to resolve the audit quickly in order to accept a position as an Assistant United States Attorney. Hoyt, however, could not resolve the audit quickly because Lahey had refused to supply records of the gross receipts from his law practice. Rather than provide Hoyt with these records, Lahey invented undocumented and nontaxable sources of cash from family members during the years in question. For example, Lahey told Hoyt that his father, James Lahey, gave him $1,500 in cash in 1986 and $2,000 in cash in 1988. James Lahey, however, testified at trial that he did not give any cash gifts to the Laheys from 1986 through 1988, and he gave the Laheys only $300 by check each year during this time. Lahey also destroyed client files containing records of fee payments both shortly before and after being served with a grand jury subpoena in May 1992. Lahey did not produce any receipt books, client ledgers, billing statements, files, or payment cards in response to the subpoena. When the IRS searched Lahey's office in July 1992, his receipt books from 1986 through 1988, and hundreds of client files and payment cards, were missing. The jury could have easily concluded that Currens' false grand jury testimony was consistent with Lahey's efforts to conceal his taxable income from the IRS and thereby inferred the existence of an agreement between Lahey and Currens.

The defendants' history of using each other as sources of cash when convenient also supports an inference that Currens' lies to the grand jury were coordinated with Lahey. When Lahey needed to resolve the IRS audit quickly and without penalties, he told Hoyt that he received a $7,500 loan repayment from Currens in 1988 based on an undocumented debt from the 1970s. Similarly, Currens, while attempting to resolve his own tax liability with the IRS, filed a financial statement in July 1990 which reported that Currens owed Lahey $20,000 and that Currens had repaid $7,500 of this debt in 1988 and $7,500 in 1989. This purported $20,000 debt was more than two-thirds of the total liability which Currens claimed on the IRS form. Yet in October 1991, when Currens was attempting to purchase a house, Currens submitted a mortgage application to a bank which stated that Jennifer Lahey owed him $15,000 and which did not include any purported debt owed by Currens to the Laheys.

The defendants assert that evidence that Lahey destroyed records of fee payments and invented sources of nontaxable income was inadmissible as to Count Six under Federal Rule of Evidence 404(b).[8] The defendants did not object to the admission of this evidence at trial, did not move to strike this evidence after the district court had granted Lahey's motion for judgment of acquittal on Counts One through Five, and did not request that the district court give a limiting instruction to the jury that this evidence should not be considered with respect to

---

8. Rule 404(b) provides in relevant part: (b) Other crimes, wrongs, or acts. Evidence of other crimes, wrongs, or acts is not admissible to prove the character of a person in order to show action in conformity therewith. It may, however, be admissible for other purposes, such as proof of motive, opportunity, intent, preparation, plan, knowledge, identity, or absence of mistake or accident.

Count Six. We therefore review the defendants' claim for plain error only.

No error was committed, plain or otherwise. "[E]vidence of uncharged criminal activity is not considered 'other crimes' evidence" under Rule 404(b) if the evidence is "inextricably intertwined with the evidence regarding the charged offense," or is "necessary to complete the story of the crime [on] trial." United States v. Roberts, 933 F.2d 517, 520 (7th Cir.1991) The conspiracy between Lahey and Currens to provide false testimony to the grand jury was the culmination of Lahey's continuous efforts to conceal the gross receipts from his law practice from 1986 through 1988 from the IRS and the grand jury. The evidence that Lahey destroyed records of fee payments and created fictitious sources of nontaxable income was clearly "necessary to complete the story of the crime [on] trial" and "inextricably intertwined" with the conspiracy. Id. The admission of this evidence was therefore not subject to Rule 404(b) analysis. The district court also did not abuse its discretion in concluding that the probative value of this evidence outweighed any possible prejudice under Federal Rule of Evidence 403.

* * *

For the foregoing reasons, the convictions of Lahey and Currens are AFFIRMED.

Notes

Recall footnote 6 where the court opines that the evidence presented at Currens' trial would have been sufficient to support a perjury conviction under § 1621 (perjury before a tribunal "in which a law of the United States authorizes an oath to be administered") or § 1623 (perjury in a grand jury proceeding). Why do you think the government did not charge Currens with one of these offenses in addition to conspiracy to violate § 1503 (corruptly endeavors to obstruct the due administration of justice)?

The next case, United States v. Atkin, 107 F.3d 1213 (6th Cir.1997), could also fit easily into section B of this chapter concerning attorneys' deception of clients. Because of the nature of this deception, however, this attorney faced obstruction of justice charges.

UNITED STATES v. ATKIN

United States Court of Appeals, Sixth Circuit, 1997.
107 F.3d 1213.

MILES, DISTRICT JUDGE.*

Defendant Sanford I. Atkin, an attorney, appeals his conviction and sentence on multiple charges arising out of his acceptance of $550,000

* The Honorable Wendell A. Miles. United States District Judge for the Western District of Michigan, sitting by designation.

from Reuben Sturman, a defendant in a federal tax prosecution. In the indictment, the government alleged, among other things, that Atkin had obtained the money from Sturman by falsely representing that he, Atkin, would bribe the United States District Judge presiding over Sturman's criminal case. Atkin never did bribe the judge, and he now challenges the sufficiency of the evidence to support his convictions on two counts of obstruction of justice. * * *

I

On November 4, 1994, a federal grand jury sitting in the Northern District of Ohio returned a 30–count indictment charging Sanford Atkin, a Cleveland attorney, with various offenses including two counts of obstruction of justice, in violation of 18 U.S.C. § 1503; seven counts of interstate transportation of property obtained by fraud, in violation of 18 U.S.C. § 2314; 11 counts of engaging in a monetary transaction in criminally derived property, in violation of 18 U.S.C. § 1957; one count of witness tampering, in violation of 18 U.S.C. § 1512; four counts of income tax evasion, in violation of 26 U.S.C. § 7201; four counts of filing false tax returns, in violation of 26 U.S.C. § 7206; and a final count which sought criminal forfeiture of $230,202, pursuant to 18 U.S.C. § 982, based on the involvement of the funds in Atkin's violation of 18 U.S.C. § 1957. The charges arose out of Atkin's acceptance of large sums of money from Reuben Sturman, a world-wide distributor of "adult" materials who was a defendant in a federal tax evasion case in Cleveland, Ohio. Atkin ultimately accepted a total of $550,000 from Sturman under the pretense that Atkin would give the money to the United States District Judge to whom the tax evasion case was assigned.

Atkin did not represent Reuben Sturman in the tax evasion case; Sturman had retained other counsel who had successfully represented him in a number of obscenity prosecutions. Instead, Atkin's only official role in the tax evasion case consisted of serving as local counsel for Sturman's son David, who was also a defendant in the case.[1] However, Atkin performed little work on behalf of David Sturman who, like his father, had other counsel. When the case went to trial in September, 1989, Atkin did not participate.

At the conclusion of a two-month trial on November 17, 1989, the jury in the tax evasion case reached a verdict finding both Reuben and David Sturman guilty on all charges. Reuben Sturman, who had apparently predicted such an outcome, attempted to ensure that he would remain free on bond pending sentencing and an appeal. Believing that Atkin was a close friend of the district judge presiding over the case, Sturman sought Atkin's assistance in bribing the judge to rule in Sturman's favor on the bond issue. Atkin agreed to help, and between

---

1. David Sturman testified at trial that his father had instructed him to hire Atkin as local counsel because Atkin was "close" to the district judge and it would be beneficial to have Atkin serve on the case.

November 6, 1989 and January 11, 1990, he accepted a total of $300,000 from Sturman for the purpose of bribing the district judge. Unbeknownst to Sturman, Atkin did not in fact use Sturman's money to bribe the district judge, although the judge did, coincidentally, allow Sturman to remain free on bond pending sentencing and appeal. The district judge sentenced Sturman to 10 years imprisonment. Sturman's appeals did not succeed, and he ultimately began serving his sentence, which was to run concurrent with a second four-year sentence imposed after Sturman entered a guilty plea on separate obscenity charges brought in federal court in Las Vegas, Nevada.

Subsequently, Sturman again sought Atkin's assistance in bribing the district judge to secure a ruling in Sturman's favor in the tax evasion case, this time on a motion under Fed.R.Civ.P. 35 seeking a reduction of his 10–year sentence to three years. Atkin again agreed to help, and during May, 1992, Sturman made additional payments to Atkin totaling $250,000 for the purpose of bribing the judge to grant Sturman's Rule 35 motion. However, although Atkin did at one point approach the district judge in chambers and attempt to engage him in a discussion of Sturman's situation, the district judge refused to discuss the case.[2] Once again, Atkin kept all of Sturman's money for himself. Sturman, through his trial counsel, subsequently filed three separate Rule 35 motions; not surprisingly, all three were denied. In December, 1992, only days after his third motion was denied, Sturman escaped from a federal prison. He was subsequently recaptured, and he and others associated with him ultimately cooperated in the government's investigation of Atkin.

On June 21, 1995, the jury found Atkin guilty on 28 of the 29 counts in the indictment, acquitting him only of witness tampering. In a bifurcated proceeding, Atkin was also required to forfeit $230,202 worth of property, pursuant to Count 30 of the indictment. On September 14, 1995, the district court sentenced Atkin to 63 months imprisonment, three years of supervised release, and a fine of $12,500. Atkin filed this timely appeal.

II

* * *

Atkin argues that the evidence presented was insufficient to convict him of the two charges of obstruction of justice. * * *

Atkin appears to concede that the government established that Sturman transferred money to Atkin based on Atkin's representations that he would use the money to influence the district judge.[4] However,

---

2. At trial, the district judge testified that Atkin approached him in chambers, asking "can anything be done for Mr. Sturman." According to the district judge, he abruptly responded that he "[did not] rule on things that aren't before me." Atkin dropped the matter and left chambers. The district judge testified that he was subsequently investigated by both the Federal Bureau of Investigation and Internal Revenue Service. He was not charged with any wrongdoing.

4. In his brief, Atkin concedes that the evidence at trial "may have established" that he received money from Sturman; that Atkin claimed he could influence the district judge; and that Sturman transferred

Atkin's challenge to the sufficiency of the evidence focuses primarily on one uncontroverted fact: that Atkin never bribed the district judge. Because he merely defrauded a criminal defendant and did not actually bribe the judge, Atkin argues, he is not subject to conviction for violation of 18 U.S.C. § 1503.

* * *

Atkin was charged and convicted under the third clause of * * * section 1503, known as the "omnibus clause," which applies to one who "corruptly ... influences, obstructs, or impedes, or endeavors to influence, obstruct, or impede, the due administration of justice[.]" " 'The omnibus clause is essentially a catch-all provision which generally prohibits conduct that interferes with the due administration of justice.' " Being "far more general in scope than the earlier clauses of the statute," United States v. Aguilar, 515 U.S. 593, 598 (1995), the omnibus clause does not require proof that the defendant actually influenced an officer of the court. Instead, to sustain a conviction under this clause, the government must prove that the defendant acted with an intent to influence judicial proceedings. *Id.* Moreover, the defendant's actions need not be successful; an "endeavor" suffices, so long as that endeavor has the natural and probable effect of interfering with the due administration of justice. *Id.* In other words, the defendant "must at least undertake action 'from which an obstruction of justice was a reasonably foreseeable result.' "[citations omitted].

Atkin's principal arguments in support of reversal address his lack of success in influencing the district judge. Because the evidence showed that the district judge rebuffed Atkin's only effort to engage in an ex parte discussion of Sturman's case, Atkin argues that the government failed to show that he was attempting to influence the judge, and similarly failed to show that any endeavor was reasonably likely to succeed. However, this argument overlooks other key evidence of Atkin's intent, namely, Reuben Sturman's testimony that Atkin promised that Sturman's money would find its way to the district judge, as well as Sturman's testimony that Atkin agreed to approach the district judge to obtain a reduced sentence for Sturman. Atkin's lack of success is simply not controlling. Had Atkin succeeded in influencing the judge as promised, an obstruction of justice would have resulted.

Although this circuit has not yet determined whether participation in a scheme to defraud which has the potential for interfering with pending judicial proceeding constitutes a violation of § 1503, other circuits have resolved this question in the affirmative. [citations omitted] As stated by the Fourth Circuit in United States v. Neiswender, 590 F.2d 1269, 1273 (4th Cir.1979), "the defendant need only have had knowledge or notice that success in his fraud would have likely resulted in an obstruction of justice. Notice is provided by the reasonable foreseeability of the natural and probable consequences of one's acts." Under the line

money to Atkin based on those representa-   tions. Appellant's Brief at 11.

of decisions following *Neiswender*, a false promise to a criminal defendant that his case will be fixed has the natural and probable effect of interfering with the administration of justice not only because of the possibility that an unlawful solicitation, if made, will be accepted, but also because a false promise that a case will be "fixed" can lull a defendant into abandoning lawful attempts to achieve a desired result, or can otherwise interfere with legal proceedings.

Finding the reasoning of these cases to be sound, we now adopt it, and conclude that it was foreseeable that Sturman would act or fail to act in reliance on the false promise of a bribe, resulting in an obstruction of the due course of the underlying judicial proceeding. If nothing else, Atkin's act of accepting money from Sturman under the pretense of making a bribe, which was disclosed to others by Sturman, caused a thorough investigation of a federal judge's finances and could foreseeably have led to his recusal from the Sturman case. Because we think Atkin's actions had the natural and probable effect of interfering with or influencing the due administration of justice, we conclude that the evidence was sufficient to support his convictions for violation of § 1503.

* * *

Notes

1. Do you agree with the court that Atkin's actions (taking the money from Sturman; telling Sturman that he would bribe the judge; attempting to talk to the judge about the case) were sufficient to constitute obstruction of justice? If so, which of these actions was more disruptive to the due administration of justice.

2. Note the district judge's response when Atkin approached the judge in chambers and attempted to engage him in a discussion of Sturman's situation. The judge's response was a model of propriety and worth remembering by those of you who will sit as judges.

In the next case, United States v. Richman, 944 F.2d 323 (7th Cir.1991), two attorneys attempt to falsify facts to obtain a settlement for the firm's client. As you read it consider what you know about torts: does Mr. Bluhm have a cause of action against Richman?

UNITED STATES v. RICHMAN
United States Court of Appeals, Seventh Circuit, 1991.
944 F.2d 323.

COFFEY, CIRCUIT JUDGE.

* * *

Fred Richman, an attorney practicing in Chicago, Illinois, was charged with mail fraud and wire fraud as a result of his involvement in two separate schemes to defraud Wausau Insurance Company.

The first of Richman's schemes to defraud the insurance company arose from Richman's legal representation of Herbert Bluhm in an accident claim against the owner of Tinley Park Plaza, a shopping mall in Tinley Park, Illinois, and its insurer, Wausau Insurance Company. On October 20, 1984, Bluhm, an elderly man fell to the sidewalk or pavement[3] outside the Cozy Corner Restaurant in the Plaza and fractured his hip, resulting in significant medical expenses. After reporting the accident to Coldwell Bankers Real Estate Company, the leasing agent for the Tinley Park Plaza, Bluhm's son, Richard, retained Fred Richman's law firm to represent Herbert Bluhm in Herbert's claim for damages.

In early 1985 Wausau's regional office referred the investigation of the Bluhm case to Michael Wachala, one of their adjusters. When Wachala attempted to interview Herbert Bluhm on February 1, 1985, concerning his injury, Bluhm advised Wachala that he was represented by the law firm of Richman and Evins. Wachala made several attempts to contact the law firm through phone calls and letters, but was unsuccessful in reaching anyone until December 18, 1985, when he received a phone call from an individual who identified himself as Gil Lande, a legal assistant with Richman and Evins. Lande stated that he was calling about the Bluhm case and during the conversation asked whether "with the holidays coming up, you might be able to use a little something extra in your pocket, and one hand can help the other." Wachala reported this comment to his supervisor, Jim Ebel, who in turn contacted the company's home office, and it was suggested that Wachala speak with Lande again to determine the meaning of Lande's statement.

Lande and Wachala met at the offices of Richman and Evins in early January 1986. At this meeting, Lande said: "[s]o you decided to make yourself some 'buckie-wuckies,' "and thereafter proceeded to outline a plan in which Wachala would receive five percent of the compensation if he settled the case. Lande showed Wachala two photographs of the accident site, one photo displaying a wheelchair ramp and the other a crack in the parking lot pavement. Pointing to the wheelchair ramp, Lande stated: "This is where the accident happened, but it doesn't look good there. Let's move it over here to where there is a crack in the pavement, and let's say that the accident happened there." Lande initially suggested a settlement amount of $50,000, but then said, "[n]o, make yourself look good. Let's go for $40,000." After this discussion Lande introduced Wachala to attorney Fred Richman who told Wachala that he "would have to use [his] imagination" to settle the case and reminded Wachala that he "did not have to announce this to the world."

Wachala likewise reported this information to his supervisor, Ebel. Thereafter, it was arranged for Ebel and Wachala to meet with Postal Inspector John Joyce to inform the federal authorities of the pay-off

---

3. There was conflicting evidence as to whether the accident occurred at the curb as Bluhm attempted to enter a car or on a wheelchair ramp leading to the parking lot. But it is undisputed that Richman's legal assistant who stated that the injury occurred at the wheel chair ramp, proposed fraudulently reporting it as happening at a crack in the parking lot to enhance the claim.

scheme. Wachala agreed to assist the postal inspectors in their investigation of the fraudulent scheme at the Richman and Evins law firm and at the suggestion of the federal authorities, he allowed his conversations with members of the Richman law firm to be recorded. Except for one unrecorded telephone conversation of January 16, 1986, between Wachala and Lande, subsequent meetings and telephone calls were taped and recorded as part of the mail and wire fraud investigation.

In the unrecorded telephone conversation of January 16, 1986, Wachala informed Lande that he wished to procure a signed statement from Bluhm describing the accident.[5] Lande suggested to Wachala that Lande and Wachala meet and that the two of them prepare a statement for Bluhm's use concerning the events surrounding Bluhm's injury. When Wachala expressed concern about whether Bluhm might say something different than what was contained in the fabricated statement, Lande advised Wachala that Bluhm would say exactly what he (Lande) wanted him to say.

Pursuant to the plan described during the phone conversation of January 16, 1986, Lande and Wachala met at Richman's office on January 20, 1986. In this meeting Lande conducted a telephone interview of Bluhm. During the call Lande asked Bluhm questions and contemporaneously repeated to Wachala what Bluhm supposedly was telling him. Lande stated that Bluhm declared that he walked from the wheelchair ramp to the parking lot using a metal walker, and at this time his walker became lodged in a crack in the parking lot, thereby causing him (Bluhm) to be thrown off balance and catapulted to the pavement. Wachala recorded the statements Lande was making as if they were personal statements of Bluhm. Wachala later testified that while he was listening to the phone conversation between Lande and Bluhm he gained the impression that Lande was putting words in Bluhm's mouth, as Lande didn't give Bluhm enough time to respond to the questions prior to informing Wachala of Bluhm's alleged answers. Bluhm's purported "personal statement" recorded by Wachala during the telephone conversation between Lande and Bluhm was in contradiction to Lande's earlier statement to Wachala that the fall had taken place at the wheelchair ramp rather than at the crack in the parking lot, but the "personal statement" was consistent with Lande's devised scheme revealed at the earlier meeting that Wachala should misrepresent the location of the accident.

The Bluhm settlement was finalized on February 3, 1986, during Wachala and Lande's next meeting when Wachala presented Lande with a draft in the amount of $40,000. Richman entered the room and told Lande and Wachala that his partner, Sam Evins, would work with them to complete the transaction. When Evins arrived he handed Lande an envelope containing $2,000 in cash, and Lande turned the money over to Wachala. During the meeting Lande made clear to Wachala that he and

---

5. As is the usual practice, prior to settling a claim, Wachala desired to obtain a signed statement from the claimant setting forth his version of the circumstances surrounding the accident as well as his injuries.

the law firm partners were interested in similar deals and made it clear that Wachala would be compensated if he provided information about other unrepresented claimants.

* * *

After the postal inspectors' investigation of Richman had been completed and the information turned over to a grand jury, an indictment was issued on November 17, 1988, charging Richman with two counts of wire fraud under 18 U.S.C. § 1343 and one count of mail fraud under 18 U.S.C. § 1341 concerning the Bluhm claim. The two counts of wire fraud arose from the transmission of a message (in accordance with Richman's scheme) from Wausau's regional office in River Forest, Illinois to the home office in Wausau, Wisconsin and thereafter from Wausau to Chicago, Illinois requesting a wire transfer of $40,000, both of which took place over interstate telephone lines on February 6, 1986. The mail fraud relevant to the Bluhm case arose from Richman's mailing the letter containing Bluhm's release and settlement from his office in Chicago, Illinois to Wausau Insurance Company in Wausau, Wisconsin on February 17, 1986. The grand jury further indicted Richman with seven other counts of mail fraud in the Williams' case.[6]

* * *

Richman challenges his convictions on all counts, arguing that the government failed to demonstrate that the schemes he was involved in constituted schemes to defraud the Wausau Insurance Company of money or property under the United States Supreme Court's decision in McNally v. United States, 483 U.S. 350 (1987). Specifically, he alleges that the evidence presented fails to support his conviction as a matter of law, since

> "*McNally* stands for the proposition that, unless money is obtained (or one intends to obtain money) in excess of an amount one is entitled to, there is no fraudulent taking and thus no scheme to defraud or obtain money under the Mail Fraud Statute. The burden is on the Government to present evidence that a defendant intended to receive an unlawful sum, i.e., an amount over and above what was lawfully due to the defendant."[7]

The thrust of Richman's *McNally*-based challenge to his convictions is that the government was required to demonstrate that his conduct resulted (or was intended to result) in a monetary loss to Wausau which

---

6. Richman was charged with one count of obstruction of justice under 18 U.S.C. § 1503, which was dismissed prior to trial. The indictment also charged Gil Lande with the two counts of wire fraud associated with the Bluhm case. Lande pled guilty to the two counts pursuant to a plea agreement.

7. Richman relies on the language in McNally that states "[i]t was not charged that in the absence of the alleged scheme, the Commonwealth would have paid a low-

er premium or secured better insurance," McNally, 483 U.S. at 360, for this argument. As we have previously noted, this statement in *McNally* was merely a "suggestion that a property deprivation might occur where, absent the scheme, the victim 'would have paid a lower [price]' for the goods or services received.... " Ranke v. United States, 873 F.2d 1033, 1039 (7th Cir.1989).

otherwise would not have occurred. He asserts that the government failed to establish that Richman would have been unable to achieve a $40,000 settlement in the Bluhm case through honest means and that the government did not demonstrate any fraudulent deprivation of Wausau's funds in the Williams claim.

In Ranke v. United States, 873 F.2d 1033, 1038–40 (7th Cir.1989), we dealt with a similar fraudulent scheme and contention in a case where a subcontractor paid "kickbacks" to an executive of a general contractor from funds the subcontractor received pursuant to a contract with the general contractor. In appealing his mail fraud conviction the executive argued that the "subcontract was not 'padded'—i.e., that [the subcontractor] absorbed the cost of the kickbacks—that [the subcontractor's] prices were fair and reasonable, and that [the subcontractor] did in fact perform the services for which [the general contractor] contracted." *Id.* We stated "[i]n essence, [the executive] claims that the [the general contractor] was not hurt in its pocket book.... " *Id.* In response, we held that the executive's

> "claim that [the subcontractor's] prices were not padded is of no avail. It does not matter that [the subcontractor] might have settled for a lower profit to 'absorb' the cost of the kickbacks. We can assume that [the general contractor] bargained to pay [the subcontractor] for what one would consider its 'legitimate' expenses (labor, materials, permit fees, etc.) and its profit (whatever profit [the subcontractor] was willing to accept). But, regardless of whether [the subcontractor's] price appeared to be reasonable and competitive, we cannot assume that [the general contractor] bargained to also pay money to its own employee, Ranke. As we stated in [United States v.]. George, [477 F.2d 508 (7th Cir.1973)], 'it is preposterous to claim' that [the general contractor] would accept such a payment as part of the deal. To paraphrase the words of the Fifth Circuit, [the general contractor] was induced to part with its money on the basis of the false premise, implicitly represented to it by [the general contractor's executive and the subcontractor], that [the general contractor's executive] would not receive a portion of that money."

Id. at 1039–40. The establishment of a mail fraud does not include a requirement that the defendant receive or intend to receive money or property "in excess of an amount [he was] entitled to [receive]." *Ranke* makes clear that inducement for a company to part with money based upon an implicit false premise violates the mail fraud statute when any portion of the money the company is induced to pay is fraudulently given to the company's own employee without the company's knowledge and/or consent. Richman's conduct in regard to * * * the * * * Bluhm cases involved fraudulent schemes in which a Wausau employee was to receive funds under the table from the claimant's attorney, in the Bluhm case for facilitating a settlement * * *.

* * *

Notes

1. Note the reference in footnote 6. Why do you think the count of obstruction of justice charged under 18 U.S.C. § 1503 was dismissed?

2. From the recitation of facts in the above opinion, do you believe Fred Richman or Gil Lande was more culpable?

3. In United States v. Craft, 105 F.3d 1123 (6th Cir.1997), the Sixth Circuit affirmed the convictions of an attorney who was attempting to conceal an error he thought he had made in representing a client:

"On February 8, 1987, Ivan Michael Cook was killed in a car accident in Kentucky. Ten days later, Patricia Sparks, Cook's mother, hired the defendant to represent Cook's estate in an action to recover for Cook's death. Exactly two years after Cook's death, on February 8, 1989, defendant filed a wrongful death action in Letcher Circuit Court on behalf of Patricia Sparks as the administratrix of the estate. The case was removed to federal court on March 23, 1989. In July 1989, the defendants in the wrongful death action filed a summary judgment motion to dismiss the action because Patricia Sparks had not been formally appointed administratrix of her son's estate and therefore had no standing to bring the action under Kentucky law. The defendants also contended that even if Patricia Sparks were now appointed, the action would be barred by Kentucky's statute of limitations.

"At this point under the allegations of the indictment, defendant Craft—apparently unaware that the doctrine of tolling might save his case and believing that his case would be dismissed—enlisted the aid of Judge Larry Collins of the Letcher County probate court to 'fabricate' and backdate documents showing that Patricia Sparks had been duly appointed administratrix of her son's estate as of February 18, 1987. These so-called 'fabricated documents' were filed in the federal civil case in November 1989. The federal judge assigned to hear the civil case, Judge Hood, ruled that although the documents in question were purportedly signed by the state judge in February 1987, the documents were not properly filed at that time with the clerk of the probate court. (No tolling justification was raised.) Judge Hood therefore dismissed the wrongful death action on that ground. In Sparks v. Marshall, Civ. Act. No. 89–79 (E.D.Ky. May 31, 1990), the court noted, 'The unusual twist to this case is that no formal petition for appointment of an administrator was filed [in the state probate court] until November 1989. . . . The order of appointment was not entered by the clerk of the court until that time. The question here is, thus, whether the order was valid when signed by the court on February 18, 1987.' Judge Hood ruled that it was not a valid appointment and that the plaintiff lacked standing under Kentucky law.

"Defendant filed a notice of appeal of that ruling to this Court—the only act in the chain within the five year period preceding the indictment— but the appeal was dismissed because it was filed one day too late. Defendant Craft was subsequently sued for malpractice by Patricia Sparks.

"On August 24, 1995, more than five years after the 'fabricated' documents were filed in the federal case and more than five years after Judge Hood dismissed it, defendant was charged with two counts of conspiracy to defraud the United States in violation of 18 U.S.C. § 371, two counts of obstruction of justice by intimidation of witnesses and jurors in violation of 18 U.S.C. § 1503, one count of perjury in violation of 18 U.S.C. § 1621 and one count of subornation of perjury in violation of 18 U.S.C. § 1622."

If you were a prosecutor, would you seek charges against Craft? Against Judge Collins?

Chapter 12

ENVIRONMENTAL CRIMES

The past few years have seen an explosion in criminal prosecutions for environmental crimes.[a] In fiscal year 1996, $76.7 million in fines were assessed for environmental crimes, and a record high 262 cases were referred to the Department of Justice for criminal prosecution by the Environmental Protection Agency. This increase is due to the growth in EPA's criminal enforcement program and increasing success in "piercing the corporate veil," which enables prosecutors to build cases against a group of people within an organization, rather than against a single wrongdoer.[b] EPA officials also attribute EPA's success in prosecuting more individuals to the greater number and expertise of agents now investigating environmental crimes.[c]

Every indication is that the increased emphasis on criminal prosecutions will continue. In recent statements, EPA officials "predicted greater use of targeted criminal investigations, more criminal prosecutions of individuals, and more federal interaction with local and state investigators."[d] As one expert explained, "The deterrent effect of criminal enforcement is far greater than that of administrative and civil-judicial enforcement because imprisonment cannot be passed onto consumers or otherwise rationalized as a cost of doing business."[e]

a. Discussing this trend are: Richard J. Lazarus, *Meeting the Demands of Integration in the Evolution of Environmental Law: Reforming Environmental Criminal Law*, 83 Geo. L. J. 2407 (1995). Dick Thornburg, *Criminal Enforcement of Environmental Law—A National Priority*, 59 Geo. Wash. L. Rev. 775 (1991); Note, *Criminal Intent in Federal Environmental Statutes: What Corporate Officers and Employees Should "Know,"* 20 Am. J. Crim. L. 359 (1993); Note, *Environmental Criminal Cases: The Dawn of a New Era*, 21 Seton Hall L. Rev. 1125 (1991); Note, *"Knowing" Environmental Crimes*, 16 Wm. Mitchell L. Rev. 987 (1990); Note, *Criminalizing Occupational Safety Violations: The Use of* *"Knowing Endangerment" Statutes to Punish Employers Who Maintain Toxic Working Conditions*, 14 Harv. Envtl. L. Rev. 487 (1990).

b. Env't. Rep. (BNA) (Feb. 26, 1997).

c. *Id.*

d. Env't. Rep. (BNA) 1957 (Mar. 18, 1994) (statement of Steve Herman, EPA Assistant Administrator for Enforcement.)

e. James M. Strock, *Environmental Criminal Enforcement Priorities for the 1990s*, 59 Geo. Wash. L. Rev. 916, 922 (1991). (Mr. Stock served as the Assistant Administrator for Enforcement at the EPA.)

There are four major federal environmental statutes and scores of state statutes. The Resource Conservation and Recovery Act (RCRA)[f] was enacted in 1988 to address the management of solid waste disposal.[g] The Comprehensive Environmental Response, Compensation and Liability Act (CERCLA)[h] was passed in 1988 primarily to address the clean up of abandoned hazardous waste sites, estimated in 1979 to be between 30,000 and 50,000.[i] The Clean Air Act (CAA), originally passed in 1963 and recently amended[j] is designed to prevent and control air pollution.[k] The Clean Water Act (CWA), recently amended,[l] is designed "to restore and maintain the chemical, physical, and biological integrity of the Nations' waters."[m]

All four statutes contain criminal penalty provisions providing that "knowing" violations of the respective provisions of each act render the violator criminally liable.[n] The CAA and CWA also provide criminal liability for negligent violations of their provisions.[o] All statutes except CERCLA provide enhanced criminal penalties for knowingly endangering another person.[p]

This chapter presents three issues that arise in environmental crimes. Part A addresses an issue repeatedly posed by white collar criminal cases: what mens rea should be shown before criminal liability attaches. As the cases in Part A demonstrate, Congress and courts have given prosecutors a boost with the mens rea requirements governing environmental criminal statutes. As you read these cases, consider whether this reduced mens rea requirement blurs the line between civil and criminal law. Part B focuses on efforts by prosecutors to hold individuals liable for environmental crimes while Part C presents one court's resolution of the difficulties presented when the same conduct is pursued criminally as well as civilly. Because of the availability of civil and administrative actions, parallel proceedings arise often in the environmental context.

---

f. 42 U.S.C. §§ 6901–6975 (1983, Supp. 1993).

g. *Id.* at § 6902(b) (Supp. 1993).

h. 42 U.S.C. §§ 9601–9675 (1983, Supp. 1993).

i. H. R. Rep. No. 96, 96th Cong., 2d Sess. 17 (1980) *reprinted in* 1980 U.S.C.C.A.N. 6119, 6120.

j. 42 U.S.C. § 7401–7491 (1983, Supp. 1993).

k. *Id.* at § 7401(b).

l. 33 U.S.C. §§ 1251–1376 (1986, Supp. 1993).

m. *Id.* at 1251(a).

n. RCRA: 42 U.S.C. § 6928(d) (Supp. 1993); CERCLA: 42 U.S.C. § 9603 (1983, Supp. 1993); CAA: 42 U.S.C. §§ 7413(c)(1)(2) (1983, Supp. 1993); CWA: 33 U.S.C. § 1319(c)(2) (Supp. 1993).

o. CAA: 42 U.S.C. § 7413(c)(4) (Supp. 1993); CWA: 33 U.S.C. § 1319(c)(1) (Supp. 1993).

p. RCRA: 42 U.S.C. § 6928(e) (Supp. 1993); CAA: 42 U.S.C. § 7413(c)(5)(A) (Supp. 1993); CWA: 33 U.S.C. § 1319(c)(3) (Supp. 1993).

A. INTENT IN ENVIRONMENTAL PROSECUTIONS

UNITED STATES v. WEITZENHOFF[q]

United States Court of Appeals, Ninth Circuit, 1993.
1 F.3d 1523.

FLETCHER, CIRCUIT JUDGE.

Michael H. Weitzenhoff and Thomas W. Mariani, who managed the East Honolulu Community Services Sewage Treatment Plant, appeal their convictions for violations of the Clean Water Act ("CWA"), 33 U.S.C. §§ 1251 et seq., contending that * * * the district court misconstrued the word "knowingly" under section 1319(c)(2) of the CWA; * * *.

We affirm the convictions and sentence.

In 1988 and 1989 Weitzenhoff was the manager and Mariani the assistant manager of the East Honolulu Community Services Sewage Treatment Plant ("the plant"), located not far from Sandy Beach, a popular swimming and surfing beach on Oahu. The plant is designed to treat some 4 million gallons of residential wastewater each day by removing the solids and other harmful pollutants from the sewage so that the resulting effluent can be safely discharged into the ocean. The plant operates under a permit issued pursuant to the National Pollution Discharge Elimination System ("NPDES"), which established the limits on the Total Suspended Solids ("TSS") and Biochemical Oxygen Demand ("BOD")—indicators of the solid and organic matter, respectively, in the effluent discharged at Sandy Beach. During the period in question, the permit limited the discharge of both the TSS and BOD to an average of 976 pounds per day over a 30–day period. It also imposed monitoring and sampling requirements on the plant's management.

The sewage treatment process that was overseen by Weitzenhoff and Mariani began with the removal of large inorganic items such as rags and coffee grounds from the incoming wastewater as it flowed through metal screens and a grit chamber at the head of the plant. The wastewater then entered large tanks known as primary clarifiers, where a portion of the organic solids settled to the bottom of the tanks. The solid material which settled in the primary clarifiers, known as primary sludge, was pumped to separate tanks, known as anaerobic digesters, to be further processed. Those solids that did not settle continued on to aeration basins, which contained microorganisms to feed on and remove the solids and other organic pollutants in the waste stream.

From the aeration basins the mixture flowed into final clarifiers, where the microorganisms settled out, producing a mixture that sank to the bottom of the clarifiers called activated sludge. The clarified stream then passed through a chlorine contact chamber, where the plant's sampling apparatus was, and emptied into the plant's outfall, a long underground pipe which discharged the plant's effluent into the ocean

q. This opinion was amended on denial of rehearing and rehearing en banc, 35 F.3d 1275 (9th Cir.1993). No changes were made in the opinion reproduced herein.

through diffusers 1,100 to 1,400 feet from shore (the "Sandy Beach outfall").

Meanwhile, the activated sludge that had settled in the final clarifiers was pumped from the bottom of the clarifiers. A certain portion was returned to the aeration basins, while the remainder, known as waste activated sludge ("WAS"), was pumped to WAS holding tanks. From the holding tanks, the WAS could either be returned to other phases of the treatment process or hauled away to a different sewage treatment facility.

From March 1987 through March 1988, the excess WAS generated by the plant was hauled away to another treatment plant, the Sand Island Facility. In March 1988, certain improvements were made to the East Honolulu plant and the hauling was discontinued. Within a few weeks, however, the plant began experiencing a buildup of excess WAS. Rather than have the excess WAS hauled away as before, however, Weitzenhoff and Mariani instructed two employees at the plant to dispose of it on a regular basis by pumping it from the storage tanks directly into the outfall, that is, directly into the ocean. The WAS thereby bypassed the plant's effluent sampler so that the samples taken and reported to Hawaii's Department of Health ("DOH") and the EPA did not reflect its discharge.

The evidence produced by the government at trial showed that WAS was discharged directly into the ocean from the plant on about 40 separate occasions from April 1988 to June 1989, resulting in some 436,000 pounds of pollutant solids being discharged into the ocean, and that the discharges violated the plant's 30–day average effluent limit under the permit for most of the months during which they occurred. Most of the WAS discharges occurred during the night, and none was reported to the DOH or EPA. DOH inspectors contacted the plant on several occasions in 1988 in response to complaints by lifeguards at Sandy Beach that sewage was being emitted form the outfall, but Weitzenhoff and Mariani repeatedly denied that there was any problem at the plant. In one letter responding to a DOH inquiry in October 1988, Mariani stated that "the debris that was reported could not have been from the East Honolulu Wastewater Treatment facility, as our records of effluent quality up to this time will substantiate." One of the plant employees who participated in the dumping operation testified that Weitzenhoff instructed him not to say anything about the discharges, because if they stuck together and did not reveal anything, "they [couldn't] do anything to us."

Following an FBI investigation, Weitzenhoff and Mariani were charged in a thirty-one-count indictment with conspiracy and substantive violations of the Clean Water Act ("CWA"), 33 U.S.C. §§ 1251 et seq. At trial, Weitzenhoff and Mariani admitted having authorized the discharges, but claimed that their actions were justified under their interpretation of the NPDES permit. The jury found them guilty of six of the thirty-one counts.

Weitzenhoff was sentenced to twenty-one months and Mariani thirty-three months imprisonment. Each filed a timely notice of appeal.

* * *

Section 1311(a) of the CWA prohibits the discharge of pollutants into navigable waters without an NPDES permit. 33 U.S.C. § 1311(a). Section 1319(c)(2) makes it a felony offense to "knowingly violate[ ] section 1311, 1312, 1316, 1317, 1318, 1321(b)(3), 1328, or 1345 ... , or any permit condition or limitation implementing any of such sections in a permit issued under section 1342."

Prior to trial, the district court construed "knowingly" in section 1319(c)(2) as requiring only that Weitzenhoff and Mariani were aware that they were discharging the pollutants in question, not that they knew they were violating the terms of the statute or permit. According to appellants, the district court erred in its interpretation of the CWA and in instructing the jury that "the government is not required to prove that the defendant knew that his act or omissions were unlawful," as well as in rejecting their proposed instruction based on the defense that they mistakenly believed their conduct was authorized by the permit. Apparently, no court of appeals has confronted the issue raised by appellants.

* * *

As with certain other criminal statutes that employ the term "knowingly," it is not apparent from the face of the statute whether "knowingly" means a knowing violation of the law or simply knowing conduct that is violative of the law. We turn, then, to the legislative history of the provision at issue to ascertain what Congress intended.

In 1987, Congress substantially amended the CWA, elevating the penalties for violations of the Act. Increased penalties were considered necessary to deter would-be polluters. S. Rep. No. 50, 99th Cong., 1st Sess. 29 (1985). With the 1987 amendments, Congress substituted "knowingly" for the earlier intent requirement of "willfully" that appeared in the predecessor to section 1319(c)(2). The Senate report accompanying the legislation explains that the changes in the penalty provisions were to ensure that "[c]riminal liability shall ... attach to any person who is not in compliance with all applicable Federal, State and local requirements and permits and causes a POTW [publicly owned treatment works] to violate any effluent limitation or condition in any permit issued to the treatment works." *Id.* Similarly, the report accompanying the House version of the bill, which contained parallel provisions for enhancement of penalties, states that the proposed amendments were to "provide penalties for dischargers or individuals who knowingly or negligently violate or cause the violation of certain of the Act's requirements." H. R. Rep. No. 189, 99th Cong., 1st Sess. 29–30 (1985). Because they speak in terms of "causing" a violation, the congressional explanations of the new penalty provisions strongly suggest that criminal sanctions are to be imposed on an individual who knowingly engages in conduct that results in a permit violation, regardless of whether the polluter is cognizant of the requirements or even the existence of the permit.

* * *

The criminal provisions of the CWA are clearly designed to protect the public at large from the potentially dire consequences of water pollution, and as such fall within the category of public welfare legislation. The government did not need to prove that Weitzenhoff and Mariani knew that their acts violated the permit or the CWA.

* * *

Notes

1. Other courts also have struggled with the mens rea element in reviewing criminal convictions for violations of other environmental crimes. As the *Weitzenhoff* court noted, the Ninth Circuit previously held that the Resource Conservation and Recovery Act ("RCRA")'s criminal provision required only proof that the defendant knew of his conduct, not that the defendant knew his conduct violated the law. *See* United States v. Hoflin, 880 F.2d 1033, 1038 (9th Cir.1989). Other circuits have agreed, United States v. Laughlin, 10 F.3d 961, 965–66 (2d Cir.1993) (summarizing positions of other circuits addressing the "knowing" mens rea of RCRA).

2. The Sixth Circuit addressed the mens rea issue in the context of the Clear Air Act (CAA) in United States v. Buckley, 934 F.2d 84 (6th Cir.1991), and similarly held that the CAA requires only knowledge of one's conduct, not knowledge that one's conduct violates the law for one to be found criminally liable of violating the CAA. At issue in *Buckley* was whether to affirm the defendant's convictions under the CAA for releasing asbestos into the air. The following jury instructions on intent were given:

> "All the government must prove is that the defendant knew the general nature of the asbestos material on pipes. * * * The government does not have to show that the defendant knew the legal status of the asbestos materials or that he was violating the law.

* * *

> "The government is not required to prove a wrongful intent or awareness of wrongdoing. The question whether the defendant acted in good faith is not material. It is the responsibility of persons who voluntarily associate themselves with asbestos demolition operations as supervisors or persons in charge to comply with the law."

Id. at 87.

The defendant objected to the jury instructions as "eliminating knowledge as an element of the crimes." The Sixth Circuit rejected the defendant's challenge, finding that the CAA requires "knowledge only of the emissions themselves, not knowledge of the statutes or of the hazards that emissions pose." *Id.* at 88. The court explained: "Because of the very nature of asbestos and other hazardous substances, individuals dealing with them have constitutionally adequate notice that they may incur criminal liability for emissions-related actions." *Id.*

3. The Second Circuit addressed the mens rea requirement for failure to report a release of a hazardous substance in violation of the Comprehensive Environmental Response, Compensation and Liability Act (CERCLA) in United States v. Laughlin, 10 F.3d 961, 966 (2d Cir.1993). The defendant challenged his CERCLA conviction on the ground that the court failed to instruct the jury that the government was required to prove that the defendant knew that his release violated CERCLA. *Id.* The Second Circuit rejected the defendant's argument, analogized to its interpretation of RCRA, *supra*, and found that both statutes were regulatory schemes, "intended to protect public health and safety." *Id.* Therefore, according to the Second Circuit, "section 9603(a) does not demand knowledge of the regulatory requirements of CERCLA; it demands only that the defendant be aware of his acts." *Id.* at 967.

As the next case demonstrates, a prosecutor cannot take anything for granted, even that the defendant knew what he was doing.

UNITED STATES v. AHMAD

United States Court of Appeals, Fifth Circuit, 1996.
101 F.3d 386.

SMITH, CIRCUIT JUDGE.

Attique Ahmad appeals his conviction of, and sentence for, criminal violations of the Clean Water Act ("CWA"). Concluding that the district court erred in its instructions to the jury, we reverse and remand.

I.

This case arises from the discharge of a large quantity of gasoline into the sewers of Conroe, Texas, in January 1994. In 1992, Ahmad purchased the "Spin–N–Market No. 12," a combination convenience store and gas station located at the intersection of Second and Lewis Streets in Conroe. The Spin–N–Market has two gasoline pumps, each of which is fed by an 8000–gallon underground gasoline tank. Some time after Ahmad bought the station, he discovered that one of the tanks, which held high-octane gasoline, was leaking. This did not pose an immediate hazard, because the leak was at the top of the tank; gasoline could not seep out. The leak did, however, allow water to enter into the tank and contaminate the gas. Because water is heavier than gas, the water sank to the bottom of the tank, and because the tank was pumped from the bottom, Ahmad was unable to sell from it.

In October 1993, Ahmad hired CTT Environmental Services ("CTT"), a tank testing company, to examine the tank. CTT determined that it contained approximately 800 gallons of water, and the rest mostly gasoline. Jewel McCoy, a CTT employee, testified that she told Ahmad that the leak could not be repaired until the tank was completely emptied, which CTT offered to do for 65 cents per gallon plus $65 per hour of labor. After McCoy gave Ahmad this estimate, he inquired whether he could empty the tank himself. She replied that it would be dangerous and illegal to do so. On her testimony, he responded, "Well, if I don't get caught, what then?"

On January 25, 1994, Ahmad rented a hand-held motorized water pump from a local hardware store, telling a hardware store employee that he was planning to use it to remove water from his backyard. Victor Fonseca, however, identified Ahmad and the pump and testified that he had seen Ahmad pumping gasoline into the street. Oscar Alvarez stated that he had seen Ahmad and another person discharging gasoline into a manhole. Tereso Uribe testified that he had confronted Ahmad and asked him what was going on, to which Ahmad responded that he was simply removing the water from the tank.

In all, 5,220 gallons of fluid were pumped from the leaky tank, of which approximately 4,690 gallons were gasoline. Some of the gas-water mixture ran down Lewis Street and some into the manhole in front of the store.

The gasoline discharged onto Lewis Street went a few hundred feet along the curb to Third Street, where it entered a storm drain and the storm sewer system and flowed through a pipe that eventually empties into Possum Creek. When city officials discovered the next day that there was gasoline in Possum Creek, several vacuum trucks were required to decontaminate it. Possum Creek feeds into the San Jacinto River, which eventually flows into Lake Houston.

The gasoline that Ahmad discharged into the manhole went a different route: It flowed through the sanitary sewer system and eventually entered the city sewage treatment plant. On January 26, employees at the treatment plant discovered a 1,000–gallon pool of gasoline in one of the intake ponds. To avoid shutting down the plant altogether, they diverted the pool of gasoline and all incoming liquid into a 5,000,000–gallon emergency lagoon.

The plant supervisor ordered that non-essential personnel be evacuated from the plant and called firefighters and a hazardous materials crew to the scene. The Conroe fire department determined the gasoline was creating a risk of explosion and ordered that two nearby schools be evacuated. Although no one was injured as a result of the discharge, fire officials testified at trial that Ahmad had created a "tremendous explosion hazard" that could have led to "hundreds, if not thousands, of deaths and injuries" and millions of dollars of property damage.

By 9:00 a.m. on January 26, investigators had traced the source of the gasoline back to the manhole directly in front of the Spin–N–Market. Their suspicions were confirmed when they noticed a strong odor of gasoline and saw signs of corrosion on the asphalt surrounding the manhole. The investigators questioned Ahmad, who at first denied having operated a pump the previous night. Soon, however, his story changed: He admitted to having used a pump but denied having pumped anything from his tanks.

Ahmad was indicted for three violations of the CWA: knowingly discharging a pollutant from a point source into a navigable water of the United States without a permit, in violation of 33 U.S.C. §§ 1311(a) and 1319(c)(2)(A) (count one); knowingly operating a source in violation of a pretreatment standard, in violation of 33 U.S.C. §§ 1317(d) and 1319(c)(2)(A) (count two); and knowingly placing another person in imminent danger of death or serious bodily injury by discharging a pollutant, in violation of 33 U.S.C. § 1319(c)(3) (count three). At trial, Ahmad did not dispute that he had discharged gasoline from the tank or that eventually it had found its way to Possum Creek and the sewage treatment plant. Instead, he contended that his discharge of the gasoline was not "knowing," because he had believed he was discharging water.

One of the key pieces of evidence Ahmad attempted to introduce in support of this theory was the testimony of Mohammed Abassi and Shahid Latif, who would have told the jury that Ahmad was at the Spin-N-Market only until 7:30 or 8:00 p.m. on January 25, and not the entire evening as the government contended. The gist of this was an attempt to show that Ahmad did not knowingly discharge gasoline himself, but rather only negligently left the pump in the hands of his employees. The district court found Abassi's and Latif's testimony irrelevant and excluded it. The jury found Ahmad guilty on counts one and two and deadlocked on count three.

II.

Ahmad argues that the district court improperly instructed the jury on the mens rea required for counts one and two. The instruction on count one stated in relevant part:

For you to find Mr. Ahmad guilty of this crime, you must be convinced that the government has proved each of the following beyond a reasonable doubt:

(1) That on or about the date set forth in the indictment,

(2) the defendant knowingly discharged

(3) a pollutant

(4) from a point source

(5) into the navigable waters of the United States

(6) without a permit to do so.

On count two, the court instructed the jury:

In order to prove the defendant guilty of the offense charged in Count 2 of the indictment, the government must prove beyond a reasonable doubt each of the following elements:

(1) That on or about the date set forth in the indictment

(2) the defendant,

(3) who was the owner or operator of a source,

(4) knowingly operated that source by discharging into a public sewer system or publicly owned treatment works

(5) a pollutant that created a fire or explosion hazard in that public sewer system or publicly owned treatment works.

Ahmad contends that the jury should have been instructed that the statutory *mens rea*—knowledge—was required as to each element of the offenses, rather than only with regard to discharge or the operation of a source.

* * *

The language of the CWA is less than pellucid. Title 33 U.S.C. § 1319(c)(2)(A) says that "any person who knowingly violates" any of a number of other sections of the CWA commits a felony. One of the provisions that § 1319(c)(2)(A) makes it unlawful to violate is § 1311(a), which, when read together with a series of definitions in § 1362, prohibits the addition of any pollutant to navigable waters from a "point source." That was the crime charged in count one. Section 1319(c)(2)(A) also criminalizes violations of § 1317(d), which prohibits the operation of any "source" in a way that contravenes any effluent standard, prohibition, or pretreatment standard. That was the crime charged in count two.

The principal issue is to which elements of the offense the modifier "knowingly" applies. The matter is complicated somewhat by the fact that the phrase "knowingly violates" appears in a different section of the CWA from the language defining the elements of the offenses. Ahmad argues that within this context, "knowingly violates" should be read to require him knowingly to have acted with regard to each element of the offenses. The government, in contrast, contends that "knowingly violates" requires it to prove only that Ahmad knew the nature of his acts and that he performed them intentionally. Particularly at issue is whether "knowingly" applies to the element of the discharge's being a pollutant, for Ahmad's main theory at trial was that he thought he was discharging water, not gasoline.

The Supreme Court has spoken to this issue in broad terms. In United States v. X–Citement Video, Inc., 513 U.S. 64 (1994), the Court read "knowingly" to apply to each element of a child pornography offense, notwithstanding its conclusion that under the "most natural grammatical reading" of the statute it should apply only to the element of having transported, shipped, received, distributed, or reproduced the material at issue. The Court also reaffirmed the long-held view that "the presumption in favor of a scienter requirement should apply to each of the statutory elements which criminalize otherwise innocent conduct." *Id.* at 72.

Although *X-Citement Video* is the Court's most recent pronouncement on this subject, it is not the first. In Staples v. United States, 511 U.S. 600, 619–20 (1994), the Court found that the statutes criminalizing knowing possession of a machinegun, 26 U.S.C. §§ 5845(a)(6) and 5861(d), require that defendants know not only that they possess a firearm but that it actually is a machinegun. Thus, an awareness of the features of the gun—specifically, the features that make it an automatic weapon—is a necessary element of the offense. More generally, the Court also made plain that statutory crimes carrying severe penalties are presumed to require that a defendant know the facts that make his conduct illegal. *Id.*

Our own precedents are in the same vein. In United States v. Baytank (Houston), Inc., 934 F.2d 599, 613 (5th Cir.1991), we concluded that a conviction for knowing and improper storage of hazardous wastes under 42 U.S.C. § 6928(d)(2)(A) requires "that the defendant know[ ] factually what he is doing—storing, what is being stored, and that what is being stored factually has the potential for harm to others or the environment, and that he has no permit.... " This is directly analogous to the interpretation of the CWA that Ahmad urges upon us. Indeed, we find it eminently sensible that the phrase "knowingly violates" in § 1319(c)(2)(A), when referring to other provisions that define the elements of the offenses § 1319 creates, should uniformly require knowledge as to each of those elements rather than only one or two. To hold otherwise would require an explanation as to why some elements should be treated differently from others, which neither the parties nor the caselaw seems able to provide.

In support of its interpretation of the CWA, the government cites cases from other circuits. We find these decisions both inapposite and unpersuasive on the point for which they are cited. In United States v. Hopkins, 53 F.3d 533, 537–41 (2d Cir.1995), the court held that the government need not demonstrate that a § 1319(c)(2)(A) defendant knew his acts were illegal. The illegality of the defendant's actions is not an element of the offense, however. In United States v. Weitzenhoff, 35 F.3d 1275 (9th Cir.1993), the court similarly was concerned almost exclusively with whether the language of the CWA creates a mistake-of-law defense. Both cases are easily distinguishable, for neither directly addresses mistake of fact or the statutory construction issues raised by Ahmad.

The government also protests that CWA violations fall into the judicially-created exception for "public welfare offenses," under which some regulatory crimes have been held not to require a showing of mens rea. On its face, the CWA certainly does appear to implicate public welfare.

As recent cases have emphasized, however, the public welfare offense exception is narrow. The *Staples* Court, for example, held that the statute prohibiting the possession of machineguns fell outside the exception, notwithstanding the fact that "[t]ypically, our cases recognizing such offenses involve statutes that regulate potentially harmful or injurious items." Staples, 511 U.S. at 607.

Though gasoline is a "potentially harmful or injurious item," it is certainly no more so than are machineguns. Rather, *Staples* held, the key to the public welfare offense analysis is whether "dispensing with *mens rea* would require the defendant to have knowledge only of traditionally lawful conduct." *Id.* at 618. The CWA offenses of which Ahmad was convicted have precisely this characteristic, for if knowledge is not required as to the nature of the substance discharged, one who honestly and reasonably believes he is discharging water may find himself guilty of a felony if the substance turns out to be something else.

The fact that violations of § 1319(c)(2)(A) are felonies punishable by years in federal prison confirms our view that they do not fall within the public welfare offense exception. As the *Staples* Court noted, public welfare offenses have virtually always been crimes punishable by relatively light penalties such as fines or short jail sentences, rather than substantial terms of imprisonment. Serious felonies, in contrast, should not fall within the exception "absent a clear statement from Congress that *mens rea* is not required." *Id.* at 618. Following *Staples*, we hold that the offenses charged in counts one and two are not public welfare offenses and that the usual presumption of a mens rea requirement applies. With the exception of purely jurisdictional elements, the *mens rea* of knowledge applies to each element of the crimes.

Finally, the government argues that the instructions, considered as a whole, adequately conveyed to the jury the message that Ahmad had to have known that what he was discharging was gasoline in order for the jury to find him guilty. We disagree.

At best, the jury charge made it uncertain to which elements "knowingly" applied. At worst, and considerably more likely, it indicated that only the element of discharge need be knowing. The instructions listed each element on a separate line, with the word "knowingly" present only in the line corresponding to the element that something was discharged. That the district court included a one-sentence summary of each count in which "knowingly" was present did not cure the error.

The obvious inference for the jury was that knowledge was required only as to the fact that something was discharged, and not as to any other fact. In effect, with regard to the other elements of the crimes, the instructions implied that the requisite *mens rea* was strict liability rather than knowledge.

There was at least a reasonable likelihood that the jury applied the instructions in this way, so we conclude that the instructions misled the jury as to the elements of the offense. Because the charge effectively withdrew from the jury's consideration facts that it should have been permitted to find or not find, this error requires reversal.

III.

Having found reversible error in the instructions, we need not consider Ahmad's other arguments. Given that this case likely will be tried again, however, we will address, in the interest of judicial economy, the exclusion of two of Ahmad's witnesses.

Ahmad argues that the district court improperly excluded the testimony of two individuals who would have testified that he was not at the Spin–N–Market from approximately 7:30 or 8:00 p.m. on January 25 through 12:45 a.m. on January 26. These witnesses, Mohammed Abassi and Shahid Latif, were intended to support Ahmad's theory that he started the pump and left the Spin–N–Market shortly thereafter, in contrast to the government's theory that he was there all evening. They were not intended to show that he had been completely uninvolved in the incident. Whether Ahmad pumped at least *some* of the fluid was not in issue; his counsel conceded at trial that "he started it [the pump] off."

The first of these witnesses was Abassi, to whose testimony the government objected on the ground that it tended to establish an alibi. After some confusion over whether the defense was required to give the government notice of alibi under Fed.R.Crim.P. 12.1(a), Ahmad's counsel settled on the argument that Abassi's testimony was not being offered as an alibi, but rather only to show that Ahmad had left the store during the evening in question. This, he argued, would support the theory that Ahmad's violation had been negligent rather than knowing, in the sense that he negligently left the store in the care of his untrained employees. The court responded that because it did not intend to give an instruction on the lesser included offense of a negligent violation, Abassi's testimony was irrelevant, and excluded it on that ground.[4]

Our examination of the exclusion of evidence is limited to the grounds that were proffered for its admission at trial. Given the basis on which Abassi's testimony was offered, the only way in which it could have been relevant was to support a theory of negligent rather than knowing violation. This in turn means that the testimony was irrelevant unless Ahmad was entitled to an instruction on the lesser included offense. If he was not so entitled, the evidence was properly excluded. We conclude to the contrary.

In Sansone v. United States, 380 U.S. 343, 350 (1965), the Court held that a defendant is entitled to have the jury instructed on a lesser included offense if there is an evidentiary basis that would allow a finding of guilt of the lesser offense and "the charged greater offense requires the jury to find a disputed factual element which is not required for conviction of the lesser-included offense." Thus the test we apply for whether the instruction should be given is two-pronged: "(1) [T]he elements of the lesser offense must be a subset of the elements of the charged offense; and (2) the evidence at trial must be such that a jury could rationally find the defendant guilty of the lesser offense, yet acquit him of the greater."

---

4. Ahmad ultimately requested, and the court denied, a lesser included offense in-struction on each of the charged crimes.

It is self-evident that Ahmad met the first prong of the test, for knowing violations of §§ 1311 and 1317(d) require everything that negligent violations do, and more. The second prong, however, is less easily disposed of.

The district court's instructions and its rulings on Ahmad's proposed instructions indicate that it thought "knowingly" modified only the element that something was discharged. Were this the correct interpretation of the CWA, the lesser included offense instruction would have been correctly denied, because no rational jury simultaneously could have found both (1) that Ahmad did not know that he was operating the pump and (2) that he was *negligent* with regard to whether he was operating it. Indeed, on the facts as presented, the idea that Ahmad could have been negligent with regard to whether a pump was being operated is almost nonsensical.

With regard to the other elements of the crime, however, there is a vivid and sensible distinction between negligence and knowledge. Having held that the district court's interpretation of the CWA was incorrect, we also must conclude that it erred in refusing to give the lesser included offense instruction. Because the statutory *mens rea* applies to multiple elements of the offense, such as whether what was being discharged was a pollutant, there was ample evidence to support the lesser violation.

Most of Ahmad's defense, after all, was built around the idea that he thought water, rather than gasoline, was being discharged. A rational jury could so have found, and at the same time could have found that he did *not actually know* that he was pumping gas. Because the lesser included offense instruction was improperly denied, Abassi's and Latif's testimony was improperly excluded as well. We remand with instruction that, if this case is retried, the admissibility of this testimony be reconsidered in light of the foregoing.

IV.

Because we reverse Ahmad's convictions, we need not address his sentencing claims. The convictions are REVERSED and the case REMANDED.

Notes

1. The court held that the government must prove that Ahmad knew he was discharging gasoline. In reaching this conclusion the court characterized the government's argument as requiring only proof that Ahmad knew he was discharging *something*. Is this a fair characterization of the government's argument?

2. After reading this opinion, do you think the prosecutor could have proven that Ahmad knew he was discharging gasoline? What evidence would the prosecutor rely upon?

As noted, *supra*, the four major environmental statutes carry an enhanced criminal penalty. The Clean Water Act (CWA) for example, provides for imprisonment of not more than 3 years and a fine of $5,000–$50,000 per day of violation for a first offense and imprisonment of not more than 6 years and a fine of $5,000–$100,000 per day of violation for a second offense (33 U.S.C. 1319(c)(2)). It further provides imprisonment of not more than 15 years and a fine of not more than $250,000 if the violator knowingly "places another person in imminent danger of death or serious bodily injury" by violating the CWA.

———

As the next case discusses, additional proof of intent must be shown to convict a defendant of knowingly endangering another person.

UNITED STATES v. VILLEGAS

United States District Court, Eastern District, New York 1991.
784 F.Supp. 6.

KORMAN, DISTRICT JUDGE.

On May 26, 1988, a teacher at the Saint John's Lutheran School took her eighth grade class on a field trip to the Alice Austin House, a museum on Staten Island that overlooks Pebble Beach on the Hudson River. While playing on the beach after touring the museum, the students came upon numerous glass vials containing what appeared to be human blood lying in the sand. The New York City Sanitation Department later collected approximately seventy of these vials scattered along the shoreline and floating in the incoming tide. The broken remains of others were found among clusters of rocks in the shallow water. Tests later revealed that five of the vials contained blood infected with hepatitis B, an infectious virus that causes inflammation of the liver and can lead to chronic illness, including cancer, or to death.

Four months later, a maintenance employee at the Admirals Walk Condominium Association (Admirals Walk), an apartment complex bordering the Hudson River in Edgewater, New Jersey, noticed a plastic bag full of blood vials wedged into the rocks of the river bulkhead. Edgewater Police Officers eventually collected at least one hundred vials floating loosely in the river or packed in containers wedged into the bulkhead. Fifty-five of these vials were tested for disease and at least five were found to be infected with hepatitis B.

State investigators traced the vials by the identifying information on their labels to Plaza Health Laboratories, a facility that tests blood for disease and other medical conditions in Brooklyn, New York. The defendant, Geronimo Villegas, was co-owner of Plaza and lived at the Admirals Walk complex when the vials were found. When questioned by state investigators, Mr. Villegas admitted to placing vials in the bulkhead in June, 1988 to make room in his laboratory for incoming blood samples.

Although he did not admit to hiding vials there on an earlier occasion, expert evidence on tides and currents established that the vials found in Staten Island could also have originated from the Admirals Walk bulkhead.

* * * This case involves difficult questions of statutory construction that arise primarily from the effort of the United States Attorney to apply the Clean Water Act to circumstances that Congress may not have specifically contemplated when it enacted this statute.

* * *

Under the Clean Water Act's knowing endangerment provision, a person acts with the requisite degree of knowledge if he possesses "actual awareness" or an "actual belief" that he is placing another person in imminent danger.

* * * [T]he language of 33 U.S.C. § 1319(c)(3) * * * provides for an enhanced sentence only where "at [the] time" the defendant discharges a pollutant into navigable waters he "knows . . . that he thereby places another person in imminent danger of death or serious bodily injury."

These words imply that the discharge must actually place another person in imminent danger of death or serious bodily injury and not merely that such result be a "potential" consequence of the defendant's act. Indeed, unless so read, the word "imminent" has no meaning at all. Cases have held that the phrase "imminent danger" does not mean immediate danger. Because the word danger means risk or peril, the phrase "imminent danger" must connote something more than the mere possibility or risk that death or serious bodily injury is a foreseeable consequence of a discharge. Thus, at the very least, "imminent danger" must mean danger that is a highly probable consequence of a discharge. It is this particular level of danger that the defendant must have known existed when he discharged the blood vials into the Hudson River.

* * *

This evidence is sufficient to support a jury finding that the defendant acted with knowledge of the dangers of hepatitis, and that some of the discharged vials contained hepatitis-infected blood. The evidence, however, does not support the conclusion that when he placed the vials in the Hudson River, Mr. Villegas knew there was a high probability that he was thereby placing another person in imminent danger of death or serious bodily injury. Of particular significance is the testimony of Dr. Alfred M. Prince, an expert in virology called by the United States Attorney. Dr. Prince suggested that the principal risk of hepatitis infection as a result of exposure to a vial of contaminated blood would arise "[i]f that vial is broken and if a piece of broken glass were to penetrate the skin . . ." While Dr. Prince testified that the likelihood of contamination in those circumstances was "very high," he also testified that the risk of this happening was "low":

The Court: Doctor, if three or four or five vials like—of the kinds we have been talking about were dropped in the Hudson River, would you say that that would place any person in imminent danger of death or serious bodily injury?

Dr. Prince: If those vials were to land on the shore and someone were to step on them and puncture their skin, they would be in danger of infection, hepatitis B, yes. Those vials that were infected, of course. They all were not.

The Court: Of course, one would have to know that that was going to happen. Or sooner or later everything floats to shore?

Dr. Prince: The risk of this happening is low but it is a risk.

This testimony was elicited outside the presence of the jury, and the defendant's trial counsel declined an invitation to have it repeated to the jury.[6] Nevertheless, the testimony does suggest the need for caution in inferring that the defendant must have known that he was placing another person in imminent danger of death or serious bodily injury merely because he knew that the vials contained a dangerous virus. Yet this is essentially the theory underlying the prosecution's case. The Assistant United States Attorneys trying the case argued that "from the evidence regarding the currents and tides the jury could infer that the defendant knew or should have known that the—anything thrown into [the] waters would be swept out into the sea and eventually be lodged on a beach," and that the defendant "knew that people walked on the rocks [at] Edgewater." Consequently, they argued, the defendant should have been aware of the risk to those who walk along Hudson River beaches or climb on the Admirals Walk bulkhead.

There was, however, no evidence introduced at trial showing that the defendant knew "that people walked on the rocks [at] Edgewater" where the vials were hidden, or that such activity even occurs. Moreover, there was no evidence introduced that showed the defendant's knowledge of the tides and, specifically, that the vials would be swept out into the sea and eventually wash ashore in an area where they could cause the kind of injury Dr. Prince described. Indeed, if Dr. Prince, an expert in virology who has a more sophisticated understanding of these matters than Mr. Villegas, viewed the danger of such serious bodily injury or death as remote, it is hard to know what Mr. Villegas should have known it to be highly probable or even likely.

There is no doubt that the defendant's conduct was irresponsible and that it had the potential to cause serious bodily injury. These factors may provide a basis for an upward adjustment of the guideline range applicable to the offense of discharging pollutants into the water. The evidence, however, is insufficient to justify the enhanced penalties provided for cases where a polluter knows that there is a high probability

---

6. Wayne Pizzuti, another prosecution expert, testified in the presence of the jury that it was also unlikely that a person swimming in the area where a vial had broken would contract hepatitis B. Trial Tr. at 356.

that he is placing another person in imminent danger of death or serious bodily injury.

Notes

Compare the "knowingly" mens rea of *Weitzenhoff* (aware of one's conduct, not necessarily aware that one's conduct violated the law) with the "knowingly endanger" mens rea of *Villegas* (actual awareness that one is placing a person in imminent danger). What is the difference? Are the different mens rea standards appropriate?

B. CRIMINAL LIABILITY FOR INDIVIDUALS

In recent years, the EPA has concentrated its investigative efforts on prosecuting more individuals who work within organizations. The rationale for this is deterrence. As Professor Brickey explained:

"In the context of regulatory crimes, the threat of criminal penalties provides the business community strong incentives to comply with the law. That is particularly true with respect to corporate officials, who belong to a social group that is exquisitely sensitive to status deprivation and censure. Stated differently, jail time is one cost of business that cannot be passed on to the consumer."[r]

The following case reveals how the environmental statutes, and the way they have been interpreted by courts, enable this.

UNITED STATES v. CARR
United States Court of Appeals, Second Circuit (1989).
880 F.2d 1550.

PIERCE, CIRCUIT JUDGE.

Appellant David James Carr appeals from a judgment of the United States District Court for the Northern District of New York (Munson, J.), convicting him under section 103 of the Comprehensive Environmental Response, Compensation and Liability Act of 1980 (CERCLA), 42 U.S.C. § 9603 (1982 & Supp. IV 1986). Under section 103, it is a crime for any person "in charge of a facility" from which a prohibited amount of hazardous substance is released to fail to report such a release to the appropriate federal agency. Appellant, a supervisor of maintenance at Fort Drum, New York, directed a work crew to dispose of waste cans of paint in an improper manner, and failed to report the release of the hazardous substances—the paint—to the appropriate federal agency. At appellant's trial, the district court instructed the jury that appellant could be found to have been "in charge" of the facility so long as he had any supervisory control over the facility.

---

r. Kathleen F. Brickey, *Environmental Crime at the Crossroads: The Intersection of Environmental and Criminal Law Theory,* 71 TULANE L. REV. 487, 506 (1997) [internal quotation marks and citations omitted].

Appellant contends on appeal that this instruction was erroneous because (1) it extended the statutory reporting requirement to a relatively low-level employee, and (2) it allowed the jury to find that appellant was "in charge" so long as he exercised any control over the dumping. For the reasons stated below, we hold that the statutory reporting requirements were properly applied to appellant. We also hold that the jury instruction challenged on appeal, viewed as a whole, was not erroneous.

Appellant was a civilian employee at Fort Drum, an Army camp located in Watertown, New York. As a civilian employee at a military installation, he was supervised by Army officers. His position was that of maintenance foreman on the Fort's firing range, and as part of his duties he assigned other civilian workers to various chores on the range. In May 1986, he directed several workers to dispose of old cans of waste paint in a small, man-made pit on the range; at that time, the pit had filled with water, creating a pond. On Carr's instructions, the workers filled a truck with a load of cans and drove to the pit. They backed the truck up to the water, and then began tossing cans of paint into the pond. After the workers had thrown in fifty or so cans, however, they saw that paint was leaking from the cans into the water, so they decided instead to stack the remaining cans of paint against a nearby target shed. At the end of the day, the workers told Carr of the cans leaking into the pond, and warned him that they thought that dumping the cans into the pond was illegal. Two truckloads of paint cans remained to be moved the next day, so Carr told the workers to place those cans alongside the target shed.

Approximately two weeks later, Carr directed one of the workers to cover up the paint cans in the pond by using a tractor to dump earth into the pit. Another worker, however, subsequently triggered an investigation by reporting the disposal of the cans to his brother-in-law, a special agent with the Department of Defense. A 43–count indictment was returned against appellant, charging him with various violations of federal environmental laws. The indictment included charges under the Resource Conservation and Recovery Act of 1976, 42 U.S.C. § 6928(d)(2)(A), 18 U.S.C. § 2 (Counts 1–4), the CERCLA charges here at issue (Counts 5–6), and multiple charges under the Clean Water Act of 1977, 33 U.S.C. §§ 1311(a), 1319(c)(1), 18 U.S.C. § 2 (Counts 7–43). Appellant pleaded not guilty, and a 6–day trial before a jury began on October 3, 1988.

After the government had presented its evidence, it filed with the court various proposed jury instructions, including one regarding the definition of the term "in charge." Over appellant's objection, the district court gave the government's proposed instruction to the jury, essentially unchanged, as follows:

There has been testimony that the waste paint was released from a truck assigned to the workers by the Defendant David Carr. The truck, individually, and the area of the disposal constitute facilities within the meaning of [CERCLA]. So long as the Defendant had supervisory control or was otherwise in charge of the truck or the area in question, he is responsible under this law. The Defendant is not, however, required to be the sole person in charge of the area or the vehicle. If you find that he had any authority over either the vehicle or the area, this is sufficient, regardless of whether others also exercised control.

The jury acquitted appellant of all charges except Counts 5 and 6, the CERCLA charges. The district court imposed a suspended sentence of one year's imprisonment, and sentenced appellant to one year of probation. This appeal followed.

* * *

Appellant raises two claims on this appeal, both of which arise out of the district court's instruction quoted above. The first claim turns on the meaning of the statutory term "in charge." Under section 103, only those who are "in charge" of a facility must report a hazardous release. There is, however, no definition of the term "in charge" within CERCLA. Appellant argues that the district court's instruction was erroneous because Congress never intended to extend the statute's reporting requirement to those, like Carr, who are relatively low in an organization's chain of command.

Our analysis of appellant's claim requires a review of the statute and its legislative history. The language of the statute itself sheds little light on the meaning of the term "in charge." Section 103 of CERCLA states only that:

> Any person in charge of a vessel or an offshore or an onshore facility shall, as soon as he has knowledge of any release (other than a federally permitted release) of a hazardous substance from such vessel or facility in quantities equal to or greater than those determined pursuant to [42 U.S.C. 9602], immediately notify the National Response Center established under the Clean Water Act [33 U.S.C. 1251 et seq.] of such release. * * *

* * * When CERCLA was enacted in late 1980, Congress sought to address the problem of hazardous pollution by creating a comprehensive and uniform system of notification, emergency governmental response, enforcement, and liability. The reporting requirements established by section 103 were an important part of that effort, for they ensure that the government, once timely notified, will be able to move quickly to check the spread of a hazardous release * * *.

The legislative history of CERCLA makes clear that Congress modeled the reporting requirements of section 103 on section 311 of the Clean Water Act, 33 U.S.C. § 1321(b)(5) * * *.

The legislative history of section 311 bears out appellant's argument that CERCLA's reporting requirements should not be extended to all employees involved in a release. "The term 'person in charge' [was] deliberately designed to cover only supervisory personnel who have the responsibility for the particular vessel or facility and not to include other employees." H.R.Conf.Rep. No. 940, 91st Cong., 2d Sess. 34 (1970), *reprinted* in 1970 U.S. Code Cong. & Admin. News 2691, 2712, 2719. Indeed, as the Fifth Circuit has stated, "to the extent that legislative history does shed light on the meaning of 'persons in charge,' it suggests at the very most that Congress intended the provisions of [section 311] to extend, not to every person who might have knowledge of [a release] (mere employees, for example), but only to persons who occupy positions of responsibility and power." United States v. Mobil Oil Corp., 464 F.2d 1124, 1128 (5th Cir.1972).

That is not to say, however, that section 311 of the Clean Water Act—and section 103 of CERCLA—do not reach lower-level supervisory employees. The reporting requirements of the two statutes do not apply only to owners and operators, but instead extend to any person who is "responsible for the operation" of a facility from which there is a release, Apex Oil Co. v. United States, 530 F.2d 1291, 1294 (8th Cir.1976). As the Fifth Circuit noted in *Mobil Oil*, imposing liability on those "responsible" for a facility is fully consistent with Congress' purpose in enacting the reporting requirements. Those in charge of an offending facility can make timely discovery of a release, direct the activities that result in the pollution, and have the capacity to prevent and abate the environmental damage. *See Mobil Oil*, 464 F.2d at 1127.

Appellant's claim that he does not come within the reporting requirements of section 103 fails because we believe Congress intended the reporting requirements of CERCLA's section 103 to reach a person—even if of relatively low rank—who, because he was in charge of a facility, was in a position to detect, prevent, and abate a release of hazardous substances. Appellant's more restrictive interpretation of the statute would only "frustrate congressional purpose by exempting from the operation of the [statute] a large class of persons who are uniquely qualified to assume the burden imposed by it." *Mobil Oil*, 464 F.2d at 1127.

Notes

Was the decision by the *Carr* court necessary to prevent circumvention of CERCLA? Does CERCLA, as interpreted in *Carr*, go too far in imposing criminal liability? Is there a way to prevent circumvention of CERCLA without imposing criminal liability on individuals such as Carr?

In the next case, the court addresses the knowledge element in the context of a large organization.

UNITED STATES v. MacDONALD & WATSON WASTE OIL COMPANY

United States Court of Appeals, First Circuit, 1991.
933 F.2d 35.

CAMPBELL, CIRCUIT JUDGE.

This appeal concerns the criminal liability of individuals and corporations under hazardous waste disposal laws.

Following a jury trial in the district court, appellants were convicted, inter alia, of having violated criminal provisions of the Resource Conservation and Recovery Act ("RCRA"), 42 U.S.C. § 6901 et seq. and the Comprehensive Environmental Response, Compensation and Liability Act ("CERCLA"), 42 U.S.C. § 9603(b).

The indictment originally contained 53 counts. By September 11, 1989, when the trial began, 16 counts had been dismissed and eight severed; and, during trial 12 more counts were dismissed on the government's motion, leaving 17 for submission to the jury. The submitted counts all related to the transportation and disposal of toluene waste from the Master Chemical Company. Appellants were convicted on all 17 counts, as follows:

MacDonald & Watson Waste Oil Co. ("MacDonald & Watson"), Faust Ritarossi, Frances Slade and Eugene K. D'Allesandro were convicted, on two counts each, of knowingly transporting and causing the transportation of hazardous waste, namely toluene and soil contaminated with toluene, to a facility which did not have a permit, in violation of RCRA, § 3008(d)(1), 42 U.S.C. § 6928(d)(1).

MacDonald & Watson and Narragansett Improvement Co. ("NIC") were convicted of knowingly treating, storing and disposing of hazardous waste, namely toluene and soil contaminated with toluene, without a permit, in violation of RCRA, § 3008(d)(2)(A), 42 U.S.C. § 6928(d)(2)(A).

MacDonald & Watson and NIC were convicted of failing to report the release of a hazardous substance into the environment in violation of CERCLA, § 103(b)(3), 42 U.S.C. § 9603(b)(3).

MacDonald & Watson was convicted of making false statements in violation of 18 U.S.C. § 1001 and of mail fraud in violation of 18 U.S.C. § 1341.

* * *

Located in Boston, Massachusetts, Master Chemical Company manufactured chemicals primarily for use in the shoe industry. Master Chemical had been owned by the Estate of Moses Weinman (hereinafter "the Estate"), which was the principal in transactions with appellants. Among the chemicals Master Chemical used was toluene, which it stored in a two thousand gallon underground storage tank. When Master Chemical personnel discovered in the late fall or early winter of 1982 that water was entering the tank and contaminating the toluene, the tank was emptied and its use discontinued. In 1984, Master Chemical Company was sold, and the toluene tank was excavated and removed. A Master Chemical employee testified that he found a small hole in the tank, and that the soil surrounding the tank appeared black and wet and smelled of toluene.

An environmental consulting firm, Goldberg–Zoino & Associates, Inc. ("GZA"), was retained to assist in the cleanup. GZA prepared a study of the site and solicited a bid from MacDonald & Watson for the excavation, transportation, and disposal of the toluene-contaminated soil. MacDonald & Watson, a company with offices in Johnstown, Rhode Island, was in the business of transporting and disposing of waste oils and contaminated soil. MacDonald & Watson operated a disposal facility on land in Providence, Rhode Island, known as the "Poe Street Lot," leased from appellant NIC. MacDonald & Watson operated the Poe Street Lot under NIC's Rhode Island RCRA permit, which authorized the disposal at the lot of liquid hazardous wastes and soils contaminated with non-hazardous wastes such as petroleum products. Neither NIC nor MacDonald & Watson held a RCRA permit authorizing them to dispose of solid hazardous wastes such as toluene-contaminated soil at the lot. At the Rhode Island administrative hearing held when NIC sought its permit, appellant D'Allesandro, president of MacDonald & Watson, testified that hazardous waste operations at the Poe Street Lot would be managed by MacDonald & Watson and that he would be the manager of the facility there. According to the terms of NIC's lease of the Poe Street Lot to MacDonald & Watson, NIC retained responsibility for compliance with state and federal law with respect to permitting and operating the hazardous waste treatment and storage facilities.

The Estate accepted MacDonald & Watson's bid to remove and clean up the contaminated soil. The Estate's attorney, Deborah Shadd, discussed the proposed arrangement with appellant Slade, MacDonald & Watson's employee, and sent Slade a contract under which MacDonald & Watson would remove "contaminated soil and toluene." Shadd asked Slade to review the contract. Shadd also asked Slade to have it signed for MacDonald & Watson, which she did. Thereafter, appellant Ritarossi, another employee of MacDonald & Watson, supervised the transportation of the toluene-contaminated soil from Master Chemical to the Poe Street Lot in nine 25–yard dump truck loads and one 20–yard load. A Massachusetts hazardous waste manifest accompanied each truckload, bearing the Massachusetts hazardous waste code M–001.[2] Four of the manifests bore Ritarossi's signature. Prior to acceptance of the waste at the Poe Street Lot, MacDonald & Watson employees received an "Authorization to Accept Shipment of Spill Cleanup Material" form bearing Slade's typed name, describing the spilled material as "toluene," and

2. "M–001" is a Massachusetts code designating waste oil, which is considered hazardous under Massachusetts law but not under RCRA or Rhode Island law. Mass. Regs.Code tit. 310, § 30.131 (1986) (Hazardous Waste from Non–Specific Sources). No RCRA hazardous waste identification number was assigned to the waste.

describing the "petroleum product and the material spilled into" as "toluene and gravel." At this point, a MacDonald & Watson employee stamped the manifests "Non-hazardous in Rhode Island, Accepted for Processing at Asphalt Production Plant." Neither NIC nor MacDonald & Watson reported the disposal of the Master Chemical wastes as a release of a hazardous substance into the environment pursuant to CERCLA § 103(b)(3).

A. Sufficiency of the Evidence

Appellants argue that the evidence was insufficient to support their convictions.

* * *

Appellant Frances Slade challenges the sufficiency of the evidence to convict her under § 3008(d)(1) of RCRA, which penalizes, "Any person who ... (1) *knowingly* transports or causes to be transported any hazardous waste identified or listed under this subchapter to a facility which does not have a permit under this subchapter.... ". (Emphasis supplied). She contends that the evidence was insufficient to prove that her actions on behalf of MacDonald & Watson were taken with knowledge that the material involved was a RCRA hazardous waste. She complains that the prosecution relied "exclusively" on the testimony of the Estate's lawyer, Deborah Shadd, who dealt with Slade and sent her the contract covering transportation and disposal of the Master Chemical waste. This evidence, Slade contends, does not establish that Slade actually reviewed the contract and specifications, or would have learned from these the specific nature of the contaminated soil. Further, she argues that neither the contract nor the attached specifications identified the contaminating substance as commercially pure toluene.

We disagree that the evidence was insufficient for the jury to infer Slade's knowledge concerning soil contaminated with commercial chemical product toluene, the hazardous waste charged. There was testimony from a former MacDonald & Watson employee that Slade was "in charge of material coming in and coming out of MacDonald & Watson to Narragansett Improvement." There was evidence that Slade had attended state compliance inspections. The jury could infer that she was knowledgeable as to what substances were allowed, and what were disallowed under NIC's permit. It could also infer from her responsibilities and her dealings with Deborah Shadd that she reviewed the contract and specifications Shadd sent to her, and learned therefrom the nature of the substance. Attorney Shadd's May 29, 1986, letter of transmission to Slade requested her to "review the enclosed agreement, particularly the first four pages," and then arrange for it to be signed before a Notary Public by an authorized representative of MacDonald & Watson. Shadd's letter to Slade also requested her to send copies of MacDonald & Watson's licenses to transport and dispose of hazardous waste, further indicating that hazardous waste was involved and that the question of legality and a proper permit was critical. The first page of the enclosed agreement recited that the contractor "agrees to remove and dispose of contaminated soil and toluene," and would do so "in accordance with all applicable federal, state, and local laws, regulations, and requirements." The specifications attached stated that soil "contaminated with toluene and lesser amounts of other volatile organic compounds has been identified ... at the site of a formerly existing 2,000 gallon underground storage tank used *for the storage of toluene*." (Emphasis supplied.) Clearly, Slade was on notice that more than a mere petroleum by-product was involved. The specifications also conditioned disposal of the contaminated soil at MacDonald & Watson's facility upon soil characteristics meeting "criteria for disposal at this facility." The jury could reasonably infer that Slade received Shadd's letter and the enclosed contract, and followed Shadd's directions, including her directions to review it, especially since the contract was thereafter executed by the firm's controller, Naples, who returned it to Shadd. We find the evidence sufficient, therefore, for the jury to have inferred that Slade knew the material was the hazardous waste in question.[4]

* * *

D'Allesandro and NIC contend that the evidence was insufficient to support their convictions. D'Allesandro was the manager and principal of MacDonald & Watson. There was evidence that he participated actively in the firm's day-to-day management, and that he had been warned on other occasions that his company had disposed of toluene-contaminated soil and that this was illegal. There was no direct evidence, however, of his knowledge of the particular shipments at issue. Since we vacate his conviction because of fundamental defects in the court's jury instructions, *see infra*, we do not reach the question of evidentiary sufficiency in his case.

NIC contends that the evidence was insufficient to support its conviction for the crimes of its purported agents. "A corporation may be convicted for the criminal acts of its agents, under a theory of respondeat superior ... where the agent is acting within the scope of employment." [5][citations omitted] NIC denies that either D'Allesandro or two

---

4. Slade also contends that the evidence was insufficient to prove that she caused the transportation of the material under 42 U.S.C. § 6928(d)(1). Based on her position of responsibility with MacDonald & Watson (in particular her being, as testified, in charge of material coming into the NIC facility), and the fact that the contract she reviewed and handled with Master Chemical called for MacDonald & Watson to remove and dispose of contaminated soil and toluene from the original site to the MacDonald & Watson facility, the jury could reasonably conclude that Slade's role in negotiating, reviewing and facilitating the contract on behalf of MacDonald & Watson directly assisted in causing the transportation of the material. Additionally, Slade's

typed name appeared on documents in connection with the shipment and delivery.

5. The district court's instructions on corporate liability were as follows:

Two of the Defendants as you know, are corporations. A corporation is a separate entity and it may be guilty of a criminal offense. A corporation, of course, cannot act for itself. It functions through officers, employees and agents. Accordingly, a corporation is chargeable with knowledge of any facts known to its officers, employees and agents and it's responsible for the actions or inactions of those officers, employees and agents at least to the extent that such knowledge, actions or inactions relate to the conduct of the corporation's business. A person need not

other MacDonald & Watson clerical employees, Giagio Cefala and Brenda Santaniello, were NIC's agents for purposes of imposing criminal liability. We do not reach this question, however, since even assuming all or some of these three MacDonald & Watson employees were agents of NIC, NIC's convictions cannot stand given our determination that D'Allesandro, one of the three, was improperly convicted. We are unable to tell what part the finding of D'Allesandro's guilt played in the jury's determination of NIC's guilt. It is at least conceivable that, without finding D'Allesandro guilty, the jury would have acquitted NIC. Further, while the government proffered evidence that Santaniello signed the name of NIC's president to the waste manifests for the Master Chemical project and received the Authorization to Accept Shipment, the government's evidence of Santaniello's involvement in all elements of the crimes charged to NIC under RCRA, 42 U.S.C. § 6928(d)(2)(A) and CERCLA, 42 U.S.C. § 9603(b)(3) was slight. Indeed, the government did not contend that Santaniello, a clerical employee, was "in charge" of the facility within the meaning of the CERCLA provision. *See* United States v. Carr, 880 F.2d 1550, 1554 (2d Cir.1989) (term "person in charge" does not extend to every person who might have knowledge of release, but only to supervisory personnel who occupy positions of responsibility and power). In any case, given our uncertainty as to D'Allesandro's role in NIC's convictions, they must be vacated.

* * *

D.   The Responsible Corporate Office Doctrine

D'Allesandro, the President and owner of MacDonald & Watson, contends that his conviction under RCRA, § 3008(d)(1), 42 U.S.C. § 6928(d)(1), must be vacated because the district court incorrectly charged the jury regarding the element of knowledge in the case of a corporate officer. Section 3008(d)(1) penalizes "Any person who.... (1) *knowingly* transports or causes to be transported any hazardous waste identified or listed under this subchapter.... to a facility which does not have a permit..... ". (Emphasis supplied.) In his closing, the prosecutor conceded that the government had "no direct evidence that Eugene D'Allesandro actually knew that the Master Chemical shipments were coming in," i.e., were being transported to the Poe Street Lot under contract with his company. The prosecution did present evidence, however, that D'Allesandro was not only the President and owner of Mac-Donald & Watson but was a "hands-on" manager of that relatively small firm. There was also proof that that firm leased the Poe Street Lot from NIC, and managed it, and that D'Allesandro's subordinates had contracted for and transported the Master Chemical waste for disposal at that site. The government argued that D'Allesandro was guilty of violating § 3008(d)(1) because, as the responsible corporate officer, he was in a

be an employee of a corporation to be its agent. Anyone authorized to act for the corporation is its agent with respect to matters of the type for which such authority is given. Consequently, a corporation is liable for the acts of its agents as long as those acts are within the scope of the authority given to that agent.

position to ensure compliance with RCRA and had failed to do so even after being warned by a consultant on two earlier occasions that other shipments of toluene-contaminated soil had been received from other customers, and that such material violated NIC's permit. In the government's view, any failure to prove D'Allesandro's actual knowledge of the Master Chemical contract and shipments was irrelevant to his criminal responsibility under § 3008(d)(1) for those shipments.

The court apparently accepted the government's theory. It instructed the jury as follows:

> When an individual Defendant is also a corporate officer, the Government may prove that individual's knowledge in either of two ways. The first way is to demonstrate that the Defendant had actual knowledge of the act in question. The second way is to establish that the defendant was what is called a responsible officer of the corporation committing the act. In order to prove that a person is a responsible corporate officer three things must be shown.

> First, it must be shown that the person is an officer of the corporation, not merely an employee.

> Second, it must be shown that the officer had direct responsibility for the activities that are alleged to be illegal. Simply being an officer or even the president of a corporation is not enough. The Government must prove that the person had a responsibility to supervise the activities in question.

> And the third requirement is that the officer must have known or believed that the illegal activity of the type alleged occurred.

The court's phrasing of the third element at first glance seems ambiguous: it could be read to require actual knowledge of the Master Chemical shipments themselves. We are satisfied, however, that the court meant only what it literally said: D'Allesandro must have known or believed that illegal shipments *of the type* alleged had previously occurred. This tied into evidence that D'Allesandro had been advised of two earlier shipments of toluene-contaminated waste, and was told that such waste could not legally be received. For the court to require a finding that D'Allesandro knew of the alleged shipments themselves (i.e., the Master Chemical shipments), would have duplicated the court's earlier instruction on actual knowledge, and was not in accord with the government's theory.[13]

D'Allesandro challenges this instruction, contending that the use of the "responsible corporate officer" doctrine is improper under

---

13. Thus the prosecutor said, in his closing, "We can concede, Ladies and Gentlemen, that we have no direct evidence Eugene D'Allesandro ... actually knew that the Master Chemical shipments were coming in. But there is another way the Government can show that Eugene D'Allesandro was responsible for these shipments.

The court will tell you what the law is but listen for the court's instruction that a corporate officer who is in a position in a company to insure that these types of actions don't occur and who knew that the company was engaged in such types of activities and did nothing to stop it can be held responsible for these actions."

§ 3008(d)(1) which expressly calls for proof of knowledge, i.e., requires *scienter*. The government responds that the district court properly adapted the responsible corporate officer doctrine traditionally applied to strict liability offenses to this case, instructing the jury to find knowledge "that the illegal activity of the *type alleged* occurred,"—a finding that, together with the first two, made it reasonable to infer knowledge of the particular violation. We agree with D'Allesandro that the jury instructions improperly allowed the jury to find him guilty without finding he had actual knowledge of the alleged transportation of hazardous waste on July 30 and 31, 1986, from Master Chemical Company, Boston, Massachusetts, to NIC's site, knowledge being an element the statute requires. We must, therefore, vacate his conviction.

The seminal cases regarding the responsible corporate officer doctrine are United States v. Dotterweich, 320 U.S. 277 (1943), and United States v. Park, 421 U.S. 658 (1975). These cases concerned misdemeanor charges under the Federal Food, Drug, and Cosmetic Act, 52 Stat. 1040, 21 U.S.C. §§ 301–392, as amended, relating to the handling or shipping of adulterated or misbranded drugs or food. The offenses alleged in the informations failed to state a knowledge element, and the Court found that they, in fact, dispensed with a *scienter* requirement, placing "the burden of acting at hazard upon a person otherwise innocent but standing in responsible relation to a public danger." *Dotterweich*, 320 U.S. at 277, 64 S.Ct. at 135. The Court in *Park* clarified that corporate officer liability in that situation requires only a finding that the officer had "authority with respect to the conditions that formed the basis of the alleged violations." But while *Dotterweich* and *Park* thus reflect what is now clear and well-established law in respect to public welfare statutes and regulations lacking an express knowledge or other *scienter* requirement, we know of no precedent for failing to give effect to a knowledge requirement that Congress has expressly included in a criminal statute. Especially is that so where, as here, the crime is a felony carrying possible imprisonment of five years and, for a second offense, ten.

The district court, nonetheless, applied here a form of the responsible corporate officer doctrine established in *Dotterweich* and *Park* for *strict liability* misdemeanors, as a substitute means for proving the explicit knowledge element of this RCRA felony, 42 U.S.C. § 6928(d)(1). As an alternative to finding actual knowledge, the district court permitted the prosecution to constructively establish defendant's knowledge if the jury found the following: (1) that the defendant was a corporate officer; (2) with responsibility to supervise the allegedly illegal activities; and (3) knew or believed "that the illegal activity of the type alleged occurred." As previously stated, the third element did not necessitate proof of knowledge of the Master Chemical shipments charged in the indictment, but simply proof of earlier occasions when D'Allesandro was told his firm had improperly accepted toluene-contaminated soil.

Contrary to the government's assertions, this instruction did more than simply permit the jury, if it wished, to infer knowledge of the Master Chemical shipments from relevant circumstantial evidence including D'Allesandro's responsibilities and activities as a corporate executive. With respect to circumstantial evidence, the district court properly instructed elsewhere that knowledge did not have to be proven by direct evidence but could be inferred from the defendant's conduct and other facts and circumstances. The court also instructed that the element of knowledge could be satisfied by proof of willful blindness.[15] These instructions allowed the jury to consider whether relevant circumstantial evidence established that D'Allesandro actually knew of the charged Master Chemical shipments. These would have sufficed had it merely been the court's purpose to point out that knowledge could be established by circumstantial evidence, although the court could, had it wished, have elaborated on the extent to which D'Allesandro's responsibilities and duties might lead to a reasonable inference that he knew of the Master Chemical transaction.

Instead, the district court charged, in effect, that proof that D'Allesandro was a responsible corporate officer would conclusively prove the element of his knowledge of the Master Chemical shipments. The jury was told that knowledge could be proven "in either of two ways." Besides demonstrating actual knowledge, the government could simply establish the defendant was a responsible corporate officer—the latter by showing three things, none of which, individually or collectively, necessarily established his actual knowledge of the illegal transportation charged. Under the district court's instruction, the jury's belief that the responsible corporate officer lacked actual knowledge of, and had not willfully blinded himself to, the criminal transportation alleged would be insufficient for acquittal so long as the officer knew or even erroneously believed that illegal activity of the same type had occurred on another occasion.

We have found no case, and the government cites none, where a jury was instructed that the defendant could be convicted of a federal crime *expressly requiring knowledge as an element*, solely by reason of a conclusive, or "mandatory" presumption of knowledge of the facts constituting the offense. [citations omitted]

* * *

15. The court instructed the jury generally regarding the element of knowledge as follows:

An act is said to be done knowingly if it is done voluntarily and intentionally and not because of ignorance, mistake, accident or some other reason. The requirement that an act be done knowingly is designed to insure that a Defendant will not be convicted for an act that he did not intend to commit or the nature of which he did not understand.

Proof that a Defendant acted knowingly or with knowledge of a particular fact does not require direct evidence of what was in that Defendant's mind. Whether a Defendant acted knowingly or with knowledge of a particular fact may be inferred from that Defendant's conduct, from that Defendant's familiarity with the subject matter in question or from all of the other facts and circumstances connected with the case.

In determining whether a Defendant acted knowingly, you also may consider whether the Defendant deliberately closed his eyes to what otherwise would have been obvious. If so, the element of knowledge may be satisfied because a Defendant cannot avoid responsibility by purposefully avoiding learning the truth. However, mere negligence or mistake in not learning the facts is not sufficient to satisfy the element of knowledge.

We agree with the decisions discussed above that knowledge may be inferred from circumstantial evidence, including position and responsibility of defendants such as corporate officers, as well as information provided to those defendants on prior occasions. Further, willful blindness to the facts constituting the offense may be sufficient to establish knowledge. However, the district court erred by instructing the jury that proof that a defendant was a responsible corporate officer, as described, would suffice to conclusively establish the element of knowledge expressly required under § 3008(d)(1). Simply because a responsible corporate officer believed that on a prior occasion illegal transportation occurred, he did not necessarily possess knowledge of the violation charged. In a crime having knowledge as an express element, a mere showing of official responsibility under *Dotterweich* and *Park* is not an adequate substitute for direct or circumstantial proof of knowledge.

* * *

In sum, we affirm the convictions of Faust Ritarossi, Francis Slade and MacDonald & Watson. We vacate the convictions of Eugene D'Allesandro and of NIC and remand for a new trial or such other action as may be consistent herewith.

So ordered.

Notes

1. Did you agree with the court's distinction of *Park* and *Dotterweich*? Would you have reversed the convictions of D'Allesandro and NIC?

2. Note the argument made by the attorney, Frances Slade: I did not know what I was signing and I did not review pertinent contract and specifications. What do you think about this defense?

C. PARALLEL PROCEEDINGS

As noted in Chapter 6 of the casebook, the grand jury has broad investigatory powers. In addition, unique difficulties for the white collar criminal defendant arise from the fact that civil or administrative proceedings may track the potential criminal liability. The next case discusses both of these issues in ruling on the defendant's request for a stay of grand jury proceedings.

IN RE GRAND JURY PROCEEDINGS
(U.S. STEEL—CLAIRTON WORKS)

United States Court of Appeals, Third Circuit, 1975.
525 F.2d 151.

HUNTER, CIRCUIT JUDGE.

This is an appeal from a district court's order staying all further proceedings before a federal grand jury pending a final judgment in a civil contempt action brought against the United States Steel Corporation by state and county officials in a Pennsylvania state court. Because we conclude that the district court erred in granting the stay, we vacate that stay and remand for such further proceedings as may be required consistent with this opinion.

* * *

The roots of the instant controversy are, to a great extent, found in a September 25, 1972, consent decree entered in an action by the Commonwealth of Pennsylvania and Allegheny County against United States Steel Corporation (U. S. Steel) in the Court of Common Pleas of Allegheny County [regarding] limitations on emission of particulate matter and sulfur oxides from the coke ovens of U.S. Steel's Clairton, Pennsylvania Coke works. * * *

* * *

On March 27, 1973, the Commonwealth of Pennsylvania and Allegheny County instituted a civil contempt action against U.S. Steel for failure to comply with the limitations set forth in the consent decree. In that action, U.S. Steel asserted that the limitations were technologically impossible of achievement and asked the state court to modify the September 25, 1972, consent decree by adopting new coke oven door emission standards. The state action was still pending at the time the district court entered its stay on March 6, 1975.

* * *

* * * The federal grand jury here involved was empaneled on October 22, 1974, for an 18–month term, to investigate the possible criminal violations of the Clean Air Act, 42 U.S.C. § 1857 *et seq.*, by U.S. Steel at its Clairton Works. On November 27, 1974, subpoenas duces tecum were served by the Government on sixteen employees and executives of U.S. Steel. The subpoenas directed the sixteen individuals to appear before the grand jury and ordered them to produce numerous documents relating primarily to the level of smoke emissions from the coke oven doors at the Clairton Works.

U.S. Steel produced the requested documents on January 7, 1975 but continued to resist those parts of the subpoenas that required the appearance of the U.S. Steel employees before the grand jury.

* * *

A hearing was set for February 3, 1975 by the district court on U.S. Steel's motion to "modify, limit or quash" the subpoenas or to stay the grand jury proceedings pending a final judgment in the state civil contempt action. The asserted bases for U.S. Steel's motions were that: * * *

the prior pending state proceedings were a bar to simultaneous federal enforcement of the coke oven door emission standards * * *.

The district court filed a memorandum opinion on March 6, 1975, in which the court granted U.S. Steel's motion to stay the grand jury's proceedings.

* * * After reviewing the legislative history of sections of the Clean Air Act, the court held that Congress "did not intend to authorize dualistic enforcement proceedings against polluters based upon the same violations of emission limitations which are incorporated in the same implementation plan." Thus, ruled the district court, since the Commonwealth of Pennsylvania had already instituted proceedings to enforce the coke oven door limitations at the Clairton Works, the United States was completely prohibited from continuing its investigation before the grand jury pending a final judgment in the state suit.

* * *

The district court's indefinite stay of the grand jury's proceedings has the practical effect of dismissal of the proceedings. This grand jury's term expires in April 1976. The state court action already has consumed more than two years and, due to the complexity of the issues presented, likely will continue beyond the grand jury's April 1976 expiration date. Investigation and possible prosecution of criminal violations of the Clean Air Act is effectively precluded by the district court's stay.

* * *

The special role of the grand jury in the history of Anglo–American jurisprudence has been amply documented by other courts and commentators and need not be reviewed by this court. The investigative function of the grand jury is at the foundation of effective law enforcement in the United States, and accordance of the broad powers to the grand jury in the conduct of its investigations is essential to the proper execution of its functions * * *.

Traditionally the grand jury has been accorded wide latitude to inquire into violations of criminal law. No judge presides to monitor its proceedings. It deliberates in secret and may determine alone the course of its inquiry. The grand jury may compel the production of evidence or the testimony of witnesses as it considers appropriate, and its operation generally is unrestrained by the technical procedural and evidentiary rules governing the conduct of criminal trials. "It is a grand inquest, a body with powers of investigation and inquisition, the scope of whose inquiries is not to be limited narrowly by questions of propriety or forecasts of the probable result of the investigation, or by doubts whether any particular individual will be found properly subject to an accusation of crime."

The district court's stay constituted an unwarranted encroachment upon this plenary historical authority of the grand jury * * *.

We are not unmindful of recent decisions by this court which have delineated the procedural rights of those summoned to appear before grand juries. These decisions have sought to preserve the proper balance between the grand jury's need to know and the rights of witnesses summoned before it. However, the issues raised in those cases are not now before this court. We are presented only with the narrow issue of whether the district court erred in indefinitely staying all proceedings of this grand jury with regard to its investigation of U.S. Steel's Clairton Coke Works. We conclude that it did err.

Notes

1.   If you represented U.S. Steel–Clairton Works in the civil contempt proceedings, would you advise individuals representing the corporation to take the fifth amendment during the contempt proceedings? (Recall Chapter 6: corporations have no fifth amendment right not to incriminate themselves.)

2.   Are greater problems presented by parallel proceedings for individuals who may retain a fifth amendment privilege, than for corporations or other fictional entities, that do not?

———

The next case raises the reverse problem raised in *U.S. Steel–Clairton Works*.

BARRY FARM RESIDENT COUNCIL v. UNITED STATES DEPARTMENT OF THE NAVY

United States District Court, District of Columbia, 1997.
1997 WL 118412.[s]

GREENE, DISTRICT JUDGE.

The plaintiffs, two neighborhood associations of citizens who live at the edge of the Anacostia River, and two environmental organizations, brought this action to compel the Department of the Navy and the General Services Administration to comply with the Clean Water Act and to remedy hazardous contamination of the river. The conditions sought to be remedied are said to stem from the history of manufacturing at the Washington Navy Yard. The government has moved to stay the proceedings pending the conclusion of an investigation into potential criminal violations of federal environmental laws at the same federal facility. The Court will deny the stay, largely on two grounds: first, the two federal agencies have studied the underlying problems for many years without taking action, and a stay would further delay solutions to the problem; and second, there is no reason why the civil action should pose significant problems to the progress of the criminal investigation.

* * *

The Washington Navy Yard, which became operational as a shipbuilding site in 1799, was the site of weapons manufacturing for over

———

s.   Not reported in F.Supp.

one hundred years, but it is now used primarily as a federal office complex. Studies by the Environmental Protection Agency, and the Navy and GSA themselves, have revealed contamination of soil, groundwater, and river sediment in the Anacostia River in the vicinity of the Navy Yard and the Southeast Federal Center. Indeed, both the Navy and GSA have been aware of the contaminated conditions at these sites since the late 1980s. Although the United States commendably, finally did initiate an investigation of potential criminal violations at these sites, it does not follow that civil proceedings should be stayed pending completion of this investigation.

Nothing in the Constitution or the laws requires a stay of civil proceedings pending the outcome of parallel criminal proceedings. SEC v. Dresser Indus., 628 F.2d 1368, 1375 (D.C.Cir.1980). As our Court of Appeals recognized in *Dresser*,

> The civil and regulatory laws of the United States frequently overlap with the criminal laws, creating the possibility of parallel civil and criminal proceedings, either successive or simultaneous. In the absence of substantial prejudice to the rights of the parties involved, such parallel proceedings are unobjectionable under our jurisprudence.

Id. at 1374. Moreover, "[t]he case for staying civil proceedings is 'a far weaker one' when [as here] '[n]o indictment has been returned.'" FSLIC v. Molinaro, 889 F.2d 899, 903 (9th Cir.1989).

In determining whether to stay a civil proceeding pending the outcome of a related criminal proceeding, courts customarily weigh the following factors: the interests of the plaintiffs in proceeding expeditiously with the civil litigation as balanced against the prejudice to them if it is delayed; the public interest in the pending civil and criminal litigation; the interests of and burdens on the defendant; the interest of persons not parties to the civil litigation; and the convenience of the court in the management of its cases and the efficient use of judicial resources. The Court considers first the factor of delay.

* * *

As indicated, plaintiffs are two neighborhood associations, Barry Farm Resident Council and the Kingman Park Civic Association, composed of citizens who live at the edge of the Anacostia River, and two environmental organizations, the Anacostia Watershed Society and the Friends of the Earth, dedicated to restoring the Anacostia River. Plaintiffs enjoy park lands adjacent to the river for family outings, viewing wildlife, and walking, and use the river itself for boating, kayaking, and fishing. If this civil suit is stayed pending the outcome of criminal proceedings when no indictment has as yet been filed, plaintiffs may well have to wait for a long time before they are able to enjoy the river in an uncontaminated state. Indeed they claim risks to their health and their children's health from contact with contaminated soil and water for a considerable period of time if the suit is stayed.

Numerous studies have demonstrated that the soil and groundwater at the Navy Yard and Southeast Federal Center contain hazardous substances which have serious environmental and health effects. The government argues that the Navy and GSA are voluntarily engaged in resolving the environmental problems related to the complaint and that the stay would therefore not prolong the period of time before the area is cleaned up. However, the progress of the Navy and GSA in addressing the contamination at the Navy Yard, of which they have been aware for years, has been extremely slow.

A review of the documents reveals that at least as early as September 1989 GSA was aware of PCB contamination at the Southeast Federal Center site. The GSA has completed three environmental impact statements and numerous environmental assessments of the contamination at the Southeast Federal Center site. Similarly the Navy has completed study upon study of environmental contamination at the Washington Navy Yard. For example, the Navy's 1988 Preliminary Assessment Report indicates that the Navy was aware of oil-contaminated soil and ground water. The Navy now proposes to begin a Remedial Investigation/Feasibility Study on one area of concern in Fiscal Year 1997, two additional areas of concern in Fiscal Year 1998, and the remaining five areas in "later years."

In filing this lawsuit, plaintiffs have attempted to compel the Navy and GSA to act upon their studies and actually to clean up the contaminated sites. The Court refuses to be a participant in further delay by granting defendants' motion to stay the proceedings. Based on the history of this matter, the Court is simply not convinced that the defendants will "voluntarily" address the hazardous waste situation to the same extent and in the same time period that would be required under a court order. At bottom, the grant of the stay motion will provide the Navy and GSA with yet a new excuse for not proceeding forthrightly and with diligence.

* * *

The Navy and GSA also claim that to deny the stay will prevent them from presenting an effective defense in the civil case. The harm that the Navy and GSA allegedly face is that employees at the Navy Yard with information relevant to the defense of the civil case may choose to invoke the Fifth Amendment's protection against self-incrimination, and may refuse to cooperate with government defense counsel's investigation. The two departments similarly claim to be concerned that statements made to those investigating the civil cases could be deemed "coerced statements" that violate the Fifth Amendment protection against self-incrimination, and that they, therefore, would be excluded from evidence in a later criminal proceeding.

The Court finds this entire line of argument disingenuous and farfetched. It is worth repeating that no criminal indictments have been filed as yet. The alleged harm to these non-parties (i.e., the Navy and GSA employees) and to the civil defendants is entirely speculative. If and when criminal indictments are filed, and Fifth Amendment issues arise, there will be time enough to deal with the problems they might cause.

As the defendants themselves have proposed, to avoid the possibility that a court might deem any statement made in the course of the civil investigation to be coerced, the Navy and GSA could inform its employees about the pending criminal investigation and advise them that they may exercise their privilege against self-incrimination without fear of dismissal.

Navy and GSA employees will not face an inherently coercive situation because the exercise of Fifth Amendment rights cannot lead to dismissal from employment. These circumstances are unlike those in Garrity v. State of New Jersey, 385 U.S. 493, 496 (1967), where the Supreme Court found unconstitutionally coercive a state statute mandating that a state employee who invoked the Fifth Amendment and refused to testify in a criminal proceeding about employment-related matters would automatically be terminated.

Although some employees who invoke the privilege against self-incrimination may perceive that they have identified themselves as criminally culpable, this does not rise to the level of "coercion":

> There is no violation of due process where a party is faced with the choice of testifying or invoking the Fifth Amendment.... Any witness in a civil or criminal trial who is himself under investigation or indictment is confronted with the dilemma of choosing to testify or to invoke his privilege against self-incrimination. Nevertheless, he must make the choice despite any extra legal problems and pressures that might follow.

SEC v. Grossman, 121 F.R.D. 207, 210 (S.D.N.Y.1987). Furthermore, "the extent to which Fifth Amendment rights [of Navy and GSA employees] are implicated is a significant factor for the [Court] to consider, but it is only one consideration to be weighed against others." Keating v. Office of Thrift Supervision, 45 F.3d 322, 326 (9th Cir.1995).

In similar cases, the courts have refused to stay civil proceedings pending the outcome of related criminal proceedings, finding unpersuasive defendants' arguments that the exercise of their Fifth Amendment rights would somehow prejudice them.

Defendants also argue that the civil proceedings should be stayed because potential criminal defendants could obtain more information through civil discovery than they are entitled to under the criminal rules of discovery. However, there is no need for discovery as yet as plaintiffs have filed for summary judgment on the public record. If discovery becomes necessary, the Court has the ability to impose protective orders to prevent potential future criminal defendants from obtaining information to which they are not entitled. A concern with an abuse of liberal civil discovery arises if a criminal defendant later initiates a civil suit in a "tactical maneuver to enable [him] to gain advance information of the criminal case." [citations omitted] This is clearly not the situation here, where the first legal proceedings were initiated by private plaintiffs in this civil case.

The government further contends, in a similar vein, that if employees are warned that they may exercise the privilege against self-incrimination without fear of dismissal, they are confronted with the perceived unfairness of either answering questions and perhaps incriminating themselves, or exercising their Fifth Amendment rights and thereby identifying themselves as targets of the criminal investigation. Although this may indeed lower the morale of some employees, the choice between testifying or invoking the Fifth Amendment, as earlier stated, "may be unpleasant, but it is not illegal." SEC v. Grossman, 121 F.R.D. at 210.[2]

Upon consideration of the relevant factors, the Court determines that the harm plaintiffs will incur should this action be stayed and the public interest[3] in restoring the Anacostia River to a more pristine form greatly outweighs any burden on the defendants or defendants' employees. The motion for a stay of the civil proceeding will therefore be denied.

* * *

ORDERED that defendants' motion to stay these proceedings be and it is DENIED.

Notes

1. Note the irony in the above case: federal agencies which are being sued by citizens for violating federal law seek a stay of the citizens' lawsuit in federal court because of a parallel criminal investigation of the agencies by another federal agency.

2. Note the arguments presented by the Navy and GSA about the problems an ongoing civil suit will pose for them and their employees during the criminal investigation (Employees will invoke their Fifth Amendment protection against self-incrimination and refuse to talk to defense counsel. This will make it difficult to defend in the civil suit). Do you agree with the district court's dismissal of these arguments?

3. The citizens in the *Barry Farm* case sued under the "citizen suit" provisions of RCRA. This provision provides

"any person may commence a civil suit on his own behalf * * * against any person * * * who is alleged to be in violation of any permit, standard, regulation, condition, requirement, prohibition, or order which

---

2. The Court has also weighed the factor of the efficient use of judicial resources. The Court finds that it would be more efficient to proceed with the civil case than to stay it for at least six months, as the defendants have requested, and probably much longer, when the Court cannot be certain that the criminal investigation will ever result in any indictments.

3. There is a significant public interest in the enforcement of all criminal laws, including environmental laws. By contrast, the public interest in a civil lawsuit between private parties, such as a contract dispute, is usually quite small. However, there is a considerably greater public interest in a civil proceeding to compel compliance with the environmental laws. Indeed, the public interest in these civil environmental proceedings is virtually identical to the public interest in enforcement of the criminal environmental laws.

has become effective pursuant to this chapter; or * * * against any person, * * * and including any past or present generator, past or present transporter, or past or present owner or operator of a treatment, storage, or disposal facility, who has contributed or who is contributing to the past or present handling, storage, treatment, transportation, or disposal of any solid or hazardous waste which may present an imminent and substantial endangerment to health or the environment."[t]

However, "[n]o action may be commenced * * * if the Administrator or State has commenced and is diligently prosecuting a civil or criminal action in a court of the United States or a State to require compliance with such permit, standard, regulation, condition, requirement, prohibition, or order." Furthermore, no action may be commenced if the State "is actually engaging in a removal action under section 104 [of CERCLA] or has incurred costs to initiate a Remedial Investigation and Feasibility Study under [CERCLA]."[u]

t. 42 U.S.C. § 6972. u. *Id.*

Chapter 13

COMPUTER CRIME

A. INTRODUCTION

"Computer crime ... creates opportunities for modern criminals beyond anything we've previously experienced."[a]

"The Internet has opened up a whole new vista for fraud activity."[b]

The Internet is a network of more than 5,000 regional, state, federal, campus and corporate networks in the United States with links to international computer networks.[c] Utilizing telephone lines, the Internet has an estimated fifteen to twenty-five million users in ninety-two countries and is estimated to be growing at a rate of five to eight percent per month.[d]

The Internet began in 1969 at the Advanced Research Projects Agency (ARPAnet) of the United States Department of Defense (DOD) as a legacy of the cold war. It joined together computer networks and allowed communication directly between computers, without a need for transmissions to pass through a center network. Thus, if part of the government's computer system was destroyed by nuclear attack, the government could still communicate as transmissions went alternative ways to their destinations. Within twenty years, the National Science Foundation (NSF) used ARPAnet's model and created a network of five

---

a. DAVID ICOVE, ET AL., COMPUTER CRIME: A CRIMEFIGHTER'S HANDBOOK 15 (1995) [hereinafter COMPUTER CRIME]. Various definitions and categories of offenders and computer crimes are reprinted in this Introduction with permission from COMPUTER CRIME: A CRIMEFIGHTER'S HANDBOOK, Copyright © 1995, O'Reilly & Associates, Inc. For orders or information call (800) 998–9938.

b. Timothy Huber, *California: Legislature Ponders Consumer Safety Net for "Net Fraud Victims,"* 1996 WL 282954, May 24, 1996 (*quoting* Ronald A. Reiter, California Attorney General's Office.)

c. James Evans, *Cruising the Internet,* CAL. LAW., 67–71 (July, 1994).

d. Catherine Thérèse Clarke, *From CrimINet to Cyber–Perp: Toward an Inclusive Approach to Policing the Evolving Criminal Mens Rea on Internet,* 75 OR. L. REV. 191, 195–96 (1996) [hereinafter *CrimINet*]; Comment, Jo–Ann M. Adams, *Controlling Cyberspace: Applying the Computer Fraud and Abuse Act to The Internet,* 12 SANTA CLARA COMPUTER & HIGH TECH.L.J. 403, 406 (1996) [hereinafter *Controlling Cyberspace*] (Internet has over five million users in more than 65 countries and is growing at a rate of more than 10% per month.) Anne Meredith Fulton, Comment, *Cyberspace and*

regional supercomputer systems. NSF encouraged universities and research institutions to use this Internet. Initially NSF discouraged commercial traffic.[e] By the mid–1980s, however, things were beginning to change. Commercial Internet Xchange circumvented the NSF's restrictions on commercial use by leasing data circuits from telephone companies and leasing them to institutions at a fixed cost.[f]

With the advent of personal computers, the Internet has been revolutionized. Anyone can access the Internet with the purchase of a computer, modem, software, and payment of a minimal monthly fee.[g] And, the monthly fee has been dropping dramatically: "In 1987 the cost per megabyte was ten dollars. * * * By 1993 [the cost was] thirteen cents."[h]

With this growth have come changes in Internet users and uses. No longer are Internet users comprised solely of reputable and trusted academic and governmental institutions. The Internet is now a panacea for crime as well as for education, convenience and governmental functions. It is not surprising that explosive use of and access to computers leads to crime. There is, after all, a huge amount of money to be stolen by computer wizards. In fact, the computer has become the "weapon of choice" by white collar criminals.[i] In addition, the Internet affords anonymity to all users—legitimate and illegitimate. As one expert stated, "When people are free to behave in anonymous ways, you will see a rise in the anti-social behavior."[j] The anonymity available on the Internet may even increase as more businesses and financial institutions move to the Internet and seek to protect their information. Techniques such as "encryption" (encoding data so only those authorized may access it) are increasingly available for ensuring absolute security.[k] The problem, of course, is that encryption is also available to criminals who exploit such

the Internet: Who Will Be the Privacy Policy? 3 COMM. LAW CONSPECTUS 63, 63 (1995).

e. *CrimlNet, supra* note d at 194.

f. *Controlling Cyberspace, supra* note d at 406. The Internet was not viewed as a valuable communication tool. "Developer Severo Ornstein's initial reaction to DOD's request for proposals was: 'Sure we could building such a thing, but I don't see why anybody would want it." *Id.* at 407.

g. Prices in most urban areas range from $10 to 20 per month. One service in Northern California costs only $20 per year. James Evans, *Cruising the Internet*, CAL. LAWYER, at 71 (July 1994).

h. *Controlling Cyberspace, supra* note d at 407–408.

i. Glenn D. Baker, note, *Trespassers Will Be Prosecuted: Computer Crime in the 1990s.* 12 COMPUTER L.J. 61, 62 (1992) [hereinafter *Trespassers*]. In fact, "[t]he concept of a computer crime may disappear, because all business crimes will be essentially com-

puter crimes of some form." Robert W. Steward, *Police Plug Into Computer Criminals*, L.A. TIMES, June 2, 1985, at 3 (*quoting* Donn B. Parker, "one of the nation's leading expert on the subject [of computer crime.]" *Id.*)

j. Andrew Brown, *Fears Grow of a Crime Spree in Cyberspace*, THE INDEPENDENT, April 8, 1995, at 12 [hereinafter *Crime Spree*] (quoting Kent Walker, formerly District Attorney who prosecuted Kevin Mitnick, see *infra*, and current consultant on computer crime.)

k. "Data encryption is a new technology that secretly encodes computer information between parties rendering it 'scrambled' to all others not privy to the secret code." Chris J. Katopis, *Searching Cyberspace: The Fourth Amendment and Electronic Mail*, 14 TEMP. ENVTL. L. & TECH. J. 175, 203 (1995) (Discussing constitutional and policy questions raised by encryption.); Anjali Singhal, *The Piracy of Privacy? A Fourth Amendment Analysis of Key Escrow Cryptography*, 7 STAN. L. & POL'Y REV. 189 (1996). (*Id.*)

secrecy to engage in money laundering, tax evasion, even collection of ransom.[l]

Various surveys have attempted to determine the scope of computer crime. The Advanced Research Projects Agency (ARPA) at Carnegie Mellon University reported a 498% increase in computer security incidents from 1991 to 1995. During this same time period, the number of Internet hosts increased 500%, from approximately 750,000 to more than 5 million.[m] In one survey, businesses reported that from 1985–1993, their monthly rate of incidents involving the computer theft of proprietary information rose 260%.[n] A 1995 survey of 182 corporate security directors reported that 98.5% of their businesses had been victimized by computer criminals; 43.3% reported that they had been victimized more than twenty-five times![o] All experts agree that whatever the reports, computer crime is under-reported.[p]

The impact of computer attacks is potentially enormous. Our world community has seen glimpses of this. An Italian University whose computers were attacked by a virus lost almost one year's worth of AIDS research data.[q] An American hospital lost 40% of its patient records to a computer virus.[r] In 1989, Bell South's computer in Atlanta was penetrated by a hacker group known as Legion of Doom; the attack jeopardized telephone service, emergency preparedness and national security.[s] Some experts suggest that computer crime has yet to become a problem compared to what we will see in the future primarily because computer traffic, especially sales consummated on the Internet, is still relatively slow.[t]

Computer attacks range in sophistication and potential damage and not all computer attacks are crimes. Commonly recognized computer attacks include "dumpster diving,"[u] eavesdropping on "electronic ema-

---

l. *Crime Spree, supra* note j at 12.

m. Scott Charney & Kent Alexander, *Legal Issues in Cyberspace: Hazards on the Information Superhighway*, 45 EMORY L. J. 931, 935 n.9 (1996) [hereinafter *Hazards*].

n. RICHARD POWER, CURRENT AND FUTURE DANGER: A CSI PRIMER ON COMPUTER CRIME AND INFORMATION WARFARE, 1, 1–2 (1995). [hereinafter DANGER]

o. DAVID L. CARTER & ANDRA J. KATZ, A NATIONAL SURVEY ON COMPUTER–RELATED AND TECHNOLOGY CRIME 1 (Oct. 1995) (unpublished summary findings of survey, Michigan State University)

p. Under-reporting may be less of a problem in the future. Computer programs known as Computer Anomaly Detection Systems (CADS) have been developed to identify suspicious activity. "One recent test proved that for each intrusion identified by a system administrator, CADS identified over 100 more." *Hazards, supra* note m at 936.

q. Christopher Elliot, *Experts to Classify Computer Viruses*, DAILY TELEGRAPH, Mar. 10, 1996, at 2.

r. Laura DiDo, A *Menace to Society (Computer Viruses May Begin to Take Their Toll in Lives as Well as Dollars)*, NETWORK WORLD, Feb. 6, 1989, at 71, 84.

s. United States v. Riggs, 967 F.2d 561 (11th Cir.1992).

t. For example, although a lot of products are shown on the Internet, customers are directed to place telephone orders. "As such, online sales were approximately (estimated) at $350 million in 1995 while catalog sales were approximately 53 billion." Timothy Huber, *California: Legislature Ponders Consumer Safety Net for Net Fraud Victims*, WEST'S LEGAL NEWS (May 24, 1996) (1996 WL 282954).

u. "Dumpster diving" occurs when the perpetrators scavenge trash. As Icove et al explain:

"Computer facilities are especially good places for scavengers who are looking

nations,"ᵛ "masquerading,"ʷ "IP spoofing,"ˣ harassment,ʸ software piracy, "traffic analysis" of data,ᶻ "trap doors,"ᵃᵃ "session hijacking,"ᵇᵇ "tunneling,"ᶜᶜ "timing attacks,"ᵈᵈ "Trojan horses,"ᵉᵉ

around for information that might help them penetrate a system. . . . Around the offices and in the trash, crackers can find used disks and topes, discarded printouts, and handwritten notes." COMPUTER CRIME, *supra* note a at 31–32.

Another type of computer "trash" which hopeful "crackers" may seek is the files on a computer that have been deleted but not erased from the system. In most computers, even when an author deletes a file, it is not gone but can be retrieved just by running an "undelete" command. *Id.*

v. Like all electronic equipment, computers emit electronic signals. These signals can be picked up and decoded, revealing the information stored in the computer. COMPUTER CRIME, *supra* note a at 33–34.

w. "Masquerading" occurs when one person assumes the identity of another to gain access to a computer. This may be through use of the other person's password or by disguising the caller's identity, claiming to be someone who might be given access to equipment (for example, an alleged repair person) or information (when a questioner claims to be a reporter gathering information for a story). The most common type of masquerading is when one person uses the password of another. *Id.* at 36. Studies have shown how easy it is to acquire the password of another: "One Chicago consultant recently broke into dozens of local—areas files merely by using the word Bulls—the name of the city's basketball team—as a password." Gary Gaston & Charles Harris, *Minimizing the Threat of Hackers*, NAT'L L.J., Feb.3, 1997, C1 at C15.

x. "IP spoofing" is a type of masquerading. It gets its name from Internet Protocol, which is one of the protocols underlying the Internet. Some computers grant access based upon the Internet Protocol. So, an attacker forges the Internet address and gains access to the computer. This was the type of attack used by Kevin Mitnick on Tsutomu Shimomura, a computational physicist at the San Diego Supercomputer Center. COMPUTER CRIMES, *supra* note a at 49–50.

y. Sending threats of inappropriate personal or slanderous messages over the Internet to others. COMPUTER CRIME, *supra* note a at 38.

z. "Traffic analysis" of data occurs when an unauthorized person monitors the "traffic" of electronic data. For example, a number of people guessed that the United

States was about to engage in battle, before Operation Desert Storm was announced, simply by observing the unusually large number of late night calls for take out food from the White House and other governmental offices. *Id.* at 41–42.

aa. Trap doors are installed in software by the programmers to allow programmers to skip the usual steps in using a program, thus making it easier for programmers to access the program for repairs of modifications. If these "trap doors" are not properly closed or if they are penetrated, outsiders may gain access to the program. *Id.* at 42–43.

bb. "Session hijacking" occurs when an outsider waits until a computer user takes a short break then begins using the computer while the authorized user is gone. Another way of committing this same act is to "connect a covert computer terminal to a line between the authorized terminal and the computer. The criminal waits until the authorized terminal is on line but not in use, and then switches control to the covert terminal. The computer thinks it is still connected to the authorized user, and the criminal has access to the same files and data as the authorized user." *Id.* at 43.

cc. "Tunneling uses one data transfer method to carry data for another method. Tunneling is an often legitimate way to transfer data over incompatible networks, but it is illegitimate when it is used to carry unauthorized data in legitimate data packets." *Id.* at 44.

dd. Timing attacks can occur because "[o]ften computers are not capable of performing commands in the order in which they are given, especially if there are multiple users. A sophisticated programmer can intervene and interfere with data waiting to be processed or printed, change the order of data, change the user's commands, even erase data." *Id.* at 44–45.

ee. "A Trojan horse is a program that appears to perform a useful function and sometimes does so quite well but also includes an unadvertised feature, which is usually malicious in nature. Viruses and logic bombs can be hidden in Trojan horses. The code in a well-constructed Trojan horse can perform its apparent triggering condition that prompts it to let loose its armed warriors." RICHARD POWER, CURRENT AND FUTURE DANGER: A CSI PRIMER ON COMPUTER

"viruses,"[ff] "worms,[gg] a "salami attack,"[hh] "logic bombs,"[ii] "data diddling,"[jj] "password sniffing" and "superzapping."

● Reasons for Computer Crime

David Icove et al, authors of COMPUTER CRIME: A CRIMEFIGHTER'S HANDBOOK, list at least six reasons computer criminals engage in computer crime: to obtain military and intelligence information; to penetrate business competitors' secrets; to steal money or other assets; to engage in terrorist activity; to "settle" a grudge; to have "fun."[kk]

National Security. Today, "[n]ational security is increasingly in the hands of computers."[ll] The publicly known breaches of national security through computers are sobering. In 1987, members of "Chaos Computer Club" penetrated NASA's network.[mm] In 1994, a sixteen year old hacker broke into a computer at Griffith Air Force base, NASA, Goddard Space Center, the Jet Propulsion Laboratory and the Korean Atomic Research Institute.[nn]

The most incorrigible computer criminal who threatens national security may be Kevin Mitnick. In 1981, at age 17, Mitnick was convicted for stealing computer manuals from a Pacific Bell switching station. He received parole.[oo] In 1982, Mitnick broke into the North American Air Defense Command computer, seized control of three central telephone company offices in Manhattan, gained access to all phone switching centers in California, and reprogrammed one person's telephone to ask

---

CRIME AND INFORMATION WARFARE 28 (1995) [hereinafter DANGER].

ff. "Viruses are computer programs that migrate from computer to computer and attach to the computer's operating system." *Controlling Cyberspace, supra* note d at 409, n.40.

gg. "Worms are computer programs that migrate from computer to computer without attaching to the computer's operating system." *Id.* at 409 n.39.

hh. A " 'salami attack ... causes small amounts of assets to be removed from a larger pool. The stolen assets are removed one slice at a time (hence the name salami). Usually, the amount stolen each time is so small that the victim of the salami fraud never even notices." COMPUTER CRIME, *supra* note a at 47.

ii. "A typical logic bomb tells the computer to execute a set of instructions at a certain date and time or under certain specified conditions." *Id.* at 48. The instructions could be to perform an innocuous act like displaying a humorous greeting when a user logs on or to perform something far more sinister, like telling a computer to start erasing its hard drive disk. Logic bombs, unlike viruses, do not replicate themselves; they simply wait for the trig-

gering time or event. Icove et al gave the following example of a logic bomb:

"[A] programmer told the logic bomb to destroy data if the company payroll is run and his name is not on it; this is a sure-fire way to get back at the company if he is fired! The employee is fired, or may leave on his own, but does not remove the logic bomb. The next time the payroll is run and the computer searches for but doesn't find the employee's name, it crashes, destroying not only all of the employee payroll records, but the payroll application program as well." *Id.* at 48.

jj. "Data diddling," sometimes called false data entry, involves modifying data before or after it is entered into the computer. "This could occur, for example, when the amount of hours an employee allegedly worked in a pay period is modified as the data is entered into the computer." *Id.* at 48.

kk. *Id.* at 5–15.

ll. COMPUTER CRIME, *supra*, note a at 5.

mm. DANGER, *supra*, note n at 9.

nn. *Id.* at 16.

oo. *Id.* at 4.

for a coin deposit each time the phone was picked up.[pp] In 1986, Mitnick posed as a computer technician, obtained the password of an authorized user and broke into the NCSC's Dockmaster Computer.[qq] In 1988, Mitnick received a second conviction for his computer activity. Mitnick had been secretly monitoring e-mail of Digital Equipment and MCI. Digital claimed that Mitnick caused $4 million in damage and stole $1 million in software.[rr] In 1992, Mitnick disappeared as federal agents sought him for parole violations.[ss] In 1993, California issued a warrant for Mitnick's arrest. He was accused of "wiretapping calls from the FBI to the California DMV [Division of Motor Vehicles] and using law enforcement access codes gleaned from the wire taps to illegally gain entry to the . . . [DMV] database."[tt] In 1995, Kevin Mitnick was arrested for breaking into the San Diego Supercomputer Center[uu] and leaving death threats on the home computer of a renowned computer security expert.[vv] When arrested Mitnick was in possession of $1 million in stolen data, including 20,000 credit card numbers of subscribers to an Internet service and stored data on some of California's wealthiest residents.[ww] Mitnick pled guilty.[xx]

Industrial Espionage. Most business crimes are committed by employees. Even the smallest business is vulnerable. For example, in one instance "a computer programmer for a small trucking company * * * quit his job, shut down the company's computer then demanded thousands of dollars to get the system going again so the company could find its trucks and their cargoes."[a] Other examples abound: In 1989, U.S. officials accused French diplomats of industrial espionage against IBM, Texas Instruments and Corning Glass.[b] France retaliated by deporting five U.S. officials who, French officials contended, were attempting to buy secret information on France's trade policy.[c]

The amount of industrial espionage is likely to increase. As one expert explained: "The accessibility and vulnerability of corporate networks means that industrial espionage is getting more economical and less dangerous. Thus, many companies outside the traditionally high risk areas of national security and technology may now be in peril of such covert operations on the part of their competitors."[d]

Financial Theft. "These days, our money may seem to be nothing but bits in a computer, numbers on a screen, and ink on an occasional bank statement. * * * It's only fitting that the biggest theft and fraud cases are electronic as well."[e] Examples abound: In 1973, a teller in a

pp. *Id.* at 4.

qq. *Id.* at 8.

rr. *Id.* at 10.

ss. *Id.* at 14.

tt. *Id.* at 15.

uu. *Id.* at 17.

vv. *CrimINet, supra* note d at 218.

ww. *Id.*

xx. *Id.*

a. Robert W. Stewart, *Police Plug Into Computer Criminals*, L.A. TIMES, June 2, 1985, at 3 (June 2, 1985).

b. DANGER, *supra* note n at 11.

c. *Id.* at 10.

d. DANGER, *supra*, note n at 11.

e. COMPUTER CRIME, *supra*, note a at 11.

New York bank, using a computer, embezzled over $1 million.[f] In 1978, Security Pacific National Bank lost $10.2 million in a computer heist. In 1981, Wells Fargo Bank lost $21.3 million from a computer theft.[g] In 1985, a brokerage firm margin clerk made over $30,000 by changing the selling price of 1,700 shares of stock from $2 per share into $20 per share.[h] In 1988, First National Bank of Chicago lost $70 million from a computer heist.[i]

Banks are not the only victims of financial thievery by computer. Law firms are warned to beware of employee computer theft through alterations in the ownership of client trust accounts, draining of accounts, creating phantom billing transactions, or using inside stock market information to make profitable stock trades.[j]

Terrorism. "Think about it from the terrorist's point of view: Why blow up a single utility tower—causing a rather unmemorable blackout—when you can crack the utilities system and turn out the lights in the northeastern United States for a whole day?"[k] "Outages," where computer systems fail, have given Americans a glimpse of the chaos that could result if major communication systems were targeted. For example, on Martin Luther King Jr.'s birthday, January 15, 1990, AT & T's long distance switching system crashed for nine hours leaving 60,000 people without telephone service and 70,000,000 telephone calls unanswered.[l] In 1991, AT & T's switching system in New York City failed, preventing about 450,000,000 domestic phone calls and 500,000 international phone calls from going through. In addition, Kennedy, LaGuardia and Newark airports were left without voice and data communication. More than 500 flights were canceled, and another 500 flights were delayed throughout the United States and Europe, affecting 85,000 passengers.[m]

Revenge. Computers provide a sophisticated avenue for revenge. Two journalists found out the hard way how effective such revenge can be. Shortly after writing a book about the rivalry between two groups of computer hackers, the Masters of Deception and the Legion of Doom, journalists Michelle Slatalla and Josh Quittner awoke to a strange Thanksgiving weekend. Their telephone didn't ring all weekend nor did they receive any e-mails, both of which were unusual since they are working journalists. When they tried to log on to the Internet, they couldn't. Soon they discovered why. Their telephone had been reprogrammed to forward all incoming calls to an out of state number where the calls were answered with an obscene greeting.[n] In addition, their

f. DANGER, *supra* note n at 2. *Id.* at 3.

g. *Id.* at 4.

h. *Id.* at 7.

i. *Id.* at 10.

j. Gary Gaston & Charles Harris, *Minimizing the Threat of Hackers*, NAT'L L.J., Feb. 3, 1997, at C1.

k. COMPUTER CRIME, *supra*, note a at 12.

l. BRUCE STERLING, THE HACKER CRACKDOWN 1 (Bantam 1992).

m. *Id.* at 40.

n. According to Quittner, "What's really strange is that nobody who phoned—including my editor and my mother—thought anything of it. They just left their message and hung up." Philip Elmer-De-

Internet mailbox had been jammed with thousands of unwanted pieces of mail.

Slatalla and Quittner had been "bombed": "the electronic equivalent of dumping a truckload of garbage on a neighbor's front lawn."[o] Speculation focused on the two computer hacker gangs Slatalla and Quittner had written about since an excerpt of their book had recently appeared in the magazine, WIRED. On the same day that Slatalla and Quittner were sabotaged, so was the WIRED office, with 3,000 copies of the same message which jammed the journalists' Internet address. The message, signed by the "Internet Liberation Front," railed against corporations that were turning the Internet into "an overflowing cesspool of greed," and ended with the following: "Just a friendly warning corporate America; we have already stolen your proprietary source code. We have already pillaged your million dollar research data. And if you would like to avoid financial ruin, get the [expletive deleted] out of Dodge. Happy Thanksgiving Day turkeys."[p] Although this "bomb" was little more than an inconvenience, the access by the hackers who sent it was alarming. By remote control someone had broken into computers at IBM, Sprint and a small Internet service provider, and installed a program which sent the e-mail messages every few seconds.[q]

"Fun". Often the goal of the computer criminal is not to steal money, trade or military secrets or settle a grudge. Rather it is to have "fun." These computer criminals usually "are kids, sometimes quite young ones, who think of their computers as the next step up from a video game."[r] The victims of these pranks include a CBS employee who downloaded a supposed graphics program from an electronic bulletin board to his PC. The program was a Trojan horse which wiped out all of his data and displayed, "Arf! Arf! I got you."[s] Various governmental agencies often are the victim of "jokes" by hackers. In 1989, someone re-routed calls to Florida's Palm Beach Probation office to a phone-for-sex number answered by "Tina."[t] In the summer of 1996, hackers accessed official Department of Justice files, replacing official information with a swastika, a photograph of Hitler and pornographic pictures. On another occasion, hackers accessed the Central Intelligence Agency's (CIA) Web site, renaming it "The Central Stupidity Agency." In early 1997, the Department of Defense had to shut down 80 sites on a global network because hackers inserted a sexually explicit video clip on an Air Force web site.[u]

• Types of Computer Offenders

David Icove et al describe three types of offenders: crackers, criminals and vandals.

witt, (quoting Josh Quittner, *Terror on the Internet*, TIME, Dec. 12, 1994, at 73).

o. *Id.*

p. *Id.*

q. *Id.*

r. COMPUTER CRIME *supra*, note a at 14.

s. DANGER, *supra*, note n at 7.

t. *Id.* at 11.

u. Gary Gaston & Charles Harris, *Minimizing the Threat of Hackers*, NAT'L L. J., Feb. 3, 1997, at C1.

"Crackers"[v] are drawn to computer crime for the intellectual challenge it presents. They are often loners and otherwise bored with their lives. Most are teenagers. Recently, this profile has begun to change with crackers working for hire.[w]

"Computer criminals" generally focus on two types of illicit computer activity: espionage and fraud and abuse. The espionage usually involves stealing confidential information from military, academic or industrial sources. Fraud and abuse by computer also "is a major growth industry."[x] For example, "the first time it would be relatively simple for a criminal to collect hundreds or thousands of credit card numbers. Then a thief could use each credit card only one time, making detection much more difficult."[y] Not only is the computer a lucrative, and often safer, way of stealing money, but legitimate and illegitimate computer transactions are an effective way to launder drug money.[z] One observer has described the typical computer criminal as "male, usually Caucasian, intelligent, under 30 years old, educationally or economically privileged, has or will earn a graduate degree, * * * often was raised in a single parent family [and] often brags about his most recent computer exploits."[aa] There is a view among computer experts that hackers and the independent computer criminal are evolving into "sophisticated computer crackers who seek information and financial gain."[bb]

"Vandals" may be authorized users of a system or strangers. The users may harbor a grudge and use the computer system to seek revenge. Stranger vandals are "relatively rare."[cc] According to Icove et al:

> Most often, the strangers who break into systems aren't vandals; they are either crackers, looking for fun or intellectual stimulation, or they are true criminals, trying to steal or change data for their own financial gain or the gain of others. Most acts of vandalism are perpetrated by insiders who are angry at some particular offense.[dd]

B.   COMPUTER FRAUD AND ABUSE

The Computer Fraud and Abuse Act was first passed in 1984 under the name Counterfeit Access Device and Computer Fraud and Abuse Act

---

v. Icove et al use the term *cracker* to refer to people who break into computers. The term often used by the press, *hacker*, is a misapplication, Icove et al suggest, since it is often used to apply to legitimate programmers. COMPUTER CRIME, *supra* note a at 62. "Hacker" is generally used to refer to those who "enjoy[] exploring the details of programmable systems and how to stretch their capabilities, as opposed to most users, who prefer to learn only the minimum necessary." RICHARD STALLMAN, THE NEW HACKER'S DICTIONARY 191–92 (Eric S. Raymond, ed. 1991).

w. COMPUTER CRIME *supra* note a at 62–63; *CrimINet, supra,* note d at 206–07.

x. COMPUTER CRIME, *supra* note a at 63.

y. *CrimINet, supra,* note d at 224 quoting Professor Eric Brewer, a computer scientist at the University of California at Berkeley.

z. *Id.*

aa. *Id.* at 211.

bb. *Id.* at 219.

cc. COMPUTER CRIME, *supra* note a at 64.

dd. *Id.*

of 1984.[ee] The 1984 statute contained three offenses, all geared to protecting computers and the information on computers. The statute applied only to certain computers (those "operated for or on behalf of the United States") and certain information (national security or records of financial institutions or consumer reporting agencies). The 1984 statute was heavily criticized as too vague and too narrow[ff] and has been amended five times since.[gg] There was only one prosecution under the 1984 statute, involving a computer hacker who accessed a Department of Agriculture computer system from his home computer.[hh]

Because of the problems with the 1984 act, it was amended significantly in 1986 and retitled as the Computer Fraud and Abuse Act of 1986.[ii] The 1986 statute corrected a number of the problems with the 1984 Act by providing definitions of key terms used, adding additional crimes, and expanding existing terms such as "financial institution" and "financial record."[jj] Most of the prosecutions brought under the 1986 Act have involved theft or fraud.[kk] The first person prosecuted under the 1986 Act was Robert Morris, a graduate student in computer science at Cornell. His prosecution has been described as "the most prominent and significant prosecution of a 'hacker' under the 1986 Act."[ll]

ee. Pub.L.No. 98–473, 2101(a), 98 Stat. 2190 (1984) (Codified as amended at 18 U.S.C. § 1030; Legislative History found at 1984 U.S.C.C.A.N., p. 3182).

ff. Comment, Jo–Ann M. Adams, *Controlling Cyberspace: Applying the Computer Fraud and Abuse Act to the Internet*, 12 Santa Clara Computer & High Tech. L.J. 403, 422 (1996); Glenn D. Baker, Note, *trespassers Will Be Prosecuted: Computer Crime in the 1990s*, 12 Computer L.J. 61 (1992) [hereinafter *Trespassers*]; Joseph B. Tompkins, *The 1984 Federal Computer Crime Statute: A Partial Answer to a Pervasive Problem*, 6 Computer L. J. 459 (1986).

gg. 1996 Amendment, Pub.L. 104–294, § 604(d). Legislative History at 1996 U.S.C.C.A.N. p. 4021. 1994 Amendment, Pub.L. 103–322, § 290001. Legislative History at 1994 U.S.C.C.A.N. p. 1801. 1990 Amendment, Pub. L. 101–647, §§ 3533, 2597(j). Legislative History at 1990 U.S.C.C.A.N. p. 6472; 1989 Amendment; Pub. L. 101–73, § 962. Legislative History at 1989 U.S.C.C.A.N. p. 86; 1988 Amendment, Pub. L. 100–690; 1986 Amendment, Pub. L. 99–474, § 2. Legislative History at 1986 U.S.C.C.A.N. p. 6139.

hh. Glenn D. Baker described this case: "[A] Los Angeles computer hacker, Phillip Gonzalez Fadriquela, was indicted under the 1984 law for using his home computer to gain access to a Department of Agriculture computer system. The indictment contained seven charges, four misdemeanor charges which were brought

under the 1984 Act, two counts of wire fraud and one count of making false statements to a federal agent. Fadriquela's major defense was that he was just playing with his computer and did not know he was accessing a government system. After a plea bargain, Fadriquela pleaded guilty to three misdemeanors for wire fraud, and in return, the government dropped all other charges. He was sentenced to three years of probation, fined $3000 and required to perform 200 hours of community work. In addition Fadriquela had to forfeit all his computer equipment and issue a statement which explained how he committed the offenses."

Trespassers, *supra* note i at 65–66 (1993).

ii. Pub. L. No. 99–474, § 2, 100 Stat. 1213 (1986) (codified as amended at 18 U.S.C. § 1030 (1988).)

jj. For discussions of the 1985 Act, see *Trespassers*, *supra* note i at 66–71 (1993); Dodd S. Griffith, Note, *The Computer Fraud and Abuse Act of 1986: A Measured Response to a Growing Problem*, 43 Vand. L. Rev. 453, 474 (1990).

kk. *Controlling Cyberspace*, *supra* note d at 427. *See, e.g.* United States v. Rice, 961 F.2d 211 (4th Cir.1992) (convicted of computer fraud for accessing a computer system of a government agency without authority).

ll. *Trespassers*, *supra* note i at 74.

As you read *Morris*, note the somewhat complex structure of the provision of the Computer Fraud and Abuse Act with which Morris was charged: the stated mens rea, "intentionally," applies to some but not all of the other elements of the offense. What do you think about this statutory drafting? Is it necessary, especially with sophisticated crimes, to adjust the mens rea to the various elements or, is it so confusing that the statute fails to give notice as to what is prohibited?

UNITED STATES v. MORRIS

United States Court of Appeals, Second Circuit, 1991.
928 F.2d 504.

NEWMAN, CIRCUIT JUDGE.

This appeal presents two narrow issues of statutory construction concerning a provision Congress recently adopted to strengthen protection against computer crimes. Section 2(d) of the Computer Fraud and Abuse Act of 1986, 18 U.S.C. § 1030(a)(5)(A) (1988), punishes anyone who intentionally accesses without authorization a category of computers known as "[f]ederal interest computers" and damages or prevents authorized use of information in such computers, causing loss of $1,000 or more. The issues raised are (1) whether the Government must prove not only that the defendant intended to access a federal interest computer, but also that the defendant intended to prevent authorized use of the computer's information and thereby cause loss; and (2) what satisfies the statutory requirement of "access without authorization."

These questions are raised on an appeal by Robert Tappan Morris from the May 16, 1990, judgment of the District Court for the Northern District of New York convicting him, after a jury trial, of violating 18 U.S.C. § 1030(a)(5)(A). Morris released into INTERNET, a national computer network, a computer program known as a "worm"[1] that spread and multiplied, eventually causing computers at various educational institutions and military sites to "crash" or cease functioning.

We conclude that section 1030(a)(5)(A) does not require the Government to demonstrate that the defendant intentionally prevented authorized use and thereby caused loss. We also find that there was sufficient evidence for the jury to conclude that Morris acted "without authorization" within the meaning of section 1030(a)(5)(A). We therefore affirm.

FACTS

In the fall of 1988, Morris was a first-year graduate student in Cornell University's computer science Ph.D. program. Through undergraduate work at Harvard and in various jobs he had acquired significant computer experience and expertise. When Morris entered Cornell,

---

1. In the colorful argot of computers, a "worm" is a program that travels from one computer to another but does not attach itself to the operating system of the computer it "infects." It differs from a "virus," which is also a migrating program, but one that attaches itself to the operating system of any computer it enters and can infect any other computer that uses files from the infected computer.

he was given an account on the computer at the Computer Science Division. This account gave him explicit authorization to use computers at Cornell. Morris engaged in various discussions with fellow graduate students about the security of computer networks and his ability to penetrate it.

In October 1988, Morris began work on a computer program, later known as the INTERNET "worm" or "virus." The goal of this program was to demonstrate the inadequacies of current security measures on computer networks by exploiting the security defects that Morris had discovered. The tactic he selected was release of a worm into network computers. Morris designed the program to spread across a national network of computers after being inserted at one computer location connected to the network. Morris released the worm into INTERNET, which is a group of national networks that connect university, governmental, and military computers around the country. The network permits communication and transfer of information between computers on the network.

Morris sought to program the INTERNET worm to spread widely without drawing attention to itself. The worm was supposed to occupy little computer operation time, and thus not interfere with normal use of the computers. Morris programmed the worm to make it difficult to detect and read, so that other programmers would not be able to "kill" the worm easily.

Morris also wanted to ensure that the worm did not copy itself onto a computer that already had a copy. Multiple copies of the worm on a computer would make the worm easier to detect and would bog down the system and ultimately cause the computer to crash. Therefore, Morris designed the worm to "ask" each computer whether it already had a copy of the worm. If it responded "no," then the worm would copy onto the computer; if it responded "yes," the worm would not duplicate. However, Morris was concerned that other programmers could kill the worm by programming their own computers to falsely respond "yes" to the question. To circumvent this protection, Morris programmed the worm to duplicate itself every seventh time it received a "yes" response. As it turned out, Morris underestimated the number of times a computer would be asked the question, and his one-out-of-seven ratio resulted in far more copying than he had anticipated. The worm was also designed so that it would be killed when a computer was shut down, an event that typically occurs once every week or two. This would have prevented the worm from accumulating on one computer, had Morris correctly estimated the likely rate of reinfection.

Morris identified four ways in which the worm could break into computers on the network:

(1) through a "hole" or "bug" (an error) in SEND MAIL, a computer program that transfers and receives electronic mail on a computer;

(2) through a bug in the "finger demon" program, a program that permits a person to obtain limited information about the users of another computer;

(3) through the "trusted hosts" feature, which permits a user with certain privileges on one computer to have equivalent privileges on another computer without using a password; and

(4) through a program of password guessing, whereby various combinations of letters are tried out in rapid sequence in the hope that one will be an authorized user's password, which is entered to permit whatever level of activity that user is authorized to perform.

On November 2, 1988, Morris released the worm from a computer at the Massachusetts Institute of Technology. MIT was selected to disguise the fact that the worm came from Morris at Cornell. Morris soon discovered that the worm was replicating and reinfecting machines at a much faster rate than he had anticipated. Ultimately, many machines at locations around the country either crashed or became "catatonic." When Morris realized what was happening, he contacted a friend at Harvard to discuss a solution. Eventually, they sent an anonymous message from Harvard over the network, instructing programmers how to kill the worm and prevent reinfection. However, because the network route was clogged, this message did not get through until it was too late. Computers were affected at numerous installations, including leading universities, military sites, and medical research facilities. The estimated cost of dealing with the worm at each installation ranged from $200 to more than $53,000.

Morris was found guilty, following a jury trial, of violating 18 U.S.C. § 1030(a)(5)(A). He was sentenced to three years of probation, 400 hours of community service, a fine of $10,050, and the costs of his supervision.

DISCUSSION

I. The intent requirement in section 1030(a)(5)(A)

Section 1030(a)(5)(A), covers anyone who

(5) *intentionally accesses* a Federal interest computer without authorization, *and* by means of one or more instances of such conduct alters, damages, or destroys information in any such Federal interest computer, or *prevents authorized use* of any such computer or information, *and thereby*

> (A) *causes loss* to one or more others of a value aggregating $1,000 or more during any one year period; ... [emphasis added].

The District Court concluded that the intent requirement applied only to the accessing and not to the resulting damage. Judge Munson found recourse to legislative history unnecessary because he considered the statute clear and unambiguous. However, the Court observed that the legislative history supported its reading of section 1030(a)(5)(A).

Morris argues that the Government had to prove not only that he intended the unauthorized access of a federal interest computer, but also that he intended to prevent others from using it, and thus cause a loss. The adverb "intentionally," he contends, modifies both verb phrases of the section. The Government urges that since punctuation sets the "accesses" phrase off from the subsequent "damages" phrase, the provision unambiguously shows that "intentionally" modifies only "accesses." Absent textual ambiguity, the Government asserts that recourse to legislative history is not appropriate.

With some statutes, punctuation has been relied upon to indicate that a phrase set off by commas is independent of the language that followed. However, we have been advised that punctuation is not necessarily decisive in construing statutes, and with many statutes, a mental state adverb adjacent to initial words has been applied to phrases or clauses appearing later in the statute without regard to the punctuation or structure of the statute. In the present case, we do not believe the comma after "authorization" renders the text so clear as to preclude review of the legislative history.

The first federal statute dealing with computer crimes was passed in 1984, Pub.L. No. 98–473 (codified at 18 U.S.C. § 1030 (Supp. II 1984)). The specific provision under which Morris was convicted was added in 1986, Pub.L. No. 99–474, along with some other changes. The 1986 amendments made several changes relevant to our analysis.

First, the 1986 amendments changed the scienter requirement in section 1030(a)(2) from "knowingly" to "intentionally." The subsection now covers anyone who

> (2) intentionally accesses a computer without authorization or exceeds authorized access, and thereby obtains information contained in a financial record of a financial institution, or of a card issuer as defined in section 1602(n) of title 15, or contained in a file of a consumer reporting agency on a consumer, as such terms are defined in the Fair Credit Reporting Act (15 U.S.C. 1681 et seq.).

According to the Senate Judiciary Committee, Congress changed the mental state requirement in section 1030(a)(2) for two reasons. Congress sought only to proscribe intentional acts of unauthorized access, not "mistaken, inadvertent, or careless" acts of unauthorized access. S.Rep. No. 99–432, 99th Cong., 2d Sess. 5 (1986), reprinted in 1986 U.S.Code Cong. & Admin. News 2479, 2483 [hereinafter Senate Report].

Also, Congress expressed concern that the "knowingly" standard "might be inappropriate for cases involving computer technology." *Id.* The concern was that a scienter requirement of "knowingly" might encompass the acts of an individual "who inadvertently 'stumble[d] into' someone else's computer file or computer data," especially where such individual was authorized to use a particular computer. *Id.* at 6, 1986 U.S.Code Cong. & Admin. News at 2483. The Senate Report concluded that "[t]he substitution of an 'intentional' standard is designed to focus Federal criminal prosecutions on those whose conduct evinces a clear intent to enter, without proper authorization, computer files or data belonging to another." *Id.*, U.S.Code Cong. & Admin. News at 2484. Congress retained the "knowingly" standard in other subsections of section 1030. See 18 U.S.C. § 1030(a)(1), (a)(4).

This use of a mens rea standard to make sure that inadvertent accessing was not covered is also emphasized in the Senate Report's discussion of section 1030(a)(3) and section 1030(a)(5), under which Morris was convicted. Both subsections were designed to target "outsiders," individuals without authorization to access any federal interest computer. The rationale for the mens rea requirement suggests that it modifies only the "accesses" phrase, which was the focus of Congress's concern in strengthening the scienter requirement.

The other relevant change in the 1986 amendments was the introduction of subsection (a)(5) to replace its earlier version, subsection (a)(3) of the 1984 act, 18 U.S.C. § 1030(a)(3) (Supp. II 1984). The predecessor subsection covered anyone who

> knowingly accesses a computer without authorization, or having accessed a computer with authorization, uses the opportunity such access provides for purposes to which such authorization does not extend, and by means of such conduct knowingly uses, modifies, destroys, or discloses information in, or prevents authorized use of, such computer, if such computer is operated for or on behalf of the Government of United States and such conduct affects such operation.

The 1986 version changed the mental state requirement from "knowingly" to "intentionally," and did not repeat it after the "accesses" phrase, as had the 1984 version. By contrast, other subsections of section 1030 have retained "dual intent" language, placing the scienter requirement at the beginning of both the "accesses" phrase and the "damages" phrase. *See, e.g.*, 18 U.S.C. § 1030(a)(1).

Morris notes the careful attention that Congress gave to selecting the scienter requirement for current subsections (a)(2) and (a)(5). Then, relying primarily on comments in the Senate and House reports, Morris argues that the "intentionally" requirement of section 1030(a)(5)(A) describes both the conduct of accessing and damaging. As he notes, the Senate Report said that "[t]he new subsection 1030(a)(5) to be created by the bill is designed to penalize those who intentionally alter, damage, or destroy certain computerized data belonging to another." Senate Report at 10, U.S.Code Cong. & Admin. News at 2488. The House Judiciary Committee stated that "the bill proposes a new section (18 U.S.C. 1030(a)(5)) which can be characterized as a 'malicious damage' felony violation involving a Federal interest computer. We have included an 'intentional' standard for this felony and coverage is extended only to outside trespassers with a $1,000 threshold damage level." H.R.Rep. No. 99–612, 99th Cong.2d Sess. at 7 (1986). A member of the Judiciary Committee also referred to the section 1030(a)(5) offense as a "malicious damage" felony during the floor debate. 132 Cong.Rec. H3275, 3276 (daily ed. June 3, 1986) (remarks of Rep. Hughes).

The Government's argument that the scienter requirement in section 1030(a)(5)(A) applies only to the "accesses" phrase is premised primarily upon the difference between subsection (a)(5)(A) and its predecessor in the 1984 statute. The decision to state the scienter requirement only once in subsection (a)(5)(A), along with the decision to change it from "knowingly" to "intentionally," are claimed to evince a clear intent upon the part of Congress to apply the scienter requirement only to the "accesses" phrase, though making that requirement more difficult to satisfy. This reading would carry out the Congressional objective of protecting the individual who "inadvertently 'stumble[s] into' someone else's computer file." Senate Report at 6, U.S.Code Cong. & Admin. News at 2483.

The Government also suggests that the fact that other subsections of section 1030 continue to repeat the scienter requirement before both phrases of a subsection is evidence that Congress selectively decided within the various subsections of section 1030 where the scienter requirement was and was not intended to apply. Morris responds with a plausible explanation as to why certain other provisions of section 1030 retain dual intent language. Those subsections use two different mens rea standards; therefore it is necessary to refer to the scienter requirement twice in the subsection. For example, section 1030(a)(1) covers anyone who

(1) knowingly accesses a computer without authorization or exceeds authorized access, and by means of such conduct obtains information that has been determined by the United States Government pursuant to an Executive order or statute to require protection against unauthorized disclosure for reasons of national defense or foreign relations, or any restricted data ... with the intent or reason to believe that such information so obtained is to be used to the injury of the United States, or to the advantage of any foreign nation.

Since Congress sought in subsection (a)(1) to have the "knowingly" standard govern the "accesses" phrase and the "with intent" standard govern the "results" phrase, it was necessary to state the scienter requirement at the beginning of both phrases. By contrast, Morris argues, where Congress stated the scienter requirement only once, at the beginning of the "accesses" phrase, it was intended to cover both the "accesses" phrase and the phrase that followed it.

There is a problem, however, with applying Morris's explanation to section 1030(a)(5)(A). As noted earlier, the predecessor of subsection (a)(5)(A) explicitly placed the same mental state requirement before both the "accesses" phrase and the "damages" phrase. In relevant part, that predecessor in the 1984 statute covered anyone who *"knowingly accesses a computer without authorization, ... and by means of such conduct knowingly uses,* modifies, destroys, or discloses information in, or prevents authorized use of, such computer. ...." 18 U.S.C. § 1030(a)(3) (Supp. II 1984) (emphasis added). This earlier provision demonstrates that Congress has on occasion chosen to repeat the same scienter standard in the "accesses" phrase and the subsequent phrase of a subsection of the Computer Fraud Statute. More pertinently, it shows that the 1986 amendments adding subsection (a)(5)(A) placed the scienter requirement adjacent only to the "accesses" phrase in contrast to a predecessor provision that had placed the same standard before both that phrase and the subsequent phrase.

Despite some isolated language in the legislative history that arguably suggests a scienter component for the "damages" phrase of section 1030(a)(5)(A), the wording, structure, and purpose of the subsection, examined in comparison with its departure from the format of its predecessor provision persuade us that the "intentionally" standard applies only to the "accesses" phrase of section 1030(a)(5)(A), and not to its "damages" phrase.

II.   The unauthorized access requirement in section 1030(a)(5)(A)

Section 1030(a)(5)(A) penalizes the conduct of an individual who "intentionally accesses a Federal interest computer without authorization." Morris contends that his conduct constituted, at most, "exceeding authorized access" rather than the "unauthorized access" that the subsection punishes. Morris argues that there was insufficient evidence to convict him of "unauthorized access," and that even if the evidence sufficed, he was entitled to have the jury instructed on his "theory of defense."

We assess the sufficiency of the evidence under the traditional standard. Morris was authorized to use computers at Cornell, Harvard, and Berkeley, all of which were on INTERNET. As a result, Morris was authorized to communicate with other computers on the network to send electronic mail (SEND MAIL), and to find out certain information about the users of other computers (finger demon). The question is whether Morris's transmission of his worm constituted exceeding authorized access or accessing without authorization.

The Senate Report stated that section 1030(a)(5)(A), like the new section 1030(a)(3), would "be aimed at 'outsiders,' i.e., those lacking authorization to access any Federal interest computer." Senate Report at 10, U.S.Code Cong. & Admin. News at 2488. But the Report also stated, in concluding its discussion on the scope of section 1030(a)(3), that it applies "where the offender is completely outside the Government, ... *or where the offender's act of trespass is interdepartmental in nature.*" *Id.* at 8, U.S.Code Cong. & Admin. News at 2486 (emphasis added).

Morris relies on the first quoted portion to argue that his actions can be characterized only as exceeding authorized access, since he had authorized access to a federal interest computer. However, the second quoted portion reveals that Congress was not drawing a bright line between those who have some access to any federal interest computer and those who have none. Congress contemplated that individuals with access to some federal interest computers would be subject to liability under the computer fraud provisions for gaining unauthorized access to other federal interest computers.

The evidence permitted the jury to conclude that Morris's use of the SEND MAIL and finger demon features constituted access without authorization. While a case might arise where the use of SEND MAIL or finger demon falls within a nebulous area in which the line between accessing without authorization and exceeding authorized access may not be clear, Morris's conduct here falls well within the area of unauthorized access. Morris did not use either of those features in any way related to their intended function. He did not send or read mail nor discover information about other users; instead he found holes in both programs that permitted him a special and unauthorized access route into other computers.

Moreover, the jury verdict need not be upheld solely on Morris's use of SEND MAIL and finger demon. As the District Court noted, in denying Morris' motion for acquittal.

> Although the evidence may have shown that defendant's initial insertion of the worm simply exceeded his authorized access, the evidence also demonstrated that the worm was designed to spread to other computers at which he had no account and no authority, express or implied, to unleash the worm program. Moreover, there was also evidence that the worm was designed to gain access to computers at which he had no account by guessing their passwords. Accordingly, the evidence did support the jury's conclusion that defendant accessed without authority as opposed to merely exceeding the scope of his authority.

In light of the reasonable conclusions that the jury could draw from Morris's use of SEND MAIL and finger demon, and from his use of the trusted hosts feature and password guessing, his challenge to the sufficiency of the evidence fails.

Morris endeavors to bolster his sufficiency argument by contending that his conduct was not punishable under subsection (a)(5) but was punishable under subsection (a)(3). That concession belies the validity of his claim that he only exceeded authorization rather than made unauthorized access. Neither subsection (a)(3) nor (a)(5) punishes conduct that exceeds authorization. Both punish a person who "accesses" "without authorization" certain computers. Subsection (a)(3) covers the computers of a department or agency of the United States; subsection (a)(5) more broadly covers any federal interest computers, defined to include, among other computers, those used exclusively by the United States, 18 U.S.C. § 1030(e)(2)(A), and adds the element of causing damage or loss of use of a value of $1,000 or more. If Morris violated subsection (a)(3), as he concedes, then his conduct in inserting the worm into the INTERNET must have constituted "unauthorized access" under subsection (a)(5) to the computers of the federal departments the worm reached, for example, those of NASA and military bases.

To extricate himself from the consequence of conceding that he made "unauthorized access" within the meaning of subsection (a)(3), Morris subtly shifts his argument and contends that he is not within the reach of subsection (a)(5) at all. He argues that subsection (a)(5) covers only those who, unlike himself, lack access to any federal interest computer. It is true that a primary concern of Congress in drafting subsection (a)(5) was to reach those unauthorized to access any federal interest computer. The Senate Report stated, "[T]his subsection [(a)(5)] will be aimed at 'outsiders,' i.e., those lacking authorization to access any Federal interest computer." Senate Report at 10, U.S.Code Cong. & Admin. News at 2488. But the fact that the subsection is "aimed" at such "outsiders" does not mean that its coverage is limited to them. Congress understandably thought that the group most likely to damage federal interest computers would be those who lack authorization to use any of them. But it surely did not mean to insulate from liability the person authorized to use computers at the State Department who causes damage to computers at the Defense Department. Congress created the misdemeanor offense of subsection (a)(3) to punish intentional trespasses into computers for which one lacks authorized access; it added the felony offense of subsection (a)(5) to punish such a trespasser who also causes damage or loss in excess of $1,000, not only to computers of the United States but to any computer within the definition of federal interest computers. With both provisions, Congress was punishing those, like Morris, who, with access to some computers that enable them to communicate on a network linking other computers, gain access to other computers to which they lack authorization and either trespass, in violation of subsection (a)(3), or cause damage or loss of $1,000 or more, in violation of subsection (a)(5).

Morris also contends that the District Court should have instructed the jury on his theory that he was only exceeding authorized access. The District Court decided that it was unnecessary to provide the jury with a definition of "authorization." We agree. Since the word is of common usage, without any technical or ambiguous meaning, the Court was not obliged to instruct the jury on its meaning. See, e.g., United States v. Chenault, 844 F.2d 1124, 1131 (5th Cir.1988) ("A trial court need not define specific statutory terms unless they are outside the common understanding of a juror or are so technical or specific as to require a definition.").

An instruction on "exceeding authorized access" would have risked misleading the jury into thinking that Morris could not be convicted if some of his conduct could be viewed as falling within this description. Yet, even if that phrase might have applied to some of his conduct, he could nonetheless be found liable for doing what the statute prohibited, gaining access where he was unauthorized and causing loss.

Additionally, the District Court properly refused to charge the jury with Morris's proposed jury instruction on access without authorization. That instruction stated, "To establish the element of lack of authorization, the government must prove beyond a reasonable doubt that Mr.

Morris was an 'outsider,' that is, that he was not authorized to access any Federal interest computer in any manner." As the analysis of the legislative history reveals, Congress did not intend an individual's authorized access to one federal interest computer to protect him from prosecution, no matter what other federal interest computers he accesses.

CONCLUSION

For the foregoing reasons, the judgment of the District Court is affirmed.

Notes

1. Although no actual damage to computer hardware or software occurred, Morris' worm caused an estimated 6,200 computers to shut down. Estimates of the labor costs to clear out the memories of the affected computers ranged from $96 million to $11.1 billion.[39]

2. Morris testified at trial. He stated:

"[My] purpose was to see if [I] could write a program that would spread as widely as possible. The worm spread on the network far faster than [I] expected.' I * * * realize [my] experiment had turned into a 'dismal failure' and that '[it] was a mistake, and [I am] sorry.'

Morris went on to testify that when he first realized the extent of what he had done he 'was scared; it seemed like the worm was going out of control.' After his failed attempt at warning programmers, he rejected an idea to write a second program to kill the first: 'I didn't do that because I had messed up with the first one and it didn't appear that I would be able to do any better the second time.' "[40]

It seems apparent that while Morris clearly intended to access federal interest computers he did not intend to do any damage. Yet, Morris' conviction is consistent with the law as interpreted by the Second Circuit. As a policy matter, however, do you think Morris' conviction is wise? Is conviction fair to Morris?

3. Recall that Morris was convicted of "intentionally access[ing] a Federal interest computer without authorization and * * * damag[ing] information in any such * * * computer." In 1994, the Computer Fraud and Abuse Act was amended and the crime of which Morris had been convicted was separated into three separate crimes. As amended, § 1030(a)(5)(A) makes it a crime to:

"knowingly cause[ ] the transmission of a program, information, code, or command, and as a result of such conduct, intentionally causes damage without authorization; to a protected computer."

This offense is punishable by a fine under title 18, United States Code, and a term of imprisonment of not more than five years, or ten years, if the defendant has been convicted previously of violating § 1030.

39. Glenn D. Baker, Note, *Trespassers Will Be Prosecuted: Computer Crime in the 1990s*, 12 COMPUTER L. J. 61, 75 (1993).

40. *Id.* at 75–76.

As amended, § 1030(a)(5)(B) makes it a crime to:

"intentionally access[ ] a protected computer[41] without authorization, and as a result of such conduct, recklessly causes damage."

The punishment for this offense is the same as for a violation of § 1030(a)(5)(A).

As amended, § 1030(a)(5)(C) makes it a crime to:

"intentionally access[ ] a protected computer without authorization, and as a result of such conduct, causes damage."

This offense is a misdemeanor only. The punishment for violating it is a fine under title 18, United States Code, and a term of imprisonment of not more than one year.

If the above provisions existed when Morris created his worm, which would best apply to his behavior?

4. Recall the second argument Morris made on appeal: that he was an "authorized" user who simply exceeded his authorization. This argument arises from the statutory language. Of the eleven different offenses currently set forth in the Computer Fraud and Abuse Act, three apply to outsiders, i.e., those who lack authorization to use the computer system. Five offenses apply to insiders, i.e., those who have authorization but exceed it. Most offenses apply to both. Had Morris successfully demonstrated that he was an "insider" because he had authorization to access the computers which received his "worm," he could have avoided prosecution because § 1030(a)(5), the offense with which he was charged, applied only to outsiders. Do you agree with Morris' argument that he was acting within his authorized access?

5. One element of § 1030(a)(5), as applied to Morris, was accessing a "federal interest" computer. One of the changes made in the 1996 amendments to the Computer Fraud and Abuse Act was substituting the term "protected computer" for "federal interest computer." This is a significant change because a "protected computer," as defined in the Act, applies to computers wholly owned and operated by private parties but used in interstate or foreign commerce or communication.[42] A "federal interest" computer was not as broad; it covered privately owned computers only when the computers used to commit the offense were located in different states or when the conduct at issue affected the use of a financial institution's operation or the Government's operation of the computer.[43]

---

41. 18 U.S.C. § 1030(e)(2) provides:

(2) the term "protected computer" means a computer—

  (A) exclusively for the use of a financial institution or the United States Government, or, in the case of a computer not exclusively for such use, used by or for a financial institution or the United States Government and the conduct constituting the offense affects that use by or for the financial institution or the Government; or

  (B) which is used in interstate or foreign commerce or communication.

42. 18 U.S.C. § 1030(e)(2).

43. Pub.L. 103–322, Title XXIX, § 29001(b)-(f) at § 1030(e)(1).

The *Morris* decision was viewed as answering affirmatively the question whether the 1986 Act was broad enough to cover all aspects of computer crime. The next case, United States v. Czubinski, 106 F.3d 1069 (1st Cir.1997), raises questions about this.

UNITED STATES v. CZUBINSKI

United States Court of Appeals, First Circuit, 1997.
106 F.3d 1069.

TORRUELLA, CHIEF JUDGE.

Defendant-appellant Richard Czubinski ("Czubinski") appeals his jury conviction on nine counts of wire fraud, 18 U.S.C. §§ 1343, 1346, and four counts of computer fraud, 18 U.S.C. § 1030(a)(4). The wire fraud and computer fraud prosecution that led to the conviction survived serious challenges put forward by Czubinski in various pre-trial motions. Given the broad scope of the federal fraud statutes, motions charging insufficient pleadings or selective prosecution generally deserve careful consideration. We need not scrutinize the lower court's rejection of the defendant's arguments in favor of dismissing the indictment, however, because we reverse the conviction on the clearer ground that the trial evidence mustered by the government was insufficient to support a guilty verdict, and hold that the defendant's motion for judgment of acquittal should have been granted on all counts. Unauthorized browsing of taxpayer files, although certainly inappropriate conduct, cannot, without more, sustain this federal felony conviction.

BACKGROUND

* * *

On an appeal from a jury conviction, we review the relevant facts in the light most favorable to the government. The evidence in this case, so presented, is inadequate to support convictions on either the wire fraud or computer fraud charges.

For all periods relevant to the acts giving rise to his conviction, the defendant Czubinski was employed as a Contact Representative in the Boston office of the Taxpayer Services Division of the Internal Revenue Service ("IRS"). To perform his official duties, which mainly involved answering questions from taxpayers regarding their returns, Czubinski routinely accessed information from one of the IRS's computer systems known as the Integrated Data Retrieval System ("IDRS"). Using a valid password given to Contact Representatives, certain search codes, and taxpayer social security numbers, Czubinski was able to retrieve, to his terminal screen in Boston, income tax return information regarding virtually any taxpayer—information that is permanently stored in the IDRS "master file" located in Martinsburg, West Virginia. In the period of Czubinski's employ, IRS rules plainly stated that employees with passwords and access codes were not permitted to access files on IDRS outside of the course of their official duties.[1]

In 1992, Czubinski carried out numerous unauthorized searches of IDRS files. He knowingly disregarded IRS rules by looking at confidential information obtained by performing computer searches that were outside of the scope of his duties as a Contact Representative, including, but not limited to, the searches listed in the indictment.[2] Audit trails performed by internal IRS auditors establish that Czubinski frequently made unauthorized accesses on IDRS in 1992. For example, Czubinski accessed information regarding: the tax returns of two individuals involved in the David Duke presidential campaign; the joint tax return of an assistant district attorney (who had been prosecuting Czubinski's father on an unrelated felony offense) and his wife; the tax return of Boston City Counselor Jim Kelly's Campaign Committee (Kelly had defeated Czubinski in the previous election for the Counselor seat for District 2); the tax return of one of his brothers' instructors; the joint tax return of a Boston Housing Authority police officer, who was involved in a community organization with one of Czubinski's brothers, and the officer's wife; and the tax return of a woman Czubinski had dated a few times. Czubinski also accessed the files of various other social acquaintances by performing unauthorized searches.

Nothing in the record indicates that Czubinski did anything more than knowingly disregard IRS rules by observing the confidential information he accessed. No evidence suggests, nor does the government contend, that Czubinski disclosed the confidential information he accessed to any third parties. The government's only evidence demonstrating any intent to use the confidential information for nefarious ends was the trial testimony of William A. Murray, an acquaintance of Czubinski who briefly participated in Czubinski's local Invisible Knights of the Ku Klux Klan ("KKK") chapter and worked with him on the David Duke campaign. Murray testified that Czubinski had once stated at a social gathering in "early 1992" that "he intended to use some of that information to build dossiers on people" involved in "the white supremacist movement." There is, however, no evidence that Czubinski created dossiers, took steps toward making dossiers (such as by printing out or recording the information he browsed), or shared any of the information he accessed in the years following the single comment to Murray. No

---

1. In 1987 Czubinski signed an acknowledgment of receipt of the IRS Rules of Conduct, which contained the following rule:

> Employees must make every effort to assure security and prevent unauthorized disclosure of protected information data in the use of Government owned or leased computers. In addition, employees may not use any Service computer system for other than official purposes.

In addition, Czubinski received separate rules regarding use of the IDRS, one of which states:

> Access only those accounts required to accomplish your official duties.

2. The indictment charged ten counts of wire fraud for accessing the return information of ten different entities; the four computer fraud counts (counts eleven through fourteen) identified unauthorized searches that also underlay four of the ten wire fraud counts (counts one, two, eight and nine).

other witness testified to having any knowledge of Czubinski's alleged intent to create "dossiers" on KKK members.

The record shows that Czubinski did not perform any unauthorized searches after 1992. He continued to be employed as a Contact Representative until June 1995, when a grand jury returned an indictment against him on ten counts of federal wire fraud under 18 U.S.C. §§ 1343, 1346, and four counts of federal interest computer fraud under 18 U.S.C. § 1030(a)(4).

The portion of the indictment alleging wire fraud states that Czubinski defrauded the IRS of confidential property and defrauded the IRS and the public of his honest services by using his valid password to acquire confidential taxpayer information as part of a scheme to: 1) build "dossiers" on associates in the KKK; 2) seek information regarding an assistant district attorney who was then prosecuting Czubinski's father on an unrelated criminal charge; and 3) perform opposition research by inspecting the records of a political opponent in the race for a Boston City Councilor seat. The wire fraud indictment, therefore, articulated particular personal ends to which the unauthorized access to confidential information through interstate wires was allegedly a means.

The portion of the indictment setting forth the computer fraud charges stated that Czubinski obtained something of value, beyond the mere unauthorized use of a federal interest computer, by performing certain searches—searches representing a subset of those making up the mail fraud counts.

* * *

On December 15, 1995, the district court denied Czubinski's motion for judgment of acquittal on all counts except for count 3,[3] and on that day the jury returned a verdict finding Czubinski guilty on all thirteen remaining counts. * * *

We reverse on the ground that the district court erred in denying Czubinski's motion for acquittal, and therefore bypass Czubinski's other claims.

STANDARD OF REVIEW

* * *

In determining the evidentiary sufficiency of a guilty verdict, "the relevant question is whether, after viewing the evidence in the light most favorable to the prosecution, any rational trier of fact could have found the essential elements of the crime beyond a reasonable doubt." Jackson v. Virginia, 443 U.S. 307, 319 (1979), * * *

DISCUSSION

I. The Wire Fraud Counts

3. On count 3, the district court ruled that there was insufficient proof showing that the search alleged in count 3 was not requested by the taxpayer whose files were browsed.

We turn first to Czubinski's conviction on the nine wire fraud counts. To support a conviction for wire fraud, the government must prove two elements beyond a reasonable doubt: (1) the defendant's knowing and willing participation in a scheme or artifice to defraud with the specific intent to defraud, and (2) the use of interstate wire communications in furtherance of the scheme. Although defendant's motion for judgment of acquittal places emphasis on shortcomings in proof with regard to the second element, by arguing that the wire transmissions at issue were not proved to be interstate, we find the first element dispositive and hold that the government failed to prove beyond a reasonable doubt that the defendant willfully participated in a scheme to defraud within the meaning of the wire fraud statute. That is, assuming the counts accurately describe unauthorized searches of taxpayer returns through interstate wire transmissions, there is insufficient record evidence to permit a rational jury to conclude that the wire transmissions were part of a criminal scheme to defraud under sections 1343 and 1346.

The government pursued two theories of wire fraud in this prosecution: first, that Czubinski defrauded the IRS of its property, under section 1343, by acquiring confidential information for certain intended personal uses; second, that he defrauded the IRS and the public of their intangible right to his honest services, under sections 1343 and 1346. We consider the evidence with regard to each theory, in turn.

A.   Scheme to Defraud IRS of Property

The government correctly notes that confidential information may constitute intangible "property" and that its unauthorized dissemination or other use may deprive the owner of its property rights. Where such deprivation is effected through dishonest or deceitful means, a "scheme to defraud," within the meaning of the wire fraud statute, is shown. Thus, a necessary step toward satisfying the "scheme to defraud" element in this context is showing that the defendant intended to "deprive" another of their protected right.

The government, however, provides no case in support of its contention here that merely accessing confidential information, without doing, or clearly intending to do, more, is tantamount to a deprivation of IRS property under the wire fraud statute. We do not think that Czubinski's unauthorized browsing, even if done with the intent to deceive the IRS into thinking he was performing only authorized searches, constitutes a "deprivation" within the meaning of the federal fraud statutes.

Binding precedents, and good sense, support the conclusion that to "deprive" a person of their intangible property interest in confidential information under section 1343, either some articulable harm must befall the holder of the information as a result of the defendant's activities, or some gainful use must be intended by the person accessing the information, whether or not this use is profitable in the economic sense.[7] Here, neither the taking of the IRS' right to "exclusive use" of

7.   For example, had the government es-   tablished that Czubinski disclosed or in-

the confidential information, nor Czubinski's gain from access to the information, can be shown absent evidence of his "use" of the information. Accordingly, without evidence that Czubinski used or intended to use the taxpayer information (beyond mere browsing), an intent to deprive cannot be proven, and, a fortiori, a scheme to defraud is not shown.

All of the cases cited by the government in support of their contention that the confidentiality breached by Czubinski's search in itself constitutes a deprivation of property in fact support our holding today, for they all involve, at a minimum, a finding of a further intended use of the confidential information accessed by the defendants. The government's best support comes from United States v. Seidlitz, 589 F.2d 152, 160 (4th Cir.1978), in which a former employee of a computer systems firm secretly accessed its files, but never was shown to have sold or used the data he accessed, and was nevertheless convicted of wire fraud. The affirming Fourth Circuit held, however, that a jury could have reasonably found that, at the time the defendant raided a competitor's computer system, he intended to retrieve information that would be helpful for his own start-up, competing computer firm. In the instant case, Czubinski did indeed access confidential information through fraudulent pretenses—he appeared to be performing his duties when in fact he used IRS passwords to perform unauthorized searches. Nevertheless, it was not proven that he intended to deprive the IRS of their property interest through either disclosure or use of that information.

The resolution of the instant case is complex because it is well-established that to be convicted of mail or wire fraud, the defendant need not successfully carry out an intended scheme to defraud. The government does not contend either that Czubinski actually created dossiers or that he accomplished some other end through use of the information. It need not do so. All that the government was required to prove was the intent to follow through with a deprivation of the IRS's property and the use or foreseeable use of interstate wire transmissions pursuant to the accomplishment of the scheme to defraud. In the case at bar, the government failed to make even this showing.

The fatal flaw in the government's case is that it has not shown beyond a reasonable doubt that Czubinski intended to carry out a scheme to deprive the IRS of its property interest in confidential information. Had there been sufficient proof that Czubinski intended either to create dossiers for the sake of advancing personal causes or to disseminate confidential information to third parties, then his actions in searching files could arguably be said to be a step in furtherance of a scheme to deprive the IRS of its property interest in confidential information. The government's case regarding Czubinski's intent to make any use of the information he browsed rests on the testimony of one witness at trial who stated that Czubinski once remarked at a social

tended to disclose taxpayer information, then the deprivation or intended deprivation of property rights would have been shown.

gathering that he intended to build dossiers on potential KKK informants. We must assume, on this appeal, that Czubinski did indeed make such a comment. Nevertheless, the fact that during the months following this remark—that is, during the period in which Czubinski made his unauthorized searches—he did not create dossiers (there was no evidence that he created dossiers either during or after the period of his unauthorized searches); given the fact that he did not even take steps toward creating dossiers, such as recording or printing out the information; given the fact that no other person testifying as to Czubinski's involvement in white supremacist organizations had any knowledge of Czubinski's alleged intent to create dossiers or use confidential information; and given the fact that not a single piece of evidence suggests that Czubinski ever shared taxpayer information with others, no rational jury could have found beyond a reasonable doubt that, when Czubinski was browsing taxpayer files, he was doing so in furtherance of a scheme to use the information he browsed for private purposes, be they nefarious or otherwise. In addition, there was no evidence that Czubinski disclosed, or used to his advantage, any information regarding political opponents or regarding the person prosecuting his father.

Mere browsing of the records of people about whom one might have a particular interest, although reprehensible, is not enough to sustain a wire fraud conviction on a "deprivation of intangible property" theory. Curiosity on the part of an IRS officer may lead to dismissal, but curiosity alone will not sustain a finding of participation in a felonious criminal scheme to deprive the IRS of its property.

B.   Honest Services Fraud (Section 1346)

In McNally v. United States, 483 U.S. 350, 107 S.Ct. 2875, 97 L.Ed.2d 292 (1987), the Supreme Court held that the mail and wire fraud statutes do not prohibit schemes to defraud individuals of their intangible, nonproperty right to honest government services. Congress responded to *McNally* in 1988 by enacting section 1346, the honest services amendment, which provides:

> For the purposes of this chapter, the term "scheme or artifice to defraud" includes a scheme or artifice to deprive another of the intangible right of honest services.

18 U.S.C. § 1346 (effective Nov. 11, 1988). We have held, after considering the relevant legislative history, that section 1346 effectively restores to the scope of the mail and wire fraud statutes their pre-*McNally* applications to government officials' schemes to defraud individuals of their intangible right to honest services.

We recently had the opportunity to discuss, at some length, the proper application of the section 1346 honest services amendment to the wrongful acts of public officials. See United States v. Sawyer, 85 F.3d 713, 722–26 (1st Cir.1996). The discussion and holding in *Sawyer* directly guide our disposition of the instant appeal. First, as a general matter, we noted in *Sawyer* that although the right to honest services "eludes easy definition," honest services convictions of public officials typically involve serious corruption, such as embezzlement of public funds, bribery of public officials, or the failure of public decision-makers to disclose certain conflicts of interest. Second, we cautioned that "[t]he broad scope of the mail fraud statute, however, does not encompass every instance of official misconduct that results in the official's personal gain." *Id.* at 725. Third, and most importantly, *Sawyer* holds that the government must not merely indicate wrongdoing by a public official, but must also demonstrate that the wrongdoing at issue is intended to prevent or call into question the proper or impartial performance of that public servant's official duties. (citing pre-*McNally* precedent to demonstrate that even where public officials violated state laws, their actions were not found to defraud citizens of their right to honest services, because the officials did not actually fail to perform their official duties properly). In other words, "although a public official might engage in reprehensible misconduct related to an official position, the conviction of that official cannot stand where the conduct does not actually deprive the public of its right to her honest services, and it is not shown to intend that result." *Id.*

Applying these principles to Czubinski's acts, it is clear that his conviction cannot stand. First, this case falls outside of the core of honest services fraud precedents. Czubinski was not bribed or otherwise influenced in any public decisionmaking capacity. Nor did he embezzle funds. He did not receive, nor can it be found that he intended to receive, any tangible benefit. His official duty was to respond to informational requests from taxpayers regarding their returns, a relatively straightforward task that simply does not raise the specter of secretive, self-interested action, as does a discretionary, decision-making role.

Second, we believe that the cautionary language of *Sawyer* is particularly appropriate here, given the evidence amassed by the defendant at trial indicating that during his span of employment at IRS, he received no indication from his employer that this workplace violation—the performance of unauthorized searches—would be punishable by anything more than dismissal. "To allow every transgression of state governmental obligations to amount to mail fraud would effectively turn every such violation into a federal felony; this cannot be countenanced." *Sawyer*, 85 F.3d at 728. Here, the threat is one of transforming governmental workplace violations into felonies. We find no evidence that Congress intended to create what amounts to a draconian personnel regulation. We hesitate to imply such an unusual result in the absence of the clearest legislative mandate.

These general considerations, although serious, are not conclusive: they raise doubts as to the propriety of this conviction that can be outweighed by sufficient evidence of a scheme to defraud. The third principle identified in *Sawyer*, instructing us as to the basic requirements of a scheme to defraud in this context, settles any remaining doubts. The conclusive consideration is that the government simply did not prove that Czubinski deprived, or intended to deprive, the public or his employer of their right to his honest services. Although he clearly committed wrongdoing in searching confidential information, there is no suggestion that he failed to carry out his official tasks adequately, or intended to do so.

The government alleges that, in addition to defrauding the public of his honest services, Czubinski has defrauded the IRS as well. The IRS is a public entity, rendering this contention sufficiently answered by our holding above that Czubinski did not defraud the public of his honest services. Even if the IRS were a private employer, however, the pre-*McNally* honest services convictions involving private fraud victims indicate that there must be a breach of a fiduciary duty to an employer that involves self-dealing of an order significantly more serious than the misconduct at issue here. Once again, the government has failed to prove that Czubinski intended to use the IRS files he browsed for any private purposes, and hence his actions, however reprehensible, do not rise to the level of a scheme to defraud his employer of his honest services.

II.   The Computer Fraud Counts

Czubinski was convicted on all four of the computer fraud counts on which he was indicted; these counts arise out of unauthorized searches that also formed the basis of four of the ten wire fraud counts in the indictment. Specifically, he was convicted of violating 18 U.S.C. § 1030(a)(4), a provision enacted in the Computer Fraud and Abuse Act of 1986. Section 1030(a)(4) applies to:

> whoever ... knowingly and with intent to defraud, accesses a Federal interest computer without authorization, or exceeds authorized access, and by means of such conduct furthers the intended fraud and obtains anything of value, unless the object of the fraud and the thing obtained consists only of the use of the computer.

We have never before addressed section 1030(a)(4). Czubinski unquestionably exceeded authorized access to a Federal interest computer. On appeal he argues that he did not obtain "anything of value." We agree, finding that his searches of taxpayer return information did not satisfy the statutory requirement that he obtain "anything of value." The value of information is relative to one's needs and objectives; here, the government had to show that the information was valuable to Czubinski in light of a fraudulent scheme. The government failed, however, to prove that Czubinski intended anything more than to satisfy idle curiosity.

The plain language of section 1030(a)(4) emphasizes that more than mere unauthorized use is required: the "thing obtained" may not merely be the unauthorized use. It is the showing of some additional end—to which the unauthorized access is a means—that is lacking here. The evidence did not show that Czubinski's end was anything more than to satisfy his curiosity by viewing information about friends, acquaintances, and political rivals. No evidence suggests that he printed out, recorded, or used the information he browsed. No rational jury could conclude beyond a reasonable doubt that Czubinski intended to use or disclose that information, and merely viewing information cannot be deemed the same as obtaining something of value for the purposes of this statute.

The legislative history further supports our reading of the term "anything of value." "In the game of statutory interpretation, statutory language is the ultimate trump card," and the remarks of sponsors of legislation are authoritative only to the extent that they are compatible with the plain language of section 1030(a)(4). Rhode Island v. Narragansett Indian Tribe, 19 F.3d 685, 699 (1st Cir.1994). Here, a Senate co-sponsor's comments suggest that Congress intended section 1030(a)(4) to punish attempts to steal valuable data, and did not wish to punish mere unauthorized access:

> The acts of fraud we are addressing in proposed section 1030(a)(4) are essentially thefts in which someone uses a federal interest computer to wrongly obtain something of value from another. ... Proposed section 1030(a)(4) is intended to reflect the distinction between the theft of information, a felony, and mere unauthorized access, a misdemeanor.

132 Cong. Rec. 7128, 7129, 99th Cong., 2d. Sess. (1986). The Senate Committee Report further underscores the fact that this section should apply to those who steal information through unauthorized access as part of an illegal scheme:

> The Committee remains convinced that there must be a clear distinction between computer theft, punishable as a felony [under section 1030(a)(4)], and computer trespass, punishable in the first instance as a misdemeanor [under a different provision]. The element in the new paragraph (a)(4), requiring a showing of an intent to defraud, is meant to preserve that distinction, as is the requirement that the property wrongfully obtained via computer furthers the intended fraud.

S. Rep. No. 132, 99th Cong., 2d Sess., reprinted in 1986 U.S.C.C.A.N. 2479. For the same reasons we deemed the trial evidence could not support a finding that Czubinski deprived the IRS of its property, we find that Czubinski has not obtained valuable information in furtherance of a fraudulent scheme for the purposes of section 1030(a)(4).

CONCLUSION

We add a cautionary note. The broad language of the mail and wire fraud statutes are both their blessing and their curse. They can address new forms of serious crime that fail to fall within more specific legislation. On the other hand, they might be used to prosecute kinds of behavior that, albeit offensive to the morals or aesthetics of federal prosecutors, cannot reasonably be expected by the instigators to form the basis of a federal felony. The case at bar falls within the latter category. Also discomforting is the prosecution's insistence, before trial, on the admission of inflammatory evidence regarding the defendant's membership in white supremacist groups purportedly as a means to prove a scheme to defraud, when, on appeal, it argues that unauthorized access in itself is a sufficient ground for conviction on all counts. Finally, we caution that the wire fraud statute must not serve as a vehicle for prosecuting only those citizens whose views run against the tide, no matter how incorrect or uncivilized such views are.

For the reasons stated in this opinion, we hold the district court's denial of defendant's motion for judgment of acquittal on counts 1, 2, and 4 through 14, to be in error. The defendant's conviction is thus reversed on all counts.

Notes

1. The offense for which Czubinski was convicted was § 1030(a)(4) of the Computer Fraud and Abuse Act of 1986. At the time of the Czubinski's conduct this provision provided:

> [W]hoever * * * knowingly and with intent to defraud, accesses a Federal interest computer without authorization, or exceeds authorized access, and by means of such conduct furthers the intended fraud and obtains anything of value, unless the object of the fraud and the thing obtained consists only of the use of the computer.

Since Czubinski's conviction, § 1030(a)(4) has been amended in two respects. First, the type of computer covered by the statute is broader. As noted *supra*, instead of applying to "federal interest computers," the current statute applies to a "protected computers." The second change concerns the requirement that the defendant must obtain a thing of value before there is a violation. The current statute provides that the "object of the fraud and the thing obtained" consist of the use of the computer *if* the value of such is "more than $5,000 in any 1–year period." Do you think the outcome in *Czubinski* would have been different if the current version of § 1030(a)(4) had been in place when Czubinski reviewed the tax records at issue?

2. Harry Donald Rice was an IRS employee who accessed IRS criminal investigation files to help a friend. As you read about Rice's activities from the following excerpts of United States v. Rice, 961 F.2d 211 (4th Cir.1992) (unpublished), determine how his conduct differs from Czubinski's. Is Czubinski's conduct more, or less, blameworthy than Rice's?

> "Rice was an agent of the Internal Revenue Service (IRS) for many years. In 1987 he became aware that a longtime friend, Walter Dennis Purser, who was heavily involved in drug dealing, was attempting to avoid a possible forfeiture of his house by transferring it for no consideration to the name of Coy Allred, another old friend of both Rice and Purser. When Purser asked Rice's opinion of the transfer, Rice told him it was a good idea, but suggested that Purser and Allred draw up a promissory note to protect Allred by making the deal appear legitimate. Eventually, Rice prepared the promissory note himself.

> "Sometime later, worried that he might be the subject of a criminal investigation, Purser asked Rice to find out whether he was being investigated by the IRS and gave Rice his Social Security number. Although Rice was not in the criminal division of the IRS and was not authorized to obtain information about Purser, he did so. Rice showed the confidential computer printout he obtained to Purser, and later

talked to the agent who was investigating Purser to find out what the codes on the printout meant. He subsequently told Purser that he was being investigated and that his garbage was being checked. Rice also disclosed the identity of the agent conducting the investigation. After this time, the investigating agent noticed that Purser's garbage no longer contained names or phone numbers.

Rice was convicted by a jury of conspiracy to launder drug profits (18 U.S.C. § 1956); conspiracy to defraud the United States of forfeitable property (26 U.S.C. § 7214); computer fraud (18 U.S.C. § 1030(a)(3)); and unauthorized disclosure of confidential information (18 U.S.C. § 1905). His friend, Purser, testified against him at trial.

At the time of Rice's conduct § 1030(a)(3) provided:

> (3) intentionally, without authorization to access any computer of a department or agency of the United States, accesses such a computer of that department or agency that is exclusively for the use of the Government of the United States or, in the case of a computer not exclusively for such use, is used by or for the Government of the United States and such conduct affects the use of the Government's operation of such computer.

Could the above section apply to Czubinski's conduct? If you were the prosecutor, how would you argue that it did?

3. Apparently, "browsing" by IRS employees is something of a problem. In 1997, the General Accounting Office issued a report concluding that despite the fact "unauthorized and improper browsing of taxpayer records has been the focus of considerable attention in recent years, * * * the IRS still does not effectively monitor employees actively, accurately record browsing violations, consistently punish offenders, or widely publicize reports of incidents detected and penalties imposed. * * * "[rr] In fiscal year 1995 the IRS' records showed 869 reported cases of browsing by IRS employees.[ss] "One employe was found to have browsed through the tax records of Elizabeth Taylor, Tom Cruise and Elvis Presley."[tt]

The IRS has stepped up its efforts to stop browsing but, as the following Congressional testimony from the Deputy Commissioner of the Internal Revenue Service demonstrates, decisions such as *Czubinski* make it harder for the IRS to crack down on browsing:

> "One taxpayer security area of particular concern to this Subcommittee and to us is the unauthorized access to taxpayer data by IRS employees—or 'browsing.' The IRS does not tolerate browsing. We consistently stress both within and outside the IRS that unauthorized access of taxpayer accounts by IRS employees will not be tolerated. However, recent court cases, especially one in the First Circuit Court of Appeals (United States v. Czubinski, No. 9–1317, 1997 U.S.App. LEXIS 3077 (1st Cir. February 21, 1997)), are very troubling to employees who violate our policy against unauthorized access.

---

rr. GAO, IRS Systems Security and Funding: Employee Browsing Not Being Addressed Effectively 1 (April, 1977).

ss. *Id.* at 5–6.

tt. Daniel Schorr, National Public Radio: Weekend Sunday (April 13, 1997) Transcript #97041306–215.

"In the past several years, the IRS has taken a number of steps to ensure that unauthorized access of taxpayer information by IRS employees does not occur. For example, each time an employee logs onto the taxpayer account data base (the Integrated Data Retrieval System) (IDRS), a statement warns of possible prosecution for unauthorized use of the system. All new users receive training on privacy and security of tax information before they are entitled to access the IDRS. The Service has also installed automated detection programs that monitor employees' actions and accesses to taxpayers' accounts, identify patterns of use, and alert managers to potential misuse.

* * *

"In addition to the internal actions, the IRS has recommended and supported legislative efforts to amend the Internal Revenue Code and Title 18 to clarify the criminal sanctions for unauthorized computer access to taxpayer information. A recent amendment to 18 U.S.C. § 1030(a)(2)(B) provides criminal misdemeanor penalties for anyone who intentionally accesses a computer without authorization or who exceeds authorized access and thereby obtains information including tax information, from any department or agency of the United States. Although the recent amendment to 18 U.S.C. will hopefully serve as a significant deterrent to unauthorized computer access of taxpayer information, this statute only applies to unauthorized access of computer records. It does not apply to unauthorized access or inspection of paper tax returns and related tax information. Legislation such as S.670, introduced in the 104th Congress, would achieve that result. By clarifying the criminal sanctions for unauthorized access or inspection of tax information in section 7213 of the Internal Revenue Code, whether that information is in computer or paper format, the confidentiality of tax information and related enforcement mechanisms would be appropriately found in the Internal Revenue Code."[uu]

C. COMPUTER TECHNOLOGY AND THE CONSTITUTION

1. COPYRIGHT PROTECTION AND ARTICLE I

Industry groups estimate that copyright holders of computer software, compact music discs, and movies lose $20 billion each year in sales because of copyright piracy.[vv] Copyright protection for material sent over the Internet presents constitutional and logistical hurdles. Article I of the Constitution envisions a free flow of ideas by declaring that the purpose of copyright protection is to promote science and the arts: Congress is given the power "to promote the progress of science and the useful arts, by securing for limited times to authors and inventors the

---

uu. *Hearing before House Comm. on Gov't Reform and Oversight, Subcomm. on Gov't Management, Information and Technology* (Apr. 14, 1997) (Testimony of Michael P. Dolan, Deputy Com'r, IRS).

vv. John Gibeant, *Zapping Cyber Piracy,* ABA JOURNAL 60, 61 (1997).

exclusive right to their respective writings and discoveries." Thus, under the Copyright Act only creative expression, not facts or ideas are protected.[ww] Protection of databases on the Internet blurs this distinction, however. In addition, because of the speed, anonymity and quality of reproductions ("indistinguishable from the original"),[xx] it is logistically difficult to protect copyrights on the Internet.

The next case, United States v. LaMacchia, 871 F.Supp. 535 (D.Mass.1994), highlights some of the difficulties encountered when copyright laws meet computer technology. As you read this case, determine whether you would rule the same way as Judge Stearns. If not, why not?

UNITED STATES v. LAMACCHIA

United States District Court, District of Massachusetts, 1994.
871 F.Supp. 535.

STEARNS, DISTRICT JUDGE.

This case presents the issue of whether new wine can be poured into an old bottle. The facts, as seen in the light most favorable to the government, are these. The defendant, David LaMacchia, is a twenty-one year old student at the Massachusetts Institute of Technology (MIT). LaMacchia, a computer hacker, used MIT's computer network to gain entree to the Internet. Using pseudonyms and an encrypted address, LaMacchia set up an electronic bulletin board which he named Cynosure.[1] He encouraged his correspondents to upload popular software applications (Excel 5.0 and WordPerfect 6.0) and computer games (Sim City 2000). These he transferred to a second encrypted address (Cynosure II) where they could be downloaded by other users with access to the Cynosure password. Although LaMacchia was at pains to impress the need for circumspection on the part of his subscribers, the worldwide traffic generated by the offer of free software attracted the notice of university and federal authorities.

On April 7, 1994, a federal grand jury returned a one count indictment charging LaMacchia with conspiring with "persons unknown" to violate 18 U.S.C. § 1343, the wire fraud statute. According to the indictment, LaMacchia devised a scheme to defraud that had as its object the facilitation "on an international scale" of the "illegal copying and distribution of copyrighted software" without payment of licensing fees and royalties to software manufacturers and vendors. The indictment alleges that LaMacchia's scheme caused losses of more than one million

---

ww. 17 U.S.C. § 102(b) 1995; see also: Brian G. Brunsvold and William H. Pratt, *Intellectual Property Rights—What Are They and How Does a Company Secure Them?*, SB04 ALI-ABA 137, 150 (1996); Russ VanSteeg and Paul K. Harrington, *Nonobviousness As an Element of Copyrightability? (or, Is the Jewel in the Lotus a Cubic Zirconiz?)*, 25 U.C. DAVIS L. REV. 331, 341 (1992).

xx. John Gibeant, *Zapping Cyber Piracy*, ABA JOURNAL 60, 62 (1997).

1. The allusion is presumably to the North Star, a faithful astronomical reference point for mariners.

dollars to software copyright holders. The indictment does not allege that LaMacchia sought or derived any personal benefit from the scheme to defraud.

On September 30, 1994, the defendant brought a motion to dismiss, arguing that the government had improperly resorted to the wire fraud statute as a copyright enforcement tool in defiance of the Supreme Court's decision in Dowling v. United States, 473 U.S. 207 (1985). The government argues that *Dowling* is a narrower case than LaMacchia would have it, and holds only that copyright infringement does not satisfy the physical "taking" requirement of the National Stolen Property Act, 18 U.S.C. § 2314.

The Dowling Decision

Paul Edmond Dowling was convicted of conspiracy, interstate transportation of stolen property [ITSP], copyright violations and mail fraud in the Central District of California. Dowling and his co-conspirators sold bootleg Elvis Presley recordings by soliciting catalogue orders from post office boxes in Glendale, California. The infringing recordings were shipped in interstate commerce to Maryland and Florida. The eight ITSP counts on which Dowling was convicted involved thousands of phonograph albums. "[E]ach album contained performances of copyrighted musical compositions for the use of which no licenses had been obtained nor royalties paid. ..." *Dowling, supra* at 212. Dowling appealed his convictions (except those involving copyright infringement). The Ninth Circuit Court of Appeals affirmed. "[T]he [Ninth Circuit] reasoned that the rights of copyright owners in their protected property were indistinguishable from ownership interests in other types of property and were equally deserving of protection under the [stolen property] statute." *Id.*

The Supreme Court granted certiorari only as to Dowling's convictions for interstate transportation of stolen property. The Court, in an opinion by Justice Blackmun, held that a copyrighted musical composition impressed on a bootleg phonograph record is not property that is "stolen, converted, or taken by fraud" within the meaning of the Stolen Property Act. Justice Blackmun emphasized that cases prosecuted under § 2314 had traditionally involved "physical 'goods, wares [or] merchandise.' "The statute "seems clearly to contemplate a physical identity between the items unlawfully obtained and those eventually transported, and hence some prior physical taking of the subject goods" *Id.* at 216. In Dowling's case there was no evidence "that Dowling wrongfully came by the phonorecords actually shipped or the physical materials from which they were made." *Dowling, supra* at 214.

Justice Blackmun felt compelled, however, to answer the government's argument that the unauthorized use of the underlying musical compositions was itself sufficient to render the offending phonorecords property "stolen, converted or taken by fraud."

[T]he Government's theory here would make theft, conversion, or fraud equivalent to wrongful appropriation of statutorily protected rights in copyright. The copyright owner, however, holds no ordinary chattel. A copyright, like other intellectual property, comprises a series of carefully defined and carefully delimited interests to which the law affords correspondingly exact protections. *Id.* at 216, 105 S.Ct. at 3133.

A copyright, as Justice Blackmun explained, is unlike an ordinary chattel because the holder does not acquire exclusive dominion over the thing owned. The limited nature of the property interest conferred by copyright stems from an overriding First Amendment concern for the free dissemination of ideas. "The primary objective of copyright is not to reward the labor of authors, but '[t]o promote the Progress of Science and useful Arts.' Art. I, § 8, cl. 8." Justice Blackmun offered the "fair use" doctrine (17 U.S.C. § 107) and the statutory scheme of compulsory licensing of musical compositions (17 U.S.C. § 115) as examples of ways in which the property rights of a copyright holder are circumscribed by the Copyright Act. *Dowling, supra,* 473 U.S. at 217.

It follows that interference with copyright does not easily equate with theft, conversion or fraud. The Copyright Act even employs a separate term of art to define one who misappropriates a copyright: "Anyone who violates any of the exclusive rights of the copyright owner," that is, anyone who trespasses into his exclusive domain by using or authorizing the use of the copyrighted work in one of the five ways set forth in the statute, "is an infringer of the copyright." There is no dispute in this case that Dowling's unauthorized inclusion on his bootleg albums of performances of copyrighted compositions constituted infringement of those copyrights. It is less clear, however, that the taking that occurs when an infringer arrogates the use of another's protected work comfortably fits the terms associated with physical removal employed by § 2314. The infringer invades a statutorily defined province guaranteed to the copyright holder alone. But he does not assume physical control over the copyright; nor does he wholly deprive its owner of its use. While one may colloquially like infringement with some general notion of wrongful appropriation, infringement plainly implicates a more complex set of property interests than does run-of-the-mill theft, conversion, or fraud. As a result, it fits but awkwardly with the language Congress chose—"stolen, converted or taken by fraud"—to describe the sorts of goods whose interstate shipment § 2314 makes criminal. *Id.* at 217–218.

The ITSP statute, Justice Blackmun observed, had its roots in efforts by Congress to supplement the efforts of state authorities frustrated by jurisdictional problems arising from the transportation of stolen property across state lines. *Id.* at 219–220.

No such need for supplemental federal action has ever existed, however, with respect to copyright infringement, for the obvious reason that Congress always has had the bestowed authority to legislate directly in this area. ... Given that power, it is implausible to suppose that Congress intended to combat the problem of copyright infringement by the circuitous route hypothesized by the government. ... In sum, the premise of § 2314—the need to fill with federal action an enforcement chasm created by limited state jurisdiction—simply does not apply to the conduct the Government seeks to reach here. *Id.* at 220–221.

A review of the evolution of criminal penalties in the Copyright Act led Justice Blackmun to observe that:

> [T]he history of the criminal infringement provisions of the Copyright Act reveals a good deal of care on Congress' part before subjecting copyright infringement to serious criminal penalties. . . . In stark contrast, the Government's theory of this case presupposes a congressional decision to bring the felony provisions of § 2314, which make available the comparatively light fine of not more than $10,000 but the relatively harsh term of imprisonment of up to 10 years, to bear on the distribution of a sufficient quantity of any infringing goods simply because of the presence here of a factor— interstate transportation—not otherwise though relevant to copyright law. The Government thereby presumes congressional adoption of an indirect but blunderbuss solution to a problem treated with precision when considered directly. *Id.* at 225–226.

Finally, noting that the government's expansive reading of the Stolen Property Act would have the unsettling effect of criminalizing a broad range of conduct involving copyright and other intellectual property that had been historically regulated by the civil laws, Justice Blackmun concluded that "the deliberation with which Congress over the last decade has addressed the problem of copyright infringement for profit, as well as the precision with which it has chosen to apply criminal penalties in this area, demonstrates anew the wisdom of leaving it to the legislature to define crime and prescribe penalties. Here, the language of § 2314 does not 'plainly and unmistakably' cover petitioner Dowling's conduct." *Id.* at 228. Dowling's ITSP convictions were reversed.

The Copyright Law

Article I, § 8, cl. 8 of the U.S. Constitution grants Congress the exclusive power "[t]o promote the Progress of Science and useful Arts, by securing for limited Times to Authors and Inventors the exclusive Right to their respective writings and Discoveries." Thus "[t]he remedies for infringement 'are only those prescribed by Congress.'" Sony Corporation of America v. Universal City Studios, Inc., 464 U.S. 417, 431 (1984). Since 1897, when criminal copyright infringement was first introduced into U.S. copyright law, the concept differentiating criminal from civil copyright violations has been that the infringement must be pursued for purposes of commercial exploitation.

Until 1909, "[t]he crime of copyright infringement was . . . limited to unlawful performances and representation of copyrighted dramatic and musical compositions." Saunders, Criminal Copyright Infringement and the Copyright Felony Act, 71 Denv.U.L.Rev. 671, 673 (1994). The 1897 Act defined the mens rea of criminal copyright infringement as conduct that is "willful" and undertaken "for profit," a definition that remained unaltered until the general revision of the Copyright Act in 1976.

In 1909, the Copyright Act was revised to extend misdemeanor criminal sanctions to infringement of all copyrighted material with the exception of sound recordings. The 1909 amendments also made criminal the knowing and willful aiding and abetting of another's infringing activities. Performers and producers of musical recordings were not protected under the 1909 Act, and composers were given the exclusive rights to license only the first recording of their musical works. After that, a compulsory licensing provision allowed anyone to record and distribute the work so long as a two cent per copy royalty was paid to the original composer.

The framework set out by the 1909 Act remained in effect until 1971, when the growth of the recording industry following the musical revolution of the 1960's brought the problem of unauthorized reproduction and sale of musical works to Congress' attention. In response, Congress passed the Sound Recording Act of 1971, which addressed the perceived flaw in the 1909 Act by granting sound recordings full copyright protection, including criminal penalties for profit motivated infringement. In 1976, Congress revamped the Copyright Act by eliminating the crime of aiding and abetting copyright infringement. It also eased the mens rea requirement for criminal copyright infringement by eliminating the burden of proving that an infringer acted "for profit," requiring instead only that the infringement be conducted "willfully and for purposes of commercial advantage or private financial gain." 17 U.S.C. § 506(a). Criminal infringement under the 1976 Act was a misdemeanor except in the case of repeat offenders (who could be sentenced to a maximum of two years and a fine of $50,000).

After lobbying by the Motion Picture Association and the Recording Industry Association, Congress increased the penalties for criminal infringement in 1982. Certain types of first-time criminal infringement were punishable as felonies depending on the time period involved and the number of copies reproduced or distributed.[5] The mens rea element, however, remained unchanged, requiring proof of "commercial advantage or private financial gain." 17 U.S.C. § 506(a). Most criminal infringements remained misdemeanor offenses despite the new penalty structure.

In the decade following the 1982 revisions to the Copyright Act, the home computing and software industry underwent a period of explosive growth paralleling the expansion in the 1960's and 1970's of the recording and motion picture industries. In 1992, the Software Publishers Association reported in testimony to the Subcommittee on Intellectual Property and Judicial Administration of the House Committee on the Judiciary that software manufacturers were losing $2.4 billion in revenues annually as a result of software piracy. "Rather than adopting a piecemeal approach to copyright legislation and simply adding computer

---

5. While the offense of criminal copyright infringement remained defined by 17 U.S.C. § 506(a), the penalties were moved to a new freestanding statute, 18 U.S.C. § 2319.

programs to audiovisual works, and sound recordings to the list of works whose infringement can give rise to felony penalties under [18 U.S.C.] § 2319," Congress passed the Copyright Felony Act. The Act amended § 2319 by extending its felony provisions to the criminal infringement of all copyrighted works including computer software. The mens rea for criminal infringement remained unchanged, requiring prosecutors to prove that the defendant infringed a copyright "willfully and for purpose of commercial advantage or private financial gain." 17 U.S.C. § 506(a).

DISCUSSION

The wire fraud statute, 18 U.S.C. § 1343 was enacted in 1952. In its entirety, the statute reads as follows:

Whoever, having devised or intending to devise any scheme or artifice to defraud, or for obtaining money or property by means of false or fraudulent pretenses, representations, or promises, transmits or causes to be transmitted by means of wire, radio, or television communication in interstate or foreign commerce, any writings, signs, signals, pictures, or sounds for the purpose of executing such scheme or artifice, shall be fined not more than $1,000 or imprisoned not more than five years, or both. If the violation affects a financial institution, such person shall be fined not more than $1,000,000 or imprisoned not more than 30 years, or both.

* * *

As the legislative history makes clear, the wire fraud statute was intended to complement the mail fraud statute by giving federal prosecutors jurisdiction over frauds involving the use of interstate (or foreign) wire transmissions. Thus what can be prosecuted as a scheme to defraud under the mail fraud statute (18 U.S.C. § 1341) is equally susceptible to punishment under § 1343 so long as the jurisdictional element is met.

A scheme to defraud is the defining concept of the mail and wire fraud statutes. Because of the conjunctive use of the word "or" in the statutory phrase "any scheme or artifice to defraud, or for obtaining money or property by false or fraudulent pretenses, representations, or promises," the federal courts (encouraged by prosecutors) have essentially bifurcated mail and wire fraud into two separate offenses; the first, the devising of a scheme to defraud, the second, the devising of a scheme to obtain money or property by false pretenses. While the latter crime comports with common law notions of fraud, "[t]he phrase, 'a scheme to defraud' came to prohibit a plan, that is, to forbid a state of mind, rather than physical conduct." Moohr, *Mail Fraud and the Intangible Rights Doctrine: Someone to Watch Over Us*, 31 Harv.J. on Legis. 153, 161 (1994).

The incarnation of mail fraud as an inchoate crime has its most celebrated expression in federal prosecutions of state and local public officials accused of depriving citizens of their intangible right to honest public service in violation of their fiduciary duty to disclose conflicts of interest. Because of the so-called "intangible rights doctrine," mail fraud and its sister offense, wire fraud, have become the federal prosecutor's weapon of choice. "Mail fraud ... has been expanded to the point that a fiduciary, agent, or employee commits an offense when, through a material deception or a failure to disclose a beneficiary, principal or employer suffers even an intangible, constructed detriment." *Moohr, supra*. Wire fraud offers an especially pleasing feature from the government's perspective that is particularly relevant to LaMacchia's case. Unlike the criminal copyright statute, 17 U.S.C. § 506(a), the mail and wire fraud statutes do not require that a defendant be shown to have sought to personally profit from the scheme to defraud.

While it is true, as LaMacchia contends, that the denial of a writ of certiorari "imports no expression upon the merits of the case," United States v. Carver, 260 U.S. 482, 490 (1923), the more interesting issue is whether the Ninth Circuit's mail fraud analysis (the significant portions of which the Supreme Court left intact) is applicable to the facts of his case.

Dowling brought himself within the orbit of the mail fraud statute by mailing catalogues advertising his bootleg phonograph records. So, too, the government argues, LaMacchia subjected himself to the wire fraud statute by advertising infringing software via computer transmissions. The government in *Dowling* (as here) did not argue any more than jurisdictional significance for Dowling's mailings, that is, the mailings themselves did not make any false or misleading representations. They did, however, serve as an obvious means of furthering Dowling's scheme to defraud.

The Ninth Circuit nonetheless focused on the fact that Dowling had "concealed his activities from the copyright holders with the intent to deprive them of their royalties." United States v. Dowling, 739 F.2d 1445, 1449 (9th Cir.1984). "It is settled in this Circuit that a scheme to defraud need not be an active misrepresentation. A nondisclosure or concealment may serve as a basis for the fraudulent scheme." *Id.* at 1448. The Ninth Circuit rejected Dowling's argument that non-disclosure can serve as the basis of a scheme to defraud only when a defendant has a fiduciary duty to make an affirmative disclosure. It also rejected the government's contention that "the presence of illegal conduct alone may constitute the basis of the 'fraud' element." 739 F.2d at 1449. "Rather, we conclude that a non-disclosure can only serve as a basis for a fraudulent scheme when there exists an independent duty that has been breached by the person so charged." *Id.* This duty, the Ninth Circuit noted, could be fiduciary in nature, or it could "derive from an independent explicit statutory duty created by legislative enactment." *Id.* In Dowling's case, the duty located by the Ninth Circuit was the duty implicit in the compulsory licensing scheme of the Copyright Act, 17 U.S.C. § 115, which requires vendors to notify copyright owners of the intention to manufacture and distribute infringing records.

In conclusion, we stress that the narrowness of our holding permits nondisclosures to form the basis of a scheme to defraud only when there exists an independent duty (either fiduciary or derived from an explicit and independent statutory requirement) and such a duty has been breached. To hold otherwise that illegal conduct alone may constitute the basis of the fraud element of a mail fraud conviction would have the potential of bringing almost any illegal act within the province of the mail fraud statute.

739 F.2d at 1450.

The difficulties in applying the Ninth Circuit's *Dowling* analysis to support a wire fraud prosecution in LaMacchia's case are three. First, no fiduciary relationship existed between LaMacchia and the manufacturers whose software copyrights he allegedly infringed. Second, there is no independent statutory duty of disclosure like the one that snared Dowling because there is no software equivalent to the compulsory licensing scheme. Third, even were I to accept the argument made by the government in *Dowling*, that illegal conduct alone may suffice to satisfy the fraud element of [§ 1343], the holding would not cover LaMacchia's case for the simple reason that what LaMacchia is alleged to have done is not criminal conduct under § 506(a) of the Copyright Act.

The government's second and more plausible argument relies on the unobjectionable proposition "that [the] enactment of particularized federal interest statutes does not oust a more general interstate commerce statute from application." Government's Memorandum at 11. The government cites a number of areas of specialized federal law where the mail and wire fraud statutes have been held to remain viable enforcement tools. This same argument, however, did not impress Justice Blackmun in *Dowling*, as none of the cases cited there (as here) "involved copyright law specifically or intellectual property in general." *Dowling, supra*, 473 U.S. at 218 n. 8. The government also points to 18 U.S.C. § 2319(a), which provides that "[w]hoever violates section 506(a) ... of title 17 shall be punished as provided in subsection (b) of this section and such penalties shall be in addition to any other provisions of title 17 or any other law." The government emphasizes the last four words of the statute without apparently noticing the first four. LaMacchia is not alleged to have violated section 506(a). * * *

The issue thus is whether the "bundle of rights" conferred by copyright is unique and distinguishable from the indisputably broad range of property interests protected by the mail and wire fraud statutes. I find it difficult, if not impossible, to read *Dowling* as saying anything but that it is. "A copyright, like other intellectual property, comprises a series of carefully defined and carefully delimited interests to which the law affords correspondingly exact protections." *Dowling*, 473 U.S. at 216. If, as the government contends, *Dowling* stands for nothing more than the proposition that one cannot equate copyright infringement with a "physical taking" for purposes of the Stolen Property Act, it is difficult to explain why Justice Blackmun devoted the bulk of his opinion to the issue of "whether the history and purpose of § 2314 evince a plain congressional intention to reach interstate shipments of goods infringing copyrights." *Dowling*, *supra* at 218, 105 S.Ct. at 3134. Nor can one explain why the same analysis should not be applied to the mail and wire fraud statutes, which like the Stolen Property Act, were enacted to fill enforcement gaps in state and federal law. Why is it not true of mail and wire fraud, as it is of ITSP, that "[n]o such need for supplemental federal action has ever existed . . . , for the obvious reason that Congress always has had the bestowed authority to legislate directly in this area [of copyright infringement]"? *Dowling*, *supra* at 220. Finally, why would not the government's position here produce the same pernicious result that Justice Blackmun warned of in *Dowling*, of permitting the government to subvert the carefully calculated penalties of the Copyright Act by selectively bringing some prosecutions under the more generous penalties of the mail and wire fraud statutes?

What the government is seeking to do is to punish conduct that reasonable people might agree deserves the sanctions of the criminal law. But as Justice Blackmun observed in *Dowling*, copyright is an area in which Congress has chosen to tread cautiously, relying "chiefly . . . on an array of civil remedies to provide copyright holders protection against infringement," while mandating "studiously graded penalties" in those instances where Congress has concluded that the deterrent effect of criminal sanctions are required. *Dowling*, at 221, 225. "This step-by-step, carefully considered approach is consistent with Congress' traditional sensitivity to the special concerns implicated by the copyright laws." *Id.* at 225. Indeed, the responsiveness of Congress to the impact of new technology on the law of copyright, limned [sic] earlier in this opinion, confirms Justice Blackmun's conviction of "the wisdom of leaving it to the legislature to define crime and prescribe penalties." *Dowling*, supra at 228.

The judiciary's reluctance to expand the protections afforded by the copyright without explicit legislative guidance is a recurring theme. Sound policy, as well as history, supports our consistent deference to Congress when major technological innovations alter the market for copyrighted materials. Congress has the institutional authority and the institutional ability to accommodate fully the varied permutations of competing interests that are inevitably implicated by such new technology.

Sony Corporation of America v. Universal City Studios, Inc., 464 U.S. 417, 431 (1984).

While the government's objective is a laudable one, particularly when the facts alleged in this case are considered, its interpretation of the wire fraud statute would serve to criminalize the conduct of not only persons like LaMacchia, but also the myriad of home computer users who succumb to the temptation to copy even a single software program for private use. It is not clear that making criminals of a large number of consumers of computer software is a result that even the software industry would consider desirable.

In sum, I agree with Professor Nimmer that:

The *Dowling* decision establishes that Congress has finely calibrated the reach of criminal liability [in the Copyright Act], and therefore absent clear indication of Congressional intent, the criminal laws of the United States do not reach copyright-related conduct. Thus copyright prosecutions should be limited to Section 506 of the Act, and other incidental statutes that explicitly refer to copyright and copyrighted works.

3 *Nimmer on Copyright*, § 15.05 at 15–20 (1993).

Accordingly, I rule that the decision of the Supreme Court in Dowling v. United States precludes LaMacchia's prosecution for criminal copyright infringement under the wire fraud statute.

This is not, of course, to suggest that there is anything edifying about what LaMacchia is alleged to have done. If the indictment is to be believed, one might at best describe his actions as heedlessly irresponsible, and at worst as nihilistic, self-indulgent, and lacking in any fundamental sense of values. Criminal as well as civil penalties should probably attach to willful, multiple infringements of copyrighted software even absent a commercial motive on the part of the infringer. One can envision ways that the copyright law could be modified to permit such prosecution. But, " '[i]t is the legislature, not the Court which is to define a crime, and ordain its punishment.' " *Dowling, supra*, 473 U.S. at 214.

ORDER

For the foregoing reasons, defendant LaMacchia's motion to dismiss is *ALLOWED*.

SO ORDERED.

Notes

1.   When arrested, LaMacchia was a twenty-one year old student at the Massachusetts Institute of Technology (M.I.T.). LaMacchia's response when he was apprehended after a sting operation conducted by the FBI and MIT officials was denial—that he was "just a user." Following dismissal of the charges, LaMacchia remained at M.I.T. working on a five-year master's program in electrical engineering and computer science.[yy] LaMacchia's activity cost software copyright holders more than $1 million in lost licensing fees and royalties.[zz]

2.   The dismissal of LaMacchia's prosecution "became a rallying point for those who say computer technology and the Internet are stretching U.S.

---

yy. Catherine Thérèse Clarke, *From CrimINet to Cyber–Perp: Toward an Inclusive Approach to Policing the Evolving Criminal mens Rea on the Internet*, 75 OR. L. REV. 191, 215–216 (1996).

zz. John Gibeaut, *Zapping Cyber Piracy*, ABA JOURNAL 60 (Feb. 1997).

and international copyright law to the breaking point."[a] There is no consensus on what should be done, however. In 1996, the World Intellectual Property Organization, comprised of 160 nations, agreed on broad international treaties to protect computerized works, but the details of how to provide this protection were left to the member nations. Also in 1996, Congress considered, but failed to pass, legislation addressing computer privacy. The legislation considered included a response to the *LaMacchia* ruling by substituting the requirement in the criminal copyright offense that the government must prove that the actor was motivated by profit, with the requirement that the actor "willfully" distribute works valued at $5,000 or more, regardless of whether the actor tried to make a profit. Additional provisions included in this legislation were protection of databases on the Internet against extraction, use of a substantial part of the contents of a database, or any "acts that conflict with a normal exploitation of the database or adversely affect the actual or potential market for the database." The legislation also prohibited the importation, manufacture and distribution of any product "the primary purpose * * * of which is to avoid, bypass, remove, deactivate, or otherwise circumvent * * * any process * * * which prevents or inhibits extraction * * * of the database."[b]

2. THE FOURTH AMENDMENT: SEARCHES, SEIZURES AND THE RIGHT TO PRIVACY IN CYBERSPACE

The Fourth Amendment provides, "The right of the people to be secure in their persons, houses, papers, and effects, against unreasonable searches and seizures, shall not be violated." Cyberspace crime promises to raise new and difficult Fourth Amendment issues. Simply executing a search warrant on computer generated evidence raises questions never before encountered. For example, rules of criminal procedure require that law enforcement officials seek a warrant in the jurisdiction where the property to be searched is located. But Internet searches pose problems: what is the property to be searched: hard drives, e-mail transmissions? Exactly where is the property to be searched: where the user logged in? where computer records were stored? where a transmission passed through?[c] Interestingly, development in civil lawsuits may impact on these questions. In 1996, for example, the United States Court of Appeals for the Sixth Circuit held that transmittal of 32 software files from a programmer in Texas to CompuServe in Ohio was sufficient to trigger personal jurisdiction in Ohio. According to the Court, in sending the files, the programmer "consciously reached out from Texas to Ohio."

a. *Id.* at 61.

b. A Bill to Amend Title 15, United States Code, To Promote Investment and Prevent Intellectual Property Piracy With Respect to Databases, HR 3531, 104th Cong., 2d Sess. (May 23, 1996). (Available Westlaw, Database, CONGBILLTXT 104).

c. Michael Adler, *Cyberspace, General Searches and Digital Contraband: The Fourth Amendment and the Net–Wide Search*, 105 Yale L. J. 1093 (1996). (Discussing how the property based jurisprudence under the Fourth Amendment is poorly suited to "digital contraband" and data.) Nicole Giallonardo, note, *Unauthorized Seizure of Private E–Mail Warrants More Than Fifth Circuit's Slap on the Wrist*, 14 J. Marshall J. Computer & Info L. 179 (1995).

The court noted, however, that simply subscribing to CompuServe would not establish jurisdiction.[d]

The Fourth Amendment provides that "Warrants shall * * * particularly describ[e] the place to be searched, and the persons or things to be seized." Historically courts have applied the particularity requirement with flexibility in white collar criminal investigations where many records are sought and the warrant describes the records generically. The Supreme Court has acknowledged that in fraud or complex investigations, evidence not directly relevant to the suspected offense is properly seized so as to help show "a consistent pattern of conduct highly relevant to the issue of intent."[e] Whether this flexible approach should be carried forth or even extended in investigations involving computer records remains to be seen.

As the next case, Steve Jackson Games, Inc. v. United States Secret Service, 816 F.Supp. 432 (W.D.Tex.1993), demonstrates, new technology presents privacy issues for citizens and difficulties for law enforcement when investigating crimes where computers hold evidence.

STEVE JACKSON GAMES, INC. v. UNITED STATES SECRET SERVICE
United States District Court, Western District of Texas, 1993.
816 F.Supp. 432.

Sparks, District Judge.

* * *

The Plaintiff Steve Jackson started Steve Jackson Games in 1980 and subsequently incorporated his business. Steve Jackson Games, Incorporated, publishes books, magazines, box games, and related products.[1] More than 50 percent of the corporation's revenues are derived from its publications. In addition, Steve Jackson Games, Incorporated, beginning in the mid–1980s and continuing through this litigation, operated from one of its computers an electronic bulletin board system called Illuminati. This bulletin board posts information to the inquiring public about Steve Jackson Games' products and activities; provides a medium for receiving and passing on information from the corporation's employees, writers, customers, and its game enthusiasts; and, finally, affords its users electronic mail whereby, with the use of selected passwords, its users can send and receive electronic mail (E-mail) in both public and private modes. In February of 1990, there were 365 users of the Illuminati bulletin board.

* * *

d. CompuServe v. Patterson, 89 F.3d 1257 (6th Cir.1996).

e. Andresen v. Maryland, 427 U.S. 463, 482–83 (1976) *quoting* Nye & Nissen v. United States, 336 U.S. 613 (1949).

1. While the content of these publications are not similar to those of daily newspapers, news magazines, or other publications usually thought of by this Court as disseminating information to the public, these products come within the literal language of the Privacy Protection Act.

[During 1988–1990, the United States Secret Service learned that a sensitive, proprietary document belonging to Bell South had been accessed and made available to the public. Mistakenly believing that Steve Jackson Games, Inc. was responsible for the unauthorized access and distribution; the United States Secret Service executed a search warrant on the premises of Steve Jackson games, Inc. Secret Service Agent Tim Foley coordinated most of the investigation at issue, including execution of the search warrant. Although there were errors in the affidavit,-ed.] the Court does not find from a preponderance of the evidence that the admitted errors in Foley's affidavit were intentional and so material to make the affidavit and issuance of the warrant legally improper. * * * Therefore, the Court denies the Plaintiff's contentions relating to the alleged improprieties involved in the issuance of the search warrant.

On March 1, 1990, Agents Foley and Golden executed the search warrant. At the time of the execution, each agent had available computer experts who had been flown to Austin to advise and review the stored information in the computers, the bulletin boards, and disks seized. These computer experts certainly had the ability to review the stored information and, importantly, to copy all information contained in the computers and disks within hours.

During the search of Steve Jackson Games and the seizure of the three computers, over 300 computer disks, and other materials, Agent Golden was orally advised by a Steve Jackson Games, Inc. Employee that Steve Jackson Games, Inc. was in the publishing business. Unfortunately, Agent Golden, like Foley, was unaware of the Privacy Protection Act and apparently attached no significance to this information.

By March 2, 1990, Agent Foley knew Steve Jackson Games, Inc. was in the publishing business and the seizure included documents intended for publication to the public, including a book and other forms of information. He also knew or had the ability to learn the seizure of the Illuminati bulletin board included private and public electronic communications and E-mail. By March 2, 1990, Agent Foley knew that Steve Jackson Games, Incorporated, and its attorneys in Dallas and Austin, were requesting the immediate return of the properties and information seized, that transcripts of publications and the back-up materials had been seized, and that the seizure of the documents, including business records of Steve Jackson Games, Inc., and their back-up was certain to economically damage Steve Jackson Games, Inc. While Agent Foley had a legitimate concern there might be some type of program designed to delete the materials, documents, or stored information he was seeking, he admits there was no valid reason why all information seized could not have been duplicated and returned to Steve Jackson Games within a period of hours and no more than eight days from the seizure. In fact, it was months (late June 1990) before the majority of the seized materials was returned. Agent Foley simply was unaware of the law and erroneously believed he had substantial criminal information which obviously was not present, as to date, no arrests or criminal charges have ever been filed against anyone, * * *.

In addition, Agent Foley must have known his seizure of computers, printers, disks and other materials and his refusal to provide copies represented a risk of substantial harm to Steve Jackson Games, Inc.—under circumstances where he had no reason to believe the corporation or its owner was involved in criminal activity.

The Secret Service denies that its personnel or its delegates read the private electronic communications stored in the seized materials and specifically allege that this information was reviewed by use of key search words only. Additionally, the Secret Service denies the deletion of any information seized with two exceptions of "sensitive" or "illegal" information, the deletion of which was consented to by Steve Jackson. However, the preponderance of the evidence, including common sense,[5] establishes that the Secret Service personnel or its delegates did read all electronic communications seized and did delete certain information and communications in addition to the two documents admitted deleted. The deletions by the Secret Service, other than the two documents consented to by Steve Jackson, were done without consent and cannot be justified.

By March 2, 1990, Agent Foley, Agent Golden, and the Secret Service, if aware of the Privacy Protection Act, would have known that they had, by a search warrant, seized work products of materials from a person or entity reasonably believed to have a purpose to disseminate to the public a "book" or "similar form of public communication."

The failure of the Secret Service after March 1, 1990, to—promptly—return the seized products of Steve Jackson Games, Incorporated cannot be justified and unquestionably caused economic damage to the corporation.

By March 1, 1990, Steve Jackson Games, Incorporated was apparently recovering from acute financial problems and suffering severe cash flow problems. The seizure of the work product and delays of publication, whether by three weeks or several months, directly impacted on Steve Jackson Games, Incorporated. Eight employees were terminated because they could not be paid as revenues from sales came in much later than expected. However, it is also clear from a preponderance of the evidence that after the calendar year 1990, the publicity surrounding this seizure and the nature of the products sold by Steve Jackson Games, Incorporated had the effect of increasing, not decreasing, sales. In fact, Steve Jackson Games, Incorporated developed a specific game for sale based upon the March 1, 1990, seizure. The Court declines to find from a preponderance of the evidence there was any economic damage to Steve Jackson Games, Incorporated after the calendar year 1990 as a result of the seizure of March 1, 1990.

As a result of the seizure of March 1, 1990, and the retention of the equipment and documents seized, Steve Jackson Games, Incorporated sustained out-of-pocket expenses of $8,781.00. The personnel at this corporation had to regroup, rewrite, and duplicate substantial prior

5. The application and the search warrant itself was worded by Foley and Cook so that all information would be "read" by the Secret Service.

efforts to publish the book Gurps Cyberpunk and other documents stored in the computers and the Illuminati bulletin board, explain to their clientele and users of the bulletin board the difficulties of their continuing business to maintain their clientele, to purchase or lease substitute equipment and supplies, to re-establish the bulletin board, and to get the business of Steve Jackson Games, Inc. back in order. The Court has reviewed the evidence regarding annual sales and net income of Steve Jackson Games, Incorporated for 1990 and the years before and after and finds from a preponderance of the evidence there was a 6 percent loss of sales in 1990 due to the seizure and related problems. The evidence was undisputed that there was a 42 percent profit on sales of publications of Steve Jackson Games, Incorporated. Thus, Steve Jackson Games, Incorporated sustained damages in loss of sales in 1990 of $100,617.00 for a loss of profit of $42,259.00 as a direct and proximate result of the seizure of March 1, 1990, and the retention of the documents seized. After 1990, the net sales of Steve Jackson Games, Incorporated continued to increase annually in a traditional proportion as the sales had been increasing from 1988. Thus, from a preponderance of the evidence, the loss of $42,259.00 is consistent with the net income figures of Steve Jackson Games, Incorporated in the years immediately following and preceding 1990.

Regarding damages to Steve Jackson, personally, his own testimony is that by 1990 he was becoming more active in the management of Steve Jackson Games, Incorporated, and spending less time in creative pursuits such as writing. Steve Jackson Games, Incorporated was in such financial condition that Chapter 11 proceedings in bankruptcy were contemplated. Thereafter, the testimony clearly established that Steve Jackson Games reasserted himself in management and was spending substantial time managing the corporation. The Court declines to find from a preponderance of the evidence that Steve Jackson personally sustained any compensatory damages as a result of the conduct of the United States Secret Service.

Elizabeth McCoy, Walter Milliken and Steffan O'Sullivan also allege compensatory damages. These Plaintiffs all had stored electronic communications, or E-mail, on the Illuminati bulletin board at the time of seizure. All three of these Plaintiffs testified that they had public and private communications in storage at the time of the seizure. Steve Jackson, Elizabeth McCoy, Walter Milliken and Steffan O'Sullivan all testified that following June of 1990 some of their stored electronic communications, or E-mail, had been deleted. It is clear, as hereinafter set out, that the conduct of the United States Secret Service violated two of the three statutes on which the causes of action of the Plaintiffs are based and, therefore, there are statutory damages involved, but the Court declines to find from a preponderance of the evidence that any of the individual Plaintiffs sustained any compensatory damages.

* * *

PRIVACY PROTECTION ACT

(First Amendment Privacy Protection)

42 U.S.C. 2000aa et seq.

The United States Secret Service, by Agent Foley and Assistant United States Attorney Cox, sought and obtained an order from a United States Magistrate Judge to search for and seize and thereafter read the information stored and contained in "computer hardware * * * and written material and documents relating to the use of the computer system * * *, documentation relating to the attacking of computers and advertising the results of computer attacks * * *, and financial documents and licensing documentation relative to the computer programs and equipment at the business known as Steve Jackson Games which constitute evidence, instrumentalities, and fruits of federal crimes, including interstate transportation of stolen property (18 U.S.C. 2314) and interstate transportation of computer access information (18 U.S.C. 1030(a)(6))."

* * *

The evidence establishes the actual information seized, including both the primary source and back-up materials of the draft of *Gurps Cyberpunk*, a book intended for immediate publication (within days to weeks), drafts of magazines and magazine articles to be published, business records of Steve Jackson Games, Incorporated (including contracts and drafts of articles by writers of Steve Jackson Games, Incorporated), the Illuminati bulletin board and its contents (including public announcements, published newsletter articles submitted to the public for review, public comment on the articles submitted and electronic mail containing both private and public communications). [T]he evidence is clear that * * * "work product materials," as defined in 42 U.S.C. 2000aa–7(b), were obtained as well as materials constituting "documentary materials" as defined in the same provision.

The Privacy Protection Act, 42 U.S.C. 2000aa, dictates: "Notwithstanding any other law, it shall be unlawful for a government officer or employee, in connection with the investigation ... of a criminal offense to search for or seize any work product materials possessed by a person reasonably believed to have a purpose to disseminate to the public a newspaper, broadcast, or other similar form of public communication.... " See, 42 U.S.C. § 2000aa(a).

Assuming Agent Foley was knowledgeable of the Privacy Protection Act (which he was not), neither he nor Assistant United States Attorney Cox had any information which would lead them to believe that Steve Jackson Games, Incorporated published books and materials and had a purpose to disseminate to the public its publications. Their testimony is simply they thought it a producer of games. As heretofore stated, the Court feels Agent Foley failed to make a reasonable investigation of Steve Jackson Games, Incorporated when it was apparent his intention was to take substantial properties belonging to the corporation, the removal of which could have a substantial effect on the continuation of business. Agent Foley, it appears, in his zeal to obtain evidence for the criminal investigation, simply concluded Steve Jackson Games, Incorporated was somehow involved. In any event, the Court declines to find from a preponderance of the evidence that on March 1, 1990, Agent Foley or any other employee or agent of the United States had reason to believe that property seized would be the work product materials of a person believed to have a purpose to disseminate to the public a newspaper, book, broadcast or other similar form of public communication.[8]

During the search on March 1, and on March 2, 1990, the Secret Service was specifically advised of facts that put its employees on notice of probable violations of the Privacy Protection Act. It is no excuse that Agents Foley and Golden were not knowledgeable of the law. On March 2, 1990, and thereafter, the conduct of the United States Secret Service was in violation of 42 U.S.C. 2000aa *et seq.* It is clear the Secret Service continued the seizure of property of Steve Jackson Games, Incorporated including information and documents through late June of 1990. Immediate arrangements could and should have been made on March 2, 1990, whereby copies of all information seized could have been made. The government could and should have requested Steve Jackson as chief operating officer of the corporation to cooperate and provide the information available under the law. The Secret Service's refusal to return information and property requested by Mr. Jackson and his lawyers in Dallas and Austin constituted a violation of the statute. Regarding any information seized that would constitute "documentary materials" (whereby the defensive theory of 42 U.S.C. 2000aa(b)(3) might apply) there would have been no problem as the property was in the possession of the United States Secret Service and their experts and Steve Jackson were present to ensure no destruction, alteration or concealment of information contained therein. In any event, it is the seizure of the "work product materials" that leads to the liability of the United States Secret Service and the United States in this case. Pursuant to 42 U.S.C. 2000aa–6, the Court finds from a preponderance of the evidence that

---

8. The legislative history to the Privacy Protection Act states:

> ... the Committee recognized a problem for the law enforcement officer, who seeking to comply with the statute, might be uncertain whether the materials he sought were work product or nonwork product and that they were intended for publication. Therefore, in the interests of allowing for some objective measure for judgment by the office, the Committee has provided that the work product must be possessed by someone "reasonably believed" to have a purpose to communicate to the public.

S.Rep. No. 874, 96th Cong., 2nd Sess., 10 (1980), reprinted in 1980 U.S.C.C.A.N. 3950, 3957. As the Court has stated, Agent Foley with only a few hours of investigation would have "reasonably believed" Steve Jackson Games, Incorporated had "a purpose to communicate to the public." Therefore, under an objective standard, assuming a reasonable investigation, Agent Foley and the Secret Service violated the statute on March 1, 1990. However, Agent Foley was not aware of the Privacy Protection Act and was therefore not "seeking to comply" with its requirements. Consequently, the Court found on March 1, 1990 neither Agent Foley nor any other employee or agent of the United States "reasonably believed" the materials seized were work product or Steve Jackson Games, Incorporated had a "purpose to disseminate to the public."

Steve Jackson Games, Incorporated is entitled to judgment against the United States Secret Service and the United States of America for its expenses of $8,781.00 and its economic damages of $42,259.00. The Court declines to find from a preponderance of the evidence other damages of Steve Jackson Games, Incorporated or liability of the United States Secret Service or the United States of America to any other Plaintiff under the provisions of the Privacy Protection Act.

* * *

WIRE AND ELECTRONIC COMMUNICATIONS INTERCEPTION
AND INTERCEPTION OF ORAL COMMUNICATIONS

18 U.S.C. 2510 et seq.

The Plaintiffs allege the United States Secret Service's conduct also violated 18 U.S.C. 2510, et seq., as it constituted intentional interceptions of "electronic communication." They allege the interception occurred at the time of seizure or, perhaps, at the time of review of the communication subsequent to the seizure. There is no question the individual Plaintiffs had private communications stored in Illuminati [the e-mail service] at the time of the seizure and the court has found from a preponderance of the evidence the Secret Service intended not only to seize and read these communications, but, in fact, did read the communications and thereafter deleted or destroyed some communications either intentionally or accidentally. The Defendants contend there is no violation of this particular statute under the facts of this case because there never was any unlawful "interception" within the meaning of the statute. Alternatively, the Defendants contend that the "good faith reliance" on the search warrant issued by the United States Magistrate Judge is a complete defense under Section 2520.

The Government relies on the 1976 Fifth Circuit case of United States v. Turk, 526 F.2d 654 (5th Cir.1976) and its interpretation of the statutory definition of "interception." In *Turk*, police officers listened to the contents of a cassette tape without first obtaining a warrant. The court concluded this was not an "interception" under 18 U.S.C. § 2510 et seq.

Whether the seizure and replaying of the cassette tape by the officers was also an "interception" depends on the definition to be given "aural acquisition." Under one conceivable reading, an "aural acquisition" could be said to occur whenever someone physically hears the contents of a communication, and thus the use of the tape player by the officers to hear the previously recorded conversation might fall within the definition set out above. No explicit limitation of coverage to contemporaneous "acquisitions" appears in the Act.

We believe that a different interpretation—one which would exclude from the definition of "intercept" the replaying of a previously recorded conversation—has a much firmer basis in the language of § 2510(4) and in logic, and corresponds more closely to the policies reflected in the legislative history. The words "acquisition . . . through the use of any

... device" suggest that the central concern is with the activity engaged in at the time of the oral communication which causes such communication to be overheard by uninvited listeners. If a person secretes a recorder in a room and thereby records a conversation between two others, an "acquisition" occurs at the time the recording is made. This acquisition itself might be said to be "aural" because the contents of the conversation are preserved in a form which permits the later aural disclosure of the contents. Alternatively, a court facing the issue might conclude that an "aural acquisition" is accomplished only when two steps are completed—the initial acquisition by the device and the hearing of the communication by the person or persons responsible for the recording. Either of these definitions would require participation by the one charged with an "interception" in the contemporaneous acquisition of the communication through the use to the device. The argument that a new and different "aural acquisition" occurs each time a recording of an oral communication is replayed is unpersuasive. That would mean that innumerable "interceptions," and thus violations of the Act, could follow from a single recording.

Id., at 657–658 (footnotes omitted). While the Fifth Circuit authority relates to the predecessor statute, Congress intended no change in the existing definition of "intercept" in amending the statute in 1986. The Court finds this argument persuasive when considering the Congressional enactment of the Stored Wire and Electronic Communications and Transactional Records Access Act, 18 U.S.C. 2701, et seq.

The Court declines to find liability for any Plaintiff against the Defendants pursuant to the Wire and Electronic Communications Interception and Interception of Oral Communications Act, 18 U.S.C. 2510, et seq., and specifically holds that the alleged "interceptions" under the facts of this case are not "interceptions" contemplated by the Wire and Electronic Communications Interception and Interception of Oral Communications Act. It simply has no applicability to the facts of this case.

* * *

STORED WIRE AND ELECTRONIC COMMUNICATIONS
AND TRANSACTIONAL RECORDS ACCESS

18 U.S.C. § 2701 et seq.

Prior to February 28, 1990, Agent Foley, Assistant United States Attorney Cox, and the computer consultants working with them were cognizant of public computer bulletin boards and the use of electronic communications and E-mail through them. Each of the persons involved in this investigation, including Agent Foley, had the knowledge and opportunity to log into the Illuminati bulletin board, review its menu and user lists, obtain passwords, and thereafter review all information available to the public. When Foley applied for the search warrant on February 28, 1990, he knew the Illuminati bulletin board provided services to the public whereby its users could store public and private electronic communications. While Foley admits no knowledge of the

Privacy Protection Act and its provisions protecting publishers of information to the public, he testified he was knowledgeable regarding the Wire and Electronic Communications Interception and Interception of Oral Communications Act. But, Foley never thought of the law's applicability under the facts of this case. Steve Jackson Games, Inc., through its Illuminati bulletin board services, was a "remote computing service" within the definition of Section 2711, and, therefore, the only procedure available to the Secret Service to obtain *"disclosure"* of the contents of electronic communications was to comply with this statute. *See*, 18 U.S.C. 2703. Agent Foley and the Secret Service, however, wanted more than "disclosure" of the contents of the communication. As the search warrant application evidences, the Secret Service wanted seizure of all information and the authority to review and read all electronic communications, both public and private. A court order for such disclosure is only to issue if "there is a reason to believe the contents of a [n] ... electronic communication ... are relevant to a legitimate law enforcement inquiry." See, 18 U.S.C. § 2703(d). Agent Foley did not advise the United States Magistrate Judge, by affidavit or otherwise, that the Illuminati bulletin board contained private electronic communications between users or how the disclosure of the content of these communications could relate to his investigation. * * * At Agent Foley's specific request, the application and affidavit for the search warrant were sealed. The evidence establishes the Plaintiffs were not able to ascertain the reasons for the March 1, 1990 seizure until after the return of most of the property in June of 1990, and then only by the efforts of the offices of both United States Senators of the State of Texas. The procedures followed by the Secret Service in this case virtually eliminated the safeguards contained in the statute. For example, no Plaintiff was on notice that the search or seizure order was made pursuant to this statute and that Steve Jackson Games, Incorporated could move to quash or modify the order or eliminate or reduce any undue burden on it by reason of the order. See, 18 U.S.C. § 2703(d). The provisions of the statute regarding the preparation of back-up copies of the documents or information seized were never utilized or available. *See*, 18 U.S.C. § 2704. Agent Foley stated his concern was to prevent the destruction of the documents' content and for the Secret Service to take the time necessary to carefully review all of the information seized. He feared deletion of the incriminating documents * * *. Notwithstanding that any alteration or destruction by * * * Steve Jackson, or anyone else would constitute a criminal offense under this statute, Foley and the Secret Service seized—not just obtained disclosure of the content—all of the electronic communications stored in the Illuminati bulletin board involving the Plaintiffs in this case. This conduct exceeded the Government's authority under the statute.

The Government Defendants contend there is no liability for alleged violation of the statute as Foley and the Secret Service had a "good faith" reliance on the February 28, 1990, court order/search warrant.

The Court declines to find this defense by a preponderance of the evidence in this case.

Steve Jackson Games, Incorporated, as the provider and each individual Plaintiffs as either subscribers or customers were "aggrieved" by the conduct of the Secret Service in the violation of this statute. While the Court declines to find from a preponderance of the credible evidence the compensatory damages sought by each Plaintiff, the Court will assess the statutory damages of $1,000.00 for each Plaintiff.

Summary

This is a complex case. It is still not clear how sensitive and/or proprietary the 911 document was (and is) or how genuinely harmful the potential decryption scheme may have been or if either were discovered by the Secret Service in the information seized on March 1, 1990. The fact that no criminal charges have ever been filed and the investigation remains "on going" is, of course, not conclusive.

The complexity of this case results from the Secret Service's insufficient investigation and its lack of knowledge of the specific laws that could apply to their conduct on February 28, 1990 and thereafter. It appears obvious neither the government employees nor the Plaintiffs or their lawyers contemplated the statute upon which this case is brought back in February, March, April, May or June of 1990. But this does not provide assistance to the defense of the case. The Secret Service and its personnel are the entities that citizens, like each of the Plaintiffs, rely upon and look to protect their rights and properties. The Secret Service conduct resulted in the seizure of property, products, business records, business documents, and electronic communications of a corporation and four individual citizens that the statutes were intended to protect.

It may well be, as the Government Defendants contend, these statutes relied upon by the Plaintiffs should not apply to the facts of this case, as these holdings may result in the government having great difficulties in obtaining information or computer documents representing illegal activities. But this Court cannot amend or rewrite the statutes involved. The Secret Service must go to the Congress for relief. Until that time, this Court recommends better education, investigation and strict compliance with the statutes as written.

* * *

Notes

1. The District Court's opinion was affirmed by the United States Court of Appeals for the Fifth Circuit, 36 F.3d 457 (1994).

2. If you were a federal agent executing a search warrant requiring seizure of a computer, what would you do differently in the search of Steve Jackson Games Inc.?

3. Commentators have been critical of the above court's conclusion that the Federal Wiretap Act does not apply to e-mail in electronic storage. Consider the following critique. What do you think?

" * * * [T]he [court] erred by ruling that the Secret Service did not violate the Federal Wiretap Act when it seized the Illuminati BBS [Bulletin Board System] and opened, read, and destroyed 162 pieces of private unread e-mail. The court overlooked an important exception contained with the Electronic Communications Privacy Act ("ECPA") which encompasses both the Federal Wiretap Act and the Stored Wire Act. The exception indicates that when a stored communication is vulnerable to interception, the Federal Wiretap Act preempts the Stored Wire Act. Unread private e-mail which exists on a BBS but has not been retrieved or read by the intended recipient is subject to interception because it has not reached its final destination. Thus, when unread e-mail exists as a stored electronic communication, it remains susceptible to interception. If the [court] had studied this important exception to the Stored Wire Act in conjunction with the Federal Wiretap Act and the relevant definitions contained within the ECPA, it would have determined that the Secret Service violated the Federal Wiretap Act when it seized the unread e-mail. Private e-mail that has been sent to a BBS, but remains unread by the intended recipient, is subject to interception.

"Second, * * * the [court] failed to adequately consider the legislative history of the ECPA; the court's decision is contrary to specific Congressional intent. When Congress amended the Federal Wiretap Act and enacted the ECPA in 1986, it intended to provide greater privacy protection to electronic communications, Congress aimed to provide the same privacy protection to e-mail and other electronic forms of communication as federal law recognizes for United States Postal mail and Telecommunications Systems. Regardless, the [court] indicated that e-mail is only subject to interception when it is actually in transit from one computer terminal to another. However, e-mail is transmitted virtually instantaneously; thus, the [court's] decision in Jackson games makes it highly unlikely that the interception laws could ever apply to e-mail. Because the court failed to consider the Congressional intent to protect e-mail communications in *Jackson Games*, the Federal Wiretap Act is virtually inapplicable with regard to e-mail.

"Third, * * * the [court] disregarded the plain meaning of the word "intercept" when it interpreted the definition under the Federal Wiretap Act. "Intercept" is defined in several ways. It means: "(1) to prevent or hinder; (2) to stop, seize, or interrupt in progress or course or before arrival; or (3) to interrupt communication, or connection with." In addition, "interception" is the "taking or seizure by the way or before arrival at a destined place." The Secret Service intercepted the private unread e-mail when it seized the BBS before the intended recipients took control of their private mail. The Secret Service interrupted the communication, intercepting it within the most basic meaning of the word.

"Finally, * * * the [court's] failure to consider prior case law interpretations of the word intercept as defined by the Federal Wiretap Act. The District Court, citing United States v. Turk, concluded that an interception occurs only when the communication is acquired contemporaneously with its initial dispatch. Because the unread e-mail in *Jackson Games* sat idly in electronic storage on the BBS, the district court found that the Secret Service did not intercept the e-mail contemporaneously with its transmission. However, the e-mail was in-transit at the time of the seizure because it had not completed its final transmission, which occurs once the intended recipient retrieves the e-mail from the BBS mailbox and reads it. Thus, the Secret Service acquired the unread e-mail contemporaneously with the e-mail transmission process qualifying the seizure as an interception * * *.[f]

3. THE FIRST AMENDMENT AND COMPUTER CRIMES

The next case, Cyber Promotions, Inc. v. American Online, Inc., 948 F.Supp. 436 (E.D.Pa.1996), arises under the private cause of action in the Computer Fraud and Abuse Act (CFAA). The CFAA, like RICO,[g] includes a private cause of action for any person who suffers damage or loss because of a violation of the Act. Unlike RICO, however, which provides for treble damages plus attorneys fees and costs, the Computer Fraud and Abuse Act provides only for compensatory damages and injunctive or other equitable relief, 18 U.S.C. § 1030(g). Interestingly, however, violation of the CFAA is listed as a racketeering activity under RICO so treble damages would be available through a RICO lawsuit alleging, as predicate acts, a pattern of violating the CFAA.

The next case arose when Cyber Promotions (Cyber) begin sending unsolicited e-mail advertisements to customers of American Online Inc. (AOL). AOL attempted to stop the unsolicited advertisements by sending "e-mail bombs" to Cyber's Internet service providers. Cyber brought suit against AOL alleging that AOL's "e-mail bombs" violated the Computer Fraud and Abuse Act. AOL brought a separate suit alleging that Cyber violated, among other things, the Computer Fraud and Abuse Act by interfering with AOL customers. Both parties seek injunctive relief. The cases were consolidated. As you read the case, determine whether you agree with the court's First Amendment analysis.

CYBER PROMOTIONS, INC. v. AMERICAN ONLINE, INC.

United States District Court, Eastern District of Pennsylvania, 1996.
948 F.Supp. 436.

WEINER, DISTRICT JUDGE.

These cases present the novel issue of whether, under the First Amendment to the United States Constitution, one private company has

---

f. Nicole Giallonardo, *Note: Steve Jackson Games v. United States Secret Service: The Government's Unauthorized seizure of Private E–Mail Warrants More Than The Fifth Circuit's Slap on the Wrist,* 14 J. MARSHALL J. COMPUTER & INFO. L. 183–186 (1995). Copyright ©. All rights reserved. Reprinted with permission of THE JOHN MARSHALL JOURNAL OF COMPUTER & INFORMATION LAW and

Nicole Giallonardo, Assistant State's Attorney for the Cook County State's Attorney's Office in Chicago, Illinois. Ms. Giallonardo received her J.D. from the John Marshall Law School, Chicago, Illinois (1996) and her B.A. from the University of Pennsylvania, Pennsylvania (1992).

g. 18 U.S.C. § 1961, 1964.

the unfettered right to send unsolicited e-mail advertisements to subscribers of another private online company over the Internet and whether the private online company has the right to block the e-mail advertisements from reaching its members. The question is important because while the Internet provides the opportunity to disseminate vast amounts of information, the Internet does not, at least at the present time, have any means to police the dissemination of that information. We therefore find that, in the absence of State action, the private online service has the right to prevent unsolicited e-mail solicitations from reaching its subscribers over the Internet.

* * *

[American Online Inc.] AOL has vehemently argued throughout the brief history of these suits that [Cyber Promotions] Cyber has no right to send literally millions of e-mail messages each day to AOL's Internet servers free of charge and resulting in the overload of the e-mail servers. Indeed, the court has received a plethora of letters from disgruntled AOL members who object to having to receive Cyber's unsolicited e-mail whenever they sign on to AOL despite repeated attempts to be removed from Cyber's lists. Cyber, on the other hand, has contended that without the right to send unsolicited e-mail to AOL members, it will go out of business.

Recognizing that Cyber's contention that it has the right to send unsolicited e-mail to AOL members over the Internet implicates the First Amendment and therefore is a threshold issue, the Court directed the parties to brief the following issue: Whether Cyber has a right under the First Amendment of the United States Constitution to send unsolicited e-mail to AOL members via the Internet and concomitantly whether AOL has the right under the First Amendment to block the e-mail sent by Cyber from reaching AOL members over the Internet. * * *

* * *

* * * AOL contends that Cyber has no First Amendment right to send unsolicited e-mail to AOL members over the Internet because AOL is not a state actor, AOL's e-mail servers are not public fora in which Cyber has a right to speak, Cyber's right to use AOL's, service free of charge, does not substantially outweigh AOL's right to speak or not to speak, and that AOL's restrictions on mass e-mail solicitations are tailored to serve a substantial interest. Because we find AOL is not a state actor and none of its activities constitute state action, we need not consider AOL's remaining First Amendment contentions.

The First Amendment to the United States Constitution states that "Congress shall make no law respecting an establishment of religion, or prohibiting the free exercise thereof; or abridging the freedom of speech, or of the press." The United States Supreme Court has recognized that "the constitutional guarantee of free speech is a guarantee only against abridgement by government, federal or state." Hudgens v. NLRB, 424 U.S. 507, 513 (1976). Only recently, the Supreme Court has stated that "the guarantees of free speech . . . guard only against encroachment by the government and 'erec[t] no shield against merely private conduct.' " Hurley v. Irish–American Gay Group of Boston, 515 U.S. 557 (1995).

In the case sub judice, the parties have stipulated that AOL is a private online company that is not owned in whole or part by the government.

Despite these stipulations, Cyber argues that AOL's conduct has the character of state action. As a general matter, private action can only be considered state action when "there is a sufficiently close nexus between the State and the challenged action of [the private entity] so that the action of the latter may be fairly treated as that of the State itself." Blum v. Yaretsky, 457 U.S. 991, 1004 (1982). Recently, our Court of Appeals observed that the Supreme Court appears to utilize three distinct tests in determining whether there has been state action. Mark v. Borough of Hatboro, 51 F.3d 1137, 1142 (3d Cir.1995). First, we must consider whether " 'the private entity has exercised powers that are traditionally the exclusive prerogative of the state.' " *Id.* This test is known as the exclusive public function test. If the private entity does not exercise such powers, we must consider whether " 'the private entity has acted with the help of or in concert with state officials.' " *Mark*, 51 F.3d at 1142. The final test is whether " '[t]he State has so far insinuated itself into a position of interdependence with . . . [the acting party] that it must be recognized as a joint participant in the challenged activity.' " *Mark*, 51 F.3d at 1142.

With regard to the first test, AOL exercises absolutely no powers which are in any way the prerogative, let alone the exclusive prerogative, of the State. In American Civil Liberties Union v. Reno, 929 F.Supp. 824 (E.D.Pa.1996) this Court previously found that no single entity, including the State, administers the Internet. *Id.* at 832. Rather, the Court found that the Internet is a "global Web of linked networks and computers" which exists and functions as the result of the desire of hundreds of thousands of computer operators and networks to use common data transfer data protocol to exchange communications and information. *Id.* In addition, "the constituent parts of the Internet . . . are owned and managed by private entities and persons, corporations, educational institutions and government entities, who cooperate to allow their constituent parts to be interconnected by a vast network of phone lines." As a result, tens of millions of people with access to the Internet can exchange information. AOL is merely one of many private online companies which allow its members access to the Internet through its e-mail system where they can exchange information with the general public. The State has absolutely no interest in, and does not regulate, this exchange of information between people, institutions, corporations and governments around the world.

Cyber argues, however, that "by providing Internet e-mail and acting as the sole conduit to its members' Internet e-mail boxes, AOL has opened up that part of its network and as such, has sufficiently devoted this domain for public use. This dedication of AOL's Internet e-mail accessway performs a public function in that it is open to the public, free of charge to any user, where public discourse, conversations and commercial transactions can and do take place." Cyber therefore contends that AOL's Internet e-mail accessway is similar to the company town in Marsh v. Alabama, 326 U.S. 501 (1946), which the Supreme Court found performed a public function and therefore was a state actor.

In *Marsh*, a Jehovah's Witness was convicted of criminal trespass for distributing literature without a license on a sidewalk in a town owned by a private company. The Supreme Court found that since the private company owned the streets, sidewalks, and business block, paid the sheriff, privately owned and managed the sewage system, and owned the building where the United States post office was located, the company, in effect, operated as the municipal government of the town. *Marsh*, 326 U.S. at 502–03. "[T]he owner of the company town was performing the full spectrum of municipal powers and stood in the shoes of the State." Lloyd Corp. v. Tanner, 407 U.S. 551, 569 (1972). The Court observed that "[t]he more an owner, for his advantage, opens up his property for use by the public in general, the more do his rights become circumscribed by the statutory and constitutional rights of those who use it." *Marsh*, 326 U.S. at 506. As a result, the Court found state action in "the State['s] ... attempt[ ] to impose criminal punishment on appellant for undertaking to distribute religious literature in a company town. ..." *Marsh*, 326 U.S. at 509.

By providing its members with access to the Internet through its e-mail system so that its members can exchange information with those members of the public who are also connected to the Internet, AOL is not exercising any of the municipal powers or public services traditionally exercised by the State as did the private company in *Marsh*. Although AOL has technically opened its e-mail system to the public by connecting with the Internet, AOL has not opened its property to the public by performing any municipal power or essential public service and, therefore, does not stand in the shoes of the State. *Marsh* is simply inapposite to the facts of the case sub judice.

Cyber also argues that AOL's Internet e-mail connection constitutes an exclusive public function because there are no alternative avenues of communication for Cyber to send its e-mail to AOL members. As support for this proposition, Cyber directs our attention to the decisions of the Supreme Court in United States Postal Service v. Greenburgh Civic Assn's, 453 U.S. 114 (1981); Lloyd Corp. v. Tanner, 407 U.S. 551 (1972) and Amalgamated Food Employees Union v. Logan Valley Plaza, 391 U.S. 308 (1968). Of these decisions, only the *Lloyd* decision is helpful to Cyber.

In *Greenburgh*, a civic association challenged a federal statute which prohibited the deposit of unstamped "mailable matter" in a letterbox approved by the United States Postal Service. The civic association contended that the First Amendment guaranteed them the right to deposit, without postage, their notices, circulars, flyers in such letter boxes. The Supreme Court upheld the constitutionality of the statute, finding that neither the enactment nor the enforcement of the statute was geared in any way to the content of the message sought to be placed in the letterbox. The Court also noted that the statute did not prevent individuals from going door-to-door to distribute their message or restrict the civic organization's right to use the mails. *Greenburgh*, however, did not involve the issue of whether there was state action. It therefore is inapplicable to the issue of whether AOL's conduct constitutes state action.

In *Logan Valley*, a case involving peaceful picketing directed solely at one establishment within a shopping center, the Court reviewed the *Marsh* decision in detail, emphasized the similarities between a shopping center and a company town and concluded that a shopping center is the "functional equivalent" of the business district in Marsh. As a result, the Court held that the picketers had a First Amendment right to picket within a shopping center. *Logan Valley*, however, was subsequently overruled by *Lloyd, supra*.

In *Lloyd*, a group of individuals sought to distribute handbills in the interior of a privately owned shopping center. The content of the handbills was not directed at any one establishment in the shopping center but instead was directed at the Vietnam War. The Court noted that, unlike the situation in *Logan Valley* where the protestors had no other alternative to convey their message at the single establishment in the shopping center, the protesters in *Lloyd* could distribute their message about the Vietnam war on any public street, sidewalk or park outside the mall. The Court therefore found that "[i]t would be an unwarranted infringement of property rights to require [the protesters] to yield to the exercise of First Amendment under circumstances where adequate alternative avenues of communication exist." *Lloyd*, 407 U.S. at 567. The *Lloyd* Court went on to reject the individuals' functional equivalency argument, finding that the private shopping center neither assumed the full spectrum of municipal powers nor stood in the shoes of the state, as did the private company in *Marsh*. The Court held that, "[t]he First and Fourteenth Amendments safeguard the rights of free speech and assembly by limitations on *state* action, not on action by the owner of private property used nondiscriminatorily for private purposes only." *Lloyd*, 407 U.S. at 567 (emphasis in original).

Cyber has numerous alternative avenues of sending its advertising to AOL members. An example of another avenue Cyber has of sending its advertising to AOL members over the Internet is the World Wide Web which would allow access by Internet users, including AOL customers, who want to receive Cyber's e-mail. Examples of non-Internet avenues include the United States mail, telemarketing, television, cable, newspapers, magazines and even passing out leaflets. Of course, AOL's decision to block Cyber's e-mail from reaching AOL's members does not prevent Cyber from sending its e-mail advertisements to the members of competing commercial online services, including CompuServe, the Microsoft Network and Prodigy.

Having found that AOL is not a state actor under the exclusive public function test, we evaluate whether AOL is a state actor under the remaining two tests, i.e. whether AOL is acting with the help of or in concert with state officials and whether the State has put itself in a position of interdependence with AOL such that it must be considered a participant in AOL's conduct. These tests actually overlap one another.

* * *

Rather, Cyber relies on the "joint participation" doctrine and contends that "AOL's use of the Court to obtain injunctive relief and/or damages [which it seeks in its prayer for relief in its counterclaim] and its assertions of federal and state statutory law, which if applicable to Cyber's activities, would violate Cyber's First Amendment rights."

In Edmonson v. Leesville Concrete Co., 500 U.S. 614 (1991) the Supreme Court refined the joint participation test by announcing that courts must ask "first whether the claimed constitutional deprivation resulted from the exercise of a right or privilege having its source in state authority; and second, whether the private party charged with the deprivation could be described in all fairness as a state actor." *Edmonson*, 500 U.S. at 620. Under the first prong, the inquiry is "under what authority did the private person engage in the allegedly unlawful acts." *Mark*, 51 F.3d at 1144.

In the case *sub judice*, the parties have stipulated that "[t]here has been no government involvement in AOL's business decisions with respect to e-mail sent by Cyber nor in any AOL decision to institute or reinstitute a block directed to Internet e-mail sent by Cyber to AOL members or subscribers." As a result, Cyber is unable to satisfy even the first prong of the joint participation test.

[The court then considered, and rejected, Cyber's arguments that its right to send unsolicited e-mails is protected under state constitutional law.]

In sum, we find that since AOL is not a state actor and there has been no state action by AOL's activities under any of the three tests for state action enunciated by our Court of Appeals in Mark, Cyber has no right under the First Amendment to the United States Constitution to send unsolicited e-mail to AOL's members. It follows that AOL, as a private company, may block any attempts by Cyber to do so.

Notes

1. Why isn't the e-mail "information highway" analogous to the privately owned street found to be a "public function" in *Marsh*? Isn't AOL providing access to the information highway just as the private company provided access through its private town streets? Is the court underestimating the essential nature of e-mail?

2. Will the decision in *Cyber Promotions* become obsolete as electronic communications become more prevalent? Once more individuals have access to and rely on e-mail will AOL become a state actor by performing a public function?

3. AOL and Cyber settled their suit by agreeing that AOL may choose whether to block e-mail from Cyber, but other junk mail companies may still send AOL users junk e-mail.[h] Both AOL and Cyber claim victory.

4. The president of Cyber Promotions, Inc. is known as the "Spam King" for fiercely defending his right to send junk mail (known as "spam" after the Monty Python "spam, spam, spam" TV sketch) to e-mail addresses.[i] Cyber is the largest commercial bulk e-mail company in the United States. In 1997, another e-mail vendor, Earthlink Network, sued Cyber for $3,000,000. According to Earthlink's President and CEO, "If we allowed every business to send junk mail to every member, the whole system would be brought to its knees."[j]

5. In 1996, Congress passed the Communications Decency Act (CDA) of 1996[k] in a furor over pornography available on the Internet. In 1997, in Reno v. American Civil Liberties Union, ___ U.S. ___, 117 S.Ct. 2329 (1997), the Court struck down key provisions of the CDA as unconstitutionally infringing on First Amendment rights. The Court held that the CDA violated the First Amendment because it was overly broad. The Court explained:

"Regardless of whether the CDA is so vague that it violates the Fifth Amendment, the many ambiguities concerning the scope of its coverage render it problematic for purposes of the First Amendment. For instance, each of the two parts of the CDA uses a different linguistic form. The first uses the word 'indecent,' 47 U.S.C.A. § 223(a) (Supp.1997), while the second speaks of material that 'in context, depicts or describes, in terms patently offensive as measured by contemporary community standards, sexual or excretory activities or organs,' § 223(d). Given the absence of a definition of either term,[ii] this difference in language will provoke uncertainty among speakers about how the two standards relate to each other and just what they mean. Could a speaker confidently assume that a serious discussion about birth control practices, homosexuality, the First Amendment issues raised by the Appendix to our Pacifica opinion, or the consequences of prison rape would not violate the CDA? This uncertainty undermines the likelihood that the CDA has been carefully tailored to the congressional goal of protecting minors from potentially harmful materials.

"The vagueness of the CDA is a matter of special concern for two reasons. First, the CDA is a content-based regulation of speech. The vagueness of such a regulation raises special First Amendment concerns because of its obvious chilling effect on free speech. Second, the CDA is a

---

h. Deborah Branscum, *King of 'Spam' and Proud of It*, NEWSWEEK, 90 (May 12, 1997).

i. *Id.*

j. *Id. quoting* Charles G. Betty.

k. Pub. L. No. 104–104, § 502.110 Stat. 56, 133–34 (1996).

ii. "Indecent" does not benefit from any textual embellishment at all. "Patently offensive" is qualified only to the extent that it involves "sexual or excretory activities or organs" taken "in context" and "measured by contemporary community standards."

criminal statute. In addition to the opprobrium and stigma of a criminal conviction, the CDA threatens violators with penalties including up to two years in prison for each act of violation. The severity of criminal sanctions may well cause speakers to remain silent rather than communicate even arguably unlawful words, ideas, and images. As a practical matter, this increased deterrent effect, coupled with the 'risk of discriminatory enforcement' of vague regulations, poses greater First Amendment concerns than those implicated by the civil regulation reviewed in Denver Area Ed. Telecommunications Consortium, Inc. v. FCC, 518 U.S. ___, 116 S.Ct. 2374 (1996)."

6. Jake Baker, a 20 year old sophomore at the University of Michigan, may have done more than any single person to prompt Congress into passing the Communications Decency Act.

Baker wrote five stores, "each twisted in its own sadistic way,"[l] and posted them on the Internet, in a forum "that specializes in sexually explicit fiction."[m] One of the stories, entitled "Pamela's Ordeal," "describes the gruesome torture, mutilation, rape and murder of a young woman by two men."[n] In this story, the name of the victim was the same as one of Baker's fellow students at the University of Michigan. In addition, Baker corresponded, via e-mail, with a person in Canada, describing how he would abduct the student. Baker wrote: " 'I have come upon an excellent way to abduct a b___. As I said before, my room is right across from the girl's bathroom. Wiat[sic] until late at night, grab her when she goes to unlock the door. Knock her unconscious, and put her into one of those portable lockers (forgot the word for it), or even a duffle bag. Then hurry her out to the car and take her away.' "[o]

Baker sent the stories and the communication to Canada on his personal university account. A Michigan alumnus in Moscow found out about the stories when the teenage daughter of a friend read them. The alumnus was offended by the stories and called the University of Michigan asking, "Why was garbage like this coming out of a university educational account"?[p] With Baker's consent and that of his roommates, University Security searched Baker's dormitory room, finding the correspondence with the Canadian individual, and called the FBI. Baker was charged with violating 18 U.S.C. § 875(c), which provides:

> "Whoever transmits in interstate or foreign commerce any communication containing any threat to kidnap any person or any threat to injure the person of another shall be fined under this title or imprisoned not more than five years, or both."

Baker was suspended from the University[q] held in jail twenty-nine days, securing release after psychiatrists concluded he did not pose a risk for

l. Megan Garvey, *Crossing the Line on the Information Highway*, WASH. POST P.H01 (Mar. 11 1995) [hereinafter *Crossing the Line*].

m. Peter H. Lewis, *Writer Arrested After Sending Violent Fiction Over Internet*, N.Y. TIMES sect. 1 page 10 (Feb. 11, 1995) [hereinafter *Writer Arrested*].

n. Joan H. Lowenstein, How Free is Speech in Cyberspace?, Chicago Tribune, Section: Perspective P.1 (Mar. 12, 1995) [hereinafter *Speech in Cyberspace*].

o. *Crossing the Line*, *supra* note m at H01; *Speech in Cyberspace*, *supra* note o at 1.

p. *Id.*

q. "On Jan. 31, Baker was asked to withdraw voluntarily from the university. ... Baker told the officials he would have

violence to others.[r] Finding that Baker's e-mail transmission were protected by the First Amendment, the District Court dismissed the indictment against Baker.[s]

7.   Other countries are more aggressive in prosecuting distribution of pornography over the Internet. In 1997, prosecutors in Munich, Germany "indicted Feli Somm, the director of Compurserve's German office, on charges of distributing child pornography." The indictment is the first of its kind in Germany, and is expected to add fuel to the ongoing debate over censorship of materials on the Internet. The charges arose from an order Compuserve disobeyed in 1995. German officials had ordered Compuserve to block access to approximately 200 discussion groups that appeared to contain pornographic material. Initially, Compuserve complied but it technologically could not enforce the ban in Germany only so Compuserve shut down the discussion groups internationally. Because of protests, especially in the United States, about infringing upon free speech, Compuserve lifted the ban. German officials responded by charging Somm, the managing director of Compuserve operations in central Europe, with "knowingly allowing access through internet news groups to child pornography, also to games that glorify violence and Nazis." Somm's attorney stated that "Somm * * * had no control over what materials were available to Compuserve's subscribers. Those decisions * * * are made in Compuserve's headquarters in the United States."[t]

to talk to his lawyer and his mom. . . . At 10 a.m., on Feb. 2 armed University of Michigan officers met Baker outside his class, presented him with a letter from [the] University President . . . dated Feb. 1 authorizing his suspension, and brought him to his dorm room to gather a few things." *Crossing the Line, supra*, note m at H01.

   r. Catherine Thérèse Clarke, *From CrimINet to CyberPerp: Toward an Inclu-*

sive Approach to Policing the Evolving Criminal Mens Rea on The Internet; 75 OR. L. REV. 191, 213 n.95 (1996).

   s. United States v. Baker, 890 F.Supp. 1375 (E.D.Mich.1995).

   t. Dan Charles, *National Public Radio, All Things Considered: Compuserve in Germany* (Apr. 16, 1997), transcript #97041607–212.

Chapter 14

TAX FRAUD

A. INTRODUCTION

If Al Capone, organized crime boss,[a] Heidi Fleiss, the "Hollywood Madam,"[b] and William Aramony, former President of The United Way of America,[c] were together in one room, they could discuss one thing they have in common: their experience with the IRS. All three were convicted of tax crimes. Capone was convicted of willfully attempting to evade income taxes for 1925, 1926 and 1927 and of failing to file returns for 1928 and 1929. Fleiss was convicted of income tax evasion and of money laundering. Aramony was convicted of tax fraud, mail fraud, conspiracy and money laundering. The professional efforts of this trio were, of course, largely directed at other endeavors: Capone purportedly engaged in bootlegging and murder;[d] Fleiss apparently laundered hundreds of thousands of dollars she earned managing her call girl service;[e] Aramony and his associates devised various schemes to divert hundreds of thousands of dollars from The United Way of America.[f] Their convictions demonstrate a key fact about tax offenses: they are among the most versatile weapons against crime in the government's arsenal. Tax offenses can be used to prosecute the garden-variety tax cheat who fails to report all or some of his earned income. Or, they may be used to prosecute individuals, like Capone, Fleiss and Aramony, who earn income illegally—through organized crime, prostitution or embezzlement and fail to report their ill-gotten gains. Often, when an individual is able to shield herself from her criminal activity and prosecution for such activity, it is possible to prosecute this offender for tax offenses. Although many criminals are able to distance themselves from their illegal conduct, especially when they are at the top of the criminal organization,

a. Capone v. United States, 56 F.2d 927 (7th Cir.1932).

b. *Hearing Before House Subcomm. on Treasury, Postal Service and General Government Appropriations*, 104th Cong., 2d Sess. at 487 (Mar. 12, 1996) (Testimony of Donald K. Vogel, Asst. Comm'r for Criminal Investigation; IRS) [hereinafter *Hearings Before House Subcomm. on Treasury et al.*].

c. *Id.* at 485.

d. *Hearings Before House Subcomm. on Treasury, supra* note 2 at 482.

e. *Id.* at 487.

f. *Id.* at 485.

954

few are willing to distance themselves too far from the financial fruits of their illegal activity. Once an individual lives beyond her means of legally earned income, a tax case becomes possible.

There is no lack of potential tax fraud defendants. The "tax gap" ("the difference between the amount of tax owed and the amount paid") is estimated to be in excess of $127 billion, annually.[g] Yet prosecution for tax offenses is rare. In 1995, the Internal Revenue Service ("IRS") examined approximately 1% of the individual and corporate tax returns filed.[h] However, criminal tax prosecutions were initiated on only 5,000 returns, or .0024% of the returns filed in 1995. Once charged with tax crimes a defendant's prospects are not good: in 1995, 3,355 taxpayers were charged with criminal offenses while 2,948 were convicted, giving a tax defendant almost a 90% chance of being convicted.[i] Once convicted, the bad news continues: almost 80% of convicted tax defendants serve some time in prison.[j]

1. PRE–TRIAL STAGE OF TAX CASES

The preindictment stage of federal tax cases is handled differently within the Department of Justice than most federal crimes. With most federal crimes, the ninety-four United States Attorneys make the decision whether to indict and for what offense, after reviewing the evidence gathered during an investigation.[k] There is no procedure or requirement that a charging decision be routed through a division within the Department of Justice prior to filing the charges. With tax cases, however, investigation reports, prepared by Special Agents with the Criminal Investigation Division (CID) of the Internal Revenue Service (IRS), are routed to the Tax Division of the Department of Justice (DOJ) before the case is forwarded to the appropriate United States Attorney's office.[l]

The IRS's Criminal Investigation Division has been operating as a unit for 77 years.[m] Currently this Division staffs 3,200 Special Agents who are trained in accounting and law enforcement, and 1,500 support personnel.[n] The CID seeks to "identify and investigate cases which will generate the maximum deterrent effect and thus, have the most impact

g. *Id.* at 484.

h. For the Fiscal Year 1995 (October 1, 1994 through September 30, 1995), a total of 205,747,000 tax returns were filed. In the same time period, 2,100,144 returns were examined. INTERNAL REVENUE SERVICE DATA BOOK, Tables 2, 13 (1995).

i. INTERNAL REVENUE SERVICE DATA BOOK, Table 20 (1995). This is an approximate percentage because IRS data report the number of cases charged by information or indictment (3,355) for FY 1995 and the number of cases resulting in convictions for FY 1995 (2,948) without reporting precisely which case resulted in a conviction.

j. INTERNAL REVENUE SERVICE DATA BOOK, Table 20 (1995). IRS reports a percentage

of 79.58 for convicted defendants sent to prison. This is an amazingly high percentage since presumably some of the convicted defendants are organizations which cannot be sent to prison.

k. RICO and money laundering cases must receive prior approval from the Criminal Section of the Department of Justice before charges are filed. U.S. DEP'T OF JUSTICE, UNITED STATES ATTY'S MANUAL, § 9–105.100, 9–110.100.

l. U.S. DEP'T OF JUSTICE, U.S. ATTY'S MANUAL, § 6–1.100, 6–4.010, 6–4.110 (Supp. 1996) and § 6–2.000 (Supp. 1993).

m. *Hearings Before the House Subcom. on Treasury et al., supra,* note 2 at 483.

n. *Id.* at 512.

on voluntary compliance."[o] The current priorities of CID are Bankruptcy Fraud; Motor Fuel Exercise Tax Evasion; Health Care Fraud; Telemarketing Fraud; Questionable Refund Program; Illegal Tax Protestors; Computer Fraud; Public Corruption; Financial Institution Fraud; Illegal Narcotics and related Money Laundering Offenses.[p]

Once it receives a referral from CID, the Tax Division of DOJ decides whether further investigation, including a grand jury investigation, is needed, whether anyone should be indicted, and, if so, for what offense. The reason for this oversight of tax offenses is to promote uniform enforcement of tax laws.[q] During this preindictment stage, the Tax Division affords the target of the investigation the opportunity to confer about the case. If prosecution is recommended, the Tax Division will determine which method of proof should be used to prove a tax offense and will attempt to ensure that the documentary evidence needed is included in the case file. Authorization from the Tax Division is also required in some cases not involving tax crimes. For example, Tax Division approval is needed when mail fraud is to be charged, either independently or as a predicate act of a RICO case,[r] when the only mailings are tax returns or other IRS documents, or the mailing is used to promote or facilitate what is "essentially only a tax fraud scheme."[s] When this review process is complete, the case is referred to the appropriate U.S. Attorney's office for prosecution. Some U.S. Attorney's offices will prosecute the case after referral; others decline to do so and trial attorneys from the Tax Division will travel to the jurisdiction to try the case.[t]

2. TYPES OF TAX CRIMES

There are three basic factual patterns that lead to tax prosecutions: failure to file a return; falsifying the amount of one's income; and, falsifying the amounts that reduce taxable income or taxes due (i.e., falsifying adjustments, deductions, exemptions, credits). In a few circumstances, it also becomes a crime to engage in a fourth type of conduct: unauthorized disclosing of tax or tax related information.

There are twelve statutes that are used most often to prosecute individuals or entities that engage in one of these types of conduct. The following four statutes make it a crime to engage in certain acts:

- 26 U.S.C. § 7201 (tax evasion);

- 26 U.S.C. § 7206 (filing a false tax return or tax related statement or document);

- 26 U.S.C. § 7207 (delivering or disclosing a false return or tax related statement or document);

o. *Id.* at 485.

p. *Id.* at 490–511.

q. U.S. Dep't of Justice, U.S. Atty's Manual, § 6–4.127 (Supp. 1996).

r. 18 U.S.C. § 1961 et seq.

s. *Id.* at § 6–4.211(1).

t. A helpful guide to the United States Department of Justice (DOJ) policies regarding tax offenses is the Criminal Tax Manual, prepared by DOJ, Tax Division, Criminal Section.

- 26 U.S.C. § 7212 (interfering with the administration of internal revenue laws).

Two statutes make it a crime to fail to do something:

- 26 U.S.C. § 7202 (failure to collect or pay over a tax);

- 26 U.S.C. § 7203 (failure to file a return, supply information or pay tax).

Two statutes pertain primarily to government employees and prevent various wrongful acts, primarily the unauthorized disclosure of return information:

- 26 U.S.C. § 7214; and

- 26 U.S.C. § 7213.

Two statutes make it a crime to misrepresent tax or tax related information in the context of certain business transactions:

- 26 U.S.C. § 7211 (regarding statement to purchasers and lessees);

- 26 U.S.C. § 7216 (regarding duties of tax preparers).

Of these offenses, tax evasion (26 U.S.C. § 7201), failure to file a return (26 U.S.C. § 7203), and filing a false or fraudulent return (26 U.S.C. § 7206 (1)), are the most commonly used statutes to prosecute tax fraud.

There are two ways of proving the above described statutory offenses: "direct" method of proof (also known as "specific items") and "indirect" method of proof (which includes the "bank deposits," "net worth," and "cash expenditures").

The direct method of proof is just that: a defendant's income is proven directly by showing specific amounts of income the defendant received but failed to report to the IRS. Such evidence could come from W–2's, 1099s, witnesses who paid the defendant for services, etc. If a defendant willfully did not report all of his income, tax fraud may have been committed.

The indirect method of proof is used when direct proof of a defendant's income is not available. With this method, the amount of income a defendant allegedly received is shown circumstantially by adding the amounts of money deposited by the defendant over a period of time ("bank deposits" method); calculating the increase in a defendant's visible wealth, such as new homes, automobiles, boats, etc. ("net worth" method), or simply documenting cash expenditures by a defendant ("cash expenditures" method). When these indirect methods of proof reveal an amount of income in excess of the defendant's income as reported to the IRS, a presumption arises that the defendant has not reported all of his income. The defendant is given the burden of rebutting this presumption.

B. MENS REA

A common defense in tax cases is mistake—that the taxpayer did not willfully fail to file a tax return, include false information in the return, or evade taxes—but that she did so because of her mistaken understanding of the tax laws. Given the complexity of our tax laws, such a defense is often credible. In the next case, Cheek v. United States, 498 U.S. 192 (1991), the Supreme Court discusses this "mistake" defense. Cheek was prosecuted for violations of § 7203 (failure to file tax returns) and § 7201 (evasion of taxes). Both of these statutes include a mens rea of "willfully". As you read *Cheek,* bear in mind that the other major statutory tax offenses (§ 7206(1) and § 7207, both of which make it a crime to file false tax returns) also require proof that the defendant acted "willfully."

CHEEK v. UNITED STATES

United States Supreme Court, 1991.
498 U.S. 192.

WHITE, JUSTICE.

Title 26, § 7201 of the United States Code provides that any person "who willfully attempts in any manner to evade or defeat any tax imposed by this title or the payment thereof" shall be guilty of a felony. Under 26 U.S.C. § 7203, "[a]ny person required under this title * * * or by regulations made under authority thereof to make a return * * * who willfully fails to * * * make such return" shall be guilty of a misdemeanor. This case turns on the meaning of the word "willfully" as used in § 7201 and 7203.

I

Petitioner John L. Cheek has been a pilot for American Airlines since 1973. He filed federal income tax returns through 1979 but thereafter ceased to file returns.[1] He also claimed an increasing number of withholding allowances—eventually claiming 60 allowances by mid–1980—and for the years 1981 to 1984 indicated on his W–4 forms that he was exempt from federal income taxes. In 1983, petitioner unsuccessfully sought a refund to all tax withheld by his employer in 1982. Petitioner's income during this period at all times far exceeded the minimum necessary to trigger the statutory filing requirement.

As a result of his activities, petitioner was indicted for 10 violations of federal law. He was charged with six counts of willfully failing to file a federal income tax return for the years 1980, 1981, and 1983 through 1986, in violation of 26 U.S.C. § 7203. He was further charged with three counts of willfully attempting to evade his income taxes for the

---

1. Cheek did file what the Court of Appeals described as a frivolous return in   1982.

years 1980, 1981, and 1983 in violation of 26 U.S.C. § 7201. In those years, American Airlines withheld substantially less than the amount of tax petitioner owed because of the numerous allowances and exempt status he claimed on his W–4 forms. The tax offenses with which petitioner was charged are specific intent crimes that require the defendant to have acted willfully.

At trial, the evidence established that between 1982 and 1986, petitioner was involved in at least four civil cases that challenged various aspects of the federal income tax system. In all four of those cases, the plaintiffs were informed by the courts that many of their arguments, including that they were not taxpayers within the meaning of the tax laws, that wages are not income, that the Sixteenth Amendment does not authorize the imposition of an income tax on individuals, and that the Sixteenth Amendment is unenforceable, were frivolous or had been repeatedly rejected by the courts. During this time period, petitioner also attended at least two criminal trials of persons charged with tax offenses. In addition, there was evidence that in 1980 or 1981 an attorney had advised Cheek that the courts had rejected as frivolous the claim that wages are not income.

Cheek represented himself at trial and testified in his defense. He admitted that he had not filed personal income tax returns during the years in question. He testified that as early as 1978, he had begun attending seminars sponsored by, and following the advice of, a group that believes, among other things, that the federal tax system is unconstitutional. Some of the speakers at these meetings were lawyers who purported to give professional opinions about the invalidity of the federal income tax laws. Cheek produced a letter from an attorney stating that the Sixteenth Amendment did not authorize a tax on wages and salaries but only on gain or profit. Petitioner's defense was that, based on the indoctrination he received from this group and from his own study, he sincerely believed that the tax laws were being unconstitutionally enforced and that his actions during the 1980–1986 period were lawful. He therefore argued that he had acted without the willfulness required for conviction of the various offenses with which he was charged.

In the course of its instructions, the trial court advised the jury that to prove "willfulness" the Government must prove the voluntary and intentional violation of a known legal duty, a burden that could not be proved by showing mistake, ignorance, or negligence. The court further advised the jury that an objectively reasonable good-faith misunderstanding of the law would negate willfulness but mere disagreement with the law would not. The court described Cheek's beliefs about the income tax system[5] and instructed the jury that if it found that Cheek "honestly

5. "The defendant has testified as to what he states are his interpretations of the United States Constitutions, court opinions, common law and other materials he has reviewed. * * * He has also introduced materials which contain references to quota-

tions from the United States Constitution, court opinions, statutes and other sources.

"He testified he relied on his interpretations and on these materials in concluding that he was not a person required to file income tax returns for the year or

and reasonably believed that he was not required to pay income taxes or to file tax returns," a not guilty verdict should be returned.

After several hours of deliberation, the jury sent a note to the judge that stated in part:

"We have a basic disagreement between some of us as to if Mr. Cheek honestly & reasonably believed that he was not required to pay income taxes.

* * *

"Page 32 [the relevant jury instruction] discusses good faith misunderstanding & disagreement. Is there any additional clarification you can give us on this point?"

The District Judge responded with a supplemental instruction containing the following statements:

"[A] person's opinion that the tax laws violate his constitutional rights does not constitute a good faith misunderstanding of the law. Furthermore, a person's disagreement with the government's tax collection systems and policies does not constitute a good faith misunderstanding of the law."

At the end of the first day of deliberation, the jury sent out another note saying that it still could not reach a verdict because "[w]e are divided on the issue as to if Mr. Cheek honestly & reasonably believed that he was not required to pay income tax." When the jury resumed its deliberations, the District Judge gave the jury an additional instruction. This instruction stated in part that "[a]n honest but unreasonable belief is not a defense and does not negate willfulness," and that "[a]dvice or research resulting in the conclusion that wages of a privately employed person are not income or that the tax laws are unconstitutional is not objectively reasonable and cannot serve as the basis for a good faith misunderstanding of the law defense." The court also instructed the jury that "[p]ersistent refusal to acknowledge the law does not constitute a good faith misunderstanding of the law." Approximately two hours later, the jury returned a verdict finding petitioner guilty on all counts.[6]

Petitioner appealed his convictions, arguing that the District Court erred by instructing the jury that only an objectively reasonable misunderstanding of the law negates the statutory willfulness requirement. The United States Court of Appeals for the Seventh Circuit rejected that

years charged, was not required to pay income taxes and that he could claim exempt status on his W–4 forms, and that he could claim refunds of all moneys withheld.

"Among other things, Mr. Cheek contends that his wages from a private employer, American Airlines, does not constitute income under the Internal Revenue Service Laws."

6. A note signed by all 12 jurors also informed the judge that although the jury found petitioner guilty, several jurors wanted to express their personal opinions of the case and that notes from these individual jurors to the court were "a complaint against the narrow & hard expression under the constraints of the law." At least two notes from individual jurors expressed the opinion that petitioner sincerely believed in his cause even though his beliefs might have been unreasonable.

contention and affirmed the convictions. In prior cases, the Seventh Circuit had made clear that good-faith misunderstanding of the law negates willfulness only if the defendant's beliefs are objectively reasonable; in the Seventh Circuit, even actual ignorance is not a defense unless the defendant's ignorance was itself objectively reasonable. In its opinion in this case, the court noted that several specified beliefs, including the beliefs that the tax laws are unconstitutional and that wages are not income, would not be objectively reasonable. * * *

II

The general rule that ignorance of the law or a mistake of law is no defense to criminal prosecution is deeply rooted in the American legal system. Based on the notion that the law is definite and knowable, the common law presumed that every person knew the law. This common-law rule has been applied by the Court in numerous cases construing criminal statutes.

The proliferation of statutes and regulations has sometimes made it difficult for the average citizen to know and comprehend the extent of the duties and obligations imposed by the tax laws. Congress has accordingly softened the impact of the common-law presumption by making specific intent to violate the law an element of certain federal criminal tax offenses. Thus, the Court almost 60 years ago interpreted the statutory term "willfully" as used in the federal criminal tax statutes as carving out an exception to the traditional rule. This special treatment of criminal tax offenses is largely due to the complexity of the tax laws. In United States v. Murdock, 290 U.S. 389 (1933), the Court recognized that:

> "Congress did not intend that a person, by reason of a bona fide misunderstanding as to his liability for the tax, as to his duty to make a return, or as to the adequacy of the records he maintained, should become a criminal by his mere failure to measure up to the prescribed standard of conduct."

The Court held that the defendant was entitled to an instruction with respect to whether he acted in good faith based on his actual belief. In *Murdock*, the Court interpreted the term "willfully" as used in the criminal tax statutes generally to mean "an act done with a bad purpose," or with "an evil motive."

Subsequent decisions have refined this proposition. In United States v. Bishop, 412 U.S. 346 (1973), we described the term "willfully" as connoting "a voluntary, intentional violation of a known legal duty," and did so with specific reference to the "bad faith or evil intent" language employed in *Murdock*. Still later, United States v. Pomponio, 429 U.S. 10 (1976) (per curiam), addressed a situation in which several defendants had been charged with willfully filing false tax returns. The jury was given an instruction on willfulness similar to the standard set forth in *Bishop*. In addition, it was instructed that " '[g]ood motive alone is never a defense where the act done or omitted is a crime.' " The defendants were convicted but the Court of Appeals reversed, concluding that the latter instruction was improper because the statute required a finding of bad purpose or evil motive.

We reversed the Court of Appeals, stating that "the Court of Appeals incorrectly assumed that the reference to an 'evil motive' in *Bishop*, and prior cases requires proof of any motive other than an intentional violation of a known legal duty." As "the other Courts of Appeals that have considered the question have recognized, willfulness in this context simply means a voluntary, intentional violation of a known legal duty." We concluded that after instructing the jury on willfulness, "[a]n additional instruction on good faith was unnecessary." Taken together, *Bishop* and *Pomponio* conclusively establish that the standard for the statutory willfulness requirement is the "voluntary, intentional violation of a known legal duty."

III

Cheek accepts the *Pomponio* definition of willfulness, but asserts that the District Court's instructions and the Court of Appeals' opinion departed from that definition. In particular, he challenges the ruling that a good-faith misunderstanding of the law or a good-faith belief that one is not violating the law, if it is to negate willfulness, must be objectively reasonable. We agree that the Court of Appeals and the District Court erred in this respect.

A

Willfulness, as construed by our prior decisions in criminal tax cases, requires the Government to prove that the law imposed a duty on the defendant, that the defendant knew of this duty, and that he voluntarily and intentionally violated that duty. We deal first with the case where the issue is whether the defendant knew of the duty purportedly imposed by the provision of the statute or regulation he is accused of violating, a case in which there is no claim that the provision at issue is invalid. In such a case, if the Government proves actual knowledge of the pertinent legal duty, the prosecution, without more, has satisfied the knowledge component of the willfulness requirement. But carrying this burden requires negating a defendant's claim of ignorance of the law or a claim that because of a misunderstanding of the law, he had a good-faith belief that he was not violating any of the provisions of the tax laws. This is so because one cannot be aware that the law imposes a duty upon him and yet be ignorant of it, misunderstand the law, or believe that the duty does not exist. In the end, the issue is whether, based on all the evidence, the Government has proved that the defendant was aware of the duty at issue, which cannot be true if the jury credits a good-faith misunderstanding and belief submission, whether or not the claimed belief or misunderstanding is objectively reasonable.

In this case, if Cheek asserted that he truly believed that the Internal Revenue Code did not purport to treat wages as income, and the jury believed him, the Government would not have carried its burden to prove willfulness, however unreasonable a court might deem such a belief. Of course, in deciding whether to credit Cheek's good-faith belief claim, the jury would be free to consider any admissible evidence from any source showing that Cheek was aware of his duty to file a return and to treat wages as income, including evidence showing his awareness of the relevant provisions of the Code or regulations, of court decisions rejecting his interpretation of the tax law, of authoritative rulings of the Internal Revenue Service, or of any contents of the personal income tax return forms and accompanying instructions that made it plain that wages should be returned as income.[8]

We thus disagree with the Court of Appeals' requirement that a claimed good-faith belief must be objectively reasonable if it is to be considered as possibly negating the Government's evidence purporting to show a defendant's awareness of the legal duty at issue. Knowledge and belief are characteristically questions for the factfinder, in this case the jury. Characterizing a particular belief as not objectively reasonable transforms the inquiry into a legal one and would prevent the jury from considering it. It would of course be proper to exclude evidence having no relevance or probative value with respect to willfulness; but it is not contrary to common sense, let alone impossible, for a defendant to be ignorant of his duty based on an irrational belief that he has no duty, and forbidding the jury to consider evidence that might negate willfulness would raise a serious question under the Sixth Amendment's jury trial provision. * * *

It was therefore error to instruct the jury to disregard evidence of Cheek's understanding that, within the meaning of the tax laws, he was not a person required to file a return or to pay income taxes and that wages are not taxable income, as incredible as such misunderstandings of and beliefs about the law might be. Of course, the more unreasonable the asserted beliefs or misunderstandings are, the more likely the jury will consider them to be nothing more than simple disagreement with known legal duties imposed by the tax laws and will find that the Government has carried its burden of proving knowledge.

B

Cheek asserted in the trial court that he should be acquitted because he believed in good faith that the income tax law is unconstitutional as applied to him and thus could not legally impose any duty upon him of which he should have been aware. Such a submission is unsound, not because Cheek's constitutional arguments are not objectively reasonable or frivolous, which they surely are, but because the *Murdock–Pomponio* line of cases does not support such a position. Those cases construed the willfulness requirement in the criminal provisions of the Internal Reve-

---

8. Cheek recognizes that a "defendant who knows what the law is and who disagrees with it * * * does not have a bona fide misunderstanding defense" but asserts that "a defendant who has a bona fide misunderstanding of [the law] does not 'know' his legal duty and lacks willfulness."

The Reply Brief for Petitioner states: "We are in no way suggesting that Cheek or anyone else is immune from criminal prosecution if he knows what the law is, but believes it should be otherwise, and therefore violates it."

nue Code to require proof of knowledge of the law. This was because in "our complex tax system, uncertainty often arises even among taxpayers who earnestly wish to follow the law" and " '[i]t is not the purpose of the law to penalize frank difference of opinion or innocent errors made despite the exercise of reasonable care.' " *Bishop*, 412 U.S. at 360–61.

Claims that some of the provisions of the tax code are unconstitutional are submissions of a different order. They do not arise from innocent mistakes caused by the complexity of the Internal Revenue Code. Rather, they reveal full knowledge of the provisions at issue and a studied conclusion, however wrong, that those provisions are invalid and unenforceable. Thus in this case, Cheek paid his taxes for years, but after attending various seminars and based on his own study, he concluded that the income tax laws could not constitutionally require him to pay a tax.

We do not believe that Congress contemplated that such a taxpayer, without risking criminal prosecution, could ignore the duties imposed upon him by the Internal Revenue Code and refuse to utilize the mechanisms provided by Congress to present his claims of invalidity to the courts and to abide by their decisions. There is no doubt that Cheek, from year to year, was free to pay the tax that the law purported to require, file for a refund and, if denied, present his claims of invalidity, constitutional or otherwise, to the courts. See 26 U.S.C. § 7422. Also, without paying the tax, he could have challenged claims of tax deficiencies in the Tax Court, 26 U.S.C. § 6213, with the right to appeal to a higher court if unsuccessful. § 7482(a)(1). Cheek took neither course in some years, and when he did was unwilling to accept the outcome. As we see it, he is in no position to claim that his good-faith belief about the validity of the Internal Revenue Code negates willfulness or provides a defense to criminal prosecution under §§ 7201 and 7203. Of course, Cheek was free in this very case to present his claims of invalidity and have them adjudicated, but like defendants in criminal cases in other contexts, who "willfully" refuse to comply with the duties placed upon them by the law, he must take the risk of being wrong.

We thus hold that in a case like this, a defendant's views about the validity of the tax statutes are irrelevant to the issue of willfulness, need not be heard by the jury, and if they are, an instruction to disregard them would be proper. For this purpose, it makes no difference whether the claims of invalidity are frivolous or have substance. It was therefore not error in this case for the District Judge to instruct the jury not to consider Cheek's claims that the tax laws were unconstitutional. However, it was error for the court to instruct the jury that petitioner's asserted beliefs that wages are not income and that he was not a taxpayer within the meaning of the Internal Revenue Code should not be considered by the jury in determining whether Cheek had acted willfully.

IV

For the reasons set forth in the opinion above, the judgment of the Court of Appeals is vacated, and the case is remanded for further proceedings consistent with this opinion.

It is so ordered.

JUSTICE SOUTER took no part in the consideration or decision of this case.

JUSTICE SCALIA, concurring in the judgment.

I concur in the judgment of Court because our cases have consistently held that the failure to pay a tax in the good-faith belief that it is not legally owing is not "willful". I do not join the Court's opinion because I do not agree with the test for willfulness that it directs the Court of Appeals to apply on remand.

As the Court acknowledges, our opinions from the 1930s to the 1970s have interpreted the word "willfully" in the criminal tax statutes as requiring the "bad purpose" or "evil motive" of "intentional[ly] violat[ing] a known legal duty." It seems to me that today's opinion squarely reverses that long-established statutory construction when it says that a good-faith erroneous belief in the unconstitutionality of a tax law is no defense. It is quite impossible to say that a statute which one believes unconstitutional represents a "known legal duty."

Although the facts of the present case involve erroneous reliance upon the Constitution in ignoring the otherwise "known legal duty" imposed by the tax statutes, the Court's new interpretation applies also to erroneous reliance upon a tax statute in ignoring the otherwise "known legal duty" of a regulation, and to erroneous reliance upon a regulation in ignoring the otherwise "known legal duty" of a tax assessment. These situations as well meet the opinion's crucial test of "reveal[ing] full knowledge of the provisions at issue and a studied conclusion, however wrong, that those provisions are invalid and unenforceable." There is, moreover, no rational basis for saying that a "willful" violation is established by full knowledge of a statutory requirement, but is not established by full knowledge of a requirement explicitly imposed by regulation or order. Thus, today's opinion works a revolution in past practice, subjecting to criminal penalties taxpayers who do not comply with Treasury Regulations that are in their view contrary to the Internal Revenue Code, Treasury Rulings that are in their view contrary to the regulations, and even IRS auditor pronouncements that are in their view contrary to Treasury Rulings. The law already provides considerable incentive for taxpayers to be careful in ignoring any official assertion of tax liability, since it contains civil penalties that apply even in the event of a good-faith mistake, see, e.g., 26 U.S.C. §§ 6651, 6653. To impose in addition *criminal* penalties for misinterpretation of such a complex body of law is a startling innovation indeed.

I find it impossible to understand how one can derive from the lonesome word "willfully" the proposition that belief in the nonexistence of a textual prohibition excuses liability, but belief in the invalidity (i.e., the legal nonexistence) of a textual prohibition does not. One may say, as the law does in many contexts, that "willfully" refers to consciousness of the act but not to consciousness that the act is unlawful. Or alternatively, one may say, as we have said until today with respect to the tax statutes, that "willfully" refers to consciousness of both the act and its illegality. But it seems to me impossible to say that the word refers to consciousness that some legal text exists, without consciousness that that legal text is binding, i.e., with the good-faith belief that it is not a valid law. Perhaps such a text for criminal liability would make sense (though in a field as complicated as federal tax law, I doubt it), but some text other than the mere word "willfully" would have to be employed to describe it—and that text is not ours to write.

Because today's opinion abandons clear and long-standing precedent to impose criminal liability where taxpayers have had no reason to expect it, because the new contours of criminal liability have no basis in the statutory text, and because I strongly suspect that those new contours make no sense even as a policy matter, I concur only in the judgment of the Court.

JUSTICE BLACKMUN, with whom JUSTICE MARSHALL joins, dissenting.

It seems to me that we are concerned in this case not with "the complexity of the tax laws," but with the income tax law in its most elementary and basic aspect: Is a wage earner a taxpayer and are wages income?

The Court acknowledges that the conclusively established standard for willfulness under the applicable statutes is the "voluntary, intentional violation of a known legal duty." That being so, it is incomprehensible to me how, in this day, more than 70 years after the institution of our present federal income tax system with the passage of the Revenue Act of 1913, 38 Stat. 166, any taxpayer of competent mentality can assert as his defense to charges of statutory willfulness the proposition that the wage he receives for his labor is not income, irrespective of a cult that says otherwise and advises the gullible to resist income tax collections. One might note in passing that this particular taxpayer, after all, was a licensed pilot for one of our major commercial airlines; he presumably was a person of at least minimum intellectual competence.

The District Court's instruction that an objectively reasonable and good faith misunderstanding of the law negates willfulness lends further, rather than less, protection to this defendant, for it added an additional hurdle for the prosecution to overcome. Petitioner should be grateful for this further protection, rather than be opposed to it.

This Court's opinion today, I fear, will encourage taxpayers to cling to frivolous views of the law in the hope of convincing a jury of their sincerity. If that ensues, I suspect we have gone beyond the limits of common sense.

While I may not agree with every word the Court of Appeals has enunciated in its opinion, I would affirm its judgment in this case. I therefore dissent.

Notes

1.   Do you agree that a defendant charged with tax offenses should be entitled to an acquittal if jurors find that his failure to comply with tax laws was due to his honest, but unreasonable, belief that he had no such duty? Does the dissent disagree with this view, or does the dissent simply believe that it is incredible that a person of Cheek's apparent intelligence would honestly believe that he was not obliged to file tax returns and pay taxes?

Do you agree with the distinction drawn by the Court that a good faith belief that tax laws are unconstitutional is not a "good faith mistake" about the laws, and should not be allowed as a defense? Or, do you agree with Justice Scalia that in an area as complex as tax, a "good faith mistake" may well be present when a taxpayer erroneously, but in good faith, misinterprets complex regulatory, statutory, or constitutional provisions?

2.   What impact will *Cheek* have? Is it possible that *Cheek* will make available a good faith mistake defense to virtually every alleged white collar criminal, since white collar crimes almost invariably involve conduct that violates complex laws and regulations?

C.   DIRECT METHOD OF PROOF

The next case, United States v. Lawhon, 499 F.2d 352 (5th Cir. 1974), demonstrates the "direct" or "specific items" method of proof. In it the court distinguishes, at least minimally, between direct and indirect methods of proof. Note that Lawhon was prosecuted both for filing false tax returns and for tax evasion, arising from the tax returns he filed for the three years in question. The court also discusses the use of summary charts.

UNITED STATES v. LAWHON

United States Court of Appeals, Fifth Circuit, 1974.
499 F.2d 352.

DYER, CIRCUIT JUDGE.

Lawhon seeks to upset his conviction for making and subscribing false income tax returns for the years 1963, 1964 and 1965, in violation of 26 U.S.C.A. § 7206(1), and for attempted tax evasion for the same years in violation of 26 U.S.C.A. § 7201.

* * *

For many years Lawhon has owned and managed citrus groves in Florida. Since about 1940 he also managed orange groves which were owned by his four children. The produce of the childrens' groves was sold to various fruit marketers through contracts in the name of "R.H. Lawhon Associates" (Associates). The checks payable to Associates from fruit buyers sometimes went directly to the children, but often were sent to Lawhon. The Associates' proceeds received by Lawhon were commingled with Lawhon's other funds, but the appellant kept a journal at his home showing his computations of the proceeds from the fruit sales and the allocation of his children of expenses and profit. From time to time Lawhon would purchase certificates of deposit for his children, make deposits in their savings accounts, or write checks to cover their personal expenses. Only a fraction of these payments, however, were reported by the children on their respective income tax returns.

The proceeds of the Associates' fruit sales were usually deposited either in Lawhon's personal bank accounts or in the accounts of family corporations which he controlled. After subtracting certain "reductions" from Lawhon's income, such as amounts of fruit income reported on the children's tax returns, the Government calculated that Lawhon was taxable on the proceeds from the sale of fruit in 1963 in the amount of $181,741.72; in 1964, $81,023.81; and in 1965, $20,106.45. In contrast to these alleged total receipts, Lawhon reported on his tax returns for those years $116,039.00 in 1963, $712.00 in 1964, and zero in 1965. The Government also asserted that Lawhon understated his income from interest in 1963 by $3,912.28; by $16,982.46 in 1964; and by $1,114.32 in 1965.[1]

Under a seven-count indictment returned in 1969, Lawhon was tried before a jury, was acquitted of making a false income tax return for 1962, but was convicted for attempted tax evasion for the three following years, as well as for making a false tax return in 1965. The jury, however, was unable to reach a decision on the charges that Lawhon had made a false tax return in either 1963 or 1964; consequently, the district court declared a mistrial on the last two charges. The court also granted a new trial on the four counts of which he had been found guilty. The primary reason given by the district court for granting the retrial was the Government's faulty evidentiary presentation of a summary chart of income reductions.[2] In the first trial, the prosecution prepared a chart listing all amounts which the Government recognized as allowable reductions from Lawhon's fruit receipts. Defense counsel successfully objected to the introduction of the chart on the ground that it was not supported by evidence in the record. A revised chart was prepared by the Govern-

---

1. Lawhon concedes that there was an understatement of interest income in 1964 and 1965 in the amounts asserted by the Government. He contends, however, that the understatement for 1963 was only $209. Even accepting Lawhon's calculations for 1963, we disagree that willfulness cannot be inferred, especially in view of our determination, infra, that the Government proved a three-year pattern of substantially understating farm income.

2. The pertinent part of the district court's order granting the new trial reads:

"The issue, then, is whether the Government had the burden of proving reduction to gross income or whether its offer to make the reduction through [the original summary chart] without proof was sufficient so that its rejection by defendant leaves the defense without a basis for complaint. This Court concludes that the Government had the burden of proving by competent evidence both the gross income and reduction so that the net income would be established by proof.

* * *

"The failure of the Government to offer evidence of the alleged gifts of certificates of deposits resulted in an incomplete picture. The evidence relative to certificate of deposit purchases should have been available to the jury; if they were not reductions as a matter of law, the question of whether they were gifts from defendant's income or distribution of his children's income should have been for the jury."

ment which did contain the requisite evidentiary backing, but both the revised chart in the first trial and the chart employed in the second trial allowed Lawhon fewer reductions from income than the original summary.[3] After a second jury trial before a different judge, Lawhon was found guilty of all six charges and was fined $9,000. This appeal followed.

* * *

The assignment of error which Lawhon presses most strongly concerns the burden of proving reduction for tax purposes from gross fruit receipts. The Government's case was based upon the specific items method of proof; that is, the prosecution first introduced all the produce receipts which it considered to be income to the taxpayer, then presented its view of the items which should be subtracted from the gross proceeds to arrive at Lawhon's taxable income. The nub of Lawhon's position is that the Government had the burden not just to show the items which it considered to be reductions, but also to introduce evidence of any item which the jury might find to be an allowable reduction. More specifically, the contention is that the Government should have introduced evidence of the amounts Lawhon gave to his children in the form of certificates of deposit, for example, even though the prosecution considered them to be not reductions but gifts. This argument seems to rely upon an analogy to a prosecution for tax evasion based on the net worth theory, see generally, Holland v. United States, 348 U.S. 121, 75 S.Ct. 127, 99 L.Ed. 150 (1954), in which the prosecution has the burden to follow up on all reasonable leads which, if true, could establish the taxpayer's innocence. Similarly, in cases based on the bank deposit method of prosecution, the Government is required to prove that it has tried to discover and exclude all non-income items from the alleged tax deficiency. None of these cases, however, undergirds the proposition that the Government must introduce those items which it does not believe entitled the taxpayer to a reduction in the alleged understatement of his taxes. We find neither precedent nor good reason for reversing this conviction because the Government failed to shoulder the burden of introducing evidence of all items which the taxpayer claims should have been allowed as reductions.

* * *

Notes

1. How does this case exemplify the "direct" or "specific items" method of proof? Can you identify the "specific items" of income Lawhon

3. Because the transcript of the first trial is not in the record in this appeal, we do not know what objection, if any, defense counsel made to the introduction of the revised summary. The record of the second trial, however, indicates that while the defense was not satisfied with the summary chart which allowed a greater aggregate of reductions than the revised chart in the first trial—but still a lesser total amount than allowed on the original chart—the district court gave the defense an opportunity to examine the chart before admitting it into evidence. The record also shows that the defense had the opportunity, not fully exploited, to impeach the agent who prepared the chart with the inconsistency between the original and the later positions of the Government.

was receiving but not reporting? What is the proper way to report income from the citrus groves?

2. To understand Lawhon's argument as to what error was made by the trial court, we must return to the "indirect" method of proof discussed in the Introduction to this Chapter. When the government is utilizing an indirect method of proof, it must show that it has followed all reasonable "leads" provided to the government by the defendant as to the source of the unreported income attributed to the defendant. Thus, for example, if the government analyzed the deposits made by a taxpayer into her bank accounts for one calendar year, and found that the deposits totalled $100,000 but that this taxpayer reported income of only $30,000, there would be a question as to whether this taxpayer filed a false tax return and evaded taxes. Assume that the taxpayer is provided an opportunity to explain this discrepancy and states that her generous Aunt Mildred gave her $70,000 during the year in question. This is a "lead" and the government is required to investigate this lead, as well as any other reasonable leads provided by the taxpayer. If the taxpayer is ultimately indicted, presumably because the Aunt Mildred lead did not prove to be true, the government must demonstrate, as part of its case-in-chief, that it followed all reasonable leads supplied by the defendant. (United States v. Scott, infra at page 398 discusses the issue of "leads" further.)

Let us return to Lawhon's claim of error—that the government was required to introduce, as part of its case-in-chief, possible explanations for Lawhon's failure to report all income from the citrus groves. As the court noted, Lawhon's argument must fail, in part, because the government is using the direct, or "specific items" method of proof, rather than an indirect method. With the direct method of proof, the government has no obligation to introduce into evidence possible explanations for the taxpayer's apparent failure to report all income.

Is there another flaw in Lawhon's argument? Is it significant whether or not Lawhon ever gave the government the so-called "lead" about the certificates of deposit?

3. Note that the convictions obtained against Lawhon in the first trial were set aside because of charts improperly introduced into evidence by the government.

Charts are often used in criminal tax cases to summarize various computations. Usually at the close of its case in chief, the Government will call to the stand a summary expert witness who has been present throughout trial and who testifies as to tax computations he has made based upon the evidence. Use of summary witnesses is based upon Federal Rule of Evidence 1006 which provides:

"The contents of voluminous writings * * * which cannot be conveniently examined in court may be presented in the form of a chart, summary, or calculation. The originals, or duplicates, shall be made available for examination or copying, or both, by other parties at a reasonable time or place. The Court may order that they be produced in Court."

The summary witness offered at the end of a tax case is offered as an expert witness under Federal Rules of Evidence 702 which provides for the use of experts who, through specialized knowledge, will assist the trier of fact in understanding the evidence. Rule 703 sets forth the evidence on which an expert may base an opinion:

"The facts or data in a particular case upon which an expert bases an opinion or inference may be those perceived by or made known to him at or before the hearing. If of a type reasonably relied on by experts in a particular field in forming opinions or inferences upon the subject, the fact or data need not be admissible in evidence."

In a tax prosecution, the summary expert witness, usually an accountant, will testify that based upon the evidence introduced, he has computed the defendant's actual taxable income. This witness will identify the sources of this income, calculate the difference in *actual* and *reported* income, and compute the defendant's tax liability for the years covered by the indictment.

To assist this summary expert witness in presenting this testimony to the jury, the witness is usually allowed to use charts, which also summarize his testimony—and thus, the evidence in the case. If the charts are based upon the evidence and are not prejudicial they usually will be admitted into evidence.

What was the problem with the government's charts in Lawhon's first trial?

D. INDIRECT METHOD OF PROOF

The next case, United States v. Lacob, 416 F.2d 756 (7th Cir.1969) (1970), demonstrates the "bank deposits" indirect method of proof, coupled with a "direct" or a "specific items" method of proof.

UNITED STATES v. LACOB

United States Court of Appeals, Seventh Circuit, 1969.
416 F.2d 756.

MORGAN, DISTRICT JUDGE.

Defendant was tried on Count III of an indictment charging income tax evasion for the calendar year 1960. He was found guilty by a jury and had prosecuted this appeal from the judgment of conviction.

Defendant is a lawyer who specialized in personal injury claims. While he was represented by his present counsel in the proceedings prior to trial in this case, he chose to defend himself at the trial and his counsel of record was permitted to withdraw.

The indictment charged a false and fraudulent return, in violation of 26 U.S.C. § 7201, reporting taxable income of $8,329.70 with a tax of $1,765.72, while defendant's correct taxable income was $30,146.15 with a tax of $9,528.69.

The Government proved by records of two banks, without dispute, that defendant deposited slightly over $99,000 in 1960. It was stipulated that in 1960 defendant received 69 case settlement checks from 29 different insurance carriers totaling $38,322.89. $36,000 of that amount was identified among the deposits to defendant's bank accounts. $1,475 was proved to have been received but not deposited. Records of the Illinois Industrial Commission, received in evidence, disclosed 22 cases handled by defendant on which checks were issued in 1960, and $17,000 from those sources was traced into defendant's bank accounts. Checks for $1,477 from these latter sources were proved to have been received but not deposited.

An Internal Revenue Service accounting expert testified that he made a bank deposit analysis and various computations from the material in evidence. Deposits of $14,569.90 were eliminated and not considered as unreported income because they represented salary which was reported and small, and unidentifiable, checks. Also, deposits of $5,415.12 were eliminated as transfers from other accounts. Deposits of currency were also eliminated. Since the defendant received a fee of 33⅓% of personal injury settlements, defendant was charged with income of $6,206.90 on $18,620.89 of deposits of identified personal injury settlement checks and $491.67 on the $1,475 of personal injury settlements received but not deposited. Since the fee on workmen's compensation settlements was 20%, defendant was charged with income of $3,420 on the $17,100 of identified workmen's compensation settlement checks deposited and $295.40 on the $1,477 workmen's compensation settlement checks which were not deposited. Of $39,356.33 of substantial checks deposited but not identified or explained, defendant was charged with income of $7,871.27, or 20%, because it was assumed, in the absence of other proof, that these were proceeds of cases and that his fee was the lower of the two fee bases used.

Defendant's 1960 taxable income was then recomputed by adding these items to the identified income shown on the return, allowing personal deductions and exemptions as claimed on the return and deducting $1,483 for bar association dues, filing fees, etc., which had not been claimed by defendant on his original return. This computation resulted in finding taxable income of defendant for 1960 of $25,131.94, with a tax due of $7,286 against the $1,765 returned, or an unreported tax for 1960 of $5,521.

Defendant's efforts at proof of a defense were somewhat abortive. A judge of the Circuit Court of Cook County, Illinois, was not able to testify to defendant's good reputation for truth and veracity in the community in which he resided, and two attorneys who did so thought that he lived in a community other than his place of residence as shown on his income tax return. Defendant sought to have his wife identify checks which he had made out, and, upon Government objection, the court did not permit her to do it, so the defendant took the stand to identify them himself. Based upon defendant's admissions that many of such checks covered expenditures which were charged to and, ultimately at least, paid by clients, and that he couldn't relate them directly to case files or other records, and upon Government objection that no proper foundation had been laid for their admission without invoices, files or book records showing that they were business connected expenses actually borne by defendant, the trial court excluded all the checks except some few to which such objection was not raised and for which defendant was given credit. A Certified Public Accountant was not permitted to testify about, or analyze, the checks which had not been admitted into evidence. Defendant testified that the checks which were excluded did represent expenses of his law practice for 1960 and that his expenses that year totaled more than his income. Accordingly, he argued that he had no net law practice income in 1960, and hence had reported none because he said he was advised that it was not necessary to detail the actual income and expenses.

* * *

It is * * * clear that the Government's employment here of the so-called "bank deposit theory" of proof of unreported income was correctly applied without any violence to defendant's rights. The plan of proving the existence of a business and the practice of making of deposits of business income into a bank account or accounts, and then adjusting total deposits thereto to avoid inclusion of transfer, redeposits, deposits otherwise explained, etc., and giving credit for ascertainable expenses, deductions and exemptions, has been long recognized. The law is likewise clear that, once the Government proves unreported receipts having the appearance of income, and gives the defendant credit for the deductions he claimed on his return, as well as any others it can calculate without his assistance, the burden is on the defendant to explain the receipts, if not reportable income, and to prove any further allowable deductions not previously claimed. The cases cited by defendant are not inconsistent with these principles and the trial court's instruction adopting these principles was thoroughly sound. The defendant here was not called upon to come forward with evidence to rebut a presumption as proscribed in Barrett v. United States, 322 F.2d 292 (5th Cir.1963), but had the opportunity to prove any additional allowable deductions he might have had to offset proven income or to explain why what appeared to be income was not. Here it should be noted that almost two-thirds of the income charged to defendant was, in fact, proved by the specific-item method. It should be noted also, as the Government points out, that *Barrett* was reversed by the Supreme Court sub nom. United States v. Gainey, 380 U.S. 63 (1965), and hence is depreciated as persuasive authority.

Defendant argues as a paramount point that he was compelled to testify in violation of his constitutional right not to do so. This point is completely without merit, especially when viewed in relation to his completely voluntary and unsworn "testimony" while handling his own defense throughout the trial. As such, he told his life story, as well as his whole defense that he had no profit from his law practice, in his opening statement to the jury, frequently promising the judge to prove his statements by evidence later. This was not done to any substantial degree, but there is no question on this record that the jury had the benefit of defendant's theory of defense and assertions of the "facts" from his viewpoint from his own lips, repeatedly, long before he took the stand. In his examination and cross-examination of witnesses, defendant also frequently "testified" by unsworn statements purporting to be facts. This amounts to voluntary testimony and a waiver of the constitutional privilege not to testify.

Defendant then took the stand as a witness when his wife was not permitted to testify about his checks which he had made out and collected for use as evidence of expenses. He identified the checks and testified as fully as he could about what they had been issued for as expenses of his law practice in 1960. The cross-examination of defendant, which he contends went beyond the scope of the direct testimony, was concerned with why the checks hadn't been produced before, how they could be directly related to his law practice, that they represented expenses actually borne by the clients, etc. Defendant's constitutional privilege was not asserted with respect to any question, and we do not believe that it was violated by questions on cross-examination here, nor do we believe that defendant was compelled to testify in any way by the Government or the trial court. His right not to testify did not destroy the large deposits proved by the Government nor permit him to offset them by incompetent evidence. The dilemma of permitting the Government evidence go unexplained and without offset, or attempting to offset it by his own testimony, which apparently was all he had, was no doubt a difficult choice, but it was clearly a choice available to the defendant. The fact that he chose to testify and his story didn't stand up very well before the jury, after cross-examination, is hardly a basis for reversal of his conviction.

Defendant's argument that exclusion of most of his canceled checks from evidence denied him jury consideration of his defense is frivolous.

It is clear that most of them were excluded because no proper foundation had been laid to relate them to the case. All they tended to prove was that defendant spent this money in 1960, but this is vastly different from constituting evidence that such expenditures were proper offsets against his law practice revenue in the computation of taxable income for 1960. The record is clear that it would have been highly prejudicial to the Government to admit the checks which were excluded if the jury believed that they had probative value as proof of law business expenses to be offset against the receipts proved. They had no such value without much more precise connection with the law practice through invoices, files, book records, etc., none of which was offered. The defendant simply cannot offer several hundred canceled checks, claim they all present law business expenses, and have them admitted into evidence as such. The bulk of them were clearly properly excluded by the trial court on the Government's objection of no proper foundation. Any lack of opportunity for the jury to consider the defense with regard to these checks was due to defendant's failure to relate them to the case under the rules of evidence.

* * *

Defendant's fourth alleged trial court error is the admission of Government summary sheets into evidence with caption "Total Net Unreported Income," which is called "irreparable prejudice." While the observation in Lloyd v. United States, 226 F.2d 9, 17 (5th Cir.1955), cited by defendant is thoroughly sound, that such sheets should be factual and should not be encumbered unnecessarily with impressive conclusionary captions, it is noted that six such captions possibly so characterized in that case were held not to be reversible error. We do not think the captions here were any more conclusionary or impressive than required to make the summaries understandable. It is noted that they were amply justified by the testimony which laid the foundation for their admission.

* * *

We have found no error in this record in any wise sufficient to justify reversal of the judgment of conviction.

It is accordingly affirmed.

Notes

1. The government used the "bank deposits" indirect method of proof in its case against Lacob. This method of proof is based on the theory that if a taxpayer is engaged in income-producing activity, and makes regular and periodic deposits of money into bank accounts in his own name or into bank accounts under his dominion or control, there is sufficient evidence for a jury to infer that the funds deposited represent income. This inference is not raised simply from proof that a person has received money or deposited it into a bank. The government must also show that the deposits were regular and periodic and that the total amount of deposits exceeds the total sum of exemptions, deductions, and reported income. Thus, in order for the bank deposits method to be accurate, it is necessary for the Government to eliminate non-income items. Once the Government establishes that the defendant is engaged in income-producing activity and eliminates non-income items, unidentified deposits may be presumed to be taxable income.

Because the bank deposits method of proof is an indirect method of proof, the government has a duty to investigate "leads" provided by a taxpayer regarding non-taxable sources of income. Such leads must be relevant, furnished prior to trial, and reasonably susceptible of being checked.

2. Can you prepare the summary chart which the government's summary expert witness would use at the trial of Lacob?

3. Lacob argued that with the "bank deposit" indirect method of proof, once the government demonstrated that more money was deposited than was reported, the burden of proof switched from the government to him to rebut the government's inference that this difference was unreported in-

come. He objected that this improperly switched the burden of proof from the government to a defendant. Do you agree with Lacob that the indirect methods of proof improperly shift this burden of proof?

The next case, United States v. Scott, 660 F.2d 1145 (7th Cir.1981) (1982), demonstrates another "indirect" method of proof: the "net worth" method (coupled with a few specific items of income). As you read this case, note the discussion of the "leads" issue and the type of evidence that was admitted to show whether the government complied with its duty to follow leads.

UNITED STATES v. SCOTT

United States Court of Appeals, Seventh Circuit, 1981.
660 F.2d 1145.

Fairchild, Senior Circuit Judge.

On April 9, 1979, defendant William J. Scott, Attorney General for the State of Illinois, was indicted for wilfully understating his adjusted gross income on his personal income tax returns for the calendar years 1972 through 1975 and for filing a false amended return for 1974. His trial began on January 8, 1980. On March 19, 1980, after five days of deliberations, the jury returned a verdict finding Scott guilty of Count One of the indictment, relating to his 1972 return, but not guilty on Counts two through five, relating to his 1973, 1974 and 1975 returns. It is from judgment on this verdict that Scott appeals.

In reviewing Scott's arguments on appeal, we have followed the Supreme Court's admonition that prosecutions such as this should be analyzed "bearing constantly in mind the difficulties that arise when circumstantial evidence as to guilt is the chief weapon of a method that is itself only an approximation." Holland v. United States, 348 U.S. 121, 129 (1954). Nevertheless, we have found no error, constitutional or otherwise, in Scott's trial. Accordingly, we affirm.

I.   The Government's Case Against Scott

Count One of the indictment charged Scott with violating 26 U.S.C. § 7206(1)[2] by wilfully and knowingly preparing and filing a false United States Individual Income Tax Return (Form 1040) for the calendar year 1972 and then verifying this return as true under penalties of perjury. The indictment charged that although Scott stated in his return that his

---

2.   26 U.S.C. § 7206 provides:

"Any person who—

(1) Willfully makes and subscribes any return, statement, or other document, which contains or is verified by a written declaration that it is made under the penalties of perjury, and which he does not believe to be true and correct as to every material matter * * * shall be guilty of a felony and, upon conviction thereof, shall be fined not more than $5,000, or imprisoned not more than 3 years, or both, together with the costs of prosecution."

adjusted gross income was $31,643, he knew and believed that his adjusted gross income for 1972 was substantially in excess of that sum.

To sustain a conviction under 26 U.S.C. § 7206(1), the proof must show: (1) that Scott knowingly prepared and filed a Form 1040 for the year 1972 which he verified as true; (2) that the return was false in some material way—in this case, that Scott falsely reported his adjusted gross income for the year 1972; and (3) that Scott's actions in falsifying his return were wilful.

In this case, the Government relied on two types of proof that Scott falsely reported his adjusted gross income for 1972: the net worth and expenditures method of proof, as approved by the Supreme Court in *Holland,* and the specific-items approach.

Under the net worth method of proof, the government was first required to establish Scott's "opening net worth" or total net assets at the beginning of the prosecution year, here, January 1, 1972. The government was then obliged to prove that Scott's net worth increased between January 1 and December 31, 1972, the end of the prosecution period for purposes of this appeal. This it did by calculating the difference between net worth at the beginning and end of the year. To that figure, the government added Scott's expenditures for the year, yielding putative income. The government was then required to show that the likely source of the difference between Scott's reported adjusted gross income and his putative income was taxable income, or that no nontaxable source for the difference existed. Finally, because the net worth method of proof rests solely on circumstantial and indirect evidence, the government was required to negate all reasonable explanations offered by Scott which were inconsistent with his guilt.

Pursuant to the specific items approach, the government attempted to show that Scott excluded several material items of his 1972 income from his 1972 Form 1040. Proof that Scott wilfully omitted any one of these items would be sufficient to sustain a conviction under 26 U.S.C. § 7206(1).

The Government's net worth proof combined with one of the specific-items of income, the Wirtz—Cooper payments, indicated that Scott understated his 1972 adjusted gross income by more than $22,153, for an adjusted gross income of at least $53,796.

A. Scott's 1972 Form 1040

There can be little doubt that Scott had personal knowledge of the contents of his 1972 tax returns. His accountants prepared his return from worksheets he personally completed. Scott signed the return after verifying it in a private meeting with his accountant. According to Scott's 1972 Form 1040, he earned $30,887 in wages, salaries, tips and other employee compensation, and $756 in interest income, for a total adjusted gross income of $31,643. His itemized deduction totaled $13,-237, including $12,000 in alimony payments, $150 in medical and dental expenses, $996 in deductible taxes (general sales, state and local income taxes), $140 in charitable contributions, $100 in casualty or theft losses, $175 for the preparation of this tax return, and $62 for the maintenance of his safe deposit boxes. According to Scott's calculations, $5,448 had been withheld for federal income taxes, but he was required to pay only $4,296. He thus claimed that he was entitled to a $1,198 refund.

B.   Evidence that Scott's 1972 Form 1040 Was False: The Net Worth Case

The government's net worth proof indicated that Scott's net worth increased from approximately $30,253 at the close of 1971 to approximately $51,420 at the end of 1972.[3] The government claimed that the likely source of this increase was campaign contributions which Scott converted to his personal use in 1972. Accordingly, it argued that these contributions became taxable income in 1972 which Scott should have reported on his Form 1040. Scott, on the other hand, introduced evidence from which the jury could have inferred that the source of the cash expenditures relied on by the government in establishing his net worth increase was nontaxable cash "gifts" he received prior to and during 1972. The government attempted, largely by cross-examination, to bring out that most of the so-called, "gifts" were motivated by concern for Scott's needs because of his political career, and, in some instances, as a reward for official action beneficial to the donor.

1.   Opening Net Worth

As its starting point in proving Scott's net worth, the government offered a letter dated April 16, 1968, that Scott wrote to his first wife, now Dorothy Humphrey, from whom he was then separated. In this letter, an apparent effort to arrange a property settlement, Scott described his assets and liabilities in detail. The letter indicated that the Scotts, together, had total assets of approximately $122,000. Their assets included their home, personal furnishings, savings and checking accounts, and stock in Holiday Travel House, Inc., a travel agency they owned jointly. Their only liability was a $28,000 mortgage on their home. Scott proposed that he transfer $93,000 of these assets to Dorothy, including the house, automobiles and bank accounts totaling $10,-000, and keep $29,000 in assets for himself, consisting of $18,000 in bank deposits and cash, and the $11,000 worth of stock in Holiday Travel House, Inc. Scott offered to retain the $28,000 mortgage on their

---

3. The discrepancy between the government's proof of Scott's adjusted gross income according to the net worth method and its total claim of Scott's adjusted gross income for 1972 is due to attributing to Scott the salary paid Ellen Cooper by Chicago Stadium Corporation during 1972. See infra.

A summary of the government's proof is as follows:

	December 31, 1971	December 31, 1972
Net worth	$30,253.12	$51,419.93
Increase in net worth		$21,166.81

Add: expenditures	30,123.90
Subtotal	51,290.71
	December 31, 1972
Subtract: nontaxable items and adjustments	8,551.60
Remainder	42,739.00
Reported adjusted gross income	31,643.06
Remainder	11,096.05
Add: Wirtz payments to Ellen Cooper attributed to Scott as Income	11,057.10
Amount under reported	$22,153.15
Adjusted gross income	53,796.21

house as a liability, which left him with a total net worth in 1968 of $1,000. Scott stated in his letter that he would place this remaining $1,000 in their children's savings accounts.

The government then traced Scott's net worth from April 16, 1968 to December 31, 1971, the eve of the prosecution period. The government's evidence indicated that at the end of 1971, Scott had a net worth of approximately $30,253.

2. The Net Worth Increase

Between December 31, 1971, and December 31, 1972, the relevant year for purposes of this appeal, Scott's net worth increased by approximately $21,000, giving him a total net worth at the end of 1972 of approximately $51,420. The evidence showed that most of this increase was reflected in increased savings: in 1972 Scott deposited $21,877 in savings accounts and certificates of deposit. The primary source for these deposits was Scott's paycheck. Indeed, the evidence showed that Scott did not cash a single paycheck in 1972. Instead, he deposited each paycheck in one of his checking accounts or invested them in certificates of deposit, savings accounts or interest bearing securities. Another source for Scott's investments was his reimbursement warrants for state travel, which totaled $2,657 in 1972. When he received them, he generally deposited or invested them: that year, he cashed warrants for only $265.82.

Having introduced proof that Scott's net worth increased between the close of 1971 and 1972, the government then traced Scott's expenditures during 1972. These expenditures would be added to the net worth increase to complete the government's proof of Scott's putative adjusted gross income. This proved to be a difficult task, however, as Scott left few records of his expenses. He wrote no checks to cash during 1972; he used his checking accounts only for expenses mandated by his divorce decree or for his savings and certificates of deposit. Neither did Scott write any 1972 checks for his ordinary living expenses, such as rent, food, clothing, entertainment and gifts for friends and family. Nor did Scott pay for his living expenses by credit card; in 1972 he used only a Holiday Travel House personal credit card for occasional travel expenses.

From this information alone, it can be inferred that Scott paid for almost all of his day to day expenses in cash, cash which he was not reporting as income. This inference is supported by Scott's state travel vouchers which showed that he usually spent cash when he traveled on behalf of the state. As previously indicated, however, he almost always deposited his travel reimbursements in his bank accounts rather than cashing them for future expenses.

Because Scott used cash for most of his expenditures in 1972, the government was forced to calculate the total amount of those expenditures. The government's evidence showed that Scott spent at least $13,000 in cash during 1972. According to the government's analysis, however, only $3,400 of that total amount was from legitimate sources such as the reimbursement warrants for state travel that he cashed, other cash reimbursements and nontaxable "gifts." Almost $10,000 therefore came from undocumented sources.

Scott spent a large portion of the undocumented income on personal travel. Although he was running for reelection as Illinois Attorney General in 1972, he traveled to Ft. Lauderdale in January; Miami in February; the Bahamas in April; England and Scotland in May; Copenhagen, Nice and Nevada in June; California and Texas in July; Ft. Lauderdale, Miami and Orlando in August; New Orleans, Miami, Ft. Lauderdale, San Diego and Beverly Hills in November; and San Diego, Beverly Hills and Ft. Lauderdale in December. On only six of these trips did Scott pay for any expenses by check. Nor are there credit card records for any of the travel expenses he most likely incurred. Few of Scott's travel expenses on these trips were charged to or reimbursed by the state, his campaign committee, Holiday Travel House, Inc., or the William J. Scott Host Fund. Only the cash travel expenses that the government was actually able to document were added to the government's calculations of Scott's total cash expenditures and hence to the net worth schedules. Therefore, any undocumented expenditures Scott made during his 1972 travels increased his unreported income for that year over and above the government's proof.

In addition to documenting certain of Scott's travel expenses, the government offered evidence of other large cash expenditures. Scott paid cash for $3,000 worth of traveler's checks in 1972. Additionally, on May 3, 1972, Scott purchased a stamp collection from Malden Jones, a retired news reporter living in Springfield, Illinois. He paid for this collection with a check for $650 and $1,950 in cash. At trial, Scott argued that the cash came from the paycheck he received on May 3, 1972. The evidence showed, however, that he deposited to his bank accounts, or directly invested, every paycheck he received in 1972. He deposited his paycheck of April 26, 1972, on May 3 or 4, 1972, to his account at Illinois National Bank in Springfield, Illinois. The evidence also showed that in December, 1972, Scott paid for a $950 diamond ring in cash.

Many of Scott's ordinary living expenses, such as rent and clothing, were not included in the government's net worth analysis because they could not be documented. For example, although 1972 was an election year, there were no records of Scott's expenditures for clothing. Nor could any rent payments be traced, although the evidence suggested that Scott was living in the Outer Drive East apartment belonging to Leonard Golan. No expenditures for gifts for friends or family could be traced, nor could the Government find any records indicating that Scott spent any money on his two children in addition to his monthly child support payments.[10] Finally, the government could trace no expenditures for household goods or services, personal entertainment, or personal care items. The jury could properly have concluded that Scott incurred some

10. During child support hearings in 1977, Scott testified under oath that he spent approximately $184 a month on his children, over and above his child support payments.

expenses for these items which would have added to Scott's net worth increase and expenditures, beyond what the Government proved.

The only daily living expense the government included in its net worth calculations was food. Although the government was unable to document any of Scott's food expenditures, his state travel vouchers provided a basis for projecting such expenses. These state travel vouchers indicated that in 1972, Scott spent an average of $8.47 per day on food and drink for each of the 83 days he submitted vouchers. The Government then applied this average mean cost to the 283 non-vouchered days for a total $2,397.01. This amount was then added to the government's net worth schedule. Of course, anything Scott spent on food over the amount would have further increased his net worth and thus the amount of unreported income.

3. The Likely Taxable Source

Having documented the increase in new worth and the cash expenditures, and thus an excess of putative income over reported income, the government was then obliged to show either a likely taxable source for this increase or that no nontaxable source for the expenditures existed. The Government introduced evidence from which the jury could infer that Scott consistently acquired political contributions and then converted them to his own personal use, making these converted contributions taxable income. In this sense, the campaign funds are analogous to trust funds, they are not income when received but become income if and when converted to personal use.

The Government's proof indicated that Scott kept the campaign funds he spent for his personal use in several safe deposit boxes. Mrs. Humphrey, Scott's former wife, testified that during November 1967, she entered two safe deposit boxes she maintained with Scott at the Harris Trust and Savings Bank in Chicago and at the Evans Bank. She found cash in these boxes totaling $48,900. She put this money into a new box at the Northern Trust. A few days later, after Scott had discovered that the money was missing, she told him what she had done. Scott demanded that she return the money. He told her, she testified, that the money was for his political campaigns and not for his personal use. She then agreed that Scott could become a joint signatory to the Northern Trust box, thereby giving them both access to the box.

The money from the safe deposit boxes was not treated as an asset in Scott's 1970 divorce proceedings because Scott insisted that it was campaign money to be used only for political purposes. Therefore, the divorce decree entered in 1970 provided that the safe deposit box money would go to Scott. The day the decree was entered, Scott and his former wife together surrendered the Northern Trust box. Scott refused to inventory the contents of the box in her presence. That same day, Scott visited Box 5457D at the Harris Trust. He had opened this box in 1970, the day before the start of the meeting of the National Association of Attorneys General held in St. Charles, Illinois.

The $48,900 Mrs. Humphrey testified about was not included in the government's net worth calculations because Scott testified in his 1970 divorce proceedings and again in his 1977 child support hearings that the $48,900 was for political use only.[12] The jury could have inferred, however, that some of Scott's documented cash expenditures came from these funds. Scott entered Box 5457D at the Harris Trust 11 times between January 1, 1972, and June 30, 1972. On May 30, 1972, for example, Scott entered the box, and the next day, May 31, he left on a trip to London, Stockholm, Nice and Copenhagen. If Scott spent any of this $48,900 for his personal use in 1972, then he was required to report that amount as income for that year.

The evidence indicated, however, that the $48,900 Mrs. Humphrey testified about was not the only cash available to Scott. First of all, bank records for 1972, an election year, show a significant increase in Scott's safe deposit box activity. According to Harris Bank records, Scott surrendered Box 5457D on July 18, 1972, for "a bigger box." During the remainder of the election year, Scott opened two more safe deposit boxes, giving him a total of five open safe deposit boxes, including one in Springfield, Illinois. Scott entered his safe deposit boxes 34 times in 1972, often within days before he left the state or his whereabouts were unknown.[14] Due to the remarkable correlation between Scott's entries to these safe deposit boxes and his out of state trips, it can easily be inferred that he kept cash in these boxes which he used for personal expenditures. Even Scott's own expert witness conceded that Scott kept cash in his safe deposit boxes and was spending it.

Second, Scott himself stated, in a 1977 interview with Chicago Sun–Times reporter Edward Pound, that he often received cash contributions from supporters:

"Scott explained: There are people who like to make campaign contributions in cash. It was not an unusual thing for people to do in those days before the state campaign reporting law (which took effect in October 1974). * * * A guy would say to me, I know you got expenses; here, $1,000. There were people who gave me $500, $1,000

12. During the child support proceedings initiated by Mrs. Humphrey in 1977, Scott testified under oath that these safe deposit box funds "were not gifts, they were campaign contributions." Scott told the same thing to Chicago Sun–Times reporter Edward T. Pound, as reported on October 8, 1977.

14. A trip in November 1972, exemplifies the pattern of safe deposit box entries, travel and personal expenditures. On November 9, 1972, shortly after his reelection as Illinois Attorney General, Scott entered Harris Box 117F. The next day he purchased $1,000 in travelers checks in cash at the First Federal Savings and Loan of Chicago. The same day, he paid cash for another $500 in travelers checks at the Harris Bank. On November 12, Scott rented a car in New Orleans. From November 13 to 16, his whereabouts are unknown. On November 17, he called his office from Miami. On November 18 and 19 his whereabouts are unknown, but on November 20 and 22 he called his office from Ft. Lauderdale. On November 24, from Ft. Lauderdale, he called Jack Wallenda, an employee who often picked Scott up at the airport. The government could trace only one expenditure from this entire trip which could be attributed to any source other than cash or traveler's checks: a one day rental bill totaling $19.11, which Scott charged to Holiday Travel House.

in cash. They considered them gifts. Fundamentally, I treated them as campaign contributions."

Both Scott and the Government treated Pound's article, without objection, for the truth of the matter asserted.

That Scott converted many of these campaign contributions to his own use can be inferred from the specific instances in which he failed to give his fund raising committee the campaign contributions he had received. Edward Barrett, a government witness, testified that he and his law partner, William J. Kiley, now deceased, gave Scott $5,000 in cash in the summer of 1972. Barrett, whom Scott had appointed Special Assistant Attorney General to handle state condemnation matters, testified that he called Scott and told him that he had a $5,000 campaign contribution. Scott came to Barrett's office to accept the contribution. When he arrived, Barrett and Kiley told him how grateful they were for the business he had given them and that they wanted to contribute to his campaign. Each of them then handed Scott an envelope containing $2,500 in cash. Scott then said "It's nice to know who your friends are," and pocketed the money. Kiley responded, "Okay, Bill, don't forget where that came from."

Barrett and Kiley were not given receipts from Scott's campaign committee, and their contributions do not appear on any campaign records. Neither did Jack Wallenda, who handled Scott's campaign contributions, receive this money. Moreover, Scott did not report it pursuant to the Disclosure of Economic Interests Law, Ill.Rev.Stat. Ch. 127 § 604A et seq. (1973), which requires state officers to disclose any gifts of over $500.

Scott diverted checks meant for his campaign to his personal use as well. On or about April 19, 1972, William Shaffer, an investigator employed by the Attorney General's Office, gave Scott a personal check for $500. A memo at the bottom of the check stated "Campaign Use." Scott endorsed the check and on May 17, 1972, he deposited it in his personal account at First Federal Savings and Loan in Chicago. He did not report this money on his 1972 tax return.

The Government also introduced evidence showing that Scott had previously converted campaign contributions to his personal use. Mr. Harry Ash, of Inheritance Abstractors, Inc., testified that on November 6, 1968, his company purchased a $4,000 cashier's check made payable to "Scott Campaign Committee." The government showed that Scott personally endorsed this check and negotiated it at the American National Bank for cash on October 3, 1969. In April, 1970, Inheritance Abstractors again purchased a cashier's check, this time in the amount of $2,500 and payable to Scott's Campaign Committee. The evidence showed that Scott gained possession of this check and endorsed it "Citizens for W.J. Scott for Public Office." He negotiated it with the Investment Department of National Boulevard Bank, where he had formerly been a vice-president, on May 15, 1970, as part payment for a $7,000 U.S. Treasury Note he purchased for himself on that date.

Ash testified that he and Inheritance Abstractors, Inc., intended these checks to be used solely by Scott's Campaign Committee, and that he never imparted any contrary intention to Scott. Nevertheless, the evidence showed that Scott converted these funds to his own use. He did not report the proceeds of these checks on his tax returns.

The government also argued that no nontaxable source for Scott's cash expenditures existed. See United States v. Massei, 355 U.S. 595, 78 S.Ct. 495, 2 L.Ed.2d 517 (1958). The government showed that during the net worth period, Scott had received no inheritance, other than stamps and coins from his father which he had not sold, and no insurance benefits. He did receive the proceeds of a single loan in 1970, totaling only $1,500 and reflected in the Government's net worth figures. For this argument to succeed, however, the jury would have to reject Scott's interpretation of the testimony of the 33 witnesses as establishing nontaxable cash "gifts" to Scott, during or before 1972.

4. Investigation of Leads

After introducing proof that Scott's net worth increased during 1972 due to campaign contributions diverted to his personal use, the government demonstrated that it had investigated all reasonable leads provided by Scott as to nontaxable sources of income which, if true, would establish his innocence. Scott presented various leads to the Tax Division of the Department of Justice in a conference held on March 27, 1979, with the Division lawyers. A letter submitted shortly after the conference, on March 30, 1979, detailed these leads. The government spent considerable time at trial proving that these leads had been investigated and accounted for in the net worth analysis. Some leads were shown to be false exculpatory statements made by Scott or through his counsel.

* * *

* * * [B]etween March 27, 1979, and April 2, 1979, Scott provided the Tax Division of the Department of Justice and the U.S. Attorney with the names of 100 persons who allegedly made cash "gifts" to Scott. Prior to the indictment, various Internal Revenue Service agents attempted to contact these people on these lists for information about their purported "gifts." The government introduced memoranda reporting these contacts as evidence of its efforts to investigate leads. The memoranda stated that of the persons contacted, seventy-five reported that they gave only nominal amounts to "pass-the-hat" funds for Scott's birthday or Christmas presents. Two of the people Scott listed did not exist, and sixteen could not be reached prior to the return of the indictment. The remaining individuals reported several different things. One stated that he had loaned $1,500 to Scott in 1970 which had never been repaid. This sum was already reflected in the government's net worth figures. One remembered making one payment of $500, which the government showed was deposited into Scott's campaign account. Another could recall giving Scott no money after the late 1960s, and yet another reported making no contributions of any nature. Two persons refused to talk to the government agents. Only one person said that he gave "gifts" between the early 1960s through 1976 which perhaps totaled $1,000. He was called as a government witness.

C. Evidence That Scott's 1972 Form 1040 Was False: The Specific Items of Omitted Income

The government introduced several specific items of income that Scott failed to report on his 1972 Form 1040. The largest of these were: the $5,000 Edward Barrett and William J. Kiley gave Scott in the summer of 1972; the payments Arthur Wirtz, a Chicago businessman, made to Ellen Cooper, whom Scott married in 1974; and the $500 check for "campaign use" which William Shaffer gave Scott in April, 1972, and which Scott converted to his own use in May, 1972. Proof that Scott willfully failed to include any one of these specific items in his adjusted gross income as reported on his 1972 Form 1040 would be sufficient to sustain Scott's conviction, regardless of the government's net worth proof.

The government used the $5,000 Barrett payment in its net worth proof as a likely source for some of Scott's cash expenditures. Standing alone, however, there was sufficient proof from which the jury could infer (1) that this payment was a campaign contribution Scott converted to his own use in 1972, thereby rendering it taxable income he was required to report; or (2) that it was a payment made for the improper purpose of influencing official conduct. If the jury concluded that it was a payment made for the purpose of influencing official conduct, Scott was required to report it as income in the year he received it—1972. It was clear from Scott's 1972 Form 1040 that he did not report it under any label.

The second item of specific income Scott omitted from his 1972 Form 1040 was the $11,057.10 in payments Arthur Wirtz [a Chicago businessman] made to Ellen Cooper during 1972. The government contended that Wirtz made these payments as a favor to Scott because as Attorney General, Scott possessed regulatory and enforcement powers over many of Wirtz' businesses. Therefore, Scott should have reported these payments, as "the first principle of income taxation [is that] income must be taxed to him who earns it," United States v. Basye, 410 U.S. 441, 449, 93 S.Ct. 1080, 1085, 35 L.Ed.2d 412 (1973), and not some other person who receives or spends it.

* * *

Wirtz testified that in either late 1971 or early 1972, Scott approached Wirtz and told him that "he had a friend named Ellen Cooper for whom he would like to find a job with one of the Wirtz companies." Wirtz told Scott that he "would be glad to find a spot for her" and that she should call his executive secretary, Gertrude Knowles. Cooper was placed on the Chicago Stadium Corporation payroll, which Wirtz described as a "confidential" account. Wirtz personally signed her payroll checks, which in 1972 totaled $11,057.10.[29] Wirtz testified that he saw

---

29. Cooper declared these payments on her 1972 and 1973 tax returns, and payroll deductions were made by the Chicago Stadium Corporation.

Scott again in late 1973. At that time Scott told him that he was going to marry Ellen Cooper. Although Wirtz couldn't recall the details of the meeting, they agreed that "she ought to terminate our services." She was then removed from the Wirtz payroll.

The evidence indicated that Cooper did nothing to earn these payments. Wirtz did not meet Cooper until some time after he put her on his payroll. None of the other Wirtz employees could remember meeting her until 1979. Neither could Wirtz find any attendance records, work product, employment application, or any other personal or corporate records related to Cooper. Moreover, throughout 1972, while Cooper was purportedly employed by Wirtz, she received a salary for serving as secretary to Scott's re-election campaign. She often traveled with Scott during this period, and numerous campaign documents prepared during 1972 contain references to her campaign role.

On cross-examination, Wirtz flatly denied making the payments to Cooper out of fear of Scott. Wirtz admitted, however, that he knew that Scott, as Attorney General, had enforcement powers over many of the Wirtz businesses.

Based on the evidence surrounding the Wirtz payments to Cooper, the government's tax expert concluded that this money should be attributed to Scott. Scott made all the arrangements enabling Cooper to receive the money and it could be inferred that he had earned it. There is no evidence that Cooper did anything to earn the money.

* * *

D.   Evidence Regarding Scott's Wilfulness

The final element necessary to the government's case against Scott is evidence of Scott's wilfulness in underreporting his adjusted gross income for 1972.

> "[Willfulness] may be inferred from conduct such as * * * making false entries or alterations, or false invoices or documents, * * * concealment of assets or covering up sources of income, handling one's affairs to avoid making the records used in transactions of the kind, and any conduct, the likely effect of which would be to mislead or conceal." Spies v. United States, 317 U.S. 492, 499, 63 S.Ct. 364, 368, 87 L.Ed. 418 (1943).

In this case, the government argued that wilfulness could be inferred from the manner in which Scott handled his financial affairs. Scott, a lawyer and an experienced banker who was once Treasurer of Illinois, invested almost all of his money derived from ordinary and legitimate sources, such as his paychecks or his state travel reimbursements, in high yield interest bearing securities or certificates of deposit. All of these funds were perfectly traceable, and from the evidence, it is obvious that Scott seldom let such funds remain idle, without earning any interest.

The very fact that Scott kept any money, regardless of its source, in safe deposit boxes seems out of character for a man who so carefully invested and earned interest on his other funds. The secreting of large amounts of cash in safe deposit boxes can itself be evidence that the cash did not come from legitimate sources simply because of the evident motivation to avoid records. This fact, coupled with his lack of records for living and travel expenses, as well as the unreported but taxable sources the jury could properly find, provides a sufficient basis from which the jury could infer that Scott was wilfully concealing his income. Scott's original defenses to the charges against him, as evidenced by the leads he submitted to the Tax Division of the Department of Justice on March 30, 1979, are further evidence of wilfulness, as the jury could have believed these to be false exculpatory statements, evidencing an intent to mislead or conceal.

II. The Defense Case

The burden of persuading the jury beyond a reasonable doubt that the defendant had income which he wilfully failed to report remains with the Government at all times. Holland v. United States, supra.

In a net worth case, however, the government is deemed to have established a *prima facie* case when it has proved putative income in excess of the income reported, the existence of a likely source of taxable income, and an effective negation of reasonable explanations by the taxpayer inconsistent with guilt. The government does not have the burden of disproving every possible nontaxable source of available funds. This is a reasonable rule, for if there is in fact such a source, evidence to demonstrate it is usually within the defendant's possession and control. At this point in the trial, the defendant, unless he elects to rely solely on the jury's finding some reasonable doubt, remains quiet at his peril.

Accordingly, Scott presented 32 witnesses who testified that they made cash "gifts" to Scott prior to and during 1972. He also presented his own expert witness on net worth computations. These witnesses, together, testified to giving Scott approximately $25,930 in cash between 1968 and 1975. If their testimony was believed, and accepted as establishing nontaxable "gifts," Scott would have had approximately $10,162 in cash on hand at the end of 1971, all from nontaxable "gifts." These witnesses testified to giving Scott another $5,187 in cash during 1972. The cash on hand at the beginning of 1972 and received during 1972 would have been sufficient to offset the government's calculations of Scott's net worth expenditures deficit of $11,096 plus the unsubstantiated travel and personal living expenses established by circumstantial evidence.

From our reading of the record, however, the jury could have perceived serious problems with these witnesses' testimony. Only one of them had records of the "gifts" and none of them could testify to the exact amount given Scott in any one year. Without exception Scott's estimates of the available cash on hand from these "gifts" was based on the witnesses' highest estimate, even though that estimate may have been reduced on cross-examination. Of the 33 "gift" witnesses, only seven had been included in the list of more than 115 names submitted to the Department of Justice in March and April of 1979. One of those seven had testified as part of the Government's case, and one had given contrary testimony to the grand jury. None of them was mentioned in Scott's accounting of his assets for his divorce proceedings in 1970 or child support proceedings in 1977.

* * *

Conceivably the jury disbelieved some of the testimony of the "gift" witnesses. Or it may have interpreted their testimony as showing campaign contributions. Or it may have concluded that payments were so motivated as to constitute compensation for official acts. Or the jury may have decided, at least to the extent of reasonable doubt, that these payments were in fact nontaxable gifts, made from a "detached and disinterested generosity." See Commissioner v. Duberstein, 363 U.S. 278, 285, 80 S.Ct. 1190, 1196, 4 L.Ed.2d 1218 (1960).

The latter determination as to all such testimony would mean rejection of the government's net worth case, and would be consistent with acquittal on other counts, but, as will be pointed out, would not require acquittal on Count One.

Scott's net worth expert witness adopted some of the government's own calculations but made several crucial assumptions in arriving at his estimate of Scott's adjusted gross income for 1972, which was equal to that reported by Scott. First of all, the defense expert calculated Scott's net worth as of December 31, 1971, to be $49,583.30 rather than the $30,253.12, calculated by the government. Much of the difference between the two starting points is explained by the testimony of Scott's witnesses, who, if believed, gave Scott $10,162 in unrestricted "gifts" between 1968 and the end of 1971. Moreover, he assumed that $12,000 in Scott's bank accounts had not come out of Scott's available cash or any other source disclosed by the evidence. Second, the defense expert assumed that every one of the "gifts" witnesses testified honestly and accurately, and that none of the money they gave Scott constituted campaign contributions or income. This assumption was made in spite of the circumstances under which many of the payments were made or the witnesses' contrary testimony before the grand jury or on cross-examination. This assumption also meant that Scott had lied during his divorce proceedings and child support proceedings. Third, Scott's expert assumed that Scott spent no money on food between 1968 and 1975, other than that accounted for on the travel vouchers he submitted to the state.
* * *

III.   Questions on Appeal

The government had fulfilled the requirements of a net worth and expenditures case by the time it rested. It had produced proof from which the jury could determine Scott's net worth at the close of 1971 and the increase in his net worth during 1972. It had shown substantial cash expenditures. Necessarily from these facts Scott must have had substantial receipts not reported as income. The government had shown that the likely source of such receipts was the conversion of campaign funds, making it taxable income. The Barrett and Shaffer items not only were shown to be converted campaign funds, but could well have been found to be taxable income as a payment motivated by defendant's official position. The government showed that it had conducted a reasonable investigation of any leads suggesting an exculpatory explanation, and had found none.

At trial, Scott offered testimony in an effort to show that the money the witnesses gave him prior to and during 1972 was not restricted to use in his political campaigns. To the extent the jury relied on the government's net worth proof, it must have either disbelieved the testimony as to restriction, or as to 1972 payments, must have found that the intent which would make the money nontaxable "gifts" was lacking.

* * *

Scott further contends that the government unfairly commented on his failure to produce and to stipulate to certain evidence, thereby implying that he had the burden of producing exculpatory evidence.[42]

Scott stops short of claiming that the government commented on his failure to testify, and the record shows no such comment, direct or indirect. The statements and arguments to which Scott objects were appropriate and justified when considered in the context of this case.

Scott first directs attention to the prosecutor's summation, merely citing 12 pages of the transcript, suggesting that the prosecution pointed to Scott's failure to supply evidence the prosecution wanted.

We have carefully examined these references and find them legitimate argument based on the evidence. In part, they questioned the credibility of defense witnesses, pointed out inconsistencies between the defense at trial and the pre-indictment explanations to the Department of Justice, argued that false explanations demonstrated wilfulness, commented on the failure of evidence to support theories advanced by the defense, and commented on Scott's practice of spending cash to avoid creating records.

Scott next cites 14 pages of the transcript in support of an assertion that the government improperly showed that Scott had failed to supply leads for investigation.

---

42. Criminal defendants are not usually required to produce documents requested by the government. In a criminal tax prosecution such as the present case, however, if the government cannot prove that it investigated all leads provided by the defendant, the court may prevent the government's case from going to the jury. Holland v. United States. Moreover, once the government has presented its *prima facie* case, the defendant "remains quiet at his peril," as he is usually the individual most able to come forward with evidence of his nontaxable income.

Each of these instances took place during the testimony of defense witnesses called to testify regarding cash gifts to Scott. Either before or after cross-examination of the defense witness, the government asked for a stipulation that this particular witness was not on the list of donors Scott provided to the Justice Department in March and April, 1979. Each time, a defense attorney, Mr. Thomas, so stipulated, although Mr. Barnett, another defense attorney, stated a continuing objection. The court allowed the government to request these stipulations, stating that the government had the burden to prove that it tracked down all leads.

The Government had a clear right to show that the witnesses produced at trial were not on the list furnished by defendant before indictment. In a net worth case, the government was required to show that it investigated leads provided by defendant to show availability of cash inconsistent with guilt. Holland v. United States.[44]

Moreover, the Government may properly comment on the inconsistencies in a defendant's case. It was legitimate to point out that although defendant had offered alleged explanations before indictment, he had offered different ones at trial.

Under the circumstances, we do not deem it an abuse of discretion to permit the government to use the technique of requesting a stipulation. It was clear that the government was in a position to establish the fact suggested, and the stipulation technique was expeditious.

* * *

We have examined the record in this case carefully. We have found no error, constitutional or otherwise, in either the proof admitted at trial or in the government's opening and closing arguments. The evidence Scott complains of was properly admitted as necessary for proving Scott's net worth, corroborating certain expenditures, rebutting defense testimony, and proving intent. The court was clearly within its discretion in determining that its probative value was not substantially outweighed by the danger of unfair prejudice. Fed.R.Evid. 403. The court carefully limited the jury's use of testimony having to do with financial transactions prior to the indictment years, both when the evidence was admitted, and during its final charge to the jury. That the jury carefully followed these instructions is evidenced by its refusal to return a conviction for the year 1975, a year for which the most potentially prejudicial proof was admitted.

Notes

1. Note the chart reproduced in footnote 3 of the *Scott* opinion. This chart outlines the net worth case. As prosecutor, how and when during the trial would you attempt to use this chart? What are the most effective

---

44. In this regard, the jury was instructed as follows:

"If you find that the government has not adequately investigated the leads or ex-

planations offered by the defendant, you must take those explanations being as true."

objections that could be made by defense counsel to keep this chart out of evidence? It may be helpful to review Fed.R.Evid. 1006 (summaries), 701 (use of experts) and 702 (bases for expert opinion).

2. Note that the government did not include in its calculations of Scott's income for the years in question any amounts spent on ordinary living expenses such as housing, gifts, personal entertainment and expenses. Scott had no records that he had paid any such expenses for the years in question, implying that he must have paid these expenses, if he had any, with cash. Is this a reasonable inference? Did it hurt the government's case not to include these figures?

3. Recall that Scott was acquitted on four counts (regarding tax returns for 1973–75) and convicted on one (regarding the 1972 tax return). Recall also that three specific items of income (the Wirtz–Cooper payment, the $5000 Barrett–Kiley payment and the $500 Shaffer payment) were part of the 1972 income calculations. Did you agree with the court's reasoning in affirming the attribution of the Wirtz–Cooper payment to Scott? In light of these specific items of proof, was the indirect method significant in securing the conviction on the 1972 count?

4. Note that on the leads issue, through the testimony of a government agent, the government was able to introduce testimony of 80–plus people, none of whom were present in the courtroom, placed under oath, or subject to cross examination. What was the court's rationale for admitting this apparent hearsay? How influential do you believe it was in securing a conviction on the 1972 count? If you had represented Scott during the pre-indictment investigation stage, what advice would you have given Scott about furnishing leads to the government?

Chapter 15

CRIMINAL LIABILITY OF CORPORATIONS AND CORPORATE EXECUTIVES

A. CORPORATE CRIMINAL LIABILITY

1. HISTORICAL DEVELOPMENT[a]

Whether corporations should be held criminally liable is one of the most hotly debated issues in modern criminal law.

Scholars have long decried the inability of our current standards of corporate criminal liability to address corporation intent. According to Gerhard O.W. Mueller, "[m]any weeds have grown on the acre of jurisprudence which has been allotted to the criminal law. Among these * * * is corporate criminal liability * * * Nobody bred it, nobody cultivated it, nobody planted it. It just grew."[b] John Braithwaite is more succinct: "A criminology which remains fixed at the level of individualism is the criminology of a bygone era."[c] Brent Fisse calls the inability to address corporate fault "the blackest hole in the theory of corporate criminal law."[d]

American jurisprudence has employed two major standards to determine when a corporation should be criminally liable. Both impose vicarious liability by imputing the criminal acts and intent of corporate agents to the corporation. The traditional, or respondeat superior, approach is a common law rule developed primarily in the federal courts and adopted by some state courts. Derived from agency principles in tort law, it provides that a corporation "may be held criminally liable for the

---

a. Portions of this section are reprinted with permission from Pamela H. Bucy, *Corporate Ethos: A Standard for Imposing Corporate Criminal Liability*, 75 *Minn.L.Rev.* 1095–84. Copyright © 1991 by the Minnesota Law Review Foundation.

b. Gerhard O. W. Mueller, *Mens Rea and the Corporation*, 19 *U.Pitt.L.Rev.* 21 (1957).

c. John Braithwaite, *Crime, Shame and Reintegration* 148 (1989).

d. Brent Fisse, *Restructuring Corporate Criminal Law*, 56 *S.Cal.L.Rev.* 1141, 1183 (1983).

acts of any of its agents [who] (1) commit a crime (2) within the scope of employment (3) with the intent to benefit the corporation."[e]

The American Law Institute's Model Penal Code (MPC) provides the major alternative standard for corporate criminal liability currently found in American jurisprudence. In the 1950s, the American Law Institute addressed the issue of corporate criminal liability, ultimately agreeing on three standards for such liability. The type of criminal offense charged determines which standard applies. The option that applies to the majority of criminal offenses provides that a court may hold a corporation criminally liable if the criminal conduct was "authorized, requested, commanded, performed or recklessly tolerated by the board of directors or by a high managerial agent acting in behalf of the corporation within the scope of his office or employment."[f] This standard still uses a respondeat superior model, but in a limited fashion: the corporation will be liable for conduct of only some agents (its directors, officers, or other higher echelon employees).

2. THE STANDARDS OF LIABILITY

In the next case, Commonwealth v. Beneficial Finance Co., 360 Mass. 188, 275 N.E.2d 33 (1971), the Massachusetts Supreme Court rejected the Model Penal Code standard in favor of a broader, respondeat superior, standard of liability.

COMMONWEALTH v. BENEFICIAL FINANCE CO.

Supreme Judicial Court of Massachusetts, Suffolk, 1971.
360 Mass. 188, 275 N.E.2d 33.

SPIEGEL, JUSTICE.

We have before us appeals emanating from two separate series of indictments and two separate jury trials of various individual and corporate defendants.

* * * The corporations convicted in the first trial were Beneficial Finance Company (Beneficial), Household Finance Corporation (Household) and Liberty Loan Corporation (Liberty). The individuals convicted in the first trial were John M. Farrell, Francis T. Glynn, Nathaniel W. Barber, James S. Pratt, Lyle S. Woodcock, Morris Garfinkle and Martin J. Hanley. In the second trial the corporate defendants convicted were Beneficial, Household and Local Finance Corporation (Local). The individuals convicted in the second trial were Hanley, Farrell, Glynn, Barber, Pratt and Edward R. Newhall.

These cases have become generally known as the "small loans" cases. In each case the defendants were charged with various offenses

e. *Developments in the Law—Corporate Crime: Regulating Corporate Behavior Through Criminal Sanctions,* 92 Harv. L.Rev. 1227, 1247 (1979). Commonwealth v. Beneficial Finance Co., 360 Mass. 188, 275 N.E.2d 33 (1971), exemplifies this approach.

f. American Law Institute, Model Penal Code § 2.07(1)(c) (Proposed Official Draft 1962).

under numerous indictments returned in 1964 by a special grand jury. The offenses charged were offering or paying, or soliciting or receiving, bribes, or conspiring to do so * * *.

* * *

* * * This evidence tends to show that during the year 1962, several licensed small loans companies (corporate defendants), together with certain of their officers and employees (some of whom are defendants), conspired to bribe Hanley and Garfinkle in their capacities as public officials. The purpose of the alleged conspiracy and the payment of the bribe money was to insure the maintenance of a maximum interest rate which companies licensed to do business in the Commonwealth were permitted to charge. * * *

* * *

[The court reviewed the evidence and] concluded that the evidence was sufficient to establish that the defendants Pratt and Woodcock were part of a conspiracy joined in by Farrell, Glynn and Barber to bribe Hanley and Garfinkle. [The court then turned] to the question of whether there was sufficient evidence to support a finding that Beneficial, Household and Liberty were parties to the conspiracy. Each of the corporate defendants raised this issue by means of a motion for a directed verdict. In view of the fact that this issue is discussed extensively in the briefs of the respective corporate defendants as well as in the Commonwealth's brief, and because the legal principles involved permeate these cases, * * * we discuss at length the applicable legal standards concerning the extent to which a corporation may be held criminally responsible for the acts of its directors, officers and agents. * * *

With this in mind, perhaps it would be helpful at this point to briefly summarize the relationships between the various corporate defendants and individual defendants: (1) Household was held criminally responsible, in part, for the criminal conduct of Barber and Pratt. Barber and Pratt were employees of Household, but were neither directors nor officers. (2) Liberty was held liable, in part, for the criminal acts of Woodcock, who was 1 of Liberty's 2 executive vice-presidents and one of its 11 directors. (3) Beneficial was held criminally responsible, in part, for the conduct of Farrell and Glynn who were neither directors, officers nor employees of that corporation. Farrell was a vice-president and Glynn was an employee of Beneficial Management, a wholly owned subsidiary of the defendant, Beneficial.

* * *

The defendants and the Commonwealth have proposed differing standards upon which the criminal responsibility of a corporation should be predicated. The defendants argue that a corporation should not be held criminally liable for the conduct of its servants or agents unless such conduct was performed, authorized, ratified, adopted or tolerated by the corporations' directors, officers or other "high managerial agents" who are sufficiently high in the corporate hierarchy to warrant the assumption that their acts in some substantial sense reflect corporate policy.

This standard is that adopted by the American Law Institute Model Penal Code, approved in May 1962. Section 2.07 of the Code provides that, except in the case of regulatory offenses and offenses consisting of the omission of a duty imposed on corporations by law, a corporation may be convicted of a crime if "the commission of the offence was authorized, requested, commanded, performed or recklessly tolerated by the board of directors or by a high managerial agent acting in behalf of the corporation within the scope of his office or employment." The section proceeds to define "high managerial agent" as "an officer of a corporation * * * or any other agent * * * having duties of such responsibility that his conduct may fairly be assumed to represent the policy of the corporation."

The Commonwealth, on the other hand, argues that the standard applied by the judge in his instructions to the jury was correct. These instructions, which prescribe a somewhat more flexible standard than that delineated in the Model Penal Code, state in part, as follows: "[T]he Commonwealth must prove beyond a reasonable doubt that there existed between the guilty individual or individuals and the corporation which is being charged with the conduct of the individuals, such *a relationship that the acts and the intent of the individuals were the acts and intent of the corporation.* Or, to put it differently, the Commonwealth must prove beyond a reasonable doubt that when the individuals were acting criminally in committing the acts which constitute the crime, and in having the intent required for the crime, *the corporation was actually so acting and intending,* and therefore is criminally liable. The Commonwealth must prove that."

"How is that to be shown? How is the jury to determine whether the Commonwealth has proved that? First let me say that the Commonwealth does not have to prove that the individual who acted criminally was expressly requested or authorized in advance by the corporation to do so, nor must the Commonwealth prove that the corporation expressly ratified or adopted that criminal conduct on the part of that individual or those individuals. *It does not mean that the Commonwealth must prove that the individual who acted criminally was a member of the corporation's board of directors, or that he was a high officer in the corporation, or that he held any office at all.* If the Commonwealth did prove that an individual for whose act it seeks to hold a corporation criminally liable was an officer of the corporation, the jury should consider that. *But more important than that, it should consider what the authority of that person was as such officer in relation to the corporation.* The mere fact that he has a title is not enough to make the corporation liable for his criminal conduct. The Commonwealth must prove that the individual for whose conduct it seeks to charge *the corporation criminally was placed in a position by the corporation where he had enough power, duty, responsibil-*

ity and authority to act for and in behalf of the corporation to handle the particular business or operation or project of the corporation in which he was engaged at the time that he committed the criminal act, with power of decision as to what he would or would not do while acting for the corporation, and that he was acting for and in behalf of the corporation in the accomplishment of that particular business or operation or project, and that he committed a criminal act while so acting.

"The Commonwealth must prove all that beyond a reasonable doubt before you can hold a corporation criminally liable or guilty by reason of the criminal acts or conduct of an individual.

"You will note from what I said that it is not necessary that the Commonwealth prove that an individual had any particular office or any office at all or that he had any particular title or any title at all. It isn't the title that counts. *It isn't the name of the office that counts, but it's the position in which the corporation placed that person with relation to its business, with regard to the powers and duties and responsibilities and authority which it gave to him which counts.* If it placed him in a position with such power, duty, authority, and responsibility that it can be found by you that, when he acted in the corporation's business, the corporation was acting, then you may find the corporation equally guilty of the criminal acts which he commits and of the intent which he holds, if you first find that the individual was guilty of the crime.

"Now, this test doesn't depend upon the power, duty, the responsibility, or the authority which the individual has with reference to the entire corporation business. The test should be applied to his position with relation to the particular operation or project in which he is serving the corporation." (emphasis supplied).

The difference between the judge's instructions to the jury and the Model Penal Code lies largely in the latter's reference to a "high managerial agent" and in the Code requirement that to impose corporate criminal liability, it at least must appear that its directors or high managerial agent "authorized * * * or recklessly tolerated" the allegedly criminal acts. The judge's instructions focus on the authority of the corporate agent in relation to the *particular* corporate business in which the agent was engaged. The Code seems to require that there be authorization or reckless inaction by a corporate representative having some relation to framing corporate policy, or one "having duties of such responsibility that his conduct may fairly be assumed to represent the policy of the corporation." Close examination of the judge's instructions reveals that they preserve the underlying "corporate policy rationale of the Code by allowing the jury to infer corporate policy" from the *position* in which the corporation placed the agent in commissioning him to handle the particular corporate affairs in which he was engaged at the time of the criminal act. We need not deal with the Model Penal Code in greater detail. Although we give it careful consideration as a scholarly proposal, it has not been enacted in Massachusetts and does not purport to be a restatement of existing law. It is not clear that if the Code had been in effect in Massachusetts, when the acts alleged and proved were committed, the corporate defendants would have been in a better situation, in view of the proof here of concerted criminal conduct (in a "program" designed to be of benefit to finance companies) by plainly significant representatives of three or more competing financing companies and the sums involved. We do not consider whether the circumstances would permit inferences of facts constituting a violation of the Code. The judge correctly charged the jury on the basis of decided cases, rather than on the basis of a proposed model code.

It may also be observed that the judge's standard is somewhat similar to the traditional common law rule of respondeat superior. However, in applying this rule to a criminal case, the judge added certain requirements not generally associated with that common law doctrine. He further qualified the rule of respondeat superior by requiring that the conduct for which the corporation is being held accountable be performed *on behalf of the corporation*. This factor is noted as important in the commentary to § 2.07(1) of the Model Penal Code. It may well be that there is often little distinction between an act done *on behalf of a principal* and an act done *within the scope of employment*, which is the traditional requirement of the doctrine of respondeat superior. Nevertheless, in the circumstances of this case it might reasonably be concluded that the explicit instruction of the judge that the jury look to the authority vested in the agent by the corporation to act within the particular sphere of corporate affairs relating to the criminal act, together with the explicit instruction that such act be performed on behalf of the corporation, required, in effect, the type of evidence which would support an inference that the criminal act was done as a matter of corporate policy. We deem this to be a valid conclusion, especially in view of the quantum of proof required in a criminal case in order to prove guilt beyond a reasonable doubt.

* * *

[The court reviewed a number of cases involving criminal liability of corporations, corporate executives, or employers for acts of employees.]

The thrust of each of the cases cited above involving a human principal is that it is fundamental to our criminal jurisprudence that for more serious offenses guilt is personal and not vicarious. "One is punished for his own blameworthy conduct, not that of others." Commonwealth v. Stasiun, 349 Mass. 38, 48, 206 N.E.2d 672, 679.

* * * [However] the very nature of a corporation as a "person" before the law renders it impossible to equate the imposition of vicarious liability on a human principal with the imposition of vicarious liability on a corporate principal. "A corporation can act only through its agents. [C]orporate criminal liability is necessarily vicarious." Note, *Criminal Liability of Corporations for Acts of their Agents*, 60 *Harv.L.Rev.* 283 (1946). Since a corporation is a legal fiction, comprised only of individuals, it has no existence separate and distinct from those whom it has clothed with authority and commissioned to act for it whether such individuals are directors, officers, shareholders or employees. Thus, the issue is * * * whether the acts and intent of natural persons, be they officers, directors or employees, can be treated as the acts and intent of the corporation itself. * * *

* * *

Household argues that in applying the foregoing standard of corporate criminal responsibility, we are merely applying the rule of respondeat superior as it is applied in civil cases and that we are "reaching out to state a completely new rule of law." We agree that * * * the judge's instructions to the jury, essentially employed the rationale underlying the doctrine of respondeat superior. However, we do not agree that application of this doctrine to a criminal case involving specific intent is a "completely new rule of law." The courts in the New York Cent. & H.R.R. Co. v. United States, 212 U.S. 481 (1909) * * * and the other federal cases * * * especially in Egan v. United States, 137 F.2d 369 (8th Cir., 1943) unequivocally focus their inquiry on the scope of authority which the corporation has conferred upon its agents to act on behalf of the corporation in managing the particular activities in which the agents were engaged when they committed the criminal act.

It may be that the theoretical principles underlying this standard are, in general, the same as embodied in the rule of respondeat superior. Nevertheless, as we observed at the outset, the judge's instructions, as a whole and in context, required a greater quantum of proof in the practical application of this standard than is required in a civil case. In focusing on the "kinship" between the authority of an individual and the act he committed, the judge emphasized that the jury must be satisfied "beyond a reasonable doubt" that the act of the individual "constituted "the act of the corporation. Juxtaposition of the traditional criminal law requirement of ascertaining guilt beyond a reasonable doubt (as opposed to the civil law standard of the preponderance of the evidence), with the rule of respondeat superior, fully justifies application of the standard enunciated by the judge to a criminal prosecution against a corporation for a crime requiring specific intent.

The foregoing is especially true in view of the particular circumstances of this case. In order to commit the crimes charged in these indictments, the defendant corporations either had to offer to pay money to a public official or conspire to do so. The disbursal of funds is an act peculiarly within the ambit of corporate activity. These corporations by the very nature of their business are constantly dealing with the expenditure and collection of moneys. It could hardly be expected that any of the individual defendants would conspire to pay, or would pay, the substantial amount of money here involved, namely $25,000, out of his own pocket. The jury would be warranted in finding that the disbursal of such an amount of money would come from the corporate treasury. A reasonable inference could therefore be drawn that the payment of such money by the corporations was done as a matter of corporate policy and as a reflection of corporate intent, thus comporting with the underlying rationale of the Model Penal Code, and probably with its specific requirements.

Moreover, we do not think that the Model Penal Code standard really purports to deal with the evidentiary problems which are inherent in establishing the quantum of proof necessary to show that the directors or officers of a corporation authorize, ratify, tolerate, or participate in the criminal acts of an agent when such acts are apparently performed on behalf of the corporation. Evidence of such authorization or ratification is too easily susceptible of concealment. As is so trenchantly stated by the judge: "Criminal acts are not usually made the subject of votes of authorization or ratification by corporate Boards of Directors; and the lack of such votes does not prevent the act from being the act of the corporation."

It is obvious that criminal conspiratorial acts are not performed within the glare of publicity, nor would we expect a board of directors to meet officially and record on the corporate records a delegation of authority to initiate, conduct or conclude proceedings for the purpose of bribing a public official. Of necessity, the proof authority to so act must rest on all the circumstances and conduct in a given situation and the reasonable inferences to be drawn therefrom.

Additional factors of importance are the size and complexity of many large modern corporations which necessitate the delegation of more authority to lesser corporate agents and employees. As the judge pointed out: "There are not enough seats on the Board of Directors, nor enough offices in a corporation, to permit the corporation engaged in widespread operations to give such a title or office to every person in whom it places the power, authority, and responsibility for decision and action." This latter consideration lends credence to the view that the title or position of an individual in a corporation should not be conclusively determinative in ascribing criminal responsibility. In a large corporation, with many numerous and distinct departments, a high ranking corporate officer or agent may have no authority or involvement in a particular sphere of corporate activity, whereas a lower ranking corporate executive might have much broader power in dealing with a matter peculiarly within the scope of his authority. Employees who are in the lower echelon of the corporate hierarchy often exercise more responsibility in the *everyday operations* of the corporation than the directors or officers. Assuredly, the title or office that the person holds may be considered, but it should not be the decisive criterion upon which to predicate corporate responsibility.

The validity and soundness of these considerations are especially reflected in the activities of public relations men in the employ of many large corporations. * * *

* * * It approaches the incredible for us to conclude from the evidence in the instant case that the public relations men, in their constant and prolonged communications with Hanley, were engaging in independent endeavors. The inference is obvious that their concerted

activities along the lines outlined in our summary of the facts could not have been carried on without the knowledge or at least the reckless toleration of highly placed corporate executives.

To permit corporations to conceal the nefarious acts of their underlings by using the shield of corporate armor to deflect corporate responsibility, and to separate the subordinate from the executive, would be to permit "endocratic" corporations to inflict widespread public harm without hope of redress. It would merely serve to ignore the scramble and realities of the market place. This we decline to do. We believe that stringent standards must be adopted to discourage any attempt by "endocratic" corporations' executives to place the sole responsibility for criminal acts on the shoulders of their subordinates.

We believe that our decision is supported by basic considerations of public policy. The President's Commission on Law Enforcement and Administration of Justice, Task Force Report—Crime and Its Impact— An Assessment (1967) provides a sound rationale for imputing criminal responsibility to the corporation for the acts of lower echelon corporate officials who have the authority to act on behalf of the corporation. The report states that " * * * It is very difficult to obtain the conviction of the true policy formulators in large, complex corporations. The top executives do not ordinarily carry out the overt criminal acts—it is the lower or middle management officials who, for example, attend price-fixing meetings."

* * *

Considering everything we have said above, we are of the opinion that the quantum of proof necessary to sustain the conviction of a corporation for the acts of its agents is sufficiently met if it is shown that the corporation has placed the agent in a position where he has enough authority and responsibility to act for and in behalf of the corporation in handling the *particular* corporate business, operation or project in which he was engaged at the time he committed the criminal act. The judge properly instructed the jury to this effect and correctly stated that this standard does not depend upon the responsibility or authority which the agent has with respect to the entire corporate business, but only to his position with relation to the particular business in which he was serving the corporation. Some of the factors that the jury were entitled to consider in applying the above test, although perhaps not in themselves decisive, are the following: (1) the extent of control and authority exercised by the individual over and within the corporation; (2) the extent and manner to which corporate funds were used in the crime; (3) a repeated pattern of criminal conduct tending to indicate corporate toleration or ratification of the agent's act.

* * *

[The court then applied these criteria to the present case and found all corporations to be guilty.]

Notes

1. The court in Beneficial Finance opted for a respondeat superior standard to assess criminal corporate liability. Why would the government prefer this standard to the MPC standard? Why would the corporate defendant prefer the MPC standard?

2. **"On Behalf of the Corporation":** To convict a corporation for the acts of its agents under the standard of liability approved in *Beneficial Finance,* the government must prove that the individual who committed the offense was "placed in a position by the corporation where he had enough power, duty, responsibility and authority to act for * * * the corporation [and] * * * that he was acting for and in behalf of the corporation * * *." Acknowledging that this standard is "somewhat similar to the traditional common law rule of respondeat superior" employed in civil cases, the appellate court noted in *Beneficial Finance* that the trial court added two requirements to this common law rule: that the conduct at issue was performed "on behalf of the corporation" and that all elements of this standard must, as in all criminal cases, be proven beyond a reasonable doubt. Note that the requirement "on behalf of the corporation" is included in the MPC standard of liability as well as in the traditional respondeat superior standard.

The court in *Beneficial Finance* may well be correct that requiring that the conduct at issue be undertaken "on behalf of the corporation" prevents improper imposition of criminal liability on a corporation. The problem is that courts have interpreted "on behalf of the corporation," almost out of existence. As one court noted, "[t]here have been many cases * * * in which the corporation is criminally liable even though no benefit [to the corporation] has been received in fact." Standard Oil Co. v. United States, 307 F.2d 120, 128 (5th Cir.1962).

Should corporations be convicted without proof that the illegal conduct benefitted the corporation? Is it appropriate to require proof that the illegal conduct was undertaken to benefit the corporation (even if actual benefit was not realized)? Are there problems in requiring proof of benefit before a corporation can be convicted? For example, from whose point of view should benefit be assessed? What if there is some benefit to a corporation because of illegal conduct by its agents—and some harm: how is the benefit and harm to be weighed? Could these problems in measuring benefit be the reason this element has little significance in practice? If this requirement can not be enforced, is respondeat superior, developed for use in the civil arena, an appropriate standard for assessing criminal liability, even if all other aspects of the standard must be proven beyond a reasonable doubt?

3. **In Search of Corporate Mens Rea.** Especially in light of the diluted interpretation given to the "on behalf of the corporation" requirement, one must question whether corporate criminal liability is appropriately assessed by either of the currently used standards of liability. One could argue that the critical weakness in both the traditional respondeat superior and MPC standards is that by imposing vicarious liability, they fail to sufficiently analyze corporate intent.

As the court noted in *Beneficial Finance,* "it is fundamental to our criminal jurisprudence that for more serious offenses guilt is personal and not vicarious." Yet, current corporate criminal liability standards make no effort to assess "corporate intent." Cases where a corporate employee acted contrary to express corporate policy and the corporation was held liable best exemplify this failure of the current standards to require corporate intent.

United States v. Hilton Hotels Corp., 467 F.2d 1000 (9th Cir.1972), is an apt example. The purchasing agent at a Hilton Hotel in Portland, Oregon, threatened a supplier of goods with the loss of the hotel's business if the supplier did not contribute to an association that was formed to attract conventions to Portland. Id. at 1002. The corporate president testified that such action was contrary to corporate policy. Id. at 1004. Both the manager and assistant manager of the Hotel testified that they specifically told the purchasing agent not to threaten suppliers. Nevertheless, the court convicted the Hilton Hotel Corporation of antitrust violations under the respondeat superior standard of liability.

The MPC standard was not used to assess Hilton's criminal liability, but if the factfinder determined that the purchasing agent had "duties of such responsibility that his conduct may fairly be assumed to represent the policy of the corporation or association" (MPC 2.07(4)(c)), the purchasing agent would be a "high managerial agent" and Hilton would be criminally liable under the MPC standard.

Arguably, the corporate criminal liability that results from a failure to assess a corporate intent is too broad. Under both the MPC and respondeat superior standards, a corporation's efforts to prevent illegal conduct become irrelevant and all corporations, honest or dishonest, good or bad, are convicted.

The MPC standard, which requires that a higher echelon employee commit, or recklessly supervise, the criminal conduct, does of course, slightly narrow corporate criminal liability. Recognizing the unfairness of holding a corporation liable for the acts of *all* its agents, the MPC views the corporation as the embodiment of the acts and intent of only its "high managerial agent[s]." High managerial agents are those individuals "having duties of such responsibility that [their] conduct may fairly be assumed to represent the policy of the corporation or association." MPC § 207(4)(c). Do you believe this limitation in the MPC standard adequately remedies the potential for holding "good," law-abiding corporations criminally liable for the criminal act of a "maverick" employee who is acting contrary to corporate policy?

4. **Further evaluation of the Model Penal Code Standard for Assessing Corporate Criminal Liability.** In rejecting the MPC standard of corporate criminal liability, the court in *Beneficial Finance* focused on evidentiary problems inherent in the MPC approach. The court noted that because illegal activities rarely are conducted openly, it would be difficult to obtain proof that a high managerial agent conducted, or even recklessly tolerated, the activity. The court also noted the size of modern corporations, reasoning that titles should not be determinative in assessing corporate criminal liability.

In addition, the court referred to the internal corporate policy fostered by the MPC standard—that corporations are encouraged "to conceal the nefarious acts of their underlings by using the shield of corporate armor to deflect corporate responsibility." This is a problem commonly, and deservedly, identified with the MPC standard. Commentators argue that the MPC standard encourages higher echelon officials to insulate themselves from knowledge of corporate employee activity.

The MPC standard also has been criticized for allowing inappropriately narrow criminal liability. Under this standard even if a clear corporate policy encouraged a lower echelon employee to commit an offense, the corporation is liable only if there is evidence that a specific "high managerial agent" authorized or recklessly tolerated this conduct. In such an instance, a corporation is not held liable despite the clear corporate policy.

For critiques of the MPC standard, see, e.g., Kathleen Brickey, *Rethinking Corporate Liability Under the Model Penal Code,* 19 RUTGERS L.J. 593, 626 (1988); Note: *Developments in the Law–Corporate Crime: Regulating Corporate Behavior Through Criminal Sanctions,* 92 HARV.L.REV. 1227, 1254 (1979).

Which standard, respondeat superior or MPC, do you believe is preferable to assess corporate criminal liability? Can you devise an alternative standard? Commentators who have suggested alternative standards for assessing corporate criminal liability include *J. Braithwaite, Crime, Shame and Reintegration* (1989); Bucy, *Corporate Ethos: A Standard for Imposing Corporate Criminal Liability,* 75 Minn.L.Rev. 1095 (1991); Fisse, *Restructuring Corporate Criminal Law,* 56 S.Cal.L.Rev. 1141 (1983).

5. **Collective Intent.** Some courts have employed an interesting fiction to hold corporations criminally liable when it is not possible to identify specific individuals within the corporation who have adequate criminal intent which can be imputed to the corporation. To employ this approach, courts combine the bits of information held by several different corporate agents into a "collective intent" which is then imputed to the corporation.

United States v. Bank of New England, 821 F.2d 844 (1st Cir.1987), demonstrates this approach. In this case the Bank of New England ("Bank") was convicted for willfully failing to file Currency Transaction Reports (CTRs) on 31 deposits made by one of its customers, James McDonough. As noted in Chapter 4, *supra*, regulations promulgated under The Bank Secrecy Act, 31 U.S.C. § 5313 ("Act"), require banks to file a CTR for any customer currency transactions exceeding $10,000. The Act imposes felony liability when a bank willfully fails to file such reports. 31 U.S.C. § 5322(b). The United States Court of Appeals for the First Circuit discussed the notion of "collective intent" and applied it to find the Bank of New England guilty:

"The bulk of the indictment alleged that the Bank, as principal, and McDonough, as an aider and abettor, willfully failed to file CTRs on thirty-six occasions between May 1983 and July 1984. Five counts were dismissed because, on those occasions, McDonough received cashier's checks from the Bank, rather than currency. McDonough was acquitted of all charges against him. The Bank was found guilty on the thirty-one remaining counts. We affirm.

* * *

"The evidence at trial revealed that from 1978 through September 1984, McDonough was a regular customer at the Prudential Branch of the Bank of New England.

* * *

"McDonough's practice was to visit the same branch of the same bank on only one occasion in a single day. He simultaneously would present to a single bank teller two to four checks, all made payable to cash, for varying amounts under $10,000 which, when added together, equalled a sum greater than $10,000. In return, the same bank teller would transfer to him in a single motion a wad of cash totalling more than $10,000.

* * *

"On each of the charged occasions, the cash was withdrawn from one account. The Bank did not file CTRs on any of these transactions until May 1985, shortly after it received a grand jury subpoena.

* * *

"We have no trouble categorizing such conduct as a single physical transfer of currency in excess of $10,000 from the Bank to McDonough.

* * *

"The judge instructed that the knowledge of individual employees acting within the scope of their employment is imputed to the Bank. She told the jury that 'if any employee knew that multiple checks would require the filing of reports, the bank knew it, provided the employee knew it within the scope of his employment, * * *.'

"The trial judge then focused on the issue of 'collective knowledge':

> 'In addition, however, you have to look at the bank as an institution. As such, its knowledge is the sum of the knowledge of all of the employees. That is, the bank's knowledge is the totality of what all of the employees know within the scope of their employment. So, if Employee A knows one facet of the currency reporting requirement, B knows another facet of it, and C a third facet of it, the bank knows them all. So if you find that an employee within the scope of his employment knew that CTRs had to be filed, even if multiple checks are used, the bank is deemed to know it. The bank is also deemed to know it if each of several employees knew a part of that requirement and the sum of what the separate employees knew amounted to knowledge that such a requirement existed.'

* * *

"The Bank contends that the trial court's instructions regarding knowledge were defective because they eliminated the requirement that it be proven that the Bank violated a known legal duty. It avers that the knowledge instruction invited the jury to convict the Bank for negligently maintaining a poor communications network that prevented the consolidation of the information held by its various employees. The Bank argues that it is error to find that a corporation possesses a particular item of knowledge if one part of the corporation has half the information making up the item, and another part of the entity has the other half.

"A collective knowledge instruction is entirely appropriate in the context of corporate criminal liability. The acts of a corporation are, after all, simply the acts of all of its employees operating within the scope of their employment. The law on corporate criminal liability reflects this. Similarly, the knowledge obtained by corporate employees acting within the scope of their employment is imputed to the corporation. Corporations compartmentalize knowledge, subdividing the elements of specific duties and operations into smaller components. The aggregate of those components constitutes the corporation's knowledge of a particular operation. It is irrelevant whether employees administering one component of an operation know the specific activities of employees administering another aspect of the operation:

> '[A] corporation cannot plead innocence by asserting that the information obtained by several employees was not acquired by any one individual who then would have comprehended its full import. Rather the corporation is considered to have acquired the collective knowledge of its employees and is held responsible for their failure to act accordingly.'

United States v. T.I.M.E.–D.C., Inc., 381 F.Supp. 730, 738 (W.D.Va. 1974). Since the Bank had the compartmentalized structure common to all large corporations, the court's collective knowledge instruction was not only proper but necessary."

As you read the next case, United States v. One Parcel of Land, 965 F.2d 311 (7th Cir.1992), consider whether the "collective intent" approach is an appropriate recognition of the way large business entities conduct business, or is further evidence that criminal liability for corporations (especially closely held corporations) is inappropriate?

UNITED STATES v. ONE PARCEL OF LAND

United States Court of Appeals, Seventh Circuit, 1992.
965 F.2d 311.

MANION, CIRCUIT JUDGE.

Pursuant to 21 U.S.C. § 881(a)(7), the government filed a complaint for forfeiture *in rem* against a parcel of land located in Oneida County, Wisconsin, alleging that the property had been used to facilitate a violation of Title II of the Controlled Substances Act, 21 U.S.C. §§ 801 et seq., punishable by more than one year's imprisonment. Modernaire

Three, Inc. ("Modernaire"), owned the property in fee simple and contested the forfeiture in district court. After Modernaire and the government filed cross-motions for summary judgment, the district court granted the government's motion. Modernaire appeals claiming that the district court improperly rejected its innocent owner defense. We reverse and remand for entry of summary judgment in favor of Modernaire.

I. BACKGROUND

The parties agree that this case presents no material issues of fact. Since the legal issue presented focuses on the innocent owner defense, the relevant facts concern the ownership and operation of the res in this forfeiture action.

Incorporated in 1972, Modernaire owned the defendant property in a resort community in northern Wisconsin. The property consists of a parcel of land and five buildings: a tavern, a house, two cabins, and a garage. Only three individuals own stock in Modernaire. Harry R. Seymer, Jr., and his wife, Dorothy B. Seymer, own two-thirds of the shares. Their son, Harry R. Seymer, III ("Harry III"), owns the remaining one-third. Harry and Dorothy Seymer provided the original capital for Modernaire and for the purchase of the real estate by selling a tavern they owned personally, contributing $25,000, mortgaging other property, and mortgaging the property purchased. Harry III made no contribution to capitalize Modernaire or to purchase the property. Harry III's shares were a gift from his parents who wanted to provide their son with a start in life. Harry Seymer serves as president and Dorothy Seymer serves as vice-president of the corporation. Harry III served as corporate secretary-treasurer at all times relevant to this appeal.

From 1972 until the government seized the property in 1990, Harry III directed the day-to-day operations of the property and the tavern business. Between 1972 and 1977, Mr. and Mrs. Seymer lived in Milwaukee and would visit the property on weekends to check on business and help Harry III with maintenance, repairs and improvements. Before Modernaire purchased it, the property had been an auto court. The buildings had fallen into disrepair, so the Seymers would spend from Friday night through Sunday cleaning and repairing the premises. In 1977, Mr. and Mrs. Seymer moved to property next to the defendant property. In spite of a physical disability, Mr. Seymer visited the property daily spending anywhere from a half hour to the whole day doing ministerial and janitorial tasks. After being diagnosed with an aneurysm in 1979 at the age of 62, Mrs. Seymer was unable to participate in the day-to-day operations of the tavern but remained in touch with how it was run.

From the inception of Modernaire, Mr. and Mrs. Seymer attended informal monthly meetings and monitored Harry III's management of the business. They did rely on Harry III, however, to relay relevant financial information to them. Harry III had full authority to handle tax and financial matters and deal with vendors, government agencies, professionals and third parties on behalf of Modernaire. In exchange for managing the property, Harry III and his wife (also an employee of Modernaire) resided rent-free on the property and collected rental proceeds from a cabin on the premises. While the property no doubt appreciated over the years and the business grew (Harry III estimated that the annual gross income between 1980 and 1985 was around $70,000 or $80,000), Mr. and Mrs. Seymer apparently received no profit or dividends from Modernaire. Since the original purchase, however, Mr. Seymer invested approximately $25,000 more into the business. He had planned for Modernaire to sell the business eventually so that he could recover his investment and divide the proceeds with Mrs. Seymer and Harry III.

Without the knowledge or consent of Mr. or Mrs. Seymer, however, Harry III began engaging in drug transactions, some of which occurred on the defendant property. Federal and state agencies were suspicious of Harry III and began investigating him for drug-related activities in the early 1980s. A series of investigations by the Internal Revenue Service, the Oneida County Sheriff's Department, the Wisconsin Division of Criminal Investigations and the Federal Bureau of Investigation, however, failed to catch Harry III. The record indicates that Harry III conducted all of his drug transactions surreptitiously, particularly since he feared the wrath of his father, an ex-Marine. Concealing the drugs was not difficult since Harry III never possessed more than an ounce of cocaine at a time, and he would keep the drugs in his bedroom in a locking bank bag or in a safe. The record shows at the most three people who came to the defendant property to engage in drug transactions with Harry III.[1] Those transactions never took place in the bar but rather in Harry III's residence on the defendant property. Harry III even placed all phone calls related to his drug transactions from the phone in his residence. Harry III never used corporate funds to purchase drugs and never put any money obtained from drug sales into the corporation. His clandestine methods gave his parents no reason for suspicion and frustrated the extended investigation efforts of federal and state agencies.

Finally, in November 1989, the FBI interviewed Charles Richardson. Richardson stated that between the late 1970s and the mid–1980s Harry III bought large quantities of cocaine in Milwaukee for distribution, that Richardson had purchased cocaine from Harry III on several occasions, and that Richardson had sold cocaine for Harry III at locations other than the defendant property.

---

1. The dissent states that Harry III turned the corporation into a "criminal enterprise ... using the stream of visitors to the tavern on the property to mask his drug business...." The record does not support this characterization. In his deposition, Harry III recalled that only Charles Richardson had come to his residence (located on the defendant property) to purchase or exchange drugs. The FBI agent who had investigated Harry III could identify only two other individuals who visited the defendant property for drug transactions. Although the Assistant United States Attorney who questioned Harry III alluded to other transactions, there is no testimony regarding those transactions from either the FBI agent or Harry III. Furthermore, although some of the deposition testimony suggests that Harry III may have carried on transactions at other locations, the only transactions relevant to this forfeiture action are those facilitated by the defendant property.

On April 5, 1990, the government filed its Complaint in this case alleging that Harry III had used the defendant property to facilitate a conspiracy to distribute controlled substances. In the Complaint, the government relied on the information that Richardson had supplied. On June 14, 1990, the court ordered the Clerk to issue a warrant for the seizure and arrest of the defendant property, and on July 19, Modernaire filed its Notice of Claim to the property. On December 6, 1990, in a separate criminal action, Harry III pleaded guilty to violations of 21 U.S.C. § 846 (conspiracy to distribute controlled substances) between the late 1970s and the mid–1980s. On December 14, 1990, both the government and Modernaire filed motions for summary judgment in this forfeiture action.

Both parties agreed that there were no material issues of fact, but Modernaire raised the innocent owner defense provided in 21 U.S.C. § 881(a)(7). Section 881(a)(7) provides for forfeiture to the United States of the following:

> All real property, including any right, title, and interest (including any leasehold interest) in the whole of any lot or tract of land and any appurtenances or improvements, which is used, or intended to be used, in any manner or part, to commit, or to facilitate the commission of, a violation of this title punishable by more than one year's imprisonment, *except that no property shall be forfeited under this paragraph, to the extent of an interest of an owner, by reason of any act or omission established by that owner to have been committed or omitted without the knowledge or consent of that owner.*

21 U.S.C. § 881(a)(7) (emphasis added). Modernaire argued that it qualified for the innocent owner exception of 21 U.S.C. § 881(a)(7) because Harry III's knowledge of his own activities could not be imputed to Modernaire.

The district court disagreed and granted summary judgment to the government for two reasons. First, because Modernaire had abdicated general corporate authority to Harry III, there was no limit on the extent to which Harry III's knowledge could be imputed to the corporation. Second, overseeing the premises was within the scope of Harry III's duties, and the knowledge he gained while carrying out his duties could be imputed to Modernaire.

On appeal, Modernaire asks us to resolve one question: Under 21 U.S.C. § 881(a)(7), can Harry III's knowledge of his own unauthorized criminal conduct be imputed to Modernaire to defeat the corporation's innocent owner defense?

II. Analysis

* * *

Under section 881(a)(7), once the government establishes probable cause to believe that property was used to facilitate the distribution of controlled substances in violation of Title II of the Controlled Substances Act, the burden shifts to the claimant to prove by a preponderance of the evidence either that the property was not used to facilitate the alleged illegal activity or that the claimant was an innocent owner. Rather than dispute that Harry III used the defendant property to facilitate his drug transactions, Modernaire seeks the protection section 881(a)(7) affords to innocent owners.

To establish the innocent owner defense, the claimant must show by a preponderance of the evidence that the illegal activity took place on the property without the claimant's knowledge or consent. Section 881(a)(7), however, harbors a latent ambiguity that has split the circuits. Some circuits hold that to avoid forfeiture a claimant must establish *both* lack of consent *and* lack of knowledge. Others hold that even if a claimant has actual knowledge, the claimant may avoid forfeiture by establishing lack of consent. The Seventh Circuit has not taken a position on this issue, and we need not do so here. Since we conclude *infra* that Modernaire did not have actual knowledge of Harry III's activities, it logically follows that Modernaire could not consent. Thus we need not decide whether Modernaire could have established the innocent owner defense by showing that Modernaire did not consent to Harry III's activities even if it knew about them.

We also note that courts disagree about whether a claimant must prove not only that it did not know of or subjectively consent to the proscribed activity but also that it did all that he could reasonably be expected to do to prevent the proscribed use of the property. This issue arises, however, as a subissue to the question of the claimant's consent to the illegal activity. Because we do not reach the issue of whether Modernaire consented, we need not decide whether consent is determined by subjective or objective criteria.

* * *

Our inquiry must focus on Modernaire's knowledge. The language of section 881(a)(7) constrains courts to employ a subjective rather than an objective standard for assessing the claimant's knowledge. A claimant may secure the benefit of the innocent owner defense by establishing that the illegal conduct occurred on its property "without the knowledge or consent of" the claimant. Nothing in section 881(a)(7) suggests that the court must determine whether the claimant should have known of illegal activities taking place on the claimant's property. Instead, section 881(a)(7) focuses on the claimant's actual knowledge. Accordingly, if Modernaire shows that it had no actual knowledge of Harry III's activities, then the innocent owner defense shields Modernaire's property from forfeiture even if Modernaire conceivably should have known what Harry III was up to.

The task then becomes to ascertain the extent of Modernaire's actual knowledge, and therein lies the rub. As a legal fiction, a corporation cannot "know" like an individual "knows." We treat corporations as separate legal entities and enable them to own property and enter contracts by relying on agency precepts. A corporation and its agents relate to one another like a principal to its agents. A corporation acts through its agents. Similarly, a corporation "knows" through its agents. But contrary to the government's contention, a corporate principal's knowledge is less than the collective knowledge of its corporate agents. To distinguish knowledge belonging exclusively to an agent from knowledge belonging to the corporate principal, courts rely on certain presumptions. Where a corporate agent obtains knowledge while acting in the scope of his agency, he presumably reports that knowledge to his corporate principal so the court imputes such knowledge to a corporation. However, where an agent obtains knowledge while acting outside the scope of his agency, the standard presumption is unfounded, and the court will not impute the agent's knowledge to the corporation.

Corporate criminal and civil cases reflect the application of agency principles.[3] Only knowledge obtained by corporate employees acting within the scope of their employment is imputed to the corporation. See, e.g., United States v. Bank of New England, N.A., 821 F.2d 844, 856 (1st Cir.1987). Acting within the scope of employment entails more than being on the corporate employer's premises. This circuit has indicated that acting within the scope of employment means "with intent to benefit the employer." Therefore, the agent is outside the scope of his employment when he is not acting at least in part for the benefit of the corporation, and any knowledge the agent obtains is not imputed to the corporation. Other cases divide the analysis differently and reason that knowledge is imputed only if the agent is acting within the scope of his employment and for the benefit of the employer. In any event, the knowledge that a corporate agent acquires while not acting at least in part with the intent to benefit the corporation is not imputed to the corporation.

Relying on these general principles of agency and their underlying presumptions, we will not impute Harry III's knowledge of his own illegal activities to Modernaire in spite of the extent of Harry III's authority. Harry III was dealing drugs to benefit Harry III not as part of his job at Modernaire. Harry III testified that no proceeds of his illegal conduct went to Modernaire in any way, and the government offered no conflicting evidence. Harry III's interest indisputably lay in concealing his own drug deals from Modernaire thus undermining the presumption that an agent reports his knowledge to his principal. Consequently, we will not mechanically attribute Harry III's knowledge of his own drug deals to Modernaire to defeat Modernaire's innocent owner defense.

After examining the general principles of agency law, the government reached a contrary conclusion in this case. Jumping to the conclusion that Harry III's knowledge could be attributed to Modernaire simply because of the extent of Harry III's authority, the government discussed the adverse agent exception to the imputation of knowledge

---

3. Granted, the forfeiture statute at issue in our case is not a criminal statute, and the government has not attempted to hold Modernaire criminally liable for Harry III's drug transactions. Nevertheless, we are focusing on Modernaire's knowledge, and the issue of corporate knowledge usually arises in criminal cases. The agency principles employed, however, are equally valid in a civil case.

and explained that Modernaire could not qualify. Under the adverse agent exception, where an agent is involved in matters damaging to the corporation, his knowledge is not imputed to the corporation even if he obtains the knowledge while acting within the scope of his agency because the presumption that the agent will report information of his activities to the corporation is invalid. The government contends that Harry III's activities were not adverse to Modernaire. The government need not have considered the adverse agent exception, however, because the general rule disposed of the issue in this case. Regardless of whether Harry III constituted an "adverse agent," Harry III did not deal drugs with the intent to benefit Modernaire in any way. Therefore, notwithstanding the extent of Harry III's authority, since Harry III did not obtain knowledge of his activities while acting to benefit his principal, his knowledge cannot be imputed to Modernaire.

Similarly, we find the government's argument regarding the "sole actor" exception superfluous. The sole actor exception functions as an exception to the adverse agent exception. "Where an adverse agent is also the sole representative of the principal in the transaction in question, the principal may once again be charged with the agent's knowledge." First National Bank of Cicero, 860 F.2d 1407, 1417 (7th Cir. 1988). Through the sole actor exception, courts protect third parties who unwittingly deal with adverse agents if the corporation abdicated responsibility to the adverse agent. The sole actor exception to the adverse agent exception has no place in our analysis since we need not reach the adverse agent exception itself. Furthermore, since we do not have an innocent third party injured by an unsupervised adverse agent, we need not engage in the equity considerations that the sole actor exception addresses.

* * *

Since we cannot attribute Harry III's knowledge to Modernaire through the application of agency principles, Modernaire has no actual knowledge of proscribed activities facilitated by the defendant property. Accordingly, Modernaire has established by a preponderance of the evidence that it is an innocent owner, and the government may not appropriate Modernaire's property. Even if a court concluded Modernaire should have known through Mr. or Mrs. Seymer that Harry III sold drugs from his residence on the defendant property, that finding would be irrelevant. Section 881(a)(7) demands actual knowledge not constructive knowledge. Therefore, Modernaire had to show only what was, and we need not consider what should have been.

* * *

Congress intended to use the forfeiture statutes as a powerful weapon in the war on drugs. "Clearly if law enforcement efforts to combat racketeering and drug trafficking are to be successful, they must include an attack on the economic aspects of these crimes. Forfeiture is the mechanism through which such an attack may be made." [citation omitted] Nothing in this opinion should vitiate the intended use of forfeiture statutes. The result in this case turns closely on the facts. If the corporation had derived more than a speculative benefit from the drug transactions, then we could have imputed Harry III's knowledge of his activities to Modernaire. If the corporation was Harry III's alter ego, if Harry III established the corporation to serve his drug business, or if Harry III had given title to the property to the corporation in order to protect his assets, then we could have imputed Harry III's knowledge of his drug dealings to the corporation. But here a corporation has presented undisputed evidence that its corporate agent surreptitiously conducted his own drug deals with no ties to the legitimately established corporation except that three individuals purchased drugs at some time on corporate property. * * *

* * *

III. CONCLUSION

For the foregoing reasons, the district court's grant of summary judgment is REVERSED and the case is REMANDED for entry of summary judgment for Modernaire.

POSNER, CIRCUIT JUDGE, DISSENTING.

Harry R. Seymer, III dealt drugs on a resort property owned by Modernaire Three, Inc., a corporation of which he is a one-third owner and the manager. The other two owners are his parents. They play no active role in the management of the corporation. It's Harry III's baby. The property was forfeit, unless the drug dealings were committed "without the knowledge or consent of [the property's] owner." 21 U.S.C. § 881(a)(7). The owner of course was Modernaire. My brethren are correct that a corporation is not to be charged with knowledge of every furtive misdeed of employees who misuse corporate property for ends not only private but contrary to the corporation's interest. But Harry III was not only a corporate officer and major shareholder; he was the manager of the corporation—the only manager. He controlled the use of its property. If he decided to turn the corporation into a criminal enterprise—as he did, using the stream of legitimate visitors to the tavern on the property to mask his drug business—there was, as a practical matter, no one to say him nay.

What the court has done is to pierce the corporate veil and deem the parents the owners of the property that Harry III used for drug trafficking. But they are not the owners; the corporation is. And if the veil is to be pierced, the spear should touch Harry, for he is one of the owners: one might have supposed that, at the least, Harry III would be required to forfeit his one-third interest. But no; he forfeits nothing. At argument Modernaire's lawyer said that the case should be decided the same way even if Harry had had a two-thirds rather than a one-third share. Why stop there? On the logic of the court's opinion Modernaire would win this case even if Harry owned all the corporation's stock.

Yet at the end of its opinion the court flinches, and tries to reassure us that "nothing in this opinion should vitiate the intended use of forfeiture statutes" because Congress could rewrite the statute and anyway "the result in this case turns closely on the facts." What facts? That Harry III's parents, people of modest means, mortgaged their property so that they could "provide their son with a start in life" that he did not deserve? That Harry III's father had a physical disability and his mother an aneurysm? That there were only three drug buyers? (I don't believe it and neither should the court, which, while emphasizing that Harry III's "clandestine methods frustrated the extended investigation efforts of federal and state agencies," credulously accepts his deposition evidence concerning the limited scope of his operations.) That the other stockholders didn't know? That the government neglected to prove what is obvious without proof, that the tavern was a convenient cover for Harry III's drug business?

The court is critical of fictions but says without blushing that "Modernaire has no *actual* knowledge of proscribed activities taking place on its land." We must ask what it means to speak of a corporation's "knowledge." A corporation is not a living being. It has no mind. When we say a corporation "knows" something, for example that it has a claim against someone (and hence that the statute of limitations is running), we mean that a *responsible* agent of the corporation knows the thing. There is no more responsible agent of Modernaire than Harry, its manager. If he knew that Modernaire had a claim against someone, the corporation could not defeat a defense of statute of limitations on the ground that Harry's knowledge could not be imputed to the corporation. Likewise the drug dealing of Harry the employee was, of course, known to Harry the manager, the responsible agent, and this knowledge the law treats as the knowledge of the corporation. The court says that "where a corporate agent obtains knowledge while acting in the scope of his agency, he presumably reports that knowledge to his corporate principal so the court imputes such knowledge to a corporation." We must be alert to the fallacy of personifying the corporation and ask what concretely it means to report to one's "corporate principal." Necessarily the agent reports not to "the corporation" but to a human being—in fact to another corporate agent, but one at the management level. Harry the drug dealer "reported" his drug dealings to Harry the corporate manager. No more was necessary to "impute such knowledge to [the] corporation" under the formula that my brethren quote.

It is not surprising that the court wants to shift the plane of analysis from whether Modernaire is to be deemed to have known of Harry's drug dealings to whether, if prosecuted for a criminal offense, Modernaire would be guilty in the absence of proof that the crime had been committed for the corporation's benefit. That is not the issue but let me go along with the court far enough to suppose that Harry III's criminal proclivities ran to monopolizing rather than to drug trafficking and that Modernaire were prosecuted for a criminal violation of the antitrust laws. If the government proved that Harry III had caused Modernaire to engage in a monopolistic practice, Modernaire would be found guilty and forced to pay what might be a ruinous fine, but the black-letter rule of corporate criminality would require the government to prove that Harry III had in some, though perhaps only a very attenuated, sense been acting "for the benefit of the corporation" (even if his action was contrary to corporate directives).

The court clings to this principle. But the statute here is different. For one thing it is not a criminal statute, and in a civil antitrust case, or for that matter any other civil case, the plaintiff need not show that the corporation's agent acted with an intent to benefit the corporation. [citation omitted] These cases emphasize the agent's "apparent authority": "the agent's position facilitates the consummation of the fraud, in that from the point of view of the third person the transaction seems regular on its face and the agent appears to be acting in the ordinary course of the business provided to him." Restatement (Second) of Agency § 261, comment a, at p. 571 (1958), quoted in American Society of Mechanical Engineers v. Hydrolevel Corp., 456 U.S. 556, 566 (1982). This is not a fraud case, but neither was Hydrolevel; it was a boycott case. Apparent authority can facilitate wrongdoing other than just that of the fraudulent variety. No doubt the fact that Harry III appeared to be—in fact, was—in control of the resort property made persons in quest of illegal drugs more willing to buy from him than they would have been had they thought him a mere tenant trying to conceal his illegal drug dealings from his landlord and his landlord's agents as well as from the police. The majority opinion derides this point as speculative, but judges need not put off their common sense when they put on their robes.

I have strayed from the central point, which is that the property was forfeit regardless of the motives or apparent authority of the person actually responsible for putting it to a criminal use, subject to a defense if the owner did not know of or consent to that use—and Harry on behalf of the corporation of which he was the manager and one-third owner knew and consented. The court has confused criminal cases in which a prosecutor must establish the liability of the corporation and to that end prove that the crime was committed on the corporation's behalf with civil cases under a forfeiture statute under which liability is presumed and the corporation must prove its innocence. All that we must—all that we may—consider is whether Harry's misconduct fits the defense. It does not, because his misconduct was known to and consented to by the corporation's responsible agent—Harry himself.

But it is a fair question to ask me what rule I would apply to this case. A simple rule springs to mind: a corporation is not an innocent owner within the meaning of the forfeiture statute if an officer of the corporation causes its property to be used in drug trafficking. It may be too simple. Suppose Harry III were an officer of General Motors and sold cocaine from his office. Would all the assets of General Motors be forfeited to the government? Surely not. The norm of proportionality of sanctions, whether or not it has any constitutional provenance or dignity, would require a limiting interpretation. So would the sheer arbitrariness of corporate organization—the size of the forfeiture in my hypothetical case might depend on whether General Motors was organized in divisions or corporate subsidiaries.

I do not have a clear idea of the form the necessary limiting interpretation would take. But I know this: if the sole manager and one-third owner of a corporation deals drugs from the corporate premises the corporation is not innocent even if the other shareholders have health problems. And I fear that if this decision stands, the cannier drug dealers will rush to incorporate in order to protect their assets. I take it that my brethren would permit that unless the government undertook to prove a specific intent to evade the statute.

Notes

1.   Note the majority's interpretation of *Bank of New England* (only the knowledge of employees *acting within the scope of their employment* may be integrated into a "collective intent" and imputed to a corporation). Is this what the First Circuit held in *Bank of New England*? Does this seem like a reasonable limit on the "collective intent" doctrine?

2.   After interpreting the above limit on the collective intent doctrine, the majority finds that Harry III was not acting within the scope of his employment; thus, his knowledge is not imputed to the corporation, Modernaire and, the property is not forfeited. Judge Posner's dissent is especially strong. He argues that Harry III's knowledge (as corporate officer, major shareholder and only manager of the corporate property) should be imputed to the corporation. Judge Posner further accuses the majority of being swayed not by applicable legal principles but by the equities (Harry's parents, now elderly and ill, sacrificed to "provide their son with a start in life that he did not deserve"; they should not suffer because the corporate property they purchased is forfeited). What do you think? How would you resolve this case?

3.   Recall what you learned about forfeiture in Chapter 5, especially Professor Guerra's remarks about the impact of forfeiture on families. Is the above case an example of forfeiture law run amuck or is it an appropriate wake-up call to American citizens not to engage in illegal activity and not to allow others to do so?

---

3.   SENTENCING OF CORPORATIONS

The United States Sentencing Commission was created under the Sentencing Reform Act of 1984, as amended, 28 U.S.C. §§ 991–998 (West 1968, Supp.1990). It is an independent commission within the judicial branch charged with establishing determinative sentencing guidelines for the federal judicial system and reviewing and revising the guidelines as needed. 28 U.S.C. § 994; Mistretta v. United States, 488 U.S. 361, 368–69 (1989). The guidelines are "binding on the courts, although * * * the judge [has] the discretion to depart from the guideline applicable to a particular case if the judge finds an aggravating or mitigating factor present that the Commission did not adequately consider when formulating guidelines." 488 U.S. at 367. The Sentencing Commission began its work on sentencing guidelines for corporations and other organizations in 1986. After many revisions and public hearings, final guidelines for organizations went into effect on November 1, 1991.

According to the Sentencing Commission, the organizational guidelines

> "reflect[] the following general principles: First, the court must, whenever practicable, order the organization to remedy any harm caused by the offense. The resources expended to remedy the harm should not be viewed as punishment, but rather as a means of making victims whole for the harm caused. Second, if the organization operated primarily for a criminal purpose or primarily by criminal means, the fine should be set sufficiently high to divest the organization of all its assets. Third, the fine range for any other organization should be based on the seriousness of the offense and the culpability of the organization. The seriousness of the offense generally will be reflected by the highest of the pecuniary gain, the pecuniary loss, or the amount in a guideline offense level fine table. Culpability generally will be determined by the steps taken by the organization prior to the offense to prevent and detect criminal conduct, the level and extent of involvement in or tolerance of the offense by certain personnel, and the organization's actions after an offense has been committed. Fourth, probation is an appropriate sentence for an organizational defendant when needed to ensure that another sanction will be fully implemented, or to ensure that steps will be taken within the organization to reduce the likelihood of future criminal conduct."[g]

A. *"Remedying the Harm"*

"As a general principle, the court should require that the organization take all appropriate steps to provide compensation to victims and otherwise remedy the harm caused or threatened by the offense. A restitution order or an order of probation requiring restitution can be used to compensate identifiable victims of the offense. A remedial order or an order of probation requiring community service can be used to reduce or eliminate the harm threatened, or to repair the harm caused by the offense, when that harm or threatened harm would otherwise not be remedied. An order of notice to victims can be used to notify unidentified victims of the offense."[h]

B. *"Determining the Fine–Criminal Purpose Organizations"*

"If, upon consideration of the nature and circumstances of the offense and the history and characteristics of the organization, the court determines that the organization operated primarily for a

g. United States Sentencing Guidelines (U.S.S.G., Ch. 8, Introductory Commentary).

h. *Id.*, Introductory Commentary, Part B.

criminal purpose or primarily by criminal means, the fine shall be set at an amount (subject to the statutory maximum) sufficient to divest the organization of all its net assets. * * *

"This guideline addresses the case in which the court, based upon an examination of the nature and circumstances of the offense and the history and characteristics of the organization, determines that the organization was operated primarily for a criminal purpose (e.g., a front for a scheme that was designed to commit fraud; an organization established to participate in the illegal manufacture, importation, or distribution of a controlled substance) or operated primarily by criminal means (e.g., a hazardous waste disposal business that had no legitimate means of disposing of hazardous waste). In such a case, the fine shall be set at an amount sufficient to remove all of the organization's net assets. If the extent of the assets of the organization is unknown, the maximum fine authorized by statute should be imposed, absent innocent bona fide creditors."[i]

C. *"Determining the Fine–Other Organizations"*

"[For other organizations, the court will first ascertain whether the organization is able to pay a fine, then it will assess a fine based upon a 'base amount' set forth in the guidelines, as adjusted by the presence or absence of the following factors:] Involvement in or tolerance of criminal activity * * *; Prior regulatory and criminal history * * *; Violation of an judicial order * * *; Obstruction of justice during the investigation; Installation of an effective program to prevent and detect violations of law * * *; Self-reporting, cooperation, and acceptance of responsibility * * *.

"[Increasing the culpability scores with the above factors is] based on three interrelated principles. First, an organization is more culpable when individuals who manage the organization or who have substantial discretion in acting for the organization participate in, condone, or are willfully ignorant of criminal conduct. Second, as organizations become larger and their managements become more professional, participation in, condonation of, or willful ignorance of criminal conduct by such management is increasingly a breach of trust or abuse of position. Third, as organizations increase in size, the risk of criminal conduct beyond that reflected in the instant offense also increases whenever management's tolerance of that offense is pervasive. Because of the continuum of sizes of organizations and professionalization of management, [these guidelines] gradually increase

" * * * Departure [from the guidelines] may be warranted if the court finds 'that there exists an aggravating or mitigating circumstance of a kind, or to a degree, not adequately taken into consideration by the Sentencing Commission in formulating the guidelines that should result in a sentence different from that described.' * * *

---

i. *Id.,* Introductory Commentary, Part C.

In deciding whether departure is warranted, the court should consider the extent to which [a] factor is adequately taken into consideration by the guidelines and the relative importance or substantiality of that factor in the particular case. The factors that may warrant a departure from the guidelines include: substantial assistance to authorities by the organization; risk of death or bodily injury; threat to national security; threat to the environment; threat to a market; official corruption; public entity; members or beneficiaries of the organization as victims; remedial costs that greatly exceed gain."[j]

D. Imposition of Probation–Organizations

"The court shall order a term of probation:

- if such sentence is necessary to secure payment of restitution, enforce a remedial order, or ensure completion of community service;

- if the organization is sentenced to pay a monetary penalty (e.g., restitution, fine, or special assessment), the penalty is not paid in full at the time of sentencing, and restrictions are necessary to safeguard the organization's ability to make payments;

- if, at the time of sentencing, an organization having 50 or more employees does not have an effective program to prevent and detect violations of law;

- if the organization within five years prior to sentencing engaged in similar misconduct, as determined by a prior criminal adjudication, and any part of the misconduct underlying the instant offense occurred after that adjudication;

- if an individual within high-level personnel of the organization or the unit of the organization within which the instant offense was committed participated in the misconduct underlying the instant offense and that individual within five years prior to sentencing engaged in similar misconduct, as determined by a prior criminal adjudication, and any part of the misconduct underlying the instant offense occurred after that adjudication;

- if such sentence is necessary to ensure that changes are made within the organization to reduce the likelihood of future criminal conduct;

- if the sentence imposed upon the organization does not include a fine; * * *.

"[Suggested conditions of probation include requiring] the organization, at its expense and in the format and media specified by the court, to publicize the nature of the offense committed, the fact of conviction, the nature of the punishment imposed, and the steps that will be taken to prevent the recurrence of similar offenses; to

j. *Id.*

submit to periodic visits and to make periodic reports to the court; and, to develop an effective program to monitor internal breaches of the law.

"In determining the conditions to be imposed when probation is ordered the court should consider the views of any governmental regulatory body that oversees conduct of the organization relating to the instant offense. To assess the efficacy of a [plan] submitted by the organization, the court may employ appropriate experts who shall be afforded access to all material possessed by the organization that is necessary for a comprehensive assessment of the proposed program. The court should approve any program that appears reasonably calculated to prevent and detect violations of law, provided it is consistent with any applicable statutory or regulatory requirement."[k]

B. LIABILITY OF CORPORATE DIRECTORS OR EXECUTIVES

1. CRIMINAL LIABILITY

Corporate executives may be held criminally liable, just like any criminal defendant, for their own criminal behavior. Unlike most criminal defendants, however, corporate executives sometimes may be held criminally liable for actions by other corporate employees, even when the executive did not know of the employee's conduct. The following case, United States v. Park, 421 U.S. 658 (1975), addresses this issue.

UNITED STATES v. PARK
Supreme Court of the United States, 1975.
421 U.S. 658.

Mr. Chief Justice Burger delivered the opinion of the Court.

We granted certiorari to consider whether jury instructions in the prosecution of a corporate officer under § 301(k) of the Federal Food, Drug, and Cosmetic Act, 52 Stat. 1042, as amended, 21 U.S.C. § 331(k), were appropriate under United States v. Dotterweich, 320 U.S. 277 (1943).

Acme Markets, Inc. is a national retail food chain with approximately 36,000 employees, 874 retail outlets, 12 general warehouses, and four special warehouses. Its headquarters, including the office of the president, respondent Park, who is chief executive officer of the corporation, are located in Philadelphia, Pa. In a five-count information filed in the United States District Court for the District of Maryland, the Government charged Acme and respondent with violations of the Federal Food, Drug, and Cosmetic Act. Each count of the information alleged that the defendants had received food that had been shipped in interstate commerce and that, while the food was being held for sale in Acme's

k. *Id.*, Introductory Commentary, Part D.

Baltimore warehouse following shipment in interstate commerce, they caused it to be held in a building accessible to rodents and to be exposed to contamination by rodents. These acts were alleged to have resulted in the food being adulterated within the meaning of 21 U.S.C. §§ 342(a)(3) and (4)[1] in violation of 21 U.S.C. § 331(k).[2]

Acme pleaded guilty to each count of the information. Respondent pleaded not guilty. The evidence at trial demonstrated that in April 1970 the Food and Drug Administration (FDA) advised respondent by letter of insanitary conditions in Acme's Philadelphia warehouse. In 1971 the FDA found that similar conditions existed in the firm's Baltimore warehouse. An FDA consumer safety officer testified concerning evidence of rodent infestation and other insanitary conditions discovered during a 12–day inspection of the Baltimore warehouse in November and December 1971. He also related that a second inspection of the warehouse had been conducted in March 1972. On that occasion the inspectors found that there had been improvement in the sanitary conditions, but that "there was still evidence of rodent activity in the building and in the warehouses and we found some rodent-contaminated lots of food items."

The Government also presented testimony by the Chief of Compliance of the FDA's Baltimore office, who informed respondent by letter of the conditions at the Baltimore warehouse after the first inspection. There was testimony by Acme's Baltimore division vice president, who had responded to the letter on behalf of Acme and respondent and who described the steps taken to remedy the insanitary conditions discovered by both inspections. The Government's final witness, Acme's vice president for legal affairs and assistant secretary, identified respondent as the president and chief executive officer of the company and read a bylaw prescribing the duties of the chief executive officer. He testified that respondent functioned by delegating "normal operating duties," including sanitation, but that he retained "certain things, which are the big, broad, principles of the operation of the company," and had "the responsibility of seeing that they all work together."

At the close of the Government's case in chief, respondent moved for a judgment of acquittal on the ground that "the evidence in chief has

---

1. Section 402 of the Act, 21 USC § 342 [21 USCS § 342], provides in pertinent part:

"A food shall be deemed to be adulterated—

"(a) * * * (3) if it consists in whole or in part of any filthy, putrid, or decomposed substance, or if it is otherwise unfit for food; or (4) if it has been prepared, packed, or held under insanitary conditions whereby it may have become contaminated with filth, or whereby it may have been rendered injurious to health * * *."

2. Section 301 of the Act, 21 USC § 331 [21 USCS § 331], provides:

"The following acts and the causing thereof are prohibited:

* * *

"(k) The alteration, mutilation, destruction, obliteration, or removal of the whole or any part of the labeling of, or the doing of any other act with respect to, a food, drug, device, or cosmetic, if such act is done while such article is held for sale (whether or not the first sale) after shipment in interstate commerce and results in such article being adulterated or misbranded."

shown that Mr. Park is not personally concerned in this Food and Drug violation." The trial judge denied the motion, stating that United States v. Dotterweich, was controlling.

Respondent was the only defense witness. He testified that, although all of Acme's employees were in a sense under his general direction, the company had an "organizational structure for responsibilities for certain functions" according to which different phases of its operation were "assigned to individuals who, in turn, have staff and departments under them." He identified those individuals responsible for sanitation and related that upon receipt of the January 1972 FDA letter, he had conferred with the vice president for legal affairs, who informed him that the Baltimore division vice president "was investigating the situation immediately and would be taking corrective action and would be preparing a summary of the corrective action to reply to the letter." Respondent stated that he did not "believe there was anything [he] could have done more constructively than what [he] found was being done."

On cross-examination, respondent conceded that providing sanitary conditions for food offered for sale to the public was something that he was "responsible for in the entire operation of the company," and he stated that it was one of many phases of the company that he assigned to "dependable subordinates." Respondent was asked about and, over the objections of his counsel, admitted receiving, the April 1970 letter addressed to him from the FDA regarding insanitary conditions at Acme's Philadelphia Warehouse. He acknowledged that, with the exception of the division vice president, the same individuals had responsibility for sanitation in both Baltimore and Philadelphia. Finally, in response to questions concerning the Philadelphia and Baltimore incidents, respondent admitted that the Baltimore problem indicated the system for handling sanitation "wasn't working perfectly" and that as Acme's chief executive officer he was responsible for "any result which occurs in our company."

At the close of the evidence, respondent's renewed motion for a judgment of acquittal was denied. The relevant portion of the trial judge's instructions to the jury challenged by respondent is set out in the margin.[9] Respondent's counsel objected to the instructions on the ground

---

9. "In order to find the Defendant guilty on any count of the Information, you must find beyond a reasonable doubt on each count * * *.

* * *

"Thirdly, that John R. Park held a position of authority in the operation of the business of Acme Markets, Incorporated.

"However, you need not concern yourselves with the first two elements of the case. The main issue for your determination is only with the third element, whether the Defendant held a position of authority and responsibility in the business of Acme Markets.

* * *

"The statute makes individuals, as well as corporations, liable for violations. An individual is liable if it is clear, beyond a reasonable doubt, that the elements of the adulteration of the food as to travel in interstate commerce are present. As I have instructed you in this case, they are, and that the individual had a responsible relation to the situation, even though he may not have participated personally.

that they failed fairly to reflect our decision in United States v. Dotterweich, and to define " 'responsible relationship.' "The trial judge overruled the objection. The jury found respondent guilty on all counts of the information, and he was subsequently sentenced to pay a fine of $50 on each count.

The Court of Appeals reversed the conviction and remanded for a new trial. That court viewed the Government as arguing "that the conviction may be predicated solely upon a showing that * * * [respondent] was the President of the offending corporation," and it stated that as "a general proposition, some act of commission or omission is an essential element of every crime." It reasoned that, although our decision in United States v. Dotterweich construed the statutory provisions under which respondent was tried to dispense with the traditional element of " 'awareness of some wrongdoing,' "the Court had not construed them as dispensing with the element of "wrongful action." The Court of Appeals concluded that the trial judge's instructions "might well have left the jury with the erroneous impression that Park could be found guilty in the absence of 'wrongful action' on his part," and that proof of this element was required by due process. It held, with one dissent, that the instructions did not "correctly state the law of the case," and directed that on retrial the jury be instructed as to "wrongful action," which might be "gross negligence and inattention in discharging * * * corporate duties and obligations or any of a host of other acts of commission or omission which would 'cause' the contamination of food."

The Court of Appeals also held that the admission in evidence of the April 1970 FDA warning to respondent was error warranting reversal, based on its conclusion that, "as this case was submitted to the jury and in light of the sole issue presented," there was no need for the evidence and thus that its prejudicial effect outweighed its relevancy under the test of United States v. Woods, 484 F.2d 127 (4th Cir.1973).

We granted certiorari because of an apparent conflict among the Courts of Appeals with respect to the standard of liability of corporate officers under the Federal Food, Drug, and Cosmetic Act as construed in United States v. Dotterweich, and because of the importance of the question to the Government's enforcement program. We reverse.

I

The question presented by the Government's petition for certiorari in United States v. Dotterweich, and the focus of this Court's opinion, was whether "the manager of a corporation, as well as the corporation itself, may be prosecuted under the Federal Food, Drug, and Cosmetic

"The individual is or could be liable under the statute, even if he did not consciously do wrong. However, the fact that the Defendant is pres[id]ent and is a chief executive officer of the Acme Markets does not require a finding of guilt. Though, he need not have personally participated in the situation, he must have had a responsible relationship to the issue. The issue is, in this case, whether the Defendant, John R. Park, by virtue of his position in the company, had a position of authority and responsibility in the situation out of which these charges arose." Id., at 61–62.

Act of 1938 for the introduction of misbranded and adulterated articles into interstate commerce." In *Dotterweich,* a jury had disagreed as to the corporation, a jobber purchasing drugs from manufacturers and shipping them in interstate commerce under its own label, but had convicted Dotterweich, the corporation's president and general manager. * * *

* * *

* * * [T]his Court looked to the purposes of the Act and noted that they "touch phases of the lives and health of people which, in the circumstances of modern industrialism, are largely beyond self protection." *Dotterweich,* 320 U.S. at 280. It observed that the Act is of "a now familiar type" which "dispenses with the conventional requirement for criminal conduct—awareness of some wrongdoing. In the interest of the larger good it puts the burden of acting at hazard upon a person otherwise innocent but standing in responsible relation to a public danger." Id. at 280–81, 64 S.Ct. 134.

Central to the Court's conclusion that individuals other than proprietors are subject to the criminal provisions of the Act was the reality that "the only way in which a corporation can act is through the individuals who act on its behalf." Id. at 281. The Court also noted that corporate officers had been subject to criminal liability under the Federal Food and Drugs Act of 1906, and it observed that a contrary result under the 1938 legislation would be incompatible with the expressed intent of Congress to "enlarge and stiffen the penal net" and to discourage a view of the Act's criminal penalties as a " 'license fee for the conduct of an illegitimate business.' "Id. at 282–83.

At the same time, however, the Court was aware of the concern * * * that literal enforcement "might operate too harshly by sweeping within its condemnation any person however remotely entangled in the proscribed shipment." *Id.* at 284. A limiting principle, in the form of "settled doctrines of criminal law" defining those who "are responsible for the commission of a misdemeanor," was available. In this context, the Court concluded, those doctrines dictated that the offense was committed "by all who * * * have * * * a responsible share in the furtherance of the transaction which the statute outlaws." *Id.*

The Court recognized that, because the Act dispenses with the need to prove "consciousness of wrongdoing," it may result in hardship even as applied to those who share "responsibility in the business process resulting in" a violation. It regarded as "too treacherous" an attempt "to define or even to indicate by way of illustration the class of employees which stands in such a responsible relation." The question of responsibility, the Court said, depends "on the evidence produced at the trial and its submission—assuming the evidence warrants it—to the jury under appropriate guidance." The Court added: "In such matters the good sense of prosecutors, the wise guidance of trial judges, and the ultimate judgment of juries must be trusted." *Id.* at 284–85.

II

The rule that corporate employees who have "a responsible share in the furtherance of the transaction which the statute outlaws" are subject to the criminal provisions of the Act was not formulated in a vacuum. Cf. Morissette v. United States, 342 U.S. 246 (1952). Cases under the Federal Food and Drugs Act of 1906 reflected the view both that knowledge or intent were not required to be proved in prosecutions under its criminal provisions, and that responsible corporate agents could be subjected to the liability thereby imposed. Moreover, the principle had been recognized that a corporate agent, through whose act, default, or omission the corporation committed a crime, was himself guilty individually of that crime. The principle had been applied whether or not the crime required "consciousness of wrongdoing," and it had been applied not only to those corporate agents who themselves committed the criminal act, but also to those who by virtue of their managerial positions or other similar relation to the actor could be deemed responsible for its commission.

In the latter class of cases, the liability of managerial officers did not depend on their knowledge of, or personal participation in, the act made criminal by the statute. Rather, where the statute under which they were prosecuted dispensed with "consciousness of wrongdoing," an omission or failure to act was deemed a sufficient basis for a responsible corporate agent's liability. It was enough in such cases that, by virtue of the relationship he bore to the corporation, the agent had the power to prevent the act complained of.

The rationale of the interpretation given the act in *Dotterweich*, as holding criminally accountable the persons whose failure to exercise the authority and supervisory responsibility reposed in them by the business organization resulted in the violation complained of, has been confirmed in our subsequent cases. Thus, the Court has reaffirmed the proposition that "the public interest in the purity of its food is so great as to warrant the imposition to the highest standard of care on distributors." Smith v. California, 361 U.S. 147, 152 (1959). In order to make "distributors of food the strictest censors of their merchandise," the Act punishes "neglect where the law requires care, or inaction where it imposes a duty." Morissette, 342 U.S. at 255. "The accused, if he does not will the violation, usually is in a position to prevent it with no more care than society might reasonably expect and no more exertion than it might reasonably exact from one who assumed his responsibilities." Id. at 256. Similarly, in cases decided after Dotterweich, the Courts of Appeals have recognized that those corporate agents vested with the responsibility, and power commensurate with that responsibility, to devise whatever measures are necessary to ensure compliance with the Act bear a "responsible relationship" to, or have a "responsible share" in, violations.

Thus *Dotterweich* and the cases which have followed reveal that in providing sanctions which reach and touch the individuals who execute the corporate mission—and this is by no means necessarily confined to a single corporate agent or employee—the Act imposes not only a positive duty to seek out and remedy violations when they occur but also, and primarily, a duty to implement measures that will insure that violations will not occur. The requirements of foresight and vigilance imposed on responsible corporate agents are beyond question demanding, and perhaps onerous, but they are no more stringent than the public has a right to expect of those who voluntarily assume positions of authority in business enterprises whose services and products affect the health and well-being of the public that supports them.

The Act does not, as we observed in *Dotterweich,* make criminal liability turn on "awareness of some wrongdoing" or "conscious fraud." The duty imposed by Congress on responsible corporate agents is, we emphasize, one that requires the highest standard of foresight and vigilance, but the Act, in its criminal aspect, does not require that which is objectively impossible. The theory upon which responsible corporate agents were held criminally accountable for "causing" violations of the Act permits a claim that a defendant was "powerless" to prevent or correct the violation to "be raised defensively at a trial on the merits." United States v. Wiesenfeld Warehouse Co., 376 U.S. 86, 91 (1964). If such a claim is made, the defendant has the burden of coming forward with evidence, but this does not alter the Government's ultimate burden of proving beyond a reasonable doubt the defendant's guilt, including his power, in light of the duty imposed by the Act, to prevent or correct the prohibited condition. Congress has seen fit to enforce the accountability of responsible corporate agents dealing with products which may affect the health of consumers by penal sanctions cast in rigorous terms, and the obligation of the courts is to give them effect so long as they do not violate the Constitution.

III

We cannot agree with the Court of Appeals that it was incumbent upon the District Court to instruct the jury that the Government had the burden of establishing "wrongful action" in the sense in which the Court of Appeals used that phrase. The concept of a "responsible relationship" to, or a "responsible share" in, a violation of the Act indeed imports some measure of blameworthiness; but it is equally clear that the Government establishes a prima facie case when it introduces evidence sufficient to warrant a finding by the trier of the facts that the defendant had, by reason of his position in the corporation, responsibility and authority either to prevent in the first instance, or promptly to correct, the violation complained of, and that he failed to do so. The failure thus to fulfill the duty imposed by the interaction of the corporate agent's authority and the statute furnishes a sufficient causal link. The considerations which prompted the imposition of this duty, and the scope of the duty, provide the measure of culpability.

Turning to the jury charge in this case, it is of course arguable that isolated parts can be read as intimating that a finding of guilt could be predicated solely on respondent's corporate position. But this is not the way we review jury instructions, because "a single instruction to a jury may not be judged in artificial isolation, but must be viewed in the context of the overall charge." Cupp v. Naughten, 414 U.S. 141, 146–47 (1973).

Reading the entire charge satisfies us that the jury's attention was adequately focused on the issue of respondent's authority with respect to the conditions that formed the basis of the alleged violations. Viewed as a whole, the charge did not permit the jury to find guilt solely on the basis of respondent's position in the corporation; rather, it fairly advised the jury that to find guilt it must find respondent "had a responsible relation to the situation," and "by virtue of his position * * * had * * * authority and responsibility" to deal with the situation. The situation referred to could only be "food * * * held in unsanitary conditions in a warehouse with the result that it consisted, in part, of filth or * * * may have been contaminated with filth."

Moreover, in reviewing jury instructions, our task is also to view the charge itself as part of the whole trial. "Often isolated statements taken from the charge, seemingly prejudicial on their face, are not so when considered in the context of the entire record of the trial." United States v. Birnbaum, 373 F.2d 250, 257 (2d Cir.1967). The record in this case reveals that the jury could not have failed to be aware that the main issue for determination was not respondent's position in the corporate hierarchy, but rather his accountability, because of the responsibility and authority of his position, for the conditions which gave rise to the charges against him.

We conclude that, viewed as a whole and in the context of the trial, the charge was not misleading and contained an adequate statement of the law to guide the jury's determination. Although it would have been better to give an instruction more precisely relating the legal issue to the facts of the case, we cannot say that the failure to provide the amplification requested by respondent was an abuse of discretion. Finally, we note that there was no request for an instruction that the Government was required to prove beyond a reasonable doubt that respondent was not without the power or capacity to affect the conditions which founded the charges in the information. In light of the evidence adduced at trial, we find no basis to conclude that the failure of the trial court to give such an instruction as sponte was plain error or a defect affecting substantial rights.

IV

Our conclusion that the Court of Appeals erred in its reading of the jury charge suggests as well our disagreement with that court concerning the admissibility of evidence demonstrating that respondent was advised by FDA in 1970 of insanitary conditions in Acme's Philadelphia warehouse. We are satisfied that the Act imposes the highest standard of care and permits conviction of responsible corporate officials who, in light of this standard of care, have the power to prevent or correct violations of its provisions. Implicit in the Court's admonition that "the ultimate judgment of juries must be trusted," *Dotterweich*, however, is the realization that they may demand more than corporate bylaws to find culpability.

Respondent testified in his defense that he had employed a system in which he relied upon his subordinates, and that he was ultimately responsible for this system. He testified further that he had found these subordinates to be "dependable" and had "great confidence" in them. By this and other testimony respondent evidently sought to persuade the jury that, as the president of a large corporation, he had no choice but to delegate duties to those in whom he reposed confidence, that he had no reason to suspect his subordinates were failing to insure compliance with the Act, and that, once violations were unearthed, acting through those subordinates he did everything possible to correct them.

Although we need not decide whether this testimony would have entitled respondent to an instruction as to his lack of power, had he requested it, the testimony clearly created the "need" for rebuttal evidence. That evidence was not offered to show that respondent had a propensity to commit criminal acts, that the crime charged had been committed; its purpose was to demonstrate that respondent was on notice that he could not rely on his system of delegation to subordinates to prevent or correct insanitary conditions at Acme's warehouses, and that he must have been aware of the deficiencies of this system before the Baltimore violations were discovered. The evidence was therefore relevant since it served to rebut respondent's defense that he had justifiably relied upon subordinates to handle sanitation matters. And, particularly in light of the difficult task of juries in prosecutions under the Act, we conclude that its relevance and persuasiveness outweighed any prejudicial effect.

Reversed.

MR. JUSTICE STEWART, with whom MR. JUSTICE MARSHALL and MR. JUSTICE POWELL join, dissenting.

Although agreeing with much of what is said in the Court's opinion, I dissent from the opinion and judgment, because the jury instructions in this case were not consistent with the law as the Court today expounds it.

As I understand the Court's opinion, it holds that in order to sustain a conviction under § 301(k) of the Federal Food, Drug, and Cosmetic Act the prosecution must at least show that by reason of an individual's corporate position and responsibilities, he had a duty to use care to maintain the physical integrity of the corporation's food products. A jury may then draw the inference that when the food is found to be in such condition as to violate the statute's prohibitions, that condition was "caused" by a breach of the standard of care imposed upon the responsible official. This is the language of negligence, and I agree with it.

To affirm this conviction, however, the Court must approve the instructions given to the members of the jury who were entrusted with determining whether the respondent was innocent or guilty. Those instructions did not conform to the standards that the Court itself sets out today.

The trial judge instructed the jury to find Park guilty if it found beyond a reasonable doubt that Park "had a responsible relation to the situation * * *. The issue is, in this case, whether the Defendant, John R. Park, by virtue of his position in the company, had a position of authority and responsibility in the situation out of which these charges arose." Requiring, as it did, a verdict of guilty upon a finding of "responsibility," this instruction standing alone could have been construed as a direction to convict if the jury found Park "responsible" for the condition in the sense that his position as chief executive officer gave him formal responsibility within the structure of the corporation. But the trial judge went on specifically to caution the jury not to attach such a meaning to his instruction, saying that "the fact that the Defendant is pres[id]ent and is a chief executive officer of the Acme Markets does not require a finding of guilt." "Responsibility" as used by the trial judge therefore had whatever meaning the jury in its unguided discretion chose to give it.

The instructions, therefore, expressed nothing more than a tautology. They told the jury: "You must find the defendant guilty if you find that he is to be held accountable for this adulterated food." In other words: "You must find the defendant guilty if you conclude that he is guilty." The trial judge recognized the infirmities in these instructions, but he reluctantly concluded that he was required to give such a charge under United States v. Dotterweich, 320 U.S. 277, 64 S.Ct. 134, 88 L.Ed. 48, which, he thought, in declining to define "responsible relation" had declined to specify the minimum standard of liability for criminal guilt.

As the Court today recognizes, the *Dotterweich* case did not deal with what kind of conduct must be proved to support a finding of criminal guilt under the act. *Dotterweich* was concerned, rather, with the statutory definition of "person"—with what kind of corporate employees were even "subject to the criminal provisions of the Act." The Court held that those employees with "a responsible relation" to the violative transaction or condition were subject to the Act's criminal provisions, but all that the Court had to say with respect to the kind of conduct that can constitute criminal guilt was that the Act "dispenses with the conventional requirement for criminal conduct—awareness of some wrongdoing."

* * *

* * * [T]his Court has never before abandoned the view that jury instructions must contain a statement of the applicable law sufficiently precise to enable the jury to be guided by something other than its rough notions of social justice. And while it might be argued that the issue before the jury in this case was a "mixed" question of both law and fact,

this has never meant that a jury is to be left wholly at sea, without any guidance as to the standard of conduct the law requires. The instructions, given by the trial court in this case, it must be emphasized, were a virtual nullity, a mere authorization to convict if the jury thought it appropriate. Such instructions—regardless of the blameworthiness of the defendant's conduct, regardless of the social value of the Food, Drug, and Cosmetic Act, and regardless of the importance of convicting those who violate it—have no place in our jurisprudence.

We deal here with a criminal conviction, not a civil forfeiture. It is true that the crime was not but a misdemeanor and the penalty in this case light. But under the statute even a first conviction can result in imprisonment for a year, and a subsequent offense is a felony carrying a punishment of up to three years in prison. So the standardless conviction approved today can serve in another case tomorrow to support a felony conviction and a substantial prison sentence. However highly the Court may regard the social objectives of the Food, Drug, and Cosmetic Act, that regard cannot serve to justify a criminal conviction so wholly alien to fundamental principles of our law.

The *Dotterweich* case stands for two propositions, and I accept them both. First, "any person" within the meaning of 21 U.S.C. § 333 may include any corporate officer or employee "standing in responsible relation" to a condition or transaction forbidden by the Act. Second, a person may be convicted of a criminal offense under the Act even in the absence of "the conventional requirement for criminal conduct—awareness of some wrongdoing."

But before a person can be convicted of a criminal violation of this Act, a jury must find—and must be clearly instructed that it must find— evidence beyond a reasonable doubt that he engaged in wrongful conduct amounting at least to common-law negligence. There were no such instructions, and clearly, therefore, no such finding in this case.

For these reasons, I cannot join the Court in affirming Park's criminal conviction.

Notes

Was Park held strictly liable, or as Justice Stewart suggested, liable for negligent supervision of employees? Does it matter which standard of culpability was employed—are not both exceptions to the criminal law's customary insistence upon a finding of intent?

The Court emphasized the policy reasons for imposing a burden on persons who had the "authority and responsibility" to prevent a situation of potential harm to the public. Are you persuaded that imposing strict liability (or liability for negligence) will effectuate this goal? It may be helpful in considering this question to review what Professor Hart had to say about strict liability crimes.

HART, THE AIMS OF THE CRIMINAL LAW
23 Law & Contemp. Probs. 422–25 (1968).[1]

* * *

A large body of modern law goes far beyond an insistence upon a duty of ordinary care in ascertaining facts, at the peril of being called a criminal. To an absolute duty to know about the existence of a regulatory statute and interpret it correctly, it adds an absolute duty to know about the facts. Thus, the porter who innocently carries the bag of a hotel guest not knowing that it contains a bottle of whisky is punished as a criminal for having transported intoxicating liquor. The corporation president who signs a registration statement for a proposed securities issue not knowing that his accountants have made a mistake is guilty of the crime of making a "false" representation to the state blue-sky commissioner. The president of a corporation whose employee introduces into interstate commerce a shipment of technically but harmlessly adulterated food is branded as a criminal solely because he was the president when the shipment was made. And so on, ad almost infinitum.

In all such cases, it is possible, of course, that a basis of blameworthiness might have been found in the particular facts. Perhaps the company presidents actually were culpably careless in their supervision. Conceivably, even, the porter was culpably remiss in failing to ask the traveler about the contents of his bag, or at least in failing to shake it to see if he could hear a gurgle. But these possibilities are irrelevant. For the statutes in question, as interpreted, do not require any such defaults to be proved against a defendant, nor even permit him to show the absence of such a default in defense. The offenses fall within "the numerous class in which diligence, actual knowledge and bad motives are immaterial * * *." Thus, they squarely pose the question whether there can be any justification for condemning and punishing a human being as a criminal when he has done nothing which is blameworthy.

It is submitted that there can be no moral justification for this, and that there is not, indeed, even a rational, moral justification.

1. People who do not know and cannot find out that they are supposed to comply with an applicable command are, by hypothesis, nondeterrable. So far as personal amenability to legal control is concerned, they stand in the same posture as the plainest lunatic under the M'Naughten test who "does not know the nature and quality of his act or, if he does know it, does not know that the act is wrong."

2. If it be said that most people will know of such commands and be able to comply with them, the answer, among others, is that nowhere else in the criminal law is the probable, or even the certain, guilt of nine men regarded as sufficient warrant for the conviction of a tenth. In the

1. Reprinted with permission from Hart, *The Aims of the Criminal Law,* 23   *Law & Contemp. Probs.* 422–25. Copyright © 1968 by Duke University School of Law.

tradition of Anglo–American law, guilt of crime is personal. The main body of the criminal law, from the Constitution on down, makes sense on no other assumption.

3. If it be asserted that strict criminal liability is necessary in order to stimulate people to be diligent in learning the law and finding out when it applies, the answer, among others, is that this is wholly unproved and prima facie improbable. Studies to test the relative effectiveness of strict criminal liability and well-designed civil penalties are lacking and badly needed. Until such studies are forthcoming, however, judgment can only take into account (a) the inherent unlikelihood that people's behavior will be significantly affected by commands that are not brought definitely to their attention; (b) the long-understood tendency of disproportionate penalties to promote disrespect rather than respect for law, unless they are rigorously and uniformly enforced; (c) the inherent difficulties of rigorous and uniform enforcement of strict criminal liability and the impressive evidence that it is, in fact, spottily and unevenly enforced; (d) the greater possibilities of flexible and imaginative adaptation of civil penalties to fit particular regulatory problems, the greater reasonableness of such penalties, and their more ready enforceability; and (e) most important of all, the shocking damage that is done to social morale by open and official admission that crime can be respectable and criminality a matter of ill chance, rather than blameworthy choice.

4. If it be urged that strict criminal liability is necessary in order to simplify the investigation and prosecution of violations of statutes designed to control mass conduct, the answer, among others, is that (a) maximizing compliance with law, rather than successful prosecution of violators, is the primary aim of any regulatory statute; (b) the convenience of investigators and prosecutors is not, in any event, the prime consideration in determining what conduct is criminal; (c) a prosecutor, as a matter of common knowledge, always assumes a heavier burden in trying to secure a criminal conviction than a civil judgment; (d) in most situations of attempted control of mass conduct, the technique of a first warning, followed by criminal prosecution only of knowing violators, has not only obvious, but proved superiority; and (e) the common-sense advantages of using the criminal sanction only against deliberate violators is confirmed by the policies which prosecutors themselves tend always to follow when they are free to make their own selection of cases to prosecute.

5. Moral, rather than crassly utilitarian, considerations re-enter the picture when the claim is made, as it sometimes is, that strict liability operates, in fact, only against people who are really blameworthy, because prosecutors only pick out the really guilty ones for criminal prosecution. This argument reasserts the traditional position that a criminal conviction imports moral condemnation. To this, it adds the arrogant assertion that it is proper to visit the moral condemnation of the community upon one of its members on the basis solely of the private judgment of his prosecutors. Such a circumvention of the safe-

guards with which the law surrounds other determinations of criminality seems not only irrational, but immoral as well.

6. But moral considerations in a still larger dimension are the ultimately controlling ones. In its conventional and traditional applications, a criminal conviction carries with it an ineradicable connotation of moral condemnation and personal guilt. Society makes an essentially parasitic, and hence illegitimate, use of this instrument when it uses it as a means of deterrence (or compulsion) of conduct which is morally neutral. This would be true even if a statute were to be enacted proclaiming that no criminal conviction hereafter should ever be understood as casting any reflection on anybody. For statutes cannot change the meaning of words and make people stop thinking what they do think when they hear the words spoken. But it is doubly true—it is ten-fold, a hundred-fold, a thousand-fold true—when society continues to insist that some crimes are morally blameworthy and then tries to use the same epithet to describe conduct which is not.

7. To be sure, the traditional law recognizes gradations in the gravity of offenses, and so does the Constitution of the United States. But strict liability offenses have not been limited to the interpretively-developed constitutional category of "petty offenses," for which trial by jury is not required. They include even some crimes which the Constitution expressly recognizes as "infamous." Thus, the excuse of the Scotch servant girl for her illegitimate baby, that "It was only such a leetle one," is not open to modern legislatures. And since a crime remains a crime, just as a baby is unalterably a baby, it would not be a good excuse if it were. Especially is this so since the legislature could avoid the taint of illegitimacy, much more surely than the servant girl, by simply saying that the "crime" is not a crime, but only a civil violation.

2. CIVIL LIABILITY OF DIRECTORS FOR CRIMINAL ACTS.

Recall from the United States Sentencing Guidelines for Organizations[m] that the fine or other punishment imposed upon an organization is determined by the organization's "culpability" score.[n] Factors relevant in assessing the culpability score are "whether high level personnel participated in, condoned, or were willfully ignorant of the offense; prior offenses by the organization and how the organization responded; obstruction of justice during the investigation; and, presence of an effective program to prevent and detect violations of the law."[o] Thus, an effective internal compliance plan is essential in minimizing the sentence handed out in any criminal conviction. As the next case demonstrates, in addition to reducing a sentence upon a conviction, an effective corporate compliance plan can protect directors from personal liability in shareholder derivative suits.

m. Chapter 15, Section A and Chapter 17.

n. U.S.S.G. § 8C2.5.

o. U.S.S.G. § 8C2.5.

IN RE CAREMARK INTERNATIONAL INC. DERIVATIVE LITIGATION

Court of Chancery of Delaware, New Castle County, 1996.
698 A.2d 959.

ALLEN, CHANCELLOR.

Pending is a motion pursuant to Chancery Rule 23.1 to approve as fair and reasonable a proposed settlement of a consolidated derivative action on behalf of Caremark International, Inc. ("Caremark"). The suit involves claims that the members of Caremark's board of directors (the "Board") breached their fiduciary duty of care to Caremark in connection with alleged violations by Caremark employees of federal and state laws and regulations applicable to health care providers. As a result of the alleged violations, Caremark was subject to an extensive four year investigation by the United States Department of Health and Human Services and the Department of Justice. In 1994 Caremark was charged in an indictment with multiple felonies. It thereafter entered into a number of agreements with the Department of Justice and others. Those agreements included a plea agreement in which Caremark pleaded guilty to a single felony of mail fraud and agreed to pay civil and criminal fines. Subsequently, Caremark agreed to make reimbursements to various private and public parties. In all, the payments that Caremark has been required to make total approximately $250 million.

This suit was filed in 1994, purporting to seek on behalf of the company recovery of these losses from the individual defendants who constitute the board of directors of Caremark.[1] The parties now propose that it be settled and, after notice to Caremark shareholders, a hearing on the fairness of the proposal was held on August 16, 1996.

A motion of this type requires the court to assess the strengths and weaknesses of the claims asserted in light of the discovery record and to evaluate the fairness and adequacy of the consideration offered to the corporation in exchange for the release of all claims made or arising from the facts alleged. The ultimate issue then is whether the proposed settlement appears to be fair to the corporation and its absent shareholders. In this effort the court does not determine contested facts, but evaluates the claims and defenses on the discovery record to achieve a sense of the relative strengths of the parties' positions. * * *

Legally, evaluation of the central claim made entails consideration of the legal standard governing a board of directors' obligation to supervise or monitor corporate performance. For the reasons set forth below I conclude, in light of the discovery record, that there is a very low probability that it would be determined that the directors of Caremark breached any duty to appropriately monitor and supervise the enterprise. Indeed the record tends to show an active consideration by

---

1. Thirteen of the Directors have been members of the Board since November 30, 1992. Nancy Brinker joined the Board in October 1993.

Caremark management and its Board of the Caremark structures and programs that ultimately led to the company's indictment and to the large financial losses incurred in the settlement of those claims. It does not tend to show knowing or intentional violation of law. Neither the fact that the Board, although advised by lawyers and accountants, did not accurately predict the severe consequences to the company that would ultimately follow from the deployment by the company of the strategies and practices that ultimately led to this liability, nor the scale of the liability, gives rise to an inference of breach of any duty imposed by corporation law upon the directors of Caremark.

I. Background

For these purposes I regard the following facts, suggested by the discovery record, as material. Caremark, a Delaware corporation with its headquarters in Northbrook, Illinois, was created in November 1992 when it was spun-off from Baxter International, Inc. ("Baxter") and became a publicly held company listed on the New York Stock Exchange. The business practices that created the problem pre-dated the spin-off. During the relevant period Caremark was involved in two main health care business segments, providing patient care and managed care services. As part of its patient care business, which accounted for the majority of Caremark's revenues, Caremark provided alternative site health care services, including infusion therapy, growth hormone therapy, HIV/AIDS-related treatments and hemophilia therapy. Caremark's managed care services included prescription drug programs and the operation of multi-specialty group practices.

A. Events Prior to the Government Investigation

A substantial part of the revenues generated by Caremark's businesses is derived from third party payments, insurers, and Medicare and Medicaid reimbursement programs. The latter source of payments are subject to the terms of the Anti–Referral Payments Law ("ARPL") which prohibits health care providers from paying any form of remuneration to induce the referral of Medicare or Medicaid patients. From its inception, Caremark entered into a variety of agreements with hospitals, physicians, and health care providers for advice and services, as well as distribution agreements with drug manufacturers, as had its predecessor prior to 1992. Specifically, Caremark did have a practice of entering into contracts for services (e.g., consultation agreements and research grants) with physicians at least some of whom prescribed or recommended services or products that Caremark provided to Medicare recipients and other patients. Such contracts were not prohibited by the ARPL but they obviously raised a possibility of unlawful "kickbacks."

As early as 1989, Caremark's predecessor issued an internal "Guide to Contractual Relationships" ("Guide") to govern its employees in entering into contracts with physicians and hospitals. The Guide tended to be reviewed annually by lawyers and updated. Each version of the Guide stated as Caremark's and its predecessor's policy that no payments would be made in exchange for or to induce patient referrals. But what one might deem a prohibited quid pro quo was not always clear. Due to a scarcity of court decisions interpreting the ARPL, however, Caremark repeatedly publicly stated that there was uncertainty concerning Caremark's interpretation of the law.

To clarify the scope of the ARPL, the United States Department of Health and Human Services ("HHS") issued "safe harbor" regulations in July 1991 stating conditions under which financial relationships between health care service providers and patient referral sources, such as physicians, would not violate the ARPL. Caremark contends that the narrowly drawn regulations gave limited guidance as to the legality of many of the agreements used by Caremark that did not fall within the safe-harbor. Caremark's predecessor, however, amended many of its standard forms of agreement with health care providers and revised the Guide in an apparent attempt to comply with the new regulations.

B. Government Investigation and Related Litigation

In August 1991, the HHS Office of the Inspector General ("OIG") initiated an investigation of Caremark's predecessor. Caremark's predecessor was served with a subpoena requiring the production of documents, including contracts between Caremark's predecessor and physicians (Quality Service Agreements ("QSAs")). Under the QSAs, Caremark's predecessor appears to have paid physicians fees for monitoring patients under Caremark's predecessor's care, including Medicare and Medicaid recipients. Sometimes apparently those monitoring patients were referring physicians, which raised ARPL concerns.

In March 1992, the Department of Justice ("DOJ") joined the OIG investigation and separate investigations were commenced by several additional federal and state agencies.

C. Caremark's Response to the Investigation

During the relevant period, Caremark had approximately 7,000 employees and ninety branch operations. It had a decentralized management structure. By May 1991, however, Caremark asserts that it had begun making attempts to centralize its management structure in order to increase supervision over its branch operations.

The first action taken by management, as a result of the initiation of the OIG investigation, was an announcement that as of October 1, 1991, Caremark's predecessor would no longer pay management fees to physicians for services to Medicare and Medicaid patients. Despite this decision, Caremark asserts that its management, pursuant to advice, did not believe that such payments were illegal under the existing laws and regulations.

During this period, Caremark's Board took several additional steps consistent with an effort to assure compliance with company policies concerning the ARPL and the contractual forms in the Guide. In April 1992, Caremark published a fourth revised version of its Guide apparently designed to assure that its agreements either complied with the ARPL and regulations or excluded Medicare and Medicaid patients altogether.

In addition, in September 1992, Caremark instituted a policy requiring its regional officers, Zone Presidents, to approve each contractual relationship entered into by Caremark with a physician.

Although there is evidence that inside and outside counsel had advised Caremark's directors that their contracts were in accord with the law, Caremark recognized that some uncertainty respecting the correct interpretation of the law existed. In its 1992 annual report, Caremark disclosed the ongoing government investigations, acknowledged that if penalties were imposed on the company they could have a material adverse effect on Caremark's business, and stated that no assurance could be given that its interpretation of the ARPL would prevail if challenged.

Throughout the period of the government investigations, Caremark had an internal audit plan designed to assure compliance with business and ethics policies. In addition, Caremark employed Price Waterhouse as its outside auditor. On February 8, 1993, the Ethics Committee of Caremark's Board received and reviewed an outside auditors report by Price Waterhouse which concluded that there were no material weaknesses in Caremark's control structure.[3] Despite the positive findings of Price Waterhouse, however, on April 20, 1993, the Audit & Ethics Committee adopted a new internal audit charter requiring a comprehensive review of compliance policies and the compilation of an employee ethics handbook concerning such policies.

The Board appears to have been informed about this project and other efforts to assure compliance with the law. For example, Caremark's management reported to the Board that Caremark's sales force was receiving an ongoing education regarding the ARPL and the proper use of Caremark's form contracts which had been approved by in-house counsel. On July 27, 1993, the new ethics manual, expressly prohibiting payments in exchange for referrals and requiring employees to report all illegal conduct to a toll free confidential ethics hotline, was approved and allegedly disseminated.[5] The record suggests that Caremark continued these policies in subsequent years, causing employees to be given revised versions of the ethics manual and requiring them to participate in training sessions concerning compliance with the law.

During 1993, Caremark took several additional steps which appear to have been aimed at increasing management supervision. These steps included new policies requiring local branch managers to secure home office approval for all disbursements under agreements with health care

---

3. At that time, Price Waterhouse viewed the outcome of the OIG Investigation as uncertain. After further audits, however, on February 7, 1995, Price Waterhouse informed the Audit & Ethics Committee that it had not become aware of any irregularities or illegal acts in relation to the OIG investigation.

5. Prior to the distribution of the new ethics manual, on March 12, 1993, Caremark's president had sent a letter to all senior, district, and branch managers restating Caremark's policies that no physician be paid for referrals, that the standard contract forms in the Guide were not to be modified, and that deviation from such policies would result in the immediate termination of employment.

providers and to certify compliance with the ethics program. In addition, the chief financial officer was appointed to serve as Caremark's compliance officer. In 1994, a fifth revised Guide was published.

D.   Federal Indictments Against Caremark and Officers

On August 4, 1994, a federal grand jury in Minnesota issued a 47 page indictment charging Caremark, two of its officers (not the firm's chief officer), an individual who had been a sales employee of Genentech, Inc., and David R. Brown, a physician practicing in Minneapolis, with violating the ARPL over a lengthy period. According to the indictment, over $1.1 million had been paid to Brown to induce him to distribute Protropin, a human growth hormone drug marketed by Caremark. The substantial payments involved started, according to the allegations of the indictment, in 1986 and continued through 1993. Some payments were "in the guise of research grants", Ind. ¶ 20, and others were "consulting agreements", Ind. ¶ 19. The indictment charged, for example, that Dr. Brown performed virtually none of the consulting functions described in his 1991 agreement with Caremark, but was nevertheless neither required to return the money he had received nor precluded from receiving future funding from Caremark. In addition the indictment charged that Brown received from Caremark payments of staff and office expenses, including telephone answering services and fax rental expenses.

In reaction to the Minnesota Indictment and the subsequent filing of this and other derivative actions in 1994, the Board met and was informed by management that the investigation had resulted in an indictment; Caremark denied any wrongdoing relating to the indictment and believed that the OIG investigation would have a favorable outcome. Management reiterated the grounds for its view that the contracts were in compliance with law.

Subsequently, five stockholder derivative actions were filed in this court and consolidated into this action. The original complaint, dated August 5, 1994, alleged, in relevant part, that Caremark's directors breached their duty of care by failing adequately to supervise the conduct of Caremark employees, or institute corrective measures, thereby exposing Caremark to fines and liability.

On September 21, 1994, a federal grand jury in Columbus, Ohio issued another indictment alleging that an Ohio physician had defrauded the Medicare program by requesting and receiving $134,600 in exchange for referrals of patients whose medical costs were in part reimbursed by Medicare in violation of the ARPL. Although unidentified at that time, Caremark was the health care provider who allegedly made such payments. The indictment also charged that the physician, Elliot Neufeld, D.O., was provided with the services of a registered nurse to work in his office at the expense of the infusion company, in addition to free office equipment.

An October 28, 1994 amended complaint in this action added allegations concerning the Ohio indictment as well as new allegations of over billing and inappropriate referral payments in connection with an action brought in Atlanta, Booth v. Rankin. Following a newspaper article report that federal investigators were expanding their inquiry to look at Caremark's referral practices in Michigan as well as allegations of fraudulent billing of insurers, a second amended complaint was filed in this action. The third, and final, amended complaint was filed on April 11, 1995, adding allegations that the federal indictments had caused Caremark to incur significant legal fees and forced it to sell its home infusion business at a loss.[8]

After each complaint was filed, defendants filed a motion to dismiss. According to defendants, if a settlement had not been reached in this action, the case would have been dismissed on two grounds. First, they contend that the complaints fail to allege particularized facts sufficient to excuse the demand requirement under Delaware Chancery Court Rule 23.1. Second, defendants assert that plaintiffs had failed to state a cause of action due to the fact that Caremark's charter eliminates directors' personal liability for money damages, to the extent permitted by law.

E.　Settlement Negotiations

In September, following the announcement of the Ohio indictment, Caremark publicly announced that as of January 1, 1995, it would terminate all remaining financial relationships with physicians in its home infusion, hemophilia, and growth hormone lines of business. In addition, Caremark asserts that it extended its restrictive policies to all of its contractual relationships with physicians, rather than just those involving Medicare and Medicaid patients, and terminated its research grant program which had always involved some recipients who referred patients to Caremark.

Caremark began settlement negotiations with federal and state government entities in May 1995. In return for a guilty plea to a single count of mail fraud by the corporation, the payment of a criminal fine, the payment of substantial civil damages, and cooperation with further federal investigations on matters relating to the OIG investigation, the government entities agreed to negotiate a settlement that would permit Caremark to continue participating in Medicare and Medicaid programs. On June 15, 1995, the Board approved a settlement ("Government Settlement Agreement") with the DOJ, OIG, U.S. Veterans Administration, U.S. Federal Employee Health Benefits Program, federal Civilian Health and Medical Program of the Uniformed Services, and related state agencies in all fifty states and the District of Columbia.[10] No senior officers or directors were charged with wrongdoing in the Government

---

8. On January 29, 1995, Caremark entered into a definitive agreement to sell its home infusion business to Coram Health Care Company for approximately $310 million. Baxter purchased the home infusion business in 1987 for $586 million.

10. The agreement, covering allegations since 1986, required a Caremark subsidiary to enter a guilty plea to two counts of mail fraud, and required Caremark to pay $29

million in criminal fines, $129.9 million relating to civil claims concerning payment practices, $3.5 million for alleged violations of the Controlled Substances Act, and $2 million, in the form of a donation, to a grant program set up by the Ryan White Comprehensive AIDS Resources Emergency Act. Caremark also agreed to enter into a compliance agreement with the HHS.

Settlement Agreement or in any of the prior indictments. In fact, as part of the sentencing in the Ohio action on June 19, 1995, the United States stipulated that no senior executive of Caremark participated in, condoned, or was willfully ignorant of wrongdoing in connection with the home infusion business practices.

The federal settlement included certain provisions in a "Corporate Integrity Agreement" designed to enhance future compliance with law. The parties have not discussed this agreement, except to say that the negotiated provisions of the settlement of this claim are not redundant of those in that agreement.

Settlement negotiations between the parties in this action commenced in May 1995 as well, based upon a letter proposal of the plaintiffs, dated May 16, 1995. These negotiations resulted in a memorandum of understanding ("MOU"), dated June 7, 1995, and the execution of the Stipulation and Agreement of Compromise and Settlement on June 28, 1995, which is the subject of this action. The MOU, approved by the Board on June 15, 1995, required the Board to adopt several resolutions, discussed below, and to create a new compliance committee. The Compliance and Ethics Committee has been reporting to the Board in accord with its newly specified duties.

After negotiating these settlements, Caremark learned in December 1995 that several private insurance company payors ("Private Payors") believed that Caremark was liable for damages to them for allegedly improper business practices related to those at issue in the OIG investigation. As a result of intensive negotiations with the Private Payors and the Board's extensive consideration of the alternatives for dealing with such claims, the Board approved a $98.5 million settlement agreement with the Private Payors on March 18, 1996. In its public disclosure statement, Caremark asserted that the settlement did not involve current business practices and contained an express denial of any wrongdoing by Caremark. After further discovery in this action, the plaintiffs decided to continue seeking approval of the proposed settlement agreement.

F. The Proposed Settlement of this Litigation

In relevant part the terms upon which these claims asserted are proposed to be settled are as follows:

1. That Caremark, undertakes that it and its employees, and agents not pay any form of compensation to a third party in exchange for the referral of a patient to a Caremark facility or service or the prescription of drugs marketed or distributed by Caremark for which reimbursement may be sought from Medicare, Medicaid, or a similar state reimbursement program;

2. That Caremark, undertakes for itself and its employees, and agents not to pay to or split fees with physicians, joint ventures, any business combination in which Caremark maintains a direct financial interest, or other health care providers with whom Caremark

has a financial relationship or interest, in exchange for the referral of a patient to a Caremark facility or service or the prescription of drugs marketed or distributed by Caremark for which reimbursement may be sought from Medicare, Medicaid, or a similar state reimbursement program;

3. That the full Board shall discuss all relevant material changes in government health care regulations and their effect on relationships with health care providers on a semi-annual basis;

4. That Caremark's officers will remove all personnel from health care facilities or hospitals who have been placed in such facility for the purpose of providing remuneration in exchange for a patient referral for which reimbursement may be sought from Medicare, Medicaid, or a similar state reimbursement program;

5. That every patient will receive written disclosure of any financial relationship between Caremark and the health care professional or provider who made the referral;

6. That the Board will establish a Compliance and Ethics Committee of four directors, two of which will be non-management directors, to meet at least four times a year to effectuate these policies and monitor business segment compliance with the ARPL, and to report to the Board semi-annually concerning compliance by each business segment; and

7. That corporate officers responsible for business segments shall serve as compliance officers who must report semi-annually to the Compliance and Ethics Committee and, with the assistance of outside counsel, review existing contracts and get advanced approval of any new contract forms.

II. LEGAL PRINCIPLES

A. *Principles Governing Settlements of Derivative Claims*

As noted at the outset of this opinion, this Court is now required to exercise an informed judgment whether the proposed settlement is fair and reasonable in the light of all relevant factors. On an application of this kind, this Court attempts to protect the best interests of the corporation and its absent shareholders all of whom will be barred from future litigation on these claims if the settlement is approved. The parties proposing the settlement bear the burden of persuading the court that it is in fact fair and reasonable.

B. *Directors' Duties To Monitor Corporate Operations*

The complaint charges the director defendants with breach of their duty of attention or care in connection with the on-going operation of the corporation's business. The claim is that the directors allowed a situation to develop and continue which exposed the corporation to enormous legal liability and that in so doing they violated a duty to be active monitors of corporate performance. The complaint thus does not charge either director self-dealing or the more difficult loyalty-type problems arising from cases of suspect director motivation, such as entrenchment or sale of control contexts. The theory here advanced is possibly the most difficult theory in corporation law upon which a plaintiff might hope to win a judgment. The good policy reasons why it is so difficult to charge directors with responsibility for corporate losses for an alleged breach of care, where there is no conflict of interest or no facts suggesting suspect motivation involved, were recently described in Gagliardi v. TriFoods Int'l, Inc., Del.Ch., 683 A.2d 1049, 1051 (1996) (1996 Del.Ch. LEXIS 87 at p. 20).

1. *Potential liability for directorial decisions*: Director liability for a breach of the duty to exercise appropriate attention may, in theory, arise in two distinct contexts. First, such liability may be said to follow from a board decision that results in a loss because that decision was ill advised or "negligent". Second, liability to the corporation for a loss may be said to arise from an unconsidered failure of the board to act in circumstances in which due attention would, arguably, have prevented the loss. The first class of cases will typically be subject to review under the director-protective business judgment rule, assuming the decision made was the product of a process that was either deliberately considered in good faith or was otherwise rational. What should be understood, but may not widely be understood by courts or commentators who are not often required to face such questions, is that compliance with a director's duty of care can never appropriately be judicially determined by reference to the content of the board decision that leads to a corporate loss, apart from consideration of the good faith or rationality of the process employed. That is, whether a judge or jury considering the matter after the fact, believes a decision substantively wrong, or degrees of wrong extending through "stupid" to "egregious" or "irrational", provides no ground for director liability, so long as the court determines that the process employed was either rational or employed in a good faith effort to advance corporate interests. To employ a different rule—one that permitted an "objective" evaluation of the decision—would expose directors to substantive second guessing by ill-equipped judges or juries, which would, in the long-run, be injurious to investor interests. Thus, the business judgment rule is process oriented and informed by a deep respect for all good faith board decisions.

Indeed, one wonders on what moral basis might shareholders attack a good faith business decision of a director as "unreasonable" or "irrational". Where a director in fact exercises a good faith effort to be informed and to exercise appropriate judgment, he or she should be deemed to satisfy fully the duty of attention. If the shareholders thought themselves entitled to some other quality of judgment than such a director produces in the good faith exercise of the powers of office, then the shareholders should have elected other directors. Judge Learned Hand made the point rather better than can I. In speaking of the passive director defendant Mr. Andrews in Barnes v. Andrews, Judge Hand said:

> True, he was not very suited by experience for the job he had undertaken, but I cannot hold him on that account. After all it is the

same corporation that chose him that now seeks to charge him....
Directors are not specialists like lawyers or doctors.... They are the
general advisors of the business and if they faithfully give such
ability as they have to their charge, it would not be lawful to hold
them liable. Must a director guarantee that his judgment is good?
Can a shareholder call him to account for deficiencies that their
votes assured him did not disqualify him for his office? While he may
not have been the Cromwell for that Civil War, Andrews did not
engage to play any such role.[17]

In this formulation Learned Hand correctly identifies, in my opinion, the
core element of any corporate law duty of care inquiry: whether there
was good faith effort to be informed and exercise judgment.

2. *Liability for failure to monitor*: The second class of cases in
which director liability for inattention is theoretically possible entail
circumstances in which a loss eventuates not from a decision but, from
unconsidered inaction. Most of the decisions that a corporation, acting
through its human agents, makes are, of course, not the subject of
director attention. Legally, the board itself will be required only to
authorize the most significant corporate acts or transactions: mergers,
changes in capital structure, fundamental changes in business, appointment and compensation of the CEO, etc. As the facts of this case
graphically demonstrate, ordinary business decisions that are made by
officers and employees deeper in the interior of the organization can,
however, vitally affect the welfare of the corporation and its ability to
achieve its various strategic and financial goals. If this case did not prove
the point itself, recent business history would. Recall for example the
displacement of senior management and much of the board of Salomon,
Inc.; the replacement of senior management of Kidder, Peabody following the discovery of large trading losses resulting from phantom trades
by a highly compensated trader; or the extensive financial loss and
reputational injury suffered by Prudential Insurance as a result its
junior officers misrepresentations in connection with the distribution of
limited partnership interests. Financial and organizational disasters
such as these raise the question, what is the board's responsibility with
respect to the organization and monitoring of the enterprise to assure
that the corporation functions within the law to achieve its purposes?

Modernly this question has been given special importance by an
increasing tendency, especially under federal law, to employ the criminal
law to assure corporate compliance with external legal requirements,
including environmental, financial, employee and product safety as well
as assorted other health and safety regulations. In 1991, pursuant to the
Sentencing Reform Act of 1984, the United States Sentencing Commission adopted Organizational Sentencing Guidelines which impact importantly on the prospective effect these criminal sanctions might have on
business corporations. The Guidelines set forth a uniform sentencing
structure for organizations to be sentenced for violation of federal

---

17.   298 F. 614, 618 (S.D.N.Y.1924).

criminal statutes and provide for penalties that equal or often massively exceed those previously imposed on corporations. The Guidelines offer powerful incentives for corporations today to have in place compliance programs to detect violations of law, promptly to report violations to appropriate public officials when discovered, and to take prompt, voluntary remedial efforts.

In 1963, the Delaware Supreme Court in Graham v. Allis–Chalmers Mfg. Co.,[23] addressed the question of potential liability of board members for losses experienced by the corporation as a result of the corporation having violated the anti-trust laws of the United States. There was no claim in that case that the directors knew about the behavior of subordinate employees of the corporation that had resulted in the liability. Rather, as in this case, the claim asserted was that the directors ought to have known of it and if they had known they would have been under a duty to bring the corporation into compliance with the law and thus save the corporation from the loss. The Delaware Supreme Court concluded that, under the facts as they appeared, there was no basis to find that the directors had breached a duty to be informed of the ongoing operations of the firm. In notably colorful terms, the court stated that "absent cause for suspicion there is no duty upon the directors to install and operate a corporate system of espionage to ferret out wrongdoing which they have no reason to suspect exists."[24] The Court found that there were no grounds for suspicion in that case and, thus, concluded that the directors were blamelessly unaware of the conduct leading to the corporate liability.

How does one generalize this holding today? Can it be said today that, absent some ground giving rise to suspicion of violation of law, that corporate directors have no duty to assure that a corporate information gathering and reporting systems exists which represents a good faith attempt to provide senior management and the Board with information respecting material acts, events or conditions within the corporation, including compliance with applicable statutes and regulations? I certainly do not believe so. I doubt that such a broad generalization of the *Graham* holding would have been accepted by the Supreme Court in 1963. The case can be more narrowly interpreted as standing for the proposition that, absent grounds to suspect deception, neither corporate boards nor senior officers can be charged with wrongdoing simply for assuming the integrity of employees and the honesty of their dealings on the company's behalf.

A broader interpretation of Graham v. Allis–Chalmers—that it means that a corporate board has no responsibility to assure that appropriate information and reporting systems are established by management—would not, in any event, be accepted by the Delaware Supreme Court in 1996, in my opinion. In stating the basis for this view, I start with the recognition that in recent years the Delaware Supreme

---

23. Del.Supr., 41 Del.Ch. 78, 188 A.2d 125 (1963).

24. Id. 188 A.2d at 130.

Court has made it clear—especially in its jurisprudence concerning takeovers, from Smith v. Van Gorkom through Paramount Communications v. QVC[26]—the seriousness with which the corporation law views the role of the corporate board. Secondly, I note the elementary fact that relevant and timely information is an essential predicate for satisfaction of the board's supervisory and monitoring role under Section 141 of the Delaware General Corporation Law. Thirdly, I note the potential impact of the federal organizational sentencing guidelines on any business organization. Any rational person attempting in good faith to meet an organizational governance responsibility would be bound to take into account this development and the enhanced penalties and the opportunities for reduced sanctions that it offers.

In light of these developments, it would, in my opinion, be a mistake to conclude that our Supreme Court's statement in Graham concerning "espionage" means that corporate boards may satisfy their obligation to be reasonably informed concerning the corporation, without assuring themselves that information and reporting systems exist in the organization that are reasonably designed to provide to senior management and to the board itself timely, accurate information sufficient to allow management and the board, each within its scope, to reach informed judgments concerning both the corporation's compliance with law and its business performance.

Obviously the level of detail that is appropriate for such an information system is a question of business judgment. And obviously too, no rationally designed information and reporting system will remove the possibility that the corporation will violate laws or regulations, or that senior officers or directors may nevertheless sometimes be misled or otherwise fail reasonably to detect acts material to the corporation's compliance with the law. But it is important that the board exercise a good faith judgment that the corporation's information and reporting system is in concept and design adequate to assure the board that appropriate information will come to its attention in a timely manner as a matter of ordinary operations, so that it may satisfy its responsibility.

Thus, I am of the view that a director's obligation includes a duty to attempt in good faith to assure that a corporate information and reporting system, which the board concludes is adequate, exists, and that failure to do so under some circumstances may, in theory at least, render a director liable for losses caused by non-compliance with applicable legal standards. I now turn to an analysis of the claims asserted with this concept of the directors duty of care, as a duty satisfied in part by assurance of adequate information flows to the board, in mind.

III. ANALYSIS OF THIRD AMENDED COMPLAINT AND SETTLEMENT

On balance, after reviewing an extensive record in this case, including numerous documents and three depositions, I conclude that this

26. E.g., Smith v. Van Gorkom, Del. Supr., 488 A.2d 858 (1985); Paramount Communications v. QVC Network, Del. Supr., 637 A.2d 34 (1994).

settlement is fair and reasonable. In light of the fact that the Caremark Board already has a functioning committee charged with overseeing corporate compliance, the changes in corporate practice that are presented as consideration for the settlement do not impress one as very significant. Nonetheless, that consideration appears fully adequate to support dismissal of the derivative claims of director fault asserted, because those claims find no substantial evidentiary support in the record and quite likely were susceptible to a motion to dismiss in all events.

* * *

Notes

1. What does the *Caremark* decision tell corporate directors about the need for corporate compliance plans?

2. One expert has identified the following seven elements of an effective corporate compliance plan:

● Element 1. The organization must have established compliance standards and procedures to be followed by its employees and other agents that are reasonably capable of reducing the prospect of criminal conduct.

● Element 2. Specific individual(s) within high level personnel of the organization must have been assigned overall responsibility to oversee compliance with such standards and procedures.

● Element 3. The organization must have used due care not to delegate substantial discretionary authority to individuals whom the organization knew, or should have known through the exercise of due diligence, had a propensity to engage in illegal activities.

● Element 4. The organization must have taken steps to communicate effectively its standards and procedures to all employees and other agents, e.g., by requiring participation in training programs or by disseminating publications that explain in a practical manner what is required.

● Element 5. The organization must have taken reasonable steps to achieve compliance with its standards, e.g., by utilizing monitoring and auditing systems reasonably designed to detect criminal conduct by its employees and other agents and by having in place and publicizing a reporting system whereby employees and other agents could report criminal conduct by others within the organization without fear of retribution.

● Element 6. The standards must have been consistently enforced through appropriate disciplinary mechanisms, including, as appropriate, discipline of individuals responsible for the failure to detect an offense. Adequate discipline of individuals responsible for an offense is a necessary component of enforcement; however, the form of discipline that will be appropriate will be case specific.

● Element 7. After an offense has been detected, the organization must have taken all reasonable steps to respond appropriately to the offense and to prevent further similar offenses—including any necessary modifications to its program to prevent and detect violations of law.[p]

What role does inside counsel play in establishing a corporate compliance plan? What role does outside counsel play?

p. Edward J. Hopkins, *Compliance Programs in the New World*, 1997 ABA National Institute on Health Care Fraud B–1. Copyright © 1997. American Bar Association. All rights reserved. Reprinted with permission, Edward J. Hopkins, Steel, Hector & Davis, L.L.P. and ABA.

Chapter 16

SENTENCING AND RESTITUTION

A. THE UNITED STATES SENTENCING GUIDELINES

1. INTRODUCTION

Since the passage of the Sentencing Reform Act of 1984,[a] the federal criminal justice system has employed determinative sentencing. The Sentencing Reform Act established an independent commission within the judiciary branch to develop and monitor determinative sentencing guidelines for the federal judicial system.[b] The Sentencing Guidelines are designed to standardize sentencing practices in the federal courts by "avoiding unwarranted sentencing disparities among defendants with similar records who have been found guilty of similar criminal conduct."[c]

a. *Sentencing Individuals*

Once an individual defendant has been convicted in the federal courts, the sentencing court is to ascertain a defendant's "Guideline." The Guideline determines the actual term of imprisonment and fine a defendant will be assessed, within the maximum specified by the statute. Most of the federal offenses which apply to white collar crimes provide for maximum terms of imprisonment not to exceed five years, per violation;[d] fines not to exceed $250,000, per violation; and, sometimes, as noted in Chapter Five, *supra*, forfeiture of assets.[e]

To calculate a defendant's Guideline, a sentencing court begins with Chapter 2 of the Sentencing Guidelines. Chapter 2 is divided into nineteen parts, based on the type of offense.

a. 18 U.S.C. §§ 3551–3742; 28 U.S.C. §§ 991–998.

b. 28 U.S.C. § 994; Mistretta v. United States, 488 U.S. 361, 368–69 (1989).

c. 28 U.S.C. § 991.

d. 18 U.S.C. §§ 286, 287, 371, 1001, 1341, 1343 and 42 U.S.C. § 1320a–7b all provide for five year maximum terms of imprisonment. Title 18 U.S.C. §§ 1956 and 1957 (money laundering) provide for a 20 year maximum term of imprisonment and 10 year maximum term of imprisonment, respectively. The maximum term of imprisonment for obstruction of justice ranges from 1 year to the death penalty.

e. 18 U.S.C. § 3571(c).

The first step in calculating a defendant's Guideline is to determine the defendant's "base offense level." Conviction on one count of most fraud offenses, for example, gives a defendant a base offense level of 6.[f]

After a court has determined the base offense level, the court is to consult Chapters 2 and 3 of the Sentencing Guidelines to determine whether "adjustments" in the base offense level are warranted. The most significant of these adjustments in most white collar cases is likely to be the amount of money at issue. A base offense level may be increased by 1 to 20 levels, depending upon the amount of money involved in the crime.[g] In some instances, courts estimate the loss by extrapolating from known facts.[h]

Various conditions surrounding the crime may increase the base offense level under the Guidelines. For example, the base offense level may also be increased by 2 levels if the offense involved misrepresentations regarding charitable, educational, religious or political organizations or governmental agencies.[i] Similarly, if the offense involved "the use of foreign bank accounts or transactions to conceal the true nature or extent of the fraudulent conduct," and the offense level is less than 12, the base offense level may be increased to 12.[j] Also, if the offense involved more than minimal planning or a scheme to defraud more than one victim, the base level may be increased by 2 levels.[k] In addition, if the offense "involved the conscious or reckless risk of serious bodily injury," the base offense level will be increased by 2 levels.[l] This particular adjustment will apply in few white collar offenses.

f. UNITED STATES SENTENCING COMM'N, SENTENCING GUIDELINES MANUAL, § 2F1.1(a) [hereinafter U.S.S.G. MANUAL]. There are some interesting base offense levels. The conspiracy offense is treated less severely than is the commission of the underlying substantive offense under the federal sentencing guidelines, unless the conspiracy has almost reached fruition. The base offense for a conspiracy charge is the base offense for the substantive offense, plus any adjustments established with "reasonable certainty." This base offense level is then decreased by 3 levels, "unless the defendant or a coconspirator completed all the acts the conspirators believed necessary on their part for the successful completion of the substantive offense or the circumstances demonstrate that the conspirators were about to complete all such acts but for apprehension or interruption by some similar event beyond their control." U.S.S.G. § 2X1.1(b)(3)(A).

The base offense for money laundering is higher than most white collar crimes. The statutory scheme sets forth this dichotomy: whereas the maximum term of imprisonment set forth in most fraud offenses is five years, the statutorily-set maximum term of imprisonment for money laundering is twenty years. The sentencing guidelines continue this distinction. Whereas the base offense level for most white collar crimes is 6, the base offense level for § 1956 violations ranges from 20 to 23 and for § 1957 violations is 17. U.S.S.G. § 2S1.1.

g. Section A(3), Chapter 17, *infra*, presents some of the issues involved in calculating the amount at stake.

h. United States v. Marrero, 904 F.2d 251, 262 (5th Cir.1990).

i. U.S.S.G. § 2F1.1(b)(3).

j. U.S.S.G. § 2F1.1(b)(5).

k. U.S.S.G. § 2F1.1(b)(2). "More than minimal planning is deemed present in any case involving repeated acts over a period of time, unless it is clear that each instance was purely opportune." U.S.S.G. § 1B1.1, Application Note 1(f) cited in United States v. Abud–Sanchez, 973 F.2d 835, 837 (10th Cir.1992). By its nature, white collar crime will almost always qualify for an increase under the sentencing guidelines as involving more than minimal planning.

l. U.S.S.G. § 2F1.1(b)(4); United States v. Laughlin, 26 F.3d 1523, 1530 (10th Cir. 1994).

After ascertaining whether any of the Chapter 2 adjustments in the base offense level apply, a sentencing court is to consult Chapter 3 of the Guidelines to determine whether adjustments related to victim, role of the defendant or obstruction of justice apply. If the victim of the offense was "unusually vulnerable due to age, physical or mental condition," the court is to increase the offense level by 2.[m] Also, if the defendant was an organizer or leader in the criminal activity, her base offense level could be increased by 4 levels.[n] If the defendant abused a position of public or private trust or used a special skill, his base offense level could be increased by 2 levels.[o] Lastly, if the defendant "willfully obstructed or impeded the administration of justice during the investigation, prosecution or sentencing" of the offense, her base offense level could be increased by 2 levels.[p] However, if the defendant "clearly demonstrates acceptance of responsibility for his offense," his base offense level could be decreased by 2 levels.[q]

After a court has made adjustments from Chapter 3, it consults Chapter 4 of the Sentencing Guidelines pertaining to defendants' criminal history. According to the Guidelines, "[a] defendant with a record of prior criminal behavior is more culpable than a first offender and thus deserving of greater punishment."[r] Chapter 4 directs courts to increase a defendant's offense level from 1 to 3 points for each prior offense.[s]

The Sentencing Guidelines provide discretion for a court to depart, upward or downward, from the base offense level. If a court finds that the case presents "unusual features," and specifies the reasons for departure, the court may depart.[t] Grounds for downward departure include whether the defendant provided "substantial assistance to authorities,"[u] whether the victim's conduct contributed to the offense,[v] and whether the defendant was coerced[w] or suffered from diminished capacity.[x] Grounds for upward departure focus on the harm caused by the defendant's conduct including death, physical injury or extreme psychological injury.[y]

Once a sentencing court has determined the final offense level (base offense level plus any departures), the court consults Chapter 5 of the Guidelines for the sentencing range for the final offense level. If, for

---

m. U.S.S.G. § 3A1.1.

n. U.S.S.G. §§ 3B1.1 and .2.

o. U.S.S.G. § 3B1.3; United States v. Garfinkel, 29 F.3d 1253 (8th Cir.1994); United States v. Custodio, 39 F.3d 1121, 1125–26 (10th Cir.1994); United States v. Gandy, 36 F.3d 912 (10th Cir.1994).

p. U.S.S.G. § 3C1.1.

q. U.S.S.G. § 3E1.1.

r. U.S.S.G., Chapter 4: Part A, Introductory Commentary.

s. U.S.S.G. § 4A1.1.

t. 18 U.S.C. 3553(b). (Excellent sources on federal sentencing policies include: THOMAS W. HUTCHINSON, DAVID YELLEN, DEBO-

RAH YOUNG & MATTHEW R. KIPP, FEDERAL SENTENCING LAW AND PRACTICE (1994); JED S. RAKOFF, LINDA R. BLUMKIN AND RICHARD SAUBER, EDS., CORPORATE SENTENCING GUIDELINES: COMPLIANCE AND MITIGATION (1993)).

u. U.S.S.G. § 5K1.1.

v. U.S.S.G. § 5K2.10.

w. U.S.S.G. § 5K2.12.

x. U.S.S.G. § 5K2.13.

y. U.S.S.G. §§ 5K2.1, 5K2.2, 5K2.3. Section A(4), Chapter 17, *infra*, addresses adjustments and departures.

example, the court determined that a provider's offense level was 6, the court would be required to sentence the defendant to 0–6 months of imprisonment. If, however, a provider's offense level was 36, the court would be required to sentence the defendant to 188–235 months.[z]

b. Sentencing Organizations

The Guidelines for sentencing organizations are found in Chapter 8 and apply to persons "other than an individual" including "corporations, partnerships, associations, joint-stock companies, unions, trusts, pension funds, unincorporated organizations, governments and political subdivisions thereof, and nonprofit organizations."[aa] The Organizational Sentencing Guidelines reflect the following general principles:

> "First, the court must, whenever practicable, order the organization to remedy any harm caused by the offense. The resources expended to remedy the harm should not be viewed as punishment, but rather as a means of making victims whole for the harm caused. Second, if the organization operated primarily for a criminal purpose or primarily by criminal means, the fine should be set sufficiently high to divest the organization of all its assets. Third, the fine range for any other organization should be based on the seriousness of the offense and the culpability of the organization. The seriousness of the offense generally will be reflected by the highest of the pecuniary gain, the pecuniary loss, or the amount in a guideline offense level fine table. Culpability generally will be determined by the steps taken by the organization prior to the offense to prevent and detect criminal conduct, the level and extent of involvement in or tolerance of the offense by certain personnel, and the organization's actions after an offense has been committed. Fourth, probation is an appropriate sentence for an organizational defendant when needed to ensure that another sanction will be fully implemented, or to ensure that steps will be taken within the organization to reduce the likelihood of future criminal conduct."[bb]

As can be seen from the principles governing the sentencing of organizations, the Guidelines provide that the "death penalty" (divesture of corporate charter) is reserved for organizations "operated primarily for a criminal purpose or primarily by criminal means."[cc] In all other situations, the Guidelines encourage sentences that require the offending organization to remedy the harm caused. To this end, a court may order restitution, require the organization to repair the damage, take steps to ensure that such harm does not reoccur, establish a trust fund sufficient to address expected harm, or perform community service and notify

---

z. U.S.S.G., Ch. 5, Part A (Sentencing Table); "Legislative history ... suggests that the phrase 'maximum term authorized' should be construed as the maximum term authorized by statute." U.S.S.G. § 4B1.1 Comments. *See* S. Rep. No. 98–225, 98th Cong., 1st Sess. 175 (1983). Thus, if the 188 months is higher than the statutory maxi-

mum, the statutory maximum would be the sentence.

aa. U.S.S.G. § 8A1.1, Comment (n.1).

bb. *Id.*

cc. U.S.S.G., Introductory Commentary, Chapter 8.

victims.[dd] The Guidelines encourage "good corporate citizenship" by permitting organizations to reduce substantially any fines otherwise applicable upon a showing that the organization engaged in certain acts of good corporate citizenship. By engaging in these acts (such as having an effective corporate compliance plan) a convicted organization can reduce its base fine (which could reach $72.5 million per count for organizations) by 400%.[ee]

The first step in determining the amount of fine a convicted organization will pay is to calculate the "base fine", which is the greatest of the following: (1) the pecuniary gain to the organization from the offense, (2) the pecuniary loss from the offense to the extent the loss was caused knowingly, intentionally or recklessly, (3) an amount ranging from $5,000 to $72,500,000, depending upon which statutes were violated.[ff]

The next step is to assess the organization's "culpability score."[gg] The culpability score determines the range of multipliers for the base fine. An organization's culpability score is increased if there is evidence that high level personnel were involved in or tolerated the criminal activity; the organization has a prior history of committing offenses; the organization violated a pending judicial order or injunction when committing the offense; or the organization obstructed justice or attempted to do so during any investigation. An organization's culpability score is decreased if the organization had in place an effective program to prevent, detect and discourage violations of the law; self-reported the violation; accepted responsibility for the violation; and cooperated with the government.[hh]

2. RELEVANT CONDUCT

The "related conduct" provisions of the Sentencing Guidelines are the "most controversial aspect of the Guidelines."[ii] Section 1B1.3 of the Guidelines provides that when imposing a sentence a court must consider the following:

> all acts, and omissions committed, aided, abetted, counseled, commanded, induced, procured, or wilfully caused by the defendant * * * that occurred during the commission of the offense of convic-

---

dd. U.S.S.G. § 8B1.1–.4.

ee. Jed S. Rakoff & Linda R. Blumkin, "Determining the Fine in Organizational Sentencing," CORPORATE SENTENCING GUIDE-LINES: COMPLIANCE AND MITIGATION (1993).

ff. U.S.S.G. § 8C2.4.

gg. U.S.S.G. § 8C2.5.

hh. U.S.S.G. § 8C2.5. Complex questions of strategy surround the decision to fully self report and cooperate to gain benefits under the sentencing guidelines. Excellent sources addressing these questions are

DAN K. WEBB, ROBERT W. TARUN & STEVEN F. MOLO, CORPORATE INTERNAL INVESTIGATIONS (1994); JED S. RAKOFF, LINDA R. BLUMKIN & RICHARD SAUBER, EDS., CORPORATE SENTENCING GUIDELINES: COMPLIANCE AND MITIGATION (1993).

ii. David Yellen, *Illusion, Illogic, and Injustice: Real–Offense Sentencing and the Federal Sentencing Guidelines*, 78 MINN. L. REV. 403, 428 (1993). [hereinafter, Yellen, *Illusion*]

tion, in preparation for that offense, or in the course of attempting to avoid detection or responsibility for that offense.[jj]

Thus, courts consider conduct that has not been charged,[kk] conduct provable with unconstitutionally obtained evidence,[ll] conduct for which a defendant has already been convicted,[mm] and conduct for which a defendant has been charged and acquitted.[nn] The rationale for requiring courts to consider relevant conduct is that it is pertinent when assessing a defendant's character and propensity to commit future crimes. There is also concern that not considering such conduct leads to "count manipulation," whereby prosecutors control a defendant's sentence by providing the court with only the information contained in the counts included in the indictment.[oo] Critics of relevant conduct sentencing argue that considering such conduct does little to neutralize the power of prosecutors who still determine the sentence through "fact bargaining," whereby the prosecutor discloses only some facts to the court.[pp] Critics of "relevant conduct sentencing" also point to the unfairness of punishing for acquitted or bargained-away charges.[qq]

The next case, United States v. Fox, 889 F.2d 357 (1st Cir.1989), discusses relevant conduct.

UNITED STATES v. FOX

United States Court of Appeals, First Circuit, 1989.
889 F.2d 357.

BOWNES, CIRCUIT JUDGE.

* * * Defendant began work as an Assistant Consumer Credit Officer at the Bedford Bank, Bedford, New Hampshire in April, 1987. On June 6, 1988 a bank official discovered two questionable loans authorized by defendant. In reviewing these loans it was found that defendant had made a loan to a Lorraine Duclos. This loan was unusual because the loan payment book was kept by the defendant. After investigation the bank found out that defendant had made a $1500 unsecured loan to Duclos in March of 1988 that became overdue on May 18, 1988. On that day a $3250 unsecured loan was made to Duclos, the proceeds of which were used to pay the principal and interest on the $1500 loan. The bank concluded that Duclos was a fictitious person and that the money had gone to defendant.

---

jj. U.S.S.G. § 1B1.3.

kk. United States v. Galloway, 976 F.2d 414, 419 (8th Cir.1992).

ll. United States v. McCrory, 930 F.2d 63, 67 (D.C.Cir.1991).

mm. Witte v. United States, 515 U.S. 389 (1995).

nn. United States v. Concepcion, 983 F.2d 369, 387 (2d Cir.1992).

oo. William W. Wilkins, Jr. & John R. Steer, *Relevant Conduct: The Cornerstone of the Federal Sentencing Guidelines*, 41

S.C.L. REV. 495, 500 (1990); Michael H. Tonry, *Real Offense Sentencing: The Model Sentencing and Corrections Act*, 72 J. CRIM. L. & CRIMINOLOGY 1550, 1562 (1981).

pp. Yellen, *Illusion*, supra, note ii, 78 MINN. L. REV. at 446.

qq. Kevin R. Reitz, *Sentencing Facts: Travesties of Real–Offense Sentencing*, 45 STAN. L. REV. 523, 531–35, 573 (1993).

On June 9, 1988, bank officials confronted defendant with the information they had. She admitted that Duclos was a fictitious person and signed a statement to that effect. Defendant agreed to made restitution in the amount of $3,279.74. She told the bank officials that she had not made any other loans to herself. Defendant was discharged by the bank.

On June 13, 1988, bank auditors discovered four additional fictitious loans with outstanding balances. Proceeds from the loans were either taken in cash or in cashier's checks payable to different banks. The cashier's checks were used to make payments on personal loans and credit accounts of defendant. On June 14, two bank officials met with defendant. She admitted making five fraudulent loans to herself in the total amount of $21,650. She made full restitution on the same day as the meeting with the bank officials.

* * *

On December 14, 1988 the defendant was indicted. The indictment charged that, while an employee of the Bedford Bank, defendant made a fictitious loan in the amount of $3,250 and retained the proceeds, in violation of 18 U.S.C. § 656 (theft, embezzlement or misapplication by bank officer or employee).

On February 13, 1989 the defendant entered into a plea agreement and then pled guilty to the indictment. * * *

* * *

At the sentencing hearing defendant made no objection to the facts stated in the presentence report. The district court found that the sentencing recommendation of the probation department was correctly calculated and adopted it. The recommendation contained in the presentence report was based on defendant's obtaining five fraudulent loans, four in addition to the one to which she pled guilty. The offense level computation was as follows: The base offense level pursuant to section 2B1.1(a) of the Guidelines is four. The court, following the presentence report, took into account the four loans not mentioned in the indictment as "relevant conduct." Six levels were therefore added under section 2B1.1(b)(1)(G). * * *

* * *

Defendant's * * * argument, that the four fraudulently obtained loans not charged in the indictment should not have been factored into the sentencing determination as "relevant conduct", has some substance. There was a great deal of discussion among the members of the Sentencing Commission as to whether all relevant conduct or only the offense charged should be a sentencing factor. The relevant conduct viewpoint prevailed. Section 1B1.3(a) of the Sentencing Guidelines provides:

§ 1B1.3. Relevant Conduct (Factors that Determine the Guideline Range)

(a) Chapters Two (Offense Conduct) and Three (Adjustments). Unless otherwise specified, (i) the base offense level where the guideline specifies more than one base offense level, (ii) specific offense characteristics and (iii) cross references in Chapter Two, and (iv) adjustments in Chapter Three, shall be determined on the basis of the following:

(1) all acts and omissions committed or aided and abetted by the defendant, or for which the defendant would be otherwise accountable, that occurred during the commission of the offense of conviction, in preparation for that offense, or in the course of attempting to avoid detection or responsibility for that offense, or that otherwise were in furtherance of that offense;

(2) solely with respect to offenses of a character for which § 3D1.2(d) would require grouping of multiple counts, all such acts and omissions that were part of the same course of conduct or common scheme or plan as the offense of conviction;

(3) all harm that resulted from the acts or omissions specified in subsections (a)(1) and (a)(2) above, and all harm that was the object of such acts or omissions; and

(4) any other information specified in the applicable guideline.

The four fraudulent loans not charged in the indictment fall within (1) and (2) of this section.

In United States v. Wright, 873 F.2d 437, 441, (1st Cir.1989) we addressed the "relevant conduct" issue:

Insofar as appellant complains of the court's taking account of conduct relevant to the offense in question, or past behavior relevant to determining an appropriate penalty for the crime, he complains of a practice in which all sentencing courts have engaged in the past and in which they will continue to engage in the future. Guideline § 1B1.3 requires courts to take account of "relevant conduct"—conduct that, very roughly speaking, corresponds to those actions and circumstances that courts typically took into account when sentencing prior to the Guidelines' enactment. Past practice, and authoritative case law, indicates that the Constitution does not, as a general matter, forbid such consideration.

There can be no question here that the conduct factored into the sentence was relevant and related. Defendant started obtaining money from the bank for which she worked by means of fraudulent loans in March of 1988 and continued this course of conduct until it was detected by the bank. That she was indicted on only one fraudulent loan does not insulate the other loans from sentencing consideration. This would be contrary to sentencing practice that long predates the guidelines. * * *

Notes

According to the Supreme Court, the relevant conduct provisions of the Sentencing Guidelines are consistent with longstanding sentencing practices:

"The relevant conduct provisions of the Sentencing Guidelines, like their criminal history counterparts and the recidivism statutes ... are sentencing enhancement regimes evincing the judgment that a particular offense should receive a more serious sentence within the authorized range if it was either accompanied by or preceded by additional criminal activity."

Witte v. United States, 515 U.S. 389, 403 (1995). Consider Professor Yellen's criticism of the relevant conduct provisions:

"[Considering "relevant conduct"] in sentencing means that [d]efendants ... are sentenced based on facts not proved at trial or admitted as part of a guilty pleas. Indeed, the sentence may be aggravated based on conduct for which the defendant has been acquitted. The sentencing judge may have found these sentencing facts by a mere preponderance of the evidence, without many of the procedural protections applicable to determinations of guilt or innocence. The defendant may be deprived of the anticipated benefit of a plea agreement, as dismissed charges are reintroduced at the sentencing stage.

"This sacrifice of fairness is particularly hard to justify if a [relevant conduct] system fails even to achieve its stated aims [of reducing disparity in sentencing]. Critics suggest that the promise of real-offense sentencing is illusory because such a system is unworkable. Real-offense sentencing can easily lead to unmanageable complexity as judges must determine all of the 'real' facts relevant to sentencing. Errors in the application of complex sentencing rules can reintroduce disparity. Prosecutors and defense attorneys may 'circumvent the guidelines by developing new plea bargaining patterns.' [Relevant conduct] sentencing also depends upon the judge receiving complete and accurate information concerning the offense and the offender. Accordingly a [relevant conduct] system is vulnerable to inadequate information gathering, which may be caused by a lack of resources or a willingness by the parties to 'hide' facts from the court. * * *

"[Relevant conduct] sentencing is not a creation of the Sentencing Commission. It has long been a part of traditional American sentencing systems, such as the federal regime that existed before the introduction of the Guidelines. This fact has led some to suggest that the Sentencing Commission's adoption of real-offense sentencing simply formalizes the pre-existing judicial approach to sentencing. This argument is misleading and understates the radical nature of the Sentencing Commission's compromise.

"Federal sentencing before the Guidelines, like the systems that continue to exist in many states, is best described as incorporating discretionary or permissive [relevant conduct] sentencing. One of the defining features of the pre-Guidelines federal system was that judges exercised largely unfettered discretion in selecting a punishment within broad statutory limits. This discretion extended to deciding which, if any, [relevant conduct] would be considered. * * *

"It is important to note the limited nature of this [relevant conduct] sentencing. A judge in the former federal system was not *required* to take into account any [relevant conduct] behavior, as would be the case with binding sentencing guidelines incorporating [relevant conduct] sentencing. * * *[rr]

What do you think about including relevant conduct in sentencing?

3. CALCULATING THE AMOUNT OF LOSS

The amount of loss caused by a defendant's crime is crucial in determining the defendant's sentence. One expert explained:

"Ben Franklin's Poor Richard's Almanac warns that 'a little neglect may breed mischief: for want of a nail, the shoe was lost; for want of a shoe the horse was lost; and for want of a horse the rider was lost.'

"If the nail was lost fraudulently, and the person who lost it was charged under the Federal Sentencing Guidelines, should he be charged with the value of the nail, the lost wages of the rider or the harm caused by the rider's failure to get there on time? The answer is critical under the Guidelines, where the length of a sentence often depends on the loss that results from fraudulent conduct."[ss]

The next case, United States v. Carrington, 96 F.3d 1 (1st Cir.1996), provides a straight-forward example of the analysis courts employ in calculating loss under the Sentencing Guidelines. As you read *Carrington* consider what, if anything, you would have done differently if you had been the defense counsel.

UNITED STATES v. CARRINGTON

United States Court of Appeals, First Circuit, 1996.
96 F.3d 1.

TORRUELLA, CHIEF JUDGE.

On March 28, 1995, Defendant Kerr Carrington ("Carrington") pleaded guilty to four counts of interstate transportation of property taken by fraud (Counts I through IV), see 18 U.S.C. § 2314, and two counts of wire fraud (counts V and VI), see 18 U.S.C. § 1343. On August 21, 1995, Carrington was sentenced to a term of 50 months incarceration, followed by a 36 month period of supervised release, and a mandatory special assessment of $50. He contests the validity of his plea based on Federal Rule of Criminal Procedure 11(f) and also appeals his sentence on several grounds. We affirm both his conviction and his sentence.

The case arises from two separate sets of schemes to defraud. In the first set, charged in Counts I through IV and spanning from December 1993 to April 1994, Carrington negotiated the purchase of four expensive cars from out-of-state dealers. He then tricked the dealers into believing that they had received wire transfers in payment for the cars. All four

rr. Yellen, *Illusions, supra,* note ii, 78 MINN. L. REV. 415–19. Copyright ©. All rights reserved. Reprinted with permission David Yellen and Minnesota Law Review Foundation.

ss. Alan Strasser, *Fraud Loss, Federal Sentencing Guidelines and an Escape Hatch,* 4 BUS. CRIMES BULLETIN 1 (Apr. 1997).

cars were then shipped to Carrington in Massachusetts. Carrington was arrested on May 3, 1994, and released on conditions pending further proceedings in the district court. On or about July 8, 1994, Carrington and the government entered into a plea agreement pursuant to which he agreed to plead guilty to all four counts of the information, which was filed on July 19, 1994. Carrington did not immediately waive indictment and plead to the information. Instead, upon Carrington's motion, the Probation Office began working on the Presentence Report ("PSR") with the intention of having Carrington plead and be sentenced upon its completion.

In the second set, charged in Counts V and VI, which he executed while on release in connection with Counts I through IV, Carrington sought to obtain and deposit bank drafts drawn against the corporate bank accounts of various companies. The conduct charged as Count V took place in November 1994. On or about November 14, 1994, while the parties were awaiting the preparation of the PSR, Carrington, identifying himself as Chad Littles ("Littles"), the Accounts Receivable/Payroll Manager of Quorum International, Ltd. ("Quorum"), opened an account with International Banking Technology, Inc. ("IBT"), of Springfield, Virginia. IBT provides a bank drafting system that allows creditors to collect payment over the phone by having the debtor pre-authorize a one-time debit to his or her account. When IBT is provided with the debtor information by its client, it prepares bank drafts (or permits the client to produce the bank drafts by means of its software) that are deposited by IBT's client into its bank account. When these drafts are processed, the debtor's account is debited and the creditor receives payment. On or about November 16, 1994, Carrington faxed thirty completed Bank Draft Sales Forms ("draft forms") to IBT. These draft forms are used to provide IBT with the information necessary for it to produce the bank drafts for the one-time pre-authorized debits. The draft forms that Carrington faxed to IBT provided all of the necessary information including the name of the company to charge, its checking account number, and the amount of the draft requested to cover the purported pre-authorized one-time debit. Carrington requested that IBT prepare 30 bank drafts of $5,000 each for a total of $150,000, which purportedly was to constitute payment for attendance at a seminar allegedly held by Quorum. Carrington's attempt failed, however, when as part of IBT's fraud control system, it attempted to verify the authorization for some of the bank drafts, and it found that some of the phone numbers were incorrect. Because IBT suspected fraud, it never completed processing Carrington's request, and Carrington failed to obtain the funds he sought.

The conduct charged in Count VI took place in December 1994. On or about December 5, 1994, Carrington, identifying himself as Paul Epstein ("Epstein"), Chief Financial Officer of Citibank, phoned IBT, faxed them an application for bank draft forms, and requested IBT software that would permit him to transmit his requests for bank drafts to IBT by modem. This software also allowed Carrington to receive from

IBT, by modem, the instructions necessary to print the bank drafts at his home. On December 29, 1994, Carrington sent to IBT by modem 80 forms for printing bank drafts at his residence, which were to be used to debit 80 different companies' accounts in varied amounts totaling $583,-443.50. He failed to obtain the total amount sought, receiving and depositing $268,000 into a personal account before the U.S. Secret Service discovered his actions.

Based on the events of November and December 1994, the government filed a superseding information adding two counts of wire fraud, Counts V and VI, to the previous Counts I through IV. Pursuant to a second plea agreement, Carrington waived indictment and pled guilty to all six counts of the superseding information on March 28, 1995. He was sentenced on August 21, 1995.

* * *

Carrington disputes the values assigned by the PSR–that is, the values represented by the prices he promised to pay the dealers he contacted—and adopted by the district court in sentencing, to the four cars that were the subjects of Counts I through IV, respectively. He contends that the district court should instead have valued the car in Count I at $30,000—the amount of money he obtained in the sale of the car—and for Counts II through IV the court should have used the fair wholesale value of the vehicles. Carrington points out that the only reference to valuation in the record, apart from references to "an agreed upon price," is in the FBI agent's affidavit of the car dealer's statements. He adds that the only information on personal knowledge as to the value of any car was the $30,000 willingly paid by a car dealer for the car in Count I. Carrington notes that while the Guidelines use "fair market value" as the measure of the value of stolen property, that rule is not absolute, and in fact, if market value is difficult to ascertain or inadequate to measure the harm to the victim, alternative methods of valuation may be used. U.S.S.G. § 2B1.1, n. 2.

* * *

Carrington's essential contention, without record support, is that the prices he negotiated in relation to the vehicles involved in Counts II through IV were overstated in order to induce the dealers' agreement. But in fact, the PSR suggests that Carrington negotiated the price of each vehicle in an arm's length transaction. Under section 2B1.1, comment. (n.2), a product's fair market value is ordinarily the appropriate value of the victim's loss. Here, it was reasonable, particularly in light of the bargaining between Carrington and the dealers, for the district court to calculate the market value of each vehicle to be the price Carrington negotiated with each dealership. Loss need not be determined with precision, and in fact may be inferred from any reasonably reliable information. Furthermore, it was reasonable for the court to adopt the retail rather than the wholesale values of the cars, since all of the dealerships from whom Carrington obtained the cars were engaged in retail sales of automobiles. As a result, we conclude that the district court did not commit plain error in determining the market value of the vehicles in Counts I through IV.

* * *

Carrington [further] contends that the sentencing court erred in concluding that Counts V and VI were both completed crimes, with a total intended loss of $583,000. He argues that the lack of actual loss counsels for the proposition that Counts V and VI should be classed as mere attempts, pursuant to the Guidelines. *See* U.S.S.G. § 2X1.1(b)(1) (mandating a decrease by 3 levels for an attempt). Thus, he posits, the offense levels for those counts should be lower than those the district court attributed to them.

In making this argument, Carrington confronts our opinion in United States v. Egemonye, 62 F.3d 425 (1st Cir.1995). In that case, the district court calculated loss pursuant to section 2F1.1 based on the total aggregate limits of the credit cards that the defendant wrongfully obtained. The defendant argued that because section 2F1.1 references section 2X1.1 regarding "partially completed offense[s]," and because he had actually inflicted a loss of only about 53 percent of the aggregate credit limit before his scheme was interrupted by arrest, the district court erred in denying him the lower offense level attendant to an only "partially completed" crime.

We rejected the application of section 2X1.1 to the defendant's conduct in *Egemonye*. We noted that there were two competing views of section 2X1.1. It could be viewed as offering a reduction for potential versus completed harm; alternatively, its provisions could be read literally to direct its application only where the defendant has not completed the actions necessary to the substantive offense. In siding with the latter view, we stated that

> [t]here would be nothing irrational in deciding that actual harm is worse than intended harm and providing a three-level discount wherever the sentence for a completed offense is measured in part by intended harm. But this is not in general the philosophy of the guidelines; if it were, possession of drugs with intent to distribute would be punished less harshly than the actual sale of an equivalent amount. . . .

> [T]he cross-references in section 2F1.1 are easily explained; they do invoke the discount, or the possibility of a discount, where the underlying crime is merely an attempt or conspiracy. . . . Here, by contrast, all 51 of the cards were the subject of completed crimes.

Id.

To be sure, Carrington tries to distinguish *Egemonye* from his case. In his brief, Carrington contends that the defendant in *Egemonye* had the credit cards and the present ability to turn the cards into cash, while, with respect to Count V, Carrington would still have had to actively negotiate the drafts even had he received them from IBT. He asserts that he never came close to being in a position to negotiate the drafts. However, Carrington does not dispute that IBT's own fraud control unit prevented him from receiving those drafts. Furthermore, Carrington also does not dispute that he did in fact transmit a wire communication pursuant to a scheme to defraud. As a result, Carrington had completed the necessary elements of the charged offense, wire fraud, just as the defendant in Egemonye had. Thus, we conclude that Egemonye is squarely on point.

In light of *Egemonye*, section 2X1.1 is simply not applicable as Carrington contends. Carrington was convicted under Counts V and VI of wire fraud, not attempted wire fraud or wire fraud conspiracy. The crime of wire fraud does not require that the defendant's object be attained. It only requires that the defendant devise a scheme to defraud and then transmit a wire communication for the purposes of executing the scheme. Here, Carrington completed the necessary acts for the crime of wire fraud in Count V when he faxed thirty bank draft sales form requests to IBT in furtherance of his scheme to obtain $150,000, and in Count VI when he sent by modem eighty transaction requests to IBT in furtherance of his scheme to obtain $583,443.50. Because section 2X1.1 does not apply to completed substantive offenses, we conclude that the district court correctly denied a reduction in offense level pursuant to section 2X1.1. As a result, we find no error of law or application that justifies such a reduction.

* * *

Notes

1. What did you think of Carrington's argument that Counts V and VI should have been treated as attempted offenses for purposes of sentencing? If, as the court pointed out, wire fraud includes inchoate offenses, doesn't Carrington's argument have merit?

On a more basic point, do you agree with the position taken in the Guidelines that attempted offenses should be treated more leniently than completed crimes? Isn't a defendant's intent the same when attempting an offense as when completing an offense, especially in a situation such as *Carrington* where the crime is halted only because the defendant was caught?

2. Consider the calculation of loss in United States v. Galbraith, 20 F.3d 1054 (10th Cir.1994), where the defendant also attempted to commit a fraud:

"Defendant Gary E. Galbraith appeals from a judgment of conviction for one count of wire fraud as an aider and abettor, in violation of 18 U.S.C. § 1343 and 18 U.S.C. § 2(a), (b).

"Defendant and others became involved in a scheme to obtain control of the majority of stock of a public corporation, drive up the price, then sell it to a European pension fund. However, the scheme was, in fact, an undercover sting operation, and the pension fund did not exist. An undercover agent paid defendant $50,000 as a "fee" for his services, although the defendants requested $80,000. The FBI terminated the investigation before any stock was bought or sold.

* * *

"Defendant [contends] * * * that the district court erred in finding, for purposes of sentencing, that the intended or probable loss of the scheme was $80,000, which resulted in a five-level increase in the base offense level of six. * * *

"The government argued that the probable or intended loss should be $623,920, which represented the number of shares owned or controlled by the defendants multiplied by the price at which they intended to offer the shares. Instead, the district court found the probable or intended loss was $80,000, which was the amount defendants requested from the undercover agent as a fee for their services.

* * * Defendant contends that because his offense was committed in response to an undercover sting operation structured so there was no possibility of loss to a victim, the intended or probable loss was zero. He relies on United States v. Sneed, 814 F.Supp. 964 (D.Colo.1993).

"In *Sneed*, the defendant was also caught in an undercover sting operation involving a scheme to manipulate the value of stock. The district court concluded that "the correct loss figure in an undercover 'sting' operation—at least one structured such as this one was—is zero." *Id.* at 969. The court reasoned that it would be a misapplication of the guidelines to rely on the loss that the defendant subjectively thought he was inflicting, as opposed to the loss that his activities probably would have caused in the normal course of events. *Id.* at 970–71.

[U]se of 'intended' loss as a measure of harm under section 2F1.1 is limited by a requirement that a sentencing court examine the circumstances objectively to see whether it was realistically possible for defendant to inflict the intended loss.... Where the scheme could not possibly have resulted in the intended loss under any circumstances, then 'intended' loss should not be used."

Based on the above reasoning the Court revised the sentence, finding that because the loss was zero since Galbraith could not possibly have caused any loss since he was dealing only with an undercover operation. Do you agree? At what amount would you set the loss in Galbraith's case: zero, $80,000., $50,000., or $623,920.? Why?

———

Recall the *Pinkerton* doctrine from conspiracy law (Chapter 1). Observe how this doctrine can affect the calculation of loss when assessing the sentence.

UNITED STATES v. LAFRAUGH

United States Court of Appeals, Eleventh Circuit, 1990.
893 F.2d 314.

HILL, SENIOR CIRCUIT JUDGE.

* * *

In May, 1988, Mr. John Vanucci, the regional security manager at the U.S. Sprint Corporation ("Sprint") received information from Mr. Ron Kaufman, a customer of U.S. Sprint, regarding the unauthorized sale of U.S. Sprint long distance access code numbers. Mr. Kaufman explained that an individual named Ms. Linda Duntley had provided him with two U.S. Sprint long distance access codes for a fee of $125.00 a month; she also informed him that she would provide him with new access codes on a daily basis for unlimited long distance telephone service. Based on this information, Sprint initiated an internal investigation, and learned that from between March 15, 1988 and May 2, 1988, callers had used a total of 57 different long distance access code numbers to make approximately 400 calls from Ms. Duntley's telephone. Sprint brought the results of this investigation to the attention of the United States Secret Service, who obtained a search warrant for Ms. Duntley's business establishment.

The Secret Service executed the warrant on May 27, 1988, and, during the search, found in excess of two hundred and fifty U.S. Sprint access code numbers, indicating an extensive use of these numbers without the knowledge or authorization of Sprint. The search also disclosed Ms. Duntley's answering machine, which in turn revealed that Mr. LaFraugh was the source of these numbers.

In a subsequent interview, Ms. Duntley explained that Mr. LaFraugh first contacted her in the summer of 1987, and that she began purchasing long distance access code numbers from him beginning in December, 1987, or January, 1988. Mr. LaFraugh apparently convinced Ms. Duntley that he (and others) had purchased these numbers from Sprint, and that the numbers still had a number of minutes left on them. Ms. Duntley paid the appellant $100.00 per month, and for that fee she was able to make unlimited telephone calls.

On occasion, Ms. Duntley also received numbers from Mr. Roger LaFraugh, the appellant's brother, from Ms. Marti Matsom, the appellant's girlfriend, from an individual named Tom, and from an individual named Stephen Hayes in New York. Mr. LaFraugh furnished Ms. Duntley with Tom's telephone number; Tom apparently furnished her with the number of Mr. Hayes. Ms. Duntley also introduced her boyfriend to the appellant, and the appellant sold him access code numbers as well.

Thus, as a result of these revelations, Special Agent Dennis Morgan, acting in an undercover capacity and using the name "Lee Murphy," asked Ms. Duntley to contact the appellant, and to have the appellant contact him. On June 7, 1988, Mr. LaFraugh contacted Mr. Morgan by telephone in California from his residence in Riverdale, Georgia. Later, the appellant offered Mr. Morgan unlimited telephone service for $300.00 a month.

As a result of this criminal activity, the government filed a criminal complaint against the appellant, and issued a search warrant for his residence at The Hometown Inn in Riverdale, Georgia. After his arrest, Mr. LaFraugh made a statement to the Secret Service in which he identified his source for the numbers, as well as the names of individuals to whom he had provided the numbers. According to Mr. LaFraugh, Stephen Hayes of Rome, New York, was at the top of the "multi-level pyramid;" however, he had also obtained numbers from both Hugh Leonard and Sue Tani of Long Beach, California, and from Tom Wynkoop of Pompano Beach, Florida.

Sprint officials later determined that the loss on only thirty-five of these numbers was $1,768,733.30. By the date of the sentencing hearing, they determined that the loss on forty-eight of the numbers was $2,012,-483.85.

* * *

On September 27, 1988, a federal grand jury filed [a] superseding indictment charging the appellant with one count of conspiracy, one count of fraud in connection with access devices, two counts of mail fraud, and six counts of wire fraud, in violation of 18 U.S.C. §§ 371, 1029(a)(2), 1341 and 1343. [The defendant pled guilty.]

* * *

The district court's presentence investigation report, in compliance with the Federal Sentencing Guidelines, computed Mr. LaFraugh's initial base offense level as 17, based on the amount of loss, resulting from not only his direct involvement, but from the acts of his co-conspirators as well. * * *

* * *

Mr. LaFraugh * * * contends that the sentencing judge incorrectly applied guideline § 2F1.1(b)(1)(J) to include *all* the losses which Sprint claimed to have sustained as a result of access code fraud. He asserts that he alone did not cause Sprint's $1.7 million loss, either directly or indirectly; he thus contends that the court should not have imputed all losses to him through his role in the admitted conspiracy. Specifically Mr. LaFraugh contends that the district court erred by using the Supreme Court's holding in Pinkerton v. United States, 328 U.S. 640, 646–647 (1946), that "the overt act of the partner in crime is attributable to all," as guidance in the sentencing process, rather than as merely a means of establishing guilt.

We begin by examining the language of the pertinent sentencing guideline. At the time of Mr. LaFraugh's offense, it provided as follows:

Relevant Conduct:

> To determine the seriousness of the offense conduct, all conduct, circumstances, and injuries relevant to the offense of conviction shall be taken into account.
>
> (a) Unless otherwise specified under the guidelines, conduct and circumstances relevant to the offense of conviction [include] acts or omissions committed or aided and abetted by the defendant, *or by a person for whose conduct the defendant is legally accountable, that [are] part of the same course of conduct, or a common scheme or plan, as the offense of conviction . . . .*

Sentencing Guidelines, § 1B1.3 (Oct. 1987). Thus, once a sentencing court determines that certain acts or omissions are "part of the same course of conduct" as the offense of conviction, it may hold the appellant responsible for all losses resulting from acts by participants for whose conduct the court deems him accountable, when applying the specific offense characteristic sections of the guideline's Chapter 2.

We hold that the standards embodied in section 1B1.3 roughly approximate those detailed by the Supreme Court in *Pinkerton*. We do not suggest, of course, that the guidelines in any sense codify the *Pinkerton* rule. We do hold, nevertheless, that the guideline's attribution to the defendant of "acts . . . by a person for whose conduct the defendant is legally accountable, that . . . are part of . . . a common scheme or plan," resembles in essence the *Pinkerton* attribution to co-conspirators of " . . . the same or other acts in furtherance of the conspiracy . . . for the purpose of holding them responsible for the substantive offense." *Pinkerton*, 328 U.S. at 647. Thus we hold that the district court correctly analyzed the factors relevant to Mr. LaFraugh's culpability.

Mr. LaFraugh next contends that, even if the *Pinkerton* doctrine was an appropriate point of reference for the district court, the court nevertheless incorrectly applied the ruling in his case. He contends, in short, that the court should not hold him responsible for the acts of co-conspirators when the evidence showed multiple conspiracies, rather than a single one.

The instant case, as noted, involved a network consisting of Mr. LaFraugh, his brother, and his girlfriend, all of whom would receive stolen access code numbers and would sell them to others. Mr. LaFraugh admitted his involvement after his arrest, and described his position as being in the middle of a "multi-level pyramid." A search of one of Mr. LaFraugh's customers produced over 250 stolen access numbers, most of which the customer attributed to Mr. LaFraugh.

Appellant now contends that, under the wheel analogy developed by the Supreme Court in Kotteakos v. United States, 328 U.S. 750 (1946), the conspiracy in his case produced a hub, (Mr. LaFraugh), and various spokes, (the central actors), but no rim (i.e. shared knowledge and common purpose) encircling the spokes. Thus, he argues, the evidence showed only a series of multiple conspiracies, leaving him responsible only for losses resulting from those in which he actually participated. Appellees, on the other hand, contend that the conspiracy can best be likened to a single chain, with responsibility flowing to each participant.

We begin in utter sympathy with the sentiments expressed by our predecessor, the Fifth Circuit, over fifteen years ago:

> As for us, the problem is difficult enough without trying to compress it into figurative analogies. Conspiracies are as complex as the versatility of human nature and federal protection against them is not to be measured by spokes, hubs, wheels, rims, chains, or any one or all of today's galaxy of mechanical, molecular or atomic forms.

United States v. Perez, 489 F.2d 51, 59 n. 11 (5th Cir.1973). We, too, prefer to examine these facts without recourse to the tempting, but ultimately confining, appeal of extended metaphors. As the Fifth Circuit has noted, "if there is one overall agreement among the various parties to perform different functions in order to carry out the objectives of the conspiracy, then it is one conspiracy." (citation omitted.) *Perez*, 489 F.2d at 62. That logic, surely, is enough to guide us in our determination today.

Here, the appellant was involved in a business called "Service Amongst Friends Enterprises," whose purpose was to distribute long distance access code numbers to others, thereby generating his profit. The appellant himself identified the source of these numbers, as well as the names of others from whom he also obtained them. According to Mr. LaFraugh, Mr. Hayes was at the top of what the appellant called a "multi-level pyramid"; others involved in distribution included Mr. Leonard, Ms. Tani, and Mr. Wynkoop. Ms. Duntley explained that she received Mr. Wynkoop's name and number from the appellant; when she contacted him, he gave her some numbers and the telephone number of Mr. Hayes. Mr. Hayes himself later provided Ms. Duntley with numbers. The appellant distributed those numbers to his brother, his girlfriend, Ms. Duntley and Mr. Jack Campbell. With this scenario in mind, we do not hesitate to find a common purpose among the various defendants. As the Supreme Court has said:

> The scheme was in fact the same scheme; the [participants] knew or must have known that others unknown to them were sharing in so large a project; and it hardly can be sufficient to relieve them that they did not know, when they joined the scheme, who those people were or exactly the parts they were playing in carrying out the common design and object of it all. By these separate agreements, if such they were, they became parties to the larger common plan, joined together by this knowledge of its essential features and broad scope, though not of its exact limits, and by their common single goal.

Blumenthal v. United States, 332 U.S. 539, 558 (1947). We hold, therefore, that the record amply supports the district court's finding that Mr.

LaFraugh was a member of a single conspiracy which was responsible for Sprint's entire loss.

* * *

Notes

What do you think about following the *Pinkerton* approach in sentencing?

4. ADJUSTMENTS AND DEPARTURES

As noted in the introductory remarks to this section, Chapters 2 and 3 of the United States Sentencing Guidelines direct courts to determine whether upward or downward adjustments in the base offense level are warranted. The first case in this section, United States v. Connell, 960 F.2d 191 (1st Cir.1992), discusses some issues which arise regarding adjustments.

Chapter 5 of the Sentencing Guidelines directs courts to consider whether a case contains "unusual features" which warrant an upward or downward departure after the base offense level and adjustments have been calculated. The last case in this section, United States v. Grandmaison, 77 F.3d 555 (1st Cir.1996), addresses departures.

UNITED STATES v. CONNELL

United States Court of Appeals, First Circuit, 1992.
960 F.2d 191.

SELYA, CIRCUIT JUDGE.

This appeal, in which the appellant complains that the government practiced "sentencing entrapment," calls upon us to venture onto *terra incognita*. Believing, as we do, that the district court did not err in accepting the fruits of the government's activities, we turn a deaf ear to the appellant's complaint. We also overrule his objection to a "special skill" adjustment made by the lower court in constructing the guideline sentencing range (GSR). Withal, an intervening change in the law leads us to remand the matter for reconsideration of the sentence originally imposed.

* * *

Defendant-appellant Gerald Connell pled guilty to a single count charging that he structured financial transactions for the purpose of evading federal currency reporting requirements in violation of 31 U.S.C. § 5324. The trial judge fixed the GSR at twenty-seven/thirty-three months (offense level 18/criminal history category I) and, on June 26, 1991, sentenced Connell to a thirty month prison term. * * *

The appellant was a stockbroker with the firm of Barrett & Company, Middletown, Rhode Island. In the spring of 1989, a Newport-area attorney introduced him to "Bill Ross." Although Ross held himself out to be a financial consultant and "front man" for anonymous persons desirous of laundering money, he was a counterfeit bill. In reality, Ross was an agent of the Internal Revenue Service (IRS), bent on investigating money laundering activities in Rhode Island. After a series of preliminary meetings, Connell began to launder money at Ross's behest.

The scheme worked this way. Connell opened a series of bank accounts in his own name at various banking institutions and established a money market account (the MMA) in Ross's name at Barrett & Company. Knowing that federal law required financial institutions to file currency transaction reports (CTRs) with the IRS for all cash transactions in excess of $10,000, Connell took cash from Ross, divided it into increments of less than $10,000, and spread the smaller increments among the bank accounts that he had opened. Connell eventually withdrew the money from the accounts, again in amounts under $10,000, and deposited the funds into the MMA. He also purchased stock in his own name, for Ross's benefit. No CTRs were filed for any of these myriad money shuffles.

Appellant did Ross's bidding on four separate occasions. He accepted $16,000 in cash on June 21, 1989; $25,000 on June 29; $15,000 on July 20; and, finally, $25,000 on March 21, 1990. Appellant's motivation seems to have been the gossamer prospect of playing a part in future business deals involving Ross and Ross's principals. In any event, he declined Ross's offer of a set fee for services rendered.

Throughout his conversations with Ross, Connell indicated an awareness that structuring cash transactions to avoid filing CTRs was a violation of federal law. Connell was not, however, aggressively inquisitive as to the origin of the funds. During their first meeting, Ross told Connell that the money was coming from an elaborate gambling operation in Atlantic City (whether legal or illegal, Ross did not specify). On three occasions in early 1990, Ross told Connell that he was laundering money derived from the illegal drug trade. All the relevant conversations were tape-recorded.

* * *

Appellant does not contest the legitimacy of the sting operation per se. Rather, his opposition to the five-level enhancement is built upon the claim that Ross gratuitously spun a yarn about the illicit origin of the funds for the sole purpose of guaranteeing that appellant's punishment would be increased. The appellant describes this conduct as "sentencing entrapment." In the relatively brief period since the advent of the federal sentencing guidelines, we have not had the occasion to analyze a comparable claim.

To be sure, appellant acknowledges that government-supplied funds, produced in the course of a sting operation, can trigger the five-level enhancement. But in this case, he contends that the vice lay in the timing: by broaching the subject of the currency's supposed origin (drug trafficking) only after Connell had fully completed three episodes of money laundering, the undercover agent forced (or lured) him into actions he would otherwise have eschewed, i.e., peripheral participation in the narcotics trade. This Machiavellian scenario, Connell adds, was orchestrated for the sole purpose of boosting the sentence he would ultimately receive. In mounting this attack, appellant relies heavily upon two cases which, while affirming sentences imposed by district judges, mention in dicta that a creature such as "sentencing entrapment" might be roaming loose in the guidelines jungle and, under certain unspecified circumstances, might warrant a downward departure from the GSR.

As a preliminary matter, we prefer to dismiss the inexact, albeit catchy, label that Connell uses. By his guilty plea, appellant freely admitted that he was predisposed to structure cash transactions. Hence, there was no basis for an entrapment defense on the merits. While it is problematic whether the appellant was predisposed to do business with drug dealers, his predisposition to engage in illegal currency transactions makes the use of the term "sentencing entrapment" both inapposite and misleading. His complaint, at bottom, is that the government practiced what might more accurately be called "sentencing factor manipulation."

By definition, there is an element of manipulation in any sting operation. The question presented here presupposes as much. It requires us to consider whether the manipulation inherent in a sting operation, even if insufficiently oppressive to support an entrapment defense, must sometimes be filtered out of the sentencing calculus. So framed, the question brings to mind much that has been written and stated about the opportunities that the sentencing guidelines pose for prosecutors to gerrymander the district courts' sentencing options and thus, defendants' sentences. It is unsurprising, therefore, that challenges to the manipulative powers available to prosecutors and investigators under the sentencing guidelines have arisen in a rich variety of situations.

At first blush, this case seems to present the problem in bold relief. But on close perscrutation of the record, appellant's argument, whatever its theoretical possibilities may portend for other cases, falters on an inadequate factual foundation. Assuming, arguendo, that prior to February of 1990, Connell did not know the funds were criminally derived, there is no doubt that he was clearly on notice thereafter. On February 28, 1990, Ross told Connell that he was "going to have cash coming in ... [that] is not very clean money. It's narcotics money." Connell inquired as to the wellspring of Ross's knowledge. Ross replied that his boss had mistakenly given him a valise containing "the pure white stuff." On March 7, 1990, Ross requested that appellant transfer some funds for him by wire. During this conversation, Ross mentioned that the funds were "payment for some narcotic[s]." Two weeks later, during a desultory discussion, Ross described his principals' business as "100% narcotics." These conversations, all of which were tape-recorded and all of which occurred prior to the final episode of money laundering, provided a sturdy predicate for the section 2S1.3(b)(1) enhancement. The only remaining question is whether the circumstances surrounding Ross's interweaving of narcotics into the fabric of an ongoing crime in some way constituted a mitigating factor for sentencing purposes. The district court thought not. We agree.

Appellant asserts that by the time the specter of drug profits surfaced, he was too far into the money laundering scheme to extricate himself, notwithstanding his aversion to facilitating the drug trade. Appellant also asserts that his newfound knowledge placed him in harm's way should he refuse to continue with the scheme. But, these assertions mix conjecture with fact. We reject them for several reasons, citing two.

First, nothing in this record suggests that Ross lured appellant into committing a lesser crime, only to exploit his vulnerability at a later date. To the contrary, dating back to appellant's earliest contact with Ross, the record is barren of any whisper of a hint of an intimation that appellant cared in the least about the breed of Ross's cash cow—and common sense counsels that, if the funds were not tainted, the need for appellant's services would never have arisen. One does not normally launder either clean clothes or clean money. In fine, the nature of the ongoing criminal activity was not materially altered by Ross's revelations. The court below was, therefore, entitled to conclude that laundering drug money came within the encincture of appellant's original decision to abandon the straight and narrow.

Second, whether Connell found the prospect of doing business with drug dealers distasteful is not the issue. The subject of narcotics was explicitly broached almost a month before the last money laundering episode occurred and was discussed on three occasions prior to the delivery of the final cash installment. Ross did not embellish his announcement of the money's source with any sort of threat. There is absolutely no indication that Ross coerced Connell in any way or tempted him with promises of greater rewards. Similarly, there is no indication that Connell was more at risk midstream than was the case at the outset of the venture.

We need not paint the lily. Appellant was given ample time and opportunity to ponder his newly acquired knowledge and, should he so elect, bow out of the scheme. The facts clearly show that he made a different choice: to carry out the March 1990 assignment with full awareness that he was handling drug money. For aught that appears, appellant continued to participate in money laundering to the bitter end for the same reason that he participated originally—his hope that Ross (and Ross's principals) would some day steer legitimate business his way. On the facts of this case, the sentencing court's decision to apply the five-level enhancement was not clearly erroneous.

Although we find no grounds for concern in the circumstances at bar, we think it advisable to reflect upon the ramifications of Connell's basic premise. It cannot be gainsaid that the sentencing guidelines, by their very nature, may afford the opportunity for sentencing factor manipulation, particularly in sting operations. We can foresee situations in which exploitative manipulation of sentencing factors by government agents might overbear the will of a person predisposed only to committing a lesser crime. This danger seems especially great in cases where the accused's sentence depends in large part on the quantity of drugs or money involved. There is, however, another side to the story. By their nature, sting operations are designed to tempt the criminally inclined, and a well-constructed sting is often sculpted to test the limits of the target's criminal inclinations. Courts should go very slowly before staking out rules that will deter government agents from the proper performance of their investigative duties.

While noting the existence of this inevitable tension, we make no effort today to chart the line between permissible and impermissible conduct on the part of government agents insofar as that conduct may have an impact upon the district court's sentencing options. We are confident that, should a sufficiently egregious case appear, the sentencing court has ample power to deal with the situation either by excluding the tainted transaction from the computation of relevant conduct or by departing from the GSR.

* * *

Appellant's second assignment of error implicates U.S.S.G. § 3B1.3. The guidelines authorize a two-level enhancement if the defendant "abused a position of public or private trust, or used a special skill, in a manner that significantly facilitated the commission or concealment of the offense." *Id.* The prosecution has the burden of proving, by a fair preponderance of the evidence, that section 3B1.3 applies in a given situation. In the case at hand, the lower court decided that the prosecution had carried the devoir of persuasion twice over, finding that appellant had both abused a position of private trust and employed a special skill in order significantly to facilitate his crime. We determine the legal meaning of the term "special skill" de novo. Thereafter, since the district court's application of section 3B1.3 to a given set of circumstances is likely to involve drawing sophisticated inferences from a web of interconnecting facts, we review the district court's findings only for clear error.

We begin, and end, by addressing the special skill issue. We must ask two questions: Did appellant possess a special skill within the purview of the guidelines? If so, did appellant use that skill in order significantly to facilitate the commission or concealment of his crime? The court below answered both of these queries in the affirmative. We find no fault with the court's answers.

The application notes define a special skill as "a skill not possessed by members of the general public and usually requiring substantial education, training or licensing." U.S.S.G. § 3B1.3, comment (n.2). As examples of individuals who possess special skills, the application notes list "pilots, lawyers, doctors, accountants, chemists, and demolition experts." *Id.* In this instance, the appellant is a registered stockbroker. As such, he has undergone specialized training. He has met certain licensing requirements. His field of endeavor (the securities industry) is subject to stringent regulation. We hold that the specialized knowledge required of a stockbroker, when combined with the ability to access financial markets directly, can qualify as a special skill within the meaning of U.S.S.G. § 3B1.3.

Thus, the issue reduces to whether the special skill that Connell possessed "significantly facilitated the commission or concealment" of his crime. U.S.S.G. § 3B1.3. The question is not free from doubt. On the one hand, the money laundering system that Connell used was relatively straightforward. The opening of multiple bank accounts, the division of the initial sums into smaller increments, and their subsequent deposit into the accounts required no special skill. And, while a person who was not a stockbroker would have needed a stockbroker (or a banker) to open a money market account, this feat could have been accomplished by a layman without undue difficulty and without arousing any suspicion. Standing alone, such activity would not justify a section 3B1.3 enhancement.

Appellant's ability to make and process deposits to the MMA without having to explain the origin of the funds to a third party is a horse of another hue. In a matter of months, Connell laundered $81,000 through the MMA. We think this to be a substantial enough sum that any third party would have been curious as to its source. Because Connell was able to process these transactions himself, he was able to avoid inquiring eyes and embarrassing questions, thereby substantially lessening the chance that he would be caught. He was also able to buy stock in a way that shielded the identity of the true owner. We doubt that a layman could have done as much, as effectively. In the last analysis, the availability of a section 3B1.3 enhancement requires only that the use of the defendant's special skill has "significantly facilitated the commission or concealment of the offense"; it does not require a showing that, but for the use of a special skill, the defendant would have been unable to perpetrate the crime. On balance, we conclude that Connell's special skill was sufficiently facilitative to support an upward adjustment. *See id.* (facilitative conduct occurs whenever defendant's special skill makes it significantly easier to conceal the offense of conviction).

Finding that appellant possessed a special skill and used it to conceal his crime does not end our inquiry. The guideline specifically provides that the special skill "adjustment may not be employed if ... [the] skill is included in the base offense level or specific offense characteristic." U.S.S.G. § 3B1.3. In such a situation, enhancing the defendant's sentence would constitute impermissible double counting. Because it is crystal clear that the special skill possessed by stockbrokers, as a class, was not factored into the base offense level for the crime of conviction, our focus centers on the specific offense characteristics.

The essence of illegally structuring monetary transactions is the defendant's ability to convert large sums of cash into smaller sums, thereafter passing the smaller sums through a bank account or investment medium in a way that avoids the need for filing CTRs. In its simplest form, the crime does not demand any detailed or specialized knowledge of financial markets or banking practices. Appellant's use of his skill as a stockbroker to conceal his crime was not a necessary concomitant to the commission of the offense; it merely made matters easier (and less risky) for him. It was, a fortiori, not a specific offense characteristic within the meaning of the sentencing guidelines.

For these reasons, we decline to disturb the district court's assessment of a two-level enhancement under U.S.S.G. § 3B1.3.

Notes

1. "Ross" conducted four transactions with Connell. In conversations with Connell, Ross left it unclear whether the funds involved in the first three transactions were from legal or illegal sources (Ross represented that the funds came from an elaborate gambling operation in Atlantic City). By the last transaction, however, Ross clearly represented that the funds were derived from an illegal activity (drug dealing). Why do you think Ross changed his story on the last transaction? Was it to see how crooked Connell truly was, or was it to enhance the sentence? Does it matter why Ross changed his story to Connell? In your opinion, is a stockbroker who is willing to launder drug money deserving of greater punishment than a stockbroker who balks when the laundering changes from legally derived funds to illegally derived funds?

2. A defendant bears the burden of establishing sentencing entrapment (also called "sentencing manipulation") by a preponderance of the evidence. Although "sentencing entrapment" is raised regularly, few defendants have been successful in producing sufficient evidence that the government engaged in sentencing entrapment.[tt] Some courts reject, as a matter of law, the possibility of sentencing enhancement or manipulation.[uu] The Seventh Circuit explained its skepticism about a claim of sentencing manipulation:

> "If we are willing to accept the assumption apparently approved by Congress that [for example] dealing in greater quantities of drugs is a greater evil, it is not clear to us what the precise legal objection to governmental behavior based on cognizance of relative penal consequences in this area could be (so long as it does not rise to the level of true entrapment or [outrageous government] conduct)."

United States v. Okey, 47 F.3d 238, 240 (7th Cir.1995). Is this a "do the crime, do the time" argument? Do you believe sentencing entrapment can occur?

In the next case, United States v. Grandmaison, 77 F.3d 555 (1st Cir.1996), which involves a mail fraud prosecution for breach of fiduciary

---

tt. *See, e.g.*, United States v. Gibbens, 25 F.3d 28 (1st Cir.1994); United States v. Shephard, 4 F.3d 647 (8th Cir.1993); United States v. Richardson, 925 F.2d 112 (5th Cir.1991). *Compare* United States v. Staufer, 38 F.3d 1103, 1106 (9th Cir.1994) (Ninth Circuit remanded for resentencing after finding that the defendant had been entrapped to engage in a larger drug transaction than was his custom).

uu. *See, e.g.*, United States v. Williams, 954 F.2d 668, 673 (11th Cir.1992).

duty, the defendant sought a downward departure on three grounds. As you read the opinion of the Court of Appeals, determine whether you agree with the trial court or the appellate court.

UNITED STATES v. GRANDMAISON

United States Court of Appeals, First Circuit, 1996.
77 F.3d 555.

BOWNES, SENIOR CIRCUIT JUDGE.

On February 8, 1995, pursuant to a plea agreement with the government, defendant-appellant Philip Joseph Grandmaison ("Grandmaison") pled guilty to a one count information charging him with utilizing the mail system to defraud Nashua, New Hampshire, citizens of their right to the honest services of their public officials, in violation of 18 U.S.C. §§ 1341, 1346. Grandmaison now appeals the eighteen-month sentence of imprisonment he received, contending that the district court failed to depart downward from the minimum prison term mandated by the Sentencing Guidelines ("Guidelines") because of the erroneous view that it lacked authority to do so. We agree that the district court misapprehended its authority to depart downward on aberrant behavior grounds. * * * Accordingly, we vacate the sentence and remand to the district court for a determination of whether a downward departure on the basis of aberrant behavior is warranted in this case. * * *

I. THE FACTS

We consider the facts as set forth in the unobjected-to portions of the Presentence Investigation Report ("PSR"), the information to which defendant pled guilty, and the sentencing hearing transcript. Grandmaison served as an "at-large" member on the Nashua Board of Alderman ("Board") from 1986 to 1993. The Board consists of fifteen members—six of whom are elected at-large and nine of whom are elected from one of Nashua's nine electoral wards—and functions as Nashua's chief legislative arm, enacting municipal legislation and approving all financing and municipal construction projects. Grandmaison served on the Board's Secondary School Coordinating Committee ("SSCC") and the Joint Special School Building Committee ("JSSBC").

Like many of his aldermanic colleagues, Grandmaison also had a full-time job. He was employed as Marketing Director of the Eckman Construction Company ("Eckman Construction"), a Bedford, New Hampshire-based company, from 1989 to 1993. In addition to his job as Eckman Construction's Marketing Director, Grandmaison participated in a number of charitable activities.

In 1990, the Board began seeking construction bids for a $6.3 million project, the renovation of Nashua's sixty-year old Elm Street Junior High School. Both the SSCC and the JSSBC, the two committees on which Grandmaison served, play integral roles in selecting a school construction contractor and in overseeing the construction process. The SSCC, *inter alia*, preselects school construction contractors, oversees school construction or renovation work, and makes recommendations concerning contractor expenditures and payments. The JSSBC, which is comprised of both aldermen and Nashua School Board members, reviews the SSCC's recommendations regarding contractors, payments, and contract modifications.

Eckman Construction submitted a bid for the lucrative Elm Street School Project contract. In spite of the conflict in interest, Grandmaison remained on both the SSCC and the JSSBC for months after Eckman Construction submitted its bid. He publicly excused himself from both committees on January 9, 1991, but only after questions were raised about his connections to Eckman Construction. The subcommittee vacancies created by Grandmaison's departures were filled by Alderman Thomas Magee ("Magee"), an at-large member of the Board and purported construction aficionado.

After recusal from the SSCC and JSSBC, Grandmaison continued as an at-large member of the Board. He also secretly took steps to manipulate the contacts he enjoyed as an alderman to Eckman Construction's advantage. From February 1991 until shortly before the Elm Street Project was completed, Grandmaison lobbied three of his aldermanic colleagues—Magee, Steve Kuchinski ("Kuchinski"), and Anne Ackerman ("Ackerman"), SSCC chairperson—on Eckman Construction's behalf. Grandmaison distributed informational materials and video cassettes about Eckman construction to both Ackerman and Magee. At the behest of Hal Eckman ("Eckman"), president of Eckman Construction, Grandmaison gave gratuities, gifts, and other things of value to Kuchinski, Magee, and Ackerman before and after major contract selection votes. These gratuities and gift items included pay-per-view sporting events, dinners, money, campaign contributions, and promises of future political support. Grandmaison also extended Ackerman a personal loan and steered Eckman Construction printing jobs to the printing business she owned.

These lobbying efforts eventually bore fruit. In June 1991, the Board awarded the Elm Street Project contract to Eckman Construction by a vote of eight to seven, with Kuchinski casting the tie-breaking vote. The project contract, which the Board subsequently mailed to Eckman Construction, served as the basis for the charges brought against Grandmaison. The government charged Grandmaison with violating 18 U.S.C. §§ 1341, 1346, the mail fraud statute. Specifically, it maintained that Grandmaison utilized the mail system to forward a fraudulent scheme in violation of the oath of honest, faithful, and impartial service he took before becoming an alderman and a host of state and local laws pertaining, inter alia, to conflicts of interest, influencing discretionary decisions by public servants, and acceptance of pecuniary benefits by public officials. The government also prosecuted Magee and Kuchinski for their roles in this case.

Pursuant to a plea agreement with the government, Grandmaison pled guilty to a one count information charging him with utilizing the mail system to defraud Nashua citizens of their right to the honest services of their public officials. The district court scheduled a sentencing hearing and prior thereto received a PSR from the Probation Department. The PSR prepared by the Probation Department recommended a total adjusted guideline offense level of fifteen. This recommendation reflects an eight level increase in the base offense because a public official in a decision making position committed the crime and a three level decrease for acceptance of responsibility. * * *

II. THE SENTENCING HEARING

At the sentencing hearing, Grandmaison requested a downward departure to an offense level of eight, which corresponds to a sentencing range of zero to six months. Grandmaison based this request on three interrelated grounds: 1) his criminal conduct constituted "aberrant behavior" within the meaning of Guidelines Manual Ch. 1, Pt. A, Introduction ¶ 4(d); 2) his extraordinary contributions to family, friends, and the community were not adequately addressed by the Guidelines; and 3) the facts of his case warranted a downward departure by analogy to section 2C1.3 of the Guidelines. The defense also submitted one hundred letters attesting to Grandmaison's good deeds and character at the sentencing hearing. Based on these letters and Grandmaison's prior record, the government agreed that downward departure on aberrant behavior grounds was appropriate and recommended a reduced prison sentence of twelve months and one day.

The district court declined to depart downward on any of the three grounds advanced by Grandmaison. The court, citing our decision in United States v. Catucci, 55 F.3d 15, 19 n. 3 (1st Cir.1995), as support, found that a "downward departure based on 'aberrant behavior,'"though generally available under the Guidelines, "was not available as a matter of law" in this case. It concluded that Grandmaison's conduct did not fall within the definition of aberrant behavior. The definition adopted by the court required a showing of first-offender status, behavior inconsistent with otherwise good or exemplary character, and spontaneity or thoughtlessness in committing the crime of conviction.

Next, the court concluded that the facts did not warrant downward departure on the basis of Grandmaison's contribution to family, friends, and the community. It did not make a specific finding on the section 2C1.3 claim raised by Grandmaison, but did state that "no other grounds ... advanced [by defendant or the government] ... would justify departure downward." Accordingly, the court adopted the PSR's factual findings and offense calculations in full. Honoring the government's request for leniency, the court selected the lowest end of the applicable guideline range and sentenced Grandmaison to an eighteen month term of imprisonment and two years of supervised release. The court also assessed Grandmaison $50.00, as required by statute.

III.   REFUSALS TO DEPART FROM THE GUIDELINES

Before addressing the three grounds on which defendant rests his appeal, we briefly discuss the rules pertaining to refusals to depart from sentences prescribed by the Guidelines. Under the Sentencing Reform Act, sentencing courts are expected to apply the Guidelines, adjust the base offense level as the facts require, calculate a sentencing range, and impose a sentence within the identified range. In general, sentencing courts are to regard "each guideline as carving out a 'heartland,' a set of typical cases embodying the conduct each guideline describes." Guidelines Manual Ch. 1, Pt. A, Introduction comment 4(b). Departures are warranted only where a case is atypical or where the facts are significantly outside the norm.

Decisions to depart generally fall into one of three categories: forbidden, discouraged, and encouraged. Forbidden departures are those based, *inter alia*, on race, sex, national origin, creed, religion, or socioeconomic status. The Sentencing Commission ("Commission") has expressly precluded departure on these grounds, even where they make a case atypical or extraordinary. Discouraged departures involve factors which were considered by the Commission—such as age, family ties and responsibilities, employment record, good works, or physical condition—but which present themselves to an extraordinary degree in a particular case. Encouraged departures, in contrast, involve considerations not previously taken into account by the Commission.

Because the Commission intended departures on any grounds to be the exception rather than the rule, a district court's refusal to depart—upward or downward—is ordinarily not appealable. The well-established rule is that appellate courts lack jurisdiction to review discretionary district court decisions not to depart from sentences imposed under the Guidelines.

There are, however, certain exceptions to this rule. Appellate jurisdiction attaches, for example, where the record indicates that the trial court's failure to depart was the product of a mistake of law. If it appears that a misapprehension of the applicable guideline or miscalculation of the authority to deviate from the guideline range prevented the court from departing downward, appellate review is appropriate.

Our review as to whether such a misapprehension of judicial authority occurred is plenary. Plenary review also governs where the issue on appeal pertains to the scope or interpretation of a guideline.

IV.   DISCUSSION

The crux of Grandmaison's appeal is that the district court misunderstood the scope of its departure authority. He argues that the court erroneously concluded that it was precluded from departing downward on the grounds of aberrant behavior and extraordinary offender characteristics. Additionally, he maintains that the court misapprehended its power to depart downward by analogy to section 2C1.3 of the Guidelines, which concerns conflicts of interest. * * *

A.   Aberrant Behavior as a Basis for Downward Departure.

* * *

The record reveals that the district court understood its general authority to depart on aberrant behavior grounds, but adopted the wrong standard in determining whether defendant's behavior was "aberrant" under the Guidelines. The court erroneously held that an aberrant behavior departure in this Circuit requires an initial finding of "spontaneity" or a "thoughtless act." Anticipating our review, the court also made it clear that it would have granted the departure requests entered by both defendant and the government had it not believed itself bound to this standard:

> THE COURT: And so I'm going to sentence you at the lowest end of the guidelines range that otherwise is applicable in your case. If the Court of Appeals disagrees with my interpretation of aberrant behavior and the case is returned, if it helps the Court of Appeals in terms of imposing sentence on appeal or resolving the question on appeal, assuming you do appeal, I will say on the record that if I thought I could depart on a principled basis and consistent with the law, I would follow the U.S. Attorney's recommendation and I would sentence you to one year—12 months and one day.

Based on this statement, we think it plain that the court misunderstood its authority to depart downward under the law of this Circuit.

* * * The district court's misapprehension of its departure authority confers jurisdiction on this court. The de novo standard of review governs our review of this aspect of defendant's claim.

* * *

The Guidelines refer to "single acts of aberrant behavior," but neither define that phrase nor provide any insight into what the Commission might have meant when it used it. Defendant's claim presents an issue of first impression in this Circuit. We have considered cases involving departure requests based on aberrant behavior, but have not had occasion to define that term with specificity until now. United States v. Catucci, 55 F.3d 15, 19 n. 3 (1st Cir.1995), which the district court erroneously regarded as foreclosing departure, did not require us to define "aberrant behavior." In that case, we acknowledged disagreement among the circuits as to what type of conduct aberrant behavior entails but did not deem it necessary to articulate a definition for our own Circuit because we found that the defendant had waived his departure claim. Grandmaison's claim, in contrast, hinges on an articulation of an aberrant behavior standard. We, therefore, turn our attention to that task.

Two cases establish what have come to be recognized as the outer boundaries of the aberrant behavior spectrum. United States v. Russell, 870 F.2d 18 (1st Cir.1989), stands at one end of the spectrum and United States v. Carey, 895 F.2d 318 (7th Cir.1990), at the other. *Russell* involved criminal conduct which was impulsive and unpremeditated. Tempted by the prospect of instant wealth, a Wells Fargo armored truck driver and his partner decided to keep an extra bag of money mistakenly handed them. The driver, who had no prior criminal record, returned the money almost immediately after committing his crime and cooperated in the subsequent police investigation. In contrast, *Carey* involved a premeditated criminal scheme carried out over a long period of time. There, a trucking company president engaged in a check-kiting scheme over a fifteen-month period. Each work day during this period the company president concealed his two over-drawn bank accounts by having his bookkeeper prepare checks to cover the fund shortage. He signed each check and frequently deposited them himself. The Seventh Circuit held that this behavior was not "aberrant." Uncertainty about the reason for the district court's refusal to depart precluded this court from deciding that issue in Russell.

Circuit courts are divided over where criminal conduct must fall on the aberrant behavior spectrum to justify downward departure. As we noted in *Catucci*, some have adopted an expansive view of what aberrant behavior means in the context of the Guidelines, whereas others require a spontaneous or thoughtless act of the sort committed by the defendant in *Russell*. The Seventh Circuit's decision in *Carey* provided the moorings for the latter group of circuits. The *Carey* court held that "[a] single act of aberrant behavior ... generally contemplates a spontaneous and seemingly thoughtless act rather than one which was the result of substantial planning because an act which occurs suddenly and is not the result of a continued reflective process is one for which the defendant may be arguably less accountable." 895 F.2d at 325. The Seventh Circuit later reinforced this tight interpretation in United States v. Andruska, 964 F.2d 640, 645–46 (7th Cir.1992), a decision reversing a district court's decision to depart downward in a case involving a woman found guilty of concealing her fugitive paramour from arrest.

The Third, Fourth, Fifth, and Eighth Circuits have embraced the Seventh Circuit's view of aberrant behavior. For example, in United States v. Marcello, 13 F.3d 752 (3d Cir. 1994), the Third Circuit explained that "there must be some element of abnormal or exceptional behavior" before adopting the Seventh Circuit's spontaneity requirement and reversing the district court's decision to depart downward. The *Marcello* defendant was an attorney who, on seven separate occasions, structured bank deposits to avoid tax reporting requirements in violation of 31 U.S.C. §§ 5322(a), 5324(a)(3). He committed these offenses over the span of seven consecutive working days.

* * *

In contrast, the Ninth and Tenth Circuits have eschewed any focus on spontaneity and thoughtlessness, opting instead for a broad view of aberrant behavior. They require reviewing courts to employ the totality of the circumstances test in making aberrant behavior determinations. Under this test, courts consider a variety of mitigating factors, such as pecuniary gain to the defendant, prior good deeds, and an effort to mitigate the effects of the crime in evaluating whether a defendant's conduct was unusual or, more specifically, "aberrant." *See, e.g.*, United States v. Takai, 941 F.2d 738, 741 (9th Cir.1991).

In *Takai*, the Ninth Circuit affirmed the district court's decision to depart downward after finding that the defendants who pled guilty to bribery of and conspiracy to bribe an Immigration and Naturalization Service official, *inter alia*, received no pecuniary gain, had no criminal record, and had been influenced by a government agent. A convergence of factors, such as the defendant's manic depression, suicidal tendencies, and recent unemployment, also led the Ninth Circuit to affirm downward departure in United States v. Fairless, 975 F.2d 664 (9th Cir.1992), an armed robbery case. Similarly, in United States v. Pena, 930 F.2d 1486, 1494 (10th Cir.1991), a drug possession case, the Tenth Circuit held that downward departure was appropriate because the defendant's behavior was an aberration from her usual conduct, which was highlighted by long-term employment, no abuse or prior distribution of controlled substances, and economic support of her family.

We are persuaded, after reviewing the cases decided by our colleagues in other circuits, that the approach taken by the Ninth and Tenth Circuits achieves the balance between uniformity in sentencing and district court discretion the Guidelines were intended to strike. We, thus, hold that determinations about whether an offense constitutes a single act of aberrant behavior should be made by reviewing the totality of the circumstances. District court judges may consider, *inter alia*, factors such as pecuniary gain to the defendant, charitable activities, prior good deeds, and efforts to mitigate the effects of the crime in deciding whether a defendant's conduct is aberrant in terms of other crimes. Spontaneity and thoughtlessness may also be among the factors considered, though they are not prerequisites for departure.

That aberrant behavior departures are available to first offenders whose course of criminal conduct involves more than one criminal act is implicit in our holding. We think the Commission intended the word "single" to refer to the crime committed and not to the various acts involved. As a result, we read the Guidelines' reference to "single acts of aberrant behavior" to include multiple acts leading up to the commission of a crime. Any other reading would produce an absurd result. District courts would be reduced to counting the number of acts involved in the commission of a crime to determine whether departure is warranted. Moreover, the practical effect of such an interpretation would be to make aberrant behavior departures virtually unavailable to most defendants because almost every crime involves a series of criminal acts. Even the Russell defendant, whose spontaneous actions are widely regarded as a classic example of aberrant behavior, could be understood to have committed more than a single act of aberrant behavior. He conspired with his partner to take money from the armored truck he drove; took the money; and then kept the money for a short period of time. Thus, we think that focusing on the crime of conviction instead of the criminal acts committed in carrying out that crime best comports with what the Commission intended.

The approach we now adopt does not unnecessarily expand opportunities for departure under the Guidelines. The totality of the circumstances test, though admittedly broader than the spontaneity test employed in *Carey*, is consistent with the Commission's intention to limit applications of the aberrant behavior principle. Concerns that it ensures every first offender a downward departure from their Guidelines-imposed sentence are without foundation. As the Ninth Circuit explained in United States v. Dickey, 924 F.2d 836, 838 (9th Cir.1991), "aberrant behavior and first offense are not synonymous." Without more, first-offender status is not enough to warrant downward departure.

* * *

The question now becomes whether defendant's conduct falls within the ambit of aberrant behavior under the standard we have articulated. We leave this to the district court's discretion. It occupies the best vantage point from which to make the decision. We, therefore, vacate defendant's sentence and remand for resentencing.

B. Extraordinary Offender Characteristics as a Basis for Downward Departure.

Defendant's second argument on appeal is that the district court misunderstood its authority to depart on the ground of his extraordinary characteristics. We agree that extraordinary characteristics such as unusual family obligations or exceptional charitable activities may, in certain circumstances, provide a basis for a downward departure. We disagree, however, that the district court misunderstood its authority to depart. It appears clear that the court found that defendant's family obligations and charitable activities, though noteworthy, were neither extraordinary nor exceptional.

The best indicator of the district court's unwillingness to depart downward on the basis of extraordinary characteristics is the stark difference between the court's sentencing-hearing statements about departure on this basis and on the grounds of aberrant behavior. When asked to make a finding about defendant's extraordinary offender characteristics claim, the district court stated:

THE COURT: To the extent you've asked me to depart based on that, I would find that those, extraordinary commitment to family and extraordinary offender characteristics, don't rise to the level that would justify a departure out of the heartland of the guidelines ... So to the extent I have discretion in that regard, I exercise my discretion not to depart downward.

These statements make it plain that the district court's refusal to depart stemmed from an exercise of discretion. And even if we were to assume that these statements are ambiguous, that ambiguity, without more, would not be enough to make the district court's refusal to depart appealable. Our review of this matter is, thus, at an end. We lack jurisdiction to review the district court's refusal to depart downward on the basis of extraordinary offender characteristics.

C.   The Heartland of Section 2C1.7 of the Guidelines.

Defendant's final argument on appeal concerns the scope of section 2C1.7 of the Guidelines, which corresponds to 18 U.S.C. §§ 1341, 1346, the mail fraud statute to which he pled guilty. Without disputing section 2C1.7's general applicability to his conduct, defendant maintains that the district court misapprehended its authority to impose a shorter prison term by departing downward, by analogy, to the sentence prescribed under section 2C1.3 of the Guidelines. For individuals in Criminal History Category I, section 2C1.3—which concerns conflicts of interest by present and former federal officers and employees—carries a sentencing range of zero to six months. Section 2C1.7 imposes a sentencing range of eighteen to twenty-four months for individuals in the same category.

Though cast as a claim relating to the district court's refusal to depart, defendant's argument, at its core, primarily concerns the heartland of section 2C1.7 of the Guidelines. Defendant essentially argues that his conduct falls outside the heartland of section 2C1.7 and within the scope of section 2C1.3 because it primarily involved a conflict of interest, not fraud. * * *

To determine whether defendant's conduct is of the sort which generally falls within section 2C1.7's "heartland," we must determine the nature of the underlying crime of mail fraud. We look in part to the language of the mail fraud statute and to the legislative history which accompanies it. Id. In relevant part, section 1341 provides:

> Whoever, having devised or intending to devise any scheme or artifice to defraud, or for obtaining money or property by means of false or fraudulent pretenses, representations, or promises ... for the purpose of executing such scheme or artifice or attempting so to do, [uses the mail system or causes it to be used] shall be fined under this title or imprisoned not more than five years, or both. If the violation affects a financial institution, such person shall be fined not more than $1,000,000 or imprisoned not more than 30 years, or both.

Congress enacted this statute in 1872, as "a general proscription against using the mails to initiate correspondence in furtherance of 'any scheme or artifice to defraud.' " McNally v. United States, 483 U.S. 350, 356, 359 (1987). The legislative history suggests that Congress intended the mail fraud statute to protect people from "schemes to deprive them of their money or property." Id. at 356. Before 1987, section 1341 was read as a broad shield, protecting individuals against schemes to deprive them of intangible, as well as tangible, property. Then, in 1987, the Supreme Court held that the statute did not embrace intangible rights. McNally held that the mail fraud statute does not prohibit schemes to defraud individuals of their intangible rights to the honest services of government. 483 U.S. at 359–60.

In 1988, Congress enacted section 1346, the honest services amendment, to reverse the Supreme Court's decision in *McNally*. Section 1346 became effective on November 18, 1988 and provides:

For the purposes of this chapter, the term "scheme or artifice to defraud" includes a scheme or artifice to deprive another of the intangible right of honest services.

It restores mail fraud convictions to their pre-McNally status by allowing the government to predicate mail fraud prosecutions on deprivations of the intangible right of honest services. An offense under section 1346 is established when the evidence demonstrates that the use of the mail system played a role in executing the deprivation of the honest services of government.

Section 1346 includes cases in which the mail system plays an integral role in the scheme to defraud citizenry of the honest services of government, as well as schemes in which use of the mail system is only incidental to the larger plan. The Eleventh Circuit recently affirmed a defendant's conviction on twenty-two counts of mail fraud even though the defendant only used the mail system to receive payments from his partner in a money laundering the scheme. In United States v. Waymer, 55 F.3d 564, 569 (11th Cir.1995), the court rejected claims that section 1346 is vague and over broad and reiterated the Supreme Court's conclusion in Schmuck v. United States, 489 U.S. 705 (1989), that "[i]t is sufficient for the mailing to be 'incident to an essential part of the scheme' or 'a step in the plot.'" In *Waymer*, the defendant was an elected member of the Atlanta Board of Education who failed to fully disclose his relationship with the contractor who provided pest control services to Atlanta's public schools. Unbeknownst to the other school board members, the defendant received fifteen percent of all the proceeds from the contractor's contracts with the school system.

Courts have read section 1346 to include efforts by public officials and employees to conceal their fraudulent acts from the public "by means of false or fraudulent pretenses, representations, promises, or other deceptive conduct." For example, the Fourth Circuit recently upheld the conviction of a public official on such grounds in United States v. Bryan, 58 F.3d 933 (4th Cir.1995). In that case, the Director of the West Virginia Lottery orchestrated a scheme whereby he secretly ensured that lottery contracts and contract bids were awarded to companies with whom he had a personal relationship. The Fourth Circuit held that section 1346 applied to the defendant's conduct. Similarly, United States v. Alkins, 925 F.2d 541 (2d Cir.1991), a Second Circuit case, upheld the section 1346–based convictions of six Department of Motor Vehicles employees because they failed to disclose their fraudulent activities to department officials. The defendants in that case secretly processed improperly documented applications for driver's licenses, identification cards, and vehicle registrations in return for monetary disbursements.

We hold that the conduct to which Grandmaison pled guilty falls within the range of conduct Congress intended 18 U.S.C. §§ 1341, 1346 to encompass and, concomitantly, rests squarely within the heartland of section 2C1.7. Grandmaison continued to lobby Board members on behalf of Eckman Construction after his recusal from the SSCC and JSSBC. He secretly delivered gratuities to Magee, Ackerman, and Kuchinski to secure favorable votes on Eckman Construction's bid. He distributed informational materials about Eckman Construction to Magee and Ackerman without disclosing his actions to other Board members. And he caused the Elm Street Project contract to be sent to Eckman Construction via the mail system. Though there is no evidence that Grandmaison received direct monetary benefit from his actions, there can be little doubt that under cases such as *Waymer*, *Bryan*, and *Alkins* he deprived the citizens of Nashua of the honest services of their government under section 1346. This is not an unusual case.

Defendant maintains that he is mainly guilty of not revealing a conflict of interest. To be sure, his conduct involved some element of such a violation. It does not follow from this, however, that he should not be sentenced pursuant to section 2C1.7, the guideline corresponding to the mail fraud statute to which he pled guilty. First, we are convinced that 18 U.S.C. §§ 1341, 1346 encompasses crimes of the sort committed by defendant. Second, even if the applicability of section 1346 were suspect, we are not at all certain that downward departure to the sentence prescribed by section 2C1.3 would be appropriate. This is principally because section 2C1.3 linguistically does not apply to defendant or his conduct; that guideline only addresses conflicts of interests by present or former federal officers and employees and, therefore, does not reach state or local officials such as defendant. In the final analysis, defendant has managed to persuade us of only one thing: that had he been a federal employee or official, the government might have been able to charge him with violating other statutes as well. Because this argument clearly does not merit the application of a lower sentencing range defendant seeks, we affirm the district court's refusal to depart downward by analogy to section 2C1.3.

V. Conclusion

For the foregoing reasons, we vacate Grandmaison's sentence and remand for resentencing under the aberrant behavior standard formulated in this opinion. Defendant's appeal for downward departure on the basis of his extraordinary offender characteristics is dismissed for lack of jurisdiction. And we affirm the district court's refusal to depart downward by analogy to section 2C1.3 of the Guidelines.

Notes

1. Do you agree with the First Circuit's adoption of the "totality of circumstances" test for deciding whether an aberrant behavior departure is warranted?

2. Do you agree with the First Circuit's analysis of Grandmaison's "heartland" argument?

B. THE VICTIM WITNESS PROTECTION ACT OF 1982

The Victim Witness Protection Act of 1982 (VWPA) provides that in sentencing a defendant convicted of an offense in title 18, United States Code, the court "may order * * * that the defendant make restitution to any victim of such offense."ᵛᵛ The next case, United States v. Lampien, 89 F.3d 1316 (7th Cir.1996), provides a discussion of the VWPA in a simple white collar prosecution for embezzlement. As you read *Lampien*, note that despite the considerable powers courts are given to enforce restitution orders, these powers are not as broad as the court may need, or thinks it needs. Note also the interplay of federal and state law.

UNITED STATES v. LAMPIEN

United States Court of Appeals, Seventh Circuit, 1996.
89 F.3d 1316.

ROVNER, CIRCUIT JUDGE.

Pursuant to a written plea agreement, Carol J. Lampien pleaded guilty to a one-count information charging her with embezzling funds from an insurance company in violation of 18 U.S.C. § 1033(b)(1)(A). Lampien was sentenced to twenty-four months in prison, to be followed by a three-year term of supervised release. Pursuant to the Victim and Witness Protection Act of 1982 ("VWPA"), the district court ordered Lampien to pay full restitution to the victim, Wausau Insurance Company (Wausau), in the amount of $498,972.94. In addition to requiring Lampien to make monthly payments of $350 in partial satisfaction of the restitution obligation, the court also directed her to make a lump sum payment that included the execution of a quitclaim deed conveying her interest in her home to Wausau. The court further ordered Lampien to provide it with a copy of her mother's will and of Lampien's disclaimer of interest in her mother's estate, by which she had allowed her share of the estate to pass to her son, Terry J. Lampien. During the pendency of this appeal, it was determined that Lampien's disclaimer of interest was invalid, and both Lampien and her son were subsequently held in civil contempt for refusing to relinquish assets that were ordered transferred to the victim as part of Lampien's restitution obligation.[1] Carol Lampien appeals the district court's restitution order on the grounds that (1) her interest in her home is protected by the Wisconsin homestead exemption, Wis. Stat. § 815.20 (1994), which prevents the court from ordering her to relinquish that interest in favor of any creditor, with certain

vv. 18 U.S.C. § 3663(a)(1).

1. Terry Lampien appealed the district court's contempt citation in case no. 96–1902, consolidated for disposition with the present case. Terry's appeal was subsequently dismissed at his own request pursuant to Fed.R.App.P. 42(b) by this court's order of June 5, 1996.

enumerated exceptions she asserts are inapplicable to this case, (2) the district court had no authority under the Victim and Witness Protection Act of 1982, as amended, 18 U.S.C. §§ 3663–3664 (1990), to order Lampien to quitclaim her home to Wausau, and (3) the court abused its discretion in ordering the payment of full restitution, and in requiring Lampien to make monthly restitution payments that are clearly beyond her means. For the reasons that follow, we vacate the restitution order and remand for further proceedings.

I. Background

At the time that Wausau discovered the embezzlement, Lampien had been employed in the company's Milwaukee branch office for forty-two years. In early August 1993, Lampien held the position of Claims Services Representative in the Workers' Compensation Claims Unit when she began misappropriating funds by issuing checks to fictitious payees on existing workers' compensation accounts and having the checks mailed to her home. To complete the fraudulent scheme, Lampien forged the signatures of the nonexistent payees, endorsed the checks over to herself, and cashed them. The embezzlement escaped detection until mid-March 1995, when it was accidentally discovered by two of Lampien's co-workers. At that time, Wausau determined that 521 fraudulent checks totaling $498,972.94 had been negotiated by Lampien in this manner. When confronted with evidence of the embezzlement, Lampien freely admitted what she had done, and explained how she was able to conceal her activities from Wausau for a period of approximately nineteen months. Lampien then entered into a plea agreement with the government, conceding responsibility for the total amount of loss that had come to light as a result of Wausau's investigation. On July 19, 1995, she pleaded guilty to embezzlement from an insurance company in violation of 18 U.S.C. § 1033(b)(1)(A). The district court ordered the preparation of a presentence report and advised Lampien that she would be required to cooperate in its preparation by providing the probation department with further information concerning her offense.

Lampien's sentencing hearing took place on September 27, 1995. At the hearing, the government advised the court that Lampien had been highly reluctant to cooperate with the probation department in disclosing her assets, and that she had failed to inform the probation department that her mother had died and had left an estate. Although the sentencing report was quite vague in accounting for Lampien's disposition of the embezzled funds, the government did not indicate that any part of those funds remained in Lampien's control. In addition to sentencing Lampien to a twenty-four month term of imprisonment and three years of supervised release, the district judge, over defense counsel's objections, ordered Lampien to make full restitution to Wausau in the amount of $498,972.94. The restitution obligation took the form of a lump sum payment due within thirty days, followed by a series of installment payments of at least $350 per month, set to begin thirty days from the date of sentencing and to terminate six months prior to the expiration of Lampien's supervised release. To satisfy the initial lump sum payment, the district court ordered Lampien to execute a quitclaim deed conveying her interest in her home to Wausau.[2] The court also ordered Lampien to transfer the value of her ITT-Hartford variable rate annuity to Wausau and to pay Wausau $7,500 in cash, all within thirty days of the sentencing hearing. The district court estimated the value of the assets Lampien was ordered to relinquish to be $99,172, or approximately one-fifth of the total restitution owed to Wausau, thus leaving approximately $400,000 to be paid in monthly installments over a period of fifty-four months.

In setting the minimum monthly installment payment of $350, the judge relied on the budget submitted by Lampien to the probation department and incorporated in Lampien's presentence report. Accepting the accuracy of the figures in the presentence report, the court noted that Lampien was due to receive a monthly pension benefit from Wausau of $920.69, and that Lampien would also be eligible to receive $716 per month in Social Security benefits upon attaining the age of sixty-two. According to the items listed in the budget, Lampien would thus receive a gross income of $1,636.69 per month, and incur expenses of $1,345.53 per month, leaving substantially less than the requisite $350 per month the court had allocated as the minimum restitution payment. Although noting that neither party had anticipated that the initial lump sum payment would include the relinquishment of Lampien's home, the district judge nevertheless ordered Lampien to quitclaim her home to Wausau. When counsel pointed out that Lampien's monthly budget had been computed on the assumption that Lampien would retain ownership of her home free of any mortgage payments, and that her housing expenses would thus entail property taxes, homeowner's insurance and maintenance costs rather than rental payments, the district court replied that when relieved of the expenses associated with owning a home and an automobile, Lampien would be able to afford approximately $380 per month in rent, and that in any event, Lampien could live with her son Terry in her late mother's house for a period of time after her release from prison. In response to counsel's objection that the restitution obligation would be impossible to fulfill given Lampien's lack of earning capacity and limited means, the district judge asserted that "this defendant does have the earning potential and the capacity to pay full restitution." (Sentencing Tr. at 30.)

During the pendency of this appeal, it was determined that Lampien had failed to transfer the amount of her ITT–Hartford annuity (less taxes and penalties for early withdrawal) to Wausau as ordered by the court. At a contempt hearing held on February 8, 1996, it was established that Lampien had provided her attorney with a nonnegotiable check, ostensibly representing the funds in the annuity account. Meanwhile, Lampien had gained access to those funds without her attorney's knowledge by negotiating a different instrument. She then retained the

---

2. Pending resolution of this appeal, the district court granted a partial stay of sentence, relieving Lampien of the obligation to quitclaim her home to Wausau within thirty days of sentencing.

funds from the annuity rather than turning them over to Wausau as required by the court's restitution order. The district court accordingly held Lampien in civil contempt. Following oral argument, this court was advised that Lampien's disclaimer of interest in her late mother's estate had been held invalid under state law, and that Lampien's share of the estate thus did not pass to her son as had been assumed at the time the district court entered the restitution order.

II. Discussion

A. The Victim and Witness Protection Act and homestead property

Lampien challenges the district court's order directing her to execute a quitclaim deed to her homestead on two grounds. First, Lampien maintains that the VWPA does not authorize a court to force an involuntary disposition of homestead property considered exempt under state law, and that the applicable Wisconsin statute, Wis. Stat. § 815.20 (1994), provides that $40,000 of the value of her home is beyond the reach of the court's restitution order. Second, Lampien contends that if her homestead may be used to satisfy the restitution order, the district court nevertheless exceeded its authority under the VWPA when it ordered her to execute a quitclaim deed to the property in favor of Wausau. In response, the government contends that the Wisconsin homestead exemption is preempted by the VWPA, which expressly allows the district court to reach any property belonging to the defendant for the purpose of making restitution to the victim. The government further argues that the court's decision to order Lampien to execute the quitclaim deed was well within the broad discretion accorded the district judge by the VWPA, and was particularly appropriate in this case in view of Lampien's persistent efforts to evade her restitution obligation. Although we agree that the Wisconsin homestead exemption does not limit the government's power under the VWPA to enforce a lien against the full value of Lampien's home for the purpose of ensuring compliance with a valid restitution order, we also conclude that the enforcement provisions of the VWPA do not authorize the district court to direct Lampien to quitclaim her homestead in favor of Wausau.

The Victim and Witness Protection Act provides that in sentencing a defendant convicted of an offense under Title 18, a district court "may order ... that the defendant make restitution to any victim of such offense." 18 U.S.C. § 3663(a)(1). * * * To determine whether the district court exceeded its authority in formulating the order, we look to 18 U.S.C. § 3663(h), which outlines the procedures that may be invoked to enforce compliance with a restitution order. According to the first subpart of that section, "[a]n order of restitution may be enforced—(1) by the United States—(A) in the manner provided for the collection and payment of fines in subchapter B of chapter 229 of this title; or (B) in the same manner as a judgment in a civil action." 18 U.S.C. § 3663(h)(1). Subchapter B of chapter 229, codified at 18 U.S.C. §§ 3611–3615, and governing the collection of fines as well as restitution, in turn imposes "a lien in favor of the United States" that arises at the time of judgment and may be enforced "upon all property belonging to the person fined." 18 U.S.C. § 3613(a). Moreover, section 3613(c) incorporates a number of the enforcement tools of the Internal Revenue Code that are available to the United States for the collection of unpaid taxes, making them applicable "to [enforce payment of] a fine and to the lien imposed by subsection (a) as if the liability of the person fined were for an internal revenue tax assessment." 18 U.S.C. § 3613(c). The authority to collect an unpaid fine, and thus also to initiate collection of an unsatisfied order of restitution as provided in 18 U.S.C. § 3663(h)(1)(A), is delegated to the Attorney General under section 3612(c). Yet in cases where a defendant fails to satisfy a restitution order, the sentencing court also retains certain powers to enforce compliance, which include revocation of the defendant's term of supervised release and holding the defendant in contempt of court.

We turn first to Lampien's claim that the Wisconsin homestead exemption, Wis. Stat. § 815.20, shields her homestead property from involuntary disposition for the purpose of meeting her restitution obligation. Under the plain language of section 3613(a), upon the court's entry of the restitution order, a lien arose in favor of the United States upon all property belonging to Lampien, presumably including her homestead. Furthermore, as discussed above, 18 U.S.C. § 3613(c) incorporates a full array of procedures available to the United States to enforce a lien against the property of a delinquent taxpayer, making these enforcement mechanisms equally available to ensure compliance with a restitution order. In particular, § 3613(c) incorporates section 7403 of the Internal Revenue Code of 1954, which provides in relevant part that

> the Attorney General or his delegate ... may direct a civil action to be filed in a district court of the United States to enforce the lien of the United States under this title with respect to such tax or liability or to subject any property, of whatever nature, of the delinquent, or in which he has any right, title, or interest, to the payment of such tax or liability.

26 U.S.C. § 7403(a) (1981). The Supreme Court has held that this broad language allows the government to enforce a lien upon any property owned by a delinquent taxpayer, including homestead property in which the taxpayer's spouse (or any other third party) shares an ownership interest with the taxpayer. The incorporation of § 7403 of the Internal Revenue Code into 18 U.S.C. § 3613(c) thus reiterates the basic premise of section 3613(a), which, when read in conjunction with section 3663(h)(1)(A), provides that upon the district court's entry of a valid restitution order, a lien against all the property belonging to the defendant arises in favor of the United States, and is enforceable to the full extent necessary to satisfy the defendant's restitution obligation.

In light of our discussion of the provisions that govern the enforcement of a restitution order, Lampien's argument that Congress did not intend that the federal statutory scheme preempt the Wisconsin homestead exemption appears singularly implausible. On its face, the statutory language reveals that Congress meant to reach every interest in property that a defendant has, in order to ensure that the defendant's obligation to make restitution to the victim of her offense is fulfilled. It is, of course, axiomatic that under the Supremacy Clause, "a state statute is void to the extent it conflicts with a federal statute," such as where compliance with both would be impossible, or where the state law " 'stands as an obstacle to the accomplishment and execution of the full purposes and objectives of Congress.' "Maryland v. Louisiana, 451 U.S. 725, 746–47 (1981). A state law that exempts any property belonging to a defendant from execution to satisfy a restitution order is in conflict with the enforcement provisions of the federal statute, and would thwart the essential objective of the statute, namely, to provide restitution to the fullest extent possible for losses that were sustained by the victim and were the direct result of the defendant's crime. Thus, if the Wisconsin homestead exemption applies to shield Lampien's home from the government's lien, or to prevent any part of the proceeds from the sale of her home from being used to satisfy her restitution obligation, the homestead exemption is void under the Supremacy Clause.

Moreover, we are not entirely convinced that the Wisconsin homestead exemption would apply in this case to prevent the United States from enforcing a valid restitution order, as Lampien maintains. The portion of the Wisconsin statute on which Lampien relies to claim the exemption reads as follows:

> An exempt homestead ... selected by a resident owner and occupied by him or her shall be exempt from execution, from the lien of every judgment and from liability for the debts of the owner to the amount of $40,000, except mortgages, laborers', mechanics' and purchase money liens and taxes and except as otherwise provided. The exemption shall not be impaired by temporary removal with the intention to reoccupy the premises as a homestead nor by the sale of the homestead, but shall extend to the proceeds derived from the sale to an amount not exceeding $40,000, while held, with the intention to procure another homestead with the proceeds, for 2 years.

Wis.Stat. § 815.20(1) (1994). According to Lampien, the homestead exemption thus operates to allow her to retain $40,000 of the value of her homestead notwithstanding the fact that her restitution obligation to Wausau greatly exceeds this sum.

On its face, the state statute appears to exempt homestead property "from the lien of *every* judgment," *id.* (emphasis added), without making any distinction between civil and criminal judgments, and thus arguably includes restitution orders. Yet as the Wisconsin Court of Appeals recently observed, the homestead exemption was enacted pursuant to Article I, Section 17 of the Wisconsin Constitution, which allows the state legislature to enact laws "exempting a reasonable amount of property from seizure or sale for the payment of any debt or liability hereafter contracted." Wis. Const. art. I, § 17. Because the homestead exemption was enacted in order to preserve a judgment debtor's home as against her contractual obligations, rather than to permit the avoidance of a debt that was incurred under entirely different circumstances, such as where the debt arose as a result of a defendant's criminal conduct, we find it somewhat doubtful that the Wisconsin state legislature intended the homestead exemption to apply to prevent the United States from enforcing a valid restitution order entered by a district court as part of a defendant's criminal sentence. Furthermore, the state statute contains an exception clause (i.e., a homestead is exempt from a judgment lien "except as otherwise provided," see Wis. Stat. § 815.20(1)) that is arguably applicable here, since the VWPA provides that upon the entry of a restitution order, all property owned by a defendant is subject to the government's lien. In sum, Lampien's contention that she is entitled to invoke the protection of the Wisconsin homestead exemption to avoid the government's lien is not particularly persuasive. In any case, as we have already discussed, the state statute is void under the Supremacy Clause to the extent that it may create an impediment to the government's enforcement of a valid restitution order entered pursuant to the VWPA.

We turn next to the means the district court has chosen to enforce its restitution order. Lampien maintains that the court exceeded its authority in ordering her to execute a quitclaim deed to her homestead, and we agree. As the First Circuit most recently observed in United States v. Gilberg, "[a] federal court has no inherent authority to order restitution in a criminal case; it may do so only as expressly provided by statute." 75 F.3d 15, 22 (1st Cir.1996). In fashioning a restitution order, a district court is therefore circumscribed by the substantive and procedural limitations outlined in the VWPA. As we have explained above, section 3663(h)(1) specifies the procedures that may be invoked by the United States to enforce compliance with a restitution order, and incorporates by reference the procedures available for the collection of fines, which in turn allow the government to utilize a number of the remedies provided under the Internal Revenue Code for the collection of unpaid taxes. Furthermore, in addition to the formidable enforcement tools that may be invoked by the government to ensure that a restitution obligation is met, the district court also retains the authority to revoke a defendant's term of supervised release and to hold her in contempt of court should she refuse to honor the court's restitution order. Our review of the relevant portions of the VWPA thus leads us to conclude that Congress' careful enumeration of the means by which a restitution order may be enforced, and its designation of those parties authorized to proceed with that enforcement, is intended to be exhaustive. We therefore hold that a district court is limited to effecting the enforcement of a restitution order only as expressly provided by the VWPA. Moreover, because the VWPA does not authorize the enforcement mechanism chosen by the district court in this case, we vacate its order requiring Lampien to quitclaim her interest in her homestead in favor of Wausau.

B.   The amount of restitution ordered

Lampien also maintains that the district court abused its discretion in ordering her to pay restitution in the full amount of $498,972.94, and in requiring her to make monthly restitution payments that are plainly impossible for her to meet. The government counters that under our deferential standard of review, the restitution order should be sustained provided it is clear from the record that the district judge considered the factors mandated by 18 U.S.C. § 3664(a) when he entered the order.

Under section 3664(a), in determining whether to order restitution and setting the appropriate amount of restitution, the district judge "shall consider the amount of the loss sustained by any victim as a result of the offense, the financial resources of the defendant, the financial needs and earning ability of the defendant and the defendant's dependents, and such other factors as the court deems appropriate." 18 U.S.C. § 3664(a). As this court explained in United States v. Mahoney, 859 F.2d 47, 49 (7th Cir.1988), the VWPA thus requires the district judge "to balance the victim's interest in compensation against the financial resources and circumstances of the defendant—all while remaining faithful to the usual rehabilitative, deterrent, retributive, and restrictive goals of criminal sentencing." As the *Mahoney* court recognized, although the statute places the burden of demonstrating the defendant's financial resources and needs squarely on the defendant, it also mandates that the sentencing judge consider those resources and needs prior to entering an order of restitution.

Moreover, although a restitution order is reviewed only for an abuse of discretion, we observe that appellate courts have not been hesitant to vacate a restitution order where it is clear from the record that the defendant is unable to satisfy the order. This willingness to vacate facially impossible restitution orders rests on significant policy considerations, as was explained by the *Mahoney* court and echoed by numerous others * * *.

Thus, as the Ninth Circuit observed, "[i]t is vital to the success of rehabilitation that the restitution obligation imposed upon the defendant ... be one the defendant is capable of satisfying." [citations omitted]

In this case, the record raises serious doubts as to whether the district court accurately assessed Lampien's financial resources and capability to fulfill the terms of its order when it directed Lampien to make full restitution. As in *Mahoney*, the restitution order itself, which requires Lampien to pay $498,972.94 to Wausau over a period of fifty-four months, despite the fact that the only income she can reasonably expect to receive during that period consists of pension and Social Security benefits totaling approximately $19,650 per year, appears on its face to be impossible to satisfy. Moreover, the judge's statement at sentencing that "this defendant does have the earning potential and the capacity to pay full restitution," appears to be directly contradicted by the probation department's findings in the presentence report. The report reveals that Lampien, who at the time of sentencing was sixty years old, began working for Wausau upon finishing high school, that she has never held any other job, and that her adjusted gross income during the years preceding her arrest averaged approximately $19,000 per year. Furthermore, Lampien suffers from "severe asthma, high blood pressure, and arthritis in her lower back," and appears to have significant emotional problems, leading both the probation department and the district court to recommend to the Bureau of Prisons that Lampien receive a full mental health evaluation while in custody. We also cannot ignore the fact that Lampien's offense against her life-long employer creates a very serious impediment to her ever being able to obtain remunerative employment in the future. In light of these undisputed facts, it is highly unlikely that Lampien will ever be capable of earning any income beyond her vested pension and Social Security benefits. And finally, we observe that the district judge did not consider any part of the embezzled funds as being available for restitution. We therefore discern no reasonable basis for the judge's assertion that Lampien has the ability to pay full restitution.

Our view that the district court did not accurately assess Lampien's financial condition is further bolstered by the fact that it ordered Lampien to make minimum installment payments of $350 per month. Apart from the fact that Lampien could never fulfill her restitution obligation at this rate of payment, the budget contained in the presentence report (and relied on by the district court) indicates that Lampien would have substantially less than the requisite $350 per month available to allocate to restitution payments. Moreover, this budget was calculated on the assumption that Lampien would retain possession of her residence, which she owned clear of any mortgage, and that her housing needs would thus be relatively easily met. In ordering Lampien to relinquish ownership of her home as part of her initial lump sum payment, it is clear from the sentencing transcript that the judge did not fully consider the financial repercussions of that course.[6] For these reasons also, the restitution order must be vacated.

We are not, however, unmindful of the dilemma facing a district court in fashioning an appropriate restitution order for an uncooperative defendant who has given the court ample reason to believe that she is hiding assets. The difficulty of the court's task is further compounded where there is some possibility that the defendant could be in control of a portion of the funds she has embezzled. As vital as it may be to the rehabilitative process that a defendant not be ordered to make restitution payments that are impossible for her to meet, it is equally important that she not be permitted to profit from her crime. Harmonizing these policy considerations is most problematic in a case where the defendant has not been forthcoming with the district court concerning her resources. We believe that the approach recently adopted by the Third Circuit, which has support in our own law and in the statutory language, may assist the district court in resolving this difficulty. In United States

---

6. As discussed above, although the order directing Lampien to quitclaim her home to Wausau is invalid, the government may proceed to enforce its lien on any property owned by Lampien, including her homestead.

v. Copple, 74 F.3d 479, 484 (3d Cir. 1996), the Third Circuit held that "the responsibility for accounting for funds misappropriated [belongs] squarely on the individual who misappropriated them." The court in that case found strong support in the statute for assigning this burden to the defendant, since section 3664(d) requires the defendant to demonstrate his financial resources. Thus, as a starting point for calculating the total amount of restitution, the Third Circuit held that the sentencing court may take the total amount of the victim's loss for which the defendant had not yet accounted. Before arriving at a final figure, the district court should give the defendant an opportunity "to prove that [s]he is, in fact, not in possession of any part of that total amount." *Copple*, 74 F.3d at 484.

Applying this reasoning to our case, if Lampien is unable to prove to the satisfaction of the district judge that she no longer possesses any part of the nearly one-half million dollars she embezzled, the judge may, in his discretion, consider the resulting amount as being available for purposes of restitution. We believe that this approach strikes a just balance between the interests of rehabilitating the defendant, assuring that the defendant's financial resources and needs are duly considered, and providing restitution to the victim. And, in a case where there is evidence that the defendant has attempted to hide her resources, this approach provides an added incentive to the defendant to be forthright with the court in accounting for all of her assets.

III. CONCLUSION

For the foregoing reasons, the restitution order is VACATED, and this case is REMANDED to the district court for further proceedings consistent with this opinion.

MANION, CIRCUIT JUDGE, concurring.

I concur with the court's decision to vacate the order of restitution and remand the matter to the district court for entry of a more appropriate order. I write separately to make two points. First, I agree that the district court exceeded its authority in requiring Lampien to deed her home to Wausau as part of its restitution order. Except where the court is directing the return of property to its rightful owner, *see* 18 U.S.C. § 3663(b)(1)(A), which is not the case with Lampien's home, an order of restitution should generally be a dollar amount payable with whatever financial resources are at the defendant's disposal. (An exception would arise where the victim consents to services in lieu of money under 18 U.S.C. § 3663(b)(5).) Thus if Lampien has other means of paying the required restitution (e.g., helpful family members, lucky lotto number, etc.), she should be allowed to keep her home. However, there is no question that Lampien's home can be sold in a foreclosure action to enforce the order of restitution if she is otherwise unable to meet her obligations. *Id.* §§ 3663(h)(1) & (2) and 3613(a) & (e); 26 U.S.C. § 7403(c).

Second, I agree that an order of restitution cannot be impossible. I'm sure the district court understood that as well, but it faced a difficult situation. Lampien stole nearly half a million dollars in a relatively short period of time. A garage full of apparently worthless clothes seems to be the only proceeds recovered. Either she blew a lot of money in a hurry in some other way (e.g., gambling) or she has a pile of cash stashed somewhere. There should be some mechanism to ensure that if any of the stolen money surfaces, it can be recovered. Perhaps the statutes could countenance a contingency order requiring payment against a lump sum due in the event the stolen money reappears, or some other mechanism to ensure appropriate restitution. That is for the district court to decide in the first instance.

As for the order to pay $350.00 per month, when all the facts are known, such a payment may not be an abuse of discretion.

* * *

There are of course limits to the amount of restitution that can be ordered. There must be at least some possibility of payment, either immediately or down the road. But one who steals almost $500,000 cannot complain if as part of making restitution for her crime she must live in a small inexpensive apartment, perhaps with a roommate, limit herself to $50 a month in clothing, forego cable television, and field only one call at a time. That is hardly penury.

I concur on this point because the total amount of restitution ordered was impossibly large given Lampien's present and (likely) future resources. And as one of several parts of the restitution order, the $350 monthly payment cannot be viewed in isolation. We vacate the entire order and remand for the district court to reformulate an appropriate (i.e., not impossible) order. In so doing the district court must decide whether to establish a time limit with a schedule of installments under the limitations of 18 U.S.C. § 3663(f)(2), or to order payment of a specified amount without a deadline or payment schedule, subject to the dictates of a subsequent enforcement action. These are matters for the sound discretion of the district court.

Notes

1.   If you were the District Court Judge handling Lampien's case on remand, what would you do?

2.   Compare the above decision to United States v. Miller, 900 F.2d 919 (6th Cir.1990), excerpted below:

"Defendants Evan Miller and his brother Jonathan, Michigan attorneys, were indicted on multiple counts of conspiracy, bankruptcy fraud, mail fraud, and obstruction of justice. Jonathan Miller was additionally charged with bank fraud, fraudulent use of a social security number, and credit card fraud. Most of these charges grew out of a series of incidents in which the brothers defrauded numerous clients of large sums of money. Each brother pled guilty to two counts of mail fraud, 18 U.S.C. § 1341, pursuant to a plea agreement. The remaining counts were dismissed. The plea agreements were silent on the issue of restitution but did provide for a maximum prison sentence of five years and a maximum term of probation of five years. The plea agreements stated that the parties had reached no agreement on the maximum fine that could be imposed by the court. Section 3571 of Title 18 provides for a fine of up to $250,000 on each count. At the time of plea, defendants acknowledged that they were subject to fines in that amount.

"The District Court sentenced each defendant to five years in prison on one of the counts to be followed by five years probation on the second. Additionally, they were ordered to pay, jointly and severally, $465,272.98 in restitution to their former clients for all of the counts of the indictment in which restitution was appropriate, including the counts dismissed as a result of the plea agreements. * * *

* * *

"The Millers argue that under the VWPA, 18 U.S.C. § 3580, the District Court could not impose orders of restitution or deny their motions to amend or vacate their sentences without first holding a hearing on the defendants' earning ability, assets, family obligations, and other factors related to the orders of restitution. We believe the hearings held by the court in these cases were sufficient.

"The defendants were given a copy of their respective presentence reports which outlined their assets, income, general financial status, family status, and discussed the injuries sustained by the victims of their crimes. The presentence reports also stated that the District Court must decide what restitution, if any, should be ordered and suggested that restitution far in excess of that ordered was possible. The factual findings of the presentence reports went unchallenged at the sentencing hearings. Further, both the Millers and Evan Miller's attorney spoke of restitution when they addressed the court just prior to imposition of sentence, though they did not mention specific amounts or discuss their financial status. Evan Miller's attorney stated that 'it appears, within sixty days Mr. Miller will have a substantial amount of money, in six figures, I would say in order to make restitution.' Having chosen not to challenge the information contained in the presentence reports, although clearly aware of the possible restitution orders that might be imposed, the defendants cannot now claim that they were not given the opportunity to be heard.

* * *

"The Millers' final argument concerning the restitution awards is that the awards are per se unreasonable, since they exceed by several times each of the Millers' annual incomes and ignore their other financial obligations. On balance we cannot say that the amount of restitution payments ordered by the court was unreasonable based upon the financial information before it. This Court has consistently found, and the VWPA specifically provides, that a defendant's ability to pay is only one factor to be considered in an order of restitution. Further, both the presentence reports and statements made at the sentencing hearings indicate that the Millers have assets to satisfy the orders. The District Court stated that it had considered this factor both at the time of sentencing and in rejecting the defendants' post-sentencing motions.

Finding no abuse of discretion, we reject the defendants' argument that awards of this size were per se unreasonable.

* * *

Is the *Miller* court's approach different from the *Lampien* court's approach? Or, were facts sufficiently different? If you had been the Millers' attorney, what would you have done differently at the sentencing phase of their case?

Chapter 17

THE JURISPRUDENCE OF WHITE COLLAR CRIME

White collar crime raises fundamental questions about the nature of criminal law because its prosecution, unlike the prosecution of street crime, regularly compromises basic principles of criminal jurisprudence—conduct and intent.

Traditionally, criminal conduct is *mala in se*, conduct that is universally viewed as wrong by a society that is willing to punish it with the ultimate sanction—loss of liberty, or life. A corollary flows from criminalizing such obviously evil conduct: everyone is on notice that if he engages in such conduct, he is committing a crime. Such notice is essential to the criminal law. As the Supreme Court has noted, "fair notice of precisely what acts are forbidden is * * * the first essential of due process of law,"[a] for "no one may be required at peril of life, liberty or property to speculate as to the meaning of penal statutes."[b] The last decade has seen criminalization of conduct previously viewed as permissible: "smurfing," insider trading, and decriminalization of conduct historically prosecuted. Determining where to draw the line between criminal conduct and legitimate activity raises jurisprudential questions: What are, and should be, the goals of the criminal law? Does prosecution of white collar crimes further—or frustrate—these goals?

Similarly, white collar criminal prosecutions often assault our notion of intent, which is perhaps the major distinguishing characteristic of the criminal law. As the Supreme Court has noted: "The contention that an injury can amount to a crime only when inflicted by intention * * * is * * * universal and persistent in mature systems of law." Morissette v. United States, 342 U.S. 246 (1952). Yet, recall that Adamson, *supra* at Chapter 9, and Weiner, *supra*, Chapter 1, were convicted for "recklessly disregarding" interests they were obliged to protect. Recall also, Park, the CEO of ACME, and Beneficial Finance Inc., *supra* at Chapter 15, both convicted without proof of intent. Again, the basic question is

a. Parker v. Levy, 417 U.S. 733 (1974).   b. Lanzetta v. New Jersey, 306 U.S. 451, 453 (1939).

raised: does prosecution of white collar crime where there is no—or minimal—intent further or hinder the goals of the criminal law?

The existence of the many collateral civil and administrative sanctions that flow from—or could perhaps substitute for—criminal prosecution gives us reason to raise these questions with every decision to prosecute.

A. THE NATURE OF CRIMINAL LAW

The following trilogy of essays focus on the goals of the criminal law. In the first essay, Professor Hart argues that the ultimate objective of the criminal law is to communicate the moral condemnation of the community. In the second essay, Judge Posner focuses on efficiency and suggests that "pricing" white collar crime is preferable to punishing it. In the third essay, Professor Coffee synthesizes much of these two views by suggesting a new approach to prosecuting white collar crime.

HART, THE AIMS OF THE CRIMINAL LAW
23 Law & Contemp. Probs. 401 (1968).[c]

In trying to formulate the aims of the criminal law, it is important to be aware both of the reasons for making the effort and of the nature of the problem it poses.

The statement has been made, as if in complaint, that "there is hardly a penal code that can be said to have a single basic principle running through it."[1] But it needs to be clearly seen that this is simply a fact, and not a misfortune. A penal code that reflected only a single basic principle would be a very bad one. Social purposes can never be single or simple, or held unqualifiedly to the exclusion of all other social purposes; and an effort to make them so can result only in the sacrifice of other values which also are important. Thus, to take only one example, the purpose of preventing any particular kind of crime, or crimes generally, is qualified always by the purposes of avoiding the conviction of the innocent and of enhancing that sense of security throughout the society which is one of the prime functions of the manifold safeguards of American criminal procedure. And the same thing would be true even if the dominant purpose of the criminal law were thought to be the rehabilitation of offenders rather than the prevention of offenses.

Examination of the purposes commonly suggested for the criminal law will show that each of them is complex and that none may be thought of as wholly excluding the others. Suppose, for example, that the deterrence of offenses is taken to be the chief end. It will still be necessary to recognize that the rehabilitation of offenders, the disable-

c. Reprinted with permission from 23 *Law and Contemp. Problems,* 401–441 (1958). Copyright © 1958 Duke University School of Law.

1. *L. Hall & S. Glueck, Cases on the Criminal Law and Enforcement* 13 (3d ed. 1958).

ment of offenders, the sharpening of the community's sense of right and wrong, and the satisfaction of the community's sense of just retribution may all serve this end by contributing to an ultimate reduction in the number of crimes. Even socialized vengeance may be accorded a marginal role, if it is understood as the provision of an orderly alternative to mob violence.

The problem, accordingly, is one of the priority and relationship of purposes as well as of their legitimacy—of multivalued rather than of single-valued thinking.

* * *

The question posed raises preliminarily an even more fundamental inquiry: What do we mean by "crime" and "criminal"? Or, put more accurately, what should we understand to be "the method of the criminal law," the use of which is in question? This latter way of formulating the preliminary inquiry is more accurate, because it pictures the criminal law as a process, a way of doing something, which is what it is. A great deal of intellectual energy has been misspent in an effort to develop a concept of crime as "a natural and social phenomenon" abstracted from the functioning system of institutions which make use of the concept and give it impact and meaning. But the criminal law, like all law, is concerned with the pursuit of human purposes through the forms and modes of social organization, and it needs always to be thought about in that context as a method or process of doing something.

What then are the characteristics of this method?

1.   The method operates by means of a series of directions, or commands, formulated in general terms, telling people what they must or must not do. Mostly, the commands of the criminal law are "must-nots," or prohibitions, which can be satisfied by inaction. "Do not murder, rape, or rob." But some of them are "musts," or affirmative requirements, which can be satisfied only by taking a specifically, or relatively specifically, described kind of action. "Support your wife and children," and "File your income tax return." * * *

2.   The commands are taken as valid and binding upon all those who fall within their terms when the time comes for complying with them, whether or not they have been formulated in advance in a single authoritative set of words. They speak to members of the community, in other words, in the community's behalf, with all the power and prestige of the community behind them.

3.   The commands are subject to one or more sanctions for disobedience which the community is prepared to enforce.

Thus far, it will be noticed, nothing has been said about the criminal law which is not true also of a large part of the noncriminal, or civil, law. The law of torts, the law of contracts, and almost every other branch of private law that can be mentioned operate, too, with general directions prohibiting or requiring described types of conduct, and the community's tribunals enforce these commands. What, then, is distinctive about the method of the criminal law?

Can crimes be distinguished from civil wrongs on the ground that they constitute injuries to society generally which society is interested in preventing? The difficulty is that society is interested also in the due fulfillment of contracts and the avoidance of traffic accidents and most of the other stuff of civil litigation. The civil law is framed and interpreted and enforced with a constant eye to these social interests. Does the distinction lie in the fact that proceedings to enforce the criminal law are instituted by public officials rather than private complainants? The difficulty is that public officers may also bring many kinds of "civil" enforcement actions—for an injunction, for the recovery of a "civil" penalty, or even for the detention of the defendant by public authority. Is the distinction, then, in the peculiar character of what is done to people who are adjudged to be criminals? The difficulty is that, with the possible exception of death, exactly the same kinds of unpleasant consequences, objectively considered, can be and are visited upon unsuccessful defendants in civil proceedings.

If one were to judge from the notions apparently underlying many judicial opinions, and the overt language even of some of them, the solution of the puzzle is simply that a crime is anything which is *called* a crime, and a criminal penalty is simply the penalty provided for doing anything which has been given that name. So vacant a concept is a betrayal of intellectual bankruptcy. Certainly, it poses no intelligible issue for a constitution-maker concerned to decide whether to make use of "the method of the criminal law." Moreover, it is false to popular understanding, and false also to the understanding embodied in existing constitutions. By implicit assumptions that are more impressive than any explicit assertions, these constitutions proclaim that a conviction for crime is a distinctive and serious matter—a something, and not a nothing. What is that something?

4.   What distinguishes a criminal from a civil sanction and all that distinguishes it, it is ventured, is the judgment of community condemnation which accompanies and justifies its imposition. As Professor Gardner wrote not long ago, in a distinct but cognate connection:[13]

> "The essence of punishment for moral delinquency lies in the criminal conviction itself. One may lose more money on the stock market than in a court-room; a prisoner of war camp may well provide a harsher environment than a state prison; death on the field of battle has the same physical characteristics as death by

---

13.   Gardner, *Bailey v. Richardson and the Constitution of the United States,* 33 B.U.L.Rev. 176, 193 (1953). It is, of course, to be understood that Professor Gardner's statement and the statements in the text do not accurately describe the significance of a criminal conviction under many modern regulatory and other statutes which penalize people who have had no awareness nor reason for awareness of wrong-doing. The central thesis of this paper, to be developed below, is that a sanction which ineradicably imports blame, both traditionally and in most of its current applications, is misused when it is thus applied to conduct which is not blameworthy.

sentence of law. It is the expression of the community's hatred, fear, or contempt for the convict which alone characterizes physical hardship as punishment."

If this is what a "criminal" penalty is, then we can say readily enough what a "crime" is. It is not simply anything which a legislature chooses to call a "crime." It is not simply antisocial conduct which public officers are given a responsibility to suppress. It is not simply any conduct to which a legislature chooses to attach a "criminal" penalty. It is conduct which, if duly shown to have taken place, will incur a formal and solemn pronouncement of the moral condemnation of the community.

* * *

Seen in this light, the criminal law has an obviously significant and, indeed, a fundamental role to play in the effort to create the good society. For it is the criminal law which defines the minimum conditions of man's responsibility to his fellows and holds him to that responsibility. The assertion of social responsibility has value in the treatment even of those who have become criminals. It has far greater value as a stimulus to the great bulk of mankind to abide by the law and to take pride in so abiding.

* * *

If the legislature does a sound job of reflecting community attitudes and needs, actual knowledge of the wrongfulness of the prohibited conduct will usually exist. Thus, almost everyone is aware that murder and forcible rape and the obvious forms of theft are wrong. But in any event, knowledge of wrongfulness can fairly be assumed. For any member of the community who does these things without knowing that they are criminal is blameworthy, as much for his lack of knowledge as for his actual conduct. * * *

POSNER, OPTIMAL SENTENCES FOR WHITE–COLLAR CRIMINALS
17 Am.Cr.L.Rev. 409 (1980).[d]

I have agreed to participate in this symposium because it gives me an opportunity to argue a favorite plank in the economist's platform for reforming the legal system, in a context in which the economic position can be simply but persuasively stated without elaborate argument and evidence. The plank is the substitution, whenever possible, of the fine (or civil penalty) for the prison sentence as the punishment for crime; the appealing context in which to argue the case for such substitution is the punishment of the white collar criminal.

The coiner of the term "white collar crime" defined it "as a crime committed by a person of respectability and high social status in the

d. Reprinted with permission from Posner, *Optimal Sentences for White–Collar*   *Criminals,* 17 Am.Cr.L.Rev. 409–18. Copyright © 1980 American Bar Association.

course of his occupation,"[1] but this is not a good definition. The terms "respectability" and "high social status" are ambiguous, and the definition arbitrarily excludes certain white collar crimes, such as evasion of the personal income tax, which is the focus of this article.

I shall instead, for reasons that I hope will soon become clear, use the term white-collar crime to refer to the nonviolent crimes typically committed by either (1) well-to-do individuals or (2) associations, such as business corporations and labor unions, which are generally "well-to-do" compared to the common criminal. White-collar crime in the sense I use it is illustrated by the criminal offenses created by the securities laws, the labor laws, the antitrust laws, other regulatory statutes, and the income-tax laws. But not every offender under such laws is a white-collar criminal as I use the term. A waitress, for example, could commit a criminal violation of the tax laws by not reporting her tips as income; but because, as we shall see, the affluence of the offender is very important to the correct punishment for the offense, I would not describe her offense as a white-collar crime. Nor would a murder committed by a wealthy person—or by a criminal gang seeking to monopolize the garbage-collection business of a city, for example—be a white-collar crime; the reason, as again we shall see, is that the proper punishment for a crime of violence raises special questions. To summarize, white-collar crimes are those more likely to be committed by the affluent than by the poor criminal—crimes that involve fraud, monopoly, and breach of faith rather than violence. The white-collar criminal is the affluent perpetrator of those crimes.

The point I wish to argue in this article, an application of the economic analysis of crime and punishment pioneered by Gary Becker,[2] can now be stated simply: the white-collar criminal as I have defined him should be punished only by monetary penalties—by fines (where civil damages or penalties are inadequate or inappropriate) rather than by imprisonment or other "afflictive" punishments (save as they may be necessary to coerce payment of the monetary penalty). In a social cost-benefit analysis of the choice between fining and imprisoning the white-collar criminal, the cost side of the analysis favors fining because, as we shall see, the cost of collecting a fine from one who can pay it (an important qualification) is lower than the cost of imprisonment. On the benefit side, there is no difference in principle between the sanctions. The fine for a white-collar crime can be set at whatever level imposes the same disutility on the defendant, and thus yield the same deterrence, as the prison sentence that would have been imposed instead. Hence, fining the affluent offender is preferable to imprisoning him from society's standpoint because it is less costly and no less efficacious.

---

1. E. SUTHERLAND, WHITE COLLAR CRIME 9 (1961). *See also* H. PACKER, THE LIMITS OF THE CRIMINAL SANCTION 534 (1968), * * *.

2. See Becker, *Crime and Punishment: An Economic Approach*, 76 J.POL.ECON. 169

(1968); for a nontechnical discussion, see R. POSNER, ECONOMIC ANALYSIS OF LAW 164–72 (2d ed. 1977). Becker argues that the use of fines as punishment minimizes the social loss resulting from crime.

The reason that the fine is the cheaper sanction is that, unlike imprisonment, it is a transfer payment. Because the dollars collected from the criminal as a fine show up on the benefit side of the social ledger, the net social cost is limited to the costs of collecting the fine. A term of imprisonment, on the other hand, yields no comparable social revenue if we disregard the negligible, and nowadays usually zero, output of the prisoner. On the contrary, to the social costs of imprisonment must be added the considerable sums spent on maintaining prisoners. To be sure, for a middle-class offender, a short prison term might be the deterrent equivalent of a large fine. But it would not follow that the social costs of the short prison term were correspondingly low, because the greater one's income, the greater is the cost of imprisonment in lost earnings. As long as these are earnings in legitimate occupations, their loss is a social cost similar to the cost of the prison guards. The large fine avoids these costs.

I anticipate relatively little disagreement with the proposition that fines are cheaper to society than imprisonment when the offender can pay the fine. I expect great resistance, however, to the proposition that the social benefits of punishment are no greater when punishment takes the form of imprisonment than when it takes the form of a fine. It will be argued that there is no money equivalent to the pain of imprisonment, perhaps especially to the affluent, educated, "sensitive" person—the white-collar criminal—that would be within his power to pay. (The offender here is necessarily an individual: a corporation or other "artificial" person cannot, of course, be punished by imprisonment.) But whether this is so depends, in a theoretical analysis, on the gravity of the crime in relation to the probability of apprehension and conviction, and, in a practical analysis, on the severity of the prison sentences actually imposed for white-collar crimes. As to the first it is no doubt true that very few people would consider a fine of any size to be as severe a punishment as death, or imprisonment for life, or, perhaps, imprisonment for twenty years. Thus, if these are optimal punishments (putting aside the consideration that imprisonment is more costly to administer), it might indeed be difficult to find a monetary equivalent. Perhaps these are optimal punishments for some white-collar crimes. * * * If so, my proposal to substitute fines for prison for white-collar criminals is in serious difficulty—but only in a rather academic sense. For whatever may be theoretically optimal, white-collar criminals, at least in this country, are not punished by death or long prison terms. * * *

Perhaps, as I have suggested, these prison terms are too short given the gravity of the crimes and the difficulty of detecting them. That is a large question that I do not propose to investigate here. I shall instead treat the existing level of imprisonment for white-collar crime as part of the background of the analysis. Given that level, it is highly improbable that there is no fine equivalent to a prison sentence in the amount of disutility it imposes on the offender. An individual who has the boldness, the effrontery, to commit a crime—even of the white collar variety—will have the capacity and inclination to consider realistic trade-offs between

90 days, or even a year or two, in one of the federal system's minimal security prisons and a hefty fine. If he would be deterred by the threat of such a prison sentence, he would be equally deterred by the threat of a $50,000 or $100,000 or $250,000 fine. (And fines could be indexed to prevent inflation from reducing their bite.)

It should be noted also that the affluent offender presents interesting opportunities for society to exercise its ingenuity in the collection of fines. For example, a penalty that takes the form of barring the defendant from pursuing his occupation—a penalty frequently used by the SEC in dealing with securities fraud and by state authorities in dealing with misconduct by lawyers—is the equivalent of a fine. The amount of the "fine" is simply the difference between the defendant's future income in the occupation from which he is barred and the income in his best alternative occupation, discounted to present value. This device offers a means of collecting a large fine from an individual who has a large fine in periodic installments. The availability of these devices enables one to contemplate realistically the possibility of levying very large fines in lieu of the present prison sentences for white-collar crimes.

* * *

I turn now to what seems a separate, but is really the same, objection to substituting fines for imprisonment in white-collar crimes: namely, that a system in which poor offenders were usually imprisoned and rich offenders usually fined would be a system that discriminated against poor people. This argument is just a variant of the fallacy that imprisonment is inherently more punitive than fines. It gains some plausibility only from the ridiculous "rates of exchange" that used to be commonplace in crimes where the criminal had the option of paying a fine or going to jail, a practice that has been invalidated by the Supreme Court under the Equal Protection Clause of the fourteenth amendment. The assumption behind this argument, however, is false. For every prison sentence there is some fine equivalent; if the fine is so large that it cannot be collected, then the offender should be imprisoned. How then are the rich favored under such a system?

A possible answer is that the rich could "buy" more crime under a fine system than under an imprisonment system. Suppose that the expected cost to society of a crime is $100, the probability of apprehension and conviction is 10 percent, and therefore the fine is set at $1,000 so that expected punishment cost will be equal to the expected social cost. A rich man would not be deterred from committing this crime as long as the expected benefits to him were greater than $1,000. But now suppose that instead of a fine of $1,000, a prison term of one month is imposed for this crime based on a study which shows that the disutility of a month in prison to an average person is $41,000. Since the disutility of imprisonment rises with income, this form of punishment will deter the rich man more than the poor one. Stated differently, a nominally uniform prison term has the effect of price discrimination based on income.

But this is not to say that a system of fines discriminates against the poor. It is rather that a uniform prison term discriminates against the rich compared with a uniform fine. If we want to discriminate against the rich through a fine system, that is easily done by progressively varying the fine with the offender's income. If we want not to discriminate against the rich through an imprisonment system, we can make the length of the sentence inverse to the offender's income. In either case the choice to discriminate is independent of the form of the punishment.

* * *

Where fines are trivial, it is natural to suppose that only substantial jail sentences will carry a "stigma" effect which adds to deterrence. Yet even if, improbably, imprisonment produced a stigma effect which no magnitude of fine could duplicate, only the rate of exchange between fine and imprisonment, and not the principle of equivalence, would be affected. The fine equivalent would then be higher than if a fine carried a stigma as well. But, in fact, the presence of stigma is an argument for fines rather than for prison sentences. Most students of the criminal process locate the source of the stigma in the fact of conviction rather than the form of the sentence. The more punishment society obtains simply from the stigmatizing effect of conviction, the smaller the fine that must be imposed to produce the optimal severity of punishment; and the smaller the fine, the less likely it is to exceed the white-collar criminal's ability to pay.

The existence of a stigma of conviction bears on the question, why, if a money sanction is adequate, is criminal punishment necessary at all? Why not rely entirely on money damages, as in a civil action? If the stigma arises either because the action is brought by the state and denominated as criminal, or because the higher standard of proof for criminal cases makes it less likely that a convicted defendant is really innocent, then it would be lost if civil penalties were substituted for criminal fines. Of course, the latter aspect of the stigma effect could be preserved simply by increasing the standard of proof in a civil penalty suit to the criminal level.

* * *

The economic objection to relying on stigma for deterrence is that, like imprisonment, it is more costly to society than the pure fine (or civil penalty) because it does not yield any revenue. (Stigma, unlike a fine, imposes costs on the criminal with no corresponding gain to society.) Hence, it would seem more efficient to drop the criminal label, and any stigma attached to it, and offset any loss in disutility to the criminal by increasing the size of the civil penalty. In that way, the social revenue can be increased with no loss deterrence.

COFFEE, DOES "UNLAWFUL" MEAN "CRIMINAL"?: REFLECTIONS ON THE DISAPPEARING TORT/ CRIME DISTINCTION IN AMERICAN LAW

71 B.U.L.Rev. 193 (1991).[e]

My thesis is simple and can be reduced to four assertions. First, the dominant development in substantive federal criminal law over the last decade has been the disappearance of any clearly definable line between civil and criminal law. Second, this blurring of the border between tort and crime predictably will result in injustice, and ultimately will weaken the efficacy of the criminal law as an instrument of social control. Third, to define the proper sphere of the criminal law, one must explain how its purposes and methods differ from those of tort law. Although it is easy to identify distinguishing characteristics of the criminal law—e.g., the greater role of intent in the criminal law, the relative unimportance of actual harm to the victim, the special character of incarceration as a sanction, and the criminal law's greater reliance on public enforcement—none of these is ultimately decisive. Rather, the factor that most distinguishes the criminal law is its operation as a system of moral education and socialization. The criminal law is obeyed not simply because there is a legal threat underlying it, but because the public perceives its norms to be legitimate and deserving of compliance. Far more than tort law, the criminal law is a system for public communication of values. As a result, the criminal law often and necessarily displays a deliberate disdain for the utility of the criminalized conduct to the defendant. Thus, while tort law seeks to balance private benefits and public costs, criminal law does not (or does so only by way of special affirmative defenses), possibly because balancing would undercut the moral rhetoric of the criminal law. Characteristically, tort law prices, while criminal law prohibits.

The fourth and final assertion of this Article is that implementation of the crime/tort distinction is today feasible only at the sentencing stage. Neither legislative action nor constitutional challenge is likely to reverse the encroachment of the criminal law upon areas previously thought civil in character. But, at the sentencing stage, courts can draw a line between the enforcement of norms that were intended to price and those intended to prohibit. Indeed, because a sensible implementation of the crime/tort distinction requires a close retrospective evaluation of the defendant's conduct, sentencing may be the only juncture where the distinction can be feasibly preserved.

* * *

Three trends, in particular, stand out. First, the federal law of "white collar" crime now seems to be judge-made to an unprecedented degree, with courts deciding on a case-by-case, retrospective basis whether conduct falls within often vaguely defined legislative prohibitions.

Second, a trend is evident toward the diminution of the mental element (or *"mens rea"*) in crime, particularly in many regulatory offenses. Third, although the criminal law has long compromised its adherence to the "method" of the criminal law by also recognizing a special category of subcriminal offenses—often called "public welfare offenses"—in which strict liability could be combined with modest penalties, the last decade has witnessed the unraveling of this uneasy compromise, because the traditional public welfare offenses—now set forth in administrative regulations—have been upgraded to felony status. This Article will refer to this last trend as the "technicalization" of crime and will combine departures from most of the above-described elements that characterize the criminal law's "method."

The upshot of these trends is that the criminal law seems much closer to being used interchangeably with civil remedies. Sometimes, identically phrased statutes are applicable to the same conduct—one authorizing civil penalties, the other authorizing criminal sanctions. More often, the criminal law is extended to reach behavior previously thought only civilly actionable. Either way, this practice of defining the criminal law to reach all civil law violations in a particular field of law in order to gain additional deterrence may distort the underlying legal standard. What needs to be more clearly recognized is the variety of ways in which such distortion can occur. For example, some civil law standards may be aspirational in character (e.g., the rule that attorneys should avoid any "appearance of impropriety"). Other standards may frame prophylactic rules, which prevent the possibility of misconduct, but involve no element of culpability.[22] Some recent writers in the "law and economics" tradition have theorized that society may have a particular "transaction structure" for dealing with different areas of social behavior, sometimes using rules that would trigger only civil liability and at other times using rules whose violation would be criminally prosecuted. Thus, overlaying the criminal law on the civil law may disrupt these transaction structures. Still, provocative as this concept of "transaction structure" is, it has remained an underdeveloped idea, which requires a fuller account of why society should prefer the structure of the civil law over that of the criminal law.

* * *

* * * [O]ur leading criminal law scholars—among them Henry Hart, Sanford Kadish, and Herbert Packer—have periodically warned of the danger of "overcriminalization": namely, excessive reliance on the criminal sanction, particularly with respect to behavior that is not inherently morally culpable. But one cannot meaningfully use the term

---

22. One such rule is § 16(b) of the Securities Exchange Act, 15 U.S.C. § 78(p)(b) (1988), which requires corporate insiders to disgorge to their corporation profits realized through short-swing trading in the corporation's securities. In order to eliminate the temptations faced by corporate insiders, the statute does not require proof of either possession of inside information or an intent to defraud. No criminal penalty is authorized for violations of § 16(b), which is intended to be enforced strictly by private civil suit.

"overcriminalization" without first defining the boundaries within which the criminal sanction may appropriately be used, and to answer this latter question only by saying that the behavior must be "blameworthy" simply uses an adjective in lieu of a theory.

* * *

In overview, the two principal claims made by this Article exist in some obvious tension. If true, the first claim—that the criminal law is more a system of socialization than of pricing—makes the second predictable: namely, that the criminal sanction is increasingly being used by regulators as a preferred enforcement tool without regard to the traditional limitations on its use. Almost by definition, a system for socialization will be put to new uses, as authorities attempt to harness its educational power. Thus, the very success of the criminal law as a socializing force implies the erosion of the traditional point at which the tenuous crime/tort distinction had been maintained. Indeed, traditional libertarians—such as Hart, Kadish, and Packer—have been criticized on this ground by sociologists, who have argued that the social standards of blameworthiness necessarily evolve over time along with other social attitudes.[24] These critics have found the "overcriminalization" thesis to be empty of content, because of its failure to recognize the interactive, reciprocal relationship between the content of the criminal law and the public's perception of what conduct is blameworthy. In their view, the public learns what is blameworthy in large part from what is punished.

Undoubtedly, there is some merit in this argument. Obviously, new problems may arise for which the criminal law is the most effective instrument, but which involve behavior not historically considered blameworthy. Modern technology, the growth of an information-based economy, and the rise of the regulatory state make it increasingly difficult to maintain that only the common law's traditional crimes merit the criminal sanction. In fact, historically, the criminal law has never been static or frozen within a common law mold, but has constantly evolved. This has been especially true within the field of "white collar" crime. Even the first modern "white collar" offenses to be criminally prosecuted—price-fixing, tax fraud, securities fraud, and, later, foreign bribery—were "regulatory" crimes in the sense that they had not been traditionally considered blameworthy. In short, the line between *malum in se* and *malum prohibitum* has been crossed many times and largely discredited. Today, to rule out worker safety, toxic dumping, or environmental pollution as necessarily beyond the scope of the criminal law requires one to defend an antiquarian definition of blameworthiness.

But where does this leave us? Those following in the footsteps of Hart, Kadish and Packer have a powerful rejoinder: if the criminal law is over-used, it will lose its distinctive stigma. While conceding that the criminal law is a system of socialization, they would reply that for precisely that reason it must be used parsimoniously. Once everything

---

24. *See,* e.g., Ball & Friedman, *The Use of Criminal Sanctions in the Enforcement of* *Economic Legislation: A Sociological View,* 17 STAN.L.REV. 197, 233 (1965).

wrongful is made criminal, society's ability to reserve special condemnation for some forms of misconduct is either lost or simply reduced to a matter of prosecutorial discretion. Still, valid as this response is, it does not answer fully the criticism that the traditional criminal law scholar's focus on blameworthiness is anachronistic because it freezes the criminal law's necessary evolution, like a fly in amber.

If so, what alternative is left? What substitute bulwark can prevent the criminal law from sprawling over the landscape of the civil law? One answer is to update the notion of blameworthiness, looking not only to historical notions of culpability, but to well-established industry and professional standards whose violation has been associated with culpability within that narrower community. Another answer is to focus on the temporal relationship of the civil and criminal law. At some point, a civil standard can become so deeply rooted and internalized within an industry or professional community that its violation becomes blameworthy, even if it was not originally so. Insider trading may supply such an example, where the norm has long since become internalized within the industry. The relationship of the civil and criminal law here is sequentially interactive: the civil law experiments with a standard, but at some point it may "harden" into a community standard that the criminal law can enforce. At that point, it may be appropriate to prohibit, rather than price, at least if society believes that the defendant's conduct lacks any colorable social utility.

But who makes these determinations? Ideally, the legislature should, but there is little prospect that it will; nor is it properly positioned to compare varying degrees of culpability. Thus, a "second best" answer is a sentencing commission, which in drafting sentencing guidelines should attempt to separate those instances when society should price from those when it should prohibit. Only an administrative agency can both make such determinations on a continuing and provisional basis and also attempt to determine the correct "price" when pricing is appropriate.

* * *

Public concern about a newly perceived social problem—the environment, worker safety, child neglect, etc.—seems to trigger a recurring social response: namely, an almost reflexive resort to criminal prosecution, either through the enactment of new legislation or the use of old standby theories that have great elasticity. Increasingly, criminal liability may be imposed based only on negligence or even on a strict liability basis. The premise appears to be that if a problem is important enough, the partial elimination of *mens rea* and the use of vicarious responsibility are justified. No doubt, the criminal sanction does provide additional deterrence, but what are the costs of resorting to strict liability and vicarious responsibility as instruments of social control? * * *

If the disposal of toxic wastes, securities fraud, the filling-in of wetlands, the failure to conduct aircraft maintenance, and the causing of workplace injuries become crimes that can be regularly indicted on the basis of negligence or less, society as a whole may be made safer, but a substantial population of the American workforce (both at white collar and blue collar levels) becomes potentially entangled with the criminal law. Today, most individuals can plan their affairs so as to avoid any realistic risk of coming within a zone where criminal sanctions might apply to their conduct. Few individuals have reason to fear prosecution for murder, robbery, rape, extortion or any of the other traditional common law crimes. Even the more contemporary, white collar crimes— price fixing, bribery, insider trading, etc.—can be easily avoided by those who wish to minimize their risk of criminal liability. At most, these statutes pose problems for individuals who wish to approach the line but who find that no bright line exists. In contrast, modern industrial society inevitably creates toxic wastes that must be disposed of by someone. Similarly, workplace injuries are, to a degree, inevitable. As a result, some individuals must engage in legitimate professional activities that are regulated by criminal sanctions; to this extent, they become unavoidably "entangled" with the criminal law. That is, they cannot plan their affairs so as to be free from the risk that a retrospective evaluation of their conduct, often under the uncertain standard of negligence, will find that they fell short of the legally mandated standard. Ultimately, if the new trend toward greater use of public welfare offenses continues, it will mean a more pervasive use of the criminal sanction, a use that intrudes further into the mainstream of American life and into the everyday life of its citizens than has ever been attempted before.

Several replies are predictable to this claim that there is a social loss in defining the criminal law so that individuals cannot safely avoid its application. Liberals may claim that the traditionally limited use of the criminal sanction was class-biased and that a more pervasive use of it simply corrects that imbalance. Economists may argue that the affected individuals will only demand a "risk premium" in the labor market and, having received one, cannot later complain when the risk for which they were compensated arises. Others may conclude that the anxiety imposed on such employees, while regrettable, is necessary, because it is small in comparison to the lives saved, injuries averted, and other social benefits realized from generating greater deterrence. This may be true, but the cost/benefit calculus is a complex and indeterminate one that depends upon a comparison of marginal gain (in terms of injuries averted) in comparison to other law enforcement strategies (such as greater use of corporate liability or civil penalties) that have not yet been utilized fully. Moreover, on the cost side of the ledger, one must consider not simply the consequences to those actually prosecuted, but the anxiety created within the potential class of criminal defendants. To the extent that liability is imposed for omissions (i.e., failure to detect and correct dangerous conditions), such fear will affect a broad class of employees, most of whom will never be prosecuted or even threatened with prosecution. In addition, there is a cost to civil libertarian values, because statutes that apply broadly can never be enforced evenly. Hence, some instances of "targeting" or selective prosecutions (based on whatever criteria influence the individual prosecutor) become predictable. These costs would be more tolerable if the conduct involved were inherently blameworthy, but negligence, like death and taxes, is inevitable.

Ultimately, much depends on how we define the purposes of the criminal law. If its purpose is simply to prevent crime, the costs of the broad use of the criminal sanction against corporate managers to deter pollution, negligence-caused injuries, or other social harms may be justified. But if we define the criminal law's purposes more broadly—for example, as to "liberate" society from fear, or to enable the realization of human potential—these broader goals may be seriously compromised by a pervasive use of the criminal sanction against individuals who cannot escape its potential threat. Pursued single-mindedly, a purely negative definition of the criminal law's purposes that asserts that the criminal law's only goal is the prevention of crime ultimately ends up, as Herbert Packer wrote, "creating an environment in which all are safe but none is free."

* * *

Starting from this premise that the criminal law is a powerful socializing force, one can attempt to explain some of the most distinctive doctrinal facts about the criminal law, including the central role of intent, the limited relevance of harm to the victim, and the use of incarceration as the characteristic sanction of the criminal law. The importance of intent may lie in the ability of socializing forces to work better with respect to conscious behavior than unconscious behavior (although they can have a significant effect on the latter as well). Hence, the criminal law should arguably concentrate on volitional conduct and leave other legal forces to deal with negligence and nonvolitional conduct. The irrelevance of actual harm to the criminal law can be similarly explained on the ground that socializing forces focus on the actor, not on the victim; thus, it is a sufficient justification for punishment that the individual defendant will serve as an appropriate object lesson. Finally, prison is the distinctive sanction of the criminal law because it fulfills a pedagogical function that fines do not. Not only are prisons highly visible reminders of the deterrent threat of the law, but the use of imprisonment broadcasts a special communitarian message about the equality of all citizens before the law. Because of the wealth differences among offenders and the declining marginal utility of money, fines cannot communicate this message, and, when used as an alternative to imprisonment, may undercut it. The criminal law is then a uniquely effective medium for communicating a communitarian ethic. Alone, it tells members of an audience who may identify themselves as belonging to very different communities (in terms of wealth, race, etc.) that each is a citizen of the same society, subject to the same duties and punishment. The use of imprisonment can symbolize the equality of all before the law, and thus it affirms the existence of a single community.

* * *

* * * Society is better advised to use prices, not sanctions, when it has great difficulty in specifying the precise standard of precaution to be observed. This observation may help explain the historic reluctance of Anglo–American courts to criminalize negligence. Unquestionably, it would be infeasible for society to specify the precautions to be observed across a wide variety of contexts and by very different actors with the precision necessary to justify the use of sanctions. In contrast, pricing can be done retrospectively when a court determines whether to impose liability.

* * *

The central theme in both Hart's and Kadish's critiques was that the criminal law would be devalued if it were to be used to express not society's moral revulsion, but merely its utilitarian preferences. This argument drew a sharp retort from those who favored the increased use of the criminal law against high-status offenders. Drawing on sociological studies, Professors Ball and Friedman challenged the idea that the criminal law would lose its unique status in the public's mind simply because it was employed to penalize behavior not historically thought to be "criminal" in nature.[154] They argued that the relationship between the criminal law and the public morality was interactive and reciprocal. Each affected the other, and, to a degree, the public learned what was immoral from what was made criminal.

* * * [S]ubsequent events seem to confirm [this] position. Each of the major "white collar" scandals of recent decades—the price-fixing scandals in the electrical equipment industry of the 1960s, the foreign payments scandal of the 1970s and the insider trading revelations of the 1980s—shocked and aroused the American public. In general, the public has shown little apprehension about the use of the criminal sanction in these cases, but rather has applauded its use. No one who has followed the media coverage of the Ivan Boesky or Michael Milken prosecutions can doubt the attitude of the American public: it has wanted prison sentences imposed—substantial ones. In part, this may simply reflect the public's enjoyment of the spectacle of the once mighty made humble, but the possibility at least exists that those commentators who predicted an erosion in respect for the criminal law if it was used to enforce economic regulations have either overestimated the legal sophistication of the American public or underestimated its appetite for bread and circuses. Possibly, the public is more concerned about being victimized by the underlying offenses, or possibly it simply does not believe that it will be at risk from such prosecutions. Whatever the reason, the public may not share the legal profession's unease with strict liability offenses.

The problem with the Hart and Kadish overcriminalization thesis is then that it tries to rest an essentially normative argument against overextension of the criminal law on the debatable empirical claim that the public will lose respect for the criminal law. In fact, the public's

---

154. *See* Ball & Friedman, *The Use of Criminal Sanctions in the Enforcement of* *Economic Legislation: A Sociological View,* 17 Stan.L.Rev. 197, 206–07 (1965).

image of the criminal law in operation is probably shaped by the outcomes in a few high visibility cases. In the antitrust scandals of the 1960s, the public was presented with the spectacle of middle-echelon executives at General Electric, Westinghouse and other major firms meeting clandestinely in motel rooms at night to fix prices; in the 1970s "questionable payments" controversy, payments that closely resembled bribes were made to major political and governmental leaders around the globe; and in the 1980s "insider trading" scandals, the public learned of briefcases stuffed with money moving among New York investment bankers, much as the cocaine industry moves money in Miami. Understandably, these cases looked to the public like criminal behavior. In contrast, the more marginal cases on which Part I of this Article focused, in which strict liability has been imposed or the criminal law has been overlaid on basically aspirational civil standards, have received little public attention.

Still, in the last analysis, there is no necessary contradiction between the Hart/Kadish view that overcriminalization will bring the law into disrespect and the Ball and Friedman view that the public learns what is immoral from what is prosecuted. Both could occur simultaneously, and this would simply represent an application of the psychologist's familiar principle of cognitive dissonance. That is, the public may react in both directions, lowering both its estimation of the criminal law and also its tolerance for the particular practice subjected to criminal prosecution. Ball and Friedman have focused only on the second transition in reporting that conduct that is criminally punished becomes conduct that the community thereafter deems immoral, and their research does not truly address whether there was also a concomitant erosion in respect for the law.

Even if a general decline in the community's respect for law does not result from increased use of the criminal sanction, this should not end the debate about overcriminalization. One flaw in Hart's conceptualization of the law's educational role is his reification of the community as a single, indivisible body of public opinion. American society is too large, diverse, and specialized for such a concept to be generally meaningful. Moreover, the "technicalization" of crime discussed earlier means that the broad mass of public opinion will never quite understand what the law required or why the behavior was illegal. However, it is not necessary to educate or socialize all of society. What Hart should have recognized is that the educational and socializing role of the criminal law focuses principally on specialized audiences within the broader society. While all of society cannot be educated as to the specialized requirements of the SEC, EPA, or OSHA, a relevant business or professional community can be. Sometimes this specialized community can be induced to internalize new community standards. For example, both price-fixing and insider trading represent crimes that, in my judgment, are today accepted as criminal by the relevant affected community. Conversely, when strict liability criminal statutes are used, it is less likely that the prohibited behavior will be internalized, and some possibility exists that it will generate hostility and resistance. Thus, even if there is not a general erosion in public respect for law and even if there is increased general deterrence, the criminal law may fail in its principal socializing mission—making law compliance habitual within the relevant population of potential offenders.

* * *

* * * Unlawful toxic dumping seems a clear example of a form of conduct where society's attitude has changed. Once this might have been seen as simply a regulatory matter—a *malum prohibitum* offense in the language of an earlier era—but today it is more likely to be viewed as behavior that knowingly endangers human life. Community standards have changed, and they will continue to do so.

* * *

The most feasible answers to both these problems dovetail. Put simply, the existence or non-existence of criminal intent supplies a traditional jury issue that also furnishes the most practical breakpoint at which to shift from pricing to prohibiting. To illustrate the kind of criminal intent on which the jury should be asked to focus, it is useful to return to a case briefly noted earlier: United States v. Sellers.[158] In *Sellers,* the court refused to give a jury instruction that required the jury to find that the defendant realized that his disposal of waste substances "could be harmful to others or the environment." To be sure, such a level of *mens rea* is not constitutionally required, but this focus on harm to others supplies a practical test, readily comprehensible to a jury, for determining when the defendant's conduct knowingly lacks any claim to social utility (and hence should be subject to "sanctions," rather than "prices" * * *). Ideally, criminal legislation might therefore distinguish two grades of the crime of toxic dumping: the higher grade requiring a subjective perception by the defendant of the serious risk of harm to others, and the lower grade not. The former might be "prohibited," and the latter "priced."

* * *

The line drawing problems in determining whether to price or to prohibit are obviously difficult, both because community standards may properly shift over time and because a retrospective factual examination of the particular case will frequently be necessary to see on which side of the line it should fall. Where does this leave us in terms of policy options? First, it suggests that the line between tort and crime cannot feasibly be constitutionalized. In any event, there is virtually no possibility that the Supreme Court would attempt to draw such a line. Recurrently, the Court has suggested that "a crime is anything which the legislature chooses to say it is."[161]

* * *

158. 926 F.2d 410 (5th Cir.1991).

161. Hart, *The Aims of the Criminal Law,* 23 Law & Contemp. Probs. 401, 432

If the courts will not draw a line between tort and crime, the legislature might still be asked to do so. But such an appeal seems even more likely to be unsuccessful. Criminal legislation is enacted for a variety of reasons: sometimes as an *ad hoc,* often hasty response to a perceived crisis; sometimes as an afterthought; sometimes as a means of dignifying the status of a federal agency so that knowing violations of its administrative rules can be criminally prosecuted. Whatever the reason, there is usually a constituency that wants criminalization, and seldom one that visibly opposes it. To oppose criminalization usually places an individual legislator in the exposed position of appearing not to consider the subject matter of the statute sufficiently serious to merit serious penalties. Such perceived insensitivity can be politically harmful, if not fatal. More importantly, any attempt to draw statutory lines that better distinguish "true" criminal behavior from merely tortious behavior would involve an effort of heroic complexity, and in all likelihood it would produce problems with which courts would struggle for decades. Not only would the charging and trial stages become more complex, but it is ultimately doubtful that satisfactory lines can be drawn in advance. Too many details matter, and hence a retrospective evaluation is necessary.

Another group that might be appealed to is prosecutors themselves. Prosecutorial guidelines could be adopted seeking to decriminalize negligent or strict liability offenses. Yet, for prosecutors to decide systematically not to prosecute what the legislature has deemed criminal is also a politically dangerous act, one that seems to undermine the legislature's position as the sovereign lawmaker. Thus, although such prosecutorial guidelines and policies would normally be lawful, they would undoubtedly draw criticism from the regulatory bodies whose enforcement powers would thereby be curtailed, as well as from their legislative allies.

In my judgment, this leaves one agency with an incentive to undertake systematically the task of determining when to price and when to prohibit a particular type of misconduct: the United States Sentencing Commission. Established by Congress in 1984 to draft presumptive sentencing guidelines, it cannot avoid this question without shirking its legislatively imposed duty. To be sure, the Commission cannot prevent the prosecution of offenses that do not amount to "true" crimes (under whatever criteria are used to draw that line), but it can ensure that such crimes are treated at sentencing like public welfare offenses. In truth, public welfare offenses have been a subterranean part of our law for over a century, but only in the last decade or so have substantial fines or criminal sentences been imposed for their violation. Recognizing that the world is imperfect and that a doctrinally pure distinction between crimes and torts will never be observed by lawmakers, the Sentencing Commission could still take as its task the implementation of * * * [the] distinction between prices and sanctions. Thus, for behavior that society wishes only to tax, fines should be framed so as to force the actor to

(1958) (discussing Shevlin–Carpenter Co. v. Minnesota, 218 U.S. 57, 67–69 (1910), and United States v. Johnson, 221 U.S. 488, 497–98 (1911)).

internalize costs, but for behavior that society wishes to prohibit, a deliberately sharp and discontinuous jump should be structured into the sentencing guidelines.

* * *

Although this Article has argued that the criminal law should normally prohibit, and not price, it has also recognized that the expansion of the criminal law into formerly civil areas of law and the increasing departures from the traditional "method" of the criminal law make it difficult to state this policy as an iron rule. An either/or choice is also unnecessary. Rather, pricing is appropriate precisely in those areas where the criminal law has relaxed its usual requirement of *mens rea* or has abandoned its normal hostility to vicarious responsibility. Clearly, corporate criminal responsibility straddles this line, and thus distinctions must be drawn that the current federal law of corporate criminal liability does not make.

Notes

1. Professor Hart argues that the criminal law is society's mechanism of communicating "the moral condemnation of the community." Professor Coffee suggests that "[o]ne flaw in Hart's conceptualization of the law's educational role is his reification of the community as a single, indivisible body of public opinion." What do you think? Are they both correct? Could it be that because only a portion of society generally commits white collar crimes, our educational efforts need be directed only toward this part of society? How could such educational efforts be accomplished—through the SEC? The Better Business Bureau? The Chamber of Commerce? Is this a reasonable burden to bestow on these agencies? On the other hand, if we seek to educate only the "necessary" part of society, how can the white collar defendant—or the government—get a fair trial from a jury of laypersons? And, are not all of these efforts to treat white collar crime differently than other types of crime further stratifying our society?

2. If Professor Hart is correct that the criminal law should educate, and Professor Coffee is correct that society's notion of criminal conduct is always evolving, what happens to fair notice? In other words, how can we have notice of what is criminal, if the definition of criminality is always evolving?

3. Does Judge Posner have the answer—that pricing, rather than punishing, avoids the jurisprudential problems that white collar criminal prosecutions pose for the criminal law? What is Professor Coffee's moderation of the "pricing" alternative? Do you prefer it or Judge Posner's formulation? Is it possible that both Judge Posner and Professor Coffee move too quickly to the sentencing phase: if the criminal law is being used improperly on defendants who did not have a criminal *mens rea* and did not engage in conduct generally recognized as wrong, can an enlightened sentencing policy cure the initial, improper, use of the criminal law? Judge Posner noted one objection to "pricing" white collar crime—that it leads to two systems of justice, one for the poor and one for the rich. Is this a problem? Were you persuaded by Judge Posner's response to this criticism?

B. THE EXERCISE OF PROSECUTORIAL DISCRETION

1. THE POWER OF PROSECUTORS

Individual prosecutors exercising their discretion implement juris-prudential distinctions every day when they decide whether to pursue—or decline—prosecution. Excerpts from the next three articles discuss this exercise of discretion. In the first article, Professor Gershman describes the increasing power of prosecutors. In the second article, Jed S. Rakoff, a former Assistant United States Attorney, Southern District of New York, and Chief of Business Frauds Prosecutions for that office, argues that there are currently in place appropriate safeguards on the exercise of this discretion. In the last article, Professor Vorenberg offers another view. Some of the ethical issues referred to, primarily by Professor Gershman, are dealt with later in this section.

BENNETT L. GERSHMAN, THE NEW PROSECUTORS[f]

53 U.Pitt.L.Rev. 393 1992.

The power and prestige of the American prosecutor have changed dramatically over the past twenty years. Three generalizations appropri-ately describe this change. First, prosecutors wield vastly more power than ever before. Second, prosecutors are more insulated from judicial control over their conduct. Third, prosecutors are increasingly immune to ethical restraints. Only the last point may provoke some controversy; the first two are easily documented, and generally accepted by the courts and commentators.

Several factors account for this change. The most obvious is the transition from a due process-oriented criminal justice model to a model that has placed increasing emphasis on crime control and crime preven-tion. Crime has grown more complex and sophisticated since the early 1970s, particularly narcotics, racketeering, official corruption, and busi-ness fraud crimes, requiring a coordinated, powerful, and equally sophis-ticated response. The prosecutor has emerged as the central figure with the training and experience to administer this effort.[3]

Examples of this new prosecutor can be seen in the so-called "special prosecutors" appointed to conduct major investigations such as Watergate, Iran–Contra, and local corruption probes, as well as the expanded use of undercover sting operations led by prosecutors. To support these new prosecutorial initiatives, legislatures have armed

---

f. Copyright © University of Pittsburgh Law Review. Reprinted with permission, University of Pittsburgh Law Review.

3. Ronald Goldstock, *The Prosecutor as Problem Solver, Center for Research in Crime and Justice*, 66 N.Y.U.L.REV. 11 (1991) (prosecutors "may be the best fitted to assume the leadership or coordinating role" in crime prevention). Ronald Gold-stock, a prosecutor of considerable experi-ence, is presently the Director of the New York State Organized Crime Task Force and a Professor at Cornell Law School.

prosecutors with broad new weapons such as RICO, Drug Enterprise, Forfeiture, and Sentencing Guidelines. The judiciary has cooperated in this new effort too. First, by relaxing constitutional protections embodied in the exclusionary rule and due process, and by interpreting statutory and evidentiary rules broadly in the prosecutor's favor, the courts have made it much easier for prosecutors to win convictions. Second, by their increasing deference to prosecutorial discretion in every form, the courts have stimulated a law enforcement mentality that the "end justifies the means." Finally, as resort to the death penalty increases, the prosecutor has become the most dominant figure on the question of who will live and who will die for crimes committed.

* * *

The prosecutor has always been a major player in crime investigation, but today the prosecutor occupies the preeminent role. Traditional functions have expanded, and new powers have been added. The prosecutor develops and coordinates strategies in major undercover investigations; uses the grand jury to investigate complex crimes such as narcotics trafficking, money laundering, official corruption, white collar crime, and organized crime; applies for authorization to obtain eavesdropping warrants; subpoenas records; and obtains the cooperation of witnesses through grants of immunity. Additionally, through sometimes controversial investigative methods, the prosecutor has been able to circumvent, neutralize, or even eliminate defense counsel as an impediment to effective investigation.

* * *

The undercover operations of today involve infiltration and in many cases actual participation in the unlawful activity. For example, law enforcement has established, supplied, and directed a huge array of illegal enterprises, including drug manufacturing and distribution rings, counterfeiting operations, bootleg whiskey operations, bars and restaurants as fronts for criminal activity, stolen merchandise rings, fictitious corporations, obscenity production, and many other illegal commercial activities.

The judiciary has approved such conduct, thereby encouraging even more aggressive and intrusive tactics such as the elaborate "Abscam" operation into legislative corruption, and the "Greylord" operation into judicial corruption. Indeed, the Abscam investigation of the early 1980s was a watershed in undercover investigations. The courts' approval legitimized the most intrusive form of undercover tactics that had yet been used.

* * *

A similar phenomenon of enhanced prosecutorial power and reduced judicial supervision is observable in the prosecutor's conduct of grand jury investigations. Prosecutors traditionally have assumed a highly aggressive posture when using the grand jury as an investigative weapon. In recent years, however, prosecutors, with the acquiescence of the judiciary, have used the grand jury even more aggressively, with considerably greater powers. The power to compel the appearance and interrogation of witnesses has been reaffirmed and reinforced, the power to compel the production of documents has been strengthened, and the power to dispense with fundamental protections of witnesses has been broadened. This trend toward virtually unlimited grand jury power is underscored by an increasing reluctance of courts to check prosecutorial excesses, as noted above. Thus, the decline of supervisory powers, the requirement that a defendant must await conviction and establish prejudice before he can raise a claim of prosecutorial misconduct, and the recent application of the harmless error rule to grand jury proceedings, make it unlikely that valid claims of prosecutorial abuse of the grand jury will be sustained. This is a perversion of the historic function of the grand jury as a buffer between the citizen and the state.

Added to these new developments is an even more ominous threat to the adversary system: the unprecedented use by prosecutors of the grand jury and other means to attack and cripple the criminal defense bar. One of the most alarming events during the last decade has been the prosecutor's attempt to compel criminal defense attorneys to give testimony and produce documents that might incriminate their clients. The testimony is usually sought in connection with fees, a subject that most courts have held is not covered by the attorney-client privilege. Recent statistics show that prosecutors in the United States issue subpoenas to defense attorneys at the rate of 645 per year. Further, most courts do not require any special evidentiary showing before a subpoena can be enforced against a lawyer. Attorneys have been jailed for refusing to cooperate with the prosecutor. As with grand jury subpoenas, prosecutors also have begun to use the statutory summoning power of the Internal Revenue Service to force criminal defense attorneys to disclose the identities of clients or third parties who pay fees in excess of $10,000 cash.

The new aggressive investigative tactics against attorneys are not limited to grand jury subpoenas or IRS summonses. There has been a rising incidence of law office searches, disqualification of attorneys from representing clients, forfeiture of attorneys' fees under broad forfeiture statutes, and the prosecution of attorneys under obstruction of justice statutes for giving legal advice to clients.

* * *

Mostly as a result of his crime-charging power, the prosecutor has always been regarded as one of the most powerful officials in government. Prosecutors historically have enjoyed almost unfettered discretion in bringing charges. Doctrines such as conspiracy, for example, have given prosecutors tremendous power to join parties and offenses in one indictment. The presumption that prosecutors act in good faith has made the charging power virtually immune from judicial review. However, we have witnessed recently an even larger accretion of the prosecutor's charging power through legislative enactments, bold prosecutorial initiatives, and judicial acquiescence.

* * *

To supplement the prosecutor's already considerable arsenal, Congress over the past twenty years has passed legislation providing prosecutors with more potent laws than ever before: Racketeer Influenced and Corrupt Organizations Act; Continuing Criminal Enterprises Act; Criminal Forfeitures Act; Armed Career Criminal Act; Money Laundering Act; Bail Reform Act; Comprehensive Thrift and Bank Fraud Act; Victims of Child Abuse Act. Moreover, the recent trend toward mandatory minimum sentencing has given prosecutors greater leverage than ever to compel plea bargaining, force cooperation, and effectively determine the length of sentences.

Notes

Professor Gershman appears to be outraged at prosecutors' attempts to investigate attorneys. What do you think about such investigations and tactics in light of the cases you've read in this course involving criminal acts by attorneys?[g]

RAKOFF, THE EXERCISE OF PROSECUTORIAL DISCRETION IN FEDERAL BUSINESS FRAUD PROSECUTIONS[h]

Comparatively few public officials enjoy the breadth of discretion accorded a prosecutor in deciding whether or not to commence a prosecution. The prosecutor may have to prove his case in court, but his decision to bring a case is subject to only limited review; and his decision *not* to bring a case is virtually unreviewable. * * * This * * * [essay] offers [an] examination [of the exercise of this discretion] and attempts to convey some practical feel for how prosecutorial discretion is exercised, by describing its exercise in the decision whether or not to seek a federal indictment in a typical business fraud case.

* * * [B]usiness fraud cases—by virtue of their complexity, difficulty, likeness to civil cases and (sometimes) moral ambiguity—often require a very sensitive exercise of prosecutorial discretion. * * * My central concern, * * * is whether the exercise of prosecutorial discretion should be governed by an additional regime of legal constraints.

Although there are few statutory restraints on prosecutorial discretion, the Constitution itself contains several such restraints, both ex-

g. Chapters 4, 9, 11.

h. Reprinted with permission from Rakoff, *The Exercise of Prosecutorial Discretion in Federal Business Fraud Prosecu-* *tions, Corrigible Corporations and Unruly Law* 173–86. (B. Fisse & P.A. French ed. 1985). Copyright © 1985 by Trinity University Press.

press and implied, on the exercise of prosecutorial discretion. One express constraint is the Double Jeopardy Clause of the Fifth Amendment: "nor shall any person be subject for the same offense to be twice put in jeopardy of life or limb." * * *

* * *

The Equal Protection and Due Process Clauses of the Constitution also provide certain limitations on the exercise of prosecutorial discretion, notably a bar to "selective prosecution" and "vindictive prosecution." * * * To establish a defense of "selective prosecution," a defendant must establish (often with benefit of discovery) both that she/he has been singled out for prosecution while others similarly situated have not generally been proceeded against and that the government's discriminatory selection of him or her for prosecution is based upon such constitutionally impermissible considerations as race, religion, or the desire to prevent one's exercise of First Amendment rights. Similarly, the doctrine prohibiting vindictive or retaliatory prosecutions appears to be applied only where prosecutors have retaliated against a defendant's exercise of such specially protected rights as First Amendment rights or the right to appeal.

Nonetheless, as in the case of the Double Jeopardy Clause federal prosecutors have as a matter of discretion implemented the Constitution-based doctrines of "selective prosecution" and "vindictive prosecution" in ways that go well beyond their judicially enforceable application.

* * *

The 94 United States Attorney's Offices are not governed by formal regulations but, so far as written directives are concerned, chiefly by the provisions of an unwieldy, multi-volume melange of policies, guidelines, legal analyses and helpful hints known as the United States Attorneys' Manual. The Manual is expressly for internal use only, and its provisions are not judicially enforceable. Internal enforcement of the provisions is sometimes lax and sometimes idiosyncratic; yet, most of the provisions are followed most of the time, perhaps because they generally correspond to older oral traditions of federal prosecution.

Most of the provisions applicable to the exercise of prosecutorial discretion are set forth in Chapter 2 of Title 9 of the Manual. In addition, the most important of such provisions, along with commentaries, are gathered together in a pamphlet entitled Principles of Federal Prosecution, issued by the Department in 1980 and now publicly available. Typical of these provisions are those comprising the so-called "Petite policy," mentioned above. (The name refers to Petite v. United States, in 361 U.S. 529 (1960), in which the Supreme Court expressly deferred to the Department's policy in this area.) As set forth in the Manual at § 9–2.142, the policy [is as follows:]

"The Department of Justice's policy on dual prosecution and successive federal prosecution precludes the initiation or continuation of a federal prosecution following a state prosecution or a prior federal prosecution based on substantially the same act, acts or transaction unless there is compelling federal interest supporting the dual or successive federal prosecution." * * *

* * *

The policies and guidelines affecting prosecutorial discretion which are set forth in the United States Attorneys' Manual tend to remain relatively constant from year to year and from administration to administration. But each administration has its own prosecutorial points of emphasis, or "priorities," as to a lesser extent does each individual United States Attorney. Three kinds of priorities which affect prosecutorial discretion bear mention here.

First, each recent federal administration has, with much fanfare, "declared war" on one or another kind of crime. Under the Kennedy and, to a lesser extent, Johnson administrations, the target was organized crime and labor racketeering; under the Nixon and, to a lesser extent, Ford administrations, it was narcotics; under the Carter administration, it was "white collar" crime and official corruption; * * * under the Reagan administration, it [was] once again narcotics and official corruption. [Under the Bush administration it is narcotics, with an emphasis on money laundering, and white collar crimes, especially fraud in financial institutions.] * * *

A second kind of prioritization—one with more impact on the exercise of the prosecutorial discretion—has been the attempt of both the Justice Department and individual United States Attorney's Offices to develop somewhat specific guidelines within each category of crime as to which cases to decline *ab initio*. For example, in the area of business fraud prosecutions, the Justice Department issued a report in 1980 entitled *National Priorities for the Investigation and Prosecution of White Collar Crime,* which recommended that particular kinds of business frauds not be given "priority" (i.e., not be prosecuted) unless their impacts upon victims met certain threshold limits. * * *

A third kind of priority is that formulated by a local United States Attorney or even one of his subordinates. Although such priorities create the possibility of "unequal" enforcement of the law in different parts of the United States, they are often reasonably responsive to particular local conditions. The relative concentration of criminal prosecutions for securities frauds in the Southern District of New York (itself the result of New York's position as the nation's financial capital) has been accompanied by the formulation of certain local priorities (some more enduring than others) as to which such cases should be prosecuted.

* * *

Beyond policies, guidelines, and priorities, federal prosecutorial discretion is substantially shaped, and substantially limited, by practices, customs, and traditions that are orally conveyed from Assistant to Assistant. These unwritten "rules" are remarkably uniform even from office to office. For example, in every United States Attorney's Office with which this author is familiar, it is the general practice not to commence a prosecution if the Assistant investigating the case has a reasonable doubt about the putative defendant's guilt, even if the Assistant's superiors think the evidence of guilt is sufficient. The Assistant's superiors see their role as including the power to disapprove (typically on legal or policy grounds) a prosecution proposed by the Assistant, but not as including the power to resurrect a prosecution the Assistant has disapproved on the facts, except in extraordinary cases. This practice—which is akin to the division of power between trial and appellate courts—finds its justification in the better "feel" that the Assistant investigating the facts has for the facts themselves, even if she/he does not have the same policy perspective as his or her chiefs. Incidentally, however, this practice provides an important protection for an accused, in that it tends to focus the decision to prosecute on the particular facts of the individual case as opposed to the broader "deterrence" perspectives on which the chiefs tend to concentrate.

With respect to the particular area of business fraud prosecutions, a rather more controversial practice which has become common in many offices is the tendency, mentioned above, to use the criminal law to map (or, some would say, extend) the frontiers of business ethics. From one point of view, "test" cases should have no place in criminal prosecutions; society's most stringent sanctions should not be imposed on a defendant regardless of how "immoral" his or her conduct may have been, unless he or she violated a known and certain legal duty to society. From another viewpoint, however, criminal sanctions may be viewed as the most effective deterrent against new and creative forms of fraud most likely to victimize the public, and a failure to invoke such sanctions may be seen as equivalent to giving free reign to the most artful swindlers.

* * *

VORENBERG, DECENT RESTRAINT OF PROSECUTORIAL POWER

94 Harv.L.Rev. 1521 (1981).[i]

* * * The fate of most of those accused of crime is determined by prosecutors, but typically this determination takes place out of public view—in the hallways of the courthouse, in the prosecutors' offices, or on the telephone. There is a broad and rather casual acceptance of the fact that prosecutors often exercise greater control over the administration of criminal justice than do other officials.

* * *

If accumulation of power is success, prosecutors have done well in recent years. This [essay] examines the extent to which prosecutors have

i. Reprinted with permission from Vorenberg, *Decent Restraint of Prosecutorial Power*, 94 HARV.L.REV. 1522–57. Copyright

© 1981 by Harvard Law Review Association.

acquired essentially unreviewable discretion. What I mean by discretion is the ability to make decisions about guilt and degree of punishment without the limits of rules or other constraints on freedom of action, including judicial review, generally imposed on other public officials making decisions of comparable import. The scope of discretion in any particular case is necessarily hard to measure because prosecutors respond in different ways to explicit limits and because such other constraints as custom, political accountability, and intra-office communication are intangible and elusive.

* * *

The core of prosecutors' power is charging, plea bargaining, and, when it is under the prosecutor's control, initiating investigations. Decisions whether and what to charge, and whether and on what terms to bargain, have been left in prosecutors' hands with very few limitations. As violations of existing criminal law have increased and legislatures have created new crimes without providing resources for trial and punishment of all those who could be convicted, prosecutors increasingly have been forced to allocate resources by deciding whether to charge and whether to offer leniency in exchange for guilty pleas.

* * *

Because prosecutors make decisions that can determine conviction and punishment, it is fair to test their process of decision against the standards imposed on other officials who make similarly critical judgments. Yet prosecutors are not held to anything remotely like what due process would require if they were engaged in an acknowledged rather than a hidden system of adjudication. No uniform, pre-announced rules inform the defendant and control the decisionmaker; a single official can invoke society's harshest sanctions on the basis of ad hoc personal judgments. Prosecutors can and do accord different treatment—prison for some and probation or diversion for others—on grounds that are not written down anywhere and may not have been either rational, consistent, or discoverable in advance. Because they need not and do not make known the reasons for their actions, there is not even a "common law" to guide future cases and future defendants. It is difficult to square this absence of standards with our notions of the constitutional guarantee of due process. As the Supreme Court has written, due process is subverted "[w]here, as here, there are no standards governing the exercise of the discretion * * * [because] the scheme permits and encourages an arbitrary and discriminatory enforcement of the law."[116]

The risk of unequal treatment created by standardless discretion is troubling not only as a threat to due process but in its own right as well. Giving prosecutors the power to invoke or deny punishment at their discretion raises the prospect that society's most fundamental sanctions will be imposed arbitrarily and capriciously and that the least favored members of the community—racial and ethnic minorities, social out-

116. Papachristou v. City of Jackson-   ville, 405 U.S. 156, 170 (1972).

casts, the poor—will be treated most harshly. Professor Ely has noted that "a discretionary system of selection *always* carries the potential for invidious discrimination * * *. Such systems amount to failures of representation, in that those who make the laws (by refusing effectively to make the laws) have provided a buffer to ensure that they and theirs will not effectively be subjected to them."[117] As we have seen, open discrimination against certain classes of defendants may raise constitutional issues, but the problems of proof are considerable.

The unfairness caused by an absence of enunciated standards is exacerbated by the lack of an opportunity for a suspect to be heard before the prosecutor makes his decisions. Even without articulated principles that guide prosecutorial decisions, it might be valuable to a suspect to argue on the basis of the facts and equities that he should not be charged; however, charging decisions typically are made without any opportunity to be heard. Although participation by counsel is a prerequisite to plea bargaining, plea negotiations have no set procedure and involve nothing that could be called a hearing. Lawyers or defendants whom prosecutors respect or like may be treated considerately and given ample opportunity to be heard, while others may simply be told what is available on a take-it-or-leave-it basis. In short, there is an absence not merely of standards but also of any systematic guarantee that the defendant will be heard on issues that vitally affect him, in violation of the principle that "[t]he fundamental requisite of due process of law is the opportunity to be heard."[119]

The easy answer to this criticism is that a defendant can get all the process that is due later, at the grand jury or preliminary hearing and the trial. The answer is easy but unfair, for the grand jury and preliminary hearing do not significantly limit the prosecutor's control. Moreover, prosecutors who use plea bargaining often enough to discourage most defendants from ever going to trial surely should be judged by the methods they use in the great bulk of cases and not by the very procedures they are preempting.

It is equally unfair to say that, because discretion can only exist at charging and bargaining levels lower than the authorized maximum, the prosecutor is only helping defendants when he exercises discretion. Because prosecutors often do not charge the maximum authorized and do offer leniency to most defendants through plea bargaining, a defendant is hurt in the most basic sense when treated in an unusually harsh manner.

* * *

Notes

Some commentators and practitioners see statutes such as RICO and Money Laundering as posing special problems because of the broad scope of discretion accorded prosecutors. According to the ABA:

117. J. ELY, DEMOCRACY AND DISTRUST 177 (1980).

119. Grannis v. Ordean, 234 U.S. 385, 394 (1914).

"We used to think of prosecutorial discretion as * * * the decision whether to charge. Now we think about prosecutorial discretion as * * * the decision whether to subpoena an attorney for a client in an ongoing piece of litigation. * * * What [such subpoenas] do is divert attention from the issue of guilt or innocence. They put pressure upon counsel to litigate issues unrelated to the guilt or innocence of [the] client, to fight to defend against * * * having to become a witness against [one's] client, to fight to preserve the economic base of his contract with his client, and the means by which [one] can stay in a case * * *.

* * *

"In 1970 Congress passed the Racketeer Influenced and Corrupt Organizations Act (18 U.S.C. § 1963 et seq.) and the Controlled Substances Act (21 U.S.C. § 801a et seq.). These new laws provided for criminal forfeiture as a penalty (18 U.S.C. § 1963 and 21 U.S.C. § 848) and civil forfeiture as a remedial measure (18 U.S.C. § 881). In order to protect from forfeiture the property of persons who may unwittingly become involved in economic transactions with drug dealers and racketeers, 'innocent owner' provisions were also enacted.

* * *

"The laws are well intentioned. Unfortunately, they also provide prosecutors with a tool to deprive accused (but not yet convicted) persons of the ability to use assets in their possession to retain attorneys to represent them in the pending criminal actions. * * *

* * *

"The 98th Congress enacted 26 U.S.C. § 6050I as part of the Deficit Reduction Act of 1984 (P.L. 98–369).

* * *

"The statute provides that any person who receives more than $10,000 in cash, including foreign currency, in the course of trade or business must file a return (Form 8300) with the Internal Revenue Service stating:

    1.   the name, address and tax identification number of the person from whom the cash was received;

    2.   the amount of the cash;

    3.   the date and nature of the transaction; and

    4.   such other information as the Secretary of the Treasury may require.

"These reporting requirements apply to any series of related transactions in which the aggregate cash amount is in excess of $10,000. They also apply to cash sums that are deposited with an attorney, but which are not earned fees of the attorney (e.g., cash from an estate).

* * *

"[ABA's] concerns about these reporting requirements began to become a reality in the summer of 1988. Many lawyers had filed the forms without identifying the name of the client and refusing to provide other identifying information. Several district IRS offices contacted selected attorneys and demanded that the required information be filed. When the firms refused to provide clients' identities, summonses were issued."[j]

Notes

Do you agree with the ABA that RICO and the Money Laundering reporting requirements inappropriately add to federal prosecutor's discretion?

2. ETHICAL RESTRAINTS ON PROSECUTORS

In addition to the checks on prosecutorial discretion noted by Mr. Rakoff, federal prosecutors are

> "expect[ed] to use the ABA's code of ethics as a guide for their own conduct. This expectation is made explicit in the Department of Justice Standards of Conduct at 28 C.F.R. § 45.735–1(b). Accordingly, Department [of Justice] attorneys can be subject to discipline under * * * internal rules for violating a bar ethics rule in appropriate cases. There is nothing new about this position—we have espoused it for years."[k]

To that end, Rule 3.8 of the ABA Model Rules of Professional Conduct (1984) ("Model Rules") may be most pertinent. It provides:

RULE 3.8 SPECIAL RESPONSIBILITIES OF A PROSECUTOR

The prosecutor in a criminal case shall:

(a) refrain from prosecuting a charge that the prosecutor knows is not supported by probable cause;

(b) make reasonable efforts to assure that the accused has been advised of the right to, and the procedure for obtaining, counsel and has been given reasonable opportunity to obtain counsel;

(c) not seek to obtain from an unrepresented accused a waiver of important pretrial rights, such as the right to a preliminary hearing;

(d) make timely disclosure to the defense of all evidence or information known to the prosecutor that tends to negate the guilt of the accused or mitigates the offense, and, in connection with sentencing, disclose to the defense and to the tribunal all unprivileged mitigating information known to the prosecutor, except when the prosecutor is relieved of this responsibility by a protective order of the tribunal; and

---

j. Exercise of Federal Prosecutorial Authority In A Changing Legal Environment: Hearing Before the Gov't Information, Justice and Agriculture Subcomm. of the House Comm. on Gov't Operations, 101st Cong.2d Sess. 41–55 (1990) [hereinafter "Hearings on Exercise of Federal Prosecu-

torial Authority"] (statement of Edward S.G. Dennis, Jr., Assistant Attorney General, Crim.Div., United States Dept. of Justice).

k. *Id.* at 249–250.

(e) exercise reasonable care to prevent investigators, law enforcement personnel, employees or other persons assisting or associated with the prosecutor in a criminal case from making an extrajudicial statement that the prosecutor would be prohibited from making * * *.

Another Rule from the ABA Model Rules has caused considerable controversy, however. Rule 4.2 provides:

"In representing a client, a lawyer shall not communicate about the subject of the representation with a party the lawyer knows to be represented by another lawyer in the matter, unless the lawyer has the consent of the other lawyer or is authorized to do so."

The controversy regarding Rule 4.2 arises in the context of undercover operations and concerns the extent to which government agents, under the direction of a federal prosecutor, may initiate or continue an undercover operation on a person who is represented by counsel. Consider the following scenario:

"An Assistant United States Attorney receives word that the underboss of one of the nation's most powerful organized crime families, currently incarcerated and awaiting trial on racketeering charges, wants to speak with him. The underboss has quietly let it be known that he wants to make a deal. In return for a reduced sentence and entry into the witness protection program, he is willing to plead guilty and cooperate fully with the government. His evidence could bring down an entire organized crime family, perhaps several families.

"The underboss has one additional condition: He insists that his lawyer not be informed about his desire to cooperate. His lawyer is corrupt; the lawyer's fees are being paid by the head of the family. If there is even a hint that the underboss might want to cooperate, he'll be killed. He is willing to appear in front of a magistrate and waive his rights to counsel, or do anything else the prosecutor thinks might be appropriate—but he vehemently insists that his lawyer not be told. Should the prosecutor take him up on his offer?

"The prosecutor does some quick legal research. Would a communication outside the presence of counsel violate the defendant's Sixth Amendment right to counsel? No. The defendant initiated the contact, and in any event that right (like any constitutional right) may be waived. Would it violate his Miranda rights under the Fifth Amendment? No, for essentially the same reasons. Is there a federal statute which prohibits such contract? No. A federal regulation? No. A Department of Justice policy? No.

"The prosecutor discovers, however, that the supreme court of his state has adopted a version of Model Rule 4.2 of the American Bar Association Model Rules of Professional Conduct. That rule—as interpreted by the state's bar disciplinary board—imposes a blanket prohibition on communications with represented persons by attorneys. There is no exception, even when the crime family lawyer's divided loyalties will cause the client to be murdered. The prosecutor also discovers that the federal district court in his district has adopted a one-sentence local rule incorporating the state ethical rules in their entirety.

"The prosecutor thus has two choices: Forego the promise of valuable evidence, or ignore the state ethical rule (and the local federal rule). The former option is almost unthinkable. The latter option, however, raises a substantial risk that the underboss's testimony may be excluded or that indictments—including the indictment of the underboss himself—may be dismissed. Moreover, the prosecutor may face discipline or disbarment for engaging in deliberately 'unethical' conduct. The prosecutor notes ruefully that the state bar disciplinary board that will sit in judgment on the matter consists of two criminal defense attorneys and five civil practitioners, none of whom has ever been a prosecutor. At best, the prosecutor will be battling charges of 'unethical' behavior for a long time to come."[1]

———

In 1989, in an effort to address this problem, Attorney General Thornburg issued a memorandum to Department of Justice litigators explaining circumstances under which federal prosecutors were *not* obliged to comply with Rule 4.2. Not surprisingly the criminal defense bar and some courts were outraged by the Thornburg Memorandum. When Janet Reno was appointed as Attorney General, she and other Justice Department Officials met with the defense bar. A proposed rule was published and after a period of public comment, the "Reno Rule" was adopted in 1994.[m] The "Reno Rule" provides:

"a general prohibition, subject to limited enumerated exceptions, against contacts with 'represented parties' without the consent of counsel. * * * The rule * * * generally permits investigative contacts with 'represented persons': that is, individuals or organizations that are represented by counsel but that have not yet been named as defendants in a civil or criminal enforcement proceeding or arrested as part of a criminal proceeding."[n]

Interestingly, the Reno Rule states that it supersedes any state or local court of ethical rules to the contrary:

"Communications with represented parties and represented persons pursuant to this part are intended to constitute communications that are "authorized by law" within the meaning of Rule 4.2 of the

l. F. Denis Saylor, IV & J. Douglas Wilson, Putting a Square Peg in a Round Hole: The Application of Model Rule 4.2 to Federal Prosecutors, 53 U. PITT. L. REV. 459 (1992). Copyright ©. All rights reserved. Reprinted with permission of University of Pittsburgh Law Review, F. Denis Saylor, IV, and J. Douglas Wilson.

m. 59 Fed. Reg. 10,086, 28 C.F.R. § 77.5–.6.

n. 59 Fed. Reg. 39910 (Aug. 4, 1994), 28 C.F.R. § 77.1–.12.

American Bar Association Model Rules of Professional Conduct, DR 7–104(A)(1) of the ABA Code of Professional Responsibility, and analogous state and local federal court rules. In addition, this part is intended to preempt and supersede the application of state laws and rules and local federal court rules to the extent that they relate to contacts by attorneys for the government, and those acting at their direction or under their supervision, with represented parties or represented persons in criminal or civil law enforcement investigations or proceedings; it is designed to preempt the entire field of rules concerning such contacts. When the Attorney General finds a willful violation of any of the rules in this part, however, sanctions for the conduct that constituted a willful violation of this part may be applied, if warranted, by the appropriate state disciplinary authority.''[o]

In light of the above, consider the following case where a federal prosecutor spoke with a defendant in accordance with the "Thornburg Memorandum," which was in effect at the time. Be aware that John Lyons was the federal prosecutor assigned to the *Lopez* case.[p]

UNITED STATES v. LOPEZ

United States Court of Appeals, Ninth Circuit, 1993.
4 F.3d 1455.

POOLE, CIRCUIT JUDGE.

I.

Jose Lopez was indicted for conspiracy to distribute and distribution of cocaine and heroin in violation of 21 U.S.C. §§ 846 and 841(a)(1), and for aiding and abetting in violation of 18 U.S.C. § 2. While awaiting trial, Lopez was detained with a codefendant, Antonio Escobedo, at the Federal Correctional Institution at Pleasanton.

Lopez retained attorney Barry Tarlow to represent him. Tarlow informed Lopez that he believed that the defendants had a viable entrapment defense and that, in any case, it was his general policy not to negotiate a plea with the government in exchange for cooperation.

Attorney James A. Twitty, who represented codefendant Escobedo, had agreed with Tarlow to coordinate a joint investigation on behalf of the defendants. In so doing, he often spoke to both Escobedo and Lopez by telephone and in person during visits to Pleasanton. In March or April of 1990, Escobedo telephoned Twitty and expressed his interest in reopening negotiations with the government. Concerned about his children, who he feared were being abused while in the custody of their mother, Lopez was anxious to be released from Pleasanton and thus echoed Escobedo's interest in a possible plea bargain.

o.   28 C.F.R. § 77.12.

p.   In the Matter of James Alan Twitty, 1994 WL 15609 (Cal.Bar Ct.), 2 Cal. State Bar Ct. Rptr. 664, 670 (1994).

Without informing Tarlow, Twitty twice traveled to Pleasanton in order to discuss the possibility of a plea bargain with Escobedo and Lopez. He spoke to both men about this possibility from five to nine times on the phone.

Lopez apparently did not want to retain another lawyer to negotiate with the government because he feared that doing so would cost him Tarlow's services, and Lopez wanted Tarlow to represent him in the event the case went to trial. Lopez also was concerned about the additional expense of having Tarlow conduct plea negotiations. Twitty accordingly contacted Lyons on behalf of both Lopez and Escobedo. Lyons claims that Twitty informed him that Lopez did not want Tarlow present at any meetings with the government because "Tarlow didn't represent his best interest in this particular context." Lyons avers that he did not press Twitty on this point, but instead assumed that Lopez was connected to a drug ring which was paying Tarlow's fees, and which would endanger his family if Tarlow learned about the negotiations with the government.

Twitty, however, maintains that during his first phone conversation with the prosecutor about the proposed negotiations, he emphasized that Lopez's reasons for excluding Tarlow had nothing to do with concerns about the safety of his family. He stressed that Tarlow's fees were not being paid by anyone with whom Lopez was in the drug business. According to Twitty, he informed the prosecutor that Lopez simply feared that if Tarlow knew about the plea negotiations, he would resign as Lopez's lawyer.

Recognizing the sensitivity of a meeting with Lopez without Tarlow's knowledge or consent, Lyons contacted the district court ex parte. The court referred the matter to a magistrate judge, who conducted an in camera interview of Lopez on May 21, 1990. The magistrate judge warned Lopez of the dangers of self-representation, informed him that he could have other counsel, and cautioned him that Twitty, as Escobedo's lawyer, could not represent him. Lopez insisted on going forward with the meeting, and signed a waiver prepared by the government. Lopez, along with Escobedo and his attorney Twitty, met with Lyons in the prosecutor's office.

On May 30, 1991, Lopez was taken once again before the magistrate judge, who verified that Lopez wanted to meet with the government a second time without Tarlow. The second meeting also took place in Lyons' office, and was again attended by Lyons, Lopez, Escobedo, and Twitty. Following this second meeting, Lyons sent Twitty a proposed plea agreement for Escobedo, a copy of which Twitty provided to Lopez. After talking with Twitty, the two men rejected the proposal.

Tarlow found out about his client's discussions with the government indirectly. In August 1990, Lyons talked with Harold Rosenthal, who was the attorney for a third codefendant. Lyons alerted Rosenthal to the fact that the government had been negotiating with Lopez without Tarlow's knowledge. Rosenthal contacted Twitty, who urged him to refrain from informing Tarlow for fear that doing so would "mess up the deal." Nevertheless, Rosenthal called Tarlow. On August 15, 1990, Tarlow was permitted by the district court to withdraw as Lopez's counsel.

Having retained substitute counsel, Lopez filed a motion to dismiss the indictment on September 27, 1990. Lopez alleged that the government infringed upon his Sixth Amendment rights as well as Rules of Professional Conduct of the State Bar of California Rule 2–100 (1988). Binding pursuant to Local Rule 110–3 in the Northern District of California, Rule 2–100 generally prohibits a lawyer from communicating with another party in the case without the consent of that party's lawyer.

After extensive briefing and six hearings at which Twitty, Lopez, and Lyons testified, the district court concluded that Lyons had violated Rule 2–100. The court rebuffed the government's attempts to invoke the "Thornburgh Memorandum," a Justice Department policy statement which purports to exempt federal litigators from compliance with the rule against communicating with represented individuals without the consent of their lawyers. The court also determined that Lyons had not insulated himself from blame by obtaining the approval of the district court before each meeting, since he had "effectively misled" the court regarding Lopez's reasons for requesting to speak with him.

Since Lopez had been able to obtain competent replacement counsel for Tarlow, the court declined to say that the government's misconduct rose to the level of a Sixth Amendment violation. It also found, however, that Lopez had been significantly prejudiced, since he was effectively deprived of the counsel of his choice. Refusing to evaluate Lyons's actions apart from the Thornburgh memorandum which he invoked in his defense, the court condemned both as an egregious and flagrant "frontal assault on the legitimate powers of the court." Rejecting less drastic remedies as ineffective, the district court invoked its supervisory powers in order to dismiss the indictment against Jose Lopez.

The government, on appeal, has prudently dropped its dependence on the Thornburgh Memorandum in justifying AUSA Lyons' conduct, and has thereby spared us the need of reiterating the district court's trenchant analysis of the inefficacy of the Attorney General's policy statement. The government instead argues that Rule 2–100 was not intended to apply to prosecutors pursuing investigations, that the contact with Lopez was authorized by law, that Rule 2–100 did not apply since Lopez was exercising his constitutional right of self-representation, and that Lopez waived his rights under Rule 2–100. Finally, the government contends that dismissal of the indictment was improper, even if Lyons did violate the ethical rule.

II.

* * *

Rule 110–3 of the local rules of the Northern District of California requires that:

> Every member of the bar of this court and any attorney permitted to practice in this court under Local Rule 110–2 shall be familiar with and comply with the standards of professional conduct required of members of the State Bar of California and contained in the State Bar Act, the Rules of Professional Conduct of the State Bar of California, and decisions of any court applicable thereto; maintain the respect due courts of justice and judicial officers; [and] perform with the honesty, care, and decorum required for the fair and efficient administration of justice.

Rule 2–100 of the Rules of Professional Conduct of the State Bar of California governs communications with a represented party:

> (A) While representing a client, a member shall not communicate directly or indirectly about the subject of the representation with a party the member knows to be represented by another lawyer in the matter, unless the member has the consent of the other lawyer.

* * *

> (C) This rule shall not prohibit:
>
> (1) Communications with a public officer, board, committee, or body;
>
> (2) Communications initiated by a party seeking advice or representation from an independent lawyer of the party's choice; or
>
> (3) Communications otherwise authorized by law.

Rule 2–100's prohibition against communicating with represented parties without the consent of their counsel is both widely accepted and of venerable heritage. The California rule tracks the language of Rule 4.2 of the American Bar Association's Model Rules of Professional Conduct, which in turn is nearly identical to its predecessor in the Model Code of Professional Responsibility, Disciplinary Rule 7–104(A)(1). A similar prohibition appears under Canon 9 of the ABA's Canons of Professional Ethics, which were promulgated in 1908. Not simply an American invention, the prohibition has roots which can be traced back to English common law. Today some version of the rule is in effect in all fifty American states.

The rule against communicating with a represented party without the consent of that party's counsel shields a party's substantive interests against encroachment by opposing counsel and safeguards the relationship between the party and her attorney. As Tarlow's withdrawal upon discovering the secret communication between Lopez and the government exemplifies all too well, the trust necessary for a successful attorney-client relationship is eviscerated when the client is lured into clandestine meetings with the lawyer for the opposition. As a result, uncurbed communications with represented parties could have deleterious effects well beyond the context of the individual case, for our adversary system is premised upon functional lawyer-client relationships.

* * *

The government argues, however, that Rule 2–100 was not intended to apply to prosecutors pursuing criminal investigations. Decisions of the state courts of California, which are binding on attorneys practicing in the Northern District of California through Local Rule 110–3, however, have held prosecutors to the rules prohibiting communications with represented parties. In People v. Sharp, 150 Cal.App.3d 13, 197 Cal.Rptr. 436 (1983), decided under the predecessor of Rule 2–100, the court noted that:

> [b]ecause the prosecutor's position is unique—he represents authority and the discretion to make decisions affecting the defendant's pending case—his contact carries an implication of leniency for cooperative defendants or harsher treatment for the uncooperative. Such contact intrudes upon the function of defense counsel and impedes his or her ability to negotiate a settlement and properly represent the client, whose interests the rule is designed to protect.

Id. Cal.Rptr. at 439–40. The court thus concluded that, by directing police agents to conduct a lineup without notifying the defendant's attorney, the prosecutor violated his professional ethical responsibilities.

* * *

The government next adopts the position that Lyons' conduct falls within the "communications otherwise authorized by law" exception to the rule against attorney communication with represented parties. See Rule 2–100(C)(3). The government argues that Lyons' contact with Lopez was authorized by statutes enabling prosecutors to conduct criminal investigations, and that the meetings were authorized by the magistrate judge's approval.

The government reasons that federal prosecutors operate pursuant to a "statutory scheme" that permits them to communicate with represented parties in order to detect and prosecute federal offenses. Citing 28 U.S.C. §§ 509, 515(a) and (c), 516, 533 and 547, the government argues that Justice Department attorneys fall within the "authorized by law" exception to California Rule 2–100 and its counterparts.

The comment to California Rule 2–100 notes that:

> Rule 2–100 is intended to control communications between a member [of the bar] and persons the member knows to be represented by counsel unless a statutory scheme or case law will override the rule. There are a number of *express statutory schemes* which authorize communications between a member and person who would otherwise be subject to this rule.... *Other applicable law also includes the authority of government prosecutors and investigators to conduct criminal investigations, as limited by the relevant decisional law.*

(Emphasis supplied). Thus, the "authorized by law" exception to Rule 2–100 requires that a statutory scheme expressly permit contact between an attorney and a represented party. While recognizing the statutory authority of prosecutors to investigate crime, however, Rule 2–100 is intended to allow no more contact between prosecutors and represented defendants than the case law permits. We agree with the district court that the statutes cited by the government are nothing more than general enabling statutes. Nothing in these provisions expressly or impliedly authorizes contact with represented individuals beyond that permitted by case law. As discussed above, "the authority of government prosecutors and investigators to conduct criminal investigations" is "limited by the relevant decisional law" to contacts conducted prior to indictment in a non-custodial setting. Lyons' discussions with Lopez were not so authorized.

The government also maintains that by obtaining the prior approval of a magistrate judge, Lyons brought his conversations with Lopez within the realm of the "authorized by law" exception to California Rule 2–100. We agree that in an appropriate case, contact with a represented party could be excepted from the prohibition of Rule 2–100 by court order. But, as in other areas of the law, judicial approval cannot absolve the government from responsibility for wrongful acts when the government has misled the court in obtaining its sanction. When seeking the authorization of the district court, the prosecutor had an affirmative duty to avoid misleading the court. Rules of Professional Conduct of the State Bar of California Rule 5–200(B) (1988) ("In presenting a matter to a tribunal, a member ... [s]hall not seek to mislead the judge, judicial officer or jury by an artifice or false statement of fact or law.").

The district court concluded that the magistrate judge approved the meeting between Lyons and Lopez in the mistaken belief, fostered by Lyons, that:

> Tarlow[ ] was being paid by a third party with interests inimical to those of Lopez and that Lopez feared that if Tarlow became aware of his client's interest in cooperating with the government, he would pass the information on to others who would harm Lopez and/or his family.

765 F.Supp. at 1452. The district court thus concluded that the magistrate judge's approval could not legally authorize Lyons to meet with Lopez.

The district court found that Lyons materially misled the magistrate judge regarding the facts surrounding Lopez's request to speak directly with the prosecutor. We agree that the magistrate judge apparently did not have a full understanding of the facts surrounding Lopez's request. Without that understanding, she could not have made an informed decision to authorize the communications.

Although it is not necessary to our determination in this case to decide whether the district court erred in its finding that Lyons materially misled the magistrate judge, we suggest that the finding is not sustainable without resolving certain conflicts in the testimony of Twitty, Lyons, and Lopez as to what Lyons knew and when he knew it (the district court, for whatever reason, said it was not necessary to resolve these conflicts). On remand, were the district court to consider lesser sanctions than dismissal of the indictment, resolution of these conflicts would be essential.

The government makes several related arguments regarding the effect of Lopez's waiver on its ethical obligations. We note initially that it would be a mistake to speak in terms of a party "waiving" her "rights" under Rule 2–100. The rule against communicating with represented parties is fundamentally concerned with the duties of attorneys, not with the rights of parties. Lyons' duties as an attorney practicing in the Northern District of California extended beyond his obligation to respect Lopez's rights. Consequently, as the government concedes, ethical obligations are personal, and may not be vicariously waived.

The government also argues, however, that Lopez created a form of "hybrid representation" by waiving his right to counsel for the limited purpose of negotiating with the government, while retaining Tarlow as his counsel for all other purposes. Since Lopez would be unrepresented for purposes of discussions with the government, it would presumably not be a violation of Rule 2–100 for the government to communicate with him directly. We have in the past held, however, that "[i]f the defendant assumes any of the 'core functions' of the lawyer, ... the hybrid scheme is acceptable only if the defendant has voluntarily waived counsel." United States v. Turnbull, 888 F.2d 636, 638 (9th Cir.1989). Representing a client in negotiations with the government is certainly one of the core functions of defense counsel, and there is no question that Lopez did not waive his right to counsel. In fact, the magistrate judge, following the hearing with Lopez, clearly communicated to Lyons that while Lopez was waiving his right to have counsel present while inquiring about the possibility of cooperating with the government, he was not waiving his right to counsel. The district court found Lopez did not wish to waive his right to have an attorney present. In Kimmel, we explained that:

> [w]hen the accused assumes functions that are at the core of the lawyer's traditional role ... he will often undermine his own defense. Because he has a constitutional right to have his lawyer perform core functions, he must knowingly and intelligently waive that right.

672 F.2d at 721. While we are not immediately concerned with the constitutional dimensions of Lopez's communications with the government, it is clear that the magistrate judge's intervention could not, as a matter of law, have created a form of "hybrid representation." To the contrary, Lyons was notified by the court that Lopez was still represented by Tarlow, and consequently he could not evade his duty under Rule 2–100 on this basis.

For the same reason, we reject the government's claim that enforcing the ethical prohibition against communication with represented parties would interfere, under these circumstances, with the party's constitutional rights. The government relies on the doctrine established in Faretta v. California, 422 U.S. 806 (1975), that it is unconstitutional to require a criminal defendant to be represented by an attorney. We see no conflict between *Faretta* and Rule 2–100. Of course, Rule 2–100 does not bar communications with persons who have waived their right to counsel, for by its express terms the rule only applies to "communications with a represented party." (Emphasis supplied). Because Lopez did not waive his right to counsel, Faretta is immaterial.

We therefore conclude that the district court was correct in holding that Lyons had an ethical duty to avoid communicating directly with Lopez regarding the criminal prosecution so long as Lopez was represented by Tarlow.

III.

The district court dismissed the indictment under its inherent supervisory powers. Finding the government's conduct "flagrant and egregious," and believing that Lopez had been prejudiced through loss of his attorney of choice, the district court reasoned that no lesser sanction could adequately preserve judicial integrity and deter future governmental misconduct. We review the district court's exercise of its supervisory powers for an abuse of discretion.

There are three legitimate grounds for a court's exercise of supervisory power: "to implement a remedy for the violation of a recognized statutory or constitutional right; to preserve judicial integrity by ensuring that a conviction rests on appropriate considerations validly before a jury; and to deter future illegal conduct." United States v. Simpson, 927 F.2d 1088, 1090 (9th Cir.1991). We have recognized that exercise of supervisory powers is an appropriate means of policing ethical misconduct by prosecutors. We also have expressly recognized the authority of the district court to dismiss actions where government attorneys have "willfully deceived the court," thereby interfering with "the orderly administration of justice." United States v. National Medical Enters., Inc., 792 F.2d 906, 912 (9th Cir.1986).

It was therefore within the discretion of the district court to act in an appropriate manner to discipline Lyons if he subverted of the attorney-client relationship. We have no doubt but that federal courts are empowered to deal with such threats to the integrity of the judicial process. In the words of the Supreme Court, "[f]ederal courts have an independent interest in ensuring that criminal trials are conducted within the ethical standards of the profession and that legal proceedings appear fair to all who observe them." Wheat v. United States, 486 U.S. 153, 160 (1988).

At the same time, however, even assuming that Lyons did act unethically, we question the prudence of remedying that misconduct through dismissal of a valid indictment. To justify such an extreme remedy, the government's conduct must have caused substantial prejudice to the defendant and been flagrant in its disregard for the limits of appropriate professional conduct.

In United States v. Owen, 580 F.2d 365 (9th Cir.1978), we adopted the view that, in order to justify dismissal of the indictment under the court's supervisory powers, there must "be some prejudice to the accused by virtue of the alleged acts of misconduct." *Id.* at 367. We explained that the idea of prejudice entails that the government's conduct "had at least some impact on the verdict and thus redounded to [the defendant's] prejudice." *Id.* at 368. Thus, in *Owen*, we found no grounds for dismissal where the defendant could not show any effect from the government's actions "beyond the vague claim of a strain in his relationship with" his attorney.

The district court specifically found that the attorney Lopez found to replace Tarlow following his withdrawal "is very able and will provide him with outstanding representation." 765 F.Supp. at 1456. Without in any way wishing to disparage the importance of a criminal defendant's choice of counsel, we fail to see how Tarlow's withdrawal in these circumstances could be said to have substantially prejudiced Lopez in his defense.

Consequently, even if the district court's finding that Lyons misled the court is correct, we conclude that the district court abused its discretion in dismissing the indictment. We are sensitive to the district court's concerns that none of the alternative sanctions available to it are as certain to impress the government with our resoluteness in holding prosecutors to the ethical standards which regulate the legal profession as a whole. At the same time, we are confident that, when there is no showing of substantial prejudice to the defendant, lesser sanctions, such as holding the prosecutor in contempt or referral to the state bar for disciplinary proceedings, can be adequate to discipline and punish government attorneys who attempt to circumvent the standards of their profession.

Accordingly, the order dismissing the indictment is VACATED. The case is REMANDED for proceedings consistent with this opinion.

FLETCHER, CIRCUIT JUDGE, with whom CIRCUIT JUDGE T.G. NELSON, joins, concurring:

At issue in this case is the conduct of the government. Because it does not seem to me that the story began or ended with the prosecutor's misbehavior, I feel compelled to say a few words about the actions of Mr. Tarlow, Mr. Twitty, and the magistrate judge.

Tarlow told Lopez at the outset of the representation that it was his "general policy" not to represent clients in plea negotiations that contemplate cooperation with the government. In a declaration submitted to the district court, Tarlow elaborated that he considers such negotiations "personally morally and ethically offensive," and that, while he would have conveyed an offer of cooperation to Lopez, "another attorney would be willing and better able to arrange his informant activities." Although Tarlow apparently did not say so explicitly, Lopez took Tarlow's policy statement to mean that if Lopez wanted to negotiate, Tarlow would withdraw from representing him altogether.

Concerned about the welfare of his children because he thought his wife might not be caring for them properly, Lopez decided that he wanted to explore the possibility of an earlier release by cooperating with the government. Lopez also wanted Tarlow to try the case if it went to trial. Faced with a difficult dilemma that he may not have anticipated when he retained Tarlow as counsel, Lopez decided to meet with the government unrepresented. I question whether Tarlow's "general policy" was in the best interests of his clients generally, and Lopez's specifically.

A criminal attorney who is bound by the Rules of Professional Conduct of the State Bar of California ("California Rules") and California's standards of professional conduct, as was Tarlow by virtue of the Northern District's Local Rule 110–3, is not free to terminate his or her representation of a client at will, or for mere personal considerations, or without the permission of the court. Notably, although under the ABA Model Rules of Professional Conduct ("ABA Model Rules") an attorney may withdraw from representation if the client "insists upon pursuing an objective that the lawyer considers repugnant or imprudent," no comparable provision appears in the California Rules. Because moral repugnance is not listed in the California Rules as a ground for permissive withdrawal, and because a criminal defense lawyer may not be entitled to assert moral repugnance to plea bargaining in any event, it is not certain, were a court to consider the matter, that Tarlow's general policy would prevail over a client's wish to pursue preliminary plea discussions with the government.

Ideally, sufficient candor and trust are present in an attorney-client relationship such that a defendant does not feel compelled to resort to clandestine meetings with the government. Indeed, the model of a successful attorney-client relationship, as expounded in Strickland v. Washington, is one in which "[c]ounsel's actions are ... based ... on informed strategic choices made by the defendant and on information supplied by the defendant." 466 U.S. 668, 691 (1984). Tarlow's relationship with Lopez fell far short of the ideal.

As for Twitty, counsel for codefendant Escobedo, his conduct was, undeniably, less than exemplary. Twitty had access to Lopez at Pleasanton correctional facility, where Escobedo was also incarcerated, because Twitty was responsible for what may have been an ill-conceived "joint investigation" of the two defendants' cases. In view of Lopez's problem with Tarlow, Twitty may have intervened in Lopez's affairs with benign intentions, but ultimately he ended up representing two defendants who had potentially conflicting interests. Although he informed Lopez that he could not act as his lawyer, Twitty nonetheless apparently advised both Lopez and Escobedo during the first meeting with the government, and may have pressured Lopez to provide information to the prosecutor during the second.

The Sixth Amendment contemplates that the assistance of counsel be "untrammeled and unimpaired by . . . requiring that one lawyer should simultaneously represent conflicting interests." Glasser v. United States, 315 U.S. 60, 70 (1942). When an attorney represents defendants with conflicting interests, "the evil . . . is in what the advocate finds himself compelled to refrain from doing, not only at trial but also as to possible pretrial plea negotiations. . . . [T]o assess the impact of a conflict of interest on the attorney's options, tactics, and decisions in plea negotiations would be virtually impossible." Holloway v. Arkansas, 435 U.S. 475, 490–91 (1978).

Significantly, the government had apparently taken the position that a plea agreement would be possible only in the event that both Lopez and Escobedo agreed to cooperate. *Id.* at 1439. Assuming he felt that such cooperation was in his own best interest, Escobedo thus had an incentive to pressure Lopez to cooperate as well. Under these circumstances, Twitty was the wrong person to be acting on Lopez's behalf during plea discussions with the government.

Finally, there are the actions of the magistrate judge to consider. Although at the hearing before the magistrate the prosecutor apparently did not say anything about his suspicion regarding the source of payment for Tarlow's fees, the district court found that the magistrate "was operating under the mistaken assumption" that Tarlow was "being paid by a third party with interests inimical to those of Lopez." 765 F.2d at 1452. Because the prosecutor had previously communicated such a theory to the presiding district judge and because he failed to disabuse the magistrate of her erroneous assumption, the district court found that the government "effectively misled" the magistrate. The district court further found that the magistrate did not ask Lopez certain critical questions when he appeared before her, namely, whether Tarlow's fees were in fact being paid by someone with a conflicting interest, or whether Lopez feared for his or his family's safety should Tarlow learn of the pending plea negotiations.

The magistrate was confronted with a difficult situation. Unfortunately, her decision to allow Lopez to meet with the government ultimately led to Lopez's losing Tarlow as his counsel, the very result Lopez had sought to avoid. Although, as the district court found, her actions may have been "understandable" in view of her assumption that Tarlow was being paid by an interested third party, her judgment may have benefitted from a more thorough questioning of Lopez regarding the fee arrangement with Tarlow. Some different options might have presented themselves had she been convinced that the safety of Lopez and his family were not at stake.

In this era of guideline sentencing, when the applicable guideline often assumes more importance than the crime of conviction, it is not unreasonable that a defendant would want to find out what the government might offer. Various forces conspired to render that inquiry exceedingly difficult for Lopez. Contrary to the intent of the Sixth Amendment, he was left to face the "prosecutorial forces of organized society" alone. Moran v. Burbine, 475 U.S. 412, 430 (1986). Others besides the prosecutor contributed to this regrettable result.

Notes

1. What do you think about the court's comments about Lyons? Tarlow? Twitty? the Magistrate Judge? Do you agree?

2. Note the court's complete rejection of the government's argument that Rule 2–100 was not intended to apply to prosecutors pursuing criminal investigations. Consider the following defense of the Thornburg Memorandum:

> "[Model Rule 4.2] is not intended to apply to criminal cases. This conclusion follows not only from an examination of the purposes of the rule, but also from the fact that those courts that have sought to apply the rule in criminal cases have almost uniformly refused to find that prosecutors committed an ethical violation. Second, * * * even if the rule applies in criminal cases, a prosecutor's communications with represented suspects and defendants are nearly always 'authorized by law' within the meaning of that exception to the rule. Third, * * * the federal district courts do not have authority to adopt local rules, such as the rule governing communications with represented parties, that prohibit otherwise valid extrajudicial conduct by a federal prosecutor. Fourth, * * * even if a federal prosecutor can be found to have violated such a state disciplinary rule or federal local rule, that violation does not give rise to a remedy in criminal litigation. Fifth, * * * the Supremacy Clause bars a state from disciplining a federal prosecutor who has committed a violation of the rule against communications with represented parties in the course of lawfully discharging the prosecutor's federal obligations. * * *

> "The ethical rule governing contacts with represented persons is found in ABA Model Rule of Professional Conduct 4.2 and its predecessor, Disciplinary Rule 7–104(A)(1) of the Model Code of Professional Responsibility. Both rules prohibit a lawyer representing a client from communicating with another party he knows is also represented regarding the subject of the representation unless the lawyer has the consent of the opposing counsel or the communication is authorized by law.

> "On the surface, the language of the rule does not seem to distinguish between criminal and civil cases. Instead, it appears to encompass all adversary proceedings, if not all situations in which a lawyer represents a client. A closer inspection, however, demonstrates that the rule, which has been in effect in varying formulations since 1908, was intended by its drafters to apply principally, if not exclusively, to civil litigation.

> "First, the text of the rule itself does not support the conclusion that it applies to prosecutors. In contrast to other disciplinary and model rules, neither DR 7–104(A)(1) nor Model Rule 4.2 provides that it applies to prosecutors. Furthermore, DR 7–104(A)(1) states that a lawyer shall not communicate with a represented party '[d]uring the course of his

representation of a client.' Similarly, Model Rule 4.2 begins with the phrase, '[i]n representing a client.' As commentators have noted, prosecutors do not represent a 'client' in any ordinary sense of the word. Although federal prosecutors represent the United States, their obligation is to the public at large. In prosecuting a federal offense, federal prosecutors do not seek to advance the interests of the United States. Instead, their obligation is to protect the public interest and to see that justice is done. As the Model Rules recognize, 'A prosecutor has the responsibility of a minister of justice and not simply that of an advocate.' Thus, the language of the rule fits imperfectly with the function of the prosecutor and suggests that the rule should not apply in criminal cases.

"Second, the interests protected by the rule are absent in the criminal context. The purposes of the rule generally are described in terms of redressing 'the supposed imbalance of legal skill and acumen between the lawyer and the party litigant,' 'ensur[ing] that lawyers not prey on persons known to be represented by counsel,' or guaranteeing that 'an unscrupulous attorney [does not] unfairly take advantage of an unsophisticated party.' In short, the rule rests on the premise that it would be unfair to allow an attorney to deal directly with an opposing party in litigation, because the attorney might use superior knowledge of the law to obtain a damaging concession or an ill-considered settlement from the party.

* * *

"Disciplinary Rule 7–104(A)(1) and Model Rule 4.2 remove from the prohibition against contacts with represented parties communications that are 'authorized by law.' Even if the rule applies in criminal cases, otherwise legal contacts between prosecutors and represented suspects are 'authorized by law' within the meaning of the rule.

"The commentary to the Model Rules of Professional Conduct does not explain the intent or scope of the authorized by law exception, but presumably the rules would not include such an exception if the rules were intended to impede government officials in the exercise of their duties. Thus, the exception of the rule appears to be intended to accommodate prosecutors, not to hinder them. As applied to federal prosecutors the exception should be sufficient to authorize most, if not all, legal prosecution contacts with represented parties.

"In some instances, specific federal statutes or rules authorize communications with represented parties. More generally, federal prosecutors operate pursuant to a statutory scheme that authorizes them to communicate with represented parties pursuant to their duty to investigate and prosecute federal offenses. The Attorney General has statutory authority to 'detect and prosecute crimes against the United States' and to 'conduct . . . other investigations regarding official matters under the control of the Department of Justice.' The United States Attorney in each district also has the statutory responsibility to pursue the prosecution of offenses in that district. These statutes give broad authority to federal prosecutors and their agents to pursue the investigation of federal offenses both before and after indictment. As the Second Circuit has held, 'a prosecutor is "authorized by law" to employ legitimate investigative techniques in conducting or supervising criminal investigations.' Within the bounds of the Constitution, interviewing suspects and defendants is a legitimate investigative technique.

"Federal prosecutors can obtain additional legal authorization to speak with represented defendants by following the Department's policy of involving a judicial officer when a defendant initiates contact with the prosecutor and asserts that he wishes to speak with the prosecutor without his attorney. If, after informing the defendant of his rights and obtaining a knowing and intelligent waiver of the defendant's right to counsel, the district court or magistrate-judge gives the prosecutor permission to meet with the defendant, that meeting is 'authorized by law' within the meaning of the exception to the rule.[69]

"A third source of authorization flows from the Constitution itself. As set forth above, the Supreme Court has held that the Constitution permits a prosecutor to engage in certain contacts with represented suspects and defendants. In these situations, the Court has explicitly held that a defendant may voluntarily abandon his choice to be represented by counsel by initiating communication with government officers and executing a valid waiver of his rights. In addition, the Court has recognized that defendants in criminal cases have an absolute right to represent themselves. When a prosecutor meets with a defendant at the defendant's own insistence, the contact is authorized by the Court's determination that the contact is permissible under the Constitution. To find an ethical violation when a federal prosecutor communicates with a represented defendant in a situation that may aid in the resolution of a criminal offense ignores the Supreme Court's recognition that criminal defendants are competent to make their own decisions regarding the right to counsel.

"Several federal district courts have adopted versions of Disciplinary Rule 7–104(A)(1) or Model Rule 4.2 as part of their local rules. In such a case, the district court ordinarily has incorporated by reference state bar disciplinary rules which happen to include DR 7–104 or Model Rule 4.2.[73] Thus, often without discussion or serious reflection on the rule's application to criminal cases, DR 7–104 or Model Rule 4.2 simply becomes part of the local federal district court rules. The argument is then advanced that, in making an otherwise legal contact with a

---

69. Even if such a contact is not "authorized by law," it is hard to see how a prosecutor who relies on the express authorization of a judicial officer can be found to have committed an ethical violation. As the Supreme Court held in a related context, "In the ordinary case, an officer cannot be expected to question the magistrate[]." *See* United States v. Leon, 468 U.S. 897, 921 (1984); see also Illinois v. Krull, 480 U.S. 340 (1987) (exclusionary rule inapplicable when officer acts pursuant to statute later declared unconstitutional).

73. For example, Local Rule 110–3 of the Northern District of California simply contains a one-sentence statement adopting the California Rules of Professional Conduct. N.D. CAL. R. 110–13. See also, e.g., W.D. Pa. R. 22(I)(B) (Rules of Professional Conduct adopted by this court are the Rules of Professional Conduct adopted by the Supreme Court of Pennsylvania, as amended from time to time by the state court, except as otherwise provided by specific rule of this court).

represented party, the federal prosecutor has violated, not only a state bar disciplinary rule, but also federal law.

"The threshold issue is not, however, whether the local rule has been violated. It is whether federal district courts have the authority to prescribe a rule, such as DR 7–104(A)(1) and Model Rule 4.2, that implicates sensitive policy issues relating to federal law enforcement, prohibits otherwise legitimate conduct by federal prosecutors, and expands the scope of a defendant's right to counsel. Under any reasonable construction of the local rule-making authority, federal district courts do not have such authority.

"Federal district courts are empowered to establish procedural rules governing the conduct of criminal proceedings, so long as such rules are consistent with federal statutory and constitutional law as well as the Federal Rules of Criminal Procedure. This rulemaking authority does not, however, empower the courts to make or alter substantive law in the guise of a local rule. Although federal district courts may establish ethical rules governing the conduct of attorneys in the grand jury and the courtroom, that authority does not extend to the alteration or expansion of existing federal law.

"Indeed, Advisory Committee comments to Rule 57 of the Federal Rules of Criminal Procedure make clear that local rulemaking authority is narrowly limited in scope. The comments state that local criminal rules may address 'matters of detail' such as the mode of impaneling a jury, the manner and order of interposing challenges to jurors, and other such procedural details.[78] The alteration, expansion, or abrogation of substantive law—for instance, as in the case of the rule governing communications with represented parties, the expansion of the scope of the right to counsel or the prohibition of otherwise lawful extrajudicial conduct by a federal prosecutor—goes far beyond the 'matters of detail' left to the discretion of each local federal court. Changes in matters so basic as this are properly handled by Congress, not through local rules of the district court.[79]

"Finally, there are 94 federal districts, each of which has a corresponding United States Attorney's office. Regulation of investigative and prosecutive conduct through local rules subjects these offices to widely varying standards of conduct. That kind of regulation creates an unacceptable lack of uniformity in critical areas of law enforcement.

* * *

"Proponents of the blanket insertion of ethical rules into the criminal justice process presuppose that the ethical rules are intended to create enforceable rights in criminal defendants. In fact, although many ethical

---

78. FED. R. CRIM. P. 57, advisory committee's note 2 to subdivision (b).

79. *See* Baylson, 764 F.Supp. at 345 ("Reasonable minds may differ about the exact contours of district court rulemaking authority, but there is no question that the lower federal courts cannot alter or enhance privileges in that manner."); see also Klu-

bock, 832 F.2d at 668–69 ("[L]ocal rules were never conceived to be a means of changing policies properly regulated at a federal level. Rather they are to address 'some matters of detail' left open by the criminal rules where uniformity is not required.").

rules are intended to protect the public, neither the rule governing communications with represented parties nor any other ethical rule is intended to confer enforceable rights on a party to litigation, including a criminal defendant.

"The commentary to the Model Rules explicitly makes this point. The 'Scope' note to the ABA's Model Rules of Professional Conduct states as follows:

> Violation of a Rule should not ... create any presumption that a legal duty has been breached. The Rules are designed to provide guidance to lawyers and to provide a structure for regulating conduct through disciplinary agencies. ... Furthermore, the purpose of the Rules can be subverted when they are invoked by opposing parties as procedural weapons. The fact that a Rule is a just basis for a lawyer's self-assessment, or for sanctioning a lawyer under the administration of a disciplinary authority, does not imply that an antagonist in a collateral proceeding ... has standing to seek enforcement of the Rule. Accordingly, nothing in the Rules should be deemed to augment any substantive legal duty of lawyers or the extra-disciplinary consequences of violating such a duty.

"Thus, the very source of the state ethical rules that defendants assert as a basis for relief in criminal litigation expressly states that the ethical rules are not intended to give rise to substantive legal rights for litigants.

* * *

"The drafters of the ethical rules contemplated that violations of the rules would be redressed through state disciplinary proceedings, not by giving a windfall to defendants in criminal litigation. It does not follow, however, that state bar authorities may bring disciplinary proceedings against federal prosecutors legitimately discharging their obligation to investigate and prosecute federal offenses. Instead, when a prosecutor behaves in a manner that comports with the Constitution and all applicable federal statutes, the Supremacy Clause bars a state from enforcing state disciplinary rules against the prosecutor.

"Although states have a substantial interest in regulating the practice of law within their borders, state ethical rules, like other state laws, 'must yield' when incompatible with federal legislation.' A state statute or rule violates the Supremacy Clause when it 'stands as an obstacle to the accomplishment and execution of the full purposes and objectives of Congress.' A state 'maintains control over the practice of law within its borders except to the limited extent necessary for the accomplishment of ... federal objectives.' Thus, to the extent that a state seeks to enforce an ethical rule 'to frustrate congressional ends, the Supremacy Clause [is] a bar to any such enforcement.'[111]

"Congress has legislated an extensive scheme of federal statutes defining federal offenses. As explained above, to enforce that scheme, Congress has conferred on the Attorney General and the United States

---

111. County of Suffolk, 710 F.Supp. at 1415.

Attorney in each district the authority to investigate and prosecute federal criminal offenses. As with other congressional delegations to executive agencies, those general authorizations necessarily imply the authority to take legally permissible steps to discharge the obligation to enforce federal law. Therefore, federal law manifests a congressional purpose to detect and prosecute federal offenses. Federal prosecutors who engage in legal contacts with represented parties are discharging their congressionally created obligation.

"A state's attempt to enforce ethical rules in a manner that prevents federal prosecutors from discharging these functions in a constitutionally permissible manner obviously would interfere with the congressional mandate to detect and prosecute federal offenses. The mere institution of a state disciplinary proceeding against an attorney can have an adverse effect on the attorney's career. Sanctions for violating state ethical rules include suspension and disbarment, as well as lesser penalties such as censure or reprimand. A federal prosecutor who faces the threat of disciplinary proceedings and the loss of his license to practice law obviously will be deterred from taking actions that the state bar wishes to forbid. Interfering with a federal prosecutor's legitimate investigative and prosecutive functions thus will 'stand as an obstacle' to the accomplishment of the congressional objective of obtaining the conviction of federal offenders.

"Moreover, the disruptive effect of state disciplinary proceedings will be exacerbated by the pull of conflicting jurisdictions. For example, the District of Columbia Court of Appeals has promulgated commentary to its version of Model Rule 4.2 stating that a prosecutor does not violate the rule if his or her conduct comports with the Fifth and Sixth Amendments. Courts and bar associations in other states, however, have condemned as 'unethical' conduct that is otherwise legal under the Constitution. Obviously, many Department of Justice attorneys practice in the District of Columbia, and because the Department does not require its attorneys to be a member of the bar where they practice, Department attorneys practicing in the District belong to state bars in other states. Department attorneys who belong to the District bar therefore may engage in conduct for which their colleagues in the next office or another section risk discipline."[q]

3. The facts of this case (the Magistrate Judge "did not have a full understanding of the facts") determined the outcome. If the situation had been as the Magistrate Judge believed (Lopez feared Tarlow because Tarlow "was being paid by a third party with interests inimical to those of Lopez"), would Lyons' actions have been proper? If so, does that mean that the Thornburgh Memorandum (now the "Reno Rule") supersedes state bar ethical rules?

4. The United States Court of Appeals for the Eighth Circuit weighed in on the "Thornburg Memorandum" in early 1998, holding that the

q. F. Dennis Saylor, IV & J. Douglas Wilson, *Putting a Square Peg in a Round Hole: The Application of Model Rule 4.2 to Federal Prosecutors*, 53 U.Pitt.L.Rev. 459, 462–484 (1992). Copyright ©. All rights reserved. Reprinted with permission of University of Pittsburgh Law Review, F. Denis Saylor, IV, and J. Douglas Wilson.

Attorney General had no authority to promulgate the regulation. United States ex rel. O'Keefe v. McDonnell Douglas Corp., 132 F.3d 1252 (8th Cir.1998).

C. CONSTITUTIONAL CONSIDERATIONS

In United States v. Halper, 490 U.S. 435 (1989), the Supreme Court addressed the nature of criminal and civil law in deciding whether double jeopardy results from parallel civil and criminal actions. Irwin Halper, the manager of a medical laboratory, was convicted of submitting false laboratory claims to Medicare. The claims falsely listed services rendered to Medicare patients on 65 occasions in 1982 and 1983, resulting in an overpayment by Medicare of $9 per claim. Halper was sentenced to two years imprisonment and fined $5,000.

The federal government then sued Halper under the False Claims Act, 31 U.S. C. § 3729, obtaining a judgment of over $130,000. The claims at issue in the civil lawsuit were the same 65 claims for which Halper had been convicted. Halper argued that imposing civil liability after conviction constituted double jeopardy. The Supreme Court agreed with Halper that there was a potential double jeopardy problem if the civil judgment bore "no rational relation to the goal of compensating the Government for its loss." In such a situation, according to the Court, a civil sanction could constitute punishment within the Fifth Amendment and thus, imposition of a civil judgment could violate the prohibition against double jeopardy.

The Court remanded Halper's case for a determination of whether the judgment of $130,000 bore no rational relation to the goal of compensating the Government for its loss. If so, it would constitute "punishment" within the Fifth Amendment and violate the Protection against double jeopardy. Eight years later in the following case, Hudson v. United States, ___ U. S. ___, 118 S.Ct. 488 (1997), the Supreme Court repudiated *Halper*. As you read *Hudson,* note the constitutional protections which still apply when the government seeks parallel criminal and civil sanctions.

HUDSON v. UNITED STATES

United States Supreme Court, 1997.
___ U. S. ___, 118 S.Ct. 488.

REHNQUIST, CHIEF JUSTICE.

The Government administratively imposed monetary penalties and occupational debarment on petitioners for violation of federal banking statutes, and later criminally indicted them for essentially the same conduct. We hold that the Double Jeopardy Clause of the Fifth Amendment is not a bar to the later criminal prosecution because the administrative proceedings were civil, not criminal. Our reasons for so holding in large part disavow the method of analysis used in United States v.

Halper, 490 U.S. 435, 448 (1989), and reaffirm the previously established rule exemplified in United States v. Ward, 448 U.S. 242, 248–249 (1980).

During the early and mid-1980's, petitioner John Hudson was the chairman and controlling shareholder of the First National Bank of Tipton (Tipton) and the First National Bank of Hammon (Hammon).[1] During the same period, petitioner Jack Rackley was president of Tipton and a member of the board of directors of Hammon, and petitioner Larry Baresel was a member of the board of directors of both Tipton and Hammon.

An examination of Tipton and Hammon led the Office of the Comptroller of the Currency (OCC) to conclude that petitioners had used their bank positions to arrange a series of loans to third parties, in violation of various federal banking statutes and regulations. According to the OCC, those loans, while nominally made to third parties, were in reality made to Hudson in order to enable him to redeem bank stock that he had pledged as collateral on defaulted loans.

On February 13, 1989, OCC issued a "Notice of Assessment of Civil Money Penalty." The notice alleged that petitioners had violated 12 U.S.C. §§ 84(a)(1) and 375b (1982) and 12 CFR §§ 31.2(b) and 215.4(b) (1986) by causing the banks with which they were associated to make loans to nominee borrowers in a manner that unlawfully allowed Hudson to receive the benefit of the loans. The notice also alleged that the illegal loans resulted in losses to Tipton and Hammon of almost $900,000 and contributed to the failure of those banks. However, the notice contained no allegation of any harm to the Government as a result of petitioners' conduct. "After taking into account the size of the financial resources and the good faith of [petitioners], the gravity of the violations, the history of previous violations and other matters as justice may require, as required by 12 U.S.C. §§ 93(b)(2) and 504(b)," OCC assessed penalties of $100,000 against Hudson and $50,000 each against both Rackley and Baresel. On August 31, 1989, OCC also issued a "Notice of Intention to Prohibit Further Participation" against each petitioner. These notices, which were premised on the identical allegations that formed the basis for the previous notices, informed petitioners that OCC intended to bar them from further participation in the conduct of "any insured depository institution."

In October 1989, petitioners resolved the OCC proceedings against them by each entering into a "Stipulation and Consent Order." These consent orders provided that Hudson, Baresel, and Rackley would pay assessments of $16,500, $15,000, and $12,500 respectively. In addition, each petitioner agreed not to "participate in any manner" in the affairs of any banking institution without the written authorization of the OCC and all other relevant regulatory agencies.[2]

1. Tipton and Hammon are two very small towns in western Oklahoma.

2. The Consent Orders also contained language providing that they did not consti-

In August 1992, petitioners were indicted in the Western District of Oklahoma in 22–count indictment on charges of conspiracy, 18 U. S. C. § 371, misapplication of bank funds, §§ 656 and 2, and making false bank entries, § 1005.[3] The violations charged in the indictment rested on the same lending transactions that formed the basis for the prior administrative actions brought by OCC. Petitioners moved to dismiss the indictment on double jeopardy grounds, but the District Court denied the motions. The Court of Appeals affirmed the District Court's holding on the nonparticipation sanction issue, but vacated and remanded to the District Court on the money sanction issue. The District Court on remand granted petitioners' motion to dismiss the indictments. This time the Government appealed, and the Court of Appeals reversed. That court held, following *Halper,* that the actual fines imposed by the Government were not so grossly disproportional to the proven damages to the Government as to render the sanctions "punishment" for double jeopardy purposes. We granted certiorari, because of concerns about the wide variety of novel double jeopardy claims spawned in the wake of *Halper.* We now affirm, but for different reasons.

The Double Jeopardy Clause provides that no "person [shall] be subject for the same offence to be twice put in jeopardy of life or limb." We have long recognized that the Double Jeopardy Clause does not prohibit the imposition of any additional sanction that could, in common parlance, be described as punishment. United States ex rel. Marcus v. Hess, 317 U.S. 537, 549 (1943). [quotation marks deleted] The Clause protects only against the imposition of multiple criminal punishments for the same offense, Helvering v. Mitchell, 303 U.S. 391, 399 (1938).

Whether a particular punishment is criminal or civil is, at least initially, a matter of statutory construction. A court must first ask whether the legislature, "in establishing the penalizing mechanism, indicated either expressly or impliedly a preference for one label or the other." Ward, 448 U.S., at 248. Even in those cases where the legislature "has indicated an intention to establish a civil penalty, we have inquired further whether the statutory scheme was so punitive either in purpose or effect," id., at 248–249 as to "transfor[m] what was clearly intended as a civil remedy into a criminal penalty," Rex Trailer Co. v. United States, 350 U.S. 148, 154 (1956).

In making this latter determination, the factors listed in Kennedy v. Mendoza–Martinez, 372 U.S. 144 (1963), provide useful guideposts, including: (1) "[w]hether the sanction involves an affirmative disability or restraint"; (2) "whether it has historically been regarded as a punishment"; (3) "whether it comes into play only on a finding of scienter ";

tute "a waiver of any right, power, or authority of any other representatives of the United States, or agencies thereof, to bring other actions deemed appropriate." The Court of Appeals ultimately held that this provision was not a waiver of petitioners' double jeopardy claim.

3. Only petitioner Rackley was indicted for making false bank entries in violation of 18 U.S.C. § 1005.

(4) "whether its operation will promote the traditional aims of punishment-retribution and deterrence"; (5) "whether the behavior to which it applies is already a crime"; (6) "whether an alternative purpose to which it may rationally be connected is assignable for it"; and (7) "whether it appears excessive in relation to the alternative purpose assigned." It is important to note, however, that "these factors must be considered in relation to the statute on its face," id. at 169 and "only the clearest proof" will suffice to override legislative intent and transform what has been denominated a civil remedy into a criminal penalty, Ward, supra, at 249 (internal quotation marks omitted).

Our opinion in United States v. Halper marked the first time we applied the Double Jeopardy Clause to a sanction without first determining that it was criminal in nature. In that case, Irwin Halper was convicted of, inter alia, violating the criminal false claims statute, 18 U.S.C. § 287, based on his submission of 65 inflated Medicare claims each of which overcharged the Government by $9. He was sentenced to two years' imprisonment and fined $5,000. The Government then brought an action against Halper under the civil False Claims Act, 31 U.S.C. §§ 3729–3731. The remedial provisions of the False Claims Act provided that a violation of the Act rendered one "liable to the United States Government for a civil penalty of $2,000, an amount equal to 2 times the amount of damages the Government sustains because of the act of that person, and costs of the civil action." Id., § 3729. Given Halper's 65 separate violations of the Act, he appeared to be liable for a penalty of $130,000, despite the fact he actually defrauded the Government of less than $600. However, the District Court concluded that a penalty of this magnitude would violate the Double Jeopardy Clause in light of Halper's previous criminal conviction. While explicitly recognizing that the statutory damages provision of the Act "was not itself a criminal punishment," the District Court nonetheless concluded that application of the full penalty to Halper would constitute a second "punishment" in violation of the Double Jeopardy Clause. 490 U.S., at 438–439.

On direct appeal, this Court affirmed. As the Halper Court saw it, the imposition of "punishment" of any kind was subject to double jeopardy constraints, and whether a sanction constituted "punishment" depended primarily on whether it served the traditional "goals of punishment," namely "retribution and deterrence." Id., at 448. Any sanction that was so "overwhelmingly disproportionate" to the injury caused that it could not "fairly be said *solely* to serve [the] remedial purpose" of compensating the government for its loss, was thought to be explainable only as "serving either retributive or deterrent purposes." See id., at 448–449 (emphasis added).

The analysis applied by the Halper Court deviated from our traditional double jeopardy doctrine in two key respects. First, the Halper Court bypassed the threshold question: whether the successive punishment at issue is a "criminal" punishment. Instead, it focused on whether the sanction, regardless of whether it was civil or criminal, was so grossly disproportionate to the harm caused as to constitute "punishment." In so doing, the Court elevated a single *Kennedy* factor—whether the sanction appeared excessive in relation to its nonpunitive purposes—to dispositive status. But as we emphasized in *Kennedy* itself, no one factor should be considered controlling as they "may often point in differing directions." 372 U.S., at 169. The second significant departure in *Halper* was the Court's decision to "asses[s] the character of the actual sanctions imposed," 490 U.S., at 447, rather than, as *Kennedy* demanded, evaluating the "statute on its face" to determine whether it provided for what amounted to a criminal sanction, 372 U.S., at 169.

We believe that *Halper's* deviation from longstanding double jeopardy principles was ill considered. As subsequent cases have demonstrated, Halper 's test for determining whether a particular sanction is "punitive," and thus subject to the strictures of the Double Jeopardy Clause, has proved unworkable. We have since recognized that all civil penalties have some deterrent effect. *See* Department of Revenue of Mont. v. Kurth Ranch, 511 U.S. 767, 777, n. 14 (1994); United States v. Ursery, 518 U.S. 267, ___ n. 2 (1996).[6] If a sanction must be "solely" remedial (i.e., entirely nondeterrent) to avoid implicating the Double Jeopardy Clause, then no civil penalties are beyond the scope of the Clause. Under *Halper's* method of analysis, a court must also look at the "sanction actually imposed" to determine whether the Double Jeopardy Clause is implicated. Thus, it will not be possible to determine whether the Double Jeopardy Clause is violated until a defendant has proceeded through a trial to judgment. But in those cases where the civil proceeding follows the criminal proceeding, this approach flies in the face of the notion that the Double Jeopardy Clause forbids the government from even *"attempting* a second time to punish criminally." *Helvering,* 303 U.S., at 399, 58 S.Ct., at 633 (emphasis added).

Finally, it should be noted that some of the ills at which *Halper* was directed are addressed by other constitutional provisions. The Due Process and Equal Protection Clauses already protect individuals from sanctions which are downright irrational. The Eighth Amendment protects against excessive civil fines, including forfeitures. The additional protection afforded by extending double jeopardy protections to proceedings heretofore thought to be civil is more than offset by the confusion created by attempting to distinguish between "punitive" and "nonpunitive" penalties.

Applying traditional double jeopardy principles to the facts of this case, it is clear that the criminal prosecution of these petitioners would not violate the Double Jeopardy Clause. It is evident that Congress

---

6. In *Kurth Ranch,* we held that the presence of a deterrent purpose or effect is not dispositive of the double jeopardy question. 511 U.S.,at781. Rather, we applied a *Kennedy*-like test, see 511 U.S., at 780–783, before concluding that Montana's dangerous drug tax was "the functional equivalent of a successive criminal prosecution. "Simi-

larly, in *Ursery,* we rejected the notion that civil in rem forfeitures violate the Double Jeopardy Clause. 518 U.S., at ___. We upheld such forfeitures, relying on the historical support for the notion that such forfeitures are civil and thus do not implicate double jeopardy. Id., at ___.

intended the OCC money penalties and debarment sanctions imposed for violations of 12 U.S. C. §§ 84 and 375b to be civil in nature. As for the money penalties, both 12 U. S. C. §§ 93 (b)(1) and 504(a), which authorize the imposition of monetary penalties for violations of §§ 84 and 375b respectively, expressly provide that such penalties are "civil." While the provision authorizing debarment contains no language explicitly denominating the sanction as civil, we think it significant that the authority to issue debarment orders is conferred upon the "appropriate Federal banking agenc[ies]." §§ 1818(e)(*l*)-(3). That such authority was conferred upon administrative agencies is prima facie evidence that Congress intended to provide for a civil sanction.

Turning to the second stage of the *Ward* test, we find that there is little evidence, much less the clearest proof that we require, suggesting that either OCC money penalties or debarment sanctions are "so punitive in form and effect as to render them criminal despite Congress' intent to the contrary." *Ursery, supra*. First, neither money penalties nor debarment have historically been viewed as punishment. We have long recognized that "revocation of a privilege voluntarily granted," such as a debarment, "is characteristically free of the punitive criminal element." *Helvering*, 303 U.S., at 399, and n. 2. Similarly, "the payment of fixed or variable sums of money [is a] sanction which ha[s] been recognized as enforcible by civil proceedings since the original revenue law of 1789." Id., at 400.

Second, the sanctions imposed do not involve an "affirmative disability or restraint," as that term is normally understood. While petitioners have been prohibited from further participating in the banking industry, this is "certainly nothing approaching the 'infamous punishment' of imprisonment." Flemming v. Nestor, 363 U.S. 603, 617 (1960). Third, neither sanction comes into play "only" on a finding of scienter. The provisions under which the money penalties were imposed, 12 U.S. C. §§ 93(b) and 504, allow for the assessment of a penalty against any person "who violates" any of the underlying banking statutes, without regard to the violator's state of mind. "Good faith" is considered by OCC in determining the amount of the penalty to be imposed, § 93(b)(2), but a penalty can be imposed even in the absence of bad faith. The fact that petitioners' "good faith" was considered in determining the amount of the penalty to be imposed in this case is irrelevant, as we look only to "the statute on its face" to determine whether a penalty is criminal in nature. *Kennedy*, 372 U.S., at 169. Similarly, while debarment may be imposed for a "willful" disregard "for the safety or soundness of [an] insured depository institution," willfulness is not a prerequisite to debarment; it is sufficient that the disregard for the safety and soundness of the institution was "continuing." 12 U.S.C. s 1818(e)(1)(C)(ii).

Fourth, the conduct for which OCC sanctions are imposed may also be criminal (and in this case formed the basis for petitioners' indictments). This fact is insufficient to render the money penalties and debarment sanctions criminally punitive, particularly in the double jeopardy context.

Finally, we recognize that the imposition of both money penalties and debarment sanctions will deter others from emulating petitioners' conduct, a traditional goal of criminal punishment. But the mere presence of this purpose is insufficient to render a sanction criminal, as deterrence "may serve civil as well as criminal goals." *Ursery, supra.* For example, the sanctions at issue here, while intended to deter future wrongdoing, also serve to promote the stability of the banking industry. To hold that the mere presence of a deterrent purpose renders such sanctions "criminal" for double jeopardy purposes would severely undermine the Government's ability to engage in effective regulation of institutions such as banks.

In sum, there simply is very little showing, to say nothing of the "clearest proof" required by Ward, that OCC money penalties and debarment sanctions are criminal. The Double Jeopardy Clause is therefore no obstacle to their trial on the pending indictments, and it may proceed.

The judgment of the Court of Appeals for the Tenth Circuit is accordingly

Affirmed.

Notes

1. *Hudson* is an effort by the Supreme Court to deal with some of the legal issues raised by parallel proceedings. It likely will not be last, given the trend toward increasingly punitive civil sanctions and more parallel proceedings. In the excerpt below, Professor Kenneth Mann describes the growth in "punitive civil law" and some of the questions it raises:

> "While new criminal laws are appearing with great frequency and criminal sentences are growing more severe, punitive civil sanctions are rapidly expanding, affecting an increasingly large sector of society in cases brought by private parties as well as by the government. These sanctions are sometimes more severely punitive than the parallel criminal sanctions for the same conduct. Punitive civil sanctions are replacing a significant part of the criminal law in critical areas of law enforcement, particularly in white-collar and drug prosecutions, because they carry tremendous punitive power. Furthermore, since they are not constrained by criminal procedure, imposing them is cheaper and more efficient than imposing criminal sanctions. As a result, the jurisprudence of sanctions is experiencing a dramatic shift. With more punishment meted out in civil proceedings, the features distinguishing civil from criminal law become less clear. As civil law becomes more punitive, serious doubt arises about whether conventional civil procedure is suited for an unconventional civil law.

> * * *

> "The growth of state-invoked and privately invoked punitive civil sanctions raises critical questions for current and future sanctions for illegal behavior. When should law enforcement agencies choose criminal sanctions over punitive civil sanctions? What is the role of full-fledged criminal sanctions in a legal system increasingly characterized by punitive civil sanctions? If a process labeled 'civil' metes out punitive

sanctions, should criminal-type procedural protections apply? How much can the 'punitiveness' of sanctions imposed in civil proceedings be increased to strengthen law enforcement tools without turning to the criminal law? Is there a proper place for parallel proceedings—one private and one brought by the state—seeking punitive sanctions against the same person or entity for the same conduct? Should legislation encourage private punitive proceedings to take an increasingly large part of the law of sanctions out of the hands of the state?[s]

* * *

2.   In an excellent article, Professor Cheh describes additional constitutional problems presented by parallel proceedings.

CHEH, CONSTITUTIONAL LIMITS ON USING CIVIL REMEDIES TO ACHIEVE CRIMINAL LAW OBJECTIVES: UNDERSTANDING AND TRANSCENDING THE CRIMINAL–CIVIL LAW DISTINCTION

42 Hastings L.J. 1325, 1389–92 (1991).[t]

* * *

"[P]arallel proceedings tend to raise three sets of constitutional problems. First, parallel proceedings can put special pressure on a defendant's fifth amendment privilege against self-incrimination. For example, even if the defendant is permitted to invoke the privilege, and does in fact invoke it in a civil proceeding, she may impair her ability to litigate the civil claim because she will be denied beneficial use of the evidence. Moreover, a civil court may draw an adverse inference from a party's refusal to testify on fifth amendment grounds.

"Second, parallel proceedings can weaken a defendant's due process rights because the government, as simultaneous prosecutor and plaintiff, may benefit from the more generous discovery opportunities afforded by civil proceedings. Sometimes the benefits are obtained inadvertently, but there are instances when the government has brought a civil case as a means of circumventing the limited discovery prescribed in criminal cases.

"Finally, parallel proceedings may undercut a defendant's sixth amendment right to effective assistance of counsel. This can happen when the government makes use of civil discovery provisions to gain access to information normally protected by the attorney-client

---

s.   Kenneth Mann, Punitive Civil Sanctions: *The Middleground Between Criminal and Civil Law*, 101 YALE L.J. 1795, 1798, 1801, 1870 (1992). Copyright ©. All rights reserved. Reprinted with permission, Yale Law Journal.

t.   Reprinted with permission from Mary Cheh, *Constitutional Limits on Using Civil Remedies to Achieve Criminal Law Objectives: Understanding and Transcending the Criminal–Civil Law Distinction*, 42 Hastings L.J. 1389–92. Copyright © 1991 Hastings College of the Law.

privilege. Additionally, as one commentator has argued, a defendant's sixth amendment right to effective counsel can be diluted indirectly when counsel works so vigorously on the production of materials for the civil defense that she neglects to consider how this information can hurt the defendant in a supplementary criminal case.

"Without the benefit of legislative guidance, courts have scrambled to find solutions to these difficulties. Primarily they have drawn upon their equitable powers to issue protective orders or orders staying the civil proceedings. Courts also have relied on less comprehensive solutions, such as quashing or modifying subpoenas or limiting the scope of discovery with respect to particular matters."

Professor Cheh concludes by predicting that "[b]ecause law enforcement authorities are relying more heavily on civil proceedings as part of their systematic efforts to fight crime, the constitutional pressures generated by parallel proceedings are likely to increase." *Id.* at 1393–94. She urges courts to be "vigilant, flexible, and equitable" in vigorously "identifying and preventing unfairness in the imposition of civil penalties." *Id.* at 1394. Do you believe *Halper* is a step in the right, or wrong, direction?

D. THE FEDERALIZATION OF CRIMINAL LAW

There has been an increasingly raucous debate in recent years over the "federalization" of criminal law. While some commentators question whether such federalization is occurring, most concede that it is; the discord primarily focuses on the merit of this transformation. In the next case, United States v. Lopez, 514 U.S. 549 (1995), the Supreme Court struck down a firearms offense as outside Congress' power to regulate commerce. As you read this opinion, consider its impact on white collar crime.

UNITED STATES v. LOPEZ

United States Supreme Court, 1995.
514 U.S. 549.

REHNQUIST, CHIEF JUSTICE.

In the Gun–Free School Zones Act of 1990, Congress made it a federal offense "for any individual knowingly to possess a firearm at a place that the individual knows, or has reasonable cause to believe, is a school zone." 18 U.S.C. § 922(q)(1)(A) (1988 ed., Supp. V). The Act neither regulates a commercial activity nor contains a requirement that the possession be connected in any way to interstate commerce. We hold that the Act exceeds the authority of Congress "[t]o regulate Commerce ... among the several States...." U.S. Const., Art. I, § 8, cl. 3.

On March 10, 1992, respondent, who was then a 12th-grade student, arrived at Edison High School in San Antonio, Texas, carrying a concealed .38 caliber handgun and five bullets. Acting upon an anonymous tip, school authorities confronted respondent, who admitted that he was carrying the weapon. He was arrested and charged under Texas law with firearm possession on school premises. The next day, the state charges were dismissed after federal agents charged respondent by complaint with violating the Gun–Free School Zones Act of 1990. 18 U.S.C. § 922(q)(1)(A) (1988 ed., Supp. V).[1]

A federal grand jury indicted respondent on one count of knowing possession of a firearm at a school zone, in violation of § 922(q). Respondent moved to dismiss his federal indictment on the ground that § 922(q) "is unconstitutional as it is beyond the power of Congress to legislate control over our public schools." The District Court denied the motion, concluding that § 922(q) "is a constitutional exercise of Congress' well-defined power to regulate activities in and affecting commerce, and the 'business' of elementary, middle and high schools ... affects interstate commerce." Respondent waived his right to a jury trial. The District Court conducted a bench trial, found him guilty of violating § 922(q), and sentenced him to six months' imprisonment and two years' supervised release.

On appeal, respondent challenged his conviction based on his claim that § 922(q) exceeded Congress' power to legislate under the Commerce Clause. The Court of Appeals for the Fifth Circuit agreed and reversed respondent's conviction. It held that, in light of what it characterized as insufficient congressional findings and legislative history, "section 922(q), in the full reach of its terms, is invalid as beyond the power of Congress under the Commerce Clause." 2 F.3d 1342, 1367–1368 (1993). Because of the importance of the issue, we granted certiorari, and we now affirm.

We start with first principles. The Constitution creates a Federal Government of enumerated powers. See U.S. Const., Art. I, § 8. As James Madison wrote, "[t]he powers delegated by the proposed Constitution to the federal government are few and defined. Those which are to remain in the State governments are numerous and indefinite." The Federalist No. 45, pp. 292–293 (C. Rossiter ed. 1961). This constitutionally mandated division of authority "was adopted by the Framers to ensure protection of our fundamental liberties." Gregory v. Ashcroft, 501 U.S. 452, 458 (1991) (internal quotation marks omitted). "Just as the separation and independence of the coordinate branches of the Federal Government serve to prevent the accumulation of excessive power in any one branch, a healthy balance of power between the States and the Federal Government will reduce the risk of tyranny and abuse from either front." *Ibid.*

The Constitution delegates to Congress the power "[t]o regulate Commerce with foreign Nations, and among the several States, and with the Indian Tribes." Art. I, § 8, cl. 3. The Court, through Chief Justice

---

1. The term "school zone" is defined as "in, or on the grounds of, a public, parochial or private school" or "within a distance of 1,000 feet from the grounds of a public, parochial or private school." § 921(a)(25).

Marshall, first defined the nature of Congress' commerce power in Gibbons v. Ogden, 9 Wheat. 1, 189–190 (1824):

> "Commerce, undoubtedly, is traffic, but it is something more: it is intercourse. It describes the commercial intercourse between nations, and parts of nations, in all its branches, and is regulated by prescribing rules for carrying on that intercourse."

The commerce power "is the power to regulate; that is, to prescribe the rule by which commerce is to be governed. This power, like all others vested in congress, is complete in itself, may be exercised to its utmost extent, and acknowledges no limitations, other than are prescribed in the constitution." *Id.*, at 196. The *Gibbons* Court, however, acknowledged that limitations on the commerce power are inherent in the very language of the Commerce Clause.

> "It is not intended to say that these words comprehend that commerce, which is completely internal, which is carried on between man and man in a State, or between different parts of the same State, and which does not extend to or affect other States. Such a power would be inconvenient, and is certainly unnecessary.

> "Comprehensive as the word 'among' is, it may very properly be restricted to that commerce which concerns more States than one.... The enumeration presupposes something not enumerated; and that something, if we regard the language or the subject of the sentence, must be the exclusively internal commerce of a State." *Id.*, at 194–195.

For nearly a century thereafter, the Court's Commerce Clause decisions dealt but rarely with the extent of Congress' power, and almost entirely with the Commerce Clause as a limit on state legislation that discriminated against interstate commerce. * * *

* * *

Consistent with this structure, we have identified three broad categories of activity that Congress may regulate under its commerce power. First, Congress may regulate the use of the channels of interstate commerce. Second, Congress is empowered to regulate and protect the instrumentalities of interstate commerce, or persons or things in interstate commerce, even though the threat may come only from intrastate activities. Finally, Congress' commerce authority includes the power to regulate those activities having a substantial relation to interstate commerce, *i.e.*, those activities that substantially affect interstate commerce.

Within this final category, admittedly, our case law has not been clear whether an activity must "affect" or "substantially affect" interstate commerce in order to be within Congress' power to regulate it under the Commerce Clause. We conclude, consistent with the great weight of our case law, that the proper test requires an analysis of whether the regulated activity "substantially affects" interstate commerce.

* * *

Section 922(q) is a criminal statute that by its terms has nothing to do with "commerce" or any sort of economic enterprise, however broadly one might define those terms.[3] Section 922(q) is not an essential part of a larger regulation of economic activity, in which the regulatory scheme could be undercut unless the intrastate activity were regulated. It cannot, therefore, be sustained under our cases upholding regulations of activities that arise out of or are connected with a commercial transaction, which viewed in the aggregate, substantially affects interstate commerce.

Second, § 922(q) contains no jurisdictional element which would ensure, through case-by-case inquiry, that the firearm possession in question affects interstate commerce. * * * [Section] 922(q) has no express jurisdictional element which might limit its reach to a discrete set of firearm possessions that additionally have an explicit connection with or effect on interstate commerce.

Although as part of our independent evaluation of constitutionality under the Commerce Clause we of course consider legislative findings, and indeed even congressional committee findings, regarding effect on interstate commerce, the Government concedes that "[n]either the statute nor its legislative history contain[s] express congressional findings regarding the effects upon interstate commerce of gun possession in a school zone." We agree with the Government that Congress normally is not required to make formal findings as to the substantial burdens that an activity has on interstate commerce. But to the extent that congressional findings would enable us to evaluate the legislative judgment that the activity in question substantially affected interstate commerce, even though no such substantial effect was visible to the naked eye, they are lacking here.[4]

* * *

The Government's essential contention, *in fine*, is that we may determine here that § 922(q) is valid because possession of a firearm in a local school zone does indeed substantially affect interstate commerce. The Government argues that possession of a firearm in a school zone may result in violent crime and that violent crime can be expected to

3. Under our federal system, the " 'States possess primary authority for defining and enforcing the criminal law.' " [citations omitted]

4. We note that on September 13, 1994, President Clinton signed into law the Violent Crime Control and Law Enforcement Act of 1994, Pub.L. 103–322, 108 Stat. 1796. Section 320904 of that Act, *id.*, at 2125, amends § 922(q) to include congressional findings regarding the effects of firearm possession in and around schools upon interstate and foreign commerce. The Government does not rely upon these subsequent findings as a substitute for the absence of findings in the first instance. ("[W]e're not relying on them in the strict sense of the word, but we think that at a very minimum they indicate that reasons can be identified for why Congress wanted to regulate this particular activity").

affect the functioning of the national economy in two ways. First, the costs of violent crime are substantial, and, through the mechanism of insurance, those costs are spread throughout the population. Second, violent crime reduces the willingness of individuals to travel to areas within the country that are perceived to be unsafe. The Government also argues that the presence of guns in schools poses a substantial threat to the educational process by threatening the learning environment. A handicapped educational process, in turn, will result in a less productive citizenry. That, in turn, would have an adverse effect on the Nation's economic well-being. As a result, the Government argues that Congress could rationally have concluded that § 922(q) substantially affects interstate commerce.

We pause to consider the implications of the Government's arguments. The Government admits, under its "costs of crime" reasoning, that Congress could regulate not only all violent crime, but all activities that might lead to violent crime, regardless of how tenuously they relate to interstate commerce. Similarly, under the Government's "national productivity" reasoning, Congress could regulate any activity that it found was related to the economic productivity of individual citizens: family law (including marriage, divorce, and child custody), for example. Under the theories that the Government presents in support of § 922(q), it is difficult to perceive any limitation on federal power, even in areas such as criminal law enforcement or education where States historically have been sovereign. Thus, if we were to accept the Government's arguments, we are hard-pressed to posit any activity by an individual that Congress is without power to regulate.

* * *

To uphold the Government's contentions here, we would have to pile inference upon inference in a manner that would bid fair to convert congressional authority under the Commerce Clause to a general police power of the sort retained by the States. Admittedly, some of our prior cases have taken long steps down that road, giving great deference to congressional action. The broad language in these opinions has suggested the possibility of additional expansion, but we decline here to proceed any further. To do so would require us to conclude that the Constitution's enumeration of powers does not presuppose something not enumerated, and that there never will be a distinction between what is truly national and what is truly local. This we are unwilling to do.

For the foregoing reasons the judgment of the Court of Appeals is

Affirmed.

* * *

JUSTICE BREYER, with whom JUSTICE STEVENS, JUSTICE SOUTER, and JUSTICE GINSBURG join, dissenting.

The issue in this case is whether the Commerce Clause authorizes Congress to enact a statute that makes it a crime to possess a gun in, or near, a school. 18 U.S.C. § 922(q)(1)(A) (1988 ed., Supp. V). In my view, the statute falls well within the scope of the commerce power as this Court has understood that power over the last half century.

I

In reaching this conclusion, I apply three basic principles of Commerce Clause interpretation. First, the power to "regulate Commerce ... among the several States," U.S. Const., Art. I, § 8, cl. 3, encompasses the power to regulate local activities insofar as they significantly affect interstate commerce. As the majority points out, the Court, in describing how much of an effect the Clause requires, sometimes has used the word "substantial" and sometimes has not. * * *

Second, in determining whether a local activity will likely have a significant effect upon interstate commerce, a court must consider, not the effect of an individual act (a single instance of gun possession), but rather the cumulative effect of all similar instances (*i.e.*, the effect of all guns possessed in or near schools). As this Court put the matter almost 50 years ago:

> "[I]t is enough that the individual activity when multiplied into a general practice ... contains a threat to the interstate economy that requires preventative regulation." Mandeville Island Farms, Inc. v. American Crystal Sugar Co., 334 U.S. 219, 236 (1948).

Third, the Constitution requires us to judge the connection between a regulated activity and interstate commerce, not directly, but at one remove. Courts must give Congress a degree of leeway in determining the existence of a significant factual connection between the regulated activity and interstate commerce—both because the Constitution delegates the commerce power directly to Congress and because the determination requires an empirical judgment of a kind that a legislature is more likely than a court to make with accuracy. The traditional words "rational basis" capture this leeway. Thus, the specific question before us, as the Court recognizes, is not whether the "regulated activity sufficiently affected interstate commerce," but, rather, whether Congress could have had "*a rational basis*" for so concluding.

* * *

II

Applying these principles to the case at hand, we must ask whether Congress could have had a *rational basis* for finding a significant (or substantial) connection between gun-related school violence and interstate commerce. Or, to put the question in the language of the *explicit* finding that Congress made when it amended this law in 1994: Could Congress rationally have found that "violent crime in school zones," through its effect on the "quality of education," significantly (or substantially) affects "interstate" or "foreign commerce"? As long as one views the commerce connection, not as a "technical legal conception," but as "a practical one," the answer to this question must be yes.

Numerous reports and studies—generated both inside and outside government—make clear that Congress could reasonably have found the empirical connection that its law, implicitly or explicitly, asserts.

For one thing, reports, hearings, and other readily available literature make clear that the problem of guns in and around schools is widespread and extremely serious. These materials report, for example, that four percent of American high school students (and six percent of inner-city high school students) carry a gun to school at least occasionally, that 12 percent of urban high school students have had guns fired at them, that 20 percent of those students have been threatened with guns, and that, in any 6–month period, several hundred thousand schoolchildren are victims of violent crimes in or near their schools. And, they report that this widespread violence in schools throughout the Nation significantly interferes with the quality of education in those schools. Based on reports such as these, Congress obviously could have thought that guns and learning are mutually exclusive. Congress could therefore have found a substantial educational problem—teachers unable to teach, students unable to learn—and concluded that guns near schools contribute substantially to the size and scope of that problem.

Having found that guns in schools significantly undermine the quality of education in our Nation's classrooms, Congress could also have found, given the effect of education upon interstate and foreign commerce, that gun-related violence in and around schools is a commercial, as well as a human, problem. Education, although far more than a matter of economics, has long been inextricably intertwined with the Nation's economy. When this Nation began, most workers received their education in the workplace, typically (like Benjamin Franklin) as apprentices. * * *

* * *

Specifically, Congress could have found that gun-related violence near the classroom poses a serious economic threat (1) to consequently inadequately educated workers who must endure low paying jobs, and (2) to communities and businesses that might (in today's "information society") otherwise gain, from a well-educated work force, an important commercial advantage, of a kind that location near a railhead or harbor provided in the past. Congress might also have found these threats to be no different in kind from other threats that this Court has found within the commerce power, such as the threat that loan sharking poses to the "funds" of "numerous localities," and that unfair labor practices pose to instrumentalities of commerce. As I have pointed out, Congress has written that "the occurrence of violent crime in school zones" has brought about a "decline in the quality of education" that "has an adverse impact on interstate commerce and the foreign commerce of the United States." 18 U.S.C.A. §§ 922(q)(1)(F), (G). The violence-related facts, the educational facts, and the economic facts, taken together, make this conclusion rational. And, because under our case law, the sufficiency of the constitutionally necessary Commerce Clause link between a crime of violence and interstate commerce turns simply upon size or degree, those same facts make the statute constitutional.

* * *

Notes

1.   Lopez was a 5–4 decision. There were six opinions filed: in addition to Chief Justice Rehnquist's opinion for the Court, Justice Kennedy filed a concurring opinion in which Justice O'Connor joined, Justice Thomas filed a concurring opinion, Justices Stevens and Souter each filed dissenting opinions, and Justice Breyer filed a dissenting opinion in which Justices Stevens, Souter and Ginsburg joined.

With which view do you agree: Justice Rehnquist who held for the Court that the criminal activity prohibited by § 922(q) had nothing to do with "commerce" or any sort of economic enterprise, or Justice Breyer who argued that Congress could reasonably find that the "cumulative effect" of many instances of students carrying weapons into public schools affected interstate commerce?

2.   Most commentators view *Lopez* as an effort by the Court "to redress a federal intrusion into the enforcement of criminal laws, an area traditionally reserved to the states."[u] As you consider the following thoughts, note the white collar crimes singled out as examples of the "federalization" of criminal law.

O'REILLY & DRIZIN, UNITED STATES v. LOPEZ: REINVIGORATING THE FEDERAL BALANCE BY MAINTAINING THE STATES' ROLE AS THE 'IMMEDIATE AND VISIBLE GUARDIANS' OF SECURITY

22 J. Legis. 1 (1996).[v]

* * *

Lopez, however, may not herald such a broad revision of Commerce Clause jurisprudence. Rather, it is more likely the Court is attempting to redress a federal intrusion into the enforcement of criminal laws, an area traditionally reserved to the states. As Justice Rehnquist noted in the majority opinion, this intrusion tips the fragile balance of power between the federal government and the states, undermining the federal structure of American government. The assertion of federal power in this area is especially dangerous because, as Alexander Hamilton noted in The Federalist, it touches on the states' key role as the "immediate and visible guardians of life and property." Moreover, as Justice Rehnquist

---

u.   Gregory W. O'Reilly & Robert Drizin, *United States v. Lopez: Reinvigorating the Federal Balance By Maintaining The States' Role As The "Immediate and Visible Guardians" of Security*, 22 J. Legis 1 (1996).

v.   *Id.* at 462–64, 474–78, 482–84. Copyright © 1997 by the Journal of Legislation, Notre Dame Law School. Reprinted with permission, Gregory W. O'Reilly, Criminal Justice Counsel, Office of the Cook County Public Defender, Robert Drizin, Esquire, and Journal of Legislation.

has repeatedly pointed out in his capacity as head of the Judicial Conference of the United States, federal encroachment into criminal law threatens to inundate the federal courts with criminal cases, thereby diluting or destroying their effectiveness. In addressing these concerns, the majority has sent the *Lopez* case, and potentially thousands of similar cases, back to where they started—state court.

* * *

Congress began slowly to expand the number of federal crimes based on its power to make laws "necessary and proper" to carry out its constitutionally-enumerated powers. Early federal offenses concerned acts harmful to the central government, such as customs offenses, crimes committed in federal enclaves, and crimes involving interference with the federal courts. The serious federal encroachment into criminal law began in 1872, when Congress protected its postal power by creating federal laws against mail fraud. These laws could be construed as efforts to protect the specifically-enumerated federal postal power and to fall within the scope of traditional federal power, as the British government had controlled the postal power during the Colonial era. Nonetheless, these laws were aimed at general frauds which might have been adequately covered by similar state regulation.

Around the turn of the century, Congress created more federal offenses, justifying its exercise of power through the Commerce Clause. Early statutes included the Lottery Act, banning the interstate transportation of lottery tickets, and the Mann Act, named after its sponsor Congressman James Mann (R–IL). The Mann Act, formally known as "The White Slave Traffic Act of 1910," prohibited the interstate transportation of a woman for the purpose of causing her to engage in an immoral practice. According to Congressman Mann, the law was needed to prevent "vampires and parasites" from taking advantage of "some blue-eyed girl and immersing her in dens of infamy." Concerns about federalism were swept aside by more emotional arguments. Congressman Thetus Sims (D–TN), for instance, argued: "How any man can haggle and higgle over a constitutional provision in the face of such abominations is more than I can comprehend."

Throughout this century, Congress has steadily expanded federal crimes, using the need to protect the channels of interstate commerce as its justification. The Supreme Court has been a willing ally in this expansion, upholding jurisdiction over activities "affecting" interstate commerce. Thus, Congress has been able to create federal offenses by merely adding an interstate element to state crimes such as kidnapping, theft, transportation of stolen vehicles, flight to avoid prosecution, sexual exploitation of children, firearms offenses, gambling, credit card counterfeiting, and the theft of over $10,000 in livestock. This reasoning has increased federal jurisdiction to allow the federal courts to reach local robbery offenses under the Hobbs Act, local extortion under the Extortionate Credit Transaction Act, a wide array of conduct if any interstate travel is involved aiding "unlawful activity" under the Travel Act, and a range of offenses covered under state law under the Racketeer Influenced and Corrupt Organization Act. Every horrendous state crime which gains wide media coverage now be comes the potential source of yet another federal criminal law. For example, after a brutal 1992 murder during the theft of a car in Maryland, Congress made armed car jacking a federal crime if the car had "been transported, shipped or received in interstate or foreign commerce." While this bill allowed Congress to sound "tough on crime," it was unnecessary, for this conduct was already prohibited by state armed robbery and murder laws, and both perpetrators had been sentenced by Maryland courts to life in prison. In 1994, Congress stepped up its federalization efforts, creating new federal offenses, including acts of domestic violence which cross state lines, gang offenses, drug offenses, federal "three-strikes-you're-out" provisions, and a number of federal death penalty offenses.

* * *

As the federal government assumes the states' role in controlling crime, it simultaneously becomes the focus of citizen demands for political responses to perceived crime problems and problems in the administration of criminal justice. The response is predictable: more federal laws, more federal funds, and a more federal system. In this federalized system, the federal government will assume the states' role as the "immediate and visible guardians of life and property," and as a consequence, it will be the federal government which comes to command the primary allegiance and trust of their citizens. So much for Hamilton's view of the states' one "transcendent advantage" in checking federal power.

Such a federal system would begin to close the fifty laboratories of democracy and thereby centralize America's criminal justice system. Today, the states provide manageable units of government adaptable to the changing needs of the local population. They test new laws and law enforcement policies, target local problems, and enforce local community standards. Successful experiments can be imitated and mistakes can be avoided; when one state's experiment fails, we avoid repeating the same mistake nation-wide. By their nature, states are also more accountable, responsive and flexible than the federal government. Unlike the federal government, they can quickly pass laws and readily adjust or end policies which do not work. By nationalizing criminal justice, we shift from these flexible and diverse laboratories to the monolithic federal government, and sacrifice creativity and adaptability for centralization. Under such a system, controversial experiments like the federal sentencing guidelines might be effectively imposed on the states. Instead of dealing with a disastrous, but contained policy effecting thousands of cases in one or a few states, a federalized system would, in one unified push, impose potentially catastrophic policies on millions of criminal cases.

* * *

* * * The risk posed by the wave of federalization is not merely that the Framers' intentions will be violated; it is, as Justice Rehnquist has warned, that federalization will dilute or destroy the effectiveness of the federal courts.

The federal courts have filled a unique function, quite distinct from that of the state courts. In his A.B.A. speech, Justice Rehnquist recalled that the Framers intended the federal courts to be:

> a distinctive judicial forum, performing tasks that state systems, because of political or structural reasons, could not perform. Throughout the two-hundred year history of the federal courts, they have maintained their special qualities, handling complex cases, protecting individual liberties, and adjudicating important national concerns. These are the jobs they do best—not those better suited to other forums.

* * *

In his 1992 A.B.A. speech, Justice Rehnquist warned that this onslaught of federal cases threatens to erode the ability of the federal courts to fulfill their unique functions. With huge caseloads, federal "judges will have less time to spend on marginal" cases, and "increased bureaucratization and management strictures will leave judges less freedom to exercise personal judgment," decreasing judges' "sense of personal responsibility and accountability." As a consequence, the "high quality of justice" will be degraded. Rehnquist also warned that expanding the number of federal judges would dilute the judiciary's quality, and lead to an "unmanageable number of circuits," or "appellate courts of unmanageable size," "an increasingly incoherent body of federal law," and "a Supreme Court incapable of maintaining uniformity in federal law." Already the increase in criminal cases has slowed the progress of civil cases traditionally litigated in federal court, as judges push criminal cases to the front of their docket in order to comply with the speedy trial requirements of criminal cases.

---

3. Professor Beale sees another consequence of the federalization of criminal law:

> "When Congress has chosen to legislate by adding new federal crimes, it has neither preempted state law as a formal matter nor provided sufficient resources to supplant state enforcement as a practical matter. Federal authorities typically have the resources to prosecute only a fraction, often only a tiny fraction, of the offenses that fall under the purview of many of the federal criminal statutes. The remaining offenses of a similar character continue to be prosecuted by the states. This arrangement is deeply problematic because it is increasingly clear that similarly situated offenders now receive radically different sentences in federal and state court. The mis-

match between the wide sweep of the federal criminal statutes and the relatively limited federal resources—both prosecutorial and judicial—virtually guarantees the continuation of this disparity among offenders who are similarly situated in every respect except one: whether they are prosecuted in state or federal court. This structurally produced inequality is increasing because of the expanded scope of federal criminal law and the disparity between the stringent sentences applicable under federal law and the more lenient discretionary sentencing regimes of many states.''

Sara Sun Beale, *Too Many and Yet Too Few: New Principles To Define The Proper Limits For Federal Criminal Jurisdiction*, 46 HASTINGS L.J. 979, 981–82 (1995).**ʷ**

4.   In contrast to the above views, consider the following comments. In the first article, *The Underfederalization of Crime*, Professors Stacy and Dayton challenge the view that crime has become federalized. In the second article, *The Federalization of Organized Crime: Advantages of Federal Prosecution*, Professor Jeffries and Judge Gleeson (E.D.N.Y.) discuss the advantages of federal prosecution.

TOM STACY & KIM DAYTON, THE UNDERFEDERALIZATION OF CRIME

6 CORNELL J.L. & PUB. POL'Y 247 (1997).**ˣ**

* * *

This article contends that judicial and academic complaints about the overfederalization of crime largely have matters backwards. The image of a runaway national government increasingly taking away the enforcement of the criminal law from the States is essentially false. The available evidence indicates that the national government's share in the enforcement of criminal law has been actually diminishing for more than the last half century. The national government does have concurrent authority over a greater range of criminal activity now, including much violent street crime. But, contrary to *Lopez* and the conventional wisdom it embraces, this expanded authority does not transgress constitutional principles of federalism. In fact, constitutional and policy considerations affirmatively support the opposite conclusion that the national government may (and probably should) exercise more authority, especially with respect to the street crime that plagues poor urban areas. It seems that crime, especially street crime, has been underfederalized.

* * *

The overfederalization thesis trades upon an image of a national government whose role in the enforcement of criminal law has grown and is growing dramatically. * * *

* * *

The data that permit a direct comparison of federal and state criminal case filings, although available only for 1984 and subsequent years, show a striking decline in the national share. While federal felony filings increased by about 32% from 1984–94, felony filings in state courts increased by 64% for that period. The share of the felony caseload borne by the federal courts declined from 2.15% to 1.78%. The trend is slightly more pronounced if one compares the rates of growth in filings rather than the absolute numbers of filings. According to a comparative study by National Center for State Courts, the growth rate in felony filings in state courts was 70%—more than twice the growth rate in federal felony filings (33%). In the ten years since 1984, which encompass much of the time period on which judges and academics rely to establish overfederalization, the data on criminal filings unequivocally show a declining national share.

* * *

Although one cannot directly compare the federal and state filings for the years before 1984, other measures indicate that the 1984–94 trend is not an aberration, but a part of a larger historical pattern. One such measure is federal criminal filings relative to population. * * *

Meanwhile, the nation's population increased dramatically. Between 1900 and 1995, for instance, the population of the United States increased by nearly 350%: about 76 million to more than 263 million. Over that same period, however, the total number of federal criminal prosecutions (felony and misdemeanor) rose from about 17,000 cases to somewhat less than 46,000—less than 275%. From 1940 to 1980, the population increased by 79% while federal criminal filings increased by only 15%. * * * [T]he annual number of federal criminal prosecutions has not kept pace with the rate of general population increases, as one might have expected it would. In per capita terms, the national government's crime fighting role has declined quite significantly since the turn of the century.

* * *

This decline strongly suggests that crime has been underfederalized, not overfederalized. Two paths lead to this conclusion. First, * * * [i]t is generally thought that, with the increasing integration of the United States economy, resulting from developments in transportation, communications, and production, an expanded regulatory national role is appropriate. An expanded national role would also seem appropriate for the enforcement of criminal laws, especially given crime's high costs to the national economy and the high priority the public attaches to the problem.

Second, the ever increasing sophistication and integration of the United States economy since the 1930s has strengthened the justifications for national crime fighting. More criminal activity crosses state boundaries now. Specialized law enforcement technologies and expertise have a wider application. One State's enforcement efforts have a greater impact in other States. The redistributive rationale for national authority carries greater weight because business and capital are more mobile.

JOHN C. JEFFRIES, JR. & HONORABLE JOHN GLEESON, THE FEDERALIZATION OF ORGANIZED CRIME: ADVANTAGES OF FEDERAL PROSECUTION

46 HASTINGS L.J. 1095 (1995).[y]

* * *

One way or another, federal statutes reach most major malefactions and many minor ones, and there is no realistic prospect of reversing that trend. * * * Today, federal prosecutors have substantive authority to pursue most crimes worth pursuing. It follows that the federalization of crime is increasingly in the hands of federal prosecutors and that informed debate on the respective state and federal roles in law enforcement should focus on the prosecutive function.

We believe that organized crime (broadly defined) is an especially appropriate target for federal prosecution. As we describe below, federal prosecutors enjoy advantages that their state and local counterparts do not possess. Nowhere can the advantages of federal prosecution be employed more productively than in the attack on criminal gangs and enterprises. In our opinion, the prosecution of organized crime should be largely federalized.

* * *

The most important constraint on federal prosecution is resources. In 1990 the total budget for federal prosecution and legal services was more than $1.5 billion. Twenty years earlier, that figure was only slightly over $100 million. Even when these figures are adjusted for the effect of inflation, federal prosecution dollars have more than tripled. The corresponding expansion in the effective scope of federal prosecution is obvious—and probably more consequential than any change in the substantive law during that period.

* * *

The crucial questions regarding the federalization of crime are therefore: What do federal prosecutors prosecute? What should they prosecute?

One answer is that federal prosecutors should—and probably do—bring cases in which there is a comparative advantage in federal prosecution. This statement is true but hugely uninformative. Such vacuities aside, it is probably not possible to give a global answer. There are too many differences among districts, too many competing perceptions of federal interest, and too many difficulties in assembling data about prosecutorial choice to support sweeping generalizations. In one large and important area, however, we think there is a reasonably clear answer to what federal prosecutors prosecute and—more controversially—to what they should prosecute. They should and do prosecute "organized crime."

* * *

* * * Why then, should and do federal prosecutors devote their limited resources to these cases?

The answer is that federal prosecutors do a better job. Several features of federal law combine to give federal prosecutors enormous advantages over their state and local counterparts, * * *. Nowhere are these advantages more pronounced than in the investigation and prosecution of organized crime. For a variety of reasons—many of which seem unconnected to the usual debates about federalism—federal prosecutors can conduct organized crime investigations more quickly, bring more charges, and win more convictions than state and local authorities. The chief purpose of this paper is to describe those advantages.

* * *

What are the advantages of federal prosecution? One, of course, is the main legislative tool for reaching group criminality, the Racketeer Influence Corrupt Organizations Act. A great deal has been written about the role of RICO in combating organized crime. If we slight that topic here, it is not because of its unimportance, but because it has been so well covered elsewhere. Moreover, we think the prominence of RICO has distracted attention from other important features of federal law. After all, many states have enacted provisions similar to RICO. Yet even in those states, there are important, but little-noticed advantages of federal prosecution. They range from the use of accomplice testimony and federal grand jury practice to the federal Sentencing Guidelines. A survey of these advantages supports the decision of federal prosecutors to direct their resources against organized crime.

One characteristic of organized crime is that the most culpable and dangerous individuals rarely do the dirty work. Although the organization's leaders are ultimately responsible for its crimes, they typically deal through intermediaries and limit their own participation to behind-the-scenes control and guidance. Consequently, their guilt usually cannot be proved by the testimony of victims or eyewitnesses or by forensic evidence. And they never confess. Generally speaking, successful prosecution of organized crime leaders requires the use of accomplice testimony. It is therefore enormously important to federal prosecutors that a federal defendant can be convicted on the uncorroborated testimony of an accomplice. Although the jury is cautioned to use care in evaluating the testimony of accomplices, it is also told that in an appropriate case it may convict solely on that basis.

In contrast, in New York state courts, "[a] defendant may not be convicted of any offense upon the testimony of an accomplice unsupported by corroborative evidence tending to connect the defendant with the commission of such offense." [citation omitted] The requirement is strict. Independent evidence of the defendant's presence at the scene of the crime does not necessarily suffice, nor does proven falsity of the defendant's alibi. Most importantly, the corroboration requirement cannot be satisfied by the testimony of other accomplices. Thus, not only is a single accomplice's testimony insufficient, but the interlocking testimony of several accomplices is also insufficient, no matter how corroborative the accomplices may be of one another. Similar rules are in effect in sixteen other states, including California.

As a result, many strong cases cannot be brought in state court. * * *

* * *

[Another advantage federal prosecutors have is ready access to grand juries.] A federal grand jury investigation may be commenced any time a prosecutor chooses. A formal allegation that a crime has occurred is not required; an anonymous tip or rumor may suffice. Indeed, an investigation may be commenced simply to provide assurance that the law has *not* been violated.

Once an investigation has begun, the powers of the federal grand jury are enormous (and therefore controversial). The grand jury has nationwide subpoena power over persons and documents, and the Supreme Court has protected the unimpeded use of that power. In order to insulate such investigations from delay, a motion to quash a grand jury subpoena on grounds of relevance must be denied unless the movant can satisfy the virtually insurmountable burden of showing that there is no "reasonable possibility" that the witness or documents will "produce information relevant to the general subject of the grand jury's investigation."

For the same reason, among others, the grand jury may hear evidence that would be inadmissible at trial. Consequently, federal prosecutors routinely present hearsay to grand juries. Indeed, the evidence of accomplice witnesses, civilian eyewitnesses, and victims is usually recounted by a federal agent who is familiar with the witnesses' statements. So long as the grand jurors are not misled as to the hearsay nature of the evidence and are aware of their right to request that the witnesses appear, they may return an indictment based entirely on hearsay.

The broad subpoena powers of the grand jury are enforced not only by laws against perjury and obstruction of justice, but also by the district court's contempt powers. A witness who, without lawful justification, refuses to answer questions or provide documents may be jailed civilly for as long as eighteen months, which is intended to coerce compliance with the subpoena. That confinement may be followed by a criminal prosecution, which is intended to punish noncompliance and, depending on the underlying offense under investigation, can lead to a substantial prison term. Finally, the prosecutors have at their disposal the federal immunity statute, which can be used to compel testimony in exchange for use immunity and which does not protect the witness from prosecution for perjury, obstruction of justice, or contempt.

In these and other respects, federal grand jury practice is stacked in favor of the prosecution and is often attacked on that ground. On the other hand, prosecutorial control of the grand jury proceedings may perhaps be defended as necessary and inevitable at the investigative stage, with careful protection of the rights of the accused relegated to the trial. However one resolves the overall debate, this much is clear: The distinctive features of the federal grand jury give it a peculiarly important role in the investigation of organized crime.

* * *

In many state systems, grand juries operate very differently. In some jurisdictions * * * hearsay is not allowed before the grand jury, and its usefulness in investigating criminal groups is therefore severely compromised. More widely, the use of grand juries is frustrated by the unavailability to state prosecutors of testimony coerced by a grant of limited immunity. In both of these respects * * * federal prosecutors enjoy distinct advantages over their state and local counterparts.

* * *

The fact that in some states the no-hearsay rule nevertheless applies has major adverse consequences in state organized crime investigations. For one thing, getting an indictment is far more cumbersome and time-consuming. Rather than have the agent assigned to the investigation relay to the grand jury the essence of the testimony of accomplices, eyewitnesses, and victims, each of those witnesses must testify. Since their appearances before the grand jury will produce a recorded statement of the witness that can be used in later cross-examinations, a responsible investigative team has to drop everything and engage in the painstaking process of preparing accomplice witnesses to testify about events that are often several years old and embedded in a life of crime. State prosecutors correctly regard this requirement as an unnecessary obstacle in the process of indicting organized crime targets.

The no-hearsay rule also prevents a state grand jury from keeping up with a fast-moving investigation. In a federal investigation, when an arrested defendant chooses to cooperate, time is of the essence. The new defendants identified by the cooperator's information are often arrested immediately, detained pending trial, and indicted within the ten-day time limit of the Speedy Trial Act by having a case agent summarize the accomplice's testimony for the grand jury. Often, one or more of the new defendants chooses to cooperate, producing fresh avenues of investigation and sometimes a new wave of arrests and indictments. In New York state, [for example] defendants must be indicted or released within six days of arrest, and the indictment must be based on first-hand testimony. This is simply not feasible if the accomplice must be signed to a plea/cooperation agreement, prepared to testify, and produced in the grand jury. As a result, state prosecutors cannot follow the natural course of the investigation as well as federal prosecutors can.

* * *

Another major advantage of federal grand jury practice is that federal prosecutors can coerce testimony by granting limited immunity for the use or derivative use of such testimony. In many states, including New York, California, and Illinois, prosecutors can force testimony only by granting transactional immunity, which protects the witness from prosecution for any activity mentioned in the immunized testimony. In part for the reasons described below, we think the federal rule preferable, but again, the question is controversial and has prompted substantial debate.

Whatever the overall merits of use-and-derivative-use versus transactional immunity, the difference between them is especially critical in organized crime investigations. In the course of such investigations, a federal prosecutor likely can identify persons in the organization who are at least witnesses and possibly potential defendants but who cannot be indicted because the evidence against them is insufficient. An example would be a person who is present for a conversation in which a mob boss mentions that he has ordered a particular murder. * * * [T]hat person is an ideal candidate for use-immunity in a federal grand jury.

* * *

The [United States] Sentencing Guidelines establish an elaborate mechanism to prescribe sentences for federal crimes. Judicial discretion, which was previously limited only by the statutory maximum, has been narrowly restricted by the creation of sentencing "ranges." Absent extraordinary circumstances justifying a "departure," the court must impose a sentence within the specified range. Since the ranges are narrow, and their application triggered by the formula specified in the Guidelines, federal sentences have become much more predictable. The simultaneous abolition of parole made the sentences more certain as well.

* * *

This [merit of the Sentencing Guidelines] is beyond the scope of this Article. Our goal is to examine a narrower point that has received too little attention: The Sentencing Guidelines empower prosecutors. Indeed, if federal prosecutors had been asked to create the sentencing regime that would place the maximum permissible pressure on criminal defendants to cooperate with the government, they could hardly have done better than the Sentencing Commission. The Guidelines have become a valuable tool, used by federal law enforcement authorities to turn targets and defendants into accomplice witnesses. Indeed, in ways that are not widely understood, the Guidelines have altered the way federal investigations into organized crime are conducted and have contributed significantly to the success of those investigations in recent years.

The Sentencing Commission established only one readily available escape from these essentially mandatory sentences: cooperation with the government. Sentencing Guideline section 5K1.1 allows a district court to "depart" from the applicable guideline range if the defendant's cooperation has resulted in "substantial assistance" to the government. There is no limit to the degree of departure; a defendant whose guideline range is 324 to 405 months may be sentenced to any lesser term or not incarcerated at all.

Significantly, this type of downward departure requires a motion from the government. The government has unreviewable discretion in determining whether to enter into a cooperation agreement and substantial leeway in determining whether the defendant has complied with the agreement and rendered the requisite assistance. In effect, the prosecutor holds the key to the jailhouse door.

* * *

In effect, the Sentencing Guidelines have added a new dimension to the federal effort to combat enterprise crime: plea or cooperation bargaining as an investigative tool. Many investigations reach a point where further progress requires helpful information from one of the targets. The investigative team selects a prospective cooperator, based on a variety of factors, including the strength of the case against him, an assessment of his ability to endure a lengthy prison term, and the degree of credibility-damaging baggage he would bring to the witness stand. The prosecution then offers the prospect the opportunity to plead guilty, typically to the most serious offense he has committed, and to testify for the government in exchange for a "substantial assistance motion." This motion is the witness's only means of escape from the mandatory guideline sentence. The negotiation is done as secretly as possible, so that the opportunity is preserved for the witness to cooperate proactively by wearing a "wire" among the rest of the targets. Even if the cooperation is only historical, as is usually the case in organized crime investigations, the information that the new witness provides is often the key to a successful investigation, and the cooperation is usually the direct result of the incentives created by the Sentencing Guidelines.

What do you think? Are you persuaded that federalization of criminal law has gone too far (Justice Rehnquist, Professor Beale) or not far enough (Professors Stacy and Dayton)? Are Professor Jeffries and Judge

Gleeson correct in arguing that certain offenses (those committed by organizations) should be prosecuted federally whenever possible? Would most white collar crimes fall into the category of "organized crimes" meriting federal prosecution? Is *Lopez* inconsistent with the argument offered by Professor Jeffries and Judge Gleeson?

E. WHY DO THEY DO IT?

One of the most puzzling aspects of white collar crime is why the defendants, many of whom, by the fortune of birth or hard work have achieved material and professional success, risk it all by committing a few dishonest, even stupid, mistakes. The following commentaries may shed some light on this question.

MOTIVATION AND OPPORTUNITY[z]
JAMES WILLIAM COLEMAN

* * *

The public tends to see criminals as a breed apart from "normal" women and men. The deviants among us are branded as insane, inadequate, immoral, impulsive, egocentric, or with any one of a hundred other epithets. In seeing the deviant as a wholly different kind of person from ourselves, we bolster our self-esteem and help repress the fear that under the right circumstances we, too, might violate the same taboos. But this system of facile psychological determinism collapses when applied to white-collar criminals. The embezzling accountant or the corporate functionary involved in an employer's illegal schemes conforms too closely to the middle-class ideals of American culture to be so easily dismissed.

[Ed.-Coleman evaluates the few studies which have been conducted on personalities of white collar criminals, dismissing them as follows:]

Taken as a group, these studies provide scant evidence for the proposition that white-collar criminals have significant psychological differences form other white-collar workers. The empirical evidence on this point is so weak, however, that it would be unwise to disregard the personality factor completely pending the arrival of more conclusive data.

* * *

Whether or not the personality of the offender is considered important, conventional wisdom offers an even more popular explanation of the motivation for white-collar crime. White-collar criminals break the law, according to this view, because it is the easiest way for them to make a lot of money. Robert Lane, for example, found that the business

z. WHITE COLLAR CRIME: CLASSIC AND CONTEMPORARY VIEWS, 360–371 (Gilbert Geis, Robert F. Meier; & Lawrence M. Salinger eds., 3d ed. 1995). Copyright © 1989. All rights reserved. Reprinted with permission from St. Martin's Press.

and government officials he studied saw the desire for financial gain as the principal cause of white-collar crime: "Most businessmen and most responsible government officers, at least from the sample interviewed, believe that businessmen run afoul of the law for economic reasons—they may want to 'make a fast buck.' " Those familiar with criminological theory will recognize these views as an unknowing restatement of the principles of the classical criminology propounded in the late eighteenth and early nineteenth centuries by Beccaria and Bentham. According to that school of criminology, people violate the law because they believe it will bring them more pleasure and less pain than the other courses of action available to them.

The longevity of this kind of explanation is not hard to understand. Although it may not provide a very convincing account of the reasons a woman would murder her husband in a fit of rage, it is very persuasive when applied to rational, calculating crimes. But Lane's formulation is too narrow, for although the desire to "get rich quick" is certainly a motivating factor in many white-collar crimes, other kinds of financial motivations are often equally important. Many white-collar offenders are driven by the fear that they will lose what they already have rather than the desire for more. For example, when Weisburd, Wheeler, Waring, and Bode examined the statements of a sample of convicted white-collar criminals made in their presentence information reports, they found that this "fear of falling" was a central motivating force for a large group of offenders. Such offenders would have been "... reasonably happy with the place they have achieved through conventional means if only they could keep that place. But the fate of organizational success and failure, or the changing nature of the economy in their line of work, may put them at least temporarily under great financial pressure, where they risk losing the lifestyle that they have achieved. ... The motivation for their crime is not selfish ego gratification, but rather the *fear of falling*—of losing what they have worked so hard to gain." Of course, the desire to make more money and the desire to protect what one already has are two closely related aspects of the same phenomenon, which may be termed *financial self-interest*.

But financial self-interest, even in its most general sense, is only part of a larger motivational complex that is deeply ingrained in white-collar workers. Along with the desire for great wealth goes the desire to prove oneself by "winning" the competitive struggles that play such a prominent role in our economic system. And this desire to be "a winner" provides another powerful motivation for white-collar crime irrespective of any financial gains that may be involved.

The definition of wealth and success as central goals of individual activity is part of what may be termed the *culture of competition*; a complex of values and beliefs that is particularly strong in social systems based on industrial capitalism. In addition to giving great importance to wealth and success, the culture of competition defines the competitive struggle for personal gain as a positive, rather than a negative or selfish, activity. Competition is seen not only to build the character and endurance of the competitors, but also to produce the maximum economic value for society as a whole. Not surprisingly, the competitive economic struggles typical of industrial capitalism are seen by and large as a fair battle in which the most capable and the hardest-working individuals emerge victorious. This belief in turn becomes an important legitimation for social inequality, as it implies that the poor deserve their inferior position because they are lazy or incompetent. The winners, on the other hand, are admired for the ability and drive that made them successful. And this adoration of the rich and successful and the stigmatization of the poor not only provides strong reinforcement for the drive for personal success, but also contributes to the pervasive sense of insecurity and the fear of failure that make up a powerful undercurrent in the culture of competition.

Of course, the culture of competition is only one of the many diverse strains of contemporary culture, and there are other constellations of values that reject or mitigate this kind of orientation. But how, then, do we explain why one individual comes to see the world in a way that is highly conducive to criminal behavior and another does not?

* * *

Donald R. Cressey's detailed study of the motivations for embezzlement was the first to provide an answer to this question. Based on intensive interviews with a sample of incarcerated embezzlers, Cressey concluded that three distinct elements are necessary for embezzlement to occur: the perpetrators must have a nonshareable financial problem, they must have the opportunity and the knowledge necessary to commit an embezzlement, and they must apply a suitable rationalization to "adjust" the contradiction between their actions and society's normative standards. Of these three propositions, the first is the most questionable, for there appears to be no necessary reason why an embezzlement must result from a nonshareable problem instead of from a simple desire for more money. The second proposition was widely accepted before Cressey's work, but his third proposition and his investigation of the specific types of rationalizations embezzlers use to justify their actions helped create a whole new direction for research on white-collar crime.

Most embezzlers, according to Cressey, rationalize their crimes by telling themselves they are just borrowing the money and will soon return it. As one subject put it, "I figured that if you could use something and help yourself and replace it and not hurt anybody, it was all right." Cressey found that his respondents continued to use this rationalization to justify their embezzlement while they became more and more deeply involved in crime. Eventually, they were either caught or realized they would never be able to pay back all the money they had taken and were finally forced to accept the criminal nature of their behavior. Cressey's respondents reported using several other rationalizations as well, but the borrowing rationalization was by far the most common, probably because it is so well suited to neutralize the ethical standards condemning embezzlement.

The borrowing rationalization doesn't work as well for other white-collar crimes. There are numerous studies that examine the rationalizations criminals use to justify other kinds of white-collar crimes. One of the most common is the claim that the crimes do not harm anyone. If one's actions do not hurt other people, the argument goes, then there is nothing unethical about them. When a Westinghouse executive on trial for price fixing was asked if he thought his behavior had been illegal, he responded, "Illegal? Yes, but not criminal ... I assumed that a criminal action meant damaging someone, and we did not do that." Survey data have shown that the public is more tolerant of theft from large businesses and the government than it is of theft from smaller, more vulnerable organizations—probably because theft from a larger organization is perceived as less harmful to the victim.

Those involved in business crimes frequently justify their behavior by claiming that the law itself is unnecessary or unjust. Business people complain loudly about "government interference" in their affairs, often using the ideology of laissez-faire capitalism to point out what they consider to be inappropriate statutes and regulations. According to such beliefs, it is the law that causes harm to the public and not the illegal activities of business. Given this ideology, a host of business crimes can easily be justified. Clinard's study of wartime gasoline rationing, for example, concluded that gasoline dealers used the belief that the rationing was unnecessary to rationalize their violations of the law.

Another common technique of neutralization is the claim that one's criminal behavior was necessary in order to survive or to achieve vital economic goals. Many employees use this appeal to necessity to explain why they went along with the illegal activities expected by their employer. Sutherland cited the case of an idealistic young college graduate who had lost two previous jobs because he refused to become involved in unethical activities. After taking his third job, this time at a used car dealership, he found out that they, too, expected him to become involved in shady business practices. "When I learned these things I did not quit as I had previously. I sometimes felt disgusted and wanted to quit, but I argued that I did not have much chance to find a legitimate firm. I knew the game was rotten, but it has to be played—the law of the jungle and that sort of thing." Even representatives of giant corporations also use this justification, although such firms are unlikely candidates for economic extinction. The Westinghouse executive quoted earlier went on to justify his involvement in the price-fixing conspiracy by saying, "I thought we were more or less working on a survival basis in order to try to make enough to keep our plant and our employees." Another version of this argument of necessity often used to justify occupational offenses is that the crime was required to help one's friends or family.

A justification that is often combined with the argument of necessity is the claim that "everybody else is doing it." As one of Cressey's subjects put it, "In the real estate business you have to paint a pretty picture in order to sell the property. We did a little juggling and moving around, but everyone in the real estate business has to do that. We didn't do anything that they all don't do." This kind of rationalization is frequently used to justify "fudging" on income tax returns, and Benson found it to be popular among those convicted of criminal tax fraud. According to one respondent: "Everybody cheats on their income taxes, 95 percent of the people. Even if it's ten dollars, it's the same principle." Another version of this justification is that criminal behavior must be some sort of individual choice, and that people are not responsible for their actions when they are merely conforming to the expectations of others. Corrupt employees often claim that they haven't done anything wrong, because they were merely going along with a pattern of behavior accepted among their peers.

Finally, many occupational crimes are justified on the grounds that the offender deserves the money. This rationalization is particularly common in cases of employee theft. In his study of dock workers, Gerald Mars found that pilferage was defined as a "morally justified addition to wages" or an "entitlement due from exploiting employers." Lawrence Zeitlin found similar attitudes among employees who stole from retail stores. One of his subjects felt that the "store owed it to me," while another said, "I felt I deserved to get something additional for my work since I wasn't getting paid enough."

* * *

* * * Up to this point we have been discussing the causes of white-collar crime in general, but now some special attention must be devoted to organizational crime. Although the same process of motivation and rationalization occurs in both individual and organizational crime, the structural demands of formal organizations create unique pressures that require some separate analysis. Modern organizations are, in a sense, machines for controlling human behavior. In order to survive, a large corporation must directly control the behavior of thousands of employees and indirectly influence the activities of much larger groups on the outside. And although organizations may well encounter special problems in persuading employees to engage in illegal activities, the mechanisms for achieving conformity to organizational expectations are much the same whatever the legal standing of the organization's demands.

One of the most powerful techniques to win conformity with organizational expectations is the threat of dismissal. John Z. DeLorean, a former top executive of General Motors and founder of his own unsuccessful automobile firm, gave the following description of the pressure applied to an engineer who objected to dangerous design elements in the notorious Chevrolet Corvair: "Charlie Chayne, vice-president of engineering, along with his staff, took a very strong stand against the Corvair as an unsafe car long before it went on sale in 1959. He was not listened to but told in effect, 'You're not a member of the team. Shut up or go looking for another job.'"

Of course, such threats are seldom made so blatantly, but even so, employees understand what is involved in going against the company's demands.

The fear of losing an important assignment or being passed up for the next promotion is just as much a threat for the achievement-oriented executive as the possibility of dismissal. In the social world of the modern corporation, dedication to the company and conformity to the wishes of one's superiors are seen as essential to success. Regular promotions are an expected part of the climb up the corporate ladder, and overly scrupulous managers are likely to find the promotions they expected going to those who have been more cooperative.

Organizational control nonetheless involves much more than simply handing out sufficient rewards and punishments to ensure employee obedience. A large organization harbors a unique social world all its own, and the subculture embodied in the organization shapes its members' behavior in countless ways; many times without much conscious awareness on the part of the employees. At the most fundamental level, the way an organizational subculture defines the work situation and the role of various employees creates the context for all organizational behavior. The ethos of a corporation also helps shape the moral sensibilities and perspectives of its employees—especially those in managerial positions. Any decision of its members to engage in illegal activity is inevitably affected by the social world sheltered within the organization.

Considerable research shows that one important element of this social world is its "moral tone"—that is, its ethical system and its attitudes toward illegal behavior which many writers attribute largely to the attitudes of top management. But while it is undoubtedly true that top management has a major impact on the moral tone of most companies, those managers' ethical standards are not simply their own personal beliefs. The ethics and outlook of those who come to hold the most powerful positions in an organization are molded and shaped by the same process of socialization that influences other, less successful managers. Indeed, promotion to the highest ranks generally requires a much higher degree of ethical conformity than is expected of lower-level employees. Those who refuse to change personal standards that are incompatible with the demands of their corporate employer seldom reach the top.

Much has been written about the numbing effects modern bureaucracies have upon the moral sensibilities of their employees. Numerous writers have chronicled the growth of what William H. Whyte called the "organization man," who is under such overwhelming pressure to conform that individuality and personal ethical standards must be sacrificed for the sake of a career. The organization man must be a "team player" and not an individualist who allows personal values to interfere with his or her performance. Many sociologists have argued that these amoral functionaries have become so common because they are necessary to bureaucratic organization. One of the principal strengths of a bureaucracy is that individual employees are dispensable—one employee can be replaced by another with a minimum of disruption. But this interchangeability requires that individual employees think and act in a similar fashion, and the existence of widely divergent ethical standards and attitudes among the work force might interfere with the smooth operation of the organization. Thus, the efficient bureaucracy breeds moral conformity, or perhaps more often, a kind of amoral pragmatism.

Notes

1. In another work, Coleman provides additional insights from research on the etiology of white collar crime:

"Neither the desire for wealth and success nor the fear of failure, however, can account for all the motivations behind white collar crime. Some of these crimes, for example, are clearly rooted in the desire of the offenders to live up to the expectations of the significant others in their occupational world. This is particularly true of the various functionaries who, out of an unreflective sense of obedience, carry out their superiors' orders to commit some illegal act, and of the members of occupational subcultures who go along with illegal activities in order to win the acceptance and support of their peers. In such cases, the offenders ignore the larger society's condemnation of their crimes and accept their occupational associates' definition of such actions as normal behavior."[aa]

2. After reading Coleman's views what do you think about corporate criminal liability? About prosecuting CEOs (like *Park, supra* Chapter 15) for the acts of corporate employees? What, if anything, can corporate America do to neutralize the factors encouraging executives to commit crimes?

———

Professors David Weisburd, Stanton Wheeler, Elin Waring and Nancy Bode found interesting differences among types of white collar criminals. As you read the following selection, consider the typical characteristics of each type of white collar criminal.

DAVID WEISBURD, STANTON WHEELER, ELIN WARING & NANCY BODE, CRIMES OF THE MIDDLE CLASSES

48–60 (1991).[bb]

* * * Our examination of white-collar offenses revealed a hierarchy in which antitrust and securities crimes occupied the upper range and tax evasions and bank embezzlements the lower. When we turn from the nature of the crimes to the nature of the offenders, we find some interesting similarities and differences. * * *

The eight legal categories can be meaningfully reduced to four groups. At the top again are antitrust and securities fraud offenders: middle-aged white males with stable employment in white-collar jobs,

aa. JAMES WILLIAM COLEMAN, THE CRIMINAL ELITE, THE SOCIOLOGY OF WHITE COLLAR CRIME 206 (2d ed. 1989). Copyright © 1989. All rights reserved. Reprinted with permission from St. Martin's Press.

bb. DAVID WEISBURD, STANTON WHEELER, ELIN WARING & NANCY BODE, CRIMES OF THE MIDDLE CLASSES 48–60 (1991). Reprinted with permission, Yale University Press.

more often than not owners or officers in their companies, who are well above average in socioeconomic status compared to other offenders. Of the two categories, the antitrust offenders tend to be richer and are less likely to have had prior convictions, though they are slightly less well educated and rank slightly lower on measures of social standing.

The perpetrators in the tax and bribery offenses are also predominantly white males, although a little more often unemployed, and less well educated than their antitrust and securities fraud counterparts. At the same time, they are generally steadily employed in white-collar jobs, and at least a third are owners or officers in their businesses.

At the lower end of the spectrum are the credit fraud, false claim, and mail fraud offenders. Fewer than half are steadily employed, and a quarter of each are unemployed at the time of their offenses. On average they are less likely to have substantial financial assets, to hold college degrees, or to own their own homes than those in the middle category, and more than two-fifths have prior criminal convictions. These offenders are younger on the average than the others, and they are more likely to be female or "nonwhite," although white males continue to make up the modal category.

Finally, we have the bank embezzlers, who cannot be easily subsumed under one of these other three groups (though they are much closer to the bottom of the hierarchy than the top). They are far younger on average than the others and are nearly as likely to be female as male. They are similar to the lowest of our three groups in financial assets held, but they are far less likely than those offenders to be unemployed or to have a prior criminal record.

* * *

Antitrust and Securities Offenders

Those convicted of antitrust or securities crimes more closely approximate the traditional image of white-collar criminals than offenders in any of the other crime categories. Overall, SEC violators have a less reputable, more marginal appearance than do antitrust offenders. For example, a typical securities violator, who was convicted of (among other things) selling unregistered stock for the company of which he was chairman of the board, was on his second marriage and rented his home. In contrast, the four company presidents convicted in one antitrust conspiracy all had at least some college education (one had a law degree), were married (to their original spouses) with children, and owned their homes. None of these men had a criminal record.

Antitrust offenders often present a public face of stability and uprightness based on characteristics that can take a lifetime to build, and they do this more consistently than do securities violators. For example, they are the best off financially, with median assets of $613 thousand and liabilities of only $7 thousand within the seven districts. Securities offenders are the second wealthiest group, as measured by assets alone.

Because of their substantial liabilities, however, these offenders seem less financially secure.

Education is one measure on which securities violators outscore antitrust violators. This reversal is largely a result of the type of occupations that the offenders in each group hold. The small number of professionals among antitrust offenders, and the presence of a number of businessmen who started with nothing and worked their way up, lowers the educational level of this category.

* * *

Tax and Bribery Offenders

The tax and bribery offenders are generally of lower social status than the antitrust and securities violators, but of higher status than the offenders who fall in the remaining categories. For example, a company president—who owned a retail dry goods store with six employees—was convicted of attempting to bribe an IRS agent who was auditing his firm. Although he had only a ninth-grade education, in other ways his profile was similar to that of the antitrust violators described above.

The offenders in these two categories are very similar in demographic makeup. They are mostly white males (though both offenses contain a larger number of females and nonwhites than found in antitrust and securities crimes) in their middle forties. They are also likely to be employed at the time of their offenses and on average have relatively stable employment histories, generally in white-collar occupations. A majority of the tax offenders are either sole proprietors or owners of larger businesses, and few use their occupations to commit their crimes. A relatively large number are professionals. Indeed, about 30 percent of the lawyers and 40 percent of the doctors in our sample commit tax violations. At the same time, lawyers and doctors each made up less than one in twenty of the total tax sample. Two-thirds of the tax offenders work in the manufacturing or nonprofessional service sectors.

Many of the professionals who commit tax violations have troubled pasts. The personal histories of the ten medical doctors in the sample—seven of whom committed tax violations—are telling in this regard. Three had prior criminal records, and their convictions included wife beating, and drunk and disorderly conduct. One had had his surgical privileges revoked, in part because his patients suffered high rates of complications. Another had filed for personal and corporate bankruptcy. One earned part of his unreported income by performing illegal abortions. At the same time many of these doctors lived in homes in exclusive sections of their towns and were considered models of achievement. The bribery category also includes many professionals. Indeed, this category contains a higher proportion of people employed in the delivery of professional services than does tax fraud.

The connection between bribery and tax fraud is often a substantive one, and this is particularly clear when the certified public accountants (CPAs) in the two groups are examined. Fifteen of the twenty-six CPAs in our sample fall into one of these two offender categories, and the ten CPAs involved in bribery were all seeking to influence officials of the IRS. Making up 9 percent of the bribery offenders, most of the accountants are college graduates, though few attended elite schools. Many attended state and city universities part-time, often taking five to ten years to finish. Few were ever employed by the major accounting firms.

As was the case with tax offenders, several of the accountants had drinking problems, and a number had histories of marital instability. It is interesting to note that the briberies we examined did not demand any particular accounting skills, although being an accountant put these individuals into the contact with the IRS, which led to the offering or paying of a bribe. This differs from the activities of accountants convicted of securities fraud.

* * *

Credit Fraud, Mail Fraud, and False Claims

Credit fraud, mail fraud, and false claims define the next group of offenders. The people who are convicted of these three crimes resemble each other in many ways and are quite different from the offenders described above. In particular, they are less likely to be white or male, are younger, and are less likely to have had steady employment than the offenders previously discussed. They are also less likely to fit an image of the "model citizen" than offenders in the preceding categories. For example, 13 percent of the credit-fraud offenders have histories of barbiturate use, and 5 percent are described in the PSIS as drug addicts. The median net worth of the offenders in each category is zero, and both assets and liabilities are much smaller than the figures for the four offenses already discussed.

The profile of credit-fraud offenders is typical of this group. A quarter of those who had never married are parents; this phenomenon is virtually nonexistent in antitrust, bribery, tax, and SEC categories. Twenty-five percent of the offenders convicted of credit fraud, mail fraud, and false claims were unemployed at the time of the offense; these rates are more than double that for any other of the white-collar crime categories. Many are in difficult financial situations. In sum, these three groups include a significant number of offenders who have some kind of personal or family troubles.

These offenses include people from many walks of life and from a broad range of social classes. Credit frauds include bank officers and financial advisers, as well as insurance agents and real-estate agents. Mail frauds include postal clerks, lawyers, accountants, and doctors, although there is no occupation that dominates. The wide variety of occupations is especially pronounced for false-claim offenders. About one in twelve are doctors or pharmacists, and an equal number are blue-collar workers. The prosecution of the many seemingly trivial false-claims cases[] * * * most notably those involving lying on job applications—may in some part account his variety.

It is also interesting to note that fifteen practicing attorneys in our sample committed mail fraud. Of these, nine were located in Maryland, and six were involved in a single conspiracy (with a group of medical doctors) to submit fraudulent reports and inflate bills to insurance companies. Four of the lawyers involved in mail fraud had engaged in political corruption or influence peddling. Other attorneys violated the trust given to them by cashing checks written to clients or mixing personal and client funds. Finally, three attorneys were involved in the sale of worthless products through the mail.

* * *

Bank Embezzlers

Persons convicted of bank embezzlement are generally quite different from those in other offense categories. Most are closer in background characteristics to those just discussed than to antitrust or securities criminals. The bank embezzlers are the youngest group of offenders, and most likely to be female. They usually come from stable working families without a great deal of money. Almost all of the bank embezzlers are bank employees, and they use their jobs to commit their crimes.

Among bank embezzlers there is a stark contrast between the positions that men and women occupy. Most men are managers or officers in the banks for which they work, though they often have only local managerial responsibilities. Most female bank embezzlers are bank tellers or hold other clerical positions. Clearly, banks provide clerical workers and low-level managers with many opportunities for white-collar crime. There is a fair amount of trust allotted to them, even though they hold relatively low-level jobs.

Interestingly, on one measure of education—high school graduation—the bank embezzlers are among the highest scoring groups, while on another—college graduation—they are the lowest. Whereas bank embezzlers rank relatively high on the SEI [Socio–Economic Index], on average they are least likely to own their own homes. Few bank embezzlers have prior criminal convictions, but this may be in great part due to the special character of employment background checks conducted by banking institutions. Here, as with other demographic characteristics, bank embezzlers hold a mixed position, appearing highly respectable in some ways but often holding positions of low social standing.

Notes

1. Do you think these categorizations provide insight as to why certain people commit white collar crimes? What is it about these often successful people that makes them cross the line into criminal behavior?

2. Why will economic, social and personal pressures seemingly push some people to criminal behavior while other individuals seem to thrive under such pressures? Do you think that our materialistic society somehow encourages white collar crimes by those who have been able to achieve only marginal success? If so, does that make white collar criminals more or less morally culpable?

Index

References are to Pages

0–314–21114–4

9 780314 211149

90000